UNITED STATES JEWRY, 1776-1985

UNITED
STATES
JEWRY
1776–1985

JACOB RADER MARCUS

Hebrew Union College

Jewish Institute

of Religion

VOLUME IV

The East European Period
The Emergence of the American Jew
Epilogue

WAYNE STATE
UNIVERSITY PRESS
DETROIT

Copyright © 1993 by Wayne State University Press,
Detroit, Michigan 48202.
All rights are reserved.
No part of this book may be reproduced without formal permission.
Manufactured in the United States of America.
98 97 96 95 94 93   5 4 3 2 1

Library of Congress Cataloging-in-Publication Data
(Revised for vol. 4)

Marcus, Jacob Rader, 1896–
  United States Jewry, 1776–1985.

  Includes bibliographical references and indexes.
  1. Jews—United States—History. 2. Judaism—United States—History. 3. United States—Ethnic relations.

E184.J5 M237 1989	973′.04924	89–5723

ISBN 0-8143-2186-0
ISBN 0-8143-2189-5 (v. 4: alk. paper)

TO MY DEAR ONES WHO HAVE PASSED FROM TIME TO ETERNITY

My father, my mother, my brother, my sister, my wife, my daughter

CONTENTS

MAPS

ILLUSTRATIONS FOLLOWING PAGE 252.

CHAPTER ONE

THE EAST EUROPEAN JEWS

Introduction

By 1885, East European Jews were arriving in the United States in substantial numbers, part of a massive folk immigration that brought millions and millions of Europeans to these shores. Responding to periodic wars, political upheavals, and heightened persecution, the Jews came in waves after 1881. The humble came first; the elite later. If this invasion of "barbarians" from the East was to continue, these newcomers would in the course of time outnumber both the Jewish native-born and the naturalized Central Europeans. American Jews had been experiencing social discrimination in the 1870's; the uncouth Eastern Jews, they felt, would only exacerbate the problem of prejudice. These "Russians" had an Orthodoxy of their own, one that was unacceptable to many American Jews: Don't confuse us with them. It is not at all improbable that reasoning of this sort may, in part, have prompted the Reform rabbis to call a rabbinical conference in Pittsburgh to lay down a radical, modern, Americanistic platform that would distinguish them from the arriving immigrants.[1]

WHO WERE THESE EAST EUROPEANS? WHERE DID THEY COME FROM?

Most of the newcomers had lived in the regions of the Russian Empire, which had been Poland before its dismemberment in the last quarter of the eighteenth century. The Polish Jews who were inherited by the Russians continued to live in their former homes; they were not encouraged to settle in the pre-partition Russian provinces. Thus, after a fashion, they were locked in behind a fence, a pale, where they were to remain, with few exceptions, till the revolution of 1917. Prussia, too, had appropriated a sizable chunk of the old Poland. These new Prussian subjects Germanized themselves speedily. They became Germans despite the fact that other German Jews dubbed them "Polacks" and affected to disdain them. Some historians today still call them Poles; they were no more Poles than California Jews are Mexicans because Mexico a century ago ruled the province of Upper California. The Austrians, too, had seized a substantial piece of the Polish commonwealth. Farther south in Eastern Europe lay the Turkish provinces that were to become Rumania. The East European Jews included Poles, Russians, and Rumanians. Jews here in America lumped them together as if they were an inchoate mass. Indeed, they were a conglomerate cherishing disparate religious rites, opinions, and prejudices. Most of them were Orthodox; a few were anti-religious political radicals.[2]

WHEN DID THE RUSSIANS AND POLES FIRST COME
TO NORTH AMERICA AND THE UNITED STATES?

There was no decade in all American Jewish history which did not shelter some Jews from these Eastern territories. Simon Valentine Van der Wilden, the brother-in-law of New Amsterdam's Asser Levy, was of Lithuanian origin. Some of the so-called "rabbis" who came schnorring in ante-Revolutionary War days were from the Russian and Polish provinces. Mordecai M. Mordecai, an eighteenth-century Pennsylvania frontier distiller, came from Telz in Lithuania, later the seat of a famous rabbinical academy. Haym Salomon, a truly heroic Revolutionary War patriot, was born in Lissa, Poland, and the Polish Hyamses, of Charleston and Louisiana, arrived in the United States no later than 1800 via Ireland and London; Henry M. Hyams, a pioneer Reform Jew in 1827, became lieutenant governor of Confederate Louisiana during the Civil War. These East Europeans were literally everywhere, often in perceptible numbers. Occasionally, in the second half of the nineteenth century, Poles and Russians moved into a town before Central Europeans.[3]

CONGREGATIONS OF EAST EUROPEANS IN THE UNITED STATES

Due to the gold rush, San Francisco became a large city almost overnight. Among the many Jews who flocked there hoping to do well were many "Polish" Jews. Often it is difficult to determine whether they were German-speaking Prussian citizens or Yiddish-speaking Russian Poles. Not improbably many were Russians. "Poles" had their own San Francisco congregation in the 1850's. Los Angeles also sheltered a number of these so-called Poles, or real Poles, like the Goldwaters, who came to town in that decade. Russian Jewish Americans were doing business in Alaska, Siberia, Russia proper, the Philippines, and Japan. Joel Gottlieb (Gottleib), a Russian Pole, seems to have lived in Chicago in 1837, in the Colorado Territory in the 1850's, and in the Montana and Utah territories in the 1860's. His base was Denver, where he died in 1874. Many of the transmississippi Lithuanians came from the Russian-ruled province of Suwalki. Untoward economic circumstances compelled them to leave; those who followed hoped to do as well as those who had already left. Abraham Rachofsky, of Colorado, a Suwalkian, brought over his family and in the course of time became the patriarch of a clan which documented its Americanization with the following names: Ross, Rice, Rich, Rayor, Ray. By the 1850's and 1870's, Gottlieb's Chicago was no longer a small town. More than one Russian-Polish congregation and ghetto existed on the south and west sides of town. By 1879, the Chicago East Europeans could even boast of their own Yiddish journal.

In the 1850's and 1860's, dozens of Yiddish-speaking peddlers, using Rochester, New York, as their base, established peddling centers in Iowa's Mississippi River towns. Some came from the same village in Russia; one served as a magnet to draw others. These East European peddlers had prayer groups of their own in the Iowa country in the 1860's, and several of them who elected to remain became important and affluent citizens. One who wandered north to the Dakotas became one of Deadwood's most highly respected townsmen. This man, Harris Franklin, invested successfully in mines, railroads, and banks. The antebellum East European American Diaspora found Jews not only in the Far West and in most, if not all, midwestern states and territories, but also in the Deep South. In 1820, a Lithuanian Jew with a long Russian name emerged as Mordecai Marks. Achieving influence, he joined elite Shearith Israel in New York and then in the 1830's moved south to Louisiana, where he became a plantation owner. These Russian and Polish newcomers were in Charleston, South Carolina, in the late eighteenth century. The Jew who translated the Hebrew for the 1792 synagogal charter betrayed through his phonetic spelling that he was a Russian or Pole or Lithuanian; Columbia, the capital, sheltered some of these "Russians" in the 1850's; Georgetown had its first East European no later than the 1870's, and these immigrants also made their presence known in St. Louis that same decade. Slavic Jewish prayer groups met for worship in Cincinnati, Cleveland, and Pittsburgh in the 1860's, and it was in that same decade, if not earlier, that these newcomers established conventicles in Baltimore, Philadelphia, and Boston, as well as in Maine. In Buffalo, they outnumbered the Germans, and they were very numerous in Pittsburgh. By 1881, it bears repeating, they were found everywhere, as individuals or groups, in every major town.[4]

NEW YORK CITY

If some Jewish historians estimate that, by 1880, 20 percent of all Jews here were of East European stock, this would indicate that 12,000 of the

60,000 Jews in New York City were Russians and Poles. The immigration statistics would seem to support this belief. (Actually, New York City sometimes sheltered about half of all the Jews in the country.) Certain facts are incontestable. By 1852, the newcomers had their own congregation of about eighty members; they held services, studied Talmud, and assembled a basic rabbinical library. For this small group, the Russo-Jewish religious way of life had made the transatlantic crossing successfully. In a very few years, they had a building of their own. They were fortunate in that the aged Sampson Simson, of Shearith Israel, subsidized them liberally. He was Orthodox and wealthy, for his farm holdings in Westchester County had increased in value. That the newcomers were ready to establish religious institutions of their own is documented by the legal inquiry of an Orthodox functionary. Rabbi Judah Middleman wrote to a scholar in Europe inquiring whether it was permissible to purchase a church and use it as a synagog. The answer was in the affirmative. In the next decades, numerous churches would be purchased by Jewish congregations in all parts of the country. Scholarly East European rabbis began to find their way to the American ghettos as Russians, Poles, and Rumanians settled here in ever increasing numbers. Among those who came were Joseph Moses Aaronson (d. 1874) and Abraham Joseph Ash (1821-1887).

Aaronson was learned, but an abrasive difficult person; he quarreled with his members and his colleagues. Bitter, internecine feuds were typical of rabbinic relations; they were the rule not the exception. Aaronson had no use for Ash, who was the first rabbi of the 1852 synagog and community. The congregation paid Ash $2 a week, a salary which he augmented by the customary perquisites. The two decades after 1850 saw a number of immigrants from the Slavic lands attain affluence as wholesalers and garment manufacturers. Others were shopkeepers. In 1881, James J. Hill, the railroad entrepreneur, sent the scholarly Herman Rosenthal to Japan to report on economic opportunities there. By the 1860's and 1870's, congregations and conventicles were sprouting on the Lower East Side; around the year 1880, there were about thirty of them. Even the Hassidim had found their way here and elected to live religiously as a separate enclave. In one of the prayer groups, the members fought vigorously over the title of the presiding officer. Was he a parnas or a president?—Americanization was making inroads. (Note also the Americanized name of Rabbi Middleman.)

The two decades before 1880 saw substantial Jewish cultural advances by the newcomers; the 1860's witnessed the publication of several works including a Hebrew commentary on the mishnaic "Sayings of the Fathers" and an attack in Hebrew on the Reform Jews. In 1867, a placard in Hebrew appealed to Jews, asking them to vote for Albert Joseph Cardozo as judge. (This was the father of the later Supreme Court Justice

Benjamin Nathan Cardozo.) Vote for the Jew, he is easy on you when you violate the Sunday closing law! In 1870, there was a Yiddish paper of sorts, a Hebrew bookstore, and by 1871 a Hebrew journal. Present, too, were an assortment of Russian and Polish scholarly literary Enlighteners, Maskilim, who evoked but little enthusiasm from the artisans and petty tradesmen struggling to stay alive. Among these learned immigrants was the Pole Phinehas Mendel Heilprin, talmudist and political liberal, who had fled Hungary after the failure of the 1848 revolution. The Heilprins were a highly cultured and remarkable clan. In 1879, the New York congressman, Samuel Sullivan Cox, raised his voice denouncing Russia and the Romanovs for persecuting Jews. Obviously, the East European Jews were beginning to make their presence felt politically. In the 1880's, a substantial minority of all American Jews were of Russo-Polish provenance. That there were 50,000 of them is a conservative estimate; thus they constituted a relatively large minority of the community which amounted then to about 300,000 Jews in the United States.[5]

WHY THEY LEFT

What brought these unhappy people here in antebellum days? It was a long trek from Russia to American ports. They fled because of brutal conscription laws which did not even spare teenaged youngsters. In an age when only France and Holland were free, Russia was particularly distinguished for its denial of basic human and political rights to Jews. It was a land wracked by famine, typhus, cholera, economic depressions, and agrarian crises exacerbated in the 1860's because of the emancipation of the serfs and the onset of a destructive industrialism. For the East Europeans in those early days, the lure of American opportunity loomed large. Pleading in 1824 for emancipation of Maryland's legally disabled Jews, John S. Tyson dwelt on the despotism of czarist society. Lincoln, too—this in the 1850's—pointed with scorn to the tyranny of the Muscovites, among whom there was no pretense of liberty. By the 1840's, German Jews were advising their Russian coreligionists to leave; in 1854, Leeser urged them to seek the safety of America's shores. The sufferings of Jews in those Eastern lands were notorious.[6]

In Russia, the Jews were constantly subject to restrictions in commerce, industry, the civil and military services, and the practice of the professions, especially law. It was difficult for them to make headway economically; their opportunities were limited. The Jews were also penned into the Pale of Settlement. The Polish insurrection of 1863 probably induced some Jews to leave for the West; there were riots in Odessa in 1871; the pogroms in 1881, following the assassination of Alexander II, set off a mass exodus. Most Jews were not directly affected by the pogroms, but it became the style to pick up and sail for the Golden Land across the seas. In addition, there were periods of economic distress. It was inevitable, therefore, in the 1880's and thereafter, as the Russians moved haltingly toward a manufacturing economy, that many of the peasants and artisans would be displaced. The Jews became the ideal scapegoat, and the government did little to hinder the riots in 1881. Revolution was in the air; many of the Jewish intelligentsia were numbered among the radicals. The May Laws of 1882 drove many Jews off the land; they were no longer allowed to settle in rural areas or to own or lease properties in the countryside. (In a way, these harsh prescriptions were duplicated in the United States in the twentieth century, when somewhat similar laws were enacted against Japanese aliens.) Compelled now to seek new forms of livelihood, country Jews found that prejudices, prevailing disabilities, and corrupt administrators made it very difficult for them to secure an economic foothold in the cities. Even in the Pale, not all towns were open to Jewish settlement. Thus, beginning in the 1880's, Jews were confronted with restrictions on all sides. Limitations were imposed on school and college attendance and teaching; there were restrictions on jury duty and discrimination in taxation as well as in the pursuit of trade and commerce. The rigid Sunday laws meant that observant Jews lost two days a week, Saturday and Sunday, a severe disability for those engaged in commerce.

Even after the 1881 pogroms, most Russian Jews opted to remain, but many in Russia proper—that is, outside the Pale—were stricken when in 1891 mass expulsions from Moscow and other cities became the order of the day. Certainly conditions did not improve as the twentieth century began. By that time the published judicial interpretations of discriminatory regulations filled a book of about 1,000 pages. The Panslavist Russians barely tolerated the followers of the Mosaic Law. The Jews were not the only victims of Russian Orthodox intolerance; Protestants, too, were oppressed and made miserable. The goal of the Romanov dynasty was religiocultural homogeneity. A popular statement ascribed to Konstantin Petrovich Pobedonostev, the procurator of the Holy Russian Synod and a close associate of the czar, had it that one-third of the Jews would be compelled to emigrate, one-third would be converted, and the remaining third would die off.

The Romanovs, entrenched in medievalism, refused to profit from history. As late as 1911, Menahem Mendel Beilis, a humble Jewish artisan, was charged with ritual murder—accused of killing a Christian boy in order to use his blood for religious purposes. Beilis languished in jail for two years before his acquittal. Then came the horrors of World War I and the revolution of 1917. The Jewish world breathed a sigh of relief. Finally, after a long century of discriminatory legislation, all anti-Jewish

disabilities were removed in 1917, but the new Communist rulers saw to
it that the Jewish religion was practically interdicted. For most Jews, this
was a disaster. But this was not the worst; hundreds of pogroms erupted
in the Ukraine; many thousands were murdered in 1919-1920. Oppression, constant for decades, impelled many to leave, to infiltrate the lands
of Central and Western Europe. Though often not welcomed by fellow
Jews in those countries, the refugees crawled into the interstitial spaces.
Others left for Palestine, South Africa, and South America; most turned
to the United States. The statement of Robert Beverly in his *History of
Virginia* (1722) still held true: "This may in truth be term'd the best poor
man's country in the world."

The difficulties that confronted the Jews in Russia were compounded
in Rumania, impelling Jews there also to leave for the United States.
Rumania was just emerging from feudalism; gypsies were held in a state
of slavery to 1856. The Great Powers at the Congress of Berlin in 1878
ordered the new Rumania to emancipate its Jews, but nothing helped;
Jews in that country remained aliens, deprived for the most part of naturalization, though they were native-born. Their rights were circum-
scribed. Galicia, under Austrian rule, tolerated no pogroms, but the poverty was intense. Many here, too, lifted their eyes and followed the sun
westward to the promise of a new land.

Thus East European Jews were not missing among the millions of
non-Jews who were landing in the American ports. Indeed, emigration
had become almost a fashion—a popular form of adventure that appealed
to ambitious youngsters. Practically none of the disabilities current in European lands were present in the United States. There were no pogroms,
there was no conscription. This was indeed a Golden Land. The railroads
and the steamships, lusting for the immigrant's dollar, advertised heavily
and employed solicitors, runners, to induce the masses to make the westward journey. With speedy and cheap transportation, space and time were
almost abolished.[7]

THE EAST EUROPEAN IMAGE OF AMERICA AND ITS JEWS

The Jews who turned to America had some inkling of what the United
States was like. America had been touched upon in Hebrew and Yiddish
books in Europe ever since the early nineteenth century; by the second
half of the century Jewish papers in Eastern Europe, in Russian, Hebrew,
and Yiddish, were allotting space to the United States and its Jewry.
There were difficulties, they pointed out. There was prejudice there, too,
against Jews—if nothing comparable to what Jews met in Russia, Poland,
and Rumania. It was not easy in America to be an observant Orthodox
Jew; keeping kosher was a problem. But—and this was important—
church and state were separated; religious and political liberty prevailed;

public educational facilities were open to all; there were no conscription laws; the German Jews here had established agencies for charity; and, above all, there were opportunities to work and make a living. Many Jews read the Yiddish tales of the Russian writer Isaac Mayer Dick (1814-1893), who made the United States look attractive: it was better to go there than to Palestine; individual Jews often acquired wealth. In 1870, Dick published his variant version of *Uncle Tom's Cabin*. Uncle Tom's master was a pious Jew; Uncle Tom's family was finally liberated and reunited and all became Jewish; their descendants are people of wealth, merchants of substance. Harriet Beecher Stowe never heard of Dick's Uncle Tom. She would have been very much interested, if not appalled, but she should have known that in the United States nothing was impossible.[8]

THE NUMBER OF EAST EUROPEANS WHO MIGRATED TO THE UNITED STATES, 1888–1920

It has been estimated roughly that about 4,000,000 East European Jews left their homes in the nineteenth and twentieth centuries; about 40,000 may have settled here in the decade before 1880; a little over 2,000,000 came to the United States in the forty years between 1881 and 1920. Yet these millions of emigrants did not diminish the size of the Russian Jewish community since the annual natural increase in that land was always larger than the numbers who emigrated. From 1881 to 1910, about 70 percent of all arriving East European Jews came from Russia, some 20 percent from Austria-Hungary, a little less than 4 percent from Rumania. Next to the Italians, the Jews constituted the largest body of émigrés in the years after 1880. For a variety of reasons, many of the newly arriving Jews decided to remain in New York City permanently. They had no money to travel farther and the city offered them Jewish companionship, religious institutions, and above all jobs. By 1920, about 30 percent of all the inhabitants in New York City were Jews. On the way over, the migrants had been helped, to a degree, by coreligionists, Austrians, Germans, French, and English. These European Jews were happy to speed the travelers on their way west. Over here, they were aided by a number of ad hoc societies set up by the earlier settlers or by the newcomers themselves. The national organizations established by the natives and the Germans did not always work together in harmony. There were rivalries among the supporters of the Union of American Hebrew Congregations, the B'nai B'rith, the Board of Delegates of American Israelites, and the Paris-based Alliance Israélite Universelle. The rivalries between the AIU and the IOBB here reflected the hostility between the French and German governments in Europe.[9]

CHARACTERISTICS OF THE INCOMING EAST EUROPEAN IMMIGRANTS

Certain characteristics distinguished the incoming Jews from Russia, Poland, Galicia, and Rumania. They came to stay and brought or sent for their families; a substantial number were illiterate though many were skilled workers. Jews and Italians, impoverished, brought little capital with them when they landed; they were lucky they were able to borrow money for a ticket or had a sibling who lent them something to help make the trip. Some even contracted to pay for the passage on the installment plan. Quite a number of the Jews were tailors, master workers, who had acquired experience in shops or garment factories back home; many were artisans who had learned to live by their skills. Despite governmental obstruction back home, they had been trained to cope with an urban industrial economy. The port of entry records point out that, for the period up to 1910, the degree of illiteracy among the Jewish arrivals was high, about 26 percent. Very few of the men or women who landed had ever attended a Russian elementary school; they were not welcomed there, and in any case, Christologically oriented institutions were avoided by East European ghetto Jews.

However, the figures on illiteracy merit closer scrutiny. A government study, published by an immigration commission in 1911, shows that over 90 percent of the Russian Hebrew workers could read and write. Another study in 1914 indicates that illiteracy among these newcomers was something less than 15 percent. All this is confusing. In all probability, literacy among the Jewish newcomers was *relatively* high; the refugees who came here after 1905 seem to have had some schooling. It is also true that the general average of literacy was pulled down because a substantial number of Jewish women had not been taught to read and write; there was a relatively high rate of illiteracy among them. It is by no means improbable, too, that the literacy tests were badly administered. A card was no doubt flashed and the newcomer given little time to respond. The examiners, civil servants, were often hostile to Jewish immigrants.

The men who came brought their wives or began saving to bring them over; it was often years before they had the necessary sum. This determination to stay and sink their roots they shared with the Irish. The Irish summarily rejected their English overlords; the Jews despised the Russian authorities; there was nothing for them in Russia or Rumania. Yet many of the newcomers did return. This was certainly true in periods when the mobs in Eastern Europe were quiescent. Some of the immigrants who landed were paupers; they may have been dispatched by communities eager to get rid of them. Sending the luckless to America, to the colonies, was a European tradition going back for centuries. The Jewish charities here were not hesitant to ship them back; it was a money-saving expedient. Some who were returned by agencies or went back on their own were shipped on cattle boats and had to work out their passage with hard, grueling labor. For some, factory and field labor had been too strenuous; others despaired of living a Jewish religious life here. Many, too, returned for business reasons or because of a death in the family; for others, the tempo here was unbearable. With the failure of the 1905 Russian revolution and the onset of a counterliberal trend, reaction, many Jews surely thought twice before returning to the Russian cauldron. What percentage of Jews did return to their native lands? Hungarian and Italian Gentiles returned in large numbers; over 50 percent of the Italians yearned for the solace of their beloved Italy; over 60 percent of the Hungarians bought return tickets. And the Jews? About 6 percent of the Jewish Russians, Poles, and Rumanians who landed were to return to their native lands. (Some of these came back later, many thousands of them.) The percentage is small but if 2,000,000 of the Children of Israel came over, then at least 120,000 went back, a substantial number for whom America was not the Promised Land.

An analysis has been made above of the characteristics of these refugees upon landing. They were not one huge amorphous glob. A few were Russian-speaking high school or college men; some of these were political radicals, Marxists for the most part. This was certainly true of some of the intelligentsia who came after the 1905 revolution. Among the 2,000,000 were numerous westernized Hebraists, Enlighteners, Maskilim, autodidacts; there were large numbers of petty businessmen and hundreds of thousands of artisans. With the exception of the few college men and women and a number of left-oriented workmen, the typical immigrant was a Yiddish-speaking Orthodox Jew with very little secular schooling.[10.]

KEEP THE JEWS AT HOME

PERSECUTED JEWS MUST BE EMANCIPATED IN THEIR NATIVE LANDS

For many reasons, American Jews hoped that the oppressed Jews of Eastern Europe would be emancipated in their native lands. In 1880, there were about 250,000 Jews in the United States; in 1882, the year after the Russian massacres, emigration from the Romanov Empire more than doubled. Most of the 13,000 Jewish refugees landed in New York, a city that then sheltered about 60,000 Jews. This massive wave shocked and frightened the earlier settlers; the exoticism of the newcomers dismayed them. Following the American tradition of xenophobia, Jews here have always looked askance at new arrivals. New York's haughty Sephardim of the 1680's established a separate cemetery of their own in their Ashkenazic-Sephardic community; Philadelphia's Jews in 1769 were not happy with the new arrivals from London. In no sense did this mean that impoverished émigrés were not helped. The demands of kinship prevailed, though most often Jewish natives dreaded the arrival of newcomers as a financial burden and a possible source of discredit to the established Jews who were making a place for themselves. By the mid-nineteenth century, the Jews of Europe and America felt it imperative that persecuted coreligionists be emancipated in their homelands. They would then not descend on their fellow Jews in Western Europe and the United States; all through the nineteenth and early twentieth centuries, Jews here and abroad worked to effect that emancipation.

The sufferings of the Jews in the Slavic lands pushed many to move westward in the 1840's; a Hungarian rabbi urged his flock to be supportive of the immigrants leaving Russia. The émigrés became an American Jewish problem in the 1860's because of unhappy conditions in the Russian Empire; the destitute who landed here had to be helped. The Jews of Central and Western Europe, more directly concerned, called conferences of World Jewry in the several decades beginning with the 1860's. American Jews were invited to sit in at these meetings and they did. These Jewish conferences could not always decide whether to tolerate emigration or to work for emancipation. They certainly preferred the latter, but if there was to be emigration, then let it be orderly and selective. Paupers and the unskilled were to be kept at home. When refugees persisted in leaving their homelands in Russia, Poland, and Rumania, their Western European hosts pushed them on to the United States, and when they arrived in numbers at New York, they were again pushed westward to the hinterland.

When conditions were bad abroad—and they always were—Jews in the United States turned to Washington, to the Presidents and the Secretaries of State, hoping that they would remonstrate with offending governments so that Jews would not be compelled to leave their native lands. The process of intervention began in 1840 when Martin Van Buren's Secretary of State set out to help the Jews of Damascus; the pleas for American intercession were to continue for well over a century. If Jews could be helped in their native lands, Jews here would be spared the problem of digesting the thousands of aliens; the kinship tug would be satisfied and America would have fulfilled herself as the great exponent of liberty and freedom for all peoples everywhere. Universal emancipation was the country's prime spiritual export. On the whole, the United States government has nearly always been sympathetic to the appeals of its Jewish citizens, though its European representatives, diplomatic and consular, have as a rule been uncooperative, if not unsympathetic and even hostile. Adhering to the formalities of protocol, the authorities at Washington have nearly always maintained that they could not interfere in the domestic concerns of a foreign state. There have, however, been notable exceptions when Presidents and their Secretaries of State have sincerely tried to help the distressed Jews of Eastern Europe. To be sure, political considerations —Jewish votes—were never absent. As Jews in the United States increased in numbers and as their political influence mounted, the authorities in the capital tended to be more concerned with Europe's oppressed Jews. It is interesting, if not instructive, to note that the standard histories of diplomacy have very little to say about American intervention abroad on behalf of suffering Jews.

The situation for Jews in Rumania was always bad, but in 1870 American Jewry determined to do something about it. The leaders here, the Board of Delegates of American Israelites, the B'nai B'rith executive, and other notables, induced President Grant to send Benjamin Franklin Peixotto to Bucharest as consul general. It was hoped that Peixotto would put an end to attacks on Jews and work toward emancipation, thus keeping the Jews of Rumania at home. This he set out to do. At least, there were no serious riots during the period of his incumbency (1870-1876), but even he had his moments of dismay, for in 1872 he was of the opinion that migration was the only hope for the Jews of that unhappy land. In 1878, the European powers met at the Congress of Berlin and insisted on the emancipation of all the peoples in the Balkans, including the Jews. Rumania accepted the fiat of the Congress, but evaded its obligations by declaring all Jews aliens, subject to naturalization. Of the many thousands in the land, only a relatively few were permitted to attain citizenship; the oppression continued. It is not without significance that American Jewry -one of the smallest congeries—deliberately set out in 1870 to solve an international Jewish problem. This Jewry even then was reaching out for recognition; here one sees the first faint strivings for World Jewish hegemony.

The Gentile world and Jews everywhere were shocked when in April 1881, the Russian peasants and city mobs began killing Jews. Jews here were slow to respond to these outrages, but they did mount protests in which they were joined by their Christian neighbors. Russia was always looked upon as a land of barbarians. The February 1882 protest meeting in New York City was called by former President U. S. Grant; the chairman of the protesting group in Philadelphia was General Charles H. T. Collis whose wife was a Jew, a member of the distinguished Levy-Cardozo clan of Charleston, S.C. This protest was not to be a Jewish affair. Only one Jew addressed the Philadelphia gathering, Mayer Sulzberger, already a well-known member of the bar; others who spoke were a Protestant bishop and a Catholic archbishop. European and American Jews could not stop the refugees as they fled from Russia to neighboring lands. Europe's Jewish leaders set out to regulate the flow; they directed the immigrants to London, where the Mansion House Committee sent them on to New York. There the Hebrew Emigrant Aid Society took over and, in accordance with established policy, urged and helped the newcomers to move inland. Colonization was constantly preached; close settlement would offer Jews community life and thus hinder assimilation. There were, however, some Jews who believed that ghetto-like colonies would further clannishness and hinder Americanization. The United States government in the 1880's imposed no hindrances to the entrance of Jews—they were not criminals, paupers, or insane—although the authorities preferred farmers and craftsmen to petty businessmen. In this crisis of 1881-1882, the New York elite took over leadership, but was resentful that the Cincinnati based Union of American Hebrew Congregations, with its network of synagogs reaching to the Pacific, was doing so little. The leaders were angry also that Downtown Jews with means—and there were some—were not coming to the aid of their needy brethren.

Almost a decade later, rumors reached Jews in western Europe and America that Russia was about to initiate mass expulsions from certain large cities and territories outside the Pale of Settlement. International conferences of Jews were held to stop the impending evil; Jews appealed to President Harrison and Secretary of State James G. Blaine. The government, sympathetic, rehearsed the sufferings of the Jews by sending relevant documents to Congress; the Russians denied any contemplated action and then set out to expel thousands, primarily from Moscow. The expulsions took place in March, 1891, on the first two days of Passover. The exile from Egypt was again reenacted. In 1890, about 21,000 Russian Jews landed in the United States; the following year, after the dread decree, there were 43,000; in 1892, there were 64,000. Always apprehensive, American Jewry hastened to remind Washington that these were refugees for conscience' sake; they would be no burden to the state.

In a letter to the American minister to Russia, Charles Emory Smith, Secretary Blaine, long familiar with Russia's mistreatment of its Jewish subjects, pointed out that oppression drove Jews to America. The intimation was clear: we have to interfere when the actions of a foreign state directly affect us. The Secretary of State reminded the American minister that Russia's actions had driven 200,000 Jews to America in the course of a decade. It is true, he added, that they are thrifty, orderly and law-abiding. Blaine's letter was written on February 18, 1891; a month later, the Rev. William E. Blackstone, of Chicago, dispatched a petition to President Harrison suggesting that a conference of European nations be called to arrange for the transfer of Palestine to the Jews. Many of America's most distinguished Gentiles and Jews, including the country's Chief Justice, signed this document; they were eager to help Russia's Jews. In 1894, fully cognizant of what some of the nations were doing to the

Jews, Isaac Mayer Wise wrote: "the world has sinned more against the Jew than a hundred Christs could atone for on the cross." By the early 1890's Baron Maurice de Hirsch, World Jewry's most generous philanthropist, had come to the conclusion that the situation in Russia was hopeless. He knew the government would not move to accord equality to its Jews. Accordingly, he established two multimillion dollar funds to help Jews leave and carve out new lives for themselves. The Jewish Colonization Association (ICA) and the Baron de Hirsch Fund were both chartered in 1891. The ICA set out to colonize Jews permanently in South America; the Baron de Hirsch Fund was directed to aid East Europeans who settled in the United States, the new Promised Land.

Despite the repetitive bad experiences Jews had suffered at the hands of the Romanovs and their administrators, there were many in the United States who realized that, ultimately, the fate of the East Europeans would have to be resolved in their native lands. Immigration was no real answer; the masses would have to remain—and they did. After managing to get a visa to visit Russia, the entrepreneurial Rabbi Joseph Krauskopf suggested to the Russian Minister of Finance that the government give land to the Jews and establish colonies on them. They would become "tillers of the soil and honorable citizens." The rationale for this request? The United States is stricken by a panic; the congestion in the labor market must be relieved; Russian Jews would do well to remain at home and work out a new future for themselves.

By 1900, the situation in Rumania had worsened for Jews; some turned to America. In 1899, about 1,300 refugees had come here, but in the years 1900-1902 over 6,000 passed through America's ports annually. Leaders like Leo N. Levi, of the B'nai B'rith, Jacob H. Schiff, the banker, and Oscar S. Straus, the diplomat, felt compelled to take action. They knew of the history of protests made by preceding presidents ever since the days of Grant. The signatories to the Treaty of Berlin in 1878 had insisted on emancipation in Rumania. Because of the flagrant disregard of the provisions of the treaty, which had guaranteed the creation of the state of Rumania, and because Schiff, Straus, and their friends knew that the Great Powers had intervened in lands of oppression to further justice, these Jewish notables began to pressure Theodore Roosevelt and Secretary of State John Hay to take action. They supplied ample data to buttress their request and on July 17, 1902, Hay wrote a note, a copy of which was to be presented to the Great Powers. They were to be reminded of their promise that all the Balkan peoples would be given equality. As in the days of Blaine in 1891, the United States was interested because Rumania was driving its Jews to America. Abuse was forcing them to leave; Rumania was imposing a burden on this country. The signatories of the 1878 treaty had a moral and humane obligation to compel Rumania to live up to its solemn promises and free its Jews. The John Hay note of 1902 accomplished little, if anything. It was, of course, good policy for the Republicans. Though the note was not particularly flattering to Rumanian Jews, American Jews were elated. A rabbi in Evansville wrote a Hebrew letter congratulating the Secretary of State and promised to remember him in his prayers; later, Temple Keneseth Israel in Philadelphia dedicated a beautiful stained glass window in its new sanctuary to the memory of Hay. For many Jews, Hay was a hero, a high-minded statesman. In that generation, the Jews of this land were grateful for any recognition, for a kind word, for a nod in the direction of oppressed coreligionists.[11]

DIVERTING EAST EUROPEAN JEWS TO EUROPE AND TO PALESTINE

INTRODUCTION

The Jews of Central and Western Europe did not want to absorb the Russian, Polish, and Rumanian Jews who made their way westward. They looked upon them as inferiors; they were certainly different. Central and Western Europe's acculturated Jews always hoped—often in vain—that these aliens would remain where they were born or if they migrated they would keep on moving to the Americas, South or North. The Jews of Berlin, Paris, and London were always willing to further their departure. They did feel sorry for them; these unfortunates had to be helped. For Europe's Jews, America was the favorite dumping ground. Thus it was that when international conferences were held in the second half of the century, American Jews had to be coopted. The Americans sat in because they had no desire to be overwhelmed by émigrés; theirs was a small community; they had neither the means nor the wish to cope with the huge charitative task that faced them. Writing to rabbinical colleagues in Eastern Europe, Chief Rabbi Nathan Marcus Adler of England begged them to stop immigration to his country; English Jewry could not afford to support the newcomers. The Jews of Eastern Europe paid no attention to this appeal and continued coming until the gates began closing slowly upon them in the Aliens Act of 1905. When the Russians and Poles began arriving in the United States in the 1880's, they were looked upon as a burden: What are we going to do with them![12]

DIVERTING IMMIGRANTS TO PALESTINE

By the 1870's, the Russians and other Slavic Jews had begun to find their way to Palestine. They built colonies in the 1880's supported by European Jews of traditional bent, by the rising Lovers of Zion, by philanthropists like the Rothschilds and Baron de Hirsch, and by a number of European welfare agencies. Western Europe's Jews, people of culture, were always ready to divert newcomers to the Holy Land. Practically all European Jews were at least nominally Orthodox; Palestine was the Promised Land. Many hoped that the newcomers would till the soil there; hard work would bring physical prowess and moral redemption—a philosophy that was soon to be adopted by Aaron David Gordon, who settled in Palestine in 1904. The building of colonies by these newcomers was watched closely by Isaac Mayer Wise from his vantage point in Cincinnati. By the 1890's, he feared that colonization might lead to the establishment of a sovereign state, which frightened him, implying as it did that Jews in the emancipated lands did not value their newly gained citizenship. Colonies, Wise maintained, were not really necessary; all Jews everywhere would ultimately be free, although he suspected that equality in Russia would come only through revolution. Like his fellow American Jews, he did not envisage this country as the new homeland for the refugees, but diversion to Palestine failed; the land was poor; the Turks at best were unsympathetic. Prospective immigrants from the Slavic lands knew full well that America was their best hope.[13]

MANIFESTATIONS OF HOSTILITY TOWARD EAST EUROPEAN JEWS BY THEIR FELLOW JEWS

Ever since the 1880's, the masses fleeing Eastern Europe had refused to be diverted; they came to the United States. Their reception here was not always a friendly one, neither from the government nor from the established Jewish communities. Many among the native-born Jews and the naturalized Central Europeans disliked and feared the incoming horde. Wise, in one of his frequent exuberant moments, said that the immigrants were dirty, ignorant, and superstitious. The earlier Jewish settlers here looked askance at these newcomers; their language and religious customs were deemed exotic and unacceptable. They were poor, without much secular education. The leaders of the new labor unions were radicals. The masses were slow to acculturate, to Americanize, so it was said. In short, they were East Europeans. It certainly did not occur to the Jews ensconced here that the refugees looked upon the established Jews, especially the Reformers, with dismay as little better than Gentiles with their English sermons and their ignorance of Hebrew. Sacrilegiously, they had introduced family pews where men and women sat together; they played the organ on the holy Sabbath while a Gentile choir sang church-like hymns; they disregarded the traditional head covering, discarded the prayer shawl, and ate forbidden foods. This savored of the abomination that desolateth. In short, the hostility of the "Germans" was reciprocated by the "Russians." Rabbi A. J. Ash vigorously attacked a Downtown congregation because it had invited the Reformer, Kaufmann Kohler, to address it (1884). Rabbi Eppstein, of Kansas City, deplored the unwillingness of B'nai B'rith to charter a lodge for the newcomers, but also pointed out that the very East Europeans who attacked the Reformers kept their shops open on the Sabbath. The Russian intellectuals who hobnobbed with the Yiddish playwright Jacob Gordin despised the American Jews and their strange way of life. When the Russians and the natives first encountered one another, there was something of a mutual culture shock. In reality, the Jews here now formed two disparate communities.[14]

In manifesting hostility toward newcomers, the Jews established here were following a traditional American pattern. Catholics were pogrommed in Boston in 1834 and Philadelphia in 1844; anti-Catholic prejudice was still strong and prevalent. Catholics were hated as the Jews in this land have never been hated. (Even the Irish Catholics and the German Catholics disliked one another.) Ever since the seventeenth century, Jews here have looked dubiously at later Jewish arrivals. This attitude of hostility to new Jewish immigrants dates from medieval, if not earlier, generations. In 1266, the Jewish community of Canterbury, England, had enacted ordinances to keep out Jews deemed undesirable; Spanish refugees fleeing for their lives in 1492 received a hostile reception in some Italian towns; the Sephardim in eighteenth-century Bordeaux despised the Jews from Avignon; London's respectable Jews worked closely with the authorities to hinder the entrance of Jews from the Continent. Here in the United States, Hazzan Seixas, of New York, expressed a mild contempt for some of the German newcomers; by 1801, the Germans of Philadelphia had established the first permanent Ashkenazic synagog in this country. These aliens had probably not been made welcome by the neo-Sephardim and so wanted to be on their own.

In the New York of the 1840's, Russian Jews, along with intermarried Jews, were not welcome in the Polish-German Shaarey Zedek. Joseph Jonas, of Cincinnati, thought that some of the German newcomers in his Queen City of the West were rude, bigoted, and superstitious. National, regional, and ethnic prejudices were common enough among Europe's Jews who luxuriated in mutual detestations. The Western and Southern German Jews cordially disliked the East German Jews, whom they dubbed Polacks because those Prussian provinces had once been Polish. By the 1840's and 1880's, the attacks on the Poles were already virulent: the Poles were filthy; Czar Nicholas was justified in oppressing the Russian Jews, a nauseating lot. As early as 1881, Henry Gersoni, a Russian Jew, had written a pamphlet on Jewish sectional prejudice; he called it *Jew Against Jew*.[15]

By the 1880's, when the Jews from the Slavic lands were very much in evidence, the acerbities became intense. In 1882, Simon Wolf, truly a decent individual and a devoted communal worker, assured a group of Jewish leaders that the newcomers could be raised "to the full stature of manhood as are negroes of the South." Cultured "Russian" Jewish women were, it would seem, not invited to join the "German" controlled Council of Jewish Women. There were native-born Jewish families in which marriage to a Christian was held preferable to marriage to an East European Jew; Julia Richman, District Superintendent of Schools in New York City, believed that pushcart owners on the East Side who violated city ordinances ought to be deported. According to Isaac M. Wise, the Jews from Eastern Europe were half civilized; he and his kind were Americans; the Eastern Jews were not. Milwaukee Jews were shaken when 400 émigrés descended on them. The entire Jewish community there numbered but 3,000 souls: these strangers are a potential danger which threatens us! One of the 400 who landed in 1882 had been mobbed in Odessa; he brought with him a three-year-old boy who grew up to become a rabbi at New York's Temple Emanu-El, the largest, most prestigious, and wealthiest Jewish congregation in the world.

The German-oriented B'nai B'rith lodges wrestled with the problem of admitting East Europeans. Some lodges accepted them as members; others rejected them; on occasion, they were even denied charters for a lodge of their own. Even so, there were always members who resented the discrimination against fellow Jews. This prejudice of Jew against Jew was to persist well beyond World War I; Christians sneered at Jews, and Jews, in turn, rejected one another. Moreover, there were ascending and descending degrees of "aristocracy" among the East Europeans themselves. Very little love was lost between Lithuanians, Russians, Poles, Galicians, Hungarians, and Rumanians. What these East European Jews all had in common was their geographical provenance, their recent arrival, and their rejection by earlier settlers. Judge Samuel I. Roseman, distinguished adviser to Franklin D. Roosevelt and one of the most influential men in the New Deal, was born in San Antonio, Texas, to East European parents. He refused to visit the city because he could never forget the prejudice to which he had been exposed in his childhood by other Jews.[16]

REASONS FOR HOSTILITY

There were almost as many reasons for hostility toward the newcomers as there were established settlers among the native-born and the acculturated Central Europeans. The older settlers did not want these immigrants because they were truly frightened. The reasons they gave reflect their own insecurities. Most of the objections offered had no basis in fact: these new immigrants don't want to work; they will exhaust our philanthropic resources; their synagogs won't affiliate with the Union of American Hebrew Congregations; they speak Yiddish, a "piggish jargon"; they live in ghettos—which the Germans had just left; they look different and dress differently; they have too much visibility; they are unionists, strikers, socialists; they are foreigners, proletarians, members of the lower middle class. In the main, they were poor, and poverty was a virtue in the Psalms, but not in the America of the Gilded Age. As the older settlers saw it, if there was anti-Semitism in the United States—and there was—it was due to these newcomers! Most Christians were disinclined to be philo-Semitic; they simply didn't like Jews; native-born Jews and their naturalized coreligionists aped the Christians in this prejudice against the new arrivals. The Germans deemed themselves aristocrats and feared their non-Jewish neighbors would identify them with undesirable foreigners. These Russians, Poles, and Rumanians—the old-timers believed—are slow to throw off their European ways and become good Americans; they will Russify us; they reflect no credit on us; they threaten our hard won status. (The Germans themselves were, after all, a rising middle-class group struggling for recognition.) These new arrivals have to be taught English; they need to read the Constitution—whatever that meant.[17]

RELIEF

Perhaps the caustic, cruel, and mean remarks made by Jews against Jews in the last quarter of the nineteenth century should not be taken too literally or too seriously. Despite frequent indictments of the new immigrants by communities and individuals, the newcomers were given help; the East Coast communities fought zealously to save individuals from deportation. Rabbi Max Landsberg, of Rochester, felt he had "nothing in common with those people," yet worked strenuously to save refugees threatened with deportation. Writing in his diary in 1905, David Philipson, the arch nativist, prophesied that "the future of Judaism in America will lie in the hands of the Russian Jews." Keeping one's distance socially is not necessarily a manifestation of animosity. The very individual who denigrated Jews from Slavic lands did not refuse to aid them when the need rose. As an agent for the B'nai B'rith and the Reform-funded Board of Delegates on Civil and Religious Rights, Simon Wolf in Washington fought valiantly to help all Jews. Kaufmann Kohler was no great friend of the East Europeans, but in his 1885 Pittsburgh Platform address he stressed the need to aid the newcomers.

Like Philipson, many realized very early that the future of American Jewry lay with these invaders from Russia and Poland. Rabbi Adolph Moses, an old nineteenth-century liberal and revolutionary, once said that these new Jews were different, but that their grandchildren would be teaching at the universities. They fooled him—in only one generation, their children graced chairs at American colleges. In the 1890's, Dr. Aaron Friedenwald, of Baltimore, predicted accurately that the newcomers would rule American Jewry in the course of the next fifty years. At a memorial address for the elite Jesse Seligman, Friedenwald made this statement: "You are different than these Poles and these Russians, tell that to the Christians. The Christian will listen to you and he'll go away having contempt for you, a contempt which you deserve." The aristocrat Emma Lazarus referred to the arriving refugees as the "teeming refuse of your shores," but she helped them personally, visiting them in the barracks where they were housed on arrival. A New York Jew wept when he saw the plight of the incoming immigrants: "These men, women and children are hunted down like wolves for no other crime than being of the same faith as myself." Then he wrote a check and went out to hunt jobs for them.

As early as 1869, Rabbi Bernhard Felsenthal, of Chicago, scholar and gentleman, welcomed the coming of the Russian emigrants. Not a few befriended the exiles in the 1880's. Individual Christians were on occasion more understanding of the Russians than the Jewish elite. Lincoln Steffens, the reformer, journalist, and muckraker, was sympathetic to the Orthodox Jews of the Lower East Side, as was Hutchins Hapgood, the author of the widely read classic, *The Spirit of the Ghetto.* Hapgood once almost lost his job as a reporter because he reproached an influential Uptown Jewish woman who resented his preference for the Downtown Jews. Emma Lazarus was not the only friend of the newcomers among New York's Jewish elite. The immigrants had their protagonists in almost every town of size. These included Henrietta Szold, Jacob H. Schiff, and Louis Marshall as well as Moritz Ellinger, the editor, Moritz Loth, the head of the Union of American Hebrew Congregations, and Benjamin Franklin Peixotto, the former consul to Rumania.

Henrietta Szold, Baltimore school teacher and future founder of Hadassah, opened a night school for the incoming aliens; in Philadelphia, there were friendly, earnest, hardworking social workers like Louis E. Levy, Simon Muhr, Alfred T. Jones, and the redoubtable Rabbi Sabato Morais. Speaking of the Russians, the rabbi said: Their misery is our misery, their oppression is our oppression, their freedom and happiness will be ours. Few, if any, of the established Jews did more than Michael Heilprin (1823-1888) to aid those who fled from Europe. Heilprin, the son of a scholarly father, had been born in Poland but educated in Hungary, where, like his father, he supported Kossuth, the revolutionary. After stays in France and England, he came to the United States in 1856 and was soon recognized as a scholar of encyclopedic knowledge. At home in twelve languages, he taught in the schools of Philadelphia's Hebrew Education Society, helped edit Appleton's *New American Cyclopaedia* and wrote for *The Nation* in the 1860's. In 1879 and 1880 Heilprin wrote his two-volume *The Historical Poetry of the Ancient Hebrew*; his approach was critical, reflecting the new scholarship then so popular and influential in Central European universities. Devoting himself tirelessly to the welfare of the East European newcomers, he was particularly interested in settling them on the soil. Heilprin was not affiliated with any established Jewish organizations; as a liberal, he went his own way but it was he who prepared the memorandum that probably influenced Baron de Hirsch to establish his American fund.

The old-timers "huffed and puffed," but they helped. Whether wholeheartedly or not, they had rallied ever since the late 1860's to aid the East Europeans who settled in the United States. Why were the newcomers helped? Because they were Jews, because of the concept of noblesse oblige and because of fear of what the Gentiles might say if the immigrants were thrown on the mercy of the general charities. The anti-Semitism of the Gilded Age made the Jews afraid not to take care of their own. Aiding émigrés was a religious tradition, an admonition, a mitzvah going back for centuries, if not millennia. The Jews of Central and Western Europe had been called upon to succor the Poles and Russians who fled westward after the Cossack massacres of 1648. The Jews in Amsterdam set up a society in the 1600's to support impoverished Poles and Germans. Here in the United States, German immigrants were assisted during the hard times that followed Andrew Jackson's administration; in 1849, Rabbi Aaron Guenzburg established a Support Society for Israelitish Emigrants. "I am," he said, "a modest beggar"; he asked for only two cents a week for his clients: the people need help; they have just arrived in the steerage after weeks and months on board ship; they are bereft of means, know no English, and have no friends—he wrote, appealing for the Central European foreigners.

A society to help newly arrived immigrants had been established in Philadelphia toward the end of the Revolutionary War. Crises brought new organizations to aid new arrivals. In 1873, New York's concerned Jews created an association to relieve Rumanians who sought refuge here. It is interesting to note—and it must be stressed—that American Jewish leaders knew that, when they rallied to the help of Jews both here and abroad, they were depriving their own cultural institutions of sorely needed means. It is also of significance that Jews now turned to the Christians and asked them to help in this task of aiding distressed newcomers. Wealthy, established Jewish communities in Europe had raised substantial funds to assist Jews in flight since the late 1860's, but it is by no means improbable that American Jewry, small in numbers, gave more than the communities across the Atlantic. Most Jews who arrived in this land had some money, if only a paltry few dollars; nearly all, it would seem, had relatives or friends, who met them, took them out of Castle Garden, and comforted them in their first days on these shores. It is difficult to determine how many turned at once to the charities and how long it was before they were able to fend for themselves. Extrapolating from reports of the established Jewish philanthropic societies, one can infer that very few remained on the charity rosters for years.

The welfare problems of the American Jewish community became numerous and challenging, particularly in the 1880's and 1890's when fresh persecutions drove thousands of Russians to America. In the autumn of 1881, when American Jews finally pulled themselves together and prepared to cope with the needs of the émigrés from pogrom-ridden Russia, the Union of American Hebrew Congregations urged rabbis to appeal to their congregants to aid the displaced persons. The Union hoped to settle many of them in the South and the West. A Russian Relief Fund was set up with Jacob H. Schiff as treasurer, working out of New York where most emigrants landed. Schiff's involvement is an intimation that the New Yorkers were ready to take over the leadership of this necessary philanthropic task; the Union, with Cincinnati as its center, could not cope with the problem. In the winter, a new American Jewish organization was called into being to supervise the job of making provision for the refugees from the czarist lands. The new association called itself the Hebrew Emigrant Aid Society (HEAS). The name was apparently borrowed from the New England Emigrant Aid Society, which sought in 1854 to settle antislavery forces in Kansas, a war-torn territory. The New England Emigrant Aid Society came with rifles; the HEAS came with bread. Both were interested in colonization. The HEAS set out to put immigrants to work in industry; for apologetic reasons, however, it was very eager to settle the exiles on farms or in colonies. It was not long before branches of the society were set up in many large towns.

The HEAS was, in essence, a removal organization to supervise the distribution of the refugees into the hinterland. Only pogrom victims were to be helped; incoming paupers were not welcomed. In the course of a few months, in 1881-1882, several thousands were aided and large sums were expended. Newcomers—many of them skilled artisans—were provided with jobs. Some of the men and families shipped west were returned by uncooperative communities. The HEAS was indignant: these people are the victims of brutal persecution; don't send them back to us; help them. Obsessed by the desire to colonize them, American Jews allotted sums to colonies established in Louisiana, Colorado, and New Jersey. On the whole, with the possible exception of the farming groups in New Jersey, these attempts to colonize the refugees were egregious failures.

On June 4, 1882, at a national meeting of the agencies and individuals who helped the newcomers, Moritz Loth of the Union of American Hebrew Congregations suggested that a nationwide agricultural society be created to put the Russians on the soil. He respected the immigrants, they were good Hebraists. Simon Wolf of Washington asked the Europeans to provide more money; the Americans he reminded them had always been liberal supporting causes sponsored by European Jewish charities. It was suggested that the United States government be asked for funds; it was pointed out that, among others, President Arthur's Secretary of State, Frederick Theodore Frelinghuysen, James G. Blaine, and Congressman James Brown Belfor of Colorado had been helpful. Thinking the crisis was over, the HEAS disbanded in 1883; its work was taken over by New York's federation, the United Hebrew Charities. There was still much to be done; anywhere from about 20,000 to about 40,000 Jews arrived annually after 1883. To be sure, most of these people required guidance, but little or no relief.[18]

RELIEF IN THE HINTERLAND

New York was, of course, the chief port of entry in the 1800's, but many debarked in other coastal towns, particularly Philadelphia. The "Russians" who settled in the City of Brotherly Love were determined to help themselves. Led by Jacob Judelsohn (d. 1891), a Russian who had arrived in the States in 1879, they set up an Association of Jewish Immigrants in 1884; it was soon taken over and administered by the earlier settlers led by Alfred T. Jones and Louis E. Levy, selfsacrificing communal workers and leaders. Why the East Europeans surrendered the reins is not known. Moses Dropsie, a distinguished and rich lawyer, a devotee of the French Alliance Israélite Universelle, aided the new welfare group. For many years, this organization engaged the services of Moses Klein, a scholar and linguist, who met the steamers and helped the arriving Jews. Years later, the society was eager to offer advice and aid to women in order to protect them from the advances of white slavers. Though this Association of Jewish Immigrants worked closely with the United Hebrew Charities of Philadelphia, it had a large diversified program of its own. Assistance was granted those threatened with deportation. Provided were a hospice for the newly arrived, an employment bureau, classes in English and civics, matzo and kosher wine for the observant, passes on the railroads for migrants moving west and south. By the early 1890's, prominent East Europeans like Dr. Charles D. Spivak and Rabbi Bernard L. Levinthal were invited to join the board. Inclusion of East Europeans on the board testifies to their increasing importance; they were being accepted as equals.

About six years after Judelsohn established the Association of Jewish Immigrants, the East Europeans of Philadelphia once more organized a self-help society called the Jewish Alliance of America (1890-1891). In all probability, it was established to assist Russians who came to this country after the massive expulsions of 1891. This was to be a national organization to aid in the dispatch of newcomers to different parts of the United States and, like the HEAS, put them into factories and on farms.

Unfortunately, this ambitious attempt of the East Europeans to help themselves enjoyed but a short life. Within a year, it was merged into a New York organization, a new society which accomplished little if anything. The East Europeans would not create vigorous, viable self-help societies until after the turn of the century. It would take almost a generation before they were able to stand on their own. New York, which always bore the brunt of assistance to newcomers, never hesitated to ask Jewish communities everywhere for assistance. As early as the 1870's, San Francisco responded to an appeal made to it. In 1881, a lodge in Buffalo took the lead in coopting other Jewish lodges in town to help raise funds; the Cincinnatians—solid and philanthropic—fitted out twenty-three households for refugee families that arrived that year; rent was paid, coal and food provided for all. Baltimore had trouble. Apparently, some of the displaced persons could find no jobs or were unemployable. When the decision was made to return them to Russia, a communal leader arose, recited the sacrosanct Jewish call to prayer, "Hear O Israel," and thus induced his auditors to reconsider their decision. The Milwaukeans were no doubt taken aback to discover that some of the refugees they found on their doorsteps spoke Russian, English, French, and German as well as Yiddish; these were not barbarians. Nashville Jews turned to their Christian neighbors and asked them to join in the humanitarian challenge.

The crisis of 1881-1882 was followed by a period of relative quiet. When in 1890-1891 the Russian authorities returned to their vomit, the charitative organizations had again to be reestablished in towns and cities in the country. In Washington, the national capital, a Russian Refugee Fund was organized and, apparently, to raise money for it, a Gentile professor from Georgetown College Law School was asked to make an address, "The Origin of Civil Liberty or the World's Indebtedness to Israel." Atlanta's synagog opened a school in its basement to teach English and provided a burial lot for a bereaved immigrant family. There can be little question that common efforts to assist hapless Jews intensified the sense of Jewish identity and made for unity; they were all working together for a common cause. Thousands upon thousands of dollars were doled out in the 1880's and 1890's for the exiles. A hundred years later, still faced by crises, American Jews responded generously. This time they raised billions.[19]

ACCEPTANCE OF THE NEWCOMERS

The earlier settlers learned—slowly, to be sure—that they would have to accept the fact that the "Russians" would not stop coming. In the course of time—and this took years—the charities organized themselves to live with this flood. Financial help was also forthcoming from the funds provided by Baron de Hirsch, monies which were not inconsequential. By the 1890's, the European Jewish communities were well equipped to speed the immigrants from the Russian and Polish borders to the German or English ports of embarkation. Migration activities in the several European countries were coordinated. Travelers were supplied with clothing, medicine, kosher food, and information. They were even given new names, German and English, to initiate them into America's Anglo-Saxon world. The 1903 Kishinev massacre was a devastating shock; clearly the twentieth century had not seen the end of medievalism. Now few could doubt that there was no hope abroad; this final conviction was reinforced by the massacres of 1905 and the years following.

Social integration here? Well, that was a different story. Some attempts were made to fuse the two groups, the older and the newer; such efforts were rare and unsuccessful. Back in 1882, Rabbi Adolph Moses of Louisville had expressed the hope that these "half-civilized" people would stay at home; he was speaking for most of his fellow Jews. That same year, the astute Isaac M. Wise told his readers in the *American Israelite* that, once the newcomers made a living here, they would adopt American ways; liberty works miracles; the children, going to public and Sabbath schools, would become Americanized—but these Russians would have to give up their East European forms of religion! Let the sons of these newcomers go to the Hebrew Union College and become the new leaders of the Russians. Actually, this is what happened, but it took three generations before the change was finally effectual. The numerous second-generation Litvaks, Polacks, and Galicians who were ordained in Cincinnati became classical Reformers; they had no sympathy for shtetl ceremonialism; their children, however, moving to the right, donned prayer shawls and skullcaps in the decades after World War II. By that time the East Europeans, educated and often wealthy, had compelled the Germans to accept the dictates of the first American Jewish Congress active in 1915-1920: the Jews of Eastern Europe were entitled to minority rights; Palestine must become a Jewish homeland. Nothing succeeds like success.[20]

CHAPTER TWO

DISPERSAL AND COLONIES

INTRODUCTION

In a sense, the history of British North America, the United States, and American Jewry, too, is the recital of the coming of immigrants and refugees down to the year 1924 when the gates were closed. These gates were opened frequently after that to tolerate, though not to welcome, newcomers from Mexico, the Caribbean World, and post-World War II Europe. American roots reach back to the English, Dutch, and Swedish settlements of the seventeenth century. Sectarian colonies, refugees for conscience' sake were then established on this continent. For well over a century, new communes were planted here, secular and religious, utopian and reform. In many respects, early America was a colony continent. Even Jews came here occasionally as colonists. The twenty-three refugees who created this continent's first Jewish colony, landed at New Amsterdam in 1654. When they disembarked, there was but one confessing Jew in the village. What was his reaction to the arrival of twenty-three fellow Jews in Ultima Thule, a village of fewer than 1,000? His lonely days were over. Thousands of East European Jews had been on the road since the middle of the seventeenth century; indeed, with the advent of mercantilism and the new industrialism, Jews everywhere were moving about. The trend was westward, even transatlantic; a large Jewish community rose in Dutch Brazil, and when Recife fell to the Portuguese, some of the exiles sailing north, sought refuge in Stuyvesant's New Amsterdam. As new English colonies were founded in the eighteenth century, English Jews and Gentiles, too, talked of settling Jews in North America; a colony of Spanish-Portuguese and German Jews landed at Savannah in 1733 only a few months after Oglethorpe. Fifty years later, a German magazine published a letter, addressed to the United States Congress, asking for permission to establish an enclave of 2,000 German Jewish families on American soil. (This was only a ploy to incite German

Gentiles to emancipate Jews, so that they would not be compelled to leave Prussia.)

Beginning with 1816, there was no decade in American history in which Jewish colonies were not projected or actually established. Colonization was an expedient whereby immigrants established themselves in or were diverted to the interior by earlier residents. From about the year 1816 into the next decade, Moses E. Levy, land promoter and religious visionary, played with the idea of settling Jews in Florida. Two or three years later, Mordecai Noah, America's best known Jewish layman, began talking of establishing a Jewish colony in New York State. After the 1819 anti-Jewish riots in Germany, William David Robinson urged Europe's Jewish philanthropists to colonize Jews in the New World; Christian missionaries now prepared to plant a Jewish-Christian agricultural commune in this country; a Hessian Jew urged the Rothschilds to finance a farm colony on American soil in 1832, and the irrepressible Heine looked forward to that Passover when Jewish newcomers would chew their unleavened bread on the banks of the Mississippi.

German Jews began emigrating to the United States in substantial numbers in the late 1830's. They arrived just in time to be engulfed by the post-Jacksonian panic of 1837. For the New York Jewish community of fewer than 10,000 souls, the need to provide for impoverished immigrants in an economic depression was something of a minor calamity. Colonies were the answer: help them establish themselves on the land where they can provide for themselves; get them out of town. Two colonial projects were proposed that year. Orthodox Solomon H. Jackson and Congregation Anshe Chesed, the Men of Love, wanted to ship these strangers out West where they could set up a colony. Living as a group, they would be able to practice their faith and be spared the impact of the assimilatory environment. Nonobservant Jews, Sabbath violators, intermarried families would not be tolerated in this proposed enclave. They called themselves the Tender Sheep, *Zeire Ha-Zon* ("The Helpless Ones," Jer. 49:20; 50:45), but their colony was never established: New York's congregations refused to work together. That same year, a colony was organized and located in Ulster County near the town of Wawarsing. The founders called it Sholem (Sholam, Sholom), Peace. It was small; there were fewer than fifteen settlers, but they had a congregation, a cemetery, and a synagog, called the Covenant Observers, Shomre Ha-Brit. They hoped to make a living; they were not too far from the busy Delaware and Hudson Canal. They farmed and manufactured goose quills and fur caps, but they were not destined to survive. By the early 1840's, the colonists had begun drifting away; their lands were sold to satisfy their creditors. They had little capital; they were given little aid. Colonists need help; American communities then and later were not prepared to advance the large sums needed to tide these communes over till they became self-supporting.[1]

DISPERSAL AND COLONIZATION

In the 1840's, the country was expanding to the West; people began to cross the Mississippi and to create new states. American and World Jewry knew what was going on; there were millions of acres to be tilled, cities and towns to be built. Throughout the 1840's, 1850's, and 1860's, there was talk of Jews from the United States and Europe establishing autonomous colonies and communes in the endless expanses that fascinated the pioneers. The harsh decrees of Nicholas I of Russia (1825-1855) shocked and aroused the Jews of Europe and America. Something had to be done. In 1840, a Berlin publication called for a colony in the American West; in 1843 Julius Stern, an American, wanted an agro-industrial "borough" where Jews could live a life of their own; that same year William Renau, a B'nai B'rith devotee, urged Jews to return to the soil. A handful heeded his words and farmed in Cook County—the beginning of what was soon to be the Chicago Jewish community.

Throughout the 1840's, Europe's Jews looked to America. Gabriel Riesser, German Jewry's militant emancipator, was exceptional. He was not interested in emigration as a solution for the rightlessness which still characterized the Jews in most European states. European Jewry faced a problem which would constantly recur: shall we fight for emancipation at home or take refuge in flight to the New World. Riesser was of course an emancipator. Ludwig Philipson, editor of the prestigious *Allgemeine Zeitung des Judenthums*, saw America as the haven of the oppressed. Texas loomed large in the 1830's; it was then a free republic; in the 1840's it became part of the United States. A Texas pioneer, Michael Seeligson (Seligson), invited the Jews to settle on his land along the Medina River. This was purely a business deal. He assured them that, if a group settled on his land, it would be able to muster a quorum and hold services. Seeligson later served briefly as mayor of Galveston; his descendants still live in Texas, but as Christians. Leeser, too, thought of Texas, though he encouraged Jews to come here and settle anywhere in the Middle West and South. He approved of farming; farms could well serve as agricultural schools. A Galician in 1848 dreamt that ultimately a separate Jewish state might be established on these shores; Russian Jews would certainly welcome such a polity, for it would enable them to maintain their Orthodoxy in all its purity.

The 1850's was a decade when nativism and xenophobia were fervent. Is it possible that some Jews preached the gospel of close settlement, colonies, farm enclaves, as havens where they could effectually escape the hatred against foreigners? It is by no means improbable that pushing new-comers to settle on farms reflected a desire to disperse them, to maintain a low profile, to lighten the load of the charities, to solve the problems created by depression and displacement in an age of burgeoning industrialism. Uriah P. Levy made a will in which he envisaged turning his Virginia estate—formerly Jefferson's Monticello—into a nondenominational agricultural school for Jewish and Christian orphans.

A man named Simon Berman had elaborate plans in the 1850's and 1860's to put Jews on the soil; B'nai B'rith continued to press for a Jewish peasantry. In 1855, the American Hebrew Agricultural and Horticultural Association was established, a German Jewish society meant to serve unemployed German Jews and the constant stream of immigrants, most of whom arrived with almost nothing in their purses. There was not a decade until 1900 that was not plagued by disastrous panics and depressions. A "Hebrew" society started out as a stock company hoping to raise enough money to establish a colony near New York City which would serve as its market for flowers, vegetables, poultry, wool, cattle, and silk. There would be a synagog, of course; the building could double as an agricultural school. Propaganda was made by Dr. Sigismund Waterman (Wasserman) and his B'nai B'rith friends in a pamphlet, *A Call to Establish a Hebrew Agricultural Society*. Again, nothing was done, although the failure of every colony projected does not seem to have discouraged other promoters. Farming was good for the Jews—this was the consensus of urban B'nai B'rith and a host of others, but there were some, not many, who raised their voices in protest: crafts and commerce, too, are honorable vocations.

FARMING, 1869-1880

The interest in putting Jews on the farm, so typical of American Jewry in the 1840's and 1850's, did not abate in the 1860's. From our vantage point, on the eve of the twenty-first century, this fascination with the soil seems strange. It is important, therefore, to call to mind constantly that most Americans were still farmers; the urban dwellers were in the minority. Farming, a basic vocation, was stimulated in the 1850's by the Homestead Act, which gave free land to almost anyone, and by the Morrill Act, which endowed schools of higher learning, especially agricultural colleges. Even before the passage of the Morrill Act, Jewish leaders were hammering away at the necessity of an establishment to teach farming to Jews. The goal was finally achieved in the 1890's, when two such schools were established. One of Missouri's leading Jews, a St. Louis synagog president and a state legislator, Meyer Friede, offered free land to Jewish settlers in 1860; he had German Jews in mind, since the Russians were yet to arrive in large numbers.

Jews were despised because they trafficked in merchandise. This was the sort of publicity that frightened Jews and induced them to urge their coreligionists to go back to the soil. In 1865, Rabbi Maurice Fluegel, a scholarly gentleman, urged Europe's Jews to come here and turn to farming and industry. The rabbi hoped that, with the aid of B'nai B'rith and European worthies, a Jewish immigration society would be set up to bring over hundreds of thousands of "Oriental" (East European) Jews. Succoring and Americanizing these aliens would be a patriotic act; Jewry in the United States would increase its numbers and its group influence. Jewish children would be sent back across the Atlantic as missionaries and teachers to salvage East European Jewry culturally and spiritually. All this, of course, was just talk, but appeals like Fluegel's enable the historians of today to understand the hopes of that generation, a generation that had not yet emancipated itself psychically. It was very difficult, after almost a thousand years of European disabilities, for Jews to assume a posture of self-respect and to maintain that commerce was just as productive as farming.[2]

As the Jewish population of the United States increased after the Civil War, there was a proportionate increase in the number of poor. Providing for them was a constant concern and challenge. Famine and cholera in western Russia brought a surge of new immigrants. The answer to both problems—care for the native-born poor and for the incoming impoverished from Eastern Europe—was the same. In the long generation from the 1830's to 1881 there was but one solution, so the established community thought, to these difficulties: dispatch the newcomers west; put them behind the plough. Even as late as 1860, less than one-half of the United States was settled and cultivated. With the exception of California and Washington State, all the land west of Iowa, Missouri, and Arkansas was frontier territory. It would still be half a generation before Custer died on the Rosebud. Colonization and agriculture occupied the minds of most American Jews until, in 1900, Baron de Hirsch's money made it possible to organize the Jewish Agricultural and Industrial Aid Society. There were Jewish homesteaders in Madison County, Nebraska, in the late 1860's. Two of these pioneers went out in a blizzard to feed their cattle in the barn, a few feet from their cabin. They lost their bearings and were soon frozen to death; it took an axe to chop off the ice from the body of one of them. In 1869, San Francisco's Jews, brash and eager, volunteered to raise money to help newcomers, but who would transport them across the country?

In 1872, Rumanians began arriving, only a handful to be sure. Solomon Franklin of Pine Bluff, Arkansas, was willing to take them on as sharecroppers, but the Jews in the East shied away from his proposal. Black sharecroppers, they knew, were anything but prosperous. By 1876,

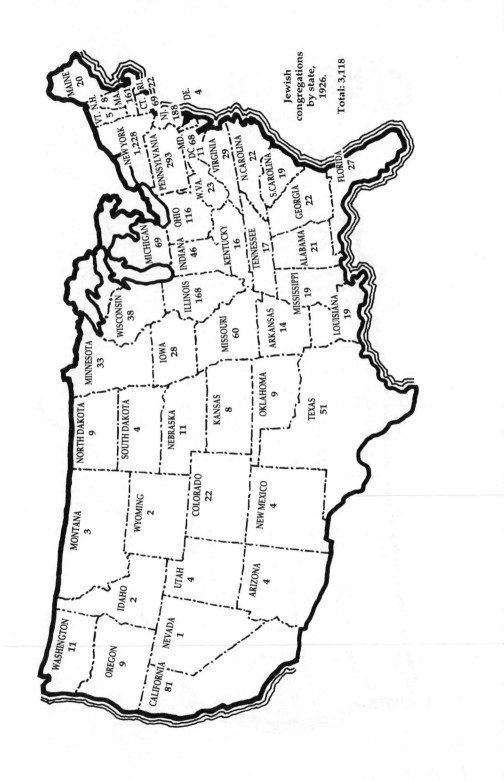

Jewish congregations by state, 1926.

Total: 3,118

MAINE 20
VT. 5 N.H. 8 MA. 161 CT. 69 R.I. 22
NEW YORK 1,228
NJ. 188 DE. 4
PENNSYLVANIA 293
MD. 68 DC 11
W.VA. 23 VIRGINIA 29
N.CAROLINA 22
S.CAROLINA 19
FLORIDA 27
GEORGIA 22
OHIO 116
MICHIGAN 69
INDIANA 46
KENTUCKY 16
TENNESSEE 17
ALABAMA 21
ILLINOIS 168
WISCONSIN 38
MISSISSIPPI 19
MISSOURI 60
ARKANSAS 14
LOUISIANA 19
MINNESOTA 33
IOWA 28
SOUTH DAKOTA 4
NORTH DAKOTA 9
NEBRASKA 11
KANSAS 8
OKLAHOMA 9
TEXAS 51
MONTANA 3
WYOMING 2
COLORADO 22
NEW MEXICO 4
IDAHO 2
UTAH 4
ARIZONA 4
WASHINGTON 11
OREGON 9
NEVADA 1
CALIFORNIA 81

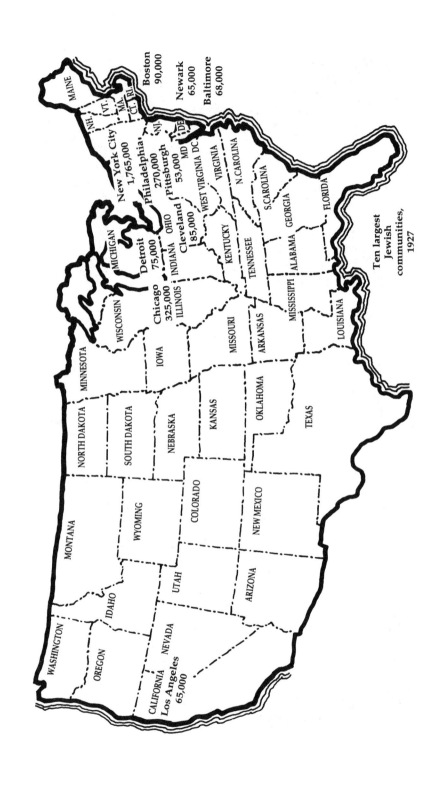

Ten largest Jewish communities, 1927

New York City 1,765,000
Chicago 325,000
Philadelphia 270,000
Boston 90,000
Cleveland 85,000
Detroit 75,000
Baltimore 68,000
Newark 65,000
Los Angeles 65,000
Pittsburgh 53,000

the Union of American Hebrew Congregations, the largest organization of its type, addressed itself seriously to the economic needs of the natives and the incoming refugees. Palestine, it realized, was no solution for the East Europeans. To deal with the problem, the Agricultural Pursuits Committee was established; some of the best men in the country were appointed members. New York soon set up a group of its own to put newcomers on the land. There were still doubting Thomases in the congregational Union, people who thought that urban jobs and an Americanization program were called for; the majority, however, could think only of farming as a solution. Apologetics always played a part in attacking all problems. What will the Gentiles think if we do not take care of our own? The elite was sensitive to Judeophobia; there was an outburst of social discrimination in New York State in 1877 and 1879, when Jews were denied admission to summer resorts. Money was needed to settle people, large sums; American Jews appealed to the B'nai B'rith, to the Alliance Israélite Universelle in Paris, to Montefiore in London. They probably got little aid from these foreign sources and had few, if any, successes here.[3]

DISPERSING THE 1881 REFUGEES

The charity needs of the social agencies seem to have increased in 1881. Polish immigration statistics for 1880 and 1881 show a huge increase; after the pogroms of 1881 Russian emigration to this country more than tripled. Most of the Poles and Russians arriving were Jews. The Jews who started coming here in goodly numbers from Poland before the pogroms may have been influenced to leave because of the upheavals occasioned by the Russo-Turkish War of 1877-1878; the flood from Russia proper in 1882 was of refugees frightened by the riots and murders. The charities responded to the need. In 1881, an Educational and Agricultural Fund was established by the Union of American Hebrew Congregations. To help the newcomers, the Union fashioned a society to raise $1,000,000. Stock certificates were sold for $5 each.

The money was to be used to tide over the new arrivals. Christians as well as Jews were to be asked to buy shares. There was, however, a qualifying clause in the articles of the organization; 10 percent of the money collected was to be used to support the students of the recently founded Hebrew Union College. Always in need of funds, the seminary was to catch a ride on the coattails of the would-be farmers. The shares sold were to be used to establish mini-colonies of twelve Jewish families. Great hopes were at first entertained for this venture; utopia was envisioned; American farming had a future; poverty and crime were to be banished; there would be no need for prisons. Living together, these farmers could observe and enjoy their faith without let or hindrance. What happened?

It would seem that very little, if any, of the money raised was used to help the Russian and Rumanian farmers. From 1881 to 1890 the fund was talked about. Farming never ceased to appeal to the shopkeepers; there was even talk of calling a national convention of Jewish yeomen. Actually only 600 to 800 shares were sold; no big giver bought more than twenty certificates; all told, no more than $4,000 was raised and most of that seems to have ended up in the coffers of the College. The year that the fund was established, a year when thousands of American Jews looked to colonization as the answer to the immigration problem, a skeptical correspondent wrote to the London *Jewish Chronicle*: this talk is like "the now proverbial Coney Island beer," it has too much froth.[4]

WHY COLONIES AND COLONIZATION?

Despite its potential power as a national Jewish organization, the Union of American Hebrew Congregations did little or nothing for the new immigrants; it had no capital, no real plan, no understanding, no capacity to meet this problem. Even so, American Jewry persisted in thinking throughout the 1880's that colonization would solve all the problems of the incoming exiles. How did American Jews define colonization? It was to be a close settlement of Jews working cooperatively under the sponsorship of an organized philanthropy. Closely allied to these colonies were the numerous farm settlements, more often than not a fortuitous gathering of neighborhood farmers working as individuals independent of each other. Between the years 1880 and 1920, there were at least 100 such congeries.[5]

By 1882, relatively large numbers of Russian Jews were arriving here; between 1882 and 1890, about 130,000 came in, descending on a United States Jewish community of about 300,000 to 400,000. From 1880 to 1900, about 600,000 Jewish men, women and children arrived in the United States. These newcomers were a problem. They had to be helped, absorbed, shipped to the hinterland. The Jewish natives and "Germans" here, convinced that farming was better than peddling or petty shopkeeping, had exaggerated ideas of the numbers they could settle. They believed that farm settlements speeded up Americanization; the newcomers would be divorced from the influence of ghettoized fellow immigrants. True, most of these refugees cherished an Orthodox lifestyle of their own, and that had to be respected; they must be kept together, preferably in colonies. Farming in 1880 was not looked upon as an unusual means of support. Over 45 percent of all Americans were still on the soil. Established Jewries here were convinced that the immigrants could live productive lives as farmers: as such they would remove the stigma from Jews as strangers; agriculture was a virtue; Jews were no par-

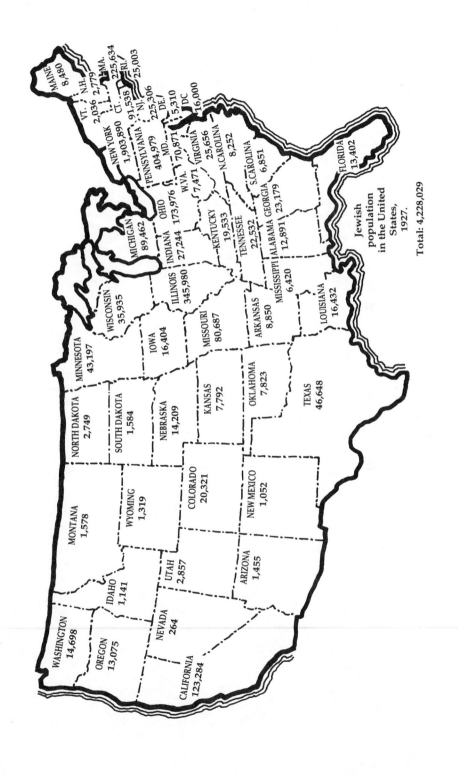

MAINE 8,480

VT. 2,036

N.H. 2,779

MA. 225,634

CT. 91,538

R.I. 25,003

NEW YORK 1,903,890

NJ. 225,306

PENNSYLVANIA 404,979

DE. 5,310

MD. 70,871

DC 16,000

VIRGINIA 25,656

W.VA. 7,471

N.CAROLINA 8,252

S.CAROLINA 6,851

FLORIDA 13,402

MICHIGAN 89,462

OHIO 173,976

INDIANA 27,244

KENTUCKY 19,533

TENNESSEE 22,532

GEORGIA 23,179

ALABAMA 12,891

WISCONSIN 35,935

ILLINOIS 345,980

MISSISSIPPI 6,420

MINNESOTA 43,197

IOWA 16,404

MISSOURI 80,687

ARKANSAS 8,850

LOUISIANA 16,432

NORTH DAKOTA 2,749

SOUTH DAKOTA 1,584

NEBRASKA 14,209

KANSAS 7,792

OKLAHOMA 7,823

TEXAS 46,648

MONTANA 1,578

WYOMING 1,319

COLORADO 20,321

NEW MEXICO 1,052

IDAHO 1,141

UTAH 2,857

ARIZONA 1,455

WASHINGTON 14,698

OREGON 13,075

NEVADA 264

CALIFORNIA 123,284

Jewish population in the United States, 1927.

Total: 4,228,029

asites; the new Jewish peasant would be Exhibit A to charm the Gentiles. And the newcomers? Very few were dirt farmers; many evinced no interest in farming or colonization; they were poor, frightened people who wanted to make a living. When dispatched to colonies, they went; often they had little real choice. Colonizers found it easier to get funds from philanthropists to settle people on the soil. The colonies were reported in the European Hebrew press of Poland and Russia in glowing terms; this may have influenced some emigrants to turn to farming and to accept colonization.[6]

There were, however, a few immigrants who really wanted to farm, to work side by side with fellow Jews. Farming as a Jewish vocation was nothing new in the czarist empire. There were numerous farmers, stewards of estates, even agricultural colonies. By 1900, most American colonies had disappeared; the number of Jews on the soil in the United States numbered then but a few thousand householders at the most, but in Russia, as late as 1900, there were still 100,000 Jews on the soil in at least 170 colonies. There might even have been more if the May Laws of 1882 had not driven thousands out of the rural districts. A number of Russian Jews had been influenced in the second half of the century by a populist movement which preached identification with the peasants. Back to the farm! These idealists were the men and women who believed in the gospel "honest toil, sweat of the brow." Farming was an ideal form of life; on the soil there were no distinctions among men; agriculture was not competitive; it offered economic security. Before coming to America in a later decade, Jacob Gordin, the Yiddish playwright, had organized a small religious group interested in manual labor. After the Russian mass riots of 1882, Jews were influenced, too, by a widely-read pamphlet of Dr. Leo Pinsker, who called for "autoemancipation"; Jews must pull themselves up by their own bootstraps; they had no future in Russia; they must have a land of their own.

Most of the pre-Herzlian Zionists of the 1880's wanted to settle in Palestine. Those who opted for America were the Am Olam congeries; the "Eternal People," they called themselves. Some of them, too, were thinking in terms of an ethnic enclave here or even an agricultural commune. Am Olam migrants who came here in 1881 were anything but homogeneous in their beliefs; they included intellectuals, laborers, Zionists, and socialists, but all of them sought a rebirth of Jewish life on the soil. Those emigrants who came with the desire to live in colonies were not deemed exotic by Americans. For generations, for centuries indeed, Americans had huddled together in communes, and eminent nineteenth-century Europeans encouraged close communal living; Francois M. C. Fourier and Robert Owen were well-known names.[7]

HISTORY OF THE DIFFERENT COLONIES

Felix Adler and his Ethical Culture followers had established some Jews in a colony near Hempstead, Long Island, in 1880. In all probability, these settlers were East Europeans. They did not remain very long in this garden town; they were unhappy living away from their friends in the ghetto. In 1881, other Jews, fleeing from Russia, were settled in a colony at a place called Sicily Island in Louisiana. These Am Olam idealists were proud to call themselves the First Agricultural Colony of Russian Israelites in America. The Hebrew Emigrant Aid Society of New York helped them, and Louisiana Jews were also most generous. As their constitution indicates, they had ambitious plans. Members were not to engage in any other business, and no liquor was to be manufactured. Setting out to be morally and intellectually exemplary, they urged the establishment of a school and a library; literary and musical evenings were scheduled; a former operatic singer entertained them with arias. Their leader, Herman Rosenthal (1843-1917), an able, scholarly man, later headed the Slavonic division of the New York Public Library. Always an ardent Jew, he would become a proud American. Before landing here, he had published a volume of German poems and had helped edit a Russian journal. Struggling to find himself in this foreign land, he played many roles. He was a bookseller, a statistician for the Edison Electric Company, an employee of the department of immigration, an expert dispatched by the Great Northern Railroad to study economic conditions in the Far East, an editor of the *Jewish Encyclopedia*, a writer for Hebrew periodicals both here and abroad, and a translator from the German, Hebrew, and Russian. Despite the émigrés' good intentions, this first colony was a failure; the land was poor —they found that they had been cheated—the climate was even worse, and the fields they ploughed were washed away in the spring flood.[8]

Colony after colony was founded in 1882, the year after the pogroms, when over 10,000 Jews landed in this country. There was a great deal of interest in the colonies established this year in the different states from New Jersey to Oregon. Some of the Sicily Island unfortunates moved north into Arkansas and planted a colony near Newport, in Jackson County, not far from Memphis, Tennessee. This settlement, too, collapsed speedily; the malaria was devastating; survivors moved still farther north into Missouri, to St. Louis. The years 1882-1884 were years of depression; thousands of Americans suffered. Unfortunately the immigrants who sought refuge here during this period and turned to farming came to a land economically stricken. Constantly looking for opportunities for the newcomers, American Jewish leaders considered Mexico as a potential haven, but the low standard of living of the peons and the intransigence of the Church precluded any serious attempt to send Jews to that land in the decades between 1880 and 1920. It was literally true that the pious peasants looked upon Jews as devils.

Am Olam enthusiasts were to be found nearly everywhere; the idealism that characterized them was not speedily dissipated. They appeared in Arkansas and even in Oregon, in the New Odessa colony founded in 1882. Here was something new, a communistic enterprise led by a Russian Gentile, Vladimir Konstantinovich Geins, who called himself William Frey (free!). This aesthete and pacifist preached a religion of humanity, but his followers worshipped at different ideological altars; there were mutually hostile factions. Men and women were accorded equal rights; some, if not most, of the comrades were vegetarian. The educational program was an ambitious one with classes in philosophy, mathematics, and English; all the colonists had the advantage of a good library. To eke out an existence, colonists supplemented their meager income by cutting ties for the railroad. Judaism was not emphasized; the Sabbath was not observed; America's rabbis were unhappy. The New Odessa colony folded before 1890.[9]

COTOPAXI

Cotopaxi was a colony established in the Rocky Mountains, in Fremont County, Colorado (1882). It was a small enterprise; all told, not more than 100 souls were assembled there. This was not a collective enterprise; these were not Am Olam adherents. Some of them were homesteaders. Most, if not all, were dependent on a Sephardic Jew, Emanuel H. Saltiel, who put them on his land and gave them jobs in his mine. Financial help had been provided by the Hebrew Emigrant Aid Society. The settlers, traditional observant Jews, were no more successful than the Sicily Island or the New Odessa visionaries. Saltiel's land proved unfit for cultivation; either he was a poor administrator or—more likely—was willing to exploit these unfortunates. In more than one instance, indeed, colonization was furthered by promoters or cheats—Jews, too—for whom immigrants were fair game. Those who worked for Saltiel were paid in scrip good only at his store. In Louisiana, the Jews had suffered from the flood; here in Colorado, they had to contend with maladministration, blizzards, and drought. Cotopaxi, too, was short-lived. The farmers began to move out; some settled in a nearby town where they had a conventicle of their own; some continued farming, some worked on the railroad, others raised stock. One man, determined to better his lot, set out for the big city, Denver, 150 miles away; he walked.[10]

Less than a decade later, a much larger colony was established at Atwood in Logan County, not far from the Nebraska border. The settlers purchased land from a Christian promoter; some of the promises he made —so they said—were not fulfilled. These farmers, too, got off to a bad start; the 1893 panic was still raging; they had a crop of melons, but no market; eggs were 10 cents a dozen; there was no kosher food; factionalism was rife. By 1899, the colony was dead. One of the men who farmed in this area was the immigrant Simon Fishman; years later, he became one of the country's great grain growers.[11]

THE DAKOTAS

The Dakota Territory—which became North and South Dakota in 1889 —lay to the north and east of Colorado. Jewish farming history in the Dakotas differed in one sense from the experience of the Russians in Louisiana, Oregon, and Colorado. Several colonies were formed in the territory in the early 1880's; sooner or later they, too, disappeared, but many of the settlers stayed on for years as homesteaders. Thus, some managed to survive; a few were even successful. Among the colonies established in 1882 in the territory was Crémieux, named after the French Jewish leader who had been active in 1848, subsequently led the Alliance Israélite Universelle, and later played an important role in the Third Republic. Numerous Jewish farmers came to the Dakotas as part of a larger stream of thousands who rushed to preempt free land. Crémieux, the colony in Davison County (South Dakota), enjoyed the guidance of Herman Rosenthal after the disaster at Sicily Island. The settlers in this new commune had a little empire of fifteen square miles—this, in the very year that many thousands of Jews were driven out of the rural districts in Russia by the anti-Jewish May Laws. The colony was not fated to survive long. Here, too, bugs, drought, hail, usurious mortgage rates, and inexperience proved the colony's undoing. Some of the colonists stayed on and opened small businesses; others went back to New York, whence they had come. They had failed even to conduct religious services, but they did have a glee club.

The colonists in Bethlehem-Judah in 1882, in the same county, included members who called themselves Bene Horin, Free Men; they were going to emancipate the Jewish people from slavery. As in Sicily Island and New Odessa, these liberals granted equality to their womenfolk, but the Bethlehem-Judah settlers, too, were no more successful than their colleagues in neighboring Cremieux. The North Dakota colonists in Burleigh, Ramsey, and McIntosh counties ran the gamut of hazards that all farmers faced breaking the sod in virgin territory. A substantial colony called Painted Woods was set up in Burleigh County, near the territorial capital, Bismarck. Rabbi Judah Wechsler, of nearby St. Paul, watched over the new colony, zealously securing funds from eastern sources. These Painted Woods venturers ran into trouble with their Christian neighbors. Nature also frowned upon them; again, it was the old story of poor soil, drought, blizzards, lack of capital, and no close markets. Painted

Woods, too, went the way of almost all the Jewish colonies. A number stayed on as individual farmers, and in the twentieth century the indefatigable Rev. Benjamin Papermaster, of Grand Forks, took them under his wing. By 1911, there are said to have been 250 families in the Burleigh County area, though this seems a very liberal estimate. A few of the old-timers assimilated and became Christians. Northeast of Burleigh County, in the Devils Lake area, several colonies were also established, beginning in 1882. Here, too, the settlements died out, but individuals remained on to plough their quarter sections or to scurry around as businessmen in the neighboring villages. Even when successful, these newcomers had little to brag about with their modest holdings, their barn, their team or two, and a few head of cattle. By contrast, Mr. Oliver Dalrymple, a Dakota farmer, had about 100,000 acres and earned about $200,000 a year.[12]

KANSAS COLONIES

Kansas in 1882 probably sheltered as many East European Jewish colonies as the Dakotas. The best known was Beersheba in the southwestern part of the state. Beersheba was the darling of the Cincinnatians and their Hebrew Union Agricultural Society. Moritz Loth, Isaac M. Wise, his son Leo, and a Davis family in Cincinnati were eager to make a success of this heavily subsidized commune. At one time, so it was said, it could muster about 200 families. The colonists had a midwife, a religious functionary who could provide them with kosher meat, and a fifty-foot-long synagog, which was built into the side of a creek and served for worship, weddings, and dances. This colony, built with so many high hopes, lasted about five or six years. The settlers were not all responsible men of integrity; supplies and even money were stolen. The Russians and Rumanians seem to have been a fractious lot. For some, if not most, of these farmers, Beersheba was only a way station; they wanted something better; they had no intention of remaining.

During the 1880's, at least seven different colonies rose in Kansas. The names borne by these settlements are interesting; they were either biblical or paid homage to famous Jews such as the late Judah Touro, Isaac Leeser, and the ancient Hebrew judge and warrior Gideon. Lasker was the name of one of the colonies established around the year 1885; it was named after the German Jewish politician Eduard L. Lasker, who had died in the United States while here on a visit. The lumber to build the houses and barns in the Lasker colony had to be hauled forty miles; the crops it grew were eaten by wild horses or dried up for lack of rain. When the opportunity presented itself, the Lasker contingent sold out and moved on. This was the fate of all the Kansas Jewish colonies.[13]

COLONIES IN MARYLAND AND VIRGINIA

Thinking of colonies and homesteads, one is transplanted in fantasy to the high plains and mountains west of the Mississippi. However, most colonies, certainly most farming settlements, were located east of the Mississippi; indeed most were north of Pennsylvania and east of the Blue Ridge Mountains. In 1882, a Baltimore philanthropist established and funded a colony in eastern Virginia, close to Chesapeake Bay and its inlets; it accomplished very little. That same year, a Hebrew-Russian Aid Committee located still another colony in Charles County, Maryland. American Jews, hopelessly romantic, would never cease to yearn for a breed of sturdy yeomen. When Russians as a body were condemned because of the collapse of this colony, Henrietta Szold rose to their defense; the Russians, she said, must not be rejected because of the sins of a few. In the early 1900's, still another Maryland colony was planted just ten miles from Baltimore; the Jewish Agricultural and Industrial Aid Society helped it. The total acreage which the settlers should have cultivated did not exceed 350 acres. They built a synagog, took in boarders, raised poultry, and quarreled with one another.[14]

THE SOUTH JERSEY COLONIES

Of the colonies established across the country in 1882, only those planted in southern New Jersey were to survive into the twentieth century. All told, about a dozen colonies and farm settlements took shape there. Some faded out only to be rebuilt and to take on new life. The reason there were so many and they held out so long before they, too, disappeared or ceased to be Jewish establishments was their proximity to Philadelphia and New York. The colonists were in constant touch with fellow Jews, both immigrants and earlier settlers, who visited them, subsidized them, and purchased their products. Good transportation and ready markets were important for survival. Liberal donors found it no problem to supervise and advise these newcomers. The colonies were bourgeois, capitalistic, individualistic ventures; utopianism, socialism, and comparable ideologies played little or no part in the development of these farmsteads. The real, the final reason why these colonies managed to hold their own was that they were agro-industrial. Industry—not agriculture—kept them alive.

Three colonies, established in 1882 stand out. These were Carmel, Rosenhayn, and Alliance. No large-scale grain farming was attempted; Rosenhayn and Carmel together owned less than 3,000 acres. For a time, Carmel did not shelter twenty families engaged exclusively in farming. Rosenhayn could count but forty-seven farming families in the colony in 1900. Vineland, something of a Jewish town which began in 1882 with about 500 souls, fared relatively well for decades; Alliance in 1901 could boast of a population of about 600 Jews. In Alliance and in the other colonies, too, people left and others took their place; replacements from the nearby cities were available; there were always some families eager to leave the cities and try their luck on a farm or in a rural village. As befitted a Jewish town of its size, Alliance had elaborate Jewish programs, several synagogs or prayer groups, a schoolhouse, a library, Sabbath schools, a dramatic club; the German poets, Schiller and Goethe, and the Yiddish poet Morris Rosenfeld were read; there were night schools for adults and lectures on ethics, the Bible, and the Talmud. The metropolitan Yiddish dailies were always at hand; living in the Jerseys meant no exile. Bearing in mind the needs of their nearby markets, these farmers sold grapes, berries, fruits, and sweet potatoes. As craftsmen, they manufactured cigars and sewed garments; they worked in a cannery. The New York philanthropist Leonard Lewisohn gave every family in Alliance a sewing machine. The Vinelanders produced sacramental wines for New York's Jews.[15]

JEWISH COLONIES IN THE 1890'S

By the 1890's, practically all of the colonies established during the 1880's in the West were gone. Hebrew readers of *Ha-Melitz* now knew that colonization was not America's answer to the Jewish problem. Enthusiasm had evaporated, yet there were always some who looked forward to a new life on the soil; individuals joined with others to create Jewish farm settlements. It is possible that incoming Russians were prompted to consider rural living in the early 1890's because the Russian authorities were in the process of expelling them from Moscow and other major towns. Emigration from Russia was unusually heavy in 1891-1892. David Lubin of Sacramento, a businessman and a thoughtful philanthropist, joined with Rabbi Jacob Voorsanger of San Francisco in 1891 in establishing the International Society for the Colonization of Russian Jews. He had his eye on Mexico, too, as a destination for the newcomers. Lubin and his brother-in-law Harris Weinstock set up a Jewish colony at Orangevale; Philip Nettre Lilienthal, son of the late rabbi of Cincinnati, transported some of the Dakota Jewish pioneers to a colony of his own at a place called Porterville. He gave them money and housing and encouraged them to become poultry specialists. Neither of these colonies could boast of any success. Quarrels helped disrupt Porterville; some of the settlers insisted on living in town rather than on their farms. Several years later, in 1897, when Ephraim Deinard, nationally known Hebrew bookman, talked of establishing a colony near San Francisco, Rabbi Voorsanger turned a cold shoulder to him. Apparently, the rabbi's experiences with the would-be farmers in 1891 had turned him off. Not to be deterred, a number of East Europeans that year bought a large ranch in Lyon County, Nevada. There is reason to believe that they were exploited; they were certainly not skilled in irrigation techniques. A year later, the bank which held their mortgage sold them out. This was the end of what was known as the Occidental colony.

In 1891, the same year that attempts were made to settle Russians on farms in Northern California, some peddlers banded together to establish a colony in Huron County, Michigan, near the town of Bad Axe. They called their settlement the Palestine Colony. By the 1890's, the Lovers of Zion movement had already captured the imagination of Jews in Europe and in America. Before long, Herzl would publish his epoch-making brochure, *The Jewish State*. Determined to survive, these Michigan farming tyros continued peddling and bartering wares and notions, dishes and tinware, for hides and rags. When success eluded them, they turned to Martin Butzel of Detroit, one of the city's leading Jews, and asked for help. He raised money, some from the Baron de Hirsch Fund, but more importantly he sent them a farm expert, Emanuel Woodic, a Jewish veteran of the Civil War. It was their misfortune to undertake their enterprise in the 1890's; the national panic of that decade lasted for about five years and helped destroy the colony, although some still continued to farm till the early 1900's.[16]

WOODBINE

Judah (Julius) D. Eisenstein was one of the best known Russian-Polish Jews in this country. He prided himself, justifiably, on being a writer and a scholar, but he was also an entrepreneur who reached out in several directions. In 1891, he sponsored a farming settlement at Mizpah, in Atlantic County, southeastern New Jersey; it was an agro-industrial undertaking, not a very successful one. This year saw new attempts to colonize in California, Michigan, and the Jerseys. As intimated above, renewed persecution in Russia and the arrival of émigrés may have stimulated interest in settling Jews on the land. Herman Rosenthal in 1892 thought that the time was ripe for a special Yiddish journal for agriculturists, *The Jewish Farmer* (*Der Juedische Farmer*), but this monthly found few subscribers and ceased to appear after a year.

A year earlier, some miles to the south of Mizpah—and not very far from the 1882 complex of Jersey colonies—a new settlement was established at Woodbine, in Cape May County. Money was available from the Baron de Hirsch Fund, and agricultural expertise, too, in the person of Hirsch Leib Sabsovich, a trained agronomist. Sixty Russian families were encouraged to settle, but most proved to be poor farmers. However, industry was speedily introduced; the newcomers manufactured locks, machines, bricks, tools, and clothing; thus, they survived. In 1895, the Woodbine Agricultural School was established under Sabsovich as a secondary, not a collegiate, institution. The agricultural commune was not successful; Simon W. Rosendale, former attorney general of the State of New York, pronounced it a failure. The town, however, flourished. It had a public bathhouse, a school, a Baptist church, and a synagog. Sabsovich in 1903 was elected mayor of this Jewish borough, one of the first of its kind in the whole world. By 1905, there were 2,000 people in town, mostly Jews engaged in industry. In 1893, Jacob Gordin, now an American and a renowned Yiddish playwright, visited Woodbine. Gordin wanted to locate his Spiritual Biblical Brotherhood in Woodbine, though his followers had no interest in Judaism or in the synagog and Sabsovich gave Gordin no encouragement. Running a Jewish colony and a town was no easy job; the colonists and the students in Woodbine were not a submissive lot. By 1919, there were 350 families in town; seventy were non-Jewish; 280 were Jewish; twenty-six families farmed.[17]

COLONIES AND COMMUNES, 1900-1920

Though, as it has already been said, the enthusiasm for colonization faded after the 1880's, it never died out completely. If colonization was inspirited in part by the desire for "community," this reaching out was still very much alive even in the late twentieth century when *havurot*, Jewish urban cultural, religious, and social fellowships, spiritual enclaves, were very much in vogue. With the coming of the new century, people still continued to organize colonies and farming settlements, frequently without sponsors; they merely clustered together; as Jews, they wanted fellow Jews about them. Thus, even in the twentieth century, they established groups of their own in a number of states from Washington on the Pacific to Happyville in Aiken County, South Carolina—all this before 1921.

By 1907, there were at least two such colonies in Washington State. One was in Ferry County near the Canadian border. The mines in the area served as a market for farm products; when the mines closed, the Jews left. Another group settled near Tacoma, where it had a built-in market. Individual farmers in this state put their money and skills into fruit orchards.[18]

CLARION AND OTHER TWENTIETH-CENTURY COLONIES

Few colonies started with as much backing as Clarion when founded in Utah in 1910. Rabbi Krauskopf of Philadelphia was interested and sent it help from the National Farm School which he had established many years earlier. The Salt Lake Jews were sympathetic, as were the Mormons and the state authorities, who were very eager to settle newcomers. About 150 colonists came out, expecting hundreds of others to follow, but by 1914 Clarion sheltered only thirty-five families who owned 6,000 acres. It is estimated that these settlers and their supporters expended about $150,000, but all in vain. Though over 1,500 acres had been planted in 1913, huge sums were needed if the land was to be cultivated properly. By 1915, Clarion was obviously just another colonial failure. The chief protagonist of this colony out in the middle of nowhere was a Mr. Benjamin Brown, who turned to the production of poultry and eggs and set up a cooperative exchange in the 1920's. His enterprise proved eminently successful and, in the 1960's, was doing over $9,000,000 worth of business annually.

Clarion had been peopled by New Yorkers and Philadelphians. The Jewish homesteaders who established neighboring settlements in southern Wyoming faced some of the same problems which had destroyed Clarion. Water was scarce or expensive. Dozens of these homesteaders settled in Goshen and Laramie counties, beginning in 1909; the Jewish Agricultural and Industrial Aid Society financed them, but here, as in other places, the farmers resented their patrons and took advantage of them. Neither these Wyoming pioneers nor those who settled in neighboring Nebraska had an easy time. There were at least two settlements of Jewish homesteaders in Nebraska in the second decade of the twentieth century. As in many other communities of this type, they were doomed before they started because of their remote isolated location; there were no nearby railroads and no towns. The Jewish stock raisers and farmers of Cherry County had to travel for two days before they came across their first town. Freighting goods was a four-day trip. Once they got title to their lands, they sold out and moved on.[19]

The Wyoming and Nebraska farmers were aided by loans from the Jewish Agricultural and Industrial Aid Society; Wisconsin's Arpin Colony, north of Milwaukee, was sponsored by the Milwaukee philanthropist, Adolph W. Rich. This Russian settlement did better than most such communes. The colonists were a small group, never numbering more than 100 souls. They moved out into the country in 1904 and a few held on for some two decades. When the children grew up, they left and the parents soon followed. Indeed, this was true of many of America's farmers; the numbers who remained on the farm were declining constantly. The Jews who left the countryside for the city yearned for a Jewish ambience, a synagog, schools, better educational institutions; they wanted their boys and girls to marry Jews; they dreaded assimilation. In 1905, some Jewish political and ideological radicals set up a colony in Aiken County, South Carolina, not far from the Georgia border. It was known as the Polish Colony; they called the place Happyville. It took but two years before they, too, disbanded. These fifty people suffered from bad weather, debts, and inexperience. Few as they were, they quarreled with one another, but because they were Jews, they had a library and staged Yiddish plays.[20]

COLONIES: FAILURES?

Sooner or later—mostly sooner—all colonies and many Jewish farm settlements faded away. Toward the end of the East European immigrant period, in 1919, only 203 farming families remained in the South Jersey colonies. All told, the little towns and farms in this eastern state, sheltered but 2,739 people—in a United States Jewry of 3,300,000. Why did the American Jewish colonies fold? Jewish leaders were trying to plant Jews on the soil at a time when Americans were leaving the farms. Even before the genesis of the Jewish colonization movement, native-born Americans were beginning their exodus from the farmsteads; in 1880, there were only about 8,500,000 men, women and children in the rural areas out of a total population of about 50,000,000. For generations, there was a gradual pull toward the city. Even the agro-industrial settlements in South Jersey could not keep the new generation at home.

For the average man, agriculture was not an inviting economic field. Farmers suffered perennially. Jewish philanthropists, indeed most American Jews, had mixed motives in pushing newcomers to follow the plough. They did want to help; noblesse oblige was a motif that was never absent. They were romantics like Baron de Hirsch, who wanted to create a new race of Jews, farmers, and stock raisers as in biblical days. Urban American Israelites wanted to make peasants of the new Jews. Anti-Semites were saying that Jews were devious traders, and the Jewish establishment took such attacks seriously; many had suffered from Jew hatred in Germany; the East Europeans were to be shunted off to the hinterland. Affluent American merchants wanted to resolve their own disquietude by pushing the new aliens out of sight. What the "Germans" here failed to understand was that the impoverished newcomers had the same ambitions that the emerging Jewish millionaires had—and some of these Russians reached their goals. The elite, thinking wishfully, failed to realize the predestined futility of colonization. Most immigrants had no desire to remain on the farms; their stay was transitional. Jews, like Gentiles who moved to the city, wanted the social, cultural, and economic advantages inherent in city living.

The reasons for the failures are many. Leadership was lacking; discipline was resisted; planning was frequently absent. There were inherent difficulties in cooperative living. Hardships out on the high plains—deserts!—were horrendous. Midwives were rare; the food was inadequate;

the work was hard; for centuries, Jews had been divorced from the soil. Back in 1824, a president of Rutgers opposed turning neophytes, Jewish-Christians, into farmers; they are not accustomed to that type of work; they don't care for it! Jews who wanted to remain Jews dreaded isolation from larger groups; they were not homogeneous; they cherished disparate philosophies and were prone to bicker. Moreover, no one could really cope with the country's frequent panics; from 1881 to 1920, there were six depressions for a total of about twelve years; collectivism had no appeal for Jewish individualists. These Jews had no capital; country banks often charged usurious rates of interest; crooks lay in wait for these naive farmers and cheated them; the soil available was invariably virgin or poor; they had no water, no good transportation, no markets; they did have cold, hail, blizzards, droughts, fire. Jews were planted in the wilderness and blamed for their failures. Ambitious American-born Jewish farm children, discontented because of their marginal existence, left home in large numbers. A Vineland youngster who had learned to roll cigars could make a better living in the city.[21]

COLONIES: SUCCESSES?

The attempt to induce the new Jews to become tillers of the soil is an interesting phase of American Jewish history—albeit a very minor one—that has to be told. It is an aspect of the desire of the American Jews to find work for the immigrants; they had to have jobs. The colonizing movement was a learning experience; the old-timers finally understood that the pages of history could not be turned back. An advanced industrial civilization offered a dim future for farmers and stock raisers. Those who slaved on the farms—and it was backbreaking work—learned the gospel of manual labor, if it is a gospel. The history of these Russian, Polish, and Rumanian colonists is a fascinating study in idealism. These few men and women, visionaries, had their brief moment in the sun. After years of trial and error, the managerial donors realized that colonies could manage to continue—for a time at least—if they were established near big cities and became agro-industrial enterprises. These farming novices were surrounded by caring Jews who patronized and bought their truck. Accessible markets made for survival. Judah David Eisenstein realized this as early as 1897 and said so. Even if a badly administered colony managed to carry on for only a few years, that was a victory; it had held out. But real successes? The colonists, who were found literally from the Atlantic to the Pacific, created a Diaspora of their own; they discovered a new America, and the few who remained and settled in nearby towns and cities became nuclei around which communities and conventicles agglomerated. In the larger frame of American Jewish history, this colonization movement is not important, yet in its day, it fired the imagination of most American Jews.[22]

AMERICA'S EAST EUROPEAN JEWISH FARMERS, 1881-1920

On a continent where the people were overwhelmingly farmers until well into the nineteenth century, it is patent that there would always be some Jews who were farmers. The Georgia Jewish colonists in 1733 had started out as farmers on the plots allotted them. In the mid-nineteenth century, Captain U. P. Levy, of the United States Navy, farmed Monticello, the old Jefferson homestead; Judah P. Benjamin owned and personally ran a sugar plantation in Louisiana. All through the 1850's, Isaac M. Wise, born and reared in a Bohemian village, hammered away at the readers of the *Israelite* to return to the soil. He himself lived on a small farm during the summer. Individuals—not many, to be sure—preempted land after the passage of the Homestead Act in the 1860's. A farmer named Altschuler had settled in the Nebraska backcountry in the 1870's; the family drove an ox team thirty-five miles to Columbus, the seat of Platte County, to buy supplies; it was a three-day trip.

Some farmers started out in organization-sponsored congeries and stayed on after the colony as such disappeared; others struck out for themselves, but their very presence—and success?—attracted others, and before long they became the core around which a Jewish farm settlement developed. Jews were always huddling together for social and religious reasons. Individual isolated farmers living among Gentiles faced almost insurmountable problems. But some Jewish farmers did make a good living; they had some capital and were driven by ambition. A few cherished the belief that life on the farm was preferable to city living, to the factory, and to peddling. Despite the contention that the frontier had vanished by 1890, thousands still continued to homestead in the West, and there were Jews among them. Unsponsored Jewish farm settlements were found in North Dakota and New England, especially in Connecticut. By the early twentieth century, Jews farmed in almost all the states. Those near the big cities specialized in truck, fruits, berries, and dairy products; toilers in the backcountry grew grain and raised stock. It was reported that in 1905 there were about 400 Jewish farmers in New England; they owned about 40,000 acres.[23]

THE NATIONAL FARM SCHOOL, DOYLESTOWN, PENNSYLVANIA

In 1894, Rabbi Joseph Krauskopf failed to induce the Russian government to put the Jews on the soil; even Tolstoi, whom he visited, thought the East European Jews would do well to emigrate. American Jewish slum dwellers, said Tolstoi, should go back to farming. Krauskopf returned and two years later established the National Farm School at Doylestown, Pennsylvania, not far from his pulpit in Philadelphia. Though it was a nonsectarian school, Krauskopf envisioned it as a training ground for the leaders of Jewish colonies; Rabbi Isaac Landman, Krauskopf's assistant, helped set up the settlement at Clarion in Utah. Krauskopf was convinced that the image of the urban Jew was a negative one; turning Jews into farmers would modify that prejudice. If Jewish newcomers became farmers, there would be no need for Palestine; in those early days, the Philadelphia rabbi was an anti-Zionist. When Krauskopf turned to Rosenwald and asked for help, the Chicago philanthropist answered that it was cheaper to send students to a general agricultural college where they would get better training; one Jewish school, Woodbine, was adequate for the needs of Jewish farmers. Wisely, Krauskopf also urged the establishment of agro-industrial villages. His school prospered, yet Rosenwald was right; the students did not as a rule become dirt farmers; the school was not instrumental in spurring an exodus to the countryside.[24]

THE BARON DE HIRSCH AGRICULTURAL SCHOOL (WOODBINE)

A year or so before Krauskopf opened his nonsectarian agricultural school —with Jewish money, of course—Baron de Hirsch money was used to fund a farm school in the Woodbine Colony; its prime purpose was to serve the colonists in an advisory capacity. The school was not without its problems; there were conflicts between students and the administration despite the devotion and technical competence of the superintendent, Hirsch Leib Sabsovich, the Russian-trained agronomist who had come to the States in 1881 and taken over the Woodbine colony in 1891. New York's Jewish social workers admired him and elected him president of their group. Like the later National Farm School at Doylestown, the Woodbine institution had set out to create a generation of farmers; this goal was never reached though its graduates often became teachers, soil chemists, and agricultural experts. The women at the coeducational school were taught domestic science, hothouse planting, and the care of poultry. The school closed in 1917 when immigrants were no longer arriving and those here were already self-sufficient. American Jews, like American Gentiles, had long ceased to seek a living in the rural areas. There was no need any more for farming as a facet of apologetics; the old-line elite was no longer apprehensive; alien newcomers had ceased to flood the country.[25]

THE JEWISH AGRICULTURAL AND INDUSTRIAL AID SOCIETY

The agricultural school at Woodbine had been financed through the Baron de Hirsch Fund. Between the years 1888 and 1891, the Baron had set up a fund of well over $2,000,000 to provide for East European Jewish immigrants coming to the United States. He had been induced to do so by Oscar Straus, the diplomat, who worked closely with other communal workers like Moses Dropsie and Michael Heilprin. The Baron may well be designated the greatest Jewish philanthropist of all times. Maurice de Hirsch (1831-1896), scion of an ennobled German Jewish family, had made an enormous fortune in Eastern Europe and the Balkans in railroads and in commodities trading. His pious parents saw to it that he received a good Jewish education. As early as 1873 he was a generous supporter of the Alliance Israélite Universelle, the world Jewish philanthropic society; he himself had a *palais* in Paris. During the 1880's, Hirsch approached the Russians and offered millions to help put Jews on farms and in factories. The Russians turned a deaf ear to him unless they could control the grants. Worried about Russian Jewry in 1890-1891, as expulsions were renewed, the Baron resolved to aid the emigration of his coreligionists from a land where, clearly, they had no future.

To further this end, he created the ICA, the Jewish Colonization Association, with a capital of about $40,000,000. In 1887, after his only son had died, he said: "My son I have lost but not my heir; humanity is my heir." As a Jew, he recognized a special obligation to his people because they had been "oppressed for a thousand years." The Baron set out to regenerate the Jews of Russia, Poland, and Rumania, morally, physically, and vocationally. To accomplish this, to make of them farmers and artisans, it was necessary that they be settled in colonies where they could have a social and religious life that would sustain them. Zangwill once remarked in his usual caustic fashion that the ICA was a charity; it could not solve the Jewish Problem. This maverick was right, but over the years the Jewish Colonization Association helped thousands. Even today there are congregations and other institutions that have taken the name "Baron de Hirsch"; his portrait, along with that of Moses Montefiore, still graces the vestry rooms of synagogs. He was Diaspora Jewry's world hero.[26]

Though the Baron was interested in helping Jews everywhere, he was conscious that the United States was the new Promised Land. He could read immigration statistics; he knew in 1890 that this country already had over 400,000 Jews and that it was growing rapidly. The ICA—his prime fund—set out to educate, to train, and to help Jews in Russia, Galicia, Rumania, and Turkey. Even more, it concentrated its efforts on sending Jews to the Argentine and Brazil. His special United States endowment, the Baron de Hirsch Fund, had multiple aims: it gave relief, pushed for removal to the hinterland, established vocational schools, fur-

thered civic education, provided classes for foreigners, funded kindergartens, and gave subsidies to organizations that labored in these fields. Its
prime interest was the return of Jews to the soil; this is why it founded
and supported the Woodbine school.[27]

In theory, the Jewish Agricultural and Industrial Aid Society embraced all the cultural, educational, industrial, and agricultural aims of the
Baron de Hirsch Fund. In actuality, it concentrated its efforts very heavily
before 1922 in putting Jews on the soil and helping them to stay there.
Through liberal infusions of Baron de Hirsch Fund and Jewish Colonization Association monies, the agricultural society trained farmers, helped
them buy land, lent them money, gave them technical advice, advised
them on sanitation, and established a test farm, a credit agency, a cooperative bank, an insurance company, a purchasing bureau, and a federation of
Jewish farmers. In some of these areas the Society was a pioneer lighting
the way for others in this country. At one time the Society included sixty
different associations. It was this Society that encouraged a fair at New
York's Educational Alliance where Jewish farmers—male and female—
exhibited flowers, cheese, butter, preserves, pastry, and bread. Again, it
was the Society that settled mechanics in the exurbs, aided industries in
the colonies, opened night schools, and stocked libraries. In 1922, after
the passage of the Immigration Act of 1921, as the gates to America began to close, the Society limited its programs; from then on, it would
work only with farmers.[28]

FARMERS IN VARIOUS STATES

Jewish farmers ploughed their lands in almost every state of the Union.
Long before the Russians and Rumanians went into farming in California, individual German Jews had distinguished themselves as agricultural
entrepreneurs in that state. Some were very successful. There were Russians, too, who made their mark in the rural areas of California. Israel
Sam Shamsky (d. 1978), who came to the United States in 1914, bought
and developed poultry ranches in Petaluma and Sonoma. This man, one
of the most successful poultry raisers in the state, became a leading citizen
in Sonoma. He joined several synagogs and was called to the board of the
Bank of America, the Red Cross, the local hospital, and the Chamber of
Commerce.

The Wyoming homesteaders who held on could boast of their farms,
their barns, their cattle and horses. Jewish farmers and settlements, too,
were not uncommon in Colorado. Some worked as dry land farmers; others became adept at irrigation; a number were successful stockmen. Those
entrepreneurs who concerned themselves with stock grazed sheep and
operated feed lots and ranches. In some instances, this was "big business";
"cattle kings" were not altogether unknown. In the early 1890's, a Jewish

immigrant who had homesteaded near Denver induced some of his friends to settle near him. He wanted company and religious services. Thus, he had a little Jewish settlement in his backyard, as it were. These particular farmers and stock raisers, however, ran into trouble for not preventing their scrub cattle from mixing with the thoroughbreds of their Gentile neighbors. The Christian ranchers were annoyed that their herds were being downgraded. Ultimately, the settlement broke up because the newcomers moved back to Denver. Even the founding pioneer's wife insisted on spending her weekends in the city. In a way, this minor settlement episode epitomizes the history of the Jewish farming movement in America.[29]

The Dakotas attracted a considerable number of Jewish homesteaders. It is difficult to know why as the land was not particularly good. Some came as colonists; some lived in Jewish settlements; others came on their own. Most had little to brag about. It was thought that by 1910 there were over 210 farm families in North Dakota. This is known: there were Jewish farm associations in the state; they gathered together to talk crops, to socialize, to enjoy a hasty religious service. Between 1882 and 1906, a dozen Jewish farm settlements existed in Burleigh County alone; there were Jewish farmers in at least eleven of the state's counties. By the 1920's, most, if not all, were gone. Nothing was left but the cemeteries, mute witnesses to a generation that had died and had little to show for its labor. Many of those who abandoned their farms had been forced out; some sold out; some went to live with their children in towns and cities.

Conditions in South Dakota were little different. By 1910 there were over seventy Jewish farm families in the state. Strangely, one of these immigrant homesteaders was not Russian, but German Jewish: the Thal family. The Thals, Orthodox in belief, preempted their lands in the 1880's. They were far out; there were still Indians about; the wolves came up to the cabin at night and howled. Supplies were freighted in by ox-team. The Thals achieved a degree of success on their section of land, for they had the only frame house in the district that could sport a chimney. The inside of their house was luxurious; they had lace curtains, Brussels carpets, a bed with a mattress, and a sewing machine. The women in the neighborhood made good use of that machine! The nearest schoolhouse was three miles away; classes were held four months a year; later, two more months were added. Mrs. Thal's Gentile neighbors taught her to make cookies and pies; she taught them the mysteries of potato salad, cottage cheese, and noodles. During the winter, when there was little to do on the place, they played cards, and if a partner was missing they hung out a lantern. That never failed to bring in a neighbor from a nearby farm. The breakfasts were substantial: biscuits, jelly, pancakes, syrup; dinner included meats and potatoes, bread and vegetables.

Southwest Michigan had a sizable number of Jewish farmers who exploited the nearby Chicago market. For similar reasons, there were farmers on the outskirts of Cleveland, Youngstown, and Cincinnati in Ohio. Jewish farmers in northern New Jersey, in the vicinity of New York, were not rare. A New York Russian settled in Union County and opened a dairy; others followed him; in much the same way, Jewish farming settlements were found in several of the New England states. There are reports that there were hundreds of Jewish farmers in Connecticut alone. Sometimes they bought neglected farms and made them pay. These newcomers clustered on the outskirts of the state's cities. Many made a living with a dairy herd; others cultivated tobacco and planted potatoes. Some of these farmers worked in the towns and factories in order to augment their incomes; others became junk collectors; some took in boarders. These Connecticut yeomen, progressive, set up purchasing and marketing cooperatives and even had a joint insurance association. Historians of the Jewish farming movement claim that by 1909 there were at least 1,000 such farmers in New England; this figure seems high.[30]

THE CATSKILL FARMERS, 1890-1920

The Catskills had good scenery and poor land. There was, however, a substantial number of Jewish farmers in the area, in Ulster, Sullivan, Greene, Orange, and Rensselaer Counties. These rural adventurers, setting out to make a living off the soil, were compelled to augment their meager incomes by peddling, dealing in cattle, and even by real estate speculations. In Sullivan County along the New York, Ontario & Western Railway lines, a few farmers began taking in boarders about the year 1900. They offered a kosher cuisine at about $5 a week. Some advertised "Hebrews Only" even before the numerous Christian boarding houses in the neighborhood limited their clientele to "Gentiles only." In those days, non-Jews never expected they would be confronted by Jewish applicants. Boarding became increasingly important for these Catskill Mountain farmers. By 1912, over 1,000 of these rural entrepreneurs lived in the mountains. Many of them turned to the Jewish Agricultural and Industrial Aid Society for advice. The Society encouraged them to take in boarders and to emphasize dairying and poultry raising. Thousands of New York Jews journeyed to the Catskills for their vacation. Rooms could be rented; cooking privileges were provided, and finally a full-blown boarding and hotel industry blossomed. As late as 1920, most hoteliers were still operating farms. This was to change in the next decade; Jewish summer resorts became big business.

Among those who switched from farming to boarding was the Grossinger clan which moved out into the country around the year 1914. A time came when the family served as many as 150,000 guests a year, among them Gentiles who learned to like matzo balls and gefilte fish. In later decades, more than 1,000 hotels and boarding houses catered to the trade; thousands of bungalows were built and rented out to summer visitors. The larger resorts had golf courses, swimming pools, night clubs, and big-name bands. The first Catskill farmers, like most Jewish farmers in all parts of the United States, did not settle on the land for ideological reasons. They did not labor on their remote homesteads to placate anti-Semites who wanted to see Jews sweat. True, they did want to get away from the ghetto and the sweatshop; farming was healthful. They went out to make a living, and when conditions improved—if they did improve—they moved back to the towns and cities. Writing to Rabbi Edward B. M. Browne in 1906, Oscar Straus said that agriculture was not the answer for the East Europeans. Most Catskill Jews would probably have nodded their heads in assent.[31]

PATRONS OF AGRICULTURE

North American Jews who were descendants of earlier settlers were wholeheartedly in favor of agriculture—for other Jews. There were, however, individuals who devoted themselves to the task of making farmers of the newly arrived Russians, Poles, and Rumanians. These patrons were fine people, in dead earnest in their zealous efforts. Rabbi Judah Wechsler, of St. Paul, mothered the Jews in Painted Woods; Rabbi A. R. Levy, the executive of the Jewish Chicago Agricultural Aid Society, busied himself helping farmers in a half a dozen states; Herman Rosenthal and Michael Heilprin were convinced that the plough was Israel's salvation. Still another advocate was David Lubin (1849-1919) of California. This Russian Pole, who had come to America as a child, received but little public school education before he left home—a runaway?—for the West, where he opened a store in Sacramento after a spell as an Arizona prospector. Emphasizing that it was a one-price institution, in a generation that loved to haggle, the business was a success. Mail orders comprised a substantial portion of its sales. Lubin was interested in farms and farming and was an active protagonist of agricultural cooperatives. As already noted above, he wanted to establish a Jewish farming colony in California. This militant reformer insisted that the railroads grant farmers equitable freight rates; he was interested in grain growers not only in the United States but all over the world, and in 1908 succeeded in establishing the International Institute of Agriculture in Italy. Over forty nations joined the nonprofit enterprise. In the sense that he urged the interdependent nations to appreciate the economic impact of what they were producing, he was furthering the concept of a United States of the World. Lubin was very much interested in Jews; he believed that farming was good for them.[32]

JEWISH NOTABLES IN AGRICULTURAL SCIENCE

Though the Woodbine School in no sense effected a revolution in farming among Jews, it did further soil sciences. There were quite a number of Jews, predominantly East European immigrants, interested in agriculture as academicians and research scholars. Among them was Joseph A. Rosen (1876-1949), agronomist and colonization expert, who had taught at the New Jersey school. A native of Russia, he had come here in 1903 and, in the course of years, furthered the planting in this country of what came to be known as Rosen rye; he was recognized for his efforts to introduce Indian corn and American farming methods into Soviet Russia. Rosen worked under Herbert Hoover in the American Relief Administration and served as the American Jewish Joint Distribution Committee representative in the Soviet Union where he supervised the resettlement on the soil of hundreds of thousands of Jews in the Ukraine and the Crimea. Because of his agrocolonization skills, he was later called upon by American Jewry to help European Jewish refugees fleeing from the Germans; it was his job to plant them in the Dominican Republic. Other agricultural scientists of note were Jacob Joseph Taubenhaus, who taught in Texas, Meyer Edward Jaffa, who worked in California, and Moses N. Levine, who served colleges in Kansas and Minnesota as a plant pathologist.

Jacob Goodale Lipman (1874-1939), the most distinguished of these scientists, was dean of Rutgers' Agricultural College and Director of the New Jersey Agricultural Experimental Station. Lipman was a leader in the field of conserving soil resources, reclaiming waste lands, and improving soils of poor fertility. He had studied at Woodbine and is acknowledged to have been one of the founders of the science of soil chemistry and bacteriology; he represented the United States at the International Institute of Agriculture and edited *Soil Science* for many years. When in 1925 Tennessee passed a law forbidding the teaching of creation theories contrary to the biblical account, a school teacher, John T. Scopes, was arrested for advocating Darwinianism and evolutionism. Scopes' lawyers, led by Clarence Darrow, relied upon Professor Lipman to prepare a defense of the evolution theories of modern biologists. Still another Rutgers scientist, one who received the Nobel Prize, was the immigrant Selman Abraham Waksman. Working in the New Jersey State Agricultural Experiment Station, he and his associates developed streptomycin and other antibiotics. The research of this soil scientist and bacteriologist has been of importance in the control of infectious diseases.[33]

NOTES ON CERTAIN FARMERS

In the monotonous litany of failures, it is a relief to report that some individuals were happy on the farm; a select few were very successful. Bennie

Greenberg, of Benzion Post Office, Ramsey County, North Dakota—this is Devils Lake country—arrived in North Dakota in 1888 with his family. His total capital was $2.50. He homesteaded and, like most others, suffered; about a decade later, he felt secure. He had five horses, nine head of cattle, poultry, all necessary implements, wagons, a sleigh, a stable, and a good frame house 18 by 24 feet (just about the length of a modern living room). He had 160 acres, free and clear; all told, his debts amounted to $250-$300. "We make a fine living," he boasted. The Russian-born Samuel Kahn, of Holt County, Missouri, on the Nebraska-Kansas border, had arrived in the United States in 1880. He turned to farming and learned his business the hard way. Ultimately, he owned 1,600 acres, where he grew grain and pastured livestock. Specializing in growing onions, he was saluted wide and far as the "Onion King." Another notable success was the Rumanian émigré, Benjamin Feldman, who had settled in the San Fernando Valley of Los Angeles County, then countryside, though now a center of the huge Los Angeles Jewish community. Feldman became a wealthy farmer, so successful that he could afford to make a gift of $200,000 to the Jewish National Fund to establish a forest of 80,000 trees in the State of Israel. An enthusiastic American, he specified that the groves in his forest be named after the American presidents. He loved this country; as a Rumanian Jew he had experienced severe discrimination in the land of his birth.

In 1908, the Sinykin family had homesteaded near the town of Quinn, in Pennington County, South Dakota, 300 miles from a synagog. The Sinykins started with a quarter section, 160 acres, and built their ranch up to 5,500 acres, about eight square miles. They called their place "The Flying Triangle." Education for the children was resolved by boarding them out in Minneapolis, where there were excellent Jewish schools. In 1955, the ranch was still in the hands of the family and was managed by L. A. (Bronco Lou) Sinykin. One of the best known of large-scale farmers was Simon Fishman (b. 1878), a Russian who had come to the United States at the age of twelve. After peddling in a number of the western states, Fishman turned to farming. Over the years, he stood out as a pioneer wheat grower on the High Plains, in Nebraska and Kansas. It is estimated that he broke more than 100,000 acres of virgin soil to the plough. After serving Sydney, Nebraska, as mayor in 1903, he moved on to Tribune, Kansas, where he represented his neighbors in both houses of the state legislature. It was Senator Fishman who shipped out the first carload of grain in this stockraising region; before long, Tribune was shipping 1,000,000 bushels of grain in the freight cars that backed up to the town's sidings.

Fishman was not alone in his success; in later decades, a New York Jew became one of America's leading raisers of turkeys; a fruit farmer grew 20,000 bushels of high quality apples in his orchards, and in 1937 a poultryman received a national award for having raised "The Hen of the Century"; she set the world record in the production of eggs. In his heyday, Fishman was recognized all over the United States as a wheat baron; Davis Rubin, of Devils Lake in North Dakota, earned no agricultural crown. His career, however, was more typical of the immigrant farmer. To encourage him, the Jewish Agricultural and Industrial Aid Society started him with a loan for which he paid 6 percent interest; the neighboring banks might have charged him as much as 22 percent. Like other homesteaders he often slept on straw and drank muddy water from a ditch. But, God be praised, after seven years he had saved enough to bring over his family. To increase his earnings, he went to work for a farmer who paid him eighty cents a day; his neighbor cheated him; he never paid him. For fifteen long years, up to 1907, he slaved, but still owed for his mortgage. The family had to be fed, and he made a little extra money herding cattle, collecting junk, buying and selling wool and hides. It was a hard, bitter way of life. There were others who suffered even more; some of the accounts of the hardships of the Jewish homesteaders are almost unbelievable.

To summarize the obvious, these colonists, homesteaders, and farmers in the years 1870–1920 moved out to the country to improve themselves; most did not succeed but were obliged to move off the land speedily; few persisted; they had no desire to establish farming dynasties. The successful ones rarely lived to see their children till the family acres; it was exceedingly rare to find a third generation of Jewish farmers. The Connecticut tobacco growers often prospered; the denizens of the South Jersey settlements survived, because they combined specialty farming with industry. They cultivated berries, vegetables, fruits, and flowers for the nearby city markets; they raised poultry and solicited summer boarders. They were not good farmers; immigrants of peasant background did better. However, it is not surprising to learn that their standard of living was higher than that of other immigrants; the house came before the barn. They were very much interested in social and educational organizations and insisted on good or better schools wherever they were; they were independent voters, not tied irrevocably to one party. All this is a brief profile of the Jews on the South Jersey farms.[34]

STATISTICS

How many Jews farmed? A United States government agency estimated in 1909 that there were about 2,700 farms in Jewish hands, in thirty-six states. This would imply a maximum of about 15,000 souls in the industry. New York State in the early decades of the twentieth century could boast of over a dozen "Jewish" farm towns. In the years between 1912 and 1914 there was talk of 18,000 to 25,000 Jews on the farms in the United States; in 1925 some experts claimed that there were about 50,000 Jews living in the rural areas. United States Jewry then numbered 3,500,000 to 4,000,000 souls. It is said that, by the middle of the twentieth century, Jewish farmers owned about 600,000 acres of land. These figures fade into insignificance when one recalls that the Floersheims, of Springer, New Mexico, could boast that they owned or controlled 60,000 acres at Las Jaritas, their cattle ranch.[35]

REMOVAL

Colonization, farming, and "removal" are closely related. America's Jewish leaders pushed hard to put Jews on the soil because they wanted them removed from the urban ghettos, which were only too often no better than slums. As early as the 1730's, London's Sephardic Jews had a refugee problem which they resolved by dispatching unassorted Jews—Spanish-Portuguese and Germans—to Georgia. Removal was a general American problem. In 1817, Hezekiah Niles, a Baltimore editor, urged that new settlers move into the interior; the maritime provinces were already crowded. Removal became an American Jewish policy in the late 1830's when, in the midst of depression, it was proposed that the Tender Sheep, Zeire Ha-Zon, be settled on Western farmsteads. By the late 1860's, when the unwelcomed Russians started arriving, it was hoped that they would be shipped out to the West and the South. In the 1870's, the Union of American Hebrew Congregations began talking of colonization —in distant regions, of course. Removal became urgent in that decade; immigration had speeded up; most of the newcomers, it was said, had decided to remain in New York City. Too many, it was felt, were staying on; they had to be dispersed. From the 1880's to the 1920's, removal was the goal of many of the country's Jewish leaders. Get them out of New York City; the ghetto encourages crime, retards Americanization, and increases prejudices against Jews. An eminent American Jewish scientist was disturbed; these masses would yet take over the community and incite anti-Semitism. Moreover, once these newcomers moved on, the charities would not be overburdened; the community would not be Yiddishized; East European Orthodoxy would not flourish; the Marxists would have departed. Vain hope! If these exotics remained in New York, immigration to this country would be restricted by the apprehensive Gentiles. What a pity if the portals to America were closed.

As early as 1881, after the Russian riots, New York's United Hebrew Charities stationed a man at Castle Garden to help the new arrivals and to encourage them to keep moving, to go to different parts of the country. When, in 1882, 3,700 Jews landed in New York, the Hebrew Emigrant

Aid Society shipped more than 2,600 to 166 cities and towns in more than twenty states. Some of thsse cities, in turn, served as centers from which Jews were distributed to nearby and even distant villages. A handful of newcomers who arrived in Buffalo were sent to a neighboring town, Brockton, New York, where a farming commune for Russian Jews had been established by the British philosemite, Lawrence Oliphant. This English philanthropist provided the little flock with kosher food and a Scroll of the Law. The Milwaukee Immigrant Relief Society members dispatched some of the Rumanians on their doorsteps to the Dakotas, but a number of them refused to remain and returned. Milwaukee shoe manufacturer, Adolph W. Rich, rustled up jobs for hundreds of these émigrés in the early 1900's. Atlanta received its quota of new arrivals in 1882. Those who established themselves brought in relatives.[36]

A decade after the 1881 pogroms, Russian Jewry was again faced with a crisis; thousands were expelled in 1891 from Moscow and other cities. Immigration to America picked up. The Hebrew Emigrant Aid Society was reorganized under a different name, and new arrivals were again told not to crowd into the New York ghetto. As the panic of 1892 hit the country, unemployed Gentiles and their labor unions wanted no competition from East European Jewish immigrants. The Secretary of State warned Simon Wolf, and he in turn urged the arriving Jews to scatter; low visibility was the better part of wisdom. The Baron de Hirsch Fund leaders, now with money in hand, provided the means for transportation out of New York; they harangued their listeners with the gospel of Americanization, vocational training, and ruralization. In the late 1890's, the newly organized National Conference of Jewish Charities worked closely with B'nai B'rith to place immigrants in the smaller towns. A special society was established by the old-timers to aid the Rumanians who were fleeing from their native land. Finally, in 1900, the Baron de Hirsch Fund and the Jewish Colonization Association—both Hirsch agencies—created the Jewish Agricultural and Industrial Aid Society to "remove" Jews and, if possible, settle them on the soil.[37]

In order to emphasize the necessity of keeping immigrants out of New York, a special committee was set up in 1901 by the Jewish Agricultural and Industrial Aid Society. It was called the Industrial Removal Office (IRO). The IRO soon made connections in the major cities of the country, particularly those on the east side of the Mississippi. It was interested in securing employment for Jews in outlying towns; its primary job was to divert immigration to the interior. Once a few Jews established themselves in a hinterland village or city, others would follow. Timid souls constantly insisted that, if Jews manifested high visibility in the cities, anti-Jewish immigration restrictions would be hastened. In 1903, the Union of American Hebrew Congregations solemnly asked its constitu-

ent congregations to help get the Jews out of New York where 70 per-
cent of the arriving Jews remained. There were hundreds of thousands of
East European Jews living within one square mile on the Lower East Side.
This it was feared would tend to breed immorality and crime. Support the
IRO! The Industrial Removal Office went to work with gusto; approximately 4,000 of the incoming "Russians" were sent to Detroit; they quarreled with their benefactors, but they remained; 2,000 were dispatched to
Nebraska, primarily to Omaha. They found jobs in the packing houses,
the smelters, the railroad shops. Artisans plied their crafts. If there were
prevailing industries, the new Jews found a niche in them, often as manual laborers. On the whole, the old-line Jewish settlers helped the newcomers. In the years 1907-1908, about 350 came to Denver either directly from the East or via Galveston. Some were given newsstands;
others a horse, a wagon, and a license and sent out to peddle; girls worked
as waitresses in restaurants; the tuberculars did what they could.[38]

THE GALVESTON MOVEMENT

The 1905 murders in Russia impelled many to turn to the United States;
in 1906, over 150,000 Jews came here in one year. This inundation
frightened many American Gentiles as well as the already established
Jews. The commissioner of immigration, Frank P. Sargent, wanted the
Jews scattered; he deplored urban congestion; the radicals among the
newcomers were deemed a menace; it was an anarchist who had assassinated President McKinley. Simon Wolf and his friends on the Board of
Delegates on Civil and Religious Rights believed that entrance through
southern ports was most advisable. Wolf and the New York financier
Schiff were in constant fear lest the anti-immigration forces become ascendant. Gentile conservative elements had been clamoring for decades to
close the ports. Schiff was hopeful that deflected Jews could build up the
more thinly populated states of the South and the West. Southern states
were eager for settlers; the Jews of Germany urged Slavic Jewish refugees
to head for South America or the less thickly settled Gulf states in North
America.[39]

American Jews, constantly apprehensive, with their own welfare in
mind, objected strenuously to ghetto congestion and the increasing crime
rate among Jews; the apparently slow rate of Americanization among the
"Russians" was troubling. In the minds of the earlier settlers, congestion
was a basic evil. The visionary Zionists thought Palestine was the answer
for all Jews; Zangwill's Jewish Territorial Organization (ITO) wanted an
autonomous enclave anywhere; Baron de Hirsch's Jewish Colonization
Association had opted for the Argentine as a haven for oppressed East Europeans. Schiff and many of his contemporaries, determining to take action, decided that Galveston, Texas, must be the port of entry for the my-

riads of arriving Jews; there was ample room in the South and the West. Schiff was willing to spend $500,000 to this end; Zangwill, the Territorialist, would have preferred some form of a Jewish state, but something had to be done. "We can only weep, sing dirges over the dead, and send round the collection box," he mourned.

Schiff knew the dangers of settlement in the South. He knew Jews could not compete with the blacks; Zangwill seems to have preferred a political enclave in Nevada. Dispersion and emancipation, he warned, made for dissolution. Sarcastically, the tough-minded Zangwill told his friends that they provided kosher food for observant immigrants moving to the South and then told them they would have to work on the Sabbath. Schiff, the American patriot, and Zangwill, the enclavist and Jewish nationalist, composed their differences for the nonce. They worked together to ship the Jews to Galveston. Zangwill's Jewish Territorial Organization encouraged the Russians to emigrate; there was even a Yiddish paper in Russia which advised prospective emigrants; it was called *Wohin*, "Whither." German steamers sailing out of Bremen filled their holds with émigrés; on the way back they loaded up with cotton; it seemed a good arrangement. Schiff organized the American end. The IRO was made a separate organization in 1907; the Galveston entry was supervised by a special committee, the Jewish Immigrants' Information Bureau; it had its own managers in New York and Galveston; the inspirational leader in Galveston was Rabbi Henry Cohen (1863-1952). This man was sui generis, a personage. He was a linguist, a social worker, a man of integrity who was recognized as one of Texas's most notable citizens. As a reformer, he sought to improve the state's prison system; he was the first historian of Texas Jewry, a contributor to the *Jewish Encyclopedia*, a Zionist, and subsequently a member of the anti-Zionist American Council for Judaism. How he built a bridge between the two disparities was his own secret. When a Catholic lass needed money to continue her education, he saw to it; when a Greek Orthodox political refugee was faced with deportation, Cohen went to Washington and interested William Howard Taft personally. The President marveled that a Jew would intercede for a man of different faith. When Cohen died, many of the stores in Galveston were closed; the whole town mourned. Speaking of his Russian charges who passed through Galveston, Cohen said that they brought brawn, sinew, and brains to America. Most of the newcomers were multilingual.[40]

GALVESTON: FAILURE

Apparently, the Galveston Movement was a failure. The differences between the Jewish Colonization Association and Zangwill's Territorialists and the harassment by the Russian government of this push to the American South was no help. All told, about 10,000 Jews passed through the city from 1907 to 1914. Brands plucked from the burning! Problems in the towns where they settled frightened off prospective emigrants. The Galveston port authorities and their Washington supporters were not helpful. The Jews felt that their medical examinations were unduly rigorous. At his post in Washington, Wolf saved thousands of Jews in New York and other ports from deportation. Indeed, relatively few Jews were sent back. "Assisted emigration" was illegal; Jews insisted that the help they gave the newcomers was permissible and proper. The depression of 1907-1908 deterred many from emigrating; labor unions wanted no competition; World War I stopped emigration on the high seas. Of all the Jews who turned to the United States as a haven, only about 3 percent came in through Galveston from 1907 to 1914.[41]

While the German steamers were unloading their cargoes of Russian Jews at Galveston, the Industrial Removal Office continued to urge new arrivals in New York to settle in distant states. In 1908 the Union of American Hebrew Congregations encouraged Rabbi Martin Zielonka of El Paso to investigate Mexico as a future home for Jewish refugees. Reaching out since the 1890's, Jews spoke of the possibilities in that land. The periodic revolutions, the poverty of the peons, and the hostility of the Catholic Church made it clear that Mexico was no option for Jews. Adolf Kraus of the B'nai B'rith thought that Jews might yet make their homes in Mexico or Brazil or Cuba. Harris Horwitz, the most learned of that Chicago Lithuanian clan, suggested politely to Kraus that, since he was affluent, he could afford to send his sons to those Spanish-Portuguese lands and give the East European Jews here in the United States a chance to prove their mettle! The Sephardic Jewish immigrant, Nissim Behar, organized the National Immigration League in 1906 to counter the anti-immigration forces; two years later, a group representative of New York's East European liberals and communal leaders established the American Jewish Society for the Regulation of Immigration. It, too, was in favor of removal with the hope that it would pacify the men in and out of Congress who were determined to keep out undesirables—East Europeans! Even the Hebrew Immigrant Aid Society, an organization favored by America's newcomers, urged Jews to get out of New York. The accusation by New York's police commissioner, Theodore Bingham, that the Jews were committing half of the town's crimes shocked all Jews in 1908. Four years later, Isaac Hourwich published his *Immigration and Labor: The Economic Aspects of European Immigration to the United States*. This magisterial work, a scientific apologia, had been subsidized by the American Jewish Committee. American Jewry was on the defensive.

It was becoming abundantly clear that American Gentiles everywhere —in the thinly settled Southwest and the Plains states, too—were not enamored of Jews. There were complaints that the personnel in the immigrant trains leaving Galveston were discourteous to the Russians. The Yiddish newspapers in New York were not eager to lose subscribers; the newcomers were not happy to settle in the American "wilderness." Some had no sooner arrived in a small town than they dreamt of removal to a bigger city, to New York. The East, not the West, was the hearth of Jewish life and of industry. Schiff was unhappy that his plan for Southern and Western settlements had failed. It had failed, yet individuals, many indeed, would make their way in those far off places. Abraham Pilicer (Pulitzer?) had landed in Galveston with about $2 when he was shipped out to Iowa. He started out as a plumber's helper; his salary was $2 a week. Ultimately, he became a master plumber and a successful businessman. Pilicer served in World War I, started an American Legion post in his Iowa town, and was selected finally as a member of the electoral college committee which informed Dwight W. Eisenhower that he had been reelected President of the United States.[42]

The congestion problem began to resolve itself while the elite was still struggling in its own way to disperse New York's immigrant Jews. As Jews attained even a modest degree of economic security, they began moving, as early as the turn of the century, to Upper Manhattan, Yorkville, Harlem, the Bronx, and Brooklyn. By 1904, there were 60,000 Jews in the Brownsville district of Brooklyn. Jews did go to the hinterland, but on their own; they avoided the villages and settled in sizeable towns; they sought economic opportunities and insisted on the solace of an organized Jewish community. A very substantial number always remained in Greater New York, enjoying its social and cultural life and valuing its economic advantages. By 1921, about 45 percent of all Jews in the country lived in America's megalopolis. From 1901 to 1917, the Industrial Removal Office had shipped out—assisted, if you will—about 74,000 individuals. They were settled in about 1,800 towns and villages. (Many of them came back to the East.) The IRO closed in 1922; the first anti-Jewish immigration act had passed in 1921; the gates were closing. The IRO was a minor success; the refugees who remained in the transHudson West brought out their families and friends. Old communities were strengthened; new communities were established.[43]

CHAPTER THREE

PART I

THE EAST EUROPEANS IN THE HINTERLAND TO 1921

INTRODUCTION

For the purpose of this work the hinterland is defined as all areas outside of New York City except Long Island and Westchester County. It is patent that the city is very important because during this period it sheltered a large percentage of America's Jews and the most important national Jewish institutions. By 1920 there were approximately 3,600,000 Jews in the United States; about 2,000,000 were in the hinterland. Most were from the Slavic lands; indeed by 1921 the majority of the Jews in this country had come from Russia, Poland, Galicia, Hungary, and Rumania. Many had come even before 1881. There was no major city in the United States that did not have an East European Jewish community by 1880. The newcomers settled in every state of the Union, primarily in cities, towns, and villages east of the Mississippi. They were not found in the South in substantial numbers; the New South of industry had yet to evidence impressive activity.

The "Russians"—thus they were lumped together by earlier settlers—started to come in large numbers after the Russian killings in 1881 and the city expulsions in 1891. They came to these shores because of the economic opportunities opened to them, and many of them flocked to the outlying areas where it was easier for aliens to survive commercially. In a number of states these newcomers organized communities before the natives and Germans; these latter were too few. Thus immigrants from the Slavic lands were the first to establish permanent Jewish settlements in Vermont, Maine, New Hampshire, the Dakotas, Idaho, Montana, Washington State and probably in other places too. If they came to a town where other Jews had already organized communities the two groups eyed each other suspiciously; nevertheless the newcomers did not hesitate in an emergency to turn to the "Germans"; after all they were Jews.[1]

How did these refugees make a living? That is important. Because of historic circumstances, in their original homelands these newcomers inclined toward trading and shopkeeping. They had come from villages and towns; they were destined here therefore to be petit bourgeois; even the artisans, working for themselves, were often shopkeepers. Many Jews would have preferred to avoid the factories here; often they had no choice. The problems confronted by them were real; they had little or no capital; they spoke no English. A Mr. Segal of Chillicothe, Ohio, was at home in Hebrew; his English at first was limited to four simple words. When a kindly client asked this peddler if he had a family he answered: "Look in the sack." (Some of his sons, university trained, were to become Phi Beta Kappas.) There was always a substantial number of men who landed at Castle Garden and Ellis Island who were artisans, craftsmen; they got jobs. Workers preferred to be self-employed; carpenters began to remodel buildings becoming small contractors. Tailors opened shops; butchers wanted to be on their own; blacksmiths were numerous. Bear in mind that prior to 1910 there were few automobiles on the streets; horses had to be shod, wagons repaired.

Peddlers were found in every town and city. New York Jews had organized peddlers associations by 1886, if not earlier; a group that came together in 1906 counted 3,000 members. In 1890, 11 percent of New York's Jews was engaged in this traffic; in 1900, 24.5 percent of the Jews in that city were peddlers, hucksters, and pushcart merchants; in 1904 about 5,000 of these businessmen were arrested in the metropolis for violating municipal ordinances; by 1912 there were over 14,000 out on the streets hawking their wares; most of them were without licenses. Many of these enterprisers became junk dealers; the lucky and the smart ones among them opened yards and made money during World War I. Immigrants west of the Hudson continued to ply their trades as urban and country peddlers till after World War I. Fast interurban transportation, mail order catalog houses, good roads, and cheap Ford automobiles put them out of business. In the towns fruit and vegetable hucksters were not easily discouraged; some became produce wholesalers. By that time, 1920, notion and garment peddlers in the big cities and small towns were opening dry goods and gent's furnishing stores; wives pitched in to help make a living. Often they were responsible for whatever success was achieved.

Individual peddlers had unique experiences. After coming to this country in the early 1880's Moses Menahem Zieve turned to peddling in Northfield, Minnesota. He was a wagon peddler who finally succeeded after six years in saving enough money to bring over his wife and his four children. Even on the road he kept kosher, carrying his own cooking utensils in the wagon. Sabbath, religiously observed, was spent with a sympathetic farmer. When on Saturday night the stars began to appear the farmer's children called out to him that he could now smoke. Sunday morning he went to the church of some German farmers and spoke to them in his German-Yiddish on the Pentateuchal portion of the week. They called him Holy Moses. Like their fellow Americans, these Jewish peddlers, shopkeepers, artisans, factory and mill workers suffered from the frequent depressions and consequent unemployment. These men worked hard struggling to make a living; it was difficult for them; their English background left much to be desired; a few became affluent; a very few became rich.[2]

EAST EUROPEAN JEWS ON THE PACIFIC COAST

WASHINGTON AND OREGON

No two Jews in the United States had identical careers. By studying communities and individuals we will be able to glimpse their struggles. This survey, however, may well show what they had in common. The geographical location determined, to a degree, the careers of individuals and communities too. There were Russian-Polish congregations in Washington State by the 1880's; some of the earliest ones began as sick-care and burial associations. The Weretnikows were among the first Jewish settlers in Seattle. Bella, one of the girls, was born about 1880 in the Ukraine. The family peddled in Canada, in Winnipeg. The Winnipeg rabbi—she recounts—was faced with a problem. One of his congregants was set on divorcing his wife but he had a child. Who was to have custody of the little one? Since there was no Solomon to help the rabbi make a decision, he told the couple to stay married, have another baby, and then each take a child. No sooner said than done, but the wife gave birth to twins. Faced with this mathematical impasse the husband decided to remain married and help raise the family of three. In the meantime Bella's family moved on to Seattle where her mama, illiterate, opened a store on Skid Road. This was about the year 1893. The mother was an excellent businesswoman; the laborers who patronized her shop trusted her and she served as their banker; when gold was discovered in the Klondike she outfitted them. Bella, determined to educate herself, became the first female lawyer in the state of Washington. Portland to the south had a Polish synagog in the 1860's but these "Poles" may well have been Prussians from Eastern Germany; it is not improbable that Russians who came to town would have been tolerated in their synagog. By the late 1880's Russian émigrés had a conventicle of their own. They managed to maintain good relations with the earlier Central European settlers who lent them a Scroll of the Law and gave them plots in the local cemetery. The new ghetto where they settled was called Little Russia.[3]

CALIFORNIA

Russians and other East European Jews were among California's Argo-
nauts. During Gold Rush days people came there from all corners of the
earth; East European Jews were no exception. Judah D. Eisenstein, the
early American Jewish historian and perceptive observer, was even of the
opinion that there were more Russian Jews in San Francisco than in New
York in the 1850's. It is true that there were numerous Jewish families
from the Slavic lands in that state at that time. Eisenstein maintained that
Jews began leaving Russia and Poland after the conscription laws were introduced in the 1820's and extended in the 1840's by the brutal Nicholas
I. Enterprising East Europeans in California of the 1850's turned to im-
porting and doing business with Alaska and Japan. In a modest fashion
Jews helped open Japan to American commerce and industry. Even in antebellum days these Russian-Polish newcomers had succeeded in founding a rigidly observant congregation which met for services on Monday,
Thursday, the Sabbath, and all fast and feast days. They called themselves
Shomre Shabbas, the Observers of the Sabbath. A visitor to their services
in the 1850's was struck by the fact that on Yom Kippur, the Day of
Atonement, these pious worshippers took off their shoes and spread straw
on the floor. Some synagogs back in Russia had stone floors; straw served
as insulation against the cold; the Russian synagog in San Francisco had a
wooden floor but it still adhered to this quaint custom. The Spanish-Portuguese Jews spread sand on the floors of their sanctuaries to remind them
of the desert which their ancestors had traversed during the Exodus.
Myth hides reality. The floor of medieval unheated synagogs and cathe-
drals were covered with sand—straw—for reasons of hygiene and sanitation! Straw and sand could always be swept up removing dirt and filth.

The refugees from the Slavic lands began to come to California in
large numbers by the turn of the nineteenth century. Few came at first because California was a long way from New York, the port of debarkation.
These new arrivals were poor and could not make the long journey. Yet
by 1900 these exiles already had six conventicles of their own and numerous auxiliary organizations in San Francisco. By 1921 there were about
30,000 Jews in the city many of whom came from Eastern Europe. Sacramento, Stockton, and San Diego could also document their presence and
the rise of their communities. It was during the 1890's that these men and
women began turning to Los Angeles, the city of the future. They were
found there as junk dealers, peddlers, clerks, shopkeepers, and garment
workers. And where there were garment workers there were socialists and
Workmen's Circle lodges. At the end of this period, 1920, the newcomers
had numerous synagogs, charities, Hebrew schools, a free loan association, two Zionist organizations, and a cemetery. That year Jews in town
estimated that they had a population of about 20,000; later in the century

Los Angeles would become the second largest Jewish community in the world with well over half a million men, women, and children.

We repeat, no two of these newcomers to Los Angeles could tell the same life story yet they had this in common—struggle and survival. Isaac Henry Goldberg (1882-1942) of Boyle Heights, a Russian, had worked in Chicago, La Porte, Indiana, Des Moines, Iowa, and Los Angeles. At times he was a junk dealer and a dry goods merchant. In the 1920's he was in the Mojave Desert buying and selling old machinery but he finally decided to become a poultry farmer. His chosen avocation was to busy himself in his Orthodox synagog and its Hebrew school. He would not let his son go to the public schools until he had first learned some Hebrew; he was determined that the boy would be a Jew. Henry Jacob Clar (b. circa 1885) came out of the Ukraine with his parents who moved from New York to Denver. Like many other lads young Henry went to school and sold newspapers to help keep the pot boiling. In 1905 he opened a shoe repair shop in Leadville; the following year he and some relatives homesteaded; each family had a half section, 320 acres. By 1922 he and his wife and children had moved on to Los Angeles. For years he worked as a waiter in a restaurant investing any extra cash in land in Colorado and Los Angeles. He reached out to other businesses, sent a daughter through high school, and a son through university. He certainly enjoyed the sociality he experienced in the Masonic order which he had joined. He died in 1970. What would have been his lot had he remained in Russia?[4]

HAWAII AND ALASKA

The Hawaiian Islands were admitted as the fiftieth state on August 21, 1959. This shows how young this country is; it is growing under our very eyes. The Islands, in the Pacific, are off by themselves about 2,000 miles distant from the California mainland. Until recently kosher meat had to be flown in; there was no problem in securing a supply of bagels; good kosher bagels could be purchased from a local Chinese baker. Throughout the nineteenth and early twentieth centuries the Jewish population fluctuated. Volume one of the *American Jewish Year Book* reported there were only twenty Jews on the islands in 1900; this was a guess. By 1985 there were about 7,500. The Children of Israel started arriving in the 1840's; they were German and English; later the Californians began to make their appearance. Intermarriage was common; this was true of all Jewish pioneer groups. A marriage between two Jews was celebrated in 1879; a San Francisco rabbi authorized a local Jewish layman to officiate.

King Kalakaua had a Sefer Torah, a Scroll of the Law, given to him as a gift, probably by a Jew. The Jews in Honolulu borrowed this Sefer Torah on occasion when they held services. There were Jews in the king's entourage. One was his "secretary of the treasury," appointed not because of his fiscal expertise but for his capacity to hold his liquor and to play poker. The Islands were annexed in 1898; two years later Hawaii became a territory. By the turn of the century two disparate Jewish communities emerged, town and uniform, a civilian and a military force congeries. The latter was more numerous. By the 1920's the National Jewish Welfare Board and its chaplains were active; they worked with the Jewish civilians too. One of the naval clergymen, Rabbi Samuel Sobel, was accorded an honorary degree by a local Christian college.

Jews began to swell the Hawaiian population after World War II. Pearl Harbor was an important station when it was bombed by the Japanese in 1941; it was a line of defense established to protect the distant mainland; among its personnel were Jewish soldiers and sailors. By the 1980's Honolulu—where most Jews lived—had become a typical Jewish community, structurally, institutionally, culturally, religiously. There were Reform and Conservative Jews; the former were more numerous. By 1960 they had built a beautiful temple. The city had its measure of cemeteries and sanctuaries, Jewish schools, a Hadassah group, a day camp, a fraternal order, men's clubs, youth societies, a community relations defense committee, a Hillel installation at the local university, and a Jewish Welfare Fund. Hawaiian Jews had been sending money abroad for a long generation. In the early days a few Jews were employed to help administer the sugar plantations; in the late twentieth century Jews were in commerce, trades, and the professions. They were at ease in the multiracial society that is distinctly Hawaiian.[5]

In January 1959, about eight months before Hawaii was admitted to the Union, Alaska became the forty-ninth state. The rise of Alaska Jewry is a fascinating story. It is a rerun—as it were—of the growth of an eighteenth-century American Jewish community; the historian turns the clock backward; he learns how frontier communities live and survive. This new state, the largest in the Union, is about seventy-five times as large as the State of Israel but the smallest in population. There are more Jews in one New York City apartment house than in the whole state of Alaska. As late as 1901, after the rush to the Klondike, Alaska did not merit an article in volume one of the *Jewish Encyclopedia*. This huge block of land was Russian till 1867–1868; its commerce was controlled by a Russian firm interested primarily in furs. Jews from the czar's empire were employed by the Russian entrepreneurs; some of their descendants, children of the native women, are still to be found in this new state. An American Jew of Russian birth also was found buying and selling his wares in Russian Alaska; his business carried him as far north and west as Vladivostok.

Deciding that Alaska was a liability, Russia sold its province to the United States for $7,200,000. A Jew by the name of Benjamin Levi claimed to be the first to hoist the stars and stripes over the new American possession. There is some evidence to the effect that Jewish businessmen in San Francisco may have engineered the purchase of Alaska by the United States; their lobbyist worked on Secretary of State Seward. They bypassed their rival, the Hudson's Bay Company, and by 1868 succeeded in establishing the Alaska Commercial Company. The prime movers in this corporation were two men, brothers-in-law, Louis Sloss and Lewis Gerstle. (There is now a Gerstle River in the state.) This company, having resources in the millions, bought out the Russian American Company. Sloss, Gerstle, and their associates, Jews and Gentiles, were intent on securing monopolistic control of the Seal Islands, the Pribilofs. The United States government gave them a twenty-year contract, 1870-1889; through this agreement the government recouped its Alaska cost; the Jews, San Franciscan entrepreneurs, made millions. The Alaska Commercial Company operated on a grand scale; its steamers and schooners ploughed the ocean highways between San Francisco, Seattle, and Alaska; it sent boats and barges up the Yukon; all told it had eighty trading posts —several in Russian Siberia—and built schools, churches, roads. Charges were made that the firm exploited the natives in its company stores—as did all colonial monopolists—but it also brought in goods, necessities; this is civilization; this, too, is progress. Life was not altogether dull on an outpost of the company, in Unalaska. Rudolf Neumann, the manager, a German Jew, staged balls every Sunday night. To the accompanying music of a wheezy pump organ, the station's personnel danced with the local Aleutian women till the early hours of the morning.

The San Francisco Jews who built the Alaska Commercial Company became wealthy but their profits were as nothing compared to the millions garnered by the Guggenheims in this huge state. This dynasty of mining entrepreneurs—aided by J. Pierpont Morgan and Jacob H. Schiff —sank enormous sums in its effort to exploit the copper mountain near Kennecott Creek, reaping a harvest that helped make the Guggenheims one of the richest Jewish families in the world. The Guggenheims owned coal mines, forests, canneries, iron deposits, railroads. Theirs was a herculean task; they lugged the twentieth century into the primeval forest; they were probably the state's largest investors; their rewards were commensurate.

Neither the Alaska Commercial Company of the nineteenth century nor the Guggenheim interests of the twentieth century controlled all of the state's Jewish commerce and industry. Dozens of other Jews went into business though on a much more modest scale. They were middle-class merchants offering goods and services. They were fur buyers, saloonkeepers, traders, shopkeepers; there were also construction workers. A few were suspected of peddling whiskey and weapons to the natives.

Jews, too, were government employees; some were part of the armed forces stationed in Alaska. The Jewish chaplains brought Judaism, schooling, to the settlers in the scattered towns and posts. Individual men made their mark in the larger Alaska community. Mount Applebaum was named after the mine owner, Samuel Applebaum; Jews served as mayors in Juneau and Nome; one town owed its library to a generous Jew; the first radio station and the first movie house in Alaska were built by Children of the House of Israel. A Jewish Federal District judge held court in a Coast Guard cutter. Dr. Ernest Gruening was territorial governor from 1935 to 1953; in 1958 he went to the United States Senate. A generation earlier the Russian Jew, Solomon Ripinski, was honored as a linguist, an artist, an amateur physician. His was a most interesting career for he came into the territory in the early 1890's, years before the Gold Rush. This newcomer helped write the codes for the territory. He passed the bar exam, became a lawyer, and, finally, was appointed a judge. The town of Haines was built around his store; Mount Ripinski bears his name.

Wherever the Jews gathered together in early America they held services—ten is a quorum—and started to build a "community." This was true, too, in Alaska. In the late 1860's, after Alaska was ceded to America the traders who had flocked there held services, and when Passover rolled around they munched matzo brought up from the lower forty-eight. In 1869 an Alaskan Jew glancing through a San Francisco newspaper saw that a group of rabbis, meeting in Philadelphia, had passed radical resolutions threatening the very integrity of Orthodoxy; he protested indignantly. The stampedes, the gold rushes beginning in the late 1890's, brought Jews to the farthest reaches of the territory; in 1901 they organized a Hebrew Benevolent Society in Nome and prepared to celebrate the High Holy Days. Somehow or other they bought or borrowed a Sefer Torah, a Scroll of the Law. Cemeteries were soon laid out in a few towns.

Despite the fact that Alaska was never blessed with a substantial migration of Jewish newcomers it began to shelter a permanent community after World War II. Jewish chaplains were in the van of the religious leaders; as air force officers they were able to move about quickly. It was not unusual for such chaplains to fly hundreds of miles to help boys and girls learn their portion of Holy Scriptures as they approached their thirteenth year. An Orthodox officer succeeded in inducing the authorities to build a mikveh so that his observant wife might take her ritual bath. Only two communities of size emerged, Fairbanks and Anchorage. Fairbanks Jewry owed much to Robert and Jessie S. Bloom, Irish Jewish pioneers, who were utterly devoted to their ancestral traditions. The husband helped establish the first Alaska college and served as a lay chaplain at the Fairbanks army base; his wife was one of a small group who organized Alaska's first kindergarten and Girl Scouts troop. In 1985 there were 210

Jewish souls in town; Anchorage could boast of 600. It also had a Reform synagog. There may have been 1,000 Jews in all Alaska; thus eighty percent of the Jews in the state were in these two towns. Here on the edge of the Arctic Circle Judaism was beginning to take firm root.[6]

THE NEW NORTHWEST: IDAHO, MONTANA, WYOMING, NEVADA

There was to be no Russian-Polish synagog in Idaho till 1912. That was three years before the German-born Moses Alexander became governor of the state. The mining booms in Montana had attracted Jewish adventurers as early as the 1860's, but when by the turn of the century the East European Jews began to make their presence felt there were still so few Jews in any town that religious compromise was imperative if a community was to be established. Out and out Orthodox services had no future on this western frontier. This state did not attract Jews; it sheltered about 2,500 of them in 1898 and about the same number two decades later. By the 1980's the Jewish population had declined precipitously; there were fewer than 700 Israelites in all of Montana.

The Rumanian Herman Fliegelman had come to Helena in 1888 where he built a large business, the New York Dry Goods Store. His two daughters Frieda and Belle grew up in the state. As children the big event in their week was to go to the local confectionery or to the swimming pool. As decorous girls in the pre-bikini age they garbed themselves properly when swimming; they wore bloomers, skirts, a top with sailor collar, and long stockings. They were well insulated against the water. For reading the girls turned to Martha F. Finley's Elsie Dinsmore books; they were pious, moralistic, well adapted to the mores and ethical standards of the age. The Fliegelman home library was more sophisticated for it included works of Dickens, Scott, Victor Hugo, Shakespeare, and an assortment of books on history and geography. Ingersoll and Twain were not missing. At night by the light of a kerosene lamp Papa Fliegelman would read Hugo's *Les Miserables*, in English, of course, to his family. The library also included an unabridged dictionary and an encyclopedia.

The girls were taught piano and dancing, taken to a matinee two or three times a year, and encouraged to join a club which included both Jewish and Gentile children. When one of the Fliegelman girls was called a sheeney the experience was traumatic. Sooner or later most Jewish children anywhere, everywhere, in the United States encountered verbal anti-Jewish prejudice. It was a shock which reverberated throughout their lives. There were few bathtubs in Montana in the early days. The Fliegelman girls used tin tubs. Adhering to some Jewish laws the girls were forbidden by their parents to sew on the Sabbath but when mother fell asleep they sewed surreptitiously. These two girls were exceptional;

they went to college. Frieda was to emerge as a pioneer in the sociology of language; Belle, a suffragist, was one of the first woman reporters in the state. That was in 1914. Three years later she served as secretary for Jeannette Rankin, the first woman to go to Congress. Belle, a poet and playwright, wrote for the *Atlantic Monthly*. She was very proud of her lampshade; it was made of rejection slips sent her by publishers and editors. The Fliegelmans were not typical; not all immigrants read Shakespeare in the original; many, however, had read the English bard in Yiddish; thousands enjoyed adaptations of his plays in the Yiddish theatre.[7]

As it has already been noted above in the chapters on agriculture and colonies there were Jewish farmers in Wyoming who hailed originally from the Slavic lands. Individual Jews from Eastern Europe lived and worked in the territory in the 1860's and 1870's, but there was to be no Orthodox congregation there till 1910. One of the territory's pioneers was Henry Altman (b. 1841) who was to become president of the Cheyenne Jewish Relief Association and state chairman of the United Jewish Campaign. Altman moved west in a covered wagon. An itinerant peddler he followed the gangs that were laying track for the Union Pacific in the late 1860's. About the year 1875 he turned rancher and with his Scottish Jewish partner, Jacob Wasserman, raised prize stock. Altman was one of the founders of the Wyoming Stock Growers' Association. He served in both houses of the Wyoming legislature and worked industriously to help place the Russian-Polish immigrants sent west by the Industrial Removal Office. In the 1920's tiny Cheyenne with its 100 or more Jewish souls also included a Workmen's Circle lodge: anti-religious proletarians, socialists, huddled together for sociability 2,000 miles from the Lower East Side. One of Altman's contemporaries in Cheyenne was Samuel Idelman (1875-1913), a Lithuanian from Pilvissok. Iowa had a "colony" of these villagers. Samuel's father brought him over as a child. The father peddled in St. Joseph, Missouri, Red Oaks, Iowa, and kept pushing west till he reached Cheyenne. Samuel built one of Cheyenne's finest shops. The race is not to the swift not even to the pioneers. The Vetas, Noem and his wife Ada, came to Wyoming in 1906 when it was already a state. Noem got a job working for the Union Pacific Railroad; they paid him 16 cents an hour and he put in a ten-hour day; that was not bad pay. Thrifty, he saved enough to open a grocery store, built up a coal business and later turned to finance and insurance. The Veta children established an oil company that had stations in 56 Wyoming towns. They finally sold it to the Sinclair Oil Company for several million dollars.

Nevada like Montana was an early boom state; there was a mining rush in the 1850's and 1860's in which Jews participated. The East Europeans there had a chance to pray in traditional fashion in an Orthodox congregation which had been established in the 1860's; it was not until

1921, however, that the newcomers had a synagog of their own; that was in Reno. In 1920 there were only about 500 Jews in all of Nevada; in the 1980's there were over 13,000 in Las Vegas alone. A hundred years earlier there was not a single Jew in that town; the gambling industry helped turn a hamlet into a big city.[8]

ARIZONA AND NEW MEXICO

Many of the western states came to life with mining booms. Arizona was no exception. Individual Jews started coming into the territory in the 1860's; they were wise enough not to go prospecting but to open stores to outfit miners. Among them were the Goldwaters (Goldwassers) from Poland. The change of name was made in England. In the 1850's they were in San Francisco and Los Angeles. Unsuccessful in the City of the Angels these Jews, capmakers, left their general store and saloon and tried their luck in Arizona (1862). The two brothers, Joseph and Michael, opened stores and finally managed to do well. Michael was the grandfather of the later United States Senator Barry M. Goldwater. Jewishly, Arizona was to grow slowly. In 1907 Douglas was the only town in the territory with a congregation; the community consisted of 90 men, women, and children. This synagogal group was probably East European in origin. There was also a Hebrew Ladies' Aid. Can there be a Jewish community without a woman's welfare organization? Holy Day services were probably held in other towns wherever ten adult males came together. Under such circumstances natives, Germans, and Russians would join together for common worship. The old Hebrew prayer book was probably the liturgy employed. In the late 1870's there were said to be 48 Jews in all of Arizona; in 1920, about 1,000; in the 1980's over 50,000; the Sun Belt had come into its own.

New Mexico also probably sheltered some of the Russian newcomers. Orthodox services were held in Santa Fe in territorial days, probably in the home of one of the Spiegelbergs, successful merchants. In the course of the late nineteenth century Jews met together on religious occasions in Albuquerque and Las Vegas. Since the services held were traditional, East European Jews could conscientiously worship at them. There were still fewer than 1,000 Jews in New Mexico in 1920.[9]

UTAH AND COLORADO

Utah in 1920 had about 4,000 Jews; it was closer to the East Coast than Arizona and New Mexico. In 1880 there were only 258 Jews in the territory, but even before 1900 there was a Russian-Polish congregation in Salt Lake (1899) with a factotum who provided for the members' religious needs; he was probably a shohet. This prayer group called itself Montefiore Congregation after the English philanthropist whom all Jews revered. Utah's East Europeans were petty businessmen; they had little capital and the Mormons were tough competition. Some of the newcomers owned small retail stores, others sold secondhand clothing; one was a butcher.[10]

Like other states in the Rocky Mountains and Great Plains area, Jewish Colorado began modestly; in 1880 there were only 400 Jews in the state, by 1920 there were over 15,000; 11,000 were in Denver. In a sense this was a metropolitan community. Beginning with the 1890's there were Slavic immigrant conventicles and congregations in Denver, Boulder, Leadville, Pueblo, and Colorado Springs. Demographically and culturally, Colorado was beginning to look like a typical eastern state. Tuberculars from the East, primarily newcomers, helped build the state's Jewish community. Colorado Springs in its early days had trouble in rounding up a quorum for religious services. There were enough Jews in town but they begrudged the two hours for services on Saturday, the best business day in the week. After a quorum was gathered in the Springs the congregational leader would lock the doors and put the key in his pocket till the service was over. Schiff visited the Springs about the year 1915 and reproached these humble shopkeepers; there was more than one congregation, but no rabbi. They solemnly promised Schiff to do better but did nothing. Mrs. Finkelstein peddled in the mines, did well, and established a clothing store in the city; she called it the Hub; there was a Hub —usually a Jewish one—in almost every town of size in the country. One wonders how the name started; was it an oblique reference to Boston, America's hub?

In Denver the East Europeans were numerous enough to enjoy the luxury of prayer groups geographically oriented. The Hassidim, too, went off by themselves; there were even synagogs for clans, extended families. One man set up a congregation of his own and to make sure he would always have a minyan, a quorum, he dispensed schnapps. These Colorado Jews, like all Jews, may have enjoyed quarreling with one another—this they did vigorously—but they insisted on pious names for their synagogs: Lovers of the Faith, Guardians of the Faith, the Pursuer of Righteousness. By 1920 there were well over a dozen congregations for the newcomers with two "chief rabbis" in town. As early as 1902 the acculturated Orthodox hired Rabbi Charles E. H. Kauvar, a graduate of the Jewish Theological Seminary; this new group wanted an English-speaking minister. Denver's East European Jews, viewed as a body, were little different from any other Russian-Polish American Jewish community. No typical institution, religious or philanthropic, was missing; they had a snug world of their own, even a Russian bathhouse and, occasionally,

Yiddish theatrical troupes from the East. Those who desired could study Talmud; there were Hebrew schools for the young, a ritual pool for post-menstruous women, cemeteries, a Ladies' Shroud Society, and a free burial society for the poor. Over the years the Free Burial Society interred about 400 people; some were tuberculars who had come to Denver only to die. Wherever there are thousands of Jews there is poverty, the need for homes for the sick, the aged, dependent children, free matzo, and kosher wine for Passover. By 1904 the newcomers even began founding institutions of their own to provide for the tuberculars. They brought into existence the National Consumptives' Relief Society; they were unhappy with the earlier hospital set up by the old-timers. In 1907 Mrs. Fannie Lorber established a home to take care of the children of the tuberculars. She solicited clothing and fed the youngsters and was finally able to buy a house to shelter them. This was the Denver Sheltering Home, later to be called the Jewish National Home for Asthmatic Children. Comfortable in their ghetto in West Colfax, the newcomers were ministered to, in 1920, by thirty different organizations. Thrifty, most Jews succeeded in buying little homes of their own; they were not plagued by the evils of tenement house living. In reaching out to make a livelihood, Denver newcomers differed little from the Jewish immigrants of any large American town. The boys sold newspapers on the streets; individuals in the countryside homesteaded or were stockmen raising cattle. Only rarely did a Jew work in the mines; they were rejected by the hard rock miners.

There were a number of interesting immigrants in Denver in the years before 1921. And, let it be interjected at once, the examples cited could be multiplied in Colorado—and all other states—manifold. The Russian, Abraham M. Blumberg (b. 1873), studied medicine in this country and at the same time supported himself by teaching in a Hebrew school. With a doctor's diploma he moved West and settled in Seibert, Kit Carson County, Colorado; it was a very small town on the Kansas Pacific Railroad. He told the villagers he would stay and practice medicine in their midst if they would respect him as a Jew. They said they would. Then he sent for the girl with whom he had fallen in love when he taught Hebrew school. When his wife bore him a son he brought in a circumciser from Denver to initiate the child into the faith. All the Christian neighbors crowded into the room for the ceremony; they wanted to see whether the boy was born with horns. He imported his kosher meat on the express from Denver. After a year in town Blumberg was elected coroner. When his children grew up, over a decade later, he moved to Denver; he wanted to be sure that they would receive a good Jewish education; one of his daughters later became the president of the Parent-Teacher Association.

Isaac Shwayder, an East European peddler who had married in England, settled in Colorado in 1879. He moved about to different towns, Central City, Black Hawk, Nevadaville, trying to save a few dollars to bring the family over. That took two years. In 1888 he settled in Denver where there were opportunities for the children who were musical. One of the girls became a pianist and played later with the Detroit Symphony; another directed the choir in a Denver Lutheran church; still another took charge of the music in the local Reform synagog. Papa opened a grocery store and later on a secondhand shop; he was not successful. One of the sons, Jesse, who played the violin and the organ, started an orchestra in high school and sang in St. John's Cathedral. Finally Jesse and his brothers—there were several—turned to the luggage business. First they retailed, then they began wholesaling and manufacturing. The firm they created, Shwayder Brothers, was known for its Samsonite Luggage; its factory would one day become the largest in the world; there were times when it grossed $50,000,000 a year; in its first fifty years it did more than $500,000,000 worth of business.[11]

THE DAKOTAS

In the Dakotas—territory till 1889—Russian and Polish Jews were pioneers in the Jewish communities, such as they were. Many of the early Jews were colonists, homesteaders. Life on the land was brutally hard. South Dakota was never to become a Jewish center of any consequence. By 1916 the newcomers had a congregation in Sioux Falls; as late as 1920 there were only about 1,300 Jews in the state. Individuals were to become notable citizens. Ben Strool, a Lithuanian, homesteaded in the state in 1908. He founded the town of Strool and served as its postmaster and storekeeper. Years later his friends elected him State Commissioner of Schools and Public Lands. Sam Bober, a Russian, arrived in South Dakota in the second decade of the century but early enough in those pre-World War I days to stake out a quarter section for himself in Butte County. For a time he was the only Jew in that part of the state. Bober was well prepared to farm for he had trained at the Woodbine Agricultural School and labored as a farm hand in Indiana and as a stockman in Montana. In his adopted state of South Dakota he organized a farm bureau, helped establish a cooperative telephone line, and introduced rust resisting strains of cereals. His expertise was such that President Coolidge consulted him and Franklin Delano Roosevelt escorted him around his farm at Hyde Park; it was planted with seeds developed by Bober.

Starting in the 1890's the Russians and Poles began setting up little communities in North Dakota, in Fargo, Minot, Grand Forks. The few "Germans" already settled in the state looked askance at the newcomers but by 1918 the state counted at least seven émigré synagog groups, all small. North Dakota's rabbi in the 1890's was the Reverend Benjamin Papermaster, a devoted shepherd of his widely scattered flocks. He traveled all over the state responsive to the needs of his people. Once in the state's western reaches he met a Norwegian woman wearing phylacteries, prayer amulets worn by devout Jews on the left arm and forehead. She had been assured by a peddler who sold them to her that they were a sure cure for headaches and rheumatism. By the early 1900's Fargo already had a congregation, a Hebrew school, a cemetery, a Ladies Aid, a Zionist association, and a burial society. The émigrés and the old-timers too resolved their differences and cooperated in establishing a B'nai B'rith lodge; here they could meet on common ground. In 1918 Grand Forks had 124 souls and ten organizations; Fargo with 600 men, women, and children had but six.[12]

KANSAS

The Industrial Removal Office started shipping refugees to Kansas in the early twentieth century. Many of them landed in Topeka where there were already a few German Jews. Apparently most of the new arrivals went into the machine shops of the Santa Fe; dozens of them were given jobs with the railroad. As soon as they had saved some money they sent for their families, first the wife and children, and then the parents. These newcomers, the first to organize a congregation, bought some land from Samuel Johnson Crawford, a governor during the Civil War days. The local German Jews helped; Gentiles, too, and a congregation was finally built. Apparently the Reformers and the Orthodox conducted separate services in the same new building. It was an uneasy alliance. By 1907 there were Russian-Polish Jews in a half-dozen towns; Wichita and Topeka each had about 150 souls; included among them were settlers who had served as a bridgehead for those preparing to cross the High Plains to the Far West. Wichita had an East European congregation in 1907; Leavenworth, the largest Kansas community, had an organized Slavic Jewish conventicle as early as 1881; indeed these newcomers may have been the largest Jewish ethnic group in the city in the late 1870's. Kansas City had two such prayer groups, both established after the turn of the century. In 1920 the state had fewer than 10,000 Jews; Nebraska to the north, about 14,000.[13]

NEBRASKA

Nebraska was not an early home for East European immigrants. In 1880 there were only about 300 Jews in the entire state, but from then on the

East Europeans became increasingly visible; in the early 1900's the Industrial Removal Office started sending recruits on to Nebraska. In 1902 there were Jews in more than 25 different towns. Lincoln soon had a Russian Jewish congregation with a school of 25 youngsters who met daily. There was even a Workmen's Circle Lodge in Lincoln which served as a rallying point for many of the nonreligious newcomers. Most of the East European Nebraska immigrants settled in Omaha which soon had a ghetto with its complement of religious, educational, and philanthropic societies.

Omaha had a large number of Jewish peddlers; most of them were urban peddlers although some certainly made their rounds in the adjacent rural areas. The typical peddler carried some women's garments in addition to notions. Yankee notions included shoelaces, soaps, dishclothes, pens, needles, combs, garters. The local hucksters sold fruits and vegetables from their wagons; some pushcart merchants sold stationery. From 1894 to 1919 Omaha's immigrant Jews organized five different peddler associations motivated by the desire to further themselves and to offer mutual-aid benefits. Peddling was a very important aspect of the immigrants' economic life in the larger towns throughout the United States. Hawker organizations were established in Chicago, Milwaukee, Cleveland, and New York. Milwaukee had at least 500 of these itinerant merchants; in 1910 in Cleveland 27 percent of all employed newcomers were in peddling. Societies to protect themselves against abuse were imperative; in the year 1905-1906 four peddlers were murdered in Denver. For the newcomers peddling was not an end in itself; sooner or later most of them abandoned that way of life. This does not mean that all or even most of them improved themselves perceptibly. Ultimately they were all forced out; they were taxed out of existence by municipalities who in turn had been pushed by angry sedentary businessmen. The children of peddlers, American born and reared, became clerks, salesmen, clothing and furniture dealers, grocers, shopkeepers of all sorts. A very small number succeeded in preparing themselves as professionals.

Observant Jews in Omaha successfully boycotted a Jewish bakery for compelling its workers to labor on the Sabbath. These newcomers who dominated the Jewish community numerically by the late 1890's set out successfully to build a Jewish hospital. It is probable that the general hospital was unsympathetic to Jews. Kosher food was always an issue for the newcomers. The local Reformers and Gentiles, too, made substantial gifts to help the project. Most generous was Abraham Slimmer, the Iowa Jewish philanthropist who gave a matching grant stipulating that non-Jews and the poor be accepted. Years later, 1930, the hospital was closed. One may assume that the general hospitals with more ample means were better equipped; what was equally important they were, probably, more cordial to Jewish physicians and more tolerant of Jewish patients. By 1905 some of the Russian-Poles were moving out of the ghetto. Natives and newcomers were also learning to tolerate one another; they joined together that year to commemorate the 250th anniversary of Jewish settlement in what is today the United States.

In 1891 Nebraska Jews could boast that their Orthodox rabbi was a competent talmudic scholar and author. This was Henry (Harry) Grodzensky (Grodinsky), an authority on female ritual ablutions. One wonders whether his writing had any relevance to the needs or interests of his Omaha congregants; certainly they respected him for his learning. One wonders, too, what degree of Americanization—if any—would flourish in the home of an old-fashioned European rabbi concerned with biblical and talmudic novellae. The answer is at hand: one daughter became a social worker; another a public school teacher; one son, a lawyer, graduated magna cum laude; another became a professor of medicine. Among the Russian exiles who found a home in Nebraska was Pincus Chaikin, father of a daughter Annis. She taught Greek at the University of Nebraska and married a Gentile, Christian A. Sorensen; three of their children, boys, became notable Americans. Philip taught law, Thomas was a journalist, banker, and civil servant; brother Theodore Chaikin Sorensen was a lawyer, politician and special counsel to President John F. Kennedy. Abram Monsky was another Russian who settled in Nebraska in the 1880's. His son Henry, a lawyer, was elected president of the state conference of social workers. It was he who brought the Community Chest to Omaha, and as a Jewish national leader assumed the presidency of the international B'nai B'rith and presided over the very important American Jewish Conference of 1943 that called for a sovereign state in Palestine.[14]

OKLAHOMA

Oklahoma included a few Jews, Russians and Poles among them, in the 1870's. Oklahoma and Indian Territory in pre-state days offered few opportunities for Jews observant of their tradition; the national Jewish census made in the late 1870's by the Board of Delegates of American Israelites and the Union of American Hebrew Congregations completely ignored these territories. A Hungarian Jew who worked as a section hand on the Santa Fe in the territories lived in Blackwell near the Kansas border, made money in gas and oil, and became the president of a bank. East Europeans met to hold religious services in Tulsa and Oklahoma City in territorial days, before 1907; both towns were to enjoy the comfort of organized congregations before 1921. Joseph Blatt, a native of Hungary, was the first ordained rabbi to serve a congregation full time in the territory. This graduate of the Hebrew Union College, a Reform Jew, was elected to fill the pulpit in Temple B'nai Israel, Oklahoma City, before the state was admitted to the Union. When Oklahoma finally became a state there were hardly more than 100 Jews in its various towns and villages. But wherever ten male adults assembled, as in Ardmore, Muskogee, and Sapulpa, and other towns, they held services during the High Holy Days; by 1920 there were several formally organized congregations in Oklahoma; most of the members were East Europeans and their children. The state then had about 5,000 Jews.[15]

TEXAS

Oklahoma was always dwarfed by its southern neighbor, the largest state in the Union before Alaska was admitted. Texas extended from the dry Great Plains in the north to the fertile lands bordering on the Gulf of Mexico. Numerous Jews settled in the Lone Star State in antebellum days. Simon Weiss of Weiss Bluff, a Galician, is a typical example of those early adventurers. Jews from the Slavic lands started coming to Texas in substantial numbers in the 1880's. By that time there were already 3,300 Jews in this vast empire; 40 years later there were about 33,000, most of East European ancestry. The Slavic newcomers established congregations and built synagogs in Corsicana, Dallas, Fort Worth, Galveston, Houston, Tyler, San Antonio, and, in all probability, met to pray together in many other towns. In the larger Texas cities the new immigrant communities had a wide assortment of supporting Jewish institutions, both male and female. There were in 1918, at least 30 Jewish "communities" in Texas that had at least one Jewish institution. Dallas, the largest town with some 8,000 souls had eight; Hallettsville, with all of twenty-seven men, women, and children, had a congregation and a Hebrew Ladies' Aid Society. Sam Reichman was secretary of the congregation; his wife, Mrs. Sam, was secretary of the Ladies' Aid.

By 1920 most of the Jews in Texas were either immigrants or the children of refugees from Eastern Europe. As these newcomers acculturated they drifted away from Orthodoxy and organized congregations or institutions that genuflected in the direction of America and its customs; they became Conservative Jews. The Mittenthals are but one example of Lithuanians who made a new life for themselves on this soil. They came, so it would seem, from the East Russian region that gave birth to so many distinguished Americans. Like many others from this area bordering on Germany they arrived here in the 1860's. This family settled in a little village, Chillicothe, in Peoria County, in Illinois; it was a core center for peddlers who bought their supplies from the Mittenthal-Ablowich clan. One branch of the family settled in Jefferson, Texas, made money and then moved on to New York to become cloak wholesalers; another branch also moved to Texas where they traded (peddled!) along the Southern Pacific Railroad line. By 1872 these Mittenthals had settled in Dallas where a goodly number of Litvaks soon established themselves. As soon as they had made a little money the Mittenthals brought their wives and kin down from Peoria where they had been left while the menfolk tested the opportunities in Texas. These newcomers branched out into retail and wholesaling. They sold clothing, shoes, dry goods, china, liquors, cigars, groceries. A few turned to livestock, even to ranching; others specialized in outfitting farmers and stock raisers.

The Jews in Texarkana, on the very border of Texas and Arkansas, met together as a Russian-Polish prayer group in 1876. When the Jews assembled that year for the High Holy Days they were addressed by Charles Goldberg, a Christian minister. Goldberg, a Pole, came to the United States in 1845 and peddled in the Middle West. When in 1847 he was nursed back to health by Christians after a sickness, he became a convert to Christianity. He studied for the ministry, was ordained, taught language in a Texas college, and preached the gospel to his auditors. When the Civil War broke out he served as a Christian chaplain; later he was called to minister to a church in Texarkana. The town had been established in 1873; he arrived there in 1874, a Pilgrim Father of sorts. His job in town was to serve his congregation and to teach in the public schools. When the Jews assembled for Rosh Hashanah and Yom Kippur in 1876, they asked him to talk to them; he did, in English and in Yiddish; he was equally beloved by Jews and Christians. When Jewish boys approached their thirteenth birthday he prepared them for bar mitzvah; he never made any conversionist approaches. When he lay dying in 1890 it is said that he called the Jews in, recited the traditional Jewish deathbed confession, and asked for a Jewish burial. The interment in a Jewish cemetery was denied him. The Christians said he died in good odor but this we know: he was buried in a nonsectarian cemetery not in the burial grounds of the church where he had served for many years.[16]

ARKANSAS

Two years after Arkansas was admitted to the Union three brothers, the Mitchells, Galician Jews, arrived in Little Rock and opened a business. These three were Jacob, Hyman, and Levi. It takes more than three adults to make a community; there was to be no congregation of East Europeans in the city until 1904; by 1918 at least four of the thirteen recorded congregations in the state were founded by Jews from Slavic lands. Individual Russians and Poles, isolated, had settled in the smaller towns. For a few years the family of Harry Jacob Warshavsky lived in Forrest City; the town held 24 Jews; 20, it is said, were members of Congregation Glory of

Israel, Tifereth Israel. Warshavsky, a scholarly man, had left for the United States in the 1880's when he saw a Jew beaten to death by the Russians. After peddling and pressing pants in a factory he saved enough to send for a girl whom he loved, Miriam Elizabeth Shapiro. As it turned out she was the head of the house; Warshavsky was never to become a merchant prince. When the family opened a store in the outback Miriam made the living. They lived in Pocohontas for a while, a village without running water. Thrifty, they bought a pig to eat the leftovers. Years later when one of the girls grew up a marriage was almost aborted because a report was circulated that here was a Jewish family that raised pigs. Mother, ever modern, took piano lessons; the children studied in the nearby convent, and to round out their education were given elocution and voice lessons. Living in the country they had their own fruit trees, a cow, a vegetable garden, and even a maid. At Passover time the local Christian pastors were invited to the festal supper. The younger generation, typically Arkansans, ate fried chicken and watermelon. During the years 1910-1914 the family lived in Forrest City; there they had a shul, in name at least. The children visited the Baptist and Methodist churches to listen to the sermons. Their Jewish education came through the Union of American Hebrew Congregations leaflets mailed to them by the Memphis Reform rabbi. When business improved the children were sent to St. Louis, New York, and Boston to study. They were interested in music.[17]

MISSOURI

Arkansas had about 1,500 Jews in 1880; a generation later they numbered about 5,000; their proportion in the general population was about 1/2 of 1 percent. Arkansas was overshadowed by neighboring Missouri immediately to the north. Missouri was a very important state; St. Louis in 1918 had 60,000 Jews; Kansas City, 12,000; St. Joseph, over 3,000. In 1880 Missouri already had over 7,000 Jews; in 1920, about 83,000. The first permanent Jewish settler in St. Louis seems to have been Joseph Philipson who may well have been a Pole. He and his brothers were cultured men, linguists and students of the fine arts. The family had made its appearance in Philadelphia around the year 1800. The East European Jews however did not begin to settle in St. Louis in numbers till the 1880's. St. Joseph had three congregations established by these newcomers; one of them was founded in the early 1880's; by 1905 they outnumbered the natives and the Germans. Kansas City in 1920 had ten Orthodox congregations and numerous auxiliary organizations; some of these "Russians," as in St. Joseph, had arrived in the city in the 1880's. By 1921 the Orthodox religious institutions of this city federated under the aegis of Rabbi Simon Glazer. The immigrants from the Slavic lands had made such progress that the Reformers joined with them in some common educational programs. It is very probable that the two groups were encouraged to cooperate by Jacob Billikopf, a native Lithuanian, who was superintendent of the United Jewish Charities of the city in 1907. Even Clinton, Missouri, with only forty-nine men, women, and children had an Orthodox shul.

The East Europeans had discovered St. Louis by the 1870's when Russian Jews from the Baltic provinces organized a prayer group. Their congregation was to become the Beth Hamedrash Hagodel. By 1890 they were able to buy a building, an old German Protestant church; the president signed the notes with an "x," apparently illiterate. By 1906 this synagog and others brought a "chief rabbi" to town, Bernard (Dov Ber) Abramowitz (1860-1926). He was already a notable because of his scholarly publications, his contributions to the Hebrew press, his participation in the founding of the Union of Orthodox Rabbis. His salary was set at $10 a month. He fostered classes in Bible and Talmud, worked to raise funds for the suffering Jews of Eastern Europe during World War I, and was a force in the religiously traditional wing of the Zionists, the Mizrachi. In 1920 he left St. Louis and returned to Palestine. He had studied there as a child when his father, a scion of distinguished rabbinical families, had settled in the country. His grandson, Dr. Abram Leon Sachar, pioneered in building the Hillel Foundation and in establishing Brandeis University; he was its first president. Volhynian Jews from South Russia flocked to St. Louis; by 1918 well over 20 congregations had been established in the city by émigrés from Eastern Europe; the Zionists were strong in St. Louis; it was certainly a source of pride to them that the blue and white Zionist flag was flown, for the first time, at the St. Louis World Exposition in 1904.[18]

LOUISIANA

South of Missouri there were only two large communities on the Mississippi; one was Memphis, Tennessee; the other, New Orleans. Louisiana and New Orleans never had a particularly large East European community; New Orleans was off the beaten track for European passenger ships and for the immigrants from Russia, Poland, Galicia, and Rumania; they preferred Atlantic coastal towns, from Baltimore north to New York City. There were few opportunities for Jewish manual laborers and artisans in the South; they could not compete with the blacks. Alexandria did not have a Russian-Polish synagog till about 1913; Shreveport, however, the second largest community in the state, had a number of immigrant Jewish associations by the middle 1880's. As in other towns these Jews from Slavic lands set out in Shreveport to create charitable and religious institutions after their own pattern; they were determined to be completely independent of the earlier settlers whose way of life they deemed to be un-Jewish. New Orleans, the state's metropolis, had an East European prayer group in the mid-1870's several years before the pogroms which induced many Jews to leave Russia. One of the outstanding cultural institutions fashioned later by these immigrants was a Hebrew school whose superintendent was the America-oriented Hebrew poet, Ephraim Lisitzky.

One of the best known Jews in New Orleans in the first half of the twentieth century was Samuel Zemurray (1878-1961), a Rumanian immigrant from Kishinev. Judging by his name it is by no means improbable that he was a descendant of the Spanish exiles who found a haven in Turkey; Zemurray is obviously a variation of Zamora, a famous medieval Jewish community in Spain. Zemurray, who came to the United States in 1892, began life here as a banana peddler. His rise to wealth was relatively rapid; he invested in tramp steamers and ultimately found himself the owner of thousands of acres of banana-producing lands in Central America. By 1930 he was the largest stockholder in the United Fruit Company; that same decade he became the president of this corporation with its 500,000 acres and its 52 ships. Zemurray stood out in state and even national politics; he was close to the Roosevelt administration during the New Deal. The Zionists and the Weizmann Institute of Science in Israel found him generous; in New Orleans he established an Institute of Mental Hygiene and Child Guidance. It is not surprising that a political activist who was sympathetic to the New Deal would initiate social welfare programs on the plantations which he controlled in Central America. He did make an effort to improve living, housing, and educational conditions for the men and women who worked on his plantations but to the progressive political forces in this country—and some Jews too—the United Fruit Company was anathema.[19]

MISSISSIPPI AND ALABAMA

Though the Russian and Polish masses who turned to America as a haven and asylum avoided the South, individuals and small groups penetrated all the states below the Mason-Dixon line even before 1881. Meridian, Mississippi, had a congregation of these newcomers by 1880; by 1906 there were at least six such organized prayer groups in the state. The Jewish historian is inclined to believe that Reformers in the South were willing to work closely with these refugees though the social gap between the two groups would not be closed for decades. The Vicksburg Reform congregation permitted the Orthodox to wear their hats in the service; ultimately these immigrants were won over. As late as 1920 there were only about 4,000 Jews in all of Mississippi; the Orthodox devout stayed in the North; they were intent on living a traditional life.

Individuals from Eastern Europe settled in Alabama in the 1870's, but there was to be no traditional immigrant congregation in Birmingham till 1889; Mobile had one in 1894, Montgomery, in the early 1900's. The old-line Jews were helpful charitatively but the newcomers had to make a life for themselves; this they desired. Individual immigrants worked hard to further themselves. Russian-born Nathan Sokol (b. 1887) came from an impoverished family; there were thirteen mouths to feed. The father died in 1903; in 1906 Nathan succeeded in reaching America after he had borrowed from kin and a moneylender. One by one the family was brought over. By 1909 Sokol was peddling in Birmingham; he hated it. Three years later he was married and had a horse and buggy to help him serve his customers; he was, it would seem, something of a customer ped-dler: he had a fixed clientele whom he sent to the wholesalers. He, in turn, collected payment in weekly installments. He bought an engage-ment ring on credit, took no honeymoon, and worked as usual even on his wedding day. In 1914 he and a brother opened a business; their total assets were less than $1400; six years later he bought a house with a mort-gage; he had now been eight years in the country. Almost a generation later he had attained affluence; it took a long time.[20]

FLORIDA

Even as late as 1921 Florida had very few Jews; it was not deemed a very desirable location; it offered few opportunities. Alabama at this time had about 11,000 Jews; Florida about 7,000. In a sense it was a frontier state. The largest city was Jacksonville, not far from the Georgia border. Jews from Hungary, Russia, and other East European lands filtered into Jack-sonville in the late 1880's; they established a congregation in 1901 and in 1907 had a building of their own; they were helped by generous Jews from out of town and sympathetic Christians in Jacksonville. Four years later a group of these Jacksonville immigrants who had come from the same little East European village was numerous enough to create a home-town mutual-aid society. This was not unusual in the hinterland. In other states, too, one daring venturer would settle in a town, induce others to follow, and then in order to help one another, they would band together into a landsmanshaft.

Miami in southern Florida was incorporated in 1896; it was an ob-scure little town, but even then there were 25 Jews there. They were real pioneers in the same sense that Meyer Hart was; he was present in Easton in the 1750's when a handful of men and women founded that Pennsyl-vania village. The Jews in early Miami were numerous enough to hold services; in 1912 they had a congregation though there were fewer than 100 Jews in the town. There was to be no permanent Hebrew school there till the 1920's; the Reformers were not to establish a synagog till 1922. By the 1980's, Miami was the fifth largest Jewish community in the United States and one of the world's important Jewish cities with its more than 250,000 Israelites. Who in 1921, at the end of the East European Jewish period in American Jewish history, could have imagined that this great community would emerge in one long generation? In the early 1920's there were fewer than 1,000 Jews in town.[21]

GEORGIA

It has been pointed out before that the closer a state was to the Atlantic Coast the larger was its Jewish community. This was certainly true of the Russian and Polish Jewish communities. In 1920 Georgia had about 23,000 Jews all told; 10,000 were in Atlanta; Savannah had 5,000. Savannah had sheltered a Jewish community since 1733; individual Jews, very few to be sure, were found in Augusta that same century. Savannah had a Prussian-Polish synagog in the 1860's. Had East Europeans come to town —as well they might—they would have worshipped with this group. The Slavic Jewish immigrants were not to have a conventicle of their own till the turn of the century. In 1921 they had three synagogs in town. Atlanta developed late but as it blossomed into a great industrial and transportation center it attracted refugees fleeing from czarist tyranny. They had a congregation in the 1880's and in the course of time established several congregations and the typical auxiliary organizations. Indeed by 1921 the newcomers were well ensconced institutionally in at least four other Georgia towns. "Russian" Atlanta was fortunate that as early as 1902 it engaged the services of the Kovno-born Rabbi Benjamin (Berachya) Mayerowitz, a learned talmudist who had been ordained by a notable Lithuanian authority. Mayerowitz dared to address his followers in English and even published a commentary on the *Ethics of the Fathers* in both English and Hebrew. Like many other traditional rabbis of his generation he realized full well that he would have to emphasize the American vernacular if he was to influence the rising generation and retain the respect of acculturating immigrants. Gradually a number of the new settlers in Georgia moved upward financially; manual laborers and hawkers began to improve themselves; a policeman might become a dentist; an itinerant umbrella repairman might open a grocery; a peddler could advance himself as the owner of a ladies' and gent's furnishings shop; clerks went into business for themselves; a secondhand furniture dealer became a manufacturer; retail establishments were numerous.[22]

SOUTH CAROLINA

South Carolina was once a very influential state; until 1820 Charleston was the largest and most important Jewish community in the country; it was, however, bypassed in that same decade by New York City. In antebellum days Charleston was distinguished for its cultured Jews; Poles who had come there in the eighteenth and nineteenth century were to become respected if not distinguished members of the general and Jewish communities. After the Civil War and its devastation Charleston and South Carolina made little progress. In the 1880's there were but 1,400 Jews in the state; forty years later about 5,000.

Charleston, of course, was always to remain South Carolina's most important city. In the 1850's a Polish (Prussian?) congregation was established, Brith Sholom; as East Europeans came in they joined it. Ultimately they dominated it as it became the state's largest congregation. Writing in 1905, Barnet A. Elzas, South Carolina's Jewish historian, said that this "element" had accomplished nothing worth recording. As a competent historian Elzas erred in ignoring this majority group; the "masses" cannot be bypassed. By 1914 Brith Sholom's new constitution was printed in both English and Yiddish. Most Orthodox constitutions in the hinterland have a sameness about them; they were essentially defensive. This one was no exception as shown by its refusal to accept members who had intermarried. Illiterates were not permitted to hold office. New is the setting up of a quick religious service in the business district; undoubtedly this was for the benefit of mourners. To make sure that they would attend and help constitute a quorum of ten, whiskey and cookies were proffered. Inasmuch as no Orthodox institution is ever meticulous enough to satisfy all extremists, secessions were inevitable; a group broke away calling itself the House of Israel, Beth Israel. Many of the members of this new association had come from the same village in Russia, Kalushin. These Kalushiners created a mutual-aid society of their own, spoke Yiddish, and kept their records in that language. Alas Beth Israel did not reckon with the assimilatory impact of South Carolina; a generation later the women in this Orthodox congregation were permitted to descend from the gallery to sit in the main hall. They were still separated by a slightly raised platform; the division was symbolic; canon law was honored. Among the Russians who became Carolinians, for a time at least, was Nicholas Eugene Lugoff, a brilliant linguist and an outstanding engineer. He was a railroad builder who had been put in charge of projects in different parts of this country ever since the 1890's; at times he worked closely with General Nelson A. Miles and his staff. He was invited into South Carolina where he was employed by the Seaboard Railroad System. For years there was a hamlet and post office in Kershaw County named Lugoff.[23]

NORTH CAROLINA

In the period before 1921 North Carolina, like its sister state to the south, sheltered no Russian-Polish community of any size. Both states were still licking wounds received in the Civil War, the Reconstruction period, and the confrontation with blacks. Jewish communities in both states were small; by 1920 North Carolina, like South Carolina, did not have more than 5,000 Israelites. North Carolina, however, was turning to industry and by the 1980's its Jewish communities were beginning to make their presence felt. Jews from all parts of the North were moving into the Sun Belt. South Carolina in the 1980's had about 9,000 Jews; North Carolina about 15,000. Perceptive writers have maintained that it was the new immigrants who were to build this state's Jewish communities. This is true but only to a degree, for some of the leading manufacturers and merchants of North Carolina were of German origin. The Russians and their associated cohorts built a prayer group in Winston-Salem in the 1890's; the Reformers in town could not organize a congregation for their followers till the 1920's. Wilmington's newcomers opened the doors of their synagog in 1906; Asheville, in the western part of the state, witnessed the founding of an East European congregation in 1891. This was really a cooperative venture of the Russians and a few farsighted Germans. The following year the members of this congregation succeeded in opening a Sunday school. It was not until 1912 that Raleigh was to have a society which conducted Orthodox services, East European style.

Durham, the home of the Washington Duke dynasty, the founders of the American Tobacco Company, was for a time the home also of a large contingent of Russians and Poles who came in to make cigarettes by hand in the early 1880's. Well over a hundred worked in town until the invention of cigarette-making machines put them out of business. While they worked they did better than the blacks and many whites—textile factory workers—who averaged anywhere from $133 to $169 a year. Two of the cigarette factories in town were managed by Jews; later these two became manufacturers. Durham had an immigrant congregation in the 1880's; associated with it in the course of years was a burial society, a hospice, a ladies' relief group, and a Sunday school. Ultimately a Hebrew school was also organized. By 1920 there were at least eight immigrant congregations in the state.[24]

TENNESSEE

Some of North Carolina's western lands became the new state of Tennessee in 1796; by 1920 Jewish Tennessee was almost three times as large as Jewish North Carolina. Before 1921 the newcomers seem to have established nine congregations where their ritual was adopted; there were then about a half-dozen Reform congregations or prayer assemblies in Tennessee. Wolfe Brody, a Polish Jew, came to Chattanooga in 1880. Others soon followed him, opened peddler supply houses, brought in cronies, and put packs on their backs. It was not long before those itinerant merchants had a congregation; that was in 1888; in 1895 they opened a Hebrew school, by 1918 they had elected a rabbi to minister to their needs. Thus it took almost forty years before these Orthodox newcomers had a full fledged Jewish community of their own, yet by 1904 a rival Orthodox conventicle was called into being; Orthodoxy was prospering. Knoxville's "Russians" had a synagog in 1890, Clarksville in 1906; Nashville and Memphis, large cities, had East European congregations much earlier; Nashville in 1920 was a community of 3,000 Jews; Memphis, 7,000. The East Europeans had built a spiritual home for themselves in Nashville in 1879; by 1895 the Hungarians there had so increased that they organized a congregation of their own. In Memphis the immigrants met together in prayer in the 1880's; in the early 1890's a group chartered the Baron Hirsch Congregation in honor of the great Jewish philanthropist who had helped Jewish immigrants to make a place for themselves in this strange new wonderful land. Secessions in Memphis brought new congregations; one of them developed out of a commune which had devoted itself to the study of rabbinic literature; another group, refusing to go along with the Reformers, left them to establish the True House of God, Beth El Emeth. For many of these Tennesseans, retailers, the core wholesale market to which they turned for goods and credit was Baltimore; the largest of their Maryland suppliers was the Baltimore Bargain House owned by a fellow emigrant from the old country.[25]

KENTUCKY

Kentucky's Jewry was not unimportant, for the state bordered on the Ohio, one of the country's chief highways to the South and West. Traditionalists in Lexington had a synagog and building of their own by the second decade of the twentieth century; it was still in use in the 1980's. There were, at times, other "Russian" Jewish communities in the state, in Covington, Newport, Ashland, but Louisville was most important. As early as 1880 there were already 2,500 Jews in the city; in 1920 there were 9,000 and eight congregations, four of which were uncompromisingly Orthodox. Asher Lipman Zarchy was accepted as chief rabbi by three of them. Prior to his coming to Kentucky he had served in Brooklyn and Des Moines. This scholarly Lithuanian, ordained by two of Russia's most noted talmudic authorities, wrote for the American Hebrew press and helped organize the Union of Orthodox Rabbis. He was highly respected. The first congregation in Louisville, established in 1836, included a number of "Polish" Jews; these Poles were probably from the Prussian Polish provinces though some of them may have been born in old Poland before that country was partitioned by the Prussians, Russians, and Austrians. A Polish synagog established in 1856 may well have included Poles from the Russian Empire. By 1893 there was a Hassidic group in town; it called itself Anshe Sphard, the Men of Spain. Of course these Jews were not of Iberian stock; they followed the ritual ascribed to the Lurianic cabalists of Palestine; the medieval roots of cabala were in Spain, hence the Men of Spain.[26]

WEST VIRGINIA

West Virginia, wedged in between Kentucky, Ohio, Pennsylvania, Maryland, and Virginia, had few Jews. Its Jewish citizens played little part in American Jewish life though the East Europeans who straggled into the state's towns and villages were an interesting lot. They, too, are part of history; corporation lawyers, bankers, clothing manufacturers, talmudic scholars do not exhaust the content of American Jewish life though they are certainly important. By the 1880's the East Europeans had already made their appearance in West Virginia as they did in most other states. They moved into tiny villages; there they could make a living for they were not too handicapped by their ignorance of English and their lack of accounting skills. There the competition they faced was not keen. Russian-Polish congregations were not established in the larger towns till relatively late; these petty shopkeepers had stayed away from the cities with their large attractive well-stocked stores.

By the early twentieth century these humble newcomers constituted the majority of West Virginia's Jews; the communities were always to remain small. By 1905 there were about 1,500 men, women, and children in all of West Virginia; by 1920 they had grown to a modest 5,500. A number of these strangers settled in Charleston. No later than 1904 the Charleston Orthodox permitted themselves the luxury of hiring a rabbi; the congregation was organized in 1889; a burial brotherhood in 1893; a Zionist society in 1899-1900; Bluefield and Keystone both had congregations by the early 1900's though prayer quorums had probably been established in these towns in the late 1890's. Keystone with less than 2,000 people in town had a Jewish community by 1904, a shohet too, a lodge of the Brith Abraham order, and an organized congregation. When the Russian Jewish "pioneers" first came to Keystone in the 1890's there were no paved streets, no electric lights, no running water. It was truly a frontier outpost for fifteen Jewish families, fourteen saloons, and numerous coal mines. It was a dangerous frontier, for some pack peddlers were murdered for their money and their packs were carried off. Huntington, a city of size, had a congregation in 1908, and finally a rabbi; Wheeling, the largest town in the state, was the scene of Orthodox Russian-type services in the early 1900's, but this group did not survive. This was not unusual; throughout the country many synagogs were established only to fade away after a few years. The men who created them were still struggling to find themselves commercially, financially. By 1907 Wheeling newcomers had a new Orthodox congregation and a factotum to serve them. Other towns and villages like Clarksburg and Fairmont, Morgantown and Kimbal had congregations before 1921. Here too, as in many other states, wherever ten adult males met—thirteen years of age or over—they would hold services at least for the Days of Awe.

What happened to the one Jewish family in a village of less than 1,000, the only Jewish family in the whole township of thirty-six square miles? The following is an example. There was but one Jewish family in all of Fairfield Township, Marion County. The one village of size was Farmington. It is not even listed in the standard gazetteers. The family was the Marcuses. The father Aaron, a native of Kovno Province, had migrated to the United States after having served the czar for five years at 45 kopecks a month—which the captain kept. The family, farmers, had been displaced by the May Laws of 1882. Marcus, arrived in New York in 1889, worked in a brickyard and in a matzo factory, but, determined to improve himself, became a garment worker. He was discharged the first day; he had sewed two right sleeves on a jacket. Marcus then picked up a basket of notions and peddled his way to Pittsburgh. There he worked in a small machine shop for George Westinghouse at a time when this industrialist knew all of his employees by name. Then came the dreadful panic of 1893; Marcus worked for a time in a steel mill and finally when everything threatened to shut down he turned again to peddling. By that time he had married a girl from his home town and he realized he had given hostages to fortune. New Haven on the Youghiogheny became his next home; it was a village across the river from Connellsville. It had become a peddlers' bridgehead for the numerous Russian and Polish Jews who peddled in the surrounding villages. These men chartered a congregation.

Around the year 1900, now a horse and wagon "merchant prince," Marcus had saved enough to go into business as a shopkeeper. He moved to Homestead, set up a retail store, and within a few years a second store in the borough of Munhall. Spurred on by ambition he moved to Birmingham, Pittsburgh's South Side, the proud possessor of a small department store. Within a year or less he was bankrupt; the panic of 1907 destroyed him. By 1909 he was operating a small clothing and gent's furnishing store in Wheeling, West Virginia, unsuccessfully. Yet, ever-mindful of his religion which was dear to him, he helped organize a congregation; he served as its president. He and his friends called it Lover of Peace, Oheb Sholom. Isaac, Aaron's oldest son, served as secretary; the minutes were kept in English; Isaac, graduate of a business college, wrote a fair, a Spencerian hand. About the year 1915, in desperation, Marcus moved once more, this time into the mountains of central West Virginia where he operated a small general store for about seven years.

He did well; the Anglo-Saxons in the village rarely darkened his door; he catered almost exclusively to the local miners, Slavs, whose languages he spoke. Isaac, who clerked for his father, went occasionally to the Sunday school classes at the Methodist Episcopal Church and fiddled for the members. The community never accepted the Marcuses; the Marcuses never accepted the Gentiles; no social relationships between the Marcuses and the local burghers were ever established though there were no overt hostilities. At no time were the Gentiles ever invited into the Marcus home; at no time did a Christian family ever invite the Jews to dine with them. The Marcuses tried to keep kosher but ultimately gave up the effort though the father would slaughter chickens ritually; the meat they ate—no pork of course—was purchased from a local butcher. In 1922 Aaron turned the business over to Frank, his youngest son, and retired to Pittsburgh where he joined a modern Orthodox congregation; he liked the dignity and decorum that prevailed; the liturgy was the centuries old traditional book of common prayer. After his first inspection of the thin Reform Union Prayer Book Marcus shook his head sadly saying, "it's consumptive." The middle son Jacob had in the meantime enrolled as a student in the Reform seminary in Cincinnati, the Hebrew Union College; ultimately he was to become a member of the faculty.[27]

VIRGINIA

By the 1890's the new immigrants had firmly entrenched themselves in Virginia, in the cities of Lynchburg, Petersburg, Danville, Norfolk, Portsmouth, Newport News, Roanoke, Richmond, and in some other towns too. The little community of Lynchburg with less than 300 Jewish souls had two Orthodox congregations but after a while they combined; the members had learned that coalescence is always the better part of wisdom, at least financially. Personal animosities had to be suppressed. Petersburg's Brotherly Covenant, Brith Achim, had a modest initiation fee of $1 but the annual dues of over $19 might well prove a burden for many. In 1915 it had a new building with the required *mehitsah*, a division separating the men from the women; it was a white sheet. Half of all the traditionalists in town belonged to three extended families; one man had come first and then sent for his family and relatives. When these settlers built a new ark it was carved and fashioned by Sabbath-observing members. This devotion to tradition is in marked contrast to the Orthodoxy of the first congregation in town in 1791. In the eighteenth century almost all members of the prayer group kept their businesses open on the Sabbath; the shohet himself bought forbidden meat. Anything can happen—and did happen—in pioneer communities.

By the first decade of the twentieth century Petersburg's Russian-Polish cultural-religious pattern differed in no whit from that of all of America's Jewish towns where the newcomers had settled and had built a community in their own image; nothing was missing. Richmond, the chief town and capital of Virginia, had a "Polish" synagog in 1856; about the year 1886 incoming Russians established a congregation which they named after Sir Moses Montefiore who had just died. The immigrants revered this grand old man of World Jewry because he was Orthodox and because he had traveled to Russia to intercede for his oppressed coreligionists. Forging ahead the new arrivals bought the old Sephardic synagog building in 1891; later when they moved again they bought the sanctuary previously occupied by the Reformers (1905). These purchases testify to the measure of their growth; they were moving up in more than one way. The local National Council of Jewish Women ran a Sunday school in the vestry rooms of the Montefiore synagog; at one time these women from the "right" side of the railroad tracks taught hundreds of youngsters; there was a library of 700 volumes, most if not all in English, of course. There were four Zionist societies in the state in 1900. Seven years later Richmond sheltered a branch of the Workmen's Circle.

In 1941 the city fathers named a street in Richmond after a Russian-born Jew, Jennie Scher. This native of Lithuania came to the United States in 1886; her husband was a tailor. Jennie helped organize the Ladies' Hebrew Aid Society (1897); later it was principally she who founded an old-folks home that also served as a hospice for helpless and impoverished itinerants. The new Jewish settlers were in most modest circumstances; there were numerous tailors some of whom had been helped to open shops of their own by the local immigrant free loan association. Numerically Virginia owes much to these men and women from Eastern Europe; in 1920 there were 16,000 Jews in Virginia, the majority of whom were new arrivals; in 1880 there were only about 2,600 Israelites in the Old Dominion state. These figures are typical; America was to grow from a community of 250,000 in the late 1870's to one of several millions by 1921.[28]

MARYLAND

Maryland had a large community of newcomers; Baltimore was an important port of entry. Before 1921 there were several well-developed communities in the backcountry built by Jews from the Slavic lands. There were modest congregations in Annapolis, Brunswick, Frederick, Frostburg, and Hagerstown. The Hagerstown group had organized itself as early as 1893; even then it had thirty members, quite a sizable congregation. It hired a Baltimore scribe, a professional, to engross the new congregational constitution which was in Yiddish of course with the usual sprinkling of English words. In the constitution the members announced their intention of hiring a shohet and of buying a cemetery. The constitution required all board members to be American citizens. Dues were 25 cents a month; congregants were eligible to borrow money from the synagog's treasury; one suspects that the amounts involved were pitifully small. In 1980 there were fewer than 300 Jews in town; in 1919, about 250. Brunswick in Frederick County near the Pennsylvania border had a number of Russian émigrés as early as 1889; the whole town sheltered less than 4,000 people. Kosher food in the early days was brought in from Baltimore. In 1917 when they opened a small synagog the congregants marched through the streets to the new sanctuary proudly carrying their sacred Scrolls of the Law accompanied by the band from the Red Men's Lodge playing such soul-stirring hymns as "Onward Christian Soldiers" and "The Old Rugged Cross." A Hebrew school was opened, a teacher was brought in from out of town. Even in those early halcyon days there were probably fewer than sixty Jews in town. After a while the young folks grew up, went to college, garnered Phi Beta Kappa keys, and did not return. The community was so tiny that in 1930 it found it advisable to sell its building. This story of the rise and fall of a small-town Jewry in the backcountry is only too typical.

Baltimore, a large clothing and manufacturing center, attracted Jewish immigrants; they found work in the factories and sweatshops. In 1880 it already had about 10,000 Jews; by 1920 they numbered over 60,000, most of them of East European provenance. The newcomers who flocked to the city in the 1880's gravitated immediately to the ghettos which had been abandoned by the Germans who were leaving for better areas of settlement. The Russians had started building communities of their own in the 1870's, if not earlier; by 1920 the city could boast of over thirty such shuls; included among them were Hassidic houses of worship. Each congregation was a separate little vibrant world with its own services, its own personnel, its burial society, and its very special mores. Many of them operated their own afternoon Hebrew schools; a few had special study classes for rabbinic literature, the Mishnah, the Talmud, and its nonlegal portions, En Yaakov; others studied the Psalms. Reading the Psalms was deemed a religious exercise; they were prayers. The very diversity made for psychic security in each bethel; there was a variant liturgy for every taste. Baltimore's womenfolk established a lying-in society; the only males included were the president and secretary; they possessed skills in parliamentary law and in the keeping of records. It would take time before these humble women—some of them were illiterate—could dispense with male administrators. As a city and mother in Israel, Baltimore was selected as the place where the Socialist Zionists, the Poale Zion, met in 1905 to effect their national American organization.

By 1889 these Baltimore devotees who cherished their brand of Orthodoxy had a Talmud Torah, an afternoon Hebrew school. Instruction was first in Yiddish. As the school developed it became a formidable institution with a corps of teachers, numerous classes, hundreds of pupils, and a curriculum that included history. Ultimately there was a separate school for girls; the language of instruction for these schools would no longer be Yiddish but English. Balking at the switch to English from the semi-Yiddish, a more punctilious group established a school where the medium of instruction remained Yiddish. Changes are a threat! Unfortunately for them time would demonstrate that the impact of the surrounding Anglo-Saxon culture was irresistible. Baltimore was to have its Yiddish and Hebrew papers, its rabbinical court of arbitration, and a free burial society which interred dozens of the poor without any charge. The town's Russian-Polish intelligentsia organized a night school to teach foreigners English. This was in 1889. One of its most devoted instructors was Henrietta Szold. It is believed that this institution taught thousands of men, women, and children English, history, and civics before the city was induced to carry on the work. In 1907 the immigrants, fiercely independent, consolidated all their charities into a federation; it was patterned on the German congeries which had been set up but one year earlier; in 1921 the two came together; the Americanization melding process was at work.

By 1900 many of Baltimore's recently arrived immigrants from the czarist lands were artisans or factory workers; they were in industry; this was true of at least half of all these newcomers in the states where they were found in large numbers. Unhappy with working conditions these Baltimore immigrants organized unions and resorted to strikes in order to improve themselves; by 1920 they forced one of the largest clothing factories in town to come to terms. Patterning themselves on the Germans, some of the émigrés became white collar workers or went into trade. This economic upward mobility manifested itself as early as the 1880's; individuals became merchants, jobbers, realtors; a few managed to enter the professions. It was not unusual for a man who labored during the day in

the garment industry to go to a school at night preparing himself to become a physician, a lawyer, an accountant. Some girls put their fiancés
through school by working. Here is the story of an immigrant who
started out as a peddler and finally became a skilled buttonhole maker. To
help make a living and raise their numerous children his wife took in
boarders. Three of the youngsters secured degrees at Johns Hopkins; one
became a heart specialist; another an economist with a national reputation; a third, who became a sanitary engineer of international repute, received an honorary degree from his alma mater. These were the Wol-
mans.

Two immigrants, the Ades brothers, Harry and Simon, devout traditionalists, started an umbrella business in 1898 when they were still teenagers; they had landed here but a few years earlier. They built a one-room
workshop into one of the largest umbrella manufacturing concerns in the
country. By 1910 they employed 750 operators who produced 3,000 umbrellas and parasols a day; fifteen traveling salesmen blazoned the virtues
of the Ades's products. Among all these newcomers the most resourceful
in those decades was Jacob Epstein who had come from Tauroggen, the
same Lithuanian village as Sol Levitan, the Wisconsin state treasurer. Epstein, arriving in Baltimore in 1881 or 1882 started his business before he
was twenty-one. It was he who built the Baltimore Bargain House into
one of the largest jobbing concerns in the country; it was a catalogue
house for small retailers. Epstein sent out a million catalogues a year,
shipped 10,000 cases of goods a day, employed more than 100 accountants, and catered to 30,000 retailers. All this by 1910. He was exceptional
in that he acquired great wealth and became a notable art collector and
philanthropist building a hospital and a sanitarium. In the clothes factory
he opened to supply his retailers he employed hundreds of Jews; these
men and women didn't "make it," but their children often entered the
sacrosanct middle class.[29]

WASHINGTON, D. C.

By the end of the East European period of American Jewish history, in
the 1920's, the nation's capital, Washington, District of Columbia, was a
relatively important city. It had a Jewish community of 10,000. The East
European Jewish community—the major group in town—had already
called into being all the institutions it needed to function fully. It sometimes happened that a welfare agency came into being as the result of a
crisis. A devoted Jew heard that an old man of about ninety had been rejected by his children; he was literally out on the street. A kindly Catholic
priest had put him in a Catholic home. The compassionate Jew took the
old man out of the Catholic institution and lodged him in a Jewish board-

inghouse. A group then came together, collected funds, bought a house, and soon had thirty-five unfortunates as residents. In a relatively short time so many others were admitted that they were sleeping in halls and on porches. The local East European community then went out and erected a million dollar home; a substantial part of the needed funds was advanced by a local bank at 2 percent interest. Thus the beautiful Hebrew Home for the Aged was built. The crisis in the life of one old man drove the community to assume responsibilities. One is reminded of the tradition that in 1820 members of Shearith Israel in New York City collected money to help a dying Jewish Revolutionary War veteran. After his death the balance left in the fund was used to establish New York's Hebrew Benevolent Society.

The capital was the home of several Jewish immigrants who were striking personalities. Among them was Nathan Ring (b. 1875) known as the shoemaker to presidents. Ring, a Pole, son of a rabbi, came to this country at the age of nineteen and went to work in Baltimore as a shoemaker; he was something of a musician and played for a while in a band in Delaware. He enlisted during the Spanish-American War and later moved on to Washington and began making shoes in a shop which he opened near the White House. Ring made shoes for Theodore Roosevelt, Wilson, and Coolidge, who liked his work so much that he sent him a box of fine cigars. Ring traded them in for a batch of five-cent cigars; the ones the president sent him did not taste like the ones to which he was accustomed. It was Ring who made the braces for the crippled Franklin D. Roosevelt and shoes, too, for members of the United States Supreme Court. He was a meticulous workman with a national reputation as a custom shoemaker.

Another well-known Washingtonian was Joseph A. Wilner who was to become one of the city's outstanding Jewish communal workers and leaders. Wilner was a joiner for he served as president of the district B'nai B'rith lodges and the town's Zionist organizations; he was a pillar of the Young Men's Hebrew Association and the National Conference of Christians and Jews. Wilner, a former student of a talmudic academy, landed at Ellis Island in 1894, moved on to Baltimore where he went to night school, and in 1897 decided to make his home in Washington. There this brilliant man—he was a gifted linguist—became a merchant-tailor making uniforms for Generals MacArthur and Pershing. Wilner went to law school, passed the bar exam, but never practiced; he was, however, active in politics as a Democrat. He was one of the founders of the Washington Jewish Community Center which was dedicated by President Coolidge. Wilner had four sons in the armed forces, one of whom was killed. He was interested in sports, read widely in American history, and loved to lead the services in his favorite Orthodox synagog. When he died his funeral was attended by over 2,000 mourners. America gave this man the opportunity to exploit his latent talents to their fullest.[30]

CHAPTER FOUR

PART II

THE EAST EUROPEANS IN THE HINTERLAND TO 1921

DELAWARE AND PENNSYLVANIA

D elaware always lived under the shadow of Pennsylvania; it was once linked to that state as the Lower Counties. Delaware was not very large; as late as 1920 it could number but 4,000 Jews most of whom were immigrants or the children of immigrants. There was but one city of size, Wilmington, and it was dwarfed by Philadelphia. Most of the Jews in the state lived in this one town; by 1919 it had eighteen Jewish institutions of religious, educational, charitative, communal, and Zionist nature. Russians and Poles were the state's Jewish pioneers; they founded its first congregation in the 1880's. The Reformers were not to organize a congregation for well over a decade after the Orthodox began to raise their voices in prayer.

Compared to New York, Pennsylvania was still a hinterland state. Yet by 1920 it sheltered about 340,000 Jews; most of them, East Europeans, had started arriving in the two decades before 1900 though individual Polish and Lithuanian Jews were doing business in the province of Pennsylvania on the eve of the Revolution. By the 1890's there was hardly a town or city in the state without one or several Jewish institutions established by newcomers from the Slavic countries and the Balkans; by the 1920's there were over 250 congregations in Pennsylvania, the overwhelming majority of which were Orthodox. Because there were so many immigrant Pennsylvanians they were able to organize according to their regional traditions and their religious inclinations. In this fashion the Russian village was, to a degree, reborn on American soil.

Eight miles east of Pittsburgh in Braddock some immigrants organized the Assembly of Brothers, Agudath Achim. Their Yiddish constitution, peppered with Germanisms and English words, was typical in that it laid stress on the rules of parliamentary procedure. Though they were still struggling to make a livelihood they made provisions for charity and,

American like, they bonded their treasurer. A ritual bath (mikveh) was built to provide for the monthly ablutions of the women. Initiation fees were high because the congregation functioned also as a mutual-aid and sick-care society. All members were expected to attend funerals; a hearse and two carriages were supplied. Criminals were expelled; non-observant Jews could not lead in prayers. Anyone proposing religious reforms would be summarily expelled! Easton sheltered both a Reform and two Orthodox congregations. The relationships between the Central Europeans and the East Europeans were not always cordial. Passing the Reform synagog, which ignored the second day of the Jewish New Year, a wag hung a sign on the door, "closed on account of holiday."

PITTSBURGH

Easton was on the Delaware in the eastern part of Pennsylvania; completely across the state at the junction of the Allegheny and the Monongahela to form the Ohio, lay the city of Pittsburgh. Jews from the Slavonic lands had made their home in the city since the 1840's; one of them was president of a German synagog in 1852. In the 1860's Lithuanians started to arrive in substantial numbers; economic conditions back home were bad. One became a manufacturer of hoopskirts, another was in the clothing business; others were liquor dealers. These Lithuanians, preferring to live off by themselves, seceded from the Tree of Life Congregation, Etz Hayyim, a Central European Orthodox commune, and created a religious association of their own; they called it the Children of Israel, B'nai Israel. Even before the 1881 Russian pogroms the Lithuanians already outnumbered the Germans. When the mass killings started, Jews from Russia flocked to Pittsburgh. Soon there were Lithuanian, Polish, Russian, Galician, Hungarian, and Rumanian houses of prayer. An immigrant headed for Pittsburgh, Kansas, where he had a cousin, was put off the railroad at Pittsburgh, Pennsylvania. Lucky man, he found a cousin in the Pennsylvania Pittsburgh and stayed there.

In 1888 the Litvaks hired Moses Simon Sivitz (b. 1858) as their rabbi. He was learned in Talmud and the author of several works in Hebrew. He had come to the United States in 1886 and after two years in Baltimore had moved west to Pittsburgh. The Hebrew afternoon school he supervised had 150 students. Sivitz was but one of several traditional rabbis in town. Aaron Mordecai Ashinsky, the minister of the Washington Street Shul, was completely Orthodox yet strongly modernist. He established a hospice, fostered Zionism, and conducted an excellent Sunday school in English. In the 1890's a group of East European Jewish women began agitating for a Jewish hospital. Sivitz and Ashinsky supported Mrs. Barnett Davis in her crusade to establish a truly Jewish hospital in Pittsburgh. They were concerned that provision be made for the indigent sick.

Led by Mrs. Davis they organized a society, collected dimes, and finally chartered Montefiore Hospital Association in 1905. They began modestly by subsidizing the poor whom they sent to local hospitals. They had to move slowly because the established Jews in town were not in sympathy with the project. Kashrut was not imperative from their point of view. There were only 15,000 Jews in town all told and the establishment felt that it was too small to equip a modern hospital. Women finally gave up control and turned the project over to the men, East Europeans also, on condition that half of the governing board would be women. They were still eager to have a hospital where the poor would be accepted, where the food was kosher, where Jewish physicians could practice freely, and where the milieu was Jewish. It was small and inadequate but it was a start. In the early days its prime concern was to serve men and women and children of the Hill District, the ghetto.

By 1900 the Pittsburgh newcomers had an extensive ghetto; it was within easy walking distance to the business section downtown. Just about the time the Russians started crowding into Pittsburgh many of the Germans forsook their homes in Pittsburgh proper and moved across the Allegheny to the North Side. That was the new genteel ghetto. As in the Lower East Side of New York, Pittsburgh's Hill District Jews had to share their terrain with others, Italians, Christian Russians, Slovaks, Americans, Lebanese, Greeks, and Chinese. Catholics in the area were numerous; they cherished their parochial school; their children feuded with Jews who attended the public schools. The streets were the ghetto playing fields; the Jewish lads played baseball and basketball; one of the basketball teams called itself the Zangwills. Zangwill had come into his own in this country in the 1890's; the Jewish Publication Society had induced him to write Jewish books. His leading role in the Zionist Movement made him a familiar figure in all American Jewish circles. Another game that was popular with the ghetto urchins was polo. One might call it the poor man's polo; they pushed a tin can around with a broomstick.

Like all other ghettos the Hill District, too, had its Christian missionaries intent on saving Jewish souls; among them was a Jewish convert to Christianity who labored in the ghetto's vineyards; for years he was a fixture; there is little reason to believe that he was successful. The best known settlement, the Irene Kaufmann Settlement House, memorialized a daughter of a local department store family. This social welfare institution taught printing, typing, domestic science, sewing. It housed a Boy Scout troop, a library, and conducted classes in Americanization. Important in every settlement was the gymnasium; the Irene Kaufmann House encouraged boxing. Youngsters of that generation were avid readers of cheap paperbacks. Aaron Marcus, owner of a small department store in Pittsburgh's South Side, bought a complete one-volume edition of Shakespeare for his four youngsters. Indignantly the boys made him return it; in its place he brought back Horatio Alger's *Phil the Fiddler*; that they read until it was tattered. Folk superstitions on the Hill were rife. An infant born on the Hill died; the physician who delivered the child could not save it. When the next baby came along the mother was wiser. She sold it symbolically to the parents of a healthy child; price, five cents; the child survived. The devil can always be circumvented.

The newcomers were grocers, butchers, barbers, bookkeepers, jewelers, soft drink dispensers, haberdashers, and clothiers. Not too many were in the real estate business; they were in plumbing and lumber; one owned a bathhouse; they sold liquors, leather goods; Fifth Avenue at the bottom of the Hill was lined with wholesalers and jobbers. Hungarian Jews in the neighboring town of McKeesport worked in the steel mills; they were accepted because they spoke Hungarian; hence it was assumed that they were "Hunkies," not Jews. A Jew who came as such might well have been turned away. There were city and rural peddlers. Horse and wagon peddlers worked six days a week; on Saturday too, but not on Sunday. Profits were small; it took years to earn and save enough to bring over a family; it might take as long as five or more years for a man to save $150, then secure a partner and open up some kind of business. Obviously the streets and roads of Western Pennsylvania were not paved with gold. On occasion—not too often—the job of making a living was the responsibility of the wife. In one recorded instance an enterprising Pittsburgh female immigrant, a linguist, got a job as an interpreter in a downtown department store. She watched the newspapers for the announcements of engagements, went to the bride and got her to buy her trousseau at the store where she worked. Her husband, a very scholarly man, was an insurance agent but incompetent; the result was that she had to go out and sell insurance for him; she saved his job. A number of Jews were in the garment trades; many were unionized by 1920 and did very well. Their pay checks were not small. Their national union was the United Garment Workers not the Jewish Amalgamated Clothing Workers of America. There was substantial Jewish leadership in the presumptive Gentile United Garment Workers; the executive personnel was largely Gentile but about half of the national executive committee was Jewish in 1907. About fifty of the locals in this country were heavily Jewish; there were tailors' locals in Pittsburgh that were, one suspects, largely Jewish.

There was a very special business in Pittsburgh in which the Jews were represented in goodly numbers as bosses and workers. This was the stogy or toby business, long thin cheap cigars. Ever since the mid-nineteenth century the tobacco industry in the United States was one in which Jews were strongly represented. It was not easy for a Jew in Pittsburgh to get a job in some of the factories, machine shops, steel mills.

Jews were not welcome. However there were a number of Jewish stogy manufacturers and they hired Jews, men, women, and children. Little girls worked from dawn to dusk for 35 cents a day. They hid from the factory inspectors; some of the little ones, hiding, worked in cellars; the children hoped they would be caught; they wanted to be sent to school. Tuberculosis was not uncommon among the workers in the tobacco industry. It was of course advantageous to work for a Jew; the shops would be closed on the Sabbath. Of the 235 tobacco factories in Pittsburgh, 133 were in the Hill District. One teenager worked in a stogy factory from the time he was fifteen until he was twenty-two; he went to school at night and finally became a lawyer. Wherever there were Jewish workers there was usually a mutual-aid Workmen's Circle, Arbeter Ring, lodge. Insurance for an emergency was necessary. There had been a W. C. lodge in town since 1904; Branch 45 had a reported 11,600 members by 1921. (Did the twenty some immigrant congregations in Pittsburgh in 1919 have many more than 1,600 paying members all told?) The W. C. people had their own building and a labor lyceum. They were not interested in religion; they worshiped at the altar of Yiddish *Kultur*. The Workmen's Circle was the first organization to rent its hall to blacks; it helped unions when they went on strike contributing to the New York cloakmakers union in 1910 and to the steelworkers in 1919. Some of the children of Pittsburgh's union workers went to college; in 1920 Jews were 12.5 percent of the enrollment at the University of Pittsburgh. The following year there were about 50,000 Jews in town; most of them were of East European ancestry.

PHILADELPHIA

The immigrants from Eastern Europe frightened the apprehensive natives and naturalized Jews of German origin; they knew that the future lay with these newcomers who outnumbered them. As early as 1897 Schiff had prophesied that the Russian Jews would ultimately dominate American Jewry. The "Germans" wanted the immigrants to Americanize themselves speedily; to develop their inherent virtues, to rid themselves of their faults, and to pattern themselves after the best in the life of the earlier Jewish settlers. These were not unworthy expectations. However these struggling émigrés from darkest Russia were primarily concerned with *parnasah*, a livelihood, with *takhlit*, achievement, results. As far as communal life was concerned they set out to create communities to please and profit themselves. The institutions they planted and nurtured, apparently completely East European, were not so in reality; they were autonomous, separatist, but American. This country offered opportunity but exacted conformity. In the 1870's these newcomers in Philadelphia had a congregation of their own; in 1919 there were at least 125 immigrant conventicles in town. Philadelphia was then the third largest Jewish community in the United States; it had 200,000 Jews; most were of East European origin. There were close to 300 institutions in the city that catered to the needs of these recent arrivals. A substantial number of all these newcomers, men, women, and children, lived in a ghetto in the southern part of town.

The Russian-Polish Jews here, as in other states, were anything but a homogeneous mass; they were vigorously disparate with their different synagogs, liturgies, societies, and prejudices. A highly respected rabbi served as a cement to give some of them the semblance of cohesion. This man was Lithuanian-born Bernard Louis Levinthal (1864-1952) who had been in the States since 1891. Like most other notable Orthodox religious leaders in the United States he came here with excellent credentials. He had studied with the best men in Russia and they had seen fit to ordain him. He succeeded his father-in-law, Eleazar Kleinberg, in Congregation B'nai Abraham. Rabbinic nepotism was not unknown in this country; it was more common in Eastern Europe and even to a degree in Central Europe of the eighteenth century. Levinthal could stand on his own two feet; he was brilliant, clever, aggressive, a good administrator who sensed full well what the times required. He was definitely Orthodox but in no sense an obscurantist. In the course of his career he organized Hebrew schools, an academy for the study of the Talmud, and helped regulate the kosher meat industry in Philadelphia. The elite natives and Germans wisely saw fit to coopt him for the American Jewish Committee; he was one of the founders of the Union of Orthodox Rabbis; he played a role in fashioning the Rabbi Isaac Elchanan Theological Seminary, and was elected a member of the 1919 American Jewish delegation to Versailles. He served the Zionist movement in a leadership capacity. America's Orthodoxy deferred to him; he was one of its leaders.

In its tolerance of immigrant women in the charities and mutual-benefit societies Philadelphia was no exception; the ladies were important and the men knew it. In a large city where there were well over 100,000 Yiddish-speaking and reading people it was inevitable that there would be a Yiddish press though it was completely overshadowed by the national newspapers that were printed in nearby New York. Modernist Hebraists in Philadelphia, the Maskilim, the Enlighteners, were few in number but active; they had established a literary society as early as 1884; it is said that they had assembled a library of 3,500 volumes. Outside lecturers were called in to talk to them; frequently the addresses were in English.

There were always a number of secular organizations in town which the younger generation of Russian-Polish origin joined; it was drifting away from Orthodoxy. Not many newcomers were accepted by the dining and leisure clubs established by earlier generations of immigrants from Central Europe; because of their ethnic backgrounds, their social status, and their lack of means they were not welcomed into the established clubs. Though these émigrés constituted an overwhelming proportion of the Jews in town their comings and goings were given relatively little space in Philadelphia's Anglo-Jewish newspapers. When Dr. A. S. W. Rosenbach said in 1905 that the East European Jews were generally prosperous, this assertion was on the sanguine side. The masses were poor, proletarians or members of the lower middle class. The pushcart peddlers were constantly being harassed by the police because they were wont to violate municipal ordinances. However, among the many thousands of these new immigrants, there were always a few who stood out for their success in business, industry, the professions, the arts and sciences. Albert M. Greenfield stands out as a Russian immigrant who built an imposing commercial empire. He achieved great wealth and exercised influence wherever he turned; he was a typical rugged individualist.

In the professions the Jews moved in the narrow range that was typical of their vocational reach; they were in medicine, law, dentistry, pharmacy. Among the professionals, Polish-born Michael Heilprin, the encyclopedist, and Max Rosenthal, an artist of national repute, stood out; both men had little in common with the Polish Jews who huddled together in Philadelphia's ghetto. Rosenthal (1833-1918) was a painter, lithographer, etcher, engraver in mezzotint. His all embracing capacities and accomplishments are most impressive. After studying in Paris he came to the United States (1849) and continued his studies at the Philadelphia Academy of Fine Arts; he may well have been the first Jew to study at this institution which Hyman Gratz served as treasurer. It was Rosenthal who helped bring chromolithography to this country in antebellum days; during the Civil War he worked as an illustrator for the United States Military Commission. Rosenthal was called upon by a publisher to illustrate some of Longfellow's poems; his lithographic portraits of American worthies included Judah P. Benjamin, the Confederate statesman.

As in New York, Baltimore, and Chicago, many of Philadelphia's Jews were also in the needle industry; they worked on garments for men and women and labored industriously in factories that manufactured shirts, overalls, wrappers, and underwear. Some of the men and women who were employed in the shops had been trained in the vocational classes of the Hebrew Education Society. Women there were taught millinery and dressmaking. Much of the work produced in Philadelphia in the early days was turned out in sweatshops run by contractors. Competition in the 1890's was keen. Bad hygienic conditions in the factories and long hours lead to tuberculosis; Philadelphia's United Hebrew Charities reported in 1898 that 40 percent of its expenditures were made in the effort to cope with this disease. Women in those days were exploited. Because of frequent layoffs many a young woman could not average more than two to three dollars a week. The sweatshop contractors made no great fortunes; they were squeezed by the factory owners for whom they worked; the contractor in turn exploited his workers in order to remain competitive; often he had no choice. The manufacturer wanted the work done as cheaply as possible. However there were times when the contractors could make anywhere from $15 to $18 a week; they specialized in men's clothing. When conditions became insupportable the garment workers in the late nineteenth century went out on strike. Jews who worked making cloaks did better than those putting suits together in sweatshops. Much of the cloak industry was centered in factories where ventilation and light were adequate; these factory workers often made as much as $20 a week. Cigar rollers did well too. Considering the times and the standards of living their pay was far from unsatisfactory. There was no field of commerce in which Philadelphia's East European Jews were not found. This was certainly true in the years after 1900.[1]

OHIO

Ohio is one of the important states of the Union, distinguished for its schools and universities. It is blessed with many good-sized Jewish communities such as Cincinnati, Dayton, Columbus, Toledo, Cleveland, Akron, Canton, and Youngstown. As early as 1880 there were already about 15,000 Jews in the state; in 1920 there were, approximately, 180,000. Jews from the Slavic lands had already organized themselves to their own liking in Elyria in the 1850's, in Cincinnati in the 1860's; Cleveland, in 1899, had over a dozen East European congregations; in 1920, at least thirty. There were then about 70,000 Jews in town most of whom were of East European origin. The early Cincinnati Russian-Polish communities owes much to the famous Isaacs family who had settled in the state no later than the 1850's. The outstanding figure in the clan in the mid-nineteenth century was Schachne Isaacs. As a compliment to him the congregation he and his associates founded was for generations known as Reb Schachne's Shul, Mr. Schachne's synagog. The Isaacses in the course of generations were distinguished by academicians who bore their name; a number of them adhered zealously to Jewish traditional practices; notable among these were Nathan Isaacs (1886-1941). After teaching law in Cincinnati, Pittsburgh, and New York, he moved on to Harvard where he became professor of business law in 1924. While professor of law in Cincinnati, 1912-1918, this devout pious Orthodox Jew set out to bore from within and bring the Reform students at the Hebrew Union College back within the ambit of ritual observance. About the year 1906 he had created a secret Hebrew letter fraternity, the Yod Kaph Taw which pledged its members—among other requirements—to observe some dietary laws. The elite students joined it, were snubbed in turn by the other students, and the fraternity accomplished little if anything. When Isaacs was born he became a breast-fed baby. Mrs. Edgar Bevis, a neighbor unfortunately could not nurse her son, Howard; Mrs. Isaacs, Nathan's mother, volunteered to serve as his wet nurse. When Nathan and Howard grew up they practiced law together briefly in Cincinnati and in later years both were on the faculty at Harvard. In 1940 Howard Landis Bevis (1885-1968) was appointed as president of Ohio State; he then invited his boyhood chum to come down for the ceremony, and knowing Nathan's scrupulosity he built him a sukkah, a tabernacle—it was the Festival of Booths. The two ate together in the hut, kosher of course, till Nathan returned to Cambridge.

In the 1890's there were not only East European congregations in all large cities but in many small towns too. The big town synagog-communes, Russian, Polish, Rumanian, Hungarian, were sustained and spiritually supported by their own economic, cultural, social, and charitable agencies. The Orthodox bethels in the small towns were often established before the natives and acculturated Germans were able to set up English-speaking Reform institutions. In 1920, Cincinnati's immigrants enjoyed the luxury of multiple prayer groups; there were many of them, several still in the downtown core areas destined soon to become slums. Cleveland at this time had about thirty-five such congregations and almost ninety other associations, most of which were established by immigrants.

The economic structure, the distribution of Jewish gainful workers in Ohio was no different from that which prevailed in most towns and states. It is not surprising therefore that in Cleveland, the largest Jewish community in the state, there would be a Jewish Peddler's Association by the 1890's and a Jewish carpenter's union around the year 1910. Economic mobility? Rags to riches? That was much more common in the Horatio Alger stories than it was in real life. Many Jews were petty retailers; they preferred to call themselves merchants. In the eighteenth century that was a word to be uttered with reverence. As soon as a "merchant" had saved a few dollars he bought a home; the children frequently, not always, were sent to high school; a favored few went to college; they were to become professionals.

Individual Jews went into industry; some were successful and became wealthy. In 1888 Dov Behr Manischewitz, a Russian, opened a matzo factory in Cincinnati. This company—still in existence though not in Cincinnati—is one of the largest processors of kosher Jewish foods in the United States. There are few people, Jews and non-Jews, who have not munched Manischewitz matzos or drunk its kosher wine. Teenage Oscar Berman (1876-1951), who had come to this country in the 1890's, worked in Cincinnati as a stock clerk for $1.50 a week, went on the road as a salesman and by 1903 had organized the Crown Overall Company. The Berman factory was one of the largest in the country. In 1920 he was president of the Stonewall Cotton Mills in Mississippi, president of a bank there, and director of a large bank in Cincinnati. Berman was to have a distinguished career as a Jewish communal worker and as an industrialist of repute. His associates and friends in the garment industry elected him chairman of the executive board of the Union Made Garment Manufacturers Association, and colleagues in the Cincinnati Jewish community rejoiced when he became a member of the governing board of the Hebrew Union College. Berman, who was at home in rabbinic literature, was a charming cultured gentleman admired by thousands.

Cincinnati's Orthodox "chief rabbi" in the first decade of the century —when there were at least several traditional synagogs in town—was Abraham Jacob Gerson Lesser (1835-1925). Three of the nine congregations accepted his leadership and contributed to his support. After serving communities in his native Russia he came to this country, no longer young (1880). Chicago Jewry, in the throes of finding itself in a strange land where Jewish Orthodoxy, Russian-style, was not entrenched, wanted him to exercise communal religious discipline. Charlatans were not unknown among the so-called leaders. While in Chicago Lesser encouraged the establishment of an afternoon Hebrew school and other communal agencies. His national repute was such that his colleagues, who respected him for his learning and integrity, elected him president of the Union of Orthodox Rabbis. After serving Chicago's East European Jewry for about twenty-four years he was brought to Cincinnati where he exercised a beneficent influence in furthering Hebrew education. In this the citadel of Reform his relationship with the older established Jewish community was a cordial one. In 1890 while still in Chicago a group of Jews and Christians came together in an interfaith conference and invited Lesser to write an apologia for Judaism and its hope for restoration. He did so in Hebrew and it soon appeared in an English translation as *It Shall Come to Pass in the End of Days.* It was an interesting essay but totally ineffective; it is hard to see how even sympathetic Christians would be impressed by what he had to say. Lesser denied that Jesus was the Messiah and denounced missionaries as despicable. What the Greeks and early Christians knew of philosophy they had taken from the Jews! Baseball was a good thing; the Christians were so absorbed by this game that they had no time to harass Jews! Lesser seems to have had some familiarity with general literature, philosophy, and history—the New Testament, too—but he spoke little English, though he was to live in this country for over forty years. It is obvious that he could not sense the need of his fellow Orthodox Jews in their relationships to the Christians of this country.[2]

INDIANA

Sandwiched in between two very populous states, Ohio and Illinois, Indiana with its modest-sized Jewish communities played no great role in American Jewish life. In 1880 the state contained 3,400 Jews; forty years later there were 27,000; 10,000 were in Indianapolis. That year, 1920, there were about twenty-four towns in Indiana which had Jewish communities, small or large. Michigan City with a Jewish population of 450 had two congregations. One held services in English, the other in Hebrew; all told there was forty-two pupils in the two local Jewish religious schools. This was in 1919. South Bend had three Russian-Polish synagogs, Evansville, two, Indianapolis six, one of them patronized heavily by peddlers. Most towns—not all—had their complement of auxiliary societies and necessary institutions. Few communities were too small to forego the pleasure of having more than one conventicle; fissiparousness is a beloved Jewish tradition. Indianapolis had no East European synagog until 1870, fourteen years after the Central Europeans established the Indianapolis Hebrew Congregation (1856). Historians tend to ignore the fact that in the smaller towns of the state relief was handled almost exclusively by the ladies. In one town there were only two institutions, a female lodge and a cemetery; in another, the only associations in town were a Ladies' Hebrew Benevolent Society and a cemetery.[3]

ILLINOIS

Because of its location, Illinois, Indiana's neighbor to the west, was an important state; Chicago, its one big town, was strategically placed on the Great Lakes; it had access to Europe and the eastern and western states. Through its rivers and canals it was able to penetrate the entire Mississippi and Missouri basin—America's heartland. As early as 1890 Chicago had a Jewish population of 10,000; in 1920, about 250,000. The Russians, Poles, Rumanians, and Hungarians outnumbered the Germans and natives by the 1890's. In 1920, it has been estimated, 85 percent of all the city's Jews were of East European background. As early as the 1850's there were Slavic Jews in town trying to live their own religiocultural life; some even found time to devote to the ancient rabbinic classics, the Mishnah and the Talmud. In the decade of the 1860's there was a sizable number of these newcomers in the city; by the next decade they were praying in no less than three congregations of their own. The Beth Hamedrash Hagodol, the Great Study House, established in 1867, was to suffer a secession. A man came to services on a scorching day in July wearing a straw hat; he was ordered out of the sanctuary; his hat was deemed improper attire. The rebel and his friends organized a mutual-aid society and since many of them were landsleit from the same town, Mariampol, the Mariampol Aid Society was born (1870). As a congregation it was later to assume the name Anshe Sholom, the Men of Peace. When it first began the Mariampoler admitted no one who was not a Sabbath observer. By 1920 there were literally dozens of these Russian and Polish prayer groups in the city; intramural hostilities and the desire for office made for constant secessions. Pragmatic seekers after social security benefits joined lodges; one East European Jewish order had thirty-three branches in Illinois. The lodge was a bargain; it provided sociability and insurance; socialization maintained and strengthened Jewish identity and permitted emphasis on a common village provenance. Though Chicago was a great Jewish city—the second largest in America—its Jewry was only one-sixth as large as that in New York.

In the twentieth century there was much cultural and ethnic ferment among the new immigrants in the country; they were faced with the problem of coming to terms with themselves both as Jews and Americans, no easy task. At the University of Illinois in Champaign a number of Jewish students had established an organization called the Ivrim Society, the Hebrews. (Hebrews always sounded better than Jews.) The woman who served as its first president was not of Russian-Polish ancestry but other members were. Some newcomers were instructors in the university. Among them were Simon Littman (b. 1873) and Jacob Zeitlin. Littman, an economist, was a native of Odessa who went abroad to study after his emigration to the United States in 1893. He attended universities in Paris and Germany and received his doctorate in Zurich (1901). While still in the United States, before he returned to Europe to secure a graduate degree, he had worked in the 1890's for the New York City Tenement House Commission; later he was to teach economics in Champaign. His colleague and a fellow immigrant Jacob Zeitlin (1883-1937) received his doctorate at Columbia and taught English at the University of Illinois. He edited textbooks in the field of English literature and wrote on Petrarch and Montaigne. He had to labor as a teacher in the department for eighteen years before he became a full professor. He was lucky; English could never be understood and taught by a Russian Jew; that was the heritage of Anglo-Saxons alone! It was very unusual in those days for Jews even to receive an appointment in a department of English; this we know from the tragic career of Ludwig Lewisohn.

The Ivrim Society was ultimately incorporated into the Menorah Society which was itself later dispossessed by the Hillel Foundation, a Jewish campus organization which devoted itself to the religiocultural and social needs of the undergraduate (1923). Littman and his wife Ray Frank were very interested in these cultural organizations. Mrs. Littman was an activist in liberal causes. She stands out in American Jewish history because she was probably the first woman in the United States to exercise some rabbinic functions, to preach in synagogs. She was not ordained, never called herself rabbi, never held a post in a synagog. As the number of Jewish students in Champaign increased—many if not most were the children of the new immigrants—Edward Chauncey Baldwin of the English department, a Gentile, set up the first Hillel Foundation; this on the Champaign campus. He wanted Jews to know more about the Bible, their classics, their heritage. He was aided by the Littmans and the gargantuan Rabbi Benjamin (Big Ben) Frankel. Out of the original Hillel Foundation there were in the course of decades to come dozens of Judaic societies in the universities of the country. In the second decade of the century, immigrant Jews in Champaign established a congregation of their own, B'nai Israel. There was already the beginnings of a Reform congregation in town but the newcomers wanted to maintain the old traditions; they identified strongly with Jewry and its sacrosanct culture.

The newcomers in Chicago had their big ghetto on the West Side. One of its distinctive characteristics was the relatively small number of saloons. There were more than 100 congregations in town by 1920; most of them served the immigrants. Among their outstanding rabbis—there were several—was Saul Silber (b. 1881), a Russian who had come to the States in 1900 after receiving a traditional education. By 1910, Anshe Sholom elected him as its rabbi. Silber was a community builder for he helped establish or furthered important West Side and national institutions and organizations which were close to the hearts of the new immigrants: an orphan home, a hospital, a Zionist interstate benefit order (the Knights of Zion), a Consumptives' Relief Society, the Mizrachi (the national Orthodox Zionist congeries), the Jewish Welfare Board in World War I to serve the men in the armed forces, the Union of Orthodox Hebrew Congregations, and the Central Relief Committee (1914) which worked to ameliorate the distress of the Jews abroad. He was one of the founders of Chicago's Orthodox rabbinical academy, the Hebrew Theological College. Identification, too, with the larger American community was one of the outstanding characteristics of a stalwart like Silber. He and his associates raised money selling Liberty Bonds and they were also active in the Red Cross despite its Christian religious symbol. Chicago's foreign-born Jews did not lack able leaders.

The city's West Side community had a plethora of institutions and societies to provide for its social, cultural, and economic needs; there were dozens of them. Among them was a federation of charities which rivaled the one created by the native German Jews. Saul Silber helped bring to birth this Federated Orthodox Jewish Charities (1912). Its first president was Bernard Horwich (b. 1863), a Lithuanian who came to this country in 1880. Chicago Jews were proto-Zionists; there had been a Lovers of

Zion (Hoveve Zion) Association in the city in 1886, and when the Zionists in Chicago organized formally Horwich became their first president. The mutual-aid Knights of Zion Order, chartered in Illinois in 1897, was one of the earliest national Zionist organizations established in this country. By 1898 Chicago's Jewish women had also fashioned a woman's Zionist society.

The chief architect of the Knights of Zion was another immigrant, Leon Zolotkoff (b. 1867). At the age of thirteen this precocious Lithuanian was already writing articles for the Russian and Hebrew press. He moved on to France, attended classes at the Sorbonne and returned to Russia where he pursued his career as a Hebrew-writing journalist and as a Russian language dramatist. Ultimately he was to be at home in four different languages. In 1888, still only twenty-one years of age, he established a Yiddish paper in Chicago; this was the *Courier*; later it became a daily. In 1897 Zolotkoff moved to New York for a brief period and served as editor of the Orthodox *Jewish Daily News*. He studied law in Chicago, became an Illinois assistant state's attorney, and was recognized by West Side Jewry as one of its beloved leaders. He was a charming person, a much sought after orator, the local community's delegate to the first Zionist Congress in Basle in 1897. It was one of his ambitions to establish a press in Jerusalem that would print Hebrew books for Diaspora Jewry; this hope was fulfilled not in his time but a generation later when the State of Israel became the Hebrew printing center for World Jewry.

Obviously, as the second largest Jewish center in the United States, Chicago's immigrants would evidence an interest in Hebrew learning and in Yiddish literature. There was a Hebrew press in town by 1877 but it achieved little. Most of these immigrants loved Hebrew but only as the language of prayer; they were not interested in furthering a literature in modern Hebrew; they had little more than a reading knowledge of the Sacred Tongue. As early as 1883, after the Russians gathered strength, they established a Hebrew Literary Society and collected a Hebrew library. Yiddish was more fortunate; it was the language of the masses; they understood it. Yiddish journalism in Chicago had its beginnings in the late 1870's; like the Hebrew it got off to a bad start but a press in the mother tongue was inevitable; by 1914 the city had witnessed the appearance of numerous Yiddish periodicals, monthlies, weeklies, and dailies. Yiddish shows had been staged since the 1880's; the Chicagoans loved the theatre in their mother tongue; many years later, in the 1980's there were still Jews in the affluent suburbs who continued to patronize visiting Yiddish theatrical troupes. Yiddish died hard.

In their efforts to make a livelihood and in the diversity of their vocational outreach Chicago's Yiddish-speaking immigrants were no different than any other group in any large American city. There was no field of craft or artisanry or business or even profession that was not participated in by these new arrivals. It is not surprising therefore that many were peddlers and hucksters, cigar workers—500 were women—and because the city was a garment industry center there was a very substantial proletarian group. It has been estimated that there were about 2,000 Jewish junk dealers in town collecting paper, bottles, and rags. There was no end to the host selling foods, dry goods, and secondhand clothing; there were tailor shops and the inevitable pawnshops. Many were clerks, some were civil service employees; more and more immigrants, men and women too, were turning to the free professions. As in Pittsburgh and other cities the Jewish bakers were organized into a union of their own; there were 400 at work in the picture frame business; others manufactured tin cans and labored in the bicycle factories.

By the last two decades of the nineteenth century Jews in the garment industry were already organizing unions and striking to win a living wage; by 1900 the work day for many had been reduced from sixteen to ten hours. Modest as were their wages in the early twentieth century, they were still doing better than some other immigrant groups. After the 1905 Russian revolution better trained Jewish labor organizers arrived in New York and Chicago; favored by the times, political liberalism, and a more sympathetic attitude on the part of the national government, Jewish labor leaders in Chicago furthered collective bargaining. They had a relatively successful strike in 1910 in the men's clothing industry; one of their leaders was Sidney Hillman. Under the American system economic upward mobility was always possible. Successful junk peddlers built iron yards and sold their scrap to the mills; peddlers often became small retailers; cloakmakers might even become garment manufacturers. But even so it took ten to fifteen years for a working man to advance in commerce and industry. Great wealth was very rarely achieved. By 1904 one of Chicago's successful cloak manufacturers was reputed to be worth $10,000; that was a respectable sum in those days. There was a Russian Jewish cigar manufacturer in town (Samuel Paley of the later Columbia Broadcasting System) with a fortune of about $20,000 (1904). He could have lived on the interest of his money. There was a wholesaler in town—so it is said— who employed 1,000 people; this was indeed unusual, paralleled only by the remarkable success of Jacob Epstein and his Baltimore Bargain House.[4]

IOWA

Iowa to the northwest of Illinois was once an important state for those moving across the prairies and the Great Plains on the way to the ever beckoning West. By the late 1840's there was already a number of Russian and Polish peddlers living in Iowa's Mississippi River towns which served them as bridgeheads as they hawked their wares in the surrounding countryside. Among these towns were McGregor, Dubuque, Burlington, and Keokuk. In 1855 Keokuk was to have a charity organization called the Benevolent Children of Jerusalem; Christians also made contributions to it. During the decade of the 1860's Keokuk had the largest Jewish community in Iowa; in the 1870's it was already in a synagog building of its own. After the turn of the century Iowa began filling up; the Industrial Removal Office dispatched dozens of newcomers to sixty-four different towns and hamlets; by 1903 there were nineteen congregations in the state; in addition High Holy Day services were held in nine other towns. Thus there were twenty-eight different communities and prayer groups in Iowa in the early 1900's; most of them were fashioned by humble newcomers from Eastern Europe.

In 1880 there were only 1,300 Jews in all Iowa; forty years later the state could count 16,000 most of whom were newly arrived immigrants. There were about forty small villages and hamlets with at least one Jew, usually a shopkeeper. The economic contributions which they made in the villages where they settled cannot be overestimated; they were harbingers of civilization, of comfort, indispensable in their own way. Des Moines in 1880 was Iowa's largest community with 260 Jews; in 1920 the state's Israelites were concentrated largely in fourteen towns; most congregations were Orthodox. As late as 1920 the two ethnic Jewish communities in Des Moines, the "German" and the "Russian," were still separate and distinct. In some towns the Germanic group was not always the older. It is interesting, too, that some of the so-called "Germans" were Americanized Lithuanians, pioneer settlers, acculturated. Among them was Marcus Younker who was born in Polotsk in 1839; there he received a traditional Hebrew education and was bar mitzvah. In the early 1850's he peddled in New York and in rural Missouri. It was not long before he and his brothers—there were several—opened a store in Keokuk. Decades later they started a branch in Des Moines; they believed that town had a future. Among the clerks they employed was a saleswoman; apparently she was the first female in town hired for that purpose. Younker's became the town's important department store. A generation later Marcus Younker served as president of the Des Moines Reform congregation yet he always remained rooted in Orthodoxy; his wife kept a kosher home.

Although in its early days Dubuque had but twenty Jewish householders it rejoiced for a time in having two separate immigrant congregations; the seceding group called itself the Jewish Protective Club. Did the dissidents set out to protect themselves from hoodlums? Ottumwa had but one synagog, a traditional one; the Torah was owned by one man; consequently he ruled with an iron hand. By 1920 Sioux City held about

2,500 Jews. The Slavonic Jews here were the first to organize; they were conducting services in the 1880's years before the Reformers established a temple of their own. Among the Russians were a number of skilled artisans; one carved the ark for the community; others did much of the painting and decorating; theirs was a labor of love and devotion. The Sioux City sanctuary was also called the Kefulier (Kapulier) Shul after the European village from which a number of the worshippers hailed. When first organized these traditionalists said that they wanted to promote the Orthodox Hebrew religion; later on they merely said that they wanted to propagate the Jewish faith; America was making inroads! By the early 1900's one of Sioux City's Orthodox shuls had moved over to the west side of town where the earlier settlers, the elite, had established themselves. It introduced family pews, a Friday evening service, and started looking for an English-speaking minister. Here we see the beginnings of Conservative Judaism on the transmississippi prairies no later than the first decade of the new century. In free America acculturation never ceased making its imperious demands. Russian villagers, rooted in medieval tradition, had no choice but to accede; many gave way willingly. By the 1920's Sioux City had forty-four Jewish societies most of which were created by the newcomers. Many of the newspaper boys in town were children of the congregants; these young vendors had an association of their own; they seemed to have been a tough lot for the Jewish community was concerned about juvenile delinquency. There is a local tradition that almost sixty of these street wise striplings volunteered during World War I to fight in the Jewish Legion on the side of the British.

Des Moines's newcomers had a ghetto of their own in a different part of town than the earlier settlers. Many of the new immigrants came from the province of Suwalki in western Russia, actually from three little towns that were to become very well known in American Jewish circles, Kalvary, Volkovisk, Pilvissok. These Lithuanians started coming in the late 1860's. Some reached Iowa by way of Rochester. There they had lived and peddled till a Rochester wholesaler sent them out West to Iowa. That was an adventure. Among these immigrants from Pilvissok was a daring entrepreneur by the name of Harris Franklin (b. 1849). (Be assured that was not his name in his native village.) By 1867 this teenager was in the United States. After a stay in Rochester, Davenport, and Burlington he took root in 1876 in Deadwood, in Dakota Territory. There he became one of the town's outstanding businessmen, a financier, and an industrialist. Des Moines had an immigrant prayer group in the 1870's, followed shortly by a congregation; by 1881 the almost inevitable breakaway took place. The secessionists felt that the older Orthodox B'nai Israel, the Children of Israel, was not sufficiently traditional; the rebels called their congregation Beth El Jacob. A permanent seat in the new congregation was not cheap, $50 a year, but there were advantages; the owner had the right to determine who would be his neighbor on his right and on his left; there could be no sale if the immediate neighbor was an enemy. These ardent souls were good haters; the location of cemetery lots was also very important; newcomers in that generation wanted to be buried near their friends.

Individual Hebraists of exceptional competence strayed as far west as Iowa. Among the newcomers who joined his fellow townsmen from Pilvissok was A. Markson (b. about 1864), a talmudist, a linguist, and a poet. After living in Koenigsberg, Germany, for a time, Markson moved on to the United States. He peddled and clerked in the Omaha neighborhood, kept books for a Jewish merchant in Ames, Iowa, and when the spirit moved him wrote Hebrew poetry; by 1903, still a relatively young man, he passed away in Des Moines. Markson had no future in his native Lithuania; it is a question how much he achieved in free America. How many brilliant, learned, sensitive men came to this country only to suffer and perish. America was not always the answer. Some of the Iowa congregations had their complement of hired officials, a cantor, a beadle, a rabbi; they also had a synagog building and a mortgage too. Salaries were very low; on occasion the rabbi received no fixed honorarium; he had to live primarily on the fees given him for supervising the production of kosher foods. In Iowa—and this was true, too, of other states and of Russia—the rich exercised a disproportionate control in the local community. Dissidence was not unknown among the Protestants of that day; administrative arbitrariness made for dissension in many churches and synagogs.

One of the Orthodox rabbis in Iowa, in Des Moines in 1903, was Simon Glazer (1876-1938). This native of the province of Kovno came to America with a rabbinic diploma. Here he moved about from community to community seeking a congregation that he would please and one that would please him. Glazer, a man of strong literary interests, was scholarly, learned, enterprising, able; he wrote for the Hebrew, Yiddish, American-Jewish press and succeeded in producing a number of works in English on Judaism and Jewish history. In his *Guide of Judaism* that he was to publish later in New York (1917) he maintained that Reform Judaism could not solve the problem of the Jew in the United States; education in traditional Judaism was the answer.

Consequently, in this religious *Guide* he dealt in some detail with theology, liturgy, and the ceremonies; he discussed the dietary laws, the status of women, the Sabbath mourning customs, and the messianic era. It was almost a code for American Jews of the Orthodox persuasion. It is hard to see how his hodgepodge of Jewish law and tradition could win the loyalty of young Americans. In 1904 he wrote his *Jews of Iowa* in English. It is a valuable work because he interviewed many of the pioneers who were still alive. His is one of the earliest histories of a Jewish community in the United States; it is significant that it was written by an immigrant. It is also worthy of mention that only a few years later the first large-scale narrative history of the Jews of the United States was published by a Russian newcomer. This was Peter Wiernik's *History of the Jews in America* (1912). Barnett A. Elzas's *History of the Jews in South Carolina* was published in 1905. Elzas, too, was an immigrant. He was born in a village on the Prussian-Russian border. As natives of foreign lands, where right and tolerance, too, were often of a lesser degree, these immigrant authors who wrote of American Jewry, may well have been appreciative of American privileges and immunities. From 1907 to 1918 Glazer officiated as chief rabbi of various synagogs in Montreal and in Quebec; in 1923 he moved on to New York City where he played a part in Zionist and Orthodox circles. There can be no question that Glazer was committed to traditionalism yet he evidenced modernity in all that he wrote, and this in the early 1900's. His prime goal was to salvage Orthodoxy on American soil, in an open society.

There was little new or really exceptional in the economic life of the newcomers in pre-1921 Iowa; here, too, they were peddlers and small businessmen; grocers by the dozen abounded in Des Moines. A detailed study of the vocations of these incoming aliens before 1904, made by Glazer, shows that very many of them were in dry goods or clothing; this was particularly true of those individuals who had settled in small towns. Indeed this is typical for the country at large. Since Iowa was a meat producing state it is not surprising that individual Jews worked in the packing houses. In order to make both ends meet a Hebrew teacher also ran a kosher boarding house for the newly arrived. A Sioux City pioneer, who had come there by 1869, advertised as "Old Kirk, King of the Jews"; that same year one of his competitors informed his customers that his firm made "no distinction in prices on account of race, color or nationality. They have only one price for everybody." This town, the second largest Jewish community in Iowa, after Des Moines, became a core town for newcomers who reached out to the neighboring states of South Dakota and Nebraska. A Suwalki province Jew—this one from Kalvary—who made good in Des Moines was Falk Brody. After coming to New York City (1881) and working as an itinerant glazier putting windows in the city's tenement houses, he moved on to Des Moines where he opened a peddlers' supply house; he made a fortune. Brody kept his wholesale house closed on the Sabbath; this entailed no great sacrifice, for the country merchants preferred coming in on Sunday to replenish their stocks. Saturday they kept open; that was the biggest day of the week. One of Brody's sons settled in Elliot, Iowa, where he became a merchant and sat on the local city council. He owned a 600-acre farm.

One of the most remarkable Jews in the Iowa of that generation was Abraham Slimmer (1835-1917). This Pole, one of a family of nine children, came to the United States in the 1850's, settling first in Little Rock, Arkansas. Some time in that decade, shortly before the Civil War, he moved north; by 1865 he had made a niche for himself in the little town of Waverly, Iowa. He then sent for his old-country sweetheart, but when she refused to sit at the same table with the hired help he sent her back to Poland; he never married. Slimmer engaged in stock raising, farming, and in other enterprises; it would seem, however, that he made his money placing mortgages for insurance companies. By 1885 he was in all probability the richest Jew in Iowa worth, so it is said, close to a half-million dollars. Rumor would have it that in the course of his lifetime he gave $3,000,000 to charity. This is difficult to determine. But this is certain: he helped establish a hospital on Chicago's South Side, an old-folks home in Cedar Rapids, two homes for the aged in Chicago, a nonsectarian hospital in Omaha, a nonsectarian orphanage in Chicago, a Jewish orphanage in this same city, a home for the aged in Des Moines, a nonsectarian hospital in Milwaukee, a Jewish hospital in Chicago, a nonsectarian hospital in Dubuque. Milwaukee's Jewish charities received a gift of $50,000 from him; his beautiful home in Waverly was turned over to the Catholic Sisters of Mercy to be used as a hospital. His early gifts were directed to non-Jewish institutions but when he discovered that Gentiles in Chicago had turned their backs on Jews he began making liberal gifts also to his own people. When he died at the age of eighty-two he was buried by a Reform rabbi from St. Paul; he was not Orthodox. Like Judah Touro of New Orleans, Slimmer, too, was something of an eccentric but his generous giving is very impressive. He was certainly a humanitarian. Like Touro, too, he avoided publicity, lived modestly, and helped wherever there was a need regardless of religion. He gave large sums during his lifetime; most of his gifts were matching grants. One wonders if he may have influenced his younger contemporary Julius Rosenwald who made it a practice to insist on matching grants.[5]

MINNESOTA

Minnesota had a larger Jewry than Iowa. This is strange for Minnesota was isolated, tucked away in the new Northwest. There is no easy explanation for this anomaly. By 1920 Iowa had but 16,000 Jews, Minnesota, about twice that number, close to 34,000. The largest town in Iowa included fewer than 4,000 Jews; Minneapolis in 1920 had about 15,000, St. Paul about 10,000, Duluth about 3,000. By 1920 there were close to thirty congregations in Minnesota; most were manned by Jews from the lands of Eastern Europe. In 1882 large numbers of East European refugees were shipped out to St. Paul by the New Yorkers and London's Mansion House Committee. Somehow or other the Jews and sympathetic Gentiles made provision for the numerous newcomers. They were put to work on farms, on the railroads, in factories; others, craftsmen, plied their trade. Most of them managed to find jobs. At the turn of the century the East Europeans who had been pouring into the state since 1882 outnumbered the natives and Germans. In Minnesota, as in other states, the newcomers drifted into small towns in order to survive commercially. Life in some of these villages was primitive. The Jewish family that called Marshall its home had no running water, heated with stoves, and depended on kerosene lamps for light. In the winter the temperature sometimes fell to forty below zero. This Jewish family celebrated Passover with the usual festal meal, the seder, inviting some Jews from a neighboring village to sit down with them. They never failed to distribute matzos, unleavened bread, to their Gentile friends. In order that the children not grow up as heathen the family in Marshall sent to Chicago for Jewish Sunday school materials.

In the Mille Lacs area, the Thousand Lakes region, one of the outstanding citizens was a Jew by the name of Emmet Mark, whose father Aaron had come to St. Paul in 1873 and worked as a peddler collecting scrap iron. Before Aaron died in 1905 his yard had become the core of an iron and steel company that a generation later was to stand out as one of the city's important industries. Emmet bore the Hebrew name Moses. How he equated this with the Irish Emmet, only he would know. Gentiles who knew Emmet called him Easy Mark. On his own Emmet became a livestock dealer and ran successfully for sheriff. Falling in love with a Gentile girl, he took her to St. Paul and arranged for her conversion. She emerged from her ritual ablutions as Esther. A good Republican, Emmet induced his friends to send him to the state legislature in the early 1900's. The Marks hailed from Lithuania; so did Solomon Sax, born in Tauroggen, the home of several notable American Jewish newcomers. Young Sax, who had come to this country at the age of fifteen, settled in the Iron Range region and made some successful investments in land. For decades he lived in a village called Wallace; in 1917 its name was changed to Sax as a compliment to its Jewish resident.

Duluth's first permanent Jewish settler was a Hungarian, Bernard Silberstein (b. 1848), who had come there in 1870 from Detroit. A decade earlier Duluth had been little more than an Indian trading post. Fifty years later the East Europeans could point to immigrant congregations. All that was required in any town in the United States to establish an Orthodox prayer group was to assemble ten adult males, borrow a Scroll of the Law, and find a pretext for secession, if there was already a congregation in town. The oldest Jewish community in Minnesota had been established by German immigrants in St. Paul during territorial days in 1856. Jews were adventurous, rarely hesitant to crawl into the interstitial spaces. Close on the heels of the Central Europeans, the Russians had a commune of their own in the 1870's; by 1879 they had a building and later they collected a fine rabbinic library. A constitution adopted in the 1890's made it clear that the newcomers would tolerate no reforms. In 1900 there were five traditional assemblies in St. Paul; by 1918 there were ten. As in most other towns the women assumed the responsibility for administering most of the charities. In 1888 Rabbi Herman Simon led one of the local traditional groups. Back in Europe he had pored over the pages of the Talmud; here in St. Paul he bowed the knee to Kant and Spinoza; for relaxation he repaired old watches that were brought to him. One is reminded of Dr. Solomon B. Freehof, the distinguished Pittsburgh rabbi, Reform's authority on talmudic law, who relaxed by rebinding old books for himself and his friends.

Minneapolis Jewry blossomed later than its neighbor in St. Paul; by 1918 the Minneapolitan Israelites far outnumbered the St. Paulinians though they had fewer synagogs. The Russians had come to the city as early as the 1870's but opened no prayer room until the 1880's; by 1900 they had six congregations. The largest of these synagogs, Kenesseth Israel (1889) maintained an afternoon Hebrew school for boys and a Sunday school for girls where the instruction was in English. The older folks had a sodality whose members read Psalms and studied the codes. One of the houses of worship established in 1901 originally called itself Anshei Russia, the Men of Russia; later, the members changed the name, reminding themselves that it was wrong to memorialize a land which had abused them. Of the immigrant assemblies in town five were under the tutelage of Rabbi Solomon Mordecai Silber (d. 1925)—not to be confused with Saul Silber of Chicago. Silber realized that if he was to exercise any influence in Minneapolis he would have to be active in the larger Jewish and general community. This impelled him to assume the role of a leader; he dressed the part with a top hat, went to all important civic functions, and appears to have been accepted and respected by both Jews and Gentiles.

Silber's attitude was by no means unusual; he was one of many Russian-born rabbis who realized that integrating Orthodoxy with the American way of life was essential. This new approach involved educating boys and girls in a more modern fashion; no longer could the heder be patterned on the traditional Russian Hebrew school. English not Yiddish must be the language of instruction; modern pedagogical methods had to be adopted. If the youngsters were bored they would not come to classes; Jewish identity would fade. Traditional rabbis who could not—would not—accommodate themselves to the American scene, who would not learn English and the American approach, had little or no influence on the younger generation. Some of those proud talmudists were not inclined to make any concessions because they were not prepared to cope with the many problems that confronted them. One is reminded of the Reformer, Rabbi David Einhorn, who insisted on retaining German and never learned to preach in English. A number of these learned Russian rabbis enjoined constant intensive study of the Hebrew legal codes; preaching but rarely and then only in Yiddish on recondite themes, they did little to modernize their talmudic schools.

The problem that faced Jews educationally in this country was fully understood by George Jacob Gordon (1874-1943). This native of Lithuania, after receiving a talmudic education, came to the United States at the age of eighteen. He worked in a paper box factory, and graduated from high school when twenty-two, supporting himself in the meantime by giving lessons in Hebrew and Latin. Leaving Minneapolis for a few years, he studied medicine in Philadelphia and received his medical degree from the Jefferson Medical College in 1900—only eight years after his arrival in this country. In the early 1900's Gordon became interested in the Minneapolis Talmud Torah, the afternoon Hebrew school. With his help it became a showpiece, one of the best institutions of its kind in the United States. Gordon, one of Minneapolis's most respected communal leaders, was sympathetic to Reform. (His son Theodore became a Reform rabbi.) In his role as a physician, he served as chief of obstetrics in a local hospital until 1928, when he abandoned his practice to become the full-time director of the Talmud Torah. One is reminded very much of his contemporary, Dr. Samson Benderly, also a physician, who left medicine in the attempt to revitalize and modernize Jewish education in New York City.[6]

MICHIGAN

Minnesota enjoyed limited exposure to the Great Lakes through Duluth at the western end of Lake Superior. Farther east, Michigan was more advantageously located with easy access to Lakes Superior, Michigan, and Huron. It was almost completely surrounded by important water highways, a decided economic advantage. Before the Russians started coming in numbers in 1882 fewer than 4,000 Jews lived in Michigan. Detroit, in those days the only town of size, could count about 2,000 Israelites. It is doubtful if there were then more than a dozen synagogs and prayer groups in the whole state; two of them seem to have been frequented by the newcomers. Shaarey Zedek, the Gates of Righteousness, founded in 1861, certainly had some members who stemmed from Eastern Europe. By the 1880's there was a "Russian" congregation in almost every city in the state; by 1920 there were at least forty such conventicles in Michigan. Detroit then, with an estimated population of about 50,000 Jews, was one of America's notable Jewish communities; the state sheltered, all told, about 70,000 Jews.

The newcomers went to any place where they had a chance to make a living. There was even a small group of them in Newberry, in Luce County on Lake Superior, in the Upper Peninsula near Canada. Adventurers from Poland started moving into Newberry in the 1880's—Luce County itself had a total population of 1,500 souls—opening clothing and dry goods stores; some of these businesses specialized in supplies for hunters. There seem to have been enough families in town to hold services for the Holy Days; a teacher was brought in to prepare the children for bar mitzvah; one pious soul was courageous enough to keep his shop closed on the Sabbath. Kosher foods were imported from Minneapolis and Detroit. The Rosenthals, one of the outstanding families in Newberry, had settled there in 1887; when they left for Los Angeles, in 1910, the elementary and high schools were closed to say goodbye to them. Some of Newberry's Jews were peddlers who had come in from New York; they were compelled to buy their stocks from distant wholesalers in Detroit. Jewish girls in town engaged in sports; one of them was on the local basketball team; the boys played both football and basketball. After going through the schools the younger generation left town and did not return; there were no opportunities for it in Luce County. Some settled in Chicago and in New York, whence their families had come originally.

Michigan's "Russians," coming from isolated Slavic villages and towns, were faced with the double problem of adjusting to one another and to the larger American community and culture. By 1904 Shaarey Zedek in Detroit wanted an English sermon for its late Friday services. This desire, of course, reflected strong American, Protestant, and Reform Jewish influences. Shaarey Zedek was well on the way to fitting into Jewry's Conservative mold; by the early twentieth century some of its members were already native-born Americans. The intramural acerbities never absent among newcomers in almost every town are obviously reflected in the tiny Jewish community of Mt. Clemens, a resort town near Detroit; there were seventy-seven souls in town, but there were three different congregations. Of the seventeen immigrant synagogs in Detroit in 1918, four of them accepted the tutelage of Judah B. Levin (b. 1863). The rabbi, a native of Lithuania, was the son of pious and learned Jewish parents; his father, a farmer, never doffed his phylacteries even when working in the fields. Even as he followed the plough, he recited a tractate of the Mishnah which he knew by heart. Young Levin was a brilliant student and, after studying at some of Russia's distinguished yeshivot, he received ordination from two eminent rabbis, Isaac Elhanan Spektor and Naphtali Zevi

Judah Berlin, the head of the academy at Volozhin. After ministering to communities in Russia Levin came to the United States in 1892, first to Rochester, then to New Haven and finally, in 1897, to Detroit. He called his little federation the Orthodox Congregations of Detroit; included among them was prestigious Shaarey Zedek. Years later in 1916, when a new Hebrew academy was opened, the community honored him by calling it the House of Judah, Beth Yehudah; it was an afternoon Hebrew school. Its support came from a variety of sources, including a female auxiliary. More and more immigrant women were reaching out to support not only the charities but schools and other institutions. They are the unsung heroes who helped make possible American Jewish culture, philanthropy, and many of its institutions.

For many of these émigrés the United States was most of all a land of opportunity, a country where they could make a living and, what was equally important, educate their children. This is reflected in the story of the Lipsitz-Mincer clan of Detroit. Charles (Ezekiel in Hebrew) Mincer and his wife Gitel had three boys, all born abroad; two of them became optometrists traveling around in the countryside, examining eyes, and fitting glasses. Apparently they did well. The youngest son went South to Texas with a circus; he was a juggler; ultimately he became a cotton broker.

In the course of years the Detroit East European junk peddlers controlled the scrap metal trade of the state; others turned to the clothing trade as retailers or wholesalers. A Yiddish directory which appeared in Detroit in 1907 illuminates the business life of the newcomers in considerable detail. The advertisements were alluring. Readers were most cordially invited to use the Russian and Turkish steambath; they were offered the services of a graduate Russian midwife renowned for her noble care of poor and rich alike, so she said. Advertisements proclaimed the virtues of tea and coffee with that special Jewish flavor, and Sol Wolfson informed the public that he was not only well known as the best horseshoer in Detroit but as a man prepared to make a wagon to order. An analysis of the ads in this Yiddish directory discloses that few areas of economic life were unexplored by Jews. The following is a list of Jewish occupations and vocations: printing, livery stables, butcher shops, delicatessens, groceries, and dry goods; steamship tickets were purchasable on time payments; they could even be bought in a drugstore. Eager entrepreneurs sold hay, coal, fish, bags. They lent money, ran shirt and cloak factories, and operated stores that sold wine, liquors, shoes, ladies' and gents' clothing; they were cobblers, barbers, movers, fire insurance salesmen, tailors, tobacconists, dairymen. Religionists were informed where they could buy Hebrew books and unleavened bread for Passover; there was a mikveh for the women's monthly ritual ablutions. There were bakers, carpenters, house

painters, paperhangers, circumcisers, and a shohet, who was also competent to chant the prayers. Peddlers and hucksters informed the readers
that they sold dry goods, notions, fruits, and vegetables.

During the bitter national political campaigns of the 1890's, when
the battle for free silver was being fought between the Democrats and the
Republicans, Jews—many of them were businessmen and identified with
the Republican Party—were denounced as Shylocks. There seems to have
been considerable prejudice against peddlers; consequently around the
year 1900 they organized themselves into the Jewish Peddlers Protective
Union; making a living even in free America was plagued with hazards.
There were also Jews who worked in the factories and when Ford offered
$5 a day—a very attractive wage—some sought employment. They
found it difficult to get on the payroll, however, because they could not
speak English; English-speaking workers were usually preferred. Hebrew
schools, heders, abounded in Detroit. There were some teachers in these
private schools who peddled part of the day and taught Hebrew in the afternoon. Tuition at one of these schools was 25 cents a week. Large
classes were profitable and some Hebrew instructors made as much as $15
a week—good pay, if one recalls that a full-course meal at a Jewish restaurant could be purchased for fifteen cents. Improved Talmud Torahs,
public afternoon Hebrew schools, were not lacking; there were parents
who insisted on modern institutions for their children. One Hebrew
teacher advertised that he was at home in the various areas of Jewish
studies, that he knew English and could teach in that language. There
were some Talmud Torahs which taught not only Hebrew reading, but
also biblical and Jewish history. A good teacher at a Talmud Torah might
be given a two-week vacation, with pay no doubt. There is no question
that by 1920 the drive toward modernity—accommodation to American
culture—had reached the Hebrew schools not only in Detroit, New
York, Minneapolis, but in many other cities. For many denizens of the
ghetto, Sunday, the Christian Sabbath, was a holiday, a time for outings,
when Jews relaxed in their clubs and social organizations singing Hebrew
and Yiddish songs. By 1917 Detroit had a Hebrew-speaking club in town
of ten boys and two girls; in time it grew to seventy members. The Yiddishists brought Sholem Aleichem to town in 1915 for a lecture under the
auspices of an organization called the Progressive Literary and Dramatic
Club.

The 1907 Detroit Yiddish directory published an ad by Charles Cas-
per Simons, attorney-at-law, and also one by his father who headed the
Simons Realty Company. Charles was born in 1876 in Detroit, one of
eight children; David W. Simons, the father, a native of Suwalki, had
come to this country in the early 1870's. He borrowed enough money to
buy a horse and wagon and became a junk peddler; in later years Judge

Simons, with a twinkle in his eye, would tell his friends that his father had been "a metallurgist from Kalwarya." David started modestly but rose to become a paper manufacturer, a real estate operator, a builder, and finally a banker. He was an important person in Detroit Jewry, one of the pillars of Congregation Shaarey Zedek, a leader in the United Jewish Charities, an activist during the Liberty Loan Drives of World War I, and a 33rd degree Mason, no small distinction. His friends elected him to Detroit's city council. The father was thus in a position to further his son's career. David saw to it that Charles was well educated; he studied law, received his degree at the University of Michigan, and began practicing in Detroit in 1900. He served in the State Senate during 1903 and 1904; in 1923 he was appointed a federal district judge, and was elevated in 1931 to the circuit bench; ultimately he became a chief judge. Charles Simons died in 1963.

Among the Russian Jews who settled in small towns in the northern part of the state were the Steinbergs. Julius Steinberg, like David W. Simons, had come from Suwalki. After fleeing Russia in the 1860's to avoid conscription, Steinberg (b. 1847) settled down in Traverse City—merely a lumber camp at the time. He started out as a pack peddler, bought a horse and wagon when he had saved a little, and finally opened a dry goods store. It took him about four years to save enough money to bring his wife and children over. Ultimately he would raise a family of seven. The business was called the Reliable Dry Goods, Carpet, and Clothing House. It was a small department store with ladies' and men's goods, trunks, and valises. In 1891 Julius built the Grand Opera House. (Such a theatre was to be found in most towns; some were built by enterprising Jews.) Stock companies used his theatre until the cinema began to appeal to people in the early twentieth century; then he began showing motion pictures and finally built a special movie theatre. Like most of his small town fellow Jews in the northern states Steinberg was a Republican.

A few East European families made notable successes; they pulled themselves up by their own bootstraps. Aaron Cohodas came to this country in 1900 settling in a Wisconsin village; the family followed him three years later, his wife and six little children fourteen and under. When the father died everyone had to pitch in to help make a living. They peddled newspapers, sold milk—they had a cow—clerked in a store and received some help from an uncle. They went into the motion picture business but made no money. Jewish tradition has a slogan: change your town, change your luck. In 1915 they moved on to Houghton, Michigan, near Lake Superior. This was almost the end of the world. Deciding to go into the retail and wholesale produce business, they opened stores also in Hancock and Calumet. Their business expanded during World War I. Sam, the business genius in the family, settled in Ishpeming in nearby

Marquette County. Convinced that the wholesale produce business was
its métier the family pushed hard until it had built one of the largest produce companies in the United States, the Cohodas Brothers Company.
These settlers made a great success in an obscure part of the country.
Busying themselves in general and Jewish causes they were acclaimed for
their many philanthropies.[7]

WISCONSIN

The United States sheltered a relatively small Jewry before the coming of
the Russians, Poles, and Rumanians from the 1880's on. There were then
only six states that had sizable Jewries, California, Illinois, Maryland,
New York, Ohio, and Pennsylvania. Even New York State at that time
did not have a community of 100,000 Jews. Wisconsin had but 2,600
Jews in 1880; Milwaukee, Madison, and La Crosse were the only cities in
the state that had congregations. Individual Jews were found in numerous
other towns but no other community in Wisconsin had as many as 150
souls. East Europeans as a body had not yet discovered the state; as late as
1898 there were only nine towns with congregations although by that
time the Russians and Poles were beginning to make their presence felt;
twelve of the fifteen Jewish religious societies in the state had been established by the new immigrants, most of these in small towns. Milwaukee
and Superior then were the only two cities with more than one congregation; in 1906 Superior, with 250 souls, had four congregations of newcomers; during the 1890's Milwaukee's immigrants hastened to establish
new congregations. In 1920 Wisconsin had something over 30,000 Jews;
Milwaukee sheltered 20,000 of them; most were immigrants. The East
Europeans then had thirty congregations in the state; Milwaukee had six,
three of which, ethnic in a narrow sense, catered proudly to Hungarians,
Poles, and Rumanians. These three had no desire to be overwhelmed religiously by the preponderant Russians.

To know one town is in a way to know all; differences were often interesting but not really important; Manitowoc and Sheboygan on Lake
Michigan were in a sense typical of the East European communities in all
American states. Refugees drifted into Manitowoc during the mid-1890's;
some were peddlers, others were junk collectors; some had small retail
shops, a few worked in factories. By 1900 one of the congregations was
able to hire a shohet to provide the members with kosher food; kosher
meat is always important because it is a prime device in establishing and
maintaining Jewish identity—on the theory that, with all due apologies
to the German philosopher Ludwig A. Feuerbach, "a man is what he
eats." In 1918 there were about 800 Jewish souls in Sheboygan and three
congregations of newcomers; one had thirty members and twenty He-

brew school youngsters; another had forty-five members and sixty pupils; the number of members in the third community is not documented but it had 110 students. It may well be that some of the immigrants in town were not affiliated with any of the synagogs. Sheboygan had a Zionist society and a mutual-aid association; there was also a Hebrew Library Society with all of seven members. It is probable that some mutual-aid members saw no need to belong to a congregation. There was also a woman's Hebrew School Society whose purpose was to help support the school of one of the three congregations. It becomes more and more patent as one studies town life that if the women had not taken over the charities and had not supported other institutions, too, the Jewish communities would have suffered egregiously; women were the indispensable fund-raisers; more than that they spurred the community to be institutionally active and creative.

How does a Jewish community grow? The Sweet family will help the reader understand. Solomon Sweet came to the United States to live with his son in Madison. Papa Sweet had twelve children. After a few years he brought them all over. He returned to Russia three times where he had left his wife and youngsters. It would seem he liked Russia. On the third trip he came back with the last of his progeny. In the course of time several of Solomon's brothers also came over with their dear ones; they saved and sent money or tickets to bring their families here. This is how Madison grew and became a community. Other immigrants in other towns did likewise. Another East European who came to Madison was S. B. Shiner. Back in Europe his father was a rabbi who saw to it that his son received a good Hebrew education. After living in the South for some time Shiner had moved North to Madison in 1915 where he served the community as a shohet, hazzan, and teacher. He worked for a year at this job while studying and preparing for the bar. No doubt his talmudic studies helped him think juristically. When he passed the examination he resigned his position with the congregation and began to practice law. In 1917 he received an interim appointment in one of the county courts; later he was elected to the bench. Another man in town also served as a shohet; he was an ardent Zionist and a leader in the Orthodox synagog. This, of course, would itself excite no comment—but this same devoted Jew was also a member of a local church! In no sense a Christian, he helped support the church as an interfaith activist; there may have been other reasons too. Admiring him, the Christian members put him on their executive board but he refused to serve because he was a Jew; he had no intention of telling the Christians how to behave and how to run their institution. Their response was that it was anybody's church not exclusively a Christian one. He finally dropped his membership; his Christian friends were too insistent.

Madison's newcomers had their own building by 1906 although they had conducted services long before that. It is worthy of comment that this small congregation had a formal rabbinical court, a bet din, to hear cases involving the members; they were required to come to the bet din before resorting to secular tribunals. Some of the complaints cited involved charges of physical violence by Jew against Jew. By 1915 the socialists— non-religionists and anti-Zionists—had established a Workmen's Circle lodge; the Labor Zionists countered with a society of their own to preach the gospel of a return to Palestine. By 1917 the women had introduced Hadassah. This may be due to the fact that they were influenced by Mrs. Joseph Jastrow at whose house they met for musicales. Her husband was a professor of psychology at the state university; she was a sister of Henrietta Szold one of the original founders of Hadassah in New York City. The local female Zionist group formed sewing circles, organized a Sabbath school, and labored to help orphans in Palestine. Many of Madison's Russians and Poles were multilingual. They knew Yiddish, at least one of the Slavic languages, and English. Practically all of them could read Hebrew though not all knew the meaning of the words in the prayer books. Most of them were Orthodox; they kept some form of kashrut at home, but many of them ate nonkosher on the outside. They were all opposed to intermarriage; very few of them observed the Sabbath in the traditional fashion. A study of 242 business people in Madison in 1930 revealed that fifty-three operated retail stores and twenty-nine were peddlers.

By the first decade of the twentieth century the East Europeans, the overwhelming majority of Milwaukee's Jews, had established the many and diverse institutions which they needed to function as a complete community. A learned rabbi was brought in during the 1890's; he was paid $50 a year; as in other towns he was expected to live on fees. Kosher meat markets were very much in evidence; during the Feast of Tabernacles families built sukkot, little huts in their yards; free burials were provided for the impoverished; famous cantors were imported to help pay off the mortgages. By the early 1900's Milwaukee had a Yiddish weekly. The town's ghetto was not a very appetizing or romantic place; no ghetto was. Some people kept chickens in the basement; cobblers worked in cellars which stank of discarded shoes. Peddlers' yards were filled with junk, old iron, rags. The community had its complement of artisans such as carpenters, blacksmiths, locksmiths, tanners, bricklayers, cabinet makers, bookbinders. There were many tailors; some had hired out to subcontractors who received their bundles from Chicago's clothing manufacturers. There was a capmakers' union in Milwaukee; most of its members were Jews. Jewish bakers and house painters also had unions of their own. A few immigrants were wholesalers; many were in petty trading, retailers.

There were some country peddlers although this form of trade was becoming increasingly difficult because of the mail-order houses, better roads, and the new cheap automobiles which brought farmers and villagers to the towns and the big stores. There were a number of urban peddlers who, as in many other towns, were often molested by juveniles and gangsters. These men hawked dry goods, notions, fruits, and collected junk. The Progressive Rag Peddlers' Union, a mutual-aid society, had 200 members; it set out to fix the price of junk sold to the wholesalers. In addition there was a Milwaukee Junk Dealers' Association, and it in turn was countered by a Wholesale Junk Dealers' Association. It is said that there were ninety Jewish retail grocers and delicatessens in town at one time; other immigrants were clothiers, hardware dealers, jewelers, restaurateurs, and booksellers. There were pharmacists, a few physicians, lawyers, and opticians; as a rule these professionals were the children of immigrants. Like the peddlers, members of various trades and businesses organized to further their interests; there was thus a Jewish Grocers' Club, an Independent Fruit Dealers' Association, a Jewish Milwaukee Shoe Repairers' Protective Association, and a similar society established by the Jewish butchers. Some of these organizations may well have been mutual-benefit congeries. One of their functions was to watch and limit the hours that stores did business. In part this was an attempt to control competition; some of the grocers were wont to keep open for twenty hours a day. Those who closed on Saturday—and there were some—kept open on Sunday; the first day of the week, Sunday, was not sacred to Jews. In summary it is believed that by 1910 there were 500 householders in Milwaukee who supported themselves by peddling; 500 others were artisans, craftsmen, retailers. Difficult as conditions were for these lowly newcomers they lived better than Milwaukee's Poles and Italians.

It was not always easy for Jews to get credit; big banks and rating agencies were not enamored of Jewish petty tradesmen; accordingly a Jewish bank was started. The Socialist Zionists had a credit union which they had established. Because work conditions and sanitation were bad in some places and tuberculosis was not uncommon, the local Hebrew Relief Association was compelled to allocate much of its resources to provide for sick and stricken immigrants; the victims, the tuberculars, were sent to city sanatoria. By the time of World War I tuberculosis was more or less under control. With sickness and economic distress came desertion; this threat to the family has always been a problem in every immigrant community. Milwaukee's chief Jewish welfare agency, the Hebrew Relief Association, tried to make desertion unattractive by refusing to give dependent women with children liberal grants; this deterred some husbands from leaving home since they realized their wives and children would suffer. When in the course of the twentieth century workers managed to make a better living, desertion diminished. The National Desertion Bureau pursued deserters relentlessly; there was no escape.

One of Milwaukee's immigrants who rose in the world was Golda Mabovitch (1898-1978). This Kiev-born Jew came to Milwaukee in 1906, a child of only eight years of age. In essence she was an American. She did very well in American schools. They helped make her what she was to become; she graduated from high school, worked for a time in a public library, went to the local Normal School, and became a teacher. An ardent lover of Palestine she busied herself in the local Zionist organization. When only a teenager she had joined the Socialist Zionists. People admired and respected her as a Yiddish and English orator. In the early 1920's Golda and her husband, Morris Meyerson, became members of a collective farm in Palestine; at times she worked as a washerwoman while her husband labored at carpentry. It was in Palestine that she turned to politics and became a force in the powerful labor federation. She was a very clever woman. Golda Meir—as she eventually called herself—served as a Zionist emissary in the United States, 1932-1934, as the new state's envoy to Russia, as minister of labor in an Israeli cabinet, as foreign minister, and finally as prime minister. When as premier she visited Milwaukee she said: "Here I found freedom, kindness, and cleanliness."

During her years in Milwaukee Golda Mabovitch was in no sense an important person; she was a school teacher, a socialist, a Zionist; when she left for Palestine she was only twenty-three years of age. By the time Golda went with her husband to settle on a kibbutz, Solomon Levitan (1862-1940) had become a very important Wisconsin politician. Levitan, a native of Lithuania, studied as a youngster in Hebrew schools, worked for a time in the Crimea, and there, according to a popular story, after helping his employer during a pogrom, was rewarded with a ticket to America. In 1880, after coming to Baltimore, he labored at several jobs including paving streets. He saved up enough money to buy a basket of notions and peddled westward to Maryland, Pennsylvania, and West Virginia; in 1882 he came to Wisconsin. At first he continued as a pack peddler; later, with some money saved, he bought a horse and wagon, and when he had enough capital opened a general store in the tiny Wisconsin village of New Glarus. His wife whom he married in 1887 bore him three children. He opened branch stores in the neighborhood of New Glarus and for a time served as a justice of peace. Levitan turned to politics, as a Republican, and worked closely with Robert M. La Follette, one of the best known political figures in Wisconsin. Levitan is reported to have said of La Follette, "I sold him a pair of suspenders and I supported him the balance of his life." In 1905 he moved to Madison so that his children might receive a good general education and be prepared for college. When he first came to Madison he did not join the Orthodox community; he waited a few years and because of this some local Jews looked askance at him; they believed he was catering to the Gentiles. He pleaded poverty but his fellow Jews were skeptical; he was already a man of some means. In Madison he did well; by 1914 he had become a successful banker.

Levitan, who now went into politics, was very popular with the voters. He was a consummate vote getter. As a Republican he voted for Taft; later he became a Progressive, ran twice for the office of state treasurer and lost. Success came to him in 1922 when he was elected treasurer and was reelected for several terms. He was finally defeated in the Democratic landslide of 1932, but in 1936 was reelected, this time on the Progressive Party ticket. All told he had served six complete terms of two years each, a Wisconsin record. As a politician he supported the universities and the Normal School, and served on the Board of Regents of the state university, on other college boards, too. He was highly intelligent, a clever, witty person. Some of Wisconsin's Indians, Winnebagos and Chippewas, elected him twice as their chief; he was known as White Deer and Roaring Thunder. The voters called him Uncle Sol. Like all politicians he was a joiner; a member of B'nai B'rith, he became the head of the Madison lodge and was appointed honorary president of the District Grand Lodge. He remained an Orthodox Jew and on occasion would even lead in prayer on the High Holy Days. When he died he was given a state funeral, the second in Wisconsin's history; the only other man to be thus honored was his friend Robert M. La Follette. He lay in state in the capitol. Despite the fact that he was Orthodox, Louis Binstock, the Chicago Reform rabbi, was brought in to conduct the funeral services. When in 1936 this seventy-four-year-old stalwart was running for office, his opponents said he was too old. Uncle Sol's answer was that handling people's money was no job for a politician; there was too much temptation; it was wise to elect an elderly man to safeguard the state's funds. As he put it, he was looking for the golden gate not the golden calf. He learned German and Norwegian and told jokes in those languages when he politicked for votes. As an immigrant and a Jew he assumed the role of a humble, simple man, shrewdly playing to the gallery.[8]

CHAPTER FIVE

PART III

THE EAST EUROPEANS IN THE HINTERLAND TO 1921

New England

MAINE

I t is not such a far cry from Wisconsin to New England; New England-
ers, those in the Connecticut Land Company and the Ohio Company of Associates, had been very active in land promotions in the Old
Northwest Territory of which Wisconsin was to be a part. As late as
1920, however, the three northern tier states in New England did not
play a large part in the life of Jewish immigrants from Russia and Poland.
By 1921, the year of the first fateful racially-motivated immigration act,
the Jewish East Europeans in Maine, New Hampshire, and Vermont did
not number 14,000 souls. As late as 1904 the America-oriented *Jewish Encyclopedia* did not include a separate article on Maine. Individual East European Jews had wandered into that state in the 1860's; some had come
from Poland and Lithuania; they increased in numbers in the 1870's and
1880's. Portland had a shohet in 1872 and a burial confraternity, too; that
was all Jews really needed to constitute themselves a community. The
Jews of the state were almost all from Slavic lands, but even for them
Maine, New Hampshire, and Vermont were something of a frontier. The
Jewish founding fathers of these communities were often peddlers; by
1883 there were two rival congregations in Portland; in the next decade,
the 1890's, prayer groups were established by these recent arrivals in three
other Maine towns; the total membership in the three new communities
numbered less than 100.

Wherever they went the newcomers brought their old home cultural
institutions with them; thus there was a Hebrew school in Portland in the
1880's; by the 1890's talmudic studies were being pursued by a few
learned men who had frequented the academies back in Europe. Before
1920 Portland had two burial confraternities; the one buried only Sabbath

observers; the other buried any Jew regardless of his orthodoxy. By 1908 modern-oriented Hebrew schools had made their appearance in the state; not only Hebrew but history and religion were taught (teaching religion as a separate discipline is very definitely a Protestant approach). Between 1916 and 1919, the first attempt of the modernists to organize and maintain a less than traditional Orthodox synagog failed; the local Orthodox rabbi would not even talk to an "Americanized" Jewish minister. By 1921 a moderate traditional Conservative congregation had made its appearance in Portland; there was a late Friday evening service, family pews, and congregational singing. By the 1920's the city's Jews had built a small but substantial community with synagogs, schools, and auxiliary societies for men and women in which practically all ideologies were represented. Sons and daughters of immigrants were already holding office in the general community, serving in the state House and Senate, as municipal judges, as civil service commissioners, and as members of the Board of Education. The vocational pattern of these Jews differed but little from that of Jewish newcomers in practically all the other states. In 1920 there were few towns that did not have at least one Jewish institution; Bath, in 1916, with its ninety-three Israelites, had only one Jewish organization, the Naomi Club, a women's society of twenty members. In 1920 Portland had at least 1,000 Jewish souls, most of them immigrants or their children. The state then included seventeen congregations; apparently none of them was Reform; the East Europeans dominated Maine Jewry completely.[1]

NEW HAMPSHIRE

In this northern tier of New England states, the number of Jews tended to diminish in the interior. By the end of the second decade of the twentieth century Maine had 7,600 Jews; New Hampshire, 3,400. It may well be that the Jews sensed that they were not entirely welcome in New Hampshire. As late as 1876 the Jews were still disabled politically and when finally the last barriers to office were removed many thousands of good Christians still voted to retain the proscriptive articles. New Hampshire's Jewish newcomers had probably moved north from Massachusetts hoping that they would meet with less competition in the villages as they struggled for a livelihood. There is no question that the first Jewish settlers in this state were poor; they joined the Jewish mutual-aid societies and lodges; paying dues in a congregation was something of a luxury; the benefits there were spiritual not financial. It is equally true that for the same reason many of the first German Jewish immigrants in antebellum United States joined benefit societies on their arrival in this country. New Hampshire before 1921 had five "Jewish" towns and six congregations. Manchester, the largest community in the state with about 600 souls, had two synagogs and at least three women's organizations. The males were only too happy when the women moved in to help the community; the men preferred staying close to their shops. The ladies were given little or no credit and even less authority.[2]

Vermont has never had very many Jews; in 1880 there were probably not 150 of them in the whole state; twenty years later, there were only about 700; in 1920, no more than 2,300. Though Vermont has no sea coast— the immigrants did not have easy access—there were five congregations in four towns by 1905; most of them were small. In 1918 Montpelier with fewer than 100 Jews had two congregations; Burlington was by far the largest Jewish town in Vermont that year; it had four prayer groups. Among them were men who belonged to a society dedicated to the study of the Mishnah, the third century Hebrew code; there was another group in Burlington that read Psalms. No matter how remote the corner, how small the group, scattered Jews remained one with World Jewry through the Bible and the codes. This was the real cement that held them together, the essence of their ethnicity. Burlington had seven charities, two administered by women. The city had its first prayer group in the 1870's but there was to be no congregation in town till 1883 when the local devotees hired a religious factotum; he did everything needed to conduct services, to hold the Jews together. This communal servant also operated a kosher meat market and an ice house; he had to reach out in all directions in order to survive. The hazzan-shohet-teacher had an Irish lad who aided him in his various callings. He was given a Yiddish name, Yankle Motke (Jakie Moses). There is a tradition, too, that the Jewish atomic scientists at Los Alamos gave Hebrew names to their Gentile colleagues. While sitting in the Hebrew school helping his employer, Jakie Moses learned Yiddish and memorized some of the standard Hebrew prayers. When a member of Burlington's devout community shocked everyone by marrying out, his name in the congregational records was not spelled out; he was referred to as "the forgotten one." A mutual-aid burial society was also established in the decade of the 1880's (1886); members had to pay dues of 20 cents a month and when they met at their first anniversary banquet the confraternity had so little in the treasury that every member was asked to bring his own food and dishes.

It is difficult today when most Jews are in the affluent middle class to comprehend the poverty and thrift of earlier generations, when it was imperative for those immigrants to rely on various benefit societies providing some protection against calamities. One of the mutual-aid societies in town was a totally Jewish Knights of Pythias lodge; when a burial society was established in Burlington, a Yiddish-speaking group, it took a page out of the Jewish Knights of Pythias ritual and appointed an officer whom it called the "Prelate." This Knights of Pythias lodge required that its members state their vocation; most of them recorded themselves as merchants—in truth, they were small shopkeepers. Some declared that they were travelers; this seems to have been a euphemism for peddlers. The selfsame Jewish Knights of Pythias gave charity to both Jews and non-Jews; they contributed funds for victims of the Kishinev pogrom and to the sufferers of the Galveston flood and the San Francisco earthquake. A second congregation was organized in Burlington in the 1880's; it called itself the Life of Man, Hai Odom; it probably began as a confraternity to study a code called Hai Adam. It was set up by secessionists from the first congregation, The Lovers of Righteousness. Why a secession in this particular instance? A congregant was denied the privilege of leading the services at the altar because he kept his store open on the Sabbath, so it is said. One of the local "rabbis," it is also recalled, wrote Hebrew with his right hand and English with his left; obviously like a good Jew he was making a distinction between the sacred and the profane. Still another religious group came into being in town in 1906; it called itself The Love of Strangers, Ahavath Garim; feeling alienated from the older synagog these rebels, newcomers, created a burial fraternity of their own.

A town rabbi was secured for all three synagogs in 1909; he was Israel Rosenberg (b. 1875), a scholarly Pole who had come to the United States in 1903. When called upon he could address his flock in Yiddish, Hebrew, or English. He once lectured on the life of Lincoln. Such acculturational ventures were not too frequent in the Orthodox rabbinate. Later, as president of the Union of Orthodox Rabbis, he excommunicated the dean of the Teachers' Institute of the Jewish Theological Seminary of America, Mordecai M. Kaplan, denouncing him as a heretic. While in Burlington Rosenberg received a salary of $18 a week; some of this was raised by a tax of two cents on each pound of kosher meat. Despite his condemnation of the radical Kaplan, the Burlington rabbi was no obscurantist; he encouraged girls to study. Rosenberg was very much interested in establishing a good Hebrew school. The Talmud Torah which was incorporated in 1909 had a fine school building; it called itself the Free Hebrew School but there was a tuition charge of fifty cents a week for boys and twenty-five cents for girls. One wonders what prompted the discount for females; it was certainly not the Christian concept of chivalry. When the building fund was collected bricks were "sold" at $15 a piece to help pay the cost of the new edifice. One man bought one and then walked around looking for his brick with his name on it. Not finding it he demanded his money back. A committee was appointed to adjudicate the complaint and it finally awarded him a rebate of $7.50.

In Burlington, and this was true in many other towns throughout the country, individuals among the immigrants found jobs as common laborers toiling in mills or as craftsmen working in their shops. Petty shopkeepers were numerous; they always had high visibility. This first generation managed to survive though very few became affluent; the newcomers were a humble lot. One member of the Burlington community was a peddler of laces and handkerchiefs; his wife helped him out by selling baked goods and serving as a midwife; she delivered well over 200 children. Another member made a living by financing peddlers and by running a rental library for Jewish books. The young folks—and this is quite typical—were always creating youth organizations which were not destined to survive. These societies, whether created by the boys or girls, were "literary" and social; the social aspect prevailed.

Many of the associations fashioned by the immigrants were sympathetic to Zionism. Some youngsters conjured up a secret society calling themselves the Young Patriots of Sinai; the password was: "If I forget thee, O Zion, let my right hand forget its cunning" (Ps. 137:5). In one of the synagogs in town the youngsters had ball teams. Early after services on the Sabbath the boys would sneak off to a nearby farm without telling their elders and then proceed joyfully to desecrate the Sabbath. Such a disregard for the sanctity of the Sabbath would never have been tolerated in a village back in the old country. Fort Ethan Allen was five miles out of Burlington. It was a well-known cavalry post with numerous Jews among the enlisted men. Most of them were probably immigrants; all of them, it would seem were Zionists. Their leader was Sergeant Max Pilzer, a devout Jewish immigrant, a good Hebraist, who never failed to don his tefillin, his phylacteries. He kept kosher and on the High Holy Days would bring in over twenty soldiers to the services. They had their own Jewish cavalry society, the Riders of Zion.

The youngsters in Burlington had an amateur theatrical group which, in 1906, staged *The Massacre of Kishinev*; it was a melodrama in five acts. Aided by the local Episcopal bishop they raised over $500. In one of Burlington's public schools practically all the pupils were Jewish, no doubt because the school was located in the Jewish neighborhood; on the High Holy Days no one was left in the entire school but a few Christians. The Jewish students, all Orthodox, were meticulous in observance of the traditional customs. When there was thunder outside they would excuse themselves, go to the cloak room, don their caps, and recite the requisite blessing. Burlington Jews, eager to see that their youngsters were well educated, sent them on to high school; a few even went to college. By 1905 the principal of the high school was a Jew; he it was who was invited to speak at a local celebration of the 250th anniversary of the settlement of the Jews in America. The immigrants identified with this country; it was their ancestors who had confronted Peter Stuyvesant in 1655.

Among the local Jews who saw to it that the children received a Jewish education was Abraham Nehemiah Lamport (1854-1928). Here in the United States this native Pole called himself Nathan Lamport. He was well versed in Hebrew for he had gone to a talmudic academy. Beginning with the 1870's he peddled for years in and around Burlington. In order to make a living Lamport reached out in more than one direction; he had a junk yard, a peddlers' supply house, and was sexton, too, of the local synagog. He served as the regional circumciser traveling to the outlying towns when needed. When he set out on a religious mission he carried with him kosher food prepared by his wife for the mother of the newborn babe. For years he was president of a local congregation but finally turned his face toward New York City. Tradition would have it that he moved on because his daughter was being courted by Christians; Orthodox Jews were opposed to intermarriage. After he went to New York in the 1890's he engaged in real estate speculation and in the manufacture of textiles. Ultimately he was to become a rich man and with wealth came philanthropy; he gave $200,000 to help build Yeshiva College. One of his sons, Samuel Charles Lamport, also Polish-born, received a college education; another son, Arthur, became an important investment banker. Samuel, the older brother, was a leading figure in the American textile industry, representing the United States government at various conferences. Like his father he, too, was active in New York's philanthropic circles; he concerned himself with Beth Israel Hospital and Jewish education, and was close to Franklin D. Roosevelt whose policies he furthered. He was also active in the councils of the American Jewish Committee. When the Germans started killing Jews he helped open the Dominican Republic to Jewish refugees. And the next generation? Arthur Lamport had a son named Harold who was an eminent research physician.

The Lamports went from Vermont to New York; Isaac Gilman went from New York to Vermont. Gilman, who was born in Eastern Europe, came to Hamburg when he was thirteen years of age looking for a way to get to America. Because he had nothing he had to earn the money to make the crossing. It took him three years to save a few dollars and it was only because there was a rate war among the steamship companies that he could afford the trip. The ticket was Hamburg to St. Louis; the price was $10. He was all of sixteen when he landed in New York in 1880; he sold the St. Louis part of his ticket for $2. Gilman set out to become a cigarmaker, apparently without success; he then turned to peddling; later he tried his hand at selling job lots of paper; now he was in his element. He soon had a store of his own, did well for a while, but ended up as a bankrupt. Ultimately he was able to repay all of his creditors although legally he was not obligated to do so. He invited all his creditors to a kosher dinner at the old Broadway Central Hotel, served them a good meal, and paid them.

At the age of thirty-seven he was doing very well; he had a company in New York which he called the Gilman Paper Company. He continued buying job lots and at times had some of his paper made up for him at a factory in Fitzdale, Vermont. Gilman specialized in kraft paper, a new product which had been perfected in Sweden. He helped introduce it to the American trade, manufacturing it at the Fitzdale mill. The Fitzdale people did well until the panic of 1907 and then because they were heavily in debt to him he was compelled to take over the company. Gilman eventually became one of the country's important paper manufacturers; his mill was the largest in the state; it had branches in Maine and an affiliate in Georgia. He was very good to the people in Fitzdale, helped them build homes, a railroad station, a hotel, a hospital, water works, a community center, a fire department, a skating rink, and an athletic field. He was also generous to the Protestant and Catholic church; the town owed him much. Apparently he was the only Jew in Fitzdale. In 1914 while he was still alive the villagers changed its name from Fitzdale to Gilman. Because conditions were very bad during the 1930's, the men cut their wages in order to keep the mill alive; it worked all though the depression. When better times dawned Gilman paid the workers the wages which they had lost.[3]

RHODE ISLAND

If the three northern tier New England states were of little importance in American Jewish history, this was not so of the three states to the south— Massachusetts, Rhode Island, and Connecticut—which sheltered metropolitan communities. By 1920 Rhode Island alone had many more Jews than all of Maine, New Hampshire, and Vermont, yet it was always to be limited in its development and influence because of its small size. In 1905 when the *Jewish Encyclopedia* published the article on Rhode Island, it was accorded a modest fourteen lines. Historic Newport was important in colonial days but this Sephardic congregation died in the early nineteenth century, about the year 1800. Even before the 1800's Ashkenazim from East Europe had begun drifting into town. It was not long before they had a confraternity of sorts and even a sizable rabbinic library. By 1902, after bickering with New York's Shearith Israel, which controlled the historic synagog building, the Russians succeeded in creating a formal community; they were given permission to use the sanctuary but were required to employ the Sephardic liturgy; this was imposed on them as it was on the Ashkenazim who joined the original Shearith Israel in New York City in 1729.

The Orthodox immigrant community in Rhode Island grew steadily. Practically all newcomers in the state were from Slavic lands; by 1900 there were four towns with at least one Jewish institution. There were then thirteen benefit lodges in Rhode Island; the one in Central Falls held services also; thus for a simple fee one could enjoy a religious service and social security; the immigrants in this society had the best of both worlds. As late as 1920 there were fewer than 22,000 Jews in the state; there were 20 congregations in eight towns. With 15,000 Jews, Providence was one of the country's substantial communities, with the usual complement of institutions and societies in the areas of religion, philanthropy, self-help, education, and sociality. No later than 1875 a congregation of Orthodox newcomers had been established in the city. To judge from statistics for the year 1906, 75 percent of the newcomers were Russian, 14 percent, Galician, 2 percent, Poles, and 4 percent, Rumanians. One of the Jewish mutual-aid lodges in the city called itself the Roger Williams Lodge; it was large, numbering over 350 members. Americanization had so impressed itself on these Yiddish-speaking newcomers that they worshipped at the altar of this Christian notable. Equally important in almost every community were the young people's social groups; with the dawn of the twentieth century young men and young women were given their chance to breathe free air. The right of assembly was a privilege not always enjoyed by the Jews of Russia and Rumania. Providence's congregation, the Russian Lovers of Peace, had 150 children in its Hebrew school. A young men's society, a young ladies' association, and a female auxiliary helped keep the Lovers of Peace on an even keel. In order to remain Jewish the immigrants were quick to build the institutions that they needed.

An analysis of the vocations of these Providence newcomers in 1878 discloses that there were 16 peddlers, 14 men in the clothing business, 17 clerks, 11 in provisions (groceries?). In 1900 Providence had 311 peddlers, 152 in the jewelry factories, 134 tailors, 129 clerks, 69 grocers, 66 shoemakers, and 53 manual laborers. Other studies show that in that year 38.7 percent of the Russians in town were in industry and the crafts; 42 percent were already in commerce as peddlers and modest traders. The tendency in the smaller towns was to move away from blue collar jobs to white collar opportunities. By 1915 about 76.8 percent of the immigrants in Providence were in trade; seven out of every ten of these newcomers were self-employed. All this is typical of most non-metropolitan East European Jews in the United States. The hinterland immigrants were gradually moving up the economic ladder. Before 1906 there was a Jewish local of the United Cloth Hat and Cap Makers of North America with all of twenty members; for a brief period there was also a painters' union in that city. By 1918, so the records disclose, there were at least four workmen's mutual-aid societies; one called itself the Rhode Island Shoemakers'

Association. In addition there was the Union Ladies' Aid Society, apparently an auxiliary of a labor group—or was the word "union" merely used to indicate that here was a group of women "united" to do good? That pre-1921 generation worked hard. Youngsters went out to shine shoes; they might make as much as ten cents a day. Precious little? In 1900 that would buy two loaves of bread. A young girl might slave for ten hours a day at a job that paid $3 a week but if she changed and got piece work in a factory she might make $12 a week, good money.

In order to get started at almost anything a man needed some capital, cash. This was provided by the Providence Free Loan Association, Gemiluth Hesed. One could borrow from $5 to $25 if one had good cosignors. This Free Loan Association had 197 applications the first year it started and lent $4,300; in 1920 it had 389 applications and lent $47,700. Defaults were few. Why did people borrow: to pay the doctor or lawyer, to start a small business, to take care of a funeral, to pay off someone else where the interest was high. Living conditions in Rhode Island were not bad; one must constantly bear in mind how most Americans lived in the early twentieth century. There were tenements in Providence but there was running water although not yet hot water. When needed, water was heated on a coal stove and poured into a portable or stationary bathtub. More than one person might use the same hot water in bathing. First there was a kerosene lamp, then gas mantle lighting, and finally electricity. Eight people could live comfortably in a five-room flat and room could always be found for an uncle and his family of four when they came to spend the Holy Days and be near a synagog.

A Providence immigrant bought a drugstore in 1911; he waited on customers fifteen hours a day, seven days a week. His wife Esther helped him, clerking in his store; she raised a family and at the same time attended the Rhode Island College of Pharmacy; she was its first female graduate. The first Jewish lawyer made his appearance in 1885; there may well have been immigrant physicians before that date. In the early twentieth century a Jewish ghetto doctor delivered over 1,100 babies, all in the home. If a child came prematurely he kept it alive by warming it in the oven. He told his patients that if they had another baby within the year the delivery was free; in other words two for the price of one. Often he was called in to attend a woman who was already in labor; that was the first time he had seen her. One of the best known men in the Providence ghetto was Abraham Bazar. He ran a steamship ticket agency and maintained that he did not care how little he made; he wanted to get people out of Russia, Poland, Rumania. It is said that he helped two or three thousand immigrants come to this country. He also ran a bank of sorts that loaned people money to purchase the tickets to bring the family over. Bazar was an entrepreneur who moved out in many directions. He had a public hall which he rented out, a celluloid comb factory, a bowling alley, pool tables, a laundry. He never discharged a man who worked for him; over the years he employed thousands. He was the richest Jew in South Providence. An American success story? Alas he died a poor man. Enterprise does not always bring its reward; one must also be lucky; this is good Judaic doctrine.

A grocery store owner in the Jewish section asked his son to print a sign for him. It was well done. A cobbler in the neighborhood liked it so much that he asked the boy to make one for him; this the lad did painting a girl with some of her leg showing in order to display the shoe. A policeman had the sign removed for indecent exposure. Many of the immigrants made from $10 to $12 a week; they were doing better than other ethnic newcomers. By 1910 quite a number of these Russian and Polish Jews were moving into the middle class; they now had homes and maintained a relatively high standard of living. An investigator visiting the homes that year found them to be clean. By that time many Providence houses had gas, sometimes electricity, bathrooms, hot and cold water. Many of the town's Jews were working in the jewelry factories where they were well paid. On Sunday, their day off, they enjoyed picnics or drives in the country. Where there were thousands of men and women at work or in business some were bound to become affluent, even wealthy.

Harry Cutler (1875-1920) is an example. This native Russian came to the United States at the age of eight with his widowed mother; his father had been killed in one of the 1882 pogroms. The mother worked in New York State for a while and then the family moved on to Providence where young Cutler got a job in a jewelry plant, and finally succeeded in setting himself up in his own business. Later he became the chairman of the Jewelry Manufacturers Association of New England. In 1908 he was elected to the state assembly and rose in the National Guard to become the colonel of a regiment. He served in Mexico with Pershing and did what he could to help the Jewish soldiers during that campaign. The Colonel was to have a distinguished career; in 1920 he was one of the state's outstanding citizens and a recognized American Jewish leader. There were few national Jewish organizations in which he did not play a role; he sat with the executives of the Jewish Welfare Board—it looked after the Jewish soldiers in World War I—he worked closely with the American Jewish Committee, the Union of American Hebrew Congregations, the Zionists, and the American Jewish Congress which sent him to Versailles in 1919 to help the East European Jews and to speed the implementation of the Balfour Declaration which promised Jewry a home in Palestine. Cutler was one of the few Russian-born community leaders who succeeded in bridging the gulf between the immigrants and the American-born Jews. He demonstrated that it could be done without surrender of principles or loss of self-respect; he prefigured the future.[4]

CONNECTICUT

Connecticut had but 1,500 Jews in 1880; by 1920 there were about 72,000 and a number of towns with substantial Jewish communities: New London, Meriden, Stamford, South Norwalk, Norwich, Waterbury; three cities had large Jewries: Bridgeport, 12,000, Hartford, 16,000, New Haven, 18,000. Some of these cities had two or three Russian or Galician or Rumanian synagogs; Hartford had numerous prayer communities. Practically all towns of more than 1,000 Jews had a series of supplementary organizations to provide for all communal needs. Norwalk and Stamford had sheltered Jewish families since the second half of the eighteenth century; New York's Jews had found a haven there during the sad days of the American Revolution. There was however no continuous Jewish settlement in these two Connecticut towns. The Central Europeans—a handful at best—did not make their appearance in Connecticut until the early 1840's. Jews from the lands east of Germany did not filter into Norwalk till the 1870's; Stamford was to be aware of their presence in the 1880's. Kosher meat was brought in from New York City. By 1922 the newcomers in Stamford had a completely Jewish Masonic lodge; they named it after the ebullient Theodore Roosevelt. When the New Britain Jews lacked a tenth man for a religious quorum they hired one to come in from Hartford; Bridgeport's Talmud Torah was supported by a group of women dedicated to that purpose. New London had a benefit society that doubled as a congregation. The first Jews in that town were Lithuanians; they were there by 1885; less than a generation later a son of one of these immigrants was admitted to the Connecticut bar.

New London newcomers who wanted to learn English could meet in a basement where Dora Schaefer taught them, charging ten cents a lesson. The town's congregation, the Love of Kindness, Ahavath Chesed, established in 1892, dedicated a building of its own in 1905. The leaders in the community raised enough money to buy two Scrolls of the Law. The dedication was a grand affair; there was a band and an address by an Orthodox American-born rabbi from New York City. The mayor and two Protestant ministers also participated in the ceremonies. The local woman's society took the Hebrew name Bnais Cheen, the Gracious Ladies; the English spelling reveals a Lithuanian mistransliteration from the classical Hebrew. The rabbi was the Russia-born Abraham Nathan Schwartz; his son Joseph Joshua, brought to this country at the age of eight, went to college, studied and taught Semitics, but turned to social work and community administration. Ultimately as director general of the Joint Distribution Committee he supervised relief operations for Jews in thirty countries, helped over a million people, and rescued 100,000 victims of World War II. Among the cantors in a New London synagog was the Russian Lazar Kahn, the father of Reuben Leon Kahn who was brought over to this country as a child. Because of his skills in bacteriology young Kahn was appointed director of laboratories at the hospital of the University of Michigan in 1928; a few years earlier he had succeeded in perfecting a blood test for the detection of syphilis.

One of the several congregations in Hartford in the early 1900's was in reality a lodge which conducted daily services; when ten adult Orthodox Jews gathered together it was inevitable that they would hold religious services. As in some other towns Hartford's Free School for the study of Hebrew was supported by a female society. By 1920 there were at least nine East European congregations in town and a host of other organizations, including the Hebrew Painters' Union, a Peddlers' Protective Association, and a Labor Educational Alliance, a workmen's cultural institution. At least one of the synagogs was a hometown society catering to émigrés from a specific Russian or Polish village; another took the name of a donor who had bought its building for the congregation. By 1900 Connecticut could boast of two Jewish political clubs; the one in Norwich, the Hebrew Independent Political Club, sounds almost like a contradiction in terms. The Jewish farmers around Colchester and Chesterfield established societies to meet their economic needs. One of Hartford's immigrant congregations had almost 100 members, and if rumor is correct most of them were on the edge of indigence. One family took in twelve boarders all of whom slept on the floor; the extra money was needed to pay the rent. Yet despite this obvious poverty, this was a generation that gave birth to doctors, lawyers, accountants, and other professionals. It is difficult to understand how the younger generation achieved what it did. How much could these newcomer parents help their children? They themselves were struggling to survive.

We have a breakdown of the business occupations of every Jew in Norwich in 1900; practically all of them were immigrants from Russia and Poland. A very substantial number were peddlers; others ran retail stores, groceries for instance; some owned clothing and tailoring establishments; the town had a laundry, a confectionary, a bakery, a leather shop, all owned by these immigrants. There was a cobbler, a cattle dealer, a painter, clerks, salesmen, watch repairmen, and a number of factory hands who worked in the cotton and small arms mills. One man sold secondhand furniture; others were casual laborers. A number of these proletarians were socialists, members of a mutual-benefit Workmen's Circle. Ambitious entrepreneurs rose only to fall and then to resume the struggle once more. Nathan Gilman (1879-1978), who had worked as a farm laborer in his native Russia, came to America with an aunt at the age of seventeen and went to work in a shirt factory. The pay was $3 for a 55-hour week. Later he became a mattress worker; the pay was no better but he learned the business. He opened a bedding company of his own in 1895 and made enough money to bring his siblings over. In 1905 Nathan sold his factory, bought a small mill, including the workers' houses, in Bozrahville, Connecticut, and changed the name of the new enterprise to Gilman Brothers Company. The firm manufactured shoddy to fill mattresses. Ruined by the panic of 1907 and numerous fires, he had to start all over again; ultimately he paid all of his creditors. In his new factory he turned to the manufacture of cotton batting; it was one of the first businesses of its type in the country. He had already founded the Bozrah Electric Company which brought life and light to the villages in the surrounding area. The government appointed him postmaster of his little town; in 1932 it changed its name to Gilman. It is amazing—but it is pure coincidence—that during the very years that Nathan Gilman was struggling to build an industry in Bozrahville, Isaac Gilman in Vermont was laboring to save the declining community of Fitzdale. Each town adopted the name of its patron. The Gilmans, apparently, were not related.

In 1919 a Conservative or modernistic Orthodox congregation was established in Hartford; it called itself Emanuel Synagog. As it has already been noted Orthodox Jews who had been living in the United States for decades were beginning to move to the left religiously. The impact of the Americanization process was irresistible. One of the founders of this new synagog was Herman Paul Kopplemann (1880-1957). Herman's family came to the United States in 1882 when he was two years old. His mother, Jessie Minz Kopplemann, was one of the town's most dedicated welfare workers. She founded a hospice and a home for children. Since help in the orphanage was lacking she did much of the menial work herself. She was also a founder of the Hebrew Ladies' Old People's Home; its constitution adopted in 1917 was written both in Yiddish and in English. Males who supported the home paid $3 a year dues; women, $2.40. All meetings were conducted according to *Roberts Parliamentary Rules of Order.* This is interesting when one bears in mind that most of the women who supported this institution were Yiddish-speaking immigrants. The constitution specified that the kitchen must be kosher and that the home be kept clean. No one was admitted who was self-supporting or had children with means. Mrs. Kopplemann also aided Father Flanagan's Boys Town, an Iowa Catholic institution.

Herman, her son, went to work at eight as a newsboy and ultimately organized the largest magazine distributing company in the state. Going into politics he became a member of the Connecticut House and Senate; in 1932 he was sent to Congress where he distinguished himself furthering liberal legislation; he was interested in widows' pensions, workmen's compensation, child labor, social security, low-cost housing, deposit insurance, the elimination of slums, public health, the eight-hour day for women. He worked ardently for the Jewish community both locally and nationally, not only as president of Emanuel Synagog but as vice president of the United Synagogue, the umbrella organization for America's Conservative congregations; he was also invited to sit on the Board of Overseers of the Jewish Theological Seminary of America.[5]

MASSACHUSETTS

Massachusetts was the most important state in New England; indeed one of the most important in the Union; in 1920 only New York, Pennsylvania, and Illinois provided a haven for more Jews; only New York City, Philadelphia, Chicago, and Cleveland had larger Jewish communities than Boston; like Ohio, Massachusetts had many substantial "Jewish" towns. In 1880 the state sheltered about 9,000 Jews, in 1920, 200,000. This growth is due to the newly arrived Jews from Russia, Poland, Galicia, and Rumania. Boston, the largest Jewish congeries in Massachusetts, had about 78,000 Israelites in 1920. The East Europeans began arriving in the 1860's and 1870's; by that time they had established about eight congregations in Boston. Pittsfield in Berkshire County was quite typical of the twenty some Jewish communities in the state. (The "trees" may be different, but the "forest" is essentially the same.) It had two East European congregations (1918), a Young Men's Hebrew Association, five charities of which two were female, a social club, two Zionist societies both of which were female (!), and, of course, a cemetery. These were all Russian-Polish institutions. One of the earliest Poles had come to the county in 1857; he peddled and later opened a store; his late twentieth-century great grandson, one of the best known and most respected citizens in Pittsfield, was the librarian of the Berkshire Athenaeum. Pittsfield's newcomers, so it would seem, were in no hurry to organize; their first congregation was not established till 1906, the second, in 1911. It is by no means improbable that the second was formed because of the ambition of dissidents seeking office. When the first synagog was opened a local paper manufacturer, a Gentile, gave the Jews the pews they needed; this man had business relations with peddlers who supplied him with the rags he needed for his mill. Harry Blank was the first president of the shul. Pittsfield tradition—for whatever it is worth—would have it that his original name was Russian and almost unpronounceable and that "Blank" was the compromise adopted.

One of the Orthodox groups in town rented space in the Reform temple and opened a Sunday school for its own youngsters; tuition was two cents a Sunday. Other folks, Hebraists, met on Saturday afternoon in their synagog and studied classical rabbinical literature. There were always some men, if only a few, in almost every town of size in the country who wanted to continue the talmudic studies they had pursued in the

Russian and Polish academies (yeshivot). (This was more than an intellectual challenge, more than religiosity; it was ego fulfillment; talmudists
were always deemed elite.) Louis Evzerow who had moved into the
county in 1914 worked as a junk dealer collecting paper. He lived in the
nearby hamlet of Lebanon. When he became the shammash, the beadle,
in one of Pittsfield's congregations he heightened the status of his position by donning a stovepipe hat and by wearing a Prince Albert in the
shul; the president and the rabbi resented this very much; they believed
that he was trying to high hat them. A member of the congregation
brought in a Hebrew teacher, a capmaker from Hoboken. He taught half
the day and collected junk the other half. In 1901 a Hebrew Ladies' Aid
Society was established; dues were twenty-five cents a month. In order to
raise money the members gave card parties supplying supper at thirty-five
cents. They succeeded ultimately in establishing a hospice in a room
rented for that purpose. Bear in mind this was in the Berkshire Hills, in
the western part of the state.

Most of the newcomers were not affluent even as late as 1920. Some
of them needed their children to help them eke out an existence. In the
summer the youngsters went into the hills and collected blueberries earning a dollar for every twelve quarts they collected. Quite a number of
Pittsfield's Jews were then peddlers, artisans, and shopkeepers. Some of
the few farmers and dairymen in the county took in summer boarders.
Mr. and Mrs. Herman H. Braun ran a bottling works and a liquor store;
on Hanukkah and Purim the Brauns gave a party for the Jewish children,
on Christmas for the Negro youngsters. One of the shuls in Pittsfield had
a free loan association; it lent $5 to $10 to a peddler; that was capital
enough to get started.

In some towns, as in Lynn, there were newsboys unions that were
almost completely Jewish. Around the year 1900 many of Boston's Jewish newcomers were in industry, workingmen. Whenever they could, as
necessity drove them, they organized unions to further themselves, especially in the garment trade. A Boston Jewish tailors' union in the 1880's
was part of the Knights of Labor; conditions in the needle trades in the
city were as bad as they were throughout the country; sweatshops were
prevalent. Some tailors worked for themselves; they avoided the factories
and the sweatshops preferring to be masters in their own little world. Julius Seltzer (1874-1952) was such a man. He lived in Lexington near Boston. As a tailor he did repair work, cleaning and pressing of clothes. He
opened his shop in 1904 and continued to live in this historic city for just
about a half century. For his religious needs this native of Russia turned to
a synagog in Boston. Seltzer was a member of the Lexington Minutemen
and accompanied them whenever they went to services in the Protestant
and Catholic churches. Years later this respected and beloved Jew was

commander of the Lexington Minutemen; indeed he was active in a number of local public associations, in the Chamber of Commerce, and in the Red Cross, too. Because of his devotion to civic needs he was cherished by the Salvation Army, the United Service Organizations, the Combined Jewish Appeal, and the National Catholic Community Services. Seltzer was always ready to solicit money for any good cause, Jewish or Gentile; he was one of the towns outstanding communal workers and when a bronze plaque memorializing the Minutemen of 1775 was unveiled he was called upon to make the address.

During the decades 1880-1920 many of these men from Eastern Europe were artisans, carpenters, painters, masons, plumbers, tinsmiths, paperhangers, and bakers; Jewish unions and clubs were organized in some of these crafts by Boston tradesmen. Jewish farmers in Bristol County, uniting to help one another, created the Jewish Farmers' Cooperative Credit Union. Peddlers also organized. East Boston's Hebrew Protective League (1901) was typical of the associations the peddlers created in many cities and states. It was ready to go to the courts to protect peddlers—and other Jews—who had been assaulted. That Jews had to organize to protect body and limb is a grim commentary of the hazards faced by them. In 1900, 53 percent of the Jews in Boston were in manufacturing, about 37 percent were in trade, and 2.4 percent in the professions. As in Connecticut and other states some of the immigrants here found work in the mills; in Massachusetts this meant they were on occasion employed in the shoe factories. Bench workers even became manufacturers but this was at a time when the industry was declining in Massachusetts. These Jewish latecomers in the industry managed to survive for a while. In 1910, only 3 of the 76 manufacturers in Lynn were Jews; in 1930, twenty years later, 47 of the 88 shoe factory owners were Jews.

In Massachusetts as in other states individual immigrants became physicians, lawyers, dentists, and even eminent businessmen. Two early Jewish settlers in Boston were physicians. Morris Kinstler, a graduate of the University of Warsaw who was practicing medicine in Boston in 1867, served as a physician to the Hebrew Mutual Relief Society, Gemiloth Chesed. It paid him $41 a month, a good wage, but in 1868 he had to sue for his hire. Dr. Fanny Berlin (1852-1921), a revolutionary, left Russia and studied medicine in Berne, Switzerland, receiving her degree in 1875. In 1880 she was in Boston serving as a resident physician in a hospital; later she was appointed a visiting surgeon. She was a pioneer in securing recognition for women in the field of medicine. Boston had shopkeepers who opened better stores in the city and, later on, expanded into neighboring areas. Working people became contractors; ragpickers developed large businesses in waste paper and scrap metal. The Jews of Boston owned property worth millions. As they became affluent they moved their homes to better areas and, later, to the suburbs. Some joined political clubs. Boston had at least two such organizations, both established in the first decade of the twentieth century. One was the Hebrew Citizens' Club of Ward Nine, the other was the Hebrew Independent Club in the same ward. These new settlers in Boston also had an association which they called the Hebrew Library and Civic Club. It was fashioned in a day when the Protestant Republicans were running the city; some Jews now lined up with the Irish (Catholic) Democrats to dispute Protestant Republican control. There were Jews—usually among the elite —who were very much annoyed by these new political associations; they denied angrily that there was a Jewish vote and that it could be controlled. By the end of the East European Jewish period, 1920, individual immigrants and their children were themselves seeking political office. A few were elected to the state legislature; a Lithuanian Jew was already presiding over the city council in Springfield, the second largest town in the state.

No matter how poor these Boston Jews were many of them were engaged in some form of charity; they were also members of social and cultural societies. The Ladies' Auxiliary of the Helping Hand Home supported this refuge for destitute children; it sheltered sixty-four youngsters in 1907; the Auxiliary then had 1,100 members. Patently it was a favorite charity of the women. However, the administration of the Home and the Society seems to have been entirely in the hands of the men. Of the numerous relief societies in Boston set up by the "Russians," many were founded by women. Boston also had a dowry society; this was unusual among American Jews although common abroad. In 1906-1907 Boston Jewish émigrés had at least thirty different charities to say nothing of about twenty mutual-benefit associations. Several were landsmanshaften, home town societies. After the 1903 Kishinev pogrom a branch of the Hebrew Immigrant Aid Society was established in Boston; it met the boats at the dock; in a three-month period in 1905 it helped over 700 newcomers.

One of the most assiduous workers was Abraham Alpert (1869-1939) who lived in East Boston where the Jews had a ghetto of their own. It was a complete village enclave with its own shops, artisans, doctors, lawyers, and Hebrew book store. Alpert, a native of Lithuania, came to the United States in 1882; he was then thirteen. In the course of time he became the spokesman for the Yiddish-speaking community of East Boston; he was well educated, at home both in Hebrew and in English. Between 1890 and 1910 Alpert ran a small lunch room where he sold newspapers, soft drinks, sandwiches, tobacco, and tea. His living quarters were above the store; since his was the only place in the neighborhood with a telephone his clients and friends made good use of it. He was not only the village orator but also its literary oracle for he wrote letters to the English newspapers and contributed to the Yiddish press. When writing in Yiddish he called himself the Man from Kovno, Ish Kovno. During World War I he served as president of one of Boston's Negro associations; the city's Gentile Lithuanians also turned to him for counsel. The assumption is warranted that in all immigrant communities of size, in those years, there was always one Jew willing to assume leadership. As a type Alpert does not seem to have been unusual.

Making a living was difficult—this cannot be stressed too often— many could not afford to join a congregation. (Others were overly thrifty.) Ghetto inhabitants were kept Jewish by their ambience; there was no need to join a congregation to maintain their identity as members of the tribe. As early as 1903 there were already over sixty mutual-aid lodges in Boston alone. Their endowment funds provided for the needs of the members when misfortune struck. One lodge had such substantial reserves that a member could not resist the temptation to make off with $39,000. Congregational memberships were usually small, even in big cities, but let there be no doubt most East European Jews were religiously committed; there were more than 200 conventicles, organized prayer communes, in Massachusetts; eighty-five were in Boston (1920). One of the best known religious leaders in the state was Rabbi Moses Zebulon (Sebulon) Margolies (1851-1936) known by many through his acronym as the Ramaz. He came to Boston in 1889 and served till 1906 as a "chief rabbi." This is a title that must not be taken too seriously; it merely indicates that a rabbi was a recognized spiritual leader of more than one congregation. It was a title used not infrequently by rabbis in large American Jewish communities.

In 1906 the Ramaz went to New York City to Congregation Kehilath Jeshurun; there he attempted to bring some order into the chaos of the kosher meat industry. Later he served as president of the Union of Orthodox Rabbis, helped found the Zionist Mizrachi organization, and worked actively in the Kehillah Movement and for the Central Relief Committee, both of which will be described in some detail below. He was a good administrator and because of his interest in furthering Jewish education he played an important role in such institutions as the Rabbi Isaac Elchanan Theological Seminary (RIETS). For a brief period in the first decade of the 1900's he served as its president. His intervention was needed; there was trouble in the school because the students were eager for instruction in secular disciplines; the difficulties were to a degree surmounted by Margolies because he was patient and gentle. In 1908 it was decided to permit—if not to encourage—the students to explore the world of the secular sciences. In 1915 the Etz Chaim Yeshivah, an intermediate Talmud school and the Isaac Elchanan Seminary, an advanced rabbinic academy, joined together to become the Rabbinical College. The new president was Bernard Revel; Margolies and Rabbi Bernard Levinthal helped put him in. It is very significant that these Orthodox leaders were wise enough to realize the importance of secular education in English for America's next generation of traditional Jews. These men could read the handwriting on the wall; acculturate or perish; they heeded the warning.

In 1889 the year that the Ramaz came to Boston one of the outstanding Orthodox laymen was a man by the name of Alfred A. Marcus; he had arrived in the city about the year 1867 from South Africa, hence the name by which he was known, Marcus der Afrikaner. He hailed originally from London. His wife was a Belasco, apparently a Sephardi. He came with a daughter and a son, arriving in a sailing vessel which almost foundered in a terrible storm. He ascribed his escape to the fervent reading of Psalms. Marcus, a wealthy man, set out, it would seem, to pattern himself on Moses Montefiore who was still alive. Generous to a fault, Marcus distributed Scrolls of the Law to needy congregations; a handwritten Scroll was no small gift. Marcus had a synagog of his own; simulating the heavens the ceiling was painted blue; it had a silver moon and golden stars. This newcomer was at his height in the 1870's and 1880's but it would seem his fortune faded in the 1890's, possibly in the depression. By that time he had lost his daughter, his wife, and his son; he was left bereft. When his family died he erected the largest tombstone in the cemetery. His ending was sad for he died a pauper and was buried by public subscription under the tombstone which he had provided for his dear ones when fortune still smiled upon him. In 1889 Marcus the Afrikaner installed one of the first telephones in that part of the city so that his daughter at home could say kaddish, the prayer for the dead, for her mother. The telephone was in the synagog and when the time came to recite the kaddish it was taken off the hook and she recited this treasured traditional prayer; for some reason the daughter could not leave the house. This particular incident, which is authentic, was typical of the adjustments then being made to the American way of life in some Orthodox sanctuaries. Marcus was no religious rebel; he was devoutly Orthodox.

Religious observance was relaxed if not neglected here in the United States by many newcomers, particularly the children. Because of the permissive American milieu the parents were compelled to be less exacting in such matters; English not Hebrew education was of paramount importance. In a way the parents were at fault; they set the pattern; they wanted to make money and to become American. This adjustment to the mores of the land reached its climax everywhere in the rise of the Conservative Movement; there was, to be sure, formal adherence to traditions but in practice the injunctions of the codes were frequently disregarded. A religion of salutary neglect was developing. In their minds these immigrants, though moving away from the Orthodoxy of their fathers, were convinced that they were loyal observers. In one area their devotions did not lessen; they loved the familiar liturgical melodies. America was a mecca for European cantors; all Russian and Polish Jews, whether traditionalists or Marxists, flocked to hear the great chaunters who visited Boston. Some had come here to settle; others visited America merely to make guest appearances and to return home richly ladened. Even youngsters enjoyed the magnificent rendition of a Sirota, a Quartin, a Rosenblatt. Those who loved Yiddish and its rich idiom crowded the halls to listen to Zevi Hirsch Masliansky, American Jewry's "national orator."

Despite the neglect in observance there was nearly always a devotion to Orthodoxy, in principle at least. The children had to learn to read Hebrew; that was minimal. Some youngsters were taught by the siddur peddler, the itinerant Hebrew teacher who came around with a siddur, a prayer book tucked under his arm; he charged ten cents a lesson to teach the children to read and recite the traditional orisons. Most congregations had an afternoon school where Hebrew was taught; it was often called the Talmud Torah, the Teaching of the Law. Some of these institutions referred to themselves as Hebrew Free Schools; actually they were not always free; tuition was required of those who could afford to pay. With the dawn of the twentieth century these afternoon institutions in Boston, as elsewhere, tended to improve pedagogically. In 1906 there was a Hebrew Literary Association in town which sponsored a modern type school. This group called itself the Shohare Sefat Ever, the Furtherers of Hebrew. Similar societies were established in New York, Philadelphia, Chicago, and probably elsewhere too. This Boston association had 365 supporters who paid dues; well over 100 pupils attended; the language of instruction was Hebrew itself; Hebrew through Hebrew was the new vogue. In addition to the sacred tongue Jewish history was also taught. This extension of the traditional curriculum reflects western cultural influences. In Boston, as in many other towns of size, devout men who had gone to talmudic academies abroad continued their studies when they had a leisure moment. As early as 1891 there was an educational association in town with a library of 600 Jewish books. By 1920 the city-wide Bureau of Jewish Religious Education was established; the following year the Hebrew Teachers' College was opened; in the course of decades it became an accredited Jewish college empowered to award degrees. Attending advanced Hebrew schools was, however, exceptional; the typical Jewish lad was interested in secular disciplines not in religious studies.

For the younger generation English was the preferred language of communication. In the Boston of 1906, 30 percent of the Ben Franklin scholarship medals awarded in the grammar schools went to Jewish children. During the same year, nine Harvard men graduated summa cum laude; four were Jews. In 1906 Henry Hurwitz and Allan Davis created the Menorah Society at Harvard for the study of Jewish history; they began with fifty-seven members; a decade later the Menorah Movement was making a strong effort to embrace thousands of American Jewish college youth within the ambit of Jewish cultural studies. Yiddish was spoken in the homes of these bright young men of East European parentage and was understood by all but the responses were often in English. Thus many American-born youngsters did not learn to speak Yiddish even though it was literally their "mother tongue." In the early twentieth century a Boston passerby noticed several children quarreling; one of them was a Jew, one a black, one was Irish; they were berating each other in Yiddish.

The Young Men's Hebrew Associations in Boston and other Massachusetts towns combined education—secular for the most part—with leisure and amusement; they furthered Jewish cultural clubs, public lectures, plays, concerts; some had summer camp programs. The children were completely acculturated in a Western, Anglo-Saxon sense. For the youngsters there were numerous debating societies, literary, social, and civic groups; one social congeries called itself the Puritan Associates. Shades of Cotton Mather! Worcester youth had three literary bodies; one was the Grace Aguilar Society, named after the beloved English writer whose novel *The Vale of Cedars*, dealing with the Marranos, was one of the most popular Jewish books read by America's Jewish youth of that generation. Boston, too, had its Hebrew Industrial School to train the "Russian" and "Polish" youngsters to ply a trade. Mary Antin was brought there to learn how to sew. She refused to apply herself; she wanted to write books. Strangely enough, she was encouraged to do so; the elite Jews sensed that she had something to give, to say. Out of this experience came her first book, *From Plotzk to Boston*, published just five years after she landed in this country. This book marked the beginning of her career as a writer.[6]

New Jersey

New Jersey is a far distance from Massachusetts but there is a link that ties them together; Newark, the largest city in the state, was settled in the 1660's by colonists from New England. One of the many proprietors of West Jersey before 1702 was the London capitalist, Benjamin Levy. He never visited America; his share of West Jersey was but one of his numerous investments. Russian and Polish Jews were not to settle in the state till the middle of the nineteenth century. As early as 1855 some East Europeans who had seceded from Bnai Jeshurun—a Central European congregation—established a synagog of their own, B'nai Abraham, the Children of Abraham. The new prayer association was not named after the biblical patriarch but Abraham Newman, a secessionist who had organized them. The new group bought and rededicated a Baptist church in 1861; in the 1880's it opened a Hebrew school; the earlier German and Bohemian settlers helped the dissidents establish themselves. By the 1880's Jews from the Slavic lands started coming to New Jersey in large numbers; a few settled around Camden opposite Philadelphia; still farther south lay the agricultural colonies, although numerically and commercially they were not significant despite the interest they aroused.

The important area of Jewish settlement in New Jersey was in the north, on the outskirts of New York City. The Jewish towns there were satellites of the metropolis. Many if not most of the northern New Jersey Israelites had come from New York's ghetto. Trying to improve themselves they had moved into nearby Jersey counties such as Bergen, Essex, Hudson, and Union; few moved down the coast to the resort towns. Some Russians and Poles settled in Bergen County, north of New York City in the 1890's. South of Bergen County lay Newark, in Essex County, into which thousands of the newcomers poured in the 1880's. They were so numerous that they could joyfully organize themselves according to the regions from which they had come in Europe. By 1920 Essex County was a haven for one of the country's largest Jewish communities. At that time the state had eighteen important "Jewish" towns; there were 163,000 Jews in New Jersey; they worshipped in about 120 synagogs and prayer rooms; they were overwhelmingly of East European origin. The larger places were well stocked with Jewish institutions; Newark had over sixty in 1918. Jersey City in Hudson County had a substantial Jewish community; among its several Jewish organizations was a Ladies' Free Loan Society (1903); the president was a female but the secretary was a man; the men also had their own loan societies to which they could turn.

Bayonne Jews had a Thespian Club which for some strange reason was listed as a charity. In 1918 some youngsters in that town organized a boys' club calling themselves the Cadets of Temperance. It would seem that they were part of a larger Christian denominational organization. The constitution called for temperance but drinking had never been a problem among Jews. The constitution also urged its members to cultivate literature and practice brotherhood. This the youngsters understood although in all probability the Cadets were concerned primarily with sociality. By 1911 Bayonne's immigrants had been in the country long enough to start moving to the left, to establish a somewhat modernist congregation which they called Temple Emanu-El. They began with very few resources; indeed they were so poor they had to rent a Scroll of the Law and a shofar (a ram's horn to sound the call during the Holy Days), and borrow an ark to house the sacred Scroll. Their ladies' auxiliary raised money by staging affairs like a raffle offering a new automobile which had cost about $1807. The raffle tickets were sold at $1 a piece. Gala balls were also arranged; one that was held in the local opera house was not a notable financial success; it netted $18. This congregation persisted however; by 1913 these Conservatives had a building of their own, augmenting their income by renting it out for dances and weddings.

In Union County, south of Essex County and Newark, there were a number of villages and towns where Jewish immigrants had planted themselves. One of these towns was Elizabeth. Eager to keep kosher the first settlers brought meat in from New York; they were miles from the big city and in the 1880's that was a real problem because they had to travel by horse and buggy, by railroad, and by ferry. The thrifty pioneers had mutual-aid societies which also conducted services; one of their organizations had a library and a reading room. For Orthodox religionists a school was imperative; the Hebrew Free School they established in 1913 was quite progressive; history was taught in English. Some teachers volunteered; others were paid. Two of the paid instructors were a husband and wife team; these were the Menuhins, Moshe and his wife Martha. Having a little baby—and no sitter of course—they brought the infant to school in a basket and deposited it on a billiard table while they taught in an adjoining room. The baby, none the worse for his perch, grew up to be one of the world's greatest violinists; he was Yehudi Menuhin.

In the same county there was a small town called Roselle. It could be that it had a Jewish constable and that it was the first place in the world to have electric lighting. Thomas A. Edison, who had a laboratory in town, built the first electric lighting plant there. Roselle's Jewish community was an interesting one. One of its first settlers was an immigrant who moved out of New York City and bought a farm in the country. This man, a tailor by trade, was lonely for Jewish neighbors. He subdivided his property and started selling lots. Two years later there were enough coreligionists in town to set up a congregation; by 1907 they had their own building. The community had a Jewish tonsorial artist known as Benny the Barber; his assistant, who sported an impressive mustache, was known as Henry the Banker. The barbershop with a pool room in the rear served as a social center for the Jews. A number of the early settlers in Roselle were tailors who worked in New York's garment industry; they commuted for they liked to live in the country. In order to spare themselves a difficult trip they set up a small garment factory in town in 1912 manufacturing knee pants for children. The town had its Jewish grocer and its mason who did its stone work, also a carpenter and dry goods merchant. One of the men who made the daily trek to New York had a little dairy; he took milk, eggs, and chickens back to the city for sale. Some Brooklyn Jews came out and settled in town because a Jewish real estate agent had

induced them to buy lots. This was Mrs. Goldstein. She gave the Brook-
lynites free railroad tickets, a free lunch, and horse and buggy transportation to the lots. Thus Roselle grew.

South of Roselle and Union County lies Middlesex County; its chief
Jewish town is New Brunswick. By 1889 the Russians and the Poles were
already established in New Brunswick; they had probably come there in
the first years of the 1880's. Brotherly Love, Ahavas Achim, was the
name of their congregation and it was sufficiently fraternal to embrace a
number of German Jews, older settlers, no doubt. These East Europeans
were a modest lot; as they put it, "our members are all of a poor class of
Hebrews." The Raritan Valley in which they lived was an important industrial area. The earlier Jewish settlers started out as junk peddlers; other
refugees from New York's ghetto turned to farming, helped by the Jewish Agricultural and Industrial Aid Society. The Galicians were among
the first in town to organize; their congregation made its debut as a mutual-aid and sick-care society. The prayer group called itself Workers of
Righteousness, Poile Zedek; many of the members were fruit and vegetable peddlers. One of the foreigners who settled in town was Selman Abraham Waksman (1818-1973) who was putting himself through Rutgers by
tutoring English to foreigners. Waksman had but recently come to America and inasmuch as he always retained his Russian brogue the accent to
which his pupils were exposed was anything but classically Harvard,
Princeton, or Oxford.

By 1910 the good ladies of New Brunswick had already created two
very active charities; the one established in 1905 succeeded in building a
hospice; the other was primarily a relief society helping the poor and the
aged. It operated also as a free loan society, lending as much as $200 to an
individual if he could muster the necessary cosigners. Among the women
who did so much to carry on the charitative program was Amelia Marks;
she left a substantial sum to provide dowries for brides without means.
Bar mitzvah boys whose parents had little were given clothing and food
for this important life cycle ceremony. Thus it was that by the second decade of the new century New Brunswick's East Europeans had its ladies
charities, three congregations, and an active YMHA amd YWHA. By
1913 this sociorecreational organization had its own building; in later
years it housed the Jewish Boy Scout troop. There were at least ten Jewish organizations in town in 1918 in a community of 3,000 souls. Among
the associations was one founded by Hungarian emigrants; they kept their
records not in Yiddish but in Hungarian. This was certainly rare. The
Raritan Valley also had a number of Jewish settlers who had come from
the Balkans and the Levant. This was around the year 1910. Some of
these Spanish-Portuguese Ladino-speaking Jews were manual laborers; a
few worked for the drug firm of Johnson & Johnson; others opened small

grocery stores. This Levantine community was rather substantial in size; it had almost ninety householders in the synagog which it established. The customs to which it adhered were traditionally Sephardic. When a father or an older brother was called to the Torah all members of the family rose out of respect. During the procession when the Torahs were carried around at Simhat Torah rose water was sprayed on everyone. Some of the members, patterning themselves on the Turks, smoked water pipes; children were named after living grandparents, a custom sedulously avoided by Ashkenazim. They had their reason; if there were two people of the same name the Angel of Death might erroneously carry off the youngster instead of the grandfather.

The farm colonies tucked away in the southern part of the Jerseys maintained a traditional Jewish way of life. Their cultural achievements leave much to be desired. In 1907 Vineland had two congregations and—this is interesting—they both bore the same name, Brotherly Love, Ahavas Achim. This affection had not prevented them from splitting apart. In 1906, Alliance, one of the earliest of the colonies, could muster 200 souls; it had three prayer rooms and an equal number of educational societies. It had a night school, lecture and music programs, and a library. The library was not well patronized; the records show that it lent only twenty-eight books a month. This was certainly nothing to brag about but understandable; farmers were too tired, too dispirited, to do any reading at night by the light of a kerosene lamp. Carmel, Rosenhayn, and Norma—all colonies—also possessed libraries. Their lending records were not much better. Rosenhayn did a little better than the others; its borrowers drew thirty-five books a week; most were in English. In 1918 this colony had a literary society named after the federal judge Julian Mack. That year his name was very much in the news for he was the head of the American Jewish Congress and of the Zionist Organization of America.

In 1906 Norma had a library of 300 volumes and a boys' group called Work and Play Club; these youngsters were interested in nature studies. The farmers in the hamlet had organized themselves into the Norma Produce Growers Association, a shipping and sales farm cooperative. Norma must be praised for its cultural drive; it seemed to have done a little better than the neighboring colonies; in 1907 it could count but 200 men, women, and children. With the exception of Woodbine none of the colonies was impressive in size. Alliance, Rosenhayn, and Norma, all told, embraced less than 1,000 souls. In 1918 Woodbine numbered about 1,900 inhabitants but many of these were non-Jews. The rooms of the Baron de Hirsch Agricultural and Industrial School were used for a Sunday school. The Jewish children had separate societies but they joined together in a common Zionist association.[7]

THE NEW YORK HINTERLAND

The northern half of New Jersey was part of New York City's exurbs; it was a satellite area. Indeed many of the Jews in the northern New Jersey counties commuted daily to the big city, especially when transportation facilities improved. On the other hand Westchester County and the western half of Long Island are really part of America's megalopolis. But there were several large cities in New York State which were in no sense satellites; by 1921 there were about 200,000 Jews outside of New York City cultivating communal autonomy. The natives and Central Europeans in New York's back-counties were small in number. In 1880 the state contained the most populous Jewry in the country; outside of New York City there were about 21,000 Jews in the state; 13,000 were in Brooklyn; that leaves 7,000 Jews in the entire New York City hinterland. Only two cities had more than 1,000 Jews, Albany and Rochester. By the 1890's New York State's Jewry was overwhelmingly Russian and Polish. The important towns by 1921 were Poughkeepsie with 1,600, Albany, 7,000, Schenectady, 3,500, Binghamton, 1,500, Syracuse, 12,000, Rochester, 20,000, Buffalo, 20,000. Patently they were all substantial communities.

Moving north in the direction of Albany one encountered first the Jewish farmers and resort entrepreneurs in the Catskills. As early as 1904 there were reportedly dozens of farmers in Ulster County; they were establishing tiny Jewish communities. Ultimately the Catskills would house a very solid resort industry. In the next few years New York's yeomen and hoteliers would have eight farmers' associations and a credit union. Most of them were immigrants who had come up from New York's Lower East Side. The state's Jewish hinterland did not blossom in a hurry; immigrants, whether they were mid-nineteenth century Central Europeans or late arriving Russians, preferred to remain in metropolitan New York. There was however a Polish family in Kingston as early as the 1840's. Kingston's Agudas Achim (1864), the Assembly of Brothers, may have been an immigrant shul. Troy's Beth Israel, established in the 1870's, was an amalgamation of three earlier Orthodox prayer groups all of whose members were very probably émigrés from Slavic lands. In 1880 there were only six towns in the state that sheltered more than 500 souls. They were Rondout-Kingston, Troy, Albany, Rochester, Syracuse, and Buffalo. Beginning with the 1890's, possibly with the 1880's, the newer immigrants began moving up the Hudson in sizable numbers; they fanned out all over the state. Newburgh in Orange County had a synagog no later than 1891. The cantor was a man named Yoelson, probably the father of Al (Asa) Jolson, the famous jazz singer, the first actor to star in a talking movie. That same year the tailors in Albany organized a mutual-aid association and bought land for a cemetery; these men were all East Europeans.

Utica on the Mohawk River numbered almost 2,000 Jews by 1920. The Slavic newcomers who had been there early probably controlled the Orthodox congregation of the 1870's; it was known as the House of Jacob. It was expensive to join; entrance fees were $20, but they could be paid quarterly. The congregation kept records of births, marriages, and deaths charging a shilling for an entry, 12½ cents. It is difficult to determine why the English form of monetary accounting was retained but it was quite common in some American East European synagogs as late as the twentieth century. Burial plots were $4 and $18, $4 for a small family, $18 for a larger one. Funeral expenses were extra. If a Jew in town refused to join and to pay dues he was not allowed to attend the High Holy Day services. The synagog executives were empowered to give 50¢ in charity without consulting the board. By 1882 this congregation had its own building. The year 1919 saw the appearance of a modernist synagog in Utica; the attempt made a decade earlier to move to the left religiously had been unsuccessful.

In Utica, as in other towns, many immigrants preferred to join benefit societies because they got more for their money. Utica's garment workers were wont to join the socialistic Workmen's Circle; there were two such lodges in town; their membership was large for the benefits were substantial. These non-religionists opened a kosher butcher shop for the benefit of those members who were observant; they had discovered that their local butcher was cheating them by selling non-kosher meats. Obviously these lodges were not intransigently anti-religious. They had a Yiddish cultural program which included dramatic readings and theatrical presentations. On Friday night they met in their rented rooms where they conducted a labor lyceum. They sang folk songs, held classes in civics, and taught English. During World War I when the Joint Distribution Committee was established, they sent money to Europe and allied themselves with the Hebrew Immigration Aid Society. They supported it financially; 50¢ of a man's dues to the lodge went to the national HIAS. The Brith Abraham order—the most successful of the East European fraternities—had a branch in town which was founded in 1900; it called itself the Spinoza Lodge. Spinoza would not have been flattered by having a Russian-Polish society named after him; he had very little interest in Jews or Judaism. Another lodge was named after Roscoe Conkling who was once mayor of the city and had served in the United States Senate. He was a conservative Republican; so were many of the Jews in town. Probably most of the substantial Jewish citizens voted the straight Republican ticket, not the Workmen's Circle members of course. Many of them were Socialists.

The Utica community had numerous welfare agencies including a hostel and several women's charities. Among the non-Marxists, cultural work was carried on by the Graetz Circle, named after the German historian Heinrich Graetz who had written a multivolume history of the Jews available in an English translation issued by the Jewish Publication Society. The rise of the Young Men's Hebrew Association and the Young Women's Hebrew Association with their emphasis on sociality put an end to the Graetz Circle. Earlier, in 1907, the Orthodox rabbi Simon Glazer had come down from Montreal where he officiated and had urged the Uticans to establish a YMHA and YWHA. It is significant that this committed traditionalist spoke in English, not in Yiddish. In order to raise money for the proposed new institution, the Ladies' Hebrew Aid Society, together with the "Ys," ran a minstrel show in 1908. The women sold tickets and secured advertisements. The rooms they rented were large enough to include a gymnasium, an auditorium, a club room, and a library. At their literary meeting the speakers invited were frequently Gentiles who spoke on general not Jewish topics. This approach is an aspect of the Americanization process to which newcomers were exposed.

The "Y" finally bought a house, remodeled it, and opened it to various Jewish clubs and the Hebrew school. When the building was dedicated in 1915 Masliansky was brought in from New York; he spoke in Yiddish of course. Others who participated in this important communal ceremony were Gentile officials and a Jewish alderman. Since there was never enough money to balance the budget a Hebrew fair was held and a popularity contest for men and women staged. There was an annual oratorical contest held in the Hebrew Community Building. The orations had no specific Jewish content. Only boys participated; there were no girl contenders. During World War I one prize winner dealt with the Last of the Hapsburgs, another orator spoke on the Enslavement of the Belgians. Utica's Jews supported the Jewish Home for the Aged in Central New York (1912), located in Syracuse; people from Utica, however, were put on the board of this regional institution. The town benefited from the services of three female philanthropic organizations.

By 1918 there were numerous congregations manned by East Europeans in Syracuse. One was founded in 1872; included among these conventicles was one dedicated to the study of Talmud. One of Syracuse's congregations was Ahavath Achim, Brotherly Love; Yudel Rabinowitz, the kosher butcher, served as its president and, if tradition is accurate, brooked no opposition. In 1919 young Rabbi Samuel Yalow, all of twenty-six, took over the pulpit. It is indicative of a trend already manifest that this scholarly man, who had studied in European talmudic academies, was within a few years to receive his bachelor's degree from Syracuse University. Like many other European-born proponents of Orthodoxy he realized the need for modern methods in the field of Hebrew education. Yalow's wife Esther, a native of Lithuania, had come to the United States as a child, gone to college, and had taught school in Virginia. She busied herself in Jewish communal charities, joined the National Council of Jewish Women, and encouraged the ladies in her husband's synagog to make use of the town's ritual bath. She embraced and harmonized the world of Orthodoxy and modernity. The Yalows had two children; the boy Aaron received his Ph.D. from the University of Illinois and then served as a medical physicist in New York. Aaron's wife was the well-known Nobel Prize winner, Rosalyn Yalow. Syracuse's Workmen's Circle lodge opened a cooperative bakery in order to provide Jewish laborers with cheaper bread; profits were to be turned over to the lodge for its cultural programs. Local directories indicate that most Jews in Syracuse were peddlers, craftsmen, and shopkeepers. The bank records identified many of the depositors as "Jew peddlers" and in some instances describe the clients by height and color. Why this procedure? Was it a device to expedite identification? Was it a manifestation of distrust?

In Auburn, not too far from Syracuse, the only congregation was B'nai Israel founded in 1898. There were 40 members in a Jewish community of less than 100 souls. Obviously about every Jew in town joined. The Hebrew school had a teacher and about a dozen pupils. In 1903 this small East European congregation welcomed an additional immigrant into its midst. The newcomer, Samuel Schwartz, a Lithuanian, had studied in a talmudical academy back home; in Auburn he became a junk peddler; his brother-in-law helped him buy a horse and wagon. Two years later he had made enough to bring over his wife and children. Though his wife busied herself in the work of the local Jewish community she and her husband made sure that their youngsters went to high school. One of the boys never went to the university; this was Maurice, called Morrey. He took over his father's junk business, expanded it, worked loyally in B'nai Israel, and served as its president. Morrey ran for public office, was elected to the Board of Education, and finally became the mayor of the city.

In the third quarter of the nineteenth century Rochester sheltered the largest Jewry in the state west of Albany. As early as the 1860's a "Russian" peddler supply house here dispatched some of its clients to the transmississippi West. Rochester in 1880 had about 1,200 Jews; some were Poles and Russians; in 1920 the Jewish community numbered about 20,000; most were of East European birth or ancestry. They worshipped in many different congregations; some in hometown synagogs; one group, as in Albany, catered to tailors, for Rochester was a garment manufacturing center specializing in men's suits. In 1900 well over 60 percent of these Russians were working in industry, primarily in the needle trades. The tailors who worked in the factories and sweatshops, like their comrades in other cities, met together in their Workmen's Circle lodges, preached the gospel of socialism, and voted the Socialist ticket. In 1917 as American participation in World War I loomed large these tailors succeeded in electing a socialist alderman from their ward. They were anti-war and anti-Russian; the unconscionable Russians were abusing Jews. It was but a step from tailoring men's suits for some to open a clothing store but these Rochester newcomers reached out in all directions. Grocers organized into a Hebrew Retail Butchers' Association; their children hoped to succeed in the professions. Mr. Benjamin Forman landed in New York a teenager. He became a tailor. Years later he moved to Rochester and opened a woman's specialty shop; by 1918 the Forman stores were grossing $2,000,000 a year.

The first East European congregation in town, founded about the year 1870, started out as a burial society. In order to maintain order during the Holy Days and to keep out families with babes in arms and strangers who had no tickets a policeman was stationed at the door. Women were given tin alms boxes, *pushkes*, to collect pennies to help pay for the building. Dues were 75¢ a month. The officiant, a cantor-reader-teacher, was paid about $400 a year. It wasn't until 1883 that the synagog hired an ordained rabbi, one competent to render legal decisions; he received but $150 a year; the beadle was paid the same salary as the rabbi. The reason the rabbi was given so little was the expectation that the other Orthodox synagogs in town would help support him; he was looked upon as a communal ecclesiastical judge. In addition it was thought that he would live on perquisites. In general American Orthodox rabbis were paid a bare subsistence wage; only in the twentieth century did conditions improve somewhat. The salaries paid Reform rabbis served as a standard which some Orthodox synagogs sought to emulate. But it must not be forgotten that most immigrant congregations were small and without means; their members were not affluent. Thrift in all things was deemed a prime virtue. In 1886, in a day when New York City could boast of about 130 conventicles, there were—it is said—only three full-fledged rabbis in the metropolis.

There were Sephardic Jews from the Levant in Rochester in the early twentieth century; these Turkish and Ladino-speaking Jews came from Serbia, from Monastir, and like many Ashkenazic newcomers they, too, went to work as tailors in the factories. They sent for their wives and children as soon as they had saved a little and organized a congregation of their own. It was called the Light of Israel of Monastir. And like the Russians, Poles, and Rumanians they established social and cultural agencies that bore their ethnic impress. A time would come when they would have their own clubhouse. Leaving the factory some turned to retailing; they became grocers, vendors of vegetables and fruits. By the early 1900's some Ashkenazic immigrant congregations, exposed to the American way of life and to liberal Judaism began to move leftward religiously. They joined the Conservative Movement; their modified services were a happy compromise between Russian Orthodoxy and American classical Reform.

A number of Polish Jews were already living in Buffalo in 1860; one married couple had two children though the wife was only seventeen years of age; another Pole had a daughter who had also married young; after the wedding she was seen out on the sidewalk skipping rope. In the variety of economic pursuits which characterized it Buffalo differed little from most other large Jewish communities. The ghetto was never without a few professionals. Ludwig E. Schroeter was a Polish Jewish revolutionary who had fled Russia, studied medicine in Switzerland, and practiced in Buffalo since the late 1880's. When his wife landed in Buffalo on a cold day and saw the huge drifts of snow she turned to her husband, the former revolutionary, saying: "now we are in Siberia." Buffalo's newcomers were in everything from junk to millinery. There was an occasional policeman, several clothing manufacturers, numerous workers in the needle trades, unions, and the inevitable Workmen's Circle lodge. With trade unions came socialism and its Russia-based variations. The workers brought in Abraham Cahan to lecture on socialism. When Buffalo's laborers, following a pattern set by others, organized a cooperative bakery, the furious Jewish bakers responded by locking out the community and closing their shops. No bread, no cake! Disciples of Chaim Zhitlowsky talked of Diaspora nationalism; Territorialists, present too, were willing to accept a homeland outside of Palestine; for the Socialist-Zionists, the Poale Zion, the Holy Land alone was God's promised country. To further their philosophy and indoctrinate their children these ideologues set out to establish non-religious Yiddish afternoon schools.

The years 1881-1920 were years of nonaffiliation for the newcomers. They were poor. No post-eventum maudlin sentimentality about the ghettos can ignore or wipe out stark reality. Many Jews in Buffalo earning from $8 to $11 a week had families to support. Tuberculosis was not uncommon. A study made in 1911 revealed that the average Jewish householder made about $468 a year. Where there are immigrants and poverty there is also deliquency among the young. The Jews had their share. The youngsters gathered in the streets, in the saloons, in the poolrooms. The family was threatened. Desertions were commonplace around the year 1910. They abated later as fathers improved their economic lot. Drunkenness was not totally absent. Every ghetto had its drunkard. Buffalo's favorite had a horse named Chaim who exhibited a considerable degree of horse sense. According to local folklore Chaim stopped automatically in front of the beer parlor frequented by his master. This may not be remarkable but on the Passover, when leaven, beer, is taboo, Chaim would not stop but continued on his way. And where there was a ghetto and problems there were invariably settlement houses. These welfare institutions helped Buffalo's Jews; some of them were established by philanthropic, socially-minded Christians without any ulterior motive; they were not conversionists. Programs included scouting, music, domestic arts, the teaching of English, and even the study of the Bible. The 1890's was a great decade for these helpful institutions.

Buffalo's ghetto Jews tried to take care of their own and were very proud of what they accomplished. By 1915 they had established a home for the aged; some old people had no family to provide for them; on occasion children refused to support their parents. Synagogs and special associations provided free loans; when a peddler needed a horse to replace one that had fallen in the shafts there was no need to turn to the pawnbroker or the loan shark. Hometown societies, lodges, mutual-aid associations were a tower of strength to their members. The newcomers bypassed the B'nai B'rith of the acculturated Germans; by 1915 the Brith Abraham order, which catered to the newcomers, had hundreds of branches in the United States. Impoverished as the Russians and Poles were, and dependent as they were on their benefit societies, they were always ready to help their fellow Jews in Russia, Poland, and the Balkans.

Social intercourse played a great role in the life of ghetto Jews. Its forum was often the landsmanshaft, the lodge, and the synagog, many of which, as it has been pointed out, catered to newcomers of a specific region or town in Russia, Poland, Hungary, Rumania. Not infrequently these immigrants organized an all-Jewish branch of a general lodge such as the Red Men. Even burial societies emphasized the social aspect especially in their annual banquet. Children built a life for themselves on the streets, in the public and Hebrew schools, in the clubs they founded. The Buffalo youngsters loved to play soldier. It was an age of military clubs; boys' brigades were encouraged by the Jewish elite; patriotism flourished at the time of the Spanish-American War. We Jews are no ghetto weaklings! David killed Goliath! Buffalo gave birth to two such military congeries for youngsters; one was called the Star of David; the other called itself the Young Stars of David.

Like others, the Jews, too, loved excursions; the railroads seeking business made it possible for groups to travel for little money. In 1904 fifty delegates making the trip to a Zionist convention in Cleveland chartered a railroad coach. The Hebrew-reading intelligentsia met in Harry Singer's store where he sold religious articles. Joshua H. Singer (1848-1925)—Harry—was a beloved Buffalo cantor who had emigrated from Russia when he was no longer young. His admirers in the synagogs he served heard him sing not only the traditional melodies but the art music of the great European Jewish cantors Sulzer and Lewandowski. He was an excellent choirmaster and a scholar, too, who published two works in

Hebrew; these included comments on the Bible and Talmud and stories of the rabbis of old.

By 1920 Buffalo had at least seven Orthodox congregations, most, if not all, with cemeteries of their own. Even the Workmen's Circle had a burial ground. It had sought a plot from a congregation but was turned down; even in death the religionists would have no truck with the atheistic socialists. Relations between the Hassidim, the Pietists, and the Orthodox masses (the Mitnaggedim, the Opponents) were not always the best. These were hostilities rooted in the distant past; in the eighteenth century the Opponents had fought the Pietists vigorously and vindictively. Buffalo's Hassidim, followers of Shneor Zalman, had their own congregational rabbis and burial societies. They had been part of Buffalo Jewry since the 1880's. The perennial president of their synagog was Jacob Rosokoff, a jeweler and local pioneer in the penny arcade, nickelodeon, and cinema industry. During the panic of 1907 Rosokoff, it is said, distributed 200 loaves a day to the unemployed. Most congregations had traditional afternoon Hebrew schools where the students—boys primarily— were taught to read Hebrew. There were also a few good afternoon schools, private enterprises, run by men who were learned and fully conscious of the needs of young American Jews. The Pole, Morris Diamond (d. 1944), spoke English well and taught in that language. The youngsters would have had little respect for teachers whose only medium of communication was Yiddish. Children of the poor were admitted free to the so-called public Talmud Torahs but even schools attached to synagogs demanded fees. Buffalo charged girls more than boys.

Conservatism, the middle denomination of the American Jewish religionists, comfortably at home between the Orthodox and the Reformers, had its followers in Buffalo as in most American towns of size after 1900. Beth El, Prussian-Polish (and Russian-Polish?) which went back to the 1840's, moved slowly away from a strict and rigid Orthodoxy. This change was not the work of a day; ultimately it was to become completely modern and yet traditional. Congregation Love of Peace, Ahavas Sholem, was established in 1892; by the middle 1890's this synagog began pressing for mild reforms. It staged dances, opened a Sunday school, and rejoiced in the elite Orthodox whom it attracted. The officers of Ahavas Sholem were seen in cutaway coats and high silk hats on Saturdays and Holy Days. Conservatism was beginning to become a factor in American Jewish religious life. These Conservatives were distancing themselves from Orthodoxy, not in theology but in practice, ritual. That meant a break that was real, definitive.

In their visual patterns these gentle rebels were moving closer to Reform despite the fact that they continued to retain the traditional book of common prayer. It was America rather than Reform that was making its presence felt. One of Buffalo's leaders in this move away from Russian-Polish Judaism was Charles Polakoff, later to serve as president of Beth El. As an entrepreneur he wholesaled coal and ice, sold insurance, and speculated in real estate. He was successful. As a Jew he worked to build an old-folks home and encouraged students at Cornell to remain loyal to the faith of their fathers. When his congregation Beth El moved into its new home in 1911 it was committed to modernism; it was very much a synagog center and an American Jewish "church," for it had mixed seating, a library, a gymnasium, a Boy Scout troop, a young men's club; it presented musical comedies; its women organized strawberry festivals and sponsored Hanukkah banquets. Conservatism came into its own when the East Europeans and their children, economically mobile, moved out of the downtown ghettos to better areas of settlement. Acculturation, modernization, westernization came quickly.[8]

SUMMARY

INTRODUCTION

In 1920 there were almost 2,000,000 Jews in the hinterland; most of them were immigrants or children of newcomers from the Slavic lands. Because of their numbers, if for no other reason, they are an important part of American Jewish history. Many Jews went into the smaller towns of America's hinterland but hesitantly; often they had no choice. If there were no Jews, no Jewish institutions, they might lose their identity; they faced, and feared, assimilation. Not infrequently they came as peddlers selling clothing or dry goods or notions, collecting junk and hides. It was not long, measured in years, before many peddlers became shopkeepers. Artisans, too, hoped to move up and become business people, merchants of a sort; the carpenter wanted to be a builder. These newcomers never ceased to hope that they would live in a Jewish community, preferably in a good-sized city. Cities were preferable, for work was available, opportunities were larger; one could maintain a Jewish way of life; this was important. The immigrants were compelled to be mobile; like the Jewish Germans who had preceded them by three or four decades these Russians kept moving about until they found a town where they could make a living; there they settled more or less permanently, finally developing a vocational pattern that was normal for them, certainly in the hinterland. In 1900, most of Atlanta's male Russian Jews were in some form of trade. This may well be typical for most East Europeans in the American hinterland although no two émigrés would have exactly the same experiences and careers as they struggled to support their families. These strangers survived because they were content with small profits, because they were thrifty; their standard of living was austere.

It is exceedingly difficult, however, to determine how many were ever modestly affluent. By 1920 immigrants had had thirty to forty years in which to advance themselves; quite a number—individuals—stood out as achievers. In general, however, looking at the masses, these new arrivals were not important in commerce, manufacturing, building, real estate, the professions, and the sciences. Though making something of an impression in commerce and in the needle trades they were certainly not vital to the American economy, certainly not in the hinterland. They had come over as refugees with nothing, no capital, little schooling; they had to learn a new language and to start at the bottom. They were not a degraded people. They were men and women willing to work hard; they had courage, morale, self-respect. They were proud of their lineage, of their background, rising above the misfortunes and the difficulties which almost all of them were to experience.

Here is the story of one Jewish immigrant businessman who lived in an American village; it is not necessarily typical. Jakie Per settled in the small Pennsylvania town of Hughesville around the year 1895. Originally he had begun his career as a peddler; he married a Jewish girl from a neighboring village. Per prospered and began opening branches in surrounding towns. He was successful because he carried a relatively large stock and he knew how to get along with people. Credit was extended and when there was no cash he resorted to barter. After a while he became a director of the local bank and burgess of the borough. In October before the onset of a winter he would charter a passenger train to run from neighboring towns to Hughesville; hundreds of people were brought in; there was no charge for the train fare; they would arrive about 10:00 in the morning and leave in the evening after doing their winter shopping. Per employed a seamstress in the store to make necessary alterations. In the 1920's, wealthy, he sold his business and moved to Atlantic City where he lived in one of the best hotels, but after the stock market crash of 1929 wiped him out he returned to Hughesville impoverished. About six years later he passed away. Most immigrants who came from Russia, Poland, and Rumania managed somehow or other to survive but they rarely admitted how much they had suffered and how hard they had struggled.

EAST EUROPEAN JEWS AND THE COMMUNITIES THEY ESTABLISHED

East European Jews started to come in large numbers in the 1880's; in many towns they organized the first Jewish institution. There had been individual Germans or natives in those places before them but only too often there had been too few Jews in town to set up a formal community. If a "German" synagog already existed in the place it was very difficult for the two groups, the old and the new, to work together; there were cultural disparities, social distance, mutual hostilities. Obviously the older settlers who spoke English would patronize the newcomers; their backgrounds were different. Many of the East European immigrants lacked a knowledge of American amenities; they had little secular education because of the disabilities imposed upon them by the tyrannical Russians and Rumanians. The newcomers who came to a town of size kept away from the older Jewish settlers. Humble though these new immigrants were they speedily took on the racial and ethnic prejudices of the town's people; they looked down upon the Negroes, the Irish, and the Slavs. The latter were all "Hunkies." However, the new Jews looked up to the Anglo-Saxons; they were Americans; they hoped to become like them.

Individual Jews in the hinterland cities, towns, and hamlets frequently had Gentile friends but in general the Gentile masses were anything but friendly to the Jewish immigrants in their midst. Here is a brief description of Jewish-Christian relations in Detroit after 1881. In this city both Gentiles and acculturated Jews tended to reject the new arrivals; they were poor, sometimes unskilled, secularly uneducated; they were exotics. Many thought these new Jews were not law abiding. There were always one or two old-line Jews in every town who set out to be helpful to their displaced coreligionists. The Anglo-American press, evaluating these refugees from the Slavic lands, was often quite objective. It reported that these Jews had a love of learning; they were good family people, willing to work; they had a low crime rate. In some towns, and this was particularly true of Detroit, they were denied work in the factories; in the early twentieth century it was not easy for them to get jobs in the automobile plants. Jewish peddlers in this city—and in most other towns, too —were constantly harassed and attacked. Thus it was that in 1900 Detroit's peddlers were compelled to set up a defense league; in 1906 it had 460 members. Some Gentiles looked askance at Jews because they refused to intermarry; others turned away from them because they were not Christians. During depressions hostilities were heightened; anti-Jewish prejudice in Detroit was exacerbated in the 1920's when Henry Ford initiated a ruthless national campaign to crush all American Jews. In the 1930's the fires of anti-Semitism were stoked by Father Charles E. Coughlin who relentlessly attacked Jews in his radio programs. The hatred directed against the Jew speeded up his acculturation; he was pathetically eager for anonymity. In general one is inclined to hazard the opinion that Jews west of New York City adapted themselves rather quickly to the American way of life because they lived in an overwhelming Christian Anglo-Saxon setting. This was certainly true in the smaller towns and cities. The hinterland children, too, exposed to the public schools where they were always a tiny minority, speeded up the Americanization process in the home. The youngsters spoke English almost exclusively.

The ambience in the backcountry states tended to push the Jew to the left, in a religious sense, away from the traditional Russian-Polish Orthodoxy which he had brought with him and which had meant so much to him. Inevitably Orthodoxy moved toward modernistic "Conservatism" in every town of size in the United States. In the Atlanta of 1900 practically none of the Orthodox Jews kept their places of business closed on the Sabbath. Some acculturated immigrants even skipped the Conservative synagog and made the leap to Reform; theologically they were latitudinarians; they hoped to be numbered with the socially elite. Jewish business people in the hinterland were often Republicans because that was America's dominant political party; in towns where the Democrats were well organized many voted that ticket. This was certainly true in the South; the Jews there overwhelmingly voted Democratic; as a tiny minority they dared not do otherwise. By 1912 the idealism of Wilson appealed to many Jews, especially the young Jews of East European background, and they started voting Democratic; Jews were always eager to identify with the majority; it gave them a sense of security. They belonged.

Most Jews in the hinterland—and in New York City too—were not influenced by the Russian and Polish radicals who were organized in, or dominated, the Workmen's Circle lodges which were found in practically every town of size. These Marxists were always a minority. These radicals were looked upon with dismay by the town's Jewish majority, but even in these very lodges the workmen moved slowly to the right. After a decade or two the members, not all, began to swim in the American mainstream. These Jews, too, did not want to stand out, to be different. Many, petty bourgeois, continued to remain in the radical lodges for social reasons and for the financial benefits in store for them.

As a rule when an immigrant came to town he helped establish a congregation; if there was one already there—Orthodox of course—he usually joined it unless there was a mutual-aid lodge; that was often preferred for its potential benefits. As Jewish towns grew in numbers the newcomers divided religiously along geographical lines; they always wanted the comfort of being with people from the same hometown or region or country. As towns grew Jewishly they had a synagog, a cemetery, an afternoon Hebrew school, and a variety of philanthropic organizations. Many of the charities were initiated and managed by women. The larger towns, almost without exception, were replete with an orphanage, a hospice, a hospital, a free-loan society, and several literary and social clubs. There was an East European-oriented institution or organization for everyone regardless of one's religious, non-religious, or even anti-religious views. Zionist societies were found in every town; formal membership was minimal, yet Zionism as a movement was very popular. Why?

The liturgy spoke constantly of a return to Palestine; a reborn homeland was part of the belief of every religionist. Yet Zionism was more, much more. The new Zionism was a mythical utopia. The myth appealed to the men and women who were struggling to make a living; despite the opportunities which America offered it was no utopia. They would do better in an ideal Palestine.

All "Russian" Jewish communities in the United States were very much alike. The congregation, the synagog, was most important for it offered opportunity to the individual to express piety, if he was so prompted to continue a way of life in which he was rooted. Equally important it guaranteed identification as a Jew; it gave all Jews a feeling, a sense of continuity, security. The smallest Jewish commune, no matter how few its institutions, was a microcosm of New York City; it offered him in essence all that the megapolitans demanded and enjoyed—religion, education, philanthropy, sociability. A weird ambivalence was unmistakably apparent in every East European community of size. Centrifugality was the norm; every group of *Yidn*—East European Jews—wanted its own life. It was wary not only of the established Jews, of their organizations and institutions, it looked askance at its East European Jewish neighbors if they came from a different Slavic or Balkan region. Ethnic xenophobia or wariness was the rule in America's East European Jewish communities. Yet centripetality was also always present, all-powerful, for these newcomers were encompassed by a cultural-religious tradition which enveloped them, from which they could never really escape. It homogenized them, held them together in an amorphous fashion as they moved toward Americanization and a common Judaization, one that they would ultimately share with most Jews in this land. Before the 1920's, however, the East European community, wherever found, was distinct and separated from the older native-German religious establishment. America sheltered two disparate Jewish entities, even cultures; the ultimate fusion of the two is the main theme of mid and late twentieth century American Jewish history.[9]

CHAPTER SIX

THE EAST EUROPEANS DECIDE TO STAY

IN THE EAST

INTRODUCTION

There were more Jews outside of than in New York City; when the year 1920 rolled around less than half of all the Jews in the United States lived in the metropolis. Nevertheless no one can question its importance; most national Jewish organizations were located here though there were some exceptions; a number of important religious cultural and fraternal associations had their home offices in the hinterland. The "Russians" started settling in the big city during the gilded age of commerce and industrialism. New York was the country's largest entrepôt, commercial center. New York offered jobs; the immigrants needed work; they had no money to move on farther. New York was synonymous with education, sociality, opportunity; here the old hometown could be relocated, rebuilt with its synagogs, its kosher foods, its schools. Here a woman could find the work that was denied her in Russia; there were more men around, too; that was very important. The newcomers were determined to stay in the East; they were wiser than Schiff the millionaire. He and his friends wanted the impoverished immigrants to keep moving, to go on the farm. The immigrants knew that the future lay in the big cities; indeed it was an age when thousands were leaving the farmsteads and moving into the towns. The cities were growing; there were twice as many Jews in Brooklyn as there were in Warsaw.[1]

SELF-HELP

The transoceanic crossing into a strange culture and a radically different economy created problems; new or modified institutions were necessary if one was to survive; self-help associations were imperative if the new Jew was to be fortified with a sense of security. These timorous strangers had to help themselves; they were proud, pious; they wanted to hold on to religion as they knew it and loved it. Because they were clannish they set out to create their own institutional milieu, to fashion a world that would encompass and protect them. The world they now created in this new country was a reborn old world; organizations were established, rooted in geographical provenance. Thus it was that all these Jews went their own way, Balts, Lithuanians, Russians, Ukranians, Poles, Galicians, Bukovinians, Hungarians, Rumanians. They were but patterning themselves on earlier migrants; the Spanish-Portuguese kept to themselves; the English, the Bavarians, the Poseners (German Polacks!), the Bohemians, and even a few French had their own congregations and institutions. But they were all Jews, all these that flourished in the mid-nineteenth century. It was therefore perfectly right and proper that the Russians plant a synagog of their own in New York no later than 1852. Yiddish was the cement that tied all these newcomers together; it was a tongue that evoked sympathy, understanding. But the institutions which they brought to birth here were in no sense completely old world; some were patterned on the German organizations that had flourished here for generations; others were borrowed from the Gentiles. Assorted non-Jewish ethnic societies go back, at the latest, to the mid-eighteenth century.

Even before individual East European Jews were firmly established in commerce, industry, and trade, they often turned to help others. An immigrant who achieved a modest degree of success might well send a load of coal to a family in dire straits. Some individuals, apprehensive, belonged not to one mutual-benefit society but to several. Jews already here were set on providing a proper social and cultural ambience for newcomers. However, charity, help, relief—so necessary for immigrants—was provided primarily by societies, not by individuals. There were few if any organizations that did not engage in philanthropy. The synagog often gave small sums to petitioners; it might even serve temporarily as a hospice. The House of God was the core institution in the community but there were also schools, burial societies, and a host of men's and women's relief organizations of every genre. Very few societies restricted themselves solely to the goal described in their title; they all reached out to help unfortunates in more areas than one; an organization to bury the dead might take time out to feed the living. These struggling aliens established institutions to clothe the naked; they built dispensaries, hospitals, homes for the aged, orphan asylums, hospices, YMHA's. They opened libraries, taught English to foreigners in night schools, created culture societies, social clubs, a Yiddish and a Hebrew press; they had their own theatres, their own restaurants, their own coffee houses. A group of Rhode Island doctors established a modest clinic to service the immigrants on a yearly fee basis, but this was no charity; this was business.

Almost everyone made a contribution, no matter how modest, to a philanthropy of his choice. No occasion was too sacred to forbid the collection of funds for charity; the hat was passed around at circumcision feasts. Many societies had special collectors; some of them were paid. Individuals working gratis for a charity went out into the streets soliciting nickels and dimes. Often they sallied forth in pairs; that was traditional. Money collected was distributed secretly. Philanthropy, making provision for the needy, was but one aspect of community building. In Chicago, for example, there were about 50 immigrant synagogs by 1900; there were 39 charities, hospitals, and asylums, 60 lodges, 13 free loan associations, 11 social clubs, 4 Zionist societies, 2 mutual-benefit organizations, a Hebrew literary association, and a rabbi's council. Most of these institutions catered almost exclusively to the émigrés from Eastern Europe. Albany had a small congregation established in 1902 called the Assembly of Brothers. This group of humble immigrants offered a variety of services though most members earned a bare $5 a week. It rented a room for worship—itinerants could always sleep on the floor; dues were 10 cents a week; a loan fund enabled peddlers to purchase a basket of notions. The Scroll of the Law was rented and housed in an old fruit box lined with colored papers. Nine years later the congregation had its own building. Some of the other Orthodox congregations in town looked down upon this Assembly of Brothers; they dubbed the members Cossacks; this was no compliment.

The women among the new immigrants were notable as founders of self-help agencies. No one can exaggerate their influence in the area of relief and social welfare. Frequently they organized auxiliaries to serve male organizations but there were probably as many autonomous congeries, lodges, free loan societies, even female landsmanshaften, all of them mutual-aid institutions. At times an individual, a man or a woman, would constitute himself or herself a committee or a society of one to go out and collect money for philanthropic purposes. Denver had its Hannah, the Boss; she would accost Jews on the street and literally, vituperatively demand gifts for her charges. Women were particularly eager to raise money to establish homes for the aged. In one of Chicago's Orthodox synagogs Jewish women were allowed to come down from their segregated gallery, stand in the pulpit, and plead for funds for a home for the old and helpless.[2]

LODGES

Lodges were self-help agencies. The immigrants joined them by the hundreds of thousands because of sociality and, more importantly, because of the benefits accorded the sick, the unemployed, widows of deceased members. Some men belonged to several lodges and were out several nights a week. They loved the mysterious pretentious rituals; they treasured the ethical injunctions. Lodges were typically American; the B'nai B'rith had been established in 1843 by the Germans; these Central Europeans fashioned numerous other fraternities of this type. Although the B'nai B'rith was at first not at all cordial to the Jews from the "East" there was a Russian branch of the order in Philadelphia as early as 1890. These aliens moved but slowly into this well-established order; they were far from ready to participate happily in this German American organization. Because of the popularity and the need for fraternities of their own the East Europeans either founded or refashioned a dozen orders. They spoke Yiddish and learned to use if not to abide by, Robert's *Rules of Order*.

Chicago's Zionists founded a Zionist order and benefit society in 1898. They called themselves the Knights of Zion; several years later, 1907, the Sons of Zion came into being, meeting in "camps." The benefits were substantial ranging as high as $2,000. It was never a large organization; at one time it had 4,500 members, 1,350 of whom were in New York City. It pleaded for a knowledge of Hebrew; one wonders what if any success it had in this area. Another Zionist fraternal group was more popular. This was the Socialist-Zionist Jewish National Workers Alliance of America, popularly known as the Farband (the "union," the "association"). Its appeal was to Zionist proletarians and petty businessmen. Before the end of the second decade of the twentieth century it finally mustered a membership of 6,000; only about 20 percent lived in New York. The Farband pioneered in establishing non-religious afternoon Yiddish classes for the children of the members; as Zionists, Palestinian nationalists, these Yiddishists deemed it necessary to teach some Hebrew. Clearly the Zionist lodges were not important numerically; Zionism had relatively few followers before the Balfour Declaration convinced many that a dream might become a reality.[3]

WORKMEN'S CIRCLE

Unlike the Zionist orders, the Workmen's Circle (Arbeter-Ring)—a popular immigrants' fraternity—was socialist, pure and simple; for about a decade it was somewhat distant from the Body of Jewry. Culturally it was Yiddishist; it manifested a secular, non-theistic relationship to Jewish history and the Jewish people, but not to Jewish religion. Numerous followers of the Workmen's Circle were Bundists in that sense. They began their work in 1905; the *Jewish Encyclopedia* of 1906 carried no separate entry under Workmen's Circle; it was too young, too un-Jewish. The Arbeter-Ring was a pro-union benefit order blatantly schismatic. When it organized a branch in Albany—something of a garment center—no Jews would rent it a room; the members were denounced as "missionaries"—a dirty word—and the pietists even attacked some of the members when they caught them distributing propaganda material. In Buffalo, at the other end of the state, the Workmen's Circle did join with an Orthodox congregation to buy a cemetery. Both were poor and had to pool their funds; economics sometimes makes strange bedfellows. This order flourished; the Milwaukee branch, 500 strong in 1916, had an active labor lyceum where for five cents one could hear a lecture by a distinguished Yiddish speaker brought in from New York City. These intellectuals talked to them on Spinoza, Bergson, child rearing, ancient Greek literature, Darwinism, the Jewish national question, and, of course, socialism. When an aroused American Jewry called a Jewish Congress into being in the second decade of the twentieth century to deal with the eventual peace conference and the fate of Europe's oppressed Jews, the Workmen's Circle remained apathetic. International socialism, not the Great Powers, was the answer to injustice. The Ring members were excited by their Marxist ideals though in the pre-millennial meantime they offered their followers the standard welfare benefits. By the 1920's, these socialists were veering slowly to the right.

Like the Farband they, too, were interested in matters cultural. They established afternoon Yiddish classes for their children; in later decades they could boast of 150 such schools where the younger generation was indoctrinated with Marxist ideals and concepts of social justice. The national organization published works on hygiene, physics, geology, and botany, and opened a sanitarium in the Catskills. They were Enlighteners, Maskilim after their own fashion, trying to educate the masses through the medium of the vernacular. In a way they had something in common with those idealists who were trying to bring culture to the benighted Jews of Russia through the medium of Hebrew. By 1920 the Workmen's Circle had hundreds of branches in New York City alone, over 600 in the United States. At one time this organization was numerically larger than the B'nai B'rith. Typically East Europeans, rooted in traditional Judaism, looked askance at the order; the members were looked upon as separatists because of their rejection of religion and Zionism. With the passing of time, as the older folk died or were more drastically Americanized, the order began to decline.

BRITH ABRAHAM

The largest Jewish order in the United States was the Brith Abraham, the Abrahamitic Covenant. This was an immigrant order that had been founded in 1887 after seceding from a Central European fraternity. The Brith Abraham people were no schismatics; they swam in the Jewish mainstream; they fought anti-immigration bills and were sympathetic to Zionism. Sedulously they avoided theology and politics as divisive. Newcomers flocked to their banner. Like the older B'nai B'rith and other orders they, too, had their female auxiliaries. By 1930 there were over 30 Jewish orders in the United States, a nation of joiners proud of its over 500 fraternal societies. Like all other Jewish orders the Brith Abraham was to decline as its members and their children began to seek other outlets for sociability and more stable forms of insurance. In order to remain viable some of the Jewish orders began to emphasize cultural programs.[4]

LANDSMANSHAFTEN

In essence the lodge was a mutual-benefit society; some were originally landsmanshaften. And the landsmanshaft? It was a hometown association uniting people from the same village, city, province, or region. It was certainly not uniquely East European. The social clubs of the German Jewish immigrants and their prejudicial exclusion of Germans from other regions partake, to a degree, of the characteristics of a landsmanshaft. Ethnic self-help societies were common in Gentile North America of the eighteenth century. Though abused in their native towns, the Russian and Polish newcomers loved the villages whence they came. Nostalgia was ascendant. New York in 1880 had a German or Yiddish hometown society that called itself Forget-Me-Not (Vergissmirnicht). There was a Slavic landsmanshaft in the metropolis as early as the 1850's; others in the 1860's and 1870's. Philadelphia in the 1890's had a Hungarian association that took the name of a Hungarian Christian nationalist and patriot; another Jewish society in town bore the name of the Austrian Emperor Francis Joseph who had crushed the Hungarian rebellion. All landsmanshaften offered mutual-aid. Later generations set up "family circles"; these were not necessarily benefit organizations. As early as 1911 distant Jacksonville in Florida sheltered a Slavic village hometown society; Jewish Detroit had many such groups in the 1920's; New York may have had as many as 1,000 embracing 100,000 members. By the late 1930's it is said that there were some hundreds of female landsmanshaften in the city.

Psychically the landsmanshaft had more to offer than the lodge. In the lodge one could expect to meet almost anyone; in the hometown society one was sure to meet kinfolk or old friends. The landsmanshaft gave the newcomer instant identity, advice too, and friendship. There was always a religious quorum for services in addition to all the benefits offered by the mutual-aid organizations. In a landsmanshaft one could negotiate a loan and, rarely to be sure, even get help in setting up a dowry for a beloved daughter. One was always assured of a proper burial; a Jew must have a good funeral! During World War I as kin were being crushed, murdered across the seas, the landsmanshaft gave money to the Jewish national relief societies and, more specifically, hovered benevolently over the village whence the members all hailed. The Plishkover Association of Pittsburgh may be deemed a typical landsmanshaft. After the post-World

War I pogroms in Russia the members of this Pittsburgh hometown society sent a man abroad to take care of their kin who had sought refuge in
neighboring unfriendly Rumania. The American agent armed with funds
arranged for American visas and bribed the Rumanian bureaucrats not to
expel the Plishkover exiles before their departure for the United States.

The landsmanshaft was an Americanization agency for it taught the
new arrivals how to understand this country, how to get ahead, how to
make the transition from the old to the new. As the members Americanized themselves their organization printed constitutions both in Yiddish
and in English. For many the landsmanshaft was more than an insurance
device. Morris Raphael Cohen's family loved its hometown association
and poor as it was—and it was very poor—it never failed to pay its 10
cents a month dues. The Cohens were proud to belong. Like the press and
the theatre the landsmanshaften, too, were threatened when restrictive
legislation locked out the Jews of Eastern Europe. Many members, rising
economically, had moved up and out; now acculturated they ventured
into the larger America. Possibly more viable than the theatre or even the
press the hometown societies held on for decades. They refused to die because they had vested interests, funds. Some native-born children, too,
had signed up to enjoy their financial benefits. Chicago in 1948 still had
hundreds of societies; New York, so it is reported, had over 1,900 in
1938. Some still persisted at the dawn of the twenty-first century.[5]

THE VERBANDS

By the early twentieth century the numerous landsmanshaften began to
federate into larger "unions" (verbands). American Christian denominations had united nationally in the late eighteenth century; the natives and
German Jews had established national associations, orders, and religious
combines in the decades from 1843 into the 1880's. These unions are
reflected in the rise of the B'nai B'rith, the Board of Delegates of American Israelites, the Union of American Hebrew Congregations, the Jewish
Theological Seminary Association, and the Central Conference of American Rabbis. The eighteenth-century old-line Sephardic natives were held
together by Shearith Israel of New York City. The East European masses
here, originally Russian subjects, did not set up a federation of their own;
they were too large, too inchoate, torn by regional prejudices; verbands
were established only by minority groups among the new arrivals. The
following East Europeans federated into national associations: the Galicians and neighboring Bukovinians—Austrian subjects; there were two
Rumanian federations, a Polish union, a Hungarian one, and an Oriental
association.

Why did these Jewish ethnics organize? They joined together to insure group survival. Bear in mind that they still had one foot in Europe;

they were set on maintaining their regional identity; they were determined not to be overwhelmed by the preponderant Russian masses. But there were other reasons; they sought strength, influence, the funds that would enable them to reach certain goals; they wanted political power if only to influence the United States government to help suffering Jews back home.

Sociopolitically they were eager to create organizations, institutions, in their own image. Only a strong federation could support synagogs, schools, hospitals, tuberculosis sanitaria, homes for convalescents, the infirm, the aged, orphans. And still another reason: they needed substantial sums to help or rescue kin exposed to the ravages of World War I and hostile governments. Ultimately by the 1920's the verbands started to fade as had many landsmanshafts; the stream of immigrants became but a trickle, and the old folks were dying off or had become a more integral part of America's mainstream. The verband movement, however, was resurrected in the 1930's as the Germans seized power all over Europe. Jewish exiles created new federations here in the United States, Jugoslavians, Lithuanians, French, Germans, and others too. These unions were ephemeral; they declined with the fall of the German Nazi empire.[6]

THE LEVANTINE FEDERATION

The year 1911 was to witness the appearance of the Federation of Oriental Jews of America; about thirty societies representing some 3,000 people came together. They are a minuscule lot but they wanted their own Jewish schools, cemeteries, charities; they were determined to have a life of their own. The adjective "Oriental" was not a felicitous one; they were Levantines from the Balkans and cities and islands as far east as Syrian Aleppo and Damascus. Many were descendants of the Jews exiled from Spain in 1492, hence Sephardim; others were the children of Jews who had lived in the Near and Middle East since time immemorial. During the Middle Ages the majority of all the Jews in the world were in the Levant; Jewry was not to become predominantly European till the sixteenth or possibly even the seventeenth century. These Levantines, all subjects of the Ottoman Empire or its successor states, were not a unified homogeneous group; they reflected three different cultures: some were Ladinos speaking Spanish-Portuguese; others spoke Greek; the language of the Syrians was Arabic. These immigrants had started coming to the United States in the 1890's; more came in the early 1900's after the Young Turk revolution which imposed conscription on them but really gave them little opportunity to become an integral part of the new state. They were not Moslems; de facto they were doomed to play a lesser role in the new Turkey. Rumania had always abused its Jews; the Greeks were more sympathetic. Dislocations in the Ottoman Empire, political and economic, Balkan wars, and worsening conditions drove many of these men and women to the United States. They were poor, downtrodden; they were looking for opportunities for real freedom.

Where did these Jews from the Ottoman lands settle? There were a few in almost every major American city but unlike the Russians and Poles there was no pattern to their settlements. Some of the urban colonies they established were due purely to fortuitous circumstances; thus some made their homes in relatively obscure towns. One Ladino would come to a city and others would follow; he was the core around which they agglomerated. One of the towns in which a few early Sephardim chanced was Seattle (1903); in the course of years they grew to become a substantial colony. It was not long before they had several different congregations which may well have started as mutual-aid associations. In the course of time each congregation had its schools, social clubs, and charities. Like the East Europeans these newcomers divided according to geographical provenance and like Jews from the Slavic lands they did not suppress their mutual acerbities. Settlements were established by them in San Francisco, Portland, Oregon, Seattle, Indianapolis, Cincinnati, Philadelphia, Washington, D. C., and the Jersey resort coast; Montgomery, Alabama, had a substantial community whose members spread to other towns; a few migrated west to Los Angeles. Some, it seemed went to Atlanta and to Birmingham. New Orleans, too, had a Sephardic congregation; a number of its young men served in World War I. It was an Americanizing experience; army chow, mess hall banter, and close order drill have an alchemy all their own.[7]

For obvious reasons New York and Brooklyn sheltered the largest Jewish Levantine colonies; New York was the country's largest port of entry. The newcomers began to make their presence felt there in the early twentieth century; they had a little ghetto enclave of their own on two streets of the Lower East Side and, like their neighbors, the Ashkenazim, they, too, succeeded after a time in moving on to Harlem, the Bronx, and different sections of Brooklyn. They were sufficiently numerous to preserve their regional integrity; thus they remained loyal to their respective Ladino, Greek, and Arabic heritages. They were however not the first Syrians here; Christian Syrians, peddlers, had preceded them. By 1925 there were about 25,000 of these Jewish Levantines in the country; in the New York and Brooklyn of 1940 they had 10 synagogs, 14 burial societies, and numerous social and charitative organizations. Their social life was distinctly Near Eastern; they had their own coffee houses and their pool rooms where they played cards. Each of these several groups had its own liturgy, folk songs, synagogal chaunts, and customs. The Ladinos were fond of the theatre. In 1914 the Seattle colony put on a Molière comedy in Ladino; more typical was a play on the condemnation and vindication of Captain Alfred Dreyfus. Anti-Semitism was a torment which they had all experienced. It is not surprising that they staged a play on the theme of Joseph and his brethren. For centuries Ashkenazim had dealt with this fascinating story of the sorry betrayal of a brother and his rise to power in a Pharaonic empire.

Like their earlier Yiddish-speaking and reading neighbors in the New York-Brooklyn area they, too, had their press. By 1925 they had published at least eight Ladino periodicals; one was socialist. The Greeks and the Arabic-speaking Syrians never had a paper of their own; the Ladino press could serve those only who spoke the Spanish-Portuguese vernacular. *La America* was published by Moise S. Gadol who set out to unite his readers for social and cultural purposes; it was an uphill battle at best. The centuries old Moslem blight made it very difficult for these refugees to pull themselves up by their own bootstraps, to work cooperatively for common cultural goals. Like many immigrants who had not been exposed to Western culture these "Orientals" were religiously devout, observant; they avoided the Ashkenazim; intermarriage with the "Russians" was rare.

Poor though many of the Russians and Poles were they looked down upon these humble strangers from the Eastern Mediterranean. Intra-Jewish prejudice was a luxury which all Jews could afford. There was no occupation too humble for these new immigrants. Montgomery's Levantines made a living selling ice cream, fruits, soft drinks, and tobacco. One of them had a restaurant. In a way this facet of economic activity was typical of the first generation of Sephardic émigrés; they were often in peripheral occupations. In the different towns where they had found a home for themselves they were peddlers, lace and embroidery purveyors; they sold flowers, post cards, rugs; some worked in factories, a few had small shops. There were Greek-speaking Jews in New York who were modest manufacturers of kimonas and aprons; the poorest among them were bootblacks; others were washroom attendants. Some worked in cigarette factories. Before 1920 there were a few, but very few, who were affluent. Exceptional was a Seattle real estate speculator who made millions. Another Levantine who was distinguished for his wealth and philanthropy was the cigarette manufacturer Morris Schinasi who died leaving substantial legacies to Jewish and Christian welfare institutions. He had emigrated from Magnesia in Asia Minor in 1893.

Unlike the Russians and Poles and Galicians who had frequented talmudic academies these aliens were no devotees of rabbinic studies; the western arts and sciences attracted but few. Centuries of oppression had left them culturally deprived. The Americanization process among them was slow, slower than among the Jews from the Slavic lands for they evinced a fierce loyalty to their old way of life. They were more tenacious than the Ashkenazim in holding on to their household gods. They had no intention of allowing the Russians, or the Americans either, to overwhelm them. The Sephardim of Shearith Israel of New York with their tricentennial American traditions could not refrain from patronizing the newcomers. The dear ladies of this Central Park West congregation told the struggling Levantines to teach their daughters to play the piano; they urged these humble hewers of wood and drawers of water to jettison their Iberian patois and to speak a pure Castilian. These well-meant admonitions are reminiscent of the suggestions of the acculturated Germans who constantly urged the Yidn of the Lower East Side to forget their Yiddish and to speed up their Americanization. A generation later Cincinnati's native Jews—many of East European ancestry—were unhappy with the German exiles from Nazi Germany who read German newspapers publicly in the town's street cars. New York's Uptown Sephardim were truly eager to help the East Side Levantines. To effect their purpose they set up a settlement house Downtown and encouraged the immigrants to organize clubs for themselves and their children. If the Sephardic elite was on occasion impatient with these "Orientals" it would have been well had it borne in mind that Aaron Cardozo, the first of this family in eighteenth-century British America, was a humble tailor. It took generations, well over a century, to produce a Benjamin Nathan Cardozo who graced the United States Supreme Court.

The first generation Levantines could to a large degree manage their own lives; they were not able in many instances to determine the mindset of their sons and daughters; native-born children began moving up the economic ladder slowly; the public schools opened new vistas to them. In the meantime the sharp distinctions which separated the different Levantine subgroups began to fade; they came closer to one another, closer later to the larger American Jewish community, closer to the common American way of life. By the 1920's the second and third generation Mediterraneans were marrying Ashkenazim; their children were American Jews in the full sense of the term. Not untypical of an American Jewish Levantine family is Richard Ben-Veniste, chief of the Official Corruption Section of the Department of Justice in Washington in 1972. His father was a Levantine; his mother was of German and Russian background.

In all probability the most distinguished, the most innovative Levantine on these shores was a man who worked independently of his fellow-immigrants. His interests were anything but parochial; in his grand designs he embraced all Jews here and their oppressed brethren abroad. This was Nissim Abraham Behar (1848-1931). The Behar clan was originally domiciled in Rumania; Nissim, who was born in Jerusalem, studied in Paris in the 1860's and taught in Syria, Turkey, Bulgaria, and Jerusalem. In both Constantinople and Jerusalem he pioneered in the instruction of modern Hebrew which he taught as a living language, Hebrew through Hebrew (ivrit be-ivrit). Through a Jerusalem trade school where he worked for years he influenced others like Eliezer Ben Yehuda, a lexicographer, who was one of the founders of modern spoken and literary Hebrew. Behar hoped that Hebrew would become the language of all the Jews in Palestine; it could well serve as the cement to unite the disparate hostile Sephardim and Ashkenazim. The bold Behar made enemies among obscurantist religionists in the Holy Land. At the age of fifty-three, in 1901, he came to the United States with the blessing of the Alliance Israélite Universelle; he came to New York to begin a new life, a second career.

Behar worked in the field of immigration. He sought the abrogation of the Russian-American treaty of 1832 which was honored in the breach by the Russians who refused to respect the American passport when presented by a Jew. He became an apostle of Americanization; he set out to organize all Jews politically to fight anti-immigration bills and to further the human rights of all Jews everywhere, but he accomplished little; he was decades ahead of his time. His vigorous propaganda was resented by the Jewish establishment; this newcomer had no right to assume a leadership role; he was an interloper. Here in the United States, as in the Ottoman Empire, Behar worked to further modern Hebrew; he helped establish the Histadruth Ivrith of America, a national Hebrew language and culture association (1916-1917), and it is by no means improbable that he influenced Dr. Samson Benderly—a fellow Palestinian—who, as the director of New York's Bureau of Jewish Education, insisted on teaching Hebrew through Hebrew. Behar was both a Zionist and a cosmopolitan, a political liberal, a civil rights activist, and an Americanizer.[8]

VARIOUS SELF-HELP AGENCIES

Since earliest days immigrants to North America have surrounded themselves with self-help institutions to make life more endurable, to round out the community which they had planted. The East Europeans, it is obvious, were no exception. After these aliens came here from Russia, Austria-Hungary, and Rumania they found many societies and institutions that had been established by earlier Jewish settlers. These Jews from the Eastern lands were not innovative in the sense that they conjured up new and different organizations; they built on what they found here. The "Germans" had already made provision for the quick and the dead; for day nurseries, child care, correctional institutions, hospitals, for a wide variety of welfare needs. The Slavic newcomers were resolved to see to their own needs; they duplicated many of the Jewish agencies that had already been created. They resolved to emancipate themselves from the old-timers and to a great degree they succeeded in this effort; the preponderant majority of these foreigners never had recourse to any charity. The East Europeans reached out in all directions to build a world of their own. In 1890 they fashioned the Russian-American Hebrew Association. It met at the Educational Alliance and was led by the Rev. Dr. Adolph Radin, a native Pole. Members paid no dues; everybody was welcome. The goals were education, Americanization. One suspects that the ultimate patronage here was elitist: the adjective "Hebrew" as a substitute for Jewish points to an apologetic source and motivation. Later the unions, the Jewish socialists, the Forward Association sponsored a Naturalization Aid League to help immigrants acquire citizenship.

To avoid the costly procedure of resorting to the courts the Yiddish-speaking émigrés of New York set up a bet din of sorts, a voluntary court of arbitration; a rabbi, an attorney, and a businessman constituted a judicial body of three. Actually most cases brought in were settled by a staff member before resort was had to a trial by the panel of judges. Thousands of cases were presented and adjudicated. There were similar voluntary courts of arbitration in other towns. In 1916 a group of academicians, all observant Orthodox Jews, set up a national society which it called the Jewish Academicians of America. These pious men wanted to harmonize tradition and the new sciences; they knew that Orthodoxy would have to come to terms with the challenge of the natural and social sciences; they were cultured scholarly men who believed in the ultimate validity of the sciences and disciplines which they had studied and taught. They wanted to resolve their ritual problems, to remain loyal to the ancient Jewish Law, yet live and think in conformity with the mandates of science. Bernard Revel of the Orthodox theological school was president. Nathan Isaacs, lawyer and college lecturer, was a member, as was the Jewish literary historian, Meyer Waxman, the American-born Orthodox rabbi Bernard Drachman, and David I. Macht, the Johns Hopkins pharmacologist. Macht believed that the Jewish dietary laws could be justified scientifically. These men knew that this confrontation between Orthodoxy and modernism—science—had to be resolved if Orthodoxy was to survive. In a way this modest group of some twenty-four members set out to inaugurate an Orthodox counterreformation based on modernism.[9]

Not long after the immigrants began arriving in New York in numbers in the 1880's they opened a hospice. It was established by the Hachnosas Orchim Society, Travelers' Aid. It was to serve as a temporary shelter for the newly arrived who had no one to offer them hospitality. Like its counterpart in Europe, the *hekdesh* (the Sanctified Place), it also gave shelter to older folks. The English name of this East Side institution was the Hebrew Sheltering House. A Jewish wanderer might well turn to the local hospice not only for lodging and food but also for help in locating a job, an address of a relative, some sound advice. No later than 1890 Philadelphia, too, had a Wayfarers' Lodge which not only offered a night's lodging to the newcomer but also functioned as a relief society dispensing food and clothing to the poor. In a two-year period it served over 10,000 meals to the needy; it housed eighty to a hundred people in a single day. Its support came from 600 dues-paying members.

All major American Jewish communities had a hospice or a room that served in lieu of one. Among the clients were tramps, hoboes, deserting husbands, and the ubiquitous collectors for Palestine's talmudic academies. After the turn of the century, as the Jews began moving out to secondary areas of settlement, the hospice followed; there could be no Jewish quarter without one.[10]

FREE LOANS

Free loan societies were patronized by thousands. Their names varied; at times they carried the traditional phrase Bestowing Love (gemilut hasadim). Like most other institutions support came from dues-paying members. These free loan associations were very important for the struggling immigrants because credit was frequently denied them at the banks. They had no collateral; if they could not secure cosigners they had to turn to relief societies which occasionally advanced them funds. Peddlers, hucksters, and shopkeepers often needed small loans to tide them over. A man might borrow to finance a wedding, to start a small business, to bury a dear one, to buy clothing for the High Holy Days, to pay taxes, a medical bill, a lawyer's fee, the price of a ship ticket. Artisans, students, married women, people without jobs were frequently among the borrowers. Long before the East European immigrant masses made their appearance, German Jewish free loan societies had been established. Congregations also lent their surplus monies to members but they usually charged interest. New York's immigrant loan society started with a capital of less than $100; 227 loans were made the first year; about $1,200 all told was parceled out. In later decades this free loan group lent to thousands, even to Gentiles. In the late twentieth century Cleveland's free loan institution found that about one-third of all its clients were non-Jews, mostly blacks. In the early days the amounts lent by a free loan society often might not be more than $5; that was a respectable sum in the early twentieth century, a week's salary for a girl in the garment industry. Before 1921 the New York society was to have several branches; one was Downtown; others were in Harlem, the Bronx, and Brownsville in Brooklyn. By that time there were twelve Jewish free loan institutions in New York.

Women, too, had the need to borrow. To take care of them, particularly where confidentiality was imperative, women created their own loan organizations. In the typical immigrant home women had no access to the family's funds; the husband controlled all expenditures. A woman, however, might well want to send a few dollars to her family back in Europe without telling her spouse; a daughter might need a new coat; Passover foods had to be purchased. There was a well-run woman's loan society in Chicago which may have been established as early as the 1890's. Women alone ran it in a very businesslike fashion. By the 1920's this organization had made 10,000 loans aggregating about $400,000. As their names indicated, the free loan societies charged no interest while credit unions usually lent funds at 6 percent. In the early decade of the twentieth century there were ten Jewish credit unions in New York City; like the free loan societies they were found in many large towns; Milwaukee boasted of many such institutions. Socialists—and Milwaukee was a socialist town—favored cooperative enterprises. The Los Angeles Free Loan Association was established in the early 1900's. By September, 1972, it had lent $30,000,000 to 60,000 borrowers. Because of the system of no loans without responsible cosigners the losses in most free loan societies were minimal.[11]

HOSPITALS

The immigrants who congregated in big city ghettos were often compelled to endure bad housing; light, ventilation, sanitation often left much to be desired. The sweatshops were unhealthy, people worked hard for long hours; illness was frequent; consequently dispensaries, hospitals, were important. Fighting for a healthy place in which to work was one of the prime goals of the apparel unions. Immigrants threatened with sickness, tuberculosis, wanted good sick care, institutions which they could supervise, a place where they were welcome. Mount Sinai in New York was a good hospital but it was the domain of the Jewish elite, the older settlers; there was no kosher kitchen and the authorities were in no hurry to coopt the services of Yiddish-speaking physicians and surgeons from the "East." The public hospitals would admit no patient unless he had lived in the city for a year. The proud East Europeans wanted their own medical institutions. That required money. The *Jewish Encyclopedia* reports in 1905 that some of the immigrants were affluent. As early as 1889 New York's ghetto denizens had established a modest dispensary; by the early 1890's it had become a hospital, Beth Israel; by 1902 this institution had more than 100 beds and serviced about 900 patients a year. Beth Israel, kosher to be sure, began to grow. In 1916 its dispensary took care of over 75,000 people and issued over 70,000 prescriptions; convalescent care was provided for 2,500 patients. Much of the success of this hospital in its early days may be ascribed to the vigorous leadership of the cloak and suit manufacturer, Joseph H. Cohen, who served as president of the board. Cohen, an immigrant, came to the United States as a boy of ten. He was interested not only in the hospital but also in Hebrew education and worked closely with the local Talmud Torah. Lay leaders in the Jewish hospitals built by East Europeans were not secularists; they were Orthodox religionists. By 1920 the new immigrants had established a number of hospitals, dispensaries, lying-in institutions, and convalescent homes in all sections of the metropolis. Many of these hospitals had female auxiliaries.

The Brownsville and East New York Hospital in Brooklyn was one of the numerous health care institutions established by the newcomers. It was called into being in that section of Brooklyn in 1910. One of the founders harangued his fellow Jews from the back of a wagon lit by a gaslight reflector as he implored passersby to establish a kosher hospital. Dues were 5¢ a week. A constitution published in 1918 was printed in English and Yiddish. Gentiles, too, were admitted. Annual dues were graduated from $2.50 to $10; members received preference in admission; the more one paid the more privileges one was accorded. In the course of time there was a hospital, a dispensary, a school for nurses, and the usual female auxiliary. In the matter of good works men could not dispense without the aid of women; no major charitative task was undertaken without them. What was true of the New York area was true of almost every major town in the country; hospitals were founded by émigrés from Eastern Europe. In some instances women were the prime initiators. The new Baltimoreans made their presence felt in 1908 through the generosity of Jacob Epstein of the Baltimore Bargain House. This millionaire was the most generous donor to the Jewish Home for Consumptives erected on a seventy-acre farm. The cuisine was kosher. Yet here, too, most of the money for this hospital came from the earlier settlers. Nurses visited tuberculars in their homes. In Providence, Rhode Island, in 1903, Mrs. Mary Grant and her friends established the Miriam Society, a women's mutual benefit organization. Sociality was envisaged but their hope was to provide for sick Jews admitted to the general hospitals. They raised money to pay for the care of indigent patients in those institutions. Mary Grant ran a millinery shop and between customers cooked chickens in the back of the shop. This food, kosher, was dispatched to the hospitals for Jews without means. Out of this benefit society came the Miriam Hospital of Providence, Rhode Island.[12]

HOMES FOR THE AGED

These new Jewish settlers were very determined to build homes for their aged. Helpless old people moved them to compassion. They were often concerned about their own future; they knew too well that some children could not or would not take care of aged and helpless parents. The immigrants were frightened; for them an old-folks home was an imperative need. In 1897—almost two decades after the refugees started coming in substantial numbers from the Eastern lands—a group of women established the Home of the Daughters of Jacob. It was founded largely through the exertions of Russian-born Mrs. Bertha Devorsky who had come to New York at the age of eight. She collected and housed 32 old needy people; by 1918 there were 204 in a home on East Broadway; later it was moved to the Bronx. Chronic invalids were admitted; husband and wife were taken in and given a room of their own. In the early days the per capita cost of providing for a patient was fifty-six cents a day. With the dawn of the twentieth century came similar homes in Manhattan and some of the other boroughs. Ultimately, during this period, there were about eight such institutions. New York City had hundreds of thousands of Jews! Every section in town wanted a home of its own. The money to build many of them and support them was raised by women; the bazaar was a favorite device to secure funds. But even in those early years of the twentieth century social workers were already pointing out that old-age pensions and social legislation would obviate the need for such homes. Government subsidized pensions for the aged and social security grants would come later through state and federal legislation, but it would take decades.[13]

BURIALS

Practically all Jewish charitative agencies in every Jewish community were concerned if only remotely with proper burial, a Jewish burial. Ever since colonial times every effort was made to establish cemeteries and provide for decent interment. A handful of Jews landed in New Amsterdam in 1654; after a little more than a year they received or bought ground for an Eternal Home, Bet Olam, as the Jews call their last resting place. It was a problem, and an expensive one, to bury deceased paupers; some of New York's congregations in the nineteenth century attempted to evade their responsibility. The East European landsmanshaften and other mutual-aid societies considered burial and the payment of funeral expenses one of their basic benefits. Not infrequently the name which burial associations adopted was the Hebrew Hesed Shel Emet, True Love; interring the dead is the truest form of love, for the dead cannot repay this act of kindness. New York's new immigrants established free-burial societies as early as the 1880's; here, too, the women organized as auxiliaries to help in this pious task. By 1901—it was almost a generation later—the Russians and Poles felt it was no longer necessary to turn to the prestigious United Hebrew Charities for help in burying the impoverished. The newcomers, now well organized, could take care of their own. By 1917 there were at least five free-burial societies in Manhattan and Brooklyn. It is curious but there was a free-burial society in Harlem led by a woman, a native of Russia.[14]

NURSERIES, KINDERGARTENS, ORPHANS

There was, it would seem, no section of Greater New York which did not have nurseries and kindergartens which the "Russians" had established to mind their little ones. Day nurseries, which took care of infants while the mothers went to work, sprang up in the early twentieth century. Some of these institutions were willing to admit children up to the age of eight and even to teach them some Hebrew; mothers' meetings, too, were occasionally held in the nurseries. Supporting societies which included men and women taxed their members twenty-five cents a month. One auxiliary organization made its business the buying of shoes and clothing for the tots. Orphan asylums were designed to house older infants and youngsters. By 1920 congregate care of infants was deemed inadequate. Some of the little ones were placed in nurseries by the agencies; others were farmed out to foster parents, in most cases to Gentiles. All this in Greater New York. There was a Federation of Bessarabian Societies, a Rumanian verband, which set up its own orphan asylum, eager to take its youngsters out of Christian homes. Chicago's orphan asylum had been founded with the aid of a modest bequest by an immigrant who had made some money in the scrap metal business. This was the Marks Nathan Jewish Home. After it was established a man by the name of Morris Katz set up a trust fund of $100,000 to educate children who evinced an aptitude for learning. There was an orphans' home in almost every major American Jewish community.[15]

HIAS

An important New York organization that was to assume national and international proportions was the Hebrew Sheltering and Immigrant Aid Society (HIAS). American Jewry was worrying about its incoming immigrants as early as the 1760's; Jewish Philadelphia, Mikveh Israel, had an immigrants' aid association in the early 1780's, this was American Jewry's first documented welfare society. New York's Jewish communal leaders did what they could to help impoverished immigrants, Germans, in the late 1830's. The Board of Delegates of American Israelites, an early congregational union, was interested in the immigrants arriving in the 1860's; many of them were East Europeans. American Israelites were represented in international conferences held in Europe since the 1870's to regulate the flight of immigrants from lands where they were persecuted. Organizations involved in the welfare of incoming Jews were controlled in the mid-nineteenth century by natives or acculturated Germans. However, it was the East European Jacob Judelsohn who organized the Association of Jewish Immigrants. With or without his consent the Jewish establishment took over and stationed an agent at the Pennsylvania port who did good work taking care of the thousands of Russians, Poles, and Rumanians who began to debark. It was in Philadelphia, too, that the Jewish Alliance of America was organized. It started out with a bang and soon had over thirty branches in this country. It seems to have done little if anything. Nevertheless it is obvious that American Jewry faced with the arrival of large numbers of alien Jews was trying to organize itself and attack the problem as a national one in order to cope with it properly. Actually American Jewry was never to establish one organization that would do the job of acculturating the masses from Rumania and the Slavic lands.

Most Jewish immigrants coming here since the 1880's landed at the port of New York. Various ad hoc agencies tried to help them, to Americanize them, and to absorb them. The Baron de Hirsch Fund of the early 1890's supplied most of the necessary funds; it worked also through the Jewish Agricultural and Industrial Aid Society and the Industrial Removal Office. The National Council of Jewish Women also did what it could by stationing a woman at New York's port of arrival. All these agencies were part of the Jewish establishment; they were working from the top down. The Russians wanted to help themselves; they could do little; they were poor; thus there were no organizational successes by them till the early twentieth century. The HIAS was to cope with this problem successfully in the early 1900's. The newcomers incorporated themselves as the Hebrew Immigrant Aid Society in 1905. (The name was a modification of the elitist Hebrew Emigrant Aid Society of the early 1880's.) In 1909 the HIAS took over the New York hospice, the Sheltering House, which served as a *Nachtasyl*, a temporary shelter for immigrants who had no place to go. The new organization thereupon took the full name, the Hebrew Sheltering and Immigrant Aid Society.

This type of organization is in nowise unique in American history. Different ethnics had their own immigrant societies in the nineteenth century. The old established Jews were never unmindful of their ties to the new arrivals. Thus it was that when the HIAS started it had the moral and financial support of the United Hebrew Charities and of such men as Schiff, Marshall, and Straus. These leaders were on the board and the constitution might well have been written by the "Germans" since it reflected their thinking. The immigrants were to go to the backcountry, to the soil; they were to become good Americans! The HIAS maintained a low profile to avoid antagonizing the port authorities some of whom were not sympathetic. The anti-immigration forces, especially in Congress, must not be provoked. The new society, however, was determined to stop the port officials from deporting Jews unless there was no recourse. "They want to send me back to Kletsk. For God's sake! Help!" This was the plea of a desperate man writing from Ellis Island. Success for the HIAS was slow in coming. When the *Jewish Encyclopedia* was finished in 1906 there was very little recognition of this immigrant aid group which had already been doing some work. HIAS cooperated with the organized charities of large cities to find homes in the backcountry for the newly arrived. It was the consensus that it was easier to survive and get ahead outside of New York; this was probably true.

As the years passed HIAS grew stronger, more autonomous, and reached out to do many things. In order to help immigrants it established branches, offices in Seattle, San Francisco, Boston, Philadelphia. This expansion came during the World War I period; newcomers were given advice, relatives were located; lodging was provided in Father Abraham's Hotel, the Sheltering House (in Jewish tradition the patriarch Abraham was noted for his hospitality). Newcomers were helped to find a job and urged to take out their first papers. After the war the HIAS searched in the European channels for relatives of Americans; funds were dispatched across the seas, families were brought over and reunited. HIAS had become an important international immigration agency. German and Austrian Jewish soldiers imprisoned in Siberia were rescued; exercising the quality of mercy it even succored the Russian Christian family of A. S. Suvorin, the publisher of the reactionary, anti-Semitic, *Novoye Vremya, New Time*, under the czars. From 1909 to 1919 HIAS helped about 500,000 refugees in many lands. Later, in the 1930's, as the Germans began persecuting and destroying Jews it rallied to do what it could before the Holocaust took its toll of millions.[16]

CHAPTER SEVEN

MAKING A LIVING

PART I: THE GARMENT INDUSTRY

INTRODUCTION

WHY JEWS WENT INTO THE APPAREL INDUSTRY

The economic life of the East European Jews in the New York area was important; a substantial percentage of the country's Israelites lived in this city; by the 1890's the majority of its Jewish inhabitants had come from Slavic lands and Rumania. The city was an industrial center, well-calculated to absorb newcomers who were willing to work. The new Jews had to make a living. Because of fortuitous circumstances they turned to the apparel industry making men's and women's and children's clothing, cloaks, shirtwaists, skirts, wrappers, underwear, men's shirts, hats, and caps. They had little or no capital to engage in commerce. The clothing industry in all its branches was prospering in the 1880's when the newcomers began to arrive. America had to be clothed. Many of the Jewish immigrants had been tailors back home; the unskilled could learn in a hurry to become operatives in the needle industry, for all they had to do was to master one phase of the manufacturing process. These are not custom tailors, master workmen, qualified to make an entire garment. Among those who became "Columbus tailors"—who learned the trade here—were young girls, teenagers. It was a day when 20 percent of all American women were gainfully employed. Because these men and women flocked to the needle trades it became a Jewish industry. Yiddish was spoken, many of the bosses were Russian Jews; some shops were even closed on the Sabbath, others allowed the laborers time out to say their prayers. The work was hard, very hard, but the shops were places where Jews could be Jews.[1]

THE NEEDLE INDUSTRY: BACKGROUND BEFORE 1881

In no sense did these newly arrived Jews create the needle industry; its roots reach back into the eighteenth century. Aaron Lopez, the merchant-shipper, was a garment manufacturer in a modest fashion in the last quarter of the eighteenth century; Hayman Levy engaged in the making of apparel during the Revolutionary War producing garments for the armed forces. America's ready-made clothing industry developed noticeably in the second quarter of the nineteenth century; German Jews began to play a part in the new needle trades industry in the 1850's; as far as it is now known they were not pioneers; they had little capital and were just beginning their rise into the middle class. Strikes and unions were not uncommon even in that decade; Jews, very probably German immigrants, participated in tailors' strikes in the 1850's and 1860's; among the leaders organizing the cigarmakers in the 1870's were Adolph Strasser and Samuel Gompers. Strasser, indeed, was the president of the International Cigarmakers Union. Among the workmen who sought to improve their lot were both German and Polish Jews. Jews—again probably Germans—had organized a laborers' association in 1873; there was a capmakers strike at this time when the men went out seeking better pay and a ten-hour day. They knew that many employees of the federal government were already on an eight-hour day.

Unions now began to come into their own. For decades strikes had been forbidden by the courts and the common law; trade unions were deemed combinations in restraint of trade. This basic ruling had been made in 1806 in the notable Cordwainers' Case, Judge Moses Levy presiding. Through most of the nineteenth century, workers—men and women—were exploited. Jewish manual laborers, both Central Europeans and East Europeans, too, suffered along with the others who fought to improve their lot. The mid-nineteenth century Jewish establishment had little if any sympathy for strikers whoever they were. Rebecca Gratz, the country's most eminent antebellum Jewish woman, had no understanding of the motives that impelled the workingmen to fight for more pay and fewer hours (1837). In the late 1860's New York's *Jewish Messenger* deplored the fact that unions would put capitalism at the mercy of labor; the paper wrote that the demand for an eight-hour day was "outrageous and unjustifiable . . . sixteen hours daily upon an ignorant man's hands! It is a deliberate wrong," a "dangerous waste of time." Yet it is to be noted that when the capmakers went on strike in 1874, they set up their headquarters in Covenant Hall, the home of New York's B'nai B'rith.[2]

EAST EUROPEAN JEWS IN THE NEEDLE TRADES IN NEW YORK CITY IN THE 1870's AND 1880's

Though immigrants from the Slavic lands had turned to the needle trades in the 1870's it was not to be the chief source of livelihood of these proletarians until the 1880's. Now the employers—Germans first, later Russians—and the workers were most often Jews. New York was but one of a series of garment centers though it was by far the largest. There were Jewish owners, workers, and operatives in Boston, Philadelphia, Baltimore, Syracuse, Rochester, Buffalo, Cleveland, Cincinnati, and Chicago. It was unfortunate for these newcomers that they had come to America at a bad time. The farmers, unhappy, were espousing populism; they wanted radical reforms. In 1886 someone—workers?—had thrown a bomb into the ranks of the police in Haymarket Square, Chicago; seven were killed, seventy were wounded. The national sentiment against labor was bitter, vindictive. Bad working conditions in the garment industry in the 1880's induced Jews to organize unions and go out on strike in order to better themselves; the struggle thus begun was to continue for a long generation.

Jews felt the need to set up their own locals; they were not welcome in older established unions; they were Jews, foreigners. In turn, the Jews wanted their own organizations where they would be accepted and permitted to speak Yiddish, their mother tongue. In those unhappy decades, the Jewish workers went out on strike frequently; employers, at times, resorted to lockouts; there was violence on both sides; the politicians were unfriendly; the police were often brutal; the public hostile. Yet in 1887 when there was a bad strike in Pittsburgh, the two congregations Rodeph Shalom and the Tree of Life—both thoroughly bourgeois—opened soup kitchens to feed the hungry. It is said that they were the only churches in town to do so. The Jewish newcomers were good strikers but poor unionists in those early days; once a strike was won they saw no need to support a union by paying dues; it would take years before they would learn that a strong union was the only instrumentality that could preserve gains and successfully confront employers' associations. Confusion in the Jewish workers' ranks was compounded by factionalism among the leaders. Political ideology was sacrosanct; socialists fought socialists; both together frowned on anarchism; the workers of Orthodox provenance were nonpolitical in the main. There would be no strong unions till the second decade of the new century.[3]

WORKING CONDITIONS: THE SWEATSHOPS

The statement has been made above that working conditions in the garment industry in the late nineteenth century were bad. This is a bland remark. What does it mean? Conditions were then bad for most laborers in the United States. Wages were low; the hours were long; sanitary conditions in the small factories and slum workshops were unsatisfactory. Light was poor; there was heat, overcrowding, dirt. People worked in basements, in attics; disease and tuberculosis threatened the men, women, and children who labored. Unhealthy surroundings were almost traditional in industry, both in England and in the United States. Children were exploited; in 1791 Alexander Hamilton recommended that children "of tender years" be employed. The ambience in the American textile factories of the early nineteenth century was notorious. In the 1830's women worked in the Connecticut factories for thirty-five cents a day; children received twenty-one cents and worked twelve long hours; in Pennsylvania youngsters were putting in thirteen to fourteen hours a day. Some girls worked twelve to fourteen hours a day and received but $1 a week and their board. Rachel Mordecai of Wilmington, North Carolina, writing to her friend Maria Edgeworth, maintained defensively that slaves in the South lived better than Irish poor in their native land. The sweatshop is not a Lower East Side innovation; it is rooted in American working conditions going back for almost a century. Child labor was to continue; in 1900 it is said that there were 2,000,000 children at work in the United States. In 1907 there were still 60,000 youngsters laboring in New York's tenement workshops.

Poverty was endemic in this country in the late nineteenth century, exacerbated by recurring depressions and chronic unemployment. Evictions of the poor were common; in the years 1891-1892 more than 11,000 dispossess notices were issued in New York's ghetto. In some factories work was doled out to contractors; they in turn harnessed subcontractors; contractors and subcontractors bidding against each other lowered wages; the immigrants pouring in, desperate for jobs, were not in a position to bargain, nor were the contractors who underbid one another. In 1883 women working at tailoring could make seventy cents in a twelve-hour day; in 1913 a girl making bows would take home ten dollars a week but her quota was 1,690; this was grueling labor. Though sweatshops declined in number in the early twentieth century they were never totally eliminated; there are some even today in our big city ghettos. As late as 1920 the sixty to seventy-hour week with low pay was not uncommon; laborers in the steel mills were putting in an eighty-four-hour week. The Jewish immigrants were not the only ones who slaved hard; most Americans lived close to the poverty level. Bad as it was, the pay in the garment industry was certainly as good as that received by many natives in the country's factories. In season, skilled Jewish garment workers made good money. One thing is certain; most Jewish immigrants were better off than they had been in the hamlets and towns of their native lands.[4]

UNITED HEBREW TRADES

Conditions may have been better for the workers here; this they seldom mentioned but they were determined to improve on them. Their radical socialist leaders had convinced them that they were being egregiously exploited; to a large degree they were. The 1880's was a decade that saw the sweatshops in full bloom. Influenced by the Central Labor Union of New York, an umbrella type organization that had brought more than 200 city locals together, the socialist leaders of the Yiddish-speaking proletariat organized the United Hebrew Trades in 1888. Three years earlier a Jewish Workers Union had been founded to help make the single-taxer Henry George mayor of the city. This central union did not survive; the United Hebrew Trades did. The adjective "Hebrew" represents an apologetic English translation of the original which calls for a United Jewish Trades Association. The new Jewish overall union was as much political as it was economic; it was determined to change the present exploitive capitalist system and to replace it with a purely socialist one, universal in scope and reach, which would see that the laborer received a full reward for his work. There was to be no compromise with capitalism. The workers were to be educated, the eight-hour day was to become standard, the sweatshop, contract and child labor, were to be abolished. A child was defined as anyone under fourteen. The land and its profits belong to the people. This was the distilled doctrinaire socialism of the Socialist Labor Party; a new political and economic polity was to be brought to birth; "the world is our fatherland and socialism is our religion," said one devotee.

The United Hebrew Trades (UHT) began modestly; there were in those days very few Yiddish-speaking locals; it would be a generation before the Jewish trade unions would learn not only to fight but to organize on a permanent basis. The UHT could be no stronger than its affiliates; they did move forward. During the 1890's East European Jewish trade union centrals were organized in Philadelphia and Chicago. By 1906 the New York umbrella organization had coopted about 35 locals with about 21,000 members; 15,000 were East European Jews; the balance were non-Jews. With the rise of permanent and successful Jewish unions the UHT blossomed; by 1920 it had enlisted more than 100 locals with a total membership of about 250,000. Like all Jewish left-wing societies the socialist United Hebrew Trades came closer to World Jewry during World War I; it supported the Jewish overseas relief organizations and worked with the Hebrew Immigrant Aid Society. Despite its commitment to internationalism, to socialism, and rejection—at the top—of Judaism, it sought shelter within the perimeters of an ethnic Jewry. Among its leaders in the early days was Morris Hillquit (Moses (?) Hilkowitz) who was destined to become a leader in the Socialist Party in the first quarter of the twentieth century. In 1918 the president of the United Hebrew Trades was Reuben Guskin, a barber; the secretary—more important than the president—was Max Pine (1866-1928). In many respects Pine was a typical American Jewish labor leader. Like almost all others he was Russian born but did not come to the United States until he was twenty-four years of age. When he landed he went to work as a laborer; he became a tailor, a union organizer, a strike leader, a staff member of the *Forward*, a printer, and secretary of the United Hebrew Trades for many years. This socialist, beloved by his followers, identified himself with relief work in Russia, Poland, and the Soviet Union, but he also shared the aspirations of many that Palestine would one day be restored to the Jewish people and become a socialist state.[5]

JOSEPH BARONDESS

Among the Russian newcomers who worked closely with the United Hebrew Trades and supported its efforts to organize an umbrella organization of New York's Jewish locals was Joseph Barondess (1867-1928). There is an almost startling monotonelike similarity in the lives of the country's Jewish labor leaders. They were Russians; they received a traditional Hebrew and talmudic education; they came to this country as relatively young men, and they began life here as casual laborers till they became activists in the Jewish labor movement. Barondess fitted beautifully into this pattern. He was a peddler, a laborer in a sugar refinery, a painter, a farm hand, a sweatshop operative, even a night law school student, and finally a union organizer. Barondess, the leader of a cloakmakers' union, 1888-1892, led it in a successful strike and made the owners pay damages. They retaliated by suing him successfully for extortion, but he was exculpated by the district attorney and pardoned by the governor. Union organizers functioned in a rough and nasty milieu in the 1890's. In the course of the next decades Barondess helped found the International Ladies' Garment Workers' Union, ran for state assembly on the Socialist ticket, edited a trade union journal, and wrote for the *Forward*. He was one of the darlings of the East Side masses; he browbeat them with love and told them repeatedly that they would win if they were not such jackasses. He was not brilliant; he was a simple, kind man. When John Paley, one of the ghetto's most distinguished Yiddish journalists, committed suicide, his wife opened a restaurant to support the children. Barondess would come around and wait on trade to encourage his friends to patronize the place.

Unlike other labor notables he finally tired of being a union leader and turned to the insurance business though he always retained interest in the welfare of the working people. His popularity brought him political power; Mayor William Jay Gaynor put him on the Board of Education and he fought for the right of women to continue teaching in the schools after marriage. Like all Jewish leaders he, too, opposed restrictive immigration laws. Unlike many socialists, however, he joined the Zionists, raised money for the self-defense groups in Russia after the massacres, encouraged the Sons of Zion, furthered the Hebrew Immigrant Aid Society, and approved of the Kehillah Movement which set out to coordinate all major institutions and organizations on the Lower East Side. And like the Orthodox he, too, supported the Talmud Torahs, the afternoon Hebrew schools. He looked with favor upon the Jewish war relief committees and the American Jewish Congress. He had become a joiner—he was an insurance salesman; no Jewish cause was alien to him. Maybe this is the outstanding characteristic of every "good" American Jew. And the socialistic class struggle? It was no longer *actuel*. He loved Jews, all Jews, and wanted to help them. Edwin Smith King, journalist and poet, wrote a roman à clef about him when he was an embattled labor leader. The novel is called *Joseph Zalmonah* (1893).[6]

SAMUEL GOMPERS

When the United Hebrew Trades was fashioned it met with the approval of Samuel Gompers (1850-1924) who had just organized the American Federation of Labor and would one day become America's most influential labor leader. Gompers, London born, child of a humble Dutch-English cigarmaker, received an elementary education at the Jews' Free School from the age of six to ten. Impoverished, the family put him to work but even then he nourished hopes of improving himself by emigrating to the United States. Like others who dreamt of coming here he sang with fervor Russell's favorite song:

> To the West, to the West, to the land of the free . . .
> Where a man is a man, if he's willing to toil,
> And the humblest may gather the fruits of the soil.

Like his father he, too, became a cigarmaker, still only a teenager, and was already a competent journeyman when he accompanied his parents to the United States in 1863. At age fourteen, he joined the cigarmakers' union and because of his facility as a reader—he was an accomplished autodidact —he was called upon by the men in the shop to read to them as they rolled their cigars. There it was that he became familiar with the work of Engels, Marx, and Lasalle. It may well be that he read these socialist classics in the original German. Even if he did not join the Socialist Party of the 1860's it is hard to believe that he was unsympathetic to its doctrines. Gompers was to play an active and important part in his cigar union in the 1860's and 1870's; its battles, its strikes were the training ground which prepared the young trade unionist for leadership. He was a vice president of the Cigarmakers International Union in the 1880's and 1890's. As early as 1881 he had participated in the new Federation of Organized Trades; he was chairman of the committee on the constitution; five years later he helped establish the American Federation of Labor (AFL). With the exception of one year when his political skills failed him he was to remain president till his death in 1924.

Gompers helped serve as an accoucheur for the United Hebrew Trades just two years after he had brought to birth his American Federation of Labor. Thousands of Jews were pouring into this country; many of them would enter the labor market. Gompers felt it was imperative that they be encouraged in order to help achieve and maintain high standards for the workmen already here. He was wise enough to realize that the Jews would have to be incorporated into the labor movement in their own fashion. He set out to help them, not as a Jew, but as a labor statesman. Though many of the unions in the United Hebrew Trades were later affiliated with the AFL, Gompers differed radically with most leaders of Yiddish-speaking unions. He was no advocate of foreign language or ethnic unions and wary of involving unions in party politics; he was no friend of government sponsored social insurance largesse. Gompers wanted craft unionism, pure and simple; most Jewish union leaders favored industry-wide unions that would embrace also the unskilled and the semi-skilled. To keep wages high Gompers, a newcomer himself, pleaded for immigration restriction; he, too, announced his intention to maintain "racial purity and strength." No one could question his Americanism. This man was no "Jewish" labor leader; he had no interest in Judaism or any religion; he joined the Ethical Culture Society. Certainly he felt comfortable with these humanitarian sophisticates; many of them were Jews. It is also worthy of note that when Cyrus Adler and Henrietta Szold compiled their vignettes of notable American Jews in 1904, in volume six of the *American Jewish Yearbook*, they include Barondess—still a hot socialist —but not Gompers. Interesting!

Gompers survived without the approval of "official" Jewry. By 1900 he had become a vice president of the National Civic Federation, an association of labor leaders, industrialists, and financiers. The president of the American Federation of Labor was no enemy of capitalism; he was prepared to work with Marcus A. Hanna of the Civic Federation. This willingness of Gompers to cooperate with capitalists was to a large degree shared decades later by Sidney Hillman of the Amalgamated Clothing Workers of America. Most labor leaders have but one concern, that of advancing the welfare of their labor clients. Gompers was a devoted labor unionist. In order to keep the AFL strong and happy he tolerated no dual unions; thus Hillman's clothing workers were excluded from the AFL because of the regnant United Garment Workers; there could be but one union for each trade or industry. Gompers never wavered; he wanted higher wages, fewer hours of work, more advantages for his charges. He carefully steered his federation through the shoals of national politics; he was nonpartisan. He survived the hostility of Daniel DeLeon's Socialist Labor federation and avoided confrontations with Hillquit's socialists; thus he held his millions of followers together. After the passage of the Clayton Antitrust Act of 1914—unions are no monopolies—he had clear sailing. In World War I Gompers sat on the Advisory Commission to the Council of National Defense (1916). Three of the seven members were Jews. Few can question that Gompers did much to raise the standard of living of American workmen. He was a clever politician; he enjoyed power and he managed it judiciously. Like his colleagues who led the Jewish apparel unions he was determined to stay on top; by the time of his death his American Federation of Labor had 3,000,000 members.[7]

THE GARMENT WORKERS AT THE TURN OF THE CENTURY

Around the year 1900 the New York Jewish workforce was sui generis. About 60 percent—immigrants—were in the needle trades; 15 to 20 percent were in commerce; the percentage of those in trade in the hinterland was higher. The garment industry, highly diversified, was an empire including well over a dozen different trades. The number of newcomers who were manufacturers, factory owners, was relatively small. During the 1890's strikes in New York and the other garment centers were common; workers and their families suffered. The exploited operatives felt that they had no recourse but to walk out. In the next decade most would have been content with a sixty-hour week. As in other towns Jewish garment workers left their shops in order to improve themselves, to secure compliance with their demands. During a cloakmaker strike in Philadelphia in 1890 some of the rabbis in town were troubled; Jews were fighting Jews; for the poor Jews it was a matter of bread and butter. Rabbi Sabato Morais of Mikveh Israel did what he could to bring the parties together. He was in no sense a protagonist of the unions. His conservative congregation never would have sanctioned a pro-union stance by its minister. Morais, a humanitarian, pitied his fellow Jews who were undergoing severe privations. In the nineteenth century no strike was really won even when the owners capitulated to the demands of the laborers, for no strong permanent unions were built to keep the employers in line.

Some Jewish leaders of the garment workers attempted in 1890 to establish a nationwide Hebrew Federation of Labor to include all American Jewish trade unions; they accomplished nothing. Yet—perspective must be retained—bad as conditions were for Jews in the industry they were better off than the Irish, Italians, Negroes, and millions of American natives, too. Not all Jews in the needle trades were members of the various Jewish unions which rose only to fall and then to rise again. Many Jewish locals allied themselves with the United Garment Workers of America (UGW); they knew that their salvation lay in a strong disciplined organization. The UGW, an apparel union established in 1891, was nonsocialist and an integral part of the American Federation of Labor. Its leaders evinced little interest in the United Hebrew Trades and its officers, committed Marxists. During the crucial years from 1904 on, the president of the UGW was wary of the Jewish foreigners. Yet there were thousands of Jews in Jewish locals of this national union; several served on the executive board. One of the founders of the UGW was a Jew, a native Baltimorean, Henry (Harry) White (b. 1866) who was for a time the general secretary of this national organization. White, probably of Central European origin, began as a clothing cutter, rose to power in the Knights of Labor and the American Federation of Labor, and even became a member of the prestigious National Civic Federation. Like Gompers he belonged to Felix Adler's Ethical Culture "church."

Conditions for all workers in the United States improved somewhat in the Progressive Age of the new century, though America's conservative forces—in alliance with God himself—were still strong. Speaking for the anthracite mine owners in 1902, George F. Baer, president of the Philadelphia and Reading Coal and Iron Company said: "the rights and interests of the laboring man will be protected and cared for, not by the labor agitators, but by the Christian men to whom God in his infinite wisdom had given the control of the property interests of this country." With the dawn of the new century there came an amelioration of the harsh conditions under which the workers labored. The hours of work were reduced; Washington inaugurated a Department of Commerce and Labor (1903); the muckraking magazines, the liberal urban press, and all the Yiddish newspapers were sympathetic to the working classes. The Women's Trade Union League—which brought factory hands and middle-class women together—the churches which preached the social gospel, and even a few synagogs fought to improve conditions for manual laborers. Rabbi Stephen S. Wise in his Free Synagogue thundered every Sunday morning to large crowds against the inequities of the bosses. Reinforcements came to the aid of men and women in the needle trades; Bundists, better trained Jewish unionists, began arriving after the failure of the revolution in Russia (1905); these men were able, experienced. Jewish socialist groups, the Workmen's Circle, the United Hebrew Trades, the Socialist-Zionists always rallied around strikers as they pushed hard to advance their cause. Slowly the Jewish unions were gathering strength, the Jewish proletarians who had been here for more than two decades were making an effort to establish viable vigorous unions. Out of this push for effective durable protective labor organizations there came the International Ladies' Garment Workers' Union in 1900; the United Cloth Hat and Cap Makers of North America (1901) fell more than once till it took on new life finally in the days of Roosevelt's New Deal; the International Fur Workers' Union of the United States and Canada, a small group catering to a luxury clientele, was firmly established in 1913; the Amalgamated Clothing Workers of America, makers of men's garments, would come into being in 1914.[8]

NOTABLE STRIKES, 1909–1910

THE UPRISING OF THE TWENTY THOUSAND

In November 1909 about 20,000 shirtwaist makers—mostly young women—went on strike to better themselves. Many of them worked from 45 to 59 hours a week; with layoffs in the off season some did not average more than $5 a week. In the opinion of some historians this protest inaugurated the "golden age" of the union in the needle trades. The "golden age" is a rather sanguine approach: the unions now became stronger, improved their lot, but the setbacks were constant, at times almost disastrous. When the leaders at a public meeting in 1909 hesitated to push the shirtwaist operatives into a general strike with its attendant consequences—unemployment and hunger—a young girl Clara Lemlich made an impassioned appeal in Yiddish. She sparked the final decision to fight: "I am tired of listening to speakers who talk in general terms. What we are here for is to decide whether we shall or shall not strike. I offer a resolution that a general strike be declared now." Charles K. Harris, the Jewish songwriter, encouraged the girls as he published "Heaven Will Protect the Working Girl." They needed divine intervention; Magistrate Olmstead told the girls who were brought before him: "You are on strike against God and nature." Hundreds of pickets were arrested and fined.

Some gains were made; the small shops acceded to the demands of the workers; the larger shops, at the final settlement in February, 1910, still refused to recognize the unions. There were liberals who sympathized with the plight of the women; the Women's Trade Union League, the socialist parties, and the United Hebrew Trades did what they could to help and encourage the young strikers; the National Civic Federation under its conciliation committee chairman, Marcus M. Marks, labored hard to effect a compromise. Most of the people involved in the strike were Jews, the employers and a large number of the shirtwaist hands. Marks (b. 1858), a native American and a college graduate, was a retired clothing manufacturer who devoted himself to communal work. He was interested in the well-known Downtown settlement house, the Educational Alliance; he helped support a tuberculosis sanatorium that sought to aid children; he introduced daylight-saving time into this country, and served as borough president of Manhattan. The strike was successful in that it taught the Jewish proletarians the importance of an effective union; they had the satisfaction of knowing that they had fought hard, heroically; they could nurse the hope that a day would come when they would reach their goal.[9]

THE GREAT REVOLT OF THE CLOAKMAKERS

About four months after the shirtwaist makers went back to work the cloakmakers, about 55,000 strong, walked out in a general strike. This was the largest strike the city had ever seen; by this time the apparel industry was the largest in the city. Here, too, the fight was between Jews. On one side were the employers, organized into the Cloak, Suit, and Skirt Manufacturers' Protective Association. They were not ogres; they were fighting to salvage their gains in a highly competitive industry. On the other side were the workers who slaved hard to support their families. As in the shirtwaist strike there were important public groups, socialist associations, and humanitarians, who rallied to help the cloakmakers. The strikers fought valiantly; a Yiddish writer wrote that thousands of zeroes were becoming heroes. New York's Jewish leaders were apprehensive as Jew was arrayed against Jew. They believed in low visibility for Jews. The times were out of joint. This was an age of strong anti-immigrant sentiment in the country and in Congress; it was an age of increased nativism and racism. Many Jews worked earnestly to bring the two parties together. Meyer London, the Socialist labor lawyer, was devoted to his clients; Lillian Wald was concerned; Henry Moskowitz, the settlement worker, Rabbi Judah L. Magnes, and Meyer Bloomfield all wanted an equitable settlement. The counsel for the employers, the civic reformer Julius H. Cohen, was no ruthless rugged individualist.

No one labored harder than Rumanian-born Meyer Bloomfield, a social worker, to end the strike. He had worked his way through Harvard as a carpenter. It was he who probably brought in A. Lincoln Filene, a department store businessman with a strong social conscience. Filene in turn brought in the Boston corporation lawyer, Louis D. Brandeis; Louis Marshall was asked to step in and through their joint efforts—people of integrity and distinction—a compromise was reached. It pleased neither party; it was only a truce but historically an important one. It was called the Protocol of Peace, September 1910. Marshall wrote much of the text but this final agreement was hammered out by the numerous interested parties. Brandeis was not unfriendly to labor but he believed that employers had rights. A fifty-hour week was agreed upon, wages were raised, a minimum wage rate was established; ten legal holidays were granted the employees; outside contract work was prohibited (sweatshops), but the union was not permitted to dominate employment; it received a preferential status. Important because of the impact on American industry at large was the establishment of a series of committees that dealt with grievances and compulsory arbitration. The public was involved; the impartial chairman method of settling disputes was inaugurated. Important, too, was the joint board of sanitary control. After a few years the Protocol of Peace was scrapped; the workers wanted the right to strike and to improve themselves further; the employers did not want to be hamstrung by arbitration; they wanted to be the bosses in their businesses.[10]

It was obvious of course that the Revolt of the Cloakmakers would be supported by the socialist pro-union *Forward*. The general manager of the paper, under Cahan, was Benjamin Schlesinger (1876-1932). Schlesinger is important because he was typical of the men who supported the cloakmakers. This foreigner came to this country as a youngster and worked for years before he rose to power. He peddled matches in the streets, slaved for a long time as a garment worker in a sweatshop, and suffered from tuberculosis. Schlesinger, one of the founders of the International Ladies' Garment Workers' Union, was elected as its president in 1904 and served again as its chief executive in 1914; his initial salary was $35.00 a week. This autodidact was recognized as a man of culture, a student, a lover of good music and literature. He was at home in American history; one of his heroes was Daniel Webster. He was domineering but shrewd and able. Schlesinger led the ILGWU in 1916 in a strike when the Protocol of Peace was abrogated. This socialist propagandist did not hesitate when the union was without funds to turn to Julius Rosenwald, Herbert H. Lehman, and Felix Warburg for money to save the union. In a 1916 strike of the cloakmakers he won the sympathy of the public when he announced that the conflict was not a battle between the haves and the have nots but a struggle to bring about peaceful collective bargaining.[11]

Another interesting example of an outstanding unionist—a lesser leader but a very interesting personality—is Isaac A. Hourwich (1860-1924). For a brief period Dr. Hourwich administered the Protocol as the chief clerk of the International Ladies' Garment Workers' Union. However, he was not the man to conciliate capital and labor. Unlike most of his contemporaries Hourwich had acquired an excellent education in Russia where he had also passed the bar examination, but, like many other Russian Jews, he was a socialist, a revolutionary; indeed he had been exiled to Siberia. When he came to the United States in 1890 he was already a mature man, highly educated. It took him only three years after he landed to get his Ph.D. from Columbia; this was quite a feat. In the course of the next thirty-four years before he passed away he was to stand out as an economist, a statistician, an educator, a social reformer, and something of a maverick. Hourwich taught at the new University of Chicago in the early 1890's but was not kept on because of his radical political views. He was admitted to the bar, practiced in Illinois and New York, but actually made his living working for the United States government in Washington as a statistician. No college would give him a job; he was a Jew, an immigrant, a socialist. When the Russian Revolution erupted in 1905 he returned to his homeland, was elected to the parliament, but was not to serve after the reaction had set in.

He came back to America where he wrote several learned works and became an authority on immigration. In 1912 Putman's published his *Immigration and Labor*. It was an important book, an apologia, in which he set out to demonstrate scientifically that the immigrants had built America, that they were no threat to the country and its workers, and that admitting them would not injure the economy. This very substantial monograph was published shortly after the congressional Immigration Commission had overwhelmed America's researchers with a forty-four volume report unsympathetic to immigrants and immigration. Anti-immigration bills came before Congress constantly; it was obvious to many that restrictive legislation was impending. In 1921 when an anti-immigration law was about to be enacted a second edition of the Hourwich book was issued; it could not stop the myth of the superiority of the Nordic race steamroller: dolichocephalics, blonde hair, and blue eyes were at a premium. Hourwich was a man of many talents and many interests. He wrote in English, Yiddish, and Russian; he was a journalist who popularized works on socialism, economics, and the natural sciences. The *Jewish Encyclopedia* coopted him; many of his articles in the Yiddish press were published under a pseudonym for he was then an employee of the government in Washington; under the circumstances discretion was certainly the better part of valor. But he was not an obdurate ideologue; when the Bull Moose Party was organized he ran unsuccessfully for Congress. This pragmatic social scientist became president of the Socialist-Zionist fraternal order in 1918. After the Bolsheviks seized power in Russia and moved toward an autocracy reminiscent of the czars he turned against them; he was opposed to regimentation. However he did not get along well with leaders either of the right or the left; the East European masses admired him.[12]

UNION HEALTH CENTER

One of the terms of the Protocol of Peace which Hourwich was administering on the union's side was the establishment of a joint board of sanitary control by the employers and the garment workers; its purpose was to make sure that the shops would remain clean, sanitary. Dr. George Moses

Price was appointed the director of the board, a job for which this quiet competent physician, a Russian emigrant, was eminently qualified. Price had worked for the New York Health Department, was an expert in the field of public health, and had written on industrial hygiene. Three years later Price became the executive head of what was known as the Union Health Center. This was a diagnostic clinic established by the International Ladies' Garment Workers' Union. For a small fee a trade unionist was given sound medical advice. Price also helped set up an insurance plan for the sick and the unemployed, all this a generation before the New Deal and its medical programs.[13]

THE TRIANGLE FIRE

After a destructive fire at the Triangle Waist Company in 1911 a commission to study the physical condition of factories in New York was established. Dr. Price became the chief investigator. A fire had broken out in the company's loft on March 25; more than 150 workers, mostly young girls, were killed. Some factory doors could not be opened; there were no adequate fire escapes. This was one of the greatest tragedies in American industry. Public opinion was aroused and concern for workers heightened. Following the recommendations of the investigating committee laws were passed designed to protect the men, women, and children in the industry. The newspapers, sympathetic, demanded action; the Tammany-controlled State House and Senate, with the aid of Al Smith and Robert F. Wagner, dealt effectively with the problem. Laws were adopted governing factory safety, child labor, sweatshops, workmen's compensation, tenement house regulation, hours of labor. Tammany's concern induced many Jews on the East Side—most indeed—to vote the Democratic ticket. At a memorial meeting held at the Opera House for the victims of the fire a woman labor leader spoke: "the life of men and women is so cheap and property is so sacred."[14]

ROSE SCHNEIDERMAN

The woman labor leader who memorialized the Triangle dead was Polish-born Rose Schneiderman (1882/1884-1972) who was brought to this country as a child of about eight. After her father's death she was put into an orphanage; the family was poor. At thirteen she went to work in a department store as a cash girl; she was paid a trifle over $2 a week, sometimes putting in seventy hours in order to earn her $2. Ambitious to improve herself she went to work in a cap factory. Mama was disappointed; clerking in a department store was genteel. Rose organized the women cap workers into a local and when only twenty-two years of age was put on the board of the national union. She was moving ahead; she was a dynamic speaker. In 1905, still young, she reached out in a different direction, for she joined the Women's Trade Union League, an organization dedicated to the welfare of women in industry. Many of its members were middle-class Gentile women. A day would come when she was to lead not only the New York section of the League but also the national organization itself. She was eager to help her fellow Jews in the needle trades; there were many thousands working in the factories. Schneiderman knew —and this was confirmed by the reports of the 1911 Immigration Commission—that women were receiving but little more than half the pay given men for the same jobs; it was a crying injustice.

One of the reasons Rose moved over to the Women's Trade Union League was because the International Ladies' Garment Workers' Union dragged its feet in according equality to females. Schneiderman worked for years organizing women for the union; she was one of the leaders during the Uprising of the Twenty-Thousand but women suffered discrimination, neglect, at the hands of the union executives. The female organizers—there were several notables among them—were for years rebuffed by the males who believed that a woman's place was in the kitchen. Women were only temporary workers; they would get married soon, the men believed. Women leaders were looked upon as rivals; if there were jobs the men were to come first. Women like Schneiderman who worked to build the unions were not feminists though they approved of the vote for women; they were class conscious unionists; the union was more important than the ballot. Emancipating the worker was more important than emancipating the female. In the course of years Rose placed her hope on a benevolent, paternalistic government: it would bring salvation to women. The authorities must watch over wages and working conditions. She wanted a welfare state that would give females the ballot, prohibit child labor, usher in the eight-hour day, and provide a decent minimum wage for the girls. She lived to see all this come to pass. Turning to politics she ran for the United States Senate on the New York Farmer-Labor ticket and when Roosevelt came to power in the 1930's she sat on the Labor Advisory Board of the National Recovery Administration; in 1937 Governor Herbert H. Lehman appointed her Secretary of the State Department of Labor. She had come a long way from the Russian-Polish hamlet in which she was born.[15]

THE AMALGAMATED CLOTHING WORKERS OF AMERICA (ACWA)

In 1912 while Rose Schneiderman was busy organizing unions and recruiting members for the International Ladies' Garment Workers' Union, the New York tailors in the men's clothing industry went on strike. New unions were flowering; Wilson had just been elected president; it was thought he would be a friend of labor. This general strike called by crafts-men, the Brotherhood of Tailors, brought close to 70,000 workers out on the streets; about one-third were women. Substantial numbers went out on strike in other towns. Again the union was not recognized by the fac-tory owners though some concessions were won after months on the picket lines. Many of the tailors were pleased with what they had accom-plished in this struggle; many, too, were not overly happy with the exec-utives of their national organization, the United Garment Workers, under whose aegis they had fought. There were problems. Two different cul-tures were embraced within the international union; the Gentiles made work clothing; the Jews made dress clothing, men's for the most part. The hostilities were partially ethnic in origin; there was a silent battle of native against immigrant. In a way, too, it was a conflict of the pure craft unions of cautious conservatives who looked down their noses at the left-wing Jewish leaders who advocated industry-wide associations. There were sharp ideological differences. The leaders of the Jews wanted more than benefits in wages and hours; messianically and socialistically they were eager to save the world—according to the gospel of Karl Marx. The workers must prepare to take control of the economy. A power struggle was brewing. The Jewish leaders were ambitious. At a national conven-tion in 1914 the United Garment executives would not seat some of the Jewish delegates and their allies. The next step was secession; in Decem-ber, 1914, the rebels set up the Amalgamated Clothing Workers of Amer-ica. Thus there were now dual international unions in the clothing indus-try, and although Gompers would not admit this rival organization into the American Federation of Labor the Jews did not hesitate to move for-ward. The new union flourished and though in the course of years the number and percentage of Jewish workers declined the leadership re-mained Jewish.[16]

JOSEPH SCHLOSSBERG

One of the men who helped build the ACWA in 1914-1915 was Joseph Schlossberg (1875-1971). After his hegira from Eastern Europe in 1888, this teenager became a cloakmaker. In 1890, if not earlier, he began to stand out as an active unionist and a strike leader; his influence grew. Po-litically he was a Socialist Laborite, genuflecting in the direction of Dan-iel DeLeon. At an early age he evinced literary and journalistic ability and edited a socialist labor paper for years. To sharpen his skills he took courses in political science at Columbia; in 1913 he was Secretary of the Joint Board of New York's United Brotherhood of Tailors. No friend of the United Garment Workers he, too, joined the ACWA in 1914 and be-came its new secretary-treasurer. Schlossberg also served as editor of the

English and Yiddish edition of the *Advance*, the official journal of the secessionists. Unlike DeLeon, Schlossberg never strayed too far from Jewry's mainstream; in his later years certainly he stayed close to the Jewish people favoring Zionism and serving as an associate editor of the Labor-Zionist *Jewish Frontier*. It was his hope that when the new Jewish state would rise in Palestine it would take on a socialist coloring. The World Jewish Congress admitted him to its council; HIAS, the immigrant society, enjoyed the benefit of his patronage, and the political powers in New York City appointed him to the Board of Higher Education. Much in his career reminds one of Joseph Barondess; ultimately both men were completely integrated into the new all-embracing American Jewish way of life.[17]

SIDNEY HILLMAN

If the Amalgamated Clothing Workers of America became a very successful union—and it did—it was due in no small part to efforts of Sidney Hillman (1887-1946). This native of Lithuania came from good rabbinical stock; the genes of talmudists are not to be decried. His parents gave him the name of Simhah, Joy; this explains the change to Sidney in this country. His family was related by marriage to the Herzogs now so distinguished in the State of Israel; Chaim Herzog was one of that country's presidents. Like other typical Jewish lads he attended a rabbinical academy as a youngster and then turned to the Social Democratic Bund. He became a revolutionary and like others found it wiser if not necessary, to learn Russian. He came to America by way of England (1907). Chicago became his home for the time being; he worked for Sears, Roebuck (Julius Rosenwald) but desiring to better himself became an apprentice cutter for Hart, Schaffner & Marx, America's largest manufacturer of men's clothing. For the first eight weeks while learning he received no pay; after that he earned $6 a week. He was doing better than many of the other workers; they put in 60 to 70 hours a week and might make anywhere from $2.50 to $4 for their labor.

In September 1910, some of the female workers at Hart, Schaffner & Marx went out on strike; after some hesitation the men, including Hillman, joined them; all told about 40,000 men and women walked out. Before a settlement was reached seven people were killed. As in New York earlier that year, before the Protocol of Peace brought an uneasy truce to that city's industry, Chicago Jewish leaders sought to bring the two sides together. Judge Julian Mack and Rabbi Emil G. Hirsch joined with Jane Addams and Reverend Jenkin Lloyd Jones in appealing to the contesting parties. Peace was finally established through arbitration; Joseph Schaffner of the firm was a man with a social conscience. The union was not recognized but the workers won a fifty-four-hour week and better wages; more importantly, as in the New York Protocol, grievance and arbitration machinery was established. Other manufacturers were influenced by the settlement accepted by this leader in the industry. This was the strike that prepared Hillman for leadership in the men's clothing unions. A new local was set up and he became its business agent. He was working out his philosophy of worker-employer relations, encouraging arbitration but always with an eye to union participation in management. By 1914 his competence had attracted the attention of the leaders of the International Ladies' Garment Workers' Union in New York City and he was brought in as chief clerk of the Joint Board, the office once occupied by Isaac Hourwich. Hillman was more successful than the learned doctor and when the ACWA was born he became its president. He was now twenty-eight years of age. He organized strikes in the country's chief garment centers, induced others by peaceful means to come to terms with the union, and began building ACWA into an important national institution. World War I and its need for clothing and uniforms strengthened the organization; tailors were at a premium because of the draft. Only six years later, 1920, this new organization had over 175,000 members and a forty-four-hour week. This was a real advance.

As the decades passed Hillman honed his skills and refined his approach to the bosses. His outlook on labor-employer relations was not original with him; some of the craft unions of the 1890's preferred to cooperate with the owners rather than do battle with them. At all events Hillman was determined to win over the wary employers. He believed that capitalism and labor must work together; the employer is not the enemy. When the need arose Hillman did not hesitate to lend a manufacturer money to salvage his business. He wanted the employers to organize nationally so that he could negotiate with them as a body; he wanted to stabilize the industry nationally convinced that mutual benefits would ensue. Hillman worked closely with the owners but he wanted a voice in management. This was the new unionism; some termed it industrial democracy. Hillman was ready to improve the quality of the work done; he was prepared to tolerate, even encourage, technological changes in order to increase output. If the business prospered the union would benefit. It is by no means improbable, too, that Hillman, the Jew, working with Jewish employers, was able to advance his cause. This, however, is moot. He convinced the owners to go along with him because he talked in terms of efficiency, profits.

But this quondam Russian revolutionary and good unionist knew that his prime objective was to secure more rights on the job for his men and women. Over the years Hillman also tried to make provision for his followers in ACWA after the power was shut off and the workers set out for their homes. He offered his people recreational, social, and educational programs and advantages. Cooperative low rent apartments were built, banks were opened, and the workers were offered unemployment, sickness, and death benefits—all this before the New Deal. The ACWA may not have been aware of its odyssey; it may not have been entirely successful in its efforts, yet in a way, unconsciously of course, it was reaching out to become a vast "landsmanshaft" that embraced all its members benevolently. Hillman believed that the unions and industry, too, were responsible for the welfare of the worker even after his stint at the sewing machine or the cutting table. In many respects Hillman was a labor statesman; he wanted to help his members; he knew it was wise to keep the employers satisfied. In this sense he was more farseeing than Gompers; both men, however, exerted an influence on American labor. Their joint contributions—organization, higher living standards, concern—are of historic significance. Hillman's social programs furthering the union members were innovative and in part antedate the New Deal. Did the ACWA and the ILGWU influence the men in Washington who fleshed out the humanitarian aspects of the New Deal? This is a historical query that merits study.

Like Gompers, Hillman became an important national figure. In 1935 he stood out as one of the founders of the Committee for Industrial Organization; this was to become the Congress of Industrial Organizations (CIO), a rival of the American Federation of Labor (1938). Going into politics in the 1930's as a partisan of Franklin D. Roosevelt, Hillman was active in New York's American Labor Party. Later in 1940 he became a member of the National Defense Advisory Commission whose job it was to produce armaments; that same year he became Associate Director General of the Office of Production Management. He was now America's most influential labor leader. Mutatis mutandis he was doing the same job on the eve of World War II that Gompers did in World War I. In 1942, after war had been declared and the War Production Board was constituted, Hillman lost much of his administrative influence; for reasons of his own the canny Roosevelt had pushed him out but used him a year later as chairman of the Political Action Committee of the CIO. Hillman worked faithfully to reelect Roosevelt and was influential in the negotiations that eventuated in the nomination of Truman as Roosevelt's running mate. Thus again he made history.

Still pushing and moving on to bigger things, so he hoped, he became one of the founders of the World Federation of Trade Unions, an international organization (1945). This immigrant was indeed a new type of unionist; he was melding the social goals of the Yiddish-speaking socialists with the bourgeoislike hopes of the conservative craft union leaders. One suspects, that in his later years the Revolution, as the doctrinaire socialists envisaged it, was not an important item on his agenda. Like many other Jews who had begun life with visions of an international world where social justice would be regnant, German brutality in the 1930's pushed him in the direction of Zionism. He was friendly to the new Jewish nationalism. His importance in American history—not American Jewish history—lies in his success in organizing the laborers who built America's men's clothing industry; the ACWA is his monument, his immortality. Because he enriched his followers with many middle-class comforts he became a typical American labor leader.[18]

POSTSCRIPT: THE JEWISH UNIONS, 1920's–1940's

Hillman lived to exercise great power and to see important changes. As late as 1914 only about 6 percent of the American work force was unionized. Before he died the men and women in the Jewish-led unions were enjoying a work week of less than forty hours. Much has happened since this young Russian working for Hart, Schaffner & Marx joined the striking women in 1910. Wages were higher, the hours of labor were reduced radically; the factories were cleaner; unions were feared if not respected. Sweatshops had diminished, arbitration had been introduced, and the national government, by grace of the Clayton Antitrust Act and the Wagner National Labor Relations Act, was less hostile to the unions. It is estimated that as early as 1918 there were 250,000 Jewish unionized workers in the country. Yet there was no decade without its problems for the four "Jewish" unions. Depressions wreaked havoc, but conditions improved markedly under Roosevelt and his New Deal; the President needed Jews —both middle-class liberals and unionists—to put together the urban coalition that kept him in office. Actually the Jewish garment workers had wandered in the wilderness for fifty years after they landed in 1881; they entered the Promised Land led by Roosevelt in the 1930's. In the 1940's manufacturing women's garments had become a billion dollar industry; the workers who produced men's clothing had improved themselves substantially; the unions set out to pamper them in their postprandial hours.

In the 1920's and 1930's these Jewish unions were Americanizing themselves in the craft union sense. Their leaders and a substantial minority of the rank and file were socialist, treasuring social ideals. Nominally they were still schismatic, anti-religious Marxists. They had a Yiddish world of their own, their own fraternal orders, afternoon schools, and a leftist press. But history was pushing them back into the particularism of World Jewry; America anti-Semitism in the 1920's and German inhumanity warned them they could not escape their heritage. By the 1920's Jewish membership in the four unions was declining radically; Jews had been moving out of the Lower East Side for decades; they now began moving out of the factory. Many went into trade; a few became garment manufacturers; immigration from Russia and the adjoining lands was sharply curtailed by Congress; in 1914, 138,000 Jews came in; in 1925, 10,000. The first native-born generation refused to follow their fathers into the factories. True, the leaders were Jews; they still held on exercising a paternalistic authority but on the whole they conducted the affairs of the union in exemplary fashion. Even the Marxist-bred leaders stopped working to usher their people into a socialist paradise; they were content with business unionism, American style.[19]

SOCIALISM

The Jewish labor movement was inextricably bound up with socialism. Marxism, socialism, was the philosophy that would lead the workers into a different, a better world. The theoreticians were the generals; the unionists were to be the army who, when the time was ripe, would vote out the old capitalist system and ring in a new universalist era of social justice. The politically active Jewish socialists were not often union executives; they set out to catch larger fish; the unions were but one aspect of their program. Socialism, in relation to unions and their leaders, has already been treated above albeit lightly. It is necessary to review the history of this social movement in the American ghettos, primarily in New York City. There, socialism had a life of its own; its tangential relation to the unions was but one of its facets. Socialism, a system of terrestial salvation was important to many immigrant Jews in this country whether they were in the needle trades or in other walks of life. Scientific socialism, so called, began with Karl Marx. Though born a Jew he was converted as a child. He grew up in a German atmosphere of Judeophobia; he may have succumbed to it. This brilliant student identified bourgeois society with Jews and Judaism; his attacks on the Jew and his faith are important, for his socialism was—is—not infrequently anti-Jewish; it has spawned attacks on Jews in many countries. The German government, 1933-1945, was National Socialist; it murdered millions of Jews. Though the word Jew was for Marx a term of denigration he had many Jewish followers in Europe and in the United States. His desire to modify the modern state appealed to thousands of Jews; with the abolition of the modern state, nationalistic anti-Jewish prejudices and disabilities would disappear; so they thought.

The Russians were not the first Jewish socialists here; the Germans had preceded them by a generation. Dr. Abraham Jacobi (1830-1919), a "Communist," had participated in the uprising against the monarchists in Germany; he had been jailed but finally escaped reaching this country by way of England. After landing here in 1853 he practiced medicine on the Lower East Side; his fees were 25 or 50 cents. Once here he took little interest in socialism; pediatrics was his medical specialty in the United States. A fellow socialist and 1848 German revolutionary, Sigismund Kaufmann, had preceded him to this country; he was here in 1849. Kaufmann remained a socialist, for a time at least; he organized a politically radical turnverein and edited its paper. In Brooklyn where he lived he was attracted to the new Republican Party; as a liberal he was an anti-slavery man. Kaufmann thus became one of the founders of the new party in Brooklyn and as a presidential elector voted for Lincoln in 1860. He was no philosophical anti-religionist, for he was a trustee of a synagog and a director of the prestigious Hebrew Orphan Asylum. There is reason to believe that there were other non-Russian Jewish socialists in this country at that time. By the 1860's there were Jewish socialists in Russia also. That is understandable, for it was a land of oppression where millions suffered from political, economic, and cultural disabilities. Socialism promised to bring an end to all these evils. Jews in that land turned to this new cure-all early. By 1897 the Yiddish-speaking Jewish Labor Federation—the Bund, the League—of Lithuania, Poland, and Russia had been established; it was socialist. Eight years later this organization proclaimed widely its concept of cultural pluralism; it sought to further a Jewish national culture; the Yiddish language was the medium. There were other Jewish socialist factions in the country, all ethnically anchored, to a greater or lesser degree, within the ambit of Jewry. Followers of all these groups made the transatlantic crossing to America, the land of opportunity.[20]

SOCIALISM AND ANARCHISM

The Russian leftist émigrés established socialist organizations here; they were intellectuals, humanitarians, ideologues; very few had Jewish interests, loyalties to the old beliefs and traditions. In 1895 a group of Socialist Laborites strung a banner in their convention hall which proudly proclaimed that "we are not Jews; rather we are all Yiddish-speaking proletarians." Here in America where they were free to express themselves these radicals set out to politicize, to indoctrinate their fellow East Europeans; the instrumentalities were socialism, anarchism, special fraternal orders, a Marxist press, control of Jewish trade unions. The Jews whom they wished to mold were not of the same clay. Most of them were religionists, followers of East European schools of Orthodoxy. They were by no means homogeneous. Nor were the socialists of one mind; the followers of Karl Marx were divided into two basic groups, socialists and those with Jewish leanings, cultural autonomists, territorialists, Zionists, each with his own solution to the "Jewish Problem." Among these socialist refugees was one who landed in January, 1917; this was Leon Trotsky. He was given the red carpet treatment; the superintendent of the United

Immigrant Aid Society met him, an apartment was furnished for him in the Bronx, provided with telephone, electric lights, and a bathtub. What a fortunate man. A vegetarian, he ate his meals in a nearby Jewish restaurant. He made a living as a journalist and as a lecturer, addressing his audiences in Russian and German; he was a sought after notable. The furnishings of his apartment had been guaranteed by the litterateur Sholem Asch. A few months later Trotsky left for Russia; the Bolshevik revolution was in the making and he knew that he would be one of the leaders. And the apartment furniture and furnishings? Sholem Asch was left with the bill.

The anarchists and socialists are usually bracketed; they are different. The socialists wanted a new government, their style; anarchists wanted no government; they believed that there was no true justice and equality under any form of the traditional state; they wanted a new system, one that would clean out the Augean stables which were filled with corruption. With rare exception, very rare indeed, the Jewish anarchists did not advocate or practice violence. They were pacific idealists. They had their own Yiddish press; it was small but not without influence; their leaders were educated cultured men. They were strongly anti-religionist and like many socialists they held religion—as they knew it—in contempt. In the late 1880's and 1890's the anarchists organized annual balls on Kol Nidre night, on the eve of the Day of Atonement, the most sacred moment in the Jewish religious calendar. They scoffed at all that was holy in Judaism. To the late twentieth-century Jew this flaunting of their views smacks of immaturity; the psycho-historian will probably come up with an explanation of their conduct. A Gentile in Grand Forks, South Dakota, owner of a woolen mill, imported his workers, Jews, cutters, operatives, and pressers. As radicals they set out to hold a ball on Yom Kippur. The indignant local rabbi made a public address denouncing them in no uncertain terms. They were let off from work, he pointed out, to observe a Holy Day and they used the opportunity to attack the United States as a capitalist land. They had fled from Russia where they had suffered and it was this capitalist country that accorded them shelter. Here they had opportunities which were denied them in their native Russia; they were using a religion which they hated for their own personal advantage; they were a pack of hypocrites.

New York's Jewish anarchists were members of the Pioneers of Freedom, *Pioniere der Freiheit*, in the 1880's. This was probably a mixed group of Jews and Gentiles. The Jews, too, seem to have been organized about the same time in an association of their own; their Yiddish paper, a weekly, was *The Workers' Free Voice (Die Freie Arbeiter Stimme)*; in the next decade they published *Free Society (Die Freie Gesellschaft)*, a monthly. Though they were as a rule a docile well behaved group, they were disliked and even hated by Jews and Gentiles. The bombing and killing of several people in Haymarket Square in Chicago in 1886 turned the American people against them though there is no substantial evidence that anarchists were the culprits. Among the Baltimore anarchists in the early 1890's was the Johns Hopkins medical student Michael Cohn. He worked his way through school writing Yiddish letters for illiterates. When in a public debate he denied that there was a God a riot broke out; he was arrested, put into solitary confinement, and excommunicated by the Orthodox. He forgot that he was in Maryland which at one time threatened a "blaspheming" Jew with the death penalty. Some of America's most distinguished citizens had no compassion for radicals, no understanding of their point of view. The kindly William Howard Taft, who would one day become president of the United States, thought that some strikers and anarchists ought to be killed. Theodore Roosevelt was of like mind. In 1908 George Shippy, Chicago's chief of police, shot down the anarchist, Lazar Averbuch. It was the contention of the chief that Averbuch, heavily armed, had come to kill him. Here, too, there is no proof that the Jew had a deadly weapon; it is not improbable that the panicky chief executed him. After the assassination of President McKinley in 1901, the country turned bitterly against all anarchists. The disparate socialists and anarchists were constantly at each others throats verbally; their factionalism hurt them both, delaying the development of strong Jewish trade unions. The number of anarchists in the early twentieth century was inconsequential. It was very difficult even for liberals and radicals to conceive of a viable anarchist society. More and more the Jewish leftists pinned their hopes on socialism and its goal of ushering in a new and better polity by grace of the ballot.[21]

SOCIALIST FRATERNAL ORDERS

THE WORKMEN'S CIRCLE AND THE FARBAND

Two important national benefit societies were established by socialists to help proletarians financially and to inspirit them ideologically. Founded in 1900 the Workmen's Circle imposed discipline on its members; they had to belong to a union, vote the Socialist ticket, and reject Zionism. This opposition to Palestine nationalism they had in common with Reform Jews. Both groups indeed were internationalists; the one stressed the sociopolitical, the other the religious. Some Workmen's Circle members took their articles of faith very seriously. Branch 179 in Cincinnati refused to cooperate with the local ghetto Settlement House; the Settlement, it said, was a religious institution. Time betrays people; after World War I America's Workmen's Circle groups became more and more bourgeois, Jewish. Despite their assimilation views they were determined to remain culturally autonomous but Jewish; the Yiddish language seduced them; it was emphasized at the expense of socialism; political ideology was not all powerful; the Yiddish vernacular was to become the ethnic cement; this beloved language—not Hebrew—was now cultivated in numerous afternoon schools. By 1921 the Workmen's Circle devotees were Diaspora nationalists; cultural pluralists, their political doctrinairism was less pronounced. The Farband (the Union), the Jewish National Workers' Alliance (the Farband-Labor Zionist Order) had established their fraternal order in 1912. Years earlier they had founded a Socialist-Zionist group (1903); in 1905 a national association came into being; it called itself the Labor Zionist Organization of America-Poale Zion. The concept of restoration was too much a part of Jewry for almost two millennia to be dismissed cavalierly. The views of Poale Zion were rejected by the internationalist socialists, by the territorialists—who would go almost anywhere for a Jewish home—and by the Workmen's Circle whose non-Palestine nationalism was ethnocultural. The Socialist Zionists were the first to establish Marxist afternoon Yiddish schools (1910); five years later they joined American Jewry in its effort to rescue the East European victims of World War I. The Zionists of America, bourgeois oriented, were ready to work with all Socialist-Zionist groups.[22]

THE RADICAL PRESS

In most social movements the press obviously is important. The American Jewish radical papers and journals, developed in the 1890's as a propaganda medium, were probably influenced by similar journals in London. Jewish socialists and anarchists had made their appearance in the English metropolis in the 1870's. Bear in mind Great Britain in that Victorian decade was the most powerful financial and industrial empire in the world. The London Jewish radicals then had a press and associations of their own; they even had their Yom Kippur balls where they set out to twitch the beards of the Orthodox. As early as 1876 Aaron Lieberman, who was to come to the United States in 1880, had founded a socialist group in London and had attempted to establish a union of Yiddish-speaking workers. Here in the United States there was a Yiddish socialist labor daily in 1894 (the *Abend Blatt*) and a rival socialist paper in 1897 with Abraham Cahan as its first editor (*The Forward*). With the exception of the several years that he worked and wrote for New York's English journals Cahan was to remain the editor of *The Forward* (*Forverts*) till his death. *The Future* (*Di Zukunft*), a propagandistic magazine, appeared in 1892 but it very quickly became a literary journal; it was still being published in the late twentieth century. *The Forward* was the most important socialist Yiddish paper in the country; it was very much involved in the efforts of the laborers to improve their lot but it was not a union organ. The various socialistic papers, movements, and fraternal orders had a substantial following, though they were always a minority of New York's Jewish newcomers. Until the first decade of the new century the Marxists papers were essentially political instrumentalities. By 1909, however, the socialist leaders turned very seriously to the realistic task of establishing permanent unions; in this effort they had the support of their press. The radical Yiddish journals held many of the immigrants together by teaching civics, emphasizing humanitarian and cultural objectives, and by reaching out for social goals.[23]

SOCIALISTS AND UNIONS

It would seem that the German Jewish participation in American socialism was not particularly significant; there is no question however that the subject merits further study. "Jewish" socialism assumed a dimension of its own when hundreds of thousands of Russians, Polish, and Rumanian immigrants made their appearance on America's proletarian horizon. Perspective in this matter must be maintained however. It is not easy to know with any degree of accuracy how many of the newcomers were socialists either in New York City or in the hinterland. In 1912 the Socialist Party mustered in all America, but 118,000 members, Gentiles and Jews; this in a country of well over 90,000,000 inhabitants. The East European Marxists, leftist leaders, set out deliberately to effect political and economic changes; through constitutional means they hoped to create a new society. They established Russian and Yiddish-speaking branches of the Socialist Labor Party; these go back to the 1880's; the United Hebrew Trades was closely integrated with DeLeon's political party.

That the already organized unions were still floating about in misty realms is reflected in the preamble to the constitution of the International Ladies' Garment Workers' Union (1902); the goals of the new institution were to bring together all workers regardless of race, nationality, creed, and sex; the new union was to engage in a humanitarian crusade. The stolid craft unions, out for higher wages and less time on the job, talked a different language. More and more Jews of ability began to make their presence felt nationally in the socialist parties; DeLeon, the Sephardi, dominated the Socialist Laborites in the early 1890's; he soon founded his own national federation of labor unions; many Jewish workers were not happy with him; the man was not concerned with the problems of the Jews as such; for him socialism was a panacea that would cure all ills. In 1897-1898, Victor Berger helped organize the new Social Democratic Party and by 1901 with Hillquit and others called into being the new Socialist Party of America (SLP). Thus in that decade alone three of the country's Marxist leaders were men of Jewish origin. These two socialist parties were reinforced by the arrival of numerous Russian Jewish Marxists who fled to America after the failure of the Revolution of 1905.

The American people were not unaware of the social welfare programs in Germany and in England; they followed the progress of the Russian Revolution; the new Soviets frightened them and the militancy of the Industrial Workers of the World might well have served as a warning to insightful politicians. There were already intimations by 1910 that the people and the government were truly concerned with the welfare of the country's rank and file. In other words they were becoming increasingly conscious of labor's demands and of the needs for some form of social security. Among those laying the foundations in this country for social insurance were two East European Jews, Isaac M. Rubinow (1875-1936) and Abraham Epstein (1892-1942).[24]

FATHERS OF SOCIAL SECURITY LEGISLATION

Rubinow was a physician, economist, statistician, actuary, social worker; he was concerned, too, with humanity at large. This brilliant teenager came to the United States in 1893; five years later he had earned a doctorate in medicine. It was in 1910 that he presented a two-volume report to the Department of Commerce and Labor; it was published a year later. The work, *Studies in Workmen's Insurance in Italy, Russia, Spain* served also to help him secure his Ph.D. at Columbia. In 1913 Rubinow published his authoritative *Social Insurance*. Before 1920 several states passed workmen's compensation laws based on his research. A few years earlier (1916) Rubinow was appointed secretary of the Social Insurance Commission of the American Medical Association. As secretary he recommended that there be a compulsory system of insurance that would cover health, unemployment, accidents, old age; the workers did not want charity; the laborer was worthy of his hire and the state must make provision for him. In general Rubinow made little progress in furthering the concept of social security insurance, even in the American Medical Association; vested interests were arrayed against him, industry and labor tool. Vocationally Rubinow moved about; his many abilities opened opportunities for him; he headed a Zionist medical unit in Palestine toward the end of the second decade; later he was to serve as the chief executive officer for the American Zionists. Social agencies made him their director and finally the B'nai B'rith called him to administer its far-flung order. Like many Russian intellectuals, Rubinow was a socialist; the arbitrary harsh rule of the Bolsheviks in Russia disillusioned him; American democracy was preferable. This outstanding expert in the field of social insurance served as one of the consultants when the Social Security Act was drafted in Roosevelt's

New Deal days. Rubinow was not too happy with the Act as passed; like many other national laws it was a compromise.

In 1927 he was a vice president of the American Association for Old-Age Security, an organization established by Abraham Epstein. Like Rubinow, Epstein, another Russian newcomer, was an expert and pioneer in the field of social and health insurance, old age pensions, unemployment benefits. Here in this country he was not as fortunate as Rubinow; he had a tough row to hoe. Back in Eastern Europe he had grown up in poverty; there he had eked out an existence as a Hebrew teacher and here, too, he taught children to find their way through the prayer book. Even as a youngster he had read Marxist literature; he was eager to help the under-privileged. Despite the fact that he made but little as a Hebrew teacher, a clerk, and a factory worker, he finally succeeded in securing a university education; he even taught for years in institutions of higher learning. By the 1920's, as an expert in his field, he was working for the Pennsylvania Commission on Old Age Pensions; Epstein wrote several works on social security and established a national organization to propagandize the need for this type of insurance. He called upon the United States government to finance and administer the program. When the Social Security Act was in preparation his advice was not sought; he had made enemies. It is worthy of note that neither Rubinow or Epstein were initially called upon to play an active role in drafting this very important legislation, regardless of the fact that they were acknowledged authorities. Epstein and Rubinow brought European—and socialistic—concepts of social security to the United States; their contributions to the New Deal social legislation are significant. Both men were Marxists, social idealists: the poor have a right to be helped. Epstein hewed to the line all the time, writing books and urging the need for the state to make provision for the aged and unemployed.[25]

SOCIALISM AND THE JEW

Rubinow and Epstein were not in politics unless every socialist who expounds or lives his philosophy is a politician by intent at least. Many socialists however were determined to exert influence on their fellow citizens in order to introduce their form of government. The year 1911 which saw the publication of Rubinow's two volumes on workmen's compensation was the year that witnessed the election of the first socialist to Congress. The new congressman was Victor Luitpold (Louis) Berger (1860-1920), a Jew. The socialists were making progress. That year there were hundreds in office in this country in hundreds of towns; very few were Jews. The following year, when about 15,000,000 votes were cast in the election for the presidency—Wilson was elected—Eugene V.

Debs, the Socialist candidate, received 900,000 votes. Many Jews were in the Socialist Party; a relatively small number were members of the Jewish Socialist Federation which in 1912 could boast of some 5,000 or more members in the United States in its 100 or less branches in twenty some states—this at a time when there were about 2,000,000 Jews in the country. It is very probable that there were some Jews, not Socialists, who shared the social hopes of the Jewish Socialists. The Jewish Socialist Federation was Bundist in its sympathies. Though completely disinterested in Orthodoxy, the members were very much interested in a secular, non-Palestinian national Jewish culture. Working with it was a Young People's Socialist League; its numbers could not have been very large. The Jewish Socialist Federation had the moral support of the socialist Yiddish press and the radical fraternal orders. Some of the branches of the Federation had libraries which were well patronized. The members supported the trade unions and developed a social life of their own; socialism for these devotees of Yiddish was a secular religion.

The socialist leaders were not free agents in their Yiddish-speaking Socialist Federation and in their unions; they had to cater to the mores, the prejudices of the masses or otherwise lose them as potential followers. The Jewish loyalties of the East European immigrants had been intensified since the Russian pogroms of the early 1900's. Another problem faced the Marxists after the great strikes beginning in 1909; Americanization rather than political socialism made headway. Radical ideology was still cherished but there was a process of gradual deradicalization if not deproletarianization as conditions improved. Union leaders now were less eager to save the world; they wanted to save the unions, to insure better working conditions; the workers seeking to improve themselves had for years been moving out to second, more comfortable areas of settlement. Leaders like Barondess, an old-timer, and Hillman of more recent vintage, were slowly inching to the right, to the center, without surrendering their interest in social and reform ideals. Many if not most socialists retained anti-Orthodox or anti-Reform prejudices. The socialists and the Orthodox, too, enjoyed belaboring the Uptown Reform Jews, capitalists; this shared prejudice was a tie that united them and made them both feel righteous. The radicals were careful, however, never to cut themselves off from the Yiddish-speaking multitudes. They touched each other if only lightly; their common Yiddish vernacular and the Zionism of the Farband were ties. After some hesitation these socialist led workers finally joined the Joint Distribution Committee in 1915 to help bring relief to the suffering Jews of Eastern Europe. This was a formal alliance with the elite American Jewish Committee crowd and the Orthodox. The socialists were rejoining the Jewish people! By 1918 labor union leaders, socialists—normally anti-war—were supporting the government in its struggle with the Germans. At this time it was obvious that many Marxists were also beginning to align themselves with Jewry because of the incessant Russian pogroms, because of the subversive impact of liberalism which gave them what they wanted, because of the appeal, the advantages inherent in American democracy. Anti-Semitism, never absent in the United States, brought them closer to all Jews. Following the trend of the Jewish masses, some left-wing dissidents voted for Wilson; later they flocked to the banner of Franklin D. Roosevelt.

By 1917 there was something of a Yiddish culture efflorescence; there were twenty-eight Yiddish journals in New York City; four were dailies; there were 600,000 Yiddish readers in New York. There was an avid interest in literature, in the novel, in poetry, in drama and the theatre. Many of the participants were socialists. The Yiddishists had been influenced affirmatively by American culture, its insistence on schools and schooling. Well educated socialist Bundists sought refuge in the United States after the czarist reaction in the early 1900's. Several of the labor leaders were themselves litterateurs. The socialistic *Forward* was the largest Yiddish paper in town and at its height it may have had as many as 200,000 subscribers. Chicago, in the hinterland, had three dailies. Before 1920 the non-religious, secular, afternoon schools of the socialists, the Socialist-Zionists, and the secularist political neutrals set out to win their children for Yiddishism, not Judaism. Cultural linguistic nationalism was their prime concern and goal. The schools were very modest in size and statistically insignificant; they constituted but a tiny minority of lower Manhattan's Jewish youngsters. Let it be repeated, in the 1920's the socialist Yiddishists were still a community within a community, a disparate cultural enclave. The New Deal and the German murders of the 1940's pulled leftists back into the orbit of American Jewry and into the mainstream of the American labor movement. Ultimately the impact of America transformed most Yiddish-speaking radicals into American Jews at one with all Jews in this land. The process was certainly complete by the end of World War II. And the children of the ghetto? They had moved far from the socialist world of their parents. The cultural, social, economic, and even political gap between the two was wide, not easily bridged. While the parents were experiencing deradicalization, the children, of their own accord, were moving or aspiring to move into the middle class. The radical Yiddish afternoon schools which the socialist youth attended did not in the slightest hinder their Americanization; in the mornings they went to the public schools; indoctrination there was irresistible.[26]

CHAPTER EIGHT

MAKING A LIVING

PART II: NOTABLE JEWISH SOCIALISTS,

AMERICAN JEWRY, AND THE LABOR MOVEMENT

INTRODUCTION

A number of the East European Jewish labor leaders in the United States stand out. None was a religionist; some were Jewish only by the accident of birth; they were all cosmopolitans, humanitarians; a number were politicians; a few would never, could never divorce themselves from the Jewish people. These unionists come to the fore in the second decade of the twentieth century when the rank and file Jewish socialists were backing into the parameter that included all Jews concerned about the welfare of American and World Jewry. As a group, East Europeans did not play a major role in American socialism; they had high visibility but were always just a minority in the party. There were a few on the national scene, however, who were notable leaders; they were important. A description of their activities as socialists is not the task of the American Jewish historian; the description of their relations to American Jewry is relevant.

DANIEL DELEON

The first Jewish socialist to play an important role nationally was Daniel DeLeon (1852-1914); he was a lawyer, an editor, a politician. In one respect he was exceptional, he was no East European but a Sephardi who had come from the Islands, the Caribbeans. His father was a physician, a dentist, a Reform Jew. DeLeon had a file of *Shemah Israel* in his library; this was a Reform Jewish magazine published in Curaçao. This journal is one of his few links to the faith of his father. In Curaçao where he was born he attended a school where he received some training in Hebrew.

When asked about his antecedents he said that he was descended from an aristocratic Catholic family. It is not easy to fathom why he denied his Judaic past unless the rising Judaeophobia in Germany took its toll of him; he had studied in Germany and Amsterdam before coming to the United States in the early 1870's. He was well educated for he knew languages and the classics; very few if any of the East European labor leaders had a comparable background in the secular disciplines. DeLeon studied at Columbia, received a degree there in 1878, and even taught at the school for a time. In 1879 he took issue with Felix Adler who had written an article urging Jews not to celebrate Christmas for it was a truly Christian holiday commemorating the birth of Jesus in whose name Christians had persecuted Jews. DeLeon in his essay expressed admiration for the "sublime" character of Jesus; Christmas was an attractive nature festival that brought people together.

Like Israel Zangwill, DeLeon believed in a melting pot that would fuse together all American races and peoples, both Christians and Jews. After Kishinev when the Russian mobs started killing Jews, DeLeon wrote that when socialism came to power there would be no anti-Semitism; he opposed Socialist-Zionism; it was nationalist. In the late 1880's before he turned to socialism he supported the single-taxer Henry George when the latter ran for mayor of New York; DeLeon was also in sympathy with Edward Bellamy who wrote of nationalizing industry in his Looking Backward (1888); that same year DeLeon enlisted in the Knights of Labor; about two years later he joined the Socialist Labor Party. He was now a Socialist. In 1891 this brilliant man had made such headway in party circles that he ran for governor on its ticket; this was but the beginning of his many attempts at elective office. The man was a prolific writer; he translated European works, fiction and nonfiction, brochures on economics and socialism. It was in that same decade of the 1890's that he emerged as the dominant and dominating leader of the party. He gave it vigorous leadership as long as he lived.

In 1895, in opposition to Gompers's American Federation of Labor, DeLeon built a rival umbrella union federation which he called the Socialist Trade and Labor Alliance. His aim was to control American labor and use it politically to make America a socialist state. In pursuit of this goal he later helped the Industrial Workers of the World (IWW) establish itself; unlike Gompers he believed in industrial, not craft unionism. Strong unions as such were not a primary goal for him; they were to be the instruments to bring about the social revolution, though not through violence. In this aim he influenced Jewish socialists and their leaders as late as the first decade of the new century; the party not the union came first. His doctrinaire consistent philosophy made its impress on the United Hebrew Trades; it joined his national Alliance. He refused to compromise with capitalism like the pragmatic craft unions. And like all Jewish socialists he was an American patriot; the Declaration of Independence was a challenge to tyranny; socialists are the spiritual descendants of the American Revolutionary leaders; socialism is American in its desire for change, for improvement. This land would one day become the first socialist republic. Uncompromising, imperious, he turned off many of his followers who left him in 1897 and 1901 to create new socialist parties. He was not a happy man; his home life was joyless; he lived on the edge of poverty.[1]

ABRAHAM CAHAN

Abraham Cahan (1860-1951) was much more fortunate than DeLeon in his career. He was not easygoing but, unlike DeLeon, he held his people in line and grew more influential and powerful with the years. Over the decades as Cahan's readers—humble workers and petty entrepreneurs—drifted slowly away from classical socialism he moved with them. Again like DeLeon he was an ardent Americanizer. Cahan was born in a Lithuanian village. Fortunately for him his family moved to Vilna where as the grandson of a rabbi he secured a talmudic training in a rabbinical academy. It was his good fortune also to receive a secular education; he mastered Russian and graduated from the Vilna Teachers Institute, a government school, in 1881. By that time he had already become a revolutionary; the following year he found it advisable to leave the country; he landed in New York in 1882. For a time he worked in a cigar factory and in a tin shop but, it would seem, actually made his living in the initial years by teaching English to foreigners, to Russians. Cahan flirted briefly with anarchism but soon anchored himself in socialism, preaching his political gospel and helping unions in the garment trades.

All through the 1880's and 1890's he busied himself editing Yiddish socialist journals; he was wise enough to realize that the only way to reach the masses was through an earthy Yiddish and he cultivated it despite the indignant remonstrances of classicists who resented his "potato-chicken" language. In 1890 he was a founder and editor of the Socialist Labor *Arbeiter Zeitung* (*Workers' Press*), the organ of the United Hebrew Trades; in 1897 he revolted with others against DeLeon and set up the rival *Forward*. Early in the 1890's he had worked on *The Future* (*Di Zukunft*), a Yiddish magazine that was to have a long and distinguished career. After a few months on the *Forward* as editor he left and worked for the next several years as a reporter for New York's English press. Cahan had turned to writing English shortly after he came to this country; in 1896 he published *Yekl: A Tale of the New York Ghetto* which so impressed William Dean Howells that he took an interest in the literary career of the young immigrant. From 1897 until 1902, Cahan, a reporter for Lincoln Steffens's muckraking New York *Commercial Advertiser*, scoured the city for stories. One of his friends on the paper was Hutchins Hapgood who, under the guidance of Cahan, wrote *The Spirit of the Ghetto*, one of the most interesting and honest studies of the Lower East Side (1902). Cahan continued to write in English even after he left the Steffens paper; in 1917 he published *The Rise of David Levinsky*. The wry comment that it is a Yiddish work written in English is apt. Whether it is a classic is certainly moot; there is no question that it is a literary document of prime importance and a source for American Jewish history. It tells the story of the Russian Jew as a clothing manufacturer; even more, it describes the problems that confronted hundreds of thousands of émigrés who had to come to terms with the New World—emotionally, psychically, culturally —after loosening their ties with an Old World that they could never forget.

In 1903, Cahan went back to the *Forward* on his own terms. It became a great newspaper. He had learned his trade well as an apprentice with one of New York's aggressive newspapers. The *Forward* was much more than a socialist organ; it was an instrument he used to instruct, to entertain, to goad his readers. He helped guide the immigrant labor unions and came to their rescue generously when they went on strikes. Like his contemporary Hearst, Cahan also gave the people what they wanted. The Socialist Labor press of DeLeon dismissed the Dreyfus Affair as intra-capitalistic bickering; Cahan told his readers that Dreyfus was the symbol of the suffering which every Jew experienced. The *Forward* took a stand on the issues that confronted the multitudes: religion, fashion, sex, hygiene, evolution, the Negro. As an Americanizer he published biographies of the great men in this country; he discussed the Declaration of Independence, the Constitution; he told his readers to vote and how to vote. The writings of the English and American classicists were serialized. He hired and paid outstanding Yiddish writers like Sholom Asch and I. J. Singer; he criticized bad theatre, encouraged realistic drama, and lauded good writers. The *Forward* was a mass educator, a significant cultural intermediary. His paper faced the same dilemma that confronted all Yiddish dailies in World War I: How could it support pogromist Russia despite its alliance with the Allies? It was easier in 1917 when the Russian monarchy collapsed and the liberals came to power, but he was no friend of the Bolsheviks. He visited Palestine in the 1920's to see what the Zionists were accomplishing and he lived to record the rise of the State of Israel but he was no devotee of the new Jewish nationalism. Cahan had come a long way since he first landed, since the early days when he told an audience to take axes and chop down the palatial homes of the American rich. He cooled off quickly; time and circumstance made him one of the most influential Russian Jews in the United States. Yet one final word of caution. Though the *Forward* was the largest of the Jewish immigrant dailies it was never read by a majority of the newcomers; they turned to their own nonsocialist papers.[2]

MORRIS HILLQUIT

Though Abraham Cahan worked for socialism he had a good word for the New Deal administration in the 1930's; he always had an ear to the ground; he never forgot that he was an editor of a paper; he was not an intractable Socialist Party politician. Morris Hillquit (Hillkowitz, 1869/1870-1933) was different. He was an active party leader; one of the most important socialists in the United States. Cahan was tied up with Jews, with his people; Hillquit was concerned with the movement, its ideals. Cahan was the better "Jew"; Hillquit was not a Jewish socialist; he worked with Jews who happened to be socialists. For him Jews were merely ammunition in a war for a righteous cause; first and last he was a Marxist, as Gomper was a unionist. He was a Socialist Party spokesman and an organizer. As early as 1903 he had written a *History of Socialism in the United States*; it was to go through several printings in a few years. One suspects that he had no real understanding of Jews, their inner sentiments; he had no commitment to their culture and was not interested in stressing Jewish ethnicity. Speaking of Magnes he once wrote: "This Jewish rabbi was one of the few divines who took the spirit and teachings of Christ seriously." A Jew would not have written that sentence. If he touched on his Jewish background it was a spade to dig with politically; he was a politician who wanted Jews to vote for him. Zionism did not appeal to him; it was a reaction to persecution; religious and racial prejudice would disappear in a socialist state. In the meantime, he was willing to work with the bourgeois forces through the ballot; there was to be no violence. In 1924 he supported the candidacy of Robert M. LaFollette of the Progressive Party, a liberal and socialist fusion group. Despite his somewhat doctrinaire approach Hillquit was sufficiently practical to bargain for social reform. If he happened to be an assimilationist in principle he was not motivated by any mundane reasons; his ideology left him little choice. Hillquit was a man of integrity, a highly respected socialist both here and abroad. Like most Jewish socialists he was an Americanizer.

What was the background of this man? He was born in Latvia which borders on Germany; his cultural background was German and Russian; he was well educated. Hillquit came to the United States in 1886 well over a decade before the Bund evolved its concept of cultural nationalism. This is important. Yiddish was not his tongue; he learned it in the United States; that was imperative if he was to reach the East European masses.

After coming to this country he worked for a while in the garment industry, learned English in the night schools, and finally in 1895 became a lawyer. In 1888 as a Socialist Laborite he had helped to establish the United Hebrew Trades and its newspaper. As a typical Marxist and anti-religionist he, too, attended the Yom Kippur balls; it was a symbol of intellectual emancipation. As a politician he ran for office frequently on a Socialist platform, always unsuccessfully. Ultimately he broke with De-Leon and the Socialist Labor crowd and helped organize the new Socialist Party of America (1901). His concern was to help the workers; it is not surprising therefore that he was not opposed to restrictive immigration legislation; the less immigrants, the less competition, the higher the wages. For political reasons he went along reluctantly with the Jewish Socialist Federation though he was not happy with such ethnic divisions in a party that preached universalism. As a socialist and an able lawyer he was counsel for Jewish labor unions; no one could question his devotion to the cause.

In 1917 during World War I he ran for mayor of New York City and garnered 145,000 votes. This is impressive. Many who voted for him were not socialists; they were Germans or Irish who were pro-German and anti-British. Hillquit was anti-war. Numerous Jews in Lower Manhattan supported him politically because their sons had been conscripted. His election program offered socialism and peace to a people at war, medical care for the masses, meals for the hungry, better schools, municipal ownership of street railways and subways. The earlier Populists would have approved of him. In this election Judah Magnes and Sholem Asch supported him, but not Barondess. Anti-war sentiment, said Barondess, was a betrayal of our sons in the camps. In this mayoralty election the Socialists were not altogether unsuccessful; they elected a municipal judge, ten assemblymen, and seven aldermen. Three years later when the state assembly refused to seat five Socialists who had been properly elected Hillquit was in the forefront of those who protested vigorously. This was during the period of the Red Scare. To refuse to seat the Socialist legislators, said Hillquit, was a "lynching of the Constitution." Marshall, the Republican, agreed with him. In 1919 when the communists split off from the socialists, Hillquit sided with the more conservative group. He had no sympathy for communists and anarchists. He always remained loyal to the party seeking reform through political action. He wanted results, *takhlit*; in this respect he was a good Jew.[3]

Victor L. Berger

Hillquit ran for Congress and never made it; Victor L. Berger (1860-1929) of Milwaukee, as it has been pointed out above, was elected on a

Socialist ticket and served from 1911 to 1913. Berger was a secular Jew with no interest in Jews and Judaism. True, he did not cut himself off from his people, for he taught Sunday school in a Reform synagog and was a long-time member of a Jewish mutual-aid society. The Sunday school was a pay job; the mutual-aid society offered benefits. Berger was well educated and seems to have attended some classes at universities in Budapest and Vienna; he was a native Hungarian. After landing here in 1878 he worked at several jobs as a laborer and finally was employed in the Milwaukee school system teaching German. Once, he almost lost his job because he attacked the Bible. Berger made his career as a journalist, as editor of the Milwaukee *Leader*, one of the largest socialist papers in the United States. Like Hillquit and most other notable New York Marxists, he, too, joined the new Socialist Party of America when many of the stalwarts rebelled against DeLeon and left the Socialist Laborites (1897-1901). Like Gompers and some other socialists he was an immigration restrictionist.

Because Berger was highly respected in the larger Milwaukee community he was reelected in 1918 and 1920. However he was not seated. The Espionage Acts made it relatively simple to indict him. In 1918 he was charged with disloyalty and sentenced to serve twenty years in jail. The Supreme Court, however, reversed the decision; in 1923 he was back again in Congress to remain there for additional terms. For many years Berger was a member of the National Executive Board of the Socialist Party of America.[4]

MEYER LONDON

In 1914 Meyer London (1871-1926), a New York ghetto denizen, was elected to Congress on the Socialist ticket defeating the Tammany candidate. Socialists, trade unionists, and discriminating Jewish voters sent him to Washington. This East Side Jew was loved and respected; he was a man of honor, and a true humanitarian. He had no interest in traditional Judaism but he was devoted to Jews. As a socialist he was an assimilationist only in the sense that he believed that every Jew should remain a Jew as long as there was any discrimination against him. London was opposed to the erection of barriers to Jews fleeing from lands of oppression; he wanted Russia to honor the American passport when carried by a Jew; he was one of the men who supported the work of the People's Relief Committee in 1915 when it began collaborating with the religionists and the old-timers in the effort to succor suffering Jews in the war zones. When the American Jewish Congress was established by the country's "Russians" after 1914 to lobby for Jewish rights in a European postwar world, London supported it; some consistent socialist internationalists did

not. Like Hillquit and Berger, London was a staunch socialist, an internationalist who nursed messianic hopes. This meant he would have little
sympathy for Zionists, nationalists; he refused to introduce a resolution in
Congress endorsing the movement and its hope for a free state.

Lithuanian born, son of a free-thinking talmudist, he came to the
United States in 1891, a man of twenty; seven years later he had already
passed the bar exam; he was a lawyer who never made much money despite his competence. Employed as counsel during the cloakmaker strike
in 1910, he played an important role in the negotiations. He had been a
Socialist since the 1890's and had run for the office of state assemblyman
as soon as he was naturalized. London served three terms in Congress, in
1914, 1916, and 1920, to the dismay of at least one of his fellow congressmen. After he made his first speech in Congress a Republican member crossed the House and peered into London's face. He wanted to see
what this weird character, this Socialist, looked like; maybe he was crazy.
London was not reelected in 1918; it was a year of reaction exacerbated by
the obsessive fears of the American people after the communists came to
power in Russia. London himself had no sympathy for the Bolsheviks. As
a congressman, he fought against lynching and injunctions in labor disputes; he was opposed to child labor and was eager to further legislation
that would provide unemployment insurance, old-age pensions, maternity
allowances. The coal mines, he believed, should be nationalized. When
war was declared in Europe in 1914 he pleaded for neutrality. Much more
than Berger and Hillquit he was a Jewish labor leader; he did not approve
of the cautious policies of Gompers but the two men were friendly. Despite his objections to the involvement of the United States in World War
I he was, like other socialist notables, a fervent American. The East Side,
the city, never forgot him; Public School No. 2 was renamed The Meyer
London School.[5]

Baruch Vladeck

Along with Berger, Hillquit, and London, Baruch Vladeck (1886-1938)
stands out as notable socialist politician, party activist, and leader. He was
less doctrinaire than the other three; from a socialist point of view that
may not be a compliment. The first and original name of this Russian was
Baruch Nachman Charney. In Russian Charney means black; that is why
his brother Samuel, a distinguished Yiddish literary critic, took the name
Niger. Vladeck was Charney's name in Russian revolutionary circles.
This socialist began life as a Hassidic pietist; at the age of fifteen he went
to Minsk to study in a rabbinic academy. It was not long after that he
emerged as a political rebel, for in 1904 he was jailed by the authorities.
On his release he became active in the Bund. For years he traveled about

the country as an agitator and organizer; in 1908 he came to the United States and carried on here as a lecturer; Vladeck was a brilliant orator. While living in Philadelphia he served as the editor of the local edition of the *Forward* and perfected his education at the University of Pennsylvania. His rise in radical circles in this country was rapid; during World War I he was involved in the People's Relief Committee and after he shifted his base to New York City became chief of the *Forward* under Cahan. In 1917 he served on the city's Board of Aldermen, as a Socialist of course. When in 1919 the break came with the Jewish communists he was on the side of the angels. By 1920 he was recognized by New York Jewry's elite, by Marshall et al; he worked well with the establishment. In the 1930's he lent his support to the ORT and the Jewish Labor Committee (1934). The ORT, originally a Russian-based artisan training philanthropy, now reached out to help the Jews vocationally in many lands. The acronym, from the Russian, was now spelled out as the Organization for Rehabilitation and Training. The Jewish Labor Committee was organized in New York to oppose fascism both in the United States and in Europe, particularly in Germany.

Under Mayor LaGuardia, Vladeck began to come into his own; after the mayor appointed him a member of the city's Housing Authority, Vladeck saw to it that in the slum clearance that followed there would be adequate housing for workers. This was one of the first undertakings of its type in the country. In 1936 he and David Dubinsky helped establish New York's American Labor Party in order to rally voters for Roosevelt; he was able to recruit socialist support for the Democratic ticket. Like the first Roosevelt, Theodore, Vladeck was also a writer, a litterateur, a poet. He had known some of the Yiddish literary giants before he fled to America. The Charney family was gifted; one brother, Daniel, was a poet. Vladeck was one of the few Yiddishists who knew that the language had no real future in this country and he had the courage to say it. Americanization would take over; in the meantime it was the job of the leaders to inculcate the workers with socialist ideals; Americanism was too materialistic. Like many of his coworkers in the party, Vladeck had made his peace with American liberalism and social reform. He had become an East Side hero and when he died hundreds of thousands—so it is said—lined the streets to do him honor. It is the measure of the man and the growing influence of the East Europeans that the city's political elite spoke at his funeral: Governor Herbert H. Lehman, Senator Robert F. Wagner, and Norman Thomas, the socialist; delegates, party delegates, too, came in from other cities. By 1938, the year that Vladeck died, there were ten Jews in the House of Representatives; several were of East European ancestry; two were born in Russia. After two long generations the Russian, Polish, and Rumanian Jews and their children were rising to power.[6]

CHAIM ZHITLOWSKY

Chaim Zhitlowsky (1865-1943) was sui generis. Here was a man who was a socialist, a brilliant orator, a scholar who introduced philosophic thinking and terminology into the Yiddish-reading world. He played no part in American Jewish politics, yet he was very influential. He was unique because he insisted that one could be both a good socialist and a good Jew; ethnos and internationalism could be reconciled. Zhitlowsky is outstanding among those Marxist ideologues who embraced Jewish nationalism, his version. He was not a Zionist. Zhitlowsky, a publicist, wrote in Russian, English, German, and Yiddish. In Russia in the 1890's he achieved recognition, distinction indeed, as one of the founders of the Social Revolutionary Party. It was in that same decade that he began expounding his belief that Jews, a distinct national group wherever they lived, were entitled to minority rights. Thus socialism could be multinational; the Jews are to be a nation among nations emphasizing culture, not their religion. America could thus be a complex of nationalities; this is cultural pluralism. He was a member of the Bund in Russia. Did he influence it? Over here since 1904, on and off, he may have influenced Horace Kallen, Mordecai M. Kaplan, and the cultural Yiddishists. All this is moot and bears further scrutiny. National rights were being advocated by minority ethnic groups in Russia long before Zhitlowsky's time.

In 1908 Zhitlowsky went back to Russia and was elected to the Duma, the parliament, but was not permitted to take his seat. When he returned to this country to settle down permanently he made a living as a journalist and as a lecturer. For many years he was on the staff of *The Day* (*Der Tog*). Though he was no Zionist he was not unsympathetic to the Zionist-Socialists and the American Jewish Congress. It was this latter group that in 1915 insisted on minority rights in the East European lands where Jews were always subject to abuse and persecution. His teachings certainly influenced many Jewish socialists to reach out to Jews as fellow ethnics. In his later years he lectured frequently to Jewish communist groups to the dismay of his socialist colleagues. They found it hard to forgive him.[7]

EAST EUROPEAN WOMEN WORKERS

Even before the mid-1880's when the Russians and Poles started coming to the United States in large numbers, millions of women in this country were pouring into industry and commerce. Indeed from that decade on there were more women than men employed in the needle trades; many females, too, went to work in the cigar and shoe factories. In New York a large percentage of young women at work were what the United States government called Hebrew Russian females. Many of them were of a tender age; some actually were children; once they were married they did not return to the factories. They did keep house; often they had to take in boarders and make provision for them. Among the many problems the women faced in the sweatshops and factories were lack of work in the off-seasons and during hard times and the generally low pay; the average wage of women in the needle trades was considerably less than the men's. There were numerous exceptions; some women brought home substantial pay envelopes. East European Jewish girls did better than other women from the same part of Europe.[8]

As early as the 1890's women were already being organized into locals by women who led them. They wanted to better themselves; very few of the newcomers went into domestic service although back home in the Slavic lands many had worked as house servants. Here in the Golden Land, they upgraded themselves. By the early 1900's these working women set out to help one another; with few exceptions, the leaders who stepped forward were socialists; all of them were dedicated to social reform. After 1900 when the Women's Trade Union League, with its substantial quota of middle-class Americans, dedicated itself to furthering these immigrant female toilers, the male union leaders dragged their heels; the men did little to help them organize. One of the early women union leaders was Theresa Malkiel, a sweatshop worker; she set out to establish a woman's trade organization in infants' wear in the 1890's. Malkiel did receive recognition from her fellow socialists; after the turn of the century she was put on the Women's National Committee of the Socialist Party. In later years she ran for office in the state assembly on a Marxist ticket; she was an ardent advocate of suffrage for women. A feminist? After a fashion, model early 1900's; she believed that a woman's prime job was to be a homemaker.[9]

COHN, PESOTTA, AND NEWMAN

It was around the year 1909, when the garment workers began to strike with a degree of success, that the International Ladies' Garment Workers' Union reluctantly began to use women organizers; among these women there was a substantial number of competent, dedicated workers; Pauline Newman, Rose Pesotta, and Fannia Cohn stand out. Their task was difficult; most Americans were anti-union; many still are. The task of the woman organizer was fraught with hazards; on the picket line she could be beaten by thugs; the union's male leaders were suspicious; they wanted no competition. The men who ran the unions looked with jaundiced eye on the middle-class women of the Women's Trade Union League who set out to help the girls. Discouraged by lack of cooperation, the WTUL changed its goals somewhat and entered the battle for equal suffrage hoping in this fashion to help female operatives. Pesotta, Cohn, and Newman labored in the garment industry. No matter the industry, women had trouble; the problems of long hours and underpayment were exacerbated by the sexual harassment to which they were exposed. The unions made little effort to cope with this problem.

Fannia Cohn (b. 1885/1888-1962) left Russia, a young woman, on the eve of the social revolution (1904). She was a Social Revolutionary before she arrived in America. Here she became an organizer for the ILGWU. Unlike other women who made a name for themselves in the industry she was not a proletarian; her family had some means; union work was a deliberate choice, a labor of love; she wanted to help the workers culturally. By 1914 she was the head of an important union. Because of her interest in educating the workers she was made the executive secretary of this department of the ILGWU (1918) and remained at this post for over forty years. It was because of her that the Brookwood Labor College was established and the ILGWU built the largest workers' education department in the United States. She was bypassed in her later years as new concepts of workers' education were adopted, but she is important historically because she wanted the workers to have learning, to think, to plan their future intelligently. Cohn was finally given recognition on a national level by the union, for she was appointed vice president in 1916. It would not be long before the ILGWU, realizing the importance of organizing female workers, addressed itself to this task vigorously.

Russian-born Rose Pesotta (1896-1965) was already a follower of anarchist ideas when she came here in 1913. In this country she became such an excellent organizer for the ILGWU that it often loaned her to other unions for their organizing drives. Throughout her long association with the ILGWU she battled against its anti-female bias, once going so far as resigning for a time. She was incensed that a union whose membership was overwhelmingly female was dominated by males; like Cohn, she, too, eventually became a vice president. Pesotta personally benefited from some of the union's social programs. Not only did she take advantage of some of its schools to further her education, she also lived in a union-sponsored cooperative apartment.

Pauline Newman (b. 1887/1891), came to this country as a child and almost immediately was put to work at the Triangle Waist Factory; she was paid $1.50 a week; it was a seven-day work week; there was no overtime pay. As a child, so she reports, she was hidden in hampers when the inspectors came around. Later, as she grew up, she, too, became an organizer—of women, of course—for the ILGWU; she traveled to different parts of the country to do her job. She was competent. She even took time out to lead a rent strike against a gouging landlord. She educated herself, for she wrote for the English and Yiddish press, and as an ambitious socialist went into politics. She ran for Congress and for the office of Secretary of State in New York; she played a role in the local and national affairs of the Women's Trade Union League and joined forces in the 1930's and 1940's with the American Labor Party and the Liberal Party. As early as 1909, she had been conscripted to work for the Joint Board of Sanitary Control in the women's garment industry; she knew all the evasion tricks of the employers; in 1913 she was an aide to Dr. George M. Price when he established the Union Health Center; by the 1920's this had become a full-time job for her. It was in no small part due to her efforts that the Center prospered. She was able, efficient, tactful, a good fund-raiser. Many thousand of workers were helped, advised, in its ambulatory clinic.[10]

DOROTHY JACOBS BELLANCA

Of the several Russian and Polish women who made a name for themselves in the union movement—the needle trades to be more exact—there was no more successful organizer than Dorothy Jacobs Bellanca (1894-1946). In a way she was more fortunate than the other women engaged in this type of work because she came to the fore at a time when workmen were no longer on the defensive, when unions and what they stood for were on the upswing. Dorothy, a Latvian immigrant, was the head of a buttonhole union in Baltimore when only twenty years of age. When she started out as a buttonhole apprentice, age thirteen, she worked the first four weeks for nothing; when she learned the art she was paid $3 a week. In 1916 the newly created Amalgamated Clothing Workers of America, recognizing her ability, put her on its executive board. This was an unusual honor for a woman. For the rest of her life she devoted herself to the job of organizing female operatives for the growing ACWA. Like other women who were union notables she also moved into politics running for city and state office; she, too, was accorded recognition in New York's American Labor Party. Dorothy had married out; few of the women union activists were ardent Jews; their first loyalty was to labor, Marxism, and nonsectarian ideals.

Individual women organizers did a good job but it took time before their contributions were recognized and rewarded. By the 1920's the Jewish female workers in industry, in the apparel trade, were doing better. They were laboring fewer hours and receiving more money than they had a decade earlier. One may well doubt, however, if they were given the pay which their work and skills merited. Immigrants had a hard lot. Conscious of its obligations to fellow Jews, to the newcomers, the Jewish community developed welfare agencies to help young women. Even staid Shearith Israel organized an Emma Lazarus Working Girls' Club which met in its vestry rooms. One may be sure that discussions of unions and strikes were not encouraged. In the shops young Jewish girls were not overwhelmed by the chivalrous conduct of their male fellow workers. Immigrant girls of a tender age were put to work; they were expected to help support themselves and the family, too, at least until they married. Marriage was important to the youngsters; for the females the unions and the shops offered little future. They were happy to quit work; men had it better; the unions, dominated by males with European (American?) traditions, looked down upon women; they were not deemed equals. All this in 1920.[11]

BELLE LINDNER ISRAELS MOSKOWITZ: POLITICAL LIBERAL AND SOCIAL REFORMER

Belle Lindner Israels Moskowitz (1877-1933) was cut from a different piece of cloth than Pauline Newman and her fellow organizers. Moskowitz began life as Belle Lindner, a native American, daughter of a Polish Jewish Harlem watchmaker. Belle went to Columbia's Teachers' College for a year. That was the extent of her formal college education. In 1903 she became Mrs. Charles Henry Israels; in 1914 after the death of her husband she married Henry Moskowitz. As a young woman, working for the local section of the National Council of Jewish Women, she did what she could to keep an eye on the public dance halls, nurseries of vice; she was interested also in providing pure milk for infants and housing for girls. Moskowitz worked in the Travelers Aid Society and had some experience as an editorial assistant on a socialist workers' paper. She was learning her job as a social reformer but she was no socialist. When the shirtwaist manufacturers took over the Protocol system first developed by the cloakmakers, she was given the important job of grievance clerk; ultimately she was to be in charge of the labor policy of the manufacturers in this industry. With respect to unions she was on the other side of the fence. She lost her job when the Protocol system began falling apart. In 1916 she was out of work. In 1918 she joined Alfred E. Smith, becoming one of his political aides. Smith, then running for governor, needed her to get out the women's vote. It was not long before she was an important part of his kitchen cabinet. During the years 1924-1928 she was a member of the National Democratic Committee's Advisory Board, the only woman appointed. When Smith was governor she was very influential, a national figure in the field of politics; he leaned very heavily on her; she helped materially to shape his sociopolitical policies. There was no other Jewish woman in her generation comparable to her with the possible exception of Anna Rosenberg. Sophie Irene Loeb and Lillian Wald, reformers, operated on an entirely different level although, to be sure there is no social reform without political involvement.[12]

ANNA ROSENBERG

Anna Rosenberg (b. 1900/1902), Belle Moskowitz's younger contemporary, had a very distinguished career; she rose to power after Moskowitz's sun had set. Newman may be the most earthy of the left-wing East European women in the union movement, Bellanca and Pesotta the most distinguished organizers, Cohn the most ambitious culturally, Moskowitz the most influential as a political advisor, Schneiderman the most successful woman in the world of labor and politics, Anna Rosenberg, however, held the highest political office among all these women of East European ancestry. This native of Hungary, who came here as a child, made a name for herself during World War I selling bonds. It took time, however, before she found herself; that was later in the days of the New Deal; in 1934 she was appointed director of New York's National Recovery Administration; her influence expanded nationally under F. D. Roosevelt. She was to serve on a host of boards and commissions, state and federal, until she became an Assistant Secretary of Defense (1950-1953) under Truman. As a public relations consultant she worked closely with agencies that raised funds for Palestine, for the Joint Distribution Committee, and the New York Federation of Jewish Philanthropies. For this thirteen-year-old Hungarian immigrant girl America was to spell opportunity. After her arrival here on these shores her native Hungary experienced a disastrous war, the domination of anti-Semites, Nazis, and communists. Her lines had indeed fallen in pleasant places.[13]

EMMA GOLDMAN

Fannia Cohn was an educator; Emma Goldman (1869-1940) was an educated woman, one of the best read and critically equipped and learned Jewish women of her day. Politically she was an anarchist. This native Lithuanian received some secular training in her home country, in Koenigsberg, Prussia, and in St. Petersburg, the capital of the Russias, where she tarried for a while; she was attracted to the opera. For the most part though she was self-educated. She was still a young girl when she emigrated to America, to Rochester, where she married, but it was not long before she was divorced; it was not a good marriage. A year after she landed in 1885, the Haymarket bombing and the execution of men who were not given a fair trial, disturbed her as it did thousands. Here in the United States she had already become a socialist; the Haymarket case and the American form of government, as she saw and experienced it, impelled her, after a few years, to turn to anarchism. In New York City to which she had moved she met Alexander Berkman, an anarchist writer and an excellent public speaker. Berkman who had come here in 1887 had been a revolutionary in Europe; here he joined the Anarchist Pioneers of Freedom. Other anarchist influences in this country made their impress; he was a follower of Johann Joseph Most, a former member of the German national parliament. Berkman, the intellectual—and that he was —made his living as a printer and cigarmaker. The two, Goldman and Berkman, fell in love; they lived together, a devoted couple.

The year 1892 was a bad year for the working classes. Early in July the steelworkers at the Homestead, Pennsylvania, mills of the Carnegie Steel Company engaged in a battle with detectives and strikebreakers. After several people were killed, the state militia was called out. Then it was that Berkman, with the help of Emma, decided to kill Henry Clay Frick, the superintendent of the mills. Frick was an enemy of society! A biography has referred to Berkman as the "Assassin as Saint"; a better title would have been the "Assassin as Schlemiel." Armed with both a dagger and a revolver, Berkman wounded Frick twice and stabbed him several times but did not succeed in killing him. He affirmed the old Yiddish aphorism that a Jew is no murderer. The attack was make on July 23, 1892; in order to finance the attempt Emma tried to become a prostitute for a night but her effort was a fiasco. Berkman languished in prison for fourteen years; Frick became a very wealthy man and left millions to further the arts. After Berkman was released he and Emma edited an anarchist monthly called *Mother Earth* (1906-1907). It was during these editorial years that he wrote *Prison Memoirs of an Anarchist*; it was dedicated "To all those who in and out of prison fight against their bondage." During World War I Berkman was sent back to prison because of his attack on conscription; in 1919 he was deported to the new Russia, but after three years fled. Communist domination was no better than capitalist oppression. In a work that he wrote in 1925 he damned the Bolsheviks who imprisoned people for their political views. In Germany and in France where he now settled he made a living as a translator and writer. His troubles all came to an end in 1936 when he committed suicide in Nice, France.

Emma, too, had her problems; she spent a year at Blackwell's Island for inciting to riot: during the 1893 panic she told unemployed workers to take bread if they were hungry. After her release from jail she studied nursing in Vienna but her real job as she saw it was to speak to the multitudes on social problems. Because of an address she made in favor of birth control she was arrested and had to serve fifteen days in a New York jail; her open opposition to the 1917 Espionage Act brought her two years in prison. It was under this congressional statute that the Socialist Debs was sentenced to prison for ten years and Berger for twenty. Berger, fortunately, never had to serve. Among the hundreds of victims of the Espionage Act were several Jews; one of them was Jacob (Jack) Abrams. In 1918 Abrams and some of his friends had distributed English and Yiddish pamphlets protesting the intervention of American troops in Russia and Siberia; there had been no declaration of war against Russia. Six Russians, including a girl, all Jews, were arrested in connection with this protest; one, tortured and badly beaten in jail, died of injuries; the girl was sentenced to fifteen years imprisonment; three others, including Abrams, received sentences of twenty years. When in 1919 the case was sent to the United States Supreme Court the sentence was affirmed; Holmes and Brandeis dissented. Four of the offenders were finally released in 1921 but had to leave the country; they went to Russia. Unhappy Abrams fled from the Soviet state and finally found refuge in Mexico.

Two years before Abrams and his friends went to Russia, Goldman and Berkman and a host of others were formally deported to that country by the United States government. This was at the time of the Red Scare when the Department of Justice, led by Attorney General A. Mitchell Palmer, arrested thousands of political radicals and labor activists; the aliens among them were deported. The U. S. transport *Buford* sailed with 249 of these unfortunates including Goldman and Berkman. Emma Goldman, unhappy in the new Russia, left after two years, and attacked it as a totalitarian state. Exiled from the America which she loved she died in Canada in 1940. Freedom as she interpreted it meant everything to her and there was no freedom in any modern state. All governments are bad; people must govern themselves; she was opposed to all dictatorship whether of the right or of the left; the ideal society was a blending of individuals and organizations, all ethically motivated. There must always be free speech; she was an egalitarian but no suffragist per se. Anarchism as a philosophy did not insist on equality for women. She was a rebel who decried violence, certainly after the Berkman fiasco (she was only twenty-three when the *attentat* was made). Like Berkman she was a good speaker. Here in the United States she had lectured since the 1890's; she spoke on anarchism, on social problems, on freedom for women, on free love: a man and a woman with mutual regard and affection can live together without the blessing of the state. American litterateurs respected her critical judgment in the areas of the fine arts; as she traveled about the country lecturing she popularized Ibsen, Shaw, Strindberg. In 1922, *The Nation*, the magazine, in an enthusiastic moment, wrote that she was one of the twelve greatest living women.[14]

ROSE HARRIET PASTOR STOKES

Rose Harriet Pastor Stokes (1879-1933) was not the most distinguished and effective of the radical women of her generation but she was an attractive appealing person; her devotion to her beliefs merits respect. She was a socialist and later a communist. Rose was born in Russian Poland into an impoverished unhappy family. After her father ran away her mother remarried; Rose took the name of her stepfather. She and her mother moved on to London where as a four-year-old she was kept busy sewing bows on ladies' slippers. She had to help where she could. Fortunately she went to the Jews' Free School for two years and was given the elements of an education. This was the institution where a generation earlier Samuel Gompers had learned to read and write. When about twelve years of age Rose found herself in Cleveland (1890) where her stepfather had moved. She was put to work in a cigar factory and labored there for twelve years; the family was large; for a time she was the sole support of the lot. About the year 1901 she began to write for the *Jewish Daily News* (the *Tageblatt*), New York's outstanding Orthodox organ. In 1903 she went on to New York and was put on the staff of the paper writing for the English page. The well-known Yiddish writer Zevin (Tashrak) was in love with Rose and helped bring the family to the city; they lived in the Bronx. Rose wrote two columns; one, signed Zelda, was titled "Just Between Ourselves Girls"; the other was called "Ethics of the Dust Pan."

Two years later the press of the country was given a juicy morsel; proletarian Rose married the social reformer James Graham Phelps Stokes, a scion of one of the most distinguished and wealthy American families. Here was a real life Cinderella story. Had he been still living Horatio Alger would have gaped in astonishment and gratification, "Rags to Riches." It was a church wedding; Rose had no religion. She left out the word "obey" in the ceremony and wore a cross for the occasion, no doubt to please her husband's family. Both she and her husband in those idyllic days were socialists. The two worked together for liberal causes; she was an activist in strikes though never a leader in the trade union movement. Rose had many interests, among them birth control and suffrage for women. She was eager to make a literary career for herself; she helped translate some Yiddish poems, wrote poetry herself, a proletarian play, and did some acting.

In 1917, the year war was declared, she and her husband left the Socialist Party; in 1918 she was back again. It is patent that she would look with favor on the fall of the Romanovs in Russia and the rise of a liberal state in that unhappy land. All Jews rejoiced when Russia was freed; years earlier Isaac M. Wise had prophesied that a day of judgment would come for that country with its "Tartarian brutality and despotism." Its only salvation would be revolution. That same year the Espionage Act trapped her in its net; she was indicted and sentenced to ten years in prison for saying that the government was supporting profiteers. Fortunately for her the conviction was later reversed. When in the aftermath of the Russian revolution a communist party was called into being here in the United States (1919) she became an enthusiastic member. Despite occasional divagations she was essentially a radical; she was true to her proletarian origins and she had the courage of her convictions. In 1925 Rose broke formally with her husband; they had grown apart personally and ideologically; he was a social reformer; she was a Marxist, a pro-Russian Bolshevik. A few years later she married a man who shared her political views; in 1933 she died of cancer in a German hospital where she had gone for help. Cinderella had come to a sorry end; not infrequently East European heroic sagas turn out to be tragedies.[15]

WERE THE JEWISH GARMENT WORKERS SOCIALISTS?

Were the Jewish garment workers in New York City and in other metropolitan centers socialists? Many if not most of the men and women who bent over their machines were not; many of the leaders were. It is not easy to determine how the masses voted. One did not have to be a socialist to demand social justice, to criticize the capitalist system. As early as 1891, in his encyclical "Rerum Novarum," Pope Leo XIII appealed for better relations between capital and labor. As a conservative he condemned liberalism; it was an ally of Judaism. Some of the Jewish newcomers were radicals; still smarting under Slavic and Rumanian persecution they did not realize that they were striking out at European tyrannies when they preached radical changes here in the United States. Even a modicum of prosperity tended to water down the leftist political-economic views of some. As early as 1905 an astute observer pointed out that the radical Jews were already moving to the right. On the Lower East Side it was not unusual for Jews to vote for radicals because they were men of integrity. It was not easy to foretell the size of the socialist vote in a national election. Post-World War I bitterness and disillusionment brought Debs, the Socialist presidential candidate, 900,000 votes in 1920. At the next election the Progressive Robert M. La Follette captured much of the "socialist" vote; in 1928 Norman Thomas, the Socialist who aspired to become president, received 268,000 votes; during the depression, 1932, almost 900,000 people voted for him but in 1936 with the New Deal in full sway, less than 190,000 men and women in the United States chose the Socialist Thomas.

One suspects that the number of hard core Jewish socialists was small. The garment workers may have read the *Forward* but the majority were not committed Marxists. Internal factionalism hurt the socialists; after 1901 the new Socialist Party of America feuded with the older Socialist Laborites; the anarchists were at odds with both groups. During the period of the Red Scare, 1919-1920, government prosecutions—persecutions—of radicals intimidated thousands. By 1921 many of the immigrant leftists departed this scene; it was then, as the workers began to harvest the fruits of a relatively successful unionism, that many evinced their indifference to Marx and the class struggle. There is some truth also in the caustic remark that many socialists wanted to live like capitalists. Trade unions did bring a fuller dinner pail; for most workers that was their prime concern. Conditions were better here; don't complain; you never had it so good! Did socialism—Jewish socialism, if you will—have any successes? Its successes were the unions' successes; if Jewish unions made advances in wages, fewer hours, a cleaner shop, a share in the administration of the industry, they were certainly indebted in large measure to the devotion of their socialist leaders. America's East European masses? Most of these men were nominally Orthodox; they were anti-socialism, anti-anarchism, anti-atheism. More often than not they detested these dissidents; they were outside the pale. Typical Orthodox Jews wanted no revolution over here—not even an evolutionary one; they had suffered in Russia, Poland, Lithuania, and had hungered in Galicia; they yearned for peace, quiet, opportunity, a chance to make a dollar. They desired bread, not ideology. Committed socialists were always few in numbers, never a majority on the Lower East Side or in any American Jewish ghetto.

What sort of Jews were socialist Jews? They were Jews; they had little choice; Gentiles on the whole rejected them because they were Jews. Even Gentile socialists both here and abroad often expressed their dislike of Jews. The unions, too, in the United States were prejudiced against them. The persecutions in Eastern Europe from the 1880's on into the twentieth century and the new racism convinced Jewish socialists that at best they would only be tolerated by the Gentile masses. This realization, sensed by the Jewish Social Democrats in Russia in the 1890's, induced them to make compromises; they conjured up a comforting philosophy of a non-religious Yiddish culture. Indeed it was not long before there was a yiddishkeit, a Jewishness, to suit every Jewish socialist palate, both here and abroad: Bundist ethnicism, Diaspora nationalism, Territorialism, Socialist-Zionism. Most socialists remained loyal to Jewry as they defined it. There is this too; both socialism and Judaism exult in their mission to make the world a better place for every human being; this they have always had in common.[16]

COMMUNISM AND THE JEWS

Russia-style communism achieved recognition here as early as 1918. Many Jewish intellectuals looked upon the new Soviet state as a messianic fulfillment; revolutionary Russia heralded the dawn of a new world of justice, equality, humanity; religion and "racial" prejudice would vanish. Communism attracted some, too, because they wanted emancipation for their dear ones in Eastern Europe. For many it was a political philosophy, more liberal, more vigorous than socialism. As the communists gained followers here there was a split in the Jewish Socialist Federation, a Jewish Communist Federation came into being (1919); by 1929-1930 America's communists created a fraternal order of their own with a Jewish section; it was called the Jewish People's Fraternal Order. In 1944 this mutual-benefit society announced that it had 43,000 members, an impressive number, if accurate. The hostilities that broke out in the country between socialists and communists were, to say the least, acrimonious; factionalism threatened for years to destroy some of the apparel unions. As was to be expected the Yiddish-speaking communists put out their own daily; it was called the *Freiheit* (*Freedom*, 1922); at its height it had a circulation of about 22,000. There are some estimates in the 1920's that about 15 percent of the Communist Party in America was Jewish; the percentage among the leaders was high. During the long depression of the 1930's the communists won adherents; people were desperate and were looking for a solution to their economic problems. When World War II erupted Russia sponsored a Popular Front policy; the Russians were the allies of the Free World. It was then that communism won Jewish members and sympathizers but the 1939 Stalin-Hitler pact and the alliance with the German anti-Semites almost destroyed Jewish communism in this country. Destruction was practically complete after World War II when reports reached the West of Stalin's murders of Jews and the rise of an anti-Jewish policy on the part of the government itself. How many Jews were card carrying members of the Communist Party? This is difficult to determine. The party never polled more than 102,785 votes in a national election out of a total of close to 40,000,000; it is obvious that the number of Jewish communist voters was minuscule.[17]

THE JEWISH TRADE UNION MOVEMENT: A SUMMARY

What did the unions, the trade union movement, and the Marxist leaders do for the Jewish working people in metropolitan areas in the years before 1921, before the first anti-Jewish, anti-immigration act was passed? One may also ask what the trade unions did—if anything—for the larger American Jewry; and finally what did these "Jewish" apparel unions do for the country, the American people? In the decades before 1921 the majority of the Jews here were "Russians," people of East European background; very many of them were in industry, wage earners. These newcomers, comfortably settled in their various American ghettos were the first—and the last—Jewish mass proletariat in American history. The garment industry which they developed to its present height was very important, particularly in New York City; by the end of the second decade of the 1900's it may have given work to 200,000 men and women—and some children too. There were also many thousands in other crafts and occupations. By 1900 the apparel trade was a billion dollar industry; the Jews were then still the largest ethnic group in the needle trades. The trade unions in the garment industry came into being in order to protect the men and women who were being exploited, largely by fellow Jews. For the first time in American history there was a substantial number of Jewish trade union organizations led by secularists. The movement was idealistic; it emphasized traditional concepts of justice, concepts that were very real and meaningful. These Jewish operatives resented deeply the oppression which they had experienced in Russia and to which their kin in that land were still exposed. They resented any injustice here in a land of presumptive freedom for all. Whatever their personal political views and prejudices were, they were ready to follow their socialist leaders who sought to improve their lot. Culturally, structurally, the Jewish trade union movement was autonomous, separatist too, cordoned off from the mass of newcomers in this land. The total movement was a complex that included locals, leftist fraternal orders, house organs, a sympathetic press, and central union federations. It was an almost self-sufficient world, a relatively large one, for there were more Jews in the needle trade unions than in any other form of industry in this country. It would be interesting to determine to what extent, in 1920, the Jewish masses of New York City in their several ghettos were involved in the movement in all its ramifications, auxiliary services, and institutions. One suspects that the majority of all Jewish immigrants kept themselves aloof from the world of the unions and their satellite associations. This was certainly true in the hinterland where half of all the newcomers dwelt. It has been pointed out above that many Jewish trade unionists were practicing Orthodox Jews; there can be no question that the members of the socialist-led unions were not of one piece. By the 1930's, when the racist Germans in Europe began persecuting Jews all American Jewish unionists and socialists had no choice but to align themselves with the totality of World Jewry, with their own people.[18]

As late as 1921 the Jewish trade union leaders were still loyal to their pristine socialist ideals; they still talked of fostering a strong Marxist movement in order to change the American political system; their attitude to Judaism, the religion, was a negative one; class identification was for them more important than Jewish identification, so they said. After the strikes beginning in 1909 the leaders set out to build powerful unions. This in a way was their undoing ideologically. As the unions gained strength and brought the workers monetary and other rewards, political socialism tended to recede into the background. During World War I the United States government, desperate for supplies, material goods, furthered the unions; the authorities encouraged them to bargain collectively and thus paved the way for higher wages and better working conditions. After a fashion the Wilson government was a precursor of the New Deal of the 1930's; government beneficence was the answer to radicalism. Segments of the larger American community, liberals, humanitarians, were increasingly friendly to the workers and their unions. Though the powerful craft unions were not sympathetic to the Jewish unions—or to Jews either—they tolerated them both when convinced that they were willing to fit into the scheme of traditional American unionism. Leaders in the powerful American Federation of Labor could not be unmindful that their overall chief was of Jewish birth.

There was no question; the Yiddish unions were becoming Americanized. Whether they knew it or not the socialist leaders were drifting away from doctrinaire Marxism and were becoming pragmatic executives. When in 1919 the socialist Jewish chiefs fought the communists they came that much closer to the conservatism of the American Federation of Labor; a day would come when the Jews and their left-wing officers in the unions would move into the New Deal. In the meantime continuous persecution of the Jews by the Russians in World War I kept the secular leaders "Jewish." With the rise of the Joint Distribution Committee which rallied labor, the economic elite, and the Orthodox, the secularist unionists were ready to work with all Jews; their schismatic characteristics began to fade. Time and circumstance were molding them Jewishly; they were becoming part of World Jewry, empathetically. By 1921 the unions were much better off than they had been in the decades from 1870 to 1910. To be sure it was not all easy sailing; the unions ran into serious problems in the 1920's; it was a prosperous but reactionary decade which ended in a disastrous depression that lasted for many years. The unions still had to cope with strikes and socialist-communist civil war. The Republican Party, now in power, was no great friend of organized labor. It was not until the days of Franklin D. Roosevelt that the unions were able to anchor in a safe harbor; the president needed their votes and their help as he faced the threat of a Nazi Germany that was moving toward the conquest of all Europe. A decade earlier—in the 1920's—the number of Jewish workers in the Jewish unions was already on the decline; some of the operatives were moving out of the industry; the older hands were dying or had retired; the children sought other avenues for economic advance. As all students of American Jewish history have always pointed out, the Jewish labor movement was a one-generation phenomenon. The members of that generation, which extended from 1880 to 1920, had suffered greatly—and further study will confirm this statement—yet in human rights, economic opportunity, in actual earnings, in their standard of living, they were much better off than they had been in Russia, Poland, Galicia, and the Balkans.[19]

WHAT DID THE JEWISH GARMENT UNIONS DO FOR THE WORKERS?

The Jewish needle unions were important; they are an integral part of Jewish history, of American history. No chronicle of the American labor movement can be written without recounting the story of these apparel workers. The garment industry employed hundreds of thousands of men, women, and children; its gross national product amounted to hundreds of millions of dollars. As unionists what did the Jewish leaders want? They wanted better working conditions for their followers; this Hillman and Gompers had in common. There was a constant struggle with depressions, unemployment, intractable employers, unsympathetic municipal and federal authorities. It took over thirty years, from about 1880 on, before the union leaders learned to function effectively and to begin to make substantial gains; it was a fifty-year struggle before they achieved security under Franklin D. Roosevelt. The successes that were chalked up were due to exceptional leaders. They were brilliant, well read, devoted, politically astute, aggressive; they were professionals. It is true, too, that American presidents of the Progressive Age were not unsympathetic to labor unions. Because productivity was imperative in World War I labor was encouraged; but the leaders made their own luck. The workers supported their elected heads sacrificially when strikes were called; they fought with demonic tenacity. The achievements of the Jewish rank and file were heroic as they created socially oriented unions. The Health Center, for instance, was a distinct if not unique contribution. After two generations the struggling American Jewish unions—as far west as Los Angeles—had won notable victories in wages, hours of work, and shop sanitation. Sweatshops were almost eliminated or subject to supervision.

By the 1920's the majority of the workers in the industry were encouraged; the hours of labor had been radically reduced; the unions had some say in the hiring and firing of workers; they had a voice in determining their economic fate. Unions, too, were beginning to cooperate with the owners and to assume some responsibility in management. These years witnessed the first beginnings of unemployment benefits, arbitration, impartial grievance machinery. In the course of the next few decades employees were to receive further benefits and forms of insurance. On its own initiative one of these international garment unions moved into labor banking, cooperative housing and introduced innovative educational programs. Most of these East European wage workers could boast of but little secular culture; the unions and their allies, the labor press and the socialist fraternal orders, educated them, opened new economic, social, and cultural worlds to them. They encouraged these social idealists to envisage a messianic age. This was a concept with which they were somewhat familiar because of their Orthodox religious background. The Jewish labor movement with its various associations and institutions built an emotional haven for its followers; unionism became a way of life for many; it fashioned a snug world of its own. This was "social security." By 1921 the needle workers were part of one of the best organized congeries in the country, and this at a time when a relatively small percentage of laborers in American industry were organized.[20]

WHAT THE UNIONS AND THE LABOR MOVEMENT DID
FOR AMERICAN JEWRY

The Jewish trade union movement, at least until World War I, never set out to do anything for American Jewry; that was not its original concern, its goal. Its hope was to create an ideal society; the world community was far more important than the few million Jews, their bourgeois hopes, their petty Diaspora or Palestinian nationalisms. In the 1880's and 1890's, and in the early 1900's many Jewish radicals rejected their East European past, Orthodoxy, which they identified with obscurantism. It is probable that some may even have held Judaism and the misfortune of Jewish birth responsible for the sufferings they had experienced in the czarist empire. Because of the disabilities under which they had suffered in that land and because of new concepts of "national minority rights," some socialist Jews —and other Jews too—nursed hopes for Jewish forms of Diaspora na- tionalism, of Territorialism, cultural and political autonomy. These ideas were carried to the United States by their protagonists; in this fashion these mavericks forged a link to Jewry as a whole. They remained within the perimeters of American and World Jewry. Socialism and communism had to compete with various forms of Jewish nationalism; many radicals could never cut themselves off completely from their past. What is "Jewish" about the labor movement: its leadership, its members, its foods, its language, its ethnicity. One hesitates to denominate its aggressive fighting spirit, its social hopes, as Jewish; these qualities were demon- strated by many other ethnic groups in the American labor movement. The gestalt is Jewish even though it sometimes took years before the radi- cal Jewish unionists became an integral part of the Body of Israel.

The leaders set out to help the Jewish masses; the clay they molded was Jewish. By using Yiddish they furthered Jewish culture and shackled themselves to the Jewish people. The Hebrew alphabet—it can be insidi- ously Jewish—gave the leftwingers an opportunity to help develop a Yid- dish literature of prose and poetry which influenced the Jewish reading of most Jews from the Slavic lands, millions. A number of the labor union leaders were themselves men of literary bent. In 1922 there were several socialist Yiddish periodicals. The trade union movement did little for Jews as Jews,but inasmuch as the dissident leaders were soon to be reinte- grated into Jewish life, beginning with World War I, the movement was important Jewishly for it held radicals together until they returned openly and avowedly to their people, albeit, to be sure, as secularists. By 1915, through the Joint Distribution Committee they were working together with all other Jews, the bourgeois masses; this is indeed a sharp about-face. The unions helped people who were Jews; it gave the workers a sense of identity, unity, well-being, as they nestled comfortably within the movement itself. They gave their followers a modern rationale, an idealistic substitute for the Judaism of their Russian childhood which some had rejected completely. After their socialism had begun to fade, so-cial,cultural and mutual-aid institutions remained. The labor crusade helped them all to an emotionally fuller life. One suspects that these union comrades were better off culturally than hundreds of thousands, possibly millions of other humble Americans, especially the farmers with small holdings whose horizons were limited to their evangelical rural churches.[21]

WHAT THE UNITED STATES DID FOR THE JEWISH UNIONS

America gave the refugees, including socialist activists who fled to this country, a chance to speak freely, to propagate their liberal and radical views, to further their efforts to raise the level of the Jewish working peo-ple economically and culturally. Over the years, almost unconsciously, these leftist leaders found themselves integrating their organizations into the mainstream of American unionism. Through resort to parliamentary law, which was adopted and practiced in the Jewish labor unions and their auxiliaries, the émigrés were taught some of the basic principles of a functioning representative democracy; they were subjecting themselves to discipline. American opportunities ameliorated their Marxism, their belief in the class struggle and revolution. America tended to make them revi-sionists, social revolutionary reformers; it shifted their devotion from the Communist Manifesto to the American Constitution. Most of the leaders and those of their followers who were Marxists made the shift slowly but contentedly. The prospect of the good life made them American patriots; American freedoms, despite their limitations, were precious to them. Here in this land they and their families could move forward; their mod-est successes were a tribute to this country; America was helping their children to a better life. This was certainly true of those who took advan-tage of the country's educational, cultural, and commercial opportunities. That same America which swallowed them in its slums gave them the chance to flee the deteriorating ghettos and to make a better life for them-selves in the newer areas of resettlement. The typical workman lived bet-ter here than in Russia. Many of the parents and all the children adopted much of American culture and rejoiced in its invitation to the good life. By the 1920's some of the workers and most if not all of their children

ILLUSTRATIONS

Polish-born Michael Heilprin (1823–1888), a political liberal and an encyclopedist who fled to the United States, was a devoted friend of the incoming East European refugees. Courtesy, American Jewish Archives.

Fort Bragg, California, a small town, sheltered a handful of Jews.
Courtesy, H. M. Shafsky and *Western States Jewish Historical Quarterly*,
Oct. 1976.

In 1904, Milwaukee Jews organized a Jewish agricultural colony in Arpin, Wisconsin; it lasted till 1910. Some families remained. Courtesy, American Jewish Archives.

Lower East Side, 1905. Courtesy, Amalgamated Clothing Workers of America.

Abraham Goldfaden (1840–1908), the founder of the
Yiddish theatre in Europe, wrote plays, operas, and
operettas. He lived and worked also in the United States.
Courtesy, American Jewish Archives.

Abraham Cahan (1860–1951). America's most eminent
Yiddish journalist, editor of the Socialist *Forward*, wrote
English novels. Courtesy, American Jewish Archives.

Judah L. Magnes (1877–1948), charismatic American Jewish
leader, builder of the Hebrew University in Jerusalem.
Courtesy, American Jewish Archives.

Joseph Rosenblatt was America's most famous and beloved
cantor. Courtesy, American Jewish Archives.

Solomon Schechter (1850–1915), rabbinic scholar and leader in
Conservative Judaism. Photo by Mandelkern.

Abraham Krotoshinsky (b. 1892), a private in the 77th
Division during World War I, received the Distinguished
Service Cross for bringing relief to his Lost Battalion then
facing capture or annihilation by the German enemy,
October 6, 1918. Courtesy, American Jewish Archives.

Professor Israel Friedlaender (1876–1920), scholar, teacher
in Jewish Theological Seminary of New York. Martyred in
Russia while bringing relief to poor. Photo in *Menorah
Journal* archives.

Family in Eastern Europe, after World War I, receiving relief from the American Jewish Joint Distribution Committee. Courtesy, American Jewish Archives.

Edna Ferber (b. 1887) was one of America's most popular novelists. In 1924 she won a Pulitzer Prize. Courtesy, Anti-Defamation League.

Meyer London (1871–1926), a Socialist member of Congress, was legal counsel for "Jewish" trade unions. Photo by Edmonton, Washington, D.C.

Sophie Irene Loeb (d. 1929), journalist, social and civic reformer, Zionist.
Courtesy, American Jewish Archives.

Lower East Side sweatshop, New York City. Courtesy, International Ladies Garment Workers Union.

Albert Einstein (1879–1955). The physicist and Nobel Prize laureate was interested in Zionism and the peace movement. Courtesy, American Jewish Archives.

Emma Goldman (1869–1940) was one of America's leading anarchists.
This cultured woman believed in a cooperative ethical society. Courtesy,
American Jewish Archives.

Leopold Mannes and Leopold Godowsky were the inventors of the
Kodachrome color process (1935). Courtesy, Eastman Kodak Company.

Rabbi Stephen S. Wise (1872–1949), distinguished liberal rabbi, Zionist leader, great orator. Founder of Jewish Institute of Religion. Photo by Halsman.

Russian-born Sidney Hillman (1887–1946), a labor leader, was active in the Amalgamated Clothing Workers, the Congress of Industrial Organizations, and Roosevelt's War Production Board. Photo by Blackstone Studios, New York.

Irving Berlin (b. 1888) was America's most distinguished songwriter. Courtesy, Abraham J. Feldman.

Chaplain Alexander D. Goode (1911–1943) was lost at sea when the transport *Dorchester* was torpedoed during World War II. Courtesy, American Jewish Archives.

Henrietta Szold (1860–1945), Zionist, founder of Hadassah, helped rebuild modern Palestine. Courtesy, American Jewish Archives.

Nelson Glueck (1900–1971), president of the Hebrew Union College—
Jewish Institute of Religion, was an eminent Palestine archaeologist.
Courtesy, American Jewish Archives.

Yeshiva University, New York City, an Orthodox Jewish institution. Its roots go back to 1886. Courtesy, Yeshiva University.

Rabbi Mordecai Menahem Kaplan (1881–1983). Founder of the Reconstructionist Movement. Courtesy, Jewish Reconstruction Foundation.

The Hebrew Union College—Jewish Institute of Religion, Cincinnati, Ohio, a Reform Jewish institution, was founded in 1875. Courtesy, American Jewish Archives.

Selman Abraham Waksman (1888–1973), microbiologist. Awarded
Nobel Prize in medicine and physiology in 1952 for his work in
antibiotics. Courtesy, American Jewish Archives.

Mrs. Beatrice Sanders of Trinidad, Colorado, volunteered, about the year
1952, to lead the congregation, to act as a "rabbi." Courtesy, American
Jewish Archives.

Albert Bruce Sabin (1906–1993), a Polish immigrant, developed the live vaccine which halted polio. Courtesy, University of Cincinnati Medical Library.

On June 21, 1964, three civil-rights workers were lynched by natives in Neshoba County, Mississippi; Andrew Goodman and Michael Schwerner were Jews; James E. Chaney was a Black. Courtesy, American Jewish Archives.

Rosalyn Sussman Yalow, a medical physicist, received a Nobel Prize for medicine and physiology in 1977. Courtesy, Medical Media Production Service, VAMC, Bronx, New York.

The library of New York's Jewish Theological Seminary is one of the countries academic treasures. Courtesy, Armstrong World Industries, Lancaster, Pennsylvania.

Ben Shahn (b. 1898) was brought as a child to the United States by his Russian parents. He became a notable artist and muralist. Courtesy, American Jewish Archives.

High Holyday services on board ship. Courtesy, Bernard Postal.

Samuel Goldwyn (1882–1974), motion-picture producer
and pioneer in feature-length films, raised the artistic level
of the cinema. Courtesy, American Jewish Archives.

Saul Bellow received the Nobel Prize for Literature in 1976.

Polish-born Isaac Bashevis Singer (1904–1991), a Yiddish writer, was awarded the Nobel Prize for Literature, 1978. Courtesy, American Jewish Archives.

The Wayne State University Press Building was named in honor of
Leonard Norman Simons (b. 1904), an outstanding leader in Detroit's
general and Jewish community. Photo by Patricia Clay.

were deproletarianized; the native born were moving up into the white-collar class. The first generation of natives had little desire to embrace or retain a strident socialism; they were determined to become affluent members of the body politic; that was the goal on which their eyes and their souls were fixed.[22]

WHAT THESE UNIONS DID FOR THE UNITED STATES

And what did these unions do for the United States? In establishing viable unions they advanced the well-being of thousands of new Americans, men and women. Reluctantly to be sure, the Jewish apparel unions were among the first, if not the first, to integrate women into their organizations. These unions ushered in no messianic age but they took Yiddish-speaking immigrants and whipped them into shape as good unionists so that by the 1930's, at the latest, they had become an integral part of American's trade union complex. The Jewish garment workers and artisans were organized into substantial unions many years before the steelworkers succeeded in forcing their employers to recognize them and give them a chance to make a decent livelihood. And when the steelworkers went on strike in 1919-1920, the Jewish garment workers, a fraction of America's unionists, donated half as much as all the craft unions in the American Federation of Labor whose membership outnumbered theirs twenty-five times. As early as the first decade of the twentieth century the garment workers of New York City, "Russians" for the most part, were manufacturing much of the country's ready-made clothing. The achievements of these immigrant employers and operatives were notable. By the 1920's women's garments were being manufactured in twelve major American cities, two of which were in California. The value of their product in New York City alone amounted to about $760,000,000. Through the technology of mass production and distribution the needle workers were making Americans the best dressed people in the world—at a modest price. They were destroying the distinctions between rich and poor, between commoner and gentry. Thus they were helping to build a democratic world. As early as 1903 Isaac Rubinow wrote: "There is no doubt that the neatly dressed American public is indebted to the tattered, sometimes soiled Jewish masses." Fourteen years later Abraham Cahan wrote in *The Rise of David Levinsky*: "Indeed the Russian Jews had made the average American girl a tailor-made girl." These unions, socialist led, bent on change, were in the van of reform movements. Committed socialist trade union leaders consistently and continuously fought entrenched political bosses; at times they were not unsuccessful. They attacked slum landlords, often their own landsleit; they crusaded to end child labor and worked to drive the sweatshop and unsupervised contractors out of the industry. They kept the factories clean. The unions were an important agency supplementing, heightening the impact of the cultural environment as it moved to Americanize these immigrants despite their disparate cultures. The Jewish immigrants paid homage to at least a half-dozen different cultures and subcultures. East European Jewish labor leaders, like Hillman, Americanized immigrants from the Mediterranean and the trans-Vistula world, even as another immigrant Jew, Gompers, whipped the natives and the older West and Central European immigrants into line. Much more than the American Federation of Labor, the Jewish unions set out to Americanize their followers, to advance them culturally. These unions always stressed secular education. Ultimately the International Ladies' Garment Workers' Union printed its paper *Justice* in four different languages; the Amalgamated in later years was to publish editions of its *Advance* in seven different tongues. These are cultural contributions worthy of note.

The Jewish unions in the needle trades are today noted for their innovative approaches in many areas of socioeconomic endeavor. If they did not always initiate these changes they were certainly responsible for their advocacy, development, and adoption; this testifies to their social vision. They cooperated with management, encouraged and raised production standards, assumed a degree of responsibility for the success of the factory, avoided strikes, pioneered in furthering arbitration and settling grievances through the establishment of continuous functioning peacemaking instrumentalities. They strove sincerely to effect harmony in the administration of the factories where they were employed; labor and bosses must work hand in hand equitably; this was a form of industrial democracy, an ideal envisaged but not frequently attained. Patterning themselves on social security practices in England, Germany, and other Continental lands, the Jewish unions were pioneers in introducing, testing, and furthering various forms of accident, sickness, retirement, unemployment, and death insurance. This was not accomplished in a moment but the unions never lost sight of these goals; all this before the coming of the New Deal. The four Jewish apparel unions, governed during the years before 1921 by Jewish socialists and political radicals, emphasized the universality of men's common brotherhood. Their struggles and their idealism may have helped stimulate the social consciousness of intelligent liberal Americans; they may have had some effect in socializing the craft unions of the American Federation of Labor, not distinguished for their devotion to humanitarian ideals.[23]

POLITICS

Jewish leaders of the unions, socialists, were politically minded but these radicals never succeeded in inducing the masses to vote the Socialist ticket. A substantial number of the Jews never even bothered to vote; naturalization required an effort; voting could be a chore; *parnasah*, livelihood, was imperative; politics was a luxury. After decades some of the socialist union leaders may not have been intent on increasing the party vote; they helped build New York's non-socialist American Labor and Liberal parties in the 1930's and 1940's. The East Europeans were not here in the United States in large numbers until the 1880's. How did these newcomers vote, particularly in New York City? To be sure, there were "Russians" here before 1880, but it is very difficult to determine how they cast their ballots. The choice in postbellum days was obviously between the Republicans and the Democrats; the popular vote for either party was always close. In the South before the Civil War—when there were very few Russians there—Jews had a choice between the Democratics and the Whigs; here, too, in national elections the popular vote was almost equally divided. After the Reconstruction period Jews below the Mason-Dixon line certainly voted Democratic; they would not have dared do otherwise in view of the political climate. In the northern hinterland very many Jews seemed to have voted Republican in the presidential elections. As in the South the Jews went along with the majority; they wanted to "belong." From the 1880's on, the presidents, catering to the slowly increasing Jewish vote, made modest, half-hearted, and ineffectual approaches to the Russian government asking it to ameliorate the disabilities imposed on Jews. All American Jews—natives, acculturated Germans, and East Europeans—were grateful for the sop thrown them. Since the 1880's New York City's East Side "Russians" tended to vote Democratic; many had close ties to Tammany to whom they could turn for personal favors; a minority opted for Republican, fusionist, reform, and Socialist candidates. That the New York City Jewish vote was split was noted as early as 1905 by a competent Jewish social worker who then edited an authoritative work on the Russian Jew. The newcomers, he wrote, did not vote en bloc like the Irish. Tammany, never sure of the Jews on the Lower East Side, was in no hurry to appoint Jews as district leaders; they could not deliver the vote.

Though they were a minority group the Downtown Socialists succeeded at times in winning a substantial number of the votes cast, about 15 percent. In a congressional election in 1908 they garnered 21 percent of the vote. This was at a time when there was a Jewish candidate on all three ballots, on the Republican, the Democratic, and the Socialist; the Democrats won. Morris Hillquit ran then on the Socialist ticket. He lost many Jewish votes because he did not identify strongly with his people and was equivocal on the issue of immigration restriction. His critics believed that he was not sufficiently vehement in his attacks on Russia for its persecution of Jews and its refusal to honor the American passport when carried by a Jew. As the complete socialist, Hillquit was convinced that socialism would not only save the Russian Jews but all oppressed people. As a truly committed internationalist he would under no circumstance stress Jewish ethnicism.

At its height the Jewish Socialist Federation of America with all its branches in twenty-six states never had more than 5,000 members. From 1900 to 1912 in the very heart of the Lower East Side, in the Eighth Assembly District, the Socialists received but a relatively small percentage of the vote cast for presidential candidates. In 1908 they won about 16 percent. In that same Eighth Assembly District, in the presidential elections of 1912, the Socialists received 683 votes, the Republicans, 686, the Democrats, 2211, and the Progressive, 2313. The Progressives, the Bull Moose insurgents, were trying to reelect Theodore Roosevelt as president. Oscar Straus was running for governor on the same ticket. In this one district Roosevelt and Straus collected more votes even than the successful Wilson. Some socialists may well have voted for Roosevelt and Straus; the former was well-liked because he had appointed the Jew Straus to his cabinet in 1906; Straus was popular and respected because he had represented the United States as a minister and ambassador in Constantinople. In 1912 some conservative Jews, Jacob H. Schiff among them, had deserted the Republican ticket because William Howard Taft had waffled on the Russian passport issue.

The year 1913 saw Woodrow Wilson come to power. It was a good year for the Democrats. Four Jews went to Congress. As intimated above Jews have a tendency to vote as the masses vote. Many flocked to the Wilson banner. Wilson, the professor, the idealist, was a Jewish type of hero. The immigrants liked him and they liked him even more when he appointed Brandeis, the Zionist, to the Supreme Court. In other words the new president was "good for the Jews." The Socialist Meyer London was first elected in 1914. In 1917 the Socialist Hillquit had run for mayor and garnered 22 percent of the entire city vote, an excellent showing. Other Socialists elected were ten assemblymen, seven aldermen, and one municipal judge, Jacob Panken (1879-1968). The Russian Panken, who had come to the United States as a child, grew up on a Connecticut farm, near Chesterfield. This was Jewish farming country. In the course of his long life he had worked in a leather goods factory, had organized unions, studied law, and had represented Jewish unions who were affiliated with the United Hebrew Trades. Years back he had helped found the International Ladies' Garment Workers' Union; later he helped establish the Amalgamated Clothing Workers of America. In the decade of the 1920's he would try his luck running for mayor, governor, and United States senator, on the Socialist ticket. Panken was active in the workmen's section of the Joint Distribution Committee; the landsleit back home had to be succored. And—this is typical of socialist notables—he had literary interests; he wrote short stories and published books. Here was a socialist who always worked with Jews as Jews. The handsome vote that Hillquit received in 1917 in the mayoralty race was not altogether a compliment to Hillquit the Socialist. Unquestionably many non-socialists voted for him because he was opposed to the war, because he was a pacifist; pro-Germans, Jews, Irish, and people of diverse hue favored him. The Jews objected to the United States allying itself with despotic Russia and shoring up the Romanov dynasty; the Irish of New York were anti-British, Gentile German Americans and German Jews loved their homeland. These groups were not happy when the United States entered the conflict on the side of the Allies.[24]

In 1921 when the Republicans again came to power there was no Jew in the Senate but eleven in the House; nine were Republicans, one, a Socialist, one, a Democrat. New York City and Brooklyn sent six Jews to the House; five were Republican; London, the Socialist, was the sixth man. Obviously the Jews, then about 25 percent of the city's population, were voting for the party of Lincoln. Most of these Jewish voters of East European descent were already living in different parts of Greater New York. The Lower East Side was giving its vote to London, voting for the man, not the party. There can be no question that newcomers in the Downtown ghetto were divided in their political preferences. These political divisions are reflected in the Yiddish newspapers which they read. *The Jewish Daily News*, the *Tageblatt* and the *Jewish Morning Journal* were Republican; the *Warheit* (*The Truth*) and *Der Tog* were Democratic or liberal; the *Forward*, the most successful of them all, was socialist. Thousands read Cahan's paper because of its appeal, not its politics; it was aggressive, sensational; it was interesting. From the 1890's on the national socialist vote fluctuated radically; it might run anywhere from 21,000 to over 900,000. The closing of the doors to East Europeans, 1921-1924, meant that the proletarian reservoir would no longer be refreshed; no more oppressed Jews were arriving; there were to be no Russian-bred angry men striking out at what they conceived to be autocratic authority here in the United States. The radicals and their followers already here were beginning to die out or to move upward economically and start voting for the traditional American parties. Socialism declined because many of the liberal voters made their compromises; they wanted a better, bourgeois type world here, not pie in the sky by and by, in a future socialist state—the misty tomorrow of international humanitarianism.

The socialist trade union leaders who emerged by 1910 wanted results, tangible immediate improvement for their followers; they made their peace with the capitalist owners. Some, if not many of the socialists and anarchists—ostensibly still internationalists—abandoned militancy; a few even became "Jewishly" national, for their new concern was the immediate welfare of the Jew as such. Jews are nearly always quick to respond to the threat of Jewry imperiled. Their sensitivity to universalism and cosmopolitanism was to a degree satisfied by a heightened awareness of the international character of a World Jewry; the radicals were sufficiently latitudinarian to embrace all Jews, from the non-affiliated Nobel Prize winner to the black Falashas of Ethiopia. The newly arrived Jewish immigrants speedily became American patriots; they accepted the political system though many were always eager to improve it, reformingly. They were Republicans or Democrats; they looked confidently to upward occupational, social, cultural, mobility; some of them, and most of their children, turned to trade and white-collar vocations.

Socialism had always faced problems here in the United States. It suffered frequently from factionalism; it was repressed on occasion by the federal authorities; it had to cope with the typical aversion of most Americans to all forms of Marxism, particularly after the rise of the Bolsheviks in Russia. The greatest threat to socialism, however, lay in the enticing appeal of the American—capitalist—system. Socialism, internationalism, cosmopolitanism was a counsel of perfection. Jews like the Irish, Italians, and other ethnics refused to surrender their particularism. The Jewish newcomers enjoyed the divisiveness, the comfort of ethnos, religion, Yiddish, culture, and their own neighborhood. Hence they rejected socialism and joined the Republican or Democratic parties where fewer ideological demands were imposed. Jewishness—the right to be Jewish—took precedence over class consciousness. America's Jewish natives and the American German Jews hammered away at the newcomers to vote for a "respectable" party, Republican or Democrat; these appeals were not without effect. Over the years the Jewish socialists turned to liberalism; slowly but surely the leaders, the leftists in the unions, the fraternal orders, the press, became deradicalized. F. D. Roosevelt, the Democrat, overwhelmed the socialists in 1936; his social reform offers were irresistible. Hillman, the typical socialist revolutionary who had been imprisoned in Russia ended up in the United States as a Rooseveltian stalwart. Jewish workers flocked to the charismatic president; he helped their unions in exchange for their votes.

The majority of the Jews in Downtown New York were always non-socialist; only a minority of the workers were involved in radical programs; the East European masses like the "Germans" and the natives were repelled by socialism, anarchism, atheism. Large segments of the new immigrants had little interest in unions. Actually the Jewish masses were not radical, not class conscious, had no proletarian political traditions; they stemmed from the all-encompassing middle class and were bourgeois in aspiration. As 1921 dawned the immigrants—apparently a solid indistinguishable glob—were in reality a heterogeneous complex; they were Republicans, Democrats, atheists, socialists, Bolsheviks, Zionists, Yiddishists, Hebraists, Orthodox Jews—Conservatives and Reformers, too—Diaspora nationalists, Territorialists, and assimilationists. The newcomers wanted to be real Americans, just like their Gentile neighbors.

In America's backcountry, Russian and Polish Jews frequently went into local politics serving in a variety of offices. America spelt opportunity for many of them. Not untypical is the story of Samuel Hyman Borofsky (b. 1865), a native of Suwalki Province in Russia. His formal English education was limited to two years of instruction in Manchester's Jews' Free School. Borofsky was also given some training in cabinet making in England before coming to Boston as a young lad (1879). He became a wanderer. In the course of an adventurous career, primarily in South America, he was a tailor, a seaman, a peon captive, a salesman, and even a cantor in a Caribbean synagog. Back in Boston in the 1890's he served as a justice of the peace, a member of the city council, a militia officer during the Spanish-American War, a representative in the state legislature, where he sponsored a bill permitting Jews to keep their businesses open on Sunday if they kept closed on Saturday. By 1908 this autodidact had been admitted to the bar. He was active in Boston's Jewish social-welfare institutions and played a role in the national Federation of American Zionists. Borofsky wrote Zionist songs and published several works in English, including a directory of lawyers. Similar stories of Russian, Polish, and Rumanian Jews who were accorded civic recognition by their fellow citizens can be duplicated in almost every state of the union.[25]

CHAPTER NINE

MAKING A LIVING

PART III: JEWS IN THE LOWER, MIDDLE, AND UPPER

CLASSES PRIMARILY IN NEW YORK CITY AND

SURROUNDING AREAS

INTRODUCTION

Though, as it has been pointed out above, a very substantial percentage of New York's Jews were in the apparel industry, a very perceptible minority—many thousands—were gainfully employed in other industrial and commercial pursuits. Many of the nineteenth-century émigrés were in commerce; they were brokers, traders, shopkeepers in the lands whence they came. Many were craftsmen and artisans. Statistics for a twelve-month period in 1902-1904 indicate that among the Jewish arrivals there were 19,000 tailors and seamstresses, over 24,000 craftsmen, about 3,400 merchants and clerks, about 9,000 female servants, 850 professionals, 8,000 unskilled laborers. The vocational breakdown is interesting, illuminating. At the turn of the century over 50 percent of the East Europeans here in the United States were in industry; the percentage of Gentiles in industry was lower. Actually the percentage of Jewish skilled laborers was three times as large as that of the non-Jews. By 1900 the Jews here were already beginning to shift from industry to commerce. More than 2 percent were in the professions; about 7 percent had clerical jobs; anywhere from 20 to 30 percent were in trade; they were peddlers, hucksters, shopkeepers. A small number was in wholesale.

ARTISANS AND OTHER LOWER INCOME WORKERS

There were Jews in mines and on the railroads but their numbers were minimal. Jews wanted to be near a community where they could practice their faith. There was no craft in which Jews were totally absent. Many were engaged in the manufacture of cigars and cigarettes. In the 1890's Jews were to be found in the tobacco factories in New York City, Newark, Philadelphia, Connecticut, Massachusetts, and in Portland, Maine. Indeed in Pittsburgh there were more Jews in the tobacco industry than in the manufacture of garments; throughout the United States there were more women than men in this industry. Jewish women were numerous in the making of cigars and cigarettes almost everywhere, but they were also found occasionally in machine shops and in the hosiery mills. East European Jewish craftsmen were bookbinders, watchmakers, and coppersmiths engaged in the manufacture of candlesticks, kettles, and samovars. They made cabinets. Some worked in factories that manufactured paper bags; in Paterson they labored in the silk mills. Many were in the building trades; they were bricklayers, masons, plumbers, carpenters, roofers; they were structural steel craftsmen; they made gates, fire escapes, and fashioned artistic ironwork. Abraham Dreier (1889-1979) is a striking example of an East European immigrant who made a fortune as a steel artificer. The business he built was called the Dreier Structural Steel Company. Dreier came from Poland in 1911. He was then a locksmith, a man of very little education. He went to work for steel fabricators and it was not too long before he owned the business. He lived on the East Side and specialized in the manufacture of fire escapes for tenement houses. By World War II he was so successful that he built invasion barges for the United States Navy. He had also specialized in real estate; he built and operated hotels in different parts of the country. When prosperity smiled he moved to Long Island.

As craftsmen these new arrivals were engravers, jewelers, upholsterers, pocketbook makers, tanners, and glaziers. Some worked in the glass factories in Western Pennsylvania, in the textile mills of Lawrence; they made boots and shoes in New England. The building industry in its many facets appealed to them. Many were painters; a goodly number were alteration painters. These latter, tyros, were not welcome in the painters' union where natives and Irish dominated; they did not like Jews. Alteration painters who worked on cheap jobs often put in a 9 to 10-hour day and received as little as $1.50 for all their effort; some made but $5 a week. Frugal and ambitious workmen bought apartment houses, mortgaged themselves to the hilt, managed and maintained the buildings themselves or hired cheap labor. Many a painting job was shoddy in the extreme.

One of the well-known apparel organizations was the International Fur Workers' Union. It was never able to brag of its numerous locals; furs were always a luxury. Furriers had their ups and downs; Herman Kirschbaum is a case in point. This Libau youngster came to America on the money he had stolen from his father. His stock of cash lasted for a while; in those days he could buy a five-course meal for fifteen cents. When his money ran out he peddled shoelaces on Broadway. Then eager to better himself he apprenticed himself to a furrier; in two years he was a master workman and during World War I, when money was not scarce, he made from $50 to $60 a week—a handsome salary. He lived high on the hog for he moved to Riverside Drive, bought expensive clothes, ate at good restaurants, and smoked fine cigars. When the crash came in 1929 he was out of a job and went on relief.

The four Jewish apparel unions in no sense exhausted the labor protective associations. Jews who were skilled journeymen frequently joined the general, non-Jewish unions. Because they were immigrants, often with a limited knowledge of the English vernacular, they were not always happy surrounded by other workmen who looked down on them. They preferred Jewish locals and there were many in the amusement, the food, the transportation, the leather industries. Jews set up their own unions for milkwagon drivers, restaurant workers, jewelers, janitors, billposters, barbers, paperbox makers, trunk artificers, mineral water bottlers, bookbinders, locksmiths, and teamsters. In 1929, when fifty New York City locals were studied it was found that 34 percent of their members were Jewish. There were numerous Jewish baker locals; by 1914 there were thirty-two such unions in the United States. Jews were concerned about the bread they ate; it had to be kosher; lard shortening was abhorrent. Baking was a very special Jewish industry; both the owners and the workers were invariably Jews. There were kosher bakers on the East Side ever since the 1880's; not infrequently they were housed in dirty cellars. In those early days a seventy-four hour, six-day week was not unusual; wages were low; strikes not uncommon. On occasion, when there was a need, the men worked a twenty-hour shift. That same decade some of these bakers had their own Yiddish language union label. In 1907 a few of the locals joined the radical Industrial Workers of the World (the Wobblies) who favored industry not craft unions. A few years later the bakers had their own periodical, *Der Yidisher Beker*. An interesting characteristic of the Jewish bakers' unions is that they shared the work. When there was unemployment the steady men voluntarily surrendered time to those journeymen out of a job. Ultimately, because the owners were so dependent on their men and the Jewish masses so insistent on "Jewish" bread, the bakers' unions became powerful and prosperous; the hours were cut down; the wages were high.[1]

PEDDLERS

By the twentieth century there were still a few New York city-based country peddlers. They were declining in number because access to the city was easy thanks to the interurban traction lines and accommodation trains, good roads, and autos. These factors were to put rural and village peddlers out of business. Normally rural peddling was only a temporary vocation for city-based peddlers. The itinerant hawker left peddling as soon as possible but there were exceptions. Morris Horowitz is such an exception; Horowitz is a real person; the name, however, is fictitious. This "Russian" had come to Chicago as a teenager and soon became a country peddler. This was to be his lifelong vocation. The farmers who knew him and trusted him helped him keep kosher; they fed him milk, bread, and butter. The first two years as he trudged the road he was a pack peddler; then he bought a horse and wagon. Horowitz never opened a store. What did he accomplish? He raised a family of six children, took care of his aged father and his wife's parents, and sent his children to college. Even for a peddler America can be a *goldne medina*. Most peddlers in the twentieth century were city peddlers, street and house hawkers, customer peddlers. These were different categories. There were several thousand hucksters and hawkers in New York City around 1900. The street peddlers hugged the pavement selling notions, shoe polish, knives, handkerchiefs, small light items. In 1905 a responsible social worker said that these street peddlers were little better than beggars; customer peddlers were swindlers. This judgment seems unduly harsh. Another historian has pointed out that in New York City there were very many pushcart merchants. A pushcart peddler was really a sedentary merchant in miniature. These pushcart princes handled literally everything: stationery, foods, bake-goods, vegetables, chinaware, notions, shaving materials, hardware, paint, wallpaper, men's furnishings, artificial and real flowers, Catholic religious pictures, pocket watches, candles, collar buttons, and genuine Palestine earth to accompany the pious deceased to the grave. Every now and then—not too often to be sure—a pushcart merchant lifted himself by his own suspenders. The most unusual example is Louis Borgenicht ("Don't Borrow"!). This Galician who came to the United States in the 1880's was a fish peddler, a pushcart entrepreneur, an occasional dispenser of men's socks, of pots and pans. Then he turned to the manufacture of children's aprons, this in a modest fashion. His wife helped him; she probably did much of the sewing; he peddled the dresses from house to house. Then he turned to the making of children's dresses; they were stylish and cheap. In the course of years he became a manufacturer on a large scale. There was a demand and he responded to it; he was a pioneer in the children's dress industry; some people referred to him as the "King of the Children's Dress Trade." Customer peddlers are the royalty of peddlers; they were at the top of the heap. Mr. Customer Peddler developed a following who bought from him. He carried no wares with him but referred his clients to wholesalers. The purchasers paid him off in installments; the wholesalers billed the peddler. One could make an excellent living if the clientele was numerous. An occasional peddler of this type even became a wholesaler, a peddler supply house. Female customer peddlers were by no means unknown. There is Aunt Rachel, for instance, who followed the talmudic injunction (*Sayings of the Fathers*, 2:6): "In a place where there are no men strive to be a man." Her husband Yankel, Jake, stayed home and made suspender straps. Obviously he was something of a *luftmensch*; she was compelled to make the living. Rachel had worked hard back in Europe; there she shouldered a pack and peddled among the Irish. They taught her to speak English with an Irish lilt. They became her customers and she sold them anything from a pack of pins to a set of furniture. On Saturday night the customers came to her home and paid their installments. She lived well.

Two of Cincinnati's most respected Russian immigrants were the Schiff brothers, devout, scrupulously observant, both thoroughly at home in the Talmud, no mean achievement. One of the brothers sent a son to college where he became a physician, an international authority on the liver, and the editor of a standard book on the subject. The other, a customer peddler, had a following: his daughter visited the clients and collected the weekly installments. One of her brothers, Robert W. Schiff, started as a clerk in a shoe store; by 1922 he and his siblings had built the Schiff Shoe Company, which later became SCOA, the Shoe Corporation of America. This was a multimillion dollar shoe business and a department store complex which included nine manufacturing plants, 700 shoe stores, and about ninety small department stores. In his memoirs, Abraham Cahan recounts how he taught English for a living. Some of his students were customer peddlers; it was imperative that they speak or write English if they were to relate to their clients. His landlady on Monroe Street was also a customer peddler. It was a small apartment; it sheltered the widow, two small children, a married daughter and her husband, and another guest, a young woman. Cahan's customer peddler pupils were an interesting lot. One was a talmudist who liked arithmetic but thought talmudic dialectics were far more interesting; another of his students took advanced instruction in geography and mathematics, went to a college, and became a successful physician; a third pupil was an exuberant lusty fellow who bought a large wardrobe from his suppliers, spoke fractured English replete with slang, sported a diamond stickpin, and told dirty stories. All peddlers began to lose out by 1920; workmen patronized established shops and department stores where they had a large assortment to choose from.[2]

POVERTY

How widespread was poverty in the lower income group? There is no question that manual laborers, many artisans, and most peddlers had to struggle to survive. It is equally true that there was much poverty among all recent immigrants; they were often on short rations. During the heyday of the sweatshop where many labored, the pay was inadequate. As late as 1920 children of six to seven years of age were often put to work. Poverty is reflected in living conditions; it was not uncommon in the first decade of the twentieth century to house as many as ten people in a small apartment; there was someone sleeping in every room. In some homes the furnishings were very primitive; a bed might well be an old spring on the floor on some form of wooden support; a barrel with a board over it could serve as a table; a newspaper spread over a box constituted a chair. The fear of being totally without means induced the poorest of the poor to pay a few cents a week to a landsmanschaft, a benefit society. In a real emergency one could request help as of right, not charity. The typical immigrant turned to the charities only when desperate. Some went to the general welfare agencies; most Jews preferred to turn to Jewish institutions when they needed help. Unhappy poverty-stricken women frequently sought abortions.

The fact that there were many philanthropic associations doling out money or food or clothes to the poor is adequate evidence that poverty was extensive. The Jewish charities always had a host of petitioners; relatively few, however, remained on their roster for a period of years. In the early 1900's it was by no means uncommon for New York City's United Hebrew Charities to interview about 10,000 people a year. What caused people to seek help? There might be a disastrous death in the family; the breadwinner was gone; widows needed help. Desertions were common, in some years there were reports that 2,000 husbands had left their families. There was illness, disease, hospital expenses. Alcoholism and venereal disease played little part in depriving people of support; insanity, however, was not infrequent. There were beggars around; many of them were professionals. Some no doubt had begged in Europe; they hoped to find greener fields here. There were paupers, the exact number is not known; these are the permanent clients of the Jewish charities. Yet there is ample evidence that despite the poverty that stalked them these Jewish newcomers did better than the typical Gentiles who came from Eastern Europe and the Mediterranean lands.[3]

JEWS IN THE LOWER MIDDLE CLASS

It is difficult to define the lower middle class. One may say that it included those gainfully employed who were leaving the factories and moving out of peddling. Many had small stores where their income was very limited. These were people who aspired to rise financially, culturally, and took steps to improve themselves. They made the effort to raise their standard of living. The men and women in this class were a mixed lot. Maybe the garment cutters and the furriers should be included though they were well paid. Customer peddlers could be very successful; those with a large following may be deemed entrepreneurs on the fringe of the middle class. It would not be inaccurate to maintain that many in the lower middle-class income group were an integral part of an extended middle class. Thus this lower middle-class group included successful artisans, a variety of white-collar workers, petty businessmen, but certainly not those who were obviously affluent. Jews in the lower middle-class category were turning away from hard manual labor. This was a time when Americans in general were moving away from the pick and shovel, and the Jews were moving with them. Jewish men and women wanted to be in the white-collar class; they were reaching out to the service industries, to clerical activities, managerial jobs, to little businesses of their own such as newsstands, groceries, candy shops. Included among this category are the Hebrew teachers, cantors, and synagog personnel.

Some New York statistics for the year 1899 reveal that among 2,900 people there were 182 different vocations; 631 of them were in the food business—these were the grocers, butchers, bakers, and milk dispensers. Soda water stands were frequent; Jews were addicted to seltzer water, not hard liquor; burping was deemed a pleasant experience. As early as 1902, so it is said, half of the young Jews up to the age of twenty-five had white-collar jobs; many were salesmen; some of them were native born. Jewish girls born abroad were also moving out into the world of commerce; back home in Eastern Europe few opportunities would have offered themselves. Here they became saleswomen, milliners, bookkeepers. There was even a handful of female saloon keepers. A favorite occupation, genteel and respectable, was public school teaching. A study made in Steelton, Pennsylvania, reveals that practically every Jew in town was in the apparel or food business. In New York City, in 1900, according to census reports, 3,256 of the male immigrants were in sales; 1,306 women were sales personnel. Given the large Jewish population of the city these statistics are not impressive but they are indicative of a trend. Around the year 1902 Morris Michtom owned a small candy and toy shop in Brooklyn. Hearing that President Theodore (Teddy) Roosevelt had gone bear hunting in Mississippi and refused to kill a bear cub, Michtom turned to his wife and asked her to make a small plush brown bear with movable limbs and button eyes. This Teddy bear was then put into a window and offered for sale. This started a craze for Teddy bears. Here was a man and a wife who showed ingenuity and enterprise.[4]

FLIGHT FROM THE GHETTO:
NEW AREAS OF SETTLEMENT IN NEW YORK AND THE SURROUNDING AREAS

Some Jews who increased their income were in no hurry to move out of the ghetto; they were comfortable there; they felt at home. This, however, was not the typical response of those who were inching upward economically. Many Jewish artisans and small shopkeepers started leaving the Lower East Side and other American ghettos, their *Nachtasyl*, as soon as they could. Pittsburgh is typical. The Hill District, Downtown, was the ghetto. By 1920 many had left heading for the suburbs and finally the exurbs. This was a process that was to continue all through the twentieth century. Pittsburgh's Jews moved out to Oakland, the East End, and finally to Squirrel Hill, the Golden Ghetto. Two generations earlier the Germans had crossed the Allegheny River to Allegheny City, the north side; now, many years later, the new trend in the mid-twentieth century was the South Side, across the Monongahela, to the beckoning hills. Jews who left the Hill wanted better housing, a yard, indoor plumbing. One of these men who trekked to a more elite section of town flushed the toilets for hours just to enjoy the magic of this wonderful invention.

Why did the New York City immigrants start leaving their Lower Manhattan ghetto? Upper economic mobility accounts for many if not most departures. The National Council of Jewish Women had been pushing Jews to move ever since the early 1890's. Better pay due to stronger unions made it possible for thousands to move; World War I brought prosperity. Some moved because they wanted healthier surroundings, better quarters for the same cost; a house was preferable to a tenement. Even the poor who left the ghetto were confident that the charities would follow them to the distant boroughs. By 1900 half of the members of New York's first ghetto synagog (1852) had already settled Uptown. Relocation to all parts of the metropolis was synchronous. By 1890 there were about 13,000 Jews in Brooklyn; most of them were "German"; a few may have been Russians and Poles. In the 1880's the East Europeans started crossing the Brooklyn Bridge (1883); by the 1890's Brownsville, Brooklyn, had a Russian-type Hebrew school; in 1897 a Yiddish weekly made its appearance in that growing city. Williamsburg and Brownsville were important Yiddish-speaking towns in 1900. The eastward move on the Island carried the immigrants as far as Greensport in Suffolk County.

There is an avenue in that town named after Nathan Kaplan. By 1907 Brooklyn had at least 90 synagogs and bethels; most were Orthodox shuls; there were numerous Hebrew schools, lodges, Zionist societies, and charities. There were almost 100,000 Jews in the city, and the population was further augmented when the Queensboro Bridge designed by a Russian Jewish immigrant opened in 1909. The subways and elevated brought the Brooklyn Jewish masses speedily to all sections of the metropolis.

In the 1890's the Jews of Lower Manhattan started to move outward. Some had been in the country for almost a decade. They now moved to midtown New York, to Yorkville, Harlem, the West Side, the Bronx. The new settlers included not only those who were faring well economically but also large numbers of factory operatives. From the Bronx, the adventurers reached still farther north to Westchester County, to Mount Vernon, New Rochelle, White Plains, Yonkers, Peekskill. Some continued traveling, crossing the Hudson to Rockland County, to Spring Valley. It is believed that by 1905, 50 percent of all New York Jews were in the white-collar class. The move away from the ghetto was perceptible by 1910; in 1916 only 23 percent of all Jews in the metropolis were living in the lower reaches of the city. New York in 1920 had 1,643,012 Jews; they were then about 29 percent of the population; Manhattan borough though had but 657,101 Jews; in 1910 there were over 350,000 Jews on the Lower East Side. And the other sections of town? The Bronx had 278,169; Queens, 86,194, Richmond (Staten Island), 17,160(?); Brooklyn, 604,380. The new Jewish ghetto was now Brownsville; it was a reborn East Side replete with pushcarts that sold anything from a dishpan to a bar of kosher soap. In the 1940's Brooklyn had 1,000,000 Jews; it was the largest Jewish city in the world.

Greater New York and the city's boroughs were not able to contain all the new Jews. No later than 1900 they started crossing the Hudson, establishing satellite communities; they moved over into Staten Island and into northern New Jersey. As early as 1905 there were more than a dozen sizable Orthodox shuls in the northern New Jersey area, in Bayonne, Jersey City, Elizabeth, Hoboken, Newark, Passaic, and Paterson. Paterson and Jersey City had about 6,000 Jews; Newark, 20,000. One may turn to Rahway, Union County, New Jersey, as an example of how a Jewish community began and grew. (To be sure no two Jewish towns had exactly the same beginnings.) In 1900 Rahway was a country village. Now and then Jews would travel there, hire a horse and buggy, and drive out from town to the beach, to picnic for the day, swim, and ride the carousel. One could also reach the beach on a horse-drawn streetcar. One of the drivers was a Jew. If the day was hot he would stop at an ice-cream parlor —owned by a Jew—and refresh himself. The passengers would wait. In

1907 Rahway had an Orthodox congregation; in 1912 it had daily services conducted by the shohet in the back of his shop where he also taught Hebrew and trained boys for bar mitzvah. If the requisite quorum of ten could not be put together a tenth man would be coopted from a nearby village. By 1914 there was an established Hebrew school; five years later Rahway had a synagog. Part of the money to buy the new shul was raised by a raffle; some lucky person won a touring car. When, God forbid, a Jew died in Rahway, each member of the shul had to contribute $1 for the family of the deceased. Even in 1919 this was not an affluent synagog.[5]

EAST EUROPEAN MIDDLE-CLASS JEWS

When is a shopkeeper in the middle-middle class and not in the lower-middle class? When he moves to a larger store, when he makes more money and raises his standard of living. In their daydreams most workers aspired to be in the middle class, more exactly in the upper-middle class; they hoped to become rich. A few of them succeeded in reaching the very top. The fact that thousands, many thousands, left the East Side—or the ghetto in every American metropolis—is a positive indication that they wanted to improve themselves. They were determined to do so. A historian has said that they were driven by a daemon; this is true; they wanted to be their own boss; and they drove themselves and their children encouraging them to become white-collar people. They were willing to work hard; they were courageous, ambitious. The basic intelligence was there; frequently there was a talmudist in their background.

By 1900 the East European middle class was growing; a few newcomers were already in the professions, or retailers, wholesalers, garment manufacturers. The German Jews had moved up; the East Europeans, too, hoped that they would have their day in the sun. By 1901 there were over 140 Jewish policemen in the city. This was certainly better than nursing a pushcart or climbing a thousand steps and peddling to make a sale. Some of these policemen had probably been recruited in the days when Theodore Roosevelt was president of the New York City Board of Police Commissioners (1895-1897); he liked athletic Jews. By 1900 there were 9,000 East European retail shopkeepers in New York City; many were in clothing and gents' furnishings; thousands were office personnel; male and female salespeople were numerous; 2,000 were dressmakers. Statistics indicate that Jewish white-collar workers outnumbered the Italians two to one. There is an estimate that by 1905 about 45 percent of all gainfully employed Jews were in the white-collar category. The Immigration Commission reported that in the large cities Jewish immigrants were pushing into trade rapidly, more so than non-Jews. This was even more characteristic of the newcomers in the hinterland. If these newcomers could not advance themselves by brilliance, they improved themselves by thrift; they were frugal. As early as 1890 hundreds of Philadelphia's Jewish immigrants owned homes—with a mortgage to be sure. In Pennsylvania's Steelton there were 37 foreign-born Hebrews who owned property; there was an equal number of Italians but the assessment value of the property owned by Jews was almost twice that of the Italians.

Many of the Russians and Poles who came in the 1880's turned to "banking." The term—one used by government statisticians—should not be taken too seriously. These bankers were ship ticket agents and money forwarders; they served the incoming masses who dispatched money and tickets to the dear ones left behind. These so-called banks were formed in many cities of the country, wherever there were immigrants in number. New York is said to have had 1,000 such institutions; a number of them catered to the needs of the "Russians." One immigrant was actually a full-fledged banker. This was the Pole, Sender Jarmulowsky (1841-1912). There were rumors that this East Side banker was about to build a twelve-story office building; the first two floors were to be occupied by his bank; the other ten floors were to be rented out. He did have a big bank on East Broadway. Jarmulowsky was a self-made man; orphaned at the age of three by the time he was twenty-six he had a bank of sorts in Hamburg where he catered to immigrants; by 1873 he had established a branch of his Hamburg enterprise on Canal Street; in 1914 during World War I, he had another office in Leipzig. Jarmulowsky continued to live Downtown until 1891 and then moved north to Yorkville. This same year J. D. Eisenstein, garment manufacturer and Hebrew scholar, moved north to Harlem. Jarmulowsky, like Eisenstein, was not baffled by a page of the Talmud. He studied it daily. He was president of a synagog and a founder of a kosher-kitchen hospital. He was an East Side community activist, a friend of Judah L. Magnes who was trying to bring unity into the East Side communal chaos. A Hebrew magazine reported that Jarmulowsky left an estate of $5,000,000; taking a liberal discount there is still no question that Jarmulowsky died a wealthy man.

The rise of a growing immigrant Jewish middle class is attested by the creation of a number of employers' associations. An association of entrepreneurs usually reflects strength and a degree of affluence. Kosher butchers, retail grocers, jewelry shop proprietors, mineral water dealers united to further themselves. The apparel manufacturers—an elite of sorts —organized primarily to cope with the unions. There were "Russian" garment manufacturers in many of America's large towns. Making apparel, as it has been mentioned, was New York City's big industry; the gross national product ran into the hundreds of millions of dollars; the newcomers dominated it no later than 1904. By 1907 the Russians and

Poles were in control of Pittsburgh's wholesale and jobbing apparel houses that were lined up on Fifth Avenue. Real estate was everywhere a field very much favored by the daring. It was Jewish speculators who built up Brownsville and the Bronx and rebuilt Boston's North End slums in the first decade of the twentieth century. Wherever there was a Jewish community of size there were contractors and builders who remodeled old houses.

One of the most successful of these enterprisers was Harry Fischel (1865-1948). This native of Lithuania came to this country as a man of twenty; back home he had worked as a skilled cabinetmaker and had served as a foreman on building jobs. Notwithstanding his skills he arrived in this country in 1885 with only sixty cents in his pocket. In his early years here he made $3 a week but he soon started building on small lots, drawing his own plans. In the course of years he became known as one of the city's successful builders. Not infrequently, in the model tenements he erected, he employed Jewish craftsmen and generously gave them a week's pay with time off Saturday. As he moved towards affluence he distinguished himself as a Jewish communal worker; he busied himself helping Beth Israel Hospital, talmudic academies, traditional Hebrew schools, World War I relief agencies, and the Hebrew Immigrant Aid Society. He poured money into the Rabbi Isaac Elchanan Theological Seminary, endowed a fund to do research in Talmud and help set up a kosher kitchen on Ellis Island where the immigrants debarked. He dwelt in one of the large apartment houses which he built in a fashionable neighborhood and there he built a sukkah, exposed to the heavens, where he ate during the Festival of Booths. It was no problem for this man to remain a devout Jew and to become a complete American. He was an active member of the American Jewish Committee, the native and German Jewish bastion.

In the garment center vernacular the apparel industry was known as the "rag" business. Actually many Jews were in the real rag business; they were junk dealers, buyers and sellers of old iron, waste paper, bottles, rags. In many respects this was a very important facet of American commerce. The junk wholesalers and brokers shipped carloads of old iron to the steel mills. Detroit had waste dealers as early as the 1880's; at one time in the early twentieth century there were over 100 Jewish waste dealers in Detroit. Some new arrivals moved into the cigar and tobacco trade; many owned drugstores. In 1904, New York had 1,500 drugstores; 1,200 were owned by Jews mostly from Eastern Europe. It is literally true that these ambitious tradesmen were found in almost every form of business. They were florists, exporters and importers, cleaners and dyers, owners of steam laundries; many were in the liquor and food business; kosher foods were imperative for the masses who hung on to the dietary laws desperately.

The East Side was dotted with shopkeepers who sold Hebrew prayer books; the Hebrew Publishing Company was an old established firm; other enterprisers manufactured tin-ware, feather dusters, watches, matches, silver umbrella handles.

A few became caterers and resort owners. As Jews acquired means they employed caterers for the life cycle ceremonies, for weddings, bar mitzvahs, and important charity meetings. Catering was an old estab-lished vocation among the German immigrants who had staged banquets and balls ever since the early nineteenth century; the "Russians" entered into this new business with panache. The Scharys, emigrants from Latvia, built up a substantial catering business in northern New Jersey; their hall was called Schary Manor. One of the Schary boys was Isidore, later Dore (b. 1905), who became a dramatist, a film writer, and chief of production of Metro-Goldwyn-Mayer. Under his aegis about 250 pictures were made, some of them with a social message. Later he wrote for the stage. Schary, who was active in the national Jewish community, was for many years chairman of the Anti-Defamation League. Summer resorts were first established in the Catskills for Jews of modest means and as they pros-pered the Catskill hotels evolved as deluxe hostelries. Grossingers of course is a notable example. In 1914 the Grossingers, modest business people and workers, bought a run-down farm in the mountains and took in summer boarders; the first season they did little more than break even. The kitchen, of course, was kosher. Ultimately as the resort prospered Gentiles, too, flocked to enjoy its Jewish cuisine. Lox, matzo balls, gefilte fish, appealed to many. Ultimately, Grossingers had its own post office, its own air field, a night club, and a dining room that would seat hundreds. Much of the success of this famous hostelry was due to a woman, Jennie Grossinger.

Most middle-class merchants and business people were not as fortu-nate as the Grossingers. They built no empires. Samuel Rosenberg (1830-1936), a Pole, was much more typical of a Jew who achieved a measure of success. After arriving in the United States in 1853, Rosenberg reached out commercially in several directions. For a time he was a manufacturer of bow ties. By 1860, already a citizen, he cast his first presidential ballot for Abraham Lincoln. About the year 1907 he started making canvas and flannel ironholders for Chinese laundrymen and for general use. There were people who dubbed him the Patriarch of Chinatown. Rosenberg, like many of his successful confreres, was something of a communal worker, for he established a hometown benefit society and a congrega-tion. He named his synagog after the Polish village whence he stemmed. Rosenberg retired from business at the age of 98 and lived to be 106 be-fore he passed away. Sol Cohn is another illustration of a modestly suc-cessful man, a merchant. Cohn, a Russian, moved west to Illinois to join a brother in the northeastern part of the state. Tiny Flanagan, in Livingston County, was never to shelter even 1,000 souls, so it would seem. Cohn began life in town as a peddler, later bought out his brother and became a successful storekeeper, on a small scale, of course. The natives were at first not friendly but they finally accepted him and even honored him. He was elected an alderman and then mayor; he did so well as the town's chief executive he was reelected for a total of four terms. He put the finances of the town on a firm basis and endeared himself to the citizenry by sponsoring the building of a beautiful park graced with a fountain. After twenty-five years he turned his store over to a son, left Flanagan, and made his home in Chicago. There he served as a resident buyer for the business back in Livingston County. This was in the early 1920's.

To be successful one ought to have amassed a capital of at least $25,000. Put out at 6 percent this would produce $1,500 a year; one could live modestly but genteelly on that amount. By 1904 many of the immigrants owned small factories, stores of size, cafes, tenements, and even apartment houses with elevators. How long did it take to become a part of the middle-income group? One did not rise in a hurry. A study of the East European presidents of congregations in New York City in 1917 —presumably people of some affluence—indicate that these men had been in the country for about twenty years. In short one can assert that by 1920 there were many thousands of immigrants from the "East" engaged in commerce, manufacturing, retail and wholesale trade, real estate; they had white-collar jobs, served in the professions, and exerted considerable authority as union officers in both general and Jewish unions. Jake Cohen (1877-1945), for instance, was a labor leader of some influence in Tennessee where he finally made his home after his arrival from the old country. Cohen was active in the American Federation of Labor in the early days and published *The Labor Review*, the official organ of the Memphis Trades and Labor Council. Cohen and the many Jewish leaders in the labor movement were not proletarians.

Most lower-income Jewish workers never became middle-income businessmen. The individual laborer, the small shopkeeper, the factory operative—they certainly hoped to improve themselves and sometime or other may well have attempted to advance themselves. Few succeeded; by the 1920's the sons and daughters, enjoying an American education, were doing better than their parents. They became teachers, clerks, managers, professionals. Typical of the fumbling economic experiences which were the lot of many—a man who finally succeeded in becoming a somebody —was the venturesome Dr. George M. Price, the head of New York's Union Health Center. After landing in the United States in 1886/1887 he was faced with the job of making a livelihood. In the course of the next six or seven years he made baskets, paper collars, worked in a chair factory, labored in a paper mill, a boiler factory, on a farm, dug ditches, ran a grocery store, collected tickets on a railroad as a conductor, handed out money as a bank clerk, studied medicine, served as a health inspector, managed an apartment house, taught public school, and edited a weekly journal—all this before settling down as a physician. When the Immigration Act of 1921 was passed the majority of America's Russian and Polish Jews were in the lower and lower-middle income class; they never emerged, never improved themselves. This cannot be glossed over; they were not successful by the standards of the day.[6]

EAST EUROPEANS: THE UPPER-MIDDLE CLASS AND THE RICH

If by 1921 most East European Jews were in the lower and the lower-middle class, if a number even enjoyed a middle-middle income, how many, if any, were rich? There were a few. The advance guard who came here in the 1860's had forty years to prove themselves. By the third decade of the twentieth century some were on the high road to fame and fortune. Who is rich? The rabbis of old had the answer, for they said that anyone was rich who rejoiced in his portion (*Sayings of the Fathers*, 4:1). East European businessmen were not satisfied with the talmudic dictum. They wanted to make money in large amounts. In this sense they were typically American, no different than the Carnegies, the Vanderbilts, the Goulds, the Astors, the Fisks, the Morgans, or the Seligmans, the Schiffs, and the Guggenheims. These were the millionaires. Jewish millionaires among the Slavic newcomers were rare. Rich is a relative term. Any man who had $100,000 was rich. This enviable category includes literally dozens of East European immigrants. Each man's story is different. Some—not all—are well known to the historian of the American Jewish scene. Among them was Henry A. Dix (1850-1933), a Ukrainian who came to the United States in 1892. His original name was Dickstein. The clothing factories that brought him wealth were in New Jersey. In 1912 he started giving bonuses to his workers and in 1923 sold them the business and even lent them $250,000 to operate it. His large estate in New York became a home for working girls. He also gave generously to the New York federation of Jewish philanthropies and to the Young Women's Hebrew Association.[7]

Louis J. Horowitz (1875-1956) stands out as the man whose skyscrapers were to change New York City's skyline. This young man, who had come to the United States from Poland in 1892, was given a job in 1903 working for the Thompson-Starrett Construction Company, one of America's great builders. Seven years later, still only thirty-five years of age, Horowitz became president of the concern. He it was who erected the Waldorf Astoria, the Woolworth, and the Equitable building; the last was the largest office complex in the world. His company received the contract to build the powder plant at Nitro, West Virginia; 3,000 separate structures were included in this one project. In the course of his presidency Thompson-Starrett erected hundreds of large buildings in major American towns all the way from New York to Winnipeg, Canada, and south to San Francisco. During World War II, Horowitz was appointed director for tank construction. A substantial part of his multimillion dollar estate was left to New York University.[8]

The Russian, Bernard Horwich (b. 1861), settled in Chicago where he went to work in a junk yard among Irish and Poles; they threatened his life. Then he turned to peddling; this, too, was hazardous; peddlers were frequently beaten by ruffians. Finally, this brilliant and able immigrant went into the wholesale bottle business, buying and selling by the carload. Horwich also dealt on a large scale in hair; he bought property, established banks, and, as a communal worker, participated in establishing Chicago's first local Zionist organization in 1898. The Chicago Federated Orthodox Jewish Charities owed much to him as one of its principal organizers, but he was also active in the elite American Jewish Committee. It is interesting to note that this religionist belonged to both Orthodox and Reform synagogs. A member of the Covenant but not the Standard Club! The latter was the haunt of the wealthy natives and the acculturated Germans. He linked both worlds, that of the affluent natives and the aspiring East European new arrivals.[9]

Albert Monroe Greenfield (1887-1967) was a man who built a realty and department store empire and became nationally important in the areas of finance and politics. He was a multimillionaire financier and real-estate man; people said that Greenfield was a man who had changed the (real estate) face of Philadelphia. He was born in Kiev in the Ukraine in 1887 and was brought to this country as a child. His father owned a grocery store and was successful. The boy, however, left school at the age of fourteen and went to work. He borrowed $500 from his mother and established a business of his own. In 1905, still a teenager, he owned a real estate company. By the time he was twenty-three he was making $60,000 a year and it was not long before he was a millionaire. He defined luck as an accident that happens only to the competent. Ultimately he built an empire with a gross annual volume of over $850,000,000; the empire was in real estate, banking, retailing, hotel, and transportation. Most of his investments were in Philadelphia though he also owned department stores in New York; indeed he controlled chains of various types of stores, a national candy corporation, banks, hotels, and cab companies but his primary field of enterprise remained real estate and retailing. He began politically as a Republican and was active nationally but joined the Democrats during New Deal days. Greenfield was active in the Philadelphia Jewish community; because of his wealth he was accepted as a communal leader. Like many other Jewish immigrants Louis Blaustein (1869-1937) came here when young. He peddled among the farmers of eastern Pennsylvania for many years and finally went to work for John D. Rockefeller's Standard Oil Company. In 1910 he established his own modest oil company; he had a horse-drawn tank wagon making kerosene deliveries. Later on, he was to make a fortune in the gasoline business; he called his organization the American Oil Company, AMOCO. With the coming of the automobile he pioneered in gasoline filling stations and developed an anti-knock motor fuel.[10]

There were a few shining lights in the world of commerce, men and women, whose names are known to the public at large; there were hundreds of lesser luminaries who in a more limited sense illuminated the sphere in which they shone. Americans gave all immigrants opportunities; some made the most of what the country offered. The careers of hundreds of successful Russian, Polish, Hungarian, and Rumanian immigrants can be studied in *Who's Who in American Jewry, 1926*. It may be assumed that the people included in this biographical lexicon are people of consequence in their local Jewish and general communities, and in all probability affluent, to a degree at least. Their fields of communal and professional endeavor are varied. Louis Satenstein organized a bookbinding company in the 1890's and finally operated the largest printing plant in the United States, so he claimed. Israel Matz (b. 1869), a devotee of the Talmud in his native Russia, became the head of a large pharmaceutical business here in the United States. In 1917 Bernard Edelhertz (b. 1880), a lawyer, bought controlling interest in the *American Hebrew* from the native elite who had originally organized it. This purchase may well be symbolic of the transfer of influence to the newcomers. Edelhertz was well-known in the cinema industry and at one time was chairman of the Motion Picture Theatre Owners Chamber of Commerce. This native of the Ukraine was a member of Temple Beth-El, a prestigious Reform institution.

Morris Eisenman and Joseph Kalmanoff were two partners in a group of five young men who founded the Metropolitan News Company. Between them, all they had was $2,000 and a horse and wagon. They rented a basement down on Henry Street for $15 a month and began to distribute Yiddish dailies. As they prospered they encouraged the Yiddish journals to run English columns. The first year that they were in business they grossed $150,000. In time the Metropolitan News Company became the largest distributor of papers in Greater New York. The partners also delivered foreign language newspapers throughout the United States. One of their newsboys was David Sarnoff who was later to become chairman of the board of the Radio Corporation of America. The career of Nathan

E. Posner is interesting; he was a vocational deviant for here was a musician who became a businessman. Posner, who had come from Europe in the late 1880's as a child of seven, had studied the violin in St. Petersburg under the eminent Leopold Auer. Later, in America, he had given recitals and had even conducted an orchestra. Around 1920 he began to collect violins and to sell them. He limited himself to very fine instruments and in the course of his life sold about 250, among which were a few Stradivariuses; even then one of them had been sold for $100,000.[11]

Another greenhorn began life here in America like Samuel Zemurray, as a banana peddler. This was in Fort Worth; later he settled in a small town in Texas called Dublin which probably never sheltered more than 3,000 people. Morris Hoffman (b. 1890) was not to become a great industrialist like Zemurray. He was illiterate, but evidently at some time during his life, he did learn to write. Here in this little Texas town he made a career buying and selling cotton and scrap iron. When the Baptists in town needed a building they turned to him and he gave them land and a church for a nominal sum and then took the money that he received and gave it to another Christian group. Dublin was grateful to Hoffman for the swimming pool which he built for it. It elected him mayor of the town for ten years and when there was a rodeo in Dublin he rode in the parade. In all probability he was the town's outstanding citizen. Kiev-born Samuel Paley (b. 1877), son of Isaac and Zelda Lapatofskey, was brought to this country as a child of eleven. When he grew up he went into the cigar business in Chicago and made a fortune. His brand was La Palina, named of course after himself. When he moved to Philadelphia he joined the elite Jewish city and country clubs but his synagog was a traditional one. The millions he made in cigars became the seed money he and his son William used to build the Columbia Broadcasting System. Julius Klorfein was another cigar manufacturer (Garcia Grande). After this teen-age Lithuanian immigrant had learned to roll cigars he went out on his own at eighteen, manufacturing his product in the morning and peddling it in the streets at night. With the money he made he turned to real estate and was one of the important developers of Florida's Palm Beach. The measure of his wealth was his ability to buy $3,000,000 worth of government bonds during World War II.[12]

The Edison Brothers Stores, Inc., a large and important corporation, was built by a group of young men who settled in Georgia. The father, a Russian, began life in the South as a peddler in and near the town of Adel, Georgia; it was not much more than a village; it had about 2,000 people. They were the only "Hebrews" in town. To help support the family, the sons, youngsters, went down to the railroad station and sold sandwiches and candy bars to arriving travelers. From Adel they moved to Valdosta and finally to Atlanta where a venture in shoes proved to be a success; by

1920 they were on their way. Ultimately the Edison brothers company became the largest retail shoe corporation in the United States. In 1982 it operated over 2,100 different stores which handled shoes, garments for young folks, and articles for home improvement; its net sales were close to a billion a year.

What happened to the East Europeans who came here before the pogroms triggered the arrival of myriads? One of the early immigrants, David Kaufman (b. 1840) became a master furrier and did well. Later in New Jersey, he turned to junk, and in 1917 was one of the largest scrap dealers in the United States, buying and selling thousands of tons at a time. Myriads of New York's metropolitans ate Nathan's hot dogs. Entrepreneurial skills are boundless. Nathan Handwerker (b. 1892) built a nickel hot dog stand in Coney Island into a $6,000,000 a year business. In some respects he was the patron saint of Coney Island. The company was called Nathan's Famous, Inc. He set up his first frankfurter stand at the resort in 1916 and kept open for twenty-four hours a day through the year. Branches were soon established in other places. Nathan personally watched the kitchen to be sure that the food was up to standard. It came to be a tradition in the state of New York that nobody could be elected without being photographed eating a hot dog at one of his booths.[13]

Women in big business? They were also beginning to make their presence felt. Lena Himmelstein was an immigrant from the Slavic lands who had come to this country in 1897 when she was but sixteen years of age. She opened a small dressmaking shop in New York and became one of the first women in this country to design a maternity gown for pregnant women. This was in 1907; in 1916 Lena incorporated her firm under the name of Lane Bryant, Inc. In 1917 the sales in her business were over a million; by 1968 with more than 100 branches the sales rose to $200,000,000. She started out with maternity dresses and then added special sizes. Lena and her son were very philanthropic; they were generous to New York's Federation of Jewish Philanthropies, to the Hebrew Immigrant Aid Society, and to the American Red Cross.[14]

Like many others, young Benjamin Davidson (b. 1859) began life in this country as a banker. After peddling in the East, he moved west to Sioux City, Iowa. There he continued peddling until finally in 1882 he and a brother opened a small shop; in the course of time it became the largest department store in the state. Another peddler who built a department store was Louis Pizitz (1868-1959) of Birmingham, Alabama. After coming to this country in 1889 from Poland, Pizitz peddled in Georgia till he had a little capital; then he opened a store in Swainsboro, a village. Seeking to better himself he moved west in the 1890's to the growing town of Birmingham in Alabama. By 1921 his little place of business had blosssomed into a sizable department store. It was known as Louis Pizitz

Dry Goods Company. In the 1930's it had 750 employees and was the largest store in Alabama. His philanthropic interests were quite diverse. He was very helpful to the Catholics, particularly the Knights of Columbus, raising large sums for them; he worked closely with the blacks, aiding them to build a YMCA and swimming pool and a hospital; he was liberal also to Tuskegee Institute. Pizitz was a joiner for he belonged to several synagogs and helped build a Young Men's Hebrew Association center as well as a Hillel House on the campus of the University of Alabama. In Birmingham he busied himself in the city's Associated Charities. In 1908 when there was a coal mine strike he sent truckloads of food and clothing to the strikers; he opened a pit to keep the miners at work. In 1914—a depression year—when cotton was eleven cents a pound he bought the crop, stored it, and promised the growers that they would get the profits when prices rose. On Thanksgiving Day during the panic of 1929 he fed the hungry; on Christmas he sent food to the prisoners in the jails. During the bad years when the teachers were given no cash, only scrip, he accepted the emergency currency.[15]

Mention has already been made of several builders, real estate speculators. There were many others who were to make a name for themselves in these fields. Joseph Rosenthal and Samuel Rosoff, contractors, were among the largest subway builders in the city of New York. The Galician, Leon Sobel, came to the United States at the age of twenty-one. He started out in the furniture business, then became a builder, and in the course of his career constructed about 400 buildings in New York City, subways too. Like many of the newcomers he was very Orthodox and was one of the generous elect who helped establish the Isaac Elchanan Yeshivah in the 1890's. Jacob M. Hoffman, a native of Odessa, was a real estate operator and builder who constructed 2,000 homes in northern New Jersey and 800 homes in Greater New York. It has been estimated that his purchases and sales of land in New York City alone amounted to about $20,000,000. The Latvian Harris H. Uris (d. 1945) came to the United States as a boy and grew up to become a prominent New York realtor; he built office and apartment buildings and important hotels such as the St. Moritz and the Belmont Plaza. All these realtors operated on a large scale; Benjamin Winter (b. 1881), a Pole, was among the most enterprising of the lot. He built up Fifth Avenue doing business in the hundreds of millions of dollars; he bought the Vanderbilt and Astor houses and the old Temple Emanu-El synagog spending millions, but he made millions.

Henrietta or Hattie Goldberg Callner (1866-1958) was born in Latvia. When she was five years old she went to live with an older sister where she had to take care of an infant; she lived there for three years and suffered mistreatment. When she was about eight years of age she went to another town where she had a brother studying at a yeshiva; she got a job as a domestic servant receiving room, board, and about $1 a year in payment, actually a ruble and a half. While still a child a young man taught her German so by the time she grew up she could read and write German well. When about fourteen or fifteen years of age an uncle sent for her and several siblings and brought them to America. This was her Uncle Morris (Maurice) Goldberg; he lived in Salt Lake where he had made some money in mining. She lived at the home of her uncle but because the uncle's wife was jealous of her she left and went east to Chicago where she again worked as a servant. She was so unhappy living with a brother that she attempted to commit suicide. Whenever she had an opportunity she went to school; she was very eager to learn. Hattie and a brother opened a merchant tailoring shop and also ventured into the cigar and tobacco business. Apparently they were successful as merchant tailors, for a brief period at least. When fortune smiled she took dancing lessons and went to the theatre. At eighteen she married a man named Henry Callner but by that time they were both broke. Because of these constant ups and downs the young couple went to Benton Harbor—there was a Jewish colony there—where they made a living picking strawberries for about a cent a box. Then they moved north along the lake to Muskegon, Michigan, where her husband peddled. Finally they returned to Chicago where Henry got a job paying him $9 a week; Hattie became a seamstress. She bought a machine on installments and started making children's dresses. Hattie then moved into dressmaking and was quite successful; at one time she had nineteen women and three tailors working for her but there was a fire and she lost everything; she had no insurance. Then she opened a grocery store; in the meantime she was constantly having babies.

In 1893 her Uncle Morris, the mining entrepreneur, came to Chicago to see the World's Fair and to renew his friendship with Hattie. When he died in 1894 he left her $8,000 and with this capital she built an apartment building, one of the first in town with steam heat. At the same time she was constantly studying, for she took courses in biology, botany, and zoology. She also studied at a local industrial institute; this ambitious young mother and family breadwinner concentrated on architecture. She sold her apartment house and started building others. She made her own plans and supervised the construction. From now on she was very successful; she bought an electric car and in 1926 she and one of her sons, Milton, began building apartment houses; that year they made their first million. A year later they had a second million and in 1928 a third. She made friends; among them were Clarence Darrow, the lawyer, and Jane Addams, the social worker. She became active in the charities; Hattie was a notable patron of Hadassah. It was believed that just before the depression came along she and her family owned a hundred buildings. Like others, however, during the long financial panic that began in 1929 the Callner empire was threatened. She had overextended herself, but she made deals with her creditors and managed to survive.[17]

The wise author of Proverbs wrote (31:30) that "favour is deceitful and beauty is vain." Helena Rubenstein (1871-1965) was not disheartened by the biblical admonition; she specialized in "beauty" and as a result became one of the country's richest Jewish businesswomen. She was a successful cosmetician. This woman who had come from a humble impoverished Galician family immigrated to Australia, manufactured a cold cream there, made some money, and moved on to London seeking new worlds to conquer. She opened beauty salons in the English capital, in Paris, and other cities, and from all indications was constantly successful. With the coming of World War I she left for the United States shifting her base here. Rubenstein became one of the country's most important manufacturers of beauty products; she was very innovative in marketing her products. When she died in 1965 she left a large personal estate; the business was later sold for $142,000,000. Here was a woman, a Polish immigrant, who competed successfully with men in the pitiless world of commerce and trade.[18]

Lithuanian-born Meyer Leon Prentis (1886-1970) did well in this country; he became the treasurer of General Motors, the firm that was to become the world's leading automobile manufacturer. During World War II Prentis negotiated a loan of a billion dollars to finance the company's war production. While living in St. Louis he learned accounting; by the time he was eighteen he was already the auditor for a large gas utility; in 1911 he went to work for General Motors and by 1919 he was the corporation's chief accountant; that same year he became the treasurer. General Motors had its problems, but he helped it survive in its most difficult days. Like many other successful businessmen he was generous to the Jewish community and its overseas philanthropies.[19]

Prentis came to the United States at the age of six; David Sarnoff (1891-1971) was nine. In 1906, after a few years of public school, he went to work as a messenger for the Commercial Cable Company. When the High Holy Days came around he took three days off not only because of the sanctity of the occasion but because he was the soloist in the synagog choir and he wanted to make some money; the company fired him. Sarnoff then became an office boy for the Marconi Wireless Telegraph Company and, later, a telegraph operator (1907). When in 1919 the company was taken over by the Radio Corporation of America he became one of its junior executives; he had come up the hard way. Two years later he was made the general manager; in 1926 he established the National Broadcasting Company; in 1930 he was president of the Radio Corporation of America. By this time he was one of the most important men in the United States in the field of radio; ultimately he was to serve as the chairman of the board of the National Broadcasting Company. Sarnoff improved radio programs, particularly in the realm of music; the Metropolitan Opera Association elected him as one of its directors. He developed coast to coast broadcasting and later pioneered in color television. The Radio Corporation of America became one of the largest electronic companies in the world; in 1960 it was a $2,000,000,000 corporation employing in the course of time 100,000 people. His first honorary degree came in the 1920's; ultimately he received degrees and awards from more than a dozen colleges, countries, and institutions. The army made him a brigadier general in the reserve. The blurb on the dust cover of a biography—*David Sarnoff*—written by Eugene Lyons, boasts that Sarnoff probably affected the daily life of more people than anyone since Edison. There is an element of truth in this puff. By the 1940's he was such a factor in American life that this man from Minsk was accepted as a member of the Harmonie, New York Jewry's elite social club.[20]

CHAPTER TEN

MAKING A LIVING

PART IV: THE CINEMA

INTRODUCTION

Like Sarnoff, but perhaps more directly, other members of the Jewish middle and upper-income groups made their livelihood in the amusement industry: the Yiddish theatre, the English theatre in its various forms, and the cinema. Included among the rich were the cinema moguls. Some were native American; a few were born in Germany; most were immigrants, Russian, Poles, and Hungarians. Starting in the 1890's they helped build one of America's most important industries. They were "fabulous." Yet several of the most famous and prosperous did not leave huge estates; some made no fortunes; two of them went to jail; they cut corners. How did the cinema begin? It began as part of peep-shows in penny arcades. These enterprises had a multitude of attractions such as fortune telling, horoscope and weight machines, punching bags, muscle testers, and kinetoscopes. A kinetoscope is an instrument where for a few brief moments action scenes were pictured; there was the illusion of motion. Jews were prominent among the exhibitors in this new commercial venture. They moved into this business because they were ready to crawl into the interstitial spaces; it was something new; they hoped to make a living—maybe even money—in a hurry. Capital poor they could not compete in some areas of commerce and trade. In 1896 a theatre already exhibited a one-reel life-size motion picture projected on a wall screen; it lasted fifteen minutes. The usual charge to view this motion picture was five cents; hence the theatre was called a nickelodeon. In the early 1900's, in Western Pennsylvania's New Castle and in Pittsburgh the Warner brothers operated such nickelodeons; they needed little cash; all they required was an empty room; they rented some chairs.

One of the first of the movie entrepreneurs was Max Aronson, a Jewish vaudeville actor, a native of Arkansas. He changed his name to Gilbert M. Anderson. In 1903 he acted in one of the very first cinema plays, *The*

Great Train Robbery; he probably got fifty cents an hour. It was the first movie with a plot; the audience could gape at their first story of some length; it ran for thirteen minutes. Later Anderson acted and directed in a series of westerns in which he starred as Bronco Billy; he produced as many as 400 in the period between 1908 and 1916. There is no question the West was won with movies. In 1907 he and a partner named George K. Spoor had established a company called the Essanay Film Manufacturing Company; Essanay of course embodies the initial letters of their names. Many of their pictures were made in Niles, California; they could often churn out a picture a day. They made a lot of money; no one could fault their productions; they were moral; justice always triumphed. It's questionable, however, whether with all the money he made Anderson died a rich man. Though Anderson was born a Jew his Jewishness seems to have been limited to his refusal to eat ham. It is to the credit of Essanay that it also developed Charles Chaplin. He made *The Tramp* in its studios, under its aegis; it was the company's biggest moneymaker around the year 1915.

By 1903 a number of Jews were producing these silent films; more were opening small theatres to exhibit them; they were certainly pioneers. By 1910 there was no town of size in this country without a nickelodeon; New York had hundreds. Millions viewed the flickers; there is no question that this was an industry with a future. The entrepreneurs were, however, hampered by the monopoly of the Motion Pictures Patents Company controlled by Edison and his associates; they owned certain patents which enabled them to dominate the industry; they produced the raw film and regulated the distribution of the pictures from 1910 until about 1914-1915 when the Sherman Antitrust Law was invoked. Among the people who helped destroy the monopoly were Carl Laemmle and William Fox. The road was now open to courageous speculators and entrepreneurs. Fox and Laemmle were among the first not only to exhibit films but to produce and distribute them; the pictures were produced both in New York and in Hollywood. After 1910 the California city had become an important center for film production because of the climate, the sunshine; winter offered little interference.

A number of Jews, mostly immigrants, were already in some branch of the cinema industry in the first decade of the twentieth century. Carl Laemmle (1867-1939) was German-born. After coming here as a teenager in 1884 he nibbled at a number of businesses and jobs till he discovered his forte; he had been a clerk, a bookkeeper, a manager of a clothing store. About 1906 he found himself in the motion picture business as a nickelodeon owner and a distributor of films. A few years later he was a producer; some of the theatre owners had to become producers; they needed the shows for their audiences. By 1912 Laemmle had a company called the Universal Film Manufacturing Company and a studio; later on his organization was known as Universal Studios. This large enterprise worked and produced in Universal City in Los Angeles. That very year Laemmle began producing full-length shows employing outstanding actors and actresses recruited from the legitimate theatre. In 1913 Laemmle's studio produced one of the first sex pictures, *Traffic in Souls*; it cost about $6,000 and grossed about a half a million. Laemmle was among the few in those early days who set out to make pictures an art, not merely a business. Among the stars of the silent days were two Jewish women, Pola Negri and Theda Bara. The latter was a "vamp," buxom in the best Jewish and Howard Chandler Christy tradition. Adolph Zukor and the Famous Players imported a multireel French film that starred Sarah Bernhardt in the role of Queen Elizabeth (1912).

Adolph Zukor (1872/1873-1976), a Hungarian, had been brought here as a teenager; his education was limited. Like Laemmle and other producers of note he engaged in a variety of businesses; he sold hardware, ran an upholstery shop, and became a furrier. Later he, too, turned to penny arcades and nickelodeons; in 1904 he was associated with Marcus Loew and others in vaudeville and in the exhibition of motion pictures. In 1912 Zukor established Famous Players Film Company together with Daniel Frohman who was primarily a legitimate theatre producer. Four years later the Famous Players became the Famous Players-Lasky Corporation; in 1917 this became Paramount Pictures, Inc. Zukor, living in New York, joined the Masonic order and became a member of Temple Emanu-El; membership in this great Reform synagog was the hallmark of a successful businessman. By the 1930's he had moved on to Hollywood making that city his headquarters. In 1936 the president of Paramount Pictures was Barney Balaban (1887-1971), a native of Chicago, a child of Polish immigrants; his father was a grocer. Balaban went to work at twelve as a Western Union messenger. About the year 1907, already grown up, he and his mother took a night off and went to a nickelodeon. Mamma was very impressed because the customers had to pay five cents before even seeing what they were getting for their money. The motion picture business seemed inviting. The family pooled its resources and rented a theatre for about $100 a month, hiring a violinist for music and cooling the place with a fan. By 1910 the Balabans had a theatre that seated 700, an orchestra, an organ, and a ventilating system. Barney had once worked for a cold storage plant and he liked things to be cool. He was innovative. Vaudeville and pictures were linked; Balaban hired stellar players for his houses; among them was Sophie Tucker, the singer, and Groucho Marx, the comic. In 1917 Balaban had a theatre in New York that could seat 2,000; in the 1920's he and his associates had 125 theatres, many were air conditioned, some had 3,000 seats and uniformed ushers.

In the 1920's he sold out to Paramount which he was later to head as chief executive.

Many years ago Professor Marcus, an historian teaching at the Hebrew Union College in Cincinnati, called on Dr. A. S. W. Rosenbach, the bookman, and asked him if he had any important documents in the field of American Jewish history. Dr. Rosenbach answered, yes, that he owned the most important document in all American Jewish history. When Marcus asked him if he could examine it Rosenbach went to his vault and picked up a framed document lying on the floor and showed it to Marcus. Recognizing it immediately the historian turned to Dr. "R." saying, "You are right; this is the most important document in American Jewish history." It was an original copy of the Bill of Rights. It was this copy that Balaban bought; he made sure that it was given a home of its own, one commensurate with its importance.

As a child in Kiev, Russia, Lewis J. Selznick (Zeleznick, 1870-1933) worked in a factory. Here in America he became a jeweler and a diamond salesman. Around the year 1912 he went to work for Laemmle at Universal. After a few years he established his own company, the Selznick Company. He was able to recruit stars. He and Zukor were rivals although the two joined forces when Selznick was short of funds; the new company was called Select Pictures but when Selznick no longer needed financial help he bought Zukor out and put the Selznick name back on the letterhead. By 1916 Selznick was doing very well; he was to have a twenty-two-room apartment on Park Avenue and to own a Rolls Royce. He financed some of his projects by selling franchises of pictures that were not yet finished. Among the stars in his cinema firmament was Alla Nazimova, a Russian Jew who was paid $1,000 a day when making a picture for him. In 1917 after the Russian Revolution when Czar Nicholas was deposed, Selznick sent a telegram to Petrograd addressed to him: "When I was a poor boy in Kiev some of your policemen were not kind to me and my people. I came to America and prospered . . . feel no ill will over what your policeman did, so if you will come to New York can give you fine position acting in pictures . . . signed Selznick, New York." Obviously this is a public relations ploy. Selznick did business in the millions but by 1923 he was bankrupt. Two years later he moved on to Florida hoping to make a new career in real estate. He was not successful. Despite his achievements he has not received full treatment at the hand of biographers and historians of the industry. Failure is inexcusable. Others also ran into hard times but they stayed the course till they retired, more or less graciously, or surrendered to the embraces of the bankers, always waiting on the sidelines.

Jesse Louis Lasky (1880-1958), a native Californian, was a vaudeville producer, a reporter, an Alaska prospector (1899), a pianist, and a cornet player. When he wrote his autobiography he called it *I Blow My Own Horn* (1957). In 1913 he and his brother-in-law, Samuel Goldfish, and Cecil B. DeMille, a writer, joined together in the Jesse L. Lasky Feature Photoplay Company. In 1913-1914 it produced *The Squaw Man*, one of Hollywood's first feature-length films. Later the company called itself Famous Players-Lasky Company; Lasky served as producer. In the decades of the '30's and '40's he worked for various other corporations; all told he may have been responsible for 1,000 films. Lasky was a native American Jew; Samuel Goldfish (Gelbfish? 1882-1974) was born in Poland; he had come here as a teenager (1896). He got his start as a glove salesman and a glove manufacturer; apparently he was successful. In 1916-1917 Goldfish and Edgar Selwyn established Goldwyn Pictures, Inc.; the corporation name is a combination taken from the two words Goldfish and Selwyn. Edgar Selwyn, a native of Cincinnati (b. 1875), was a well-known actor, playwright and cinema producer. Goldfish soon changed his name to Goldwyn. In 1923 he organized a company which he controlled, Samuel Goldwyn, Inc.; the following year this became part of Metro-Goldwyn-Mayer but he soon dropped out and again made pictures on his own. As a producer he insisted on high quality and artistic merit; he was meticulous, striving for perfection and seeking out the best actors and writers; he hired eminent authors to write his scripts.

In 1914 the silent cinema was well on its way although it was only a decade since the first picture was filmed. The country was building beautiful theatres; the musical accompaniments were superb. Production had its first master in D. W. Griffith who in 1915 released *The Birth of a Nation*. World War I was then raging in Europe and the United States government was soon to be involved. Determined to win at all cost, the authorities here employed the cinema as an instrument of propaganda. It was very effective. By this time the United States was making more than half of the world's pictures and was rapidly moving toward control in the industry.

During this period (1915) William Fox (1870-1952) organized the Fox Film and the Fox Theatre corporations. Fox, a native Hungarian, was brought over as an infant when his parents settled on the East Side. At the age of eleven he went to work in the apparel industry. In 1903 Fox opened a penny arcade in Brooklyn; within a year he started leasing theatres and gradually built up a chain where pictures and vaudeville were both shown. In 1912 he began to produce films in New York; later he shifted his production to Hollywood where he built a large studio. In 1926 this immigrant was to head New York's United Jewish Appeal drive for $6,000,000; this was a very prestigious assignment and honor; he was now one of the most important Jews in New York, in the country, as a matter of fact. Before the 1929 depression destroyed him he owned or controlled more than 800 theatres and had offices in about 200 cities. He was one of the early movie entrepreneurs who built ornate theatres, introduced organ music, and presented elaborate programs which combined vaudeville and full-length motion pictures. Some of his productions elicited high praise from the critics. For many the cinema had become a rival of the corner saloon. The Fox empire was a huge business running into the hundreds of millions of dollars; it collapsed during the depression. Later, bankrupt, he served five months in prison on charges of fraud and obstructing justice.

At one time Loew's, Inc. was controlled by Fox. Marcus Loew (1870-1927), the son of Viennese Jewish immigrants, was born in New York City, and like others this quondam furrier and real estate operator began with penny arcades. David Warfield, the actor, was his partner. Originally Loew was a theatre man but the need to provide pictures for his customers drove him into production. He bought Metro which was later in the 1920's to become part of Metro-Goldwyn-Mayer Film Corporation, the largest and most successful of Hollywood's cinema companies. His prime interest remained in distributing and exhibiting. Before his death he was the president of about 100 corporations; Loew's, Inc. was capitalized at $100,000,000; with its 300 amusement places it was a far cry from the penny arcade. Marcus Loew became the patron of Nicholas and Joseph Schenck who were to play a notable part in the cinema industry especially after the 1920's; the family lived on the Lower East Side and then moved up to Harlem. Both boys sold newspapers and then went to work in a drugstore which they finally bought. They leased food concessions at Fort George in Washington Heights serving holiday crowds; it was there that they met Marcus Loew and went into business with him. They worked closely with Loew, especially in his real estate ventures which included nickelodeons and vaudeville and cinema houses. After Loew died, Nicholas took charge of the theatre circuits; in the 1920's he was in control of Metro-Goldwyn-Mayer; by 1932 there were 12,000 people working for him in various operations. For years Nicholas and Joseph were partners in joint undertakings; in later decades Joseph was president of United Artists and Twentieth Century-Fox. Both men were very influential in the industry. Like Fox, Joseph, too, came into conflict with the law and served in a federal penitentiary for evading payment of income taxes. He was also charged with paying bribes to racketeers and stagehand unions. Joseph and Nicholas were not men of artistic calibre; they were, however, exceedingly able and administered a business complex successfully.

Nicholas Schenck was the majordomo who ran the Loew empire after the death of Loew; this included Metro-Goldwyn-Mayer, but even before the passing of Loew the chief of production for pictures was Louis Burt Mayer (1882/1885-1957). Mayer was the son of East Europeans who had moved to New York and Canada in the late nineteenth century. Louis worked for his father as a junk collector; his mother helped by peddling chickens from door to door. In 1904 the family moved to Boston, still in the junk business; three years later Mayer, in his early twenties, rented a theatre in Haverhill. Christmas time, 1907, he showed a French version of *The Passion Play* and made money; this was his first success. He began to build a theatre chain; by 1916 he was part of Metro Pictures, a distributing firm; he had learned the business back in Massachusetts. That year, too, he became a producer in New York but moved on soon to Hollywood; he had his own company, the Louis B. Mayer Corporation. In 1924 he became the head of production for Metro-Goldwyn, producing spectacular films, successful ones; he knew what the masses wanted. Personally he was very difficult, egoistic, aggressive, and vindictive, but he was an excellent businessman; he made good pictures and developed notable stars. He may well have been the leading film producer of his day. For years he was one of the highest paid executives in America with a salary in the seven figures; he had come a long way since he first peddled junk.

The Warner brothers—contemporaries of Mayer—were in a way both pioneers and late bloomers; they were among the first to open nickelodeons but they were not to loom large in the cinema world till the 1930's. There were four Warner brothers in the film business, Harry, Albert, Samuel L., and Jack L. They were to struggle for half a generation before they saw the light. Like the Mayers, the parents had come to Canada in the 1880's; the father was a cobbler. Later the family settled in the United States, first in Baltimore and then in Youngstown where the boys ran a bicycle shop. As early as 1903 (1905?) Harry opened a nickelodeon in New Castle, Pennsylvania, just across the border from their Ohio home. He started a film exchange but it was not very successful because of the restrictions imposed by the Motion Pictures Patents Company, the so-called Edison Trust. Ten years later Harry and his brothers organized Warner Pictures; in 1917-1918 they produced a full-length picture dealing with Ambassador James W. Gerard's *My Four Years in Germany*; this was a war propaganda film and was well received. Soon they began producing films from novels and plays; by this time the firm was known as Warner Brothers Pictures.

In the 1920's the firm began to expand; a decade later it had its own film exchanges in the United States and abroad and controlled a chain of theatres, ultimately several hundred. It was one of the largest film organizations in the United States. Its importance lay in its introduction of talking pictures; the Warners were the pioneers. The silent pictures prevailed until 1927-1928; from then on the voice and the pictures were synchronized. Warner Brothers produced *The Jazz Singer* (1927), one of the earliest movies with dialogue; a year later it produced the first all-sound cinema. *The Jazz Singer* was a picture by a Jewish firm with a Jewish story starring Al Jolson the son of an immigrant cantor named Yoelson. The theme of *The Jazz Singer* was one that would appeal to every East European Jew. It was a pathetic story guaranteed to melt the hearts of the most obdurate. The father, a cantor, was too sick on the Day of Atonement to sing the Kol Nidre, that most sacred of melodies. The son, a musical comedy star, about to open his own show that very night, made the sacrifice of repairing to the synagog to take his sick father's place.

THE CINEMA INDUSTRY: THE EARLY YEARS—A SUMMARY

What really moved these Jews to go into the cinema business? Jews are not speculative; they are usually a cautious lot. They moved into the business because it was a chance to make a living; relatively little capital was needed in the days of the penny arcades. Thus they came into the industry through the back door, through the nickelodeons and theatres where pictures were exhibited. Some of them turned to the cinema because it was not yet developed and there was no overwhelming competition from capital-rich Gentiles. The cinema was an open field particularly after the wings of the Motion Picture Patents Company were clipped. What was the extent of Jewish participation in this new and challenging field? It is estimated that there were over sixty individuals or firms making pictures in 1913; the Jews were producing almost 20 percent of the movies. In the period up to 1921 they were active but not dominant though they were constantly forging ahead. The most important film of the day, *The Birth of a Nation*, was not made by Jews. In the 1930's, out of a total of eight important companies, Jews owned three; they had partial control of three; two were entirely out of their control. The nature of the work they accomplished? They never forgot that they were merchandisers. The Jews started as exhibitors, distributors, marketers, and then turned to production; ultimately in later decades, they were in all phases of the industry; many were writers and directors. The garment industry which they saw all about them served as a paradigm; they were producers and distributors.

In the course of time they became innovative: in the exhibition of films, in picture palaces, in the musical accompaniments, in the symphony-type orchestras, in the Hollywood type of premieres with stars. Almost as important as a good film was the ambience in which it was shown. Samuel Lionel Rothafel ("Roxy") made a name for himself by his imaginative novel presentation of films. This ex-United States marine managed a theatre in his native Minnesota and then turned to New York where he became the world's most celebrated movie palace manager. It was he who introduced excellent orchestras, precision dancing choruses, good singers, uniformed and courteous ushers, and breath-taking lavishly decorated buildings. Speaking of the Hollywood executives, Dr. Hortense Powdermaker, a sociologist and writer, said that she found them as interesting sociologically as the cannibals of the South Pacific. They were with few exceptions a ruthless group, "sharp," very egotistical; most of them arranged to have their biographies written. This was self-serving to a large degree but publicity—so they thought—was their lifeblood. They could not serve as models for the Sunday school children in the Los Angeles and Hollywood synagogs. They were certainly no worse to be sure than the typical American "rugged individualist," Jew or Gentile. They were frontiersmen in a new industry which they helped develop. They were bold, tough, not always admirable human beings. Yet when they made money they were often generous to Jewish and other causes. They were imaginative, courageous, and not without an artistic sense, for when they had a choice they often opted for the better. Most of them belonged to synagogs even if they did not frequent them. They had been reared in Orthodox homes and surroundings but they had "emancipated" themselves. They lived in a Jewish world but were not truly part of it. Americanism was their Judaism, their religion.

What did these Jewish moviemakers do for America commercially? They helped develop an important facet of the entertainment industry. By the 1920's they were beginning to employ thousands of people; ultimately the industry would put hundreds of thousands to work. In the decade of the 1920's, 20,000 movie theatres were opened in the United States; there were 130,000,000 weekly admissions. In the following decade—so it is estimated—65 percent of all Americans went to the movies. Bronco Billy, Zukor, Selznick, Mayer, Fox, Goldwyn, Loew, the Schencks, Laemmle, Lasky helped make this country the production center for the world's movie industry. They helped parlay a penny arcade into a billion dollar industry. What did these Jewish immigrants do culturally for the land that gave them shelter? These early pioneers—most without any good secular education—never set out to raise the niveau of American culture. They were businesssmen eager to make a dollar, fast. They wanted to create and sell a product. If, not infrequently, these clothing, glove, fur, jewelry, salesmen, junk dealers, produced magnificent socially uplifting motion pictures, if, not infrequently, they transcended themselves, it was because they were intelligent enough to realize that these, too, were salable. They were intelligent; God had not punished them; they were not born fools.

And what did they do for the image of the Jew? Precious little. They were not concerned. In this sense they were altogether unlike the Catholics who over the decades insisted on presenting a favorable image of the Catholic Church and its clergy. Jewish subjects were occasionally treated and Jewish characters appeared on the screen, but this was incidental. The

Jew was for a time a comic, a ludicrous figure; occasionally the portrayal was anti-Jewish. Some shows savored of the melodramatic; there were pictures of suffering in Russia. Scott's Rebecca of York appeared in *Ivanhoe*, Dickens's Fagin snarled in *Oliver Twist*; there were sympathetic presentations of Disraeli and Captain Alfred Dreyfus, the French Jewish martyr. There were portrayals of peddlers, pawnbrokers, and even of a Jewish cowboy. After Ikey Rosenthal was hired on the Bar-X ranch the other cowboys threatened him with a pistol and made him do a "Yiddishe dance." Later after the Jew had become a pawnbroker and had taken the cowboy's pistols in hock he could then shoot at his tormentors. In 1911 this was deemed good clean humor! In the 1920's the Jewish Irish intermarriage theme began to make its appearance. The melting pot was a success (in the movies at least); the nice Jewish boy marries the nice Christian girl. There were no Yiddish films here in the United States before 1921.

Ever since the 1890's when the Jewish cinema entrepreneurs first turned to the penny slot machines they realized that it was their job to entertain, to amuse. This was basic. They furthered what was to become the chief form of escape, entertainment, for the American people and ultimately for almost every human being in the farthest corners of the earth; the appeal was universal. It is no sin to have entertained the world. On the whole the influence of these Jewish cinema men was salutary. Artistically, culturally, emotionally, the viewers were moved. Millions who poured into the motion picture theatres had to think, to like, to dislike, to exercise moral judgment. Whole new worlds and scenes were opened up to them, and the glorious past in all its splendor was unrolled before their eyes. Pictures, especially of historical themes, were educational. People who paid their pennies discovered the world of antiquity and the Middle Ages; they were given lessons in the geography of the continents and the distant seas. The American standards of living, of dress, of good manners, and above all of liberty and freedom were bound to be impressive, inviting. Americans were taught American history; the producers were romantically Americanistic. By the stories they pictured they encouraged the youth of America to move ahead, to achieve, to become men and women of note. They were cultural imperialists spreading the gospel of the Pax Americana. Few Jewish producers and directors can be compared to D. W. Griffith, but the beautiful artistic films that Goldwyn and others produced were aesthetic experiences that almost brought down heaven to earth. It bears repetition, the Jewish moviemakers never set out to exercise a positive, cultural influence on their fellow Americans and the people of distant continents. Despite its humble beginnings and its many poor and sordid films, despite the purely commercial motivation that prompted many of the pioneers—for it was a business, not an art—the cinema was an influence for good. It is true the movies almost destroyed the legitimate theatre. This was inevitable yet though its decline is to be deplored this cinematic world which Jews helped bring to birth was a boon. Imagine a world without it.[1]

CHAPTER ELEVEN

MAKING A LIVING

PART V: THE ARTS AND THE PROFESSIONS

THE IMPACT OF SECULAR CULTURE

The new immigrants made their presence felt in nurturing and furthering the motion picture industry. Whatever may have been the motivation that spurred on the producers and exhibitors there can be no question—as it has been pointed out above—that the cinema was a cultural medium of great importance. An apposite query is warranted; what was the attitude of these newcomers—all of these East Europeans—toward America's secular culture? In the newer areas of settlement, in Middle and Upper Manhattan, in Brooklyn, Long Island, the Bronx, Westchester, and in the satellite towns of northern New Jersey, acculturation was more pervasive than on the Lower East Side. There was an inexorable exposure to the larger non-Jewish community. True, the Jews were apparently self-contained, disparate, but they were overwhelmed on all sides by American cultural institutions, educational agencies, an Americanizing Yiddish press, the cinema. All these pounded away at the immigrants and especially their children. For the new generation there were night and day schools, libraries, theatres, concerts. The Lewisohn Stadium concerts brought them the world's most beautiful music. Bear in mind that probably less than 10 percent of the immigrants had gone to public school in their native lands; here by grace of the American educational system the children were introduced to the modern contemporary world of learning, hygiene, civics, and manners. Wherever they turned there were agencies that moved to deghettoize them, secularize them, enlighten them. The parents were not spared; they were influenced by contact with the natives, by the challenges of American politics, by the new words that crept into their Yiddish. Words are ideas. The new Jews here integrated themselves willingly into the new culture; they owed nothing to the despotic regimes which had harassed and despised them; yet most Jews here, religionists, never forgot their ancestral heritage despite the threat of a constantly advancing secularization.

In a positive sense why did the émigrés here accept the advances of the contemporary world? Many, most, were interested in learning for its own sake; their traditions taught them to respect knowledge; leaders of the unions and the Marxist radicals wanted to raise the intellectual level of the workmen. Language was an open road to economic advancement. Just because they had been denied schooling abroad it was the more welcome here. Not untypical is the Bernstein family of Rochester, the mother and siblings of Philip Bernstein, once the rabbi of the local Reform congregation. The Bernstein parents were never to be affluent. Back in Lithuania the literate mother, when still a teenager, had written letters for the women in town whose husbands had gone to America and had not yet sent for them. Many of the town's women were illiterate. When Mama came here, still a youngster, she ate black bread and herring on the three-week voyage; she kept kosher. She went to work in a clothing factory, attended night school, and struggled through all of Dickens—a liberal education in itself. When she married she insisted that her boys be well educated. Two of her sons received Ph.D's; Philip, a third was a president of the Central Conference of American Rabbis, wrote for the better American magazines, and was the recipient of several honorary degrees. The Jewish children of East European parents were most eager to attend the public schools; very few, however, went on to high school. Indeed in these days not many native Gentile children went beyond the eighth grade. As late as 1914 there was a pitifully small number of high schools in Manhattan and the Bronx.[1]

Actually formal education was not absolutely necessary for upward economic mobility. Many educated themselves as they went along; they succeeded because of sheer ability, intelligence, moral courage, hard work. The children in the public schools set their sights high. Public School No. 188 on the Lower East Side had 5,000 students; many if not most were Jewish. In one class there were 39 boys; they were asked what they hoped to become. One student had not yet made up his mind; eleven wanted to be businessmen; nine wanted to be lawyers, three dentists, three doctors, two teachers; one each wanted to become a mechanic, an engraver, a clothes designer, an electrical engineer. Six who picked their vocation after watching the building of the Williamsburg Bridge, wanted to be civil engineers. If this study of a class in Public School No. 188 is any indication, the children of the immigrants were inclined toward the professions. In 1918, 39 percent of the women attending Hunter were Jewish; 29 percent of the men in City College of New York were Jews; in both schools most of the Jews were of East European background. Impressive statistics? Not necessarily, considering the size of New York's Jewry; in those days there were 1,500,000 Jews in Greater New York. Back home in the Slavic villages a boy seeking a career would go to a talmudic academy and think seriously of the rabbinate. There were few professional openings for Jews in Russia and Rumania. Here in the United States knowledge of the Talmud was of little value; the Orthodox rabbinate was not a high prestige profession; the Hebrew codes were not actually the organic statutes regnant in the ghettos. Only secular education would lead to a profession; educational opportunities were wide open here. The interest in schools is reflected in the almost euphoric autobiography of Mary Antin. There is no question that the youngsters wanted white-collar jobs; accounting was helpful if one wanted to advance in commerce and the professions. The emergence of writers, scholars, artists, scientists in the decade of the 1930's testifies to the efficacy of orderly academic training. Not untypical is the case of the Galician youngster Isidor Isaac Rabi. In 1915-1919 he was a student at Cornell; in 1944 he was a Nobel Prize winner in the field of physics.

Prior to 1921 it was not easy for a Russian, Pole, or Rumanian to acquire higher education here in the United States; they had no means; some were illiterate. Only a small fraction opted for college training; a few of these became important in the Jewish community; still fewer made a name for themselves in the larger American body politic. These exceptional individuals became leaders in commerce and industry; they ran for office and sat in the state legislatures, in Congress. By the 1890's a handful of immigrants who had landed in the 1880's had already begun to advance themselves; Russian Jewish girls were already teaching in New York's public schools. By the year 1900 the number of gainfully employed immigrants, Jewish professionals, may have been as high as 3 percent; some of these were women. That year, according to demographic studies, there were 526 male public school teachers of immigrant background; there were 132 females, 305 physicians, 217 lawyers, 75 dentists, 37 actresses. Rubinow in 1902 said that one-half of all New York's physicians were Jews; this certainly seems to be an exaggeration but three years later it was said that there were 400 Russian Jewish physicians, 400 lawyers, 300 dentists, 1,000 druggists, and 25 architects. Immigrant women, too, were turning in increasing numbers to dentistry, medicine, pharmacy, and law.[2]

By 1910, relatively more Jewish foreign-born were going to college than their Gentile fellow citizens. In a descending order Jews majored in the liberal arts, pharmacy, law, medicine, engineering, dentistry, and veterinary science. If the number of those who opted for pharmacy was high it was because as Jews they were often denied admission to the medical schools. On the other hand East European women were securing degrees as physicians because the women's medical colleges were less prejudiced, more eager to increase their enrollment. By 1910 Jewish women were studying liberal arts, medicine, law, and pharmacy. A goodly number were turning to public school teaching; these were the students who were interested in securing a Bachelor of Arts degree. In 1918, when the Jews of New York City constituted 25 percent of the population, 38.5 percent of the college students were Jews. In terms of percentage, however, there were fewer Jewish women in the city's institutions of higher learning than Gentiles. In a descending order Jewish men were studying commerce and finance, medicine, engineering, law, and dentistry. Most Jewish male students were crowded into these five fields; women were in commerce and finance, education and law; almost as many women as men were preparing themselves to pass the bar examination. Most of these students were foreign-born or the children of immigrants.

Statistical estimates—and that is what they are—vary for 1920. A conservative guess is that 5 to 6 percent of the male newcomers was gainfully employed in the professions. Compared of course to those in commerce and industry the percentage was not high; according to some estimates over 53 percent of the immigrants at work were in commerce and in some form of manufacturing. There is no question that quite a number of the children were determined to climb the ladder to economic success and social recognition. Many advanced themselves through their own effort or through parental aid. It was a sacrifice when a father permitted sons or daughters to study and did not compel them to take a job to help the family. By the 1930's—so it is reported—over half of New York's teachers, physicians, dentists, and lawyers were Jews; many of these professionals had been born across the seas.[3]

Who are some of these foreign-born notables? In what disciplines did they distinguish themselves? A few East Europeans who were destined to exercise influence in this country had found a home here as early as antebellum days. The Pole Michael Heilprin, encyclopedist and Jewish communal worker, had come to the United States in the 1850's; Dr. Charles H. Liebermann, a Russian, was one of the physicians called in to attend President Lincoln after he was shot by John Wilkes Booth. This surgeon and ophthalmologist was one of the founders of the Georgetown Medical School. Max Rosenthal, an antebellum Polish immigrant, served as an artist with the army of the Potomac during the Civil War. Joseph Pulitzer, who served as a cavalryman in the War of 1861, and who was to emerge as one of America's leading newspaper entrepreneurs, was a native Hungarian.

There were few fields wherein Jewish newcomers did not stand out. Joseph Goldberger was to discover a cure for pellegra; Samuel Meltzer, a Lithuanian, arrived here in 1883 and before he passed away in 1920 was to be acclaimed as one of the country's outstanding medical scientists. He served as head of the department of physiology and pharmacology at the Rockefeller Institute. As early as 1906 Meltzer was honored by the University of Maryland with an honorary degree, probably one of America's first East Europeans to be so recognized. Among his colleagues at the Institute was Phoebus Aaron Theodore Levene (1869-1940); he immigrated here in 1892. Years later he was cited by his colleagues as "the outstanding American worker in the application of organic chemistry to biological problems." He was indeed a notable biochemist.

The plant physiologist, Charles Bernard Lipman—brother of the equally famous Jacob Goodale Lipman—had come to free America the same year that Goldberger landed (1888). Before Charles B. Lipman died he was to become professor and a dean at the University of California and to serve on the educational advisory board of the John Simon Guggenheim Memorial Foundation. Like his brother, Charles was a pioneer soil scientist. Albert Bruce Sabin, a native of Bialystok, landed here in 1921; through the educational opportunities afforded Sabin here he succeeded in developing a live virus vaccine that served to immunize children against infantile paralysis. In 1927 both Selig Perlman and Isaiah Leo Sharfman were full professors of economics in their respective schools, Perlman at the University of Wisconsin, Sharfman at the University of Michigan; the latter had attained the full professorial rank in 1914. The two were among the few elite Jews who had advanced in the academic hierarchy; both had been born in the czarist empire.[4]

One of the most brilliant of America's immigrants, certainly one of the most respected and admired, was Morris Raphael Cohen (1880-1947), philosopher, educator, polymath. He was in his element teaching the bright Jewish boys in New York's City College. They loved him for his iconoclasm and his devotion to Jewry. He was a dedicated man, no lawyer yet a philosopher of logic and the law. The profession of law was a favorite vocation of the ghetto dwellers. One of City College's students, Nathan D. Perlman (1887-1952), a native of Poland, was sent to the State Assembly in 1915 and to Congress in 1920. He was a Republican. The Democrat Herman Paul Kopplemann (1880-1957), a native of Odessa, served in Connecticut's legislative house and senate before going on to Congress; Alice S. Petluck, another Russian, was the first woman lawyer to practice in several of New York's most important courts.[5]

Two teenage Ukrainian lads were brought to the United States in 1881 or 1882; the one, Louis J. Pritzker became a well-known physician and surgeon in Chicago; his younger brother Nicholas J. Pritzker (b.1871) worked the streets of the city as a newsboy and a bootblack. Nicholas went to night school and became a bookkeeper, and later a pharmacist; by 1902 he had passed the bar exam, had started to practice law, and soon became a recognized Chicago Jewish community activist. Nicholas's sons have built one of America's commercial and hotel empires. By the late twentieth century the family controlled over 100 hotels both here and abroad—The Hyatt Corporation; their industries are known as the Marmon Group. In 1968 the Pritzkers gave a gift of $12,000,000 to the University of Chicago Medical School.

Nicholas J. Pritzker began his business career as a bootblack; Louis Waldman, a fellow Ukrainian, got his start in the garment industry and finally became a garment cutter; this was an elite job. Waldman went to night school, studied, and became a civil engineer; later, he made a switch, like Pritzker, and turned to law (1922). Before that—in 1919 and 1920—he had already been elected to the New York State Assembly on the Socialist ticket but his colleagues in the legislature would not permit him to take the seat to which he had been elected. He was not acceptable to his fellow assemblymen; in that reactionary period Socialists were deemed disloyal to the state; they were internationalists. As a Socialist Waldman ran for many offices; thrice he was a candidate for the office of governor. He was very successful in his chosen profession becoming an outstanding union counsel; he was the strikers' lawyer. In 1936 he was one of those who established the American Labor Party. By the 1940's and 1950's, now more conservative, he had accepted the presidency of the Brooklyn Bar Association and the chairmanship of the American Bar Association Committee on American Citizenship. This quondam Socialist had become a Republican. His wife was also a lawyer; she was counsel for the National Desertion Bureau.[6]

FINE ARTS

Two of the country's theatrical impresarios, Max Rabinoff and Solomon Hurok, were born in Eastern Europe. Rabinoff began life in this country as a teenager stripping tobacco; then he sold pianos, organized concerts in Chicago's public auditoriums, managed the Boston Opera Company, and brought the Ballet Russe and the dancer Anna Pavlova to this country. When Pavlova danced in Chicago in 1915 young Jacob Marcus and other Hebrew Union College students studying at the Divinity School of the University of Chicago occupied a box until they were politely escorted out; they had failed to buy tickets for the performance. Rabinoff was largely responsible for developing the New York City Center as a major theatrical and musical institution. Hurok became "America's impresario No. 1." The cultural impact of the dancers and ballet companies he brought to America was impressive. Some of Europe's greatest musicians were brought by him to the United States, and it was he who played no small part in arranging for cultural exchanges between this country and the Soviet Union. That Hurok had a healthy respect for his own achievements is documented by his two autobiographies. One of impresario Sol Hurok's rivals was Morris Gest. Like Hurok this native of Russia brought a Russian ballet troup to the United States. He served as the agent for the famous Italian actress Eleonora Duse and induced Max Reinhardt to stage *The Miracle* here. Gest produced about fifty plays in this country.[7]

As the decades passed more and more of the newcomers devoted themselves to the fine arts. This is particularly interesting in view of the fact that the graphic arts were rarely cultivated by Jews in the East European lands. Painting offered but little opportunity for a livelihood in the European ghettos. Although one might suspect that the East Side slums would not breed artists, there can be no question that a substantial number of America's Jewish artists in the post1920's were immigrants from Eastern Europe. Art was their vocation and their passion. The immigrant parents of Sir Jacob Epstein (1880-1959), the sculptor, were probably not happy with their son who set out to become an artist but they did not or could not stop him. Young Epstein, who was determined to become an artist, lived in the ghetto after his parents had moved out. He had been taken out of school at the age of thirteen, had turned his hand to a variety of jobs, and even worked on a farm. He took a room in the ghetto and managed to make a living selling his sketches. He lived on about $12 a month; the staples that kept him alive were tea and eggs. He set out to limn individuals and scenes as he saw them, realistically, without sentimentality. As Hapgood in his *Spirit of the Ghetto* has pointed out, there were other artists on the Lower East Side; some, like Epstein, were interested in ghetto types and scenes; others saw different challenges. *Who's Who in American Jewry* (1926) contains the biographies of a number of foreign-born Jews who had become sculptors, artists, etchers, and painters. An impressive art collector was the Latvian-born Joseph Herman Hirshhorn who made a huge fortune in uranium. His final gift to the government and people of America included about 4,000 paintings and 1,600 pieces of sculpture; the value of this treasure ran to somewhere between $25,000,000 and $50,000,000. This is a far cry from the time he sold newspapers and pretzels on the streets of Brooklyn. What stimulated his interest in art: a picture on a calendar published by a life insurance company. Why did he give his collection away: "I couldn't do what I did in any other country. What I did I accomplished here in the United States. It belongs here."

A fellow Latvian was the painter and sculptor Maurice Sterne (1878-1957). Sterne was a post-impressionist painter and sculptor who came to this country at the age of eleven or twelve. He studied art at the National Academy of Design at night and worked by day in a saloon. He moved on to Paris and was friendly with Gertrude Stein and Max Weber; Picasso, he thought, was a charlatan. He was a teacher of art for almost fifty years before he received recognition though he was never to be acclaimed one of the great. One of his best-known pieces of sculpture, *The Early Settlers*, can be seen in Worcester; he also did mural paintings in the Washington library of the Department of Justice. In 1929 Sterne served as president of the Society of American Painters, Sculptors, and Gravers.

Among the foreign-born artists who were to make a name for themselves in this generation were Max Kalish, the sculptor, Abraham Walkowitz, the impressionist painter, William Auerbach Levy, etcher and caricaturist, Ben Shahn, painter, muralist, designer of tapestries, and illustrator of a Haggadah, the Passover ritual. Another artist of note, a member of the avant-garde, was Max Weber. He was a pioneer in modern art though it was many years before he won a following. By the time he passed away in 1961 his paintings, sculptures, and abstractions had been exhibited in many galleries and museums. Bernard Berenson (1865-1959), who was himself not an artist, became an authority on Renaissance painting and in this role served to guide some of the world's greatest collectors. This young Lithuanian who was educated in Boston's Latin Grammar School and at Harvard settled in Italy and was universally recognized as a critic and connoisseur of Italian art.[8]

William Zorach, brought to Ohio as a child, grew up to become a notable sculptor, working in wood, stone, and marble. Hungarian-born Martin Birnbaum graduated from City College, learned to play the violin well, took a degree in law but made his living as an art critic and salesman. He sold paintings to millionaires who accepted him as a friend and a social equal. He entitled his autobiography, *The Last Romantic*. The Joseph B. Abrahams, who served the Jewish Theological Seminary as its secretary, was a calligrapher and illuminator who also created Hebrew type faces and designed the bronze door for New York's Temple Emanu-El. His illuminated citations were presented to different presidents; the windows and ceilings of churches and temples show his handiwork. This youngster from Lithuania, who grew up on the East Side, began his career as a news reporter. Later he was to edit an art journal and to write for the art magazines. It puzzled him that the Declaration of Independence when written was not illuminated. He failed to understand that its very simplicity was symbolic of its glory. No students of art would ever admit that Louis I. Bloom was a member of their magic circle. This Russian immigrant made his living in his early days as a hand in a Massachusetts shoe factory. Then he brought a smile to thousands of boys and girls—and their parents too—by creating a whole new world of brightly colored imaginatively shaped stuffed toy animals. The bunnies be brought to birth were pink; his elephants were yellow; his pussycats orange; his dogs were red. Who is so bold that he will deny the artistry of this gifted man?[9]

USIC

Music has always been an important element in the life of the Jews ever since biblical times. In modern days a good hazzan, the cantor, was treasured in the ghettos of Russia and America; fiddlers were loved. By the 1920's there were a substantial number of eminent foreign-born musicians in this country; they were virtuosos, conductors, composers, and critics too. It had been pointed out above that a statistical survey revealed that in 1900 there were many male and female East European musicians in New York City. It is probable that these men and women had received their training in their European homelands; a number of them made careers here as directors of symphonies before the 1920's. One of them was Joseph Alexander Pasternack (1880/1881-1940), a Pole who came to the United States in 1895. Though originally a concert pianist he played the solo viola for the Metropolitan Opera House and as an assistant conductor was in charge of its Sunday concerts. He was also visiting conductor with other symphonies. In 1916 after his appointment as director of the Victor Talking Machine Company, he broadcast concerts over the major radio networks.

Another symphony director was Nikolai Sokoloff (b.1886); he had come here at the age of fourteen from his native Ukraine. Sokoloff began his American career as a violinist with the Boston Symphony; in 1919 he led the Cleveland Symphony and later conducted orchestras in New York, London, and other cities. Because of his administrative skills he was appointed national director of Roosevelt's Federal Music Project in 1935. The Russian pianist Ossip S. Gabrilowitsch (1878-1936) started touring this country in 1900 but settled here permanently in 1914; in 1918 he was asked to conduct the Detroit Symphony. His wife Clara Clemens was the daughter of Mark Twain (Samuel Clemens). Gabrilowitsch was sympathetic to the rising Jewish community in Palestine; not all Jewish virtuosos and conductors identified themselves with Jewry; their professional careers meant everything to many of them; most of them maintained an aloof stance. Among the Jewish piano virtuosos, one of the most distinguished to settle in the United States, was the Lithuanian, Leopold Godowsky (1870/1871-1938); he was also a composer and teacher. It is said that he made his debut as an artist at the age of nine. He toured America for the first time in 1884; in 1888 he gave a command performance at the British court. He lived in America for many years but he went back to Berlin in 1900 where he achieved recognition as a musician of international stature. He, too, settled permanently in the United States in 1914 at the time of World War I.[10]

Violinists may well have been more popular here, certainly among East European Jewish newcomers. Three of the outstanding violinists who settled here were Efrem Zimbalist, Mischa Elman, and Jascha Heifetz. All three were world famous virtuosos; Elman settled here in 1908; Zimbalist in 1911; Solomon Hurok was their impresario. Efrem Zimbalist, a Russian, married the Rumanian Jew Alma Gluck, one of America's most beloved singers. This talented couple became converts to Christianity. The most distinguished of the three violinists may well be Jascha Heifetz (b.1901). At the age of seven he was already playing in public in his native Russia; at eleven he toured Europe concertizing. It was then that he appeared as a soloist with the Berlin Philharmonic Orchestra. Heifetz made his debut at Carnegie Hall in 1917 and was soon recognized as one of the world's greatest violinists. In 1925 he played for the Jewish Palestinians in order to raise money for a concert hall in Jerusalem. In the 1950's he played for the Israel Philharmonic Orchestra and included a work of Richard Strauss who had been associated with the Nazis. This caused quite a stir in the country.

Irving Berlin's music was an entirely different genre than that of the classical virtuosos. "Alexander's Rag Time Band" is not a concerto. People, however, will be singing "God Bless America" long after they stop listening to the violin recordings of Jascha Heifetz. Irving Berlin's name is attached to hundreds of songs including one that he called "Russian Lullaby." This folk singer—and he wrote songs which the masses still sing and love—was a native of the town of Mologa on the Volga. He is one of America's musical heroes. In his popularity he is comparable to Stephen Collins Foster but unlike the latter he was not doomed to poverty though he began life in this country on the East Side as a singing waiter in a Chinatown restaurant.[11]

MEN AND WOMEN IN THE PROFESSIONS

Irving Berlin was an artist; he wrote songs. Leon Solomon Moisseiff (1872-1943) was also an artist; he designed beautiful bridges. He had a creative imagination. This native of Riga designed or served as consultant for the Manhattan and Queensboro bridges over the East River and the Delaware River bridge joining Philadelphia and Camden. When the Delaware River bridge was built it was the longest suspension bridge in the world; later, the Golden Gate bridge—designed by a Cincinnati Jew, Joseph B. Strauss—was to be even larger; Moisseiff was one of the engineers who helped build it too. This Latvian was looked upon as an authority on long span bridges and was frequently called in as a consultant. When he had a little leisure he wrote articles on literature and drama for the Yiddish press. An engineer, a bridge designer, a litterateur; he was an unusual man.

Practically all the persons described in the above vignettes achieved national recognition. Thus they are not typical of the immigrant professionals who built new lives for themselves here in the United States. They were the elite, the tip of the iceberg. There were many others, thousands of men and women, who stood out at least in their local communities; they were educators, lawyers, doctors, social workers, scientists, engravers, artists, scholars. One can summarize the achievements of these many professionals by saying that they made contributions of note in their various fields. This would be inadequate, unfair; they deserve their moment in the historian's sun; they cannot be brushed aside with a genuflectic generality. The Radins were Polish Jews. Papa, Adolph Moses Radin (1845-1909), a Pole, came to the United States with a Ph.D. degree from Greifswald. Here he worked as a prison chaplain and as a preacher in the Educational Alliance, the Downtown settlement. Max and Paul, his sons, were little boys when papa emigrated in 1886, a man of forty-one. Max became a jurist and a historian; Paul, an anthropologist. Rumaninan-born Paul Klapper was to become the first (unconverted) Jewish college president in the United States when he was appointed head of Queens College (1937).[12] Quite a number of the newcomers became litterateurs and journalists. Simeon Strunsky was an editorial writer for New York's *Evening Post* and a columnist for the *New York Times*; Elias Tobenkin, a reporter on the *Herald Tribune*, was an authority on the Soviet Union; Anzia Yezierska, after an unhappy stint as an operative in a sweatshop and as a domestic cook, turned to the writing of stories and won an award as the author of the "best short story of the year." Herman Bernstein was a reporter, editor of an American Jewish magazine, founder of the Yiddish daily *Der Tog*, a translator of Russian classics, and the United States minister to Albania.[13]

Irving W. Halpern, a native of Odessa, was a criminologist recognized both in Washington and in New York as an authority on delinquency. Because of his expertise he was invited to lecture at the Fordham University School of Social Work. America's outstanding Jewish social worker was Vilna-born Jacob Billikopf (1883-1950). As early as 1911-1912 he served as president of Missouri's state conference of charities. Later he was to achieve recognition as a leader in employer-labor relations and in overseas relief work. During World War I he counselled American Jewry when it began its massive philanthropy programs in Eastern Europe; in the 1930's he advised his fellow Jews when they set out to rescue German Jews from the persecutions to which they were subjected. Early in his career as a social worker he had been appointed superintendent of the Jewish Settlement in Cincinnati (1904). When he came to that city that year the head of the United Jewish Charities was Boris David Bogen (1869-1929). Bogen had come to this country well educated; he had studied at the University of Moscow. For a time he was librarian at the Jewish Educational Alliance; he taught also at the Baron de Hirsch Trade School, and in the early 1900's was invited to become the superintendent of the Agricultural School at Woodbine, N.J. In Cincinnati he not only served as the head of the United Jewish Charities but was the field agent for the Conference of Jewish Charities. In 1917 he left to become the director general of the American Jewish Joint Distribution Committee; it was under his direction that the work of relief was carried on in Europe's eastern war zones. This was a very important assignment. In 1924 Bogen became superintendent of the Jewish charities in Los Angeles; the following year he was invited to become the executive officer, the international secretary of the Independent Order of B'nai B'rith. Bogen was the author of two books; in 1917 he wrote *Jewish Philanthropy*, the first full-length study of American Jewish welfare activity; his autobiography, *Born a Jew*, was published posthumously in 1930.

Few women or men, too, can rival the achievements of the journalist and reformer, Sophie Irene Loeb (1876-1929). She was a special feature writer for the New York *Evening World* but devoted a great deal of her time to social welfare activity and legislation. It was she who organized the campaign that produced New York State's pension law for widows. Her activity included penny lunches for the children in public schools and the enactment of legislation which required motion picture theatres to be sanitary and fireproof. She served as a mediator in a taxicab drivers strike and saw to it that New York's schools were opened to serve as community forums. Loeb busied herself with legislation furthering child welfare; it was her belief that home life for dependent children was superior to institutional care. Unlike other Jews in the public eye in the early twentieth century she was very sympathetic to Zionism. Sophie Irene Loeb was no soberside; she was noted for her *Epigrams of Eve*:

A brainless beauty is but a toy forever,
A woman purrs at being termed a kitten but scratches when called a cat.[14]

David Ely Fink was a scientist who wrote numerous articles on economic entomology. These studies were of importance for the American farmer; bugs can bring losses in the hundreds of millions of dollars. The two Goldenweisers, brothers Alexander and Emanuel, natives of Kiev, were the sons of Alexander S. Goldenweiser, a distinguished Russian lawyer and criminologist who did not emigrate. Alexander, the son, was an anthropologist and sociologist who taught at many American colleges; Emanuel was an economist and statistician who served for years on the Federal Reserve Board. The economist and statistician, Nahum I. Stone, worked for the United States Tariff Board and served as an impartial chairman in the dress industry. When Marcus Jastrow left troubled Europe in 1866 he brought his very young sons Morris and Joseph with him. They had been born in Warsaw where the father, a German, served as rabbi before he was expelled by the Russians. Morris grew up in Philadelphia to become a professor of Semitic languages at the University of Pennsylvania; Joseph became professor of psychology at the University of Wisconsin; in 1900 he was elected president of the American Psychological Association. In later years this popularizer of the science of psychology lectured over the radio to thousands and syndicated a newspaper column, "Keeping Mentally Fit."[15]

There were quite a number of eminent foreign-born workers in the field of medicine. The Lithuanian Leon J. Lascoff, who had come to the United States in 1892, was president of the New York State Board of Pharmacy in 1914; Mendel Nevin, a dentist, pioneered in block anesthesia for oral surgery; Isador Hirschfeld became the first head of the department of periodontology at Columbia University; William Salant, from Courland, served as chief pharmacologist in the chemistry bureau of the United States Department of Agriculture and then moved on to the University of Georgia where he became a professor of physiology. The Rumanian, Mark Joseph Schoenberg, taught ophthalmology at Columbia and established the New York Society for Clinical Ophthalmology. The cancer researcher at New York University, Professor Isaac Levin, was also the editor for years of the *Archives of Clinical Cancer Research*; the chemist, George W. Raiziss, was professor of chemotherapy at the University of Pennsylvania and among the first scholars in this country to develop sulfa drugs. The orthopedic surgeon Isidor S. Tunick pioneered in the injection treatment of varicose veins. Several immigrants made a name for themselves in the field of gastroenterology. John Leonard Kantor worked in the Vanderbilt Clinic at Columbia; Nicholas Dobkin was chief of the department of stomach and intestinal diseases in New York's Post-Graduate Medical School and Hospital, but the outstanding authority in this area of medicine seems to have been Max Einhorn, inventor of useful surgical instruments, author of several books in his specialty, and the donor of the Max Einhorn Memorial to the Lenox Hill Hospital. This annex was limited to patients with gastroenterologic ailments. Even Mount Sinai, the bastion of native and German Jewish aristocracy, appointed a Russian Jew chief of internal medicine at its dispensary. This was Dr. Gedide A. Friedman who had acquired his medical education in Russia; he, too, was distinguished as a specialist in the field of gastroenterology.[16]

Neurology and psychology were favorite disciplines for a number of newcomers. Isaiah Spanier Wechsler, professor of neurology at Columbia, was the author of a textbook on the subject that went through nine editions and was translated into several languages including Hebrew. He played a very active role in New York's Jewish communal life. The professor of neurology for many years at Tufts in Boston was Abraham Myerson; from 1935 on he was clinical professor of psychiatry at Harvard. Abraham Arden Brill was recognized as one of the first physicians to introduce Freud's work into this country. This brilliant Galician came to the United States at the age of fifteen eager to get away from home. After struggling in the garment industry he set out to get an education and worked his way through college and medical school. His break with the past alienated him from Jews and Judaism and inclined him toward Christianity but he later turned back to Jews and Jewry. His wife, a psychiatrist, was a Gentile. Brill became the country's first psychoanalyst building on a background of psychiatry, not neurology. In order to further the cause of psychoanalysis to which he was devoted, he founded the New York Psychoanalytic Society, translated Freud's works, and published many of them in the Modern Library Series in 1938. It was in no small measure due to his energy and enthusiasm that the United States was soon to become the world center of psychoanalytic theory and practice.[17]

One of the graduates of the Woodbine Agricultural School, Harry Aaron Marmer, called himself a tidal mathematician; he was an authority on tides and currents; Ludwik Silberstein, a mathematical physicist, found employment with Eastman Kodak. In his leisure hours he lectured at universities on the theory of relativity. Moscow-born Solomon Lefschetz, a mathematician, was a professor at the University of Kansas till he moved on to Princeton. He was distinguished in his field but was apparently content to transfer to Princeton with the title of associate; in a very short time, however, he achieved full professorial rank. Later he was to be elected president of the American Mathematical Society. The chief chemist of The International Paper Company's research division was Max Cline; Moses Gomberg became professor of organic chemistry at the University of Michigan; Martin André Rosanoff worked for some time as a research assistant for Thomas A. Edison before moving on to Clark College and then to the Mellon Institute at the University of Pittsburgh. He was director of the department of research and chemistry.[18]

There were many chess players among the men and women who landed on these shores; some were masters. The Russian Julius Finn, learned the game while living on the East Side. As early as 1901 he was the New York State champion. He was recognized as the world's champion blindfold chess player. Finn found time as a communal votary to devote himself to hospital work. The most distinguished of the Jewish immigrant chess players from the Slavic lands was the child prodigy Samuel Reshevsky (b. 1911). Reshevsky was a descendant of a distinguished cabalist; he himself lived as an observant Orthodox Jew. This brilliant child learned to play, so it is said, at four. At eight he was "concertizing" all over Europe, and at nine he came to the United States. He was very successful here. Julius Rosenwald and others made him go to school and educate himself. In the 1930's he came back to chess and became one of the world's important grandmasters winning championships several times. This young Pole was particularly expert at simultaneous play and in 1945 participated in international matches conducted by radio.[19]

Max Abelman (b.1887), who was a pioneer in the new profession of public relations, also called himself a banker and a communal worker. Meyer Bloomfield and Henry Moskowitz, like Abelman, Rumanians, may well be included in this category of men who worked in the twilight zones of social welfare, public relations, and community concern. Abelman sold $40,000,000 in bonds during World War I, brought Filippino physicians and nurses to American hospitals when there was a need for trained help, and raised money to keep the Brooklyn Academy of Music open when lack of funds threatened its very existence.[20]

In the field of the social sciences one of the most competent and scholarly of the newcomers was Lewis Levine. He was born in 1883 near Kiev; his parents' name was Levitzki. Here in the United States he or the family took a good American name, Levine. He had received a secular education in Russia but continued his studies at Columbia where he was awarded a Ph.D. in 1912. He taught at Columbia, Wellesley, and at Montana. In Montana, at the university, 1916-1919, he served as professor of economics. There he wrote a book, *Taxation of Mines in Montana*. Later he was on the editorial staff of the New York *World*. He was professor of economics at Beloit, special correspondent for the Chicago *Daily News* in Russia, and then went on to work for the International Ladies' Garment Workers' Union writing the history known as *The Women's Garment Workers* (1924). Sometime later he changed his name to Lewis L. Lorwin. He probably thought that in view of his past experiences the Levine name was a handicap. The name Levine, however, was to remain very popular in the United States among the new arrivals.

In the *Universal Jewish Encyclopedia* there are five Levines, all immigrants. One Manuel, was educated in Cleveland where he was to sit as presiding justice of an Ohio Court of Appeals; Max Levine became a judge of the General Sessions Court in New York City and is said to have been the organizer of the Grand Street Boys' Association, a society of former denizens of the ghetto who had done well in this country. Still another Max Levine was ultimately to become professor of bacteriology at Iowa State College. Victor Emanuel Levine, who was later to become head of the department of biological chemistry at Creighton University in Omaha, was an arctic explorer and the author of several books on nutrition. Isaac Don Levine became a distinguished foreign correspondent, an authority on the Soviet Union. He was nineteen years of age when he landed in this country (1911); three years later this foreigner was writing for the Kansas City *Star*. What struck his notice as he lived in a Jewish neighborhood in a midwest city? Levine craned his neck to gape at a skyscraper, ate his first banana, admired electric lights, and expressed delight when he entered a public library which encouraged the free circulation of books. He liked rocking chairs, big beds; he was not impressed with the 450 saloons in the city. Levine, a foreigner, viewed the typical American way of life objectively. He watched people chew tobacco and gum; he was well aware that people here were fascinated by baseball; the papers could not give the sport too much publicity. The game came first; obituary notices of the great were buried in a paragraph or two. The large Sunday paper! That appealed to him. Policemen in America were not tyrants. Young Levine paid his devoirs to the burlesque theatre, political bosses, graft and corruption. Foreigners here, he sententiously remarked, do all the annual labor; the Americans have the white-collar jobs; they are the clerks, salesmen, engineers, doctors, tradesmen. Levine praised the schools, colleges, and playgrounds; he was not happy when he wrote of vice, lynching, monopolistic trusts. Manicuring parlors attracted his attention; he approved of picnics, camps, and outings for poor children.[21]

It would not be difficult to write a substantial volume recounting the exotic careers of Jewish immigrants from the Slavic lands and Rumania. One wonders if the same might not also be said of the country's Gentile Slav and Italian immigrants. In studying the careers of the dozens, the hundreds of Jewish immigrants who were well within the ambit of academia in the days of World War I and immediately thereafter, one is surprised to find out how few ever received professorships in the larger colleges and universities. There can be no question of their capacity, their brilliance. The conclusion can only be drawn that native Americans, Christians, Protestants, were given the preference over these new Americans. They had three strikes against them; they were "Russians," immigrants, Jews. Many of them forged ahead despite the hurdles. *Who's Who in American Jewry, 1938-1939* contains the biographies of about 10,000 notables; most of them were East European immigrants or their children. And when one surveys the histories of many of these men and women who found themselves in this land of freedom one cannot help but agree with the writer who said that here in the United States we have "the greatest collective Horatio Alger story in American immigration history."[22]

CHAPTER TWELVE

TWO DIFFERENT COMMUNITIES: THE "GERMANS"

AND THE NEWCOMERS

EAST EUROPEANS AND THEIR RELIGION:

THE GHETTO AND ORTHODOXY

INTRODUCTION

T he old-timers and the newcomers were in conflict because they embodied two disparate cultures. Let this be borne in mind constantly. The émigrés brought with them an old-new unique world of
their own tightly packed in their impedimenta. It is obvious from the
above descriptions of notable, and less than notable immigrants from the
Eastern lands that many of them fully repaid the hospitality shown them
in their new home. With rare exceptions, however, American Gentiles
and Jews—the latter mainly of German origin—failed to recognize the
substantial contributions made by the new arrivals. They saw not the
trees, but the forest, which looked to them like a jungle of bizarre, unattractive slum dwellers. The immigrants were not welcome; they were not
acceptable. One of the reasons they were not wanted was precisely because they were newcomers. Ever since the seventeenth century, new arrivals were on the whole not made welcome by the established Jewries
here. They were seen as business rivals; as strangers, they made trouble in
the synagogs; as foreigners, they incited the native Gentiles to look critically on all Jews. The Jewish native-born and the older acculturated immigrants always felt threatened by newcomers, even by compatriots from
the same homeland. Now the "Russians" were deemed separatists. Even
before the 1880's, the East Europeans had communities of their own in
the large cities. The established Jewish synagogs kept them at arm's
length. Prejudice against Russians and Poles was traditional back home in
Germany. It became an alarming factor there after the 1880's when these
East Europeans, *Ostjuden*, settled in the country and threatened through

the ballot to take over the administrative apparatus of the *Gemeinde*, the state-recognized Jewish polity.[1]

Even the kindest and the most tolerant of the Jewish native-born looked upon the newcomers as "lowly brethren" who required uplift. Unkinder Jews here—and they were the majority—deemed them uncouth. By American standards, they were. They annoyed the established Jews with their stigmata. They were poor, ignorant, and dirty; they were beggars, schnorrers, bearded aliens; they spoke a terrible jargon; they were greenhorns! They were unamericanized, uncivilized! They were peddlers; they belonged to the lower classes; they were certainly not *salonfaehig*. The Germans, those who had been immigrants but a few decades before, disliked these new migrants; the newcomers reminded the old-timers of what they once had been; the East Europeans heartily reciprocated this dislike. Many of these immigrants from the Slavic lands kept kosher in an age when American congregations and congregants were often abandoning the dietary laws. New York's Mount Sinai Hospital, established by the Orthodox aristocrat Sampson Simson, had no kosher kitchen to bring comfort to unfortunate East European patients. Religiously, the Russians were said to be ignorant and superstitious. The Reformers—a minority elite—disdained them. But, it may be interjected, were not most American synagogs also Orthodox, and did they not use the same liturgy as the Russians? This is true—but we are well mannered, disciplined, decorous; you cannot compare us with them. (The elite forgot that Isaac M. Wise's Reform career began in 1850 at Albany with a fist fight on the pulpit on a Rosh Hashanah morning.)

The chasm between the Americanized Jew and the intruder was wide, apparently unbridgeable. Even if one might possibly ignore the permissive indecorum of the Orthodox religious service, one could never tolerate the vociferous aberrations of the political dissidents. The community was threatened. Some of these newcomers were socialists, anarchists, positivists, rebels, atheists, strikers, unionists; they were not respectable members of the established political parties. (Actually most East Side Jews voted the Democratic ticket.) What annoyed the Reformers and even more the native-born and foreign-born Americanized Orthodox were the Kol Nidre-Yom Kippur Balls of the militant radicals. In the 1890's, the radicals staged balls, festivities, and dinners on the holiest day in the Jewish religious calendar when all synagogued Jews fasted and repented of their sins. The Marxist approach was rejected summarily by most American Jews; its economic philosophy threatened the very foundations of bourgeois society. America's established Jewries failed to recognize that many of the new immigrants were versed in rabbinic literature; they had fine minds; hundreds, if not thousands, of the post-1905 arrivals, revolutionaries, were self-taught students of literature, educated and cultured.

The native-born and the Germans lumped all newcomers together and rejected them as a whole, unable to see that they were a heterogenous lot ranging from illiterates to the many who had attended universities in Russia, Austria, and Rumania, where schools were not entirely closed to Jews.[2]

By the early 1880's, many American Jews—probably most of them—would have stood out as anti-Zionists. The pre-Herzlian Orthodox Lovers of Zion (Hoveve Zion) had already made their appearance here in the early 1880's, particularly after the murderous Russian pogroms of 1881. The old-timers here were always apprehensive lest they not be accepted politically. The very thought that they might be accused of dual loyalties terrified them—though, actually, Gentiles rarely asked Jews to choose between America and Palestine. It was even thought that Temple Emanu-El had discharged its English-language lecturer, Raphael J. De Cordova, for preaching Jewish political nationalism. Certainly "Zionism" had become a real issue in 1885; the Reformers, meeting in Pittsburgh, denied that the Jews constituted a nation and said categorically that they did not expect a return to Palestine. These religious liberals felt threatened by the newcomers from Russia who were not yet Americanized. Many of the older settlers were convinced that if there was anti-Semitism in the United States, it was due to these newcomers. They preferred to overlook the fact that American Judeophobia was directed primarily against the Germans. The hatemongers and the urbane anti-Jewish muckrakers were not to discover the East Europeans until the twentieth century. The unhappy natives and their acculturated German confreres were thus plagued on two fronts, politically by the socialist and anarchist minorities among the immigrants, and religiously by an East European type of Orthodoxy which was unacceptable to American Orthodoxy. These were growing pains in the American Jewish community; "Anglo-Saxon" Jewry was at odds with Slavic Jewry. Catholic churches in every big city were plagued with the same problem; Irish, German, and Polish Catholics warred with one another.[3]

GHETTO

In the 1880's, Erasmus Darwin Beach, chief manuscript reader for New York's Sunday *Sun*, asked the young Abraham Cahan: "What is a ghetto?" Most Americans were soon to know the word and its meaning. By 1900, the majority of American Jews lived in ghettos, in a world apart. The native-born and other Uptown Jews felt threatened by these alien hordes, although the fears they felt were largely conjured up in their own minds; their Christian fellow citizens were not ready to reject American Jews because the Slavic newcomers were different and lived off by themselves in slum-like tenements and houses. These newcomers, who had clustered in their own enclaves, established a communal, cultural, and religious life of their own.

Why did Jews congregate in ghettos? Jews had always lived close together in the towns of the Diaspora since leaving Palestine in pre-Christian days and taking up residence in Alexandria, Antioch, and Rome. Compulsory ghettos by decree of the state were always relatively few. Most ghettos in Europe and, of course, those in the United States were voluntary. Jews in Eastern Europe always lived close to one another; they even had their own villages in the countryside where they might constitute a majority or a near majority. They huddled together for spiritual and emotional support; they wanted a group life; they enjoyed it. Here in the United States, they sought to recreate or transplant the Old World atmosphere; they wanted to exert social control to protect themselves from assimilation. Living together guaranteed psychic security. They were eager to maintain and cultivate their beloved mother tongue, Yiddish. Religious reasons may have been paramount. Newcomers wanted to be near their kosher butchers, their Hebrew schools, their ritual baths; it was imperative that the synagog be within easy walking distance; Jewish law implied a group life.

Jews lived in ghettos for social and economic reasons; they did business with one another; they were close to their jobs; they could help one another. The ghetto was a buffer; it softened culture shock. Living together seemed advisable; Jews welcomed the ghetto, certainly at first. There were occasions when they could have bettered themselves financially by moving out, but often they refused to do so; the advantages of close settlement outweighed its disadvantages. In no sense were Jews unusual in segregating themselves; all the people who came here had quarters of their own, the Chinese, the Italians, the Gentile Poles, the Irish, the Germans; they clustered together for the same reasons that prompted the Jews to head for the East Side as soon as they debarked. Most Jewish newcomers who landed in New York City found homes—if only for a time—on the Lower East Side. The ghetto as such might include the area as far north as Fourteenth Street; in a more limited sense, it embraced the streets south of Houston. Nor were the Jews in any sense unusual in crowding into the towns; 40 percent of all foreign-born settlers, whoever they were, preferred to remain in large cities. In the early 1900's, about two-thirds of all American Jews lived in New York-Brooklyn, Philadelphia, Chicago, and Boston. Obviously these Jews were an urban people. Back in Russia, the 1882 May Laws had driven them out of the villages. Here in the United States, once they moved into a section of a town, the non-Jews moved out leaving the invaders to remain monarchs of all they surveyed; the enclavistic nature of their settlement was then intensified. The statement has been made above that all ethnic settlements here were voluntary. That asseveration requires commentary: in a sense, they were not voluntary, since Jews had to live together if they were to survive as Jews.

Jews from Kovno, Vilna, Pinsk and Kiev did not create the New York ghetto; they inherited it. They settled there because it was the poor man's quarter and because other Jews were already there. The original slums of New York had been created by non-Jews in antebellum days. The older ghettos were bad; there was no running water in the homes. The tenement houses were miserable; thousands lived in cellars; often one single room sheltered a whole family, whether it was in a cellar or a garret. Omnipresent were darkness, fire, rodents, small pox, cholera; one is reminded of the ten Egyptian plagues. In the 1860's there were 15,000 tenement houses in New York City; over 18,000 men, women, and children lived in cellars. Conditions in Boston were equally bad. The United States, said a Bostonian in 1853, is a land where the rich are growing richer and the poor are growing poorer. During the Civil War, the Draft Riots were in part provoked by the wretched conditions under which the proletariat lived. When the Russians and Poles first moved into the area, it already had a number of synagogs and kosher butcher shops. The Germans had been there since the late 1830's, the Sephardim since the 1650's. In those days when the impoverished German Jews were dominant, the Lower East Side was no rose garden. Respectable female Jewish social workers hesitated to make their visits. When Jews from Russia started crowding into the tenements in the 1880's, they found many East Europeans; they had been there since the early 1870's. Thousands were already in the apparel industry working for the Germans; Russian and Polish synagogs were found on many streets. The East Europeans crowded out the Germans and, in the course of time, inherited some of their sanctuaries. New York's ghetto of the 1880's was not as bad as its antebellum forerunners; Jews were better tenants; if anything, they upgraded the neighborhood and there was much less disease.[4]

New York was the most important port of debarkation but it was not the only American city with a Jewish ghetto. Every town of size had a Jewish quarter where Jews stayed close together for security and comfort, and the imperative need for synagogs and other typical institutions. Baltimore's eastern section had 10,000 Jews in 1880; many of them were newcomers; in 1918 there were 60,000, most of them East European. Milwaukee's Jewish ghetto was but one of many; the Gentile Poles, Italians, Hungarians, Bohemians, and Slovaks all enjoyed the warmth and intimacy of their own quarters. Denver Jews would spread themselves in the West Colfax area; the one-story brick houses were comfortable; there was no crowding. Birmingham's Jewish enclave was replete with synagog, ritual bath, Jewish bakery, Hebrew schools, and a Young Men's Hebrew Association with a library. In 1880, Detroit had about 2,000 Jews; a minority were immigrants from Europe's East. In 1920, the city sheltered 50,000 Jews; most were newcomers. The houses here were for one or two families; there were yards and lawns. Boston's Russians settled in the North End, the West End, and the South End before they started moving southwest into Roxbury and Dorchester; Philadelphia Jews settled in the southern part of the city and set up a full complement of necessary institutions; Chicago's immigrants took possession of the West Side.

Not to be outdone by larger towns, Providence had not one but two ghettos, on the northern and on the southern side of town. North Providence Jews, who had come as early as the 1880's, looked down upon those in South Providence; they had come a decade later. During the forty years from 1880 to 1920, 200 Jewish organizations had been chartered in this Rhode Island town, almost all by the new Jewish immigrants. Many of these associations fell by the wayside. Among those chartered was the Wendell Phillips Educational Club. And who was Wendell Phillips? He was a Yankee reformer, a prohibitionist, abolitionist, lawyer, orator, a friend of labor and the Indians, a folk hero. The new Jews adopted him. St. Louis's Jewish ghetto was called Little Jerusalem. New York's ghetto was the largest and the worst. The Industrial Commission reported having surveyed a tenement house in that city which in 1886 sheltered 156 Rumanians, 198 Poles, fourteen Russians—all Jews—and a handful of Gentile Italians, Irish, Germans, and natives. The first floor was occupied by prostitutes. Twenty-five arrests were made in that house in ten months; seven of the twenty-five arrested were Jews. One of the youngest American Jewish ghettos was in Los Angeles. It was full blown in the 1920's just about the time the Lower East Side was losing its Jews. Boyle Heights nurtured a complete little world of its own, including Jewish hotels, Yiddish theatres, lodges, and a marriage broker, who was also a surgeon-circumciser cum scrivener of "Speeches in English and Jewish." Boyle Heights was the Lower East Side reborn.[5]

What is the nature of a ghetto, whether the gargantuan New York East Side or one in any other large city Jewish quarter? What was to be seen there? There would be street hawkers, pushcarts, sweatshops, cigar factories, Hebrew schools, cafes, Russian baths, retail shops, groceries, Jewish foods: pickles, herrings, rye bread. There were secondhand emporia, blacksmith forges, public halls for weddings, Yiddish theatres, newsstands, variety shops, stores for paints, wallpaper, clothing, and yard goods. There would be a photographer, a druggist who dispensed free medical advice, a travel agency, a "bank," a barber, a shoemaker, a milkman. There would be poverty, corrupt police, wily politicians. In short, one could find everything from a Jewish "priest" to a Jewish prostitute.

The many thousands of Jews who poured into America's ghettos were but part of a multimillion migration of European peoples. In 1880, when New York sheltered 60,000 Jews, a substantial minority were already Russians and Poles; by 1910, well over a million of these migrants had landed in the metropolis, and many remained there. In fifteen of America's largest towns, the immigrants and their youngsters outnumbered the natives. Over 75 percent of all New Yorkers were foreign-born or the children of newcomers. Noting this preponderance of immigrants in the urban centers, a well-known historian ventured to suggest that the newcomers would exert a profound influence on America's culture and ideals. When, in 1904, the superintendent of the Educational Alliance made a survey of the city's ghetto, he reported that the district housed twenty-two churches, forty-eight public schools, 6,000 tenement houses, and 306 synagogs, of which only a relatively few were stable institutions; the others held services only on the Sabbath and Holy Days and during the week might well be rented out as shops, factories, or dance halls. The ghetto could boast of 307 private Hebrew schools—most of poor quality —giving instruction to 8,616 boys and 361 girls. There were four Yiddish theatres. No ghetto, no Jewish quarter, lacked a bookstore, but it was not a typical American bookstore; it was a Jewish bookstore. It sold brass candlesticks to grace the Friday night table, New Year's cards, marriage certificates, possibly even printed paper amulets to be tacked up to scare the devil away from a lying-in woman. It stocked mezuzot with their citations from the Pentateuch and sold Turkish cigarettes, those with a Russian label. Hebrew prayer books could be purchased, with or without facing English translations. Yiddish devotional works for wives were always available; they were full of moralistic legendary accounts of Bible heroes. Detroit's Jewish bookstore, owned by Jacob Levin, had a circulating library and a variety of Yiddish books, romances, and histories of the French Revolution and of Russian tyrants. Levin was an intellectual, a radical, an anarchist. He was probably a very mild mannered man; most Jewish anarchists were. In 1892, it is believed, 75 percent of all New York's Jews lived on the East Side; by 1910, the masses were moving out.[6]

So many Jews lived on the Lower East Side that they were able to segregate themselves according to their country or region of origin. This was true as well of ghettos in other large cities. Thus, in Detroit, Poles, Russians, Ukrainians, Hungarians, Galicians, Rumanians—all Jews— clustered separately in mini-ghettos, on a street of their own or even on part of a street. Social lines were strongly drawn among the ghetto denizens; rabbis were at the top, while shoemakers, draymen, and tailors were at the bottom. The Denver ghetto reflected an ethnic status hierarchy that characterized most towns; the Lithuanians preened themselves; they were aristocrats; the Galicians were disdained; their social standing was low.

The Gentiles indulged in the same ethnic practices and prejudices as the Jews; immigrants from Italy, desiring to be on their own, fanned out and bunched together as North Italians, Genovese, Neopolitans, Calabrians, Sicilians.

There was more on the East Side than pushcarts, Jewish foods, Hebrew signs, and dismal cellar refuges. There were cultural institutions. Back home, a substantial minority had sharpened their minds in the talmudic academies; others had managed somehow or other to study Russian; the public schools of Hapsburg Galicia and Hungary were open to Jews. Thousands yearned to improve themselves academically. These immigrants were eager to raise their standard of living and thinking; they were exposed to cultural influences on all sides. Yet the majority were also not ready to disavow the past. They struggled to retain the Old World mores; they loved their Yiddish vernacular; thousands exulted in their Hebraic knowledge; there were also some at home in Russian literature and the secular sciences. The religionists here were trying to maintain their Old World culture, threatened as it was with disintegration. The revolt of their children was disheartening. Many were torn inwardly as they sought to effect a synthesis between the demands of the New World and their love for the old ways. A few not only persisted in holding onto the sacred traditions, but retreated into obscurantism as they faced the dominant Anglo-Saxon culture. They equated acculturation with assimilation, spiritual death, and fought in vain to reestablish here the religiocultural milieu which they had left behind in Europe. The ghetto seethed with cerebral challenge; it was a boiling Jewish cauldron; socialists, communists, and anarchists fought one another, joining together only to attack the bourgeois. There were Hebrew schools, libraries, Hebrew, Yiddish, Russian, and Ladino periodicals, clubs of infinite variety. The Jews were culture-vultures. There were Bundists (socialists), Zionists, Diaspora nationalists of variant hue, Hebraists, Yiddishists, atheists, pietists. There were journalists, students, litterateurs, musicians, and artists. Young Jacob Epstein organized an exhibition of the works of ghetto artists. People were reaching out not only to read trashy romances, but also Shakespeare, Thoreau, Tolstoy, Ibsen, Shaw. The Workmen's Circles were thriving cultural institutions; there were hundreds of cafes, restaurants, and tea rooms —salons, if you wish—where people not only ate and drank, but talked, argued, and thought. Intellectual striving and diversity stamped the ghetto.[7]

Ghettos are usually associated with slums, heavily populated, overcrowded urban areas, run-down housing, social disorganization, dirt. Being compelled to wash oneself several times a day was a bother for children. Jacob Riis tells a story of the ghetto youngster who wrote on Indians and emphasized that they did not wash. The final sentence of the essay was eloquent: "I wish I was an Indian." Disorganization? The ghetto dwellers were well organized; almost every Jew belonged to some organization, some landsmanshaft or fraternity that insured him and guaranteed him sick benefits and—God save us—a decent burial. How filthy, how evil were the Jewish ghettos? How clean were the towns, cities, and villages whence they came? Vilna was one of the great cities of Russia, a center of Jewish culture. Abe Cahan remembered it for the stench of its outhouses. Almost a century later, American Orthodox boys who studied at the Telz Talmudic Academy in Poland were shocked by the primitive toilet facilities. Hundreds if not thousands of American towns, villages, and hamlets stank because they were dependent on outhouses. This in the early twentieth century. The East European Jews who came here had suffered politically and economically. They were poor when they came and they remained poor for a long time. They were shown scant courtesy at Castle Garden or Ellis Island; they struggled to get a job, to raise the money to pay the rent. Housing was scarce because almost a million and a half Jews landed in New York City from the 1890's to World War I, and many, if not most of them, were determined to live on the Lower East Side where they could find kinsmen, Jewish institutions, work, opportunity. In 1915-1916, it was thought, about 350,000 Jews lived in this ghetto; there may have been many more. Demographers and historians are not sure exactly how many Jews were in Lower Manhattan in 1920. Practically all American Jewish population statistics are estimates.

A New York social worker describing a front and back tenement complex—two houses on one lot—said that the two buildings sheltered fifty-two families; each family included anywhere from three to ten people, and there was an equal number of boarders, some of whom slept on the floor. These boarders were young men or husbands saving to bring over their families. New York's Jacob Riis reported in 1890 that a two-room apartment on Essex Street sheltered twenty people at night. Only too often apartment rooms were used during the day as sweatshops. Rents for a tiny apartment—usually three rooms—were relatively high. Many of the owners of these apartments were themselves immigrants from the Slavic lands. Though laws were frequently passed requiring better housing, the slum dwellings always left something to be desired. From 1880 to 1920, in New York City, there were anywhere from 500 to 1,000 people living on a built-up acre; in hot weather, people slept on the roofs or on the fire escapes. Ventilation in the rooms was a real problem. There was more space for the immigrants in Philadelphia; it is estimated that there were only about 200 souls to an acre; in the better sections they averaged about fourteen persons to an acre. The masses in London, too, were packed together like sardines; there were about 100,000 men, women, and children squeezed into some two square miles.[8]

Where large numbers of poor people compete for housing—poor housing—they must be prepared to live in slums. When writers described the ghetto, they often spoke of dirt, garbage on the streets, rats, gangsters, prostitutes. The ghetto was not quite that bad. It is true that, with poverty, begging in the ghetto was not unknown; some of the adept, the professionals, made a good living. Writers dwell on the "obscene poverty" in the United States. The poverty that existed was obscene only in the eyes of the beholder. The critics spoke from the vantage point of a house, a bathtub, a job. Poverty was not obscene for the Jew in the American ghetto when he had an apartment and a pay envelope; some garment workers, indeed, were well paid; there were thousands of such fortunates. William Dean Howells wrote of the ghetto dwellers as captives but he was wrong; they were not in exile; only a minority returned back home, defeated economically or dismayed by the persistent religious pluralism. It is true, too, that the housing was poor; large numbers lived in a few rooms; fires were not uncommon; in 1905, nineteen died in a fire; forty were badly burnt. Most stoves were coal burning, producing soot; lighting was inadequate. There was some electricity, but for a time people turned to kerosene lamps, then to gas mantles. Many rooms were in constant darkness unless they faced the street or backyard. Toilets were a problem. In time, flush toilets were installed in the tenements, but for decades outhouses were found in the yards, as they were in hundred of thousands of homes throughout the country. Bathtubs were scarce in the American ghetto. In 1904, there were 373 bathtubs in the houses occupied by 10,000 Chicago Jewish immigrants. Some of the bathtubs may even have served as storage bins. There were public baths, Russian baths, too, but they were not inexpensive. The fortunate few who had friends or relatives in Harlem would descend on them and one after another make use of the tub. Telephones were scarce; if the local drugstore had one, it became a neighborhood resource.

Running water in the apartments had to wait its turn; the tenants depended on the hydrant in the yard, and if water had to be hauled up several floors, cleanliness became a burden. Because of lack of means and the relatively high rent, many had to take in boarders. Where income was inadequate, children ran around half naked; this was certainly true in families where the husband had left and the mother was dependent on the charities. It is obvious that, with so little room in a small apartment, many grew up on the streets, where they grew old before their time and learned to cope with the non-Jewish gangs in the next neighborhood. On occasion, Jews resorted to clubs to protect the old men harassed by roving juveniles. Bad housing, lack of fresh air, miserable sanitation facilities, all these brought disease. Tuberculosis was very much feared by Jews. It was not uncommon in the mid-twentieth century to watch prominent East

European Jews, successful professional men, carefully examine their handkerchiefs after hawking; they were looking for a telltale drop of blood. Jews were quick to run to the doctor if ill; landsmanshaften and fraternities had their contract physicians. In every ghetto there was a Jewish doctor to whom the masses turned. One of Detroit's favorites in the 1890's was Dr. Joseph Beisman (1863-1927). Patients did not pay for each call; their doctor was hired by the year, a not uncommon practice in many non-Jewish communities, too. Beisman lived with his clients in the heart of the ghetto. A native Russian, he came to this country in 1881 and went to work at once. He put in time at several jobs before he finally began his career as a physician; he was a cigarmaker, a basket weaver, a cotton mill hand in Maine, a bookkeeper, but whenever he could, he went to night schools. Nine years after he landed, he was licensed to practice medicine. Unlike most physicians who kept their noses to the grindstone, Beisman found time to become a very active figure in the Jewish community. He raised money for the Kishinev victims, busied himself in Zionist organizations, and joined both a Conservative and a Reform congregation.[9]

THE "VIRTUES" OF THE JEWISH GHETTO

The evils, the suffering in the ghettos, cannot and should not be glossed over; they were real. That is why the Uptown Jewish social workers and reformers, hosts of them—dedicated sisterhood members, too—were solicitous of the welfare of the newcomers. Uptown social workers were determined to help the Lower Manhattan toilers. The idealistic East Side Civic Club of Christians and Jews set out to serve the masses who lived in the tenements. They wanted better school buildings, cleaner streets, more parks and playgrounds. Nevertheless, there was a lot of happiness in the Lower East Side; the quarter did not destroy its residents, it sustained them; it was an enclave that had much to offer them; they survived and lived to move on to better things. Despite the dirt in the streets, the one square mile core of the ghetto was "the healthiest spot in the city," said Jacob Riis, the social worker and photographer. Their surroundings notwithstanding, Jews in the New York Jewish quarter—and in the ghettos of other large cities—were less prone to tuberculosis; they had a lower mortality rate; their children, however dirty, had a much better chance to survive than the scions of the silk-stocking wards. The evidence is convincing. As far back as 1890, Dr. John Billings in his very important survey pointed out that in Ward Ten, the most heavily settled section of New York, the death rate among the Russian and Polish Jews was low—this in a part of town which sheltered 544.36 persons per acre.[10]

Regardless of the relatively low incidence of tuberculosis in the Jewish quarter, it was a scourge with which the immigrants had to cope. Statistics indicate that they were less exposed than their neighbors to the dangers of syphilis, morphinism, and alcoholism. There is evidence, however, that they suffered more than their Gentile neighbors from diabetes; they were faced, too, with an adverse balance when they had to cope with neurasthenia, rheumatism, hernia, neuroses, psychoses, and a proneness to suicide. According to Dr. Charles H. Bernheimer the Jewish home tended to be cleaner than the homes of Gentiles who lived in the ghetto. Personal hygiene and cleaning up for the different Holy Days were mandated by Jewish religious law. Jewish children born or reared here in the American ghetto were better physical specimens than their Russian-born parents. One may venture the opinion—and it is nothing more—that Jewish economic mobility in the ghetto was marked because Jews suffered less from disease than their fellow citizens; prolonged illnesses can be devastating.

The typical ghetto Jew was not sorry for himself; he disdained the pity and the patronage of the Uptown Jews; he did not look upon himself as a deprived slum dweller. He lived in a tight, all-embracing world of his own; he was relatively comfortable, even psychically secure, if not happy. As in the village back in Europe, the newcomer was surrounded here by a familiar ambience, one he himself had fashioned. Had he moved out to the hinterland, he would have had more elbow room, better and cheaper housing, but he preferred New York City with its obvious metropolitan advantages. The Lower East Side slum was a concept, a reality, a fluid everchanging physical area, a demographic setting. Lower Manhattan in the mid-nineteenth century was not a pleasant place; conditions there, however, began to improve materially after the Jews arrived in large numbers. Because of the impact of these newcomers, the authorities moved legislatively to upgrade the tenements. After the 1890's—even to a degree before that decade—the quality of the housing was improved; there was more light, more fresh air, more running water. As in London, the Jews who moved into Lower Manhattan served as moral scavengers. After the Jews began invading the Lower East Side in the 1880's, hundreds of barrooms had to be closed; the Irish saloonkeeper had to leave; he was no longer a social and political force and could not relate to abstemious immigrant Jews.

The overwhelming mass of East European Jews in the ghetto survived economically. The proof? The number of suppliants who applied to the charities. According to the census of 1890, the percentage of paupers among the newcomers was six-tenths of 1 percent; the rate was higher among other foreign-born. To be sure, the Jews had their hundreds of mutual-aid societies which served as a buffer. What do charity statistics show? The numbers of those who remained on their rolls, paupers, were very small. If the husband could not make a living, the wife often stepped into his shoes and became in effect, the provider. She managed. Hinda Fagelson Matzkin's husband was a cutter; because he would not work on the Sabbath, his boss fired him. He stifled his principles and went to work on that sacred day; he still could not support the family. Hinda kept boarders, six of them. Mr. Matzkin moved to New Haven where he was well paid; cutters nearly always did well—but when there was a strike, there was no money. In New Haven "there was but one God and one manufacturer," and when he closed up, Hinda had to gird her loins. Her husband became ill and the agent who collected the rent offered to lend her money; the grocer gave her unlimited credit. When she left and moved to another city, they all wanted to advance her funds or even give her money; ultimately she paid off all of her debts.

Living conditions for workers improved in the second decade of the twentieth century as the unions became stronger and more successful. World War I brought prosperity. People even saved enough money to spend time in the Adirondacks, hiring rooms with cooking privileges. There were pianos, phonographs, and good furniture in some homes. If they moved to Brooklyn, they had hot water and a bathroom. Some moved not because they were unhappy with their ghetto homes, but because it was the thing to do. Moving out was moving up; mobility brought status. Some girls rejected the factory and opted for jobs in department stores; a select few went to high school; it was a long walk, miles; a few, a very few, even went to normal school and became teachers. On Saturday afternoon, the lucky child who had a nickel went to the movies; there were places where two youngsters were admitted for the price of one. The public library was warm, pleasant, well lighted; it was a good place to do one's homework. William Dean Howells, visiting the East Side, found the Jews there noticeably clean. Lillian Wald said that they were sober, affectionate, grateful, courteous, interested in educating their young. She recalled the young immigrant, a fervent patriot, who came to her and played the "national anthem" on his violin. She grinned: it was not "The Star Spangled Banner," but Charles K. Harris's "After the Ball Is Over." The whole American world was singing the song of the Milwaukee Jew; a generation later, it would sing Irving Berlin's "God Bless America."

The ghetto families were moving ahead. Avrum K. Rifman's father came to America and went to work in a Baltimore sweatshop for $5 a week; he put in sixty hours. When little Avrum was born, his mother made him a nightgown out of a floursack advertising Pillsbury, or it might have been another Minnesota flour. The family saved money and with the first $50 made a down payment on a house; it was a modest home; the privy was outdoors. These strangers from East Europe were thrifty, but they never stinted on the Sabbath dinner. Friday night found a table laden with fresh baked white bread, gefilte fish, chicken soup, chicken, vegetable stew, tea, lemon, sugar, and compote. The father who spoke Russian, Lithuanian, Polish, and English opened up a men's cleaning and tailoring shop in a Polish neighborhood. Ultimately, Father Rifman bought a larger house and lived on the income. Now free of economic worries, Papa spent more time in his synagog where he served as president and helped the Free Burial Society, his favorite philanthropy. Before her death, Mama set aside her savings with the injunction that they be distributed to her favorite charities. When the women in Mama's circle discovered an unfaithful husband, they descended upon him and beat him with umbrellas until he promised to behave. Avrum, the son, was determined to make a career in athletics; he had earned some money umpiring a game between two Catholic baseball teams. Accordingly, he made up his mind not to go beyond high school. When Mama heard this, she wept and pleaded till he promised to remain in school; he became a lawyer and a judge. This is a true story. Equally true is the story of a man, grandson of a notable Lithuanian talmudist, who informed his mother that he intended to leave the professional school where he was about to graduate. His mother went down on her knees and in her English-Yiddish patois begged him piteously not to quit. She exacted a solemn promise that he would continue; he did. Years later, long after Mama had died, his features graced the cover page of Time magazine. In his later years, Judge Rifman, as a Jew, sat on a Roman Catholic diocesan court.[11]

THOUGHTS ON THE GHETTO

By 1920, the New York ghetto had declined perceptibly. People began moving out in large numbers to better quarters during and after World War I; immigration came to a halt in the 1920's; higher wages and better transportation made it possible for newcomers to establish themselves in several boroughs of the city and maintain an improved standard of living. Ultimately, with the rise of a generation of native-born Jews, all Jewish ghettos in the United States faded away—except, of course, the golden ghettos. The new problem was not economic survival, but survival as committed or identifiable Jews. The ghetto was for everyone something different. To the outsider, at first glance, it was a smelly place; to some middle or upper-class native-born, be they Jew or Gentile, it was an exotic and dirty quarter, a cultural aberration; others discovered in it the abode of intellectuals, social idealists. It was a kaleidoscope of noise, crowds, clotheslines, and foreign tongues. Who would have suspected that some of the little "pishers" they saw running around would one day become corporation presidents, distinguished lawyers, eminent physicians, pontificating judges? A perceptive student of the Lower East Side phenomenon once referred to it as the Heroic Age. The decades from 1870 to 1920 were marked by courage and daring. Dogged determination could be grand, noble, impressive. The ghetto was often bad; people struggled and were unhappy; there were hardships, loneliness, alienation; human beings struggled to stay afloat in a sea of despair. If the Hebrew teacher beat his charges in his cellar schoolroom, it was not because the youngsters were dumb; it was because he felt miserable, frustrated, embittered. Family life in the ghetto was often anything but idyllic. For many, it was a sad generation, but if they had remained in Russia, it would have been worse, even more tragic. The unhappy operative here cried out: To Hell with Columbus, but here at least he was free to say it publicly.

Was the ghetto a community? Was there a sense of "community," gemeinschaft? There was a "community" back in East Europe. The Pale of Settlement, the hostile churches, the distrustful peasants, the indifferent governments guaranteed that the Jews would think of themselves as a distinct and separate group. The rabbis, the synagogs, the Jewish traditions, customs, and prejudices reinforced this feeling of uniqueness. Spiritually, commercially, culturally, the Jews were a people apart. Seemingly, the East European immigrants in America were galloping off in different directions; they were religionists, Marxists, unionists, petty bourgeois. What, if anything, held them together: a common past, a common plight, the struggle to eke out an existence; the hope for something better? They were joined together by a common physical neighborhood, by an ardent ethnicity, by their determination to help the Jews they had left behind. Was there real unity in the ghetto? Not until World War I and the need to rally to the defense of kin at the mercy of the German, Russian, and Austrian armies. There was no final unity among these diverse elements until the 1940's when the Germans annihilated the European Jewish masses. This was almost a generation after they had left Delancy Street for Brooklyn, Harlem, and the Bronx.

In a negative sense, they were a community. These Jews had been ghettoized by force in the provinces of Russia, and they voluntarily ghettoized themselves here in order to survive. To meet every eventuality in this foreign land, they established institutions from orphanages to cemeteries. Despite its multifarious associations and societies, the ghetto was distinctly a community if only by rejection; Americans have never welcomed foreigners with any enthusiasm. As a community, did the ghetto cherish any specific ideals and envisage any common goals? It is difficult to maintain that the members of this ethnic group embraced any other goal but that of survival, the right to live their own disparate lives as religionists or secularists but always as Jews. These refugees met challenges here; a minor one was to come to terms with the Jews already here. This they ultimately did, but it would take another generation—after World War II. The immediate confrontation was survival as something of a Jew in an American world. This was a different universe, one of machines, factories, tenement houses, seductive tolerance, a strange language. They had to learn to live in a non-Jewish culture, yet maintain their own. Though the Jew never acknowledged it—even to himself—he came to accept his ghetto existence not as a tragedy, but as an opportunity.

The mass of Jews who lived south of Houston Street were never really conscious of the fact that they had to come to terms with the American way of life. This much they knew: they were East Europeans; their problem was to transport the Old World to the New. This was a prime concern. They believed in yiddishkeit—that is, Orthodoxy, its rituals, its customs, its liturgy, its foods, its traditions, its culture. Many were conscious that they were fighting a losing battle with America; it was a war that they would never win. Even though New York's ghetto dwellers constituted a sizable percentage of the city's total population, their yiddishkeit had no future; the Anglo-Saxon environment would not be denied. Even the most Orthodox Jews were happy to wear a derby, the very symbol of the English gentleman. The parochial world of foods and folkways would have to give way to an America of tolerance and permissiveness. It could not be sustained, as in Russia, Poland and Rumania, by resentment. Still, here in the United States, ties to the past could not and would not be cut; the immigrants never lost their prepossessions, their prejudices, their theology. They held on to their praying shawls and prayer books; their kin back home stretched out their arms to them in supplication. The Yiddish press helped them hold back the tidal waves of speedy acculturation. Nevertheless, they knew that they were here to stay; this was home, they were better off here; few returned after the pogroms of 1903 and 1906, for there was no Russia to which they could go back. Many had already broken with the past, though this did not dawn upon them. Working on the Sabbath was yiddishkeit's first defeat. The old ethos was doomed; sooner or later, they would have to develop a new synthesis, one that would embrace America and all that it meant. The slum in which they dwelt was to become the road to a new life; when the French conquered Padua in the 1790's, they renamed the ghetto Via Libera. American culture swept all before it. That a new Jewish community, a community of sentiment and identification would rise was guaranteed by the intelligence, the essential yearnings, the ideals, the respect for learning that characterized many of the bearded newcomers. The privileges of American citizenship would move them to action if they were to survive as Jews.

The Jewish newcomers were compelled to build a new world for themselves here on these shores. They were determined to be "Jews," though the interpretation of that noun was to include an infinite variety of nuances. They would have to come up with some amalgam of Judaism and Americanism. Ultimately, they did as Zionists, socialists, traditionalists, liberal religionists, secularists, careerists. All children with any ability set out to make a future for themselves; some of their immigrant parents had already climbed the first steps of the commercial and professional ladder. And, as they climbed, they carried their Jewishness with them; it was their treasured baggage. A government report said that some of the Russian Hebrews, as the report called them, owned tenements and sent their children to schools and colleges. It added that they were eager to make their way commercially; they were quiet, orderly, industrious—and dirty. This was in 1901. Running water in the new tenements and the new Brooklyn and Bronx homes would serve as a solvent. For hundreds of thousands of Jews, the acreage in Lower Manhattan—less in area than three North Dakota Jewish homesteads—proved to be neither an insurmountable barrier nor a legend embroidered with posteventum nostalgia and fantasy. It was a generational stopover, a training ground, a forty-year trek, where Jews sloughed off the past and made a new start. A new Jewry would arise; a new Judaism would appear. It is true, as it has been well put, that the ghetto was not only a mass in transit, it was a world in becoming. Before the first decade of the twentieth century had come to an end, 4 percent of Detroit's Jews were already professionals or semiprofessionals; 13 percent were proprietors and managers; 26 percent were white-collar workers. They had begun to climb. A new generation was ready to take over, one that experienced no difficulty in savoring both kugel and apple pie. Lincoln Steffens tells this story of an eleven-year-old child. When Mama, who was in charge of a large tenement house, took sick, her little girl took over. At home, she did the cooking and washing and looked after five younger children including an infant. Another little youngster—a girl, too—handled the renting of a large apartment house, collected the rents, and conducted the interview with the Board of Health.[12]

ORTHODOXY

The overwhelming percentage of the ghetto Jews were Orthodox. One must not be misled by the clamor of the radicals, the socialists and anarchists; they were decidedly in the minority. What is the meaning of the word Orthodox when applied to Jews? They were believers in a traditional faith that included a credo and an intricate system of practices and observances. On the whole, the Maimonidean Thirteen Principles printed in the Orthodox daily prayer book were accepted by synagog worshippers. They believed in an all-powerful omniscient Deity who had revealed himself to the biblical Hebrews, the ancestors of the Jews. They believed in a Messiah yet to come, in resurrection, in the Ten Commandments, in the Jewish Sabbath and the Holy Days, and in numerous ceremonies associated with the rites of passage. Thus they observed the customs associated with circumcision, bar mitzvahs, marriage, divorce, and death. (The traditional rituals, to be sure, were in no sense dead among the natives and the Germans; almost all of them were retained and respected, but the "style" of observance pursued by the Russians was different and deemed unacceptable. That was important.) The East Europeans as traditionalists were convinced that their ethics were superior to all others, that the divinely revealed moral imperatives were immutable. They loved the Yiddish language and reserved Hebrew for sacramental matters. They were dedicated to the observance of a standard code, a common law, and a customary praxis that made for a completely disparate East European way of life. Despite its universalism—and it was that—their Judaism was a folk religion, a civilization, a sense of kinship, a common destiny. Religion, culture, and ethnos were one and indissoluble. Intermarriage was summarily rejected as a calamity. The total ensemble of creed and practice, of pride and prejudice, was yiddishkeit, a term which may be inadequately translated as "Jewishness." It was this Slavic Jewish Orthodoxy that was transported here to the United States and was ultimately to exercise a profound influence on late twentieth-century Judaism.

Most of American Jewry's native-born and the older migrants among the Uptown Jews were also Orthodox, but it was an Americanized, acculturated form which they cherished. Actually, all Orthodox prayer books were practically identical. But the temperamental differences between the two groups were pronounced. Mutual contempt was characteristic and was to continue well past World War I. There was a social chasm between "Russian" and "German," between "kikes" or "Yidn" and "Yahudim," that was hard to bridge. The Germans, even those who professed Orthodoxy, often pretended that the newcomers did not exist, although the immigrants had come to outnumber the natives and old-timers by at least five to one. In 1887, in one of his angry moments, Isaac Mayer Wise wrote that America—the real America—began west of New York and Philadelphia. "Besides the name [Jew] we have very little in common with them." Yet, these immigrants were to bring a resurgence of Orthodoxy to American Jewry. Three years later, Rabbi Aaron Wise, of New York, excoriated a fraudulent "rabbi" who issued religious divorces before a civil divorce had been obtained. These so-called rabbis, Russians and Poles, said Aaron Wise, are members of a group which accepts our char-

ity, fills our hospitals, and loads its aged, infirm, and paupers on us. They
never contribute a cent to charity, even when they have the means. They
are Slavs and will never become Americans. They cannot be saved; but let
us work with their children. The new arrivals denigrated both Reformers
and Conservatives. The latter may have been nominally Orthodox in belief, but the East European Orthodox rejected them summarily; their rabbis were not real rabbis. Even so, notwithstanding their common beliefs
and style, the East Europeans also fought one another religiously. At the
slightest provocation, new synagogs were established. Pronunciation of
Hebrew was a bar that kept Poles and Lithuanians apart. Even before the
outbreak of Russian pogroms in the 1880's, the very special sect of Hassidim had followers here. Many more came in the 1880's and thereafter.
Efforts to establish Hassidic dynasties here failed, although it was estimated that there were about 30,000 of these "Pietists" in the United
States by 1917. They would, however, penetrate American Jewish life
very successfully after World War II. The attempt at a renascence of Orthodoxy led by Young Israel in 1912 made relatively little progress; they
were too unyielding in their demand that congregational officers be Sabbath observers, though they were determinedly Americanistic in their insistence on decorum and the use of English.[13]

PROBLEMS

As the East Europeans came over, Orthodox for the most part, they made
a gallant attempt to naturalize their ancestral way of life here in the
United States. Thus, a group of these newcomers in New York City organized a synagog of their own. Some baked their own matzos to be sure
that they were prepared properly without leaven. By the early 1870's,
study groups for the rabbinic classics were established; a modest hospice
was set up for newcomers. The truly observant who wanted to maintain a
European type of community were still faced with many problems. Back
home, they had had the support of an autocratic state that would brook
no innovation. Russian tyranny served as a bulwark for Jewish Orthodoxy; here, however, state and church were divorced. The permissive
American environment made it easy for the children to rebel against the
fathers; leadership in the synagog was in the hands of laymen who were
not scrupulously observant; rabbinic leadership was ineffectual; there was
a substantial and vociferous minority of politically radical secularists who
dared to scoff at the most precious sancta of the religiously observant. Between the Orthodox stalwarts and the belligerent left stood the mass of
newcomers, who realized that they would have to make compromises;
somehow or other, they would have to synthesize Orthodoxy and Americanism; they stumbled haltingly. Ultimately, of course, a modified Judaism would emerge. Unlike the uncompromising believers in the Law,

these Jews did not resist Americanization. Many of them turned to the new Jewish Conservatism, thereby making their peace religiously with the new America; a few even embraced Reform, which deliberately broke with the traditional codes. Protestants and Catholics, too, were faced with the same problem of coming to terms with modernity. Protestant evangelicals preached a return to fundamentals and gave birth to "fundamentalism"; Catholics flirted with what Rome condemned as "Americanism." In order to survive in the new American milieu, most Orthodox Jews compromised some of their Old World practices; they knew that here, in this permissive land, their identification as Jews was not seriously threatened.[14]

What threatened the new Orthodoxy here was the need to come to terms with a polity in which church and state were separate. Orthodoxy was on its own; there was no Jewish "authority." The Orthodox rabbinate, powerful in East Europe through its alliance with a learned and affluent laity, was most often brushed aside here. Lay leaders had taken virtually complete control here; some were unlearned and autocratic. Democracy at times put the bottom rail on top. The talmudists were unhappy that in America, unlike Russia, they were not on top. America law, not talmudic law, was regnant in this country; that made all the difference. Laxity was widespread because social controls were weak, at times almost non-existent. The women were lax about using the ritual bath after menstruation; some rabbis were disturbed that the ritual bath accommodations did not meet the most scrupulous specifications, an important matter to the legalists. America, a religious frontier, confronted meticulous observers. A board established in the 1880's presumed to exercise authority in matters of circumcision, marriage, and divorce; the qualifications of its members were suspect; some of them were less than honest. Many ritual slaughterers and butchers were unfit, corrupt, offering a product which was not truly kosher.

The greatest breach occurred in the disregard for the sanctity of the Sabbath. In all probability, more than 50 percent of the Jews here violated the prohibition not to work on the seventh day of the week. They had no choice; they had to make a living. It was so easy to strike a match and light the gas on Saturday. Many made a real effort to keep that day holy, but it was not easy. A Pittsburgh Jew who sold food on passenger trains was not allowed to get off on Rosh Hashanah; he went over his boss's head. When not working, he was very observant; he would not even strike a match on the Sabbath. His associates respected his beliefs and, when they had company get-togethers, served him cheese, not forbidden meats. When he had a Sabbath off—and this is interesting—he stayed home to take care of the youngsters and let his mother go to the synagog. Orthodox leaders, led by an American-born rabbi, Bernard Drachman, a rabbinical paragon of devotion to the Law, established the Jewish Sabbath Association of America in 1905. They helped secure employment for Jews who would not work on the Sabbath; they defended the thousands of religious artisans who were arrested for working on Sunday after resting on Saturday. There were some Jews to whom Judaism meant so little that they renounced their faith; their numbers, however, were very small. In Boston, a number of Jews were intermarried with the Irish; in some instances, the Christian wife would go along with the husband's Jewish traditions and conduct herself as if she were a proselyte.[15]

For the Orthodox, the spiritual transatlantic passage from the Pale of Settlement to the big city ghettos was difficult, often truly traumatic for some individuals. They fought shy of the settlement houses which made Americans of their children first, and only then encouraged them to remain Jews; they were dismayed with bar mitzvah parties where the addresses were in English, not Yiddish, and where citizenship rather than God and his Law was stressed. They saw their children drifting away from them religiously, avoiding the synagog, smoking on the Sabbath. There were Russian rabbis—some who never left Europe and others who visited here—who believed that, religiously, this land was "unclean." One could not be a Jew here. Some adherents of the Law returned to Russia; they were persecuted there, but at least they could remain good Jews under the czar. Some diehards fought to maintain the age-old injunctions, but it was most often a losing struggle. It was very hard to cope with secularism, the jettisoning of tradition, the Law, the halakah. Rabbi Moses Weinberger, an unreconstructed adherent of the Torah, wanted to solve New York's religious problem by establishing a hierarchy, a chief rabbinate, and a supporting body of learned rabbinical leaders. He failed entirely to understand the American democratic tradition, its hostility to an establishment of religion.

There is no question that Orthodoxy initially could not meet the challenge and the threat of America, its free choices, its democracy, its separation of church and state. For a long generation, traditional Judaism fought a losing battle before it began to find itself, to fight back constructively and thus learn how to survive. It took decades before the synagog-goers discovered that decorum was more valued than boisterous prayer and disorder. Synagog officials were slow in discovering that it was not unwise to station a policeman at the door to maintain order during the festivals and High Holy Days. All pioneers are plagued with exuberance. The Sephardim of eighteenth-century New York City had to penalize vituperative members; the Germans, in their immigrant days here, were anything but quiet and well behaved; the East Europeans, too, spent a generation toning down their voices and discovering that conversation in services lent nothing to prayerful reverence. Even in well-behaved Cincinnati, some members of the Great Study Hall (Beth Midrash Hagadol) emerged one evening with blackened eyes and bloody noses; "serve the Lord with joy!" (Ps. 100:21). What hurt the newcomers from the Slavic lands was the loss of their best youths; the Reform-sponsored Hebrew Union College gained such precious and brilliant souls as Hyman G. Enelow, Abba Hillel Silver, Solomon B. Freehof, the Raisin brothers, Israel Bettan, Samuel S. Cohon, Levi Olan, and a host of other notables-to-be.[16]

Yet traditional Judaism was by no means dead. It was changing radically, reaching out and learning how to maintain itself in an open society. By 1917, there were over 1,100 synagogs and temporary meeting houses in New York where the masses—some socialists, too—would gather for the Holy Days and shed a tear. Even the Yiddish theatres, the Windsor and the Thalia, were commandeered for the solemn services on the Days of Awe; churches, too! About 100,000 worshippers flocked to these rented premises. When in 1902 on a Yom Kippur morning Dr. Isaac Rubinow needed a tie, he had to walk twenty blocks before he found an open haberdashery; the Jewish stores were all closed. Let it not be forgotten that the strictly Orthodox and Europe-oriented Etz Chaim Yeshivah was founded on the East Side in 1886—the very year that the Conservative Jewish Theological Seminary Association was formed.

Despite the fact that only a minuscule number of New York Jews were members of congregations in 1917, the masses were religious Jews and found a spot to worship on the New Year and the Day of Atonement. The percentage of affiliated was higher in the smaller cities; the smaller the town, the higher the rate of affiliation; social pressure made membership in those places imperative. As early as 1872, there were about thirty East European prayer halls and sanctuaries in New York City; in 1920, there were at least 2,000 such immigrant synagogs in the United States. Here in America, the old Russian Jewish Orthodoxy was declining; there was laxity in practice and disregard for custom, even on the part of some officiants. True, the prayer book was untouched, but the exacting laws of marriage, divorce, and ritual bathing were not infrequently violated. The Sabbath prohibitions were disregarded egregiously. Yet, there was devotion to kashrut, the dietary laws. Most Jews realized or believed that a kosher kitchen was the essence of yiddishkeit, of identification as traditional Jews. In short, if one may attempt to summarize the Orthodoxy of the newly arrived, there was much devotion, but a definite turning to the left. The East European type of observance began to decline. Even those who affirmed their allegiance to the European religious way of life were compromising with modernity; those who moved farther to the left were beginning to build the Conservative movement. Both segments were to insist on decorum, on anglicization in language and manner, but—and this is important—the prayer book was still the traditional one. Jewish bookstores did a brisk business selling prayer books when the Holy Days rolled around. Decades later, after World War II, right-wing East European Orthodoxy would rise reborn, militant, aggressive. It would include only a small percentage of American Jewry, but it would be very much alive in its aggressiveness, its salesmanlike approach, its slick paper magazines; it would be very American.[13]

KASHRUT

In many immigrant homes—how many, will never be known—the daily prayers were no longer said; the phylacteries were no longer donned, yet a determined effort was made to keep kosher. Many rationalized their observance by saying that kosher meant clean, fresh; kosher meat, they insisted, was better. The examination of the lungs of the carcasses certainly eliminated tubercular animals, which may account, in small part, at least, for the fact that ghetto Jews were less prone to tuberculosis than Gentiles. Observing the dietary laws kept the Jew separate; it never let him forget that he was different; kashrut was all important as a basic form of identification during the sixteen waking hours of the day. Kashrut, eating kosher food, is enjoined by the Bible in a number of verses. The rabbis of later generations expanded the biblical injunctions and built an elaborate code of dietary prescriptions. Because of the extra expense entailed in kosher meat, it sold at a premium and invited cheating and corruption on the part of the unscrupulous. Kashrut was a multimillion dollar business, and where huge sums are involved, fraud is almost inevitable.

It is believed that, in 1915, at least 20 percent of the kosher butchers sold nothing but forbidden meat. In the early 1920's, so it is said, practically all the "kosher" delicatessen shops sold only unkosher products. Had the masses really revolted, something might have been accomplished, but their prime concern was to make a living. Social controls in matters religious were notoriously feeble, but individuals rallied to the aid of the exploited masses. Elhanan Kelson, one of Pittsburgh's pious Jews, brought in a carload of matzos from Chicago to break the monopoly of the Jewish grocers who had raised prices. Determined to help observing Jews, the Workmen's Circle in one town opened a kosher butcher shop. These Jewish anti-religionists wanted to protect the masses, to give them what they wanted; they did not trust the local kosher butchers. Led primarily by enraged housewives who believed that they were being gouged by the butchers, food riots and boycotts marred the peace of the Jewish community in Boston, Paterson, and Philadelphia during the early twentieth century. The big riots occurred in New York City in 1902, when the butchers raised the price of a pound of meat from twelve to eighteen cents. Riots broke out all over the city directed against the butchers and the "meat trusts." The women believed that Rabbi Adolph M. Radin, of the

Educational Alliance, was not sympathetic; the Uptown elite who controlled the Alliance frowned on women who raided and burnt butcher shops. An editorial in *The New York Times*, May 24, 1902, denounced these "dangerous" and "ignorant" women. The police were called out; women were beaten, but the price of meat was pushed back down to fourteen cents. The strike and acts of violence paid off, for the time being at least.

The Orthodox Yiddish dailies, the widely-read socialist *Forward*, and the unions were helpful. Observant Jews in America have had to cope with fraud ever since the eighteenth century. Little could be done to remedy the situation, and by the early nineteenth century, it was obvious to many that kashrut was a real problem. The secular authorities rarely intervened; they dreaded breaching the wall between church and state. Orthodox leaders, conscious of the scandals in the production and sale of kosher products, made desperate efforts to give their followers meat that was ritually fit. The problem was exacerbated in the late nineteenth and in the twentieth century by the rivalries of local rabbis who set out to control the appointment of the ritual slaughterers. Some of these rabbis were struggling for power; others derived financial benefits from the slaughterhouses. These authorizing rabbis were often poor, embittered, unhappy men. In the final analysis, the rabbis had no authority and could impose no effective sanctions. In the course of the twentieth century quite a number of states and municipalities have passed laws and ordinances regulating kashrut. Whether they have eliminated fraud is questionable, but they have helped maintain standards. Were Jews alone plagued by these problems? In 1906, Congress passed the Pure Food and Drug Act to protect the whole country against adulterated or unfit products.[18]

New York's traditional Jews were themselves frequently lax in observance of the ritual laws laid down in the standard codes, but realizing the psychological importance of kashrut, they pushed hard for the introduction of kosher foods in Jewish and other institutions. In April 1911, the 2,000 Jewish pupils in Public School No. 9 enjoyed meals prepared in a kosher kitchen; each lunch cost them 3 cents. The members of Maccabee Lodge of the B'nai B'rith started pushing the board of the Yonkers Home for the Aged and Infirm to provide its clients with kosher food—in November 1914, in a day when most Jewish leaders in the old established institutions scoffed at kashrut. Seventy years later, most Jewish public dinners in the United States guaranteed that the dietary laws would be observed. With the exception of a devoted few, kashrut will decline, but for large numbers of American Jews the hankering will never die. Kosher foods and kosher style morsels have made inroads into the hearts and stomachs of the American people. In the years before 1921, there was hardly a town without its kosher restaurant. By the second quarter of the twentieth century, they began to disappear even in metropolises, displaced by the "kosher style" restaurant that cheerfully ignored the kosher laws as it catered to nostalgic palates. (It is of no consequence to latitudinarian Jews that one may also order a ham sandwich in these "kosher style" establishments.) There are still quite a number of kosher restaurants in New York City, that last stronghold of Russian and Polish Orthodoxy. The town at times has supported not one but two kosher Chinese restaurants; in one of them the Chinese waiters wore yarmulkes, ritual skull caps sported by the pious.

Jewish food is in the ascendancy. There is something for every gourmet: borscht, corned beef, chopped liver, pickled and creamed herring, potato pancakes (latkes), matzobrei (crumbled matzo fried in an egg batter), blintzes, matzo ball soup, and the Jewish K.K.K. Jewish K.K.K.? Kishke (stuffed intestines), kreplach (three-cornered stuffed crepes), and kasha (groats). These may be called Jewish "soul foods." Many Jews are devotees of the bagel cult; bagels may now be purchased in almost any supermarket in the United States. New York in 1962 had its independent Bagel Bakers Union and it was no light matter when Local 338 went on strike in February of that year. Bagels are important, especially on Saturdays and Sundays when relaxed businessmen and women look forward to a late and leisurely breakfast of lox and bagels. It was reported somewhere that the bagel baker in Honolulu was Chinese; more important is the fact that one can buy a green bagel in New York City on St. Patrick's Day. Judy Blau, of Eastchester, New York, is an artist who drys, hardens, and shellacs bagels to serve as ornaments, necklaces, napkin holders, Christmas wreaths, and candle holders. What a sacrilege! Let the curious Gentile epicure be warned. The Reuben sandwich is not kosher. This curious compound of corned beef, swiss cheese, sauerkraut, and rye bread is definitely a violation of Jewish law despite the fact that it was invented by a Jew. Some say it came out of New York; others stoutly insist that it first flourished on the Great Plains, in Omaha.[19]

Kosher food, authentic or otherwise, was a big business in the ghetto; it still is in Jewish life. In 1897, in one slaughter house alone in New York, 1,800 head of cattle might be kosher slaughtered every week; in another abattoir 15,000 chickens were killed every day. In 1969, it was said that Hebrew National (wurst and sausages) rang up about $18,000,000 a year in sales. The company employs an aggressive and expensive advertising company and spends huge sums to publicize its products. Many of the consumers of kosher products are Gentiles who like these foods because they are full-bodied and full-flavored. In a Dallas delicatessen, the largest in all Texas, 95 percent of the customers were Gentiles. This was in 1962 at a time when there was no kosher restaurant in town. Kosher Palestinian wines were purchased by Jews in this country as early as the first decade of the century. They were popular because they were produced in the Holy Land colonies. East European Jews, Zionist or not, drank the Carmel wines. Today, only about 10 percent of Manischewitz's kosher wines are sold to Jews; more of them are vended at Christmas time than at Passover. Jewish foods are found in almost all American supermarkets. This is transculturation; the immigrants have imposed their cuisine on the natives, both Jews and Gentiles.

Acceptance of Jewish wines and foods may be due, in part at least, to advertising campaigns; it is far more probable that they achieved wide acceptance because they are tasty. Because they are good, can one assume that they further philosemitism? One can love enchiladas, tacos, chili, tortillas without loving Mexican Americans. Chicken paprikash, goulash, and stuffed cabbage have not enhanced the status of Communist Hungary. Actually, most if not all East European Jewish foods are Slavic, possibly of relatively recent origin. It is sad, but the "Jewish" food of yesteryear may ultimately vanish even from Jewish tables. Heine drooled over carp in brown raisin sauce seasoned with garlic; Gershom Seixas, the Revolutionary War rabbi, loved his Spanish-Portuguese albondigas (meatballs); Esther Levy's Jewish Cookery Book (1871) does not even mention gefilte fish. From all indications, however, kosher Jewish foods are here to stay. The Union of Orthodox Rabbis puts its *hekhsher*, stamp of approval, on millions of cans of truly kosher food. Many buy them because of their freshness and their quality. These foods strengthen and fortify Orthodoxy. Kashrut in cans reflects the synthesis of two cultures, the American and the Jewish. Is it hard to be a Jew? Not gastronomically; all that one needs is a can opener.[20]

SYNAGOGS

Keeping kosher, or what passed for kosher, was a cement that tied Jews closely together. For about fifty weeks a year, the synagog was ignored, yet without it there could be no Jewish community or continuity. It was the foundation on which Judaism rested and on which Jewry stood. People are rarely conscious of the foundations of their homes or the walls that enclose and protect them. In 1905, studying the metropolitan synagogs, Charles Bernheimer said that the Orthodox congregation was a house of prayer, a mutual-aid society, a cultural center, and even something of a literary club. He was guilty of exaggeration, but what, in fact, was an East European style synagog? It was most frequently a room or two with a Hebrew manuscript Scroll of the Pentateuch (Sefer Torah), a table or two, and enough chairs or benches to seat ten males, the minimum quorum for prayer. A few congregations or prayer groups did offer some elements of mutual-aid, still fewer had study circles where men pored over two major rabbinic codes, the Mishnah and the Babylonian Talmud. In some congregations, they met to read Psalms. Did they understand the Hebrew they read? This is moot; some surely did, but how many? No distinction should be made between the religious, the social, and the cultural functions of these conventicles. In Judaism, the religious and the profane are inextricably woven together; that has always been the Orthodox pattern. Any layman could lead in chanting the services. The privilege of standing by as the portion of the week was read was auctioned off in shillings. Shillings? Was this an eighteenth century American survival, or an importation from the London ghetto?

Why a synagog? The Jews knew that without a synagog they could not survive as Jews. It was home; the ghetto was built around these primitive sanctuaries. Wherever Jews went, they established these conventicles. True, only a hard core of devotees rushed to establish a synagog; others more practical, turned to the mutual-aid societies and fraternal orders where sociability as well as financial relief received emphasis. In the larger cities, many synagogs were village-oriented, frequently appealing to émigrés who hailed from the same hamlet or town; most often, the determining impetus in organization was regional or national provenance. Thus, the Russians, Rumanians, and Poles huddled separately in a synagog which was usually comparable to the one they had attended in the Old Country. With acculturation, regionalism as a factor in agglomerating Jews would disappear; men would build large synagogs, spurred on primarily by denominationalism, by the degree to which they were prepared to accept or reject changes in religious services.[21]

By the 1860's and 1870's, there was not a major city north of the Mason-Dixon Line and east of the Mississippi that did not shelter at least one East European conventicle. Multiplication of synagogs was encouraged by governmental indifference to the churches and by the Protestant example of constant fission—all this before the pogroms of the 1880's. By 1909, Baltimore had twenty-five conventicles; very few allowed themselves the luxury of employing a rabbi; Providence had three synagogs and prayer meeting groups; Pittsburgh sheltered over twenty of these "Russian" sanctuaries in the Hill District. One was called the Rags Peddlers' Shul, but it was not a synagog for ragpickers; it was the sanctuary for a group engaged in the dry goods and clothing business. Colloquially, people in the retail garment industry were said to deal in "rags" (shmates). Lynn, Massachusetts, a small community, had four Orthodox congregations in 1913. In towns where there was only a handful of Jews, multiple synagogs were a luxury which the regionalists could not afford; the disparate East Europeans buried their differences and united in a common synagog. But even in the larger cities, in the metropolises, membership before 1921 was pitifully small. Struggling immigrants could not afford to join or would refuse for reasons of thrift to support a synagog. The largest Orthodox congregation in Chicago in 1905 had but 200 members. Typical to a degree of all these prayer groups was Congregation B'rith Sholem in Buffalo. Established in the 1860's and reorganized decades later, it had a total of twenty-three members, eight of whom were officers. An entrance fee was imposed, and in addition dues were $12 a year—a substantial amount for a struggling businessman or artisan. Originally, so it would seem, B'rith Sholem was a mutual-aid association and some of the provisions of a tightly knit society were retained. Applicants for membership could be blackballed; special committees watched over the sick, buried the dead, and recited prayers for their souls annually. The congregation was to have a rabbi, a beadle, and a cantor, who doubled as the ritual slaughterer. No marriage could be performed without permission from the congregation as a whole. Members who gossiped about synagogal affairs could be fined; the reasons why are not clear.[22]

In New York of the 1850's, all the synagogs in town, Sephardic, Reform, and Orthodox Ashkenazi, were on the Lower East Side. Of course it was here, too, that the East Europeans settled and established their first worship societies. By the turn of the century, after the coming of the East European masses, there were about 250 conventicles; by 1920, there were at least 700 of these places of worship, mostly small, all on the Lower East Side, practically all of them in rented rooms. Personal ambitions and petty rivalries were often the real cause for the establishment of new conventicles. Small synagogs were important psychologically; the individual counted for something. Western style decorum in the conventicles and synagogs of the newcomers was conspicuous by its absence, but these Jews were not barbarians; the synagog was home, a familiar place, an associational center. There was no need to speak in hushed tones; the shul was not a dimly lit Protestant church, where an all-powerful stern Deity was ready to judge and condemn all sinful men and women. God was a friend; a little conversation improved the services. Permissiveness had always been traditional in the house of God. Fighting and quarreling in the sanctuary can be documented in the eighteenth century Sephardic synagogs and in the German shuls.

Before the immigration act of 1921 would be passed by Congress, of the 1,000—more or less—East European congregations and religious meeting-houses in New York, about 100 were already in the Bronx, over 130 in Harlem, and almost 300 in Brooklyn. It would seem that the first formally organized synagog of the East European newcomers was called the Beth Hamidrash, The House of Study, established in 1852. It was a small organization; the members were mostly Poles, but included also were Lithuanians, two Germans, and an Englishman. By 1856, they not only had a good Hebrew library, but also a building of their own through the generosity of that Orthodox stalwart, Sampson Simson, whose family had come to New York in the early 1700's. In a circular which they broadcast appealing for funds, they made it clear that they were determined to resist the encroachments of the Reformers, whose teachings were a threat to true believers. By 1859, another congregation had emerged; calling itself the *Great* House of Study, Beth Hamedrash Hagodol, it assumed leadership and for years struggled to advance itself. The beadle served as collector of dues and augmented his modest salary by working as a glazier. In addition, he was allowed to operate a buffet in the vestibule of the synagog for mourners who came to recite kaddish. For ten cents one could buy a small brandy and a piece of sponge cake. Hassidic émigrés, who originally formed part of the synagog, seceded and celebrated on Saturday night by feasting with fish, meat, liquor, and song. By the 1870's, the Beth Hamedrash Hagadol sheltered coteries who studied Mishnah and Talmud; by the 1880's, it had purchased a large Methodist church and dedicated it as a synagog.[23]

The activities of the Beth Hamedrash Hagodol were not unique; other congregations aspiring to greatness bought large, beautiful churches from departing Protestants. Was it proper to use a former church? Certainly, said a prominent Galician religious authority; you are helping to usher in the messianic age. Quoting Zephaniah, 3:9, the European pundit wrote:

> For then I will make the peoples pure of speech, So that they all invoke the Lord by name, And serve him with one accord.

Why these large impressive sanctuaries? In Europe, Jews were building magnificent edifices. Jews here could do no less to convince themselves, if no one else, that they had "arrived." World Jewry had been too small too long. And here in the United States to compete with one another and to pay off huge mortgages they hired the best and most costly European cantors.[24]

CANTORS-HAZZANIM

Rabbis would serve for as little as $1 a week, nor were run of the mill hazzanim overpaid, though often they did much better than the rabbis financially. Cantors filled the synagogs and attracted new members; rabbis made no contributions to the exchequer. Distinguished hazzanim, brought in from Europe since the 1880's, were given very large salaries. Some of them, brilliant musicians with magnificent voices, came here because they refused to tolerate the autocratic rule of their synagogal boards back home. The fancy salaries which they received here were, of course, an additional incentive to emigrate. A number of these accomplished artists returned to Europe; for them the United States was exile, but others remained and made great careers as cantors, composers, and concertizers. The competitive bidding for the greatest voices finally stopped when the congregational leaders realized that the cantor alone could not pay off the mortgage. Among the famous singers, two stand out. Pinchos Minkowsky (1859-1924), who sang in the Eldridge Street shul in 1886, and Josef (Yosele) Rosenblatt (1882-1933), who was invited to prestigious Ohab Zedek, Dr. Philip Klein's synagog. Rumor had it that Minkowsky was paid $5,000, which might well have been a "Jewish" exaggeration. There is no question that he was a superb musician, a cultured man, at home in Hebrew, Russian, and German. As a litterateur, he wrote for the scholarly press in all three languages; Abraham Cahan taught him English.

Rosenblatt, who started concertizing as a child in Russia and Europe, came to the United States in 1912. Though a competent musician and composer, he was not as scholarly as Minkowsky. Rosenblatt had a gorgeous tenor voice that permitted him to sing in the coloratura and falsetto range. When, in the late 1920's, Al Jolson appeared in "The Jazz Singer," the voice was that of Rosenblatt. His liturgical "sob" stirred the hearts and souls of all who heard him. American Jews of Russian and Polish background were utterly devoted to him. He cut numerous phonograph records and gave concerts in all parts of the United States and in Europe, too. After some disastrous investments, he worked hard to pay off his debts and appeared in a concert in Carnegie Hall. His religious scruples did not permit him to sing in opera, although lucrative offers were made to him. He was a charming, kindly person with a gentle sense of humor. When he discovered that some of his son's friends were smoking on the Sabbath, he said nothing until once he saw them smoking on a Sunday. Jokingly, he said to them: "You must not smoke today, only on the Sabbath."

Jacob Koppel Sandler (1856-1931) came to these shores in 1888, no longer a youngster; he had made a living as a chorister and a choir leader in Russia. It was hard work, for he had to support a wife and six children; he had married at seventeen; his wife was only fifteen. Life was no easier here as he tried his luck as a customer peddler, a salesman, a choir leader, a messenger. He finally secured a modest job with the *New York Times*, where he remained. Before this, in 1896, while composing music for a Yiddish play, he had written the heartrending appeal of a Jewish girl about to be crucified. In her agony, she cried out with the psalmist: My God, my God why hast thou forsaken me? Was this, too, stolen—this time from the gospels, quoting the dying Jesus as he hung on the cross? (Math. 27:46.) The song in its day had a remarkable appeal. No one could fail to be thrilled by the words and melody of *Eli Eli lamah azavtoni*. The show ran for weeks. Then the song was forgotten. Years later, after a new arrangement by a skillful musician, it was sung again at the Metropolitan Opera House by Sophie Braslau. Sandler lived to hear his reborn classic, but the courts refused to acknowledge his authorship. Today it is a folk song. Among the Russian cantors who came here seeking his fortune was Moses Baline. When he landed in 1893, he brought with him his son Israel (b.1888). Later, as Irving Berlin, he became one of America's most popular composers.[25]

RABBIS

The spiritual head of an Orthodox synagog or community was the rabbi. In Eastern Europe, he was not a pastor or counsellor; he was not even a preacher in the modern Protestant sense, although he occasionally addressed himself publicly to a fine point of law—which most of his auditors could not appreciate. The rabbi was regarded as a canon law expert and as an authority on marriage, divorce, and the ritual slaughter of cattle and fowl. All this had been the role of the rabbi in Europe for centuries. When he picked up stakes and moved to the United States, he found to his dismay that American Jews did not really need or want him. The rabbi was a greenhorn. He did not dress like an American; often enough, he spoke only Yiddish. Slowly, inevitably, many if not most of the people were to break with many treasured traditions, customs, and taboos. They now had little need for rabbis; after all, any layman could conduct services. The rabbi was not oriented to America and its problems; his knowledge was not relevant. Devout, traditional leaders were miserable here. Jews here summarily rejected hierarchial control, blind submission to authority. On the whole, most rabbis were treated shabbily. The observant masses were not affluent; many were poor; the rabbi was deemed a luxury. To be sure as will be noted below, there were outstanding rabbis who refused to be ignored, who made a place for themselves and who could and did adapt themselves to conditions here in this country.[26]

The first Orthodox rabbi to serve in America—in this case, in a congregation maintained by German immigrants—had not come to America until 1840: Abraham Rice, who settled in Baltimore. As the New York congregations grew in number, the need for an authoritative "hierarchy," customary in Europe, began to reflect itself here. In the 1840's, an unsuccessful attempt was made to appoint Leo Merzbacher some sort of local spiritual head in New York City. About the same time, Max Lilienthal actually led three German congregations, but his rule lasted but a year or two and he resigned in disgust. Both Merzbacher and Lilienthal ultimately found a haven in Reform. Rice in Baltimore in the 1840's and some Orthodox rabbis in Philadelphia in the 1870's sought in vain to establish effective ecclesiastical courts. The first East European rabbi was

Abraham Joseph Ash (1813-1888), who arrived in the United States about 1851 and a year later became a founder of New York's first Russian synagog. Ash served the congregation for many years—except during the Civil War period, when he became briefly a successful hoopskirt manufacturer. After he lost his money, he reassumed his rabbinical post. By 1879, he was receiving $25 a month salary. Other learned rabbis soon followed Ash to this country. Among them was Moses Aaronson (Joseph Moses Aaronson), who came to the United States in 1861 and is remembered as the first American rabbi to publish a volume of responsa dealing with the religiolegal problems that plagued the American faithful. It appeared posthumously in 1878. Aaronson, made his living by rendering decisions in matters of marriage and divorce.[27]

By 1879—even before the mass immigration from Russia—it was obvious that some form of hierarchical authority was imperative if the East European newcomers were to cope with laxity, ritual neglect, and internal dissension. About twenty-six synagogs met as the United Hebrew Orthodox Congregations (American Orthodox Hebrew Congregations) in 1879 and prepared to extend a call to a European notable, Meir Loeb Malbim (b. 1809), but he died that very year. There was no question that he was a distinguished scholar, although, like some Russian rabbis, he was also a controversial personality. Though schooled in Western studies, he was not ready to make concessions to modernists and liberals; he was committed to traditional Orthodoxy and was vigorously opposed to reformist innovations. By the late 1880's, as the East Europeans poured in after the pogroms and as abuses manifested themselves in the misdeeds of incompetent and irresponsible religious officials, it was manifest that something had to be done. Rabbi Ash, who had exercised some authority, if only symbolically, died in 1888. A large measure of uniformity, order, and authority was seen as imperative. There was a welter of religious leaders: rabbis, reverends, cantors, ritual slaughterers, preachers. The meticulous were often shocked at what they saw in the area of divorce and marriage. There were clergymen who would agree to divorce a husband in America from his wife in Poland for the sake of the fee; there were others who would license ritual slaughterers who were unqualified.

A chief rabbi could remedy all this, so it was hoped. Thus it was that a large number of New York synagogs met in 1887 as the Association of American Orthodox Hebrew Congregations—all East European, of course—and in 1888 elected Jacob Joseph, of Vilna (1848-1902), as their Chief Rabbi. No American rabbi was even considered. They wanted an East European whom they could respect. They promised Rabbi Joseph a large salary, hoping that he would establish an ecclesiastical court, proper schools, and well-regulated charities—and made sure that he would be subject to lay control. Jacob Joseph was a good man, a brilliant preacher, a competent talmudist, but he lacked administrative skills. He could not cope with the problems he faced here; he suffered a stroke and died neglected. His salary, based on a tax on matzo and kosher meats and on their purveyors, was not forthcoming. The whole effort was an egregious failure. His coming was marked by enthusiasm. When he spoke in New York after his arrival, hundreds, if not thousands, of his compatriots turned out to greet him. There was a minor riot; over thirty policemen rushed to preserve order, and some of the throng, a woman among them, were jailed. When he died, the masses who had first acclaimed him and then shamelessly neglected him gathered to do him honor in the funeral procession. As they passed the foundry of R. H. Hoe & Company, the workers pelted the Jews down below with stones, pieces of metal, and refuse. The chief rabbinate of Jacob Joseph failed for many reasons. Joseph, a decent, honorable man, was a greenhorn in a land and situation where everyone prided himself on being "American." No one could really unite and control all these Jews; no one ever did. The situation, not the man, was at fault. In retrospect, the fact that Isaac Mayer Wise could unite his "Germans" to the extent that he did sheds light on his true greatness. The ultimate control of the New York East European communities lay in the hands of the lay leaders. There was inadequate financing; rabbinical rivalries were constant; ethnic and regional particularism hindered unity. There could be no compulsion, legal or moral, in a land where the authorities would not breach the wall between church and state. Congregationalism and voluntarism were characteristic of American religious institutions. Vested economic interests prevailed in the end; the kosher butchers would brook no effective supervision; they felt that their profits were at stake.[28]

Though the attempt to create a local hierarchy of sorts, both among the German Orthodox in the 1840's and among the Russians since the 1870's, had failed, individual East European rabbis in New York and in other major cities and towns made a determined effort from the 1880's on to bring order out of chaos; occasionally, success rewarded their efforts. No Orthodox rabbi before 1921 dominated all the East European congregations in his "diocesan" seat, yet there were competent and capable leaders in every big town and in most small cities. In the larger towns, these rabbis usually served a number of synagogs. In general, however, the smaller the town, the more extensive the authority; he was the "rov," the rabbi of the community. Somehow or other, he eked out a living despite his small salary. Perquisites were important: marriages, divorces, kashrut supervision, gifts from the affluent. Since he did little pastoral work, he was not always loved, but if he was a scholar and noncontentious, he was respected; he survived. As the pogroms and the reaction increased in Russia and Rumania, more and more rabbis came to these shores, especially after the turn of the century. There were good men in all the Jewish communities stretching from San Francisco to New York and Boston.

Morris Bloch (b.1869), of Oakland, California, may have received rabbinical ordination back in Russia. His first job here in America was in Oakland, where he was paid $7.50 a week, but he had to go out collecting junk in order to augment his salary. Six years later, he moved to a congregation in San Francisco where his salary was doubled—he now received $15 a week. But he was also a butcher, shohet, circumciser, and, during prohibition days, a source for sacramental wine. His afternoons were devoted to schooling the children in Hebrew. One of his friends was a Catholic priest, whom he visited often. The rabbi's children were enjoined to say nothing of this; one never knew how the congregation would respond to such ecumenism. In the late nineteenth and early twentieth centuries, Denver had two traditional spiritual leaders. One was Elias Hillkowitz, who had left Cincinnati because of asthma to settle in the mile-high city. He was highly respected and probably listened to because he was not financially dependent on any of the dozen or so prayer societies in town. The other Orthodox rabbinical émigré was Isaac A. Braude. When he died, the masses turned out in huge numbers; indeed, it was said to have been the largest Jewish funeral ever seen in Colorado. In one of his addresses, he denounced those Jewish mothers who desecrated the Sabbath by rushing to the stores to take advantage of bargain sales. Bernard Abramowitz was one of St. Louis's best known Orthodox rabbis.[29]

Chicago, as the second largest Jewish community, was too big, too divided, to meld its Jews together under the leadership of one man. Of course, it was attempted, but the effort failed. Chicago's would-be chief rabbi was the Ridbaz (1845-1913), "Rejoice O" Jacob David Willowski, the son of Zeev. When he came to America in 1900, he was already a renowned rabbinic scholar, possibly the world's leading authority on the Palestinian or Jerusalem Talmud. He had been a child prodigy and apparently could easily locate any passage in both the Babylonian and the Palestinian Talmuds. He was so erudite that few could follow him when he lectured. He was elected to head several congregations in Chicago in 1903, but the city had several other East European rabbis of learning and distinction; they refused to accept his leadership and fought him vigorously. After a brief sojourn in Chicago—this was his second trip to America—Ridbaz settled in Palestine where he continued his talmudic studies and publications. There was no question where he stood and what he wanted. The Bible, he said, must be studied in Yiddish, not English. Preaching in English is taboo, because ethics, not Jewish lore, will be stressed. Emphasis on morality alone leads to Reform. When a liberal preaches or sermonizes, walk out on him; don't get dressed on Sunday and go to the park or the Yiddish theatre; stay home and study the Law. He frowned on the American Jewish religious school system which merely taught the boy to read; he wanted knowledge in depth; he favored talmudic academies. The Ridbaz saw no reason to teach women to read Hebrew. Yiddish, yes! Let them read the pious ethical works written in the vernacular. Willowski was probably sympathetic to the teachings of the Hungarian notables, Rabbis Moses Sofer and Hillel Lichtenstein, men who frowned on public schools, secular education, music, chess, and checkers and saw the Talmud as all important. The Sabbath had to be observed; kashrut had to be carefully supervised; only qualified rabbis were to officiate at marriages and divorces; the community was to be united under one head; the charities were to be extended and improved. Had he remained in Chicago it is questionable if he would have been able to cope with the problems of his followers. While in Chicago, he saw a Jew hawking his wares in the Jewish quarter on the Sabbath and was so angered that he threatened to lay him under a ban. He desisted only when told that the peddler was impoverished and was desperately striving to support a wife and children. The Ridbaz was a compassionate man.[30]

Louisville had its Rabbi Asher Lipman Zarchy, a gentle soul; Cincinnati treasured the venerable Abraham Jacob Gerson Lesser (1834-1925), who had once served in Chicago. Rabbi Lesser officiated in Reb Shakhne Isaacs's synagog. Isaacs, the patriarch of a distinguished Cincinnati clan, was right-wing Orthodox; he had once burnt a heretical Reform prayer book. Pittsburgh had two Orthodox leaders, the modernist Aaron Mordecai Ashinsky and the quiet retiring Morris Simon Sivitz, who presided over the spiritual destinies of three of the local Orthodox synagogs. Among the numerous Baltimore talmudists was Rabbi Isaac B. Isaacson, who came to the city in the early 1900's and, when he had saved enough money, sent for his wife and children. In the course of time, he became an outstanding member of the city's Orthodox rabbinate.[31]

The Children of Abraham, the Men of Russia, as it was called, was one of the best known Orthodox congregations in Philadelphia. It began with seventeen members in 1882 and by 1894 had 200 supporters. Its first rabbi was Israel Moses Sachs, an excellent talmudist and a fine Yiddish orator. When Sachs was buried, so many people crowded around the grave that it caved in and had to be redug. After serving for about four years, he was succeeded by Rabbi Eleazer Kleinberg, who had officiated as a judge in Vilna's rabbinical court. He, too, passed away after a very short reign and was succeeded in 1891 by his son-in-law, Bernard L. Levinthal, who was to become the town's most eminent Orthodox leader, even though he exercised supervision over only a few of Philadelphia's East European synagogs. In 1894, a number of the city's religious societies joined together as the United Congregations (Agudat Ha-Kehillot). Its goals were ambitious; it wanted to foster charitable and educational institutions in the ghetto and make sure that the kosher food had been properly prepared. Here in the United States, one of the most distinguished rabbis of the old school was the Ramaz, Rabbi Moses (Morris) Zebulon Margolies (1851-1936). After serving for many years in Russia and Poland, he came to America about the year 1889, to Boston, where he officiated for a while as the spiritual leader of three congregations. He was particularly zealous in his support of Russian talmudic academies and Palestine's philanthropies and schools.[32]

SOME REFLECTIONS ON ORTHODOX RABBIS

The tendency of the critical historian is to brush these foreign-born Orthodox rabbis aside and to say that they had little influence on their people in the first two decades of the twentieth century. They could not cope with the challenge of America and were unsuccessful in transporting East European Orthodoxy to the United States. This is true in part. They were distinguished by their rivalries and factionalism; many were embittered, frustrated, unhappy men. But they were by no means unaware of their problem. They knew that, if the people were observant of the details of the Law, Orthodoxy would survive. This is why they hammered away at kashrut, the Sabbath, Hebrew education, and scrupulosity in all matters touching on marriage and divorce. Respect and tenure for these right-wing spiritual leaders was to come decades later with Americanization. Reform rabbis were treated respectfully like Protestant ministers; ultimately Orthodox rabbis would be shown the same consideration and given adequate support, financial and otherwise.[33]

ORTHODOX NATIONAL ORGANIZATIONS

The Ramaz, undeviating in his Orthodoxy, was concerned with the religious, cultural, and philanthropic welfare of fellow Jews in the United States, Eastern Europe, and the Holy Land. Margolies and his ideological contemporaries were convinced of the need for organization, centralization, to maintain Orthodox standards and ensure Orthodoxy's ability to survive the attacks of modernity. What they contemplated was not especially extravagant; after all, federation, no matter how tenuous, was never beyond the reach of Jewish religionists here in the United States. In the late eighteenth century, the American congregations, all of them traditional, had worked together to provide for foreign visitors; they had been in touch as they collected money for the needs of Palestinians. From the 1840's on, at the latest, a national organization of welfare activities and a federation of communities were goals for Leeser, Wise, and others. The

Board of Delegates of American Israelites was born in 1859, and after the Civil War, the word "union" attained an almost sacrosanct character. The Union of American Hebrew Congregations came into being in 1873; it set out initially to embrace all religious groups, even the Orthodox. After 1883, when the Union of American Hebrew Congregations blundered, unintentionally, by serving forbidden foods at its national celebration, the Orthodox, long distrustful of the Union's liberal tendencies, set up the Jewish Theological Seminary Association of America. They had a model in Orthodox Jews in Germany who had already established a union of their own in 1885. That year, the Reformers at Pittsburgh once more shocked the traditionalist majority by promulgating a radical platform. In 1887, the Jewish Theological Seminary opened its doors; it was an Orthodox institution—let there be no question about that. At that same time many traditional synagogs in New York City came together to invite a chief rabbi here, one who could, they hoped, bring order out of chaos. Almost from the very beginning, the 1887-1888 Association of American Orthodox Hebrew Congregations was ineffectual, and two years later in 1890, J. D. Eisenstein records talk of a new national organization of Russian Jews. It was not, however, until 1898 that a new permanent national federation of congregations was effectuated: the Union of Orthodox Jewish Congregations of the United States and Canada.

The new union was created by Henry Pereira Mendes (1852-1937), a Sephardi and a native Englishman, brought to the United States in 1877 to serve as hazzan of Shearith Israel in New York. His was a notable family; an ancestor had already served Shearith Israel as its religious functionary in the 1740's. Mendes was very active in the American Jewish community. He helped reopen the old colonial synagog in Newport and was distinguished for his aid in establishing such important New York Jewish institutions as the Montefiore Home and Hospital for Chronic Diseases, a guild for crippled children, and the all-inclusive new Board of Jewish Ministers. The rabbi had a literary bent, for he wrote novels, essays, stories, and poems, some of which were set to music. The Jewish Theological Seminary owed much to him, for in 1886-1887 he was one of the founders of what was, in essence, an Orthodox rabbinical college dedicated to the preservation of the old way of life. It was determined to stop the inroads of the new Reformist Hebrew Union College. The first meeting of this new traditional religious association was held in the halls of Shearith Israel. The seminary itself was opened in 1887, as the East Europeans were organizing a congregational union to bring a Russian chief rabbi to the city. It was obvious that these Jews from Eastern Europe would not accept guidance from the new seminary of the Americanized Orthodox, and so two disparate tradition-oriented cultures confronted each other here: Mendes was rooted in Anglo-American thinking; Isaac

M. Wise, the Reformer, was actually closer to the East Europeans than this Occidental Sephardi who spoke no Yiddish and had never swayed over a Talmud in a yeshivah.

Unlike Wise, however, Mendes and his associates wanted to commit the new American generation of Jews to the age-old traditions of the fathers. He held Hebraic education important; equally important to him was secular schooling and all that it implied: knowledge of the amenities, the mores of Angle-American society. Something had to be done if the Judaism of the rabbinical sages was to be salvaged. By 1897, Morais of Philadelphia, the head of the Seminary, was dead; the school itself was almost ready to close its doors; a new leadership, a new presence, a new institution was necessary in New York City if Orthodoxy was to survive. It was now almost a generation since the floundering East European masses had begun arriving in sizable numbers. The Reformers had dozens of congregations flouting God's laws. Now, however, Jewish protestants, to save Judaism, organized the Union of Orthodox Jewish Congregations of the United States and Canada. It was established primarily to unite the Orthodox synagogs of the natives and the "Germans," though it hoped also to win the East Europeans. At its first biennial convention in 1900, the Union listened to addresses by the people's preacher, Hirsch Masliansky, and by the great Ridbaz. Could Mendes and Lewis Dembitz—Brandeis's uncle—understand these speakers as their eloquence and erudition gushed forth—in Yiddish?

The program of the Orthodox congregational union was aimed directly and deliberately at the articles of the Pittsburgh Platform. This new Orthodox association insisted on emphasizing the Bible as the prime source of revelation; Jews were called on to believe in the old ceremonies, the codes, the Maimonidean credo. (It is ironic that Maimonides (1135-1204), a "liberal" in his day and an acculturated Arabist, had by the late nineteenth century become a symbol of an unyielding Orthodoxy.) We Jews, it was affirmed, await a personal Messiah. As citizens, we are certainly willing to work with Gentiles for common goals, but religiously we will remain separate in a world of our own. Male converts must undergo circumcision and perform the customary religious ablutions. We are sympathetic to the new Zionism; in no sense does it conflict with our loyalty to our beloved America. Still, the new Orthodox Union congregations balked at convoking a synod, a legislative body of clergy and laymen. Did they contemplate changes? They were certainly completely and utterly American. Mendes was a prime mover in 1905 as American Jewry celebrated the 250th anniversary of the settlement of Jews in his land. No breach could be tolerated in the wall that separated church and state; Mendes and his friends fought all attempts to introduce Christian influence, ceremonies, carols, teachings, into the public schools. The

Union of Orthodox Congregations and the Jewish Theological Seminary set out to fight the Reformers, yet both institutions had accomplished but little by 1902. The Orthodox seemed unable to do much to bring order into the religioeducational life of the East Side youngsters; they did not even set out to clean the Augean stables of kashrut. Unification of the East Side masses was not even attempted; in truth, it was an impossible task. The Seminary was moribund; the Union of Orthodox Congregations, little more than a paper organization. When Schechter came to the Seminary in 1902, many Orthodox synagogs had already started moving to the left; by 1913, the modern Orthodox had created a union of their own, the United Synagogue of America. The Union of Orthodox Congregations was isolated, impotent, unimportant. Indeed, it was not to take on new life till after World War II, when, renascent, it would campaign vigorously for kashrut and begin to establish a parochial school system.[34]

True believers from trans-Vistula Europe kept their distance from the new Orthodox union of congregations. Though both groups cherished the same theology and practice, the social chasm that separated them was too wide; there was no religiosocial bridge leading from Russia, Galicia and Rumania to middle or upper Manhattan. The East European worthies made this clear by the creation in 1902 of the Union of Orthodox Rabbis of the United States and Canada. Troubled by violations of Jewish Law of which its Orthodox practitioners were guilty and realizing full well the educational needs of the younger generation of immigrants, Mendes, in 1896, had stressed the need to unite the Orthodox rabbis into a union. This effort, too, failed. A few years later, in 1902, the European *rabbonim* took the bit between their teeth and established their Union of Orthodox Rabbis of the United States and Canada. The effort was furthered not only by perceptive rabbis in the East, men like Margolies of Boston and New York, and Levinthal of Philadelphia, but also by a number of able clergymen in the Middle West. These transallegheny rabbis realized that the Jews in their communities were almost totally enveloped by masses of Gentile Americans; they knew that Reform was in the ascendancy, that the younger East European generation was almost lost. Something had to be done; it was "a time to work for the Lord." Without any surrender of principle, it was imperative to adapt Orthodoxy to the pressing demands of the American milieu. The English language and secular education had to be encouraged. This was a very realistic appraisal. The Union of Orthodox Rabbis moved to the left very slowly. Its members had no intention of destroying themselves. Very few of them could hope to become English preachers. They insisted on the exclusive use of Yiddish, the only vernacular they employed. They tried to make it a sacrosanct tongue even as the Sephardim had done with their Spanish-Portuguese language. Setting up their Torah-true Judaism, they refused to make any compromises;

the East European religious way of life was to be maintained; all-day schools, afternoon Hebrew schools, and talmudic academies were to be furthered. The Sabbath, the dietary prescriptions, and the laws of marriage, divorce, and ritual bathing were all to be maintained as zealously as they had been in the villages and towns of Russia and Poland. No rabbi was to be accepted into their guild unless he was as highly qualified as they were; they, of course, would determine the criteria for admission. If talmudic studies lost their primacy, then these talmudists were nobodies! Such goals for American Orthodox Jewry meant little to most of the younger generation and many older immigrants, too, but these European-born and trained rabbis had no choice; they hewed to the line.

A substantial number of rabbis might have qualified for membership. Some refused to join the new Orthodox union; they were too poor even to pay the nominal dues; personal rivalries were common and bitter. In the early twentieth century, two groups of ministers, preachers, and Orthodox rabbis created separate rabbinical associations. These men—primarily New Yorkers—cherished the same religious goals as the bearded *rabbonim,* but they were more realistic. They were preachers who had constant relations with the immigrant masses. They emphasized the need for a court of arbitration to settle disputes between a congregation and its rabbi; they wanted an employment bureau; they worked for a five-day work week which would make it possible for observant laborers to attend Sabbath services. By 1904, the Union of Orthodox Rabbis had broken with the Jewish Theological Seminary; it would not accept Solomon Schechter and his thoroughly Western faculty. The Seminary, it asserted, was not Orthodox; it taught the Higher Criticism of the Bible; its students were not rabbis in the accepted sense. The professors knew no Talmud—these critics claimed, incorrectly—and, in any case, how could anyone teach Talmud in English and not Yiddish. As they saw it, the new union of the Conservative congregations affiliated with the Seminary was nothing but Reform hiding under the mask of Orthodoxy. This attack by the Orthodox rabbis was made in the Spring of 1914, yet that very year the Orthodox worked closely with the Reformers and the Conservatives to feed thousands of fellow Jews abroad, threatened by the invading and counter-invading German, Austrian, and Russian armies.

By 1921, the new Orthodox unions of rabbis and congregations had accomplished little of note. As late as 1906, the *Jewish Encyclopedia* deemed neither union worthy of a separate article. Yet the unions had been established; that was a gain. At least they realized that they were faced with serious problems here in America. Organization, unity, was essential if any progress was to be made in creating a viable American Orthodoxy. Little was done because the Orthodox masses were scrabbling for a living; they were too poor to support their rabbis or to maintain

their congregations adequately. So far as ritual, ceremonies, and observances were concerned, American latitudinarianism was devastating. The
children of the immigrants were smothered in the embrace of the public
school system with its gospel of Americanism. The younger generation of
East Europeans was pulling away from a Russo-Polish type of Judaism.
The Orthodox unions had yet to come up with programs that would synthesize Judaism and American culture. It was unthinkable that Rabbi
Mendes, president of the Union of Orthodox Congregations of the
United States and Canada, could bring salvation to the East Side Yiddish
immigrants with his message:

> God, let Thy blessings come
> On us of Saxondom.
> O save us all![35]

MODERN ORTHODOX

The very men who were fulminating against Reform and the new deviant
Orthodoxy—Conservatism—were trying to adapt the old country religious practices to America's demands. They were too intelligent, and too
grateful, not to do so. They were desperately eager to save their Judaism
in this new country with its inexorable challenges. By the 1880's, the
leaders of Orthodoxy—laymen in this instance—knew that their rabbis
would have to be men with good secular backgrounds in order to win the
respect of cultivated Jews and Gentiles here. If, as pointed out above, Jacob Joseph was chosen, it was because New York's Jewry had no choice:
the Westernized European rabbis had no desire to exile themselves to the
United States. It is not without significance that 12,000 of the 218,000
synagog seats in New York City were occupied by Orthodox Jews whose
rabbis preached to them in English. Most of these 12,000 auditors were
native-born or Germans; many were certainly of East European provenance. There was a growing demand by Russians and Poles for modern
rabbis, secularly educated and aesthetically inclined. By 1917-1920, the
leaders, the officers of the Union of Orthodox Rabbis, included not only
the old-line Russian clergy, who had never gone to a secular school, but
men like Philip Klein of New York and Schepsel Schaffer of Baltimore,
rabbis who had earned their Ph.D. degrees in Europe. Schaffer was born
in Russia; Klein in Hungary. Even the venerable Lesser had one foot in
the modern world, if only by courtesy of the post-renaissance Azariah dei
Rossi, whose scholarly *Light of the Eyes* he had read. In one of his writings
Isaac Leeser wrote that the restored Hebrew state in messianic times
would be ruled over by an elected president. Leeser tacitly ignored the
explicit injunction of the daily prayers which besought God to restore the
(autocratic!) David Dynasty. Later, as the Orthodox leader in Cincinnati,

Rabbi Abraham J. G. Lesser would use Hebrew Union College Library, though the later "Chief Rabbi" Eliezer Silver refused as a matter of principle to set foot on the campus of the Reform seminary. Israel S. Rubinstein, a chief rabbi of Rhode Island, busied himself in the World War I relief movement, served as a delegate to the American Jewish Congress, wrote articles for Eisenstein's Hebrew encyclopedia *Ozar Yisrael*, worked to organize a local university Menorah Society, and accepted office on the boards of several charities. He had certainly come to terms with America.

The uncompromisingly Orthodox Schaffer, who got his degree at Leipzig and ordination from Isaac Elchanan, of Kovno, had once studied in Russia with Dr. Philip Klein. The latter, a brilliant talmudist, had come to the United States in 1891 after serving congregations in the czarist empire; his synagog in New York was one of the most prestigious in the country. No man was more respected in New York's Orthodox world. Hirsch Masliansky, "the national Jewish orator," as he called himself, was completely and thoroughly Americanized, yet no one could call his Orthodoxy into question. For many years he preached in Yiddish at the Jewish Educational Alliance, an institution dedicated to the Americanization of Lower East Side Jewry. It was his prayerful hope that he might salvage the souls of the younger generation and help their immigrant parents learn to live happily in this country. After he landed in the United States in the 1891's—already a famous man—the police escorted him to his pulpit through massive crowds; in Russia, the police had dragged him off pulpits. He was an American patriot; he had every reason to be so. Aaron Mordecai Ashinsky, another Russian who had come here without benefit of secular schooling, had served as a chaplain in Canada and conducted one of the most modern Sunday Schools in Pittsburgh in the vestry rooms of his synagog, the chief seat of Orthodoxy in Western Pennsylvania.

Bernard Louis Levinthal is to be numbered among the five or ten most influential Orthodox rabbis of North America. He was on the executive committee of the Americanist Union of Orthodox Jewish Congregations, honorary president of the right-wing Union of Orthodox Rabbis, yet also one of the founders of the elite American Jewish Committee. He led the Orthodox cohorts in Philadelphia as they set out to sell Liberty Bonds in World War I. When Marxist intellectuals turned to him, he did not repulse them, but spoke learnedly—in Yiddish, of course—on the labor laws of the Talmud. This highly intelligent man was faced with a quandary. He knew that if he encouraged or even tolerated secular studies, traditional Orthodoxy would suffer impairment, yet he felt he had no choice. Sensing what the future would bring, he cast no stumbling blocks in the paths of those who moved into the American world of acculturation. Levinthal hired a scholarly litterateur, Albert Mordell, to tutor a son in English and took lessons himself, though he never ventured to preach in that tongue; he was not secure enough in his knowledge of the new language. He permitted his children to teach in non-Orthodox religious schools; he was no bigot. In as much as they had to pronounce the Ineffable Name, the hatless children resolved their problem by hastily running a hand over their heads when the divine letters appeared in the text! (This they had learned from the pious Sabato Morais.) At times Levinthal was almost latitudinarian in his conduct. Summering at Atlantic City, he went into the water in a bathing suit that covered him completely from neck to ankles, but there were women swimming on the same beach. This shocked the ladies back home; the rabbi bathed with women! When the ebullient, irrepressible Stephen S. Wise spoke in laudatory terms of Jesus, some of his Orthodox confreres threatened to resign from the Zionist organizations with which Wise was identified. Levinthal poured oil upon the troubled waters to pacify irate pious Zionists; it was all a mistake, said the Philadelphia rabbi.

Individual rabbis, natives of Slavic Europe, learned English to impress their congregants and to win the confidence of American-born children. Some opened Sunday schools patterned in conduct and in content on those established by the Reformers. These conformists knew that they had to make their peace with America's religiocultural milieu. If they had scruples, they suppressed them. Some New Yorkers, devoted to their faith but rebelling against the disorder that characterized too many religious services, created Young Israel in 1912. They set out to counter the inroads of Reform, socialism, and a rising tide of delinquency among the youth. They wanted decorous services and succeeded in this effort. In the course of the next generation, the movement gained adherents not only in metropolitan New York, but in other cities too. Theologically and liturgically, they held firm to their traditional moorings; they made few, if any, concessions to innovators. By the 1941's the National Council of Young Israel had thousands of members with branches throughout the country. Over the years, Young Israel had become an autonomous Orthodox movement with its own social and educational programs. By 1915, a renewed, militant American Orthodoxy began to resolve the problem of synthesizing the ancestral faith with Americanism; in that year, Rabbi Bernard Revel (1885-1941), a European talmudist with an American graduate degree, was elected president of the Rabbi Isaac Elchanan Theological Seminary, as it was to be called. Orthodoxy had come a long way. Conscious that traditional Judaism must always put its best foot forward, a Cincinnati Jew, H. Liberman, published a forty-seven page pamphlet in English, Yiddish, and Hebrew, *The Path of Israel* (1899); it excerpted the choicest ethical epigrams of the Talmud. Apparently he believed that a collection of beautiful ethical aphorisms was more appropriate to the needs of the younger generation than a disquisition on some fine point of rabbinic law. Was all this a step toward Conservatism? Reform? Not necessarily. When the Reformers and the National Council of Jewish Women attempted to set up religious services in the Philadelphia ghetto, its Orthodox Jews, both young and old, refused to respond to the overtures of the natives. Socially and religiously, the natives and the "Germans" were suspect. In their own way and in their own time, the true believers would independently work out their salvation.[36]

CHAPTER THIRTEEN

HEBREW AND THE EAST EUROPEAN JEWS

INTRODUCTION: THE VERNACULARS OF THE EAST EUROPEAN JEWS

The Jews from the Slavic lands were multilingual. Some knew Polish and Russian; the Hungarians spoke German and Magyar; some Rumanians spoke Yiddish and the language of their native country—imperative if they were to do business with Gentiles in the villages and towns. Here in the United States, however, the languages of the masses from the East were Hebrew, Yiddish, and English. Relatively few newcomers were ever to master English; there were, of course, notable exceptions, writers, journalists, scholars of distinction. Russian was not a popular vernacular for, back home, Jews lived in close settlements and were not encouraged or even permitted to go to the Russian public schools in large numbers. Unlike the German Jews, who were patriots and constantly spoke German, the Russian Jewish masses had no love for a land or a people that had rejected them. In 1890, probably not more than one in twenty of the Jewish denizens of the East Side could speak Russian, and this is a liberal estimate. There was, however, a solid core of intellectuals who gloried in their knowledge of the Muscovite vernacular. To that extent, these radicals—most were Marxist—were Russophiles. They spoke Russian when they assembled socially and wrote reports in that language for the Russo-Jewish newspapers back home. There was a rather extensive Russian press in the United States reflecting diverse political philosophies. It was not a Jewish press despite the fact that some of the editors were Jews, East Side notables, who were to distinguish themselves as Jewish writers, social workers, and labor leaders. The Russian-speaking newcomers who came in the 1880's built a tight little social world of their own. They would meet on New Year's Eve to sing Russian songs and talk of the day when Russia would be free. Many had a mild contempt for the Uptown social workers and do-gooders whose answer to the social problem was religion, athletics, and a good hot bath. These

Russians were a proud lot; they did not like to be patronized. They were politically liberal or radical, poor synagoggoers, devotees of secular education.[1]

HASKALAH, "ENLIGHTENMENT"

Exceedingly few employed modern Hebrew as a living language; there were exceptions, of course. Modern Hebrew was still laboring to be born; Eliezer Ben Yehuda (d.1922), the most notable of the founders of Hebrew as a spoken language, was still at work. Practically all East European Jewish newcomers knew some Hebrew. It was the language of the liturgy, of the prayer books, of the Bible. Prayers had to be in Hebrew; it was the only language acceptable to God, so it was believed. It is true that most Jews did not know and never would know what the words meant. That was not important; the words had a mystical, magical meaning all their own; God was at home in Hebrew and loved the Holy Tongue. In 1911, an old Christian minister came to the Hebrew Union College to study Hebrew; he knew it was the language that would be spoken in Heaven. Hebrew and Aramaic were also the legal languages of the Jews, of the Talmud, of the codes which were still in force wherever Orthodoxy prevailed. Among the millions of observant Jews were many thousands with some knowledge of rabbinic Hebrew. They knew what the "Law" was, what men and women had to do if they were to live the Jewish life. Hebrew was the language of religion, the second language of the Jewish masses. Without it, the content of the codes could not be transmitted.

The nineteenth century found some Jews in Russia, Poland, Galicia, and Rumania determined to employ Hebrew as a living language in order to bring European culture to the benighted Jews in the European ghettos. Orthodoxy frowned on the Western arts and sciences. Superstition, bigotry, was not uncommon in the Slavic lands; the masses were not "educated." The Russian language could not serve as a vehicle of culture. Not only were few allowed to go to the Russian schools, but most had no desire to send their children to study the language of the oppressors. Most East European Jews were well aware of what the West had to offer. A few turned to German as the key to the new knowledge; some believed that Hebrew could be employed. These Hebraists wanted to "enlighten" Jewry, to fight Orthodoxy and obscurantism, to emancipate the young spiritually and culturally and introduce them to the glorious new secular world of science and literature. Modern Hebrew was to serve as the medium of instruction for these Maskilim, these "Enlighteners." They wrote and published in Hebrew; they created a press and literature in that language as they worked toward a Hebraic renascence. This rebirth of "Enlightenment" is called the Haskalah. By the 1870's, a few of the Maskilim turning to Jewish nationalism as proto-Zionists, were determined to make Hebrew the language of a Jewish state yet to be born. Some of these lovers of modern Hebrew literature came to the United States, hoping that here they could carve out new careers for themselves. But America had no need for Hebrew as a channel to culture; English was available to all; this was a free country. The Maskilim, consequentially, lost their raison d'être as liberals; they did an about face and stressed nationalism, Zionism, Hebrew as a living language. The Enlighteners who came here were not crusaders for free thought. If they nursed liberal ideas about religion, they found out soon enough that America frowned on atheists and agnostics, on any type of freethinking; the Hebrew readers to whom the litterateurs turned for moral and financial support were not iconoclasts. Haskalah Hebrew literature in the United States was to huddle under the sheltering wings of a nominal Orthodoxy.

Hebrew here, as in Europe, was to become a language for poetry and prose, belles letters, essays, and the whole world of scholarship, traditional and critical. No later than the 1860's, East European rabbinical scholars here in the United States were writing and publishing Hebrew responsa on legal questions, Hebrew commentaries on the Bible and talmudic tractates, Hebrew sermons, and apologias defending Judaism and proclaiming its virtues. There were afternoon schools in all major towns where the prayer book and the Bible were taught; there were even several yeshivot, rabbinic academies, where the Talmud was studied in the traditional European fashion. In New York, even before 1921, there were teachers' institutes where advanced Hebrew studies were pursued. It is interesting to note that in many congregations of the country pious Jews met daily to study Psalms or the Mishnah or the Talmud or the aggadic selections compiled by a sixteenth-century worthy (En Yaakov). In a less organized fashion, individuals studied Talmud privately, alone or with a haver, a boon companion. Books were available in the Jewish bookstores found in every large city. Polish-born Morris Diamond (1860-1944), who had stopped off in Dublin where he perfected his English, settled in Buffalo where he opened his modern private Hebrew school in 1889. He was a competent talmudist, a grammarian, and an excellent Bible scholar fully aware of the teachings of the Higher Critics. The writings of the Maskilim, both European and American, were known to him. His home was kosher; Sabbath was observed in traditional fashion, yet he was a Maskil, for he questioned the prayers for the restoration of the sacrificial system and deprecated the emphasis upon the kaddish, the prayer for the dead. Judaism, he said, never emphasized dying but life and learning. When he discovered a son smoking on the Sabbath he admonished him somewhat ironically. "If during the week you smoke a five-cent cigar, smoke a ten-cent one on Shabbos." He helped found more than one East

European philanthropic society in Buffalo and from his meager earnings sent four sons to college and graduate schools; one of them became a Reform rabbi.[2]

THE CRITICAL SCHOLARSHIP OF THE EAST EUROPEAN JEWS IN THE UNITED STATES

The Maskilim with their penchant for learning were not necessarily scholars. They lacked methodology, the leisure to do research, and the opportunity to publish. Yet many surmounted these difficulties and wrote works that met the demands of historical criticism. One may venture to assert that there were almost as many East European scholarly writers as there were litterateurs. The men who turned to research worked in the fields of Bible, rabbinics, history, philosophy, philology, grammar, and bibliography. When Funk and Wagnalls undertook to publish the *Jewish Encyclopedia*, most, if not all, of its American contributors were dependent on Abraham Solomon Freidus (1867-1923), the first head of the Jewish Division of the New York Public Library. Like many Jewish scholars who were to make their mark in the late nineteenth and early twentieth centuries, he was of East European origin. Just about the time that Freidus became the chief bibliographical resource for the *Jewish Encyclopedia*, there were a number of Jewish businessmen, Maskilim, who began to win their spurs as scholars in the field of Jewish studies. Judah David Eisenstein, a shirt manufacturer, was to publish many volumes of basic source materials and to edit a Hebrew encyclopedia. Eisenstein had come to the United States in the early 1870's and, as he sank his roots here, expressed the hope that America would become a haven for the persecuted and also an outstanding Jewish cultural center. He did what he could to further scholarship not only through his numerous anthologies, but also through his support of Jewish cultural institutions which promoted Hebrew and its literature. The numerous books and manuals which he published were not always meticulously edited but they were and still are very useful.

N. S. Libowitz, a merchant and prolific writer who had been influenced by the modernistic Azariah dei Rossi (ca.1511-ca.1578), published a critical life of the Venetian Leo da Modena. Abraham Hayyim Rosenberg (1838-1925), a printer, published a multivolume biblical encyclopedia (*Ozar Ha-Shemot*). What happened to the family of this Hebrew writer in America? A daughter of Rosenberg taught mathematics at Hunter College; one son was a chemist, another edited an American newspaper, a third became a famous physician. Ephraim Deinard (1846-1930), a bookseller, helped build the Jewish collections in the Library of Congress and at Harvard. He wrote a great deal—dozens of Hebrew books—edited a magazine and enjoyed attacking Reform, Hassidism, Stephen S. Wise, Christianity, and Karaism. Students are grateful to him for his *Koheleth America*, a bibliography of American Hebrew prints, 1735-1926. Deinard pointed out that almost 1,000 books had appeared in Hebrew in America from 1735 to 1926. Nearly 600 appeared from 1900 to 1921. Most of the works were liturgies, rabbinic monographs, and children's texts. Only about 200 volumes were scholarly works and belles lettres. One writer was of the opinion that for the period 1904-1922 there were but forty-nine original studies. Another researcher has pointed out that about 500 words in the *Webster Third New International Dictionary of the English Language* come from the Hebrew and Yiddish.[3]

Deinard, a shrewd businessman, managed to survive in the American maelstrom. Three other East European scholars struggled hard to maintain themselves: Arnold Bogumil Ehrlich (1848-1919), Phineas Mordell (1861-1934), and Michael Levi Rodkinson (Frumkin, 1845-1904). Ehrlich, who came to the United States in 1878, first made his living at hard manual labor; later he became a Hebrew teacher. He was a brilliant and original biblical exegete and lexicographer who published his comments on the Sacred Scripture in Hebrew and in German. Gone to America, like gone to Texas, was oft a wry suggestion that the immigrant's conduct had left something to be desired; America's maw was big enough to digest all newcomers. Many Jews held Ehrlich at arm's length, for he had once been a convert to Christianity, though later he returned to Judaism. It was in his early days in Europe that he helped Franz Delitzsch, head of the missionary Institutum Judaicum, make his beautiful Hebrew translation of the New Testament. Phineas Mordell, a very competent Hebrew grammarian, came to this country only a few years after Ehrlich and, like him, first turned to hard physical labor before becoming an instructor in Hebrew for children. His sons enjoyed a better life; one was a recognized and respected litterateur and critic; the other became a world renowned mathematician, lecturing in England, the United States, Germany, and for several years served as president of the London Mathematical Society. Rodkinson had edited Hebrew and Yiddish periodicals before coming to this country in 1888. He was no longer a young man; he was looked at warily in Europe, for he was also suspected of apostasy. Here in the United States he wrote books in Hebrew and in English on Jewish subjects and was known for his translation of several tractates of the Talmud into English. His renditions into the American vernacular were anything but felicitous and did little to enhance the understanding of the Talmud by non-Hebraists. Mordell once had a job as a shammash, a beadle, a most humble position. Rabbis who were scholars had it easier; they enjoyed a steady income. Benjamin Szold and Alexander Kohut, both natives of Hungary, had good posts, the one in Baltimore, the other in prestigious Ahavath Chesed in New York City. Szold wrote a commentary on Job in

Hebrew; Kohut, despite his congregational labors and his duties at the Jewish Theological Seminary, finally finished his multivolume lexicon of the Talmud in 1892. He was an insightful preacher—long-winded, to be sure—and did not hesitate to reprimand one of his members who dared to wave a watch before him reminding him that he had already been sermonizing for more than an hour.[4]

Kohut taught at the Jewish Theological Seminary before the school was rechartered with the coming of Schechter in 1902. Hebrew studies were then intensified. The critical method was tacitly introduced, and the institution slowly moved to the left. The distinguished members of the faculty were, with the exception of Alexander Marx, East European; Solomon Schechter (1850-1915) was a Rumanian; Louis Ginzberg (1873-1953) and Israel Davidson (1870-1939) were "Litvaks," Lithuanians. All three enriched Jewish scholarship in this country because of their superb research in rabbinic literature and Jewish thought. Schechter, as president of the Seminary and Ginzberg as a teacher there, did not share the fate of most Russian Hebraists who barely survived despite their linguistic and research skills. Israel Davidson was to "sweat blood" before he became a professor at the Seminary. He peddled, worked in an orphan asylum, and served as a chaplain at Sing Sing while studying to earn a graduate degree at Columbia. His doctor's dissertation on *Parody in Jewish Literature* and his four-volume opus *Thesaurus of Medieval Hebrew Poetry* are valuable contributions. It was these men who, together with Alexander Marx, built the reputation of New York's Conservative seminary. Ginzberg was more than an incomparable talmudist; he was a polymath; Schechter, as essayist and researcher, brought the vast field of rabbinic thought to the attention of cultured laymen.[5]

Ginzberg and Schechter, too, wrote for the *Jewish Encyclopedia*; Jacob Z. Lauterbach, a Galician, was an office editor. This brilliant, charming talmudist, folklorist, raconteur and gourmet was later called to teach at the Hebrew Union College. Other transoceanic Hebraists who preceded him at that school were the philosopher David Neumark and the grammarian Caspar Levias. Neumark was at home in almost every area of Hebrew learning; at the age of six he was already "swimming in the sea of the Talmud." A theologian and philosopher, he was the author of several works in English, German, and Hebrew which analyzed the teachings of medieval and modern Jewish metaphysicians. This polymath was one of the several pioneers who helped bring the Science of Judaism to the United States and made this country a center of Jewish learning. Chatting with his favorite students, Neumark spoke in Hebrew, and when Emil G. Hirsch visited the College and paced the corridors, the two men conversed in the language of their Israelite ancestors. Curious students trailed the two notables trying to catch the drift of their Hebraic discussion.

Both Neumark and Levias were particularly eager to publish some of their writings in modern Hebrew. Both as ardent Zionists were devotees of the Jewish national vernacular and contributed to the Hebrew press in Europe as well as in the United States. Levias was one of the group who in 1891 succeeded in producing Hebrew and Yiddish translations of the Declaration of Independence and the Constitution. Three Maskilim who were to make names for themselves were graduates of the Hebrew Union College in the years 1900-1903: Abraham Benedict Rhine and the brothers Jacob and Max Raisin. They remained loyal Hebraists, publishing books and articles on modern Hebrew literature and other subjects. Jacob Raisin (1878-1946) wrote Hebrew articles on English literature, served Charleston's old "Sephardic" Beth Elohim, and married into an eighteenth-century aristocratic family. He was the author of *The Haskalah Movement in Russia* (1913). His younger brother Max, author of the *History of the Jews in Modern Times* (1919), in English, wrote several autobiographical works in Hebrew, among them *Leaves from a Rabbi's Notebook* (*Dappim Mipinkaso shel Rabbi*, 1941). Both Raisins were born in Poland; one of their schoolmates was the Lithuanian Rhine, whose thesis on Judah Leon Gordon, the poet, was probably the first Hebrew Union College rabbinical dissertation to achieve publication (1910); it was followed in 1919 by his five-volume amplified English edition of Graetz's *Popular History of the Jews*. He was a competent Hebraist, beloved by his classmates for his willingness to help them with a difficult passage in the Talmud.[6]

It is quite obvious that modern scientific Hebraic and Judaic scholarship, centered in the rabbinical seminaries and Jewish colleges, was almost exclusively the province of foreign-born Jews, primarily East Europeans. In its early days, Dropsie College sheltered the immigrants Joseph Reider (b.1886), a biblical philologist; Benzion Halper (1884-1924), the gifted Hebraist and Arabist; Henry Malter (1864-1925), editor of a critical edition of a talmudic tractate and the authoritative biography of Saadia, and Max Leopold Margolis (1866-1932), Bible translator and commentator, meticulous student of the Septuagint. Levias, Malter, and Margolis had once taught at the Hebrew Union College; the latter two failed to survive in the Reform atmosphere that completely enveloped that institution when Kaufmann Kohler, the theologian, assumed the presidency. The Russian Solomon Zeitlin (1892-1976) who had come to Dropsie via Paris and New York, was officially professor of rabbinics; actually he was a historian, the acknowledged authority on the intertestamental period, the era of the Second Commonwealth.[7]

The Dropsie alumnus who was to have a more notable career than his professors or classmates was the Lithuanian-born talmudic prodigy Bernard Revel (1885-1940). In 1915 Revel revamped the Rabbi Isaac Elchanan Yeshivah which was in the next decade to become Yeshiva College. It was then also that a number of East Europeans made their initial bow in the scholarly world. They were men who were to become notables in the field of Hebraic studies. Among them was Pinkhos M. Churgin (1894-1957), Hebraist, Aramaic scholar, teacher, and ultimately a founder of Bar-Ilan University in Israel. He helped bring the scientific approach in matters academic to Palestinian Orthodoxy. This was no mean achievement, although the school was to remain ideologically well entrenched in traditional theology. Henry Austryn Wolfson (1887-1974), an historian of philosophy, began teaching at Harvard; Isaac Husik (1876-1939) was beginning to write on Jewish philosophy in English. He taught at Gratz College and the University of Pennsylvania. Revolutions and war in Eastern Europe brought Reuben Brainin, the literary critic and editor, to these shores in 1910; Jacob Mann (1888-1940), the learned scholar who was to reconstruct the unknown history of the medieval Jewish Levant, arrived in 1920. America offered these scholars freedom and opportunity; in return, these men, almost all Russians, Poles, Galicians, Lithuanians and Rumanians, brought America a scientific-critical approach to almost all genres of Hebraic lore. It cannot be overemphasized that their contributions were notable, even imperative, if the United States was to develop as a Jewish cultural center.[8]

HEBREW LITERARY SOCIETIES

It is perhaps advisable to make a distinction between individual belletrists who were primarily interested in furthering their own careers and a not insignificant number of modern Hebraists who were determined to cultivate Hebrew not only as literature but as a medium to attach American youth to ancestral traditions. In order to accomplish their purposes, aficionados had been creating Hebrew literary societies in several large cities ever since 1880. Some of the organizations sponsored lectures in Hebrew and established libraries for their members. One wonders whether these devotees were influenced by the Society for the Promotion of Culture Among the Jews of Russia, which was established in that country in 1863. It is true that the Russian organization was interested in Hebrew and had maskilic support though its prime goal originally was acculturation. The societies created in this country were cultural, separatistic in the sense that they emphasized Hebrew, Judaism, and Jewish literature. In 1883 a Chicago Hebrew literary association set out to elevate Jewry spiritually, stop assimilation, further attachment of the children to Judaic values and, above all, cultivate the Hebrew language to which the group was devoted. The society talked grandiosely of establishing branches in other states; another society with the same goals appeared in Chicago in the 1890's and in Philadelphia in the early 1900's; by World

War I, some of the young members of New York's Dr. Herzl Zion Club, who had matriculated at the Hebrew Union College in Cincinnati, were meeting as a Hebrew-speaking group in that Ohio city. It was on the whole a closed corporation, a New York transplant; no effort was made to teach others to converse in Hebrew.

New York's lovers of modern Hebrew had met together as early as 1880 with the paternal blessing of the Uptown elite, Jacob H. Schiff, Henry Pereira Mendes, and Abram S. Isaacs, of the *Jewish Messenger* clan. They even succeeded in publishing a quarterly *Ha-Meassef*, which, like practically all Hebrew periodicals, was short-lived. By 1917, about a dozen such societies had made their appearance in the metropolis. They set out to sponsor Hebrew periodicals, to further modern Hebrew and to foster the Zionist ideal; their activists were Jewishly nationalist. It is worthy of mention that two of the associations were composed of workers, Poale Zion members; students at City College had their congeries, and there was even a group determined to establish a Hebrew theatre. Various afternoon Hebrew schools in New York boasted of their Hebrew-speaking groups, and there were at least two dozen such clubs in other towns. Evening courses in Hebrew were not uncommon. Perspective is important; in 1917 when there were about 1,500,000 Jews in Greater New York, all these societies could muster but a little over 500 members. Not all Hebrew-speaking Jews were joiners; however, several thousand were at home in the new vernacular and occasionally turned to it as a medium of communication.[9]

By 1916, Jews could look back upon almost forty years of activity in the field of Hebrew literature. Thus it is not surprising that, on the eve of the Balfour Declaration, after a generation of Zionist propaganda and a large number of Hebrew language periodicals and societies, the Hebraists in this country succeeded in founding the Histadruth Ivrith. The title was all encompassing, the Hebrew Organization, but in reality its goals were more limited. This Zionist society set out to federate the Hebrew-speaking groups in this country; it was determined to promote the study and speaking of Hebrew and it had some success. Hebrew as a vernacular was introduced into the afternoon Hebrew schools, into some public high schools of the country, and into some colleges. By 1917, the Histadruth boasted that it had twenty-seven affiliates throughout the country and a total membership of over 1,200. In the Mizrachi Teachers' Training School, an Orthodox institution, the language of instruction was Hebrew exclusively. It is believed that, by the 1950's, about 8,000 students were attending classes in modern Hebrew in New York high schools and colleges. The clubs that were then formed were ultimately federated in the 1950's into a National Hebrew Culture Council. During this decade, over 1,400 colleges were willing to accept Hebrew as a modern language requirement. The devotees of the new vernacular were very sanguine, but, as will be seen later, a strong national Hebrew-speaking movement was not destined to prosper on American soil. There was to be an inverse ratio in this country between the rise of the State of Israel and the flowering of Hebrew-speaking clubs. In the 1980's, the Histadruth insisted that Hebrew must be primary in Jewish life, culture, and education, but that was only a pious hope.[10]

THE HEBREW PRESS

The heart—the soul, too—of the modern Hebrew movement in this country was the press. Here the litterateurs came into their own; American Jewish scholars of East European provenance were completely at home in the Sacred Tongue, but most of them published their monographs in English. The Hebrew societies, however, expressed themselves through the periodicals which they published or patronized; their members were interested primarily in belles lettres, not in learned disquisitions. About 125 Hebrew periodicals were published in this country between 1871 and 1931. Among these Hebrew papers was a Christian missionary journal that began to appear in 1897 and was kept alive to 1898 by its patrons. Very few of the Hebrew journals survived beyond the first few issues. There was a Hebrew paper in Chicago as early as 1877, when a Hebrew supplement was incorporated into a Yiddish periodical. Five Hebrew journals appeared in that city in the next two decades; Pittsburgh and Baltimore, too, could brag that they published a periodical in the Sacred Tongue. Most Hebrew magazines, however, were printed in New York on the East Side where the Jewish masses were to be found. An occasional annual was published; more numerous were the quarterlies, monthlies, and weeklies. At times, the attempt was made to issue a daily, in 1909 and 1921; in the latter year, *The Post* (Hadoar), appeared as a daily, but folded two years later. This country could not or would not support a daily Hebrew newspaper.

What was the nature of these publications? The better papers—and there were some good ones—set out to develop the new Hebrew vernacular, to establish a forum for discussions that would appeal to the younger generation. These journals reached out in all directions; they published poems and stories; they were dedicated to Jewish nationalism, Zionism. The constant growth of the Palestine colonies and the need for a national home encouraged the Hebrew papers to devote themselves to the Herzlian ideal. Some papers dedicated themselves to humor and satire. Because of the interest in better schools and schooling, pedagogy was a recurring topic. Contributors wrote on homiletics, on the Jews in medicine, science, history. Before 1921, and particularly in later decades, there were essayists who wrote on contemporary problems and on Judaism, the religion; Max Raisin, the Maskil and Reform rabbi, insisted that the United States would one day become a center of Jewish culture. Others urged the Hebrew writers to turn for inspiration to the English classics; John Milton must not be ignored. New writers were recruited when deteriorating conditions in early twentieth-century Russia drove gifted immigrants to these shores.

Among the writers of quality was Isaac Dov Berkowitz, who came to these shores in 1913 and helped edit *Ha-Toren* (*The Mast*) and later *Ha-Miklat* (*The Refuge, The Haven*). America was a shelter for many during and after the devastating World War I. *The Mast* first began to appear in 1913, but Berkowitz did not serve as an editor until the years 1916-1919. This was a paper of real literary quality and enjoyed the guidance of almost a dozen notable litterateurs and immigrants. Its issues included fiction, poetry, and essays of import. Neumark wrote on philosophy, Max Raisin on Reform Judaism. Like many other papers it was oriented, of course, to Zionism and for two years was subsidized by the Zionist Organization of America. In 1919, Berkowitz undertook to edit *Ha-Miklat*, which was underwritten by the Jewish philanthropist and publisher, Abraham Joseph Stybel. Despite its auspicious beginnings, it put out but five issues before it came to an end. In 1916, Meir Berlin, an Orthodox Zionist leader, a Mizrachi, transferred *The Hebrew* (*Ha-Ivri*) from Berlin to New York and kept it alive for five years with the help of the Mizrachi Organization of America. Despite the fact that Orthodox sponsorship apparently limited its range of articles, it was an excellent journal.

The editor of the weekly, *Hadoar*, Menachem Ribalow (1895-1953), was to play an important role for the next three decades in America's Modern Hebrew movement. With the aid of the Histadruth Ivrith, he managed to keep the paper alive. This young Russian, who had come here in 1921, was a good newspaperman, an excellent Hebraist who learned to fit into the American milieu without the resentment that characterized many of the older, embittered Maskilim. The paper learned much from the contemporary American press; it published poems, fiction, and comments on problems that confronted the American Jew; with an eye to the religionists, it carried notes on the weekly Bible portions. It was to be and to remain staunchly Zionist. For Ribalow and the Histadruth, Palestine was to be more than a haven for the persecuted; it was hopefully to become a home for the Jewish people, all of them. In later years, *The Post* added a child's supplement, in Hebrew of course. Ribalow edited two jubilee issues, an anthology of Hebrew writers; still another collection of American Hebrew poets was published in Yiddish. Some of his literary essays also appeared in English translation. Ribalow was utterly devoted to Hebraic culture; it was his conviction that without this treasured language there could be no national culture, no Jewish people.[11]

WHY THE HEBREW PRESS FAILED

There can be no question: the Hebrew press in America was not successful. The reasons for this failure are not hard to find. Most of the editors—not all of them—were incompetent; they were not businessmen; publishing is also a business. On the whole the Hebrew style employed was good; it was simple, intelligible, devoid of neologisms. But these Hebrew periodicals that began appearing in 1871 were not mass publications; they were literary instruments. Most Jews could not understand Hebrew and they had no real interest in it. And even those immigrants who were Hebraists—there were thousands—were struggling to make a living. The price of a paper would buy two loaves of bread.

Subscribers were few. Were it not for the generosity of literary patrons like Israel Matz (Ex-Lax Company), S. Lamport (textiles) and Abraham Joseph Stybel, some magazines would never have seen the light of day. Another generous philanthropist was Louis M. Rabinowitz who made a fortune in corsets, dress trimmings, and some happy investments. He was very much interested in Jewish culture, the fine arts, and archaeology. Hebrew literary societies subsidized some journals, but their funds were inadequate. Of all the writers before 1921, it is very doubtful whether even one made a living from his pen as a Hebraist. As a vernacular, Hebrew had no future in the United States; Yiddish and English were the languages of the masses. The Hebrew journals had no American message; they looked backward to an ancient Palestine or forward to a new Palestine that was still a dream. Most of these ephemeral magazines did little or nothing to bond the Jew to his new home, to an America which meant everything to the Jew who was determined to remain here. Though in the decades of the 1920's and beyond there were writers who were more America-oriented, it was no easy task to prepare a people to speak a new tongue or to create a literature for a land yet to be born. The best of the papers struggled desperately to stay alive. In the years between 1913 and 1925, *Ha-Toren* had several series of editors and four different sponsors. Despite the exaggerated claims made for some of the papers, not one of them, it would seem, had more than 2,000 subscribers before the advent of *Hadoar* as a weekly in the 1920's. Years later when the State of Israel rose and the Tel-Aviv daily newspapers could be flown over in a few days, the American Hebrew press appeared doomed; it has a well populated graveyard.[12]

THE SUCCESSES OF THE HEBREW JOURNALS

Failure is a relative term. It was a source of pride, fierce exultant pride for the Maskilim that they were able to publish a magazine of their own in Hebrew, even though all of these individual forays ended in bitter futility. The dozens of periodicals that now grace the shelves of a few national libraries are important sources for the American Jewish cultural historian. Zionism was fostered by practically all writers; Jewish traditions were treated reverently, and this is most important—the new Hebrew literature was kept alive here till it found a more receptive home in the young Jewish republic on the shores of the Mediterranean.[13]

HEBREW LITERATURE IN THE UNITED STATES: BEGINNINGS

There was a Hebrew literature in the United States long before there was a Hebrew press. Wherever there was a community there were services in Hebrew; someone—if only the hazzan—had some familiarity with the prayer book and with the traditional literature. Such Hebraists were to be found in New York City ever since the late seventeenth century. These cognoscenti then were not necessarily East European Jews; indeed few— if any—were. There was actually Hebrew literature in the colonies before the Jews came. Some of the Pilgrim Fathers knew the basic elements of Hebrew, although it would be a mistake to overestimate the Hebraic knowledge of these Christian pioneers and their successors. The language of the Hebrew Bible was revered; it was taught in colonial colleges, but there were few men who had more than a reading knowledge of the tongue. There is some evidence that Isaac Miranda, who had settled in Pennsylvania not later than 1715, was a competent Hebraist; this convert to Christianity had a Hebrew library of sorts. Another convert, the Italian immigrant Judah Monis, had written and published a grammar of the Hebrew tongue at Boston in 1735. From this time on, born Jews—converts to Christianity and Torah adherents alike—continued to write and publish Hebrew grammars in antebellum America; they were designed for sale to Christians primarily. When, in 1786, Gershom Seixas married for the second time, an admirer of his wrote a Hebrew acrostic poem lauding him and his beloved Hannah. Later functionaries at Shearith Israel wrote Hebrew verse to enhance the services on ceremonial occasions. The tombstone of Walter J. Judah, who died of the yellow fever in 1798, bears a poetical epitaph in the sacred tongue, but there is reason to believe that this inscription and the tomb itself were prepared abroad and shipped to the United States.

By the 1820's, New York and Philadelphia Jews had begun preparing and publishing various editions of the Hebrew prayer rites. Leeser, Sephardic Philadelphia's hazzan, published not only versions of the Sephardic and Ashkenazic prayers, but also a Hebrew Reader and editions of both the Pentateuch and the Bible in the original tongue—all this in the 1830's, 1840's, and 1850's. By then, the officiating hazzanim were reenforced by immigrants from Central Europe, teachers and ordained rabbis, who were competent Hebraists. Several were able, when the need rose, to write commemorative verse. These learned men—Abraham Rice, Isaac M. Wise, Isidor Kalisch, Bernard Illowy, Bernhard Felsenthal—settled in the United States in the 1840's and 1850's. By 1849, Leeser was already printing Hebrew communications, original prayers, and letters in his *Occident*. In 1854, an Hebraist rose to the defense of Isaac M. Wise in Hebrew verse. By 1859, Isaac Goldstein had written a Hebrew poem in honor of a Louisville, Kentucky, congregation; Jacob Mordecai Netter, a traveler, wrote and dedicated some Hebrew poems to friends and benefactors whom he had met in San Francisco. Later, in 1865, Goldstein praised the martyred President Lincoln in an acrostic poem stressing his emancipation of America's blacks. A cantor who served in New York and Baltimore, Moses Aaron Schreiber, wrote a poetical history of the United States from the adoption of the Constitution and a centennial ode commemorating the Declaration of Independence.[14]

EAST EUROPEANS AND HEBREW LITERATURE, 1860-CA.1910

East European Jews had been filtering into the United States in some numbers since the early nineteenth century. Conscription, civil and political disabilities, despotism pushed them to emigrate; liberties and immunities here induced many to come. Even the ghetto denizens knew that America spelt opportunity. This image had been established in the European Yiddish and Hebrew literature at an early date. By the 1850's, there was a distinctive Slavic Jewish community in New York City. By 1860, a scholarly wanderer had already published a commentary on the mishnaic tractate *Fathers*, the *Avne Yehoshua* (*Stones of Joshua*) of Joshua Falk. This was the first Hebrew rabbinic work published in America; it appeared 211 years after the first Jew landed in Boston; by 1921, when the portals were closing to East European refugees, dozens of rabbinic works had already been written and published by Jews of Russian, Polish, and Rumanian origins. In 1867, when Albert Cardozo, father of United States Supreme Court Justice Benjamin Nathan Cardozo, presented his name as a candidate for the New York State Supreme Court, his friends printed an election circular in Hebrew asking Jews to vote for him. Obviously, this was an appeal to learned East Europeans; there was even a Cardozo political club in those days when Tammany was in the saddle. That same decade Elijah Holzman published a brochure in Hebrew damning the Reform Jews; attacks on Reform were nearly always *de rigueur* for aspiring Hebrew litterateurs and journalists. The Reformers were resented as successful acculturated businessmen who looked down upon the neo-Hebraic litterateurs. The Reform rabbis, relatively prosperous, were envied and denounced. By the 1870's, a substantial number of Maskilim, at least a dozen, lived here. Most of them had begun their literary careers abroad; all of them were to continue writing on these shores. They were poets, prose writers, editors of neo-Hebraic journals. One was to edit America's first modern Hebrew journal; another was to prepare a Hebrew translation of a work on American history; a third, James H. (Jacob Zevi) Soble, issued a thirty-six page brochure of Hebrew and Yiddish poems, the first such publication in this country; he called it *A Golden Song in Honor of Israel of Old* (1877). In another of his writings, Sobel gloried that he now lived in a land of freedom:

> Tho I have but only a cent
> My son may yet be president.

He loved Hebrew, but was less than enthusiastic about Yiddish as a literary vehicle; it was a "jargon." This prejudice against the vernacular of the masses was common among the Enlighteners. A writer, Leon (Abraham Judah Loeb) Horowitz (1847-1926), spent three years in this country before returning to Europe. There, in 1874, he wrote two pamphlets urging Rumanian Jews to emigrate to America. Important is the second half of his work, in which he described this country and, implicitly, the opportunities here. This guide book was obviously sponsored by steamship and railroad companies. Horowitz bragged about his pure, easy style; indeed, the book was well written. Before coming to America, he had studied with renowned scholars in Vienna and Paris.[15]

The Russians came in large numbers. The pogroms frightened them; later, many emigrated because it was the style to come to America. Life was no bed of roses under the Romanovs, and in Austrian Galicia and Rumania, too, poverty was the hallmark of both village and town Jews. A sizable minority of the newcomers were interested in the new Hebraic literature. Abraham Cahan used to visit the owner of a tobacco shop who had established a salon for Hebraists in his small simple apartment behind the store. The pious Hungarian Moses Weinberger wrote of New York's lovers of Hebrew who eked out a living as teachers, peddlers, or petty businessmen. One way or another, these learned men managed to survive. Alexander Harkavy (1863-1939) had a flair for the literary and academic. At fourteen, back in Russia, he had "published" a handwritten journal. Here in America after his arrival in 1882, he worked on a farm, took a job as a manual laborer, taught Hebrew, founded pre-Herzlian Zionist societies, wrote for the English, Hebrew, and Yiddish journals, and published a series of manuals, dictionaries, vocabularies, phrase books, and letter writers in at least five languages, including Hebrew, of course. Included in his writings were Yiddish biographies of Washington and Columbus. By 1903, he had already penned an autobiography. He was best known for a two-volume Hebrew-English-Yiddish dictionary. One of the well-known Russian Jewish Hebraists of the 1880's was Henry Gersoni (1844-1897), who had come to New York in 1869. He was an exceptionally able man. In his relatively brief life, he played many roles. He was a rabbi, journalist, editor of German and English papers, a research worker for Ph.D. students, a translator of stories from the Russian, and an occasional apostate. He wrote engagingly in English, Yiddish, and Hebrew. Indeed, in the early 1870's, he had been an editor of one of the first Yiddish papers in the United States. Longfellow thanked him for his Hebrew translation of "Excelsior." When Gersoni first landed, he was hired to teach in Temple Emanu-El's Sabbath school, though he had no particular love for Reform Judaism. In 1874, he was called to serve as the rabbi of the Reformist temple in Atlanta; the congregants were pleased with his services as spiritual leader and as the principal of a private Hebrew school which he conducted. In his later years, he served no congregation; his dubious past as a man who had played fast and loose with his religion caught up with him. There were other Hebraists of questionable religious loyalties in the decades before the turn of the century. America received them all; frontier America was not quick to denounce or persecute backsliders.[16]

By the turn of the century there were a number of trans-Vistula émigrés here writing Hebrew poetry. This is no surprise to the historian for there were 250,000 Jews in the city, most of them Orthodox immigrants from Europe's East. Some of these poets were writers of quality. Isaac Rabbinowitz, a man in his late forties when he fled from Russia, published several volumes of good Hebrew verse in the 1890's. In a poem lauding those of his congregants who had the courage to continue their rabbinic studies, Rabbi Abraham Braude, of Chicago, deplored the materialism of his generation, reminding them that "learning was better than earning." In distant Waxahachie, a village county seat south of Dallas, a Jewish poet wrote an acrostic poem dedicated to one of Texas's pioneer Jews, a member of the Mittenthal family; this was in 1892, when all of Texas sheltered fewer than 10,000 Jewish souls. It was a decade when even educated Central Europeans were cultivating the Hebrew muse. Moses Mielziner, of the Hebrew Union College, and Gustave Gottheil, of New York's Temple Emanu-El, were writing anniversary and congratulatory poems; Mielziner genuflected in the direction of the leaders of the Reform movement; Gottheil wrote a poem in honor of a Christian friend.[17]

Menahem Mendel Dolitzky (1856-1931) was the most famous Hebrew poet to settle in this country. When he came here in 1892 or 1893, he was already a poet of repute; Judah Leon Gordon, one of Russia's leading Hebrew litterateurs, had already saluted him as a man of the future. As with most Russian Enlighteners, America added nothing to his stature; if anything his artistic creativity tended to decline. His *Songs of Menahem*, his Hebrew poems, were published here largely through the generosity of a Baltimore German Jewish clothing manufacturer who even permitted this Zionist to take up a collection for his cause in his factory. Not infrequently the German Jewish elite supported the publication and writings of Maskilim. Samuel Benjamin Schwarzberg, one of the editors of *Ner Ha-Maaravi*, was given financial aid by a number of Reform rabbis, including Isaac M. Wise. Schwarzberg's friends reproached him for seeking aid for the magazine from Reform Jews, the enemy. It was difficult for Dolitzky to write of the glories of Zion when he had to struggle for a livelihood in a garment factory, a cafeteria, or a private school hammering Hebrew into indifferent youngsters. In desperation, he, like others, turned to Yiddish journalism, to the writing of serialized sensational romances for teamsters and domestic servants. "The Educated Murderer" was one of the dozens of thrillers that he ground out. He was a bitter, unhappy man, disillusioned as he peddled some of his writings. He had brought his Hebrew wares to the wrong market; he died in poverty.[18]

When Dolitzky came to the United States, he began writing for the Hebrew magazine *Ha-Ivri* (*The Hebrew*), whose editor was Gerson Rosenzweig (1861-1914), a native of the Russian province of Grodno. By 1888, Rosenzweig had moved on to New York and, like his literary confreres, tried his hand at a host of jobs in order to keep body and soul together; he peddled, kept books, ran a shoestore and a restaurant, and of course taught Hebrew. Like Dolitzky, he, too, became a Yiddish journalist: all this to make a living; his forte was a wry bitter humor. He has been called the "Sweet Satirist of Israel," a pun on 2 Samuel 23:1, where David is called "The Sweet Singer of Israel." This poet and prose parodist wrote a mock talmudic tractate poking fun at the immigrants, highlighting their sufferings in the land of opportunity. His *Tractate America* in the Yankee Talmud is clever; it still makes interesting reading. Modeling himself on the first of King David's Psalms, Rosenzweig wrote: "Blessed is the man that walkest not in the council of scholars, nor standeth in the way of the enlightened, nor sitteth in the seat of the learned, but his delight is money and in the accumulation of wealth does he meditate day and night." Rosenzweig's parody of the first of The Ten Commandments bitterly indicts America of the Gilded Age: "I, Mammon, am the Lord thy God who has brought thee out of thy fatherland, where thou wast a sand carrier, a chimney sweep, a vagabond, a swindler, an informer, a traitor, a horse thief, and have brought thee here into the land of gold to become a president of a synagog, a merchant, a landlord, and a politician." This was written in an age when cultured Jews and Gentiles, too, looked down with disgust on Yankees as vulgar, ill-mannered, whisky-drinking, tobacco-chewing cheats. This Maskil delighted in epigrams. The following is typical: "Alas, I lost a dear friend. Did he die? Nay, he became rich."

Yet, this dismayed critic of the American Jewish ghetto scene was apparently a patriot; he made Hebrew translations of three of the country's best-known national songs: "America," "Columbia, the Gem of the Ocean," and "The Star-Spangled Banner."[19]

The year that brought Rosenzweig to the United States also witnessed the arrival of the learned William (Wolf Zeev) Schur (1844-1910), journalist, novelist, apologete, and political Zionist. After spending years in rabbinic studies in Russia, Schur moved on to Berlin where he studied at the liberal Jewish seminary. Later, he traveled to the Far East and recorded his impressions in the European Hebrew press and in two special volumes which were published before he settled in the United States. When he came here—a mature man—he began publishing a Hebrew magazine of high quality, *Ha-Pisgah, The Summit.* His journal followed him wherever he settled, in New York, Baltimore, Chicago. Modern Hebrew literature was important to him; he hoped it would serve to unite the Jewish people. As he indicated on the title page of Ha-Pisgah, he was interested in politics and the humanities, in Jews and in Judaism. Undoubtedly, in his cultural and Zionist objectives, he was influenced by his friend and mentor Hermann Zevi Schapira, whom he met in Germany where Schapira spent several years before starting on his travels to Egypt, India, China, and the Philippines.

Schur, a man of convictions, developed a rounded-out Jewish program reflected in his writings, especially in his historicoreligious *Nezah Yisrael*, which was published at Chicago in 1896-1897. The book title, *The Eternity of Israel*, reflects his belief that Judaism was eternal and superior. The education of American Jewish youth must be based on Torah, yet reenforced by secular studies. Young Jewish children must be schooled, not given over to peddling on the streets and slaving in the sweatshops. The academic and spiritual standards of the East European Jews must be raised. Yiddish threatened the role of Hebrew. In this unrealistic approach, Schur was a typical Enlightener. Reform Judaism offered no answer; it was assimilationist. Similarly, he had no sympathy for the Jewish Marxists, nor for Christianity. Though Schur was a political Zionist, one of the first, he was wary of the Rev. Mr. Blackstone's efforts to restore the Jew to his ancient homeland. Quite correctly, Schur assumed that a missionary conversionist intent was not absent—and, indeed, Blackstone hoped as a good Christian that, once the Jews had been restored, Jesus Christ would usher in the millennium. *The Eternity of Israel* was written at the time that Herzl was writing and publishing his *Jewish State.* Schur, too, wanted a Jewish state, but more than Herzl he wanted it based on the Hebrew language and the moral message of the biblical heroes. Like Ahad Ha-Am, who was then preaching his gospel, Schur looked to a Zion which would be more than a purely political state; for

Schur it was also to be a religious center; he sought spiritual redemption as well as political salvation.[20]

SOME REFLECTIONS ON THE AMERICAN JEWISH "ENLIGHTENMENT" MOVEMENT

When the twentieth century was ushered in, the American Haskalah, the modern Hebrew Enlightenment Movement, had a history here that went back for at least thirty years. Its impact on the East Europeans in the United States was minimal. The article on the "Maskil" in *The Jewish Encyclopedia* of 1904 gave the American Haskalah seven lines; the *American Jewish Year Book* that year included about two dozen East European Hebrew literary worthies among its biographical sketches; these men—and one woman, too—described themselves as writers, Hebrew teachers, and authors; one called himself a merchant. They would have preferred to be known as poets, essayists, satirists, literary historians, belletrists, journalists. They had hoped to be supported generously on this cultural frontier. They were disappointed. Frustrated and embittered, they moved to attack. They were critical not only of the native-born and the German Jewish establishment, but also of the East Europeans who ignored them. They poured forth their wrath on the newcomers for their vulgarity, their materialism, their greed, their worship of the Golden Calf. The Maskilim failed to understand that Haskalah—the cultivation of the Hebrew language and literature—had little or no appeal to a bright boy who had his eyes on New York's tuition-free City College. They had expected to be honored if only as the clever Hebraists they were. The talmudists who came here often nursed the same hopes; both groups were egregiously disappointed. Perhaps not a real exemplar of the rejected Maskil, but a symbol, nevertheless, was Naphtali Herz Imber (1856-1909), a poet, "Bohemian," drunkard, author of the Jewish national anthem "The Hope," "Ha-Tikvah," the hope for a return to Palestine. This poet came to the United States in 1892, the same year that witnessed Dolitzky's arrival. The expulsion of Jews from Moscow in the early 1890's convinced many that, short of revolution, there was indeed no future for them in the Romanov Empire. Imber, a native Galician, received an excellent Hebrew education and then began his "travels" throughout Europe. It was in Rumania or Palestine that he wrote "Ha-Tikvah," which appeared in a volume of his Hebrew poems (1885-1886). Soon set to music it was exceedingly popular in Zionist circles, and finally became the official national anthem. Imber was an early political Zionist whose interest in Palestine colonization anticipated that of the Lovers of Zion of the early 1880's. While wandering about Europe, Imber met Laurence Oliphant, the English writer, entrepreneur, mystic, and would-be Palestine colonizer, and lived on his largesse for several years before moving on to England and the United States.

Here in the United States, Imber speedily emerged as a populist and something of a left-wing liberal, expounding his views in a pamphlet which he wrote. Moses, he said, had been a social reformer, a populist, a single taxer. Jesus, too, was a political radical; the capitalists executed him. Jerusalem fell because of a civil war between the proletariat and the monied classes. This shiftless, luckless wight wandered hobo-like all over the country from Boston to San Francisco. Judge Mayer Sulzberger gave him a small stipend, enough to keep him alive—or in drink—but personally kept him at arm's length. Imber was in no sense an admirable character. On the occasion of his fiftieth birthday, he wrote an English poem, doggerel at its worst, in which he attacked false friends, physicians, and all rabbis. He selected the Reform Jewish clergy for a very special animus, promising to serve them pork chops at his birthday dinner. He did a Hebrew translation of Edward Fitzgerald's "Rubaiyat of Omar Khayyam" which he aptly called "The Cup." Samuel Francis Smith, Baptist clergyman and author of "America," had made money autographing copies of his national anthem; Imber, bragging that he was the Jewish National Poet, exploited his authorship of "The Hope," but always remained a hapless alcoholic. In this, he resembled Stephen Collins Foster, who sold his songs for a drink or two and died in the charity ward of a hospital. Imber fared somewhat better; thousands of East Siders turned out for his funeral.[21]

America's Modern Hebrew Literati in the Early Twentieth Century

World War I effectually disrupted the development of modern Hebrew and its literature in Eastern Europe; within a few years, the dominant Marxists destroyed the Hebraic movement in Russia. In America and the nascent Jewish Palestine, however, Hebrew literature could be cultivated. Indeed, there were no other important nurseries. America was to become an asylum for writers who loved the language of their ancestors. Originally, in the czarist empire, Hebrew had been deemed an instrument to introduce Western culture and civilization to benighted Jews who were still medieval in their knowledge of the arts and sciences. In nineteenth-century America, the literary Hebraists, operating primarily through their journals and occasional writings, emphasized Hebrew as a separatist device to keep Jews Jewish, to bind them together. Some were protagonists of the language for its own sake; by the early twentieth century—certainly by the end of World War I—there was a new breed of writers here; they were concerned with Hebrew as a literature, pure and simple. They were belletrists, not cultural or Zionist propagandists. Despite the increasing persecutions in Russia and Poland, these newcomers had enjoyed educational advantages at home; they were in touch with the best cultural traditions of the Western world. Their interest in Hebrew was highlighted by the rise of Zionism, which had determined on Hebrew as the national language of the new homeland. After the Balfour Declaration of 1917, when the rise of a Jewish commonwealth appeared imminent, the Hebrew language was cultivated intensively; many, influenced by Ahad Ha-Am, were interested in furthering a Palestinian Jewish culture of spiritual, moral, and ethical quality.

ANGLO-SAXON INFLUENCES

By the end of World War I, a new school of literary craftsmen had made its appearance here. These Hebrew writers—poets, for the most part— were not uprooted dejected émigrés. Some of them had come here as youngsters; one, Reuben Grossman-Avinoam, was a native American. They were American in spirit; they loved this country and what it stood for at its best. A number of them had received their secular education in this land; one sang of Columbia his alma mater. True, they were Zionists; they were also Americans who wrote Hebrew verse. To be sure, there were nineteenth-century Maskilim who had been highly Americanistic and had translated Longfellow, the Declaration of Independence, and the Constitution, but these early writers had not been consciously Americanistic. The new generation was deeply rooted in English and American literature; it knew and loved Shakespeare, Milton, Coleridge, Byron, Keats and Shelley, Tennyson, Dickens, Wordsworth, Poe, Whitman, and later Frost, too. These writers translated English and American classics into Hebrew and made them all available to a new generation in Palestine and Israel. It is not surprising, therefore, that some of the most gifted Hebrew belletrists here wrote with sympathy of the lore and the plight of the Indian natives and the blacks. With the rise of the United States to world power, East European men of letters settled here; Hebraic literature flowered, albeit modestly. There were numerous writers of competence and devotion who had their followers and were admired by the knowledgeable. These literati, all immigrants, reached out to work in all genres; they were poets, essayists, novelists, translators from the English—and the Greek, too—editors, journalists, literary critics, teachers and administrators in Jewish schools and colleges. Among these writers was Rebecca Annetta Altman, who had received an excellent Hebrew education in her native Lithuania. In Steubenville, Ohio, she wrote in Hebrew for Rosenzweig's *Ha-Ivri* and published translations from the German, Yiddish, and Hebrew. She was of course in no sense typical.[22]

Literary judgments are inevitably relative and subjective, yet most historians and critics of early twentieth-century Hebrew literature in the United States agree that some of the belletrists made contributions of import to modern Hebrew literature. Among them were Isaac Dov Berkowitz (1885-1967), Benjamin Nahum Silkiner (1882-1933), Ephraim E. Lisitzky (1885-1962), and Israel Isaac Efros (1891-1981). These men had much in common. They developed high literary standards; they overcame the hazards and avoided the roadblocks that had crushed the early American Maskilim; they succeeded in carving out careers as Hebrew-writing litterateurs. As a man of letters, Berkowitz may well have been the ablest of this new breed. He was a short story writer, a novelist, and a translator into Hebrew of the Yiddish writings of his distinguished father-in-law, Sholem Aleichem. Though, as pointed out above, he was an editor of *Ha-Toren* for only three years and of *Miklat* for about five issues, he established literary standards which were to serve as a pattern for his admirers. One of the editors of *The Mast* (*Ha-Toren*) before Berkowitz took the reins in his hands, was Benjamin Nahum Silkiner (Silk), a Russian who came here at the age of twenty-two, young enough to become thoroughly Americanized. Silkiner, Lisitzky, and Efros were completely oriented toward the life, culture, and mores of this country. The latter two landed on these shores when still youngsters.

Silkiner, the poet, wrote an epic about the sufferings of the Indians under the Spanish in early colonial days. He emphasized American, native themes in his writings. Like his contemporaries Lisitzky and Efros, he, too, translated Shakespeare into Hebrew. The English bard had become part of their cultural heritage. Silkiner's poem on the early Indians, written in 1910, was titled "Before the Tent of Timmurah"; Lisitzky, a generation later, wrote "Dying Campfires," conceived in the unrhymed trochaic tetrameter familiar to his fellow Americans through Longfellow's Indian epic, "Hiawatha." This American Jewish poet had studied at a yeshivah in Russia and before he found himself had been a socialist, an Enlightener, a Zionist, and a pharmaceutical chemist. Young Lisitzky came to grips with himself in this New World, writing of themes that appealed to him as an American. He settled down in New Orleans as the principal of a communal Hebrew school and for decades published prolifically in Hebrew, poems, essays, and translations. Living in the Deep South, surrounded by blacks, it was almost inevitable that he would write a poem, "In the Tents of Cush" (Ethiopia), in which he mirrored what he had learned of the legends and traditions of his black neighbors. His Hebrew autobiography, in which he described his struggle to find himself as a litterateur, was translated into English and appeared in 1959; it was entitled *In the Grip of Cross-Currents*.

Israel Efros (1891-1981) was another member of this new generation who set out successfully to make a place for himself as a literary craftsman. He wrote for *Ha-Toren* in its early days, helped compile an English-Hebrew dictionary, and, like Silkiner and Lisitzky, wrote a Hebrew epic on the American Indians: *Silent Wigwams*. He was also the author of "Gold," a poem on the California of 1849. Efros, who had come to this country as a fourteen-year-old lad, became a respected academician; he helped found the Baltimore Hebrew College, enjoyed a fellowship at Johns Hopkins, and taught at a number of American colleges. As a scholar, his forte was medieval philosophy. Efros was to continue his editorial work for the rest of his life, probably the only Jew in America to live by his pen as a Hebraist. He was a publicist, essayist, and above all a literary critic. Among the books which he wrote or edited were a Hebrew annual and an anthology of American Hebrew writers. Some of his essays were translated into English. The Histadruth Ivrith of America, the national society dedicated to the furtherance of the Hebrew language and literature, elected him its vice-president.

As reflected in the careers of men like Berkowitz, Silkiner, Lisitzky, Efros, and others, too, there were Hebrew belletrists who made a name for themselves in the decades following World War I. After a few years, these men enjoyed positions of repute, if not of profit; they were successful writers. Yet, as intimated above, this upsurge of Hebrew belles lettres was to decline precipitously in the second half of the twentieth century. The new State of Israel seriously impaired this movement. Berkowitz had moved on to Palestine in 1928; Efros emigrated in the 1950's. Israel during the 1970's was to become a state of some 3,000,000 Jews; its literature flourished; Hebrew was native to the country. Talented Hebraists in the United States settled in the Promised Land. Here in America transoceanic flight brought Hebraists their favorite Israeli newspapers and periodicals in a matter of days. The United States will hardly prosper in the future as a Hebrew literary center. This is a great Jewry of over 5,000,000 souls; though thousands here read and understand the new Hebrew, Hebrew literature will not flourish in this land. Hebrew as such is daily becoming more important, more vital. Due to Zionism, to the Israeli state, to a rapidly mounting devotion to Hebraism, Judaism, and scientific studies, hundreds of American scholars were and are working in areas that require a knowledge of Hebrew. The Holocaust, the rejection of Jewry by Gentiles, Jewish resentment directed at a Christian world that tolerated the massacre of millions by the Germans have prompted Jews of today to turn to the study of the language and history of their people.

MORE REFLECTIONS ON THE AMERICAN HASKALAH

Of all the numerous Hebrew language periodicals that made their appearance between 1870 and the 1920's not one proved successful. There were very few Hebrew readers; the leading European Hebrew magazine, *Ha-Shiloah*, it was said, had but ten subscribers in all of New York; Hebrew writers here could not make a living by their pen. A correspondent in *Hamelitz* in 1894 pointed out that there were then about twenty Yiddish periodicals in this country, but only one Hebrew paper (*Ha-Ivri*) managed to stay alive. One could make a living as a Yiddishist the Maskilim discovered when they were reduced by necessity to writing for the "Jargon" press; many of them deeply resented successes in the use of Yiddish, a tongue which they affected to despise; they revered Hebrew. The Sacred Tongue, however, could not compete with English and Yiddish as a literary instrument; these were living languages used by millions; modern Hebrew was an artificial creation, an import from benighted Eastern Europe. There was, of course, use for Hebrew in this country; it was the language of prayer in the synagog; talmudic, rabbinic, and legal code studies had relevance for the Orthodox masses; scholars in the new seminaries needed and used Hebrew as they pursued scientific criticohistorical investigations into the Jewish past. Of all that was written in Hebrew in American magazines from 1870 to 1910, there is little, if anything, of quality that will find a place in the treasury of world Jewish literature. Indeed, it remains to be determined if the truly literary figures who dotted the American landscape from 1910 to 1950 have produced any piece of poetry or prose that will elicit the admiration of tomorrow's Hebrew readers. Who has written anything that will live as a classic?[23]

What did the early transplanted Enlighteners accomplish in a land that already knew a high degree of secular enlightenment? As Hebraists, they could not afford to devote themselves to American culture. Instead, they tended to ignore it; American Jewry in turn ignored them and their brave little periodicals, many of which died aborning. Since their potential readers were nearly all immigrants from the Slavic lands—Jews with an Orthodox background—the Maskilim here aligned themselves with the traditionalists at a time when Judaism in the United States was moving to the left. The early Enlighteners here did not confront acculturation constructively; they turned away from the very problem that faced every Jewish newcomer. Culturally and spiritually they vented their anger on the East Europeans who would not help them and on the prosperous Reformers who were not even aware of their existence. By contrast, the new writers who made their appearance between the two world wars were Americanizers, conscious of the need for literary standards. Coming here as young men, they could not escape their American milieu; indeed they yearned to embrace it. They constituted a cultural enclave which found solace in its own creation. They were devoted lovers of the new Hebrew medium; the pursuit and development of the new literature was its own reward; they had their raison d'être. Increasingly, the writers after World War I reflect the influence of Anglo-American literature; the translations they made of the classic writings of England and America have benefited thousands of readers in Israel and all Diaspora lands. They have channeled the English literary tradition into the mainstream of Hebraism. They are a link in that chain which goes back 2,000 years, a chain which found Jews absorbing the best in the Hellenic and Arab cultures. The latter-day Hebraists—those who began to write and teach after 1910—made their mark in the Jewish educational field. They are the men who later brought modern Hebrew into the public high schools, the afternoon Talmud To-rahs, the all-day schools, the teachers' institutions, the Jewish colleges, and the American universities. This is no small thing. For thousands of Jewish boys and girls in the post-1920 period, the Hebrew they acquired was important not only because of its intrinsic cultural value, but because it served as a prime instrument of identification; the youngsters knew that they were Jews.

It is to the credit of the early Maskilim in the United States that they cultivated Hebrew; few others did. Hebrew was a bond that tied all Jews together in all lands; these pioneers prepared the ground for the next generation of Hebraists who were not inchoate propagandists, but men of letters. By the 1940's when the State of Israel arose, there may have been as many as 100 of these craftsmen writing in this country, fostering Hebrew as a language and as a literature. They were a group apart. In the face of insuperable odds, these devotees had chosen modern Hebraic culture as their way of life, as their contribution to Jewish survival. The Reformers had their liberal theology and their critical Jewish scholarship; the Orthodox and the Conservatives were determined to live through the synagog, kashrut, the Sabbath, the Talmud and its thousand-year-old literature; the Zionists held fast to the vision of an autonomous political homeland.

To repeat, these neo-Maskilim embraced the Hebrew language and its invitation to enter the republic of letters. It was these new men, here in a budding Hebraic center, who held the fort till an indigenous literature began to develop in Jerusalem and Tel-Aviv. Their efforts here contributed to the stimulation of nationalism and the intensification of Jewish loyalties. Basing themselves on the Bible, on modern East European poets and writers, on the earlier American Maskilim, the post-World War I literary craftsmen were in the process of creating a corpus of poetry and prose that reflected strong American influences. The rise of the State of Israel and the emergence there of gifted belletrists tended to hamper the development of a Hebrew cultural center on American soil. The writers who remained here continued to cultivate Hebrew and succeeded in raising up disciples; some are native Americans. If Israel ever experiences severe political economic reverses, if its cultural advances are halted in any degree, American Jewish Hebraic literati will emerge ever stronger. United States Jewry may then well become a Hebraic cultural center of quality.[24]

RELIGIOUS EDUCATION

RELIGIOUS SCHOOLS FOR THE EAST EUROPEANS

The East European Jews who came to New York in the early 1880's were determined to remain Jewish. They were concerned about the future of their faith here in this strange land. This meant, as far as they were concerned, that they would have to educate their children in Hebrew. They would have to employ rebbes, melammeds, to come to their homes or they would have to send their children to Hebrew schools, all-day or afternoon schools. There was no need to introduce these instructional media; in general, the rebbes, the all-day school, and the afternoon classes—after public school was over—had all been characteristic of American Jewry since the eighteenth century. The newcomers of the 1880's merely continued and adapted what they found here. In essence, the system differed little from what had characterized their East European home towns. Adult education? Study of the Psalms and rabbinic literature in conventicles? That, too, had been established here no later than the 1850's, probably earlier. European Hebrew magazines were read here, though, to be sure, the subscribers were pitifully few; there had been Hebrew printers and booksellers here since antebellum days.

It is no exaggeration to maintain that in almost every town, large or small, there were immigrants interested in intellectual advancement, whether in matters religious or secular. A few examples will clarify this statement. A substantial number of the "Russian" synagogs sheltered adult groups which met to study Psalms or Mishnah, Gemara (Talmud), or the *En Yaakov*, the non-legal portions of the Talmud. When, in 1883, a branch of the New York City YMHA was established Downtown, Eisenstein, an ardent devotee of Hebrew, gave it 400 books and subscribed for one year for the European Hebrew periodicals. Philadelphians, eager to further themselves culturally, set up the Hebrew Literature Society in 1885. They had their own rented quarters, a large library, and an ambitious lecture and social program. They were not parochial in their tastes, for they listened to lectures in English by Orthodox and Reform rabbis and by Morris Jastrow, Jr., a young Jewish Semitics scholar who had received his doctorate from the University of Leipzig. Like the Philadelphians, the Chicagoans, too, early established their Self-Educational Club. Apparently they were even more latitudinarian in their tastes than the Philadelphians, for they listened to Jane Addams and Jenkin Lloyd Jones, the Liberal Christian minister. Not to be outdone, the Marxists in their Jewish Workingmen's Educational Club invited a number of speakers, all with different views. Pittsburgh's newcomers enjoyed English lectures on general themes, which they heard at the Irene Kaufmann Settlement House. The left-wingers edified their followers in Yiddish at the local Jewish Workmen's Circle Labor Lyceum; enthusiastic Yiddishists came to hear Sholem Aleichem, the writer, who had settled in this country; the Zionists propagandized for their cause in lecture courses; the traditionalists, as in New York, Philadelphia, and Chicago, swayed over the pages of the Talmud. Occasionally, too, on a Saturday afternoon a literate woman would gather some Jewish women about her and read biblical tales from a standard Yiddish work. There were intellectual delights and challenges for every Jew.[1]

THE ITINERANT REBBE

Substantial numbers of children in the large cities were taught by rebbes, itinerant teachers who went from house to house. Often the rebbe carried a prayer book (siddur) under his arm. The standard siddur published in the United States had a few introductory pages with the Hebrew alphabet and the vowels. It did double duty, serving also as a textbook for beginners learning to read the language. There were a few competent rebbes among these men who peddled their sacred wares; no two teachers were alike among these instructors, who can be traced back to the early eighteenth century in colonial New York. One thing they all had in common: they were poor. Most of them had failed to make a living in trade; wandering from home to home, giving lessons, was the last resort of these luckless indigents. They were not brutal; this the parents in the home would not tolerate. In the 1880's, they were paid as little as 10 cents a week for their instruction; others received as much as 24 cents for a five or six-day stint. It was not a happy profession for these unfortunates.[2]

THE HEDER

The peregrinating rebbe went to the homes; the sedentary rebbes made the children come to their place of business. Their schoolroom was called the heder (*the room*). The heder was thus a private school and was popular with the parents. They paid only a pittance in tuition, but they retained their pride. In Europe there were free Hebrew schools, but they were not free of the taint of charity; these were the Talmud Torahs (Learning Torah). Back in Russia, they were resorted to only by the impoverished. Here in America—and what follows applies to both the metropolises and the inland towns—the heder was often but a rented room. In New York and other large cities where rents were high, the children occasionally met in cellars. The physical ambience of the heder back in Russia was often nothing to brag about; Jews there, too, lived in ghetto-like surroundings. Yet a survey made in New York City in 1890-1893 demonstrated that the heders were not unsanitary. The heder teacher often taught the class as a group or gave each child some private instruction. While waiting their turn, the youngsters could chat or fight. Corporal punishment in the heder was not necessarily the rule. True, some of the teachers—as miserable as the rebbes—vented their unhappiness on the students. Twisting ears was not uncommon; this was painful. Other teachers would wield sticks, rattans. Instruction by violence, intimidation, was an honored American tradition. (In seventeenth-century Harvard, Nathaniel Eaton, the college head, wielded a cudgel "big enough to kill a horse." Throughout the twentieth century, some schoolmasters deemed the hickory stick the chief board of education.) The stick had no problem navigating the Atlantic in the late nineteenth century. In the heder the language of instruction was most frequently Yiddish; English was employed on occasion in New York, more often in the provinces. New York rebbes and heder entrepreneurs who were willing to improve themselves could get instruction in the American vernacular at the Educational Alliance.

For many children, the heder was a good experience. They became devout Jews. Decorum, respect, camaraderie prevailed in the Homestead, Pennsylvania, congregational heder in the first decade of the twentieth century. The vestry rooms where the children met were clean and pleasant. Young Isaac Marcus was devout, and when he rose to intone the Standing Prayer, he was all wrapped up in reading the Eighteen Benedictions. One winter evening a mischievous classmate approached him silently from the rear and jabbed a pin into him. Marcus flinched but continued to the final genuflection, then he quietly walked over to the pot bellied stove, grabbed hold of a skate and slashed at the nose of his tormentor almost severing it from the face. Isaac was never again molested as he rose to pray. Good modern heders, private Hebrew schools, were not uncommon. Hillel Malachovsky and A. H. Friedland, both respected Hebraists and litterateurs, had excellent schools and were patronized by the successful middle-class families who could afford to pay high tuition fees. Friedland taught girls—this in a day when most Hebrew schools did not encourage the attendance of females. In the New York of 1903 less than 5 percent of the students in the heders were females. In one of the heders in Pittsburgh's Hill district, the boys assembled at four after selling their newspapers. (Children helped make a living.) At 5:30 they ate out of their paper bags and then played ball in the yard till six o'clock. Classes ran from six o'clock to eight-thirty. They did not get home till nine. Were they fascinated by the stories the teachers told them? The heder rebbe in Linden, New Jersey, was a good pedagogue. He combined confection with affection. If a child was well behaved, he received a white caramel at the end of the week; if he knew something about the lesson, he got a pink caramel, and if he was very good and well behaved, he got a chocolate caramel.

The New Jersey rebbe was not typical of his confreres. The teachers were more often unhappy, distraught men; they barely made a living from the fees they received, 50 cents to $1 a month. As often as not, the students were hostile; the rebbe was a greenhorn in speech and in dress, though he invariably vaunted his Americanism by the derby perched on the back of his head. By the 1930's, the heders had begun to decline in numbers; the Talmud Torahs were better. But in their day, from the 1880's through the 1920's, the heders were popular. By 1909, there were about 470 in New York City alone; they educated thousands of Jewish children over the years. Most of them taught the boys just enough to read the prayer book, to recite a few necessary blessings, and to chant their portion of the Pentateuch and their chapter from the prophets. To be sure, they rarely knew the meaning of the Hebrew words. The teachers even provided them with a bar mitzvah speech in English or Yiddish. There were a few schools where the students were taught the meaning of the Hebrew words; some even learned to read the medieval biblical commentary of Rashi (1040-1105); a few, very few, even dipped into the Talmud. Thus, the new generation faced the world, Jewishly educated, at the age of thirteen. On the whole, the indoctrination was complete and effective. The parents—who had no standards—were happy; the child would never forget that he, or she, was Jewish. When Papa died, the son would recite the memorial prayer, the kaddish. This was imperative.[3]

THE ALL-DAY PAROCHIAL SCHOOL

The heder was a private enterprise, an afternoon-evening school, usually open from about 3 to 8 or even later. Most students in heders learned only to read Hebrew by rote. There were, however, Jews who were unhappy with the late afternoon heder and the semi-communal Talmud Torah, which also taught in the late afternoon hours. These few who rejected the heders and Talmud Torahs wanted an all-day institution where more emphasis would be laid on Hebraic studies. They wanted to train students—boys, of course—who would understand what they were reading and be prepared ultimately to study Talmud. Secular studies would be taught, as state law required, but they certainly would not be stressed; acculturation invited assimilation; taking off the cap in a public school only led to irreverence. Some right-wing European yeshivah heads were opposed to secular education. Judaism here in America had to be rescued through a thorough education in traditional Jewish sources; Bible and rabbinics would guarantee survival; so they thought. The all-day schools with their inclusion of secular subjects were not rooted in European Jewish tradition. The talmudic academies abroad evinced no interest in secular studies; they were frowned upon in most schools. In the early twentieth century, Rabbi Isaac Jacob Reines, the founder of Torah-oriented Zionism, the Mizrachi, was exceptional in looking with favor on the acquisition of the new learning by the students in his talmudic academy in Russia.

The Jewish all-day school in this country is American in origin. The early schools in the colonies were church-related schools, as was the school at Shearith Israel in New York. This Sephardic congregation had established a day school no later than the 1750's, probably earlier. The "Germans," who came later to New York and the hinterland, resorted to all-day schools to avoid Christology in the so-called public schools. The individual congregations abandoned their "parish" schools in the 1860's, by the 1870's at the latest. But even before that, flinching under the threat of Christian missionary schools on the Lower East Side, New York's Jews—not the congregations—rallied in the 1860's and set up a Hebrew Free School where Jewish and general subjects were taught. The liberal European tradition that public schools were to be free, lay, and compulsory made really little progress in New York in the mid-nineteenth century. The East European Jews of the 1880's may have been influenced here by the Catholics, who insisted on parochial schools for their young.

Dismayed at the lack of Talmud instruction in the afternoon schools of New York, some lovers of this "Learning" established what they thought would be a typical East European yeshivah, an academy to train talmudists. These devotees, humble men for the most part, founded the Tree of Life (Etz Chaim) in 1886. The Torah is the Tree of Life and all who cling to it are happy! The founding fathers were convinced that, if there was no Talmud, there would be no Judaism; the Talmud is the basic work expounding the Torah. They were set to create an institution of real learning. It is curious that it was incorporated as a charity, but this was no mistake. Their prime goal was to teach children of the poor. Charity boxes were put into homes. The children of the poor were taught, and a female auxiliary supported the naked with clothes; food, too, apples for the boys! Of course, no women were admitted. Tuition was required of those who could afford to pay, twenty-five cents a week. The curriculum included the Pentateuch, some Talmud with commentaries, and the basic codes. Yiddish writing was also included in the course of instruction. Most of the day was devoted to Hebrew studies; the English courses, taught in a very desultory fashion, were reserved for the late afternoon hours. The young immigrant Abraham Cahan was one of the English instructors. A visitor evaluating the school for Oscar Straus, the diplomat, said that some of the students could barely read English. It was hardly an American institution and, it would seem, some of its sponsors were not pleased with its accomplishments as a talmudic seminary. But it was a start; it would train no rabbinical scholars, but it did help youngsters plunge into the sea of the Talmud.[4]

The Etz Chaim bit off more than it could chew; it never became a real yeshivah in the best Russian style although it was reported to have had a substantial student body in the early twentieth century. The Rabbi Jacob Joseph Yeshivah was less pretentious and more successful. It wanted to be a good all-day school, and that it succeeded in becoming. It was founded about 1901 by Samuel I. Andron and took the name of Rabbi Jacob Joseph after the chief rabbi's death. The students were taught to translate the Pentateuch and given instruction in the Talmud. All of the Hebrew disciplines were stressed though secular studies were not neglected and many of the students experienced no difficulty in moving over to the city's high schools and colleges. The general studies were taught in English; the Jewish, in Yiddish. The youngsters and parents liked the school; by 1917-1918, there was an all-male student body of about 550. The Etz Chaim and the Jacob Joseph yeshivot served as patterns for similar schools; one was established in 1908 in Harlem, another in 1905 in Brownsville (Brooklyn). By 1918, these four day schools had a total registration of close to 1,000. Baltimore was one of the few towns— if not the only one—outside of New York that had established an all-day school. The social pressures exerted by acculturated Jews and the indifference of the Jewish masses did not then encourage Jews in the hinterland to open day schools. The Catholics and their schools were not viewed sympathetically by the Protestant public.

Toward the end of the period—in 1918, to be exact—an entirely new type of educational institution made its appearance. This was the progressive Jewish Day School, certainly no Talmud-centered yeshivah. It was a truly modern day school where secular studies were probably given more attention than Jewish disciplines, though the latter were certainly not neglected. This new institution, the Center School, part of the West Side Jewish Center, was the brainchild of Rabbi Mordecai M. Kaplan, a modern pedagogue who had been profoundly influenced by the new ideas that came out of Teachers' College, Columbia. In the next decade, there were to be other progressive all-day schools. In all such institutions, the hours were shortened, women were welcomed, good pedagogy was deemed imperative. There was even one school that admitted only women. In this period, prior to 1921, the all-day schools failed to become popular. The reasons are obvious: the immigrants wanted to become American in a hurry; the secular school was the royal road to learning and to opportunity, offering easy access to the colleges and the universities. Public schools were good and free; day schools cost money; most immigrants were poor, still struggling to get ahead. Beginning with the 1920's, old-fashioned day schools made advances in areas of dense settlement, albeit slowly. Decades later, after World War II, they were to become very popular; by the early 1980's, there were about 90,000 children in the hundreds of all-day schools that had sprung up. Why so many? The Hassidic émigrés who came to these shores after the Holocaust wanted their own cultural enclaves; they were determined to shut out the modern world which had tolerated their slaughter in Europe. Many old-line Americans became more attuned to Jewish learning after the German massacres. Actually, thousands flocked to the new all-day schools because the standards of America's public schools had fallen precipitously; the training in secular studies in the Jewish schools was often superior.[5]

TALMUD TORAHS

Prior to the closing of the gates against Slavic immigrants in 1921 and 1924, most Jews who came here were satisfied with the visits of the melammed in the home or the ministrations of the rebbe in a private heder. It was imperative that a male youngster learn to read Hebrew so that he could follow the synagog services and, God spare us, recite the kaddish, the memorial prayer when a parent died. Day schools were expensive. For the truly impoverished, even the heder was too costly; they resorted to the Talmud Torah, a school that usually met in the afternoon, Monday through Thursday and on Sunday morning. Some preferred the Talmud Torahs because they held formal classes and devoted much more time to Hebrew instruction than the heders. Important is the fact that the children could go to the free public schools in the morning and get a good general education. Talmud Torahs were definitely a cut above the heders; consequently, these afternoon schools, patronized by a substantial number of Jews in every town of size, were probably the most popular educational institution established by the East European newcomers. Essentially, the Talmud Torah school was an afternoon Hebrew school—nothing new in this country. American Jewry had conducted afternoon Hebrew classes for decades. The Hebrew Free Schools established by Uptown Jews for

Downtown Jews since the 1860's could brag of making provision for about 2,500 Lower East Siders in 1887. These classes had first been started in the 1860's, although Pesah Rosenthal, a newcomer, had operated a Talmud Torah for the children of indigent Russians and Poles a decade earlier. The Talmud Torah back in Europe, was something of a pauper's school; here in the United States it was upgraded and ultimately became a highly respected institution attended by thousands. A modest tuition was soon required, but very few were turned away if they had no means. The Talmud Torahs here, apparently, were really semi-communal schools; they were not private economic enterprises. They were started and maintained by the pious, determined to make Hebrew schools available for almost anyone, male at least. These schools, we repeat, were created by émigrés to guarantee spiritual, religious continuity in the traditional sense.

It was in part an importation, but it speedily became American. Back home, the students went to the Talmud Torah all day, here only in the afternoon. The mornings were reserved for the public school; that was imperative; that guaranteed a future. Abroad, in Russia, Poland, and Rumania, secular studies would rarely have been given precedence in the ghetto. The American Talmud Torah did not set out to prepare a student to be a talmudist; its goal was to give the boy a measure of Jewish education and then send him into the world of commerce and challenge.

Herewith, we have the odyssey of a youngster sent by his widowed Mama to get a Jewish education. First he went to a heder where tuition was twenty cents a week. He did learn to read Hebrew, but when he came home with a bloody nose, his mother blamed the rebbe and hired a melammed to come to the house. He was a good teacher, but when the poor exhausted man fell asleep while teaching Mama fired him and sent the boy to a Talmud Torah where he studied from 4 to 7 o'clock on weekday afternoons (except Fridays) and 9 to 12 on Sunday mornings. He studied Pentateuch with the Rashi commentary, knew the prayer book, and even dipped into the standard code, the Shulhan Arukh, all taught in Yiddish. But after Mama's darling provoked the principal, who slapped his face, another change was made. The youngster transferred to the Machzike Talmud Torah (Those who hold on to the study of the Torah. The name may have been Machzike Ha-Dot Talmud Torah; more or less, those who hold on to the religious Talmud Torah.). This was a good move; there were girls at this school, and this appealed to the nine-year-old. Classes for him were held only two hours a day; the extra time could now be devoted to the violin. At the school, he learned some Jewish history, read and spoke some modern Hebrew, and became adept in the daily worship ritual. Mama was happy. He knew how to don the phylacteries, kept kosher, and was prepared to recite the Aramaic prayer for the dead. This youngster remained a Jew.

Over the years, Pesah Rosenthal's paupers' school developed into the flourishing Machzike Talmud Torah, the country's best known independent afternoon school. At first, girls were not welcomed; this was changed later. Instruction was in Yiddish, but by 1899 courses were also taught in English. As early as 1886, it had its own building and could boast of 400 students; by 1901, there were 1,000 youngsters in its classes, and over the years many thousands matriculated and went on to careers by grace of the city's high schools, colleges, and commercial opportunities. Wealthy East Siders like the banker Jarmulowsky and Uptown notables like Schiff gave the school money. By 1890, the Talmud Torahs had moved into Brooklyn and Harlem, by 1906 into the Bronx. As early as 1909, there were twenty-four Talmud Torahs in the city; 20 percent of all children receiving a formal Jewish education attended these schools. The schools followed the children as they moved out.[6]

ADMINISTRATION

What was the character of these Talmud Torah schools? Until the second and third decades of the twentieth century, not many teachers were competent. They were foreigners, dealing with children who were American in spirit. The challenge was obvious. The schools themselves were undeviatingly Orthodox. The teachers had to conform. An instructor in a Syracuse Talmud Torah had to promise not to write on the Sabbath when he attended university courses. (The Hebrew Union College, too, frowned on students taking notes on the Sabbath—this, as late as 1911.) The trustees of the Machzike Talmud Torah expected its instructors to grow beards. Yiddish was most frequently the language of instruction in the Talmud Torahs. The sponsors of the schools, often immigrants, wanted no English, the language of the acculturating and assimilating Jewish natives and Germans. The trustees distrusted the religious loyalties of those who did not employ Yiddish which had now become an almost sacrosanct tongue. English, however, was more frequently employed in the Talmud Torahs after the turn of the century; it tended to placate Uptown givers who suspected that insistence on Yiddish served to ghettoize the youngsters. Textbooks were few and inadequate. The curriculum? No two schools were alike. Hebrew, of course, was primary. It had to be taught with the chaunts. The newcomers scorned the Sunday schools, where little or no Hebrew was required. For them one could not be a Jew without Hebrew.

The Talmud Torahs promised to teach the Pentateuch, in Yiddish translation, of course. They talked of imparting grammar, of familiarity with the Orthodox prayer book, of teaching history, ceremonies, customs, the blessings. They even intimated that they would make an effort to dip into the Midrash and the Talmud (Gemara) itself, a maximalist program advertised to win the support of the staunch traditionalists, but very rarely implemented. The hours, too, varied. Schedules required some seven to ten hours a week; corporal punishment was frowned upon; five years of attendance was suggested, but few ran the full course; fewer than 5 percent stayed on. Most Talmud Torahs encouraged boys, though girls were admitted in the course of time. Support came from the devout who paid membership fees; tuition was required if the parents had any means; if necessary, the principal himself might be coopted as collector. Donations were solicited; charity boxes were installed at home. One Talmud Torah sold such licensed boxes for $10 and permitted the purchasers to keep whatever they collected; the school at least had the $10. Generous benefactors were promised that the children would chaunt Psalms when the donors were ill and would join the funeral cortege. These were fringe benefits.[7]

TALMUD TORAHS IN THE HINTERLAND

And the Talmud Torahs in the hinterland? In many respects, not all, they were replicas of the schools in New York City. There were Talmud Torahs in all major American towns and in many small towns, too. As in New York, the Jews in the backcountry found out that these nonprofit semicommunal schools were better than most private heders operated for profit. Actually, privately owned heders were not too common outside of New York and some other very large towns. Chicago would seem to have had a Russian Talmud Torah as early as the 1860's. In other towns, some were opened in the 1880's after the exiles arrived in larger numbers; by the 1890's, there were Talmud Torahs almost everywhere. Foreign-born Orthodox rabbis took the lead in establishing these schools; they were concerned that the children of the poor be well-educated Jewishly. The larger town ghettos had more than one such afternoon school. Like the New York institutions, these charitably motivated schools after a time improved their status, charged tuition, and reached out for communal support. Girls, it appears, entered these schools at a relatively early time— in contradistinction to the New York practice, where the Orthodox were in no hurry to educate and emancipate their womenfolk. After a testing period, the Talmud Torahs received a degree of communal support, though this was effected more easily in smaller communities than in larger, unorganized metropolitan Jewries. One suspects, too, that English was adopted as a teaching language in these backcountry Talmud Torahs more speedily than in New York. The acculturative pressures were strong on these smaller Jewries; the English-speaking milieu was overpowering.

In 1883, as Moses Montefiore's centennial approached, the Chicago Orthodox elite established a Talmud Torah and named it after the "Torah-true" centenarian. In 1886, the German Jewish elite and their rabbis, Emil G. Hirsch and Felsenthal, led in the appeal for funds. For many years, Yiddish remained the sole language of instruction. Advanced students studied some Mishnah and Gemara. By 1911, Chicago's newly established federation of charities was subsidizing six Talmud Torahs. Among those who taught in this city's Talmud Torahs was Jacob Dolnitzky (1855-1933), reputed to be one of the country's most learned talmudists. Dolnitzky, who had studied in Lithuania, Germany, and France, was thoroughly at home in the Bible and the vast rabbinical literature. In 1887, Baer Manischewitz, of Cincinnati, known for his matzos, sold his product to the local schools at cost, encouraging them to dispose of it at retail for the benefit of the new Talmud Torah. Boston's Jewry with its several Talmud Torahs might well be proud of the Ivriah, which began in 1904 and in 1915 published a Hebrew magazine dedicated to the furtherance of the language. That year, this modern school could boast that it taught 260 boys and 160 girls. They were able to translate the Pentateuch, read the commentaries of Rashi, understand the prophets in the original, and even navigate through the pages of the aggadic *Well of Jacob* (En Yaakov). In addition, they studied modern Hebrew literature. By 1910, Baltimore had a school of 900 youngsters; many of them were clothed also, for the Baltimoreans had to compete with the Christian mission schools which offered the boys and girls books, candy, and garments. Two years later, it is reported, some advanced students were being taught Talmud. In order to make sure that brilliant youngsters would remain and not go out on the streets to sell newspapers, a female auxiliary offered them very handsome stipends if they would continue their studies. The better students among them were induced by Rabbi William Rosenau to enter the Hebrew Union College. A Milwaukee Talmud Torah supported by the old-timers was called the Milwaukee Jewish Mission. The Orthodox disliked that name; it smacked of Christian conversionism. Philadelphia, as befitted a huge city, had numerous Talmud Torahs; in 1912-1913, they reported that they sheltered 10,000 students. These figures might well be suspect. That Orthodox stalwart Rabbi Bernard Levinthal made sure that the Talmud Torahs operated efficiently. It bears repetition: the curricula in all schools west of the Hudson resembled those of the New York Talmud Torahs. Orthodoxy in America always directed its goals toward the capacity to read the prayer book and the Pentateuch. That was the minimum; everything beyond that was a windfall, and a surprise.[8]

CONGREGATIONAL SCHOOLS

Some Talmud Torahs were supported in part by congregations. Such schools were opened primarily to make provision for the children of members; children of nonmembers were admitted, too, if their parents were willing to pay tuition. The long-established Uptown Orthodox congregations had supported afternoon Hebrew schools long before the turn of the nineteenth century. In smaller towns, this congregational school was usually called a heder, and though the local omnibus functionary ran the school and derived benefits from it, it was not a private undertaking. It was a communal Talmud Torah. The Hebrew schools of the larger orphanages in the major cities were also Talmud Torahs, though limited to the children of a specific eleemosynary institution. The huge classes that met in New York's Educational Alliance from the 1890's and on constituted an institutional Talmud Torah. In all probability, no tuition charges were imposed. Unlike the typical Talmud Torahs, the Hebrew language was not stressed in the schools of the orphanages and the settlement houses; religion, ethics, morals, history, were emphasized. The total number of students in these charitative and social-welfare institutions ran into the many thousands. In a way they were a cross between a Talmud Torah and a Sunday school. As Jews moved out of the ghettos of first settlement and found homes in different parts of a metropolis, in more comfortable ghettos, they joined congregations which speedily developed congregational afternoon schools. In effect, they were Talmud Torahs. However, this shift from the afternoon Talmud Torahs to the congregational schools did not assume large proportions till the 1930's. There were only sixty congregational schools in New York in 1918; in 1944, they had grown almost 400 percent. It was cheaper to pay—or not to pay—tuition in a Talmud Torah than to join a congregation. The newcomers were still scrambling to become firmly ensconced in the lower middle class.[9]

TALMUD TORAHS: A SUMMARY

The efforts of the Jewish native-born, Germans, and the newcomers themselves to further the East Europeans educationally and Jewishly are impressive. Beginnings were made as early as the 1850's. The children of the new arrivals were taken into Sunday schools and later into settlement houses; there were Free Schools, Talmud Torahs, all-day institutions, privately run heders, and itinerant rebbes. By 1910, the secularist Zionists and socialists began to establish children's schools in the hope that they would raise a generation of young Americans devoted to the Yiddish language and culture. The typical Talmud Torah of this period projected far-reaching curricula that embraced some knowledge of talmudic literature. The parents were not sanguine in their expectations; very few were ready to make any real sacrifices to support comprehensive curricula and educational programs. They were content with minimal achievements for their progeny. Coming to the heders and the Talmud Torahs after a long hard day in the public schools, the youngsters were tired. What did they accomplish? Most of them succeeded in learning to read Hebrew rather fluently. They conned the prayer book; they were acquainted with the Holy Days; they memorized the necessary blessings. A few may have acquired some translation skills. This was the sum total of the achievements of the typical student who became bar mitzvah at thirteen. His parents were satisfied; he certainly was. For most of them, the unconscious Jewish indoctrination process was effective.

During the 1920's, the semi-commercial Talmud Torahs appeared to be doing well. The rising federations began to subsidize them, in part. The federations, representing what was then the Jewish community as a whole, moved to help finance the education of those who would not or could not do so themselves. Many of the Orthodox wanted the larger Jewish community to educate their children—in Orthodoxy—for them. Still, the Talmud Torahs which got off to such a good start had no real future. The Conservatives, destined to become the largest Jewish denomination in this country, developed good afternoon schools in order to hold their children and to build loyalties to the congregation itself. This was true, too, of the Orthodox as they built synagogs and schools after they left the ghettos of first settlement. The Talmud Torahs began to lose their students. The curricula in the congregational schools of the second quarter of the twentieth century were more varied; pedagogy made advances; the synagogs attained their minimum goals; the boys and girls were trained to read Hebrew, to be at home in the siddur, to translate portions of the Pentateuch, and to do a creditable job at bar mitzvah when they rose to chaunt from the Scroll of the Law.[10]

YESHIVOT

The so-called yeshivot were programatically more ambitious than the Talmud Torahs. Around the year 1905 there were three yeshivot on Henry Street in the Lower East Side: the Etz Chaim, the Rabbi Jacob Joseph School, and the Rabbi Isaac Elchanan Theological Seminary (RIETS). The first two institutions set out to become yeshivot, after a fashion, but were not successful in the effort. They were all-day schools that finally initiated some students into the mysteries of the Talmud. A real yeshivah, European style, taught advanced talmudic students; they were also trained in reading the codes and the responsa, the legal decisions of scholars, some of whom lived in medieval days. Many of the immigrant youngsters who attended Etz Chaim were under thirteen years of age. In the pre-1900 days, one of the instructors in secular studies in this all-day school was a public school graduate, all of fourteen. The Etz Chaim was not unsuccessful as a sort of junior high school; it sheltered 175 students in 1905.

Why yeshivot in America? In Eastern Europe, the Talmud was the source of Jewish law. Its practitioners, its judiciary, were the rabbis—miserably paid, of course, but consulted, respected, and even revered. Jews in the Pale made their careers through Torah, the Law. Devout and learned Jews—the unlearned, too—wanted to naturalize these talmudic "colleges" in the United States; rabbinic law must remain regnant. Thus it was that real yeshivot took root here not only in New York City but also in the hinterland; their numbers were small. Traditionalists here wanted to reconstitute the old Polish-Russian religiocultural community. Alas for their hopes; the immigrant masses and their children were ready, if not eager, to embrace the American legal system and the English common law in vogue here. By 1905, the attempt had already been made to found advanced yeshivot in Boston, Pittsburgh, Philadelphia, Chicago, and New York. If there actually were talmudic colleges in Boston and Pittsburgh, as has been maintained, they made little or no stir; Philadelphia had boasted of its Israel's Sanctuary, Mishkan Yisrael, since the first decade of the new century. This yeshivah had been established by the brilliant and able Bernard Levinthal, the dean of Philadelphia's rabbinical pundits. He was a power politically in American Orthodoxy to the day of his death. The old guard rallied around him, but he knew full well that the future of Orthodoxy here in the United States lay in its alliance with modernity. Mishkan Yisrael was initiated to train its students for a traditional American rabbinate. This goal was not reached. The Chicagoans were more successful. The Chicago school called itself Bet ha-Medrash l'Torah, the Hebrew Theological College of Chicago. Like Levinthal's Mishkan Yisrael, it, too, grew out of a minor yeshivah that had been established about the year 1899, Etz Chaim. The name was probably borrowed from New York's Henry Street day school. By 1922, this Chicago institution was well on its way; it had a preparatory and collegiate division and a teacher's institute, all housed in a beautiful new building which included a library, a kitchen (kashrut!), and a shower bath. The graduates soon began to fill traditional pulpits in the Middle West.

The most successful of these few talmudic schools was the Rabbi Isaac Elchanan Theological School (RIETS) named after the famous Lithuanian scholar Spektor, a man of international repute. Spektor died in 1896; the school was founded here in 1897. New York's Etz Chaim had disappointed its founders; no religious balm would come forth from this Henry Street institution. Eleven years later in 1897, the uncompromising Orthodox opened the doors of its seminary. This was a real yeshivah, yet it was also Americanistic. It announced that it would train rabbis for America and train them in the secular sciences. This was new; as yet no yeshivah in Russia had actually incorporated any of the profane subjects into its curricula permanently; the East European rabbis were soured on the arts and sciences because they had been antagonized in the past by Maskilim, Enlighteners, who frequently embraced heretical doctrines. For years, the new American college served as a half-way house for learned immigrants, young men for the most part, who wanted bread and butter while they looked around. A standard stipend in those days was $2.75 a week. One could rent a room or sleeping space for 75 cents a week; 25 cents a day would suffice for food—a modest table, to be sure—and 25 cents a week was reserved for emergencies, medicines, for instance. The school ran into trouble; the students wanted to learn English in order to cope with American congregations; the trustees in those days had no real interest in secular studies; the students waged a successful strike in the early years of the new century; they threatened the board with publicity. The trustees feared, too, that some of the students might transfer to the still Orthodox Jewish Theological Seminary where secular studies were encouraged. The talmudists were then permitted to study in secondary schools at their own expense. America was not Russia. Let the board not be condemned; the school and its rulers were truly poor. Support came from collections, donations, and the promise of prayers on behalf of the sick and the dead. A woman's auxiliary helped students financially. Very few of the students took rabbinic posts. By 1905, one of the graduates had a job, but most Orthodox congregations preferred mature European trained rabbis; no one could question their authenticity. A dour critic who visited the school in those days said that it would have benefited from the supervision of a man who lived in the twentieth century.

This was the RIETS in the first decade of the twentieth century. But all this was to change; American Orthodoxy was to be profoundly influenced—and for the better—by the arrival of a Lithuanian yeshivah student who came to these shores in 1906. This was the prodigy Bernard Revel, all of twenty-one on his arrival. Unlike the earlier talmudists who had sought refuge and a future in the United States, he had gone to a public secondary school back home and had been imprisoned for his political liberalism. Here in the United States while he was studying at RIETS, his talmudic brilliance impressed Levinthal, who brought him to Philadelphia as his secretary and encouraged him to get his Ph.D. at Dropsie (1912). He was the first to receive his graduate degree at that college. Equipped with a good degree—he had two, in fact—he was prepared to become America's first Russo-Polish Orthodox leader. (Dr. Philip Klein, New York's Orthodox notable, had his doctorate, but he was Hungarian-born. Revel's background was totally Yiddish and Slavic.) When, in 1915, New York's concerned traditionalists merged Etz Chaim and RIETS, the thirty-year-old Revel was appointed head of the new Rabbinical College of America. By this time, there was a new generation of East

European traditionalists. Among them were men of wealth, completely Americanized, who were to insist on a good English training for all graduates. Even the Union of Orthodox Rabbis went along with Revel, though some of its members were to harass him in later years. One of those who had high hopes for the Rabbinical College was the builder Harry Fischel. As early as 1928, a biography describing him rolled off the presses: Herbert S. Goldstein's *Fifty Years of Struggle for a Principle*. Fischel fought all his life, uncompromisingly, for the maintenance of the tradition which he had brought with him from his native Russia. He was completely Jewish, thoroughly American. He wanted rabbis who would be at home in the Talmud, but cultured, in an Anglo-Saxon sense, and thus able to win young American Jews for the ancestral faith. He himself was notable for his involvement in almost every good Jewish cause: the American Jewish Committee, the Kehillah Movement, overseas relief, the Hebrew Immigrant Aid Society, a Talmud Torah, a Hebrew day nursery, Beth Israel Hospital, and of course the Etz Chaim school and the Rabbinical College.

When Revel took over in 1915, Etz Chaim had already taught hundreds if not thousands of youngsters; the RIETS talmudic school had nourished and encouraged 500 students. The year 1915 saw East European Jewry devastated by brutal armies in the course of World War I. It was obvious that the United States was to become a new World Jewish center. Revel succeeded in introducing a modern, varied and balanced curriculum comparable in many respects to that of Schechter's Jewish Theological Seminary and Kohler's Hebrew Union College. This new school was thoroughly modern in its hopes; some of its teachers were Ph.D's; its talmudic instructors were learned. Before long, the new institution included also a preparatory all-day school, a Hebrew high school called the Talmudical Academy, and of course a rabbinical department. By the early 1920's, Revel had taken over the Mizrachi teachers' institute which those Orthodox enthusiasts had established in 1917. Students were no longer encouraged with a pitifully small grant-in-aid; they received as much in scholarships and loans as the youngsters at the Hebrew Union College.

There was a job to be done, and the new men at the helm of the New York Orthodox college were determined that it would be done right. Revel's goal was to produce a generation of learned and competent rabbis and in this endeavor he met with much success. He set out to train teachers, social workers, and communal leaders. His vision encompassed a new American Jewry rooted in a traditional enlightened Judaism, but it was to be undeviatingly Orthodox. That is why he provided secular training on the premises, determined as he was to protect his protégés from the assimilatory influences of the country's public schools and colleges. By 1921, the Rabbinical College had graduated about fifty men; about half had taken pulpits; the others had opted for careers in other avenues of endeavor. In 1928, Revel founded a "secular" school, Yeshiva College, which eight years after his death became Yeshiva University. Pushed by Revel and a group of Old World rabbis and wealthy businessmen who knew that radical changes were necessary, American Orthodoxy embraced American culture, modern learning, and administrative skills. It was determined to survive.[11]

STATISTICS AND A SUMMARY

Ever since the 1850's, East European adults and children had numerous opportunities here in the United States to secure some Jewish training in institutions of their own. Talmudic study circles abounded in the ghettos; rebbes had been available for generations for home instruction; heders, private Hebrew schools, were at hand everywhere. Those Jews who were concerned about Jewish education for themselves and their boys experienced little difficulty in finding schools, associations, and conventicles to fit their needs, their purses, and their prepossessions. For those who wished to walk the paths that led to eternity, there were congregational afternoon schools, Talmud Torahs, and institutions that catered to special interests such as Zionism and the education of girls. There were day nurseries and kindergartens, settlement houses, Young Men's Hebrew Associations, parochial schools, yeshivot, seminaries for the Orthodox, the Conservatives, and the Reformers. There were trade schools, "mission schools," established by Uptown Jews for Downtown Jews. Some of these were sponsored by sisterhoods and sections of the National Council of Jewish Women. Classes were also held in orphanages and in institutions set up for delinquent children. In addition, there were summer camps, teachers' institutes, and the various secular Yiddishist schools. By the beginning of the third decade there were Jewish synagogal centers, distinguished by their innovative cultural, social, and religious programs. By this time, too, a substantial percentage of the youngsters in all Reform Sunday schools were the native-born children of the Russian and Polish immigrants. They were taught Bible stories and the amenities. As already described, curricula varied. Indeed, there was no common denominator for all American Jewish schools; not all even taught Hebrew. However, the institutions controlled by the East Europeans themselves did have one thing in common; they insisted that every male child learn to read enough Hebrew so that he could be called to the Torah at age thirteen and recite the necessary blessings. Schools sponsored by Jews automatically assumed a Jewish character. This applied even to the Marxist Yiddish institutions with their diverse hues. In one form or another, all schools indoctrinated their students to be "Jewish," however that term was defined.

How many of the children of the newcomers received a Jewish education? There are statistics; they are not always accurate, but they are helpful. Prior to 1904, there is no consensus among scholars which would enable the historian to determine what percentage of young Jews was receiving a Jewish education at one time. There is a report, for whatever it is worth, that in 1900 only 18 percent of the Jewish boys and girls in the United States was being sent to Jewish schools. Some think that 50 percent of all youngsters was going to Jewish schools. This would include those at the Educational Alliance where the instruction was in English. This figure seems very high. In a survey made in 1908 of the Jewish schools in the United States, it is estimated that about 30 percent of all Jewish children was receiving some instruction; in descending order, they were to be found in heders, Talmud Torahs, congregational schools, and all-day institutions. In 1910, Benderly came up with a statement that 28.3 percent of America's young Jews were attending Jewish schools; in 1914-1915, Dr. Julius B. Greenstone, of Philadelphia, estimated that nationwide 25 to 30 percent were given Jewish instruction. Studies made in 1911 show that at one time about 20 percent of the children in New York was being educated Jewishly, about 24 percent in Philadelphia in 1912, about 16 percent in Newark in 1913-1914, and about 28 percent in Cincinnati. Baltimore and Pittsburgh did better; in the Pennsylvania city, about 80 percent of all youngsters in town was enrolled in Jewish schools, though only 20 percent was studying Hebrew; in Baltimore, over 60 percent of the city's youngsters was receiving a Jewish education. Social control and pressures were always stronger in smaller cities. Any non-Marxist parent who did not send his boy to a Jewish school invoked the censure of his peers.

By the second decade of the century, more people were concerned with this problem of Jewish instruction for the young. Let it not be forgotten that the East Europeans had been coming to this country in numbers since the 1880's. They set out finally, a generation later, to take remedial action, yet in 1914 and 1917 only about 25 percent of the Jewish children in New York and the country was receiving a Jewish education at any one time. This does not preclude the possibility that a far larger percentage did get some religiocultural schooling before their thirteenth year. It is worthy of note, too, that by 1917 more and more women were teaching in the Jewish schools. They had been teaching in the Sunday schools ever since the 1830's. Now, by the end of the second decade of the twentieth century, these women teachers documented their presence in substantial numbers in afternoon schools, in Jewish communal institutions, and even in Talmud Torahs. Women were more than 50 percent of the staff at the Sunday schools though none taught in the Jewish all-day schools.[12]

Patently the education received by the children of the immigrants was not extensive. It is estimated that some never received any schooling; they were never even bar mitzvah. Parents were content if a son could read the Hebrew prayer book without knowing the meaning of the words. At thirteen, a boy's Jewish education was complete; he went to work or to high school; he was now a "man" by the dictates of religious tradition. General education was deemed more important than further training in Hebrew. Secular studies opened the way to a livelihood, to opportunity, to status. Since most children were not enamored of their Hebrew studies and their foreign-born instructors, what then did the schools do for them? They learned little of content, of the Hebrew language and its literature. There was, however, a rude form of identification as a Jew, and that made for survival. Certain exceptions must be noted. There were some schools with intensive Jewish educational programs. They will be discussed in a later section of this work.[13]

CHAPTER FIFTEEN

YIDDISH: THE THEATRE AND THE PRESS

INTRODUCTION

The Hebrew taught in the Jewish schools was a form of identification, an important one, to be sure. Hebrew itself was not the national language of the Jews; it had not been the demotic tongue even centuries before the Christian era. Two thousand years ago, the Jewish masses spoke Aramaic and Greek; later, many Jews in Asia Minor, the Levant, and North Africa spoke Arabic. During the Middle Ages, the language of the Iberians was Arabic and, later, Spanish; the Central and East Europeans spoke Yiddish. By the early nineteenth century, Yiddish, Judeo-German, was the most popular language of World Jewry. It was the "national" tongue, basically German with reminiscences of other European parlances, and of course the Slavic. Most Yiddish-speaking Jews lived in Slavic lands; in the United States, Yiddish was profoundly influenced by English.

Among the Jews, there was no speech without its literature, oral or written. The East European Maskilim, the Enlighteners, set out to create a modern Hebrew language to make it the vehicle for the acquisition and spread of western culture. Many of them despised Yiddish—the jargon, they called it. Their prejudices stemmed from German Christians who disliked both Jews and their Germanic idiom. Aspiring German Jews adopted this denigration of Yiddish and transmitted the prejudice to Russian and Polish Jewish literati. In turn, German Jewish immigrants to the United States, and the few Maskilim here, transported contempt for Yiddish to this country. The Germans here forgot that their parents in Europe had spoken a Yiddish of their own. Very many nineteenth-century German Jews continued to employ the Hebrew cursive script, even though their Yiddish had now become good German. They forgot or did not know that, when Mendelssohn and his coworkers set out to modernize European Jewry by translating the Bible into German, they employed the Hebrew alphabet.

Yiddish in Eastern Europe

Of course, Yiddish had a literature of sorts almost since the day it became a spoken language in Central Europe during the Middle Ages. In the succeeding centuries, it produced works on ethics and education; reworked biblical stories were popular. Primitive dramas dealing primarily with the sale of Joseph into slavery began to be written and performed. Purim plays were not uncommon. Women were provided with attractive pietistic liturgical books. No later than the middle of the nineteenth century, strolling minstrels began to make their appearance in Russia, Yiddish bards, impromptu poets, who recited and sang their Yiddish doggerels in inns, at concerts, at weddings. Some enjoyed great popularity. Russia's most famous folksinger was Eliakum Zunser (1836-1913), composer of hundreds of songs. Some of them were sung by the masses in every corner of Eastern Europe; they taught a simple wholesome morality, a return to the soil, the plough, to God's Holy Land, Palestine. Zunser's popularity was his undoing. Fearing the crowds who gathered to hear him, the Russians frowned on him and in 1889 he left for the United States, the land of freedom, the land of Washington of whom he sang. His son would not be conscripted in the army! Many of his folkist creations were published; he concertized for a few years here, but his minstrelsy failed to provide a livelihood. With a grant from the Uptown Jews, he opened a small printing shop and managed to subsist. Was he rejected here? What happened? It is difficult to determine why this minnesinger, who attracted large numbers in despotic Russia, failed in free America. Was his type of entertainment untypically American? Yet English-speaking monologists prospered in this country. Were the immigrants looking forward not backward? Was English the language of opportunity? The people did flock to the Yiddish theatres!

Modern Yiddish literature was to have its beginnings in Russia with the appearance of a Yiddish periodical in the 1860's and with the rise of three classicists, Shalom Jacob Abramowitch (Mendele the Book Seller, d. 1917), Isaac Loeb Peretz (1852-1915), poet, short story writer, and novelist; Sholem Aleichem (1859-1916, Solomon Rabinowitz) writer, humorist, the "Jewish Mark Twain." Mendele, the granddaddy of modern Yiddish literature, began writing in the 1860's, Peretz and Sholem Aleichem in the 1880's and 1890's. The latter fled to America in 1914, but died two years later. He made a poor living here, though crowds flocked to greet him when he landed and still larger crowds came to his funeral. Like other East European notables, Rabbi Jacob Joseph and Eliakum Zunser, he never learned that in America God helped only those who helped themselves.

THE COMING OF THE EAST EUROPEAN JEWS

Yiddish was probably the mother tongue of many North American immigrant Jews ever since the second quarter of the eighteenth century. In those early days, quite a number of the business letters were written in Yiddish. In writing English, Cohen & Isaacs of Richmond employed the Hebrew script, not the Latin. As early as 1849, a minister who officiated in Boston's first synagog addressed the congregation in Yiddish; the year 1870 was to witness the first beginnings of Yiddish literature; a Judeo-German (Yiddish!) "newspaper" made its appearance. By 1880, there were over 250,000 Jews in the United States; a substantial minority were of East European provenance, probably as many as 20 percent. It is estimated that there were somewhere between 175,000 and 225,000 Jews in New York City in the early 1890's; a great many of these New Yorkers were recent arrivals from the Slavic lands. The language of these newcomers was Yiddish; most of them knew no other. Even the Russian-speaking Jewish intelligentsia understood it and spoke it, though they affected to disdain the "jargon." The vast majority of the newcomers loved the language and surrendered it most reluctantly. Yiddish, like the older Spanish and Aramaic languages, assumed a semi-sacred character. This determination to retain the mother tongue was common among all immigrants. Scandinavians and others in Dakota Territory, in Wisconsin, in Illinois, insisted successfully that instruction in the public schools be permitted in their ancestral tongue. The Pennsylvania "Dutch," Germans, continued speaking their patois well into the twentieth century; the Central European Jews taught German in their American all-day schools and published Hebrew prayer books here with German translations. This was true, too, of the Reform Jews. Wise and Einhorn published prayer books with German translations; Kohler, Schiff, Einhorn and other foreign-born Jewish leaders never ceased writing to their friends in German, the language they loved.[1]

EARLY YIDDISH THEATRE IN EASTERN EUROPE AND THE UNITED STATES

The Jewish masses here wanted to be amused, hence a Yiddish theatre. They were not seeking to be enlightened, challenged, or educated. To escape? Of course. Theirs was a hard lot, and the many who flocked to the theatre loved what it offered. Some may even have gone to performances back home in Russia or Poland or Rumania. Jews, as it has been pointed out above, had enjoyed theatrical productions for centuries. Most of them were simple, amateur performances. In the early eighteenth century, more interest was shown by Jews in the world of the playhouse. Central and West European non-Jews already had a well-developed theatre; the Shakespearean plays date from the 1590's. As the Jews moved into the world of modern culture, they encountered the theatre and they liked what they saw.[2]

It was in 1882, apparently, that the first Yiddish theatrical performance was staged in New York City. It was about that year that professionals made their appearance in the city; some of them had trod the boards in Rumania where the first modern Yiddish theatre was born. One of the first "modern" dramas performed—it may well have been the first —was a work of Abraham Goldfaden (1840-1908). This brilliant man is frequently referred to as the "Father of the Yiddish Theatre." That he was. When his father discovered that his young son had literary ambitions, he saw to it that he received a good education—which meant that he was at home in Hebrew, Russian, and German. Yiddish, of course, was his mother tongue. Although he had studied at a Russian rabbinical academy, the ministry did not appeal to him. By the 1860's, he had already published some of his Hebrew and Yiddish poems; he began writing Hebrew verse when he was only ten. In 1876, in Jassy, Rumania, he produced and directed the first Yiddish theatrical show. It was truly all his, for he painted the scenery, wrote the story, and directed the players. For the first time, wandering Jewish minstrels worked with prepared dialogue and a plot. Jewish entertainment was now to become more than impromptu vaudeville. Goldfaden took his company to Russia and toured the country till 1883, when the government banned the Yiddish theatre; it feared the impact of group assemblies.

The early New York theatre had its problems, too; Coroner Ferdinand Levy, a political power in New York City, disliked the new Yiddish theatre. His standards were set by the contemporary English and German stage. It was his belief that these Yiddish performances reflected culturally on the city's Jewish community. Levy, his two brothers, and his father had served with distinction in the Civil War. Goldfaden's works were being played in the East Side theatres before his arrival here in 1897. He stayed but two years, ran into rude competitors, and hastened back to Europe. He finally returned in 1903, when Russia was rife with revolution. Goldfaden had determined the format of the typical Yiddish play, which was somewhat reminiscent of the commedia dell'arte. It was to become a stereotype, a melange of music, songs and dances, humor, horse play, a touch of the risqué and a plot of sorts. In the several hundred plays he wrote—many of them adapted from Russian, German and English models—his auditors were regaled with humor, satire, melodious songs, and gobs of history tunefully served up. The expulsions and pogroms of the 1890's inspired him to recount the prowess of a Judah Maccabee and a Bar Kochba who dared to defy the Syrian and Roman empires. His most successful operetta was *Shulamis*, in which he limned the fate of an un-faithful lover and his inamorata. Goldfaden lived five years after he re-turned to New York City. Contemporary accounts state that 75,000 peo-ple came out to watch his funeral cortege; a platoon of twenty mounted policemen cleared the way for the carriages and hearse. How many peo-ple, asked a local English daily, would turn out to watch the funeral of any American poet no matter how distinguished?[3]

LATTEINER, HOROWITZ, AND SHAIKEWITZ

Although Goldfaden profoundly influenced the Yiddish theatre through his creative pioneer writings and activities, the East Side masses and the hinterland Jews were certainly more directly moved by the writings and productions of Joseph Latteiner (1853-1935), "Professor" Moses Halevi Horowitz (1844-1910), and Nahum Meyer Shaikewitz (1849-1946). One of the early arrivals in the New York ghetto, Latteiner, a Rumanian, was already staging plays on American themes by the year 1886. One of the first professional producers for the American Yiddish theatre, he is said to have written more than 100 plays and comic operas. The early stage owes much to him. Like practically all his nineteenth century Jew-ish colleagues, he borrowed and adapted his plots from others. "Professor" Horowitz, a Galician, had been a professional writer and pro-ducer back in Bucharest. His enemies spread the rumor that he had once been a convert to Christianity. This was the superlative in defamation and need not be true. There was no question, however, that he was a "sharp operator." He organized a mutual-aid organization and used the funds collected to rent a theatre, to buy a house, and to parade ostentatiously with a horse and carriage. If Latteiner could boast of 100 plays he had written, the Professor could match him with 169. It was said that Horo-witz could stage a new drama in twenty-four hours. He was adept at writ-ing historical dramas, operas, and topical plays. The ritual murder accusa-tion in Hungary in 1882, the Dreyfus Affair of the 1890's, the Kishinev massacre of 1903—all these were grist for his mill. With an eye to his proletarian followers, he also put together a show describing how the Pinkertons in 1892 had mown down the Homestead strikers at the Car-negie Steel Mill. When directing the Hungarian ritual murder play, Ho-rowitz himself played the part of the defending lawyer and spoke passion-ately on behalf of his clients for a full forty-five minutes. Unlike most productions, this eight-act drama ran for two whole nights.

A third writer of those late nineteenth-century days was the brilliant Shaikewitz, a White Russian, who had come to America in 1889. Like the others, he had worked in the theatre back in Eastern Europe. A Mas-kil, a militant Enlightener, before coming to these shores he had written novels castigating the Orthodox extremists who stood foursquare on their own gospel. Here in the United States, he was widely accepted as a journalist, a litterateur, a dramatist, a novelist distinguished for the hundreds of penny dreadfuls, comedies, and farces that he ground out. Thousands read his novels eagerly; he moved Jews to read! Unlike Latteiner and Horowitz, however, he set out to play a part in the larger East Side community; he worked closely with the Hebrew Immigrant Aid Society and was later active in the American Jewish Congress. As a publicist, he had agitated for years for the establishment of a democratically elected American Jewish Congress. His pseudonym was Schomer (Shomer), the Watchman. It is difficult to determine if he attached any particular significance to that word. It was later adopted as the family name. Latteiner, Horowitz, Shaikewitz-Shomer, and other dramatists of that generation wrote what literary critics called *shund*, a German and Yiddish word which has not yet crawled into the English dictionaries and which means trash, offal. These Jewish litterateurs wrote melodramas, sentimental, romantic, low comedies with impossible plots. Their crime was that they gave the people what they wanted, what they enjoyed. This dereliction will be discussed later.[4]

JACOB GORDIN

The modern Yiddish theatre started, so we are told, when Goldfaden put Yiddish plays together in the Rumanian town of Jassy. The next step was the rugged melodrama as developed in the United States in the 1880's and 1890's by Latteiner, Horowitz, Shaikewitz, and a number of others. Inevitably sooner or later American Jews would tolerate, if not welcome, theatrical performances more in accord with the best European and Broadway traditions. That moment came in the early 1890's when Jacob Gordin began to write for the Yiddish stage. Gordin (1853-1909) was a well-educated Russian journalist. He was more Russian than Jew, culturally. "I am not a Jewish writer," he said, "I am merely a writer writing for Jews." Influenced by a heretical Russian Christian sect and possibly by a number of East European Jewish anti-nomistic traditions, he created the Spiritual Biblical Brotherhood which, in its rejection of rabbinic tradition and in its devotion to the Bible, was somewhat reminiscent of Russian Jewish Karaism. He emphasized ethics rather than the Torah Law; he urged his handful of followers to return to the soil, to artisanry. Never tolerating dissidence, the imperial government bore down on him and he left for the United States. Here, too, he wanted to develop his agrarian oriented cult, but the Baron de Hirsch people, committed to a return to the soil, rejected him because of his unacceptable religious views. To make a living, he began to write plays.

Gordin did not set out merely to entertain. (The dramatist, of course, always hopes to win his audience.) As far as it lay in his power, Gordin—a most sober man and mind—eliminated the weird, the preposterous, the inchoate, the impromptu. He expected his actors to stick to their text; the plot was fixed; the play was meaningful. His actors were expected to portray character and mood, to explicate themes, to react like human beings. As a Russian, he tended to push his realism to extremes. However, like most good dramatists, he,too, was compelled at times to stoop in order to conquer, but in his better works he dwelt on the theme of ingratitude, the parents betrayed by their own flesh and blood; he accentuated the conflict between Old World fathers and their wayward Americanizing children. He described the conflict which ensues when religious tradition clashes with love, when the Jewish home is threatened by intermarriage and the emancipation of women. Like Goethe's Faust, his dramas confronted the insidious power of wealth and position. These are universals, problems which Gordin borrowed from Shakespeare, Goethe, Tolstoy, and the sad world about him; none of it was escapist pabulum.

Like most Yiddish dramatists of his generation, this non-Hebrew "Enlightener" adapted many of his plays and plots from the great classics, from Goethe, Shakespeare, Ibsen, Gorky, Hauptmann, Strindberg, Chekhov. He set out to preach, to educate. He even established an Educational League in New York; in this sense, he was evangelical. His record was impressive; the Gentiles, Hutchins Hapgood, Edwin C. Markham, knew of his work, his aims. In Christian circles, he was New York's best known playwright even as Morris Rosenfeld was the ghetto's best-known poet. The critics admired him and respected him; he was certainly far removed from the more popular Latteiner, Horowitz et cie. The question is: how influential was he with the Downtown Jews? One cannot doubt that he had a substantial following; he was certainly versatile. He also wrote stories and essays. Was he a great dramatist? That is at least moot. One thing is certain; he raised the cultural and literary standards of the Yiddish stage; he was a reformer, an innovator, something of a revolutionary. The more serious theatregoers learned to admire him; he furthered the sense of the true and the beautiful.[5]

LIBIN, GORIN, AND KOBRIN

Gordin came to the United States in 1891. Within a few years, other Russians would settle in the United States, men who were to maintain the Gordin tradition of concern for the stage as a vehicle to challenge the thoughtful. Z. Libin (Israel Zalman [Solomon] Hurwitz, 1872-1955), Bernard Gorin (Isaac Goido, 1878-1925), and Leon Kobrin (1872-1946) were not only dramatists, they were also litterateurs, journalists, often translators. Few, if any, made a living at writing plays. They and a host of other literati turned to anything to keep themselves alive in order to write. It was not easy. Stylistically to a large degree, they were adherents of realism. In his stories and dramas, Libin described the lot of those who labored in the sweatshops. Arriving impoverished, he suffered in the effort to survive. For a time, he was a capmaker and newspaper deliverer. His skills, however, brought him to the attention of Cahan, and he became a staff writer on the *Forward*. Libin wrote thousands of stories, many of which may well serve to document the life of the workers in the factories and in their miserable tenement homes. Bernard Gorin, a Lithuanian, came to these shores in 1894. Like Hurwitz, he employed a pseudonym; Gorin was a pen name. It is difficult to understand why these litterateurs constantly employed pseudonyms unless this was imperative in Russia, where they had to cope with censors and police. Gorin was known as a writer in Russia and Poland before he found it necessary to move on to the United States, where he found work as an editor, a writer of ghetto tales, and a drama critic. For a time, he was to edit *The Jewish Farmer*. Historians will remember him gratefully for his two-volume *History of the Yiddish Theatre* (*Di Geshikhte fun der Idishen Theater*). In this work he listed 2,000 Yiddish plays, eloquent testimony to the significance of the Yiddish stage. Kobrin, who was to become a well-known novelist, playwright, and journalist in America's Yiddish world, left Russia in 1892 to make his way in this country. He had begun to write back home in Russia when but a youngster of fifteen. Like Libin, he struggled; it was not easy to make a living as a shirtmaker, baker, or newsdealer. He wrote for the socialist papers but finally found a haven on the staff of the *Day*. Ultimately, he was to be acclaimed by Yiddishists as one of their most distinguished writers and dramatists. His plays—despite or because of their eroticism and sensationalism—were successful. His stories of slums and workshops, true to life, betrayed the realistic influence exerted on him by Maupassant and Chekhov. Aided by his wife, he made Yiddish translations from the Russian and French; a few were adapted for the Yiddish stage. Some of his own writings, too, were translated into German, Russian, and English.[6]

HIRSCHBEIN AND PINSKI

Even Gordin, Libin, and Kobrin had to genuflect occasionally in the direction of Latteiner and Horowitz; vox populi, vox Dei; no one could hope to ignore *shund* entirely if he sought the approval of the masses. However, Gordin's influence was salutary. In addition to men like Libin and Kobrin, there were dramatists like David Pinski (1872-1959) and Peretz Hirschbein (1880-1948). The latter was a relative latecomer to the

United States. He was here in 1911 and, with the outbreak of World War in 1914, decided to make this country his bridgehead. Like other Yiddishists, he was a novelist as well as a dramatist. He had written and worked in Russia before coming here. Already a respected playwright, he traveled here with a troupe which produced some of his dramas. His works, like those of many of his colleagues, were in the realm of the realistic, but he was prone to reach out also to the idyllic, the mystical, the symbolic. Here he became a writer for the middle-of-the-road *Day*. His productivity was large; by 1930, an editor of his collected works had already published nine volumes. It was a source of annoyance to him that the theatrical lords ignored his dramatic writings and preferred to reap their profits from popular melodramas. For him, *shund* was a caricature, an abomination. His plays were rarely produced; they were good literature but not good theatre; he did not appeal to the masses.

David Pinski, an older contemporary, was not much more successful as a dramatist in winning the people. He was a voluminous writer who produced novels, short stories, essays, and travel sketches. For years after he came to this country in 1899, he edited labor papers. He began life as a Bundist, a Social Democrat, a Russian deeply troubled by the fate of his fellow Jews. The Kishinev massacre moved him to the right; the Russian pogroms drove most of the East European socialists into the Socialist-Zionist or other Jewish ethnic camps. Pinski became a Zionist Socialist. He distinguished himself as a pioneer in the Labor Zionist organization and its fraternal order. His play, *The Treasure*, was accorded considerable recognition; it was produced on the Yiddish, English, and German stages. The theme was universal; it dealt with greed and the corrosive power of wealth. His career almost spanned the life of Yiddish literature; when, like a good Zionist, he retired to the new State of Israel in 1949, the glow of Yiddishism had already begun to fade. Despite his diverse literary interests, Pinski was primarily a dramatist; he wrote more than eighty plays, but very few of them were produced; like Hirschbein's works, they could never become commercial successes. They addressed themselves to the cultured few. Pinski wrote well; his writings anticipated the rise of a Yiddish art theatre.[7]

YIDDISH ART THEATRE

Dramatic clubs peopled by amateurs were staging some of Pinski's plays as early as 1913, if not earlier. Theatrical groups in the German Jewish social clubs and YMHA's were producing English and German shows, dramas, and Purim entertainments decades before the rise of the Yiddish theatre. In the early 1880's, even before the Jews came in mass numbers to the American haven, there were Yiddishists here who yearned for good drama. The number of these discriminating enthusiasts increased in the course of the decade. The socialist intellectuals appealed for interesting dramas and beautiful musical operas. The comrades pleaded for a true portrayal of life. Everything unclean, crude and immoral was to be driven from the Yiddish stage. They asked for true art, aesthetics, education. As early as 1891, a socialist group in New York City began to produce plays. The dramas staged were not necessarily Jewish. Molière—adapted of course for a Yiddish-speaking audience—was one of their selections. In the same decade, admirers of Gordin organized a "folks-theater" presenting Yiddish plays in the best Gordinesque tradition, no trash. "Progressive" dramatic clubs began to appear in New York and in the larger cities of the backcountry. Many of the participants were women reaching out for better things, slowly moving forward to take their place alongside men. Much of the material was politically left, propagandistic, but these amateurs were careful to avoid the buffoonery of the popular presentations. A visit of the 1910 Vilna Troupe taught America that there was such a thing as good theatre.

Thus the ground had been prepared for decades for a theatre that would attempt to measure up to the standards of the best on the non-Jewish stage. This new type of drama, which owed much to Gordin, was indebted also to new actors who now appeared on the scene, Jacob Ben-Ami Shieren (b. ca.1890) and Maurice (Abraham Moses) Schwartz (1889/1890-1960), the one a native of White Russia, the other a Ukrainian. Ben-Ami had a career on the European stage before coming here in 1912. Six years later, he and Schwartz established a sophisticated Yiddish theatre which rejected the sensational, the sentimental, and the attractive disorder of the traditional Yiddish stage. After a year or two, however, Ben Ami moved Uptown to Broadway's English theatres, though he continued to travel to other lands starring in Yiddish roles. He was a good actor. Schwartz stayed behind and, after some hesitation, remained faithful to the ideals of the cultured Jewish theatregoers who looked to the stage for intellectual and aesthetic challenges. There were now Americanized Yiddish audiences who began to look with dismay on the old-fashioned rough and tumble presentations.

This new instrumentality was called the Yiddish Art Theatre. In its origin it owed much to Ben-Ami. Schwartz, like Ben-Ami, made his mark as an actor and director. Despite his Russian birth, however, he was in reality an American. His father, migrating to America, was compelled to leave young Abraham in London. There the ten or eleven-year-old worked for a time as a ragpicker. After Papa made enough money to bring the youngster over, he had some schooling, sold newspapers, and finally turned to the Yiddish stage. He had a long apprenticeship in the hinterland before he and Ben-Ami joined together in 1918 in the effort to revolutionize the American Yiddish stage. In a career that was to extend for decades, Schwartz mastered a huge repertory of the best Jewish and non-Jewish classics. Yiddish audiences were to have a feast of the best in both worlds: Sholem Aleichem, Peretz, Goldfaden, Sholem Asch, Gorin, Pinski, Hirschbein, Shakespeare, Schiller, Ibsen, Gorki, Oscar Wilde, George Bernard Shaw, Arthur Schnitzler. Over the years the Yiddish Art Theatre managed to survive; it played even to non-Jewish auditors who knew no Yiddish, but preferred a Maurice Schwartz production to a Broadway banality. The Uptown theatres had their own brand of *shund*.[8]

ACTORS ON THE YIDDISH STAGE

If the golden age of the inglorious *shund* enchanted East Siders and provincials, it was due to superlative acting. The vessel, the form, the play may have been tawdry; the acting was often magnificent. The pogroms brought good actors here from Russia. In the 1890's, when the Yiddish theatre developed in New York City, there were considerably fewer than 100,000 Yiddish-speaking men and women in the city; there were millions of Jews in Russia. Eastern Europe was still the hearth and nursery of the Yiddish stage; the murders in Russia impelled the best male and female actors to come to this land; they sensed this was the market of the future. The great artists who were to thrill the thousands here had already made careers for themselves on their native soil by the time they landed at Castle Garden and Ellis Island. Among these notables were Boris Thomashefsky, the Adlers, Mogulesco, Madame Keni Liptzin, David Kessler, Bertha Rachel Kalich, Maurice Moscovitch. These are the names that stud the indices in George C. D. Odell's massive *Annals of the New York Stage* and fill the pages of Zalman Zylbercwaig's multivolume *Lexicon of the Yiddish Theatre*. The actors were very important; the theatre-loving immigrants came to hear their favorites; the Yiddish theatre was built on and around the star system.

Boris Thomashefsky (1866?-1939) saw to it that he was a star in the many productions that he featured. This brilliant actor and theatrical entrepreneur was born in Russia of a family that, like the Adlers, was to build a theatrical clan, one that was numerous and notable. The handsome Boris who had come here with his father about the year 1881 worked, so it seems, in a tobacco factory for a time before devoting himself to a career on the stage. He sang in what may well have been the first professional Yiddish production in New York City in 1882. The family had voices and were musically gifted. (One of the descendants is a well-known American symphony conductor.) Young Thomashefsky early made a career as a musical comedy star; he was good looking; the women loved him; he had such beautiful legs! In a long varied career, he demonstrated that he was a gifted actor. He often starred in his own production of a Shakespearean work; on the night before, he may well have sung in a Goldfaden opera. Occasionally, he would step before the curtain between acts and entertain his audience with recitations from Byron's *Hebraic Melodies*. In English? Yiddish? Not infrequently, he appeared as actor, manager, and director in some of the classics of the Yiddish stage. Sigmund Mogulesco (1858-1914), a Rumanian, was a famous mime, comic, and singer. Like other Yiddish singers, he reached out into the infinite world of music for his melodies; musical theft was the order of the day. This brilliant performer had a large following in Rumania and in this land, to which he brought his troupe in 1886. In the course of time, Mogulesco was to become one of the most active leaders in the theatre industry. One of the men who had worked with Mogulesco in Rumania was David Kessler (1860-1920), destined to become a star in his own right. Here in New York, Kessler was to shine in Gordin's plays and by 1913 had a theatre of his own like the Adlers and the Thomashefskys.

FEMALE YIDDISH ACTORS

Thomashefsky's wife, Bessie, who was to become a notable actor, opened a theatre of her own when she and her husband parted company. The several competent Jewish actresses on the American Yiddish stage were highly respected and admired, though they never acquired the following of the males who strutted across the boards. It is not improbable that women actors were accepted or acclaimed because there were already notable actresses in America's Uptown theatres. This was the age when women were being accepted in the larger world; they were granted suffrage in 1920. More important is the fact that practically every play required women and this need was filled by brilliant performers like Bessie Thomashefsky, Sarah Adler, Keni Liptzin, Bertha Rachel Kalich, and several others. Kalich (1872/1874-1939), a tragedienne who was compared in later years to Sarah Bernhardt and Eleonora Duse, was a native of Galicia. Before she came to the United States in the early 1890's, she had embarked on a career in Europe as a singer, appearing most frequently in Yiddish productions. By the time she arrived here, she was ready for stardom but as a singer in the opera comique. Speedily she turned to serious roles, furthered by the best ghetto playwrights, who fashioned roles for her. There is every evidence that she was a magnificent actor; Harrison Grey Fiske, the producer, ever alert to new talent, gave her a five-year contract to appear on the English stage. In the course of her career, she was to appear in more than 100 different plays in seven different languages. One critic deplored that she was never "able to shake off her own strongly remarkable racial characteristics"; others admired her very much.

JACOB ADLER

The young Cincinnati seminarian Jacob Marcus, who went to hear Kalich in the second decade of the century, thought her too theatrical, but then this adolescent from the hills of West Virginia was hardly competent to judge an actor who performed in the grand style. A historian of the American Yiddish theatre maintained that Sarah Adler (1858-1953) was America's greatest Yiddish actress. In 1890, she divorced her husband Maurice C. Heine to marry the actor Jacob P. Adler (1855-1926). Young Marcus was also privileged to hear Jacob Adler when this histrionic Zeus loosed his verbal thunderbolts. Marcus shuddered with exquisite pleasure.

There is no question that Adler was acknowledged to be one of the leading stars of the rialto. Back in Russia, he had worked under Goldfaden in the late 1870's; he was a finished actor by 1883 when the Yiddish theatre was closed by Czar Alexander III. After a stay of several years in London, Adler moved on to the United States in the late 1880's, but success eluded him. He went back to Europe and then in 1889, recrossed the Atlantic. He was ready to play any part in a tragedy or comedy, but knew that his forte lay in serious drama. He had high standards. His opportunity came when Gordin wrote *Siberia*. Here he had a heroic role and he did justice to it. Success came with the years; he controlled more than one theatre where he grandiloquently played the roles of actor, manager, and theatrical entrepreneur. As early as 1893, he appeared as Shylock in Yiddish with an English-speaking cast. When Ben-Ami and Maurice Schwartz determined in 1918 to produce dramas of high quality, their project had not sprung full blown from their brows. There was then a vigorous tradition—almost thirty years old—of the importance of good theatre. This was documented in the playing of Adler and a number of his contemporaries. Yet, an examination of the data on the Yiddish ("Hebrew") stage described in detail in Odell's voluminous *Annals* proves conclusively that notable actors, stars, were ready to shine in almost any vehicle that offered itself. Apparently, they were not discriminating; they worked with Gordin as well as Horowitz; they had to earn a livelihood.[9]

THE YIDDISH THEATRE: ITS SIGNIFICANCE, A SUMMARY

Stars in their moments of success leased or owned theatres where they held forth. By 1917, there were seven Yiddish theatres in Greater New York. For as the economically mobile immigrants moved to Harlem, the Bronx, and various parts of Brooklyn, they took their theatres with them. By 1927, there were eleven in the metropolitan area, not to speak of the houses that catered to the immigrants in the East Coast cities, St. Louis, Los Angeles, and other towns. All told, there were twenty-four theatres offering their productions. There was something for everyone—melo-drama, serious fare, vaudeville, operettas, opera. Very many of the shows were adaptations. In the Jewish version of Hamlet, the villain is a rabbi in a Russian village; Hamlet, a rabbinic student. The villainous rabbi attempts to defame Hamlet as a Nihilist, but his machinations are discovered and he himself is exiled to Siberia. This is the Yiddish version, but the unadulterated Shakespearean text was also presented—in Yiddish, of course—with electric lights burning in the castle despite the fact that it would be many centuries before Edison appeared on the scene. What would one see in the Yiddish theatre in the 1880's: *Exile in Siberia, Ten Girls and No Man, The Last Days of Zion, The Jewish Persecution in France.* Odell, in his *Annals*, chided the Jews for their self-pity, their dwelling on persecution. On a Saturday night in 1893, the management stopped a performance which had dragged on till midnight. The Sunday laws were severe. The indignant crowd, robbed of their climax, insisted that the show go on or that they be given a refund. The police had to be called. By September, 1892, *The Return to Zion*, a historical opera, was offered the patrons of the Thalia. If this was a Zionist presentation—as it probably was—it was a reflection of the Love of Zion movement current in those pre-Herzlian days.

How many people went to the Yiddish theatres? Not as many as one might think. The proof is that few shows ran for more than seven days. Programs changed during the week; sometimes there were two different presentations in twenty-four hours, one at the matinee and one in the evening. One suspects that there was a hard core of devotees who went regularly; because of them, shows had to be staged frequently. Thousands may have gone to the theatres in a week, but let it be borne in mind that, by 1920, at least a million Jews in New York City understood and spoke Yiddish. The tickets were relatively costly; theatre was a luxury. Mondays through Thursdays were "benefit" days. All the seats were bought by a union, a charity, a society which then peddled the tickets to their followers in order to raise money for the organization. A benefit performance was a social occasion; people ate candy or sandwiches or drank pop during the intermission periods and visited with friends. The head of the society would come out between acts to harangue his group; a medal was awarded the person who had sold the most tickets. The actors, stagehands, and musicians were organized. Occasionally, there was a strike; it was difficult for a stagehand to live on $3 a week.

The mortal blow to the Yiddish theatre and to Yiddish culture came with the passage of the immigration acts of 1921 and 1924, although it was to be a long generation before the effects of those racially motivated laws were really felt in this country. Cultures do not die overnight. During the Middle Ages, it took at least a century before Arabic culture faded away in the Jewish communities of Spain and the Provence. The Yiddish theatre was to continue after the East European newcomers were denied entrance. The theatregoing devotees loved their dramas and operettas. Theatre attendance flourished in the 1930's. Good theatre developed primarily after the immigration acts were enacted, but what percentage of the masses were actually patrons of the Yiddish Art Theatre? Yiddish theatre at the turn of the century was an imperative psychological necessity; the new theatre that began with the second decade of the century was an aesthetic and intellectual luxury. The depression of the 1930's—when money was tight—hurt the theatre. Out in the provinces, exposed to the impact of the overwhelmingly Anglo-Saxon environment, the Yiddish theatres felt the crunch earlier. Indeed one of Chicago's Yiddish playhouses closed as early as 1911. The Americanization of the parents was a rapid process. Some of them, militantly American, began to withdraw from all institutions that were obviously Yiddishist. Many Jews learned to appreciate the midtown English-language drama; Yiddish stars moved north to Broadway—if only for a foray: Ben-Ami, Paul Muni (Muni Weisenfreund), Bertha Kalich, and even Jacob Adler. The silent movies and the radio rose as competition to the traditional vernacular stage. By World War II, the theatre was dying. Large numbers of its votaries were already dead.

With the exception of Hapgood and a number of venturesome and sympathetic critics, the Yiddish theatre was ignored and denigrated. Odell in his *Annals* barely conceals a patronizing tolerance. Nothing of this concerned the Downtown Jewish masses. Most of them liked the theatre. They would have summarily rejected the slur of the Jewish writer who called it a cross between a synagog and a bawdy house. For the theatregoer, the show was an emotional release. *Shund*, trash, cheap melodrama? They loved it; that is why *shund* was the bread and butter staple all through this period. Odell's pedantic listing of the shows makes this abundantly clear. The theatre was a solace and a comfort to the man or woman who had labored like a demon for ten to twelve hours a day in a shop or factory. Many were not bookreaders; thousands were illiterate unless the government statistics are false. Those who spent their hard earned 25 or 50 cents for a seat loved the theatre. They were thrilled in 1896 when they first heard Jacob Sandler's heartwarming lament, "My God, My God why hast thou forsaken me?" Gordin's *Jewish King Lear* and *Mirele Efros* plucked at the heartstrings of thousands; the ingratitude of children, their rejection of the values parents cherished, moved them deeply. The sentimental, romantic, emotional dramas of the Yiddish stage constituted no evidence of "decadence," as the critics maintained. If anything, they were the golden age of the theatre; this is what the masses needed to sustain them. It pointed up their problems and gave them a brief moment to shed a tear. The historical dramas of biblical heroes, of the warriors who baited the Syrians and the Romans, who refused to bow before the Spaniards and the Russians—all these were a source of pride and exaltation. A sweatshop worker who could ill afford the cost ran to the theatre with his young son to listen to Sholem Aleichem, Jacob Gordin, Shakespeare, Gorki, Tolstoy, Schiller, and Goethe. He thrilled to the words of all the great Yiddish stars; he could recite from memory whole portions of Shakespeare and Schiller, of *The Merchant of Venice* and *The Robbers*. The classics, even some of the melodramas, were never without their message; they were a slice of life holding a mirror up to reality, exposing vice, preaching morality, evoking new intellectual concepts.[10]

THE YIDDISH PRESS

THE EARLY PRESS TO 1880

The Yiddish press made its appearance in New York City more than a decade before the first professional theatre performance was staged there. East European Jews had been coming to the United States in a steady stream since the late 1850's because of bad economic conditions, epidemics, and political oppression. It was inevitable that they would create a press in a language that they understood. In 1678 when Amsterdam apparently sheltered the largest Jewish community in Europe, the dominant Spanish-Portuguese had published a periodical in their own Iberian dialect, and the Ashkenazim there had put out a Yiddish paper of sorts in 1686, though neither journal was destined to survive. The Jews in Russia first witnessed the appearance in their country of a modest Yiddish periodical in the 1860's. It is somewhat surprising that a Judeo-German weekly would be published in New York City in 1870, at a time when at the most there were but 10,000 East European immigrants in town. Most probably, the answer is that post-Civil War America was enjoying a boom; opportunities here were deemed limitless. On March 1, 1870, J. K. Buchner, a Russian or German Pole, put out No. 1 of the *New York Judeo-German Paper, the Hebrew Times (Di New Yorker Yidish-daytshe Tsaytung)*. It was to appear weekly—and it did, sporadically—priced at six cents. This was a Judeo-German lithographed paper written in Hebrew script. The Yiddish was actually an acceptable German. The words were vocalized to make it easy reading for the untutored. In all likelihood, Buchner hoped to attract German-reading Jews, many of whom still used the Hebrew rather than the Latin alphabet. Buchner, who had already published German and Yiddish periodicals in Germany and in London, made his living on this side of the Atlantic by selling sewing machines on the installment plan and running a modest peddler supply house, where he offered New

Year cards and red woolens. He lectured at New York's folk-university, Cooper Union, on Moses Mendelssohn, on Israel Baal Shem Tov, the founder of Hassidism, and on Israel Jacobson, the German Jewish organizer of Reform Judaism. Obviously, Buchner was a modern man.

In his modest New York sheet, he offered brief news tidbits from Europe and Palestine. The Jews are suffering in the Danubian principalities (Rumania); Russia is conscripting Jews cruelly; Gentiles are giving charity to the Palestine poor; the Turks are not mistreating the Jews in Jerusalem; there are revolutionary troubles in Paris. Interesting are his comments on contemporary New York: Congregation Bnai Jeshurun has mistreated its hazzan; the Russian refugees here are suffering for lack of food and clothing; the rich Jews spend millions on new temples, but won't help the immigrant poor. Biblical scholars of today will certainly be interested to note that this issue contains a letter from Elijah the prophet, who was then visiting America. Elijah informs the editors and the readers that, as an Orthodox Jew, he refuses to attend a Reform synagog. The prophet of old also assures Editor Buchner that he would read his Jewish newspaper; he does not read Gentile languages. To entertain his readers, the editor relates the true story of a young teacher who fell in love with an attractive girl, one of his pupils. To be sure, the story continues, girls do not require much education. Though Buchner solemnly assures his subscribers that he will stay out of politics, it is not improbable that he and some of his immediate successors were financed by Gentile and Jewish politicians who hoped to garner the East Side immigrant vote. By the early 1870's, other Germanized Yiddish papers had made their appearance. A pogrom in Odessa in 1871 heightened the interest of Russian immigrants in their native land. Isaac M. Wise, of Cincinnati, denounced these new Yiddish journals as trash. Finally, in 1874, after some failures, Kasriel Hersch Sarasohn (1835-1905), America's pioneer Yiddish journalist, succeeded in publishing a weekly that survived: the *Jewish Gazette* (*Yudishe Gazeten*). Before the decade passed, there would be a Yiddish printer and a Yiddish bookstore offering their services to the newcomers.[11]

THE YIDDISH PRESS, 1880-1920

INTRODUCTION

When the Russian Jews poured into this country in the 1880's, fearing pogroms and seeking opportunity, they began to publish journals—in Yiddish, of course. They may have been influenced by the appearance of similar papers in London, where some immigrants had stopped over on the way to the Golden Land. The press was important to the newcomers here. It told them what was going on in the lands they left, where their kin still remained. Despite the disabilities imposed on Jews there, most exiles were still tied to the Eastern Europe which had been so unkind to them. The press was important for another reason; all Yiddish literature had its beginnings in the dailies, weeklies, and monthlies; here was where the writers—journalists themselves—first published their poems, their sketches, their novels, their essays. Before 1890, dozens of Yiddish periodicals had already made their appearance only to fold after a few issues. Those who hoped to attract the humble appealed to them in "potato-Yiddish," in a simple, terse, understandable lingo into which commonly used English words and phrases had crept. There were two types of periodicals which now appeared on the scene, the folk papers and the radical, the Marxist, periodicals. The latter, appealing to the so-called intelligentsia, to aspiring rebellious workingmen and women, were essentially propagandistic, preaching socialism and anarchism. Their literary level was high. Even the pre-Herzlian Zionists had begun to publish a journal of their own by 1890. They called it *Sulamit*; traditionally, Sulamit was King Solomon's sweetheart. One publisher in those early days was less than honest. He printed a notice for a naive Gentile businessman assuring readers that the suspenders manufactured by his client were kosher. He was careful not to include this deceptive advertisement in the copies he sent his Jewish subscribers—who knew that kashrut applied in the main to food.[12]

THE YIDDISH PRESS OF THE MASSES

The press read by the religious masses had subscription lists larger than those of the Marxists. In 1885, Sarasohn published the first copy of a new daily after two other ventures had failed. He called this new paper *The Jewish Daily News, Yidishes Tageblatt*. It was the first Yiddish daily newspaper that was to survive. It is nothing less than remarkable that the *Tageblatt* could be published in a city where there were only about 100,000 Jews, some of whom could not read any language. The Russian Empire with its millions was to have no daily Yiddish journal until 1905. Sarasohn was probably helped in his enterprise by the new linotype machine perfected by Ottmar Mergenthaler in 1884. The road was now open to speedy cheap printing that would make mass circulation possible. The *Tageblatt* was Orthodox; it hewed to the line. Though Sarasohn is occasionally described in the biographical lexica as a journalist, he was in reality a publisher—and a real survivor. In his successes, he is comparable to Abraham Cahan, though ideologically the two were poles apart. Sarasohn had only contempt for the anarchists and the others of his day who deliberately flouted the sancta of Judaism by staging balls on the Day of Atonement. Like many other East European newspapermen, this dogged entrepreneur had studied Talmud and remained loyal at all times to the traditions of his fathers. He was aggressive in his attempts to bring some order into the funds that were syphoned off to support the faithful in the Holy Land. His efforts may be viewed as the reaching out of American Jews for authority in the countries across the seas. The turn of the century was to witness the first hegemonic strivings of America's Jewish community. In 1901 Sarasohn had to cope with a rival, the *Jewish Morning Journal, Der Morgen Zhurnal. The Morning Journal* was Orthodox and quite Zionistic but somewhat less pietist than the *Tageblatt.* It soon attracted a substantial following and from 1906 to 1911 was probably the largest Yiddish daily in the country. Because it was a morning paper, it carried a long list of want ads eagerly read by people looking for jobs. It had foreign correspondents who cabled the news from Russia, Poland, and the Balkans.

In 1902, a year after the *Morning Journal* first appeared on the stands, Masliansky, America's notable Yiddish preacher, together with a number of associates, founded the *Jewish World, Di Yidishe Velt.* Lacking money, Masliansky turned to the Uptown Jews, to Louis Marshall and his cohorts. Masliansky, an Americanizer, knew where they stood, and they rallied to his help financially. Marshall had no respect for any of the Yiddish newspapers, certainly not the Marxist organs. This was the age of William Randolph Hearst and his sensationalism; Marshall was strongly of the opinion that the Yiddish dailies were not uninfluenced by the "yellow" press. The Uptowners wanted a clean wholesome religious paper, one that was anti-Tammany and committed to civic reform. The *Jewish World* was not successful; the East Side throngs distrusted almost everything that was controlled by the "German" elite. They even looked askance at the new Jewish Theological Seminary and the Uptown-sponsored settlement house, the Educational Alliance. By 1905, there was a new daily on the streets, *The Truth,* the *Jewish Daily Warheit,* which appeared the year that the murders in revolutionary Russia reached the thousand mark. The newspaper was politically to the left of the *Jewish Daily News* and the *Jewish Morning Journal,* both of which were Republican. The *Warheit* leaned toward the Democrats.

The workers in the vineyard of the Yiddish press had long ago organized themselves into unions; the typesetters had established a relatively strong organization as early as the 1880's; the newsdealers had come together in 1908, the deliverers in 1910. Four years later, three Americanizers announced the publication of a new daily, *The Day, Der Tog.* These three were Rabbi Judah L. Magnes, America's beloved young Lochinvar, Bernard Semel, a communal worker active in the attempt to organize the East Siders into a compact community, and the brilliant journalist Herman Bernstein. *The Day,* like the *Warheit,* was liberal and hoped to build a solid respectable paper whose standards would be exemplary.

Five years later, in 1919, it absorbed the *Warheit*. By that time, the Yiddish press had already started to decline; its days were numbered.[13]

THE RADICAL PRESS, ANARCHIST AND MARXIST

A radical Yiddish press made its appearance in the United States almost as early as the conventional, non-Marxist journals. There was a short-lived left-wing Yiddish paper in this country as early as 1878. From the point of view of modern western culture, the radical press was superior. Though its editors and some of its readers were grounded in rabbinics, they were intellectuals who were also interested in the fine arts and the sciences. They were socialists, anarchists, non-theists, Marxists—moralists, too—whose goal was to educate Jews. They were interested in the class struggle and the social revolution. Jewishly, they were schismatic; they were not concerned with Jewish survival; they opposed the Orthodox as obscurantists and the Zionists as nationalists. The radicals were internationalists, cosmopolitans. By the 1880's and 1890's, there was a press of monthlies, weeklies, and a daily, too, staffed by notable writers. With exceptions, the most notable journalists wrote for this new radical press which blossomed here on the free soil of America. These men, all East Europeans, would not have dared to express themselves publicly in darkest Russia. During the last two decades of the nineteenth century, this new left-wing press printed the best of European literature, in Yiddish translation, for the aspiring workers and the petty bourgeois of Jewish immigrant America. This was a contribution of no mean sort.

Several of these liberal periodicals were excellent. Among them were the *Arbeiter Zeitung* (*Workers' Press*, 1890), *Di Tsukunft* (*The Future*, 1892), the *Abendblatt* (the *Evening Paper* 1894), the *Forverts* (the *Forward*, 1897), and the *Freie Arbeiter Stimme*, (*The Worker's Free Voice*, 1890). The socialist *Future*, was literary and educational in its aims. Its very first issue carried a contribution by the thoughtful, heterodox Jacob Gordin, a biography of Karl Marx by Morris Hillquit, a discourse on Darwin by Abraham Cahan, and a study of the proletariat by Daniel De Leon. Here was an intellectual galaxy. Despite its Yiddish garb, the *Future* claimed not to be a "Jewish" paper. Like all radical periodicals, it set out to be a propaganda instrument. The *Abendblatt*, was the first Socialist Labor daily; the *Forward* was a later rival. The anarchistic *Freie Arbeiter Stimme* was one of the best of the radical periodicals; its cultural standards were high. The Socialist Zionists, squaring the circle of nationalism and internationalism, began to issue the *Jewish Warrior* (*Der Idisher Kempfer*) in 1906. By the early 1900's, there was a paper for every taste; for the Orthodox and socialists of different hues, for the Zionists, for the Territorialists who were willing to colonize Jews outside of Palestine, and for the Diaspora nationalists who preached the gospel of Jewish ethnicity in any land anywhere. By 1922, the Soviet

Communist influence had made itself felt in the ghettos of this land. The communist Workers' Party of America came out with *Di Frayhayt* (*Freedom*). The 1917 revolution—so thousands believed—was the fulfillment of a messianic dream, but the socialist unity, such as it was, was shattered.

After 1911, the *Forward* was the Yiddish paper with the largest circulation in the United States. Whether it was the most important Jewish periodical is moot. It was "Jewish," but not traditional and not part of the Jewish mainstream; many of its readers were indifferent to its socialism, and even some Orthodox practitioners were to be numbered among its subscribers. It was a good paper, cleverly, brilliantly edited. The success of the *Forward* was, in large part, due to Abraham Cahan, its editor. When Cahan landed at Castle Garden, there were fewer than 300,000 Jews in this land; when he died, there were about 5,000,000. The paper he first edited had about 6,000 subscribers; it was ultimately to be read by hundreds of thousands. He was fated to witness the rise and decline of the Yiddish press and Yiddish culture. When Cahan returned to the *Forward* in 1902-1903, he knew how to run a paper and, in the next forty-some years, would demonstrate that he was one of America's most enterprising editors. He had been in this country twenty years when he "went back" to the ghetto. The job that confronted him was almost disheartening. The paper had begun with small donations from devout socialist believers who were determined to build durable unions, to crush the sweatshops, and to promote social reforms. Before Cahan finished his task, his paper—and it was *his* paper—had twelve national editions, including one that circulated in Los Angeles. The *Forward* made money and succeeded in building a skyscraper on East Broadway. This was Jewish socialism, American model.

Cahan's story is also the story of a socialist who slowly, almost imperceptibly, moved to the right. In this, he was typical of a whole host, for there were thousands of Marxists on the East Side at the turn of the century. By 1911, after about thirty years in the United States, he voiced no objection to Jews—his socialist Jews—observing the Passover Seder. Obviously, he would be sympathetic to the Soviets when they first established their state, but he turned bitterly against them when he became convinced by their autocracy that there was no balm in the Soviet Gilead. By the 1920's he drew closer to the Jewish people. The gates were closed to immigrants; Jews were suffering in the new national—and still anti-Semitic—succession states of Eastern Europe; Palestine was the only hope for refugees; even Zionism ceased to be objectionable to this internationalist. He began to realize that he was not only a humanitarian; he was also a Jew. He had his finger on the pulse of the Downtown Jews. When Sholem Asch set out to do a Yiddish trilogy on Jesus, Mary, and Paul, the atheistic Cahan warned him that the Jews, victims of Christian prejudice, would deeply resent what he wrote. During the 1930's, Cahan even accepted Roosevelt and his New Deal; he had become a socialist with "common sense." A decade after Cahan's death, the *Forward* embraced the State of Israel and smiled benignly on Orthodoxy.

Cahan ran his empire with an iron hand which was not gloved in velvet. He was a good hater, not apt to forgive his enemies. Emotionally, he was a force for good in the American Jewish immigrant community. Selig Perlman, the economist, called him the greatest mass educator in American Jewish history. This may be true. He did not disdain to write an editorial on the need of a clean handkerchief for a child at school. The *Forward* once carried an article on the "Fundamentals of Baseball Explained to Non-Sports." He preached humanism, morality; he serialized translations of the finest in the European classics. Jews, he said, must become citizens; his paper published articles on American Jewish history, and ran columns on the English language. With an ironic grin, a Jewish humor paper warned Cahan that by teaching the immigrants English the *Forward* was cutting its own throat. There are times when a funeral is the measure of the man. When Cahan died, the masses thronged to salute him as he passed into eternity. They were not driven by guilt because they had neglected him. They had respect for Cahan, who had taken a struggling sheet and made it a force in the lives of myriads. It was a great funeral; the United States Secretary of Labor spoke; the ambassador from the State of Israel paid his respects. The *Forward* had traveled a far distance from *Das Kapital*. Cahan built well; his paper survived all the other dailies to 1983, when it, too, surrendered to the inevitable.

MORE ON THE *FORWARD*

The historian cannot dismiss Cahan without a further paragraph on the paper. Why was it successful? What did Cahan do that moved people as far as the Pacific Coast to welcome this newspaper into their homes? Certainly, until the 1920's at least, the *Forward* was a socialist organ. It fought for the unionization of workmen, for the underdog. It was anti-Tammany, anti-capitalist, anti-trust. It helped send Meyer London, the Marxist, to Congress; it subsidized strikers and aided an English-language socialist journal. Cahan employed the best Yiddish writers in the world, both Americans and Europeans (unless they were in his dog house); he put his novelists on a regular salary, a most unusual procedure; the *Forward* became a treasure house of the best in modern literature. Yet, this man always had an eye toward the wind; he knew how to win the masses and he catered to them. William Randolph Hearst, the successful yellow journalist, was an ever present exemplar. The *Forward* was never without its attractive romances and stories; *shund*, if you will, had been a Yiddish journalistic staple since the 1880's; it was never out of style completely.

The simple Yiddish Cahan persisted in using was an intelligible medium. He appealed to women.

His *Bintl Brief,* "Bundle of Letters," fascinated all his readers. In 1906, he started a column of letters to the editor. The paper encouraged its readers to write in, to vent their problems, to ask for help. This was a most successful innovation. Over the years, thousands wrote. The letters were carefully culled; the most interesting were published. True, some—probably many—were "improved" in the editorial office; some may even have been concocted there. Nevertheless, it is likely that the letters constituted an adequate sampling of the difficulties faced by newcomers. These missives reflect the social pathology, not the norms; they mirror the challenges faced by European city denizens and rural villagers confronting the challenges, the bitter disillusions, of an industrial metropolis. There was no end to the problems described in the *Bintl Brief.* People wrote of love, marriage, desertion, sexual freedom, intermarriage, child delinquency, Sabbath observance. The peddler beaten by hoodlums appealed for help; the freethinking socialist asked if he should recite prayers for his dead, if he could attend synagog on the Day of Atonement—only to listen to the melodies, of course. Can a non-believing cantor lead the congregation in prayer? What is a modern man to do who balks at the formality of a wedding? Over the years, millions read the *Bintl Brief* and derived comfort. By the late twentieth century, two Jewish columnists, the Friedman sisters, "Dear Abby" and "Ann Landers," were writing in English for national and international audiences of millions who also sought answer to their dilemmas.[14]

PRESS NOTABLES

Cahan was certainly the most notable of America's Yiddish journalists and editors; he had rivals, though most of them were not really comparable. They were not quite as successful. Over the years 1890 to 1920, there were literally hundreds, if not thousands, of competent Yiddish journalists. There was really no typical Yiddish newspaperman; the only characteristic common to all was that they were of East European birth and that they worked and wrote for Yiddish papers. Anyone worth his salt differed from his colleagues; he was sui generis. Saphirstein, owner of the very successful *Morning Journal,* was primarily an entrepreneur, though he wrote frequently for his own publications. Zevi Hirsch (Harris) Masliansky, the publisher of the Yiddish *World,* was famous for his oratory. The editor of the first Zionist magazine cannot be ignored for he established his periodical just about a decade before the appearance of Herzl's *Jewish State.* This proto-Zionist was Moses Isaac Mintz (1860-1930). Interesting is the fact that his paper was also socialist; he had no difficulty harmonizing the two conflicting philosophies, nationalism and internationalism.

Mintz, who had become a Lover of Zion back in his native Russia, spent some time in the Palestinian colonies before emigrating to the United States. In addition to his work as a journalist and editor, this able man earned a degree in medicine here and worked for years for the New York Board of Health. Later, he returned to Palestine. His paper was one of the very first to publish the poetry of Morris Rosenfeld. There were several Mintz brothers, gifted men, carrying on the family tradition of scholarship.

Practically all these journalists had begun life as students of the Talmud; they had whetted their minds on rabbinical literature. John Paley had come here from Lithuania in 1888 and and, within a year, turned to editorial work. Some five years later, in 1894, he went to work for the Sarasohns and their papers, building circulation through a liberal dose of sensationalism and romantic fiction. He was quite a writer of literary trash. One of his contemporaries was Jacob Adler (1874-1975), not to be confused with Jacob P. Adler, the celebrated actor. Adler, the writer, a native of Galicia, had come to America as a youngster and had worked for years as a tailor until he turned to journalism. This newspaperman might well have bragged that he had employed more than a dozen pseudonyms. He began in the late 1890's writing poetry for the new *Forward*; in 1911, he was a member of the staff. His literary output was prodigious; over the years, he contributed articles to more than fifty periodicals, wrote about a dozen books, 18,000 poems, and more than 30,000 humorous essays. Like many Jewish journalists, he was also a playwright. One of his stage shows was *Yente Telebende*. It may well be that his *Yente* popularized the word to indicate a somewhat vulgar, unattractive Yiddish mama.

Saphirstein was a Pole, Adler a Galician, David Moses Hermalin (1865-1921), a Rumanian. Hermalin, who had played a part as a journalist of repute in his native country, settled in America after he was compelled to leave. He arrived about the year 1886 and taught French and Hebrew. (Most of these Yiddish writers were multilingual; many were autodidacts.) Over the years, he edited magazines, wrote plays, made translations from the English and Russian, and achieved distinction as Jewry's most admired family page editor. Exceedingly versatile, he could write attractively on any subject and did. In addition to the thrillers he concocted, Hermalin published studies of Jesus and Mohammed, and produced a sort of Yiddish *Lamb's Tales of Shakespeare* for the delectation of his readers. Hermalin knew a little bit about everything; George (Goetzel) Selikovitsch (1863-1926) was a scholar at home in English, French, Yiddish, and Hebrew. It was Selikovitsch who translated the teachings of Buddha into Hebrew. This Kovno-born journalist, a talmudist of note even as a child, was a Semitist and an Egyptologist. In 1885, he accompanied Lord Wolseley and Kitchener when they marched to the relief of Gordon Pasha besieged by the Sudanese in Khartoum. Selikovitsch was the interpreter. Shortly after he settled in the United States in 1887/ 1889, he lectured on the Egyptians, but finally turned to the *Tageblatt*, where he reigned as literary editor for a quarter of a century. Because of his knowledge of foreign languages, the Republican party hired him to electioneer for McKinley when he ran for president.

One of the most noted of all Yiddish newspapermen went by the pseudonym of Morris Winchevsky (1856-1932); his original name was Lippe Benzion Novachovitch, and his legal name was Leopold Benedict. "Newspaperman" hardly encompasses the world of this granddaddy of Yiddish writers and social reformers. Winchevsky came to this country relatively late, in 1894, after a historically significant career in London, where he had pioneered as a Yiddish socialist and writer. He went to London because he had been driven out of Germany and Denmark. In 1884, he edited the first socialist Yiddish paper in London. This Lithuanian émigré finally settled in the United States, where he was warmly welcomed by the radicals. He was already a notable with an international following; here he wrote poetry, plays, novels, and essays. Winchevsky's translations of the works of Victor Hugo, Ibsen, and others contributed to the education, the Westernization, of his readers. He wrote for the *Forward* and served for a time as an editor of the *Future*. As a socialist, he wrote to usher in a universal free society. That was his prime goal, although he always maintained a sympathy for the Jewish people. In the 1920's, he welcomed the rise of the new Soviet state in Russia.

Like Selikovitsch, Peter (Peretz) Wiernik (1865-1936) was a child prodigy with a phenomenal memory. He is noteworthy not because he was unusually distinguished—he was not—but because of what he accomplished quietly and effectively; he was a productive journalist. After leaving Russia in 1885, he settled in Chicago and struggled there for a couple of years to make a living; he was a peddler, a stevedore. In those years, he sympathized with the anarchists; it was the time of the Haymarket Massacre. It was in Chicago that he learned English well; he read Gibbon, Hume, and Rousseau. He nursed his Hebrew knowledge by working closely with the Expounders of the Hebrew Language (Dorshe Safrut Ivrit); he had always been a lover of the Bible. Around the year 1887, Wiernik got a job on the local Yiddish newspaper, *The Courier*; he was office boy, typesetter, reporter, writer; several years later, he was appointed chief editor. After a few years in this new post, he moved on to New York, where he worked for Sarasohn on the *Jewish Daily News*. There he was in charge of the English page of this Yiddish daily. He made extra money by writing articles for *The Jewish Encyclopedia*, which paid him one cent a word. Exploitation? No! Every five words he turned in would buy a loaf of bread. By 1901, he had switched to Saphirstein's

Morning Journal; there he finally became the chief editor; his job was to write the editorials.

While working for Saphirstein in 1912, he wrote his *History of the Jews in America*, the first full-length narrative of what had happened to the Jews in the Western Hemisphere since Columbus set sail in 1492 with a Jewish interpreter on board. Isaac Markens's *Hebrews in America* (1888) is structurally and historiographically inadequate; the work of Wiernik, the immigrant, is far superior. In New York, he worked closely with the leaders of the Jewish community, aided the Joint Distribution Committee which brought relief to the victims of World War I, and looked with favor on the new Rabbi Isaac Elchanan Theological Seminary, though he was not a synagoggoing Jew. In politics, he voted the Republican ticket; yet, when during World War I the government threatened to close the *Forward* because of its socialism and anti-war policies, Wiernik joined Louis Marshall in protesting this action. Wiernik was indifferent to the demands of the Zionists for a sovereign state, yet this man—known for his intractable stubbornness—successfully edited a powerful pro-Zionist newspaper for almost a generation. Yiddish journalists were compelled to follow the line and policies laid down by the owners. Wiernik was a fervent Americanizer.[15]

THE YIDDISH PRESS: A SUMMARY
AN ANALYSIS OF SELECTED ISSUES

The Yiddish press in the early decades of the twentieth century was a penny press; later a copy of the Communist *Freiheit* cost three cents. But almost everyone could afford the few pennies to keep in touch with a very exciting world. The bourgeois papers like the *Jewish Daily News*, the *Morning Journal*, and the *Day* were similar; the socialist *Forward* and its adversary the Communist, pro-Soviet *Morning Freiheit* (*Freedom*) were different—Workers of the World Unite—yet all the papers had much in common. Every issue of every daily was interesting; the "mix" was good: there was solid instruction, learning, culture, belles lettres, news of every genre from near and distant lands. The *Freiheit* was more likely to describe the virtues of Birobidjan, the new Jewish region in the Russian Far East, a potential rival of Zionist Palestine. These Yiddish papers were influential; in 1910 the *Tageblatt* bragged that it went into 70,000 homes; the *Forward*, into 83,000 homes. The English language had penetrated almost every Yiddish paragraph; they were American papers in Yiddish.

If a press in Yiddish reflected the needs of the newcomers it is manifest that it would print news of interest to Jewish men and women who were not only Jews but East Europeans. This it did. What was news: a collection for an orphanage, a column on the doings of the unions, strikes, World War I in Russia, wounded Jewish soldiers in a hospital, oppression in St. Petersburg, the lynching of a rich Jew by the Persians, the denying to Oscar Hammerstein, the impresario, of a visa to visit the Romanov Empire. A pasha in Haifa, Palestine, intervenes to protect Jews; Socialist Meyer London, now in Congress, announces his intention to fight anti-Semitism, to oppose restrictive immigration laws, to protect proletarian workers. There is a report that Taft would help the Russian Jews (he did not); fraternal orders record their activities; a Jew living in America learns that his wife and children were murdered back in Russia; an American judge declares sententiously that Europe is sending its criminals to this country; the Joint Distribution Committee has now been organized to bring relief to the victims of World War I. There is no dearth of news on general Zionism and Socialist Zionism. But the Yiddish dailies are in no sense Jewishly parochial. The Socialists are losing elections; Commander Perry is moving on to the North Pole; the Indians of Yucatan are suffering; William Jay Gaynor, newly elected mayor of the city, is organizing his staff; gigantic trusts are being established; Tammany is important in the Board of Aldermen; Finland's freedom is threatened; Victor L. Berger, the Milwaukee Socialist congressman, discusses the need of a separate workers' party.

But solid news of this type will not satisfy the masses; they want more for their penny: bandits have held up a train; a girl returning from her vacation in the Catskills commits suicide; a powder magazine has blown up; five persons coming back from a funeral have been run over by a train; a polygamist is sent to jail; a man shoots his mother; another poisons his wife; a banker defaults; a procurer is arrested; a "bummer" who insults a girl is sent to the workhouse; a midwife dies while delivering a child; a woman throws her children out of a window as a fire rages. This is news. If one's intellectual's palate is still not titillated then there is always the *Bintl Brief*, the "Bunch of Letters": a tuberculosis victim, compelled to go to Denver, discovers that during his absence his wife has sold the store and taken the children, and run off with a stranger. What shall I do?

There were always some newcomers who had interest in culture, who were willing to reach out to new horizons of thought and knowledge. Provision was made for them. They could expect a good editorial on Labor Day; there were articles on commerce, on tariffs, on a coloratura singer, on Zangwill's *Melting Pot*, his plea for assimilation, on Conservative Judaism, on Bukharian Jews in Palestine, on Christmas and New Year's customs, on the Socialist Party. When Claude Montefiore, the English Reform Jew, wrote of Jesus with reverence, a Yiddish editor took him to task; another admonished his readers to learn English; a distinguished Semitist and Yiddishist asked his admirers: Is a college education worthwhile? What is the value of a diploma?

The girls, women, and men, too, who slaved in a factory or sweatshop wanted more than "news," more than the oracular utterances of a Sorbonne graduate; they wanted romance. This was supplied—in abundance—by all Yiddish papers; the Communists and the Socialists, too, hastened to genuflect. The *Forward*, in particular, emphasized belles lettres. All papers ran stories and serialized romances; there was no issue without some fiction. The title is the message: "The Secret of the Throne," "The White Slaves," "The Mother's Sin," "The Red Widow," "The Wild Man." For those who wanted more substantial fare there were translations from L. N. Andreyev, Count Leo Tolstoi, contributions by Sholem Asch. On New Year's day there were poems by Morris Rosenfeld and others.

Researchers in the field of Yiddish-speaking America might do well to recognize that the true history of this people cannot be written unless they read and analyze the advertisements; they are as important as the editorial page, the news columns, the feuilleton paragraphs; possibly even more revelatory. Here, one may venture to suggest, is the real history. Most of the shows, the theatrical productions, are advertised in the pages of the dailies; the great names stud the pages; there is a star and a tragicomedy for everyone. There is a "theatre" on the Bowery that offers a "show" that lasts for five hours, admission ten cents; the profit, probably, is in the beer that is sold. Zion's workers, the Poale Zion, invites you to a cultural evening of drama and recitations; there is a musical concert in the Educational Alliance settlement house; the Hebrew Publishing Company offers its clients books and New Year cards; an East Side secondhand bookstore assures browsers that it stocks 100,000 volumes (!!); the Hebrew *Ha-toren* (*The Mast*) pleads for subscriptions as did the anarchist *Freie Arbeiter Stimme*.

Because the Yiddish daily is typically American it advertises the same national products which invite buyers in the English and in all foreign language periodicals: Gulden's Mustard, Beecham Pills, Gold Medal Flour. Patent medicines? Magic Oil for rheumatism. Mining stocks! Bankers accept deposits, sell ship tickets, forward money to beloved ones abroad. The professionals invite patronage: dentists, doctors who provide free medicines. If you have a bad complexion there is a cure for you, too; oculists will fit you with glasses, frame and all, price, $1. There are always pawnbrokers; the Shoemakers Union urges you to buy only union made goods; a clever businessman offers the class-conscious garment worker, Workmen Circle cigarettes, ten for five cents. Comrade Abraham Cahan, editor of the *Forward*, urges you to buy his history of the United States. A dress goods wholesaler assures you that if you peddle his wares, you can make $30 to $100 a week. There are schools where—for a fee, of course —you can learn English, clothes designing, pass the naturalization exam.

A vacation? Go to the Catskills. Food: herring by the barrel, freshly killed poultry. John J. Rockefeller's Standard Oil advertises a variety of kosher candles. Good skilled workers are needed: buttonhole makers, operators, sleeve makers, trimmers, finishers on silk dresses. Apparently there are jobs in New York City for those who are competent, yet the Industrial Removal Office suggests politely that you leave town; skilled tailors, upholsterers, ironworkers do well in the hinterland.

Victrolas may be purchased for as little as $12; a good one costs $30. Pianos are advertised in almost every issue of every newspaper; a piano is expensive. Is all this talk about ghetto poverty poppycock? There was hardly a Saturday night without its masque and its full-dress civic ball. A prize would be awarded to the best tango dancers. The socialist *Forward* held its ball in Madison Square Garden; the prizes amounted to $1,000. The Kishinev landsmanshaft held a benefit ball for the orphaned children of that war-torn community; admission, twenty-five cents. The anarchists invited their friends to the Red Circle ball; the money made would go to help Russian political prisoners. The proletarian Workmen's Circle urged pleasure seekers to come to a full-dress ball. Advertisers offered a tuxedo for $12.50, a full-dress outfit could be purchased for $17 to $20. Patently these Marxists were not waiting for pie in the sky by-and-by. It is equally evident that we shall have to revise our stereotypes of the impoverished ghetto denizens.

Yiddish readers lived in a cosmos that included America and much more; theirs was a world of hard grinding labor, of potential culture, a world of romantic flights, of excitement. It offered them much; many, it would seem, were content with their lot; they often cursed Columbus, but they remained here. The Uptown elite, frequently superficial in its judgments, was unhappy with the Yiddish press, it wanted something better. Therefore, when Herman Bernstein published his first issue of *Der Tog* (*The Day*, 1914) America's most notable Jews rushed to congratulate him. He promised American Jewry that he would publish a paper that was absolutely independent. He was, he wrote, dedicated to the furthering of the Jewish people. It is clear that here we have an implied reflection on the dailies and the weeklies of the Orthodox, the socialists, anarchists, Zionists, and those who had made their peace with Tammany Hall. The masses, however, were content with their newspapers; they had their choice of dailies, for them their gazette was a treasured cultural instrument. Yet, future reseachers are challenged to determine the sense of civic responsibility, the degree of high-minded integrity which may or may not have distinguished its Yiddish newspaper publishers.

STATISTICS

Close to 100 American Yiddish periodicals of diverse hue had appeared and disappeared by the year 1920, among them twenty dailies. Foreign language newspapers were common in this land of immigrants. As late as 1920, there were about 1,500 foreign language papers published in the United States in thirty-three different languages with 8,000,000 readers. In the second decade of the new century, the *Forward* forged ahead as the daily with the largest circulation, although the non-Marxist papers were always to enjoy more readers than the socialist ones. America's New York Yiddish dailies recorded their highest circulation in 1917 with about 600,000 readers. (American Anglo-Jewish papers in the city could only recruit a mere 15,000 readers.) The coming of World War I, the cessation of emigration, the flare-up of Anglo-Saxon American nationalism and chauvinism frightened and silenced Americans of foreign birth and culture. In general, Americanizers were intolerant of those who read non-English papers. By 1917, the Orthodox *Jewish Daily News* was declining; in the long run, East European Orthodoxy and the Yiddish press would not survive in the United States.[16]

THE PRESS: WHAT IT WAS, TAUGHT, AND ACCOMPLISHED

The press was, and still is, important in this country. As early as 1900, there were over 17,000 periodicals in the United States; the Jews published between forty and fifty all told, in English, German, Yiddish, and Hebrew. Thus the one million Jews in this country were responsible for only a minuscule fraction of the papers that appeared. But for the immigrants from Eastern Europe, the Yiddish press was very important. One wonders what the Jewish press meant to the native-born and the acculturated "Germans"; they did not patronize their German and American-Jewish press enthusiastically nor subscribe in large numbers to the Jewish Publication Society. The native-born read few Jewish books or Jewish papers; they were on the whole an ill-educated group, Jewishly; completely Americanized, they read the English papers. The "Russians" had come from lands where they had but a tiny vernacular press of their own, one that was censored and controlled by a tyrannical regime. In America, the Yiddish press enjoyed better conditions; indeed, the press and Yiddish literature were inextricably one. Almost every Yiddish literary work made its debut first in a newspaper or a magazine. There were almost no Yiddish litterateurs who had not been journalists at one time or another. For the Slavic and Rumanian Jews, the press here was to open a new world. They had come from benighted lands; here in America the people who had sat in darkness saw a great light. For most of them, the Yiddish press was the open road—often the only road—to knowledge. The institutions which touched the lives of these newcomers revolved in general around a journal that helped them, taught them, guided them; the press made survival as Jews a strong probability. It provided them with a comforting ambience. There are some who maintain that these Yiddish journals constituted the most influential foreign language press in the country.

Why did Jews read the Yiddish press? Obviously, because it was really the only tongue they knew well. But there were other reasons. They loved Yiddish; they were desperately eager to know what was happening to their dear ones abroad. As intelligent people, they were interested in the general news too. The typical reader enjoyed his serialized novel; the intelligentsia prided itself on its interest in literature. An analysis of a sampling of editorials written during the second decade of the twentieth century discloses that, in descending order, the people—or the journalists—were interested in Palestine, relief in Eastern Europe during World War I, anti-Semitism, ethics, Jewish notables, American patriotism, socialism, and religion. Even when the subscribers were at home in English, they continued to read the Yiddish dailies; they turned to these journals because they were very much concerned about Jews and their problems.

The immigrant Jews—always individualists—had a periodical for every purpose and every taste, every ideology and every trade. The list is almost startling. The newcomers could subscribe and receive periodicals in the following areas: news, commerce, humor, literature, music, the theatre, religion, socialism, anarchism, communism from 1922 on, Zionism, Territorialism, Diaspora nationalism, politics (Republican, Democratic, independent). There was a paper for children, for women, for the grocer, the butcher, the chess player, the marriage broker (shadkhan), the farmer. The unions had papers for the fur workers, the cloakmakers, and for all branches of the garment industry, even for those who labored in neckwear. There were unions and papers for painters, knitters, moviegoers, bakers, cigarette makers, et al, et al. The Yiddish press taught the workers to organize, to cope with the industrial revolution. The radicals were determined to save the world and the Jews along with the others. For the older Marxists, Yiddish was a vehicle, not an end in itself, not a cherished language. Whether the Yiddish reader was or was not aware of the fact, his favorite newspaper was a prime instrument of Americanization. The philosopher Morris R. Cohen said that his Yiddish journal, more so than the English gazettes that he read, prepared him to be a good American. There can be no question that Yiddish dailies were eager to help their readers feel at home in this country. Many of the editorials dealt with American themes. The Jewish vernacular press Westernized and Americanized its followers; many of the new words incorporated into the "jargon" were English—and words make people think. The press explained this new country to the newcomers; and because the immigrants realized that this was a land of freedom, many listened to the editorial admonitions and opted for the citizenship that was denied them in their lands of origin. Explaining America furthered democracy.

It is something of an exaggeration to maintain, as some do, that the Yiddish press is an American one written in Yiddish, but the dictum is not without its element of truth. Influenced by the bohemian characteristics of the American newspaper fraternity, Jewish writers in the early twentieth century organized a drinking group of their own. They called themselves the Perpetual Boozers (Pi Tomid); it was hard, however, to get drunk on tea. As Abe Cahan recounts, the Americanization process was more manifest in the children than in the parents. A Jewish parent, perplexed by the steady supply of money brought home by a sturdy son, finally discovered that the young man was a professional pugilist. He was shocked that a man could make a living knocking out another man's teeth. Interested to attend a prize fight, papa was afraid that the Irish American opponent would kill his son; when the young Samson emerged victorious, papa did not know whether to be horrified by the brutality or proud of the victory!

With very few exceptions, the Yiddish press was staffed by litterateurs. In order to compete with one another, the papers were compelled to cater to the masses who insisted on their sentimental romances and their sensation-packed thrillers. On the other hand, there was a substantial minority who wanted content, material of a cultural, informative nature. They looked for news, poetry, good fiction, American and Jewish history, economics, politics, religion, popular science, manners, and mores. Because they had little secular education, they had never been book readers; the press was to become their Bible. Many developed literary interests; they found that most papers offered them a mixed diet, not only the crassly popular but also the best in the world's literature. Imitating the best non-Jewish journals the Yiddish press always offered some solid fare. Whether they were superior in this respect to the best American newspapers is questionable. The *New York Times* was no dispenser of trash. Appealing to the substantial minority of readers who had an appreciation of good literature, the Yiddish press—the magazines, in particular —published translations of the Russian classics, German, French, English, and American. Jewish immigrants could now read Tolstoi, Chekhov, Gorky, Hauptmann, Buckle, Zola, Jules Verne, Ibsen, and Darwin; there was even a translation of one of the histories of Graetz, the Jewish historian. American translations included Poe, Longfellow, Whitman, Bret Harte, and Edward Bellamy with his wonderful story, *Looking Backward*. New York City had long been a center of Yiddish culture; World War I sealed the fate of the Yiddish literary luminaries in Eastern Europe; the American Yiddish aesthetic and literary world now achieved a high degree of centrality. By 1920, Yiddish culture became an end in itself; ideology was no longer all important; propaganda did not dominate. The recurrence of brutal attacks on Jews in Russia and the threat of destruction that faced the Jews in the Eastern war zones dampened the international aspirations of the radicals and turned them inward; now they began to identify as Jews.[17]

CHAPTER SIXTEEN

YIDDISH LITERATURE

INTRODUCTION

American Yiddish literature, the writings of East European Jews in the United States, includes poetry, drama, fiction, and essays. New York was not the original home of Yiddish writing. Modern Yiddish literature had its origin in the Slavic lands and in Rumania. Indeed the three great classic writers, Shalom Jacob Abramowitsch (Mendele), Isaac Loeb Peretz, and Sholem Aleichem (Sholem Rabinowitz) were all still alive as late as the second decade of the new century. The Jews here were to develop their own Yiddish cultural center synchronously with those in Poland and Russia. In the early days, the 1880's, the Russian Jewish intelligentsia in their arrogance and naiveté evinced scant sympathy for the emerging Yiddish literature, though snobbery led them to respect the Russian and German classics. And how did non-Jewish American writers receive work by Yiddish writers? Yiddish writings were simply not welcomed into the realm of literature; of course, non-Jews had virtually no knowledge of the Yiddish language. *The Dictionary of American Biography* admitted very few Yiddishists into the sacrosanct lists of notable writers. Later, this was to change and Yiddish would become respectable. Even Yiddish-speaking Jews had few hopes for the new literature; Wiener of Harvard, the pioneer historian of Yiddish in this country, was convinced it had no future; Peter Wiernik shared this opinion; both men were native Russians. Yet Yiddish was destined to grow and win acceptance. A Yiddish book was printed in the 1870's; by the 1880's, there were textbooks, dictionaries, and a host of other writings. Over the decades, there were hundreds of Yiddish journalists producing millions of pages of reading material. In 1978, Isaac Bashevis Singer was awarded the Nobel Prize for literature; he was acclaimed for the beautiful stories he wrote in Yiddish.[1]

The Beginnings of Yiddish Prose in the United States

Until after the turn of the century, Yiddish writings here were ghetto literature. The litterateurs were immigrants, the people who surrounded them on the noisome streets were newcomers struggling to make a living. All émigrés faced hard realities, personal and financial. Ghetto literature reflected these difficulties. Stories and poems that described the problems of people who lived in ghettos, small or large, began with the "Germans," the Central European Jews. This type of literature, primarily genre fiction, was brought to this country and is reflected in the tales and romances of Isaac M. Wise and quite a number of other Jewish Germans who had settled on these shores. Among them was Martha Wolfenstein (1869-1906), the author of the charming Moravian vignettes, *Idylls of the Gass*, stories of the "Street." Isaac M. Wise, the Reformer, was all his life a journalist. Most "Russian" writers were journalists. Their only outlet was the Yiddish press. Indeed they were fortunate to be employed on a paper; otherwise they remained in the sweatshop or made a living as humble artisans or shopkeepers. These latter wrote at night when they had a moment of leisure.

Literature began with the radical press of the 1880's. The socialists and anarchists who wrote poetry and fiction were concerned with social problems, with the economic distress they saw everywhere in New York's ghetto. (They had suffered, too, in Russia, Poland, Galicia, the Ukraine, and Rumania.) They were angry people. Literature in the 1880's was incitement, propaganda; but by the 1890's, it transcended itself and became belles lettres although the artists remained faithful to their pristine political philosophies. They continued as socialists, anarchists, Zionists, Diaspora nationalists. It was then, at the turn of the century, that American Jewish literature, after a decade of struggle with itself, became an instrument not only for enlightenment but also for aesthetic challenge, intellectual enjoyment.

Numerous Yiddish translators of the world's classics now raised the cultural niveau of both writers and readers. Writing as literature was to improve and Yiddish readers as connoisseurs were to increase with the early 1900's. American classical literature made an impact on the Yiddish intellectuals; they read English and extended their cultural horizons here in this land of freedom. Many of the thousands of Russian Jews who fled after the 1903 and 1905 massacres were people of secular education; good writers began to come here, particularly during the World War I period. Sholem Aleichem, Sholem Asch, Abraham Reisen, and Peretz Hirschbein sought shelter and opportunity in this country during these years. Yiddish America was a writer's market; during World War I, it was the most important Yiddish cultural center in the world. The older immigrants, now somewhat more affluent, could afford to subscribe to the journals and buy a book.

A word of caution: the number of devotees of good literature was always small, very small. Not every garment worker—many of whom were illiterate—read Tolstoi or Buckle's *History of Civilization* in the Yiddish. Since papers are dependent on subscribers, the owners catered to the multitudes. The publishers dared not ignore the cultural capacity or incapacity of the masses. Knowing what their subscribers wanted and demanded, they gave them shund. Sentimental, romantic, gothic, sensational literature, had already been fed to Jewish readers in Russia as early as the 1860's. Isaac Mayer Dick (1814-1893) was one of the pioneers in this field. It was imported here early both for the stage and the press. By the 1890's, these thrillers had become big business; fasicules (*heftn*) of these works were issued serially and sold by the thousands on the newsstands of New York. Dozens of these novels and romances were written and gobbled up by eager readers who could hardly wait for the next installment. By the early 1900's, the newspapers—the *Forward*, too—had no choice but to follow suit; they, too, turned to this type of literature to increase circulation.

Thrillers abounded in American literature; everybody read dime novels; it was a huge business. America gloried in genres of its own: Indian wars, detective mysteries, and rags to riches success stories. The humble Jews of the ghettos and the eager housewives of the hinterland hobnobbed with kings, queens, and millionaires—on paper. The Yiddish stories were frequently devoid of any Jewish content. Readers followed the adventures of Jules Verne, the Count of Monte Cristo, the miners in the gold fields of California, and the Black Gang of New York. The readers were unaware of art and indifferent to the sneers of the literary critics and the learned Marxists. The latter were so concerned with the prevalent social evils and their own political utopias that they were wont to forget the immediate emotional, psychic needs of the workers. Serious writers as realists emphasized suffering; the throng needed no reminder: they sought escape, entertainment, some promise of better things. Pleasure is not a mortal sin; the villain will be foiled, the heroine will be rescued. "Rags are royal raiment when worn for virtue's sake." Reading even nonsensical romances was a healthy educational exercise; the literate masses polished their reading skills.[2]

In a way, the Yiddish literary world was a very narrow one composed almost entirely of journalists. There was really nothing of belles lettres outside the confines of a newspaper or a magazine. An inevitable corollary: the thesaurus of every writer included but two themes, with infinite variations he wrote of life in the old homeland and the struggle to come to terms with the America of the ghetto. (Was there any other American

Jewish world for the immigrant?) It is fascinating to trace the fortunes of the Yiddish writers who wrote in the four decades before 1921. Louis E. Bandes, who wrote under the name of Louis E. Miller, came to the United States in 1886 after a career as a revolutionary in Europe. Here he worked in a shirt factory, studied law at night, and helped found the *Forward*. When he broke with the journal and with Cahan, he established a leftwing paper of his own, the *Truth (Warheit)*, which landed finally in the Zionist camp. His later years were devoted to the practice of law, writing for the press, furthering Zionism. Bernard G. Richards—like Miller, a Lithuanian—arrived here the same year. His wanderings took him as far west as Denver, but for many years, with Boston as his base, he wrote for the Yiddish and English press. Before that, he had made a livelihood as a peddler, clerk, and English teacher. He developed an excellent English style; his English *Discourses of Keidansky* are clever feuilletons reviewing the American Jewish scene. In his later years, he played a not insignificant role as a national communal worker. Jacob Gordin, the playwright, was also a story writer; his contemporary, Shaikewitz-Shomer, after a successful literary career in Russia as a "dime-novelist," made a second career in New York, where over 200 novels poured out of his pen. The titles are their own critique: *From the Throne to the Gallows, A Bloody Adieu, Murder for Love*, etc., etc.

Bernard Gorin wrote for the *Morning Journal* reviewing plays and adapting classics for Yiddish readers. As a gifted translator, he prepared Yiddish versions of the best French, Russian, and English writings. Thus, his admirers could read Tolstoi's *War and Peace* and the stories of Charles Dickens. Like Gorin, Gedaliah Bublick (1875-1948) made his career as a Yiddish writer and journalist on the *Jewish Daily News* before it was taken over by the *Morning Journal*. Bublick, an able writer, had written in Hebrew in his native Russia before migrating to Argentina, where he lived in one of the Baron de Hirsch colonies. His editorial position with the Orthodox *Jewish Daily News* brought him influence, which he exerted on behalf of the Kehillah, Mizrachi Zionism, the American Jewish Congress, and the Joint Distribution Committee. Editors of Yiddish newspapers were leaders in the Jewish community, probably more so than the notables who presided over the destinies of the English press. Jews as "a people of the book" were impressed by the written word; editors were highly respected. By the 1910's, the collected prose writings of American Yiddish authors began to appear in book form. Today many of these works are collector's items.

World War I which prepared the way for the Holocaust, brought Sholem Rabinowitz to this country. He was popularly known as Sholem Aleichem, "Peace be unto you." People called him the Jewish Mark Twain and called Twain the English Sholem Aleichem. Rabinowitz was one of the greatest of the Yiddish writers, a classic in every sense. He was an "Enlightened" man, but no propagandist. He was content to be a humorist, to describe the life and vicissitudes of the small town impoverished, pious Jews, but always with a wry smile. He was widely acclaimed wherever Yiddish was spoken; in the course of time his stories of quaint but lovable human beings were translated into many languages. It is said that hundreds of thousands of copies were sold in China. In order to make a living, he traveled about, lectured, and wrote. *The Fiddler on the Roof,* which later carried this country by storm, immortalized one of his favorite characters, Tevye, the Milkman, the Milky One. Tevye once said: "With God's help I starved to death." Rabinovitz did not starve, but he had to hustle to support his large brood. For him, this was no land of unlimited opportunity.

Sholem Aleichem had little immediate impact on literature here, although the numerous writers who worshipped at the altar of a Jewish Comus certainly did not escape his influence. Rabinovitz did not rail against Russian injustice, for he had no desire to beat his head against the wall; the American prose writers did cry out in anguish, because this was a land of freedom with hope ever beckoning. The typical writers here, leftists, Marxists, demanded social justice. They hated the sweatshops; they were troubled by poverty, unemployment, the slum tenements, tuberculosis; they were never unaware of the conflict between the Russian parents and their American children. Possibly the mantle of Sholem Aleichem fell on Israel Joseph Zevin (1872-1926). Certainly he was one of America's beloved Yiddish humorists. People knew him as Tashrak, which is simply a word formed of the last four letters of the Hebrew alphabet spelled backwards. Here was another "newsboy" who became a candy store owner and finally rose to be an editor on the *Jewish Daily News.* One of his favorite characters—an American Tevye, if you will—was Hayyim der Kostumer Pedler, Hayyim the Customer Peddler. With a kindly but all-seeing eye and understanding heart, Hayyim records the odyssey of the petty Jewish businessman, his headaches, his joys, his little triumphs. Over the years, Hayyim brought a smile and a grin into the homes of those who were privileged to follow him in his peregrinations. On a more sober level, Tashrak collected and published volumes of stories and anecdotes that he culled from the vast rabbinic literature; publications such as these were of educational and ethical value.

Libin, Kobrin, and Tashrak remained well within the ambit of Greater New York; Isaac Raboy (1882-1944), a novelist who had immigrated here in 1904, discovered the world west of the Hudson. Tired of working in a hat factory, he enrolled in the Woodbine Jewish Agricultural School and, upon graduation in 1910, made his way westward to North Dakota. There he labored on a ranch. The novels that he wrote later dealt with life on the prairies. Despite his strong proletarian sympathies, he wrote lyrical prose about life on the farm and the enticing beauty of nature and her boundless spaces. Upon his return to New York, he went back to the factories and wrote stories and novels when he had a moment's time or was out of a job. One of his books, written shortly before his death, was called *The Jewish Cowboy*. A contemporary of his, who also wrote short stories and novels, was Joseph Opatoshu (1887-1954). More fortunate than Raboy, he became a successful writer who saw his stories and books translated into several languages, including English. For themes for his Jewish tales, he reached out in all directions, to Poland when it fought for freedom from the Russians, to the Middle Ages with its constant threats to Jewry, to New York and its teeming masses in Lower Manhattan. In this sense, he, too, was a ghetto novelist. Unlike others, he did not have to slave for years in workshops; he was a respected member of the staff of the Yiddish *Day*.

LATER NOTABLES

It is well to bear in mind that many, very many Yiddishists before 1921 were brilliant litterateurs. Each one had skills of his own; all were men of influence enjoying and meriting the admiration of their readers. The man who emerged as the most notable of them all was the Pole, Sholem Asch (1880-1957); he was a storyteller, a novelist, a dramatist. He wrote in Yiddish; his novels were translated into many languages and sold in the millions. Asch was in and out of the United States in the second decade of the new century and during the years when the Germans began exterminating Europe's Jews. Knowing America and its East Side ghetto, he was competent to write of its people and their problems. About the time that Cahan was writing his story of the garment manufacturer David Levinsky, Asch, too, set out to record this important epoch in American history when "Russians" were replacing "Germans" as America's clothiers. Both tried to describe what America did to the newcomers as they clawed their way to the top. Asch was as much an international writer as he was an American one; he lived in various lands, but he was always a Jewish writer. Through his stories, he reached back into Jewish history, to Jesus, Mary, Paul, to the early modern Poles and Cossacks who murdered Jews, to World War I where the Jewish masses of Eastern Europe were decimated, literally. He was a magnificent storyteller. If nothing else, his novels affirmed Yiddish as a language of classics that men and women will read in generations yet to come.

There were other notable writers who sought the safety of America in those sad years of World War I. New York's intelligentsia then welcomed Abraham Coralnik (1883-1937), essayist and literary critic. This journalist—he wrote for the *Day*—was typical of the new breed. They had studied at universities, were multilingual, and had trained themselves in an evaluative critical methodology. Here, as in Europe, Coralnik's votaries were many; in his generation, his written word carried weight. Revered, beloved even more, was Abraham Reisen (1876-1953), who, like Coralnik and Asch, came to the United States in the early days of World War I. Highly respected by New York's Yiddish literati, Reisen, a story writer, a lyric poet, a humorist, a fighter for social justice, a sensitive creative artist, touched the souls of thousands. Samuel Charney ("Black," 1876-1955?), who wrote under the name Samuel Niger, was another Yiddish writer whom the war—the post-war devastation—brought to this country. He was a brother of Baruch Charney Vladeck, the journalist and politician. Niger was a power in the world of Yiddish literature, because he was soon recognized as an authoritative critic. For better or worse, his pronouncements in matters literary were rarely questioned. He was competent, a scholarly litterateur who already had a distinguished career in Europe before coming here in 1919, and he was fair; his standards were high, determined by the criteria that characterized the world's classics. His influence on American Yiddish literature was salutary.

Let it be clearly understood; the world of Yiddish literature was not exhausted by the writing of the belletrists. There were dozens of American Yiddishists who, through their work, created a rounded-out body of knowledge and critical thought. They made Yiddish culture possible. All these men wrote in Yiddish before 1921. At the request of the United Hebrew Trades, Hertz Burgin prepared a *History of the Jewish Workers Movement in America, Russia, and England* in 1915; another author published works on the Talmud, the rise of Christianity, and the Jewish thinkers and poets of the Middle Ages. Books rolled off the press on astronomy, chemistry, zoology, physiology, political science, philosophy, Jewish folksongs. The well-educated Abner Tannenbaum (1848-1913), author of many romantic tales, once made his living running a candy and cigar store. Historically, he is important because he devoted himself to the popularization of scientific knowledge—which did not deter him from translating the works of Jules Verne and reputedly turning out a history of the Jews in America. The antireligionist Benjamin Feigenbaum directed his shafts against Judaism, the kosher dietary laws, and the biblical concept of creation. To aid him in his crusade, he wrote on Darwin's concept of evolution. "Philip Kranz"—born Jacob Rombro (1858-1922)—made his contribution to the developing body of Yiddish literature by writing on Aristotle, Mohammed, Spinoza, the French Revolution, the Rothschilds, and the history of culture. In his day, he worked in many lands in different fields. This student at Russian schools and the Sorbonne taught chemistry and English in the United States, yet found time to edit some of the more important Yiddish journals. The motivations that impelled him originally were socialism and propaganda; later, he settled down to become a culture expositor.

Certainly interesting and very different was the career of Leon Solomon Moissieff. He, too, like all Yiddishists, was a native of Eastern Europe, but he was not the sweatshop type or a newsstand petty entrepreneur. Here was one of the world's most distinguished bridge builders. Yet, in 1915, this engineer found time to lecture on Yiddish literature to a group of Uptown Jewish intellectuals. Moissieff published a Yiddish radical magazine, supported the work of the Jewish Publication Society, and furthered the new Hebrew University in Jerusalem. Others who addressed the Uptowners—in English of course—were the story writers, Louis Lipsky, B. G. Richards, Henry Moskowitz, and Nahum Slouschz. Yiddish was becoming respectable; the "Russians" had arrived. Moissieff had a degree from Columbia; Charles David Spivak (1861-1927) had a degree in medicine from a Philadelphia college. It took him time to fight his way up. Though he received a good education in Russia, he was compelled here to work in freight yards and mills; he was a farm hand and a typesetter. After he received his degree, he taught medicine in Colorado and there helped establish the Jewish Consumptives' Relief Society and its sanatorium—a small hospital area which became Spivak, Colorado. In 1911, together with Yehoash, the Yiddish poet, Spivak published a Yiddish dictionary which listed the Hebrew and Aramaic elements in Yiddish. Because it included proverbs and idiomatic expressions, it is a sound contribution to Jewish folklore. Articles on medicine and longevity which appeared in the *Forward* were often written by him.

Yehoash and Spivak just touched on the fringes of Yiddish lexicography; Alexander Harkavy was America's first and most prolific writer of Yiddish linguistic manuals and textbooks. This country offered him its own realistic brand of opportunity. Unwillingly, he worked as a strikebreaker on the dock; he was a farmhand, a factory worker, and a teacher of English to immigrants before his appointment as a social worker stationed on Ellis Island. He was the great Americanizer through the medium of his dictionaries and vocabularies, dictionaries that embraced Yiddish, Hebrew, English, Russian, and Polish. His first English-Yiddish manual went through many editions. What else does a Yiddish lexicographer do? He prepares works on American history and civics, issues a Yiddish edition of the Bible, edits Yiddish periodicals, and translates Don Quixote, so that his Yiddish-reading fellow immigrants can chuckle over the adventures of the peerless knight and his faithful Sancho Panza. In matters of ideology, there was probably no Yiddish writer in the United States more influential than Chaim Zhitlowsky. Zhitlowsky had no interest in Judaism or its religious tradition; he was a secular nationalist. Cul-

ture was to be built around a language, in this instance Yiddish. This was
the instrument, the medium that would unite all Jews everywhere. Zhitlowsky wanted to further Jewish life in the Diaspora; he was no assimilationist. His preachments brought many East Europeans back to Jewry.[3]

PROSE LITERATURE: A BRIEF SUMMARY

The fifty years between 1870 and 1920 mark the rise of an American Yiddish literature that was channeled almost entirely through the press. One
suspects that in those days even a Sholem Asch was practically dependent
on the press. In the 1880's and 1890's, litterateurs, strongly influenced by
radical panaceas, preached salvation through anarchism and socialism:
God cannot help us; cosmopolitanism, internationalism, is the only answer to the ills of society. The twentieth century brought a gradual turn
to the right among writers, who now embraced various forms of Jewish
nationalism. The Dreyfus Affair, the Russian murders, the devastating
experiences of Jews as Jews during World War I induced many to despair
of humanity. During those decades, the nascent Yiddish literary culture
sought to bridge the gap between the "medieval" and the modern Jew. It
was imperative that the Children of Israel from Eastern Europe catch up
with the twentieth century; some of them were centuries behind the
times. Unfortunately, it is difficult to determine how many sloughed off
those aspects of the past that hindered them from entering and embracing
the new industrial civilization which confronted them. Through the medium of the short story, primarily, all writers emphasized the differences,
the conflict between the old and the new. Those were unhappy days; a
centuries-old Orthodoxy had to cope with the sweatshop, the desecrated
Sabbath, strikes, unions, anti-Jewish radicals, and the religious threats inherent in Americanization. In the course of time, proletarianism was
modified. The bourgeoisie advanced; the newly arrived twentieth-century
East European émigrés raised their cultural sights, and out of the cauldron
of conflict and propaganda slowly emerged a new literary artistry. It was
not, however, to flower fully till the second quarter of the twentieth century.[4]

POETS AND POETRY

There were dozens of competent Yiddish professional writers who wrote
prose; there were probably many more who wrote poetry. That is why
American Jewry's most distinguished Yiddish litterateurs were poets. It
may well be that some turned to poetry because it took less time to write
verse than to labor over a story or a novelette. These men of letters were
not men of leisure; they labored in shops or factories; they sweated as arti-

sans. New York's first Yiddish poet—the first at least to document his presence in the press—was Jacob Zevi Sobel (Soble). This Enlightener had run the gamut in Russia from the traditional rabbinate to sophisticated modernism. Shocked by the pogroms in Odessa in 1871 and despairing of a Russia which had betrayed the nineteenth century, he turned to America. Arriving about the year 1875, he wrote a Judaeo-German poem which appeared in Sarasohn's weekly *Jewish Gazette*. America dismayed him; here was liberty and confusion; Poles hated Russians, and the German Jews despised them both. Unity was imperative. Superstition must be rejected, poverty overcome. The ever-present reality is chaos; the promise is paradise. In 1877, Sobel published a thirty-two page bilingual work in Hebrew and Yiddish. The Hebrew title was *The Golden Song in Honor of the Old Israel*; the Yiddish title was *The Old Israel*. In his Yiddish poems, which are little better than doggerel, Sobel emphasized the freedom and opportunity enjoyed by the newcomers who had found a sanctuary in this land, but he was disturbed by what he saw in America's East European Jewish community. The Jews quarreled in the synagogs and assimilated on the street.[5]

By the 1880's, there were many poets. Those who arrived then and in the following decade were men who worked hard for a living. Their lot was not enviable, for they were exploited in the Gilded Age of brutal industrialism; they were denounced, if not despised, because they were foreigners, disadvantaged because they were not able to express themselves in English. Most of them were autodidacts reaching out to the great in all literatures, yet their lack of educational discipline was a distinct psychological and cultural handicap. Because of their misery, that pre-1900 generation of Yiddish poets was radically oriented; these men yearned for a better world; scientific socialism and anarchism seemed to be the answer. In a way, their poetry was American, a reaction to their problems in the economy of this, their new homeland. America gave them freedom, the freedom to go hungry. They were not inner-directed masochistic narcissists weeping over their lot in life; they had a message; they wanted the world to sense the meaning of social distress and move toward social justice. Yet, most if not all of these writers who sang their song of sorrow had more than one string to their bow.

Of the many proletarian poets, only a few will be mentioned here. Some were deemed notable in their generation; others must be mentioned because they are typical. Isaac Reingold (1873?-1908?) had packed many adventures into a life that ended after thirty some years. Upon coming here, this teenage Ukrainian settled with his father in New Jersey's Woodbine Colony, quarreled with his folks over matters religious, and then took off for the midwestern prairies. By the age of nineteen, he was married and by the grace of God was blessed with five children. He worked by day and wrote by night; his lyrics of social protest were even set to music, for many sang as they labored. A man could be a socialist and love Zion, too. Back in the East to which he returned, in New York, he became a hack translating Shakespeare and adapting Broadway hits for the Yiddish theatre. Morris Winchevsky was one of the last of the proletarian poets to make his home in New York, in 1894. His verses reeked of sweat; his bread was soggy with tears as he sounded the call to revolt. Winchevsky was a superior writer, a man at home in the literatures of most European lands. In his prose-like verse, he sang of the three sisters of Leicester Square: one sold flowers, another sold ribbons, and a third sold herself. His songs of labor and suffering, like those of other proletarian poets, were set to music and were to be sung many years later, even in Soviet Russia.[6]

David Edelshtadt (1866-1892), the most militant of the proletarian poets, was posthumously acclaimed by the Soviet Union; his collected works were published in Moscow in 1935. He had begun writing his poetry in Russia at the age of nine and was publishing when he was twelve. When about sixteen, he came to the United States and, after several years in distant Cincinnati, settled in New York. Like many other radicals, he made a living in the garment industry. A few years before he died, the anarchist *Free Workers Voice* appointed him editor. By this time, he had contracted tuberculosis and went to Denver, where he died and was put to rest in potter's field. Later, the Workmen's Circle, Jewish socialists, gave him a proper burial and erected a fitting monument. The workers admired him for his utter devotion to their cause; singing of the red flags of blood and of battle, he goaded them to throw off their shackles. As a writer, he never for a moment forgot that he was an agitator, a propagandist.[7]

The day Edelshtadt died, his friend Joseph Bovshover (1872/1873-1915/1916) wrote a Yiddish poem to sanctify his memory. This is the first verse of the English translation:

> Lovely sunshine, hide your glory,
> Veil the splendor of your light
> In a broad expanse of darkness,
> Black and somber as the night.

Artistically speaking, Bovshover was superior to the comrade he memorialized. Bovshover came to the United States from his native Russia a teenager who had yet to learn his English. He was a furrier, a grocer, a farmer, and even spent a year at Yale. Nothing could tie him down. Like Edelshtadt, he, too, was an anarchist and wrote for the *Freie Arbeiter Stimme*. The Yiddish of this gifted man was excellent; he made a translation of *The Merchant of Venice*. The Shakespearean task was done at the request of the actor Jacob Adler; the money Bovshover received was squandered in a few days. That same year, 1899, he became insane and was put into an asylum where he died many years later. Bovshover was one of the very few Yiddish poets who wrote good English poetry; poor Imber could write only the most primitive doggerel; Rosenfeld's English verse was never acceptable. Here are some lines from Bovshover's writings in English under the name of Basil Dahl:

> When solitary on the cliffs I stand
> And downward gaze upon the boundless sea;
> When on the Titan clouds my glances rest
> And blend together with Infinity;
> When through the air my fancy floats and sees
> The radiant planets on their stately march,
> How forceful am I then and yet how frail!
> How insignificant and yet how grand!

He was less of a class poet than Edelshtadt, but the proletarians can rightly claim him as their own:

> To strive is to be
> We are slaves or we are free

"To the Toilers" is another one of his English poems:

> I hate your superstition, workingmen,
> I loathe your blindness and stupidity.
> Your pointed quips have never made me laugh;
> Your senseless chat is wearisome to me;
> Your shallow joy is not the joy I like.
> But when I contemplate your ceaseless toil,
> Your quiet activity and sunless life,
> Your works of splendor, and gigantic strength,
> I bow my head in reverence to you.

Influenced by Emerson, Whiteman, Poe, and Markham, this Yiddish poet reached out to every human being as he sang of nature, love, happiness, freedom. He drew the whole universe to himself, but his heart had little room for Jews; as a poet, he passed them by. The suffering which anarchists and socialists experienced as Jews rarely brought them closer to their people. If anything, they turned against their own, the presumptive cause of their misfortune. The solution to tyranny lay in a universal humanitarianism or in a love so boundless that no form of government was necessary.[8]

Morris Rosenfeld (1862-1923) was America's best known Yiddish proletarian poet. He was the poet laureate of the masses in the garment industry; his verses were set to music. Despite the recognition accorded him, most of his years were sad ones. He labored as a tailor in London, as a diamond cutter in Amsterdam, and as a sweatshop worker in New York's ghetto. Embittered by his struggles to survive, he wrote with revolutionary rancor. Years later, after he had moved politically to the right, he bought up those radical outpourings and destroyed them. He had come to America for the first time in the early 1880's, returned to Europe, and had then come back in 1886 to settle permanently on this side of the Atlantic. It was his good fortune that Russian-born Leo Wiener—then teaching Slavic languages at Harvard—"discovered" him. In 1898, Wiener published an edition of Rosenfeld's poems for the general public. The verses selected were transliterated into the orthography of literary German accompanied by English prose translations. This thin brochure-like book of a little over a hundred pages rescued him from the misery of the factory. The Uptown Jews, Schiff and others, bought him a newsstand; Gentile notables patronized him; he gave readings in America's most prestigious universities and traveled all over the United States reciting his poems to Yiddish audiences. But the new life was no bed of roses; audiences came to hear him, but hesitated to buy his five-cent package of printed verses. There were days when he did not even make his expenses from New York. True, he finally got a job grinding out poems for Cahan at the *Forward*, but that in a way was a proletarian literary sweatshop.

In 1914, he moved from the socialist *Forward* to the Orthodox *Jewish Daily News*. This was a radical return, a retreat, he was back with his people, committed religionists, Jewish nationalists. The Gentiles coddled him; he was a curiosity, like a Negro poet. Flattered, Rosenfeld turned to English poetry, like a Bovshover-Dahl, but the Anglo-Saxon spark kindled no fire; his English poems did not merit publication. He wrote voluminously, dashing off poem after poem. He finally stopped writing stark descriptions of the robot human machine. Whether he was disillusioned by the incessant hammering of socialistic verbiage or was stirred to respond to the poetry within himself, he now began to write on diverse subjects. The many-faceted Rosenfeld could even poke fun at his people on Hester Street: you live in a real paradise; you live as a Jew; you die as a Jew; who wants to speak English? As an early and ardent Zionist, he wrote "national" songs. He also write on love, on liberty, on the soaring eagle, on winged poets, on nightingales who sang in cemeteries. Certainly he was the most Jewish of the proletarian poets. His sentimentality, not untouched by self-pity, moved thousands who read his simple verses. They were easy to read, easy to understand. Let the critics decide whether he was a great poet.[9]

THE YOUNG ONES

It would be wrong to label the proletarian poets men whose literary world was tied to the misery of the working masses. Because they were poets, they soared with the genius within them; the whole world was grist for their fancy. While these radicals were still writing their lyrics— Rosenfeld and Winchevsky lived into the 1920's and 1930's—new poets arose who gave rein to their muse. The poets overcame the propagandists. The sources of this autoemancipation are difficult to determine. Did the twentieth century evoke a new spirit? Was the lot of the masses less distracting? Was the influence of modern Gentile poets all powerful? Did the new Jewish poets emancipate themselves from the shackles of their own people? Whatever the answer, the twentieth century brought to birth a generation of Yiddish poets who brushed aside the past, surrendering themselves to the dictates of their artistic impulses. Thus, there rose a new school; these writers disparate though they were in their approach— are known as the Young Ones, *Di Yunge.* They were called *Di Yunge* because some were young in years; they were young also because they were new in emphasis; their approach was different. They were interested in art for its own sake. These artists were not dedicated to a specific political philosophy; they did not set out to save the world and its Jews. In 1907, they published a magazine, *Youth (Yugend),* which failed to survive; later they published an anthology. They were a mixed lot; some were men of culture acquainted with Europe's modern classics; others were workingmen, among them a bootmaker, a paperhanger, a fur worker. Most of the Young Ones were poets—there were some women too—some wrote prose, short stories, and novels.

A substantial number of litterateurs may he included under the rubric of the Young Ones. Among them were Joseph Opatoshu, the popular novelist and short-story writer; Moishe Leib Halpern, whose poetry is sheer beauty; Moshe Nadir (Isaac Reiss), the translator of Heine, a writer with a delightful sense of humor. Still another of the Young Ones was the farmer and factory hand, Isaac Raboy, who wrote of his life as a homesteader on the high plains of North Dakota. H. Leivick (1886-1962, Leivick Halper) was highly respected as a poet and dramatist; there are some historians of Yiddish literature who believe that he was America's outstanding poet and playwright in the post World War I period. Leivick, oldest of a family of nine, grew up in poverty. His father was a Hebrew teacher; his mother helped eke out an existence by baking and selling bagels. Leivick left home at ten and went from yeshivah to yeshivah, eating in a different house each day when invited; like all yeshivah students, he had his "eating days." At night, he slept on a bench in the house of learning. The uprising in Russia in 1905 made him a revolutionary; like others, he was arrested and exiled to Siberia, where he spent years at hard labor. After he escaped, he came to the United States where he worked as a garment worker and paperhanger while writing of his Siberian anguish and the travail of humanity in exile. His life spanned the Holocaust and the rise of the State of Israel, events which were to evoke poetic responses. He was a dramatist, symbolist, and mystic whose years in Siberia and as a tubercular were to excite him intellectually and sensitize him emotionally.[10]

Di Yunge differed from the proletarian poets in the direction they took. The sweatshop poets never forgot that they were called upon to champion the workers; the Young Ones put themselves first as they surrendered themselves to their own emotions and their intellectual fantasies. The Young Ones cannot be easily delimited or classified. They reflect so many different types of philosophies that one is tempted to declare that they were simply twentieth-century poets devoted to untrammeled artistic literary expression. They were not utilitarian preachers. They felt free to disregard the national tie in Jewry, the social distress of their fellowmen; they sought and achieved aesthetic autonomy. They did not look upon themselves as the moral launderers of a decadent society. They were impressionists, individualists devoted more to imagery, tone, and form than to content. The Yiddish language was their vehicle of expression; these new practitioners of Yiddish verse were cognizant of all the schools of poetry and the literatures of Europe and America. If they were hortatory, their homiletics was subtle. They were imaginative, content to portray the mood of the moment. Yet some of the writers of this new school —if school it was—were never to cut the cord that bound them to their people. The persecutions in Eastern Europe, the ghetto ambience, their nostalgia for a world passed by guaranteed that they would never leave their people.[11]

INZICHISTEN

A new school of Yiddish writers who made their appearance about 1919-1920 moved still farther to the "left" Jewishly. They declared formally, programatically, that they desired no Jewish or social responsibility; they set out to join the universe of poetry. (Were they aware that they were speaking to but a tiny fraction of the literate East Europeans and that the very tongue that they employed locked them in to a tight little world?) *Di Yunge* were impressionists; these new writers were expressionists. They issued a manifesto and published a paper and an anthology in 1920; they called themselves the Within One's Self group, *In-Zikh*—the name they proudly adopted and gave their publication. There were three leaders, Nahum Baruch Minkoff (1893-1958), Aaron Glanz (1889-1966), and Jacob Glatstein (Gladstone) (1896-1971). All were Poles; all had studied at American colleges; they were not sweatshop poets. Minkoff had graduated from a law school and was, like his two colleagues, an advocate of individualism and cosmopolitanism. In later years, he wrote a three-volume work on the pioneers of Yiddish poetry in America. His own poems, fraught with emotion, disregarded logic and sequitur; these traditional conventions were not important. Glanz, who wrote under the pseudonym A. Leyeless, had a brilliant career in the American world of Yiddish letters and was awarded an honorary doctorate by the Reform Movement's Hebrew Union College-Jewish Institute of Religion. He had studied at the University of London and at Columbia, taught and lectured, and worked at the *Day*. Like his friends, he evinced imagination and sensitivity in his writing. These rebels were arbitrary, utterly personal, as they looked within themselves for reality. The poem for them was an outward sign of inward grace. Glanz-Leyeless turned to the universal for his themes rather than to the Jewish world which encompassed him, but even he preferred Isaiah to Homer.

Glatstein outlived the other two and was fated, from the vantage point of free America, to survive the Holocaust and to witness the rise of the State of Israel. All this was a challenge to the subjectivism and universalism which characterized him and the In-Zikh group. The Jewish fathers received the Torah on Sinai's heights; their children, Germany's murdered millions, gave it back; the dead cannot praise God. These Yiddish expressionists exulted in emancipating themselves from meter and rhyme; they were innovators, obviously influenced by the new currents among French and American writers. In the works of this new Yiddish school, the line between prose and poetry was not sharply drawn. These men experimented in form and style. Their verse was free in that they felt free to voice their moods; thought was not important; the expression of emotion was. These daring rebels—limited in numbers and followers—bursting out on the left, unleashing the personal, the subjective, the aesthetic, the unconventional, were certainly no poets for the shop workers. Pants pressers were mindful of the amenities, the conventions, restraints. These new poets of the late 1910's traveled a far distance from the humble proletarian bards and their simple rhymes.[12]

There were many good poets in the early twentieth century who remained well within the ambit of the more traditional forms of poetry. This is not to imply that they were fettered by traditional modes, that they could not soar with the angels of sound and melody. Like many of his generation, Abraham Walt (1872-1938) made the journey from the talmudic academy to the haunts of the revolutionists before seeking asylum in tolerant America. Here, under the pen name of Abraham Liessin, he blossomed out as a poet, journalist, socialist, and Bundist, writing for the *Forward* and editing the *Zukunft*, the Yiddish magazine of quality. As a socialist, he wept for the tragic fate of the laboring masses, yet, drawing on the wells of compassion within himself, he mourned, too, for the martyrs of his people, for a Judah Maccabee and Simon Bar Kochba. Some have called him the poet of Jewish history. Perhaps it is not so strange that he, like many others of his day, wrote of Jesus and the apostles. For these Yiddish writers, was Jesus, the crucified one, Jewish suffering incarnate? In one of his poems, he asks the Madonna why she does not raise her voice against those who worship at her shrine for what they have done to her people.

Walt-Liessin was certainly no member of the Introspective group, but Yehoash was claimed by the rebels; he disdained conventional versifying; he belonged to no special school; he was a poet pure and simple. Yehoash is the pen name of Solomon Bloomgarden (1870/1872-1927), a Lithuanian who came to these shores in the early 1890's. It may be that his father gave him the name Yehoash; it is more probable that he himself took the name of the king of ancient Israel who defeated the invading Syrians. Bloomgarden loved the Bible and its heroes. A talmudist of sorts like most Yiddish literati, this newcomer began his career as a Hebrew poet, but here on these shores he turned to Yiddish. There was no future, no bread, in writing verse for the Hebrew press. Anything to make a living; he worked in a bookstore fifteen hours a day for $3 a week. (There are all kinds of sweatshops.) He was a bookkeeper, an office manager, a tailor, a peddler (merchant!) and, of course, a Hebrew teacher. After ten years, tubercular, he was ripe for Denver, where he remained for another decade till he regained his health. There he pursued his career as a writer vigorously. The threat of the grave is a powerful stimulant. Sickness and the Kishinev murders made of him a concerned Jew; he worked closely with Spivak and his hospital stalwarts and concerned himself with the newcomers sent to Denver by the Industrial Removal Office. In 1909 he was back in New York, known and respected, but still sweating out a living; 1914 found him in Palestine living at Rehovot with its Russian pioneers. When the War erupted, he fled back to the safety of New York.

Through the years, this intellectual, who had taught himself to read the classics of the ancients and the moderns, turned for his grist to the literatures of all peoples. As one who had striven to survive and as a socialist, he retained his strong sympathy for the workers; for his material, he turned to the Talmud, folklore, legends, Cabala, Hassidism. Like Liessin, he could not forget the tragedy of the long Jewish exile. As one who had lived in a Palestine colony, he could not reject Jewish nationalism. No school of poetry could claim him as he thundered against American lynchers and reached out to catch a glimpse of the soul of the Japanese and the Chinese. Between the writing of volumes, he took time out to translate Hiawatha and the Rubaiyat. His lyrics reflect his love for nature and the green forests. He was stirred by the bells of the Angelus and consoled as he thought of the alien God incarnate, Jewry's gift to the world. Yehoash sang of a redemption that was yet to come, of David, old and gray, plucking the strings of his harp; he wrote of shadows and darkness and death in the night and shaped a poetic tribute to a seashell. The best and the last years of his life were spent making a Yiddish translation of the Hebrew Bible. This is his immortality.[13]

YIDDISH POETS AND POETRY: A SUMMARY

Among America's Jews, poetry was the most cultivated of the arts. The volume was huge; apparently there was a demand. The variety was almost infinite; there were traditionalists, realists, nationalists, impressionists, expressionists; there were writers who defied classification and others who embraced all schools. By the early 1920's, there were already romanticists sanctifying the dead shtetl, creating a myth that ignored the poverty, the meanness, the stupid anti-Jewish hatreds which had always characterized the Slavic states and the Rumanian provinces. Despite the nonparticularistic ideologies to which many clung, very few could escape their Jewishness; it was difficult to evade the clutch of 2,000 years of exile. Originality? Most of the writers, whether autodidacts or college men, were well acquainted with the great poets of all times: Isaiah, Jeremiah, the Psalmists, of course; but they knew and cherished the immortals of old—Homer and the Latins—and the latter day masters like Keats and Shelley, Byron and Yeats. Were their poems, their prose-verse, great literature? That is not easy to determine. The Yiddishists say yes; the non-Yiddishists, who know only the translations, may have other opinions. The English renditions reflect the virtuosity of the translators; only too often—to quote Bialik—a translation is a kiss through a veil. The future? Yiddish is dying in America. It will live for a century—centuries?—wherever refugee East European Jews have built cultural enclaves. Persecution guarantees its survival. Unlike the manuscript Arabic-Jewish lore, Yiddish is available in print in millions of pages; for centuries yet to come, scholars will confront the challenge of resurrecting the dead. Jewish scholars of the future will study Yiddish, the so-called "jargon." As a dead language, it will not threaten people who no longer fear for their status as Americans.[14]

YIDDISH IN THE HINTERLAND

INTRODUCTION

New York is not America. About the year 1920, at least 54 percent of all Jews lived west of the Hudson. A great many spoke Yiddish. In one form or another, these men and women were exposed to Yiddish culture. In the towns or villages, almost every East European subscribed to a New York daily; in the larger cities, they patronized an occasional Yiddish theatrical troupe and participated in numerous educational entertainment programs. The socialists, the anarchists, the Zionists, the Workmen's Circle, the labor lyceums, and even the "German Jewish" sponsored settlement houses all encouraged or tolerated lectures in the East European vernacular. About the year 1915, Detroit invited the recently arrived Sholem Aleichem to read from his writings. Even university students, conversant with Yiddish, came to hear him; the children from a Hebrew and Yiddish school gave him a bouquet, and he is said to have received a fee of $500. (Gossip has little respect for reality.) Other literary notables made their appearance, Abraham Reisen, Peretz Hirschbein, and Yehoash. At these affairs, there were also supplementary performers; a cantor might sing, a young lady would play piano solos of the world's great composers. Who can deny the cultural impact of these literary and musical soirees?

HINTERLAND THEATRE

By the time of World War I, as prosperity smiled on the immigrants in all parts of the country, Yiddish theatre companies were established in many of the large towns. Yiddish plays were produced as far west as San Francisco; the seasons were not long. New York companies toured the provinces, and eager theatregoers could see the great Jacob Adler in Karl Ferdinand Gutzkow's *Uriel Acosta* or even listen to Jacques Halevy's *La Juive*, all in Yiddish of course. Goldfaden's operettas were popular. In Baltimore in 1895, when Professor Horowitz's *Alexander or the Crown Prince of Jerusalem* was staged, a fire broke out and twenty-three people were killed. When Boris Thomashefsky came to Cleveland a good seat cost as much as $1.50; in Pittsburgh, a devotee of the stage could buy an admission ticket for 25 cents, but had to bring along his own box on which to sit. In that city, as in other towns, there was frequently a show on Friday night despite the fulminations of pious Rabbi Sivitz. Pittsburgh had amateur theatrical companies. Good plays were put on or read to appreciative audiences. As in New York, the theatre everywhere appealed to the masses; the Yiddish they heard linked them to the past, to their people; they admired the New York celebrities who stalked across the boards; there was always a moral to fortify the virtuous.

HINTERLAND PRESS

If there was a Yiddish literature in the interior, it manifested itself, as in New York, in the press. There was hardly a town with a large Jewish population that did not support a Yiddish periodical. (Often there was an

English page.) At one time or another, many large cities experimented with a daily Yiddish journal. Around 1921, there were at least a dozen Yiddish dailies in the United States; New York had five, and there were at least seven in other towns, three in Chicago, and one each in Philadelphia, Cleveland, Milwaukee, and Los Angeles. At times, some of these towns had two papers; the *Forward* was eager to publish local editions for the edification of its patrons. Chicago was a Yiddish cultural center; it had a very substantial East European colony; by 1920, there were about 275,000 Jews in town; most of them probably spoke Yiddish. At one time, there were ten Yiddish periodicals in the city; the socialists always wanted to make sure that their voice would be heard. The paper that persevered when others disappeared was the *Jewish Courier*. For many years its editor was Leon Zolotkoff (1866-1938) who reached out in many different directions. He even found time to quarrel with the great Emil G. Hirsch. The feisty rabbi attacked the West Side greenhorn: "You don't know English," to which Zolotkoff replied, "You don't know Russian."

The tiny "Russian" Jewish community in Atlanta—it numbered about 2,400 souls—had a Yiddish journal of its own from 1908 to 1911. This East European Jewish group was really too small and too poor to support a paper. In Providence, Rhode Island, 900 householders subscribed to New York's dailies; Philadelphia's elite Jewish citizens turned up their Sephardic and Ashkenazic noses when "jargon" papers were first published in the city; Yiddish was mistakenly thought to be only a hodgepodge of words and expressions. In 1906, in neighboring New York, William Randolph Hearst started a new Yiddish daily; he was determined to defeat Charles Evan Hughes and become governor of the state; the Jewish vote there was important; there were about 600,000 Jews in town and most of them read Yiddish. When Hearst was defeated, he immediately dismantled the staff and closed the paper. It was a good newspaper, but he had no interest in keeping it alive. He had bigger fish to fry.[15]

AMERICA AND YIDDISH

Most East European Jews found the American ambience irresistible; they could not escape the impact of the new land and the changes which it imposed. They were affected politically, socially, culturally, linguistically, and economically. Merely by virtue of being here, they were compelled to give hostages to fortune; they had become "American." Acculturation began the day they landed. Not a few of the literati had come here young; they went to the schools and colleges; little separated them from the native-born; they were Americans almost from the start. What was more Yiddish than the Yiddish theatre? Yet the programs were very often printed in English as well as Yiddish. Almost from the first day of his arrival, the immigrant turned to the want ads; he needed a job. It was the newspaper that helped every newcomer cope. In many respects, East Side dailies were American papers written in Yiddish. The editorials were concerned primarily with the problems and opportunities that faced the Jews not only as Jews but also as Americans, as citizens or as citizens in the making. Most papers at one time or another ran an English column, a section, or a page. English lessons and stories, too, were printed with explanatory notes in Yiddish. It is not improbable that some of the journals discontinued their drive for English, knowing full well that anglicized readers might turn to the Uptown dailies.

The Declaration of Independence and the Federal Constitution had been translated into Yiddish well before the dawn of the twentieth century. The outside world embraced the "Russians" with a bear-like hug. Even the "good" Jews began going to the Yiddish theatres on Friday nights, Saturday noons, and on the Holy Days. Writers, sophisticated, reached out to embrace American literature. They read the American classics; they translated them for the periodicals and journals where they worked. This was a tradition that began as early as the proletarian poets; David Pinski later felt free to write a play about Mary Magdalene. Who could be more Yiddish than Shaikewitz? Yet this man was completely at home in English and employed it in some of his writings. Many of the Yiddish writers wrote excellent English. The new literati who appeared on the scene around the time of World War I refused to be tied down to Jewish themes; they found inspiration in sheer poetry, in nature, in the village, in life on the prairies. One may be reminded again that it was Peter Wiernik, a Yiddish journalist, editor of a right-wing Orthodox paper, who wrote the first narrative history of American Jewry in English. Mastering the English idiom was not always easy. The following ship announcement appeared in an English newspaper: *The Empress of China* arrived here yesterday on her maiden voyage. Here is how the same notice appeared in a Yiddish paper: The Empress of China came here yesterday looking for a husband.[16]

YIDDISH IN ENGLISH AND ENGLISH IN YIDDISH

It took time but in the course of the twentieth century by courtesy of Jewish comedians, cartoonists, comic strip artists, the radio, and, finally, the press—even the austere *New York Times*—a few Yiddish words and phrases, too, slipped into English. There is shamus or shammash (detective); shmo (jerk); shadchan (marriage broker); blintz (Jewish crepe); matzo (unleavened bread); gonif (a thief or sharper); meshuge (crazy); kibitzer (brash observer at a card game); mazel tov (good luck); sholem aleichem (howdy). Then of course there is the choicest of tidbits—if so it may be denominated—gefilte fish, which may be purchased today in any

American supermarket in the Jewish food section. When the American Jewish Committee sponsored a banquet for President Eisenhower in New York in the 1950's, the menu daintily referred to this Jewish favorite as "traditional minced fish." Shlemiel antedates the Eastern Europe newcomers; it was common among the Germans, too. The shlemiel is the man who spills the coffee on his friend; his friend, on whom the coffee is spilled, is the shlimazel, the luckless wight.

English of course made inroads into the Polish-Russian-Rumanian Yiddish. The immigrant vernacular was Americanized rapidly. Words were introduced for which there was no Yiddish equivalent. The garment industry made substantial contributions to the newcomer's vocabulary. These are just a few words that are good Yiddish: factory, shop, dress, hat. Admitted, too, into the new Yiddish thesaurus are boy, chair, window. An allrightnick is an immigrant who has "made it." Abraham Cahan once quoted a Yiddish sentence of a woman (a yente) preparing to clean house: "Ich vel scrobbin dem floor, klinen die vindes und polishen dem stove." Of course, no European language brought here by any immigrant was spared. The German employed by Pennsylvania Christian colonial notables was replete with English nouns and verbs.[17]

YIDDISH AS A TOTAL CULTURE

The English word *Yiddish* was not coined until about the 1880's; as a language and a culture, it was something strange to Anglo-Saxon people, but for Jews it had been beloved since the High Middle Ages. Here in the United States, Yiddish was but one of a dozen different languages for the demographer; for the Jews, Yiddish was not just another statistic. The Jews had special reasons to treasure this tongue; with Yiddish in one's knapsack, one could travel all over the world; it is quite probable that more Jews spoke Yiddish than any other language. Millions in the United States understood it. This would include the American-born children of the Slavic and Balkan émigrés. By 1921 there may have been 2,000,000 Americans whose mother tongue was Yiddish. A Gentile New York manufacturer who sold medicated plasters included Yiddish in the directions printed on the packet.

For these new arrivals on American soil, Yiddish was a portable homeland embracing their language and a complete Jewish way of life, yiddishkeit. The dictionary definition of Jewishness is inadequate unless it included loyalty, culture, social ideals, identity. For many, yiddishkeit is the unexpressed conviction that the concept is not exhausted by piety. A good Jew need not always be a meticulously observant religionist. Mordecai M. Kaplan, the Reconstructionist, shared similar views. Who used Yiddish: the labor union leaders, communal workers like Joseph Barondess and B. Charney Vladeck, the secularist socialists, whether cosmopolitans or Jewish nationalists, the literati, the Jewish immigrant masses. Indeed, by the second decade of the twentieth century thousands of unsynagoged immigrants set out to create Yiddish cultural enclaves in which the language and its writings were ends in themselves. America's East European world, particularly in the New York Jewish ghetto, was riven with intramural hostilities; Yiddish, a common language, helped maintain a semblance of unity and "community." Hebrew was relegated to the synagog and the prayer book; modern Hebrew was a luxury for a few unassorted intellectuals; Yiddish was an imperative necessity. Here in a foreign milieu, the newcomers, treasuring it, held on to it with dogged determination. They loved it for its rich capacity to express every nuance of thought, every variation of emotion. Invective? The curse is the true measure of a language. Everyone must stand in awe of its startling blood-curdling imaginative imprecations.

Were these newcomers overzealous in cherishing and retaining their mother tongue? The American Jewish native-born and elite protested constantly against the use of this foreign "jargon." They felt threatened by it and denounced it; they were convinced it impugned the Americanism of Jews. When the Enlightener Judah D. Eisenstein sent Gustav Gottheil his Yiddish translation of the Declaration of Independence and the Constitution, the latter reproached Eisenstein for using this gibberish. Do you want to clothe the Constitution in rags, put the Jew on a level with Negroes and their English jargon? But a wiser Louis Marshall informed the patrician native-born and "Germans" whom he led that, thanks to Yiddish, pushcart peddlers and humble garment workers were reading the world's best literature in translation. If the immigrants persisted in holding on to their mother tongue, they were doing no more than the securely ensconced Jewish elite, the German Jews, who held on tenaciously to their language despite the fact that the German lands had refused Jews complete emancipation until 1871. A Milwaukee synagog of the 1870's adorned the ark with the Ten Commandments both in Hebrew and in German; Kohler and Einhorn wrote each other in that language; Felsenthal, of Chicago, also wrote Richard Gottheil in German despite the fact that the latter's mother tongue was probably English. Up to World War I, the older Schiffs and Warburgs wrote to one another in their beloved German. (What was true of these German Jewish immigrants was true of many others, Gentiles, who came to this land. The Midwestern Veblens, Norwegians, never ceased speaking the language which they brought with them. Thorstein, a son, a native American, a future eminent social scientist, had trouble with English when he enrolled in an academy.)

Yiddish cast its net wide and far; it was a language that embraced dramatists, novelists, storytellers, poets, and journalists; it was the life-blood of theatres, newspapers, schools, and social welfare institutions. Thousands of school children attended Hebrew schools where Yiddish was the language of instruction. In the world of the immigrant, language, culture, and folk were indissolubly united; they were all one. For a generation that was to experience travail, it was of supreme importance; it was the prime sustaining factor for traditional religionists and socialistic icon-oclasts; it gave them comfort, solace, identity, security; it helped them to survive, to rear a new generation that would find its own way culturally and spiritually; it was a bastion against overhasty acculturation. It is probable that, when World War I erupted, the United States was on its way to becoming the center of world Yiddish literature. More than ever, Yiddish welded together large numbers of Jews, linked them to one another, to a common Jewish fate.

THE PRESS

In the world of Yiddish and all that it meant, the press was the most important institution. By this we mean the world of the newspapers and all other periodicals. Due to American enterprise and means and the absence of a Russian-like censorship, the Yiddish vernacular press flourished here. The humblest workingman could allow himself a penny or two for a newspaper; books were more expensive. The typical immigrant did not build up a Yiddish library; he could not afford it. The newcomers, transferring their village culture to metropolitan industrial New York, relied on their newspapers, which sustained them in this transoceanic world and kept them in touch with the land where their dear ones still remained. What did the press teach them? It taught them democracy, America at its best. This meant much, for these Jews had come from lands of disability and oppression. The papers they read encouraged them to send their children to the public schools. This they did, since the schools were free and opened the road to opportunity, to a livelihood. Despite their disparate ideologies, all Yiddish papers favored labor unions; "bread to eat and a garment to wear"; that was all important. Frequently, the immigrant leaders urged ghetto dwellers not to overcrowd the professions, to move to the hinterland, to learn a skilled trade, to go in for physical sports. In some of these recommendations, the voice was the voice of the Russians, but the concepts were those of the Uptown Jews. Most important was the fact that journals took the immigrant Jews—a century behind the times—and introduced them to the fascinating world in which they now found themselves. Yiddish newspapers of diverse hues put the culturally backward immigrants in touch with all facets of American life; the radical journals were Enlighteners with a vengeance; the socialists, anarchists, secularists, antinomians, were enthusiastic humanists.

THE IMPACT OF AMERICAN CULTURE

No matter their form, Yiddish writings became Americanizing agents, directly or indirectly. The constant interpolation of English words into the changing Yiddish was not unimportant; words are dynamic; the words became action. America and what it stood for worked through the street, the job, the newspaper. The bourgeois newspapers never set out originally to Americanize their subscribers; their prime purpose was to make money for the publishers. This they had in common with Adolph S. Ochs, Joseph Pulitzer, and William Randolph Hearst. In the long run, however, all the Yiddish dailies, Marxist and non-radical, did a good job in helping their readers survive through cultural adaptation. Time and newsprint have an alchemy all their own. Slowly, slowly, these Jewish Slavs and Rumanians became Americans. They had to change. Let it be remembered that Yiddish—almost a thousand years old—had up to the late nineteenth century lived in a world of autocracy; now it had to learn the language of democracy. The editors were more than willing; they hammered at their readers to learn English, to become citizens, to vote on principle. Despite economic exploitation, the émigrés loved America and its ideals. Its impact was so powerful that even the internationalist, socialist, and anarchist papers gradually moved to the right. American conservatism could not be denied. Yet, despite their Americanization, the men and women who came here in the fifty years after 1870 died loving Yiddish. They loved it for what it was, even the non-romantic secularists never rejected it. For these realists, Yiddish was a cultural substitute for the religion which they had abandoned. They would have no truck with the bourgeois Reform Jews who constantly stressed English. Ultimately the East Europeans, too, moved away from Yiddish, but they did so at their own pace.

YIDDISH LITERATURE AND CULTURE:
ITS ALL-EMBRACING EXTENT

Through the medium of the theatre and the press, New York's large Jewry, complemented by other American Jewish metropolitan communities, created a noteworthy Yiddish literature. A corpus of writings developed here in the United States because of the relative prosperity of the immigrants. Even the sweatshop and factory workers were better off than they had been in Russia, Poland, Galicia, and Rumania. Some historians are convinced that these Jewish newcomers were producing the largest

foreign language literature in this country. There were hundreds of litterateurs; most of them had some tie to the dailies and magazines. One cannot but be impressed on checking the American Jewish names in the four
volumes of Z. Reisen's *Leksikon*, in the eight volumes of the *Biographical
Dictionary of Modern Yiddish Literature*, and the Zylberscweig dictionary of
the Yiddish theatre in six volumes; the literature is huge; the writers are
numerous. By 1905, New York was the largest Yiddish book market in
the world.

The literature itself is almost infinite in its variety. It was read by all,
developed by all. The authors included men and women, artisans, who
labored daily for their livelihood. There was a steady export to Russia; the
ghetto denizens there enjoyed the American penny dreadfuls. The presses
here poured out papers, magazines, books, and plays for political extremists, middle of the road religionists, and creative poets who worshipped at
the altars of the Greek Homer and the Hebrew psalmist. Yiddish culture
added a fillip to the world of the synagog and the halls of the labor lyceums; eager auditors could listen to the impassioned Zionist homilies of
an Orthodox Masliansky and the cold logic of the nontheistic Zhitlowsky. The growing Yiddish literature included much more than belles
lettres; there were dramas, memoirs, and dozens of works explicating all
the sciences. Ideologically, there were writers who lined up with the traditional religionists, with the Palestine or Diaspora nationalists, or with
the several schools of secularists. Much of the writing was rooted in European soil, inasmuch as all the writers were immigrants; a number of them
had won their spurs before making the Atlantic crossing. Culturally,
these belletrists stood astride two disparate worlds; they could not divorce
themselves from their past and had to come to terms with both Russia and
America. Their writings never escaped being Jewish, even when they
were peripheral, Americanistic, universal, and iconoclastic. Obviously,
they were all ghetto writers, trying to resolve their physical and spiritual
odysseys. Though many of the poets fled to nature, to love, to the inviting world with its endless appeal, it would be decades before they could
fully emancipate themselves from the ghetto and its clutch. They had to
confront the promises of freedom and the threats of the extreme. In cata-
loguing their writings, it is clear that they ground out both good literature and bad literature. The historian is prompted to suggest that the real
literature—the most interesting at any rate—might well be the "bad" literature, for it reflected the tastes, the desires, the mind-set and the heart-
set of the masses. If what they loved is to be dismissed with a contemp-
tuous sneer, what then is history?

In a larger sense, a study of Yiddish culture must always touch on the
songs which the masses sang. Any reader of Odell's massive volumes on
the annals of New York City's theatre cannot but be impressed by the

persistence of the musical shows, the operas and operettas that were staged. This is what the people wanted to hear; they never tired of Mogulesco's new songs, of Goldfaden's music, of Sandler's poignant song. The provenance of the material was not important; everyone "borrowed" what they could. Wagner, said the elegant and knowledgeable Goldfaden, composed but one good melody and I stole it from him.

Anyone who wishes to gauge the immensities and the opportunities afforded by the world of Yiddish must wade through the book catalogues of the house of Druckerman. The first Druckerman began his career as a bookdealer back in 1869 in Europe. By 1888, he had opened a shop here on Canal Street and the firm was to remain there for decades. The Druckermans sold everything that reinforced yiddishkeit: prayer books and phylacteries; all the standard rabbinic classics were on their shelves; there was violin and piano sheet music, there were volumes on socialism and anarchism, and no end of brochures on Zionism. There were do-it-yourself books on how to write a letter and how to become a citizen and even how to play a fiddle. The writers of the Russian and Polish Yiddish classics were, of course, at hand; and there was no lack of works of the proletarian poets, and of Gordin, Pinski, Hirschbein, and Kobrin. There was a translation for every taste: Spencer and Zola, Marx and Engels, Bellamy and Buckley. By judicious purchases at Druckerman's, one could become a truly educated autodidact; reading the catalogues was an education in itself.

THE RISE IN ARTISTRY

By the end of this period, by 1920-1921, Yiddish literature had inched into its Golden Age. In a way, the earlier proletarian poems were but prologue. This is not to imply that folk-writers of the late nineteenth century were unimportant. By no means. They wrote for the masses. It is not mawkish sentimentality to venture the thought that their verses were written with blood, the blood of tuberculars. By the 1920's, the new literature of the poets, the dramatists, the storytellers was on a different, a higher level. The times had changed; it was a long generation since the first frightened émigrés had arrived. Now there was a small body of men and women, educated, exposed to the best in the world of books; they had developed an understanding of the truly artistic. As Yiddish litterateurs burgeoned, were they accorded recognition in the American republic of letters? Who in the upper reaches of Manhattan could read Yiddish? Volume one of the *Dictionary of American Biography* first appeared on the bookshelves in 1929; the editors were chary of including Yiddishists. Their Jewish advisers would have been cautious; Yiddish was not respectable. This may well be due to ignorance, not prejudice. Despite the almost childlike enthusiasm of some Gentiles, culture adventurers, acculturated Jews and most non-Jews had little knowledge of the literary world below Fourteenth Street. There are not many writers of Yiddish included in the biographies assembled in volume six of the *American Jewish Year Book* (1904); almost fifty years later, the *Oxford Companion to American Literature* had no entry under "Yiddish"; it did carry a short article on "Jews"; Yiddish and its writers were given three lines. It was not easy for literary pundits to conceive that the Torah would come forth from Canal Street and the word of God from East Broadway.

YIDDISH AND THE JEWISH WOMAN

There were women writing in Yiddish ever since the turn of the nineteenth century. Some had written in Russia before coming here. Even in Eastern Europe, there was always a group of women well read in Russian and German literature. Some knew French; a few nursed literary ambitions. Here, the aspiring female writer had the opportunity to do something; the Russian cities and villages were no hearths of tolerance and liberalism. The women writers here in the United States, most frequently journalists, wrote poetry and fiction. Some, like Rose Pastor Stokes, were columnists. Eager to increase their subscription lists, all papers went after the women and catered to their interests; they were enticed with romances and domestic science hints. It is curious that the *Jewish Daily News*, a right-wing Orthodox paper, had no hesitation in employing Rose Pastor Stokes despite the fact that she was a socialist. (Her columns were in English, however, not Yiddish.) A small number of Yiddish-speaking women, intellectuals, radicals, frequented the cafes where their socialist, anarchist, and literary friends gathered. Some of these women worked in industry; apparently, their interests were solely intellectual; they were not coy females setting out to make themselves attractive to men. An even larger group of immigrant women here had entered the professions of law, medicine, dentistry, pharmacy, and nursing. They were culturally articulate. Male intellectuals who favored left-wing ideologies affirmed the equality of women, in theory at least. Yiddish-speaking women did come into their own in the theatre. They were needed; the time was long past when male youngsters could play female parts. There were a number of famous women stars who were enthusiastically received by their admirers. Unlike the actresses in the Uptown theatres, these women were not svelte beauties. They were pleasingly plump (zaftik, succulent); they were actors and excellent ones. The world of the ghetto was slow to move toward sexual egalitarianism. Even the liberal-minded labor leaders were in no hurry to advance women in the hierarchy of power. The Jewish Lower East Side was still a man's world; it was not easy to modify a patriarchial social system as old as society itself.

YIDDISH: RECAPITULATION AND REFLECTIONS

Yiddish embodied within itself the literature of myriads; its writings were one aspect of "Jewishness." The social ideals of its exponents were close to the preachments of the Hebrew prophets. No one who used the Hebrew alphabet could escape being Jewish. Regardless of ideologies, the goal of all Yiddishists was to live their own lives; they did not set out to conform to the cultural patterns and prejudices of the Uptown Anglo-Saxons and the Jewish elite. The real ultimate goal of the theatre and the press was to produce a profit, but there were honest secondary interests; the theatre set out to entertain, the press to educate, to Westernize. There was, of course, a distinction between the religious and the secular journals; the former wanted to maintain Orthodoxy; the latter, proselytizing, wanted to preach the gospel of Marx and to change the world. By 1921, as the portals started slowly to swing shut, literature for some had become a self-centered individualistic art, an end in itself. The degree of Jewishness varied with the individual and the occasion. Pogroms abroad intensified Jewish sympathies. Murders, rejection, hatred, have a persuasion all their own. Though standing outside the synagog, the secularists never left the fold. They were still Jews, for they spoke Yiddish and, like their bearded cousins, also stressed traditional ethics. All Jews, even government-rejecting anarchists, were good Americans. (Emma Goldman loved America.) By the 1920's, practically all Jewish immigrants here had assumed a positive attitude toward this country and the ideals of the Founding Fathers. All Jewish writers were reaching out over the ghetto walls into the modern Western world of good books. Like the Uptown Jews, the Downtown folk took what they needed to reinforce their traditional holdings. Cultural assimilation is not self-destruction; often, it is just the opposite.

Yiddish literature is not unimportant for the general American historian; it is a basic corpus of material for the historian of the American Jewish scene. The Jewish Russians, Poles, Rumanians, and eastern Hungarians have constituted the Jewish majority here in these United States ever since the 1890's. Their literature reveals their experiences, their hopes as they moved toward integration into the life of this new land. These sources, running into the millions of pages, may well be the largest collection of foreign language data in the libraries and archives of this country. It is true that little notice is taken of this vast collection of data by the general historians. There is no entry "Yiddish" in the indices of the twelve-volume *History of American Life*, none in the exhaustive two-volume revised edition of the *Harvard Guide to American History*. All this does not detract from the fact that it was the cultural-literary institutions and the communications media of Yiddish America that sustained Jewry for at least six decades. Yiddish writings were a force in the lives of large numbers of men and women, millions, who happened to be American.

As early as the second decade of the twentieth century, as Yiddish began to fade in the provinces, it was obvious that its days were numbered. The process of decline would be a slow one; Yiddish was still alive in the late twentieth century. By World War II, the Yiddish theatre was no longer a vital institution anywhere; the dailies began to close their doors one by one, though by the 1980's there were still seventeen Yiddish periodicals in New York alone. It was the racially motivated immigration acts of the 1920's which really gave Yiddish literature the coup de grace. Very few Yiddish-speaking Jews could now hope to enter this country; the immigrant reservoirs could not be replenished; the lifeline to America was cut; those left behind could find no other haven and had only to await the German Holocaust. In drama and in life, there is such a thing as the "catastrophe," the climactic last stage in tragedy. Though the catastrophe for Yiddish and Yiddish culture was already in the making in the 1920's, strangely enough this was the decade that ushered in a golden age, an age of experiment and artistry, of emotional and intellectual creativity that endured till World War II and after. By that time, the actors, the poets, and the readers were all dying; there were but few epigones. The press of these trans-Vistula exiles suffered the same fate as the German Jewish newspapers. Gotthard Deutsch edited Isaac M. Wise's German-language *Deborah* till 1903; then he, too, closed shop. There were no more readers. Yiddish was and is a transitional culture. It was a reality in the 1870's; it may persevere till the year 2000. With certain exceptions, the American-born children of the ardent Yiddishists did not cultivate the language of their ancestors. The new generation turned to an American press, to the Uptown theatres, to the English-writing poets. These children, born on American soil, but still conscious of their foreign background, were determined to become 125 percent American. As the century advanced, there was an increasing interest in the nature and character of Yiddish literature on the part of a few. Translations were frequent. Yiddish in its death achieved respectability; now it threatened no one. Because of its significance for the historians who will want to study a Jewry that grew from 250,000 to 6,000,000, Yiddish will never die. It is destined for a better fate than the Aramaic, the Judeo-Greek, and the Judeo-Arabic classics that have disappeared or languish in manuscript libraries. It is not improbable that many students will arise to study and love Yiddish for its intrinsic worth. What the parents spoke and their children derided the grandchildren will study in college classrooms.[18]

CHAPTER SEVENTEEN

WHAT IS TO BE DONE WITH THESE

INCOMING EXOTICS

WESTERN LEADERSHIP

The native-born and naturalized Jews were not happy with these Yiddish-speaking Slavic and Balkan newcomers; they were exotic; they had high visibility; they were un-American! They were different—inferior!—religiously, culturally. They lived on a lower economic level. Not sure of their own status—never to be sure—the naturalized Germans felt threatened lest they be identified with these newcomers. The problem was acute; these "Russians" were here to stay. What was to be done? They outnumbered the natives and the naturalized Central Europeans. A large percentage of these refugees opted to remain on Manhattan Island, partially because they had no money to move on, but also because these exiles were not stupid; they knew New York was the new industrial hub. With rare exception the Jews long settled here realized that they would have to help the incoming East Europeans; they had no choice but to acknowledge them as fellow Jews. This was a national problem but there were few national organizations prepared to tackle it. The Board of Delegates of American Israelites? It went out of existence in 1878 and was succeeded by a committee, the Board of Delegates on Civil and Religious Rights, an agency of the Union of American Hebrew Congregations (UAHC). The BDCRR could not cope with this immigrant horde; it wanted to help but it had no staff, no budget, no plan. Like the older Board of Delegates of American Israelites this new civil rights congeries tried to improve conditions abroad so as to obviate the necessity for emigration. It too hoped that the United States government would intercede with the inhumane governments of Russia and Rumania. It also worked to keep the portals of immigration open. Once the exiles were here the BDCRR made way for those institutions that favored colonization, agriculture, industrial retraining, or removal to the backcountry. Very few of these expedients were helpful. These displaced persons crowded the warrens of the East Side.

Though limited in size and scope the Union of American Hebrew Congregations had a moral obligation to attack the problem of these aliens. The Union was certainly not unaware of the issues but the leaders had headaches of their own; they could do little; actually there was no real leadership in Cincinnati where the Union was centered. In the crisis of 1881-1882 Isaac M. Wise taunted the Eastern elite for its inactivity; the latter rejoined sarcastically that the Westerners were do-nothings. The problem was at the doorstep of the New Yorkers; the Westerners were not threatened by the mass invasion and consequently they dragged their heels. Wise was growing old and was less of a force on the national scene. By 1900 the basic cultural institution of the Union was threatened. There was a move to get the Hebrew Union College out of Cincinnati, to unite it with the moribund Jewish Theological Seminary in New York. Schiff and Marshall were in sympathy with this proposal; a merger would save money. New York had good universities where the students could study. Working out of that metropolis the new proposed conjoint school, improved, could pull the Lower Manhattan masses into the magic circle of modernity, Americanism, so the New Yorkers thought. Loath to surrender Western leadership, Emil G. Hirsch was ready to move the Cincinnati school to a big city with a large university; he had his own Chicago in mind. It may be assumed that he would be willing to head the transferred school but continue to remain as rabbi of prestigious Sinai. The attempt to coalesce the College and the Seminary failed; it is difficult to mold Catholicism and Protestantism into one harmonious whole! Lewis N. Dembitz, the uncle of Louis Dembitz Brandeis, opposed the union of the two seminaries vigorously. The seminary, Orthodox, observed kashrut; the Reformers ate "abominations and creeping things" at their religious banquets![1]

For three years Cincinnati, the spiritual center of liberal Judaism, struggled with the problem of finding a president for the College after Wise's death. Israel Abrahams of Cambridge, England, living on a pittance, refused to take the job; several successful aggressive American rabbis shied away when the presidency was tendered them or imposed unacceptable conditions. The student body was pitifully small; the campus was a remodeled private mansion. Kaufmann Kohler, the man finally selected to head the College, was already sixty years of age. From the vantage point of distant Cincinnati he did little to lead the million or more Russians, Poles, and Rumanians out of the wilderness into the promised land of cultured America; indeed he had little real sympathy for the newcomers. He was the architect of the 1885 Pittsburgh Platform that rejected the new Love of Zion movement making itself felt here in the United States. Yet the rabbis of the Pittsburgh Conference were fully conscious of the need to come to terms with the new immigrants for at this very meeting they urged the establishment of a society in every congregation that would make advances to the émigrés, write tracts for them, educate their children, and elevate them culturally.[2]

Kaufmann Kohler's son, Max, a lawyer, devoted himself to the job of helping the East Europeans both here and abroad. This learned scholarly man was utterly devoted to his people and used his very considerable talents on their behalf. He was an ardent student and writer in the field of human rights and American Jewish history. In 1915 he and Simon Wolf —also a lawyer—wrote *Jewish Disabilities in the Balkan States.* Wolf (1836-1923) was the outstanding Jewish lobbyist in Washington. He was a shtadlan, a persuader, who devoted most of his life to the defense of American Jewry. The Union of American Hebrew Congregations and the B'nai B'rith (IOBB) used him as their Washington representative for about sixty years. This was for him a labor of love; he was not paid. This South German came to the United States with his grandparents in 1848 when he was twelve years of age. After he grew up he went to work as a salesman and a bookkeeper. He studied law and at the age of twenty-five was admitted to the bar in northern Ohio. A year later, 1862, he settled in Washington where he made his residence for the rest of his life. He was a life-long Republican politician and even found it possible to excuse General Grant, a Republican, for his General Orders No. 11 expelling Jews from the areas patrolled by his army during the early years of the Civil War.

Concerned about the sufferings of the Jews in Eastern Europe, Wolf constantly intervened for them at the nation's capital. He had influence because he was for years head of the BDCRR and for a time was president of B'nai B'rith and a power in the Kesher shel Barzel, the Iron Chain, another large Jewish fraternal order. From the 1860's on, since the time of Lincoln, Wolf had access to every president. His memoirs make interesting reading. It was he more than anyone else who saw to it that his fellow member in B'nai B'rith, Benjamin Franklin Peixotto, was appointed consul to Rumania with the hope that he might be able to help the oppressed Jews in those Danubian principalities. In order to keep the gates to America open for Europe's Jews, Wolf worked hard to convince the United States immigration authorities that the newcomers would never become a public charge; he saved many who were threatened with deportation. To counter the anti-Semites who said that Jews had not rallied to the defense of the Union during the Civil War he published a statistical work proving that thousands of his coreligionists had fought in the armed forces. In later years, in his role as Jewry's chief lobbyist, he worked for the abrogation of the discriminatory treaty with Russia and was eager to insure political equality to all Jews in Eastern Europe after World War I. He was an Americanizer and consequently an anti-Zionist; he could not conceive that a Jew could be loyal to the United States and long for the restoration of the ancient state of Israel. Despite his devotion to World Jewry it was not in him to undertake the task of serving as a leader for the recently arrived Jews from the Slavic lands.[3]

The UAHC and the B'nai B'rith were aware of the problem; they were not unsympathetic but they accomplished little in helping the Russians make their way here. Some of the leaders of the B'nai B'rith were Westerners, removed in a sense from the problems geographically and possibly emotionally. It is true that IOBB president Julius Bien, the noted cartographer, was a New Yorker but the strength of his order lay in the hinterland. Bien ruled the fraternity from 1868 to 1900; his successor was Leo N. Levi, a Texas lawyer who had moved to New York but the metropolitan elite refused to accept him; Adolf Kraus, a Chicago attorney, led the B'nai B'rith from his fortress in Chicago (1905-1925). Nevertheless the IOBB seems to have been more concerned, more effective than the Union of American Hebrew Congregations in aiding the Russians. Immigrants were helped to settle in the hinterland; social rooms and an employment bureau were opened in the New York ghetto in the early twentieth century; manuals of citizenship were published. Like all other Jewish agencies the IOBB too, harped on the virtues of Americanism. Some of the local branches of the order admitted East Europeans but there was no large-scale approach to the problem of welcoming them into the American (Jewish) fold. The immigrants did not join the B'nai B'rith; they established large fraternal associations of their own, very successful ones too.

As leaders of the only national congregational and communal organization in the United States, the lay heads of the Union of American Hebrew Congregations should have taken the lead in acculturating the newcomers, particularly in the hinterland where the acculturated Germans were all powerful. They talked of putting the émigrés on the soil and conjured up elaborate schemes which accomplished very little. They were more successful in opening their schools to the children of the new arrivals; here they did a good job. But the leaders of the UAHC and the IOBB were too parochial in their views, unimaginative on the whole, completely unprepared to offer national guidance to the thousands of immigrants from Russia and the Balkans. What could they have done for the strangers in their midst? When the Cincinnatians were approached about moving the College to New York and helping to Americanize the immigrant masses they answered indignantly, in German of course, *Wir haben auch Lokalstolz,* "We have our local pride." The Reformers did make a gallant effort to establish a conventicle in the Philadelphia ghetto. It was to be a people's synagog, Orthodox in liturgy; no overt attempt was made to proselytize. But despite the support of an ardent few among the East

Europeans nothing was accomplished. Many of the adolescent youngsters of the immigrant Russians were religiously indifferent. Philadelphia's Orthodox leaders and their followers disdained the modernizing effort; the Reformers were no better than the hated missionaries!

The problem of working closely with the Orthodox émigrés appeared insoluble to the Western leaders; they were not prepared to turn the clock back. To satisfy the incoming masses they would have been compelled to re-Hebraicize the services, keep kosher, reinstitute abandoned ceremonies, and embrace the new Jewish nationalism, Zionism, with its fearful implication of disloyalty to America. And had they done all this, it would not have availed them. They spoke no Yiddish; the social gap between the two groups could not be bridged. Is there nothing the Reform leaders, the Western elite, could have done? They could have helped the newcomers on their own terms, given them space for their Orthodox services in the Reform temples, if only in the vestry rooms. They could have helped them maintain their East European institutions and way of life allowing the alchemy of America to work at its own pace. The Reformers were derelict, doing little to further the integration of these Jewish newcomers into the larger Jewish community. In 1921 Cincinnati may have had 15,000 Russians at the most; New York at that time probably sheltered 1,000,000 of these aliens. The masses were in New York; the Union of American Hebrew Congregations could do little directly for these metropolitans. If these immigrants were to be given guidance—whether it was sought or not—it would have to come from the East. The Easterners were more than willing; the problem was theirs primarily.[4]

EASTERN LEADERSHIP

EX ORIENTE LUX

Light would have to come from the East, not from the B'nai B'rith nor from the Union of American Hebrew Congregations. The leaders of American Jewry resided in New York City ever since the late 1820's. Temporarily leadership was wrested from them in the 1870's when the Union of American Hebrew Congregations was established and the Hebrew Union College was opened. It was during that period, in 1878, that the Board of Delegates of American Israelites was taken over by the UAHC. The seventies is definitely the decade of the West; it was able to pile victory upon victory. When the Eastern and Western congregations were joined together in the Union in 1878 it was inevitable that the Eastern leaders would make the effort to control the Union; they had no choice but to assume the initiative as the East Europeans began arriving.

During the years 1883 and 1884 some individuals talked of calling a national convention to cope with the problems that faced American Jewry. Many were aware that the children of earlier settlers were drifting away from Judaism. A number of notables wanted the Union of American Hebrew Congregations to widen its scope and to incorporate the semi-secular Young Men's Hebrew Associations. This movement was led by outstanding Jews from New York (Jacob H. Schiff), Philadelphia, Boston, and Washington. In 1885, the attempt to establish a national ecclesiastical juridical body—a synod—was ruled out of order by the Union of American Hebrew Congregations. In short the efforts of the Easterners to make the UAHC an overall all-inclusive national assembly failed; the Cincinnatians were afraid of being taken over. The only overt result of the maneuverings, 1883-1885, was that Kaufmann Kohler, a New Yorker, called the conference in Pittsburgh to survey the national religious scene; a left-wing partisan religious program eventuated. Eastern efforts to control the UAHC failed. A generation was to elapse before the New Yorkers and their associates would create an instrument to attack American Jewry's problems. This was the American Jewish Committee. In one area both Easterners and Westerners were in agreement; the laymen were to dominate the UAHC; the rabbis were to play second fiddle.[5]

There was little leadership in all of American Jewry from the 1880's until the early 1900's. This was a period of crisis due to the pogroms, the expulsions in Russia, and the coming of a flood of unwanted aliens. It would take time before leaders would emerge to guide the masses. A few hardy individuals began to make their presence felt late in the 1880's; in less than three decades the elite of New York and Philadelphia would reassert their leadership. Jewish bankers and other notables undertook to deal with the problem of assimilating the newcomers; they looked upon them as a threat to their status in the larger non-Jewish community. Some old-timers were of the opinion that these aliens would evoke anti-Semitism. The very people who were fearful that this might happen were unmindful of the fact that when Jew-hatred manifested itself in the late 1870's it was directed against men like Joseph Seligman, an international banker, a pillar of the church (Temple Emanu-El), and one of the chief supporters of Felix Adler's Ethical Culture movement.

What must always be borne in mind is that these elitists were proud Jews and in this sense identified themselves with the new arrivals. They were uneasy but they sincerely wanted to help them. There was a whole host of men particularly in New York City who wanted to be of aid to the incoming immigrants. Among them was Adolph Lewisohn, a notable philanthropist and the donor of the Lewisohn Stadium at the City College of New York. This mining magnate was a concerned Jew. Other Easterners, devoted Jews, were Jesse and Isaac N. Seligman, members of the famous banking family; Nathan Bijur, a jurist and a very active communal worker; Judah Leon Magnes, a rabbi with verve, imagination and liberal views; Cyrus L. Sulzberger, a philanthropist, a civic reformer, an activist eager to promote the welfare of New York, the metropolis; Myer Samuel Isaacs—another New Yorker—was active in many New York Jewish communal institutions; William Bower Hackenburg, a Philadelphia silk manufacturer, was a leader in that city's Jewish charities. He was the head of the committee that undertook the first published census of American Jewry (1880).

Outstanding figures among the Easterners were Oscar Solomon Straus, Cyrus Adler, Louis Marshall, Jacob H. Schiff, and Mayer Sulzberger, a Philadelphian. Most of the others were New Yorkers. These men reached out for leadership. The late nineteenth century was an age of financial capitalism; it was an age when individuals exerted tremendous influence upon the political and economic life of the country. Some of the men mentioned above fitted into this mold. They felt that leadership was imperative; they were interested; they had wealth; they were concerned for the welfare of the new Jewish immigrants; their devotion to Judaism cannot be questioned. A number of them had excellent religious training; they were in no sense assimilationists. Their attitude was one of benevolent paternalism. The massive immigration of uncouth thousands with different religious patterns, the need for helping these strangers make an adjustment to American life stimulated the interest of these leaders; crises brought them out. It must not be forgotten that the 1880's was the decade of the Haymarket massacre when the American people trembled wondering what the anarchists would do to the land they loved. Fearing for their own status these apprehensive lawyers, bankers, and businessmen wanted to integrate the Russians, Poles, and Rumanians into the American mainstream. What they frequently failed to note was that very early a substantial minority of the newcomers, achievers, were already making their way economically and culturally. The older settlers set out to control the voting patterns of the new citizens, to make sure that most of them would always vote either the Republican or Democratic party; socialism and anarchism were abhorrent. The East Europeans who were pouring in were a heterogeneous group hailing from different parts of Eastern Europe and the Balkans; the natives and the German Jews wanted to homogenize them according to their own cultural pattern.

In a larger sense the men who were to emerge as the Eastern leaders had a program for the newcomers, a program that would apply not only to New York City and its ghettos but also to the country at large. They wanted to Americanize them politically and culturally, to occidentalize them religiously. They wanted to modify Orthodoxy radically, at least externally. This was an innovative, an imaginative, a daring approach, an unrealistic one. To accomplish their ends they offered to lead the masses. They hoped that their advances would be accepted and the adjustment of the newcomers to the American way of life would be speeded up. The newcomers resented any plan imposed from above. Yet in the long run it was the very same plan that the newcomers adopted but they, however, evolved it independently both in New York City and in the hinterland. Americanization was imperative. The following incident is illuminating. In June 1906, a large number of immigrant women stormed some of the East Side schools because they were told and believed that their children's throats were being cut by physicians. Actually what the doctors were doing in the public schools was performing vaccinations and, probably, in some instances, removing adenoids. When the teachers saw how frantic the mothers were they sent the children home; the rioting ceased.

Americanization as it was understood in those days meant the use of the English language, donning American garb, employing the amenities, learning the nature of the American political process, and the American way of life. There is no question that if the new arrivals wanted to be in-tegrated into the mainstream of America they would have to come to terms with this country. Did this mean that they would have to give up their past? Not at all. In reality all that Americanization demanded of them was that they conform superficially to the social standards and folk-ways of the land. They could become good Americans and remain good Jews. Turning to the newcomers the apprehensive older settlers asked the newcomers to discard their Yiddish vernacular, emphasize American manners, avoid the ghettos, move to the backcountry, and forswear radi-cal politics. They felt that one could not be a true patriot and remain a so-cialist or anarchist. The old-timers expected the newcomers to maintain a very low profile. In other words they were to become replicas of their German Jewish exemplars; they were to be undistinguishable from all other Americans except in matters of religion. They believed that if this program was adopted the immigrants would become good Americans; it certainly would diminish anti-Semitism. The East Europeans had their own concept of Americanization. Above all they did not want to be dubbed greenhorns and scorned by older East European settlers. They were eager to modify their dress, ready to trim or remove their beards, but they were certainly not willing to give up any of their folkways; they had not come to America from a land of oppression to surrender their Jewish way of life. They would make concessions but only if driven by dire eco-nomic necessity. At its highest level the editors of the Yiddish papers defined Americanism in their editorials as the love of liberty, the practice of justice and humanitarianism.[6]

Among the numerous leaders in all major cities—some were women —who reached out to help Americanize the newcomers a few stand out, not only because of their achievements but because their efforts are typical. One of the Jewish notables who helped the émigrés was Oscar Solomon Straus (1850-1926). This native of Rhenish Bavaria had come to this country at the age of four and lived with his parents in Talbotton and Columbus, Georgia, until after the Civil War. Then he was taken by his parents to New York where he studied law at Columbia. There is a family tradition—for what it is worth—that he was encouraged to study law because he was an ineffectual businessman. At all events he was a member of his father's glass and crockery firm, a very prominent business on the Lower East Side. Straus began as a Democrat when he was appointed minister to Turkey in 1887 during the first administration of Cleveland; Oscar's brother, Isidor, and the president were close friends. Later Oscar Straus moved over to the Republican party; he broke with the Democrats on the question of monetization. As a Republican he was appointed minister and later Ambassador to Constantinople. Turkey was the "Jewish" post. It was probably felt by the authorities in Washington that a Jewish diplomat would be more acceptable in a Moslem country than in a Christian land. The job of Straus in Turkey was to protect the Christian missionaries and to further American business interests. This he did. In 1902 he was appointed a member of the Permanent Court of Arbitration at The Hague; he was always interested in the peace movement. Four years later Roosevelt, seeking to secure Jewish support, appointed him Secretary of Commerce and Labor, the first Jewish cabinet appointment in American history (except, of course, for Judah P. Benjamin, who was the Confederate Secretary of State). In 1912 when Roosevelt left the Republicans and organized the Progressive (Bull Moose) Party, Straus joined him and ran for governor of New York state. He polled more votes than Roosevelt but was not to become New York's first Jewish governor. He was defeated by William Sulzer, a Tammany politician of rather dubious character. Sulzer was the idol of the ghetto because he had been very vigorous in furthering the abrogation of the 1832 treaty with Russia.

Straus had strong literary interests; he was a political idealist. In 1885 he published *The Origin of Republican Form of Government in the United States of America*; in the 1890's he wrote *Roger Williams; The Pioneer of Religious Liberty*. In this latter work he stressed the influence of Hebraism on the colonial governments and their notables. There was no question he was a prominent Jewish communal leader. His Jewish interests, it would seem, reflected the teachings of his father, Lazarus Straus. In 1892 Straus became the first president of the American Jewish Historical Society which he helped establish. It is to his credit, too, that he was one of the influential Americans who induced Baron Maurice de Hirsch to set up a special fund to assist the East European Jews who were landing in this country. This was about the year 1890 at a time when Straus was still minister to the Sublime Porte. He knew Herzl but he was no Zionist. He was, however, always eager to aid the Jews in Palestine who were exposed to a Turkish government that was frequently oppressive. In the early years of the twentieth century he was quick to aid the Russian Jews who were being murdered; in 1905 he met with Witte the Russian statesman in order to discuss the situation of the Jews in the Romanov Empire; in 1906 he became one of the founders of the American Jewish Committee, and after World War I Straus did what he could to help the Jews secure their rights when the peacemakers met at Versailles.[7]

CYRUS ADLER

Straus gave his support to many Jewish causes but his diplomatic duties, which kept him out of the country, made it difficult for him to be as active as his interests might have dictated. Among his friends who were notable leaders at this time was Cyrus Adler (1863-1940). Adler is distinguished in American Jewry as one of its best administrators. He was an Orientalist who had studied at Johns Hopkins where he was the first person to receive a doctoral degree in Semitics. At one time or another he was either president or a very important voice in the Jewish Theological Seminary, Dropsie College, the American Jewish Committee, and the Jewish Publication Society. His influence in these various organizations made him one of the country's outstanding Jews. He was born in Van Buren, Arkansas, but during the Civil War the family moved to Philadelphia where it had relatives. His mother was a Sulzberger, a family that was to play an important role in the Jewish communal life of New York, Philadelphia, and Chicago. In the twentieth century the descendants of the Sulzbergers were active in the management and control of the *New York Times.*

As a boy in Philadelphia Cyrus Adler went to a Jewish parochial school and studied Hebrew with Morais. After he received his doctorate at Hopkins he taught there for a short time before assuming an administrative post under the United States government. It was Adler who was largely responsible for the organization of the American Jewish Historical Society in 1892. Because of his interest in American history he was appointed the editor of the American history section of the new *Jewish Encyclopedia.* In a way his research in this field marks the first scientific study of American Jewry. Many of the articles on this subject in the *Encyclopedia* were written by him, certainly some of the most important ones. Together with Aaron M. Margalith he was to write on *American Intercession on Behalf of Jews in the Diplomatic Correspondence of the United States, 1840-1938.* This book was first published by the American Jewish Historical Society in 1943 after Adler's death. His work in furthering the study of American Jewry helped emphasize the importance of the American Jewish community. In 1901 when he undertook to head the department of American Jewish history in the *Jewish Encyclopedia* this country already sheltered the third largest Jewry after Russia and Austria-Hungary.

As president of the Jewish Theological Seminary, Adler was a major force in the Conservative Movement. Like most of his contemporaries he had no sympathy for political Zionism, and when the national Conservative synagogal union adopted a Zionist program he proffered his resignation as head of that body. Adler was very active in organizing the national association of YMHA's and the Jewish Welfare Board, which provided for the Jewish soldiers in World War I. In 1910 he brought the *Jewish Quarterly Review* from England to this country and together with Schechter helped edit it; this strengthened scientific Jewish scholarship in the United States. When a committee was established in 1908 to translate the Old Testament, a work done under the auspices of the Jewish Publication Society and the Central Conference of American Rabbis, he was elected chairman; it should not be forgotten that his original training was in Semitics. In 1919 he was a member of the American delegation that sought rights for East European Jews at the Peace Conference. If Jewry in this land was ultimately to assume a large degree of hegemony in the Jewish world it is no small part due to his labors as the head of important Jewish institutions. This scholarly man was tied to traditional Judaism; he understood the East European Jews though he was in no sense close to them ethnically, socially, Zionistically. Yet years later he went along with the expanded Jewish Agency which was concerned with building Palestine. After all as an Orthodox Jew he knew full well that God had promised to restore the Jews to their old homeland. He believed that the Germans had made an exemplary adjustment to American life and hoped that the East Europeans would turn to them for guidance. He was an urbane, cultured gentleman, a man who moved in the best Gentile circles yet always remained a ritually observant Jew. He was singularly fortunate that he hardly ever ran into anti-Semitism. One of the very few times that he heard an anti-Jewish remark was when he returned to his birthplace, to Van Buren. This small town had very few Jews; only too frequently there is an inverse ratio between Judeophobia and the presence of Jews.[8]

MAYER SULZBERGER

Mayer Sulzberger (1843-1923), a relative of Cyrus Adler, was the most distinguished of the Sulzberger clan. In their notable *History of the Jewish People*, Margolis and Marx made the statement that Mayer Sulzberger was the foremost Jewish layman in America. One suspects that this is hyperbolic. Alexander Marx, the librarian of the Jewish Theological Seminary, was very grateful to Sulzberger who had turned over his exceedingly valuable collection of rare books and manuscripts to the school. The collection had about forty-five incunabula, exceedingly rare fifteenth-century Jewish books. Sulzberger, knowledgeable in the field of Hebraica and Judaica, was one of the great Jewish book collectors; in later years he was to write a number of books on the Old Testament; he was not, however, a scientific scholar in the accepted sense. Among the notables who served as the leaders of American Jewish life he and Adler were the best Hebraists. Both men observed kashrut. Like Oscar Straus, Sulzberger was born in Germany and was brought over to this country when he was a child. He studied law, and became a very successful and distinguished practitioner; in 1895 he was appointed a judge and served in the Philadelphia courts until his retirement in 1916. He was an eminent and respected jurist; he could have had the post of minister or ambassador to Constantinople but did not make himself available. As a youngster he was close to Isaac Leeser, the outstanding Orthodox Jew of his day, and after Leeser's death edited the *Occident* for a brief period. Over the years he became a leader in Jewish affairs both locally and nationally. Sulzberger was an significant force in Gratz College, Dropsie, the Jewish Publication Society, the Jewish Theological Seminary, and the Baron de Hirsch Fund. He and Adler made Philadelphia an important Jewish cultural center in the early twentieth century. In 1906 the judge became the first president of the new elite national organization, the American Jewish Committee, serving until 1912. He was not an avowed Zionist but was ready and eager to make Palestine a refuge for Jews. His views were shared by most notable American Jews who refused to accept the political Zionism of Theodore Herzl. If there was a handful of men who controlled the important Jewish cultural and religious institutions of America during the first quarter of the twentieth century Sulzberger would have to be included.[9]

JACOB HENRY SCHIFF

Far more important and influential than Mayer Sulzberger was the New York banker Jacob Henry (Hirsch) Schiff (1847-1920). He was born in Frankfort on the Main and was very proud of his heritage; there was a German saying that a man would have to be crazy not to boast that he came from that famous city on the Main River. He was a scion of a distinguished rabbinic family that went back for generations; he was a *Kohen*, a "priest." One branch of the family was Geigers and included Abraham Geiger, the distinguished liberal. As a young man Schiff had studied with Samson Raphael Hirsch; this can only mean that he was a very observant Jew, a right-wing religionist. However, in the spirit of Samson Raphael Hirsch, he was educated secularly. Unlike some other extremists among the Orthodox in Central Europe, Hirsch believed in secular training. The influence of Samson Raphael Hirsch never left him. Hirsch was also the teacher of Kaufmann Kohler and when Kohler lectured to the Central Conference of American Rabbis on this distinguished founder of Neo-Orthodoxy, Schiff gave the printed address wide distribution. Later the Schiff family was to make sure that Kohler's *Theology* was sent to hundreds. In 1865 the teenage Schiff came to America and went to work; he was a Sabbath observer and would not labor on that day. It is very probable that throughout his life he observed some of the laws of kashrut; occasionally he would even lead the prayers in Hebrew at the Montefiore Home and Hospital for Invalids. After returning for a brief stay in Germany he decided to remain in this country (1875). That year he married the daughter of Solomon Loeb of Kuhn, Loeb & Company; ten years later he was the head of the firm. He was interested in financing railroads and was appointed a director of many important corporations; in the course of years he became the most influential Jewish banker in the United States.

We are primarily concerned with Schiff, the Jew, and his relations with the newcomers. He was distressed that these, his fellow Jews, were suffering persecution. As early as 1878 during the Russo-Turkish war he did what he could to help East Europeans. In 1903 after the massacres at Kishinev Schiff came to the conclusion that there was very little hope that Russia would ever develop a democratic government. As a loyal Jew with a strong sense of kinship for his people this banker would have nothing to do with the despotic Russians. When Russia went to war with Japan he helped float loans for the Japanese; he was eager to see the Russians defeated, hoping that then this tyranny would ameliorate. In 1905 when the Russian Sergei Yulievich Witte came to America to negotiate a treaty with the Japanese, Schiff, together with Straus and others, met with Witte to intercede for oppressed Jewry in the Romanov lands. In all probability it was Schiff himself who told Witte that Russia would get no loans here unless she became a democratic state guaranteeing equality to all. There is a tradition that Schiff banged the table to make his point. The Russians certainly had no love for this Jew knowing what he had done for Japan. Witte was in no position to promise the Jews anything. Realizing that the Russians would not change Schiff welcomed revolution in their land, believing that the problem of the Jews had to be resolved in Russia itself. Immigration to America was no real solution, but, as far as is known, he did not oppose the coming of the Jew to the American haven. Schiff was dismayed that Jewish bankers in Europe were floating loans to support the Russians. When in 1905 an Anglo-French mission came to the United States seeking a huge loan Schiff asked Lord Reading, a Jew, whether he could guarantee that none of the money would go to Russia. This Lord Reading could not promise. Six years later when all American Jewry went into high gear to secure the abrogation of the treaty with Russia the drive had his complete support.

Schiff was famous in his day for his philanthropy. Though Schiff, a notable capitalist, had his enemies, most East European Jews were grateful to him for his largesse. He was America's most generous Jew in the early twentieth century. He was an important philanthropist because he did not merely give cash, he gave of his time; he gave of himself. He spent hours and hours at the Montefiore Home; it was his favorite charity and he worked closely and personally and intimately with the patients there. Schiff gave large sums to non-Jewish causes, to Harvard, Barnard, Cornell, and Tuskegee. He was generous to peace organizations, the Red Cross, museums, libraries, and universities. On his seventieth birthday he gave large sums, and in his will left substantial sums to charity. Schiff had a pension list of about 100 names, friends whom he sustained through small grants; he also established liberal pension funds for rabbis. When relief for Jews was imperative he turned to John D. Rockefeller, Jr., who gave him $100,000. He helped the Hebrew Immigrant Aid Society and the Jewish Chautauqua, among many other organizations. New York's United Hebrew Charities could always count on him.

Schiff's cultural and philanthropic interests embraced almost every aspect of American Jewish life. Here is a partial list: money to the Jewish Publication Society for its first English translation of the Bible; grants to the Joint Distribution Committee, the Jewish Welfare Board during World War I, funds to build the Jewish and Hebrew sections of the New York Public Library and the Library of Congress. It was he who provided generous grants to educate teachers for the Conservative and Reform synagogs; the Schiff Hebrew Classics, patterned on the Loeb Classics, owe much to him. He financed a shelter for newly arrived immigrants on Ward's Island. He was interested in New York's Bureau of Jewish Education, the settlement work of the Jewish Educational Alliance, the craft training program of the Hebrew Technical School. In his largesse he was certainly not parochial; he gave money to Ben Yehuda to prepare his all-inclusive dictionary of Hebrew, and when Leo Frank of Atlanta was fighting for his life Schiff hastened to make a contribution. As a typical American Jewish philanthropist he wanted to settle Jews on the soil, hence his interest in the Woodbine Agricultural School. Indeed Schiff was one of the trustees of the Baron de Hirsch Fund that supported this enterprise. Yet he had little love for Krauskopf's National Farm School; he was not fond of this Reform rabbi. It may well be that Krauskopf's type of Judaism was far too radical for him; it is not at all improbable that Krauskopf, who wore a clerical collar, turned him off. Clerical collars were worn only by Catholic priests, Episcopalians, and other conservative evangelicals. On occasion Schiff would go to Woodbine to visit the school to see how it was doing although it was an arduous two-day journey and stay.

Schiff was interested in the work of the Industrial Removal Office which had set out to send Jews into the hinterland, to get them out of the New York ghetto with the hope that they would do better culturally and commercially away from the metropolis. It was he alone who was responsible for what is known as the Galveston Movement, the attempt to divert immigration from New York and direct it into the outback by way of the Texas port. When in Kansas City he asked the Jewish social worker there, the famous Jacob Billikopf, about these Galveston immigrants who had settled in that Missouri town. He visited some of them and was very pleased when they gave him a bouquet of flowers. Schiff was a man of moral courage and very strong convictions. He was disturbed by the action of government officials in Galveston whom he thought were deliberately making trouble for the incoming immigrants. Angry, he met with Charles Nagel, Secretary of Commerce and Labor, and with Attorney General George W. Wickersham. Fortified as he was by his great wealth and political power Schiff, so it is said, pointed a finger at Nagel and said: "You act as if my organization and I were on trial; you Mr. Secretary and your department are on trial." Schiff maintained that he was promoting the best interests of the country and was being throttled by unreasonable obstacles. There are different versions of this story.

Because Schiff was undoubtedly the most influential Jew in the United States his attitude toward Zionism is of historic significance. One might think that he would be interested in Zionism because of his conservative religious training. In his daily Hebrew prayers he called upon God to restore the ancient Hebrew state. His support of Palestine Jewish institutions was constant especially during World War I when they were cut off from the Diaspora dole. Like Rosenwald he gave very generously to the technical school at Haifa and supported Jewish educational institutions in Jaffa and Jerusalem. But neither Schiff nor Rosenwald was ever a convinced Zionist in the sense that they urged the recreation of a Jewish state. In 1898, after the first Congress at Basel, he wrote Sarasohn of the *Tageblatt* that he could see why Jews would want to leave Russia—where they were persecuted—but he could not understand why American Jews would be willing to forswear their citizenship and liberties here and immigrate to Turkish Palestine. He lived to see the Balfour Declaration of 1917, but he was not excited about the promise of a homeland; Zionism was not a religious movement. Essentially a modern man Schiff was fearful lest a Jewish homeland develop a religious hierarchy. (And this is what happened in the State of Israel.) However most Jews, even the anti-Zionists, were willing to further Mandate Palestine as a nursery of Jewish culture; this of course would explain why Schiff was willing to support the Hebrew dictionary of Ben Yehuda. In 1919 when Zionists were seeking the Palestine Mandate for the English, Schiff was prepared to accept

Palestine as a homeland for those who wanted to settle there. If through the force of circumstances a state were to evolve, that was their right and privilege; he had no objection. He continued to his death to contribute liberally to the upbuilding of Palestine, but he never became a formal member of the Zionist movement as did Louis D. Brandeis, the Boston lawyer. Schiff always emphasized the religious aspect of Judaism; this follower of Samson Raphael Hirsch was anything but a secularist.

People listened to Schiff because of his wealth, his generosity, his devotion to Jewry. He was in every sense of the word a committed Jew. It was his good fortune to have lived in an age when bankers were very powerful. He was not a political reactionary; he was interested in civic reform. He wanted good government and though like very many wealthy Jews a Republican, he voted twice for Wilson. He could not see his way to cast a ballot for Taft because of the latter's unwillingness to abrogate the treaty with Russia. There were some who spoke of the dictatorship of 52 William Street where he held court. If at any time he assumed a "despotic" stance it was certainly a paternal despotism. The man had no truck with Jew haters as the following incident will document. A contemporary of his, Austin Corbin, president of the Long Island Railroad and owner of the Oriental Hotel at Manhattan Beach, was an anti-Semite; at all events he disparaged the Jews in 1879. He did not want them on his beach. Realizing in the course of time that his anti-Jewish approach was hurting business he sent a check for $10,000 to aid the Montefiore Home, Schiff's pet charity, and when the Home returned the gift Schiff made good the loss.

His concept of Americanism may possibly have been a broader one, a more understanding and sensitive one, than that of some of his fellow Germans. In matters of manners and dress and speech he did not reproach the newcomers. Like many Germans he believed in "duty"; it was an important word in his vocabulary. Because he was a Jew he felt he had an obligation to help all Jews, everywhere, not only in the United States, and he conducted himself accordingly. Schiff had a tendency to play the part of a heavyhanded paterfamilias in the family circle but he was essentially a good man. He was a man of sound judgment. He was generous and genuinely interested in Jewish culture. This helped contribute to his leadership and acceptance by the "Russians." Unlike Rosenwald who was essentially a humanitarian Schiff's prime interest was in Jews. Schiff was a self-appointed leader; noblesse oblige; there was work to be done on behalf of the newcomers and he did it. His sympathetic attitude to the East Europeans was shared by many other rich Jews. On the whole the Jewish masses respected this banker and were influenced by his opinions. A man who lived in the upper Bronx wrote to Schiff that he was giving a reception in honor of his son's bar mitzvah and he would send Schiff a check for $100 for his favorite charity if the latter would attend; Schiff did. This documents the greatness of the man.[10]

LOUIS MARSHALL

Was not Louis Marshall who "ruled" a substantial segment of American Jewry under "Marshall Law" in the early twentieth century an even greater Jewish leader than Schiff? Comparisons may well be irrelevant. Fractious East Siders who resented Schiff's policies might have elected Marshall their leader and representative in a democratic election. There were very few Jews who could not identify with Jacob Schiff; there were probably many more for whom at best Marshall was but a name. The two men were different; Schiff was a financier; Marshall, a lawyer, one of the greatest in the land. This New York counselor set out on his own to lead American Jewry; to the extent that the "Germans" and the "Russians" subjected themselves to leadership, this man sought to respond to their need. When he appeared in Zurich at the Jewish Agency meeting where the leaders of World Jewry had foregathered, no one was better known or more admired than Louis Marshall (1929). One thing Schiff and Marshall had in common; they were both born to rule; this is not necessarily bad. They were not only incisive determined men, but leaders who were completely devoted to the Jewish people and their welfare. It is well to bear in mind that these two German Jewish leaders, frequently suspected of assimilation, were completely rooted in Jewish traditions and loyal to their implications.

Louis Marshall (1856-1929) was the son of humble German immigrants. The father had landed in America with ninety-five cents in his pocket; the mother had come over on a sailboat and had suffered for seventy-two days before she debarked. Louis Marshall grew up in Syracuse where he was given a smattering of the classics and some knowledge of Hebrew. But German was the tongue he learned at home; thus it was not difficult for him to read a paper in the "jargon," Yiddish. Something of an autodidact he learned to read novels in several languages. After he graduated from high school he studied law, finishing his formal training at Columbia where it took him about a year to complete the course. After he passed the bar examination he became a member of a good firm in Syracuse and was soon recognized as a distinguished constitutional lawyer. It was obvious that he was destined for great things. Markens in his *Hebrews in America*, the first hardcover history of American Jewry, saluted Marshall in a brief glowing vignette. The Syracuse lawyer was then but thirty-two years of age and had not yet moved on to New York City. In 1894, seeking new worlds to conquer, Louis Marshall became a member of a prestigious New York law firm. The important partners were all Jews. As a citizen he was interested in conservation, in parks, in forests, and in wild life. He was a fervent patriot, a conservative Republican in his politics, a man who was concerned at all times with the constitutional liberties of all groups and all religions. Determined to maintain and to further the underlying spirit of the Constitution, he fought for the rights of blacks, Japanese, and Catholics. It was due to him in large part that an Oregon Ku Klux Klan approved anti-Catholic law closing parochial schools was declared unconstitutional. As amicus curiae Marshall filed a brief with the Supreme Court which declared this Oregon statute unconstitutional. The court agreed with him that Catholics had a right to their own schools as long as they maintained public school standards in their secular studies. In 1920 Marshall spoke up on behalf of the Socialists who had been ousted from the New York Assembly by red-baiting members.

Early in the twentieth century Marshall concerned himself with the problems of Jewry at large in New York City. In 1902, already a power in the larger community, he was appointed chairman of the committee to investigate the riots at the time of the Jacob Joseph funeral. A year earlier he had already been appointed a trustee of Emanu-El and was later sufficiently influential, though not president, to prevent the election of Stephen Wise as senior rabbi of this prestigious synagog. Marshall and his associates on the temple board were fearful of the radical social outreach of this independent and intransigent minister. In 1902 Marshall, now chairman of the board of the Jewish Theological Seminary, helped reorganize the moribund theological college. Like others he had once sought to merge the Hebrew Union College and the Jewish Theological Seminary; it took some time before he realized that it would be entirely impractical to harmonize two religious denominations different in quality and character.

It was at this time, 1902, that he helped subsidize and assumed control of a Yiddish newspaper, *The Jewish World* (*Yidishe Velt*). His goal in supporting this paper was to speed up the Americanization of the East Side Jews. Though no chauvinist he was an eager Americanizer. Marshall had little sympathy for many if not most of New York's Yiddish journals; he was vigorously opposed to the socialist and the anarchist papers; the other journals, whether they were Democratic or Republican, he believed to be venal and sensational. Through a properly conducted journal he hoped to elevate the East European Jews politically, morally, religiously, and culturally. He was convinced that Tammany had too much influence in the Jewish press, that it was a corrupt institution. Though a Republican he was essentially a civic reformer. He wanted a clean press in the days when William Randolph Hearst was exerting a powerful influence on the people of the city. Marshall and his wealthy friends who subsidized this new daily did not interfere with the day-to-day administration of the paper. Competent journalists were employed despite the fact that some were socialists, anarchists, and Zionists; their views, however, were not aired. The writers of the English pages were outstanding Jewish litterateurs. The very fact that Marshall and his associates were "Germans" precluded acceptance of the paper by the Jewish masses. They wanted no rule from above.

As a concerned citizen Marshall fought for legislation to improve the status of dependent children; he was very disturbed about the problem of Jewish juvenile delinquency, and in order to further the acculturation of the newcomers supported the Educational Alliance, the outstanding Jewish settlement, and the various Young Men's Hebrew Associations. When in 1906 the natives, the acculturated Germans, and some outstanding East European Jews organized the American Jewish Committee, Marshall was not missing; six years later he became president, remaining at the helm until his death in 1929. Realizing the trend to close the gates to all East European immigrants he fought the literacy bills that came before the Congress. In 1910 he was one of the prime arbitrators in the cloakmakers' strike and together with Brandeis and a number of others helped set up the Protocol of Peace; his role in this historic strike has not been given adequate recognition.

In 1911 he stood out as a leader in the drive to abrogate the 1832 Russian treaty. In 1914 after the war broke out he assisted the Jewish Welfare Board. When that same year Jewry bestirred itself and organized the Joint Distribution Committee to relieve the distress of the Jews in Europe he became president of the American Jewish Relief Committee. These were the days when the East Europeans, revolting against old-line leadership, established an American Jewish Congress of their own. It was Marshall who led the resistance against this mass uprising and, when it failed, he loyally implemented the resolutions adopted by the conjoint body, the "Germans" and the "Russians." He accepted the proposal that Palestine was to be a home for persecuted Jews. In 1919 he went to the Paris Peace Conference and worked to secure minority rights for the Jews in Eastern Europe, rights that would in the long run guarantee them equality with the Christian leaders and masses who were determined to disable their Jewish fellow citizens politically and culturally.

Marshall fought prejudice on all fronts whether it was against Christians or against Jews. When in 1904 Melvil Dewey, the New York state librarian, explicitly excluded Jews from a club and hotel which he had established at Lake Placid, Louis Marshall was among those who successfully led the battle against this public servant who had exhibited such flagrant Judeophobia. As one of the outstanding leaders of American Jewry he reproached General Theodore A. Bingham, New York's police commissioner, for his statement that East Side Jewry supplied 50 percent of the city's criminals (1908). He was active also in defending Leo Frank when the Atlanta Jewish industrialist was unjustly accused of having raped and killed a young girl. During World War I, when chauvinism and nationalism were at fever pitch, Governor Harding of Iowa was prepared to forbid the use of any language other than English. Marshall answered in a statement that is well worth reprinting because in it he gives his definition of Americanism:

> Americanism is not the product of one but of many civilizations; not of one but of many traditions. It represents those that were brought on the "Mayflower," on the "Half Moon," and on every ship that has brought us the millions of immigrants who have sought asylum here from tyranny and persecution, who together constitute the American people and look upon our flag as the symbol of the Nation which together they constitute. To say that they may not preserve the traditions of their ancestors or speak their language is contrary to that spirit of liberality and of freedom upon which our institutions are founded, and which is exemplified in the slogan: E pluribus unum.

In the 1920's he fought the anti-Semitism of Henry Ford and wrote the retraction which the auto manufacturer was compelled to sign. Marshall, like Schiff, had helped the Haifa Technical Institute and the Jewish Agricultural Experimental Station both of which were established in Palestine but like most American Jewish notables he was in no sense a Zionist. Yet in 1929, when World Jewry met to establish the enlarged Jewish Agency because of the need for a haven to which persecuted Jews might flee, he went along with the Zionists. The wealthy New York Jews agreed to work with them to build a Jewish homeland as a cultural center. The liberality of the anti-Zionists is seen in the fact that they were ready to work with the nationalists whose goal was political rather than cultural. After the passage of the discriminatory immigration legislation of 1921 and 1924, laws designed to keep out Jews, Slavs, Italians, and other Southics, Marshall felt that it was necessary that there be some place to which a Jew could immigrate.

This New York lawyer was not enamored of the concept of collective reasoning or "democratic" procedure whereby all important matters would be settled by a vote of the majority. He believed that individuals should assume leadership by virtue of intellect, vigor, and integrity. He was supported by his wealthy elite colleagues. He exerted great influence in the American Jewish Committee, the Jewish Theological Seminary, and in many other organizations; his associates recognized his loyalty and deep concern for the Jewish people. In his approach to the problems and the needs of American Jewry he was essentially a religionist rather than a nationalist or an ethnicist. The cumulative effects of his activity were impressive. Because in America there was no formal national Jewish assembly representing all Jews this somewhat anarchic condition was an invitation to aggressive individuals to take over. Marshall responded. There was a tendency toward autocracy in his leadership but the organized opposition of the East Europeans and established institutions such as the B'nai B'rith and the Union of American Hebrew Congregations tempered his authoritative inclinations. He was a shtadlan, a leader, a quiet diplomat in the best tradition. He exerted influence beneficially. This man was no craven; he walked softly and carried a big stick; in this sense both he and Schiff had much in common. His rival for leadership in the second decade of the new century was Louis D. Brandeis. Brandeis was another important lawyer but of an entirely different genre. Brandeis owed his authority to his prestige as an outstanding attorney and to the fact that he had the enthusiastic support of the small but vigorous and articulate Zionist group. He headed the rebellion against the "German" overlords. Actually the motivation inspiring the people behind Brandeis was the desire to emancipate themselves from the leading strings of their benefactors. Brandeis went along with his followers who sought a homeland in Palestine and supported them in their push for minority rights for persecuted Jews abroad. It is ironic that the East European Jews in this country, most of whom were religiously Orthodox, rallied around Brandeis, a freethinker, a person of non-Russian ancestry.

Marshall was essentially a Puritan. He did not drink; he went to the synagog on the Sabbath, he prayed and devoted himself to his children in his home; he read Dickens to them. Here was a simple almost childlike American who read his Bible, composed sonnets and comic dialect sketches, and dwelt on the beauty of nature. When he died he left a tenth of his estate to charity. He was successful in many things but not in the ambition that he quietly if not secretly nourished. He had hoped ultimately because of his ability to be appointed to the United States Supreme Court. When David Josiah Brewer, the United States Supreme Court Justice died, Marshall hoped to succeed him. He certainly would have done a good job. Taft, however, was vigorously opposed to him; he would not appoint a man who was a partner of Samuel Untermyer, the nemesis of large corporations. Untermyer, Marshall's partner, was a Democrat and a liberal. Taft appointed Hughes. Marshall's attack on the national administration in 1911 for doing nothing about Russia's refusal to recognize an American passport when carried by a Jew may have been motivated in part by his resentment at being bypassed for a Supreme Court appointment. Schiff, too, had pushed for Marshall in vain. For the most part these two important men were friendly and worked together though they were not always in agreement.

When the Hebrew press of the Jewish Publication Society was established to reprint some Jewish classics, Schiff paid half the cost; Marshall contributed a quarter of the total needed. Marshall realized shortly before his death that the important job in America was the furtherance of Jewish education and had he lived he would have devoted himself to this very important problem. He was active in the Bureau of Jewish Education of the Kehillah (1909). As an American this very distinguished man was loyal to the best traditions of our first presidents, the Americans who made this country great. Because he was profoundly influenced by them and worked in their spirit he was nearly always on the right side of important issues. When he spoke at Zurich in 1929 expressing his willingness to work with the Zionists he stood out as the great unifier in American Jewish life; when he addressed congressional committees in Washington pleading that the gates to America remain open he was vindicating the ideals of the founding fathers; at Versailles seeking freedom for many of Europe's Jews (1919), he was an outstanding liberator. Speaking of Marshall after his death, Benjamin Nathan Cardozo, who was later to become a Supreme Court Justice, said that Marshall was a great lawyer, a great lover of liberty, a great leader of the Jews, and a lover of mankind.[11]

INSTITUTIONS

Louis Marshall was eager to Americanize the incoming Jewish refugees. He was not alone in this desire; every generation since the seventeenth century set out to Anglicize (Americanize) newcomers. The Pardos of the 1680's changed their name to the English equivalent: Brown; in the middle eighteenth century the two Gratz brothers preferred to correspond with each other in English rather than in their mother tongue, Yiddish. They reserved Yiddish paragraphs in their letters for confidential communications. Throughout the eighteenth century the problem of providing a secular education for the children of newcomers was faced; Shearith Israel of New York City always made provision for them; they were taught reading, writing, and cyphering. In the early nineteenth century the Sunday school established by Rebecca Gratz with the help of Isaac Leeser set out to work with the children of the German Jewish immigrants as well as with the native-born youngsters. Some of the original Sunday schools were philanthropic, Americanistic, as well as religious in intent. In New York in 1864 a Jewish Free School was established on the London model. Undoubtedly this parochial school made provision not only for the children of poor Jews from Central Europe but also for the children of East Europeans. Later, as the public schools improved, the children were enrolled in them for their secular studies but sent to the Hebrew schools for training in Judaism. But even in these afternoon Hebrew schools the language of instruction was in English. They were patronized by children of parents who had little or no means. In 1871 J. K. Buchner proposed the founding of an institution to educate the Russian Israelites—as he called them—in the arts and sciences; civilization was to be planted among them. Buchner hoped to establish a school that would teach the children Hebrew, English, and a craft; the sons and daughters of the new immigrants, East Europeans primarily, would have to be Americanized, educated, in order to avoid creating problems for the older settlers. Buchner challenged the establishment to underwrite this Americanization program.

Some Gentile ethnic groups were making cultural provisions for their countrymen; the Jews could do no less. For the Jews the problem was to become increasingly urgent. By the 1900's Jewish immigration constituted a very substantial percentage of the new arrivals; in each of eight years from 1904 to 1921 more than 100,000 Jews landed on these shores. For most Jewish charities, helping the poor was tied up with education and acculturation. It was thought that if impoverished aliens were taught English and a craft they would be able to make a living; they would improve themselves and move out of the slums where they reflected upon the established Jewish communities. In order to implement this philosophy of Americanization, institutions were set up all through the nineteenth century. Their goals were diverse. The refugees were to be put on farms or to be taught crafts. The girls were to work in offices; their mothers were to be trained to keep a (clean) home in the American style. All newcomers were to be taught to speak English; the schools established in the ghettos would also serve to repulse the incursions of the evangelicals; there were many Christian missions on the East Side. Were there too many Jewish institutions? As a matter of fact there were not enough to provide for the thousands and the hundreds of thousands who needed guidance, although most of the organizations that were ultimately established—if we include the self-help societies—did much to make it possible for the immigrants to survive psychically, emotionally, culturally, physically in this strange new world.

The immigrants themselves had little time, opportunity, or the means to set out deliberately to create Americanizing agencies. It would take years after the arrival of the first wave of exiles before they could help themselves by establishing associations to improve their lot here in the United States. It is true, however, that the societies they did establish were unintentionally, unwittingly Americanistic if only because of administrative needs. The American environment, the milieu, was always overpowering; it had the last word. As early as the 1890's the immigrants themselves made the effort to found institutions that would make the transition in America easier for themselves. Adolph Radin organized the acculturational Russian-American Hebrew Association. In this same decade Philadelphia's East European Jews, with the aid of natives and older settlers, created the Jewish Alliance of America; one of its prime purposes was "to instruct Hebrew immigrants in the duties and obligations of American citizenship." Established in 1902, the Hebrew Immigrant Aid Society (HIAS) was largely the creation of the newcomers themselves. The HIAS met the immigrant at the docks, helped him become settled the first day he was in this country, and aided him in the naturalization process if he sought to become a citizen. Through the employment of secret order ritual and parliamentary law the fraternal orders, too, brought the newcomer into the field and range of American culture.

By the second decade of the twentieth century the labor organizations, after initial victories, set out deliberately to educate the members of their unions. This was particularly true of the International Ladies' Garment Workers' Union which established schools—there were eight such centers in New York City—where English was taught and studied and where workers could listen to lectures on economics, hygiene, and other cultural subjects. The development of this educational program was to continue over decades. The most influential adaptational medium set up by the East Europeans themselves was of course the Yiddish press. Americanization was furthered not merely through factual information but also through editorials and deliberate formal instruction in English; English columns and sections were common. The introduction of English words and concepts into Yiddish was very important; they influenced the newcomers profoundly. More significant than the slow and unsystematic efforts of the East Europeans to come to terms with America were the programs and institutions fashioned by the older settlers; they had plans and the means and, for a variety of reasons best known to themselves, were determined to Americanize these foreigners as speedily as possible. The leaders of the Union of American Hebrew Congregations, centered in Cincinnati, urged the establishment of what they called mission schools in the large cities; instruction in English was to be primary. This suggestion bore fruit in the education which the children of the Russians, Poles, and Rumanians received in the Reform Sunday schools. The attempt of the UAHC to maintain a modern Orthodox synagog in Philadelphia failed because it was imposed from above; the Philadelphia Jewish masses would have to find the path to modernity by themselves; this they succeeded in doing and rather speedily.

The plan of the older settlers was to establish religiocultural and vocational schools in the ghettos. The approach was adopted in practically all American metropolitan areas; the newly arrived immigrants clustered in large towns; they were urban oriented. As early as 1875 the United Hebrew Charities of New York City set up a domestic arts and sewing school for girls; that same decade the philanthropies established a Downtown Sabbath school named after Minnie D. Louis, the social worker; additional schools were fashioned in the New York ghetto in the decade of the 1880's as the Russians fled from their intolerant homeland. Among the new institutions was the Hebrew Technical Institute for boys. In 1887 the Uptown women taking the initiative organized a personal service sisterhood at Temple Emanu-El. Rabbi Gustav Gottheil was the godfather of this attempt to aid the immigrants.

The rabbi was ably supported in his Downtown work by Mrs. William (Hannah Bachman) Einstein (1862-1929), the president of the sisterhood. She must be numbered among the country's notable Jewish social workers. She prepared herself by taking courses at Columbia and the New York School of Philanthropy. Mrs. Einstein worked for pensions for dependent mothers; she was no proponent of orphanages; children must be reared by the mother in a home. Hospitals hastened to put her on their boards; she was elected president of New York's Federation of Jewish Women's Organizations. More significant is the fact that she became a trustee of the prestigious United Hebrew Charities; this woman was a member of the power structure. Temple Emanu-El women soon joined with fourteen other associations to fashion the citywide Sisterhoods of Personal Service; the Lower East Side was their particular concern. Americanizational philanthropic work was the forte of the women. Clinging to their skirts, the men in Emanu-El sponsored schools and clubs Downtown to bring moral and religious "uplift" to the ghetto youngsters. There was almost a frantic desire to counter the efforts of the Christian missionaries. Americanization, secular education, modernization of religion were the goals of the Emanu-El Brotherhood and of the Uptown social welfare organizations which had a stake in Lower Manhattan. The Baron de Hirsch Fund (1891) was put into the hands of American Jews none of whom was an East European. The board members were entrusted with the task of helping the newcomers become good citizens. In 1892 the Baron de Hirsch Trade School for boys was established; a new home was built for the older Hebrew Technical Institute; later the Clara de Hirsch Home for Working Girls was opened. Rabbi Voorsanger of San Francisco established a similar boarding home for Jewish working girls in his community (1894). It was the opinion of the trustees of the Hirsch Fund that an honest trade was the answer to all problems; petty commerce and peddling were evil; the newcomers had to become part of the American people. (The adjective "honest" reflects an anti-Jewish stereotype which the Jewish leaders had adopted.) New York's Jewish notables were determined to fashion a new generation of ghetto Jews; the pattern consciously adopted was American; it in turn was strongly influenced by Protestant Christianity.

YOUNG MEN'S HEBREW ASSOCIATIONS (YMHA)—YOUNG WOMEN'S HEBREW ASSOCIATIONS (YWHA) AND THE NEWCOMERS

Accelerated immigration in the 1880's pushed New York's Jewish philanthropists to establish institutions to help new arrivals from Eastern Europe. In the year 1881, there were 5692 Jewish immigrants; in 1889 there were over 25,352. The Hebrew Technical Institute and a YMHA were opened Downtown in 1883. The new YMHA opened on East Broadway was eager to help the younger male immigrants socially, culturally. One of the English teachers in the Downtown "Y" was Abraham Cahan, the future editor of the *Forward*. Emma Lazarus, the poet, was interested in the program that was dedicated to the task of making these aliens become one with the American people. Schiff gave the "Ys" a new building; by the early 1900's some of the Russians, already old Americans, were founding "Ys" on their own. The American patterns were paradigmatic for some immigrant women. Helped by Julia Richman they organized themselves into a Young Women's Hebrew Association; thirty some years later there were 132 such female Jewish Ys in the United States out of a total of over 300 (1920). This is a revolutionary emancipatory change for Jewish women. Myriads of Russian-born young men were inducted into the United States armed forces by 1918; the newly created Jewish Welfare Board—a service organization—and the army itself made them almost instant Americans; it was a forcing house experience.

THE NATIONAL COUNCIL OF JEWISH WOMEN (NCJW) AND THE SETTLEMENT HOUSES

In 1893 America's Jewish women organized the National Council of Jewish Women, the first organization of its type to span the country. This was the second great step in the emancipation of Jewish womanhood. The first, in 1819, was the founding of Philadelphia's Ladies Hebrew Benevolent Society, brought into being by Rebecca Gratz. The 1893 constituent assembly of the NCJW was only too well aware of the need to help the immigrant women find a place and a future for themselves in this land but the number of East European women who participated in the proceedings that year was pitifully small. Fifteen years later the effort to Americanize the female newcomers and their children was in high gear. The prime medium was the week-end religious "mission school" for children but the NCJW, always helpful, reached out also to women on the farm and stationed agents at the ports.

One of the important agencies aiding the new arrivals to adapt themselves to this foreign American milieu was the settlement house. It was an institution that worked primarily, though not necessarily, in the slums; hence its clients in all large cities were often Jewish. Around the year

1920 the United Hebrew Charities established a settlement on the Upper East Side in one of the new immigrant residential areas; trailing the exodus to new neighborhoods the charities worked with the children of the émigrés. What is a settlement? It is a neighborhood social service institution. The original settlement houses were nonsectarian though they were enspirited with Christian social idealism. They were planted in a neighborhood to cement all its dwellers together with a sense of brotherhood; all encompassed by it were to be improved socially, politically, culturally; they were all to be bound together by the concept of community. Uptown and Downtown were to be united in (Christian) love. Idealists left their homes to live in ghetto settlement houses where they could reach out to the underprivileged throngs. Jewish houses were different in spirit and probably in ultimate goals. Unlike the Christians, Jews wanted salvation here on earth. The social coalescence of an entire neighborhood was not encouraged; certainly it was not primary. The Jewish ruling classes were interested in the externalities, the acculturation of the newcomers. Judaism, the religion, was borne in mind; religion could not be neglected because it was an important facet of Jewish identity. Bible history was taught; there was, however, very little formal instruction in religion for the children; the Orthodox masses would never have tolerated a purely religious approach; the Reform sponsors were unkosher; whatever the Reformers did smacked of suspect missionization. Jewish settlement houses were founded with one purpose, Americanization. Education, culture, brought economic advancement.

The impatient sponsors of Jewish settlement houses pushed for speedy integration. Jews, saving their religion, must become anonymous faceless Americans. As early as the 1880's disciples of Felix Adler and the Ethical Culture movement had established a Neighborhood Guild on the East Side (1886). Later in the 1890's and early twentieth century Felix Adler's cohorts built a bridgehead on the Lower East Side. Some of these Ethical Culture settlement residents were Jews, among them was Rumanian-born Henry Moskowitz (1879-1936). This native of the Balkans studied at City College of New York and at Columbia and earned a Ph.D. degree at a German university. In later years he stood out as a leader in Theodore Roosevelt's Progressive Party; his wife, far more influential, was Belle Lindner Israels Moskowitz. Non-Jewish sponsored settlements predominated in the Jewish ghetto but there were similar agencies set up by the Jews. The oldest was the Educational Alliance (1889); then came the separate efforts of the women and the men of Temple Emanu-El. By 1924 there were many settlement houses in Lower Manhattan.

LILLIAN WALD AND THE HENRY STREET SETTLEMENT

There was a nonsectarian settlement on Henry Street in New York City; one of its founders was a Gentile; the other was Lillian Wald, a Jew. This social-welfare agency had considerable support from Jewish philanthropists, Schiff among others. It was largely Jewishly administered but it was in no sense Jewishly motivated unless Judaism is identified with humanitarianism. Wald was a humanitarian; "religiously" she was a follower of Felix Adler. It is difficult to determine whether she had any Jewish ethnic attachments; she was born of Jewish parents. Wald may be credited with several major achievements; prominent among them was the founding of an important settlement in a major ghetto; even more notable was her work in establishing a visiting nurse service, one divorced from all religious control. This good woman was born in Cincinnati in 1867; she died in 1940. According to a family tradition she was a descendant of Saul Wahl who, according to an old legend, was King of Poland for a day. This meant that she was a member of the Katzenellenbogen clan, one of the most brilliant and learned families in all Jewish history. Karl Marx, too, was a scion of these notable talmudists. Wald was given a good education, was trained as a nurse, and spent some time in a woman's medical school. It was in 1893 that she and a friend opened their house, later to be known as the Henry Street Settlement. Years later her agency had over 200 visiting nurses making hundreds of thousands of calls. The House on Henry Street like similar welfare institutions had clubs, dancing, bowling, billiards, and a cooking school. People were encouraged to help themselves socially, culturally; instruction was given in the field of music, art, and the drama. The Neighborhood Playhouse was furthered. This remarkable woman was eager to assist those who turned to her; she patronized no one; she was no lady bountiful. She lived on Henry Street but she reached out to all people, everywhere.

Wald was much more than an everyday social worker; she was a courageous innovator, a crusader who set out to improve the world about her. Concerned for the totality of society she was eager to provide medical services for school children; she helped develop America's social conscience. Wald worked to secure good housing, cleaner streets, better parks and playgrounds, improved schools, study halls for the youngsters, vocational guidance and training, special classes for the handicapped, aid to the tuberculars, wholesome amusement for the ghetto people. She was interested in the peace movement, in reform politics, in doing away with the slums and all the evils they dragged in their wake. Like other notable Jewish women of her day she encouraged trade unions, worked to abolish child labor, and stood out among those who urged the creation of the Federal Children's Bureau. Women in industry were to be protected. This Henry Street nurse was one of the organizers of the Women's Trade

Union League; she believed in the vote for females. In 1906 she lent her prestige and support when the first settlement for blacks was opened. The nursing program which she and her friend started was ultimately taken over by the city. Her influence spread; lectures on public health nursing were introduced at Columbia's Teachers' College; the conservative Red Cross was impressed by her work in public nursing. A dedicated social worker, Lee K. Frankel, pointed out to the profit-directed Metropolitan Life Insurance Company that nursing prolonged life, hence more premiums. Thereupon the company gave this brilliant practitioner an important executive position encouraging him to carry on a nationwide health program. The list of Wald interests and accomplishments is almost breathtaking. In the 1970's she was admitted to the Hall of Fame for Great Americans.[12]

THE EDUCATIONAL ALLIANCE OF NEW YORK CITY

Although Jews constituted the majority of all those who entered the doors of the House on Henry Street in the years before 1921 it was not, as pointed out above, a Jewish institution. The Educational Alliance was. It was founded by Jews for Jews; its programs were Jewish as its sponsors defined that adjective. The roots of the Alliance go back to the 1860's when during the Civil War the Hebrew Free School Association was organized to educate impoverished Jewish youth. The youngsters then were largely of native and German Jewish provenance although there was a trickle of East Europeans. The New York Jewish community established the Free Schools under duress; Jews only too frequently take action when driven by crises. The establishment of Christian missionary schools in the ghettos frightened the local leaders. A generation later, in 1889, the Hebrew Free School Association, the Young Men's Hebrew Association, and the Aguilar Public Library worked together. Schiff was after them to consolidate their efforts. The objects of their concern were the Russian refugees who had been streaming into the city in large numbers for almost a decade. By that year New York sheltered about 200,000 Jewish men, women and children; most of them were Russians and Poles. In 1891 the Hebrew Institute, as it was then called, had a building of its own; two years later these three merged organizations called themselves the Educational Alliance. These neutral names invite a query. Is it not probable that the sponsors, seeking a low profile, did not want to emphasize the fact that they were a Jewish institution? This much is certain, their primary goal was the Americanization of the incoming Jewish aliens, particularly their children.

In a narrower sense the Educational Alliance wanted to wean parents and children away from their foreign mannerisms and their alien tongue, Yiddish. It was not long, however, before the board began to realize that acculturation did not necessarily require de-Yiddishization. The Uptown Jews began to understand that East European Judaism—a truly moral religion—and the Yiddish language were inextricably interrelated. It is probable, too, that the Uptown leaders—brilliant and able men and women—began to sense the meaning of what was later to be called cultural pluralism. In 1898 the authorities appointed a new superintendent of the Alliance, David Blaustein (1866-1912). This Russian had fled his native heath as a youngster and had found a refuge in Germany where he sought to educate himself. When Bismarck made it difficult for alien Jews to remain Blaustein moved on to Boston (1886) and soon assumed the post of rabbi in a Rhode Island Reform congregation, in Providence. At the same time he went to Harvard where he received his B.A. in 1893. Five years later Blaustein became the executive head of the Alliance, probably the largest settlement house in the country. A few years after his arrival there Zevi Hirsch Masliansky, the famed Yiddish orator, was invited to lecture regularly at the settlement house (1899); Yiddish and its culture was now recognized by the "Germans." Blaustein experienced trouble maneuvering between the Scylla of his Americanizing board and the Charybdis of an East European Jewry that was overwhelmingly Orthodox and uncooperative. Confusion was compounded by a very vocal Marxist minority that had nothing but contempt for the Uptown barons who controlled the policies of the Educational Alliance. These tensions were too much for the sensitive Blaustein who resigned in 1907 to head a similar settlement, Chicago's Hebrew Institute. Unfortunately for him there, too, he ran afoul of radicals when he refused to let the anarchist, Emma Goldman, address his charges.

Though many thousands of newcomers and their children made use of the facilities of the Alliance there were many more who never passed through its doors. When envisaging the totality of the East Europeans in Lower Manhattan, it is not easy to determine how many came under the influence of the Alliance's Americanization program. Its library was certainly used. In 1887, before the Aguilar Library became part of the Alliance, 90,000 books were drawn by its readers annually. This was in a day when the New York citywide library system had not yet been perfected. Libraries, both public and Jewish, were always heavily patronized by the children; the books drawn out were general not Jewish works. In 1903 the Chatham Square branch of the New York Public Library issued 1,000 volumes a day; in circulation it was the third most busy branch in the city but the first in the use of volumes on history and science. These youngsters and their parents, too, made use of the opportunity to educate themselves, an opportunity that had been denied them abroad. The most effective Americanizing instrument on the Lower East Side was not the Alliance and the other settlements but the public schools. These city institutions were reinforced by special Jewish schools which made educational provisions for the immigrant children and their parents. The little ones were taught English preparatory to their entry into the public schools; the parents were invited to attend night schools after finishing their stint in the factories and sweatshops. Inasmuch as the classes for adults were voluntary many did not go; they were tired and often despondent. Attendance for the boys and girls in the public schools was compulsory although the enforcement of the truancy laws was slack before 1900. Actually most children were eager to attend. There is some evidence that these youngsters of foreign-born parents were more regular in class attendance than the children of native-born parents. School clubs furthered sociality for the youngsters; their parents began joining parent-teacher associations. Many schools were overcrowded; School No. 188 sheltered 5,000 children practically all of whom were Jews. There was such a need for rooms that a hospital ship was transformed into a makeshift school where thousands were taught. It was the school system that made Americans of these little ones from the Slavic and Balkan lands; the toddlers were sent to kindergartens. As early as 1882 a kindergarten had already been established on the East Side by the sponsors of the Hebrew Free Schools. In this area of education for pre-school children Jews were among the pioneers not only in New York City but in other cities as well.[13]

PROGRAMS FOR AMERICANIZATION

All agencies established in the ghettos to help the newcomers had specific programs. They were also all doubly motivated: the immigrants wanted linguistic skills to enable them to make economic headway; the natives and the naturalized old-timers wanted to help their struggling coreligionists to Americanize themselves. That was overt; actually the Jewish ruling classes, insecure, wanted these Jews to manifest a degree of invisibility lest they stand out and make an unfavorable impression upon the non-Jewish generality. For these reasons Americanization was stressed inexorably. Be an American first, then a Jew. Even Isaac M. Wise once said this (He didn't mean it.). In the headlong drive for the use of English the Uptown sponsors of Downtown agencies first decried the use of Yiddish. Later they were to realize that it could well serve as a basic Americanization tool. Julia Richman who was in charge of many of the schools in Lower Manhattan was a rabid Americanizer; she reflected the early views of her social caste but she was no dyed-in-the-wool Philistine. She organized classes for delinquents and the mentally and physically handicapped; she believed in providing free lunches and clothes for impoverished little ones and in working with the parents of the school children. She was a very able and dedicated woman but she had no real understanding of the East European Jewish psyche. Apparently sympathy, too, was lacking. This indomitable educator ordered the teachers to follow the students even into the toilets to determine whether they spoke Yiddish. If caught they were to be given demerits. Some of the East Europeans made a determined effort to oust her. Richman believed that the old Russian and Polish Jewish traditions enslaved the mind and hindered acculturation. The ghetto was a "menace to the entire Jewish community of New York." Richman and her host of like-minded friends believed that these immigrants must be made over in the image of the American Jew; they must learn to speak English and to observe the amenities.

An ideal newcomer was one who turned to the soil or pursued a craft, and did not settle in New York City. This hope was rarely realized. In a way the settlement houses and the technical schools were substitutes for removal. Since thousands of these new Americans refused to budge—they loved New York—programs were to be developed in the city that would Americanize them as rapidly as possible. The settlement house, it was hoped, would make Anglo-Saxons of them; cultural diversity was treason to the United States. Thus programs were formulated to attain the ends desired. The problem of making Americans of millions of immigrants was faced by all older settlers, by the generality of the citizens, by the Catholics and the diverse Protestant churches. The programs adopted by the Jews were probably those employed by non-Jewish settlements and Christian institutional churches. What did the Jewish agencies set out to do? Teaching English was primary; families had to be held together; it was imperative that the children be kept in the synagog and off the streets; sociality for youth was to be furthered, but under supervision. Some of these problems would solve themselves in time; others were insoluble. The older generation would first have to die off.

The public schools served not only to educate but to further sociality; they sheltered the clubs of the students and the parent-teacher associations. Not many Jewish children went to high school till after the early decades of the twentieth century; in 1915 only 20 percent of all young Americans attended high schools, still fewer went to college, to New York University, City College of New York, and Columbia. During the World War I years more Jewish young men and women began to matriculate in schools of higher learning. Economic conditions were better for the papas and mamas; they were less dependent on the earnings of their children. Jews frequented City College of New York; the costs were minimal. In 1906 the total number of graduates, Jews and Gentiles, at CCNY was about 140; this in a city of over 600,000 Jews. There were many opportunities in this metropolis for ambitious Jews to advance themselves culturally, for there were numerous educational institutions open to im-

migrants of all faiths. There were courses in English, in the exact and social sciences, in general literature. Lectures on advanced and recondite
themes were available; in these classes one might even encounter a pushcart peddler or a tailor. Jewish institutions provided lectures or courses on
Jewish history and literature. Every effort was made, within the limitations of the institution,to help the students in the classes make a new life
for themselves in this new land. Humble Hebrew teachers were taught
English in order that they might the better serve their students; there
were special classes for those men and women preparing themselves for a
career in a profession. By the turn of the century, if not somewhat earlier,
when thoughtful social workers realized that Yiddish was vital as a medium of communication, of acculturation, Yiddish brochures were
printed describing the various institutions in town and the services they
offered.

Pamphlets taught the aliens where to look for a job, how to become a
farmer, how to register for citizenship. Resort to Yiddish was double-
edged; it was a language the immigrants knew; it was a force for Judaization though the Uptown elite was not primarily interested in furthering
Judaism the religion; its prime concern was to turn the greenhorn into an
American as speedily as possible. East Europeans, proud, hastened to
emancipate themselves from the leading strings of the Uptown Jews. To
accomplish this purpose they created the Yiddish press; it was all things
to all Jews; it kept them Jewish; it made them American, and when Louis
Marshall entered the lists with a Yiddish paper which he controlled they
brushed him and his *Jewish World* aside. They were determined to find
their own way to Americanism, to dress, speech, and patriotism. Immigrant writers built up a stock of American literature in Yiddish; using
their old-world vernacular they wrote and translated works on American
Jewish history; Yiddish-English dictionaries and manuals poured off the
presses, all written and compiled by newcomers. God helps those who
help themselves. In 1915 Paul Abelson (1878-1953) published his *English-Yiddish Encyclopedic Dictionary*. Here was a man who epitomized the
Lithuanian-born achiever. He was a lexicographer, lecturer, educator, labor arbitrator, lawyer. The City Board of Education hired him to lecture
on history and civics; the Educational Alliance chose him to lead its summer school; he even attained a degree of recognition in New Deal days.
His Ph.D. degree came from Columbia.

Urging the refugees to learn a manual trade was very deliberate on
the part of the community leaders. The Uptown personalities had their
own concepts of success; they themselves were dedicated to commerce
and the professions but they urged and cajoled the new arrivals to turn to
the crafts or to follow the plough. Americanizing immigrants through insistence on the use of English proved successful; the immigrant had no

choice. Craft training facilities were limited and it is questionable how numerous were the skilled artisans prepared in the Jewish technical schools of New York and the hinterland. Most newcomers had to be trained or retrained if they were to enter the job market. At least 90 percent of all immigrants succeeded in finding their own way. Vocational training programs provided by Jewish and non-Jewish institutions were helpful to a fortunate few. The Gentile organizations wanted to promote and encourage American industry; the Jewish leaders wanted to keep the refugees from knocking at the doors of the charities by directing the children into crafts. Since the community leaders could do very little to retrain adults they concentrated their energies on helping the sons and daughters make a living. The youngsters were taught mathematics, carpentry, plumbing, house and sign painting, metal work, printing, and the use of machines; some became electricians.

Women—and this is important—were accorded special attention. America opened new vistas to them inside and outside the home. Thousands upon thousands of Russians and Polish girls were taught the mysteries of domestic science; America's kitchen world is not that of the East European village. Women had to be retrained here in cooking and housekeeping. A New York non-Jewish settlement gave a course in kosher cooking. Many of the young women, taught to sew, made a living as dressmakers; others became milliners. Indeed there were schools where women, too, were taught to use tools. With the surge in industry and commerce and the need for office personnel women turned to bookkeeping, stenography, typing. Penny Provident Fund Banks were established in the settlement houses; most émigrés were thrifty. Civics, the facts about citizenship, was always stressed; there was more than one Yiddish translation of the Declaration of Independence and the Constitution. When the students in some civics courses finished their studies they would stage a formal celebration and sing patriotic songs. Patrons hammered away at the amenities, dress, the social graces; knowledge of these, they contended, betokened the real American. The agent of the National Council of Jewish Women at Ellis Island met a woman who had waited fourteen years for her fiance to send for her. When the engaged man saw this dumpy European-clad unattractive creature he fled. The Council women bathed and dressed her to look like a typical American girl and induced her swain to take another look. He took her back.

Among the Jewish natives bathing was deemed important. This is an old Jewish tradition. Elisha healed the leprous Naaman, general of the Syrian forces, by telling him to take a seven-fold bath in the healing waters of the Jordan; the New Testament Pharisees were excoriated for their frequent ablutions. Bathing, however, was a problem for the tenement dwellers; very few houses were equipped with baths. The house was at fault, not the immigrant renter. In some older tenement complexes water was found only in the yard; pails had to be carried up several flights. There were, however, many bathhouses on the East Side. It is literally true that some of the boys who went to the settlement house for a shower would ultimately have swimming pools in their suburban backyards. Dr. Simon Baruch, Bernard Baruch's father, brought free public baths to New York and Chicago. A native Prussian, Simon had served as a physician and surgeon in the Confederate Army. Many years later he moved on to New York where he became a professor of hydrotherapy at one of the city's medical schools. He published monographs on the therapeutic use of water although he is acclaimed in American medicine for his work in the surgery of appendicitis. American Jews, laying emphasis on hygiene and sanitation, imposed their views on the strangers who settled in the slums. On the whole they met with but little resistance. Lectures, advice on the care of babies and children were available to those who were interested. Health clinics for needy Jews studded the metropolitan ghettos, and when the immigrant, once financially impoverished, acquired some means he patronized the young Jewish physician who had ministered to him in the ambulatory clinic. A sound mind in a sound body: gymnasiums were established almost everywhere; physical training and sports were deemed important; hundreds of ambitious youngsters hoped for a career as pugilists; some were eminently successful.

It is not improbable that the diverse Americanization programs did more for the women than they did for the men. Russian and Rumanian Orthodoxy—or was it the East European milieu in general—disabled the womenfolk culturally, religiously. In America the women were to become somebodies. In the van of the Jewish women's emancipation movement, the National Council of Jewish Women played a not unimportant role. This worked to the advantage of the incoming female Jewish immigrants. Council was definitely and unabashedly feminist though not militant. Fanny Fligelman Brin (1884-1961) is a notable exemplar. This native of Rumania earned her Phi Beta Kappa at a Minnesota college and ultimately rose to head the National Council of Jewish Women. After the turn of the century (1903), the Young Women's Hebrew Association also hovered over female immigrants; Baroness de Hirsch and others established homes for these friendless and lonely girls. Indeed there was no dearth of agencies and programs helping the arriving women find a place for themselves in this country. It is no exaggeration to maintain that American Jewry did more for the Jewish woman than any other country in all the millennia of Jewish history.

Many, if not most of the leisure programs for the Jewish foreign-born were attractive facets of the Americanization process. The Lower East Side was by no means devoid of opportunities for fun and pleasure.

There were parks, games, playgrounds, roof gardens. In the summer thousands of children were sent to camp if only for a brief period. It is literally impossible to record and describe the many social clubs—most of them ephemeral—which the youngsters organized in the different settlement houses. The House on Henry Street even sheltered a grandmothers' club. The ghetto had its drama societies, orchestras, music classes, art schools, and exhibitions. Drama groups put on Purim and Hanukkah plays and even ventured to stage Shakespearean classics. The totality and variety of cultural and leisure services offered the East Siders are very impressive. The programs of the Jewish institutions were helpful to many although there can be little doubt that these foreign-born men, women, and children were Americanized primarily because of their exposure to the American milieu in which they found themselves. Even in the densely packed enclaves of Lower Manhattan the impact of the larger America was overwhelming. These Jews were determined to integrate themselves into this land of freedom and opportunity. By virtue of living in these United States these oppressed Russians, Poles, and Rumanians were well on the way to deghettoization, to Americanization, to a higher standard of living.[14]

Americanized to a degree and thus prepared to face the outside world, the ghetto Jews of New York City started moving out in large numbers when the second decade of the twentieth century brought a touch of prosperity. They left for the Bronx and Brooklyn with a heightened appreciation of secular culture; the institutions established Downtown by the Uptown Jews taught them to reach out for new worlds. There were attractive options. They could join a YMHA or YWHA where there were no religious qualifications and engage in programs that offered culture, recreation, and athletics; or, if religiously inclined, they could follow a daring innovator like Mordecai M. Kaplan and join his synagog which offered not only services and religious instruction but a variety of classes in almost all aspects of Jewish literature. Social togetherness in these new Jewish institutions was stressed. In Chicago, Rabbi Emil G. Hirsch developed an institutional church, as it were, that gave people a choice of dramatics, music, ballroom dancing, athletics, lectures on the social sciences. In this Sinai Social Center there was no credal test for membership. By the second decade of the century there was still another option in many towns. In addition to the "Ys" and their open door policy and the various types of synagog centers among Reform and Conservative Jews, there was the emerging Jewish community center. The approach of the center was new. It conceived of the community as a whole; religious affiliation was not imperative. The center set out to serve any Jew, all Jews. It was an all-embracing democratic institution; fees were charged. The programs included a wide variety of cultural courses and almost all forms of athletic activity. It was intended to cement together the disparate Jewish groups in the town's community; the smaller the city the greater the impact; the community centers in metropolitan areas were limited in their demographic grasp.[15]

AMERICANIZING THE EAST EUROPEANS IN THE CITIES WEST OF THE HUDSON

Well over 50 percent of all Jews in the United States lived beyond the confines of Greater Manhattan. All communities had leaders, if only by default; among them were natives, old-line Germans, and a few East Europeans. Foreign-born paid social workers in the backcountry, like those in New York City, usually reflected the views of their elitist employers. Outside of the New York metropolis the natives and the Germans dominated into the 1920's. Americanization, and it was always at work, was largely a byproduct of the charitative process. Here the women had much to say. The charities were on two levels; the major organizations and institutions were controlled by the earlier settlers of Central European origin; there were, however, numerous and diverse philanthropic societies set up by East Europeans, men and women. In the limited quarters of their ghetto and Jewish streets the immigrants were moving speedily to emancipate themselves from the old-timers; they were eager to provide for their own people. Very frequently the leaders in the hinterland towns —no matter their geographical provenance—were men and women of ability. All of them were eager to help the newcomers. Among them was Dutch-born Jacob Voorsanger (1852-1908), a former Orthodox hazzan who became an aristocrat and a powerful figure in the San Francisco area; Portland enjoyed the enthusiastic solicitude of David Solis-Cohen (1850-1928), a native American of Sephardic-Ashkenazic ancestry, and Benjamin Selling (1852-1931), a businessman, philanthropist, political notable. Jacob Billikopf (1883-1950), Kansas City's innovative social worker, was born in Lithuania. Chicago could with justice boast of its notables: Emil G. Hirsch, rabbi and scholar, Julius Rosenwald (1862-1932, Sears, Roebuck!), a commercial empire builder and supporter of many good causes, Hannah Greenebaum Solomon (1858-1942), founder of the National Council of Jewish Women. Bohemian-born Adolf Kraus was a lawyer, Chicago politician, and the ruler of the B'nai B'rith from 1905 to 1925. Officeholders in those halcyon days were in no hurry to surrender their posts; congregational and society presidents often served for decades before they reluctantly retired.

Chicago was fortunate in that it counted several female communal leaders. Among them was Mrs. Emanuel (Babette Frank) Mandel, a native of Germany who came to this country as a young girl and enjoyed the benefits of a high school education. She devoted her time and energies to the Maxwell Street Settlement, to a ghetto dispensary, a lying-in hospital, and the National Council of Jewish Women. Other important local communal workers were Jennie Purvin, Jennie Gerstley, Kate Levy, and Mrs. Ben Davis. Mrs. Moses L. (Jennie Franklin) Purvin (1873-1958) ran her father's cigar business when he became ill. She was a woman of many talents. Influenced by a Reform rabbi and a Unitarian minister she rose to power in the Chicago general and Jewish communities. As a Jew she helped the Zionists, a local sisterhood, the wartime Jewish Welfare Board; as a citizen of her city she worked to provide public concerts, to improve the city's library, to encourage parent-teacher associations and women's civic clubs. She was the person who cleaned up Chicago's garbage strewn lake shore and turned it into a series of beautiful beaches. All her life she worked hard to help others; "I never knew how to dress, never used powder until I was fifty or lipstick until a few months ago" (age eighty-four).

Like Jennie Purvin, Jennie Rosenfeld Gerstley, a school teacher, became an outstanding Chicago communal worker. As early as 1882 she had founded a Young Ladies' Aid Society whose members visited the sick in hospitals. Like other Chicago women she reached out to serve the newcomers through the Maxwell Street Settlement, kindergartens, and summer recreational programs. She was an early Jewish feminist. The two Jennies were German-born; Dr. Kate Levy and Mrs. Ben Davis, although both native-born, were of East European ancestry. Levy, who was born in New York, received her physician's degree at Northwestern, taught in a medical college, and interested herself in the Jewish Manual Training School and other agencies dedicated to the welfare of ghetto Jewry. Mrs. Ben Davis was the daughter of a notable Russian scholar who came to America in antebellum days, Samuel Hillel Isaacs. Jeanette Isaacs received her teacher's diploma from a normal school, married a Chicagoan, and soon blossomed out as an influential and aggressive leader of the Russian element. There were almost no associations of importance in which she did not play a part. The National Council of Jewish Women genuflected in her direction; she was an active Zionist since 1898, a leader in Hadassah, a worker in a local settlement house, a protagonist of the controversial American Jewish Congress, an officer of the Woman's League of the United Synagogue of America. She wrote and she lectured; all in all she was a striking example of the new leadership that characterized a limited number of thoroughly acculturated women of Slavic Jewish background.

The notables in Cincinnati were men, officers of the Union of American Hebrew Congregations, still the country's outstanding national religious organization. Among them were Moritz Loth and Julius Freiberg, successful businessmen, and Bernhard Bettmann, communal worker, politician, and poet. These three Cincinnatians, Reform Jews, were national leaders in building the UAHC but Cyrus Adler, a Conservative religionist, did not see fit to include their biographies in the *Jewish Encyclopedia*. They were ardent Jews, conscious of the needs of the new immigrants but their accomplishments on behalf of the newcomers were of little consequence. Two of New Orleans most respected Jews were a father and daughter; these were the Weises, a wealthy and philanthropic family. Julius Weis, cotton dealer and banker, was, it would seem, the city's outstanding Jewish citizen. Ida Weis Friend, his daughter, was one of the South's most important clubwomen. For a time she was a Democratic national committeewoman and president of the local Urban League which fought for the rights of blacks. This Wilsonian Democrat served as president of the State Federation of Women's Clubs and finally took over the reins of the National Council of Jewish Women. Her interest in the NCJW was testimony to her desire to help the Russian and Polish Jewish women who had found a haven in this country. Most of Philadelphia's Jewish leaders were involved in the struggle to make life more pleasant for the thousands of Russians and Poles who had been settling in the city even before the pogroms of the 1880's. Among them were Joseph Krauskopf, a Reform rabbi, Judge Mayer Sulzberger, a traditional religionist, William Bower Hackenburg, businessman, statistician, and tireless communal worker, Simon Muhr (b. 1845), industrialist and president of the immigrant oriented Jewish Alliance of America, Louis Edward Levy (b. 1846), graphic arts technician and friend of the newcomers, and Rabbi Sabato Morais, compassionate friend of the laboring man, Americanizer, and a founder of the Jewish Theological Seminary. It is a tribute to Morais, an Italian immigrant, that he was made an honorary member of the local Union League, a bastion of political conservatism.

The men and women mentioned above were exceptional in their leadership and their genuine concern for the Jewish immigrants. But there were hundreds of other communal workers in the backcountry who set out to help all Jews irrespective of their background. Among the anonymous many there were Russian, Polish, and Rumanian men and women, of foreign or native birth, who aided their fellow provincials find their niche in American society. Most of these East Europeans and their able children devoted themselves to their local Russian Jewish communities. It would take two generations before the émigrés were completely and totally integrated into both the American and Jewish communities. A few of the children of newcomers made a place for themselves in the larger Jewish and general world. Individuals among them were so successful, so influential, so truly American that they achieved national recognition. On the whole the types of American institutions established throughout the hinterland were similar to those already fashioned in New York City. Indeed, in all America there were very few Jewish welfare and cultural organizations which did not envisage help for the newcomers; the social clubs were an obvious exception. In some towns the local Jewish communal dignitaries, eager to make the incoming aliens feel at home, borrowed patterns for their institutions and programs from their Gentile neighbors, but in general the Jews in the backcountry leaned heavily on New York paradigms when they engaged in acculturational tasks. Most Jewish businessmen of substance went to the New York market for spring and winter buying; they knew what was going on in the metropolis; their Jewish newspapers told them what the leaders were thinking and doing. Often the institutions they founded adopted the very names of similar organizations in New York and other large cities. Hebrew Institutes and Educational Alliances flourished in the towns west of the Hudson. Some of the national societies like the National Council of Jewish Women and HIAS had branches or correspondents in many places. There were YMHA's and YWHA's and settlement houses almost everywhere.

An important institution imparting information and techniques was the National Conference of Jewish Charities (1899). Here the country's outstanding social workers, lay and professional, native and alien-born, met and discussed their problems. For them nothing was more important than the task of integrating the displaced thousands, helping them to become self-supporting, contented Americans. In the efforts to develop new welfare skills that would further the physical and psychic well-being of the immigrants no city surpassed Cincinnati. Max Senior, wealthy industrialist, was acknowledged as one of the country's most progressive social workers. Foreign-born Jacob Billikopf and Boris Bogen learned their trade in this Ohio town. Bogen, a native of Moscow, left his native city in 1891. There was no future for him in Russia; he was a Jew and a revolutionary. He left for the United States. After working in a cotton mill and at other jobs he managed like hundreds of others, to get a university education; he earned a doctorate. He made a living as a social worker, and taught in various immigrant schools before accepting an appointment as superintendent of Cincinnati's Jewish Charities. Max Senior and Dr. Lee K. Frankel taught and guided him. By 1917 he was ready to assume the task of helping and saving the Jews of Eastern Europe; he was appointed director-general of the American Jewish Joint Distribution Committee, the most challenging assignment ever undertaken by a Jewish social worker.[16]

AMERICANIZATION IN THE HINTERLAND: ILLUSTRATIVE DATA

The illustrations that now follow will give the reader some concept of
how the Americanization process manifested itself and how it was furthered by individuals. These illustrative comments could be duplicated a
hundred-fold; they are obviously selective. In an interview with the
Texas Fort Worth *Star-Telegram* for January 19, 1914, Mrs. Theodore
Mack said that the immigrants were better citizens than the natives because they know the nature of Americanism; they appreciated what they
found here. The Jewish women in Fort Worth opened a school in the Reform temple welcoming all immigrant Jews, Greeks, Germans, Italians,
and others, too. This agency had the support of the Workmen's Circle
many of whose members were socialists. The local section of the National
Council of Jewish Women supplied the teachers; one of them knew Yiddish. Pragmatically this school for immigrants taught the amenities, English, civics and—this is interesting—encouraged the children to read the
best in literature. As the name indicates—the Immigrant Night School—
many if not all the classes were held after work hours. One half of the
children at the Atlanta Orphan Asylum were of Russian and Polish ancestry. Broken homes, poverty? This institution was the darling of Simon
Wolf, Jewry's Washington lobbyist. Like most settlement houses the asylum taught the youngsters a trade, music, too, and of course some Hebrew; they had to be able to read the prayer book. Atlanta's settlement
house called itself the Jewish Educational Alliance. The Workmen's Circle, the Zionist-Socialists, and different literary and social groups used its
premises. Among the Jewish groups that met there was the Henry Grady
Debating Club. Grady (d. 1889), the editor of the Atlanta *Constitution*,
was one of the outstanding publicists of the South. The local junk dealers,
united in a protective association, convened there, and it was not long before East European Jews also graced its board. It was no light thing that
this settlement house made it possible for Orthodox religionists and non-
theistic socialists to meet on common ground, to tolerate one another. All
this before World War I.

   A boy of six who played ball in the Providence, Rhode Island, Jewish
interclub baseball league was given a glove to catch the fast ones. This
was instant Americanism. Baltimore, too, had its Jewish Educational Alliance; it was no typical settlement; the Alliance was a resident home to
house women who could not live honorably on their scanty wages. But
the Alliance, true to the exemplary New York traditions, also introduced
programs to keep boys and girls off the streets. At one time the proposal
to open a Young Men's Hebrew Association in this Maryland city met
with opposition from a distinguished rabbi; it would keep youth away
from the synagog. Indianapolis Jewry pioneered in opening an institution
that was more than a settlement house, more even than an Americanizing

agency; it was an early community center to which all Jews could turn, old settlers and new immigrants. Fees were charged; here was a place where all could meet on a plane of equality.

Cincinnatians, in the forefront of America's Jewish communities in many areas of religious, cultural, and social activity, had opened their Sunday schools in the early 1880's to the children of the refugees. In later years these very boys and girls were to shine as some of Cincinnati Jewry's beloved citizens. Ten years after New York's Educational Alliance became active, Cincinnati Jewry organized a Society for Neighborhood Work (1899). It specialized in teaching English to foreigners. Here, too, the neutral name reflected the desire of local Jewry to carry on its work with low visibility. However by 1906 the institution was known as the Jewish Settlement. It may well be that in this community Jewish identification was strengthened, as in many others, after the Russian massacres of 1903 and 1905; with the pogroms came the traumatic realization that the twentieth century was not ushering in the best of all possible worlds. Max Senior (1862-1939), the communal worker, was respected for his labors on behalf of both Jews and Gentiles; he was a leader in the international Joint Distribution Committee, in the Cleveland Jewish Orphan Asylum, and in the city's juvenile courts. In those early decades of the new century he preached the gospel of low-cost housing, mortgage loans for people of modest means, and help for underprivileged blacks. Cincinnati's Jewish federation—in some respects the first in the country —owed much to his vision. This Jewish community, through its collection and allocation of funds, may well have been exemplary when the city itself later established a Community Chest.

Cincinnati had its Max Senior; Milwaukee had its Lizzie Black Kander (1858-1940). The settlement house where she labored, the first in the city, started out as a Jewish mission school; an English vocabulary and Jewish morals were the panaceas for any ills that would ever confront a newcomer.

This settlement house prepared a cookbook to teach the immigrant women not only to prepare food but how to make a fire and clean dirty dishes. *The Settlement Cookbook* was so successful that profits from its sale helped support the settlement itself. The work of Kander and her friends was so worthwhile that the municipality was induced to open a vocational high school for girls. The National Council of Jewish Women was the preeminent Americanizing agency in Pittsburgh, though even before it had adopted its cultural and social programs, Rabbi Lippman Mayer had opened a "Russian" school in the vestry rooms of his synagog (1890). This was later taken over by the NCJW which devoted itself to the establishment of the Columbian Council School, an immigrant night school. For a time this was the only free school in town where the newcomers could learn English. Noting the successes of the Council the city opened special schools to teach immigrants. It was in the second decade of the new century that the NCJW carried on the massive task of teaching and acculturating the children of the East Europeans. Thousands of youngsters were taught in their supplementary schools; 90 percent of these boys and girls were members of the local public libraries. By the 1920's the Irene Kaufmann Settlement House, like most other similar institutions, incorporated Yiddish culture in its programs. This was possible because the immigration acts had closed the doors to America; the Russians and Poles were no longer a threat; individual newcomers, affluent and influential, now sat on the boards of the settlement house. What was true of Pittsburgh and Atlanta was very probably true of other towns, too.

The larger the city, the more numerous were its foreign-born denizens and the older were its acculturation agencies. There was a Jewish mission school for foreigners in Philadelphia in 1872, a decade before the Russian pogroms; this was a Sunday school in the Rebecca Gratz tradition. Later, in the 1890's, a branch of the YMHA was located in the ghetto; it set out to help the new immigrants; they in turn, determined to help themselves, established cultural societies of their own. It was not long before Russians and their children were entering the professions; they turned to teaching, to law, to medicine, to pharmacy, to engineering. This was in the decade of the 1890's; by this time the city's Jewish establishment had opened several city-wide Sunday schools.

For obvious reasons—noblesse oblige was never absent—the older settlers in most towns were the first to create institutions to help the recent arrivals. By 1888 Chicago's Sinai Temple elite had already aided in the founding of the Jewish Training School in the West Side ghetto; it was actually an early settlement house where vocational training was emphasized. Nominally it was nonsectarian; America's Jewish elite never denied itself the pleasure of being latitudinarian. This euphoric love for all human beings characterized European Jewry ever since it first left its ghetto in the late eighteenth century. As in other towns the Jewish Training School taught English to children and adults. Its night school, like the one in Pittsburgh, was the first in the city and enjoyed the support of the Reform congregations whose rabbis amd affluent members supported this philanthropic and cultural institution. When in the early 1890's the Chicago community was confronted with one of the largest Jewish ghettos in the world and its concomitant problems, it organized the Maxwell Street Settlement (1893). By the time it closed in 1919 the West Side Jews, Americanized, less impoverished, were moving out to other, better neighborhoods; there was no longer a need for an institution whose prime goal was Americanization.

Almost a generation earlier the Russians had started a Self-Educational Club; this became the Chicago Hebrew Institute, and ultimately, as the immigrants asserted themselves, the People's Institute. Pushed by Dr. Kate Levy and aided by notables such as Rabbi Emil G. Hirsch and Julius Rosenwald, the Institute finally had a building of its own. This organization had been in the making for a generation but made no real progress till Rosenwald lent it the money to build. It was not easy for the aspiring immigrants to emancipate themselves from the tutelage of the Germans; the newcomers rose to affluence slowly; the rich among them, mindful of their struggles to survive, were slow to give now that they were on their feet (1908). The Institute brought in David Blaustein from New York. He and his associates soon realized that the real problem of the new citizens was not Americanization but re-Judaization. Poor Blaustein lasted but two years; internal dissension destroyed him. The immigrants were an independent lot wracked by conflicting ideology. Rosenwald stepped in and took over and after a relatively short time he was succeeded by another elitist who occupied the presidential chair for many years. The old-timers gave money and service; they exercised discipline; the Institute thrived. In the early 1920's over 13,000 people attended classes; there were 37 departments, 50 clubs, a female auxiliary had 900 members; 300,000 men, women and children frequented its playgrounds in the summer.

By 1921 many of the newly Americanized citizens, began to think of themselves not only as Russians, Poles, Hungarians, Rumanians but as members of an American Jewish community. Community centers began arising; many Jews began to think of themselves as a solid undivided entity. The community centers did not set out to acculturate foreigners. Most Jews here had already been integrated into the larger body politic; the community center was essentially a sociocultural, recreational institution for all Jews, both native and foreign-born. There was no longer an urgent need to "civilize" the newcomers, to teach them civics; they had learned their lessons in the preceding decades. Americanization in the backcountry moved even more rapidly than in New York City; the impact of the environment was always stronger in the towns than in the densely packed Jewish enclaves. It is true that the process of Americanization worked differently with every individual but it is equally true that it worked for almost everyone. A Pittsburgh immigrant family of limited means took out the telephone and used the money saved to pay for piano lessons. This is Americanization. Israel Brodie (1812–1876) of Vilna came to the United States in the mid-nineteenth century. Prior to his coming he had served as a minister in various European countries including Ireland. While reading American history he had been impressed by the careers of the patriotic Warrens and even before landing began to call himself Israel Warren. Here in the United States he served in Quincy, Illinois, and in the New York ghetto. The Buffalonians who hired him were convinced that he needed a respectable Jewish name; accordingly he now became Israel Warrensky. Buffalo's Beth El called him in 1862 and there he was to remain to his death. The congregation gave him a three-year contract with an annual wage of $300 and the privilege of living in the vestry rooms downstairs. The synagogal authorities preened themselves that they had been very generous. One of his sons, Samuel, influenced no doubt by his residence in Ireland, sympathized with the Fenians here who invaded Canada in 1866. Tradition has it that Samuel was captured by the Canadians when the filibustering incursion failed. At all events Samuel married a Roman Catholic, raised a good Christian family, and took back the old name Warren. And this, too, is Americanization.[17]

CHAPTER EIGHTEEN

AMERICANIZATION

INTRODUCTION

Hundreds of thousands of alien Jews arriving in America created a problem for the established Jewish citizenry; it was imperative that these newcomers be integrated speedily for the good of the immigrants themselves and the older Jewish settlers. The attitude adopted by the majority of the old-timers here was "Follow our example." The phrase was that of an earlier immigrant, Jacob H. Schiff. Be an American both in the synagog and on the street. All Jewish leaders, whether "German" or "Russian," encouraged the outsiders to take on the ways of the New World. The New York Jews supplied most of the leaders; they were truly devoted men and women, ready to guide the exodists here in the Promised Land. Most immigrants landed in New York, the largest Jewish community in the world; the local Jews, generous within their lights, were aided by the huge sums supplied by Baron de Hirsch and his wife. Both the de Hirschs and the American Jewish elite hoped that the newcomers would turn to the soil, learn a craft, settle in the interior, and become anonymous faceless Americans. This larger program was never accepted by the immigrants with this exception, however: they did become American culturally. Attempts were made in New York and all large cities to encourage artisanry; successes were anything but notable. All Jews here, however, were grateful to the de Hirschs for their princely generosity and they repaid their debt in World War I when they sank millions, ultimately billions, in Europe, North Africa, and Asia in the effort to sustain and train fellow Jews. In the drive toward Americanization in New York and in all other cities where Jews were found settlement houses were established; the programs—first formulated in New York—were imposed from above. Louis Marshall said that over 2,000,000 men women and children crossed the threshold of the Educational Alliance every year and that there were over 300 separate activities in the building. These figures,

if accurate, are impressive; there can be no question that religion and sociality were furthered, that thousands were taught English and encouraged to pursue the arts and sciences.

In some respects the settlement house and technical school programs
were exemplary; they pioneered in classes for children, in kindergartens,
in vocational training, in language instruction for adults, in parent-
teacher associations. All these innovations were in the course of time
adopted by the municipal authorities. The settlement houses, the Hebrew
Immigrant Aid Society, the National Council of Jewish Women constituted themselves quasi-civic agencies preparing immigrants for citizenship. On the whole a respectable number of East European Jews opted for
naturalization; there were many laggards. Their children were certainly
no laggards in crowding the public libraries. It is probable that there was
no immigrant group in the United States more interested in reading than
the Jews from the Slavic and Balkan lands. With the adults in mind no
Americanizing instrumentality was more powerful than the Yiddish
press, the men and women who read these papers faithfully could hope to
become knowledgeable Americans. Lectures in Yiddish and English on all
subjects were available; Reform religious schools were open to immigrant
children almost everywhere; Westernization and Americanization went
hand in hand. Even in the Orthodox synagogs English sermons were
heard occasionally; as early as the 1910's an undeviatingly Orthodox
Young Israel insisted on the American (Protestant) concept of order and
decorum in its services. Through the programs of the settlement houses,
labor lyceums, fraternal orders, the National Council of Jewish Women,
myriads if not hundreds of thousands of immigrants moved from medievalism to modernism. In 1893 Minnie Louis, one of New York's notable
communal workers, said it would take generations to make a teacher of an
immigrant Jewish woman; undoubtedly Minnie lived to see many of
them make it in one generation. Minnie Dessau Louis (1841-1922) was
involved in many service organizations but this woman reared in the antebellum South, wealthy and educated, did not have the common touch.
A Mr. Klapper, a Rumanian, worked in the East Side University Settlement as a janitor; his foreign-born son Paul became president of Queen's
College.

AMERICANIZATION AS A PROBLEM AND A PROMISE

It was stated above that 2,000,000 people annually went through the
doors of the Educational Alliance. This is an impressive statistical datum.
Actually how extensive was the use of the settlements and similar agencies? First, let it not be forgotten that many of the 2,000,000 were the
same individuals who daily or frequently attended courses, lectures, serv-

ices, and other activities of the Alliance. The influence of the settlements was limited. Blaustein once made the statement that the settlement house was no hospital where one could point to a patient recovered. At most all institutions catered to limited segments of the ghetto masses. No one knows how many children frequented the settlement houses. Most Orthodox parents stayed away from these institutions; they were not sufficiently "Jewish"; Orthodoxy, yiddishkeit, was not stressed; the old world ambience of the landsmanshaften was missing. For many East Europeans their future lay behind them; all would move toward Americanization but at their own pace. In Portland, Maine, the acculturated Germans in B'nai B'rith kept their minutes in English; the records of the East European institutions were written in Yiddish; their children preferred English; their grandchildren knew only the Yiddish expletives, at best. Patronization in most communal agencies was unavoidable inasmuch as policies were made by acculturated Jews. When Minnie D. Louis made an address at the Jewish Women's Congress in Chicago (1893) she entitled her talk, "Mission Work Among the Unenlightened Jews." Minnie was enlightened. Jews of East European origin, whether old or young, resented what they believed to be the condescension of the earlier settlers. Protesting against the attitudes and teachings of the Educational Alliance, a group of radicals in 1901 created an organization of their own; there is no evidence that it was effective.

The numbers of people actually trained in the vocational schools were inconsequential when compared to the hundreds of thousands of ghetto inhabitants. It is even questionable how effective the actual instruction was. The Uptown Jews believed that a craft skill would enable an unskilled immigrant to make a living. Many of the older German immigrants had been compelled in their homeland to learn a trade but when they came over here many abandoned their craft and turned to commerce; they attempted, however, to impose an artisan regimen on the East European newcomers. Many successful Jewish natives believed that public relations demanded that there be a substantial number of Jews engaged in "productive" manual labor. The East Europeans paid little heed to the pleas of their patrons; they went their own way. In 1904 a Yiddish journalist of distinction, an American-born Orthodox Jew, declared baldly that the settlement houses solved no problems. He may have had in mind the dangers of juvenile delinquency. Homer, Shakespeare, chess, and checkers in a club room did not always solve the problem of a son or daughter who repudiated parental authority. The sponsors of the settlement houses, welfare agencies, personal service brotherhoods and sisterhoods set out to build bridges to the ghetto linking the Uptown and the Downtown. The question is how many Jews walked across these bridges. Social demarcation persisted; the worlds of the giver and the recipient could not be linked, certainly not in a decade of two.

Families were disrupted by the new culture. Americanization made strong demands; it was a form of compulsory assimilation. The new Jews here were asked to meld into an anonymous American mass, to change radically in dress, speech, mannerisms. Jewish agencies deliberately worked toward this end though, wisely, they rarely failed to genuflect in the direction of Judaism the religion. Adler and Sulzberger were traditionalists; Schiff was bound to Orthodoxy though nostalgia; Straus and Marshall came from homes where religious customs were still maintained. Americanization demands no departure from religion. As loyal conforming Jews—nominally at least—many of the old-line communal leaders favored a pattern of religious behavior which smacked somewhat of Protestantism in its emphasis on decorous behavior in "church." Ceremonial was not emphasized by them. To a degree this drive to adapt is reflected even in the thinking of the Orthodox hazzan-minister Henry Mendes Pereira of the Spanish-Portuguese synagog; he prided himself on his Anglo-Saxonism. One wonders how this type of swooning culture identification would be received by a pious Jew from Kovno or Kiev. The pushcart peddler on Hester Street had only to look about him to see that the United States was no Garden of Eden; the Tammany politician was no Thomas Jefferson. As early as 1903 the brilliant Russian-born publicist, Isaac M. Rubinow, admonished the lords of creation here not to press the newcomers to hasten their Americanization; every group had a right to live its own life. Rubinow, it would seem was a proto-cultural pluralist.

What did America do for the Russian, Polish, and Rumanian stranger who came to this land? It carried him on eagle's wings from an obscurantist Slavic and Balkan culture into the magical new world of literature, science, aesthetics. It educated him, if only to a degree; it pushed him toward secularism; it affected him profoundly as a religionist. Orthodoxy as a sustaining way of life began to fade; for many disregard for ritual, religious laxity, set in as soon as the ship docked and discharged its passengers. Rabbi J. D. Willowski was shocked when he saw immigrants on Ellis Island who neglected to wash their hands before eating bread and even dispensed with grace after meals. Many ignored the dietary laws, the Sabbath, the Holy Days. The younger generation lived in two worlds; the one was the Orthodoxy of the tenement home; the other began when a youngster descended the steps to the sunlit world of the great outside. Thousands of adolescents, with views of their own, walked out on their parents. Young men and women reared in the comforting embrace of Orthodoxy had to come to terms with a permissive culture that promised a glowing future; this was not always easy; for some it bred psychic distress. Perceptive Jacob Billikopf realized that the problem facing the incoming immigrants was not Americanization or Judaization but the synthesis of the two. If there was no need to stress traditional values then there was no moral justification for a *Jewish* settlement house. Though there were disruptive breaches in far too many immigrant homes filial love and parental resignation often helped to cover over if not to repair the damage. America was not only to change the minds and the manners of the incoming Jews but their bodies as well. Here the native-born son and daughter of Slavic immigrants had benefited physically; they were a stronger, taller, sturdier lot. Gymnasium exercises and playground games contributed to the well-being of the new generation.

Most parents were eager to send their young ones to school. There had always been problems in Russia in securing a secular education; the government was in no sense inclined to further Jews culturally; Jews in turn hesitated to send their children to educational institutions which nursed conversionist aims. Though Christian ceremonies and New Testament readings were common in most American schools in the early twentieth century there was no overt attempt to Christianize the Jewish children. Parents here sent the boys and girls off to school gladly; schooling would prepare them for a career; education was imperative. There is ample evidence that the youngsters, whether foreign-born or native, enjoyed going to school. Attendance of Jewish children compared favorably with that of the children of Central and Western European immigrants. This, despite the fact that, or because, these Jews had come from benighted lands. The new generation took advantage of its opportunities; for the most part they were good students learning not only the three "r's" but also cleanliness and proper dress. Relatively few went to high school prior to 1921; all American youth were taught in those days that an elementary school education was sufficient to cope with the job market and to carve out a career. There is evidence that Jewish children attended high school in larger numbers than many other ethnic groups. Gradually, beginning with the second decade of the twentieth century, more and more Jews found their way into the high schools; the somewhat improved condition of their immigrant parents made this possible; the young ones were less frequently pulled out to help support the family. Papa and mama wanted a son or daughter in the professions.

It is true, too, that the percentage of Jews of immigrant parents who went to college was always higher than most of their ethnic neighbors. In 1908 a survey of 77 colleges showed that 8.5 percent of the male students were Jews; Jewry then constituted 2 percent of the population; a survey made in 1918 of 106 large metropolitan colleges—where Jews were found in substantial numbers—disclosed that they constituted 9.7 percent of the enrollment; this was about three times their proportion in the population. The percentage of Jewish girls going to college was low, lower relatively speaking than their Gentile neighbors. The New Yorkers began to crowd into tuition-free City College; it was really a Jewish school; the

Gentiles were but a minority. But even Harvard had a Jewish student body of 7.7 percent in 1915; this was a relatively high proportion; Jews then constituted but 3 percent of America's total population. There is every reason to believe that most of the Jewish students surveyed in these various statistics were children of East Europeans. A distinguished American visiting the New York ghetto in 1895 found that the children all spoke English. What is also true is that the newcomers learned English quickly, the wives, more slowly. English, too, speedily made itself felt in American Yiddish. Many ghetto Jews began reading English papers as soon as they acquired some proficiency in the language; this did not deter them from continuing to read their favorite Yiddish journal. Children in the public schools made astonishingly quick progress. When Mary Antin was not yet thirteen and but two years in the land she wrote an ode to George Washington:

> 'Twas he who e'r will be our pride,
> Immortal Washington.
> Who always did in truth confide.
> We hail our Washington.

The schools were very important in making Americans out of the children of Russians, Lithuanians, Poles, Hungarians, and Rumanians, but there were other factors contributing to the shaping of the new citizens. This was the larger, the total milieu. When Young Israel Levinthal—later to become a distinguished rabbi—called on the noted Talmud lexicographer Marcus Jastrow, the latter politely told the young man that in America one took off his hat in a house. Lesson number one in the amenities. Russian-born children in a farm colony at Chesterfield, Connecticut, were proficient in English and playing baseball after but six months in this country. Papa, the Slavic newcomer, was Americanized by his children, by his job, and by the Yiddish press. Even the separatistic landsmanshaft was important in the process of becoming one with this land; its Yiddish meetings were conducted according to standard parliamentary rules. Jews were Americanizing themselves rapidly; settlement houses were not really indispensable; the local culture was all pervasive. This was certainly true in the smaller towns where there were no formal Americanization agencies. Making a living made Americans. In the 1890's Isaac M. Wise, president of the Hebrew Union College, said that the "Polak will be wiped out in the rising generation." He knew what he was talking about; he had a number in his student body. They were ardent patriots and World War I intensified their Americanism. In July, 1912, the borough of Manhattan set up a Fourth of July Committee to celebrate the great day. The chief officers were immigrants; Yiddish stage stars made their appearance; Lillian Wald lent her support, and Judge Otto A. Rosalsky (1873-1936) worked closely with this enthusiastic group. Rosalsky, the son of East Europeans, was an Orthodox Jew, a Zionist, and a recognized authority on criminal law.

When the cards were down every Jew made his own America; he Americanized himself if he wished, and most did. Despite the retarding impact of the ethnic ghettos here most of the newcomers succeeded in acculturating themselves. Americanization, or Anglicization, is a process that has distinguished Jewish immigrants since the seventeenth century. Louis Gratz, a peddler from the former Polish province of Posen, became commanding officer of a Civil War cavalry regiment just two or three years after he landed in New York. The newly arrived greenhorn who hastened to discard his garb and modify his mores speedily looked with disdain upon the newcomers who arrived on these shores six months later. These immigrants were desperately eager to be accepted, to attain respectability. Many of the intelligentsia who came here were already at home in Europe's finest literature; here they bought dictionaries and immersed themselves in study, lectures, class work, debates, concerts. The Brith Abraham order catered almost exclusively to the newly arrived Russians, Poles, and Rumanians. As early as 1899 about 100 of the 239 lodges conducted their meetings in English. In its editorial for July 8, 1915, a Yiddish daily said that while a Broadway theatre was featuring trained dogs, the Downtown Yiddish theatres were staging plays of Ibsen, Hauptmann, and Strindberg. Twenty-year-old David Blaustein arrived here in 1886 and graduated from Harvard seven years later. Most East European adults continued to speak Yiddish but they cherished America's political ideals. True, many wrote a phonetic English; so did Daniel Boone. America is more than good English and soap.

EAST EUROPEAN ACHIEVERS IN THE UNITED STATES

There were literally innumerable newcomers who were achievers; some of them were to stand out, nationally. Beryl Segal, an Ukrainian, was no notable. When he came here to be with his sisters he hardly recognized them; they were American, total strangers because of language, dress, and demeanor. After but a year's preparation he entered the University of Minnesota. He loved Dickens and Scott, Keats and Shelley, Lamb and Samuel Johnson. His future was dedicated to his job as a pharmacist and as a laboratory technician. Then there is Bernard Manuel Goldowsky. This Russian youngster, like Segal, read the English classics, Dumas and Victor Hugo also, and of course Robert G. Ingersoll, the freethinker. At night he would crawl up on top of the icebox and would read by the light that penetrated from a street lamp. He became a crayon artist and a peddler of sewing machines until he discovered his own métier. He went to work for the Pinkertons, the detectives, and finally set up his own agency. He bought a Willys Overland touring car in 1915; when it turned over he stopped driving. Morris Morgenstern was sui generis. This Bukovinian lad lived on Long Island where the family had a dairy. This meant he peddled milk, not notions. Ultimately he was to become a millionaire mortgage banker who made and lost several fortunes. Because he loved Orthodoxy he volunteered his services as a cantor for the High Holy Days. What did he do with his money? He purchased the original letter of George Washington to the officers of the Newport synagog (1790). This is the famous manuscript in which Washington wrote that the government of the United States "gives to bigotry no sanction, to persecution no assistance."

Then there are those who were truly notable like Sophie Irene Loeb, Jacob Epstein, and Morris Raphael Cohen. Epstein was born on the East Side, Loeb and Cohen were immigrants. Few people in the United States did more than Sophie Irene Loeb, a New York journalist, to further child welfare, to provide widows' pensions, better housing, good milk, cheaper utilities, public baths, play streets, penny lunches. Epstein read Walt Whitman; his father read Yiddish penny thrillers. Epstein was bar mitzvah at thirteen like other youngsters but the ceremony left him untouched. He studied art, listened to Eugene Debs and the socialists, went to the Metropolitan Opera House. Then he left for Europe and was one day to become one of the world's great and controversial sculptors. Was he less an American because he became an English citizen? Morris Raphael Cohen was born in Minsk in Russia, in 1880; he came here as a twelve-year-old. Like other families the Cohens struggled to make a livelihood; father had a sodawater stand in a pool room. Yet Maurice Raphael went to Harvard and became a professor at City College. In 1933 Cohen established the Conference on Jewish Relations to encourage Jewish academicians to study their own people. He was no religionist yet he was devoted to Jewish ideals. His colleagues elected him president of the Eastern Division of the American Philosophical Association; a generation after his death his students still spoke of him in worshipful admiration. Polish-born Rose Pastor, who wrote an English column for the *Tageblatt* and was to become a notable labor protagonist, socialist, and communist, married the millionaire Christian liberal social worker, James Graham Phelps Stokes (1905). This, too, is part of the saga of Americanization.

THE IMPACT OF THE UNITED STATES ON THE SLAVIC AND BALKAN NEWCOMERS

While being Americanized the Jews in the smaller cities and towns succeeded in remaining Jewish because they huddled together for comfort and security; in the metropolises, the landsmanshaften, the hometown ethnic fellowships, kept the masses Jewish while they both endured and welcomed the impact of American civilization. By 1921 there was a decreasing need for settlement houses and similar institutions. Imitating the "Germans"—whom they envied and admired—the newcomers everywhere embraced the American way of living. World War I stopped the inflow of immigrants; by the mid-1920's the gates were closed. Now that the immigration reservoirs were no longer replenished acculturation was speeded up. The economic well-being that came with World War I enabled thousands to move to new areas of settlement; the ghettos of first settlement began to lose their Jewish denizens. Many, now citizens, turned to the synagog and community centers for sociality, instruction, and education, as well as for religion. These newcomers were no longer the objects of Jewish upper-class patronization; they had paid their dues; they were equal. Culturally they were Americans. By the 1920's Yiddish was tolerated; the Jewish ruling classes had no choice; indeed Yiddish had been accepted, resignedly, for almost a generation. Stiff-necked Yiddish-speaking Jews were now no longer on the defensive. Free to make their way here they slowly affected a harmonization of yiddishkeit and an enticing Americanism. (Actually they were adapting themselves, superficially to be sure, to the standard white Anglo-Saxon Protestant way of life.) By 1921, so it would appear, there were three categories of East Europeans of the first and second generation. First came the assimilationists who had no interest whatsoever in Jews and Judaism; there is no way to determine the numbers of these escapists. Most Jewish immigrant families were religionists of diverse hue, and finally there was a small articulate group of Marxist secularists. Many of these latter were already substituting Yiddishism for Judaism. All the above categories were completely American-centered. America was home; despite occasional recriminations they loved this land; the percentage of returnees was small. The highest tribute one can pay these newcomers is that they surmounted their Slavic past; the Orthodox parents who prayed daily that they might be at ease in Zion were already at ease in this new land where opportunity beckoned and there was none to make them afraid.[1]

OCCIDENTALIZATION

It has been pointed out above that the American Jewish establishment had a threefold program as it set out to integrate the East European immigrants. They must be Americanized, Occidentalized, and be given leadership from above. The term Occidentalization is implicitly denigratory; Judaism, the religion of the Slavic and Balkan lands is Oriental, unacceptable; it must be modernized, Westernized without, however, the renunciation of any basic beliefs. The canon law, the halakah, must remain untouched. Services must be modified, refined; in a word decorum must prevail. New York's Jewish leaders were certainly not unaware of the action of Samuel Montagu in uniting and federating the smaller East European Orthodox synagogs in London (1887). What happened in the United States? In the vast hinterland, wherever the newcomers were found, they had the decorous religious behavior of the Reformers staring them in the face. They scorned this type of service but ultimately adopted many of its externalities. The immigrants in the backcountry were influenced by Jewish Americanization agencies, by the mission schools of the Jewish old-timers, and later by the all-embracing social and cultural programs of the synagog centers. Some of the Orthodox shuls were determined to have order and decorous behavior even if it meant stationing a policeman at the door on the High Holy Days. The New Yorkers of course were pioneers in organizing institutions in the ghetto designed to make "respectable" self-supporting Americans out of greenhorns—as speedily as possible. The prime thrust, however, was directed at the children. They had to be Americanized at all costs. Concerned Uptown leaders wanted a type of Orthodoxy that would tie the children to tradition and preserve the integrity of the Jewish home.

To accomplish this Schiff et al reconstituted the somnolent Jewish Theological Seminary and brought over Solomon Schechter as the seminary head. Here was a man who could do the job, so they thought. He was a Rumanian who had wandered westward in Europe, modernized himself, spoke a beautiful English, and, to boot, was a scholar of renown. He was at home in the Talmud and the later rabbinic literature; in his practice he was Orthodox. Schechter knew what he wanted to do. Through the revived Jewish Theological Seminary he hoped to train American rabbis who would establish an all-American traditional Judaism —Westernized to be sure—that would embrace the majority of the Jews in this country. Obviously he had England's United Synagogue in mind with its book of common prayer, the "Authorized Daily Prayer Book." Schechter automatically excluded the radical Reformers and the hyper-Orthodox from his hoped-for monolithic American Jewish faith. He knew that they would never accept him. He wanted an exemplary pilot Orthodox synagog to be established in the Lower East Side. Here is his program summed up by him in a letter to Schiff (1904):

> Well-regulated Hebrew and religious schools conducted according to enlightened methods of education; divine service in which order and decorum should prevail, an English sermon should be delivered, occasional English prayers be given, but conducted otherwise according to Orthodox ritual; proper direction secured in regulating the religious and moral life of the people through the appointment of a responsible and competent religious guide, whose independence should be assured by a Directorate combining stability with responsiveness to popular demand.

Schechter's plan was never accepted by the notables who supported the Seminary. They wanted immediate action to save the children of the immigrants. The youngsters must be bound to the centuries-old sancta and be subject to parental authority. Many of the youngsters had little sympathy for the religion of their fathers; delinquency was beginning to be a problem. As early as 1880 the apprehensive editors of the *Jewish Messenger* believed—as did the later Schechter—that an exemplary synagog service in the Lower East Side would "refine" the Jews. A synagog is better than a penitentiary, the paper warned. Like Schechter and the *Jewish Messenger*, the Uptown Jews believed that an attractive service with an English sermon and congregational singing would appeal to the Downtown adolescents. Although these German Jewish leaders were not missionizing Reformers and had no wish to modify the principles of Orthodox belief, the Orthodox rejected all their religious approaches as well as Schechter and his school. It was not a matter of creed but of social class, life style. Schechter, a proponent of modern learning and insistence on English, was suspect; his daily speech was not Yiddish. By the early 1900's the board of the Seminary was either German or native-born; East Europeans were conspicuous by their absence. Leonard Lewisohn (1847-1902) was typical of the men who rallied to revive the theological school. This Hamburg-born Jew was a copper magnate, wise enough to know that copper had a great future because of its use in conducting-wires. The firm of Lewisohn Brothers had been established in the 1860's. As early as 1882 brother Leonard had rallied to the help of the Alliance Colony in South Jersey and had contributed liberally to the Hebrew Sheltering Guardian Society of New York which devoted itself to the care of orphans and dependent children. Here was a wealthy industrialist and philanthropist. What did he have in common with the struggling East Side peddlers, petty shopkeepers, and factory hands?

The East Siders wanted conformity and continuity for traditional law and customs; the social and cultural chasm between them and the native American Jewish Orthodox could not be bridged. The Russian and Polish rabbinic scholars, secure in their knowledge of the Talmud, had nothing but contempt for all and any American rabbis; they were not members of the guild. However the learned rabbis and concerned laymen from the Eastern lands realized that they could not ignore the modern world in which they found themselves; on the contrary they were eager to conform. The Prince Albert frock coat and the high hat became de rigueur for a host of Orthodox leaders. What is far more significant, most old-world Orthodox rabbis realized that if they were to save the youth, hold them tight to ancestral belief, English, not Yiddish, was imperative. This was a challenge they dared not avoid. In almost every city of size in the United States there was at least one Orthodox rabbi who spoke, sermon-ized, and taught in English; Aaron Mordecai Ashinsky of Pittsburgh and Simon Glazer of Des Moines, Kansas City, Seattle, Toledo, and New York, are notable examples. Glazer joined the Masons! As early as the late 1890's Bernard Abramowitz (b.1860/1865) had already arranged to secure the publication of a Hebrew and English guide to Jewish practice and customs; he called it the *Law of Israel*. Abramowitz and Glazer based their publications on standard Hebrew codes. After 1915-1916 Gerald Friedlander's Hebrew and English code, *Laws and Customs of Israel*, published in England, was being used in the United States. All these abbreviated manuals were rigidly Orthodox. It was hoped that translations would win the attention and the devotion of the American-born children of East European parents.

Catalogs of booksellers are revelatory; they are basic sources for the historian. No later than 1908 S. Druckerman of Canal Street, New York, began offering English sermons and textbooks to the Orthodox rabbis and congregations of this country. Some of these books had been imported from England where Orthodoxy and English culture had been harmoniously fused. A number of the religious brochures advertised by Druckerman were translations of Orthodox European works. They had been used by mid-nineteenth century American traditional synagogs; Druckerman offered them for sale to the newly established enterprising Russian and Polish synagogs. By 1901 Russian-born Julius Henry Greenstone, a graduate of the Jewish Theological Seminary, had written his *Religion of Israel*; this well written, informative book was designed for Orthodox believers. In 1912 a group of zealous East Side Jews organized Young Israel which gradually evolved into a modern American-oriented Orthodox synagog movement. In short most East European leaders realized that if the American children of foreign-born parents were to be kept within the Orthodox ambit, communication with them, written or spoken, would have to be in English. As early as the 1890's some of these Russian and Polish notables began reaching out to the younger generation by employing the English medium. The settlement houses were working on one level; the wise, religiously-committed East Europeans were working on another level. The result was that many boys and girls would still cherish a love and respect for the old ways and the old beliefs; their loyalties flowered in the Conservative Movement which flourished mightily in the mid-twentieth century.[2]

LEADERSHIP

KISHINEV 1903

There can be no question that the Jewish notables in this country were determined to help the immigrants who came here from Eastern Europe. The newcomers were fellow Jews; they had to be aided in their hour of need. That was the decent thing to do; that had to be done lest they come upon hard times and reflect on us, the earlier settlers. Thus when in April 1903, American Jews heard of the murders in Kishinev, Russia, they rushed to do what they could. On Easter, April 19—according to the Western calendar—a pogrom erupted in Kishinev, the capital of the province of Bessarabia in southwestern Russia. About one-third of the city was Jewish; Jews dominated the trade and the industry of this large town. On this Easter Sunday the peasants from the countryside, the mechanics in the town, and the criminal element in the slums turned against the Jews. About 50 men, women, children, and infants were butchered; about 500 were maimed, 1,500 stores and houses were looted, over 2,000 families were harrowed.

Circumstantial evidence indicates that this mass murder was carefully engineered by local and national officials. Back of it all, so it would seem, was the Russian Minister of the Interior, Vyachislav (Wenzel) Konstantinovich Pleve, a cynical, brutal, unconscionable civil servant. His motives were mixed. He hoped to curry favor with the benighted clique who surrounded the hapless, incompetent Nicholas II. He was their agent. Russia then was an autocratic state sitting on a volcano that threatened to erupt. As head of the secret police he knew the desperate plight of millions of the Russian people; revolution was a potential threat. In order to divert the attention of the oppressed masses a scapegoat was needed. A pogrom, a truly brutal slaughter of Jews, would intimidate Jewish radicals, appeal to the bigots, and for the time being assuage the anger of the oppressed. It would divert their attention from the autocratic government under which they suffered. Kishinev, it would seem, was chosen by the St. Petersburg bureaucrats for this political divertissement. During this Easter season, which coincided with the Jewish Passover, the local—and only—newspaper accused the Jews of ritual murder. Even as the Jews had once crucified Jesus, now again they were still torturing and murdering Christians and using their blood in horrible rites. This was the message on which the anti-Semitic newspaper harped. At a given signal the mob moved to the attack. The local police and the army garrison stood idly by until orders came two days later to stop the carnage. Europe, the United States, the civilized world were shocked; this was the twentieth century! The emperors of Germany and Austria-Hungary protested. And when the whole civilized world, as it were, pointed the finger of scorn at Russia the governor of the province was removed; dozens of the killers were arrested and punished; the ringleaders were not even charged.[3]

The reaction to this massacre in the United States is our concern. The American people were outraged at the bestiality, the horrible mutilations of the living and the dead. Protest meetings, led by Christians and Jews, were organized in more than fifty cities and towns, in some thirty states. In Baltimore, for instance, over 3,000 protesting Jews and Gentiles crowded into the Academy of Music to voice their sorrow. Newspapers and magazines dwelt at length on the almost unbelievable brutality tolerated, if not abetted, by the ruling authorities. The largest meeting was held in New York City; the chief speaker, former President Grover Cleveland, condemned the Russians. About $500,000 was raised for relief throughout the world, one-fourth came from the United States; much of this came from humble Russian Jewish immigrants still living in the ghettos of the large cities. The Hearst newspapers raised large sums in New York, Chicago, and San Francisco; the cautious John Hay, Secretary of State, sent $500; President Theodore Roosevelt was warned to send nothing to avoid a diplomatic blunder; Russia was a friendly state. Schiff, the banker, led those who collected and dispatched the relief funds. Benefit performances were staged in the New York Yiddish playhouses; more than one drama was written to describe the Kishinev murders. The facile "Professor" Moses Horowitz, with his customary literary legerdemain at once produced a tragedy in five acts, "The Story of Kishineff"; the son of the governor of Bessarabia had fallen in love with a Jew and when she was murdered he committed suicide at her grave. This was the plot.

Simon Wolf in Washington alerted Hay; Washington would have to do something. The American people expected its government to take some action; American Jewry demanded it. Hay cabled the ambassador in St. Petersburg who answered that there was no occasion to do anything; a few days later the ambassador reversed himself and confirmed the reports of the mass murders; he had read about them in an English newspaper. The Russian press was censored. Wolf, speaking for the B'nai B'rith and the Union of American Hebrew Congregations and their thousands of affluent Jews, arranged a meeting of B'nai B'rith notables with Hay and the President. (This was almost two months after the bloodbath.) Hay had no use for the Russian barbarians but the Kishinev killings came at an inopportune moment. He was trying to hold down the Russian advances into Manchuria; the United States favored an Open Door policy in China. Like Hay, the President, too, was dismayed by the cruelty. Publicly he and Hay declared that this was mob action; Nicholas II was a peaceful man devoted to the highest imperative of religion. (Roosevelt and Hay knew better.) The President and his Secretary of State certainly felt that their hands were tied. No American had been killed; the United

States could not interfere in the domestic concerns of Bessarabia any more than this country would tolerate any reproach for their lynch mobs. From 1882 to 1936 almost 3,400 Negroes were lynched; in 1902, about 100. Some of them were burnt alive at the stake. Unless the administration was willing to overstep the bounds of traditional diplomatic behavior there was little that it could do, so it believed. Yet Presidents Arthur and Harrison in 1882 and 1891 had dared to do this in their annual messages to Congress in those years; they had not failed to expose the callous brutality of the Russians toward their Jewish citizens.

After a fashion, Simon Wolf, Oscar S. Straus, and Leo N. Levi, president of the B'nai B'rith, found a way to get the President and Hay off the hook. Wolf and Straus, committed Republicans, were high in the councils of the party. Congress would not act to take any drastic action that might have embarrassed Washington. The B'nai B'rith president suggested that a protest petition, signed by thousands, be addressed to the Czar. The administration went along. Roosevelt was eager to do something to please the Jews; he hoped to be reelected in 1904. American Jewry, apparently, was satisfied with the device of a humble respectful appeal to the Czar asking him to accord religious liberty to all of his subjects, both Jews and Christians. A few years later, 1907, Jews would not be satisfied with the sop of a humble petition to the throne; they then began to besiege Congress to abrogate the 1832 commercial treaty with the Romanovs. In July the government released the text of the petition. It was ultimately signed by about 13,000 Americans, many of them notable Christians. It was cabled to the embassy and then offered to the Russian authorities. The Muscovite government refused to accept it but the implied denunciation of the reactionary regime was made known to the world. The Jews here looked upon the dispatch of the petition as a victory. Roosevelt and Hay were pleased; they felt it was a coup on behalf of humanity. Henry Adams, sick with anti-Semitism, sneered, "I am so glad John [Hay] loves the Jews." Since the petition had not been accepted by the Russian authorities Hay arranged for its deposit in the archives of the State Department: "It is a valuable addition to public literature and will be sacredly cherished among the treasures of this department." Some time later, Wolf wrote a frank letter to the Russian ambassador to the United States, this at a time when revolution in Russia was already in the making. Linking the Kishinev massacre to an impending uprising of the Russian people, Wolf warned the ambassador that the country would have to clean its Augean stables.[4]

WHAT KISHINEV TAUGHT AMERICAN JEWRY

The killings in Kishinev stimulated the radicalism of the Jewish intelligentsia in Russia and pushed many into the revolutionary movement which was to culminate in the overthrow of the Romanov dynasty. Some of these left-wingers, brilliant, educated, came to the United States to raise funds and to present their cause. A few elected to remain in this country. They brought an intellectual ferment that influenced thousands in the ghetto enclaves. Among them was the Social Revolutionary Chaim Zhitlowsky, the Diaspora nationalist, the cultural pluralist. The Kishinev atrocities, condoned by the Russian authorities, turned the Rothschilds of London and Schiff of New York against the Muscovite state. These important international bankers refused to finance Russia when she was threatened by inner dissent and foreign enemies. American Jewish leaders realized finally that there was no hope for Jewry under the ancien regime; the Jewish elite in almost all lands was now convinced that only a radical political upheaval in Russia would ameliorate the condition of the Jews in that unhappy land. In the meantime emigration was inevitable; the new-comers must be accepted and integrated. All Jews here in the United States were reconciled to the coming of additional refugees. After the violence in Kishinev the Jews of Russia needed no further incentive to leave. In 1902, 57,688 came to the United States; in 1903, 76,203, in 1904, 106,236.

The two decades since 1881 had taught the Jewish natives and Germans here that the newcomers were achievers; their successes evoked commendation and respect. More than ever the Zionists in the United States, led by Richard Gottheil, were convinced that the only salvation for persecuted Jews was a homeland of their own. The cry of anguish from the Bessarabian capital fired all groups in American Jewry to give and to give liberally; working together for a common cause brought Jewish natives and immigrants closer. The events of 1903 taught American Jewry the value of political protest and its concomitant power. Little though it was, it had compelled Roosevelt and Hay to take some action if only to reproach publicly the trans-Vistula tyrants. Through protest meetings American Jewry in 1903 informed World Jewry that the Jews of this country were ready to play an important role in defense of their coreligionists abroad. Jewry in the United States began inching forward toward World Jewish hegemony. Some Jewish leaders realized, however, that in reality they had accomplished but little. They were fully aware of the need to create a strong central organization embracing all of American Jewry, one that would have the power, the authority, to influence Washington and other capitals to exert themselves on behalf of Jews wherever they were disabled.[5]

AMERICAN JEWRY IN THE POST-KISHINEV YEARS, 1903-1906

POGROMS

The reactionaries who staged or tolerated the massacres at Kishinev thought that they could divert the attention of the suffering Gentile masses from their troubles. The pogroms initiated at Kishinev would rise to a crescendo that would startle the civilized world. The B'nai B'rith petition which exposed the Russians did not deter them in their policy of holding the Jews responsible for the problems of the country. Six months after Kishinev, in September, Jews in the town of Gomel were attacked; many who dared to defend themselves were jailed. Kishinev and Gomel were a warning to all Russians that the regime would tolerate no dissidence. Monotonously it harped on the one string: the Jews who are the cause of all our troubles will be destroyed and you will share their fate if you rebel against authority. Any form of constitutionalism was damned as the machinations of Jewry. If the country suffers in war or peace the Jews are responsible. Apparently the government had no other solution for internal problems than diversionary pogroms. Between April, 1903, and June, 1906, Russia was wracked by at least 250 anti-Jewish civil disorders; at least 1,000 Jews were murdered; many more were injured; the property damage ran into the millions. The outrages reached their height in Odessa on October 31, 1905, when hundreds were killed and thousands beaten brutally. Pamphlets inciting to riot had been printed on the presses of the secret police. The soldiers and the police did nothing to stop the attacks.

Killings were not organized by the government in the same sense that they were by the Germans in the 1940's. If the Russian authorities had employed its armed forces to eradicate the Jews hundreds of thousands if not millions would have died. However, individual officials, both on a local and national level, encouraged and abetted the riots; they were often carried on with the aid of the police and the military. Count Witte, who was the premier at the height of the murderous onslaughts, certainly did not sanction them; if he knew about them before they occurred there was little that he could do. It is difficult to believe, however, that the Czar was not privy to the action of his reactionary supporters. There can be little doubt that he, too, thought that the demand for a constitutional monarchy could be drowned in Jewish blood. As an absolute monarch in command of a ruthless army he could have stopped the rioting. He did nothing. When his Minister of Foreign Affairs, Count Vladimir N. Lamsdorf told Czar Nicholas that the demand for a constitutional monarchy was a conspiracy of World Jewry and its bankers, the Czar agreed enthusiastically. This was on January 16, 1906, less than three months after Nicholas had been compelled to grant a liberal constitution.[6]

The war with Japan which lasted from February 1904 to September 1905 was a disaster for the Russians. Without effective leadership Russia faced anarchic conditions at home. While conscripted Jewish soldiers fought and died at the front their families were being ravished in the towns and villages. During the twenty months of the war there were at least ninety mob attacks on Jews. These outbreaks, tolerated by the provincial authorities, were intended to distract the attention of the people from the defeats on land and sea. In August, 1905, Theodore Roosevelt set out to bring the two warring powers to the peace table. He feared lest the Japanese dismember and control China; he wanted no socialist revolution and regime in Russia. Thus, in a way, he bolstered the autocratic Romanov state; Roosevelt, a Republican, was no flaming liberal. When in August, 1905, Count Witte repaired to Portsmouth, New Hampshire, to make peace with the Japanese, a delegation of Jewish notables waited on him. They told him bluntly that Russia must emancipate its Jews. They let him know that they would bring all their influence to bear against the Russian state. This he knew full well; Schiff, through the loans he had floated, had fortified the Japanese and helped them materially to win the war. Witte could promise nothing; he knew he had no authority.

What a contrast there was between Russia and the United States! In the month of November, 1905, alone there were at least 100 attacks on Jews in the czarist empire; here in the United States American Jews, on Thanksgiving Day, November 30, met together to celebrate the 250th anniversary of their first settlement in New Amsterdam. (Actually it was the 251st year.) A mass meeting was called at Carnegie Hall where thousands of Jews gathered, free and unhindered. Among the notables, Grover Cleveland and Schiff made addresses. Roosevelt sent a letter to be read. This time the President, less cautious, denounced the Russians though not by name; Schiff reminded his audience—who needed no reminder—that Jews were being martyred in darkest Russia. On December 4th, four days after the Jews and their friends had assembled in Carnegie Hall, there was a huge memorial march to mourn for the hundreds of innocents who had been killed in Odessa on the last day of October. This was the most disastrous of the attacks on Jews since the seventeenth century when the Cossacks and the Tatars and the Poles, too, ravaged the cities and villages killing myriads. Dressed in black, at least 50,000 Jews marched from the Lower East Side to Union Square where the gathered throng was addressed by its leaders. Churches tolled their bells in sympathy. The marchers were nearly all immigrants. Very probably this was the first American Jewish protest march.

The Uptown notables led by Oscar Straus, Schiff, and Cyrus Sulzberger collected large sums through their National Committee for Relief of Sufferers by Russian Massacres. All told over a million dollars was raised in this country from about 800 different communities. Even in distant Bisbee, Arizona, the ten or so Jewish merchants closed their stores and met to mourn and make their modest gifts. In another town the Young Men's Christian Association sponsored the anti-Russian protest. Christians gave generously. Edward H. Harriman, the railroad financier, sent $10,000, no doubt at the request of his friend Schiff. The monies collected by the Uptown Jews were dispatched to Europe, to England, for distribution. Again, as during the Kishinev appeal, United States Jewry contributed more than its share. In a world of 11,000,000 coreligionists, 1,500,000 Jews here raised more than half of the funds that were sent on to Eastern Europe. The newcomers who marched on December 4th had been led by Rabbi Judah Leon Magnes, a recent graduate of the Hebrew Union College. He was the head of the Jewish Defense Association which set out to supply arms to the Russian Jews who had organized self-defense groups. Were it not for these armed defense organizations hundreds if not thousands more would have died at the hands of the mob. In some communities there were as many casualties among the attackers as among the defenders; on occasion the rioters retreated when they saw that the Jews were armed. There was no unanimity among the Jews here as to the disposal of the funds. Many of the older settlers wanted the monies to be used solely for relief, at the most for arms and defense. The ghetto denizens and some Uptown Jews were willing to support the revolutionaries believing that emancipation for Jews would come only after the Romanovs were overthrown and a modern constitutional state established. There is reason to believe that some of the funds sent abroad were given to radical political parties who looked upon all bourgeois, Jews, too, as the enemies of an impending revolution. Some of these Marxists sympathized with the mobs. Anarchy would hasten revolution. If a socialist state was to be established then the end justified the means.

The Russian people, bourgeois and workers, had compelled the Czar to grant them a constitution on October 30, 1905; the Odessa riots began a day later and by the Spring of 1906, as the reaction set in, the government had begun to delimit the authority of the newly established parliament. By May autocracy was once more in the saddle; by June there was a full-scale massacre attack on the Jews. This was in Bialystok; the revolution had failed for the time being. The events of 1904-1906 were obviously a case of déjà vu, a Kishinev replay; murder, shock, protest, fundraising. By 1906 American Jewry had adopted a multi-pronged approach to the problem of the Jews in the Muscovite Empire. Immediate financial relief was imperative and was forthcoming. So far as they had influence affluent Jews urged that financial sanctions be applied against the Russians; revolution was favored with the hope that it would give birth to an egalitarian state. All Jewish groups here were now ready to encourage immigration to the United States. The Russian Israelites needed no encouragement to leave. They were anxious to avoid conscription during the Russo-Japanese War, to escape violence and massacres at home. There was no future for them after the failure of the 1905-1906 Revolution. A few left for Palestine; most turned to America. Schiff sponsored the Galveston Movement hoping to rescue millions though he realized full well that ultimately the Jewish problem would have to be solved in Russia proper; it would never be possible to bring them all out (1907).

By 1906 the American people had turned against the Russians because of their brutality. It was the American Congress, American public opinion, not the Jews who would take action in 1911 to abrogate the 1832 treaty with Russia. Adolph Lewisohn, the industrialist, pointed out correctly that if this country had turned against the Moscovites it was not because of its love for Jews but because of its abhorrence of injustice. Chronology is not without significance: the mass killings occurred in Bialystok on June 14, 1906; Congress passed a resolution on the 22nd excoriating the Russians; Roosevelt signed it a few days later; on December 17th, Oscar Straus assumed office as Secretary of Commerce and Labor. "I want to show Russia and some other countries what we think of the Jews in this country," said Roosevelt. Because of Russia, Jewry all over the world was cemented together; this was certainly true here in the United States despite the fact that Jewish political radicals were at each other's throats and often refused to work with one another; but this was not significant since their numbers were small. All Jews were certainly of the opinion that a more effective national central organization was needed to cope with the problems that faced Jewry both here and abroad. Such an association could work to remove disabilities in Eastern Europe, intervene when violence erupted, and speed relief to the suffering.[7]

AMERICAN JEWISH COMMITTEE

Long before Kishinev, American Jewry realized that there was a need for a really effective national organization that would guard over the Jews here and be helpful to those abroad. The first proposal to unite all American Jews—religiously—came from the pen of Isaac Leeser in 1841; Leeser and Isaac M. Wise made another effort in 1848; Wise, intoxicated with the concept of union, made still another attempt in Cleveland in 1855 to create a national religious organization. In 1857 the ambitious Wise presided over a national conference—minuscule in size—that met in Baltimore to protest a discriminatory American treaty with the Swiss; the rights of American Jewish citizens had been ignored. American Jewry, alarmed by the persecutions of Jews in Damascus (1840), the discriminatory Swiss Treaty (1855), and the abduction of a Jewish child in Bologna by the papal authorities (1858), organized the first national congregational association in 1859. Patterned on the Board of Deputies of British Jews it called itself the Board of Delegates of American Israelites (BDAI). It was never able to coopt more than a minority of the larger, stable American synagogal societies. As a defense organization it did what it could to guard the interests of Jews both here and abroad. In 1873 the congregations of the South and the West established still another organization whose goals were solely religious and educational. The new group was the Union of American Hebrew Congregations. In 1878 this union took over the Board of Delegates creating in its stead the Board of Delegates on Civil and Religious Rights (BDCRR) which functioned as a defense agency. Led for many years by its Washington agent, Simon Wolf, it made a valiant attempt to come to the aid of American and World Jewry. It kept in touch with similar national agencies in Europe.

The BDCRR was called into being in an age when all America was consolidating; this was true of big business, labor, fraternal and scientific bodies, Indians, and blacks, too, after the turn of the century. The drive to organize was constant and insistent. By 1890 the Jewish émigrés from Eastern Europe had been coming here for almost a generation; of the 400,000 Jews in the country many had fled from the Slavic lands. These immigrants wanted to free themselves from the leading strings of the Jewish natives and the established Germans; working on their own they were eager to solve their problems here in this country. Thus it was that in 1890—the year that the mass expulsions in Moscow began—Philadelphia's newcomers created the Jewish Alliance of America, hoping to put Jews on the farms and in the colonies, to train many as craftsmen, to shunt them off to the backcountry. Their enthusiasms were shared by the Russo-Jewish bard Eliakum Zunser who was now living and singing in this country. This agrarian romantic wanted Jews to throw off their peddler's packs, walk out of the sweatshops, and turn to the plow. Petty business encourages anti-Semitism; Jewish farmers would disarm the Jew-haters. This drive for self-help and self-emancipation was short-lived. In a few months, by February 1891, the Alliance had been taken over by Philadelphia's Jewish philanthropists and social workers. The newcomers were poor; they lacked the means to hire staff. It was then, that month, that Simon Muhr was elected president of the reorganized Alliance. Numerous notables appeared at the founding meeting; there was obviously a desire to organize American Jewry on a national scale. David Solis-Cohen came in from Portland; the politicians Simon Wolf of Washington and Ferdinand Levy of New York made their appearance; Henry M. Leipziger, the educator, also came down from the New York metropolis, and the young Lithuanian rabbi and Harvard student, David Blaustein, made the journey from New England. The Russians were a substantial part of the new Alliance. This society appealed to the new arrivals; dozens of branches were organized; there was even one in Ardmore, Indian Territory. The Milwaukee society opened a night school for immigrants and could soon boast of an attendance of 70 refugees, men and women. Strange, but just about a year later the Alliance was dead; it was swallowed up by a recently established New York association, the American Committee for Ameliorating the Condition of Russian Refugees. This was a Baron de Hirsch Fund adjunct; shortly after even this new organization, the American Committee for Ameliorating the Condition of the Russian Refugees, disappeared. It may well be—this is a guess—the Baron de Hirsch Fund group preferred to operate unhampered. This attempt of the East Europeans to organize themselves on a large scale was a failure.[8]

By 1900 the United States was reaching out slowly for power and hegemony. Imperialism was in the ascendancy. It was not improbable that the political and emotional climate here affected American Jewry with its million or so Jews; this was the second largest Jewish community in the world. The synagog follows the flag. By 1901 the Union of American Hebrew Congregations and the B'nai B'rith were talking of working together to help World Jewry; the National Council of Jewish Women was thinking in terms of a national Jewish assembly, and in 1903 Rabbi David Philipson and Joseph Stolz tried to induce the UAHC to sponsor a Jewish Congress that would unite and help all American Jews. The Union board made an effort to enlist support but finally decided that a congress was inexpedient. A year later Rabbi Krauskopf, president of the Central Conference of American Rabbis (CCAR), pushed for a synod, a lay and rabbinic body to legislate on matters religious. The synod was a theme on which Isaac M. Wise had dwelt ever since the 1850's; some rabbis always favored it as a device to ameliorate the immutability of Jewish law. These religious leaders continued in 1906 to promote the calling of such a legislative body. That same year some of the Reformers were talking of an all-encompassing central Jewish representative organization, based on the many hundreds of American synagogs. Stolz, president of the CCAR in 1906, pleaded for a union of all Jewish forces in the United States. He emphasized religion, the primacy of the synagog, deploring that many laymen and rabbis refused to favor a national religious organization because, presumptively, religion was by its very nature divisive. This distinguished rabbi and gentle soul took a sideswipe at anyone attempting to set up a self-constituted, self-perpetuating, mutual-admiring, aristocratic association to help and unite Jewry. The American people, he said, would never be satisfied with such an organization. This was a covert attack on the American Jewish Committee then in the process of formation. Simon Wolf joined the chorus of all those calling for a new national defense association. Just weeks after the Odessa riots of October, 1905, he pleaded for an organization that would be truly representative of all shades of public opinion; its primary job would be the scattering, the distribution of the immigrants who were arriving in large numbers.

In 1906, in the wake of the never-ending rioting and killings in Russia, there was an almost frantic demand for a truly effective national defense organization. American Jewry itself was prospering and growing rapidly. In this sense it was the best of times but structurally it was the worst, the most chaotic of times. Abraham S. Schomer, the Yiddish litterateur, talked of an international congress of All-Israel; Rabbi Jacob Voorsanger in distant San Francisco organized an International Jewish League to fight for Jewish rights; Rabbi Judah L. Magnes was interested in the Jewish Self-Defense Association and in the Federation of Jewish Organizations of New York State. Hundreds of societies, landsmanshaften and associations joined this Federation which was determined to help the Jews of Russia; the Federation talked of an elected democratic congress with international ramifications, but all it could raise in dues was a paltry $219.

One of the organizers of the Federation was Nissim Abraham Behar (1848-1931), a Jerusalem educator who had come to this country in 1901 as a friend if not as an agent of the Alliance Israélite Universelle (AIU). The Alliance, created in France in 1870 after the Mortara Affair, aspired to become the world representative of Jewry; in a sense it reflected French imperialism. As a patriotic Gallophile association it was anti-Zionist and anti-German. Thus it had no close ties to the Hilfsverein der deutschen Juden (the German Jews' Relief Association) and to the American B'nai B'rith which was German to the core. The AIU hoped to extend its influence to the United States; it had a branch in San Francisco as early as 1864. The B'nai B'rith did not want the Alliance poaching on its preserves here in this country. Let the Alliance concern itself with the emancipation of the Jews in Eastern Europe so that they will not be driven to emigrate here; these newcomers create problems for us. Behar had little confidence in the B'nai B'rith; it could not lead American Jewry. This Jerusalemite, who soon emancipated himself from the AIU, was an activist, determined to organize American Jewry to fight vigorously, politically, for the rights of Jews everywhere. To this end American Jewry must be organized on a national scale. His was a voice crying in the wilderness; in 1906 he built the National Liberal Immigration League to fight the immigration restrictionists and he had plans to federate all American Jewish associations. He was a man of vision and bold plans but the Uptown elite looked down upon him as a nuisance. Throughout most of 1906 all the talk of creating a viable American Jewish organization to include all Jews was just talk. The associations that were established were short-lived and ineffectual. There was to be one exception.[9]

Europe's Jews were just as concerned as the Americans with the problems of the Jews in Eastern Europe. The Zionists, a young and aspiring organization, called an international conference to meet in Brussels on January 29, 1906. The delegate from Odessa, the scene of the worst pogrom, was Asher Ginsberg, the protagonist of Cultural Zionism. Palestine, Zion, was of course suggested as the answer to Russian brutality but there was much talk of emigration, of colonization in other lands. Brussels provided no answers, no solutions. Here in the United States, twenty-five years after the first pogrom and the arrival of refugees from the Slavic lands, there was still no overall national Jewish organization that could command the loyalty of all American Jews. France had the Alliance Israélite Universelle (1860), England had its Anglo-Jewish Association (1871) and Board of Deputies, Austria its Israelitische Allianz (1873); Germany had its Hilfsverein der deutschen Juden (1901) which was determined to help the Jews of Eastern Europe, and aid the German Empire in its "Push to the East." These well-organized national Jewish societies were a constant silent reproach to the Americans. Schiff, as early as 1904, Cyrus Adler in 1905, wanted an overall American body that could work with its opposite Jewish numbers in Europe. There is no question that the agitation of Behar, Magnes, et al, confronted the Uptown elite and drove it to take action. The Brussels Conference, Zionist sponsored, was a threat. There was a power vacuum here in the United States; if the responsible American Jews would not step in the socialists and the Zionists here might take over. This thought frightened the older element.

The Eastern Jewish elitists had been talking about the establishment of a permanent national Jewish defense and relief establishment ever since the 1903 Kishinev massacre. The Brussels Conference may have impelled the American Jewish notables to move faster. Cyrus Adler who had been pushing for a national Jewish organization was opposed to a congress which implied the right of universal Jewish suffrage in establishing a national congeries. Such an election would give the East European masses control; the radicals, too, would assert themselves; all this was unacceptable. Louis Marshall, the New York lawyer, called for a national convention on February 3, 1906, to talk of establishing a defense organization; like all the others he and his friends wanted to stop the pogroms. He was well aware, too, of anti-Semitism in Germany and France. The anti-Jewish Dreyfus Affair in free France (1894-1906) had shocked the whole Jewish world. Wolf, American Jewry's Washington's voice, was looked upon as "an old fossil." There is no question that the New York elite did not expect much from the defense activity of the B'nai B'rith and the Union of American Hebrew Congregations. Marshall and Schiff, religionists, wanted the new national organization to be based on congregations; they were eager to further Judaism as well as Americanism. No headway was made in February, 1906, to organize American Jewry on a congregational basis. Even the rabbis feared that religion could not cement American Jewry; the religionists distrusted one another. Marshall and others had to make their peace with the non-religionists if they hoped to achieve any degree of unity. There was a consensus that the B'nai B'rith and the Board of Delegates on Civil and Religious Rights should be bypassed. The suggestion made at this meeting that a small committee of representative Jews be set up was adopted; an initial committee of fifteen was to be expanded later to fifty. This group, it was hoped, would coopt leaders from the different national societies.

The men who met in February reconvened May 19, 1906, and proceeded again to reject any religiously based national organization. In a way the rejection was typically American. The 1843 B'nai B'rith allowed no religious discussion; the Board of Delegates of American Israelites and the 1873 Union of American Hebrew Congregations, both congregationally based, discouraged all religious polemics. The protagonists of the new 1906 assembly were not necessarily anti-religious; they wanted harmony. In rejecting Marshall's religious approach and in opting for a small elite group they were in effect anti-democratic; Marshall had asked for authority from the people. On May 12, 1906, the B'nai B'rith issued what came to be known as the Chicago Manifesto. No new committee was needed; the B'nai B'rith wanted no association with radical theorists. This approach of the B'nai B'rith, wrote Marshall, was repugnant to democracy. A few days after the Westerners wrote their remonstrance the new organization coopted two of the very men who had signed the manifesto, Rabbi Emil G. Hirsch and Simon Wolf; Hirsch was even put on the all-powerful executive committee. Despite fear of the newcomers the first group of notables selected included two Russian-born clothing manufacturers. The Downtown East European leaders, however, looked askance at the new assembly; it was oligarchical. They feared that Zionists and socialists would not be welcome.

At the formal founding meeting, November 11, 1906, the new organization called itself the American Jewish Committee (AJC). The notables represented a deliberate geographical, ideological, and "social" distribution. (Not all notables are socially equal!) Joseph H. Cohen, the Russian-born cloak manufacturer wanted the Committee to embrace all groups and aspects of American Jewish life, Zionists, Orthodox, and the like. He was voted down. Despite their misgivings Wolf and Kraus attended; they were needed; they represented the German-Jewish middle class, many thousand strong; they were voters; they wielded political power. Adolph Kraus, president of the B'nai B'rith, warned those present that democracy was not attainable or even desirable. He wanted a "high class" association; there was no need to cater to the "riff-raff." About forty years earlier Kraus had landed in Chicago with two cents in his pocket. Famished, he was grateful when a kindhearted grocer gave him two apples for a penny. It is obvious that this teenage Bohemian youngster did not believe that at one time he, too, was riff-raff. Sulzberger shared Kraus's disdain for the East European newcomers. He resented the lack of verbal restraint that characterized many of their notables some of whom were not even naturalized! Not all Jews live in the ghetto, said the irate judge; there are Jews also in the South and in the West! Harry Cutler, whose father had been murdered in a Russian riot, was put on the executive and remained on it for many years. There were nearly always one or two East Europeans on the executive; the committee even invited Hannah Bachman Einstein to sit with it; she was a formidable personality, a harbinger of the new order that would begin to prevail two generations later. From the very first there were always Zionists, Conservative and Orthodox Jews—rabbis, too—on the advisory council, although the authority of these district members was limited; the executive was all powerful. Isador Sobel (1858-1939) was typical of the men who were asked to serve on the first executive committee. This native American, who made his home in Erie, Pennsylvania, was a typical successful Jew from the backcountry. He was a power in the general community, unquestionably the outstanding Jew in town. He started out as a businessman and at the age of forty turned to law; ultimately he was to become chairman of the local bar association and the town's postmaster. His fellow Jews made him president of the B'nai B'rith Grand Lodge, head of the local Jewish orphan asylum, the Jewish social club, and the Reform synagog which he had helped establish.

The American Jewish Committee drew fire from all sides; it was derided as an undemocratic institution; the Central Conference of American Rabbis, the Union of American Hebrew Congregations, and the B'nai B'rith refused to make peace with this brash intruder on the national scene. Expressing its willingness to work with all American Jewish national associations, the Committee moved quickly to enlarge its roster of notables for it was determined to build a wider geographical and "ethnic" base. Thus it was, in 1915, that nine of the fifteen people on the executive committee were from the hinterland. There was no New York majority. The goals for the society were spelled out clearly in 1906 at the time of its founding: to emancipate all rightless Jews in all lands; to bring relief to all coreligionists suffering persecution. The Committee emerged quickly as the dominant American Jewish defense organization; it became heir to the surplus monies of the National Committee for the Relief of Sufferers by the Russian Massacres. With funds it could flesh out its programs. The very emergence of the new national association was also an unequivocal declaration that American Jewry was emancipating itself from the West, from Cincinnati and Chicago.[10]

THE ACCOMPLISHMENTS OF THE AMERICAN JEWISH COMMITTEE

As soon as it was organized the Committee set out to implement its program. It was an efficient businesslike organization; this reflected its German Jewish leadership. In order to understand the problems that faced it —at least here in the United States—it began at once to collect statistical data. It worked closely with the United States Bureau of the Census when congregational data were collated. Relief was sent to the Jewish community in San Francisco after the earthquake, to Morocco when the Moslems began to raid the Jewish quarter, to Constantinople when there was need. Russian political refugees in this country who were threatened with extradition were saved and when the government here threatened to classify Jews as "Asiatics" the Committee intervened; "Asiatics" might well be barred. Along with other national groups it fought constantly and successfully against the immigration restriction bills that had been steadily fed into the congressional hopper since the late nineteenth century; the Committee carried on a delaying action. Literacy bills were also opposed; Presidents were induced to veto them. Many of the Jewish immigrants were illiterate even in Hebrew and Yiddish; the Russians had been loath to open the public schools to them; a Jewish education cost money; thousands back in Russia and Rumania were too poor even to provide religious schooling for their youngsters.

Beginning in 1907 the new organization, working closely with the B'nai B'rith and the Union of American Hebrew Congregations, began to press the government in Washington to urge the Russians to honor an American passport when presented by a Jew. In 1909 the Jewish Publication Society of America and the Committee became co-publishers of the *American Jewish Year Book*. The Committee supplied the data. This was an important cultural achievement; the *Year Book* is an invaluable reference work. That same year the Committee organized the Jewish Community of New York City, the Kehillah. This was a gallant attempt to coordinate and improve the activities of all the city's Jewish organizations and institutions. Ultimately, so it was hoped, all major Jewish communities would be similarly reorganized. It was a magnificent concept. It did what it could to aid the Russian Jew, Mendel Beilis, who was tried by the Russian courts (1911-1913) on a charge of ritual murder. This was the old medieval accusation that Jews murdered Christian children and used their blood for ceremonial purposes. When in 1912-1913 the Balkan wars came to an end, and there were shifts in sovereignty, and large numbers of Turkish Jews found themselves living in Christian lands, the AJC asked the State Department to interpose its good offices to protect the religious and civil rights of these Jews.

In 1913, the year that Beilis was exculpated, the Committee, led by its president, Louis Marshall, succeeded in amending the civil rights law in New York; it was now illegal to advertise that public places of accommodation excluded individuals for racial or religious reasons; one could no longer inform the public that Jews and consumptives were not welcome. When in 1914 World War I broke out funds were dispatched to Palestine to support the stricken community; the AJC then worked closely with the Zionists. That same year the Committee took the initiative in establishing an international relief organization, the American Jewish Relief Committee; this was part of the Joint Distribution Committee which was ultimately to send hundreds of millions of dollars to aid European, North African, and Asian Jews. The following years the leaders of this aggressive organization asked the Pope to intervene with the Poles who were carrying on a devastating economic boycott directed against Polish Jews; several years later the new Poland marked its rise as an independent republic by murdering Jews. Marshall and his Committee protested vigorously. When the United States entered World War I in 1917 and the Jewish Welfare Board was established to aid Jews in the armed forces, the leaders of the AJC were quick to support this patriotic enterprise, and when in the fall of that same year the British, through the Balfour Declaration, offered the Jews a homeland in Palestine, this anti-Zionist organization did not withhold its support. Despite its elitist character the AJC never lost touch with the Jewish people. It was certainly willing to help build mandate Palestine as a cultural center. By the 1920's at the latest the AJC was America's dominant Jewish defense agency; it still was in the mid-twentieth century. There were many problems abroad to which it addressed itself earnestly. In order to accomplish its purposes it established offices at different times in Europe, South America, and the State of Israel. After the close of the American ports by the restrictive immigration laws of the 1920's, Marshall, eager to open Palestine to refugees, drew closer to the political Zionists; it was he who made possible the extended Jewish Agency whereby non-Zionists expressed their willingness to work closely with the World Zionist Association. In the years 1933-1945 the Committee did what it could to counter the anti-Semitism and the savage pogroms of the Germans and to find homes for Europe's Jewish refugees. After World War II when Central and Western Europe's Jewish communities moved to rehabilitate themselves structurally, culturally, the Committee was quick to advise them offering American communal models that had proved their worth. The Committee still continued to use its good offices on behalf of the Jewish settlements in Palestine when the British began closing the country to Jews. The anti-Jewish acts of the Soviet Empire were brought to the attention of the world; help where possible was offered to oppressed coreligionists in the Moslem lands of North Africa; the Jews of South America were given moral support as they faced a rising tide of Judeophobia.

Despite the guarantees of the American Constitution, the common law, state and federal legislation, and executive orders, Jews in the United States faced many problems throughout the twentieth century. The Committee addressed itself to their solution or amelioration. Anti-Jewish prejudice, anti-Semitism, had to be faced. This was at a time when the virulent anti-Jewish *Protocols of the Elders of Zion* were being circulated by Henry Ford who was spending millions to incite prejudice against his Jewish fellow citizens. It would take decades before some social clubs would begin to accept Jews and the executive suites of mammoth industries were in large part still closed to Jews on the eve of the twenty-first century. The Committee did what it could to cope with discrimination against Jews in the job market. Extensive interfaith work was carried on by brilliant staff members of the Committee; the Vatican in 1965 was encouraged to issue a statement denouncing anti-Semitism. This marked a revolutionary change in papal policy. Through the medium of the radio, the press, and later the television, the effort was made to induce all Americans to accept Jews wholeheartedly as fellow citizens. *The Contemporary Jewish Record* and *Present Tense* were published to enlighten Jews; *Commentary*, it was hoped, would create a climate of liberalism and support the egalitarian hopes of America's non-Jewish intelligentsia. For decades this defense agency opposed political Zionism vigorously but when after the Holocaust the State of Israel emerged the Committee rallied to its support. It really had little choice if it hoped to continue playing an important role; with few exceptions American Jewry was dedicated to the support of the new Jewish republic, the only place in the world where a Jew could go as of right. Moving toward democracy after World War II the AJC became a mass organization recruiting thousands of members who carried on its programs in local branches. This change was imperative; the membership, affluent middle-class professionals and businessmen, was in a position to influence the local Jewish Welfare Funds to make substantial grants to the national organization. Without this financial aid the Committee would not be able to carry on its work. By the 1940's and 1950's the AJC moved to advance the cause of freedom everywhere. It raised its sights fighting prejudice and malpractice in education, housing, and employment. Together with all liberals it worked to secure social and economic rights for America's blacks. As early as 1925 Marshall, in a way, had initiated this policy of concern for all who were experiencing disabilities when he and the Committee successfully challenged an Oregon law which denied Catholics the right to educate their children in parochial schools. Influenced by the American Jewish Congress the Committee, in the mid-twentieth century, began to work vigorously to repulse all encroachments on the traditional immunities accorded all citizens; it joined in almost every effort to maintain the liberal traditions first established by America's founding fathers.[11]

SUMMARY

The American Jewish Committee was a successful defense organization; that was obvious almost from the day it started. It was aggressive; it had good leaders in Sulzberger and Marshall. The latter was one of the most brilliant and devoted communal workers in all American Jewish history. The executive secretaries who were to carry on the day-to-day tasks were competent. The AJC fortunately had enough money to ensure the implementation of its plans; it was far more fortunate than the B'nai B'rith and the Board of Delegates which were always strapped for funds; the budget allowed Wolf's BDCRR was incredibly small. The leaders of the AJC and the notables who constituted its limited membership were men of wealth and influence. Thus it was that the State Department and the President listened when they spoke. Dedicated to capitalism and rugged individualism, the Republican Party elite deferred to Schiff; it feared him. It is not improbable that the Washington administration overestimated the power of the Committee but in its anti-Russian push this defense agency worked closely with the Board of Delegates and the B'nai B'rith. These latter two national associations had mass followings, thousands of members, important when the ballots were counted. Roosevelt, Taft, and Wilson, too, were well aware of this.

The B'nai B'rith never gave up its struggle to exert power in defense of Jewry; the Union, on the other hand, waited till Simon Wolf died and then moved to abolish its civil defense arm (1925). It limited its activities solely to the support of the Union and the Hebrew Union College; it had little money and it knew it could never hope to compete with Marshall's Committee and its dedicated adherents. Though the majority of all American Jews lived west of the Hudson, leadership in American Jewish life was securely fixed in New York City ever since the early twentieth century. Marshall and his executive board made sure that all parts of the country were represented in the organization's fourteen districts, in its members-at-large, and in the invited delegates from other organizations. Even in the 1920's social distinction between Germans and Russians had not yet been erased; the old-timers always controlled the board; there were many East Europeans on the membership rosters but they remained a minority despite the fact that in population they outnumbered the older element. Was the AJC "Jewish?" The very name is the answer; as twentieth century men with a sense of pride and security there was no need to elevate themselves, to hide behind the adjective "Hebrew"; they were Jews. The logo displayed on Committee publications documented its loyalty to the Jewish people though the members were committed anti-Zionists. They needed no Jewish state; the United States was the only country they wanted. Their logo was an American type of shield with thirteen stars and bars above which was a six-corner Jewish star: Americanism and

Judaism harmoniously united. Superimposed on this shield is a Hebrew inscription from 2 Samuel 10:12: "Let us be strong and resolute for the sake of our people." The second half of the verse was deliberately omitted: "and for the cities of our God," Palestine! The Committee was never assimilationist; it was always acculturational.

THE PASSPORT PROBLEM

One of the problems the American Jewish Committee faced was the refusal of the Russian state to accept the American Jew as an American citizen possessed of the same rights as Gentile Americans. American Jewish citizens, Russian-born or native American, who visited Russia were subject to the corpus of Russian laws imposed on Jews as long as they remained in that country. No Russian-born Jew was ever recognized as an American citizen; no native of the Muscovite empire had the right to alienate his citizenship. If a Russian Jew had fled the country to evade conscription he would have to serve if he returned even if he was a naturalized American. Relations between the United States and Russia were governed by a commercial treaty ratified in 1833. It specified that Americans "shall enjoy the same security and protection as natives." Jews, said the Russians, will therefore be treated—or mistreated—as native Jews. The United States contended that an immigrant can abandon his original citizenship and that all American citizens, even if Russian-born, are entitled to complete equality wherever they went; there are no distinctions in citizenship in the United States; all are equal and must be so treated when they visit Russia. Washington never abandoned this position; the Russians never made concessions, hence an impasse. It was not resolved till 1917 when the Romanovs were driven off the throne and a liberal state was established.

The occasional American Jewish citizen of Russian origin who ventured to return home flirted with danger. When Bernard Bernstein went back in 1864 to visit his parents the Russians arrested him because he had evaded military service. The Rosenstraus brothers, Theodore and Herman, were not allowed to buy land in areas restricted to Christians (1879); Henry Pinkos was driven out of St. Petersburg (1879). The Rosenstraus affair moved their Manhattan congressman, Samuel S. Cox, to offer a resolution in the House of Representatives praying that the treaty be amended to assure Jews of equal rights when doing business in Russia. After the Pinkos expulsion the American minister in St. Petersburg was instructed by President Hayes's Secretary of State to tell the Russians that all Americans regardless of religion must be treated equally. The 1881 violence in Russia impelled many to emigrate. As in the past, when naturalized Jewish citizens returned to Russia they ran into trouble if they attempted to exercise their rights as Americans. Congressman Cox continued to introduce resolutions protesting the mistreatment of Jews in Russia on humanitarian grounds. These resolutions were politically motivated; Jews in New York and in other cities were becoming numerically important. The Secretary of State under Garfield, as under Hayes, protested to the Russians when the privileges of American Jewish citizens were restricted. President Arthur found it necessary at the time of his annual messages, 1881-1883, to remind the world and the Russians that the rights of all Americans—he meant Jews—must be respected. Isaac M. Wise in his *American Israelite* wanted more drastic action against the Russians. Neither Wise's fulminating nor Congressman Cox's resolution was effective.[12]

When the Romanov, Alexander III, expelled thousands of Jews from Moscow in the early 1890's, American Jewry was shocked. Because of Russia's inhumanity Americans, Jews and Gentiles, talked of terminating the treaty of commerce. An Ohio congressman, James Irvine Dungan, offered a resolution in 1892 that diplomatic relations with Russia be severed. This sharp attack on the Romanov empire is difficult to explain. Dungan represented an Ohio area that sheltered very few Jews. His intercession on behalf of Jewry is reminiscent of the action taken by Thomas Kennedy in Maryland in 1818. Kennedy, a state legislator, then took the lead in pleading for the complete emancipation of Maryland Jewry; there were very few if any Jews in the county in which he lived. Republicans and Democrats incorporated anti-Russian Jewish planks in their political platforms; resolutions were again introduced in the House and the Senate attacking the Muscovite government; in his 1891 message President Harrison paid high tribute to the Jews and protested against the anti-Semitism—his word—that forced Jews to immigrate to the United States. The newcomers threatened to flood the American labor market, said the president; we are remonstrating on commercial and humanitarian grounds. Cleveland too —this was in 1895—complained that Russian consuls in the United States were interrogating citizens, Jews, as to their religious faith and denying them entry to Russia. This, said the president, was an obnoxious invasion of American territorial jurisdiction. The president's patience was wearing thin. He had close Jewish friends; one of them was Isidor Straus of Macy's department store. Straus, who had been elected to Congress in 1894, was one of the several congressmen who protested the Muscovites's refusal to honor American passports when carried by Jews.

Another Jewish congressional protestant was Isidor Rayner (1880-1912) of Maryland. In his resolution he demanded rights for American Jewish citizens and if this was refused then let the president denounce the treaties of commerce and extradition. Representative John F. Fitzgerald of Boston—the grandfather of the later President John F. Kennedy—also used the word "demand" when he sought equal rights for Hebrew Americans who visited Russia. Later, in 1911, Rayner, now a United States senator, was to ask for abrogation of the treaty. This Maryland Jew, a distinguished lawyer, had also served Maryland as an attorney general and had fought for the rights of blacks. William Jennings Bryan once said that the senator was presidential material. Rayner married out of the faith; his wife reared her child as a Christian and saw to it on her husband's death that the funeral service was conducted by Gentile clergymen. Memorializing the late senator the chaplain in the House spoke of "everlasting life in a risen and glorified Christ." Though no synagoggoer the senator was a member of Congregation Har Sinai in Baltimore, the liberal synagog which his father had helped establish.

One naive American who found himself in the toils of the Russians was John Ginzberg of Glasgow, Montana, a bustling town on the Upper Missouri. As a teenager Ginzberg had fled from Russia and made the mistake of going back. The Russians clapped him in jail and kept him there for two years, 1894-1896; the American minister in St. Petersburg made clucking sounds of sympathy. Far more helpful was the cash which the Christians of Glasgow sent. Without the money to leave he would have been dispatched to Siberia. The year Ginzberg was arrested, 1894, Rabbi Joseph Krauskopf, a notable American rabbi, succeeded in entering Russia; the Russians made an exception in the case of this Jew and permitted him to travel about. In an interview which the minister of finance granted him Krauskopf informed the Russian official that the American labor market could not absorb the Jews who were emigrating. The solution for this problem, said the rabbi, was colonizing the Russians. Let the government give the Jews land. Two years after he returned Krauskopf opened the National Farm School at Doylestown, Pennsylvania. Gentiles as well as Jews were welcomed; Krauskopf was an ecumenical humanitarian.[13]

The American people in the first decade of the twentieth century continued to turn away from the Russians; the mob attacks and killings that proceeded almost uninterruptedly in 1903-1905 shocked them. Though compelled for a brief period in 1905 to genuflect in the direction of liberalism the Russian bureaucrats speedily returned to their wonted ways; absolutism was again regnant. This intransigence aroused American and Jewish leaders. A New York City Jewish congressman patiently offered resolutions asking that the old treaty be renegotiated (1902, 1909); the Union of American Hebrew Congregations wanted it terminated; the political parties in their quadrennial platforms repeated their pious pro-Jewish platitudes (1904, 1908); Roosevelt in his 1904 annual message said forthrightly that it was the duty of the American people to protest crimes against humanity. He had the Kishinev massacre in mind. The following year he wrote to Witte, the Russian peacemaker, and asked him to permit reputable American Jews to visit his country. As early as 1901 Roosevelt's state department had told America's Jews that they could not hope to enter Russia; in 1907, Secretary of State Elihu Root issued a circular informing them that he would issue no passports for Russian travel unless the Russians first gave permission. This warning was tantamount to an acquiescence in the Russian position; it implied that the American Jews were second-class citizens. America's Christians could enter Russia; American Jews, no! Louis Marshall and Edward Lauterbach, well-known New York lawyers and communal workers, compelled Root to withdraw the circular. The secretary was no anti-Jew; there was little he could do; the circular was a confession of impotence.

It was now that Marshall told Root the story of Louis J. Horowitz, the Polish Jew who in a brief span of years had succeeded in becoming the virtual head of one of the largest building contractors in the United States, if not the world. Horowitz, who had just finished the new railroad station in Washington, would now like to visit his Russia-Polish homeland and while there talk to the government about building a similar railroad depot in St. Petersburg. The Russian embassy in Washington refused to visé his passport. Delegations of old-line Jews met with Roosevelt's successor Taft and appealed to him to take action on the violations of the treaty. The East Europeans sent their own leaders to the president, the editor of the *Jewish Daily News* and the publisher of the *Morning Journal*. These two Yiddish papers exerted great influence on the Jews of the Lower East Side. Taft listened patiently, promised to do what he could, but did nothing. The American presidents in the 1850's would not terminate the treaty with the Swiss; America's exports were at stake; it was the same motivation that hamstrung Taft in the early 1900's; he was dedicated to the furtherance of American business; Russia was a good customer. All through this period the Romanovs remained adamant. Any concession to liberalism would threaten the very foundations of the autocratic state.[14]

Russia's wariness in allowing Jews to cross her borders applied of course to all of Europe's Jews. Georg Morris Cohen Brandes (1842-1927), a very distinguished Danish litterateur, was also refused a visa to enter Russia; he was a notorious liberal. His answer was to write a story, "The Confession of the Parents." Eager to visit the land of the Romanovs, St. Peter and his fellow apostles, all Jews, applied for permission to cross the Russian border; they were denied the right. (The capital of Russia was named after St. Peter.) Disappointed Peter returned to Heaven and related his experience to Jesus. Thereupon God's only begotten son decided to go down to earth and see what the Russians were doing. He saw a consul and asked that Maria Magdalena be given the right to enter the country. The answer was she could come in if she was willing to ply her old profession as a prostitute but if she enrolled in a school as a student she would be expelled. Then when Jesus asked that he himself be permitted to enter he was asked if he was Jewish. He admitted he was not a good traditional Jew but could not deny that his parents were Jewish; thereupon permission was denied him. Unhappy with the decision of the minor bureaucrats, Jesus made it his business to enter the office of the Minister of the Interior. Recognizing Jesus at once the Minister told him that he was an undesirable person; Russia wanted no agitators. Ringing a bell the cabinet officer summoned the police, ordered that Jesus be detained and severely lashed. Then the Minister himself left to attend religious services in the cathedral.[15]

By 1910 at the latest most Jewish notables were ready to believe that the administration in Washington would take no drastic action to induce the Russians to respect an American passport when carried by a Jew. Some Jewish and Gentile leaders had been convinced for decades that the only recourse left the United States was abrogation of the treaties. By 1908 Judge Sulzberger, president of the American Jewish Committee, had made up his mind that both the commercial and the extradition treaties would have to go. Jews feared that under the extradition agreement political refugees would be turned over to the Russians. Actually Washington never returned any Jew to Russia under the terms of this instrument. America's important Jews had been patient for years with the different presidents. Most of these Jewish worthies were Republicans and had no desire to push the Republican presidents too hard. This was particularly true of Simon Wolf. Finally, however, these Jewish notables made up their mind to move from diplomacy to battle. The public challenge was staged at a convention of the Union of American Hebrew Congregations in New York in January, 1911. The Speaker, Louis Marshall, reviewed the history of the struggle and asked the convention to go on record asking for abrogation of the disputed treaty; the attitude of the czarist bureaucrats was an insult to all Americans. His resolution was immediately adopted. The administration was alarmed; Taft expected to run for reelection. The UAHC represented wealth and thousands of voters. On February 15 nine distinguished American Jews were asked to lunch at the White House to confer with Taft. American Jewish Committee, UAHC, and B'nai B'rith representatives were there in force. These were America's elite Hebrews.

At the meeting the President read a prepared statement. The Jews were disappointed. They had come to argue their point of view and were now faced with what seemed to be a fait accompli. Taft told them that the treaty had been in force for decades; let it alone; it is too late to change it. Nothing can be done with the Russians. There are important financial and commercial interests at stake; why jeopardize them. He was

President of all the Americans and must look after their interests. At this point the implication was clear; he could not concern himself too much with the needs of one particular group. This was dollar diplomacy. Taft intimated that if the treaty was abrogated the Russians might even unleash pogroms. Some of the Jews back in Russia, he had heard, were revolutionaries. The President was inept, a fumbling politician but he was not anti-Jewish. He realized full well the abuse to which the Jews in Russia were subject. He was a Unitarian, a religious liberal; he had listened to Isaac Mayer Wise when he exchanged pulpits with the local Unitarian minister in Cincinnati. Later he would not hesitate to veto a literacy bill which would strike hard at incoming Russian Jews. Indeed in the Progressive Age, then in full swing, he was a liberal of sorts. He told the listening delegation that he was not moved by mercenary motives but non possumus; abrogation would accomplish nothing.

In a way he was right; the Russians were obdurate. His audience was unhappy; Schiff was intransigent; diplomatic overtures were useless; the honor of the nation required the termination of the treaty. In the Civil War, he said, we did not consider the financial cost; we were fighting for the right! The nine Jews who were present that February day were not merely fighting for their right as Americans to visit Russia; they were fighting for their status as first-class—not second-class—citizens. You have failed us, said Schiff to the President; we are now going directly to the American people who are certain to do us justice. When the banker left he did not offer his hand to the President nor did the President extend his. Bernhard Bettmann of the Union of American Hebrew Congregations muttered as they left; "Wir sind in golus." "We are in exile." His meaning was clear. What can we do? Jews have always taken a beating; that was the philosophy of resignation, of acquiescence. The feisty undersized Schiff's response was different: "This means war." In a letter to the President written a few days later Schiff reproached him. You have ignored your personal and party pledge to do something effective. Even an American Jewish ambassador—he had Oscar Straus in mind—could not secure permission to enter Russia. Schiff volunteered to help finance a campaign to secure the termination of the treaty.

Thus the battle was joined February 16, 1911. The Democrats who had been out of office in Washington since 1897 were determined to make hay while the sun shone; they attacked the Republicans for doing nothing; Jewish notables continued to appear at the White House to argue with the President; the Hearst papers thundered; Jewish delegations met with their congressmen; petitions to Congress poured in from all sides; there were eighty alone from Jewish organizations in Massachusetts. American citizens, non-Jews mostly, made this their fight. Chambers of Commerce protested; so did the American Federation of Labor.

For once Samuel Gompers, the Jew, was on the side of the angels. Church federations, the Quakers, and the Episcopal diocese of southern Ohio raised their voices. These Episcopalians were based in Cincinnati, Taft's home town. Many Cincinnatians resented him because he was a Unitarian; it was questionable if he was even a Christian. In Scranton Christian Russians, Poles, and Lithuanians assembled together and passed a resolution asking for abrogation. No one appeared at the meeting of the House Committee on Foreign Affairs to defend Russia. A huge mass meeting in New York City on December 6 listened to Governor Wood-row Wilson of New Jersey, William Randolph Hearst, and James Beauchamp ("Champ") Clark, the Speaker of the House. On December 13, 1911, Representative William Sulzer of New York City offered a resolution asking that the treaty be abrogated; the vote was 300 to 1, but there were 87 abstentions. When the resolution was being considered the New York Jewish congressmen, Henry M. Goldfogle and Jefferson Monroe Levy, were in the chair. (Levy was a kinsman of "Commodore" Uriah P. Levy.)

When it was obvious that the Senate was about to pass a similar resolution, Taft rushed to save what he could. He instructed the ambassador in St. Petersburg to inform the Russians that he intended to give notice of abrogation; the treaty was no longer responsive to the needs of the United States, he said. Then after he had informed the Russians, and the American people knew what he had in mind, Taft asked the Senate to approve his recommendation to terminate. The Senate approved unanimously; the House moved immediately to adopt the Senate's version of the resolution. The Socialist representative from Milwaukee, Victor L. Berger, a Jew, asked his fellow congressmen to recommend the cancellation of the extradition treaty; they rejected the suggestion. When Taft signed the joint resolution he gave the pen to Adolf Kraus, the head of B'nai B'rith, and a great admirer of the President. Taking the initiative the President had turned defeat into victory. Russia had failed to honor an American passport when carried by an American Jewish citizen; it had discriminated against Americans because of their religion! When the Republican and Democratic party delegates assembled in 1912 they hammered away at platforms which declared piously that they would tolerate no discrimination against Americans because of their faith. On January 6, 1913, the B'nai B'rith gave Taft a gold medal because he more than any other individual had furthered the welfare of Jewry. For the B'nai B'rith he was a moral hero. He had emerged from a political cloaca smelling like a rose.[16]

THE SIGNIFICANCE OF THE NOTICE OF ABROGATION

What did the notice of abrogation mean to the Russians? The liberals in that country who were fighting for a constitutional regime were encouraged; it was a blow to autocracy. The agitation to nullify the 1832 treaty did nothing to improve Russia's image in this country. Russia was in bad odor in the United States for many decades; she was associated with brutality. The murders of Jews in 1903 and 1905, the invasion of Persia in 1911 and the concomitant brutality only served to heighten this impression. Russian exports to America were not large; the needed imports from the United States, sewing machines and agricultural machinery, would still continue to be shipped. Thus the imminent abrogation was apparently of little concern to the Moscovites. They were convinced that they could not afford to accord equality to visiting American Jewish citizens; this might well disturb the millions of deprived Jews in the country. Jacob Schiff and some of his confreres were convinced, too, that if American Jews were given equality in the Romanov empire it would be difficult to deny equal rights to the country's second-class Jewish citizens.

One thing is certain: the Russian authorities wanted and made no change. In no sense did the nullification of the treaty help the Jewries of Russia or America; in this respect Taft was right. Extremists in Russia now reminded the Americans of their mistreatment of the Negroes; the pot had no right to call the kettle black. Russian reactionaries had no trouble explaining the drama of 1911; the Jewish bankers ruled the United States; the 1905 Russian revolution was not inspired by misgovernment; it was the result of a Jewish plot. This conspiracy theory had been gestating in Russia since the late nineteenth century. It is by no means improbable that the Russian authorities encouraged the trial of Mendel Beilis in 1911 to prove to the world that the Jews were horrible and did not deserve to be treated as normal human beings. Undeterred by public opinion in the United States, or anywhere else, the czarist reaction continued. The result was that emigration to America mounted into the tens of thousands annually. Alarmed by this inrush of the multitudes Congress closed the portals to America in the 1920's. The Jewish masses were compelled to remain penned up till the Germans in the 1940's murdered them by the millions. This was the final solution. American Jewry won a battle in 1911 but in the end East European Jewry perished. The position of the Polish and Russian Jews was not improved. One is tempted to say that if the treaty fight was waged to help, to save Jews, the Russian autocrats emerged victorious. History operated in weird ways to contrive its own horrors.

Nullifying the 1832 treaty was the work of the American people not the Jews. In this instance the country had not rushed to the defense of

Jews nor was it concerned about human rights; the self-esteem of Americans as Americans was at stake. It was this that prompted the American masses and the Congress to force the President to take action. In many instances the protest meetings throughout the country were led if not organized by Gentiles. No one can doubt that the people, the press, the political parties, and even the Catholic and Protestant churches had turned against the Romanov state. Russia barred Catholic priests and Protestant missionaries as well as American Jews. The young Cincinnati seminarian, Jacob R. Marcus, well recalls attending a local mass meeting where a Catholic priest speaking classical Hebrew called upon God to blot out the Russians. The presidents and their secretaries of state were not hostile to Jews; some were sympathetic, genuinely so, yet these men in authority rarely transgressed the boundaries of proper diplomatic behavior. Russian sovereignty and law were deemed inviolable; American presidents, cabinet officials, and most embassy personnel wanted Russia to recognize the citizenship of American Jews; they understood American Jewish misgivings; many had sympathy for the plight of the Russian Jewish masses but they hesitated to take drastic diplomatic action. And there is this irony: while America as a whole turned against the Russian government because of its cruelty to its Jews and its refusal to recognize the sanctity of the American passport yet, at the same time, most Americans were pushing hard for anti-immigration legislation that would close this country as a haven and asylum for the poor and oppressed Jews of Eastern Europe.

And what did abrogation do for the American Jew? The discerning Jew of that day would have answered that the problem was America's not the Jews. America had been insulted; invalidating the treaty was therefore a logical step for the American authorities. The Jews fought because their status as Americans, as citizens, was at stake. It is true that they relished the chance to strike out at oppressors; it was an opportunity rarely accorded them. Marshall was eager for battle toward the end; he wanted to prove that "we no longer possess the cringing Ghetto spirit"; he wanted to show the world that the Jews of the United States were respected. No one can question that the victory was important for Jewish self-esteem, certainly in this country and probably in the Jewries of Europe. The victory taught Jews that they had political power; they enjoyed employing it. There were almost 2,000,000 of them in the country in 1911; about 900,000 were in New York City; they could elect congressmen who would make their voices heard. It is true, as said before, that it was the American people who rose in righteous anger but it is equally true that the Jews triggered the uprising which forced the administration to take action. (It was more than the Jews were able to do under Franklin D. Roosevelt when the lives of millions of European Jews were at stake in Europe, but then Roosevelt was shrewder than the ponderous Taft.)

American Jewry in 1911 was far more successful in influencing the state than the national Jewish organizations of Germany, France, and England. These European Jewish communities were plagued with the same problem of having their passports ignored by the Muscovites. England and France were allied with Russia; the national governments therefore refused to press the Russians; they were girding their loins to crush the Germans who were reaching out for world power. France would certainly not quarrel with the Russians and demand rights for French Jewish citizens. Russia owed the French 10,000,000,000 francs. The world could not but be impressed that America had dared to denounce a treaty with a great power because the passports of American Jewish citizens had been disregarded. One suspects that the status of American Jewry worldwide was enhanced. The success achieved here proved to the Jewish world that from now on it would have to reckon with American Jewry. Although some Jews had not wanted to confront Washington on the issue of the treaty, most had been determined to fight. The struggle brought unity to American Jewry; the national organizations, usually at loggerheads, joined together; the crisis created a sense of community.[17]

CHAPTER NINETEEN

THE GHETTO: PROBLEMS AND SOLUTIONS

CRIME

In 1908 Louis Marshall was disturbed by an article which appeared in the September issue of the *North American Review*. In a brutally frank statement New York's police commissioner, General Theodore A. Bingham, had written that though the Jews were only about 25 percent of the population they committed about 50 percent of the town's crime. These malefactors, Russian Hebrews, brought up their children to lives of crime; 40 percent of the boys in the House of Refuge were Jewish; 37 percent of the youngsters arraigned in the children's courts were Jews; their truancy rate was the highest; some of these children started their life of crime when they were but ten years of age. New York's Jews were outraged by these accusations. The sensational Yiddish papers had a field day demanding Bingham's resignation. These journals screamed because they knew that the Uptown Jewish leaders would step up and do something effective. New York's Jews had crossed swords with Bingham before. In 1907 he had refused to let the Jewish police take a day off to attend services on Yom Kippur, the holiest day of the year. A compromise, however, was effected: New York's Jewish stalwarts were assigned to synagogs where they could both work and pray. Actually Bingham was no anti-Semite; his article in the *North American Review* was directed primarily against Italians. The Italians were fair game. In the 1890's the good citizens of Louisiana had lynched nineteen Italians. Bingham, a West Point graduate who specialized in engineering, nursed the typical prejudices which characterized a host of Anglo-Saxon Protestants. Like General U. S. Grant, Bingham had his anti-Jewish stereotypes: Jews were adverse to physical labor and prone to crime; they were anarchists and arsonists, burglars and pickpockets; some of their women were prostitutes. His police harassed Jews who violated the Sunday closing laws, yet when Julia Richman, the intolerant educator, asked Bingham to move against the Jewish pushcart peddlers who flouted the town's ordinances he told her that "they have to make a living." Marshall went to work quietly and succeeded in getting a full retraction—which Marshall probably wrote—in the November issue of the *Review*.

Were the Jews as evil as Commissioner Bingham described them? The Jews certainly did not think so; they enjoyed the delusion that Jews rarely produced scamps; the Jewish home made criminality improbable. This they believed. Actually Jews had always had a goodly share of criminals. For over a thousand years they had suffered oppression in Europe, Asia, North Africa; for most of this period they had lived impoverished in slums; poverty bred crime. There are volumes written on the subject of thieves' argot; Hebrew and Yiddish words and phrases play their part in this picaresque thesaurus. What was true of Europe is true, to a degree, of America. There were Jewish rogues here too. In 1727 Moses Sussman was hanged for theft in New York on charges brought by a fellow Jew. "Jewish" transports were not unknown in the colonies; these were criminals who were sent from London to serve out their terms here as indentured servants. There was no time in the nineteenth century when there were no Jewish criminals; to be sure their crime rate was low. A sensational case in the 1870's was that of Pesach N. Rubenstein, a pious New York Jew who was accused of murdering his cousin Sarah Alexander. In a trial where prejudice may well have played its part he was found guilty, but before he was executed he committed suicide (1875). After his death a chapbook was published treating in lurid terms of the life and career of this man. It was written by a Jew. In 1892 Alexander Berkman attempted to assassinate Henry Clay Frick. An assassin is a criminal even if, like Berkman, an anarchist, an idealist if you will, he resorted to violence to reach what he believed to be humanitarian goals. In this decade of the 1890's the East Side, where Berkman had lived and plotted, was referred to as a nursery for crime. That it was; in this slum crime and criminals flourished.[1]

In 1908, months before Bingham made his accusation, many of New York's Jews, both Uptown "Germans" and Downtown "Russians," were fully aware that they were faced with a problem of criminality in the ghetto. Edward Lauterbach, the president of the Federation of Jewish Organizations, had already started collecting statistics on Jews who had been brought before the Court of General Sessions in 1907. The data he collected demonstrated that proportionately New York's Jews had fewer criminals than the non-Jews. This was true, too, of the benign minor violations that were within the jurisdiction of the Magistrate's Court. Jews were among the chief violators of the city's ordinances; they were petty shopkeepers who kept their stores open on Sundays or peddlers who hawked their wares on the Lord's Day; they were not criminals; their offenses were not serious. A group of small businessmen organized themselves in Hartford in 1909 as the Hebrews' Peddlers Association to help one another when cited by the courts. But American Jews never lacked for hardened criminals and serious crime. "Sheeney Mike," Michael Kurtz, was a notorious burglar with a national reputation; a Mrs. Mandelbaum was well known in the trade and in the police precincts as a receiver of stolen goods. Picking pockets was a Jewish specialty; there were in fact few areas of crime in which Jews were not represented. They were strikebreakers and horse poisoners. In those pre-automobile days deliveries were made by horse and dray. Threats of poisoning the horses became a source of extortion which was not countered until the owners organized as the East Side Horse Owners' Protective Association. One of the commonest accusations hurled at the ghetto Jews in the late nineteenth century was that they were arsonists; some were. The same accusation had been directed against the German Jews in the 1860's when many insurance companies, for a time, refused to issue policies to Jewish businessmen.

Gambling was a centuries-old Jewish vice; the Italian Jews were addicts. Cardplaying characterized Jewish social life from the earliest days; eighteenth-century Newport Jews enjoyed their whist and their glass of wine. Professional gambling in the United States was a field which many Jews cultivated. In 1912 Herman Rosenthal, a gambler, was assassinated by order of Lt. Charles Becker, a New York City police officer. Rosenthal and Becker were partners and it was feared that the gambler was about to betray the policeman; practically all the men involved in the Rosenthal-Becker affair were Jews. Arnold Rothstein of New York, also a gambler, operated on a larger scale. He was suspected of having "fixed" a World Series baseball game in Chicago in 1919. His aide in this crooked scheme was said to have been Abe Attell, one of the world's greatest boxers; he was known as "The Little Hebrew." There was no proof, however, that these two men were responsible for bribing the players. When the Volstead Act and the Prohibition amendment became law Rothstein turned to bootlegging on a large scale. He was interested in nightclubs, prostitution, horse racing; he was a large-scale crime entrepreneur who reaped his reward; he was assassinated in 1928.

Jews bragged that they gave birth to no killers. It was a boast that could not be sustained, for even in 1920's there was a crop of brutal gangsters on the East Side; they became more numerous in later decades when, as the popularly denominated Murder, Inc., they killed substantial numbers of criminal competitors. A typical gangster of that day was Louis ("Lepke") Buchalter (1897-1944), a member of a large respectable family. He began life as a juvenile delinquent, probably after his father's death. Young Buchalter, a thief, was sent to a reformatory and on the expiration of his term came out to spend the rest of his life as a criminal. He worked as a mobster for unions and employers, robbed lofts, extorted funds from hapless furriers, blackmailed manufacturers with threats of strikes through the unions he controlled, and distributed narcotics on a large scale. From the 1920's on Lepke Buchalter was a widely known feared criminal. He lived well in his beautiful apartment on Central Park West until he was electrocuted for murder on March 4, 1944.[2]

In general the Jews were well behaved. In 1908, the year Bingham hurled his accusations, there were about 800,000 Jews in New York City. In such a large group there were bound to be crime and criminals, potential Lepkes. It is imperative that one constantly bear in mind that a very substantial number of all New York's Jews lived on the East Side, a slum area where crime flourished. The East Side had been a zone of physical and moral deterioration since the middle nineteenth century, long before the Russians and Poles began arriving in such substantial numbers. New York's Jewish criminals were guilty of gainful offenses; they turned to gambling, forgery, fraud, larceny, blackmail, extortion. There were frequent violations of municipal ordinances. The age in which the newcomers lived, 1870-1920, saw the emergence of great corporations and unconscionable speculators who exploited the American people on a grand scale robbing them of hundreds of millions of dollars. They managed to stay out of jail; Jewish criminals, not so fortunate, found themselves locked up in the Tombs. Alcoholism played little part in inciting Jews to misdeeds unlike the Irish and some other immigrants. Drink was not a Jewish problem then. That generation was abstemious. Alcoholics like Napthali Herz Imber, the Hebrew poet, were few. Liquor, however, assumed an important role in Jewish criminality in 1920 when prohibition was in full force. Many Jews turned to bootlegging; even some religious functionaries found it profitable to sell "sacramental" wine. The indignant Reform rabbinate maintained that grape juice was as good as wine when the Sabbath was ushered in on Friday eve.

In proportion to their population few Jews were involved in crimes of violence although the absolute numbers of felons often dismayed Jewry. It was small comfort when statisticians told them that, proportionately, there were fewer Jews than Gentiles in the jails and prisons; the crime rate among the Children of Israel was less than that of America's general population. Concerned about Jews behind bars the New York Jewish community saw to it that they were visited by chaplains ever since the 1890's. In the early 1900's the Jewish Protectory and Aid Society was established. Its job was to help rehabilitate juvenile delinquents. The National Council of Jewish Women looked after incarcerated females. Some malefactors scoffed at rehabilitation; they persisted in living a life of crime. Israel Schwartzberg is an interesting example. He was a gambler who specialized in "fixing" basketball games. While in jail he became a brilliant student of criminal law and when he emerged he lectured to lawyers and others displaying his expertise. He once made the remark that "when I was born you either died in the electric chair or you became a judge. I was the happy medium." He may have neglected to tell his audiences that he served for fourteen years in penitentiaries. Mr. Schwartzberg exaggerated; very few East Side boys were electrocuted; not many became judges. The typical East European Jew, whether a denizen of a ghetto or the owner of a modest home in the hinterland, was a law-abiding citizen. He lived an uneventful life as a member of the lower middle class. The reason these immigrants—wherever they were found—were respectable citizens and stayed out of jail was that they cherished middle-class economic and religious values; they knew what was right and they hewed to the line.[3]

PROSTITUTION

Prostitution was one of the many problems faced by Jewish immigrants; indeed it was a problem for all Americans. An enterprising citizen in New Orleans published a guidebook to the town's bordellos. Throughout the country committees and commissions were appointed to investigate prostitution; there was a large literature on the subject. After 1900 legislation was passed by federal and local authorities to abolish the trade. After the reformers closed the red-light districts whores took to the streets reinforced by protective pimps, enterprising procurers, and greedy landlords. This scourge was exacerbated because almost everywhere it was tied in with gambling, political corruption, venal police, and other assorted forms of criminality. In the early 1900's Jewish leaders like Schiff and Professor E. R. A. Seligman of Columbia helped organize the Committee of Fifteen to fight Tammany which tolerated this social plague.

When faced with the reality that there were unchaste Jewish women, Jews were unhappy. American Jewry had always insisted that the Jewish home was immaculate, glorying in this myth. But the facts were incontrovertible. In one street on the Lower East Side a house of prostitution (Jewish?) was flanked by a synagog and a public school. There were Jewish prostitutes, madams, and bordello owners. There were enough Jews in the business to have a benefit society of their own; Jewish burial was important, but no respectable mutual-aid society would accept men or women who were in the industry. It was no consolation to Jews who bragged of the beautiful Jewish traditional home that all American ethnics had their share of harlots. Jews wanted no part of the commerce; they were concerned about their image in the American world; any identification with prostitutes was bad. What they sedulously failed to recognize was that the profession was as old as the Bible and the patriarchs (Gen. 38:15). Nor were they aware of the fact that prostitution was a business in which Jews were found in Europe, South Africa, South America, and in Moslem lands, too.

For several decades white slavery distressed Jewish communal workers not only in New York City but in every major city and even in some smaller places. Very few prostitutes had come to this country from Eastern Europe; most had been recruited here; they were plying their trade in the streets of New York in the 1880's, if not earlier. The ghetto red-light district was on Allen Street. By the early 1920's prostitution by Jews and for Jews was in full swing; Jewish whores were relatively numerous. Prominent among them was Polly Adler, author of the autobiography, *A House is Not a Home.* Polly had been raped by her shop foreman and when she was rejected by her kin she turned to prostitution and ultimately to the management of a "house." Apparently she was a successful madam. The Hertzes seemed to have been more enterprising. Led by the notorious Rosie Hertz her entire family devoted itself to the business, running a string of brothels on the East Side. Rosie and some of the prostitutes were religiously observant; religion had its consolations; there were whores who found comfort and security in the practice of their faith. Researchers tell us that there were eighteen Jewish "houses" on the East Side and numerous "hotels" that served as places of assignation. Pittsburgh's Adolph Edlis, a businessman who served in the state legislature, pushed through a bill which sought to curb prostitution in the Hill District, the town's ghetto.

National Jewish organizations were very much concerned about Jewish participation in this traffic. The Council of Jewish Women met ships at the docks to protect young women from the advances of procurers; the B'nai B'rith carried on an active campaign throughout the United States to drive Jews out of this ugly business. During World War I when more work opportunities opened for women the rate of Jewish prostitution seems to have declined. Why were there Jewish prostitutes? What brought them into this profession? Some were seduced in the dance halls; the procurers offered them marriage; newcomers were fair game; a few were coerced. In all probability a pressing cause was poverty; the panic of 1893 drove girls out on to the streets. Some girls were eager to get away from unhappy homes; others wanted to improve themselves financially; most Jewish women who plied this trade went into it voluntarily.[4]

DESERTION

Desertion was much more of a problem for Jews than prostitution; it was also a problem for the American people in general. As early as 1848 Congregation Bnai Jeshurun of New York City gave money to a woman to move on to Canada to search out her absconding husband. By 1900 there were many Jewish broken homes. In 1905, of the 10,000 applicants for relief at New York's United Hebrew Charity 2,000 were women whose husbands had left them. In 1909, 11 percent of the Jewish charity cases in Chicago concerned women whose husbands had run away; in Baltimore the figure was even higher, 16 percent. By 1912 the National Desertion Bureau with headquarters in New York City reported that it had 22,000 cases in its files. Alarming as these numbers are there were still more two-parent families among Jews than among non-Jews; the Jewish rate of desertion was lower than that among others. One suspects that desertion was a social disease which Jews would have liked to have ignored; as late as 1969, at least one-third of all middle-class Americans who had left their families were Jews.

American Jewry in the early twentieth century was determined to cope with this problem. The New Yorkers moved vigorously to make desertion a felony. The East Europeans did what they could to halt this plague. The *Forward*, for instance, in its Gallery of Missing Husbands carried the pictures and biographical details of deserters and asked for information. The *Forward* and other Yiddish papers reached out to all corners of the country. The data for these dossiers had been assembled by the National Desertion Bureau which had been established in 1911; it was in touch with about seventy Jewish communities; there was really no place for a Jew to hide out. In many instances the Bureau was successful; it threatened the runaways with prosecution and pitiless publicity. Its goal, however, was not punishment but reconciliation and support for the wife and children. It is worthy of note that the National Desertion Bureau deliberately omitted the adjective "Jewish" from its name; it was embarrassed. Why did husbands leave home? Desertion was the poor man's divorce. Many men fled because they had no jobs. Some who loved their families left hoping the charities would then support the wife and children. When the charities sensed that this was the cause they refused to succor those left behind thus forcing the concerned father to return. An unhappy home induced some men to leave; often the husband was Americanized; the wife—a later arrival—was still immured in her Russian village way of life. It is curious but true that one of the chief causes for desertion was "love"; the husband was enamored of another woman.[5]

JUVENILE DELINQUENCY

Along with desertion juvenile delinquency was a serious problem for American Jewish communities. There was no town of any size in the United States where the local Jewry was exempt from this challenge. In all probability the delinquency rate was low in the smaller places, certainly for girls; social controls were all powerful. It was tragic that some of the big city delinquents blossomed out as gangsters, even murderers. Juvenile delinquency struck home; the future lay with the children. Most of the boys and girls who ran afoul of the law were native-born children of foreign-born parents. New York's East Side was to cope with the misdeeds of its youngsters as early as the 1880's; the problem was worrisome in the 1890's. A Boston Yiddish writer summed it up bitterly and brilliantly: "Father plays cards; mother amuses herself with the boarders; daughter spends her time in the dance halls; sonny sits in jail."

The statistics of delinquency for the first decades of the twentieth century are awesome. About sixty Jewish boys were arraigned every month in Chicago; the charges were larceny, holdups, gang warfare. In New York for the years 1907-1929, over 57,000 Jewish offenders were brought into court; this was about 21 percent of all who were arrested. In 1909, 30 percent of all youngsters charged were Jews; Bingham exaggerated when he wrote his article for the *North American Review* but he knew, and responsible Jewish leaders knew, that juvenile delinquency was a very real problem. Baltimore was of course a smaller town than New York but even there 965 young offenders came to the attention of the Jewish social agencies from 1910 to 1915. Many of the charges were serious. In 1917 there was a record of 1,046 youngsters who were troublemakers. In 1903, 99 of the 1,450 inmates in New York's Elmira State Reformatory were Jews; 18 were of East European ancestry. Houses of Refuge for boys and girls sheltered sizable numbers of young Jewish offenders. By 1917 New York City's Jewry had eight agencies to make provisions for its delinquents; other scamps were jailed in public institutions. Around the year 1904 a New York Jewish chaplain maintained that delinquency among young Jews in New York City was lower than that in the general population. This may well be true. It is also true that many of the violations with which youngsters were charged were of a benign nature; no moral turpitude was involved; violations of the child labor laws were frequent. All this was small comfort to the Jewish community. Among the troublemakers with a future all his own was young Arthur Flegenheimer (1902-1935); he grew up in the Bronx. His parents were German, not East European. The father, a glazier, deserted his family; his mother was compelled to take in washing. Arthur took to the streets where he sold papers, worked in a printing shop, and developed some skills as a roofer. When still a teenager he was arrested for larceny; society sent him to a reformatory from which he emerged as a gangster. He took the name Dutch Schultz. Arthur was a brilliant businessman; he built large criminal enterprises and achieved national notoriety as a labor racketeer, a gambler, a "numbers" entrepreneur, a bootlegger. Feuding with another Jewish gang was a fatal error for he was assassinated by a fellow Jew Arthur Workman; twenty-three years later Workman finally emerged from prison a free man. Dutch Schultz was but thirty-three years of age when he was killed; a pious member of an East Side psalm circle might have muttered to himself: "Bloody and deceitful men shall not live out half their days" (Ps. 55:24).

What made some young Jews turn to crime as a way of life? Every case is of course different but there are generalizations which are valid. Most important is the slum ambience; here there was an unholy alliance between politicians, police, and criminals. Unhappy broken Jewish homes, which were in part responsible for desertion and prostitution wrecked the lives of some youngsters; such homes were marked by poverty, parental conflict, the breakdown of discipline and traditional ethics. Two cultural social systems were at war with one another, American latitudinarianism and Eastern European authoritarianism. Boys were sent out on the streets to help keep the family afloat; streets could be nurseries of crime. Looking for attractive social activity youngsters loafed in pool rooms; the girls went to the dancing halls where they were exposed to the wiles of procurers. Some of the boys turned to thievery and violence.

Social workers, of course, were sure they had the solution to these problems. They harped on the importance of industrial training, on the need for settlement houses, on the value of clubs. Gymnasiums and athletics were rated high in their scale of essentials; ball parks and schools were helpful. Even the Central Conference of American Rabbis, which was slow to turn to social reform, could not ignore this problem. Three years after the Bingham affair the Conference appointed a Committee on Defectives, Dependents, Delinquents. More and more Jewish notables, both Uptown and Downtown, were convinced that a good Jewish education was the panacea for all juvenile social ills; a good student would make a proud Jew. Louis Marshall shared this conviction. This was a sanguine generation. It is a fact that cannot be gainsaid that many of these "delinquents" turned out to become solid citizens. Most of the ghetto Jews ultimately left the Lower East Side moving out to areas where they had better homes, a healthier environment. Economic conditions improved for many; delinquency tended to fade. A Denver offender did not end up in jail; he went to Harvard. One scapegrace was sui generis. This was Milton Mesirow (1899-1972). In 1917, teenage Milton was put away in a reformatory; he came out an unreconstructed social rebel; the name he now took was Mezz Mezzrow. Mezz bragged that he was a "voluntary Negro." It was not long before he became a notable jazz artist playing the clarinet and saxophone. One jaundiced critic said that he was no virtuoso; another was sure that he was the world's greatest musician. Mezz went his own way and in between leading jazz groups, recording albums, and peddling marijuana he vacationed in jails.

There can be no question, slums are bad, yet it is important to report that both in Philadelphia and New York—and probably in other towns too—Jews upgraded these areas of urban deterioration. When the immigrant Jews moved into Philadelphia's ghetto the Gentile criminals moved out; when the Russians and Polish Jews took over the Lower East Side brutal gangs and saloon keepers had to leave. It is amazing that despite the sobering statistics on juvenile delinquency and crime this East European Jewry, within the course of two generations at most, developed into one of the most affluent, intelligent, and prestigious groups of citizenry in all America. This is not filiopietistic bombast. This is a fact. Beaten down in Russia and Poland, Jewry could not make headway; here in free America Jews met the challenge of American opportunity.[6]

THE KEHILLAH

The attack by Police Commissioner Bingham frightened New York Jews: they were both angry and embarrassed. The charge that Jews were criminals was grist for the mills of the anti-immigration forces who were determined to keep out all East Europeans, Balkanites, and Italians. Many newcomers here were saving up to bring over wives, children, siblings, parents. Yet, despite their remonstrances, the ghetto Jews never fooled themselves; criminality was a grim reality. Marshall had handled the immediate problem by inducing Bingham to retract. This did not satisfy the ghetto leaders. They wanted an organization to tackle criminality, to help them cope with difficulties that confronted them on all sides. These remonstrants made one mistake; they confused organization with solution; they seemed to think that once they were organized all their problems would go away. They were not altogether wrong. The earlier settlers, the Germans, had pooled their interests successfully for decades; several national congeries had come into being and were doing effective work. The Russians and Poles had even established the Hebrew Immigrant and Sheltering Aid Society; it was moving along beautifully.

The newcomers did not wish to be dependent for help and advice on the American Jewish Committee; they resented the leadership of the old-timers; they wanted to stand on their own two feet. They were eager for an organization with leaders whom they would chose. In 1887 the Orthodox Rabbi Moses Weinberger in his *Jews and Judaism in New York* had appealed to the East Europeans to create a united community. That same year several of the city's traditional synagogs banded together to bring over a chief rabbi; a chief rabbinate would solve all problems! In 1888 the socialist-led labor unions created the United Hebrew Trades; in 1890, when the Romanovs began driving Jews out of Moscow, Philadelphia's Russians founded the Jewish Alliance of America. Toward the end of the century panicky Orthodox—led again by acculturated settlers—created a Union of Orthodox Congregations of the United States and Canada (1898); four years later the old-fashioned Yiddish-speaking Orthodox rabbis established the Union of Orthodox Rabbis of the United States. All this organizing for strength and influence was typically American. After the turn of the century there was talk of uniting East Side congregations and associations as the United Hebrew Community (1901).[7]

Then came the Kishinev murders of 1903 and the almost never-ending pogroms in the following years. All over the United States individuals and groups now began coming forward with their panaceas—local and national societies—to cope with problems both here and abroad. Rabbi David Philipson, a classical Reform Jew, suggested that a congress be called. In 1906 there were at least four different organizations of consequence which addressed themselves to the needs of American Jewry; there were Nissim Behar's National Liberal Immigration League; the Federation of Jewish Organizations of New York State; the charitative Council of Jewish Communal Institutions of New York City, and the American Jewish Committee. The demand for representative assemblies continued. Despite the rise of the prestigious American Jewish Committee, the *American Hebrew* called for still another national Jewish organization. The various landsmanshaften and ethnic groups were combining to gain their ends but their goals and interests were parochial. The multitudes below Fourteenth Street were conscious that they constituted one of the largest Jewries in the world; there were literally thousands of East European organizations; the newcomers were concerned about their youth; they were anxious to bring order out of chaos; they wanted planning! A new institution was imperative, so they believed. America's Russian and Polish Jewish leaders knew full well that Europe's Jewries were governed by powerful organized national associations. They refused to accept the American Jewish Committee with its limited representation; it was undemocratic; that damned it in their eyes. Nostalgically the Russians recalled that back home they once had a citywide community council, the kahal. They preferred to forget that it was abolished as early as 1844 and that it, too, was plutocratic and oligarchic. Ambitious Russian and Polish Jews in this country wanted an organization that would give them power.[8]

The multitudes in Lower Manhattan finally brought to birth a new organization to represent their interests. But even here they had to turn to an outsider for leadership, a man whom they adopted as their own, the Reform rabbi Judah Leon Magnes. It is almost axiomatic that in the early decades of the twentieth century new organizations of immigrants coopted old-timers, earlier settlers; the latter were efficient, competent, and willing to help. In September, 1906, even before Bingham's attack on the Jews, there was a meeting of New York's leaders intent on founding an effective association to meet their needs. The Zionists, too, were present; they were still small in number, powerless, looking for recognition. Then, in October after the Bingham exposé, the Downtown Jews, led by Magnes, came together to establish "The Jewish Community of New York," the Kehillah. A committee of twenty-five was to be appointed to represent all groups in the city; authority was to come from the people as a whole. Beginning on February 27, 1909, a constituent convention met and over a period of two months hammered out a constitution. Magnes, the chairman, brought in the American Jewish Committee because "the Jewish Community"—as its name implied—would have to include all Israelites in the city. The Kehillah became a part—an important part—of the American Jewish Committee, for the board of the Kehillah was to serve as the New York City branch of the national American Jewish Committee.

The Kehillah board members were split almost equally between Uptown and Downtown Jews; Orthodox rabbis and Zionists were not ignored. It would be the job of the board to protect the interests of the city's Jews and to represent them in their relations with the other citizens of the metropolis. Why did the American Jewish Committee go along? It had nothing to lose; it was interested in all aspects of national policy; it was more than willing to work with the immigrants out of a sense of noblesse oblige; it was eager to help, to Americanize them. (Americanization was a magic word.) Germans were well aware that ultimately the Russians and Poles would dominate American Jewish life; Schiff and Marshall knew this; they thought it wise to join the Kehillah in order to exercise a restraining influence on the so-called uncontrollable ghetto leaders. Marshall, however, made sure that the Kehillah could not control the Committee. More than 200 associations joined the Kehillah at once; later dozens of others would affiliate but the ambitious new organization would never include more than a fraction of the numerous societies in New York City.[9]

Magnes, always the democrat, wanted to bring the Uptown and Downtown Jews closer together. Just a year or so before the Kehillah was founded Israel Zangwill's *Melting Pot* was introduced on the American stage. Magnes did not envisage the social assimilation of the immigrants; he knew that this was impossible. The "melting pot" he had in mind was the working together, the coordination of all Jewish immigrant groups into a common community, joined together administratively with the institutions of the earlier settlers. In short he wanted to integrate all the Jews of the city into a Kehillah that would further Judaism and Americanize the newcomers. Let it not be forgotten that Magnes was a rabbi and though many secularists in the Kehillah had no interest in Judaism, Magnes, Marshall, and Schiff were committed religionists. For them Judaism was to be the substratum of all Kehillahs. The New York City communal enterprisers hoped that eventually all American city groups would be structured tightly as "communities." The New York congeries was to serve as a pilot project for all major and middle-size American Jewish settlements. Thus, in effect, all Jews in the United States would be tied together through the overall beneficent administration of the American Jewish Committee. Philadelphia and Denver did build such structures; Cleveland, Chicago, Detroit were interested.

Like the mother creation in New York, none of these communities was destined to survive. If these towns, like New York City, did not succeed in founding a viable Jewish city council and community, and if similar attempts to build truly democratic Jewish community councils in the mid-twentieth century failed it was because they were perforce voluntary. Affluent Jews who had to carry the burden of financing any Jewish institution never participated unless they were assured of commensurate authority. No truly democratic Jewish community council has ever functioned on the American scene. When first organized the "Jewish Community of New York City" met with vigorous opposition in several quarters. People of distinction maintained that it had no authority to speak for Jewry; here in the United States there could be no union of Church and State; the Kehillah spelt separatism, segregation; it was un-American. The *American Israelite* denounced the new association as an aspect of "crazy nationalism"; it was but "a tail to the Zionist kite"; the Central Conference of American Rabbis discountenanced any movements in Jewry other than those built on a religious basis (1911). The criticism of the opposition and the threat of law suits compelled the new organization to adopt the word "Kehillah" as a major component of its title. It had no right to call itself "The Jewish Community of New York City." The Kehillah concept of uniting all Jews in the United States, locally and nationally, was a breathtaking bold concept. There is no question that this movement is one of the most interesting episodes in all American Jewish history.[10]

THE PROGRAM OF THE KEHILLAH

As New York City's most representative and democratic Jewish institution—on paper at least—it is obvious that the executive of the Kehillah, the Kahal if you wish, was ready to defend Jewry against all forms of prejudice and discrimination. It voiced a protest against those firms that advertised that they would employ Christians only; it raised its voice against those—Jews, too—who caricatured Jews on the stage. It was just about this time that the B'nai B'rith set up the Anti-Defamation League in Chicago to fight prejudice nationally (1913). In 1919 the Kehillah opposed the efforts of Poles here who set out to boycott American Jewish businesses; the newly established Polish Republic had nothing but contempt for its own Polish Jewish citizens. The Kehillah was determined to scotch a proposal that would outlaw the use of foreign languages at public gatherings. This was the day when Wilson's attorney general, A. Mitchell Palmer, was staging raids against political dissidents and deporting those who were not yet naturalized. A number of these unhappy men and women were Jews. By 1912, the year of the Rosenthal murder, the Kehillah had established its Bureau of Social Morals. Morals in the ghetto could certainly bear watching, improvement. Criminals were to be exposed; brothels closed; gangsters, thieves, and drug peddlers fought.

In 1918 the Kehillah published a second edition of its *Jewish Communal Register*; the 1,597 page work contains a description of all important—and many unimportant—societies and institutions in the metropolis; it is an invaluable source book for the historian. Another branch of the Kehillah called itself the Bureau of Philanthropic Research; it collected statistical data, evaluated the problems of the charities, and established a modest school for communal workers. Children from broken and impoverished homes were transferred from non-Jewish institutions; a system of modern Hebrew schools was established. (This Bureau of Jewish Education will be described later.) The new Federation for the Support of Jewish Philanthropic Societies, linked to the Kehillah, was destined soon to become far mere important than the Kehillah itself. Missionaries, the eternal bane of Jewry, were stigmatized. The masses, religiously observant, watched the Kehillah as it expressed its concern for violations that infringed on canonical injunctions governing marriage, divorce, circumcision, the ritual bath. To make sure that the Jewish Law (halakah) was followed, the Kehillah set up an advisory Board of Rabbis (*Vaad ha-Rabbanim*). A prime worry of the Kehillah was the temporary houses of worship, the mushroom synagogs that sprouted during the High Holy Days. These commercial enterprises offered religious services to the unaffiliated masses. It is estimated that about 350 of these halls were opened to provide for the temporary religious needs of about 160,000 worshippers. The Kehillah did not want the pious exploited; religion was not a commodity to be bought and sold; model synagogs were provided by the "Jewish Community" during the Days of Awe.

Eager to see that observant Jews received leave of absence for the High Holy Days, the Kehillah intervened with large business firms and with the municipal and federal authorities. Trying to help Jews who did not want to desecrate the Sabbath or the Holy Days was an almost insoluble problem. Emergency funds were made available to benevolent and loan societies; Jews were urged to take out naturalization papers; complaints by some that they were not welcome in the general hospitals were investigated. The Kehillah set up a Bureau of Industry (1914) to work with labor and the employers, both Jewish. It got little help from the socialist union leaders; they shied away; the "Jewish Community" was bourgeois, capitalist, noncosmopolitan. Many union leaders were schismatic not ready to identify with the Jewish people; their roseate vision embraced a wider world of universal economic well-being. By 1918 a few unions, however, were working with the Kehillah. The Jewish Community was interested in vocational training, in helping juvenile delinquents, ex-convicts, the unemployed; they all needed jobs. Wherever the Kehillah turned it had the support of the Uptown leaders who sincerely wished to help fellow Jews. Magnes' Community was at all times Americanistic for the Uptowners were convinced, for more than patriotic reasons, that the immigrants would fare better in this new transatlantic world. It was hoped, through the programs envisaged, that all Jewish institutions in the city could be coordinated, that a spirit of community would develop. By 1917 the Kehillah was making an effort to democratize itself still further, to become representative of the masses whom it served; in this effort it was pressured by the rise of the belligerent American Jewish Congress. But then by 1917 it was already too late to save the Kehillah.[11]

SUCCESS

The Kehillah, as pointed out above, was but another effort of American Jewry to create an overall stronger Jewish community both locally and nationally. The Kehillah was not without a measure of success; hundreds of organizations did come under its influence. To a degree it paved the way for communal unity by encouraging the citywide Federation for the Support of Jewish Philanthropic Societies. City federations of charities were to constitute the closest approach to unity, to community, in most American towns, even in the late twentieth century. The Kehillah, with justice, may preen itself that it never failed to emphasize the need for the close coordination of all Jewish agencies. As a listing of its diverse bureaus would indicate, it made an effort to maintain the sanctity of the Sabbath, to guarantee kashrut, to encourage arbitration in industry. It supported all types of philanthropy both here and abroad; it combatted prostitution, crime, juvenile delinquency; it helped underprivileged children; it collected statistics in order to evaluate communal needs, and it never failed to emphasize that social work must be based on scientific principles. The Kehillah stressed the values of religion and Jewish education; it urged its clients to become citizens; it reached out in all directions to embrace the Jewish world in which it lived. In a sense it is immaterial that its successes were limited; important is the fact that it drew a blueprint for future generations.[12]

FAILURE

The "Jewish Community" failed to unite all Jews in New York City under one ethnic umbrella; it could not induce them to work together. Actually what it really set out to do was to coordinate the activities of a limited number of agencies. The failure to do so need not necessarily reflect
on the leaders; the problems were insurmountable; immigrants from
abroad were pouring into the city; from 1909 to 1921 the Jewish population just about doubled; in 1922 when the Kehillah died of inanition
there were close to 1,900,000 Israelites in the metropolis. These myriads
were scattered all over the city; there were thousands of organizations
with diverse interests; it was impossible to merge them together voluntarily. What these Jews had in common was the determination to remain
Jewish at all costs; their immediate drive was for economic survival. The
heterogeneity which the Kehillah faced was formidable; the masses were
traditionally-oriented religionists; there were minorities of multihued socialists; there was a smaller number of Zionists set on establishing a sovereign state in Palestine, and even they were divided into factions. The
dyed-in-the-wool Zionist with his eye on a future state in the land of his
fathers was not primarily interested in building a tight community here in
the United States. If the Kehillah had any hopes of melding New York's
Jews religiously—and this was very questionable—it was faced with at
least three religious denominations. Ethnically the city was split into numerous Jewish semihostile groups who were loath to surrender their prejudices; differences were rarely glossed over; marriage between a Lithuanian and a Galician was looked upon as a mésalliance. Most socialist
labor leaders warned their followers to stay away from the Kehillah; the
powerful *Forward* damned the Jewish Community as an instrument of the
Orthodox rabbis and Uptown philanthropists; both were suspect; socialism was the only answer to the problems of the ghetto; once socialism
was regnant all difficulties would disappear!

The lack of money helped destroy the Kehillah; most immigrants,
truly poor, had little to give to this new institution; only a minority of the
town's Jewish institutions joined it; unlike Europe's German Jewish communities it lacked the power to tax. For a time the Uptown Jews served as
a major source of support but they withdrew their help when their philosophy was attacked and their leadership rejected. In 1920 the total income of this community project was about $14,000, barely enough to pay
office expenses. One is inclined to believe that the attempt to unite Uptown and Downtown was nothing less than naive; most Russian and Polish society members were averse to any disciplinary control; these trans-
Vistula migrants had never submitted to regulation tamely. Rebellion,
rugged individualism was a tradition going back to anarchic biblical days
when "every man did that which was right in his own eyes" (Judges,

17:6). Jews of old and Jews of the East Side were particularistic; their loyalties were focused on institutions of immediate concern. Yet one may wonder why a formal community was not possible inasmuch as most European Jewries were well organized. The answer is simple: the state abroad intervened either directly or indirectly. The organized Kehillah, gemeinde, was a tradition in Europe but not here in the United States where there was a wide gap between Church and State. Centrifugalism was the rule here no later than the 1820's; a coordinated citywide federation of all institutions was never in the cards. Vested interests, constant, divisive, uncompromising, hampered all efforts toward unity. The businessmen who operated mushroom synagogs were struggling for their livelihood; the rabbis feared for the loss of their perquisites; butchers dreaded any supervision of kashrut; Talmud Torah boards and private school (heder) teachers would brook no interference dictating changes in pedagogy and curricula.

The formal alliance between the Downtown Jews and a handful of Uptown notables was an uneasy one. The Jewish middle class north of Fourteenth Street paid little attention to the institution which Magnes chaired. It is questionable how many even knew of its existence; it certainly did not touch on their lives. And the East European Jewish leaders south of Fourteenth Street? They were almost always suspicious of the American Jewish Committee stalwarts. This suspicion was not justified; the so-called Yehudim—German Jewish leaders—were not hostile. About one-half of New York's Kehillah-AJC district members were East Europeans; however, there could be no real unity between the two divergent groups for economic, social, and ethnic reasons; both generations would have to die off and a new "American" Jew would have to rise who would be more receptive to schemes of federation. The establishment of the Federation for the Support of Jewish Philanthropic Societies of New York City may well have diminished the stature of the Kehillah; this new charitative complex with its limited objectives was noncontroversial. Its board was homogeneous; the members were all Germans with the exception of one man, Meyer London. What was this wolf doing in the sheepfold? As a socialist he and the German anti-Zionists saw eye to eye. This Russian, admired and respected for his integrity, was ready at all times to help his fellow immigrants at the southern end of Manhattan's Isle; he was a link between the givers and the recipients. One wonders whether, unwittingly at least, the Federation cut the ground from under the moribund Kehillah. Through its largesse—resented though it may have been —the Federation helped thousands of newcomers.

World War I dealt a mortal blow to the Jewish Community. New York Jewry was faced with more pressing needs; the American based Joint Distribution Committee was called upon to send millions of dollars across the seas to the suffering Jews in the war zones. Human lives were at stake. The American government sank all its resources into an international conflict in 1917 when it declared war on Germany and Austria-Hungary; it was an age of almost hysterical chauvinism; ethnic disparities were barely tolerated. The Jewish Community of New York City was, so it seemed, a separatistic organization; it believed in cultural pluralism; there were Jews, and Gentiles, too, who were convinced that there was no place for an American secular organization that underscored its Jewish affiliations. In time of war many Jews tended to become 125 percent American though they remained loyal to Judaism and to Jewry too.

The Kehillah was hurt by the rise of the American Jewish Congress (1914). The Congress—an attempt to emancipate East European Jewry and to restore Palestine to the Children of Israel—appealed to the immigrant masses. It was their very own organization; it was the symbol of revolt against their Uptown benefactors. The ghetto dwellers were fascinated by the prospect of a real democracy. The Congress was nursed and developed by the Zionists; its romantic appeal was irresistible; it set out to help the dear ones abroad who were in desperate danger and in need. The American Jewish Committee leaders, who constitutionally and actually dominated the Kehillah, were apprehensive; their control was threatened; they detested most East Side Zionist leaders; the accusation of dual loyalties haunted them; for them a Jewish state was taboo. The Kehillah as such did not come out for Zionism because of its Uptown ties.

Thus it was that the "Jewish Community" found itself faced with a rival organization that appealed to the imagination of the newcomers and commanded their loyalty. The "Congress" diverted attention and support from the Kehillah; it rejected its important sponsors. The Zionists pushed the East European Kehillah members to break with the American Jewish Committee, to endorse the Congress; this they could not and would not do. The Zionist leaders knew precisely what they were doing; they set out to control American Jewry now overwhelmingly East European in origin; they wanted to harness the energies and the great resources of this Jewry in order to build a new Palestine. A Jewish homeland was the only solution to an immediate Jewish need; millions were suffering in Europe as the clashing armies overran the towns and villages of Russia, Poland, and Austria. The rivalry and the popularity of the Congress was a devastating blow to the Kehillah's effort to unite Downtown and Uptown Jewries. Essentially the Kehillah was America-directed; the Zionists were Palestine-directed. Magnes cast his dice for the Kehillah; he loved everything Jewish; he had been a devoted Zionist for over a decade but he was not committed to a political state. He had always hoped to forge a united American Jewish community but by rejecting the Jewish Congress, he broke with his beloved Jewish masses, with the people for whom he had labored; without them the Kehillah was doomed.

Was Magnes, chairman of the Kehillah of New York City from its birth to its death, responsible for its failure? He and his friends in Lower Manhattan saw what the Jews and sympathetic Gentile citizens were able to accomplish in forcing Washington to abrogate the 1832 treaty with Russia. All Jews joined in that fight against the Muscovites but the Kehillah had no such following even in the ghetto. Even the rise in crime among Jews, juvenile delinquency, did not induce the East Siders to enlist under the banner of this new organization. It may well be that Magnes was not the right man to build the "Jewish Community of New York City." He had the imagination, the devotion, but not the consummate skills to unite hundreds of thousands of men who were often at odds with one another. One is tempted to say that this was an impossible task yet it was during these very years and decades that titans of industry performed miracles; they created gigantic trusts, the Standard Oil Company, the United States Steel Company, the American Tobacco Company. Magnes was no titan. This charming gentleman did the Kehillah no good when the United States went to war and he turned to pacifism (1917). This repelled many who did not want to be identified with a man who was no "patriot"; pacifism was anti-American, even pro-German! Many Jews were disturbed lest his anti-war stance play into the hands of the anti-immigration forces who were determined to close the gates to America. Jews are not loyal! Writing to Magnes, his brother-in-law, in June, 1917, Marshall warned him that he was hurting the Kehillah, the American Jewish Committee, the Joint Distribution Committee; Magnes had helped found all three organizations. This charismatic rabbi was induced to remain at the head of the "Jewish Community" till 1922 when he left for a visit to Palestine; by that time the Kehillah had given up the ghost.[13]

THE KEHILLAH: RETROSPECT

The Bingham accusation in 1908 brought the Kehillah Movement to birth. There was a crisis; Jews were attacked as criminals. Crises in America—real or imaginary—have always called forth proposals to create united Jewries, either local or national. The question to ask and to answer is this: to what extent was the desire for community sparked solely by the need of the moment? Was it a continuing drive toward community, a desire for unity, security, power? Whatever its ultimate motivation the Kehillah Movement was an attempt on the part of East Europeans to create an overall organization; it was nursed by men who were convinced that an authoritative national body would be good for the Jews. By the twentieth century East European Jewry here had been working toward community, if only in a limited sense, through the federation of lodges, mutual aid, hometown, and regional associations. There were other reasons why some of New York's Russians and Poles, Galicians and Rumanians, looked forward to a strong centralized Jewish communal congeries. They were driven by a nostalgic reminiscence of Jewish city councils that once united Jewish townspeople in earlier decades and centuries. There was never any effective national community in the Russian empire; the government would not have tolerated it.

Here in the United States American Jewry was undoubtedly influenced by the tendency among the Protestants to organize along national lines. This began during George Washington's first administration. Since then Jewry here had striven—tentatively, sporadically, to be sure—for national unity. All through the nineteenth and early twentieth centuries there were men who believed that one central national body would be good for the Jews; it would bring them security, strength. Ethnicity would cement them all. This centripetal drive, however, was halted by factors that were apparently contradictory. Jews were particularistic; they were kept apart by different ideologies; Orthodoxy, Reform, socialism were at war with one another; loyalties were parochial, limited to congregations and hometown societies. Yet there was at the same time a strong desire on the part of most immigrants to become an integral part of the American totality. This tension between particularism, regionalism, and Americanism did not tear Jews apart; the American pull always won out as long as one's Jewish identity was not threatened. Judaism remained the substratum, the continuum. The typical Jew—acculturated German, native-born, or East European—was determined to remain Jewish even though Americanization was his overt goal. Every individual harmonized the variant philosophies to his own satisfaction.

JUDAH LEON MAGNES

The Kehillah and Magnes are inseparable. Who was Magnes? Judah Leon Magnes was a man who touched many associations and movements in his lifetime and they were all the better for his presence and influence. He was a catalyst; the organizations with which he was affiliated may have changed; he always remained Judah L. Magnes; he was always true to himself. The founder of the Kehillah, born in San Francisco and reared in Oakland, did not come from an affluent family; his father was a Pole; his mother came from Posen, a German province which bordered on Polish Russia. Jacob Voorsanger, the distinguished Reform rabbi of San Francisco, was certainly an influence on the young Magnes. A Dutch immigrant Voorsanger started life in America as an Orthodox cantor and became one of the most influential men in Northern California. This able aggressive leader—something of a Pacific Coast Isaac M. Wise—was interested in learning and communal work; one of his jobs was to teach Hebrew at the University of California. Though the Magnes family had suffered reverses it managed to send its son to the rabbinical college in Cincinnati. Isaac M. Wise in the 1890's was a tired old man but it is not improbable that this organizer of the Reform Movement left his impress on the young student. Moses Buttenwieser who taught Bible may have played a part in fashioning the ideals of the young Californian; Buttenwieser was an enthusiastic exponent of the social message of Israel's prophets. Young Magnes, however, was not popular with all his teachers and his fellow students; even then he lived, somewhat withdrawn, in a world of his own.

In 1900, after his ordination, he went to Germany to study; under the gemeinde system Berlin was then one of the most highly organized Jewish communities in Europe. In those halcyonic days this young American met brilliant Russians and Poles, Zionists who were studying in that city. The Germany of those years was a land of spiritual and cultural ferment. Tradition tells us that this young man came back with a beard and ate kosher; the beard can be documented. Magnes returned to his alma mater in 1903 where he taught Bible and served as the librarian. After a year he went on to New York, to Brooklyn, to a congregation.

Even in those early days he talked of a "people's synagog." Here was a man who was always reaching out; he respected the old way of life but he was not wedded to it; he was no run of the mill rabbi. In 1905, with the Russian pogroms raging, he organized a Jewish self-defense organization to provide Russian Jews with funds and arms; he led thousands as they marched to protest the massacres in Eastern Europe. That same year he became a power in the Federation of American Zionists; he led the B'nai Zion, a fraternal order. In the course of two years he had emerged as one of New York's best known personalities. A year later this Zionist, this idol of the East Side multitudes, became a founder of the American Jewish Committee; Temple Emanu-El, the country's richest synagog, called him to serve it as an associate rabbi; two years later he married a sister-in-law of Louis Marshall (1908). Magnes, young, handsome, was admired by the elite of Manhattan and the notables of the ghetto. A Reform rabbi who was a Zionist and identified with immigrant masses was certainly "kosher." When he accepted the chairmanship of the Kehillah (1909) he was the man best fitted for the post because of his friendships in all quarters. Here was a notable who could unify New York's Jewry, at least induce its factions to work together; it was his conviction that Jews had much in common; they were one people.

The same year that the Kehillah was established, Magnes helped found a society of East Europeans, with a sprinkling of Germans, dedicated to Jewish cultural pursuits. The following year he severed his relations with Emanu-El. He had presented it with an ultimatum; either it would reform Reform or he would leave. He left. The majority of the

Board of Trustees was glad to see him leave; Marshall, his brother-in-law, and Schiff, friends and admirers, attempted in vain to soften the curt resolution of the majority that he not be reelected. What happened? In no uncertain terms Rabbi Magnes told the board members to return to their roots, to teach the children more Hebrew, to restore the traditional prayer book, to encourage adult education classes, to lower fees, to recruit less affluent members, to democratize the congregation, to come into "closer communion with the whole House of Israel." (Much that he asked for in 1910 was adopted by the majority of Reform synagogs in the days after World War II; the Holocaust had a persuasiveness all its own; it made him a true prophet.) By now Magnes was moving rapidly in several directions; he furthered the Intercollegiate Menorah Association, helped fashion the Yiddish *Day*, and served as a founder of the Joint Distribution Committee (JDC), the country's most important international philanthropic agency dedicated to the rescue of war-wracked Russian and Polish Jewry (1914). Magnes went on the road to raise money for the JDC; the masses who heard him were carried away by his fervent appeals; the men emptied their purses; the women stripped rings from their fingers.

A year after the JDC had begun its work Magnes, a pioneer Zionist, broke with many of his friends; he resigned from Brandeis' Provisional Executive Committee for General Zionist Affairs; he would not go along with the Boston attorney. He was suspicious of the authoritarian thrust of the Zionist-motivated American Jewish Congress. It may well be that he looked askance at the rising Brandeis who overshadowed him. In establishing a state in Palestine one could not cavalierly ignore the Turkish authorities; it was their country. This was a realistic approach. Magnes knew where he stood; he wanted the ancient homeland to become a haven of refuge for the persecuted; it was to be a great Jewish cultural center; a political state was not the ultimate goal. In 1917 when the revolution in Russia drove the Romanovs off the throne Magnes welcomed the new liberal regime. By this time he had become a pacifist, opposed to war and chauvinism. It was not surprising therefore that he joined with Jane Addams, Roger Baldwin, and the Socialist Norman Thomas when the American Civil Liberties Union came into being. In 1922 he left for Palestine; he went to visit but he elected to remain. The Kehillah was no more; Jerusalem not New York was now the scene of his spiritual-cultural endeavors.

When Magnes came to the Holy Land in 1922 only 11 percent of the population was Jewish; it was obvious therefore that he would preach the gospel of binationalism; he wanted the Jews to be tolerated in this overwhelmingly Moslem land. After the massacre of the Hebron Jews in 1929 he was convinced that his Covenant of Peace, B'rit Shalom group was on the right track. Later in 1942-1943, when the Zionists in their Biltmore program and the American Jewish Conference came out for a sovereign Jewish Palestinian state, Magnes, Henrietta Szold, Martin Buber and others still insisted that binationalism was the only answer. This was the goal of a new association which was then established; it called itself Ihud (Unity). The Arabs, irreconcilable enemies of the Jews, would have nothing to do with his overtures; the Zionists were equally obdurate; Palestine was to be Jewish. Culturally Magnes was more effective than he was politically. In his new homeland he worked hard to further cultural Zionism. Like Brandeis he believed that good Zionists make better Americans. Starting modestly Magnes took the helm as chancellor at the Hebrew University in 1925 and built it into a scholarly institution. Unfortunately for him his opponents kicked him upstairs (1935); as president he had little real authority. Einstein had no respect for Magnes because he was not an acknowledged academician; Weizmann, Zionism incarnate, was interested in political sovereignty. Professors and students resented his binational preachments. He was unhappy when partition was proposed in 1947; he knew that even then the Jews constituted but 42 percent of the population and when, a year later, Israel proclaimed its independence he still hoped it would federate with the surrounding Arab states.[14]

THE NATURE OF THE MAN

The Bible says "for as his name is so is he" (1 Sam.25:25). The name is the man; this applies to Magnes. His original name, the one given to him by his parents was probably J. Leon Magnes; the "J" was in memory of a grandfather whose first name was Judah; the English equivalent adopted by Magnes and the family was the Latin Julian. However, they called him Leon. This was to be his name as a student at the rabbinical seminary; the University of Cincinnati knew him as Julian. At times he dubbed himself Leon J. Magnes. When appointed instructor at the Hebrew Union College he was known as J. Leon Magnes; his final decision was to call himself Judah Leon Magnes. In the Bible Judah was a lion's whelp (Gen. 49:9). Our Judah was a romantic. He knew full well the story of Judah Halevi, the medieval Spanish poet, the lover of Zion. It was Judah Halevi who wrote: "My heart is in the East and I am in the uttermost West." Magnes was acquainted with the modern Hebrew poets; among them few were more respected than Judah Leon Gordon (d.1892). But Magnes, the romantic, was not content to spin out fantasies on a distant cloud; he was determined to do things, to be somebody. Among his contemporaries were John Haynes Holmes, Jenkin Lloyd Jones, Stephen S. Wise—who was no admirer of Magnes—and a whole host of Protestant Social Gospel preachers, humanitarian activists. Magnes, a child of that generation and its aspirations, was a civil libertarian, an anti-imperialist. As a pacifist during World War I he suffered for his convictions; his Christian neighbors snubbed him. Later, when Hitler, the ultimate evil, appeared on the scene, Magnes discarded his pacifism but he always remained a social reformer concerned for society as a whole.

A Jew has many options; Magnes never forgot that he was a Reform rabbi although he had abandoned the congregational pulpit before he had lived out half his life. Jews, said he, have a mission to the world; the prophets of Israel left their mark on this preacher who had taught Bible and biblical history in a theological school. Unlike the vast majority of his Reform rabbinical contemporaries, he was a Zionist, but sui generis. Though Palestine was to become a cultural center for all Jewry the Diaspora was to have a productive life of its own. Magnes was an early cultural pluralist, a devotee of Diaspora nationalism; in his thinking he seems to have been influenced by Simon Dubnow and Chaim Zhitlowsky; he knew the latter well; they were members of the same discussion club. What was the ultimate essence of the man? He was set on preaching a nationally tinged universal Judaism. This was not easy. True, there were a number of distinguished Jews who admired him tremendously; there were others, however, who scorned him, who viewed him as a confused faddist. They referred to him as the eternal dissenter, as the vague enthusiast; they pointed out his inconsistencies and emphasized his failures.

There is no question; here was a man in search of himself; his final address to his sophisticated congregants in Emanu-El in 1910 is totally unrealistic; he was tilting at windmills. It is true too that he was ambitious; he was eager to lead, to mount a rostrum and preach to the world. (Elijah of old chose Mount Carmel.) Magnes believed in his messianic mission; justice was his ruling passion, an inner compulsion moved him to tell the truth as he saw it regardless of the consequences. It is no wonder that he ran into trouble; he would have been less than human if he had not brooded over Isaiah's Suffering Servant (53:3): "He was despised and rejected of men, a man of sorrows." No one questioned the honesty of this idealist; some of the men who condemned him made great careers and stayed on top but only after they had muted their principles and surrendered to their ambitions. This man could not and would not betray himself; that was his sin; his failures were magnificent. He was constant in his faith; history may acclaim him a latter-day prophet when it is ready to admit that spiritual heroes are not necessarily successful enterprisers. His ultimate importance? He brought a breath of fresh air wherever he turned. Pedantic factual historians will always recall that he helped establish the Kehillah's Bureau of Jewish Education and Jerusalem's Hebrew University.[15]

BUREAU OF JEWISH EDUCATION

Magnes and his Kehillah garnered very few laurels. The Bureau of Jewish Education established in 1910 may be an exception; it was not without some influence educationally in New York and in the provinces. As it has already been pointed out Jewish education in New York City left much to be desired, certainly from the point of view of modern professionally trained pedagogues. There was no communally controlled and financed educational system because there was no organized Jewish community. (Actually there was always a strong community but only by consensus.) Knowledgeable, sensitive Jewish leaders in New York City were troubled in the early twentieth century when they discovered that only about 25 percent of the town's Jewish children were receiving a Jewish education. But this was at one time only; in fact, substantially more would receive some Jewish training before they closed their Jewish books. Very few children, however, were given intensive instruction in Jewish schools. Indeed there were a few synagogs down on the East Side that would not open their buildings for the instruction of the young. When Jews spoke of "Jewish education" they meant the ability to read Hebrew by rote and to follow the time honored service in the siddur, the Orthodox Book of Common Prayer. If the Bureau was set to tackle the problem of improving Jewish schooling what then was the status of Jewish education in 1910? There were heders (private Hebrew reading schools), siddur peddlers who came to the home to give lessons, two or three parochial schools which taught some Talmud, semi-communal Talmud Torahs (afternoon Hebrew schools), and one "college" or European type yeshivah that taught Talmud. This was the Isaac Elchanan Rabbinical School—whatever its name at that particular moment.[16]

In all probability a majority of the East Side youngsters—boys for the most part—went to the heders or were taught by the itinerant teachers who came to the house. This type of teaching was inadequate; the heder ambience was often bad; the class might well meet in a cellar or over a stable. One heder teacher advertised that he wrote letters for the illiterate, that he was prepared to officiate at marriages, perform circumcisions, and, what was far more important, exorcise cancers. Not even the most learned medical professor could do this! All these Hebrew schools were influenced by their American milieu; the English language made inroads frequently displacing the Yiddish as the medium of instruction. In Eastern Europe the Talmud Torah was an all-day charity Hebrew school, a pauper's school of sorts; here it became a supplementary afternoon tuition school although in some instances poor children were provided with clothing. In 1915 New York's Etz Chaim, a parochial school, and the Rabbi Isaac Elchanan Theological Seminary, a real yeshivah, united as the

Rabbinical College of America; Dr. B. Revel, the principal, introduced secular studies; the vernacular employed for these disciplines was English.[17]

The Kehillah's Bureau of Jewish Education determined to further instruction in Judaism through the Talmud Torah, because as an afternoon school it supplemented the public schools. Magnes and Benderly—the latter was the head of the Bureau—were not protagonists of the parochial school. They avoided the afternoon congregational schools in order not to come in conflict with the rabbis who brooked no interference. The Talmud Torah was the nearest approach to a communal institution; the Bureau was set on developing Jewry in a community setting. No two Talmud Torahs were the same. The language of instruction might be Yiddish, English, or German; the Hungarians, natives of the Austria-Hungary empire preferred to teach in German. The instruction in most Hebrew schools before 1910, and after that, too, was inferior from the vantage point of an American professional educator.

Social pressure moved many Jews in Eastern Europe to send their sons to a Hebrew school. In this country, the pressure was not as strong. No one could compel a parent to enroll a child in a heder or Talmud Torah. The professional Jewish educators bemoaned the lack of standards in Jewish education. They ignored the fact that ultimately a substantial number of children did receive some Jewish schooling. They tended to forget that illiteracy was endemic in Eastern Europe and, to a degree, here, too, in the United States. As late as 1920 illiteracy among America's foreign born was over 13 percent. It has been pointed out that as late as the 1970's there were some college athletes who were functionally illiterate. More important is the fact that for the average Jew who sent his child to a religious school content was not all important. The parents realized, if only subconsciously, that association, attendance in a Jewish school was sufficient to establish identification. Boys in such schools, indoctrinated by friendships and by their Hebrew reading, were for the most part destined to remain Jewish no matter how little they learned. In addition, the home ambience, the ghetto milieu, rejection by Christians, all made for the survival of the younger generation as Jews. Thus, knowledge in itself —content—was not imperative if the child was to remain Jewish.

The parents, we repeat, were satisfied with the rebbe and the heder; they did not push Magnes and the Bureau to raise standards. Having sent their child to a neighboring Hebrew school, they felt they had done their duty by God and Jewry; then they turned to the pressing necessity of making a living. But if Mr. Cohen, a native of Kovno, was content with his son's Jewish education, the Uptowners were not. They worried about juvenile delinquency, particularly after the publicity evoked by Commissioner Bingham's attack. They wanted a type of school that emphasized ethics as well as Hebrew reading and instruction in the ceremonies; they insisted on what they called Americanization. Americanization? Many of them interpreted this in terms of soap, water, and good manners.

There were immigrants who were not satisfied with the state of Jewish education; they were fully aware that the teaching in the American public schools was superior. The newcomers who flocked to this country after 1905, after the mass murders in Russia, cherished relatively high educational standards; some had gone to the public schools. By the early 1900's there were a number of modern Hebrew schools in Russia where secular disciplines were taught; there was even one rabbinical academy which had incorporated some of the profane disciplines. Among those educated immigrants who landed in New York at this time were Socialist-Zionists, bourgeois followers of Theodore Herzl, liberals and political radicals of diverse schools of thought, Diaspora nationalists, Orthodox religionists, and tradition-true Zionists. Many of these newcomers were pushing for a type of Jewish instruction that would square with their own ideology and meet contemporary American educational standards. It is true, too, that long before the arrival of these educated East Europeans, long before the establishment of the Bureau of Jewish Education, there were individuals and organizations that pushed for more advanced forms of Jewish education. In 1886 the Reformist Hebrew Sabbath School Union set out to coordinate the instruction in America's Sunday schools. Around the year 1904 the Union of American Hebrew Congregations fashioned its Department of Synagog and School Extension. By 1906 the East Europeans here, the Orthodox, had created a Central Board of Talmud Torahs in New York City; two years later there was a Federation of Hebrew National Schools in Brooklyn; in 1909 Dr. Joseph Isaac Bluestone, head of the Machzike Talmud Torah, organized the Central Board of Jewish Education.

All these Russian Jewish organizations accomplished little if anything but the new settlers were attempting to meet the pedagogical challenges that confronted them. The Bingham Affair, the need to emphasize content and ideals in Jewish educational institutions, pushed New York's Kehillah to establish the Bureau of Jewish Education. Schooling, it was convinced, made for survival. The Uptowners believed that good schools, a proper modernized Jewish education, was a prophylaxis against crime. Though Benderly, the Bureau head, often made magniloquent gestures, he and his friends cautiously limited their goals; the Bureau remained an umbrella organization, an instrumentality to insure coordination. To influence others more directly Benderly founded model schools, Talmud Torahs which the Bureau supervised. It introduced an all-inclusive curriculum; the afternoon schools were to teach Hebrew, history, customs, religion. Above all the schools set out to integrate Jewishness—which tolerates secularism—Judaism, the religion, and Americanism. The new Bureau was outstanding in its approach but, and this bears repetition, it was in no sense a pioneer in imposing modernity on America's East European Jewish educational institutions. For decades there were many others who had anticipated the Bureau's views; they had long been working for new approaches to traditional Jewish education; they were trying to emulate the American educational system. One is tempted to say, however, that the newly established Bureau owed almost everything to the creative sensibilities of Samson Benderly; he was its inspiring and creative head.[18]

Who was Samson Benderly? Benderly (1876-1944), a native of Safed in Palestine, quarreled with his Hassidic parents; this youngster was determined to acquire a secular education. He left for Beirut where he attended the American College and studied medicine. He came to the United States in 1898 and settled in Baltimore to be near his patron, Dr. Aaron Friedenwald. He supported himself by teaching Hebrew; later reports that he tutored Henrietta Szold, founder of the Hadassah movement, will hardly bear scrutiny. In 1900 he received his medical degree; his chosen field was ophthalmology. While studying medicine he taught in a local Jewish school; education was a passion with him. To the surprise of some of his friends he speedily abandoned medicine and turned to teaching. There is a Baltimore tradition according to which he once said: "there are plenty of professionals trained to heal the Jewish body but none trained to heal the Jewish soul." Benderly had no formal training in pedagogy, but read much and was acquainted with modern educational theory. It is probable that he was aware of the writings of the men who made history at Teachers College, Columbia University.

It was during the decade that Benderly was in charge of some of Baltimore's Hebrew schools that he worked out his approach to Jewish education. He came to New York and the Bureau with a plan (1910). Even before his arrival in the metropolis he had already written to Magnes telling him what he proposed to do; in essence he was recapitulating what he had accomplished in Baltimore. The Baltimore curriculum was the one he offered New York's Talmud Torahs and which he hoped would be adopted in the afternoon Hebrew schools of the country. It included Hebrew, liturgy (the siddur), Bible, some classical Hebrew literature, medieval poetry, modern Hebrew writings, Jewish history, ethics. A modest teachers' training school had also been started. Benderly insisted constantly that teaching was a job for professionals; he urged and encouraged girls to become instructors in Jewish schools. He believed in physical exercise, in playgrounds, and clubs for the youngsters; he encouraged them to conduct religious services of their own, to organize their own choirs. Cleanliness, he enjoined, was imperative. Back in Baltimore no child could enter the classroom without showing his hands. Like most Jewish schools in the United States his Baltimore schools charged tuition. If a student could not or would not keep up his money was returned and he was dismissed and if mama objected Benderly told her to take the refund and go out and buy herself a new hat. Because he was intent on making Hebrew a modern living language he incurred the ire of some Orthodox Baltimoreans; they resented his profane use of the Sacred Tongue. A contemporary president of the Hebrew Union College in Cincinnati shared this same Orthodox hope that Hebrew would be limited to liturgical and religious uses exclusively. Benderly was a Zionist and in later years, after the Balfour Declaration opened Palestine to Jews, he took time out to become the head of the American Palestine Company, an investment corporation that sought to improve the economy of the Holy Land.[19]

The statement has been made above that the Bureau owed much to the creative sensibility of Samson Benderly. He was certainly a man of vision and something of a visionary; he had ideas, big ideas. When he joined the Kehillah and the Bureau he hoped to enlist 100,000 members and to integrate the activity of 1,000 different organizations. Benderly dreamt of a cultural renaissance, unmindful, of course, that historically there had never been a cultural efflorescence of the Jewish masses in any country at any time. In his more cautious moments he hoped to use the Bureau as a lever to move the whole American Jewish world culturally. His basic goal was to improve elementary Jewish education; the home and the synagog had lost their influence; the school must take their place. He proposed to use the Talmud Torahs to do the job; in doing this he was following his Baltimore experimental school pattern. Why Talmud Torahs? The Reformers' Sunday schools did not allot enough time to accomplish much and, from his point of view, were not particularly Jewish; the heder was obviously wanting. Most heders were private enterprises; coordination would be difficult if not impossible. Thus he pinned his hopes on progressive afternoon schools. These schools would have to be sponsored and supported by a community, a Kehillah; all educational work would be supervised; curricula would be standardized. Administration would be patterned on the American public school system. There had never been a full-fledged communal system of Jewish education which embraced all children, both boys and girls. Benderly admired the American public schools; he was eager to make the new Jewish generation an integral part of America spiritually. He knew, too, that the immigrant could not afford a separate, a "parochial" system; the immigrants had no money; the public schools were free.

Thus Benderly set out to establish model schools and to supervise others; they would all serve as examples for American Jewry. He, his associates, and a host of other notables were sure that education was the answer to all the ills of American Jewry. It was that simple. In this he was joined by Louis Marshall. This remarkable Jewish leader hoped that bureaus would be established in all major Jewish centers. Once post-World War I European Jewry had been helped to stand on its own two feet Marshall was determined to address himself to the problem of improving the American Jewish educational system. One of the reasons that Benderly staked everything on a few model schools was because of lack of funds to set up an elaborate new educational organization. Schiff had provided some money to help finance the Bureau but it merely primed the pump. A board of trustees was appointed to supervise the Bureau; all but one were Zionists; not one was a traditional Orthodox Jew. They were all in agreement that education must be religious, home ties strengthened. The model schools must be modern in all respects; teachers, college men and women, were to be instructed and licensed. The curriculum that Benderly brought with him was all-inclusive, Jewish, child centered, not content centered.

Leaning on the American public school, his constant paradigm, Benderly insisted on graded textbooks, properly printed and well illustrated. In a sense this was revolutionary; there was nothing like this in all the history of Jewish pedagogy. Quite traditional, however, was his insistence that Hebrew was important; there could be no Judaism without it; yet for Americans it was no substitute for English. In teaching the Sacred Tongue he emphasized the "natural method," Hebrew was to be taught in Hebrew. This system, in vogue in Palestine for decades, had been introduced into this country many years before the Bureau was established. One of the reasons Benderly stressed modern Hebrew was because he was a Zionist; one day there would be a Palestine Jewish homeland and Hebrew would be the language of the people. If children were taught Hebrew here, he said, they would come that much closer to their parents; the family would be strengthened. As a follower of Asher Ginsberg (Ahad Ha-Am, "one of the people"), Benderly looked forward to the day when Palestine would become a spiritual center, yet like most of the notables who led the Bureau he underscored at the same time the importance of Diaspora Judaism and Diaspora nationalism.

He was at all times an Americanizer. Benderly and his disciples looked to Columbia, to Edward Lee Thorndike, William Heard Kilpatrick, to John Dewey, the philosopher. The Jewish educationists of the Bureau shared many of the views on cultural pluralism popularized by the young Horace Kallen. Cultural pluralism has been defined as a condition of society in which diverse ethnic groups can maintain their traditional culture within the confines of a common civilization. Dewey was aware of the cultural diversity of different ethnic groups and looked upon these differences as potentially positive factors; the American body politic was clothed with a coat of many colors. Dewey was no proponent of the "melting pot" theory. Like Kallen and others, Benderly, Magnes, Israel Friedlaender, and their followers wanted to synthesize American culture and its political ideals with Judaism and Jewish nationalism. Such a harmonization would foster Jewish survival in a democratic America. They believed that by remaining Jewish, by emphasizing their own spiritual values, they were making a contribution to America. Under a system of cultural pluralism there was room for all streams in Jewry, for the Orthodox, the Conservatives, the Reformers, the Yiddishists, the Socialist-Zionists, the Territorialists, the Diaspora nationalists. They could all be loyal to their own ideologies and yet remain good Jews and good Americans.[20]

ACCOMPLISHMENTS OF THE BUREAU

The Bureau helped the lay leaders of the Talmud Torahs organize in order to discuss their administrative and financial difficulties. The Talmud Torah principals, professionals, met together in a society of their own to discuss curricula and educational ideals. They encouraged the youngsters in their school to celebrate the Fourth of July and Thanksgiving Day; thus they forged a link to the Pilgrim Fathers and to the founders of this republic. The teachers in the afternoon schools were encouraged to organize a society where they could ventilate their problems. Immigrant teachers, such as the Agudat Ha-Morim, published Hebrew magazines for themselves and their charges; American trained instructors edited *The Jewish Teacher*, in English of course. None of these papers was destined to last very long. Some teachers organized a union; the instructors in the Reform Sunday schools established a society where they could wrestle with their problems.

In 1916 the Bureau founded a school for Jewish Communal Work, the first Jewish institution of this type. Since Magnes and Benderly believed in the centrality of the community it was imperative that Jewish administrators be trained to help the immigrant myriads cope with issues raised by industry, education, religion, crime, leisure, and philanthropy. The newcomers had to be helped to make the transition from the old world to a culture, a civilization, and a polity that were new, inviting, yet not threatening. This school for Jewish civil servants had close relations with Columbia which gave credit for work done under the auspices of the Bureau. It is worth noting that this training institute was controlled by the Uptowners, by men such as Felix Warburg, the banker and philanthropist, and Judge Irving Lehman, later to become the chief justice of the New York State Court of Appeals. This in-house school closed in 1919. This brief span of activity is typical; many Jewish institutions rose only to disappear after a burst of activity; permanent institutions were built on the ruins of predecessors. Six years later, 1925, this School for

Communal Work was succeeded by the Graduate School for Jewish Social Work.

The model elementary schools supervised by Benderly were intended to be experimental. That they were, and innovative too. Benderly et al were determined to capture the interest of the youngsters; in addition to Hebrew and history they were encouraged to conduct services, taught the meaning of festivals and ceremonies, and urged to embrace the fine arts. *The Jewish Child*, the magazine which the Bureau published for its young readers, was full of poems, legends, stories, and news items. To be sure it was not the first of the children's magazines; the Reformers had begun printing *Young Israel* in the 1870's. Outstanding in the Bureau's system was the insistence on education for girls; their training had been neglected by traditional Jews for millennia. The Bureau had five graded schools where girls were taught and encouraged to become teachers. Extension courses were also provided for older adolescents who worked for a living.[21]

The fact that the elementary schools were basic to Jewish education did not deter the leaders at the Bureau from experimenting on the preschool and high school levels. High school classes were established; the students, both boys and girls, were encouraged to enter the Teachers Institute of the Jewish Theological Seminary. People who had little time during the day to go to school were directed toward the Israel Friedlaender Classes of the Seminary; here they could begin their studies and prepare to take courses in the Teachers Institute. The introduction of modern Hebrew as a discipline in the public high schools was favored by the Bureau. Paying homage to a Jewish tradition that is at least 2,000 years old Benderly and his board introduced a lecture series for adults. Back in Baltimore, Benderly had already stressed popular talks for men and women; in New York competent lecturers were invited to describe the life of Jews in other lands; thus the New York community was linked to World Jewry. Marshall, the busy lawyer, was called in and served as chairman of a committee that sponsored a series of discourses on communal problems. Despite the mission work of the Bureau there were still many thousands of youngsters who received little or no training as Jews. To reach them the Circle of Jewish Children was organized by Benderly; within the short space of two years thousands were gathered and taught the meaning of the Jewish Holy Days; older boys and girls were reached through the League for Jewish Youth. By 1919 Dr. Albert P. Schoolman, one of Benderly's disciples, had opened Cejwin, an educational camp in the Catskills. Camps were not new in Jewish life; as early as the 1880's settlement houses, "Ys," and philanthropic organizations had begun sending children into the country for a summer rest. A few, not many, had programs which included elements of informal education. There were even some camps where modern Hebrew was cultivated but Cejwin was the first one where Jewish culture and its many facets were explored; its goal was to make Jewish children proud of their heritage.

To encourage parents to work closely with the Jewish schools the Bureau constantly urged the establishment of parent-teacher associations (PTA). This much is certain: Jews did not have to be pushed to cooperate with the public schools; they were pioneers in the PTA's. According to a Jewish educator there were almost 3,700 Jewish organizations in New York City; many of them were of a religiocultural nature. The Bureau was eager to influence them. It cooperated with the Educational Alliance. Thousands of Jewish children were taught; Benderly reached out to the Sunday schools of the Jewish religious denominations; there were also hundreds of children in orphan asylums and other institutions who were aided. In a 1913 report the Bureau said that it had touched the lives of 12,000 children. This may well be accurate though there were but 2,500 youngsters in the supervised schools. In 1915 the Bureau reported that it was in touch with schools in forty different cities. Whether this boast is accurate or not it did reach out to guide and influenced many. In 1920 Louis Marshall claimed that the Bureau had influenced 25,000 young men and women; he was not the man to exaggerate.

Certainly by the beginning of the third decade of the twentieth century Jewish education had made progress; curricula were expanded; pedagogy had improved. It is difficult to determine exactly how much of the change was due to these New York educators; certainly Benderly was known for the work that he was doing. Historians of American Jewish education are agreed that the Bureau and its aggressive educators had diversified curricula; they trained teachers; they coordinated programs; they raised standards; they made communities aware of their responsibility to educate every Jewish boy and girl within the borders of their town. When the Bureau began to falter for lack of funds New York's Federation for the Support of Jewish Philanthropic Societies began to subsidize it, albeit modestly. The rationale for this financial help was that educated children would not engage in crime. It is by no means improbable, too, that the Federation was willing to help because it sought to extend its influence in those cultural and social areas which affected the lives of the immigrant masses. Jewish charity federations are by nature expansionist.[22]

SOME BUREAU ASSOCIATES

It is clear from what has been written above that Magnes and Benderly were not the only educators who had grand designs. There were several intellectuals who were interested in helping their fellow immigrants confront their problems. Apparently all these men were committed to education of a modern type; among them were Israel Friedlaender (1876-1920) and Mordecai Menahem Kaplan (18-1983). Friedlaender, a native Pole, was by training a Semitist, an Arabist; he was a German Ph.D. The Bureau of Jewish Education was close to his heart; he was the chairman of its board of trustees. Like his compeers he wanted to train a new generation of America's college youth to provide leadership in the days that lay ahead. Every aspect of intellectual endeavor that related to Judaism appealed to him. Ideologically he, too, was influenced by Simon Dubnow and Ahad Ha-Am; he was a cultural Zionist and a Diaspora nationalist; he loved both America and Palestine.

Like Friedlaender, Magnes, and Benderly, Kaplan wanted to organize Jewish communities around modernized traditional synagogs. He reached out to tie the whole Jewish world together through a common philosophy that would make for survival. It was not a common theology that he sought but a common religionationalist culture. Like others who clustered around the Kehillah and its Bureau of Education he wanted to effect a synthesis of Jewish tradition and the demands of American culture. Kaplan, a Lithuanian, came to these shores as a child, went through Columbia, and was ordained as a rabbi at the Jewish Theological Seminary in 1902. Thus he was American trained. It was inevitable that he would attack the problem of adapting East European Judaism to the ineluctable intellectual demands of this country. From 1903 to 1909 he was an Orthodox rabbi at prestigious Kehillath Jeshurun; he was never to emancipate himself completely from Orthodoxy. In 1909 Schechter summoned him to become the principal of the Teachers Institute of the Seminary. This was an important, a strategic post. Like all professors at the Seminary he had other jobs. He taught homiletics. Kaplan was also one of the leaders of the Kehillah.

He and his friends looked with favor upon the development of the Central Jewish Institute (CJI) which was established in 1912. This school, a very unusual Talmud Torah attached to a synagog, reflected many of his teachings and hopes. Although the CJI was built around the needs of the child it reached out to embrace the family too. This Institute provided clubs and societies for the youngsters, sent them to summer camp, and offered them an elaborate diversified six-year curriculum. It was determined to foster the spiritual, the intellectual capacities of its students, both boys and girls. Traditional and American disciplines were taught. There were classes which addressed themselves to the American Jewish community and its problems; the course in American Jewish history was very probably the first taught in this country. The curriculum showed what could be done by devoted, imaginative professionals. The program was so successful that the school, achieving autonomy, was given a grant by the city's Jewish welfare federation. Sometime after the CJI was established in Yorkville, at 85th Street, a somewhat similar institution made its appearance on the West Side on 86th Street. This was the Jewish Center which may be looked upon as a clubhouse built around a synagog. In matters of worship it was Orthodox but in addition to a sanctuary it included facilities for sociality, education, and physical exercise. Undoubtedly the Center was influenced by the rise of the Protestant institutional churches which had flourished since the 1890's, but unlike the Christian institutions the Center catered to immigrants who had achieved affluence. The Central Jewish Institute on the East Side reached out to the neighborhood in general; the Jewish Center made provision primarily for its own families. Neither group set out to work with the underprivileged.

In 1922 Kaplan established the Society for the Advancement of Judaism; this marks the beginnings of Reconstructionism, a fourth Jewish "religious" denomination; it was different. Reconstructionism was a movement that was to influence not only the Conservatives—with whom Kaplan was allied—but also the Orthodox and the Reformers. The new denomination was eclectic in its philosophy; it was traditional yet radical. If the challenge of modernity was to be met, if the Jew was to survive in his new milieu, Judaism must change; it must become an evolving, progressive, nationalistic, religiocultural civilization. Kaplan's God is the hypostatization of man's highest ethical hopes. The Jewish religion, as he defined it, is broad enough to embrace any Jew no matter his belief. It could be all things to all men; this could well be a boon. Like Magnes, Kaplan set out to fashion a new Jewish community to meet the challenge of a new world which offered the incoming aliens an infinitude of opportunities. Like the other notables who graced the Kehillah he, too, was a cultural Zionist and a Diaspora nationalist. All these men believed in the Jewish people; one sometimes wonders whether the "Jewish People" was not a substitute for a Jewish God. They agreed, too, that the Jewish community must be all-inclusive. Mayhap, some of them believed, if only subconsciously, that religion was too divisive to serve as a bond; hence formal theology was shunted to the side; ethnicism was pushed to the fore. And like many others, Kaplan also insisted on recognizing women; he involved them in his religious services and instituted the ceremony of bat mitzvah for girls; this was a radical innovation.[23]

THE BUREAU'S DISCIPLES

Magnes, Friedlaender, Kaplan, and Benderly especially, raised disciples, working with enthusiastic young men and women, both native and foreign-born. These were the teachers who carried the good tidings to distant cities; they were frequently referred to as Benderly's "boys" and of course that included the girls like Rivkah Aaronson Brickner. These were the people who were to put the new ideas into practice; they set the course for the bureaus they led. It is said that Benderly had 100 disciples;

certainly his admirers were many. Outstanding among them were Alexander M. Dushkin, Isaac B. Berkson, Israel S. Chipkin, Leo Lazarus Honor, Barnett R. Brickner, Emanuel Gamoran. Many of them had studied at Columbia where they had come under the influence of the new trends in pedagogy. They were all cultural pluralists who had worked out their own syntheses of Judaism, Zionism, and Americanism standing astride these three different cultural worlds.

Some of them wrote dissertations in their chosen field. Isaac Baer Berkson handed in the first Jewish doctoral dissertation in education; when published it carried the title, *Theories of Americanization: A Critical Study with Special Reference to the Jewish Group* (1920). Typical of the influence of these disciples is the work of Gamoran. In 1923 the Union of American Hebrew Congregations and the Central Conference of American Rabbis appointed him executive of their joint Commission on Jewish Education. Through the publications Gamoran supervised he reached hundreds of congregations, not only Reform but Orthodox and Conservative. He was a pioneer in publishing good textbooks for the Jewish Sunday schools of America. Gamoran directed his work toward the synagogs' religious schools for he realized that with the emergence of congregational schools the so-called Talmud Torahs had little future. His work with the Reformers was particularly important for it brought their children closer to World Jewry. Benderly's "boys" and others who shared their views built Jewish schools that were comparable in quality to America's educational institutions; they helped move the Jewish school from medievalism to modernity.[24]

TEACHERS COLLEGES

Many of the young Jewish educators who began to dot the American cultural landscape had been influenced by the Teachers Institute of the Jewish Theological Seminary where Kaplan presided. As they sallied forth into the larger American world these young educators helped establish teachers colleges in other cities. In a sense the Institute of the Conservative Seminary helped pave the way for the Kehillah's Bureau. By 1921 there were several teachers colleges in this country. With one exception —the Yiddishists' school—they were all very much involved in teaching the Sacred Tongue in which the Bible is written. The first teachers school, Gratz College, opened in 1897. The Seminary's Institute which had opened in 1909 had been financed by the ever-generous Jacob H. Schiff who evenhandedly bestowed his largesse on the Hebrew Union College also. The Cincinnati Seminary's school of education was not particularly successful; Kaufmann Kohler, the president of the Reform seminary, was a scholar not an administrator. When the Schiff gift was turned over to him Kohler was almost sixty-six years of age.

The Seminary school was more successful; Kaplan was an educator with a mission; he had a large laboratory in New York with its 1,000,000 or so Jews; Cincinnati had about 20,000. By 1917, the Orthodox Zionists, the Mizrachi, opened a teachers college where the language of instruction was Hebrew; only men were admitted. Shortly thereafter Baltimore Jewry established a similar institution; it was the first outside of New York City; Benderly's influence was probably still felt. Now it was, too, that the socialists, the anti- Zionists, opened their school. Thus there were normal schools that catered to the needs of Reformers, Conservatives, Orthodox, Hebraists, Yiddishists, and Marxists. The clashing ideologies were well represented; diversity was traditional: "every man to his tents, O Israel" (2 Sam.20:1). After the 1920's there was a substantial increase in the number of teacher training institutions in the provinces and by the year 1930 there were schools for Jewish educators in Boston, Pittsburgh, Cleveland, and Chicago. Instruction was in English, Yiddish, or Hebrew according to the prevailing ideology. All these institutions taught history and some other subjects. A number of them met at night, for their students had to work during the day. The students were usually in their teens and included many girls; they were eager to improve themselves. Before 1930 even the Orthodox had opened a school to train female teachers; this was a radical step, a reversal of Jewish tradition. In all these training institutions American concepts of pedagogy and school organization were regnant.[25]

OPPOSITION TO THE BUREAU OF JEWISH EDUCATION

The multiplicity of teacher training schools with their different educational philosophies is eloquent testimony that "community" in education was an almost visionary ideal. Indeed the New York Bureau was faced with vigorous if not vitriolic opposition from different sources. Some of the older settlers, Uptowners, thought that the Bureau was too Hebraic, Zionist, Orthodox; Orthodoxy was associated with reaction. Radicals, socialists, internationalists, frowned upon the Bureau because it was Zionist, nationalist. In this ideological area the Socialist-Zionists were an exception; they looked forward to returning to the ancient homeland. Many Torah-True Jews looked askance at the Kehillah's Bureau because they were convinced that it was not sufficiently mindful of tradition and its observances. The untutored European-born teachers resented the efforts of Benderly and his cohorts to control the Talmud Torahs. These immigrant instructors who knew little English feared that if licensing procedures were adopted they could not pass the requisite examination. Schooled in the old ways they feared that they could not cope with the demands of modernization; they denounced the supervised Talmud Torahs as heretical institutions. They dared not admit to themselves that modern education was more important than a knowledge of Talmud. If rabbinic learning was bypassed in favor of the new disciplines, ordained rabbis of the old school would have no authority. This haunted them; the only commodity they had to offer was of little value in this profane new world. Thus there were Orthodox Jews who were anti-Kehillah, anti-Bureau, anti-modern.

On one occasion when Alexander Dushkin was showing some stereopticon slides a devout believer cut the electric cord; graven images must not be shown or projected; they are forbidden in God's Ten Commandments. The Bureau was threatened, too, by the state, for during World War I chauvinism was rampant; sedition was feared. The Bureau, the Jews, were Hebraists, philo-Palestinians, cultural pluralists. Magnes, the leader, was a pacifist! Any culture except that of a militant Americanism was suspect. Marshall was furious when he encountered these patriotic heresy hunters; he believed they ought to be investigated, not the Jews.[26]

WHAT HAPPENED TO THE BUREAU?

The Bureau was not a pronounced success; the "community" did not rush to assume responsibility for Jewish education. There was little tradition for such a communal approach; there were too many centrifugal ideological biases. The three Jewish denominations certainly did not wish to be coordinated, to be aligned. The Bureau never had the money it needed even for a modest program. The old educational systems continued to satisfy most of their clients. Children continued to attend the Reform Sunday schools, the afternoon congregational classes, and the heders; the families employed rebbes who came to the home and rehearsed their charges in rote reading; the Yiddishist educational institutions enjoyed catering to their followers. To be sure it is probable that some schools, possibly many, were touched by the pedagogical and curricular innovations of the Bureau; it had high visibility. It is very difficult, however, to determine the degree of this influence. If only 25 percent of New York's youngsters received some Jewish training every year, and if only a fraction of these were under the supervision of the Bureau, then obviously its direct influence was quite limited. There is reason to believe, however, that it would make its presence felt through Benderly's disciples.

However, the immediate accomplishments of the Bureau were modest. There were few if any communal systems of education set up anywhere except possibly in the small towns where unification of effort was a painful necessity. When one reflects on the coordinating activities of the mid-nineteenth century Hebrew Education Society in New York and Philadelphia one wonders how real were the advances of the Bureau, organizationally speaking. The New York bureau had but six or seven years of intensive activity as an autonomous organization. Around the year

1917 some of the city's Talmud Torahs began to receive subsidies from the local federation of charities; the Uptown was back in the saddle. By 1941 the Bureau gave up the ghost; a new organization, the Jewish Education Committee, took over. The elite Uptowners hoped that Jewish education would bridge the gap between parents and children; the Jewish home must be strengthened, protected. It is not easy to determine the degree to which the old-timers were interested in furthering the Jewish education of the immigrants; however the philanthropies did not impose their ideology on the schools that they aided though they were always aware of Zionist indoctrination. Benderly and his cohorts went along with the federation; they had no choice; they had no money. In a way aid from the federation was a move forward; it was a form of communal recognition of the importance of Jewish schooling, of the need to help.

By 1925 very few East European immigrants were permitted to land in America's harbors; the United States was no longer to be "the asylum of all the oppress'd in Europe," with all due respect to Benjamin Franklin. The Talmud Torahs would ultimately decline; they took too much time out of the lives of boys and girls. The interest of the children was centered on the public schools, not on Hebrew or religious instruction. There was however a solid core of Orthodox who were determined to hold the line; after World War II they began building parochial schools and these increased rapidly as public school standards declined and the impact of the Holocaust was felt in this country. When the newcomers were acculturated they became conscious of the low standards of their own Hebrew schools and the inadequacies of foreign-born teachers; consequently they gradually began to reject the heders and the rebbes who taught in them. The first native-born generation of East European ancestry, graduates of the American public school system, summarily rejected the old-fashioned schools. On the way up financially, many old world parents moved out of the East Side and joined congregations in the new areas of settlement. These synagogs had organized afternoon Hebrew schools that in the course of time became effective pedagogical instrumentalities that furthered the denomination, not the concept of community. By the 1920's congregational and Sunday schools were becoming popular among the East Europeans. In the 1980's congregational schooling was still in the ascendancy although there were faint intimations of communal education.[27]

THE BURGEONING OF MODERN JEWISH EDUCATION IN NEW YORK CITY

Even as late as 1920 most Jewish youngsters were still being educated along the lines laid down by the East European parents and the ancestors of those parents. There can be no question however that the Bureau was making its presence felt, to a certain degree. If not pioneers Bureau educators were harbingers of new approaches. Intimations of modernity were present no later than the 1880's. Writing a letter to his parents in 1886 the learned Judah David Eisenstein defended his right to teach his son English grammatically and permit him to play the piano. "The present requires other measures . . . necessity impels us, so that we may mingle with the people among whom we live." As early as 1893 a Brooklynite, Zundel Hirsch Neumann had established a modern all-day school, the Gates of Zion, Shaare Tsiyyon. He taught Bible grammatically, Hebrew as a living language, mathematics, Jewish history, modern languages, and provided his students with library facilities. Even more he promised to teach them manners and the importance of cleanliness. The stress on Hebrew as a living spoken tongue owed much to the nascent Zionist movement. No later than 1910 the Hebrew schools in this country were ready to come to terms with America. There were already a number of good educational institutions staffed by excellent teachers. By the early twentieth century New York's newcomers could even boast that they had a nursery school and a kindergarten.

It is significant that these immigrants, ignoring their past, surrendered to the American demand that girls, too, be educated. Even the Machzike Talmud Torah which had been established in the 1880's finally began admitting large numbers of girls in the second decade of the twentieth century. Orthodoxy at times reflected a remarkable capacity to adapt itself; this may well explain its survival despite the vicissitudes of two tortuous millennia. A yeshivah, a talmudic rabbinical college, is usually the last bastion of Orthodoxy. Traditionally it is uncompromising. Then, in 1915, the Lithuania émigré, Bernard Revel, united two yeshivahs and gave the students a chance to study profane subjects in a thoroughly modern high school which he had organized. Seven years earlier the students had already gone on strike insisting upon their right to study secular disciplines; they won concessions. What made Revel, a devoted adherent of Orthodoxy, a modernist in education? He had gone to a secular high school in Russia; his Philadelphia patron, a notable Orthodox rabbi, encouraged him to pursue doctoral studies at Dropsie. Frequently, not always, the Orthodox, the comparatively unbending believers, learned to roll with the punches.[28]

MODERN JEWISH SCHOOLS IN THE PROVINCES

Modern teachers colleges, bureaus of Jewish education, and progressive Talmud Torahs were established in all major Jewish communities. Most of these new institutions were aimed at educating the children of immigrants from Eastern Europe. The influence of New York's Bureau of Jewish Education reached into the hinterland, frequently carried there by Benderly's boys and girls who settled in several of America's major centers. Even the more modern Orthodox attitude toward education as represented by Revel had its influence in the hinterland. In the course of a decade or two there were improved Talmud Torahs in Minneapolis, Pittsburgh, Philadelphia, Cleveland, Saint Louis, Baltimore, Boston, Buffalo, Cincinnati, Detroit, Chicago, Indianapolis, Denver, and San Francisco. In a number of these towns the traditional Jewish educational institutions were subsidized by the local philanthropy federations; they would not have tolerated the old European forms of schooling. They were quite willing to give money to Orthodox schools but they required instruction in English. In a sense these federation subsidized "communal" schools were transitional institutions; when, as in New York City, congregational schools began to flourish in the provinces the local bureaus of Jewish education declined in importance.

Individual educators stood out; it was they who made good schools possible. Independent of Benderly's Bureau—so it would seem—these men had already developed their own ideas and their own educational philosophies. As early as 1907 Rabbi Simon Glazer, staunchly traditional, had begun writing English textbooks for the Orthodox youth of this country. It is patent that old-country rabbis like Glazer—and there were several—were determined to salvage traditionalism; they were quite willing to bend pedagogically, to discard Yiddish and to adopt English as the teaching medium. Orthodox rabbis in Atlanta and other towns learned to preach in English; they were concerned about the young members of their congregations. These leaders were fully cognizant that if they could not appeal to the children in a vernacular which they respected, Orthodoxy would suffer. Early in the twentieth century the Orthodox *Tageblatt* of New York had the smallest circulation of all the Yiddish newspapers in the city; the Orthodox leaders did not need this ominous statistic to warn them of the challenge to their faith.[29]

A few notes—arbitrarily selective to be sure—will illustrate the progress of modern Jewish educational practices among the East Europeans in some of this country's major cities. Boston like other towns had traditional Talmud Torahs in the 1880's; by 1907—several years before Benderly left Baltimore for New York—Hebrew was being taught in the hub city according to the natural method. By 1917 Boston had federated twelve religious schools; it was this group that organized a teachers training course in 1918; ultimately the Hebrew Teachers College emerged from this initial pedagogical effort (1921). This new training institution built an elaborate Hebrew program in the course of years; its support came from the local Jewish charity federation, membership dues, and funds collected by devoted and devout women. Like Boston, Philadelphia, too, brought its Hebrew schools together into a federation. Bernard L. Levinthal, the dean of Orthodox rabbis, encouraged the schools to employ America's educational techniques. Baltimore got off to a good start pedagogically because of Benderly; he had taught there for many years developing his philosophy of Jewish education and perfecting his teaching skills. When one of the Talmud Torahs began instructing the children in English those who resented this innovation set up a rival institution where Yiddish was retained; the new English-speaking school had a student roster of 700. In those days popular Talmud Torahs succeeded in enrolling large classes; New York's Uptown Talmud Torah sheltered almost 1,500 boys; one of Benderly's experimental schools for girls met in the same building.[30]

The modern Talmud Torah in Pittsburgh was the very successful Hebrew Institute founded in 1916; in 1920 it had 800 pupils and branches in different parts of the city. Though it was a tuition school almost anyone in need could secure a scholarship. And like some other schools it, too, had classes for those wishing to pursue advanced studies; its high school department was named after a local Reform Jewish philanthropist. A teachers school was added; there was a kindergarten for tots and classes in cooking for the girls. The high excellence of this well-known Pittsburgh school was due to Israel A. Abrams (b.1882), a Pole who had studied in yeshivot at home and in colleges here in this country. Before coming to Pittsburgh he had honed his administrative skills directing Hebrew schools in Chicago and Baltimore. He knew of Benderly and his Bureau, and may have been influenced by the views of the Baltimore educationist. Some of Abrams's students became notable Jewish communal workers and leaders in later decades. Fifteen years before Abrams came to Pittsburgh Aaron Mordecai Ashinsky, rabbi of the Orthodox Beth Midrash Ha-Gadol, the Chief House of Learning, had already established an English-speaking Sunday school. It was an exemplary institution. One of his teachers, young Freda Davis, was a graduate of a prestigious eastern women's college. (Her brother, Allan, was a Harvard man.) She was modern and progressive in every sense of the term. The immigrants from the Hill District, the ghetto, the acculturated newcomers, and old-line Reform families joined together in Pittsburgh to support Jewish education not only for its own sake but because they, too, were worried about the threat of juvenile delinquency.

The Buffalo Jewish traditionalists were fortunate in that they were privileged to send their children to a thoroughly modern Hebrew school in the 1890's. Blind chance was responsible for this. By 1904 Buffalo's Talmud Torah was directed by a scholarly man who had received his doctorate at a German university and had perfected his academic training by attending American colleges. This Talmud Torah opened its doors on Sunday for children whose parents, so it would seem, were loath to send them to Reform weekend classes. There were Jews in town who looked with suspicion upon an Orthodox Talmud Torah where subjects were taught in English; they insisted that some of the subjects be taught in Yiddish and their wish was granted. Two of America's most noted Hebraists taught in this Talmud Torah; they were Ephraim E. Lisitzky and Hillel Bavli.[31]

It is curious but true that the Minneapolis Talmud Torah, off by itself, distant from vibrant Jewish mass communities, had a national reputation for excellence. This it owed to one man, Dr. George Jacob Gordon (1874-1943), a Lithuanian. Like most other Russian or Polish educators who came here Gordon, too, had gone to a yeshivah and filled his belly with talmudic lore. After coming to the United States at the age of eighteen he settled in Minneapolis and set out to secure an American education. It took him one year to cover the subjects in public school; it took him more time to master the high school curriculum; while studying he supported himself by teaching Hebrew. Then he moved on to Philadelphia where he worked his way through a medical school tutoring not only Hebrew but also Latin. After receiving his degree he went back to his Minneapolis home where he practiced obstetrics, teaching his specialty in a college. Minneapolis Jewry accepted him socially despite his foreign background; he became a member of the somewhat exclusive B'nai B'rith, and made a name for himself as a respected communal worker. When a black dentist was refused office space Gordon and one of the rabbis worked together to remedy his plight; for many years Minneapolis was known for its reactionary attitudes toward Jews and others.

It was 1911 before Dr. Gordon and his friends were finally able to open a Talmud Torah that was to become an exemplary institution. It offered classes for advanced students; all told the full curriculum required ten years of study. It was amazing that 36 percent of those who entered finished; normally only about 5 percent of the youngsters enrolled in Talmud Torahs stayed the course. At one time the alumni association included about 800 members. In 1928 Gordon decided to give up his practice of medicine and to devote himself full time to his Talmud Torah as its executive head. He knew what he had to do; like Benderly and others he was convinced that education, Jewish schooling, was American Jewry's most important challenge; these men were concerned with Jewish survival in an open society.

In 1887 two Cincinnatians, aided by other concerned Jews, set out successfully to open a Talmud Torah; they were Moses Isaacs and Behr Manischewitz. Isaacs, a member of the nationally-respected Isaacs family noted for its Orthodoxy, was American-born. Manischewitz was the founder of the famous matzo manufacturing corporation. This Talmud Torah announced that it would not only teach Hebrew, translation of the Pentateuch and history but would also introduce its students to the Shulhan Arukh, Jewry's popular legal code. One wonders to what extent this goal was reached. In 1904 the language of instruction was no longer exclusively Yiddish; some English was employed; girls, too, were later permitted to attend. The tuition fees charged were not sufficient to support the school; the budget was met by the proceeds from solicitations and collection boxes. Manischewitz, committed to Orthodoxy and Hebrew education, sold the Talmud Torah matzos at cost; it, in turn, sold the matzos at retail and used the profit to help maintain the school. In the second decade of the century the Talmud Torah dedicated a building of its own; the substantial mortgage was ultimately paid off by a female auxiliary.

The Downtowners, traditional of course, opened a Sabbath school for their girls; they were wary of the Reform Sunday schools though in fact most of the East European youngsters attended the Reform Sunday schools where they were welcome. When these boys and girls grew up and achieved a modicum of affluence many of them joined Reform synagogs. The Downtown Talmud Torah, in accordance with the spirit of the day, organized a Parent-Teacher Association. About a decade after the immigrants began moving out of the "bottoms"—Cincinnati's ghetto— the Talmud Torah followed it to the suburban hills of Avondale establishing its new home in the area just vacated by the more affluent German Jews (1927). The new school, now a part of the Jewish Bureau of Education, had the support of the elite "Germans" and the more affluent Russians.

Benderly, the Palestine Ashkenazi, and Louis Marshall, the Ashkenazic American, were at one tackling the same problem; they hoped to make it possible for Jews to remain Jewish in the American milieu. To a considerable degree they shared the same traditional belief: education and religion are really one; for the Jew study is worship. By the early twentieth century all Jewish forces in America were already conscious of the need to educate youth along new lines. Notable advances were being made educationally in all quarters although it was equally true there were thousands of boys and girls who were receiving little or no formal religious instruction. (However this had always been true in Jewish life in centuries past.) By 1921, as the portals to America began to close, Jews more than ever were exposed, full force, to the assimilatory impact of the country; the immigrant reservoirs of loyalty, devotion, observance were ebbing fast. All Jews, both those of the older and of the newer migrations, knew that they could no longer ignore the pressing problem of educating large numbers of the country's Jewish youth.[32]

NON-RELIGIOUS YIDDISHIST SCHOOLS

Most Jewish schools in the United States were established by religionists, many of whom were Russians; they were overwhelmingly Orthodox. The prime subject which they taught was Hebrew; it was the cement which held Orthodox Jews together. But there were notable exceptions; a vigorous minority of secularists set out before 1921 to create their own educational institutions. These dissidents were opposed to traditional Orthodoxy. They were dedicated to the humanities; politically they were left-wing; in fact many if not most of them were socialists; they supported labor and stressed social justice, ethics. Like the Orthodox they, too, wanted to bind the children to the parents and the home. The Orthodox wanted to do it through Hebrew, the heder, the Talmud Torah, the synagog; the secularists wanted to reach the same goal by the use of Yiddish.

To this end they fashioned schools of their own. Yiddish was basic, not peripheral; it was to serve not only as a medium of communication but also as an instrument for cultural growth; these East European devotees wished to create and further a distinctive Yiddish literature; Yiddish was their cherished folk tongue. The founders of this new school system were influenced by secular schools that had already been established in Russia and in Poland. America's Yiddish schools, secular and radical, were a product of the twentieth century. Why Jewish secular schools? In Russia very few Jews wanted any part of the traditional Panslavic general culture. It was no problem to turn against the Russians and their standard beliefs, for the Russians had rejected all Jews contemptuously. Back in Russia many Jews, political and cultural liberals, had also turned against the intransigent Jewish Orthodoxy that refused to compromise with modernity. These radicals were anti-religious, anti-national, cosmopolitan, eager to embrace and incorporate the teachings of science.

The cultural and political ideals and hopes cherished by these dissidents were transported to the United States. Although many of these incoming secularists, logically committed to assimilation, would not have stressed the fact that they were eager to be Jews, they were nevertheless determined to maintain themselves as a separate group on the fringes of Jewry. Here in the United States Yiddish was flourishing in 1910; there were newspapers and magazines for all schools of thought; creative Yiddish-speaking leaders were admired and read. America gave these immigrant ideologues the right to profess and cultivate their disparate philosophies, to reach out to win the New York and provincial Yiddish-speaking masses for their cultural views and spiritual beliefs. This was a freedom they had never enjoyed in Russia or Poland. The new schools these Yiddishists founded here were influenced by American educational practices; this they had in common with Benderly though he had remained cautiously within the ambit of religion. Despite their professed devotion to socialism and internationalism these men and women were Jewish survivalists; they wanted to be identified as Jews, to further Yiddish culture; they loved the language. Culturally they were humanistic, always eager to embrace the best in the world about them. They had emancipated themselves from tradition, overtly at least.

After the dust of polemics and discussion had settled these dissenters found that they had called into being four different types of Yiddish schools here in the United States. One type was the schools of the various Socialist-Zionist groups. As early as 1910 the Socialist-Zionists, the Poale Zion, had opened a weekend school; a few years later their fraternal order, the Farband, the Jewish National Workers' Alliance of America took over the support of these educational institutions. These Zionist-oriented socialists were never able to recruit many pupils—there is an inner contradiction between nationalism and internationalism; as late as 1918 the Farband only had about 6,000 members in all America. National-radical was the name given to the new weekend courses; later, when afternoon classes were set up the preferred term was folk schools; by the time of World War I, 1917, "radical" was a dirty word. The slogan adopted by these Yiddishists was an attractive one: the Jewish child belongs to the Jewish people. At first most of the children who attended these schools were girls. Despite their secularism, parents who were intent on educating their sons Jewishly sent them to heders and Talmud Torahs.

The curricula of the different Yiddish schools were quite similar; no religion was taught; using Yiddish as the medium of instruction the teachers taught history, customs, folkways and Yiddish literature; they stressed socialism, morality. The Zionist socialists were the only Yiddishists who taught Hebrew in the early days because of their ultimate hope of a return to Palestine where Hebrew would be the national tongue. The different Yiddishist groups now emerging established presses and published their own texts; their ideologies, their differences, were sacred. By 1918 the pioneer Yiddishists, Zion's Workers, had opened the Jewish Teachers' Seminary. Some Hebrew Bible was taught, even some Talmud. The powerful Workmen's Circle order which ultimately followed the Zionist socialists in opening afternoon schools, attempted originally to train their own instructors but they and another radical group joined together to support the Jewish Teachers' Seminary. Maintaining separate normal schools was a luxury which workmen could not afford.

The pioneer Yiddish schools were committed to teaching socialism and Zionism; there were other socialists who were also Territorialists; according to them it was not imperative that Jews rebuild the old homeland; a Jewish commonwealth might be established in some other country. This was the teaching of Chaim Zhitlowsky who had many admirers in this country where he had finally settled. In 1913 a small coterie of Territorialists founded a Yiddish school in the Bronx; later the group became apolitical. By 1916 the Territorialists had several small schools; two years later they established an umbrella organization and called it the Sholem Aleichem Folk Institute, Inc.; it was named of course after the famous Yiddish writer who had just died in this country. This particular group was interested in Yiddish literature; its goals were cultural, not political. More so than many other Yiddishists these men and women did not hesitate to affirm their Jewishness. They attempted to steer clear of the radical Yiddishists who warred with one another and fought the battle of communism and anti-communism.

These Sholem Aleichem devotees did not attack Zionists; in later years they even taught some Hebrew in their more advanced classes. Some knowledge of Hebrew was necessary because Yiddish employed the Hebrew not the Latin alphabet; there were several thousand Hebrew and Aramaic phrases in Yiddish. The Institute published a Passover service book, a Haggadah, in Yiddish not in Hebrew. Unlike the Orthodox the Sholem Aleichem boys did not wear the traditional skullcap nor did they learn or recite the traditional Aramaic prayer for the dead, the kaddish. The curriculum which they were the first to formulate tended to become typical for all Yiddishists; emphasis was laid on literature, history, customs, the Jewish festivals. The concept of the Jewish "folk" was stressed. This organization always remained small; there were never more than 1,000 children in all its schools. In 1922 the Sholem Aleichem Institute set up its first camp, Camp Boiberik. No kashrut was observed but there were Sabbath services where the children were entertained and edified by stories of the past; music, the arts and crafts were also taught. In later years it, too, gave courses in Hebrew. These Yiddishists observed the Ninth of Av, the anniversary of the Fall of the Temple and the Jewish state, but this was a genuflection in the direction of folkishness, nationalism, not Judaism. In later decades the various Yiddish secularists opened camps of their own; the Workmen's Circle, the largest of these Yiddishist associations, established camps near several major cities.

As indicated above the Arbeter Ring, the Workmen's Circle, also established Yiddish schools. This was the group that remained schismatic the longest; it was anti-nationalist, anti-romantic, anti-Palestine, anti-religious; its followers were good consistent socialists. They identified strongly with labor; some refused, in theory at least, to emphasize their Jewishness. Marxism was all important for them but the sufferings incurred by their dear ones in Eastern Europe during World War I brought many back to Jewry; by 1916 they began seriously to talk of the importance of Yiddish schools; by 1918 they opened their first one. Their slogan in those days was, "the Jewish child belongs to the Jewish working class." Later when they broke with the communists and when the Germans began liquidating Jews they were more willing to accept the watchword of the other Yiddishists, "the Jewish child belongs to the Jewish people." Slowly they began inching to the right; they were not avowedly nationalist yet they were no longer anti-Zionist. This rapprochement with Jewry and its sancta was reflected in their willingness finally to teach some Hebrew and to observe some of the Holy Days such as Passover, Hanukkah, and Purim. These three festivals were identified with political freedom, escape from the Egyptians, the Syrians, the Persians. Purim was also celebrated because it was a child's holiday enlivened by merrymaking and the giving of gifts.

American holidays were celebrated in the Yiddish schools; the Fourth of July and the 12th of February, Lincoln's birthday, were treasured. The anniversary of the Russian Revolution was also commemorated for then it was that the Jews were freed from Russian oppression; the first of May was another one of their holidays for it emphasized the brotherhood of all who labored. There is a relatively obscure Jewish holiday which was resuscitated by the Arbeter Ring school; this was Lag ba-Omer, the thirty-third day of the counting between Passover and Pentecost. These radical Yiddishists singled it out either because traditionally it was a child's holiday or they were aware that it might well commemorate the second-century revolt of the tiny Judaean state against the Roman Empire. The Workmen's Circle was a large order; by 1939 it could number 130 educational institutions with about 8,000 pupils. Ultimately the Yiddishists nurtured these four different secular school systems: the Socialist-Zionists, the apolitical Sholem Aleichem cohorts, the strongly socialist Arbeter Ring, and the communist Jewish Peoples Fraternal Order, part of a larger complex known as the International Workers' Order. The last group had seceded from the Workmen's Circle in the 1920's; these secessionists were completely schismatic except for the fact that Yiddish was the language employed in the numerous supplementary schools which they had set up.

YIDDISHIST SCHOOLS IN THE PROVINCES

Soon after the Socialist-Zionists opened their first weekend schools in the New York area similar institutions were founded in many American towns. A number of Socialist-Territorialists in distant Sioux City, Iowa, established a Yiddishist educational institution. These men and women were not enamored of the prospect of a Palestine commonwealth. As followers of Chaim Zhitlowsky they were willing to work for a Jewish commonwealth outside of the Holy Land; they were prepared to meld Jewish nationalism and socialism. Patterning themselves on the Socialist-Zionists, Yiddish folkists also began setting up Yiddish schools in various sections of the United States; this is in the second decade of the twentieth century. These Yiddishist school founders were well aware that most children in Hebrew schools were learning the Sacred Tongue only by rote; these radical innovators were determined to teach content in a vernacular which the youngsters understood, Yiddish. Detroit had a weekend national-radical school in 1912; a few years later a Socialist-Territorialist institution opened its doors but it was not until 1921 that the Arbeter Ring followed the others in establishing a school in that city. Milwaukee had a Poale Zion folk school in 1911-1912; not to be outdone, in 1913 the Arbeter Ring opened its own Yiddish educational classes for boys and girls emphasizing socialism and Jewish ethnicity and ignoring Hebrew and anything that smacked of religion. Aroused by these "false" teachings and determined to counter them the local Orthodox finally pulled themselves together and started a Sunday school for girls.

Chicago's first Yiddish school was opened in 1912; others soon followed. One of these radical institutions studied the lives of socialist and Jewish notables; included in what was a mixed galaxy were Robert Owen, the Baal Shem Tov, founder of Hassidism, Karl Marx, the talmudic genius Elijah of Vilna, and the renowned modernist Moses Mendelssohn of Berlin. The Poale Zion entered the list in 1914 with the Maccabean folk schools; the Workmen's Circle, usually the last to organize because of its hesitancy to stress Jewish values, established schools in 1919; it was not long before they enrolled 1,300 pupils; by 1930 the order had several schools in town. During the 1920's Chicago's Yiddish schools represented different and often competing ideologies; despairing political neutrals established a Sholem Aleichem school where they could cultivate their ideals in peace. In Providence, Rhode Island, the Workmen's Circle children met in the Labor Lyceum; the pictures they hung on their walls documented their ecumenical devotion to the world's liberals. They paid homage to Eugene V. Debs, Morris Hillquit, Meyer London, Norman Thomas—the perennial Socialist candidate for the presidency—and two European Jews, Ferdinand Lassalle (1825-1864) and Moritz Hess (1812-1875), both socialists. Hess, one of the most interesting of European Jewry's notables, was a socialist, a communist, a proto-Zionist of sorts, a cultural pluralist.

THE YIDDISHIST SCHOOLS—A SUMMARY

The student of American Jewish history must always maintain perspective in studying these non-religious Yiddish schools. They grew very slowly; the Yiddishists were swimming against the current. Statistically they were not important; the workers who sponsored them were always poor; schools are expensive. As late as 1919, about a decade after the

Workers of Zion established their first classes, there were only 10 schools in the country with a total of about 400 pupils. The Yiddish schools did grow; they were still open and active in the late 1940's. This was because many Russian and Polish immigrants were still alive; they loved Yiddish. In 1946 the socialists and non-communists reported that all told they had 217 such schools with 14,000 pupils; the communists, 94 schools with 6,000 students. These are the figures that are given; they seem high. The schools were supported primarily by their respective lodges and orders; ideology was important to the Socialist-Zionists and the Workmen's Circle; the Sholem Aleichem supporters had no fraternal order to finance them; this may explain why they had so few students. All these institutions emphasized cultural autonomy; this was precious in their sight. What they had in common—whether they admitted it or not—was their hope for survival as Jews; this bound them to World Jewry. These Yiddishists fought gallantly to build a cultural pluralistic world of their own; it was a conceptual world that could not survive. Ultimately Anglo-Saxon culture, Americanism, was to emerge triumphant because all the children attended the public schools where indoctrination was irresistible. The youngsters became American Jews not Yiddish Americans.

What has just been said about the Yiddishist schools applied equally well to the all-day parochial schools of the religionists. The English disciplines they studied in those religious institutions and the American ambience that enveloped them cemented them permanently to American culture. In the late 1940's the Socialist-Zionists and the Sholem Aleichem people attempted to establish all-day (parochial) schools in Greater New York. These schools did not prosper. After World War II the secular school movement declined. The students were all natives; some were of the third generation. American-born boys and girls could not be culturally, linguistically isolated. By this time all these schools, with the exception of those administered by communists, were nonschismatic, Jewishly speaking; their sympathies were definitely Jewish; they had rejoined World Jewry. It was not easy for Yiddish schools to maintain themselves as separatist entities; the new curricula clearly reflect their move to the right. After World War II all these schools were subject to a strong Jewish social pressure which was basically religious in nature. By this time the children in some of these Yiddish schools were blessing candles, attending High Holy Day services, conducting seders, and enjoying secularist bar mitzvahs. Their kindergartens, their elementary and high schools, were Jewishly tinted.

What brought about these changes in the 1940's? The anti-Semitism in the United States and Europe in the 1920's and 1930's, mass murders of millions abroad drove Jews back to their people. They had no place to go; the world still rejected them. This explains in large part why they modified their curriculum in the direction of yiddishkeit. Now they studied the Bible, emphasized their past history, revived old folkways, and came closer to American and World Jewry. Most of the schools had originally been opened to maintain class consciousness but these very socialist parents encouraged their children to go to college to become professionals, bourgeois elitists. Basically all the children were deproletarianized; very few were Marxists. The new generation did not want to be set apart, walled off as an ethnic minority; Yiddish schools were a transient cultural episode. Even before the Holocaust all the schools, except those of the International Workmen's Order, had become pro-Palestinian for that was one of the few lands still open to refugees. The Yiddishists all had kin who were desperately seeking asylum in the 1930's. It is true the schools persisted in the 1940's but they were soon to decline in membership.

Why did Yiddish, the language, persist into the late twentieth century? Was Yiddish a whim of its devotees? To give up Yiddish was self-destruction; it was the mother tongue, the medium that tied Jews to fellow nationals in all corners of the Diaspora. As an all-important instrument of communication it was more *actuel* than Hebrew. All linguistic cultures die slowly. At all times the schismatics who employed Yiddish were part of the Jewish people if only because of the Yiddish they loved. This is true even of the Jewish communists. Yiddish education is Jewish education even if it is non-religious, anti-religious.[33]

CHAPTER TWENTY

WORLD WAR I AND THE AMERICAN JEWISH

JOINT DISTRIBUTION COMMITTEE

INTRODUCTION

World War broke out in Europe in August 1914. It was not long before England, France, and Russia—the Triple Entente—were arrayed against the Triple Alliance, Germany, Austria, Turkey. At stake was world hegemony, world power; England was determined to dominate; Germany threatened her rule. When this European conflict erupted most Jews in the United States took sides though the country was not as yet directly involved. The Jewish socialist leaders of trade unions and their followers would have nothing to do with the war; they disdained the bourgeois capitalists; workmen in the embattled nations would gain nothing killing one another. The Zionists, few in number, were split; some, neutralists, did not wish to offend the Turks lest they destroy the Palestine colonies. The headquarters of the World Zionist movement was then in Cologne; these Zionists did not wish to offend the Germans. Other followers of Herzl, pro-Entente, hoped that with the fall of the Ottoman state the West Europeans, the Bible-loving English particularly, would aid the Zionists by establishing a commonwealth of sorts in the Land of Promise. This dream approached reality in 1917 when the British agreed—so it seemed—to restore the Holy Land to the Jews. After the United States entered the war on the side of the Allies all Zionists here in this country rallied behind the government. The Yiddish journals, however, with few exceptions, were anti-Entente because they were anti-Russian. Russia was a land of infamy; thousands had been abused and killed in that country even in the twentieth century. America's acculturated Central European Jewish immigrants, the "Germans," were also anti-Russian not only because of Muscovite brutality but also because they loved their Fatherland and its culture despite the fact that anti-Semitism was a German product. By 1871, however, the Germans had accorded their Jews equal rights. Fully aware of the social and cultural disabilities that were still regnant in Germany and Austria, American Jewish bankers like Schiff, would have been willing to float loans for the Entente if Russia would only emancipate her Jews; this she refused to do.[1]

THE SUFFERINGS OF THE JEWS IN THE WAR ZONES

The sufferings of the Jews in the East European war zones were severe; millions of Jews lived in the areas which the armies contested. The Russians invaded Germany and Austria; the Germans and Austrians pushed them back; caught in between, the Jews suffered doubly, as Jews and as war casualties. The Russians and the Poles were cruel to their fellow subjects. Hating Jews and seeking to disable them economically the Poles initiated boycotts to drive them out of business. Russian Jewish prisoners were the object of solicitude by the German Jewish charities; Jews in the Polish areas occupied by the Germans were not grossly mistreated. The invaders sought the cooperation of the Yiddish (German!) speaking masses; German Jewish chaplains—among them Rabbi Leo Baeck—were a restraining and beneficent influence. The German national Jewish philanthropic agency, the Hilfsverein, was eager to be of assistance. The Germans were by no means angelic; anti-Jewish bias was never absent; the military authorities—always looking for a scapegoat if they lost the war —set out through a census to prove that the German Jews were slackers; they never published their findings. German Jews on this side of the Atlantic were convinced—and they were probably right—that if the German allies won the war they would bring German culture and, ultimately, emancipation to the millions in Poland and Russia. Once the East European Jews were granted equal rights and given the advantages of a modern education a Golden Age would blossom built on a synthesis of modern culture and rabbinic learning.

Those Austro-Galician refugees who fled west before the advancing Russians ran into trouble. The Bucovinian Jews who moved south into Rumania were harried; like the Poles the Rumanians were rarely if ever kind to Jews. The Galicians who sought shelter in Austria proper were not welcomed though the Allianz, the national Jewish relief and defense agency, came to their aid. The Russian and Polish Jews suffered greatly during World War I. While fathers, brothers, sons, soldiers, were fighting and dying at the front their families were being deported brutally into the interior of Russia. Locked in box cars they were frequently denied food and water. When threatened with defeat the Russians suppressed the Yiddish newspapers; at times the Russian vernacular press even refused to publish the names of Jews who had been decorated for heroism; Jews were accused of spying for the enemy; the medieval accusation of poisoning the wells was revived. Russian Jewry, however, was fortunate that its well-organized relief associations helped ameliorate distress. Russian Jewry's economic losses were tremendous; thousands were murdered in the civil wars that wracked the Ukraine in 1919-1920; the agony of the years 1914-1920 was matched only by the slaughter in 1648 when the Cossacks and the Tatars ravaged the Polish provinces.[2]

THE RISE OF NEW RELIEF ORGANIZATIONS DURING THE FIRST WORLD WAR

It is not difficult to imagine how the Jews in the United States felt when they heard reports from the Eastern War zones. Of the some 3,000,000 Jews here most were Russian and Polish immigrants. Their immediate families were threatened; the parents, wives, and children of many of them were still in the villages waiting to be brought over. Something had to be done immediately. There was in this country no organized association equipped to raise funds on a large scale. When the American Jewish Committee was created in 1906 it envisaged European relief as an important component of its work. Most of the national relief societies established up to that time had done their job and then disbanded. The American Jewish Committee stayed on.

During the years 1912-1913 Turkey and the Balkan states went to war. New nationalistic Christian states were rising intent on dismembering the Ottoman Empire. Confusion was exacerbated by intra-Christian wars as the Slavs and Austrians fought for power in Southeastern Europe. In those short-lived conflicts lands and people were shifted about, Jews among them. The latter suffered more than others; they had been second-class citizens under the Turks; their position was little improved in the new states; indeed, under the Rumanians they were worse off than under the Moslems. These Jewish unfortunates were helped by the French Alliance Israélite Universelle; the American Jews, working through the B'nai B'rith and the American Jewish Committee, did what they could. The Committee employed the services of the German Hilfsverein. When World War I exploded making its demands on America's Jews, American Jewry had never been so challenged. As the largest Jewish group in the world not directly involved in the conflict the Jews here were called upon to help millions of people; over 40 percent of the world's Jews were in the path of the advancing and retreating armies. American Jewry responded to the call for help without any hesitation. The American Jewish organizations set out to help stricken civilians in the war zones. Much of the work of these associations was carried on after the war for it was not easy to help people as battles were fought. The Red Cross, the Quakers, were called upon for help. Realizing the desperate plight of Europe's masses in the postwar period the Congress voted $100,000,000 for the

American Relief Administration; Herbert Hoover was put in charge of the mission. The gargantuan task that faced American Jewry and its readiness to meet the challenge of feeding, clothing, and reconstructing the very lives of the East Europeans—the largest Jewry in the world— prompts this query. Were these American Jews unique in their utter commitment and in their accomplishments on behalf of coreligionists and fellow nationalists? One suspects that they were. Aware of the needs of stricken Palestine and Europe, Louis Marshall, head of the American Jewish Committee, issued a strong public appeal for aid as early as September 1914. Convinced that the governments in a Slavic Europe would do little for their Jews he called upon his coreligionists here to save the wretched masses. But even before he could organize American Jewry effectually Orthodox immigrants here established a national relief congeries on October 4, 1914. This was the Central Relief Committee. Its first impulse was to rescue the rabbis, the scholars, the rabbinic academies. The learned came first; this was an old talmudic tradition going back well over seventeen centuries (Baba Bathra, 8a). The Orthodox established an Ezrath Torah Fund; save those who study God's Law! But like the sages in Roman times the Central Relief Committee had second thoughts and set out to help wherever it could. These important Orthodox Jews—they looked askance at the Reformers—tried to work on their own but recognizing speedily their lack of funds and skills they turned to the natives and old-timers; they knew they would not be rejected.

Marshall was annoyed that the Orthodox had set up a separate relief society. It would seem that he hoped the American Jewish Committee would be able to unite all Jews here for this humanitarian task. He wanted one single agency; this was the efficient approach but he soon realized it was the better part of wisdom to start anew; New York's Jewry would not accept the American Jewish Committee. He and the Committee summoned American leaders to meet on October 25, 1914, at Temple Emanu-El. Representatives of dozens of organizations assembled and established the American Jewish Relief Committee (AJRC). Marshall, the president, hoped that this AJRC would serve as the all-inclusive national organization of all Jews in this country. He wanted no overlapping campaigns; he was willing to work with all factions and was moving to organize the hinterland to effect his purposes. Refusing to disband, the Central Relief Committee nonetheless joined with Marshall. Just a few weeks after the AJRC was created, the natives and the immigrants established a new organization called the Joint Distribution Committee (November 27, 1914). Most people knew it as the Joint, or the JDC. As the name makes clear it was a distribution not a fund-raising institution. It was established in the office of Magnes. This charismatic leader became the country's outstanding Jewish speaker at rallies where appeals were made and the people aroused to support the distressed in Palestine and Eastern Europe.

By the end of 1914 the JDC already represented the Orthodox, Conservative, and Reform Jews, the Zionists, and a number of immigrant fraternal orders. The socialists, at first, refused to go along; they nursed a contempt for the Orthodox and the bourgeois Reformers. Mindful of their belief in the class struggle they were determined to go their own way. By August, 1915, they, too, had created a fund-raising society, the People's Relief Committee, but by November it had become the third member of the Joint; like the Orthodox these factory hands and artisans had little money and few administrative skills. These disparate Jewish groups learned to work together; the Orthodox and the labor people knew that Marshall's American Jewish Relief Committee would carry the financial load. Both socialists and Torah-true religionists discovered that blood was thicker than theology and Marxist dialectics.

When the proletarian People's Relief Committee was first organized Meyer London was its leader; as early as October, 1914, he had worked closely with Marshall to set up the American Jewish Relief Committee. The People's Committee executive officer was Baruch Zuckerman (1887-1970), a typical learned Lithuanian who had sharpened his wits in a talmudic academy. In later years, as a journalist, this Socialist-Zionist stood out as one of the leaders of Labor Zionism. The religiously-minded Central Relief Committee was led by Leon Kamaiky (b.1864), another talmudically trained Lithuanian who, unlike many others, continued his studies here in this country. His friend Kasriel Sarasohn appointed him publisher of the daily *Tageblatt* (1890). From this vantage point he moved on to become one of Orthodoxy's notables. He played a role in the Kehillah, the Hebrew Immigrant Aid and Sheltering Society, the religious Zionists (the Mizrachi), the Isaac Elchanan seminary, and because of his power, he was also coopted by the American Jewish Committee and New York's federation of Jewish philanthropies. As an observant religionist he joined Rabbi Moses Margolies' Kehillath Jeshurun. It is significant that this congregation, one of New York's outstanding traditional synagogs, could muster but a bare 100 members. The real power in the Joint was resident in its chairman Felix Moritz Warburg (1871-1937), a banker. Warburg was no Russian student who had seesawed over a page of the Talmud. Leaving his native Hamburg he came to the United States (1894), married Schiff's daughter Frieda, joined Kuhn, Loeb & Company, and on the death of his father-in-law became the firm's senior member. As a partner in Kuhn-Loeb and as its head he was almost automatically an important factor in America's commerce, finance, and industry. As a member of the city's Board of Education he had helped bring nursing into the public schools. He knew Lillian Wald for he was a friend and supporter of the Henry Street Settlement; he also served as a trustee of Teachers College. As a scion of the noted Warburg family it was obvious that he would play an important part in many of the city's Jewish organizations. He was interested in the East Side's Educational Alliance and the Uptown's Federation for the Support of Jewish Philanthropic Societies. Warburg gave the Jewish Theological Seminary his beautiful Fifth Avenue mansion; this became the Museum of Jewish Ceremonial Objects, the finest in the country. Like his father-in-law, Warburg was a philanthropist who devoted his time and his means to help others; less parochial than Schiff he evinced a keen interest in the fine arts. Warburg, a highly intelligent, cultured man of the world was no slave to his countinghouse; he was not a flamboyant personality but because he was a gentleman, highly intelligent, and religiously tolerant he managed to cope with the divisive forces in the JDC.[3]

AMERICAN JEWS, WORLD WAR I, AND AFTERMATH, 1917-1919

In April 1917, after the war had been dragging along for almost three years in Europe the United States became a combatant. This country had tried to stay out of the conflict; many were opposed to war; some were in sympathy with Germany and Austria. Most people, it seemed, leaned toward the Entente powers; they preferred the English and the French; selling goods to them brought millions of dollars into American coffers. America's Jews wanted no part of a war which would help the Russians; that is why they voted for Wilson; "he kept us out of war." The "German" Jews, immigrants from Central Europe, were pro-German. Their devotion to Germany is not easy to understand; it is even more difficult to fathom why many Jews back in Russia, patriots, volunteered to fight for the czar. They fought and died for a Russia that denied them human rights. The answer may be that both the German Jews and the Russian Jews desperately craved acceptance by the very people who had rejected them. They wanted to "belong"; being Jewish was not enough.

Over here in the United States no East European Jew had any sympathy for the Russians. Having enjoyed the immunities of American citizenship they despised the country which had oppressed them. By January 1917, American public opinion had turned against the Central European powers. In 1915 the Germans had sunk the *Lusitania* drowning about 1,200 men, women, and children, including many Americans; two years later Germany's unrestricted submarine warfare, which brought destruction to American ships carrying supplies to the Entente, enraged this country's citizenry. When in April 1917, Congress declared war on the Germans and Austrians the problems of loyalty which confronted America's Jews had already been resolved. Jews of Central European origin were repulsed by Germany's ruthless conduct on the high seas, and when in March 1917, the Romanov Empire collapsed, and equality was accorded all its inhabitants, America's East European émigrés felt that they could support the new Russian state with a clear conscience. Thus it was that the Jewish Germans, Russians, and Poles rallied around Wilson and supported the war vigorously. Elated with the prospect of freedom a number of Russian Jewish immigrants returned there after the emancipatory revolution. These were primarily radicals, socialists; many of them had been unhappy here; America manifested little tolerance for Marxists. In May 1917, just a few weeks after this country went to war, the administration sent Elihu Root, former secretary of state, on a mission to Russia. The new Russian state threatened to make peace with the German allies. This would allow the Central European powers to fight on only one front and materially increase their chances of victory over the French, English, and Americans. It was Root's task to keep the Russians in the war thus compelling the Germans and Austrians to fight on two fronts. When the administration first thought of sending a mission to Russia there was talk of including Jews. After all there were millions of Jews in the old Muscovite Empire; a number of the revolutionaries now in power were Jews. Some suggested that Gompers, the labor leader, be sent over; that would flatter the St. Petersburg rebels; others mentioned the name of Eugene Meyer, a prominent businessman, and Oscar Straus, the former envoy to Turkey. Secretary of State Lansing had no objection to Gompers but he thought it a mistake to overplay "the Jew element."

American Jewry was eager that a Jew be included; Russian Jewry was the largest Jewish congeries in the world. There were some individuals in Wilson's Department of State who were not ready to speed the emancipation of Russia's Jews; this might move the Christian masses to protest, to pogroms; this would hinder the Russians from prosecuting the war. The government's commission of nine included no Jews; in its final report it said that Russia would stay in the war; Root and some of his associates knew better. Privately, the former secretary of state said that the mission had failed because of the criminations of American Jewish remigrants. They had hindered his task by denouncing America as a tyranny. He was looking for a scapegoat in the event that the Russians came to an understanding with the hostile armies on their flanks; actually after the Bolsheviks came to power they did sign a treaty of peace (March 1918). The French and English would now receive no help from the Russians; the war would have to be fought on the western front.

In May 1917, when Root left for Russia, Henry Morgenthau, Sr., former ambassador to the Sublime Porte, also left on a mission. Root wanted to keep the Russians in the war; Morgenthau, who had friends in high places in Constantinople, wanted to get the Turks out of the war. If the Turks were to drop out the Dardanelles and the Black Sea could be opened to the Entente; through direct access to Odessa Russia could be prevented from vacillating or defecting; she would be compelled more or less to remain loyal to the Entente. Morgenthau, a patriot, set out to help America by inducing Turkey to desert the Alliance. The Britains were not happy with the ambassador's foray; they wanted no separate peace with the Turks for they hoped soon to conquer Palestine, to sit astride the Suez dominating Egypt and the seaway to India. Chaim Weizmann and other Zionist leaders were not happy with the thought that if Morgenthau induced the Turks to defect the latter would retain Palestine; there would be no national Jewish home. This of course did not disturb Morgenthau; he was an anti-Zionist though always willing to help Palestine's Jews. Weizmann, an ardent English patriot, wanted the British to conquer Palestine and give it to the Jews. Morgenthau was ultimately talked out of his excursion into diplomacy; the cautious American state department ordered him to desist.

While Root and Morgenthau were preparing to serve their country on the eastern front New York's Yiddish editors banded together to establish a patriotic pro-Entente society, the Jewish League of American Patriots. This was in March 1917, before the United States went to war. Most Yiddish papers supported Wilson and Congress when they opted for war. The Socialists dissented; Meyer London in Congress voted no; Cahan's *Forward* saw no reason why American Jewish workers should die to enrich capitalists. The intransigent *Forward* ran into trouble; the postmaster general threatened to revoke its second-class mailing privilege; this would have forced it to shut down. The Espionage Act of June 15, 1917, gave the government the authority to close any newspaper whose editorial opinions were suspect; they were promoting the enemy's cause! Marshall now stepped into the breach though he was no friend of the *Forward*'s radical preachments; he was the friend of free speech. He was close to the East Side Jews. No Zionist himself he may have cherished a bit of sympathy for this non-Zionist newspaper. When Marshall volunteered to act as a censor the postmaster general permitted the *Forward* to appear; it was the only socialist foreign-language newspaper that was published all through the war.

Practically all Jews in this country rallied around the flag in April 1917; there were some notable exceptions. Magnes and a number of other rabbis, all Reform Jews, were pacifists. They had to keep quiet or they would have been dismissed by their congregations. When they did raise their voices they were rebuffed; few Jews had any sympathy for Rabbi Eli Mayer of Philadelphia who declared publicly that "the thought of God and the thought of war are utterly incompatible." One of Mayer's teachers at the Cincinnati seminary was Gotthard Deutsch, the historian.

Deutsch was proud of his German cultural background. Around the turn of the century, after the death of Isaac M. Wise, Deutsch had edited the German-language *Deborah*. Unlike most German Jews he was no enemy of Yiddish and enjoyed reading the East Side periodicals; he even prided himself on his ability to write in that language. Deutsch was always a political liberal concerned for the welfare of humanity; during the war he was a pacifist. As one rooted in German traditions he questioned the motives of the Entente in waging war against the Central European powers. Love for the German way of life was bred in his bones though he could not have been unconscious of the fact that his native Austria made it very difficult for him as a Jew to embark on an academic career; that was why he came to America. Though a Reform Jew, teaching at a Reform Jewish seminary, he sneered at his liberal coreligionists who gloried in the prophetic message of peace yet favored war. Deutsch linked himself to the ancient prophet Jeremiah (26:1-16) who had spoken out even when his life was threatened. The professor's antiwar convictions, which he refused to keep under a bushel, offended Cincinnati's Jews and Gentiles; he declined even in court to say that he favored victory for the United States; he would not equivocate. In November 1917, his enemies moved to expel him from his post. Many rallied around him; his favorite disciple, young Jacob Marcus, then a soldier in the First Ohio Infantry, sent a strong telegram deprecating the attacks on his beloved teacher. More to the point was a telegram from the all-powerful Louis Marshall. Deutsch was tried and censored but not deprived of his chair (December).

War hysteria prevailed almost everywhere. By 1918, in Cincinnati, a German town, the German language was excised from the curriculum of the public schools; German street names were changed; German books were no longer circulated in the public libraries; German Jewish Cohens now became Coles and Colliers.

During this First World War a Julius Kahn (1861-1924) was far more typical than a Gotthard Deutsch. Except for a brief two-year period, Kahn served San Francisco in Congress from 1899 to his death in 1924. This native of Baden, Germany, grew up in the California metropolis where he drove a bakery wagon for his father, enjoyed a not unsuccessful career as an actor, studied law, and went into politics; he was a good speaker. Shortly after he was elected to Congress he was invited to dine at the White House by President McKinley. Kahn and his wife walked to the White House; a carriage would have cost them a dollar. Turning to his wife Kahn said to her: "In what country could two poor Jews be on their way to dine with the head of state?" Though a Republican he worked with Wilson, the Democrat, and helped him push the Selective Service Act through Congress. He was a member and then chairman of the important House Committee on Military Affairs; he was an influential congressman. When in January 1918, Wilson came out with his Fourteen Points for peace even the radical Jews in this country turned to him. He promised the world that he would work for the reduction of national armaments; Russia would be free; small states and ethnic groups would come into their own; an association of nations would be established that would guarantee the independence of all countries both large and small. Entranced, even many socialists were ready to support the administration. When the Third Liberty Loan was offered the denizens of the East Side— the unions among them—rushed to make purchases; they dug into their savings and poured $12,000,000 into the government's tills. A beautiful new world was about to be made safe for democracy.[4]

JEWISH ECONOMIC CONTRIBUTIONS IN WORLD WAR I

The purchase of bonds by lower middle-class Jews during the First World War is typical of their desire to support the government. An unhappy sweatshop worker might well curse Columbus for having discovered America but he had no desire to go back to the land of his birth; he knew that he was infinitely better off in New York than in Warsaw, Vilna, or Odessa. The Jewish masses and the old-timers made their contributions in commerce, the garment industry, and, to a degree, in private banking. Individuals stood out. Felix Frankfurter, a native Austrian, served Harvard as a professor of law by 1914. Four years later Wilson appointed him chairman of the War Labor Policies Board to mediate industrial disputes and thus further the production of goods and munitions that would help guarantee victory. In 1917, during the war, Albert Davis Lasker (1880-1952) served his country in the Department of Agriculture; he was a member of a family that achieved recognition both in Germany and in the United States. Lasker was to make a very substantial fortune in advertising; indeed he was to revolutionize the industry. When he went to work for Lord and Thomas in 1898 its annual billings were about $800,000; some forty years later, after he acquired control of the company, it was authorized by its clients to spend $750,000,000. Some of America's best known products—cigarettes, foods, toothpaste—became household names because of this innovative enterpriser. Having achieved his financial goals this conservative Republican turned to politics; in 1921 after President Harding appointed him chairman of the United Shipping Board he set about the task of liquidating the 11,000,000-ton wartime merchant marine that had cost this country well over $3,500,000,000. He found time too in his role as a highly intelligent philanthropist to further medical research. Unlike some other Jews who had also acquired great wealth he identified strongly with his people; he was generous to the new State of Israel.

Eugene Isaac Meyer (1875-1959) was politically more important. During the war he served the Advisory Commission of the Council of National Defense and the War Industries Board. Secretary of War Baker asked him to investigate and stimulate aircraft production. By 1918 he was a member of the War Finance Corporation and was to serve as its head for many years. This was a very important job, for the corporation was authorized to spend billions in credits to industries producing materials for the armed forces. The Council of National Defense for whom Meyer worked had been established by Congress in 1916; apparently the government was at that time gearing up for war. Six cabinet members were assigned the task of "insuring national security and welfare." Many of the important decisions were made by the Council; they were implemented by an Advisory Commission of seven; three were Jews—Samuel Gompers, the labor leader, Julius Rosenwald, the merchandiser, Bernard Mannes Baruch, a Wall Street broker. Though possessing relatively little actual authority the Advisory Commission set out to mobilize the country's industrial resources; it, too, had the war in mind.

Baruch (1870-1965) may not have been the most capable and astute of the three Jews on the Advisory Commission; however he was certainly the most interesting of the three. The word "Jews" above might have been set in quotes. Gompers and Baruch had little interest in the people who gave them birth; Rosenwald was identified with numerous Jewish causes yet at heart his prime loyalty was to humanity, not to Jewry. Baruch's father Simon, served as a surgeon in the Confederate army. He was a German immigrant. The son was a stockbroker, a speculator who turned politician, a philanthropist. Politics and his philanthropy at times intertwined. Eager, very eager to make a career as a national figure he made good use of his wealth employing it where it would do him the most good. In 1916 Wilson appointed him to the Advisory Committee; he was in charge of raw materials for the War Industry Board and in purchases for the Allies. In 1918-1919 he became chairman of the War Industries Board assigned the challenge of mobilizing the country industrially to win the war. Given real authority the Board succeeded in bringing order and productivity to wartime industry; its work was successful. Baruch and his associates also succeeded in making powerful enemies; it is not surprising therefore that the Board was phased out in 1919. For a very brief period, Baruch, a South Carolinian, was one of the country's most influential men. For almost another half-century this ambitious notable continued to reach out for influence but he was never again to match the power he exerted in 1918. Grateful to Baruch for his generosity and conscious of his ability, Wilson appointed him a member of the American Commission to negotiate peace. In later decades presidents found it politic to consult him; Roosevelt listened to him as he prepared to confront the Germans in the Second World War. In the 1930's and 1940's Baruch exerted influence through his disciples, his friends, whom he helped secure high office.

The canny Baruch built a following in Congress and in the Washington bureaucracy; he was generous and helpful to those who furthered his career as a politician, and as "an advisor to Presidents." This political and fiscal conservative was determined to stay in the limelight no matter who was president. Some who disliked him damned him as a "man of self-inflicted self-importance." Others condemned him as a "Hebrew Wall Street speculator." These are unfair attributions. He was much more than that. True he was an opportunist but he was highly intelligent, an ardent patriot, rich enough to be honest, and certainly as devoted to his country as many of the "greats" of his generation. He was kind and generous. As a Jew who sought influence in Washington he exemplified a rather common type. He was a paradigm for other rich Israelites who were determined "to be somebody." He was one of the best known Jews in American public life.

Baruch never cut his ties to his people; prejudice kept him Jewish. As a college teenager he was denied election to a Greek letter fraternity because of his origins yet he was elected president of his class. His relation to his people was an ambivalent one; he was a marginal Jew; despite his intermarriage Gentiles never really accepted him; many Jews looked askance at him; they demanded unequivocal loyalty. This he would not avouch. Baruch was a member of a congregation; he went to services on the High Holy Days occasionally; he gave to Jewish charities; he was buried by a rabbi. In matters of immigration—the acid test—he, like Gompers, was a restrictionist. Baruch was not even willing to let the bars down when the Nazis came to power in Germany and Jews there were looking desperately for a city of refuge; he was not even willing to use his influence to open Palestine to the Jews; he was ready, however, to settle the German émigrés in Africa. He was certainly no Zionist for he was more concerned "with the stars and stripes than the Star of David." As a non-Zionist he did not hesitate to give money liberally to Zionist and other popular causes; he wanted friends in all corners. He was an ardent American of the Jewish persuasion.[5]

THE JEWISH BOARD FOR WELFARE WORK

Just about the time Bernard Baruch, Julius Rosenwald, and Samuel Gompers were working on the Advisory Commission to the Council of National Defense to prepare this country for war American Jews were bestirring themselves to establish an organization that would concern itself with the welfare of Jews in the armed forces. They knew full well that the rigors of the service could be abated by amenities, comforts, hospitality. In 1916 over 100,000 troops were stationed on the Mexican border as the army under General John J. Pershing pursued the guerrilla Pancho Villa into the interior of Mexico; Villa had been raiding into Texas and killing Americans in the border towns. The Central Conference of American Rabbis saw to it that Rabbi Isaac Landman conducted High Holy Day services in Texas and in Mexico for the Jews in this punitive force. This was the first time an American rabbi, acting as a chaplain for troops, had conducted services on foreign soil.

When America went to war in 1917 Jewry here knew that hundreds of thousands of Jewish soldiers would respond to the call to arms. Catholics and Protestants had their chaplains; it was obvious that rabbis, too, would be recruited to serve their coreligionists. To provide for the social and welfare needs of the men and to organize a Jewish chaplains corps—authorized by Congress in 1917—the Jews established the Jewish Board for Welfare Work, the JWW, but they speedily changed the acronym. JWW resembled IWW, the initials of the Industrial Workers of the World, a radical union which was feared and disliked by many Americans. A new name was therefore adopted by this national association; it became the Jewish Welfare Board, the JWB. The government recognized it as the agency that was authorized to provide for the non-military needs of the Jewish soldiers, sailors, and marines. The JWB was a federation that included the three Jewish religious denominations, the various "Ys," the Jewish Publication Society, the Jewish Chautauqua, the National Council of Jewish Women, and some other national organizations. Thus cultural institutions were represented along with religious and social societies. Here, too, Louis Marshall had made his presence felt by helping to establish this new wartime agency; the president was Harry Cutler of Providence, a well-known national communal worker.

The Welfare Board had big plans to serve soldiers in a host of military installations both here and in Europe. Large sums were needed and Jacob Billikopf who had done so much for the Joint Distribution Committee offered advice as it turned to American Jewry for funding. Actually the Welfare Board could do little to provide for the religious needs for the men at the fighting fronts. Thousands of Jewish enlisted men were scattered among a host of Gentiles; with but one exception there was no separate Jewish fighting unit. For the most part World War I was waged in pre-airplane days. Transportation for the chaplains was a problem; the rabbis could not fly from division to division and hold services for the scattered Jews. The chaplains who looked after the needs of the men in the States were stationed in installations and bases where relatively large numbers of Jews could be reached. The twelve chaplains in the American Expeditionary Forces had to remain in the larger cities of France, in the recreation areas, if they wanted to serve Jews on furlough. The one chaplain assigned to a Jewish battle unit was Captain Elkan Voorsanger. After graduating from the Hebrew Union College and taking a rabbinic post in St. Louis he had volunteered and joined a medical unit that went to France in the early days of the war. After his appointment as a Jewish chaplain was authorized—the first since the Civil War—Voorsanger was sent to the 77th Division. A very substantial minority of its men came from New York's East Side; a rabbi was needed. Ultimately he became the senior chaplain of the entire division. The rabbi, bold, aggressive, was no chair warmer who elected to remain in comfort at division headquarters. When his men moved out to battle Voorsanger marched with them; wounded he was honored with a Purple Heart.

The one Jew who served the navy officially as an acting chaplain was Rabbi David Goldberg (b. 1886), a Russian who only came to these shores as late as 1909. Commissioned a lieutenant in the navy in 1917 he ran into problems almost immediately. As a clergyman he was expected to wear the insignia which appeared on the collars of all chaplains, the cross. The cross was the symbol of Jesus. His suggestion that a shepherd's crook would be more appropriate for all the chaplains in the navy was summarily rejected; the Christians would not deny their God. When Goldberg was assigned to a ship—wearing the cross of course—he found but 8 Jews among the 800 men on board. There were not enough Jews for a minyan, a religious quorum. It is very probable that he conducted a nondenominational service; he was certainly not going to invoke the Father, the Son, and the Holy Ghost. Over fifty years earlier Rabbi Ferdinand Leopold Sarner had been elected chaplain of the 54th Volunteer New York Infantry, popularly known as the Schwarze Jaeger (Yaeger), the Black Hunters. Sarner had been chosen by the Gentiles—mostly Germans—because he spoke their language; he was a German Ph.D. No doubt his services too were nondenominational. Although Goldberg made a real effort to avoid wearing the Christian symbol on his uniform, the then president of the Central Conference of American Rabbis excoriated him for so doing; Cyrus Adler of the Seminary knowing Goldberg had no choice did not chide him but set about securing an acceptable Jewish emblem for all Jewish chaplains. Success crowned his efforts. Ultimately the rabbis who served in the armed forces were permitted to wear the two tablets of the Law, the Ten Commandments.

WHAT THE JEWISH WELFARE BOARD DID

Jewish soldiers had special needs which were met. The Welfare Board made sure that religious services were available in camp or in the nearest town. Most enlisted men were Orthodox; many of them were recent immigrants; they wanted to hear an occasional Hebrew word; some never forgot to say kaddish, the prayer for their dear departed. A special prayer book was prepared with the hope that it would satisfy all Jewish religious denominations; it was a rather crude compromise but it was adequate for those soldiers who made up a religious quorum, so it would seem. An abridged English Bible was also published; one wonders how many read it. More appealing, so it would appear, was *A Book of Jewish Thoughts* compiled by the British chief rabbi Joseph H. Hertz. It was a delightful interesting anthology. The publishing costs of the books supplied the men in the armed forces were met by the American Jewish Committee and its cohorts. These cultural works, so typically Jewish, were supplemented by books from the Jewish Publication Society. Soldiers in the base hospitals were visited by neighboring townspeople. It was the small town Jew near the army cantonments who went all out to befriend the soldiers. Girls were delighted with the abundance of Jewish young men; it was a pleasure to view the crop of prospects. In the cities, auxiliaries visited families of the enlisted men and sought to help them. The Welfare Board was most successful in its efforts to further the social relations of the soldiers in the barracks or in the tent cities. Soldiers at leisure nearly always had a place where they could while away the evening; they never hesitated to bring their Christian buddies; they, too, were welcome.

When the war was over and the men were discharged in 1919 the Welfare Board was an organization in search of a job. This it soon found for it became the umbrella agency for the numerous Young Men's and Young Women's Hebrew Associations (1921). Eventually these "Ys," influenced in part by the teachings of Mordecai M. Kaplan, became Jewish Community Centers. It was a hope of Rabbi Kaplan that the emerging centers would become the basic unifying institutions in the towns. This was the hope that was rarely realized; the centers were never able to supplant the synagog. The American ethos merely tolerates divisive social and cultural institutions; it encourages divisions along religious lines. Synagogs prospered because they offered Jews not only the religious but also the cultural, the folk, and the ethnic affiliations which they craved. Under the guise of religion the Jew can live a full life. In the Second World War the Jewish Welfare Board went back to work again in the camps and cantonments; it became part of the United Service Organizations for National Defense (USO).[6]

THE AMERICAN JEW AS FIGHTING MAN

When the President in 1917 called upon his people to go to war against the Central European powers, American Jewry responded but there were exceptions; there was a substantial number of socialists and a handful of pacifists. The Jewish pacifists were Reform rabbis, men of integrity and rare courage; the socialists, garment workers for the most part, saw no reason to die in a capitalist war where soldiers who bore each other no malice were asked to sacrifice their lives. It has been estimated that somewhere between 200,000 and 250,000 Jews served in the First World War; they constituted about 5 percent of the men in the ranks; the Jewish percentage in the general population was then about 3.2. One of the reasons that Jews exceeded their numerical proportion in the population was that they merited very few exemptions; they were not farmers, miners, nor laborers in heavy industry, the areas where exemptions were common. In addition anti-Semitism was not absent among the draft functionaries. In a government *Manual of Instructions for Medical Advisory Boards* the officers were warned that Jews were apt to malinger more than the native-born. When informed of this libel Wilson ordered the immediate recall of the induction book. About 15,000 Jews were listed as casualties; they were the sick, the gassed, the wounded, the killed. Some were immigrants but recently arrived who were given little opportunity to enjoy America's freedom. They fled Russia only to die on Europe's battlefields.

About 9,000 Jews were commissioned officers; approximately 100 were colonels and lieutenant colonels; none became generals. This is difficult to understand; a number of the regimental commanders were exceptionally able. (Several Jews were brevetted as generals in the Union army in the 1860's). The obvious answer is that here, too, prejudice was present; this was certainly a comforting rationale for ambitious Jews denied promotion. Two of the colonels may be selected for mention; it is not easy to determine whether they were typical of the others. Milton J. Foreman, a member of a distinguished Illinois family, a lawyer in civilian life, commanded a field artillery regiment in the Illinois National Guard which was mustered into federal service. After the war he and Colonel Abel Davis were among those who founded the American Legion in Paris. Later Foreman became the national commander of the Legion. Back in Illinois Foreman remained in the national guard retiring finally as a three-star general. Davis, another Chicagoan, was a Russian immigrant who was also trained as a lawyer. He served in the Spanish American War, on the Mexican border with Pershing, and finally was to command the 132d Illinois Infantry in France. The very year he was separated from the service he returned to Chicago to head a campaign for the Joint Distribution Committee. The city acclaimed him as one of its outstanding citizens.

Many things are not easy to explain; only too often the historian who asks why, can find no ready answers. It is interesting that in the navy where anti-Jewish prejudice was once traditional, Jews advanced higher than in the army. Charles Lauchheimer (1859-1920), an Annapolis graduate, made a career as a marine and as a lawyer. He was the author of a work on naval courts. This committed Jew, a synagog member, reached the rank of general, brigadier, as early as 1916. Another Annapolis man rose even higher. This was Rear Admiral Joseph Strauss. Like Lauchheimer he had served in the Spanish- American War. His competence in the area of ordnance brings to mind Major Alfred Mordecai, one of the country's leading authorities on ordnance in antebellum America. By 1918 Strauss was already a two-star naval officer; on his retirement in 1930 he was appointed a full admiral.

Before army officers Foreman and Davis returned to the States they had been singled out to receive Distinguished Service Medals. During World War I there were at least 1,100 Jews honored with awards; among them were about 150 recipients of the Distinguished Service Medal and the Distinguished Service Cross. An analysis of the awards received by these soldiers shows that they risked their lives to save wounded or served as couriers and scouts under very hazardous conditions. At least six men received the Congressional Medal of Honor, the country's highest reward for bravery; these men performed acts of heroism well beyond the call of duty. Typical of the six is the conduct of Benjamin Kaufman, a top sergeant in New York's Jewish division. Kaufman, a sergeant in the 308th Infantry, was not a native of Lower Manhattan; he was born in Buffalo. During the battle of the Argonne, October 4, 1918, he advanced on a German machine gun nest alone. Though his right arm was shattered he moved forward against the enemy throwing grenades with his left hand, charged with an empty pistol, scattered the machine gun crew, and took a prisoner before returning to his company for first aid. William Sawelson, a sergeant in the 78th Division, was a native of Newark, New Jersey. On October 26, while in battle, he heard a wounded soldier in a shell hole calling for water. Leaving his shelter the sergeant crawled through heavy machine gun fire to bring the man some water. After returning to his shell hole and then returning again to help his wounded comrade he was killed by a machine gun bullet.

The award of a Congressional Medal of Honor is to a degree arbitrary; it is not easy to measure the quality of bravery; whatever the award the hero has put his life on the line. No man was braver than Sam Dreben (1878-1925), a Russian who enlisted in the army shortly after arriving in this country. He became a professional soldier. This is by no means unusual; the army offered a home, security, comrades, acceptance; this could mean a great deal to a newcomer. In the course of his life Sam Dreben fought in the Philippine Insurrection, the Boxer Rebellion, and as a mercenary in Central America and Mexico with the rank of colonel. He was widely known as the Fighting Jew. As a soldier of fortune he had even fought under Villa but when Pershing invaded Mexico Dreben joined him as a scout. World War I found Dreben in France with the American

Expeditionary Forces. On October 8, 1918, First Sergeant Dreben received the Distinguished Service Medal for an act of heroism. Accompanied by volunteers from his men Dreben attacked a German position, killed over forty of the enemy, captured two machine guns, brought back two prisoners, and returned to his own lines without having lost a man. He was a proud Jew, a generous person, and when the Joint Distribution Committee appealed for funds he gave it $1,000 of his savings; this was a large gift from a man of modest means, a professional soldier. Damon Runyon, the American journalist, saluted Dreben in the following verse:

> Now whenever I read articles
> That breathe of racial hate,
> Or hear arguments that hold his kind to scorn,
> I always see that photo
> With the cap upon his pate,
> And the nose the size of bugler Dugans' horn.
> I see upon his breast
> The D.S.C.
> The Croix de Guerre, the Militaire,
> These too—
> And I think, thank God Almighty,
> We will always have a few,
> Like Dreben,
> A Jew.

Abraham Krotoshinsky, a soldier in the First Battalion of the 308th Infantry, also received national acclaim. He and Benjamin Kaufman were in the same regiment. Krotoshinsky's battalion, led by Major Charles W. Whittlesey, was completely surrounded by the enemy in the sanguinary battle of the Argonne Forest. Whittlesey's men are known in army lore as the Lost Battalion. For five days they were exposed to constant artillery shelling; the losses were very heavy. The major sent out numerous runners to try to get through the German lines and bring relief; all of them were either captured or killed. On October 6, 1918, Krotoshinsky volunteered to go for help. As he was crawling through the lines, hiding in bushes, a German officer tramped on his fingers but he suppressed a cry of pain. Exhausted, gassed, wounded, he finally reached the American lines and returned with the men who relieved his besieged comrades. His battalion went into battle 550 strong; when finally rescued only 194 were left. President Coolidge later saw to it that Abe Krotoshinsky was given a job with the New York Post Office. He had been in the country but a few years when he was conscripted; he probably spoke with a heavy accent.[7]

WARTIME RELIEF BY INDIVIDUALS AND ORGANIZATIONS

In 1917 and 1918 while American Jewish soldiers were engaged in combat in France their friends back home were desperately trying to reach kinsmen in the war-torn lands and offer them aid. East European émigrés had been sending money back to Russia and Poland ever since they came here by the thousands in the 1880's. In the course of the decades millions of dollars were transferred across the seas to succor dear ones; many of the newcomers had left wife and children back home; they were busy earning money to bring the family over. Beginning in 1914, when Eastern Europe was to a large degree cut off from America by the German and Austrian armies, the situation in Eastern Europe became more desperate. Agencies of various types were now established in New York and other towns to meet the needs of the men and women who wanted to help their families abroad. Individuals and others forwarded funds through numerous private banks; synagogs, fraternal orders, federations of hometown societies (verbands) did what they could to help fellow Jews and the towns whence they hailed. After the war was over, in 1919, the landsmanshaften dispatched delegates abroad with money for relief and reconstruction. On the whole the delegates worked with integrity; a few of them were tempted to speculate on the market with the dollars at their disposal. To meet the demands of the suffering masses abroad for ever mounting sums, hometown and other agencies staged benefit performances in the Yiddish theatres and if men and women turned a deaf ear to the pleas for help they were exhorted by popular Yiddish songs which tore at their heart strings. After the war it was somewhat easier to send food packages through the agency of Hoover's American Relief Administration. It is worthy of note that though kosher package food was available most food purchased was non-kosher. Inasmuch as both the donors and the recipients were largely observant Jews this is difficult to understand.

It was not easy to help dear ones caught in the war zones in the years 1914-1918; it was even more difficult in the postwar years 1919-1920 when conditions verged on the chaotic in the expanded Rumania and in the new succession states Estonia, Latvia, Lithuania, Poland. The new chauvinism was often tinged with bitter vengeful anti-Semitism. Few of those states were spared political and economic turmoil. Until the Bolsheviks finally pacified Russia there were civil wars and forays by murderous bandits, especially in the Ukraine. After the Poles had attained their independence in 1919 it became increasingly difficult for American Jews to aid their kin. Funds sent over were sometimes confiscated; delegates carrying money were harassed, and for a short time import duties were imposed on relief packages. The Poles insisted—and had their way—that relief in money and kind be shared with the Polish people. Little or no publicity was given by the Joint Distribution Committee to the fact that what was sent by American Jewry had to be shared by the Poles who never abated their hostilities to Jews. These contributions, voluntary or forced, to the Polish people were not appreciated; it is patent that the government and the Gentile masses had no desire to accept their Jewish fellow-citizens.

Conditions for Jewry in the new Polish republic were not amelio-rated by the attitude of the American minister, the consular officers, and the Department of State back home. All were less than sympathetic to the plight of the Jewish masses who once lived in the Pale of Settlement. The United States government personnel in the new Polish republic tended to reflect the prejudices of the Polish masses and their leaders. Conditions worsened for East European Jewry when the new immigration acts went into effect. People here made every effort to bring their kin over before the gates swung closed. A fortunate few came in just under the line.

<h2 style="text-align:center">HEBREW SHELTERING AND
IMMIGRANT AID SOCIETY OF AMERICA</h2>

One of the Jewish social welfare agencies with which the newcomers could identify, which helped them when they rushed to rescue their fam-ilies, was the HIAS, the Hebrew Sheltering and Immigrant Aid Society. In its early days it was an immigrant organization which set out to assist the Russian and Polish newcomers as they debarked at Ellis Island. The HIAS was incorporated in 1905; it seemed to have emerged as a distinct organization in 1902. In all of its labors, particularly when it first began its work, it enjoyed the moral and financial support of the Uptown Jews. The HIAS met the incoming steamers in the early years of the century; it doubled its efforts to be helpful in the war and postwar years. During and after the First World War, as Russian Jews began to flee eastward through Siberia, Manchuria, China, and Japan to Seattle, the HIAS strove to be present wherever it was needed. It established an office in Chicago. The officers of the HIAS were devoted, efficient, and successful, making every effort to aid those émigrés already here bring over the relatives left be-hind, and when the immigration acts of the 1920's went into effect the HIAS exerted itself to find new havens in the Caribbean and in Latin American lands. The problems of the HIAS became acute in the 1930's when the German National Socialists came to power. The erstwhile Rus-sians were now in a position to help the German émigrés as they de-barked. For years after World War I the HIAS operated a bank which sent remittances across the Atlantic. It has been estimated that by 1939, when the Polish Jews no longer left their homes, the HIAS had forwarded

$40,000,000 for its American clientele. By that time, so it is estimated, it had aided 800,000 people. It was a record of which this self-help society with its modest beginnings could well be proud.[8]

WAR RELIEF IN THE HINTERLAND

In talking and writing about the help which World Jewry received from Jews in this country during the war and postwar years there is a tendency to think only of New York City and its Jews. After all, the important relief and social agencies such as the Joint and the HIAS were located there. However the hinterland must always be taken into account because the majority of American Jews lived there. Despite the presence of Jewish garment and craft unions in the towns west of the Hudson, relatively few Jews in the backcountry were factory hands; most of them were petty businessmen, members of the lower middle class. The lion's share of the Jewish money given for relief came from the provinces. From 1918 through January 1919 over 66 percent of all funds received came not from New York but from the other cities and states of the Union.

Christians sympathetic to Jewry, or good citizens eager to please their Jewish neighbors, gave to the Jewish campaigns; the amounts were very modest. After all Gentiles found it difficult to respond to the needs of Russian village and ghetto Jews. Christian participation in campaigns throws light on Jewish-Christian relations, especially in the states where Jews were few. In 1921-1923 North Carolina fund-raising was led by Lionel Weil of Goldsboro; the Weils—an old-line family—were a power in the state not because of their wealth but because they were leaders in many good causes. In order to help the North Carolina Jews, mayors in different cities issued sympathetic proclamations; collections were taken up in churches and Sunday schools. In some towns Christian ministers chaired the relief committees; children in a Masonic orphanage offered their pennies and even tots in schools gave their mite. It is not easy to determine whether this Christian outpouring in North Carolina was typical. From Atoka, Oklahoma—population of about 2,500 in 1917—came a check to Herbert H. Lehman, from a humble missionary to the Indians. The gift was obviously a sacrifice for a poor man, a Christian, who sought to help kindred human beings. And in North Dakota with its total Jewish population of about 1,000 souls? Campaigns here, as in North Carolina, were nonsectarian. Fund-raising proceeded apace in about thirty towns and villages though in some of them there were all told but one or two Jewish families. Christian clergymen played an active part in these fund-raising efforts.

The important drives for funds were staged in large cities where numbers, wealth, and sympathy were met together. In Chicago, for instance, a judge having no ready cash on him enthusiastically surrendered his gold watch. Women gave their jewels. Then, later, an auction was held and these generous donors ransomed their personal possessions. Milwaukee offers an example of how a midwestern city set about collecting funds. In September, 1914, weeks before the New Yorkers had pulled themselves together to meet their obligations, Milwaukee's Jewry had already organized a relief society. The immigrant newcomers here responded eagerly to the cry for help; synagogs, lodges, Zionists, socialists, unions, Jewish business organizations—all answered the appeal for aid. House to house solicitations were made, collections were taken up at bar mitzvahs, circumcisions feasts, weddings. There were tag days, balls, picnics. Milwaukee's Jewish affluent natives were at first slow to give; many of them kept their distance sedulously from the ghettoized newcomers. Later a number of the elite gave generously. In general, however, the old-line German families were in the forefront of the givers; they recognized their responsibilities. After the United States went to war modern style fund-raising was introduced into Milwaukee. The charismatic Magnes made his appearance here; Albert D. Lasker, the advertising tycoon, came in from Chicago. The goal that year, 1917, was $50,000; $36,000 was raised in one night at a dinner.[9]

HELPING JEWS IN PALESTINE DURING THE FIRST WORLD WAR

The campaigns conducted in the hinterland and New York City were all ultimately directed by one organization, the Joint Distribution Committee and its three affiliates, the American Jewish Relief Committee, the Central Relief Committee, and the People's Relief Committee. But even before the Joint came into being in November 1914, America's Jews were confronted by an urgent appeal from Palestine. The Jews in the United States—all classes—answered the cry for help at once. Palestine was different; liturgical and religious tradition had always put the Holy Land in the forefront; pride demanded that the Jews in the ancient land of the patriarchs be rescued speedily; this was a sacred obligation. Jews had been sending money to Jerusalem since pre-Christian times. As early as 61 B.C.E., L. Valerius Flaccus, proconsul of Asia Minor, had confiscated large sums being sent to Jerusalem. Charged with peculation he was defended by Cicero (59 B.C.E.) For centuries most of Palestine's Jews had lived off the contributions of the Diaspora's pious; this was called the *halukkah*, the allocation. This was still true in 1914; well over three-fourths of the Jews in the land were dependent; they had no other source of livelihood. After the war broke out the Turks joined forces with the Germans and Austrians against the English, French, and Russians. France and England soon blockaded the eastern Mediterranean; food and money could no longer be brought into Palestine and the country's wines and citrus fruits could not be exported; the economic situation was critical. Much of the *halukkah* had come from Russia, the bastion of Orthodoxy; now this source had dried up. Palestine's Jewish residents, Russians and Poles, enemy aliens, fled or were deported to nearby Egypt.

In those days of despair Henry Morgenthau, Sr., the ambassador to Turkey, cabled and asked for immediate help. This was in August after the war had already begun in Europe. Though an anti-Zionist Morgenthau was eager to be of help. The United States Jewry answered the call by collecting $50,000; actually it was the rich old-timers—the American Jewish Committee, Jacob H. Schiff, and the Zionists—who provided the funds. The Zionist share was made up, for the most part, by Nathan Straus of the Macy Department Store clan. The $50,000 in gold was carried to Jerusalem by Maurice Wertheim, Morgenthau's son-in-law. When the local Jewish organizations, bitterly divided, could not agree on the apportionment Wertheim locked himself in a room saying he would not come out until they all agreed on the division. They finally did.

In 1915, with the support of the Washington authorities, the coal steamer *Vulcan* was sent to Turkish Palestine with 900 tons of food, medicine, and another substantial sum in cash; 45 percent of all this had to be given to the local Moslems and Christians; this was the price the Jews had to pay for relief. When the *Vulcan* sailed the Zionists here hoped it would fly the Zionist flag; this the American Jewish Committee would not tolerate; it recognized but one national banner, it said, the Stars and Stripes. Fortunately for the Jews at least, the British overran Palestine in 1917-1918, and although the military regime and the bureaucrats in London were not particularly sympathetic, the days of Turkish oppression had finally come to an end. During the war years, 1914-1918, $15,000,000 was raised in the United States for Jews in distress; of these moneys over $2,000,000 was dispatched to the ancient homeland. American Jewry was quick to help the Palestinians; the Orthodox particularly were insistent on this score. The Palestine Jewish settlements were numerically but a minuscule fraction of the millions in distress; the Holy Land received about 15 percent of all the funds sent abroad. Later, in the 1920's and in the decades that followed, hundreds of millions were spent in this country for relief, for the talmudic academies, for vocational schools, and in the effort to change a benighted Turkish province into a modern industrial state. The effort was successful.[10]

THE JOINT DISTRIBUTION COMMITTEE AS A RELIEF AGENCY, 1914 AND ON

The masses, the millions, who had to be succored were not in Palestine—

there were about 80,000 there—but in those East European lands that extended from the Baltic into the Balkans. As early as 1914 hundreds of thousands of Russian, Polish, Galician Jews were on the move. Huge numbers were deported from the Pale of Settlement and shipped into the interior of Russia; some fled to neighboring inhospitable Rumania. Galicians, in the path of the armies, fled into the interior of Austria and Hungary. Unfortunately many had to remain in place, in the war zones; words cannot exaggerate their plight. The prime organization that set out to relieve the distress of these Jews, that operated over the years in those stricken lands, was the Joint Distribution Committee. The American Jews were not the only ones working to help Jewry in Europe. German and Austrian Jewish social-welfare agencies did yeoman work. The Hilfsverein and other German societies were very helpful in German-occupied Poland in the early days of the war; in Austria, the Allianz, made provision for Galician refugees. Russia had well-organized Jewish associations that worked to help the Jewish masses overrun by the invading and counter-invading forces. All these efforts of the European Jewish welfare societies were encouraged and in some instances subsidized by the Joint.

Back in the States, the JDC, as its name indicates, was primarily a distribution agency; its funds were raised by its three affiliates which worked through the local committees that had been established in practically every American town of size. By December, 1915, the Joint itself decided also to go out and secure the funds it needed. Apparently the American Jewish Relief Committee, the Central, and the People's Committee were inadequate for the pressing need. In 1915, for instance, all of American Jewry had contributed only something over a million dollars; this was not enough. The change in procedure was inaugurated at a mass meeting in Carnegie Hall on December 21, 1915; Magnes spoke. A few weeks later President Wilson picked January 27th as Jewish Relief Day; large sums were raised; Nathan Straus made a notable contribution. Refining its techniques and raising its sights the Joint in 1916 and 1917 reached out to individuals in about 1,400 towns and hamlets even if there was but one Jewish resident there. Laborers called upon to donate a day's pay made the sacrifice. By the Spring of 1917, the United States found itself at war; the Joint could no longer distribute its largesse directly; it worked through neutral Holland. The Dutch, at peace with the Germans and Austrians, were thus able to distribute American Jewish funds in Berlin and Vienna for the use of Jews in the war zones.

For 1917 the goal to be reached was set at $10,000,000. In order to arouse the givers something sensational was needed. The decision was made to ask a rich man to give a million dollar gift. When Schiff refused to do so, Jacob Billikopf, the social worker, then turned to Julius Rosenwald for a matching grant, a hundred thousand dollars for every million raised by the American Jews. Billikopf repaired to Washington where Rosenwald was laboring day and night for the Advisory Commission of the National Defense Council. The interview was held late at night. According to a tradition that was widespread, after Rosenwald assented to the matching grant idea, Billikopf said to the Sears Roebuck magnate: "And now Mr. Rosenwald will you please give me a note to that effect." To this the indignant Rosenwald answered, "Don't you believe me?" and in response Billikopf answered, "I believe you but they won't believe me." There are accurate records of what actually happened on that night. Rosenwald listened, agreed, and all that he said was "alright." Rosenwald's example stimulated other Jewish donors. Simon Bamberger, the governor of Utah, agreed to give 10 percent of all that was raised in his state; Moses Alexander, governor of Idaho, made the same agreement; Ben Selling in Portland and others also came up with matching grants. The American Jewish rich were learning to give. Behind all this giving was the indefatigable and ingenious Jacob Billikopf.

Though the war years were bad, very bad, the two years 1919-1920 were worse. Conditions in the succession states were bad because of political and economic corruption, chauvinism, and traditional anti-Jewish prejudice. These were years of famine, disease, civil wars, guerrilla horrors, mass murders. In the city of Pinsk thirty-five responsible Jewish citizens were murdered by the Poles. Some historians estimate that during the years 1919-1921 as many as 100,000 Jews were killed in the Ukraine; there are no accurate figures. It is impossible to determine how many died of violence in that unhappy period. By 1919 the JDC had succeeded in sending a large unit into postwar Poland to carry on the task of helping and advising; the social workers were led by Boris Bogen. Among those who accompanied him was Captain Elkan Voorsanger, former senior chaplain of the 77th Division. Present too was another rabbi, Hyman Bernard Cantor. Writing to his teacher Gotthard Deutsch at the Cincinnati seminary, April 2, 1920, Cantor reports on his visit to the Galician town of Belz, a famed center of Orthodoxy and Hassidism. Centuries before, in the 1650's the town had gone up in flames in the war between the Poles and the Swedes; now in 1920, 600 of the 720 houses in town had been destroyed; Belz alone had 600 orphans; there was no bread; 40 people were living in two caves. On July 5, just about three months later Cantor and Israel Friedlaender, on a mission of mercy, were murdered by bandits.

RECONSTRUCTION

It is evident that under conditions such as these more than relief was needed if these unfortunates were to survive and rebuild their lives. The magic word was "reconstruction." To a degree at least "reconstruction" was a phrase which the Joint exploited to rally American Jewish givers who were inclined to give less now that the war was over; their enthusiasm had waned despite the fact that help was imperative. Even before the United States had entered the war, while the European powers were destroying one another, their lands, and their peoples, Jacob H. Schiff realized that gigantic efforts would be needed to rehabilitate Europe once the armies had stopped fighting. He talked the problem over with Rosenwald and after the armistice had been signed wrote that same month to his Chicago friend suggesting that each of them give $1,000,000 to rebuild Europe. This country, he said, would have to raise $5,000,000. Schiff also suggested that they invite other individuals to make similar grants, men like J. P. Morgan, Henry Ford, and George F. Baker of the First National Bank. Schiff asked Rosenwald to talk to Wilson and find out whether he would support this plan. I can't talk to him, said Schiff; he doesn't like me. Nothing came of Schiff's proposal.

Unfortunately, the crises in Eastern Europe continued; American Jewry was concerned. Conditions in Russia had deteriorated toward the end of 1917 when the Bolsheviks, the Communists, came to power. They were determined to destroy the capitalist structure and they succeeded. From the point of view of the Jewish bourgeois this was a disaster. Most of Russia's Jews were now declassed; they had no rights and but few chances to make a livelihood. Their only hope was to restratify, to become artisans and farmers. The Russians wanted them to till the soil, to become "productive," to raise grain to feed the country's millions. This was the challenge that faced hundreds of thousands in this new Soviet state. As early as 1919 the American government set out to help relieve distress in Russia. Hoover's American Relief Administration (ARA) and other American and European agencies now went into Eastern Europe to aid Russia, Poland, and the other war-stricken lands. Eighteen million tons of food for the hungry were shipped into the area by the Americans; in addition over 840,000,000 pounds of clothing and other goods were sent in; hundreds of thousands if not millions of food packages were distributed. The unfortunates in the areas ravaged by wars had to be fed and they were by the American Relief Administration and other agencies including the Joint Distribution Committee. In the early postwar years the JDC worked closely with the ARA; formally, at least, it was part of the Hoover organization. In 1922, still operating under the umbrella of the ARA, the Joint made provision for 90,000 children in 700 different institutions. That same year it was feeding 400,000 adults; many of these were non-Jews. The immensity of the challenge that confronted American Jewry staggers the imagination.

Dr. Joseph Rosen, the agronomist in charge of the JDC work in Russia proper, often had no choice but to work along nonsectarian lines. In 1923 he advised the Russians as they set out to plant almost 3,000,000 acres with corn. A few years later Rosen settled thousands of Jews on land, in colonies, primarily in the Crimea. Others were taught trades so that they, too, could enter the economic parameters of the Marxist state. In a formal sense "reconstruction" began in 1924, although there was often little distinction between the palliative relief of earlier years and the later reconstruction activities. In a word food, clothing, loans, medicine would have to be shipped in as long as the Joint was permitted to remain in the Slavic states. The reconstruction agency established in 1924 to aid the Russian Jews was known as the Agro-Joint, short for the American Jewish Joint Agricultural Corporation. The two parties in this bold enterprise were the American JDC and the European ICA, the Jewish Colonization Association, the creation of the late Baron Maurice de Hirsch. In Russia, the JDC, the ICA, and the Soviets worked together to rehabilitate the country's Jews. Rosenwald was now induced to give millions. There is no question that the Agro-Joint saved thousands by qualifying them as farmers and artisans. Whole villages were built, machines installed, tractors brought in, livestock purchased, seed supplied, farm schools set up, dairy cooperatives organized, agronomists enlisted, clinics and hospitals established. Civically and economically Jews were now integrated into the body politic.

Much of what was accomplished was due to the genius of one man, the Russian immigrant, Joseph Rosen, an American Ph.D. In 1938 the JDC and its Agro-Joint affiliate were asked to leave Russia; the government believed that they were no longer needed. Just three years later the Germans invaded the country; huge numbers of Jews were murdered; on September 29-30, 1941, almost 34,000 Jews were machine-gunned by the Germans at Babi Yar, a ravine near Kiev. Before these invaders retreated to their native land some two years later about 100,000 men, women and children, mostly Jews, had been executed and buried in the same place. Those left over, at least two million, were subject to forced assimilation in the course of decades. Like others in the Soviet Empire they were denied cultural and religious rights. One is reminded of the compulsory conversions in Portugal in the 1490's. The Portuguese conversions brought forth a generation of Marranos, secret Jews, and in a somewhat similar fashion Russia has been producing its Marranos, men and women who still affirm their Jewishness. Those who opted to remain Jews ultimately hoped to escape, and to go to Israel or, preferably, to the United States.

Rehabilitation in Poland and the other succession states in 1924 was carried on under the aegis of a new institution; it called itself the American Joint Reconstruction Foundation. The problems that faced the Foundation in the bourgeois states were entirely different from those that faced the Agro-Joint in proletarian Russia. In Russia restratified Jewry had to become artisans or farmers; in the Slavic states to the west the old petty capitalist economy had to be rebuilt. Four to six years of war had destroyed Jewish institutions and businesses; the Jewish artisans and trading class still remained. Local Jewish organizations arose again; these East Europeans were courageous and sanguine; they set out to help themselves although they often tended to lean on their "rich uncle" across the seas. In 1924 fund-raising in America to finance the needs of suppliant Jews became more difficult; American Jewry had been giving, and giving liberally, for ten long years, since 1914. As interest in giving ebbed the appeals became more lurid: "Babies of our blood are dying like flies; fathers beg for crusts and mothers go mad," but there were years when these maudlin appeals reflected dread reality.

As in Russia the JDC and its affiliates saved thousands of lives in the postwar states that had sprung from the loins of Russia, Germany, and Austria. Concerned primarily with the new Poland, American Jews built houses, trained nurses, established soup kitchens, founded orphanages, set up old-age homes, trained craftsmen, and supported schools. Money, clothing, medicine, food were shipped in constantly. Culturally the Americans catered to the disparate Jewish ideologues who confronted them; they had no choice; the Orthodox, socialists, Zionists, Yiddishists were determined to live their lives as their consciences and mentality dictated. The JDC was harnessed to perform a variety of services; it forwarded letters, brought together scattered families; dispatched remittances to distant Polish hamlets; established national child care and medical organizations, and organized numerous small cooperative loan banks and free loan associations.

POSTWAR PROBLEMS

Helping European Jews in the war-contested lands was not easy. There were frequent economic upheavals, a fluctuating currency, famine, disease, insensate religiosocial hatreds. Both Jews and Christians were hostile to one another. American Jewish social-welfare agencies which looked to Washington for understanding and sympathy were frequently disappointed. As early as 1915 an official in the State Department said that Jews exerted undue influence in this country; they had enough power to abrogate the old treaty with Russia; they owned important newspapers, theatres, banks; if they controlled immigration they would own the country. This was the traditional anti-Semitic line in Germany, France, and the United States. The refugee problem which became acute in 1914—

actually 1881—never abated. During the war thousands of uprooted Jews wandered about in Siberia. Many moving westward towards the United States in 1921 had nowhere to go when the quota laws went into effect; some finally found a haven in the Caribbean, in Mexico, and in South America. Thousands who had made the Atlantic crossing were worried about their wives and children left behind in Russia and Poland.

Helping immigrants to migrate was anything but a simple process; the United States government set its face against what it called "assisted immigration." The Joint maintained a low profile when it aided emigrants; it was so fearful lest it incur the wrath of the Washington authorities that it even stopped forwarding remittances to Europe for individuals; the HIAS, more resourceful, continued transmitting money for its clients; it dared to skirt the letter of the law. The tragedy of restratification in Russia was met when small town traders became artisans and farmers but the economic challenges were succeeded by anticlerical government pressures which spelt cultural and religious genocide. In Poland the virulent nationalism may well have been a rationale to displace the Jews from their entrenched positions in the country's middle class. This attempt to emasculate the Jews economically was also made in Rumania and in some of the new Baltic states. There can be no question; the Jews had to struggle in all these polities to maintain their rights that had been accorded them by the European powers when the peace treaties were signed. Most, if not all the new states carved out of Russia, persisted in looking on Jews as aliens. There was little desire to accept them as fellow citizens, to live peacefully with these infidels with whom they had been feuding for centuries. In turn, the Russian Jews, overwhelmingly Orthodox in belief, were unwilling to accept an antireligious communism; in Poland the Jews would not make their peace with a Christian-tinged anti-Jewish Polish nationalism.

The East European Jews and their American Jewish benefactors resented that they had to share their gifts of money and food with people who despised them. In the early 1920's Jewish social workers in the Soviet Union turned to the American Relief Administration and asked it to tell the Russian people that the help they were receiving also came from Jews. The problems of the JDC both in America and in Europe were compounded by the fact that there was no unity among the Jews either here or abroad. Here in America the JDC embraced at least five different cultural, economic, social, and religious groups; they did not always work in harmony. There were natives, acculturated Germans, socialists, proletarian workers, Orthodox religionists. Few disparities were completely reconciled yet the different groups worked together because the American Jewish Relief Committee had the upper hand; it collected the bulk of the funds by far. The divisive forces that threatened Jewry here were even more in evidence in Europe where relief was allocated. As early as 1914 when help was sent to occupied Poland through the agency of Germany's Jews, German Zionists of that country squabbled about the distribution of the moneys. Intra- Jewish antagonisms were virulent in Poland. Literally there were at least ten different Jewish ideological groups; party philosophy was dominant. Under these circumstances it was difficult for the JDC to bring relief and to plan reconstruction; conflict and disunity were constant. Each group wanted to manage its own institutions and their insistent demands were frequently reinforced by partisans back in the States. These were some of the problems that confronted the JDC when it set out to help the Jewish East Europeans. Given these hazards it is surprising that the American Jews accomplished as much as they did. These difficulties must not be glossed over.

NOTABLES IN THE FIELD OF RELIEF

Over the years the accomplishments of the Joint Distribution Committee were noteworthy. What it did is a tribute to the millions of Americans who answered its appeals for help. In one campaign alone, in New York City in the 1920's, 90,000 Jews made contributions. In the final analysis it was always the people who gave the money, yet leadership was important. The success of any enterprise was usually due to the workers, the brilliance, the devotion of those who stood at the head. Many notables gave time, a great deal of time to the Joint Distribution Committee; some were old-timers; others were immigrants. Among the men engaged in this philanthropic work were Felix Warburg, Louis Marshall, Jacob H. Schiff, Cyrus Adler, Boris Bogen, Joseph Rosen, Herbert H. Lehman, Jacob Billikopf. There were dozens of others who merit mention. Only two are singled out here, not because they were more important than others but because they were typical of those who rallied around the JDC as it reached out to help.

One of these workers was Herbert Henry Lehman (1878-1963), scion of a successful Alabama German Jewish family that responded to the call of noblesse oblige. Lehman's father, Mayer, attempted in the latter days of the Civil War to bring relief to Alabama war prisoners incarcerated in Northern prison stockades. Herbert, the son, was named after a well-known Alabama Gentile politician whom Mayer admired. As a young man Lehman worked in a boys' club room in Lillian Wald's Henry Street Settlement; he was also on the board of the National Association for the Advancement of Colored People. Later, after a start in textiles and in banking, Lehman went into politics. He was a Democrat and no doubt frequently received Tammany support but he never permitted the Tammany leaders to threaten his integrity. As a wealthy man he kept his skirts clean. As one always interested in the social welfare of society it is easy to understand why New York's Jewish elite picked him to head the Reconstruction Committee of the JDC in 1921. It was his job to help rebuild war-torn East European Jewry. In the late 1920's he served as lieutenant governor under Franklin D. Roosevelt and when the latter went to Washington Lehman moved up to the gubernatorial chair; he served four terms. In 1949 New York sent him to the United States Senate.

He was an admirer of the suave charismatic Roosevelt but when the President set out to pack the Supreme Court Lehman opposed him. He was not the man to make deals with anyone; he never learned the art of political compromise and thus he was never a power in the upper house. In World War II, Roosevelt made him director of the United Nations Relief and Rehabilitation Administration (1943-1946); he had learned the business in the 1920's working for the JDC. Through his job as head of UNRRA he fed millions of men, women, and children all over the face of Europe. Feeding Europe during the 1940's was not an easy task; the war was still going on; the armies had priority in all things but this New York communal worker persisted and met the demands of the task till relieved; it was a multibillion dollar enterprise. As a politician he had no dash, no color; he was naive but few dared question his honesty, his sincerity, his idealism. He gave liberally to Jewish causes and helped further the Palestine community though like most of his circle he was no Zionist. When he died the President of the United States came to pay his respects.

Lehman was born to wealth; his father was a successful commodity broker, a trustee of prestigious Temple Emanu-El. Jacob Billikopf, the brain behind the Joint Distribution Committee's fund-raising, was a Lithuanian who came to the United States as a fourteen-year-old lad. For most of his life he made his livelihood as a social worker. He was one of the men who raised the status of the profession among Jews making it a position of dignity and respect. After serving his apprenticeship in Cincinnati and Milwaukee he settled down in Kansas City where he distinguished himself by his interest in social legislation. Missouri would eventually thank him for his help in establishing public night schools, municipal baths, a legal aid bureau, a loan agency, municipal recreation facilities. Billikopf contended that he pioneered in furthering aid to dependent children (mothers' pensions). In later years he was the executive of the Jewish philanthropies in Philadelphia. Billikopf staged some of the JDC's multimillion dollar campaigns. He was an ingenious innovative fund-raiser; he thought in terms of millions and when the Red Cross spoke of raising $5,000,000 he urged it to go out for $50,000,000. Impressed by his ability Schiff offered him a job in the banking business; he did not accept. He was a man who liked to reach out to the larger world about him. He was a trustee of Howard University, a black school, and the Hebrew University of Jerusalem. Billikopf was a letter writer; he kept in touch with the great, both Jews and Gentiles; his letters are a mine of information for Jewish historians.

SUMMARY

It would seem that the most important job that the Joint Distribution Committee did in Poland and in the succession states was to set up cooperative loan banks and free-loan associations. For the numerous small-scale enterprisers, artisans, and shopkeepers, capital, credit, was their life blood. An average loan was about $20; small as these amounts were they helped keep these petty businessmen afloat. From 1924 to 1938 the American Joint Reconstruction Foundation of the JDC made over 5,000,000 loans; it lent over $580,000,000. From 1914 to 1921 the Joint Distribution Committee spent over $38,000,000 helping its European clients; more money was required in the last two years than in all four years of the war. Counting up what it had expended for European relief American Jewry discovered it was sending abroad as much as it gave to its local communal institutions; Jews discovered, too, that in war relief they gave four times as much per capita as their non-Jewish neighbors. A disproportionate percentage of their gifts went to Palestine; the Orthodox were adamant in insisting on this priority for the Jews and schools of the Holy Land; the American Jewish elite, who actually controlled the available funds, went along with them. The bounty of the Joint was not limited to the Slavic lands where suffering and poverty were most evident; the Distribution Committee reached out to serve in many lands. It responded to the appeals of Jewish prisoners of war wherever they were confined, helped Russian and Polish students studying at Swiss universities, and subvented the Jews of Morocco, Algiers, and Tunis when the tourist trade declined during the war and these North Africans were compelled to appeal for assistance.

Long after the end of World War I the JDC was still working to aid the East Europeans always hoping, however, that its clients would be able to stand alone. Then came the German National Socialists; the Slavic lands were again overrun; Polish Jewry was destroyed; Russian Jewry was decimated; the JDC had no choice but to continue its work; crisis succeeded crisis. For a time the only refuge open to European Jews was Mandate Palestine. Funds once directed toward the Baltic states, Poland, Russia, and Rumania were now poured into the old homeland. The United Palestine Appeal, a congeries of Zionist institutions, began to receive the bulk of American Jewish gifts; in 1939 the JDC and the Palestine Appeal, now joined together permanently as the United Jewish Appeal, began to direct their millions toward the new Jewish haven. East European Jewry was dead or dying; it had no future.

After the Second World War the JDC reached out to bring hundreds of thousands of Diaspora Jews to the new-old land of Palestine. Jews poured in from the displaced persons camps, from Middle Eastern lands, and from all the Moslem states of northern Africa. As of the 1980's the JDC was still at work, for the world was still in turmoil. During that decade this great American Jewish philanthropic institution was still busy in about seventy lands; since 1914 it had spent well over a billion dollars to rescue men, women and children, to bring them relief, to help them rebuild their lives and their institutions. Ever since the sad years that began in 1914 American Jewry sought to help kinsmen abroad; individuals and hometown societies poured millions into Eastern Europe; organized efforts, however, were carried on primarily by the JDC. Relatively speaking this may be deemed one of the great philanthropic feats of all times. American Jews, working as a body, made all this possible. It is ironic, pitifully so, that many of the human beings rescued were in the 1940's murdered by the Germans and their Slavic collaborators.

What did the giving of money, time, devotion do, not for the Jews of Europe but for the Jews of America, the givers, not the recipients? Giving for a common cause was a major factor in developing the national American Jewish community still in the stage of "becoming." The community began in 1840 with protests against the persecution of Jews in Damascus; its next communalizing steps were the establishment of the B'nai B'rith Order, the Board of Delegates of American Israelites, the Union of American Hebrew Congregations, and, a generation later the founding of Orthodox and Conservative congregational and rabbinical associations. Then in 1906 came the American Jewish Committee. Before 1921 the next big step forward was the establishment of the American Jewish Joint Distribution Committee. It was a step forward because the Joint reached into more than a thousand towns, villages, and hamlets to embrace and to link together American Jews and their institutions. The New Yorkers, through the Joint, built national unity by co-opting the provincials and tying them all together; the individual settlements now became an integral part of a new whole. Without surrendering their cherished prejudices, their social, economic, and cultural biases, the disparate groups learned to tolerate one another and to cooperate. Working for a common humanitarian (Jewish) purpose the powerful Jewish labor leaders, schismatics, were induced to return to their people.

The functioning Joint Distribution Committee was an exercise in democracy, limited to be sure; cooperation was attained not by the ballot but by compromise. The sense of community in this country was heightened as kinship was acknowledged. The new unity was built on charity not religion; denominationalism was divisive; in an age of advancing secularism people were turning away from religion; saving human lives appealed to all regardless of their ideologies. The crises with which American Jewry had to cope in Europe, 1914-1945, were comparable only to the East European wars of 1644-1655, the Spanish and Portuguese persecutions in the 1490's, the Crusades, and the attempt of the Jews in 66 and 132 C.E. to free themselves from the Romans. The challenge to help millions threatened with famine brought out the best in American Jewry; without hesitation the masses, all groups, assumed responsibility for their kinsmen abroad. As Jews they knew that myriads would perish if they did not respond to the cry that came out of the East. They believed—and they were not altogether wrong—that for the new governments east of Germany the Jews were expendable. Thus it was that an American Jewry set forth to rescue millions of human beings; the very concept alone was grandiose.

In helping others, Jews learned to give. In 1915 Jewry in this country collected about $1,500,000; every year thereafter it raised its sights; by 1917 under the leadership of Rebekah Kohut, the women of New York City were co-opted to go out as women and to do something for their people. The first million-dollar gift of Rosenwald created a sensation in the American Jewish world—a Gentile, George Peabody, had already given away millions before he died in 1869. Rosenwald now set the pace for Jewish philanthropists on this side of the Atlantic; a generation later million-dollar gifts by Jews were commonplace. Individual acts of farsighted generosity were not unknown. During World War I a group of New York's Uptown elite was induced to bring Eliezer Ben Yehuda to America and support him. This was the man who was busy at work developing modern Hebrew; his dictionary was to become a classic reference tool. The men who financed Ben Yehuda were, for the most part, non-Zionists but they respected Jewish tradition; they wanted to further scholarship.

It was during World War I, as all the people of this country stood shoulder to shoulder, that a common philanthropic fund was established in many major towns; it served equally Protestants, Catholics, Jews. This was the War Chest. This innovation, ascribed by many to a similar fund established by the Cleveland Jewish community in 1913, served to link Jews and Christians as they worked during the war to relieve distress at home. In postwar days the War Chest became the Community Chest. After the war, after the euphoria of fraternalism in a national crisis had abated, the Jews were called upon to decide whether they would surrender fund-raising for local Jewish needs and depend on the largesse of the Community Chest. The decision was in the negative. No Community Chest or United Fund could with good conscience support Jewish religious schools, Jewish foreign relief, campaigns against Gentile anti-Semites, sociocultural associations which were often religious in nature.

The decision to set up a separate Jewish fund was not made without some question. As late as 1917 even Julius Rosenwald and Simon Wolf were not sure that they wanted to continue the Joint Distribution Committee as it moved to support Jews in the war zones. It was the hope of men like Rosenwald and Wolf that foreign governments and nondenominational religious agencies would provide for Jews as they did for the commonality. Louis Marshall dissented from this view. He pointed out laconically that when Gentiles had been solicited by the Jews they gave less than 1 percent of the money collected; experience and statistics taught Jews that no dependence could be placed on the American Red Cross; the East European governments were hostile to their Jews; the Jews everywhere would have to depend on institutions of their own which were geared to Jewish survival. Out of the conviction that Jewry would have to help itself came the creation of Jewish Welfare Funds in the 1920's. Because of the massive funds sent abroad Jews here staked their claim to hegemony over World Jewry. This has been a fact of life since 1914; unwittingly Jews in the United States were already rising to power in 1903 when they rushed to aid Russian Jews after the Kishinev massacre. The obligation to assume leadership has been thrust upon American Jewry; it has been called upon to help Jews in distress wherever they are; it has rarely failed to respond.[11]

CHAPTER TWENTY-ONE

UNITY, CONFLICT, ZIONISM

THE EARLY YEARS

When the East European Jews began to stream into American harbors in sizable numbers in the mid-nineteenth century apprehensive Jewish communal leaders here set out to Americanize them, to occidentalize their Orthodoxy, to offer them leadership. The native and German-born notables were proud of what they were doing for the newcomers. They had rallied around these émigrés after the Russian massacres of 1881, 1903, and 1905; it was the "Germans" who put together the American Jewish Committee dedicated to defense and relief; they had worked hard to secure the abrogation of the 1832 Russian treaty and had helped organize the New York Kehillah in 1909; it was these old- timers —the established elite—who carried the financial burden of the Joint Distribution Committee as it girded its loins to save the Jews of Russia, Poland, and the Balkans. To a considerable degree unity had been achieved; the two disparate American Jewish groups were working together. The recent immigrants could not emancipate themselves from the established elite although they affected to despise it. The successful Russians—petty bankers, manufacturers, professionals—patterned themselves on America's older established Jews; the newly arrived imitated them; they wanted to be recognized socially by the Germans; they were eager to ensconce themselves within the ambit of a decorous American Jewry. The East Europeans were ready to reject the Slavic village and town singularities and to adopt the Anglo-Saxon way of life. Both congeries recognized the demands of kinship. All Jews here were shocked by the pogroms and the oppressive Russian and Rumanian legislation. With few, very few exceptions, they were determined to keep the portals to America open; the charity federations slowly began integrating Russian and Polish philanthropic agencies; the very first executive committee of the American Jewish Committee included two Russians and the son of a Pole.[1]

633

Yet there were tensions resulting in rancorous conflict. There were mutual hostilities of a social, economic, ethnic nature. Newer immigrants were despised as "kikes"; sneering at the old-timers the Russians hurled at them the Hebrew epithet "Yahudim"; emphasis was on the elongated antepenult. The "Germans": real Jews? Certainly not! The new ghetto Jews had their own way of life, their own press, language, literature, music, fraternal orders, mutual-aid societies, religious services, and, to boot, a small but vociferous militant body of sociopolitical radicals. The differences between the two communities were real; they snarled at one another from opposite ends of the social spectrum. One is tempted at times to believe that the only particular that they had in common was the designation, "Jew." Often it was a case of immigrant versus immigrant, German versus Russian. This style of Jewish ethnic hostility was nothing new in American Jewish history; it may well have manifested itself as early as the 1600's, Sephardi versus Ashkenazi. The arrival of the Germans in the 1830's dismayed the established Jewish communal leaders.

Now in the late nineteenth and early twentieth centuries the differences between the two Jewish communities were patent. The Reformers and the American Orthodox were not happy with the boisterous Russo-Polish services; the Downtown masses resented the Uptowners; it was a case of the rich versus the poor; after a fashion it was a struggle between two classes. The non-and anti-Zionists attacked the Zionists. Emphasizing the concept of democracy the denizens of the ghetto revolted against the paternalism of the older establishment; the Russians wanted a strong democratically elected national Jewish association that would move the federal authorities to intercede on behalf of suffering European Jewry. We, said the Russians, outnumber you "Germans" four to one; we want our own leadership, at least autonomy. To which the Germans countered that it was they who had created or developed most of the country's present day Jewish communal institutions, the basic local and national associations and agencies; it was they who had effected a cultural synthesis of Americanism and Judaism. They were proud of their achievements; they had earned the leadership the leaders exerted; they would not relinquish it. If American Jewry exercised World Jewish hegemony since World War I it was due to the devoted efforts of America's older established community. This apologia was not accepted by the ambitious new Jewish communal leaders; they revolted. The battle was fought on the issue of an American Jewish Congress which set out to oppose and, if possible, replace the American Jewish Committee. The Committee was anti-and non-Zionist; the new Congress was strongly Zionist. Superficially at least the battle of the Committee against the Congress implied rejection or acceptance of Zionism; in reality there was much more at stake in this conflict during the second decade of the new century. Who will rule American Jewry, the Germans or the Russians?

HERZLIAN ZIONISM

If central control, domination, was the hidden agenda, Zionism was the overt issue. Zionism was a political philosophy adopted in Switzerland in August 1897 by a group of Jews from many lands. The programs, defined in Basel at that time, expressed the determination to create a home for the Jewish people in Palestine, one that would be secured by public law and would be based on Jewish national sentiment. The movement itself was organized by cultured Central Europeans; the mass followers were Russians, Poles, and Rumanians, men and women living under hostile regimes. The desire for an independent sovereign state was not spelled out but it was probably envisaged by most of the delegates.

Zionism is a return to Zion, to Jerusalem, to Palestine. This modern restoration movement owes its origin to Theodor Herzl (1860-1904), a charismatic Hungarian-born journalist who represented the *Vienna Neue Freie Presse* in Paris. He was fully aware of the increasing impact of anti-Semitism in Eastern Europe and France. When the French Captain Alfred Dreyfus was found guilty of treason Herzl recognized that anti-Jewish hatred played its part in condemning this man whether he was guilty or not. Herzl witnessed the joy of the Paris mob when Dreyfus—later proved to be innocent—was publicly degraded (1895). Slowly Herzl came to the conclusion that the cultured western world, even liberal France, would never fully accept the Jew; the Children of Israel must return to a land of their own. With this thought in mind he published a German pamphlet in 1896, *The Jewish State: An Attempt at a Modern Solution of the Jewish Question.* Some, even friends, thought him daft, yet the idea, the hope for a Jewish state caught on. Political Zionism was born. Soon there were hundreds of Zionist societies all over the world. Zionism was to become one of the most successful movements—the most successful?—in modern Jewish life. The oppressed Russian, Polish, and Rumanian Jews welcomed Herzl's organization because it promised them surcease; many western Jews supported the Viennese visionary because the Jews of Eastern Europe had to be helped.[2]

PRE-HERZLIAN ZIONISM

Zionism pre-dates Herzl. Many Jews in all parts of the world embraced the movement immediately; they were heartsick at the almost annual reports of the sufferings of Jews in Eastern Europe and the Balkans. These unfortunates needed succor; there was no hope for them in their homelands. Indeed many questioned the future of the Jews in enlightened Europe where Judeophobia had appeared in a new pseudoscientific guise as anti-Semitism. There were some Jews—probably not many—who believed that the cost of emancipation was too high if it meant giving up a comforting Jewish way of life. If one wanted to live Jewishly, a free Palestine was the answer. Jews had always been Zionists; the Bible assured them they would yet return; for centuries they had prayed in their book of common prayer daily for the restoration of the Davidic monarchy and the reestablishment of the sacrificial system in a rebuilt Jerusalem temple. (They thought they were praying for a messianic utopia.)

Jews did not have to wait to the nineteenth century to develop nationalism; their ethnicity was inextricably tied up with their religion; they never forgot Jerusalem. Long before the advent of Christianity Diaspora Jewry had been sending its half-shekels to support the Palestine homeland and its temple. Early Christian Jews, devotees of Saint Paul (Saul of Tarsus), sent their mite to the Christian saints (hassidim) in Jerusalem (Romans 15:24ff.); the halukkah system, the Palestine dole, has an ancient history. (Today it is measured in billions.) Jewish nationalism which really needed no fillip was bolstered by European nationalism all through the nineteenth century; the Germans, the Italians, the Slavs, the Balkan peoples were coming into their own. The effect of this burgeoning nationalism was to impel some East European Jews to think of nationalism in political terms, to look to Palestine. The Jewish natives of the East European lands could not, would not, genuflect in the direction of Russian or Polish or Rumanian nationalism; the Christian citizens of these states had rejected them. Reacting to rejection and religious prejudice, the Jews of all these countries intensified their traditional ethnicity. Wilson's Fourteen Points of January, 1918, only served to bolster their own hopes for restoration.[3]

Decades before Herzl came out with *The Jewish State*, Jews moved to settle in Turkish Palestine. Some insisted that living in the country was enough; others established agricultural communities. In 1862 a German Orthodox rabbi, Zvi Hirsch Kalischer (1795-1874), had written a Hebrew essay in which he urged Jewry to colonize Palestine; he feared the assimilatory pressure of European culture. It was he who pushed the Alliance Israélite Universelle to open the first modern agricultural school near Jaffa; this was Mikve Yisrael, The Hope of Israel. As an Orthodox Jew he believed in the coming of the Messiah and the ultimate restoration of the sacrificial cult. Colonization would give the Messiah a nudge. In establishing an agricultural school in Palestine the French Alliance was not pushing for a political state; like many Jews of that century it wanted to further the economic welfare of Palestine's Jews many of whom lived on grants that came from abroad. The very year that Kalischer wrote his Hebrew monograph, *Search for Zion*, Moritz Hess (1812-1875), a brilliant writer, a socialist or communist, published *Rome and Jerusalem*—in German—appealing to Jews to return to Palestine and establish a political state where they could develop their moral and spiritual potentiality. The western world was not ready to accept Jews. His book exerted little influence in its day; the times were not ripe. By the 1870's East European Jews began moving into Palestine; in 1878 they established a colony Petah Tikvah, The Gate of Hope. It did not do well at first; more successful was Rishon le-Tsiyyon, Zion's First, a wine colony which was aided by European Jewish philanthropists who were eager to see Jews return to the soil.

On the whole, these first colonies were not politically motivated; they were farm settlements pure and simple. By 1882 when Rishon le-Tsiyyon was established the 1881 Russian pogroms had come and gone; the May Laws drove many Jews off the soil and out of the villages. Then it was that the Russians and Rumanians, too, began to think seriously of colonizing the Holy Land. In 1882 Leo Pinsker, a physician, had written a pamphlet in German: *Autoemancipation: A Warning of a Russian Jew to His Brethren* in which he stressed his conviction that Jews had no future even in emancipated lands; their only hope lay in a country of their own wherever it might be. He soon linked himself with the Lovers of Zion societies which had come into being at that time. These devotees were primarily interested in establishing farmsteads; a political state was not in their thinking. By 1882 a group of young devotees had made their way to Palestine; they were the Bilu group; the word is a Hebrew acronym taken from Isaiah 2:5: "O House of Jacob, come ye and let us go." The Love of Zion movement spread over Europe and soon reached the United States. By 1884 the several societies met together in an international convention at Kattowitz in Upper Silesia, Germany. Pinsker assumed the presidency but his plans and work were hindered by the Turks; they did not welcome aliens who bought land and established close settlements in Palestine; they were apprehensive. Nevertheless, by the turn of the century a number of Jewish colonies had been settled; some of the farmers were already speaking Hebrew.[4]

RESTORATIONISM AND PROTO-ZIONISM IN AMERICA, 1600's-1860's

Though North America was thousands of miles distant from Europe and Palestine both Christian and Jews here were always interested in a restored Jewish Palestine. For reasons of their own Jews and Christians devoutly hoped for the rebirth of the ancient Israelitish state. What did they have in common: the Bible was the work of God; He had explicitly promised that a day would come when he would restore all Jews to their ancient home, no matter where they dwelt. Anne Bradstreet (d. 1672), one of America's first poets, expressed this hope in verse:

Where now those ten Tribes are, can no man tell,
Or how they fare, rich, poor, or ill, or well;
Whether the Indians of the East, or West,
Or wild Tartarians as yet ne're blest,
Or else those Chinoes rare, whose wealth and arts
Hath bred more wonder than belief in hearts:
But what, or where they are; yet know we this,
They shall return, and Zion see with bliss.

According to the Christians the Jews would ultimately go back to Palestine, convert, and welcome Jesus as he began his rule for a thousand years
over a blissful world. This was the Millennium, the Second Advent.
(Some believed the Jews would not accept Christianity until after the
Millennium.) At all events Jews would first have to return. This is restorationism, a concept accepted by both Jews and Christians; millions of
pious American Christians still believe that the Jews will yet go back to
the land of their fathers as God and the prophets have promised. Thus
these believers were, in a way, proto-Zionists. All through the nineteenth
and twentieth centuries, there were Christian missionaries who were bent
on converting Jews to speed the reappearance of the Christian God. Many
of these Christian restorationists were pragmatically inclined. By the
early nineteenth century they hoped that Jews would return to Zion and
rebuild it as a modern industrial and agricultural state. Let the Rothschilds
buy the country; they are rich enough. John Adams looked forward to the
day when the Jew would rule in Turkish Palestine. He was no pious
evangelical; if the thirteen colonies could rise as the United States why
not a republic in ancient Israel. Numerous American Christians combined
religious restorationism and nineteenth-century nationalism to envisage a
thoroughly modern Jewish state in the ancient homeland. All this long
before the birth of Theodor Herzl.

Not untypical are the views of a Dr. Ch. F. Zimpel, a German physician, who prepared detailed plans in the 1850's and 1860's for a reborn
Judaea. This Christian Zionist advocated modern methods in farming and
envisaged railroads and good harbors for the new Palestine. He hoped for
a political and religious rebirth of Jews despite the frowns of the Reform
Jews who urged acceptance of the Diaspora. Palestine is the Jew's salvation; it is difficult to cope with anti-Jewish prejudice so prevalent in the
lands where the Jews now dwell. It is reasonable to assume that Dr. Zimpel was influenced by the nationalism engendered by the 1848 German
revolutions. His proposed new state, a binational one, was to include
Christians and Jews; the Arabs, who occupied the land, were ignored. Interesting also are the views of Dr. Zimpel's contemporary, the American
Quaker Warder Cresson (1798-1860). Eager to help the Russian Jews
suffering under Nicholas I, Cresson urged them to settle in Palestine and

engage in scientific farming. Jerusalem, he declared, was the center and joy of the whole earth. Like the Millerites who looked for the speedy advent in the 1840's of their lord and savior, Cresson, too, believed that Jesus was once more to make his appearance. To welcome him Cresson went to Jerusalem. There he became a Jew taking the name Michael Boaz Israel but when he returned home his family attempted to commit him as a lunatic. The courts decided, however, that even though he had accepted Judaism he was not crazy (1850). Back in Palestine he set up a model farm and opened a soup house to feed indigent Jews; thus he countered the enticements of the missionaries who won souls by feeding bodies.[5]

JEWISH PROTO-ZIONISM, 1700's-1860's

Here in America there has never been a time in which Jews were not interested in Palestine Jewry. As believers in the promises of the Old Testament, tradition-true Jews prayed daily for Zion, the rebuilding of the Temple, the return of the sacrificial cult, the restoration of the Davidic monarchy. Jewry in Palestine must be helped, supported; funds were constantly dispatched abroad. Such collections were already being made in North America in the second half of the eighteenth century; an authentic official "evangel," an authorized Palestine collector from Hebron, reached these shores in 1775 only to flee as war broke out between the British and the rebellious Americans. The money collected here was usually apportioned (halukkah) among the various groups in Palestine who were organized ethnically and denominationally. Jews here were ready to support them because these Palestinians prayed day and night for divine restoration. They were the real Jews; they lived in the Holy Land; they interceded with God for Diaspora dwellers.

Collectors came frequently in the nineteenth century; their integrity was not always above suspicion. They scoured the land; their traveling expenses and their commissions were high; not too much was left for the devout importunates back home. American Jews were well aware of the pitfalls of the halukkah system and its collectors. As early as the 1830's and then in the 1850's Jews here established national collection agencies to raise funds and to forward them to the holy cities of Palestine through the medium of trustworthy bankers. The most that American Jews could hope for was equitable distribution. Nineteenth-century American Jewish philanthropists wanted more; Judah Touro of New Orleans left substantial sums which were used to build housing in Jerusalem; Sampson Simson of New York City and Yonkers bequeathed funds to Palestine's Jews with instructions that they be taught the arts, sciences, and modern methods of agriculture. (His family tried to break the will.) Let it be clear, the halukkah, the dole system, is in no sense political Zionism. The recipients did nothing to build the country; Orthodox Jews maintained, however, that they studied Torah; for them this was a worthy contribution to world culture and religion. Study is service to God.

Touro and Simson were in reality a new breed; they were successful businessmen who looked at Palestine with the critical vision of moneyed Americans. Commercial advances did not leave them untouched; the changing political scene influenced others. Gershom Seixas, the Revolutionary War patriot minister, played with the thought of an imminent restoration. He and some of his American Jewish contemporaries were fully aware of the nationalistic impact of the new United States; later Seixas watched as Napoleon summoned Jewish notables to meet in an international convention; the New York rabbi hoped that the Emperor would establish a Jewish state in Palestine or at least grant Jews equality in the Holy Land so that they might develop a strong community. His younger contemporary, Rebecca Gratz, one of the country's most cultured women, was an ardent restorationist. God would restore the Jews ultimately to their old homelands; this the prophets had assured us. Mordecai Manuel Noah, Rebecca's fellow Philadelphian, was a political Zionist, one of the first on these shores. The new American and European nationalisms influenced him profoundly. Even the Negroes have been restored to Africa! For most of his life he talked and wrote of the reestablishment of a Jewish state in the ancestral homeland. It was to be a refuge for oppressed Jewry. He wanted a modern state, one that would be preeminent in industry and agriculture, patterned after the United States, important because of its location on the strategic road to Africa and the Far East. In later decades Herzl would talk of a charter; Noah wanted the rich Jews to buy the land from the Turks, or if need be seize it by force. To accomplish this the Christians—conversionists, too—would have to be co-opted. They, too, believed in God's irrefragable promise; only the Great Christian Powers can work this modern miracle; Protestant and American political idealism can accomplish wonders on behalf of the Jews.

Noah died in 1851; later in that decade Raphael J. De Cordova, a lay preacher in Emanu-El, preached on nationality and restoration. Mayhap he was some sort of Zionist; there is, however, no evidence in the minutes of this congregation to enlighten us. His contemporary, the distinguished Isaac Leeser, the country's best known antebellum Jewish cleric, had very definite ideas on the subject. By that time, at the latest, political nationalisms were blossoming in many parts of Europe. Leeser had grown up in post-Napoleonic Germany where the Prussians, enheartened by their victories, set out to build a national state. Virginia, his new home, made Leeser a nationalist, an American patriot. He extended his newly acquired Americanism to embrace contemporary Jewry nationally but always as an

Orthodox religionist. He was a biblical restorationist but like Noah he was convinced that any new state established near the Suez must be modern in every sense, even as America itself. Warder Cresson was his friend. A rebuilt Palestine would prove the Bible was right. Noah, not infrequently, published his views in Leeser's *Occident*. The two men were not always in agreement. Noah, the journalist, was no enemy of sensationalism; James Gordon Bennett of the *Herald* was a contemporary. Leeser, disagreeing with Noah, said that the Jew could not work with the Christians; they were conversionists intent on destroying the Jews spiritually. The Great Powers? They could not be trusted. Yet a Palestine refuge had to be established to offer a haven to Europe's afflicted Jews. There was no need, however, for American Jews to go back; Palestine was too small; the rebirth of a commonwealth there, however, would bring a new pride to the community here. We will be respected if we have a government of our own. Instead of peddlers, shopkeepers, bankers, we will have farmers and statesmen. Leeser hoped that the new state might even be established in his own day under the rule of a scion of the Davidic house. It was too bad that internal strife among Jews themselves made this hope somewhat illusory. Thus Leeser.[6]

CHRISTIAN PROTO-ZIONISM, 1860's-1897

The establishment of a Palestine Jewish homeland was often the subject for discussion in the Gentile secular and in the Christian sectarian press in the middle and late nineteenth century. There was no consensus; some journals were sympathetic, others questioned whether the Jews had the capacity to establish and run a government. The new nationalism and the rise of ethnic states in Europe probably stimulated this discussion. The Christian restorationists, who had been very much in evidence for centuries, continued to express themselves vigorously all through the nineteenth and the twentieth centuries. All Jews will yet go back to Palestine; this has been promised us in God's Bible; Palestine belongs to the Jews. As a corollary these evangelicals believed that the Children of Israel would ultimately accept and worship Jesus. The Jews must accept Christ; otherwise Christianity is a sham; this was inconceivable. Since God so wishes it the Jew must be helped to return.

Like their ancestors the evangelical Protestants were proto-Zionists. Americans began to travel to the Holy Land, to walk in the footsteps of their Christian God. Herman Melville was there in the 1850's, Mark Twain in the 1860's; in the 1870's James Parton, writing in the *Atlantic Monthly*, was eager to see the Jews settle in ancient Canaan. These visitors and these writers stimulated interest in a Jewish Palestine. In 1876 George Eliot's *Daniel Deronda* was reprinted here in the United States reenforcing the views of those Christians who hoped to witness the re-birth of the third Jewish commonwealth. The Jewish heroes in this book looked forward to the creation of a Jewish state where Jews would rejoice in a home of their own. Eliot's *Daniel Deronda* reflected, very probably, the views of many Christians who could only nod their heads in affirmation as they followed the appeal for a Jewish state. A Palestine re-born, peopled by cultured Jews, astride the continental crossroads, would certainly enspirit the effete East.

In the 1870's and later in the 1880's, Laurence Oliphant, the English writer, urged Jews to settle in Transjordan's Gilead and establish a thor-oughly modern state. Oliphant was certainly willing to help; he had little sympathy, however, for the prevailing religious mendicancy. The archae-ologist Lt. Col. Claude R. Conder and the English historian W. E. H. Lecky were interested in a Jewish Palestine. These men were not without influence in American Gentile circles. Oliphant's colonial plans were con-ceived with the hope of helping unhappy Russian Jewry; persecutions of Jews by the East Europeans moved many Christians both in England and in the United States. American diplomats and consuls like Lew Wallace, Oscar S. Straus, and Selah Merrill, faithful to their official obligations, in-tervened successfully with the Sultan to protect American Jewish citizens who had retired to Palestine. Some East European Jews who had been naturalized in this country moved on to the Holy Land to spend their last years there. Consul Merrill ventured the opinion that the Jews would never be able to establish a state; they were accustomed to the dole. The Sublime Porte wanted no Jewish mass settlement in the Christian and Jewish Holy Land; Turkey feared the new nationalism which had cost them much of their European possessions; they wanted no non-Moslem politically autonomous groups in a Palestine where the vast majority of the inhabitants worshipped at the shrine of Allah. The apprehensive rul-ers of the Ottomon Empire did not realize that these Jewish American newcomers who worshipped at the Wailing Wall had no immediate polit-ical ambitions. In a special issue, September 26, 1885, the Chicago *Herald* predicted—with tongue in cheek—that a wealthy Chicago clothing man-ufacturer would one day buy Palestine and proceed to modernize it with railroads and irrigation canals. They dubbed this enterprising industrialist "King Solomon"; his original name was Moses Solomon.

The Russian pogroms and expulsions of the 1880's and 1890's made the Russo-Jewish problems acute. Pious Christian restorationists and Sec-ond Adventists were disturbed; it was time that God rally to help his Chosen People. In 1891 a Chicago businessman, William Eugene Black-stone, attracted a great deal of attention by his determination to come to the aid of persecuted Jewry. He began agitating in the period when immi-gration exclusion laws in this country were first passed. Jews were coming here in large numbers; xenophobic Americans would have been delighted if the stream of newcomers could be diverted to some other land. Blackstone wanted Palestine restored to the Jews. He was a pious, evangelical Christian, a restorationist; there is little question that he hoped for the ultimate conversion of the Children of Israel. As early as 1878 Blackstone published *Jesus Is Coming*; a million copies were distributed; translations appeared in at least a dozen different languages including Hebrew. That same year a Mr. James Mitchell had written to President Hayes suggesting that the Jewish bankers—the money kings of the world—buy Palestine from the Turks, turn it over to the Jews, and elect Sir Moses Montefiore as their first president.

The memorial which Blackstone sent to President William H. Harrison and Secretary of State James G. Blaine in 1891 created quite a stir. He wanted these men, who were well acquainted with the distress of the East European Jews, to call an international conference of European states with the hope that they would urge the Turks to turn Palestine over to the Jews. The new state was to be established under the protection of the Great Powers; the Turks, of course, were to be compensated for the loss of their province. Many of America's most distinguished leaders signed this petition. Among them were John D. Rockefeller, J. Pierpont Morgan, the Chief Justice of the Supreme Court, the Speaker of the House. Even some famous Jewish non-Zionists lent their names. Emil G. Hirsch, however, refused to sign the Blackstone memorial; he wanted nothing to do with a scheme that aimed to establish a Jewish state. The Chicago *Tribune* was sympathetic; New York's *American Hebrew* was not unfriendly; Philadelphia's *Jewish Exponent* was enthusiastic; New York's *Jewish Messenger* wrote that the remedy was worse than the disease; Cincinnati's *American Israelite* was brutally frank: "The Russian Jews are not fit to govern themselves." Years later, 1916, Blackstone, still alive and active, sent a second petition to Woodrow Wilson, this at a time when the American Zionists were seeking the establishment of a legally assured home in the Palestine of their forebears.

A year after the appearance of the Blackstone memorial, Paul Haupt (1858-1926), a Gentile who taught Semitic languages at Johns Hopkins in Baltimore, published a German pamphlet recommending that Jews turn to Mesopotamia if they were eager to establish colonies; the title was *Concerning the Settlement of the Russian Jews in the Area of the Euphrates and Tigris (Ueber die Ansiedlung der russischen Juden in Euphrat und Tigris Gebiete)*. American Jews discussed this brochure with a great deal of interest; Haupt had many Jewish friends; some if not most of them were non-Zionists. Several years later his first doctoral student, Cyrus Adler, sent the brochure to Theodore Herzl, the father of Zionism. During the 1890's many Jews were interested in colonizing their coreligionists in the Middle East; anywhere, it would seem, but not in Palestine, holy alike to both Jews and Christians. It is a measure of the interest evoked by the movement to resettle the Jews in their ancient home that a new word was coined, no later than 1893, to characterize this interest in the rebuilding of the Jewish state. The new word was Zionism. It is metonymic because it included much more than Zion, Jerusalem. And Zionism? Its connotation was anything but exact; it envisaged almost any type of settlement in Palestine.[7]

Jewish Proto-Zionism, 1860's-1897

It is obvious that for religious reasons Jews were always interested in Palestine. This concern mounted in the late nineteenth century as persecution increased in the Slavic lands and in Balkan Rumania. Responding to the hostility in Eastern Europe small groups of Jews made their way to the Holy Land. Some of these immigrants—barely a trickle—were moved by the new European nationalisms, by romanticism. They were ready to begin a new life in an old homeland; there they would speak Hebrew, the language of their biblical fathers. However, most Jewish Europeans who fled sailed into American harbors. The Holy Land was no asylum for them though they were willing to help the few who since the 1870's settled in the Palestinian colonies. Most American Jews, including Reform congregations, were ready to support their Palestinian fellow Jews. Rebecca Gratz's Philadelphia Sunday School had a penny contribution box for the poor of Jerusalem. Isaac M. Wise in the 1860's was quick to help the Palestinians; he suggested that societies be established in American towns for that purpose. The United States, through its ministers to Turkey and its Jerusalem consuls, protested energetically and effectively when American citizens were threatened in Palestine by local tyrants.

Practically all American Jews, even the recently arrived East European émigrés, wanted the Palestinians to become self-supporting. It was hoped that the Jewish settlers there, in the *Yishuv*, would adopt modern farming methods; these Jews must turn to industry, develop modern social-welfare and educational agencies. As in earlier decades most Jews here looked with suspicion on the official collectors who were dispatched to America to collect funds for Palestine's poor; these agents were not trusted yet American Jewry gave and gave generously. Among the numerous collectors who came here with outstretched palms Rabbi Hayyim Zevi Shneersohn (1834-1882) stands out. As his name indicates he was a descendant of Shneor Zalman, the founder of the Lubavitch Hassidim. This Palestine agent came to this country as early as 1869. He spoke English, made public addresses, urged the modernization of the Palestine

Jewish colonies, and even met with President Grant on behalf of Europe's oppressed Jews. When Shneersohn left these shores he had opted for American citizenship.

In a modest fashion Bernhard Felsenthal, the Chicago Reform rabbi, was already a proto-Zionist in 1883, two years after the Russian mobs rose against the Jews. Palestine would serve well as a refuge for the Jews of Eastern Europe and North Africa; these men could build a thoroughly modern community tied together by a network of railroads that would reach out to all lands in the Middle East. As industrialists, Jews could become garment manufacturers. He admitted then that a Jewish commonwealth was not a realistic goal; in the next decade after Herzl's *Jewish State* appeared he emerged as a political Zionist. Even before Felsenthal preached his form of Zionism in 1883, Emma Lazarus, writing for the Jewish and general press, pleaded for a Jewish state, making clear, however, that it was to serve as a home for persecuted Jews only. She was content to remain here; East Europeans would do better in Palestine than in the United States. Maskilim, Hebrew-speaking "Enlighteners," who had settled here in the pre-Herzlian decades were enthusiastic proto-Zionists. They were thrilled at the thought that Hebrew could become the vernacular in the new colonies. America's talmudically-learned Jews, however, were not interested in modern Hebrew; they failed to support the country's Hebrew magazines; in this respect many were not proto-Zionists. William (Zev Wolf) Schur was typical of this new breed of Zionist "Enlighteners." Beginning in 1888 he edited Hebrew magazines in which he urged the reestablishment of a Jewish homeland where Jews would find spiritual redemption. He was delighted when Blackstone urged the world to restore Palestine to the Jews. After the rise of Herzl, he hammered away at the need for a politically assured home for Jews.

HOVEVE ZION, THE LOVERS OF ZION

When Schur came here from Eastern Europe he identified with the Lovers of Zion, Hoveve Zion. By 1884 the movement had already begun to make some progress in this country; ultimately branches were established in many states, in obscure Mississippi, in far off California and Nevada. These Lovers of Zion were content to support the new colonies; they themselves were determined to remain here in the United States. In some respects Hibbat Tsiyyon—Love of Zion—a romantic movement, was cultural in its aims; it hoped that concern for Zion would slow down the assimilation process. There were a number of these devotees who, in theory at least, wanted to do more than support the *Yishuv*; they thought of returning to Palestine to establish colonies where they themselves would live. They were led by a native American of German background. This was the Philadelphian Adam Rosenberg (1858-1928). This new society called itself Shave Tsiyyon, Returners to Zion (1891). Its members bought land but never developed it; their numbers were minuscule. Jews liked it here; they had no desire to leave; they hesitated to make aliyah, to go back, "up" to Jerusalem. One of the pro-Palestinian societies of that time had a charter that was written by Rosenberg but examination of this document discloses that its purpose was to establish colonies in this country. Fearful that they would be attacked on the charge of dual loyalties, Rosenberg and his friends hid their real aim—Palestine colonization—by asserting that their purpose was the establishment of farm settlements here in the United States. The Yiddish papers showed some interest in the Love of Zion movement; the socialists, internationalists, ridiculed it. There were of course Orthodox rabbis, too, who believed that any form of colonization in the Holy Land was forcing God's hands. The Holy One, Blessed be He, would send His Messiah to effect a restoration when He was ready; that day had not yet dawned. (The Christians had similar hopes; Jesus would yet return to inaugurate the Millennium.)

Dr. Joseph Isaac Bluestone (1860-1934) was an outstanding Lover of Zion. This Lithuanian had come to the United States about the year 1880 after studying in a talmudic academy. Here he eked out an existence teaching Hebrew while working his way through medical school. Along the way Bluestone published a Hebrew supplement to a Yiddish paper and in 1889 a Yiddish Zionist journal, *Sulamit*. In later years Bluestone, Orthodox, became a prominent member of the Federation of American Zionists and served as grandmaster of the Order Sons of Zion. The Hoveve Zion had numerous followers in New York City. One of them called on Rabbi H. Pereira Mendes of Shearith Israel with the hope that he would address a mass meeting. His Christian housekeeper informed the delegation that Mendes was a Jew and never attended mass. Among the Lovers of Zion was Rabbi Aaron Wise; his devotion to the ancient homeland may well have influenced his son Stephen Samuel Wise later to become one of the most eminent of American Zionists. One of Pittsburgh's Lovers of Zion, Ralph Raphael (1856-1903), published a brochure in 1893 calling upon the Jews of this country to establish a semi-autonomous state in Palestine under Turkish suzerainty. In this book, *The Jewish Question (She'elat ha-Yehudim)*, Raphael described in detail the nature of the new republic. Jews would have the right to impose taxes, set up their own courts and police force, and elect their own president. Christian settlements in the country would not be encouraged! Raphael, a Hebrew writer, made a living fashioning human hair into watch fobs and the like. His daughter Rose was permitted to make an address at a Zionist rally in Rabbi Moses Simon Sivitz's Orthodox synagog; Orthodoxy in America had come a long way.

After the rise of the Federation of American Zionists some of the Hoveve Zion societies refused to affiliate with it; the Zionist leaders of the Federation were Reformers or secularists; the Lovers of Zion were Orthodox. The Hoveve Zion was not a successful organization; all told it could muster but 2,500 members in metropolitan New York. It accomplished little except to keep alive a love for the Holy Land; by the late 1890's the movement was moribund. Nevertheless, as early as 1891 a Boston Jew had designed a "Jewish" flag: two blue stripes stretched across a white canvas; between the stripes a star of David carried the Hebrew inscription "Maccabee" painted in blue.[8]

AMERICAN ZIONISM, 1897-1914

With the publication of Herzl's *Jewish State* in 1896 many American Jews turned to Zionism. There had been numerous proposals for a Jewish state by Jews and non-Jews all through the nineteenth century but none had the appeal of Herzl's brochure. He created a worldwide movement which ultimately brought to birth the State of Israel. Post-eventum explanations for the success of his movement are rational but they prove nothing. It is sufficient to say that the idea—a Jewish state—spread like wildfire. Jews had always been Zionists since they lost their Judean state in 586 B.C.E. Their Bible and liturgy assured them that they would be restored; their tight Jewish communities in the Diaspora developed an ethnicity, a peoplehood that made for an ardent nationalism that was 2,000 years old when Herzl wrote his booklet. There had been numerous pseudo-Messiahs since the first century; even then Jesus was not the only Jew to come to the aid of his people. To be sure there were factors that encouraged Jews to turn to modern Zionism. Nationalism was in the air; Palestine could become utopia where one could live a real Jewish life; in a Jewish homeland there would be no assimilation. The public degradation of Dreyfus convinced many that no country would ever accept the Jews; even in free United States anti-Semitism reared its head all too frequently. Thus it was that when the Zionists convened for the first time in an international conference in Basel, in August 1897, several American Jews were present either as delegates or auditors.[9]

ADMINISTRATION

As early as 1897 a large number of societies—there were over thirty— came together as the Federation of Zionist Societies of Greater New York and Vicinity. Many of them leaned toward traditionalism. Their leader was the old Lover of Zion, Dr. Joseph I. Bluestone. A few years later, 1903, Bluestone presided over a group of Orthodox dissidents, Zionists, who called themselves the United Zionists. They did not go along with the Federation of American Zionists that had been called into being in 1897 by Richard J. Gottheil of Columbia and the young Reform rabbi Stephen S. Wise. Bluestone and his crowd, "Russians," were well aware that Gottheil was the son of Gustav Gottheil, for many years chief rabbi of Temple Emanu-el, the bastion of Reform. (It was immaterial that Gustav was a Zionist; he was a German and a Reformer; that made him suspect.) The Federation of American Zionists was headed by men and women like Gottheil, S. S. Wise, Magnes, Jacob de Haas, Harry Friedenwald, Louis Lipsky, Henrietta Szold. They were all educated, acculturated Americans; not one was an East Side denizen. Many Zionist organizations both in New York City and in the hinterland refused to affiliate; there were divisions, mutual acerbities; members were scarce; money was lacking. The Federation administration was completely inadequate. Later in 1918 under Brandeisian influence the Federation was succeeded by the Zionist Organization of America (ZOA); this was an improvement; discipline was tightened.

In 1901 the Zionists began publishing the *Maccabaean*, an English language magazine. It was a cultural, literary, polemical journal which enjoyed attacking the anti-Zionist Reformers, their favorite whipping boy. They reproached the right wing Orthodox who looked to God alone for a restored state. The *Maccabaean* stressed the fact that Zionism was ready to embrace all Jews regardless of their religious beliefs and unbeliefs. It wanted physical semi-military training for youth, Boy Brigades; it stressed the pursuit of the fine arts, the social sciences, as they touched the Jews. Later, in 1908, the Zionists published a Yiddish weekly, *The Jewish People* (*Dos Yidishe Folk*). In the course of time the general Yiddish press discovered that it dare not ignore the new movement. The Orthodox *Morning Journal* was sympathetic as was the more liberal *Day*; the socialist *Forward* stuck to its guns. Socialism, internationalism, would not compromise with nationalism, with a bourgeois retreat to a corner of the Eastern Mediterranean. By 1914 the Zionist Federation was all-embracing. It included at least one fraternal benefit order, libraries, clubs, youth groups, girls' and womens' organizations, congeries of college students and urban professionals, middle of the road Orthodox and Conservative Jews, in short a variety of associations with disparate and conflicting ideologies. However, they were all Zionists.[10]

THE WHEELHORSES

The Federation and later the Zionist Organization of America were administered by a few men who cannot be brushed aside although they are not to be classed with others like Brandeis, Frankfurter, Julian Mack; they were never to become national heroes. There were several workhorses who carried the national load; all with one exception were East European immigrants. These men lived for the party and often on the party. Such devotees were found in every large town in the country where there was a substantial Zionist following. Among these workers and leaders was Joseph Barondess—who might have described himself as a unionist, socialist, politician, businessman, Zionist. Barnard A. Rosenblatt rose to become a judge; he had studied at Columbia and was respected for his efforts to further the economy of the ancient homeland. Emanuel Neumann was an East Side boy who began his career as a member of the Dr. Herzl Zion Club. Years later he was to become a president of the Zionist Organization of America; outside of Zionism there was no life for him. Abraham Goldberg was a journalist, an Hebraist who undertook to edit the Zionist party Yiddish organ, *Dos Yidishe Folk*.

Like Goldberg, Bernard Gerson Richards was also a journalist. His Russian parents brought him to these shores in 1886; it was in Boston that he became a reporter for general non-Jewish newspapers. In those early days, completely Americanized, he had little sympathy for the Zionists. Jews are not to be relegated to an obscure corner of the world; they need a bigger stage; the whole world is Holy Land. In the course of time he became a socialist, a Territorialist—Palestine need not be the only Jewish haven—and finally a devout Zionist. Kishinev may have moved him to join and work for the Herzlians. He wrote well; his *Discourses of Keidansky* (1903) are amusing, instructive, and still worth reading. The most important of this group was Louis Lipsky (1876-1963); he was the only native American among them; like Richards and Goldberg, he, too, was a writer, journalist, editor. He was not born with a silver spoon in his mouth; his father was a shohet in Rochester; as a teenager he went to work in a cigar factory. (This he had in common with Samuel Gompers.) He administered and led the Federation of American Zionists and later the Zionist Organization of America. Above all he was a fervent Zionist and a politician who managed to stay on top but he was not comparable to Brandeis.[11]

Zionists in the days before the First World War belonged to diverse ideological factions; the Federation of Zionists was an umbrella organization ready—if they opted to remain—to shelter them all. Most followers of the movement—later known as General Zionists—were middle of the road travelers; they included Orthodox and Conservative religionists, a handful of Reformers, a substantial minority of secularists, East Europeans, and acculturated natives. The various factions had come into being very early in the twentieth century. Right-wing Orthodox, rabbis especially, who wanted to fashion the new Palestine after ancient Israel and Judah, called themselves the Mizrachi. The word is a Hebrew acronym and spells out as Oriental Spiritual Center. These were the men and women who were quite willing to force God's hands by building a new state now. The most noted Mizrachi was Meir Berlin (Bar-Ilan, 1880-1949). He came to the United States in the second decade of the new century and assumed control of the movement. Though very conservative, he was no obscurantist. Later, in 1926, he returned to Palestine and became the world head of the movement. Here in this country the Mizrachi established a good teachers' college and favored afternoon schools that were open to modernist influences. In addition to Talmud they encouraged biblical studies and stressed the ethical. Many of their afternoon schools employed the English vernacular. In the course of time they organized youth and female auxiliaries. After Berlin's death an Orthodox oriented university was established in Tel Aviv and named after him. There were many men and women here who sympathized with the Mizrachi. The Enlighteners were close to the Mizrachi in that they both emphasized the vernacular use of Hebrew; they hoped it would ultimately become the national Jewish tongue, at least in Palestine.

Zvi Hirsch Masliansky was a tower of strength to the Mizrachi for he ranged the length and breadth of the land eloquently haranguing his auditors in Yiddish, appealing to them to join and support the Zionist cause. He had a large following. By 1918 there were about 200 Mizrachi societies in this country; most were small. A not untypical Orthodox rabbi who was sympathetic to Mizrachi was the Palestine-born Chaim Hirschensohn (1857-1935). He is limned here because there were others who shared his modernist views. Hirschensohn's father, a Russian who had immigrated to Palestine, sent his son to a yeshivah; at seventeen he was married; the family he reared spoke Hebrew. He organized a B'nai B'rith lodge in Palestine, edited a Hebrew magazine, and even farmed a bit. Moving on to Constantinople, the capital of the Ottoman Empire, he established a Hebrew-speaking school. In 1903 he came to the United States, settling in New Jersey. He wrote only in Hebrew as he pursued his studies in Bible and Talmud, evincing a knowledge of exegesis and geography as he pursued the career of scholar and teacher. Palestine, he hoped would one day become the national home of the Jewish people, a land of culture.[12]

POALE ZION

If the Mizrachi was on the right, the Poale Zion, the Laborers of Zion, was at the opposite end of the spectrum. Its full title was the Jewish Socialist Labor Organization, Poale Zion. As with the Mizrachi its roots were in Russia. These Zionists were secularists, socialists, non- and anti-religionists, but they wanted to be Jews despite the reproaches of the

Marxists and the anarchists who scoffed at Jewish loyalties and savored the gospel of world brotherhood. These latter radicals were convinced that the revolution in Russia was inevitable; the masses would all be emancipated; there was no need for Palestine. The Poale Zion followers were devoted modernists, interested in education, music, choral groups, schools of their own. Palestine was to develop into a labor controlled Jewish socialist state; ultimately their hopes were realized; the State of Israel was ruled for decades by the Labor Party. The Poale Zion was organized here as early as 1903 and met in national convention at Baltimore in 1905. By 1906 it had begun to publish *Idisher Kemffer* (*The Jewish Warrior*), a Yiddish magazine of quality; it was still being published in the 1980's. Six years later, 1912, it had established a fraternal order of its own, the Jewish National Workers' Alliance. Among the Poale Zion were non-Marxist workmen and Territorialists as well as Palestine nationalists. Obviously here in anti-socialist America the Poale Zion was not destined to win a large following. Like the Mizrachi it had many branches, small in size, limited in their funding. In the course of years it, too, won supporters among the youth and the women. In 1918 it reported 4,000 members. Their spiritual leader over here was Dr. Nachman Syrkin (1868-1924), an early Zionist, a litterateur at home in Yiddish, Hebrew, Russian, German, and English. He came to these shores in 1907 after the failure of the uprising against the Romanovs. Here in America he asked his followers to set up cooperative settlements in Palestine, kibbutzim. He was not without influence; Israel became known for this type of close settlements. During World War II, long after his death, an American liberty ship was named in his honor.[10]

CULTURAL ZIONISTS

Practically all American Zionists, even those who were committed to a completely independent political state lived in two worlds; they were indeed pro-Palestinian but they were also pro-American. They thought in terms of two cultural centers, one in the Promised Land, another in the United States. They were Diaspora affirmers; a Jewish center can be developed in this country as well as in the land of their ancestors. Jews here could cope successfully with assimilatory impacts. The cultural Zionists had a goodly following although they established no formal organization. Many cultural Zionists were Conservative Jews agglomerating around the Jewish Theological Seminary. Magnes, no seminary man, shared their views; he was no Zionist negator who believed that the Jews of the Diaspora were destined to disappear. Other Zionist culturalists were Harry Friedenwald, a Baltimorean who served as president of the Federation of American Zionists (1904), Israel Friedlaender, Mordecai M. Kaplan, and

Solomon Schechter. Israel Friedlaender was convinced that the United States would become a great Jewish culture center; Palestine for him was primarily a "city of refuge" for the oppressed. Schechter, the head of the seminary, hesitated to cast his lot with the Zionists. Too many were secularists; he was well aware of the Reform leanings of Richard J. H. Gottheil and Stephen S. Wise. Schechter finally joined the Zionists in 1906; after all Zionism could serve as a bulwark against assimilation; as a member of the movement he could throw his weight on the side of religion and learning. Jewish consciousness must be stressed; perfervid American acculturationists frightened him. To a degree Magnes, Friedlaender, Kaplan, Schechter, went along with Ahad Ha-Am, the Russian, who had been a Lover of Zion in the 1880's but who insisted on the cultural centrality of the Jewish homeland. A great cultural renascence there would influence World Jewry; a political state in itself offered no solution to the preservation, the permanence of the Jewish people.

Ahad Ha-Am's emphasis on the importance and the right of the Jew to develop a spiritual Palestine was in a sense fortified in the United States by the teachings of Dr. Horace Mayer Kallen (1882-1974) who urged Jews here to stress Jewish cultural values. He it was who laid emphasis on the concept of cultural pluralism. Kallen was born in Germany of East European parents; his father was an Orthodox rabbi who succeeded in alienating a brilliant son; Kallen, a Harvard graduate, was bright, able; he was also aggressive; the man was no suppliant. He taught at Harvard, Clark, Princeton, and Madison but he was not accepted and advanced as his academic capabilities merited. It was his misfortune to live in a generation when Jews were not wanted on college faculties. He finally found a home in New York's New School for Social Research. Kallen was a secular nationalist; the United States, he taught, was a commonwealth of different national cultures. In a democracy all these varying spiritual values and qualities must be encouraged and exploited. We can be equal and different; diversity enriches. His views were congruent with those of America's cultural Zionists and were helpful in inducing educated Americans to turn to Zionism. It is well to recall that *Selected Essays* by Ahad Ha-Am was published in this country in 1912; two years later Richard Gottheil's *Zionism* appeared. Zionism was beginning to achieve recognition, respectability.[14]

Henrietta Szold

Henrietta Szold (1860-1945) belonged to the cultural Zionist circle. She had studied at the Jewish Theological Seminary. After the death of her father, 1902, Henrietta and her mother moved to New York where the daughter took courses at the Seminary in order to prepare herself to edit her father's Hebrew writings. (She promised the apprehensive seminary's authorities that she would not turn to the rabbinate.) In her day she was probably the country's most learned woman in Hebraica and Judaica. More and more as her life is studied the historian is inclined to believe that she was the country's most important Jewess in matters Jewish. There were of course other women of distinction who worked in the Jewish field, Hannah Greenebaum Solomon, Sadie American, Hannah Bachman Einstein, Rebekah Kohut. (Lillian Wald and Sophie Irene Loeb did not concern themselves primarily with Jewish causes.)

Henrietta was born in Baltimore to parents of Central European ancestry. They encouraged her to go to high school which was considered more than adequate at the time. She went to work as a teacher in private schools. In the 1870's she became a stringer—still a teenager—for New York's *Jewish Messenger* writing under the pen name Sulamith. In the late 1880's she began teaching Russian immigrants in a night school. Later she wrote for the *Jewish Encyclopedia* and soon had a steady job doing editorial work for the Jewish Publication Society. More than anyone else she was responsible for the appearance of its publications. She was meticulous; she was literally invaluable. By the 1890's she was already a proto-Zionist; later she was to become a high level officer in the Federation of American Zionists and in the Palestine Jewish community where she finally settled. Health care, education, social welfare were her portfolios. After Henrietta moved from Baltimore to New York she undertook to guide a Harlem group of the Daughters of Zion. She was then a woman approaching fifty. This club was the matrix out of which was to come Hadassah, the largest Jewish women's society in the world, the Women's Zionist Organization of America. Szold visited Palestine in 1909; the physical misery she saw there impelled her to do something. She returned to America where she organized Hadassah in 1912. It was a national organization whose members read, studied, sewed, and raised funds for a Palestine program. They were determined to foster Zionist ideals in this country and to rebuild Palestine Jewry.

In 1913 with the help of the Nathan Strauses and some Chicago women, two nurses were sent to Palestine; this was the beginning of a medical campaign that attacked the problems of malaria, trachoma, typhus, cholera, tuberculosis. Szold succeeded in establishing a vocational school for girls, an institution to train nurses. She was concerned to provide visiting nursing, maternity and dental care, health stations, pasteurization of milk; she fought juvenile delinquency. In her middle seventies, in 1933-1934, she girded her loins and administered a program that brought thousands of Jewish youngsters from Nazi Germany. Literally they were brands plucked from the fiery crucible. Of course she had help, but the programs were primarily hers. She was not a typical Zionist despite the fact that she was one of the important executives of the Palestine community. Like Magnes she was a pacifist and a binationalist; she lived in the country in a day when the overwhelming majority of the inhabitants were Arabs; she was concerned about their rights. Though observant in matters of ritual she had little sympathy for obscurantists. She worked hard; some days she rose at 4:30 and labored till midnight. When the Jewish Publication Society printed its first English Bible she volunteered to read proof, no small task.

What motivated this woman? This is difficult to determine. She was not a self-seeker; though she edited the Jewish Publication Society's series of biographies in 1904 she omitted mention of herself. She was constantly driven to prove herself. Her father had educated her well and expected her to do well. She wanted a family but she never married. While editing for the Jewish Publication Society she worked with Professor Louis Ginzberg and fell in love with him. It did her no good; she was much older and, it would appear, unattractive to men. She had little sense of humor. Rabbi Max Raisin who knew her said that she was "the noblest and most gifted" of American Jewish women. There is much truth in this eulogy. Hadassah was to become her immortality, her monument. By the late twentieth century, after her death, her organization numbered its adherents in the hundreds of thousands; they raised millions for their work abroad. The Hadassah Medical Center practices the best medicine in the Middle East. The organization maintains its autonomy and stays out of politics; it has but one concern: good medicine for the people of Palestine. She gave American Jewish women a cause for which they could work enthusiastically. Hadassah has shown the male Zionists what can be accomplished. In many respects these women have been more successful than the men. What Brandeis did for the Federation of American Zionists in 1914-1916, she did for the women in the movement, 1912-1945. They were both meticulous "Germans."[15]

Hadassah has had a remarkable career since it began as a woman's socioeducational club in Harlem in the early twentieth century. There was a contemporary boys' club that had a history that was also unique. This organization began, as did Hadassah, as a Zionist society. It was established at the turn of the century; it boasted of a Hebrew name, *Zion Bemishot Tipodeh*, Zion Shall Be Saved by Justice. Just a few years later it became a Greek letter fraternity calling itself ZBT; the Hebrew initials, however, were retained. Ultimately it was to become a national Jewish social fraternity; its members came from middle-class families; they had no interest in Zionism. Another boys' club was the Dr. Herzl Zion Club. It was founded in 1904 at the East Side home of Moses Silver, a Zionist and a lover of Hebrew. His sons Maxwell and Abba Hillel and a youngster named Israel S. Chipkin were the pioneer members. They were teenagers.

This was a Hebrew-speaking association, one of the first boys' clubs of this type in the country. The three youngsters had attended the same afternoon Hebrew school. Members had to be twelve to be admitted; dues were 5 cents a week; one cent was given to the Jewish National Fund, the land-buying agency of the World Zionist Organization. In 1905 Abraham Goldfaden, the playwright, wrote a Hebrew play for them which was produced in a public auditorium. Other Hebrew plays, too, were written for them; young Abba Hillel Silver frequently played the stellar roles. A number of East Side notables lent them their moral support. They met Saturday nights. After a time the Educational Alliance opened its doors to them, somewhat hesitantly to be sure; the Alliance was an Americanizing agency with little sympathy for Zionism. Dr. David Blaustein, the superintendent, encouraged their cultural endeavor. According to one story a member of the Alliance board querulously asked why they spoke Hebrew. He was silenced when one of the boys asked him if he would object if the club spoke German or French.

This group served as a paradigm to others, both boys and girls; it is not improbable that the Dr. Herzl Zion Club influenced the rise of Young Judaea. In 1914 the club began to disintegrate; the youngsters looked round for careers. Several of them received scholarships from the anti-Zionist Temple Emanu-El and went to the Hebrew Union College in Cincinnati. Reform Judaism had its points; Magnes and Stephen S. Wise were Zionists. These boys wanted to make something of themselves; they had no money; education at the Cincinnati college was free; they were ambitious and able. Quite a number of the club members made great careers for themselves becoming figures of national renown. Included among them were rabbis, educationists, journalists, a Hebrew poet, an eminent physician, Zionist leaders.[16]

ZIONISM IN THE HINTERLAND

The national headquarters of the different Zionist organizations were nearly always in New York City but at least half of their members lived in different states of the Union. If history concerns itself with people, the masses, then the Jews in the backcountry cannot be bypassed. It is a fact: wherever there was a Jewry of any size a Zionist society came into being. Many such organizations solicited women members reflecting American influence. Money was raised by distributing fund-raising boxes, little flags were sold, bazaars were held, Zionist literature was distributed. In 1904, after the death of Herzl, young Jacob Marcus in Homestead, Pennsylvania, was given large lithographs of the late Zionist leader and told to go out and collect ten cents for each. If Aaron Marcus, Jacob's father, had been asked why he was a Zionist, he might well have quoted the prophet

Ezekiel, 36:24—the father was at home in the Hebrew Bible—"I will take you from among the nations and gather you from all the countries, and I will bring you back to your own land."

There were, throughout America, Zionist clubs for boys, for girls, for women. Around the year 1905 there were Zionist organizations in Grand Forks, North Dakota; they had 96 members; 22 were women. Chicago surfaced as a Zionist center as early as New York City. It could boast of a Zionist society in 1897. A year later Leon Zolotkoff took the leadership in establishing an order, the Knights of Zion. Chicago had a western Zionist federation of its own. The Knights of Zion opened an afternoon English school where Jewish history and literature were taught. Some of the Orthodox synagogs were not friendly to the new movement; in one sanctuary where the Zionists met the lights were turned out on them to hasten their departure. By 1902 Cleveland had a woman's organization which called itself the Roses of Zion. Its president was Rose Pastor, not yet well-known. By 1904 there were a dozen Zionist groups in Cleveland; they cultivated the arts and listened to lectures. When a Zionist convention was held in town that year the streets in the Jewish quarter were decorated with blue and white banners; the store windows displayed portraits of Herzl.

A Minneapolis society established in 1898 received the moral support of David C. Bell, a Christian Zionist. His pro-Zionist argument was succinct: Palestine is a land without people; the Jews are a people without land; Jerusalem must be rebuilt. In 1910 the Milwaukee Socialist-Zionists had 124 dues-paying followers. When solicited for funds 104 gave 25 cents each; that was all they could afford; a quarter would buy 5 loaves of bread. The pious Jews of Baltimore sent their Rabbi Schepschel Schaffer to the Basel convention in 1897; he may well have been the only American delegate who was officially accredited. Among the Baltimore Zionist clubs was one where German was spoken; Harry Friedenwald, president of the National Federation of American Zionists, was a member. Philadelphia's devotees had a Zion Institute, a home of their own where cultural programs were carried on. The Zionist society in San Antonio, Texas, one of the oldest in the country, was founded in 1897 by a University of Vienna student, a Lover of Zion. When in 1917 the Balfour Declaration was issued by the British, the blue and white Jewish flag was flown on one of the city's municipal towers.[17]

Summary

Historians say that little was accomplished by the American Zionists in the period before the First World War. By common standards of evaluation and criticism they are right. Yet the movement aroused thousands emotionally and mentally; their eyes were brightened; their pulses were quickened. There was not a community in the United States that was left untouched by the Herzlian appeal. Relatively few joined the societies; most Jews were too poor or too thrifty. Survival here preempted most other interests. The newcomers were too busy trying to adapt to this new American milieu to join Zionist groups, yet in spirit most Jews, the Orthodox masses, were Zionists. In this community of immigrants it was almost inevitable that most Zionist leaders—not all—would be native Americans of Central European background. Zionist administration was normally poor; East European leadership was inadequate; there were relatively few pre-1881 families that were ready to consort with the immigrants; the movement was not quite respectable. Jews were disturbed by the fear that they would be charged with dual loyalty. This really disturbed them. Zionist propaganda was vigorous, strident, polemical, assertive.

Efforts were made to win Christians as well as Jews. In 1907 the Federation appealed to the Christian world: Help us, we have wandered for 2,000 years; we want a home for ourselves, a place where we can make a contribution to the world and make it a better place in which to live. Zionism did elicit sympathy from some Christians, especially the evangelicals. In appealing to Jews the elite leaders of America's Zionist federations made the point that a haven was desperately needed for the oppressed Jews of Eastern Europe. Palestine is our hope. If it is too small we can spread out into Syria and Mesopotamia where we once thrived and wrote the Talmud. We are already building colonies in the land of our fathers; we can once again develop a Hebraic culture. To be sure, there was a certain ambivalence in the minds and hearts of the Zionists here. It is true, America is the Golden Land, yet here, too, we suffer poverty; we have to work hard; tuberculosis strikes us down, anti-Semitism threatens us; Palestine, however, is our ideal; it is the idyllic homeland. We embrace it.

Jewish pride was coddled by Zionism. Jews were beginning to speak Hebrew in Palestine; the Hebrew language was reborn; there was a modern academy in Tel Aviv, over fifty settlements in the country. True, many of these colonies barely stayed alive but the immigrant students of American history—they were a host—knew that the early colonies in North Carolina and Virginia were anything but successes. One of the appeals of Zionism was that there was a society to suit every taste, socially, culturally; there was a group to satisfy every ideological bent. Influenced possibly by the example of the older Returnees to Zion, Palestine settlement and investment groups were established here in this country. These organizations bore such names as *Ahuza* (holdings, estate) and American Zion Commonwealth. Romantically inclined Jews invested their American dollars in Palestinian homesteads on which they would ultimately settle—in imagined comfort—and live at peace under their own vine and fig tree. There they could carry on a truly Jewish life.

Zionists here in the United States could chalk up some victories. They had participated in the 1913 language war which determined finally that the language of instruction in the Haifa Technion would ultimately be Hebrew and not some European vernacular. Actually this victory for Hebrew over German was achieved by non-Zionists, American Jews of German origin who gave the money for the support of what they hoped would become a Massachusetts Institute of Technology, Jewish style. These American Jewish philanthropists opted for Hebrew. America's Jews were happy that during World War I hundreds of Jews here had joined the Jewish Legion under British auspices in the effort to wrest Palestine from the Turks (1917-1918). Some of these legionnaires served under Allenby when the Ottoman forces were compelled to retreat. The Zionist leaders worked cautiously when the war erupted; they did not sponsor this Jewish armed force; the Turks might well destroy the young Jewish colonies. Jews, as Zionists, saw action with the advancing British forces. After the conquest of Palestine the English were eager to demobilize the Jewish Legion; Palestine was to be policed by English troops whose first loyalty would be to the authorities in London.

What did the Herzl dream do for the Jews in the United States? It united diverse immigrant groups who worked together for a common cause. Community spirit was developed, enhanced. Jewish knowledge was furthered; most Zionist societies were geared to educate their members; Hebrew, history, Jewish literature were cultivated. A Zionist Jewish press in Hebrew, Yiddish, English evolved; the Yiddish dailies—except for the *Forward*—smiled on the new movement. Little things are important; a Zionist flag was flown at the World's Fair in St. Louis on the Rosh Hashanah of 1904; a Zionist play written by a Jew was staged at Harvard. When, in late 1918 a Zionist national convention assembled in Pittsburgh, twenty-five brass bands blared as 3,000 children dressed in blue and white—the national colors—marched along singing Hebrew songs. Important is the fact that the Federation of American Zionists and the disparate but vibrant Zionist factions kept this movement alive until Louis D. Brandeis appeared on the scene. How many enrolled dues-paying Zionists were there in the United States in 1914? No one will ever know. Many if not most sympathizers were never members; many never paid the annual "shekel." In 1900, so it is reported, there were 124 societies in 66 towns; in 1914, there were anywhere from 7,400 to 12,000 members in an America of about 3,000,000 Jews; the annual budget—not the annual income—of the National Federation was then $12,000. Yet, small as the American Zionist movement was, it was probably the second largest in size among the world's national federations. Many of the members here were women in organizations of their own.[18]

CHAPTER TWENTY-TWO

THE AMERICAN HERZL:

LOUIS DEMBITZ BRANDEIS

L ike all other Jewish organizations, the Federation of American Zionists responded immediately to crises in World Jewry. The murders in Kishinev increased Zionist membership; World War I raised the number on the rosters from about 7,400 in 1914 to 149,000 in 1919. There was no future for the Jews in Russia; Jews needed a secure home of their own; immigration restrictionist bills were being fed into the congressional hopper. Refuge America was imperiled. American Zionists succeeded in enlisting the support of a notable citizen, Louis Dembitz Brandeis (1856-1941). In 1914 this captain grasped the helm at the Zionist Federation. His parents had come from Bohemia in 1849 after the failure of the anti-monarchical revolution in Central Europe. It was a day when thousands of ambitious Germans, Jews and Gentiles, were moving on to America to improve themselves. The Brandeises and their clan, the Dembitzes, Goldmarks, and Wehles, were not typical German immigrants; they were cultured; they had some means. Adolph Brandeis settled in Louisville at the falls of the Ohio, went into business, and did well, but with the coming of the depression in the early 1870's he and the family went back to Germany taking their teenage son Louis with them. The youngster had no trouble in the high school which he attended; German was his second language. His mother whom he adored wrote to him in German for many decades. Later, in the 1870's, he went to Harvard and graduated from the law school first in his class. He practiced law in St. Louis where he had kin; his sister Fannie had married a lawyer, a Christian, Charles Nagel, later Secretary of Commerce and Labor under Taft. Unhappy in St. Louis, Brandeis moved north to Boston where he very soon became a successful and wealthy corporation lawyer; by the 1890's he had a national reputation.[1]

So much for Brandeis, counsellor-at-law. What sort of a Jew was he? He was not much of a Jew; he was conscious of his ancestral background but like thousands of others he was a secularist. He had no interest in organized religion. Brandeis was, however, very much interested in his family background. He pestered his mother, Frederika, to write and tell him all she knew about her Dembitz ancestors. Over a period of six or seven years she wrote him detailing the history of the clan. In Prague they lived in a home right on the edge of the ghetto; they were near it but not part of it. The traditional Sabbath lamp with its wicks and oil spouts hung from the ceiling. They were descended from Israel Von Hoenigsberg, one of the few Austrian Jewish families with a patent of nobility, albeit a minor one. Some of the clan, generations back, had been talmudists, observant Jews, subject to the *Matrikel Gesetz*, the registration law which limited the numbers of Jewish marriages in the community (Jews were not always wanted).

Some members of the Dembitz family were Frankists, followers of the "Messiah," Jacob Frank (d. 1791). The Frankists were antinomian, anti-Talmud; some of them in Poland had converted to Christianity: the Prague Frankists remained Jews; they were an ethical high-minded lot. Living as Jews and occasionally going to the synagog did not prevent Brandeis's family from having a Christmas tree in the home. Some of Frederika's close friends were Christians; she was an autodidact who was widely-read in German and French literature. She was acquainted with Isaac Marcus Jost's history of the Jews; she had even read a philosophical work by Mendelssohn. In many respects she was akin to the Jewish salon women of early nineteenth century Berlin and Vienna. She admired the Prague preacher Rabbi Michael J. Sachs and had listened to him; some of her family leaned in the direction of a more liberal type of Judaism. She had no patience with Orthodoxy and when her brother Ludwig (Lewis) became a traditional Jew she was shocked. She herself had reverence for Jesus but no respect for orthodox Christianity; the Christians had done nothing to make this a better world. She was definitely a theist but she reared her son without loyalty to any religious system. Brandeis grew up in a generation when Felix Adler, son of a Reform rabbi, was organizing the Ethical Culture movement; many of Adler's followers were Jews. Brandeis married a Jew; Adler officiated at the wedding; the two men were brothers-in-law. Originally named Louis David Brandeis, Brandeis changed his name early to Louis Dembitz Brandeis; he admired his uncle Lewis, the lawyer; he loved his mother; both Dembitzes.

When the Federation of Jewish Charities was organized in Boston in 1895 Brandeis was a charter subscriber; ten years later he addressed a Boston club on the occasion of the 250th anniversary of the settlement of the Jews in New Amsterdam-New York. It was then that he broke a lance in defense of Americanism, attacking hyphenated Americans, including Jewish Americans. Like other Jews of Central European origin he was not satisfied just to be a mere 100 percent American! But, and this was not "Germanic," he had little use for the stereotypical German Jew; he believed that the "Russians" had a sense of reverence, idealism. By 1910 the fifty-four-year-old lawyer had begun moving closer to Jewry, to the Zionists. That was the year he served as an arbitrator in the garment worker strike fought on the streets and in the shops of New York. Something in the Jews he met there seems to have appealed to him. Two socially-minded Boston Jews had enlisted him to help settle the quarrel; he worked on a non-fee basis. One of these men who induced him to intervene in the strike, the department store owner A. Lincoln Filene, wanted the strike settled; he needed garments to sell.

That same winter, in December, Brandeis proclaimed his sympathy for Zionism in an interview: the greatest triumphs of the Jews were spiritual; they were a priest people. In 1911 he wrote of the idealism underlying Zionism; it was working to make this a better world. He attended a meeting of the National Conference of Jewish Charities. In May he addressed the Menorah students at Harvard and stressed the importance of social justice; the following year, 1912, he was thrilled as he read of the exploits of Aaron Aaronson, the innovative agronomist who had set out to bring the advantages of scientific farming to the people of Palestine. That same year Jacob De Haas, the Zionist editor of Boston's *Jewish Advocate*, succeeded in inducing Brandeis to become a shekel payer, a registered Zionist; De Haas had been working on him for two years. But let it be clear, no single person could have moved Brandeis to become a Zionist, a "Jew." He knew what he was doing and he did it deliberately; Zionism appealed to him; he had been thinking about it; it is not improbable that there were inner forces, influences, germinating in him for decades of which he himself was not aware. These induced him to come out as a Jew.

For the Jewish historian 1912 was Brandeis's crucial year. This noted lawyer campaigned for Wilson. Who can question that he would get a reward for his efforts? Here was a man with money; he had fame; he also had an ego; he wanted recognition. Wilson and his cohorts refused him high office when the final choices were made. Brandeis was not a representative Jew; he commanded no votes; a party needed people. As a sop to the Jews, Henry Morgenthau, Sr., was sent an as ambassador to the Sublime Porte. Morgenthau and the Jews were not elated; Constantinople was a "Jewish" job. The same month, after Brandeis was bypassed by the Washington Democrats, he chaired a Zionist reception in Boston in honor of Nahum Sokolow, a member of the World Zionist Executive (1913). Zionism is an ideal that can be realized, Brandeis said. He was now a publicly committed Zionist. He went to work for the movement because he believed in it. However there seems to be little question that he also sought national recognition, a federal office worthy of his talents. But he lacked followers. He turned to the "Russians," to Zionism, a progressive secular movement.[2]

AMERICAN ZIONISM, 1914-1917

The First World War brought with it a crisis that affected World Jewry; it was the worst in centuries. Millions of Jews were threatened; American Jewry had to help them; these men, women, and children were family, dear ones. The United States was the largest country not at war; there were millions of Jews here; they had means; they were concerned; if organized they could exercise influence on behalf of Jewry at the eventual peace conference. (American Jewry was convinced that the Entente would win the war.) American Jews' interest in their brethren overseas was evinced along two lines, the philanthropic and the political. Relief, aid, was administered by the Joint Distribution Committee. It did a magnificent job. Political aid presented problems. If there was to be an organized effort unity was imperative; national unity in American Jewish life materialized only at moments of great distress; when the danger passed, the unity evanesced. Efforts were made in almost every decade to create an overall national Jewish community. Until 1916 no effort was truly successful, though, to be sure, national associations came to birth in every decade. They were, however, limited in scope. They were fraternal, cultural, religious, defensive, philanthropic. The most successful and efficient of these national organizations was the American Jewish Committee established after the 1905 riots and murders in Russia.

To meet the overseas problems facing American Jewry, three Zionist activists—two were Socialist-Zionists, members of the Poale Zion—suggested, August 30, 1914, that an all-inclusive American Jewish Congress be convened. The three men were Baruch Zuckerman, Bernard G. Richards, Nachman Syrkin (1867/68-1924). All were foreign born. Syrkin was the most distinguished of the lot; his Ph.D. degree came from Zurich. He was a Territorialist, later a Zionist. When the European states resorted to war the World Zionist Organization faced structural collapse. World headquarters were in Germany; the shekel-paying masses were in Russia, an enemy land. To solve the administrative problems a bureau was established in neutral Denmark, in Copenhagen. Some American Jews suggested that international headquarters be moved here, if only temporarily, since men and money were then to be found only in America. Accordingly, in August, 1914, the Provisional Executive Committee for General Zionist Affairs (PEC) was established here.

Among those who suggested that this committee be organized in the United States was Shemarya Levin (1867-1935), a member of the World Jewish Zionist Executive. Like Syrkin, Levin, too, was multilingual; he spoke fluently and beautifully in Yiddish, Russian, and German. Back in Russia, where he had enjoyed an appointment as a government rabbi, he had been elected to the national legislature before going into exile in 1908. Here in the United States thousands turned out to hear him. As a man of culture he experienced no difficulty in making friends with America's most notable Jews. Magnes, Marshall, Julian Mack, Rosenwald, Kraus of the IOBB, all respected him. (He was a German-speaking Ph.D.!) Schiff gave him money; Emil G. Hirsch, the acerbic radical Classical Reformer liked him; Kohler, an anti-Zionist, allowed him to speak to his Hebrew Union College students. When he suggested that the PEC be established he was traveling in this country on behalf of the Haifa Technion; he had no choice but remain here; the war was raging. Levin lived a most colorful life which he has described charmingly in three volumes of memoirs. They still read well; they are important historical documents.

Brandeis was now, August 1914, appointed head of the Provisional Executive Committee. This Boston lawyer was new in the movement; Richard Gottheil's *Zionism*, which appeared in 1914, does not include his name in the Index. He was called because he was important, because he was needed; the Federation of American Zionists was run in a slipshod fashion. For the Zionists he was a catch, one of America's most notable attorneys, a somebody in the Gentile world; the Zionists—immigrants—could now shine in reflected glory. The Yiddish-speaking Zionists welcomed him enthusiastically even though he was divorced from yiddishkeit and did not lead a Jewish life. In many respects he was a repentant sinner, a *baal teshuvah*, who had returned to the fold. When he spoke in Cleveland in 1914 the Reform rabbi, Louis Wolsey—later an intransigent anti-Zionist—introduced him as the next president of the Zion Republic.[3]

There were several proposals for a national American Jewish congress in the first two decades of the twentieth century. David Philipson, the intractable anti-Zionist, had called for such a congress in 1903; in January, 1915, he once again asked American Jewry to meet through its representatives and discuss the problems of a Jewry riven by a devastating European war. This organization would have the authority to speak for American Jewry and to intercede for Jews in Eastern Europe and in Palestine too. Philipson, like most Reform rabbis, was always ready to further the welfare of Jews in the ancient homeland, but he was adamant in his objection to a Jewish political state. Several weeks before Philipson called for an American Jewish congress in 1915, a group of "Russians" in New York had already established a Jewish Congress Organization Committee

(JCOC). They wanted more rights for Palestine's Jews and minority privileges for the Jews in the Slavic lands. In Eastern Europe the Jews were looked down upon as a separate undesirable lot. These Children of Abraham could not share the nationalisms of the Poles and the Russians for these were inextricably tied to Christianity. The Jews also looked upon themselves as a separate people. Because they had no faith in the governmental authorities they wanted their own schools, their own language, the right to observe the Sabbath unhindered. They were opposed to "equal" rights; that meant they would have to live within the parameters of an anti-Jewish Christianity. They wanted "national" rights. It was a day when nationality recognition was sought by the people of Central Europe, Eastern Europe, and the Balkans.

The purpose of the Jewish Congress Organization Committee was to create an effective American Jewish agency that would have the power to induce the American government to intervene at the peace conference on behalf of oppressed Jews. A summary of the ultimate goals of the Congress Committee and the Zionists with whom it collaborated indicates their sponsors wanted control of America's East European Jewish community. It is also probable that they hoped to assume authority over all of American Jewry; these newcomers were determined to cut the leading strings that tied them to the older, the elite groups, the natives and the Germans. World War I saw America reaching out for power, world hegemony; Jews here, patterning themselves on Washington, sought to influence if not to dominate World Jewry. The aspirations of the Jewish Congress Committee disturbed the American Jewish Committee not because of what the newcomers sought but because they had set themselves up as a rival national organization. The American Jewish Committee believed it was doing a good job; it was. The Russians were different, socially, culturally, and, to a degree, religiously. Marshall and a few of his confreres looked upon many of the East European leaders as irresponsible demagogues; they were troublemakers; some were secularists; they threatened the hard won status of the older acculturated settlers. The elite of the American Jewish Committee resented the fact that the Congress Zionists were reaching out for a national homeland in Palestine. Was the United States not good enough for them?

The establishment heads were determined never to accept a permanent national American Jewish Congress dominated by Russian and Polish Jews. However, the old saw that politics makes strange bedfellows was certainly true in this bitter conflict between Committee and Congress. Many of the union leaders—socialists, radicals, secularists—allied themselves with the American Jewish Committee, bonded by anti-Zionism. The American Jewish Committee rejected a Palestine commonwealth because of its concept of American patriotism; the union bosses were cosmopolitans; they were opposed to all nationalisms. The leftwingers effected an organization of their own. This was the National Workmen's Committee on Jewish Rights in the Belligerent Lands (NWC) which maintained that it sought rights for Jews in all countries. This would certainly not exclude better conditions for Jews in the Holy Land. These immigrant workers, ideologues, were a variegated crew. Now for the first time they sat together around the table, Socialist-Zionists, Territorialists, anarchists. For the nonce they ceased their intramural squabbling.

Like the Zionists they, too, wanted a democratic convention, but like the American Jewish Committee they were determined never to tolerate a permanent congress. There was no need for such an overall body; the union leaders were convinced that a revolution would, in the not too distant future, bring equal rights to all Jews in Russia; that would solve the Jewish problem there. There was no need for a Palestine state. However these proletarian stalwarts did realize that until the Revolution dawned they would have to work with others, with the American Jewish Committee and the Zionists too. The union principals were well aware that most of their followers were traditionally-minded Jews who wanted immediate remedial action on behalf of their dear ones abroad. The Jewish masses here were impatient. They were not Marxists looking for a utopian state in the distant future. The alliance between the American Jewish Committee and the National Workmen's Committee was an uneasy one; they represented two disparate classes.

Throughout 1915 the powerful Committee and the immigrant congress negotiated hoping to come to some sort of an understanding. The talks between the two groups were acrid; the American Jewish Committee wanted a conference of national organizations and notables; the congress crowd wanted an assembly of elected delegates chosen by all the Jews of this country. The Provisional Executive Committee and the Federation of American Zionists could speak for only a minuscule number of people; they needed mass support if they were going to influence Wilson to implement their program, to intercede at the Peace Conference. The Yiddish-speaking masses were not affiliated with formal Zionist organizations though most were sympathetic to the Herzlian approach. The Provisional Executive Committee members wanted to control the proposed nationwide congress; this was the power base they needed. They were quite willing to work for Jewish minority rights in Eastern Europe but their eyes were always set on Palestine; they were Zionists.

Very soon after the Congress Organization Committee was established, the Provisional Executive Committee's head, Brandeis, took over. He knew what he was doing; if the congress could be built the Zionists would be in a better position to enlist the help of the United States government to establish a Palestinian Jewish homeland. The differences between the two groups, the Zionists and the anti-Zionists, were too stark to be glossed over speedily. The struggle was an ethnic one, Russians versus Germans, minority rights versus equal rights, Zionists versus anti-Zionists, democracy versus oligarchy. These propagandistic battle slogans were constantly repeated but behind all the turgid rhetoric were human beings fighting for power, recognition. The Zionists, Brandeis, Julian Mack, Louis Lipsky, Judah L. Magnes were born in America; Felix Frankfurter and Stephen S. Wise came over as children; they were not East Side denizens. By November, 1915, the American Jewish Committee had begun to retreat; it was willing to call a congress on a democratic basis to consider the problems of the Jews in the Slavic lands; there is no mention as yet of Palestine. It would take another year before the American Jewish Committee threw in the sponge and went along with the congress partisans.[4]

As head of the Provisional Executive Committee and the Jewish Congress Organizing Committee Brandeis tried to convert Jews to Zionism. When in October, 1914, Rabbi Philipson of Cincinnati, dean of the Reform rabbinate, heard that Brandeis threatened to invade his bailiwick he voiced a loud and strong protest; Brandeis backed off. The latter was not interested primarily in talking to immigrants—they were already sympathetic—he wanted to impress the affluent natives and Germans. Over a year later, in January, 1916, Brandeis returned to Cincinnati in triumph, and when he spoke at the aristocratic Cincinnati Woman's Club he packed the auditorium; Philipson and his anti-Zionist friends were in the front rows. Brandeis received a heartwarming reception. He was very pleased. That same night—it was a Friday—he spoke at Rabbi Jacob H. Kaplan's Reformist temple. Kaplan was an ardent Zionist; Philipson's temple was still closed to him. Jacob R. Marcus, a student at the Hebrew Union College, came out to hear Brandeis and sat up front so that he could see the great man. He remembered nothing of the talk—Brandeis was no orator—all that he recalled in later years was that the distinguished visitor fiddled with his prayer book during the services but read none of the prayers. Brandeis was no religionist. Two months later the East Europeans broke definitively with the American Jewish Committee leaders; this took courage. On March 26, 1916, the congress congeries called a Preliminary Conference in Philadelphia of the American Jewish Congress; they were now in business. Two of the featured speakers were rabbis B. L. Levinthal and Stephen S. Wise. Levinthal spoke in Yiddish; Wise, of course, in English. Wise, the nonconformist Reformer, harped on the theme of democracy. This Congress was an American crusade; we must be our own masters and free ourselves from the bondage of eleemosynary patronage. He was appealing to the galleries in his own inimitable fashion. Actually in that very same year almost half of the members of District Twelve of the American Jewish Committee—the New York City group—were of East European ancestry; most of them were foreign-born. Indeed at this time the national executive of the Committee included several Zionists.

The program adopted by the new American Jewish Congress was a most cautious one: minority rights for the Jews in Eastern Europe and consideration of the problem of Jewish development in Palestine; there was no outright call for a commonwealth. In July 1916, the American Jewish Committee beat a strategic retreat; it stooped to conquer. It called a conference of national Jewish organizations to deal with the problem of the overseas Jews. The response indicated that the American Jewish Committee was all powerful; most national Jewish organizations sent delegates: all the religious groups, many East European fraternal orders, the Hebrew Immigrant Aid and Sheltering Society, the United Hebrew Trades, and the National Workmen's Committee. The program adopted called for a national democratic congress to meet and to plead for minority rights for those European Jews who desired them. No mention was made of Palestine. The American Jewish Committee, the socialists, the unionists, and many immigrant groups were ready to work together. The Independent Order of B'nai B'rith, still a "German" organization, was conspicuous by its absence; this fraternity would never acknowledge the suzerainty of the Committee. It was at this time that the press attacked Brandeis who had already taken his place on the bench of the United States Supreme Court. Shocked, he resigned as head of the Congress; he was sensitive about his role as a justice. The well-attended July meeting of the American Jewish Committee frightened the Congress opposition; between the months of October and December, 1916, the two groups hammered out a compromise; they were agreed on rights for the Jews of Eastern Europe and Palestine. They realized they had to work together; the Committee could not be bypassed; it enjoyed the formal allegiance of many of America's Jewish national associations while the Congress commanded the loyalty of the unorganized Yiddish-speaking masses.

The compromise established a new committee; Marshall and Kraus, rivals, were sidetracked; beloved Nathan Straus, wealthy (R. H. Macy & Co.) German Jewish philanthropist and Zionist, became the head of the new American Jewish Congress. The final decision of the conjoint association was that a democratic national people's congress would convene; the non-Congress people were to be allotted one hundred delegates, one-fourth of all who would assemble. The reconstituted Congress was not permitted to commit its followers to any specific philosophy or ideology; it would not favor or condemn socialism, Zionism or non-Zionism. The Congress was to be a temporary one and was to disband after it made its presentation at the Peace Conference and had reported back to its sponsors.

Though pro-Zionist, a restored Palestine was not the prime objective of the Jewish masses. America was their home; they had no intention of returning to the cradle of their people. The newcomers won out when it was agreed that special rights would be sought for their kin in Eastern Europe. The Zionists gained their main point; a united American Jewry would back them as they pressed for privileges in the land of their ancestors. Marshall was not happy; for the time being, at least, the American Jewish Committee was no longer regnant; if the Zionists hoped through a congress to secure control of American Jewish organized life they too were sorely disappointed. Brandeis, the doctrinaire democrat, had no cause for rejoicing; there was to be no permanent democratic national American Jewish Congress. The immigrant masses who shared this disappointment with Brandeis had even looked forward to a permanent World Jewish Congress. Years later such a congress came into being but it was never to become an effective unchallenged instrument.

It is interesting to note that when the authoritative administrative committee was finally established in December, 1916, it embraced men with all points of view; it included Hillquit, the socialist, Rabbi Emil G. Hirsch, the Classical Reformer, Adolf Kraus of the B'nai B'rith, Louis Marshall of the American Jewish Committee, the Orthodox Rabbi B. L. Levinthal, and David Pinski, the socialist and Zionist Yiddish litterateur. The Congress was now truly an all-inclusive representative Jewish organization. Even women were included; there were several among New York's elected delegates; Mrs. Joseph Fels was the only woman, however, who was given a place on the administrative committee. Every group got something; none got everything for which it had fought. The newcomers had certainly won a temporary victory. Decades later, after World War II, the powerful American Jewish Committee, still going strong, incorporated Jews of East European background in its leadership and accepted their point of view; ultimately the Zionists were to come out on top.

By the spring of 1917 Reform Jewry was having second thoughts about participation in the American Jewish Congress. Mayhap the Reformers were painfully aware that they were losing ground to newcomers. The National Workmen's Committee withdrew because the new liberal regime that crushed the Romanovs in Russia had granted equal rights to Jews. Some of these trade unionists did come back to participate in the national election for delegates that took place in the summer.[5]

THE BALFOUR DECLARATION, NOVEMBER 2, 1917

Great Britain issued the Balfour Declaration on November 2, 1917. By this official pronouncement the British authorities, through their foreign secretary, Arthur James Balfour, informed the English Zionists that they viewed with favor the establishment in Palestine of a national home for the Jewish people and would use their best endeavors to facilitate the achievement of this object. However, they hedged this statement with limiting qualifications: "it being clearly understood that nothing shall be done which may prejudice the civil and religious rights of existing non-Jewish communities in Palestine or the rights and political status of Jews enjoyed in any other country." Vague as this document was it elated the Provisional Executive Committee, the Federation of American Zionists, and the majority of the American Jewish Congress.

What moved the British to make this promise? What part did American Jews play in inducing the English to issue this declaration? Balfour was the medium through which this communication was transmitted to London Jewry, but he was not its author. This English statesman was ambivalent in his attitude towards Jews. Although there were individual Jews whom he respected—Brandeis, for instance, whom he had met in Washington during the war—he was no friend of the Children of Israel. Balfour was prime minister in 1905 when the Aliens Immigration Act was pushed through parliament restricting the entrance of Jews, among others. He believed that Jews were able, patriotic, but he held it against them that they refused to assimilate completely; they would not intermarry. Like some other Englishmen he probably believed that after World War I many East European Jews would seek to rebuild their lives by moving to England; if diverted to Palestine they could do a good job rebuilding that region. This would be good for the British Empire in view of its interest in Egypt and its determination to protect the highway to India.

The Balfour Declaration was a war ploy; the British were determined primarily to benefit themselves. A proclamation of sorts had been under consideration since 1915. It was favored by a few restorationists, Bible believers; there were also a handful of English Jews who were political Zionists; some of them were notables, but it is very much to be doubted that the views of these Palestine protagonists exercised any real influence on the formulation of the Declaration. The sole motive for turning to the Jews was political. The situation for the Entente was critical in 1917; the war was not going well. The English thought that they could be helped by international Jewry; they were ready to grasp at straws. The Italians had suffered defeat; the French were immobile in their trenches; German submarines were destroying allied shipping. Great Britain was also apprehensive lest the Germans issue some sort of statement of their own to win the support of the Jews and Zionists. After all the Germans and the Turks (Palestine!) were allied. The Germans, like the English, too, wished to extend their influence in the Moslem Middle East.

The English were convinced in 1917 that they needed Jewish good will. Many Jews were not pro-ally because Russia was a member of the Entente, and Russia had never ceased mistreating its Jewish subjects. The English—credulous in this instance—had an exaggerated and naive belief in the power of World Jewry and its bankers. The myth of the all-powerful Rothschilds died hard; Rothschild was still a good name in international finance. The Balfour Declaration was addressed to Lord Rothschild, a Zionist notable. (The British did not take into account that many Jews had no interest in Zionism.) The English were well aware of what Schiff had done to finance the Japanese in their war with the Russians. The authorities in London also hoped to win over Russian Jewry through a pro-Palestinian manifesto. The revolution in the Muscovite Empire had finally broken out in the spring of 1917; there were more than 6,000,000 Jews there; many of the politicians in the new liberal Russian regime were Jews. The good will of Russian Jewry was important for the Entente if Russia was to stay in the war, maintain a second front, and threaten the Germans.

The British had nothing to lose by issuing a declaration in favor of the Zionists. They could well afford to give up Palestine; they had not yet conquered it. Not all the English were enthusiastic about the impending statement in favor of Zionism. Some were fearful of the Arab reaction; 85 to 90 percent of Palestine's population was Moslem, not Jewish. In addition there were some elite London Jews who also were unhappy with the idea of a Jewish commonwealth; they were terrified by the specter of the accusation of dual loyalty. In consequence the English kept watering down their pro-Jewish statement; they finally authorized its publication after working on it almost to the last moment.

AMERICA AND THE BALFOUR DECLARATION

The British wanted not only to win the Jews of Russia and the United States, they wanted to please Wilson; they refused to move without him. The American president was now the most powerful statesman in the world; the English needed him and American credits for supplies. They reasoned, correctly, that he would want to reward the Jews; many had supported him loyally; they had deserted the Republican Party to come into his camp contributing generously to Democratic coffers. Where did Wilson stand with reference to the British pro-Zionist announcement?

He wanted to help the Zionists; Rabbi Stephen S. Wise and Justice Brandeis were close to him; he was enough of a politician to realize he had to reward his friends but he had problems. He was in the midst of a world war. Palestine was not an important item on his agenda. France, an ally, also had pretensions to parts of Palestine. Far more important was the fact that the United States never went to war with the Ottoman Empire; Palestine was Turkish; America could not cavalierly give it to the Jews. American Christian missionaries with their millions of pious followers in this country were emotionally tied to the Holy Land; it was there that Jesus had lived and died. The Jews had crucified their Lord and Savior. Why reward them? The American State Department must not be discounted; its bureaucrats were anything but enthusiastic about the English pro-Zionist position paper; they did not think it was important. Some anti-Zionist Jews encouraged the State Department to look askance at Zionism. In general the anti-Jewish attitude of this department is not easy to explain. As a rule it was no friend of the Jews; American economic interests in the Middle East, however, were as yet not important though there was some talk of oil. It is not improbable—and this is only a guess—that some of the State Department personnel were snobs; these civil servants may well have resented Washington's rising Jewish officials; some of them occupied positions of power.

Because of their economic dependence on the United States the British would not move without securing Wilson's assent to the proposed Zionist proclamation. His approval was cabled to the English on October 16, 1917; about two weeks later the Balfour Declaration was published. However, the President moved slowly and cautiously before issuing a public statement. He waited ten months before he wrote to his friend Rabbi Stephen S. Wise on the occasion of the approaching Jewish New Year for 1918-5679, and even then he was equivocal, almost evasive, as he expressed satisfaction with the progress being made in Palestine since the release of Balfour's letter. Wilson delayed saying anything until the war was practically over, when it was obvious that the Turks were about to lose Palestine to the English. As it was to be expected there were Christians and Jewish anti-Zionists who were unhappy with the President's letter.

Though the evidence is not conclusive it seems that the reluctant Wilson supported the Balfour Declaration partly due to the intervention of Stephen S. Wise and Brandeis, Zionists. The justice's hands were tied; he had already been sworn in and he was very busy with the court duties; it was difficult for him to do much although Weizmann and others were urging him to do something to speed the publication of the proposed British paper. But the justice saw Wilson rarely and knew that the President could not be pressured. Brandeis went along with the President.

Maintaining peace with the Turks was imperative; Palestine was a Turkish province; it could not be turned over to foreigners. In his thinking
Brandeis was first an American, then a Zionist. In the same way Chaim
Weizmann, the English Zionist, who pushed hard for the statement, was
an ardent English patriot. He wanted the English to rule in Palestine; under the far-flung British Empire, still one of the world's great powers,
Jews would certainly fare better than under the Turks. A Jewish Palestine
would be good for the English Empire. Weizmann was unhappy with the
hedges which were incorporated in the British manifesto; they had been
inserted largely through the intervention of the Jew, Edwin Samuel Montagu, a cabinet member, Secretary of State for India. This man was a belligerent anti-Zionist; he would have preferred to see no pro-Zionist pronouncements; he had but little interest in Jews and Judaism.

What the Declaration Did For American Jewry

Here in the United States the Zionists and hundreds of thousands of sympathizers were elated when this controversial document was released.
When in a few months Jerusalem fell into the hands of the English many
Jews were overjoyed; the Declaration could be put into force. Thousands
of American Jews became members of the Federation of American Zionists; among them were Jewish natives and acculturated Germans; most
new Zionists, however, were of Russian and Polish ancestry. Anti-Zionists began to have second thoughts; many now became non-Zionists.
Louis Marshall lost patience with the Cincinnati hard-line anti-Zionists
led by Philipson and Max Senior, the distinguished social worker. Most
Yiddish papers were sympathetic. Zionism had become respectable. The
Jews had achieved a new status; they had a "country" of their own; now
they were like all the other nations, the Gentiles. On April 28, 1918, after careful thought, the American Jewish Committee finally came out
with a statement on the Balfour Declaration; it was friendly though cautiously worded. The country's Jewish elite took six months to decide
what it would say.

The Zionists were now ready to rebuild Palestine; conditions were
favorable. It did not require too much vision to realize in 1917-1918 that
the gates to America were about to close; a new haven for East European
Jewry was imperative; Palestine could serve that purpose. American Jewry's real problem now—World Jewry's also—was not the anti-Zionists
but the Arabs. With justice the Moslems feared the Declaration. They
began to revolt; the British hastened to renege on their promises to the
Jews. Now that English had emerged victorious from the war there was
no need to placate Jewry; the Declaration was a hindrance. Desiring a free
hand in Palestine the English began to delimit the territory which the
Jews were permitted to develop (1922).[6]

THE PHILADELPHIA AMERICAN JEWISH CONGRESS MEETING, DECEMBER 15-18, 1918

The American Jewish Congress which was called to order on December 15, 1918, in Philadelphia was the first formal meeting of this group after the armistice had been signed in World War I. It was an organization that embraced practically all of American Jewry; there had never been an assembly like this in all of American Jewish history. Included were Orthodox Jews, socialists, the American Jewish Committee, natives, acculturated influential Germans, an assortment of delegates of East European ancestry, Zionists, non-Zionists, anti-Zionists. They were all there except the leaders of the Reform Movement and some left-wing radicals who stayed at home. The Reform Jewish organizations—the Union of American Hebrew Congregations, the Central Conference of American Rabbis, the Hebrew Union College—were not officially represented; they could not reconcile themselves to the thought of working for a Jewish national home; like the socialists they may have believed that the new Russia would solve the Jewish problem; they were, however, always eager to secure equal rights for disabled East European Jews.

American Jewish notables wanted to be seen; they flocked to this gathering; some were elected vice presidents. Adolf Kraus of the B'nai B'rith made his appearance; Jacob H. Schiff was elected treasurer. There were delegates from the Far West. Among them was Ben Selling of Portland, Oregon, a distinguished and generous philanthropist. Dov Ber (Bernard) Abramowitz, a stalwart Orthodox rabbi, came from St. Louis; Rabbi Joseph Blatt of Oklahoma City represented the Jews of his state; for years he had served as the only ordained Jewish clergyman in Oklahoma. Among the others present were Professor Horace Kallen of the University of Wisconsin; Gotthard Deutsch, the Jewish historian at the Hebrew Union College; Allan Davis of Pittsburgh, the Harvard man who had staged a Jewish play on the Cambridge campus; Joseph Silverman, senior rabbi of Temple Emanu-El, New York, and Sadie American, one of the founders of the National Council of Jewish Women. Julius Rosenwald of Sears, Roebuck had also been selected as a delegate. Felix Frankfurter of Harvard, Rabbi Joseph Krauskopf of Philadelphia, the Classical Reformer, and the genial Henry Cohen of Galveston, Texas, also attended. Even the Federation of Jewish Farmers of America was there. If nothing else this assembly testified eloquently that American Jews were not a homogeneous lot. Marshall and his American Jewish Committee were there in force; the New York lawyer—a man of absolute integrity—was determined to do what he could to help his fellow Jews. Special secretaries were appointed to record the speeches in English, Hebrew, and Yiddish. This much is certain; the Russian and Polish Jews were in the saddle. The Zionist flag flew over Independence Hall.

Among the leaders—there were dozens—were Stephen Samuel Wise and Julian William Mack. Mack, a scion of an old-line Jewish family, was elected president of the Philadelphia assembly. He was a very important person, a jurist, a social worker, a communal leader, a Zionist. He was an interesting paradigm of a concerned American Jew, a classical example of this breed, a man who had completely harmonized his Americanism and his devotion to Jewry. It was patent that he believed the chasm between the Jewish natives and the émigrés could be bridged. He was active both in the American Jewish Committee and in the American Jewish Congress. Mack (1860-1943) was born in San Francisco but grew up in Cincinnati which always prided itself on being the Queen City of the West. There were numerous Macks in this Ohio town; some had been there since antebellum days but it is not certain that the pioneer Macks were kinsmen of Julian. One Mack did business with Jesse Grant, the general's father, in Civil War days. Jesse Grant secured permission to bring Southern cotton through the lines; the Macks sold the cotton to the textile mills in the North.

Julian Mack studied at Harvard where he did well; he was one of the founders of the *Harvard Law Review*. The school gave him a scholarship which permitted him to study for years at German universities. On his return Chicago became his home; there in the 1890's he taught law at the universities, sat as a county judge, distinguished himself in a juvenile court, and finally, in 1913, became a federal judge in the circuit division. He may well have been the first Jew in this country to reach this high station. During World War I he played a role as a member of a board of inquiry which investigated conscientious objectors. The judge, who was close to Jane Addams, succeeded her as president of the National Conference of Social Workers, a signal honor. The National Association for the Advancement of Colored People knew him well; he was at one time board chairman of Survey Associates, a prestigious social work group. There is cumulative evidence that he was one of the most respected men in the country in the field of social endeavor. Later he lent his name and his skills to the New School for Social Research and served on Harvard's Board of Overseers at a time when President Abbot Lawrence Lowell sought to limit the number of matriculating Jews.

The judge was very active in numerous important Jewish institutions although he was in no sense a joiner; he wanted to be helpful. Because of his interest in furthering immigrants he worked closely with Chicago's United Hebrew Charities, helped in the establishment of the Maxwell Street Settlement, served as an officer of the Jewish Publication Society of America, the National Conference of Jewish Charities, the Combined Young Men's and Young Women's Hebrew Associations, and the United Jewish Appeal. It was no real problem for him, conscientiously, to join a congregation although he was not an ardent religionist. He was a member of Chicago's Sinai, then led by Emil G. Hirsch, a radical theologian who was committed to social causes. Hirsch was the man who had introduced the social justice clause into the 1885 Pittsburgh Platform of the Reformers. In joining a temple Mack departed from the pattern that characterized his secularist friends, Frankfurter, Morris R. Cohen, and Horace Kallen. Sometime about the year 1914-1915 he moved in the direction of Zionism. It is not easy to determine exactly what motivated him to make this move. It may well have been the spurrings of his conscience. He knew the Chicago ghetto well; he had no contempt for the denizens of Halsted Street; he knew that the Russians in the United States and in Europe needed help. He was a proud Jew, inclined to accept Kallen's insistence on cultural pluralism, strongly influenced by his Zionist friends, men and women of culture, impressed by Brandeis.

Like Brandeis he came to Zionism late; Mack was over fifty when he threw in his lot with the Jewish nationalists. By 1918 he had assumed the presidency of the Brandeis-dominated Zionist Organization of America, the reconstituted and improved Federation of American Zionists. The delegates who assembled in Philadelphia on December 15, 1918, had no difficulty in accepting him as their permanent chairman. His Zionist credentials were impeccable. The following year he went to the Peace Conference where the assembled Jewish delegations chose him as their leader. During the next decade when Jewish notables from all over the world met to found the Hebrew University he made his presence felt, and when in 1922 Stephen S. Wise established the Jewish Institute of Religion, a liberal rabbinical seminary, the judge was called upon to serve as chairman of the board. By that time he was living in New York. Those men and women who were privileged to know Mack found him to be a courteous gentleman, totally devoid of arrogance and pretentiousness. American Jewry was fortunate that it was able to command the services, the leadership, of a man of his caliber.

STEPHEN SAMUEL WISE

Mack was a charming gentleman but he was neither colorful nor charismatic; Wise was. Wise exuded a personality, a magic that overwhelmed individuals and large audiences. In many respects Stephen S. Wise (1872/74-1949) was the country's most famous Reform rabbi. Certainly he was America's most influential Jewish minister in the decades between 1920 and 1949. The man was a Zionist, a social worker, a political activist, an outstanding American Jewish leader. Wise was anything but a typical clergyman; he was a humanitarian concerned with the underprivileged; this concern he shared with Julian Mack. He was a very active civic reformer; this made him a politician. Above all he was different; he was an iconoclast. This remarkable Jew was born in Hungary, son and grandson of learned rabbis. (Stephen was the name of the patron saint of the Magyars.) The father immigrated here in the 1870's bringing young Stephen with him. In New York City, where the father settled, he made a name for himself and carved out a career that brought him the respect of his colleagues. Young Wise went to City College and Columbia; in 1901 he received his Ph.D. degree; his published thesis was a study of an ethical work of the medieval Spanish poet and philosopher Solomon Ibn Gabirol. When only about twenty-one Wise had already opted for the rabbinate. He was a self-made minister; he received no formal instruction in a rabbinical seminary either here or abroad; much of his training came from tutors or learned friends. Scholars of distinction gave him private ordination; among them was the learned Henry Gersoni, an immigrant, who had helped him when he translated Gabirol's *Improvement of the Moral Qualities*.

There is no question, Wise was a young man in a hurry. After several years of rabbinical service in New York he accepted the Reform pulpit in Portland, Oregon. In New York he had leaned toward traditionalism but he was moving toward the left. According to contemporary gossip—in this instance not to be discounted—Gustav Gottheil, one of his teachers, urged him to go West, make a name for himself, and then return to New York. Gottheil, so it is said, wanted Wise to succeed him in Emanu-El. (Unfortunately, Gottheil was dead by the time the young New Yorker returned.) In Oregon, Wise distinguished himself as a social worker fighting for reform; he was in the van of those who conducted the war against gambling, prostitution. Recognizing his powers and his commitments, the state's social agencies rewarded him accordingly. The congregational board, a conservative group, was aghast at some of the things he said and did. His liberalism attracted many; some Christians wanted to become seatholders in his temple. He frightened his board members because he dominated them; his powerful personality overwhelmed them. One suspects that they were glad to see him go. After he left, the congregational leaders amended the constitution; the next rabbi was not permitted to sit with the board. The amendment was passed unanimously; Wise was indignant. It is obvious that in his case virtue was not its own reward.

The young rabbi was called back to New York City in the winter of 1905 to give a series of trial sermons at Emanu-El, the country's most prestigious congregation and probably its richest. His reputation as a stormy petrel had preceded him. When he started negotiating Emanu-El's board told him immediately that it expected no trouble from him but that in the event of any dispute the decision of the board was final. Wise's answer was that no self-respecting minister would ever subject himself to the control of a board; in Portland he had at all times maintained a free pulpit. In 1906-1907, back in New York to stay, Wise started the Free Synagogue, preaching on Sunday mornings in a public auditorium. Hundreds, thousands, flocked to hear him, Jews and Gentiles. His preaching was really nondenominational. Support came from wealthy admirers; in a relatively short time he was recognized as one of the city's most distinguished ministers. He stood out as a humanitarian, a social worker, and because he was a fighter for good government, it was not long before he turned to politics.

Theologically, morally, spiritually, his thinking paralleled that of the older Felix Adler. The latter left the faith; Wise remained well within the ambit of Jewishness preaching a Judaism rooted in the teachings of the Israelitish prophets. Nothing liberal was alien to him; he was helpful to the blacks fighting for their rights; he urged the passage of old-age pension legislation; he fought against exploitation of women and children in industry; he encouraged the unions in their struggle with their employers. Wise's support of the strikers who revolted against the United States Steel Company alienated some of his wealthy contributors; it would be years before he was able to build a synagog of his own. In the war for good government he fought the entrenched Tammany Democrats and helped oust their mayor, James J. Walker. By 1912 Wise was a political power in the country; he supported Wilson and later Franklin Delano Roosevelt. New York's votes were important to those two men. Wise had a large following, particularly among the underprivileged; the politicians respected him and listened to him.

As a Jewish crusader he struggled to help his people. Wherever there was a Jewish cause particularly one of a humanitarian nature, people turned to him. For Wise Zionism was no passing whim. In his early days he had helped found and lead the Federation of American Zionists working closely with his Columbia teacher, Richard J. H. Gottheil. For a few years, in Oregon, he had directed his energies primarily toward civic and social reform. Back in New York he threw himself wholeheartedly into the effort to build the Zionist organization. For a decade after his return to the metropolis he was overshadowed by Brandeis but when the Boston lawyer donned his judicial robes in Washington Wise found it easier to impinge his powerful personality on the American Jewish masses; by the 1920's the rabbi was recognized as one of the most influential of America's Zionists; in the 1930's he led the Zionist Organization of America and the reconstituted American Jewish Congress.

In 1922 he took a fateful step; he opened a liberal theological seminary intended deliberately to rival the well-established Hebrew Union College in Cincinnati. It was a bold move; he had limited financial resources while the Cincinnati seminary could count on support from hundreds of congregations. Wise wanted to train men responsive to the needs of second-generation Jews of East European origin. The New Yorker did not leave his imprint on the rabbis of the Central Conference of American Rabbis. He spent little time at their sessions. He did not cultivate them; he frightened them; he awed them. He was not the man to submit tamely to the decisions of a majority. This distinguished American was never the leader of American Jewry because he was too far to the left; he had no real rabbinical following until he began producing his own men; they adored him. Wise was a magnificent orator; his adherents among his coreligionists in this country were numerous. He loved Jews and they responded with an almost worshipful admiration. One may venture to assert that there was probably never a Jewish minister in this country who was so popular, so respected, so beloved as this man. Hundreds of thousands of Christians knew him and admired him. Many Jews looked upon him as an apostle to the Gentiles; politicians in Washington deferred to him.

On the Road to Paris, December 1918

Before the delegates of the Philadelphia convention dispersed in December 1918, they selected a deputation to represent American Jewry at the Peace Conference. With the exception of Marshall and Mack all the others were foreign-born. The delegation included members of the American Jewish Committee, socialists, and Zionists; a Reform and an Orthodox rabbi were also included. The members carried with them a Bill of Rights written by Marshall, the constitutional lawyer. In brief the deputies were charged to influence the powers at the Peace Conference, to induce them to grant minority national rights to the East European Jews and to help implement the Balfour Declaration. The Congress wanted Britain to secure the mandate for Palestine. When the committee departed for Paris it was understood, however, that the World Zionist Organization—the European leaders—would be given a free hand to negotiate for Palestine's future; the American delegation was to concern itself primarily with the needs of the Jews in Russia, Poland, Galicia, and especially Rumania where abuses were rampant. It was understood—this was patent—that the Palestine homeland was intended primarily for Europe's oppressed Jews; the Americans intended to remain here; the Holy Land, they realized, was in fact too small to contain all of World Jewry. Ideological debates at the convention had been ruled out but Chaim Zhitlowsky, the eminent socialist and Yiddishist was a law unto himself; he rose and spoke his mind proposing separation of church and state in the new Palestine. The indignant Mizrachi, pious and observant, insisted and obtained the right to answer the brash secularist radical. This verbal scuffle served to enliven the proceedings.[7]

THE PARIS PEACE CONFERENCE, 1919

THE ZIONISTS IN PARIS

In March 1919, Mack, Marshall, and Wise, members of the deputation chosen to go to Paris and intercede at the Peace Conference, waited on President Wilson and presented the proposals of the American Jewish Congress, the American Jewish people. These three deputies were notables; they represented millions of people. Wilson listened sympathetically as they asked for national rights for East European Jewry and the opportunity to build a commonwealth in the Promised Land. They told Wilson that the Jews would not only rebuild the waste places but would advance the land culturally. Earlier, by February, before the American Jewish deputation had sailed for Europe, the leaders of the World Zionist Organization were already in Paris pushing for the acceptance of the Balfour Declaration and the granting of the mandate for Palestine to Great Britain. The Zionists could now move with a degree of confidence for they knew they had the wholehearted support of the American Jewish Congress and the sympathy of Woodrow Wilson. Behind the President loomed the rich and powerful American state which had lent the allies billions and had thrown 2,000,000 troops into the war against the Central Powers, Germany and Austria-Hungary. The Zionists were moving from strength.

FELIX FRANKFURTER

While the European Zionist leaders were petitioning for the recognition of Palestine as a Jewish homeland, Brandeis and Mack sent Professor Felix Frankfurter of Harvard to France to act as a legal advisor to the Zionists at the Peace Conference. One suspects that he was dispatched to Europe not only to help but to keep a wary eye on Weizmann and his associates. Brandeis took his responsibility for Zionism very seriously. As early as January Weizmann had come to terms with the Arab Prince Feisal. The Arabs and Moslems were important in Palestine and the Middle East since they were the occupants of all the lands at the eastern end of the Mediterranean. Feisal assured the Zionist leaders that the Arabs would work with the Jews coming to Palestine and in turn would expect the newcomers to help them establish an independent Arab state of their own. Feisal's promise meant little. In March, Frankfurter negotiated with the Arab prince and secured his written endorsement of Zionist hopes. These promises, too, proved to be worthless; Feisal equivocated constantly; the Arabs would never reconcile themselves to the coming of the Jews. Islam taught that Jews and Christians, too, were to be treated as subject peoples.

The propaganda on behalf of the Balfour Declaration at the Paris Peace Conference disturbed not only the Arabs but also the Christian missionaries. Pro-missionary followers back in the states, numbering into the hundreds of thousands, exercised a great deal of political influence. By the summer of 1919 Wilson found it advisable to appoint a commission to determine the wishes of the inhabitants of Palestine with respect to their political future. This was in line with democratic procedure, self-determination. Thus it was that Wilson appointed the King-Crane Commission. It went to work in June, 1919. Henry C. King, an educator, was close to the Christian missionaries; Charles R. Crane, an industrialist, was friendly to the old Russian regime. It was clear that it would be difficult for either of these men to approach the Balfour Declaration with any degree of sympathy. When the Commission made its report to Wilson in the late summer of 1919 it told him that the native Palestinians were opposed to a Jewish commonwealth; Jewish immigration to the country should be curtailed. The report was not published for years by the Americans; Wilson had committed himself to help establish a Jewish commonwealth in Palestine. The King-Crane Report was of no significance except to emphasize that the Palestinians were strongly opposed to the implementation of the Balfour Declaration. They wanted no Jewish commonwealth; the Jews were not welcome. Palestine was a Moslem land.

During the summer of 1919 while King and Crane were making their study, Felix Frankfurter moved on to Poland. He was sent to that country, probably, to keep an eye on Henry Morgenthau who had been dispatched there to investigate the mistreatment of Jews. Frankfurter knew Morgenthau well. He had accompanied the latter in 1917 when this former ambassador to the Sublime Porte proposed to take Turkey out of the war by detaching it from its alliance with the Central Powers. Frankfurter was an able diplomatic pinch hitter, available when needed either by the government or his friends. In 1919 he was coming into his own. This man excites comment from America's Jewish historians because he is a paradigm of the cultured Jew who is important in the larger American world but manifests only a tangential relation to its Jewry. Such men were numerous. Unlike Brandeis, Frankfurter (1882-1965), came out of Orthodoxy. He was always to maintain ties to Jews but he was no synagoggoer. This native of Vienna was about thirteen years of age when his parents landed and settled on New York's East Side. Beginning at the bottom he started scrabbling to reach the top. Like other East Siders he went through City College and then moved on to Harvard where he was graduated from the law school in 1906. From Cambridge he went to New York serving under Henry L. Stimson, the United States District Attorney, and when Stimson was called to Washington in 1911 he took Frankfurter with him. By 1914 Frankfurter was a professor at Harvard, all of thirty-two years of age. The faculty wanted him; Schiff and other Jews helped endow his chair. During World War I he served his country in Washington, working in the War and Labor Departments; by 1918 he was chairman of the War Labor Policies Board. Four years earlier the taciturn but persuasive Brandeis had won him for Zionism and put him on the Provisional Executive Committee for General Zionist Affairs. In 1919 he was in Europe, at work in Paris and in Poland, always close to Brandeis and the Zionists. When Brandeis was pushed out by his rival Weizmann, Frankfurter left with him. Brandeis was the better Zionist; the cause was dear to him; Frankfurter never lost his interest in the movement but it was not a real force in his life.

In his early days the Harvard professor was a Progressive, a liberal for only through liberalism could Jews hope to find a niche for themselves. He and Morris Raphael Cohen, another East Sider, roomed together at college. This Viennese Jew supported the American Civil Liberties Union and the National Association for the Advancement of Colored People; he questioned the fairness of the trial of Sacco and Vanzetti (1927); he was close to the circle that published the *New Republic*. During New Deal days Frankfurter was important. He cultivated Franklin Roosevelt—whom he flattered inordinately—and he augmented his influence through numerous disciples whom he sent to Washington. In 1939 the president put him on the Supreme Court. The commonly publicized rationale for this appointment was that Roosevelt wanted to show Nazi Germany that the Jews were accepted and respected here in the United States. It is far more probable that the president chose Frankfurter because of political pressures exerted by Jews who had rallied around Frankfurter enthusiastically. Roosevelt knew, too, that Frankfurter would always support him in the court. This brilliant immigrant was determined to get ahead. He went far.

One of his biographers refers to Frankfurter as an enigma. That he was not; he was a typical frightened insecure newcomer who desperately wanted to belong, to be recognized. This is not to imply that he was a humble man; he was impressed by his own abilities and very conscious of his successes. When he reached the top in 1939 he veered to the right; he exercised "judicial restraint"; the Supreme Court was not a legislative body. It is likely that he did not wish to move too far from his colleagues on the bench because he sought their acceptance, if not their commendation. Brandeis was of sterner stuff; he hewed to his line. Frankfurter was a better Jew than Brandeis though he did not nurture his heritage; his Jewish roots were strong. When he realized that his end was approaching he asked that one of his disciples, an Orthodox Jew, say kaddish for him. "I came into the world a Jew and . . . I want to leave it as a Jew." Yet in the biography which he submitted to *Who's Who in America* the words Jew and Jewish are conspicuous by their absence. This, too, is typical.

When United States Jewry sent its American Jewish Congress delegates to Paris there were several Jewish groups already in that city who were also interested in furthering the interests of World Jewry. The Union of American Hebrew Congregations and the American Jewish Committee were represented by deputies who were eager to see that Jews everywhere were accorded the type of equal rights found in the American political system. The French Alliance Israélite Universelle and the Joint Foreign Committee of England were also present ready to help their coreligionists in Eastern Europe although they were opposed to the granting of "national rights." Barnard Baruch and Henry Morgenthau also floated around. Baruch spoke to Wilson protesting the persecutions in Poland; despite his anti-Zionism, Morgenthau was interested in protecting the Jews in all lands if they were denied the immunities of citizenship. With its own deputation as the core, the American Jewish Congress organized most of the European delegations into a Committee of Jewish Delegations at the Peace Conference (Comité des Délégations Juives auprès de la Conférence de la Paix). Mack was the overall chairman until he had to return to the States; he was succeeded by Marshall who gave up his lucrative legal practice and stayed on for months; he wanted to do a job and incidentally make sure that his American associates would adhere to the Bill of Rights adopted by the December 1918 Philadelphia Conference. It is worthy, too, of note that much of the expense of maintaining the American delegation was provided for by Marshall; the funds of the American Jewish Congress were limited. On May 10, 1919, the Comité made its presentation on behalf of East European Jewry to the allied authorities. No action could be expected on the Palestine situation because no treaty had yet been signed with Turkey.

The Comité emphasized the need for minority rights. Let it be clear that the Jews were only one of many civically underprivileged groups in Central Europe, Eastern Europe, and in the Balkans. It is estimated that there were millions of men, women, and children who required the protection which the Jews also sought. Back in the United States there were millions of immigrants, Gentiles, who were concerned about their kin in the old war zones, anxious that the new treaties include immunities that would protect their dear ones. The Jewish delegates pushed hard for national rights in 1919 because of the constant recurrence of persecution in the new states. As early as May 1919, the Paris Jewish delegates protested vigorously against the unending tragedies that afflicted their people. These excesses induced the peacemaking authorities to include minority clauses in all treaties. The promises made in these documents were calculated to protect all groups suffering disabilities. If the allied leaders in Paris sought to aid Jews it was because they were fully cognizant of the breakdown in law and order in large parts of Poland, Rumania, and Russia. There was nothing they could do in Communist Russia; they had no influence there. In Pinsk, on April 5, 1919, thirty-five Jews meeting to arrange for a distribution of Passover foods for the needy were executed by Polish soldiers. The United States Congress passed a resolution sponsored by Henry M. Goldfogle of New York deploring the Polish outrages. The estimates of death and casualties in the Polish and Ukrainian regions where anarchy was rampant for many months ranged anywhere from 30,000 to 200,000. Hundreds of towns and villages were ravaged. The concomitant economic boycott carried on by the Poles against their Jewish neighbors exacerbated an almost intolerable situation. Months later Marshall besought the Poles to work with their Jewish fellow citizens; the Jews, he told them, had the capacity to help build Poland commercially, industrially.

There is reason to believe that no Jew was more important than Marshall in inducing the allied powers to incorporate minority rights safeguards. He operated as a *shtadlan*, a lobbyist, under the aegis of the democracy that was an American Jewish Congress fetish. He won the confidence of all who were associated with him in his task. Finally on June 20, 1919, the Versailles and Polish treaties were signed. The minority treaties written and signed protected ethnics from Finland south to Turkey. On the whole the Jews succeeded in obtaining the basic rights they felt they needed to survive. They could pursue their cultural goals; they were given linguistic (Yiddish) privileges, autonomy in their communal administration, financial support in their schools; their Sabbath was to be respected, to an extent at least. It was hoped that these privileges would ultimately be guaranteed by the new League of Nations. In July, Marshall returned to New York to receive a hero's reception. He was hailed as a "martial" Jew who had fought to foster the American ideals of liberty and justice for all. Back home he encouraged his followers in the American Jewish Committee to work with the Zionists and help them build Palestine for he knew that the gates in America would soon be closed; Palestine might well become a new haven for Jewish immigrants. He believed, however, that the new treaties would materially improve the conditions of the Jews in the successor states. Now American Jewry could return to its own immediate problems, the education of its children and youth with the hope that they would learn to cherish their Jewish traditions.

THE MORGENTHAU POLISH MISSION, JULY-SEPTEMBER 1919

Wilson had set out to placate the American missionaries, the pro-Arabs, and the anti-Zionists in his entourage by appointing the King-Crane Commission. Just about the same time he set out to placate American

Jews who were shocked by the murders and looting in Poland. Cyrus Adler then in Paris representing the American Jewish Committee referred to this "carnival of hatred and persecution" as pogroms. These were not pogroms; they were not incited by the Polish leaders General Jozef Pilsudski and Ignace Paderewski. Whether these men could have done more to curb the mobs and discipline their troops is moot. Poland suffered internationally from a bad press; Paderewski turned to Wilson and asked him to dispatch a commission to Poland to make an impartial investigation. As a politician and a humanitarian, Wilson had a stake in the new anti-Communist Polish state. The president had to do something; the situation in Poland could not be glossed over. Consequently the American Commission to Negotiate the Peace and the president chose Henry Morgenthau, Sr., (1856-1946) to head a board of inquiry (July 1919).

Morgenthau was at the Peace Conference looking for chores. Wilson was very much in his debt politically. In many respects Morgenthau was a notable American in the Horatio Alger Luck and Pluck tradition. He was a German immigrant who had come here as a child and had to go to work early. He took a job as an errand boy. Morgenthau managed to finance himself in school, studied law, went into business and made a fortune in real estate and industry. This man was no reactionary capitalist; he was wealthy and generous. He was interested in social reforms, in settlement houses; that is why Stephen S. Wise chose him to serve as the first president of the Free Synagogue. In December 1918, Morgenthau was elected or appointed as a delegate to the Philadelphia conference of the American Jewish Congress but he refused to attend because he believed that the important decisions had already been made; he was right. His mind was set; he had worked hard to help the Palestine settlers when ambassador to Constantinople. The Holy Land, he believed, could develop as a center of Hebraic culture and religion but he was a resolute anti-Zionist; he wanted no Jewish state. When he resigned as head of the Free Synagogue—this was in 1918—it was because he could no longer work closely with a committed Zionist, with Wise. Because he had done so much to provide the funds for Wilson's presidential campaign, Morgenthau hoped he would be made Secretary of the Treasury. This Wilson had no intention of doing; he shunted the reluctant Morgenthau off to Constantinople as ambassador to the Sublime Porte (1913). Before Morgenthau sailed for Turkey the Zionists gave him a banquet; they knew he could be helpful; he was. Once at his post he befriended Palestine Jews and American missionaries; that was the tradition that distinguished Oscar Straus, a predecessor in the post. Years later, under a Republican administration, he took on the job of chairman of the League of Nations Resettlement Commission, 1923; he aided in the resettlement of over a million Asia Minor Greeks and European Turks who had been uprooted by the war. During New

Deal days he enjoyed good relations with Franklin Delano Roosevelt. Like Oscar Straus, Bernard Baruch, Eugene Meyer, Albert D. Lasker, and other wealthy Jews, he relished public life.

When in July of 1919 Wilson sent him to Poland he was instructed to find out what was done to the Jews and why. His report was an objective one; he described the economic boycott directed against Jews and enumerated the disorders that cost the lives of many innocent people. He did not fail to detail the prejudices nursed by the Poles against their Jewish fellow citizens. The Poles were unhappy that Jews constituted a very substantial percentage of the country's population and were concentrated in trade. It was equally true that the Poles disliked Jews cordially; the Jews reciprocated this hostility. Because the quondam ambassador did not condemn the Poles for the excesses that had alarmed World Jewry he lost his chance to become a Jewish hero. Poland in 1919 was shaky; it had in no sense consolidated its power or even determined its borders. The American authorities did not want the new republic to be denigrated; they expected Morgenthau to promote harmonious relations between Jews and Poles; they did not want his report to encourage the neighboring Russians who were about to go to war with the Poles. The Americans hoped that Morgenthau would be placatory. It is by no means improbable that a Jew had been chosen to head the commission of inquiry with the hope that he would lean over backward; his name had actually been suggested by Paderewski. Like Marshall, Morgenthau urged the Polish government to cooperate with its Jews; the Jews, he pointed out, could help rebuild the country. The ambassador did not set out to exculpate, to whitewash the Poles, to strengthen the regime of Pilsudski and Paderewski; it is equally true that he did not vigorously denounce the Poles for their brutalities.

American Jews were shocked; this refusal to condemn the Poles was in their eyes unforgivable; they wanted Morganthau to react as an outraged Jew and not as an American diplomat representing a country that was sympathetic to the new Slavic state. Frankfurter, who had ample opportunity to know Morgenthau since 1917, said the man was a decent sort but a "lot of hot air." He may indeed have been a bore but he was able. It is also reported that some people thought he was vain. That, too, may be true, but he was also kind and generous. Like American Jewry the English Jewish community was shocked by the sufferings of their Polish coreligionists. The English, too, were prompted to send a team of investigators headed by Sir Stuart Samuel, a wealthy industrialist who was president of the Board of Deputies of British Jews. Sir Stuart, a brother of Herbert Samuel who was soon to be appointed High Commissioner of Mandate Palestine, was Orthodox, as were some of his immediate ancestors; he was one of the leaders of the English Mizrachi, the religious Zionists who were determined to cultivate traditional Judaism in the new Palestine. Possibly more so than Morgenthau Samuel stressed the disabilities under which Polish Jewry labored. He pressed for their removal. On the whole he seemed to have been more concerned about the plight of his coreligionists in Poland than Morgenthau. There is no question that Morgenthau's criticisms and the more condemnatory response of Sir Stuart Samuel alarmed the Polish leaders and pushed them to suppress attacks on Jews. This was particularly true after the Poles gained full control of the lands which they occupied.

The advances made by the Jews, the Zionists, in establishing a Palestine homeland alarmed the Arabs; they began rioting in March and April 1920, attacking Jews in various parts of the country. In April of that year, the mandate over Palestine was given to England by the Supreme Council of the Allied Powers meeting in San Remo, Italy. The English were now obligated and officially empowered to implement the Balfour Declaration. The World Zionist Organization was recognized by the British as the official Jewish agency charged with the duty of developing the country. In the course of the decades the Zionists enlarged their agency to include affluent non-Zionists with the hope that distinguished bankers and businessmen would turn Palestine into a modern agricultural and industrial state. This expanded Jewish Agency failed to achieve its purpose; the Zionists refused to share authority; the coopted notables were determined to develop the country on their own terms. In 1920, a few months after the San Remo directive, Sir Herbert Samuel entered into his duties as the first High Commissioner. He took over from General Louis Bols, the military administrator. The General, something of a wit, asked for a receipt before he would surrender the country to the civil administration. Sir Herbert gave him a receipt which reads as follows: "Received from Major General Sir Louis Bols, one Palestine, complete." It was signed Herbert Samuel and followed by the initials "E. & O. E.," errors and omissions excepted. All this with tongue in cheek. Sir Herbert had been a Zionist for years but he never forgot that above all he was a British civil servant; his first obligation was to the English authorities back in London. In August Turkey signed the Treaty of Sèvres relinquishing its hold on Palestine; the British were free to carry out the terms of the mandate and the Balfour Declaration.

A few months earlier, Marshall reported to the American Jewish Congress meeting again in Philadelphia. His mission was accomplished and in accordance with the agreement that had been made in 1916 the Congress was adjourned sine die (1920). Almost immediately a group of Zionists reconvened the Congress. In May 1922, it was officially reorganized with Rabbi Stephen S. Wise as president. This new organization was called into being to watch over the minority treaties, to further Mandate

Palestine, and to fight anti-Semitism in all lands. The tasks which faced it were formidable, for the 1920's ushered in years of anti-Semitism here in the United States. This new national organization never mustered a large following. For the immigrant masses the crisis had passed; they were convinced that the minority treaties would safeguard the rights of Jews in Eastern Europe and in the Balkans; there was no need for another Congress. The American Jewish Committee was now faced with a permanent rival agency; the new organization, however, was never a threat to the older Committee for it suffered from lack of funds to carry on its program.

Some knowledgeable, cautious American Zionists were not altogether pleased with the guarantees promised the Jews in their old homelands. An American endorsement of the English mandate would mean more to them; America was all-powerful. American Zionists, therefore, were happy when in the summer of 1922 Congress voiced its approval of the Balfour Declaration by passing the Lodge-Fish Resolution. One of the reasons the Jews welcomed the passage of this statement of good will was the hope that it would influence the Council of the League of Nations to give official approval to the English mandate to govern Palestine and to further Zionist goals. Some congressmen may have voted for the Lodge-Fish Resolution because they knew that Palestine might well serve as a home for fleeing Jews who could no longer enter the United States. The exclusionary Immigration Act of 1921—directed in no small measure at Jews—limited their entrance to this country. On July 24, 1922, the mandate over Palestine was given to Great Britain by the Council of the League of Nations. This pleased the Jews eager for the assurance that the League would police the minority treaties. Actually most of the new postwar states defaulted on their obligations to their minorities; this certainly applied to their Jewish subjects. The League was destined to remain weak; it was never recognized by the United States government. The rights of American citizens in Palestine proper—Gentiles or Jews—were determined by a convention between England and the United States (1924-1925). One may doubt whether this Anglo-American treaty was motivated by the desire to help American Jews who settled in the ancient homeland. American corporations, which had now begun to evince an interest in oil, insisted on an open door policy in the Middle East, in Palestine.[8]

AMERICAN ZIONISM, 1918-1921

AMERICAN ZIONISM AFTER THE BALFOUR DECLARATION

While the American Jewish Congress and Brandeis groups were piling up victories in Paris, Versailles, and San Remo the Zionists in this country were getting ready to change leaders in midstream. At a Zionist Congress in Pittsburgh, 1918, the Federation of American Zionists became the Zionist Organization of America (ZOA); very quietly, behind the scenes, Justice Brandeis had reorganized the movement; under him it became a tighter, more efficient, national organization; it was no longer a loosely knit federation. The Poale Zion and the Mizrachi stayed out of the ZOA; they wanted to maintain their autonomy; as socialists and as religionists these two disparate groups lived in worlds of their own. The General Zionists, the larger body, were neutral in matters of politics and religion. They were wise. One is reminded that beginning with the 1840's the B'nai B'rith and later the Board of Delegates and the Union of American Hebrew Congregations trod warily where political and religious issues were debated. It was at the Pittsburgh conference that Brandeis began to outline his program for Palestine; the Balfour Declaration made it imperative that the Zionists address themselves to the nature of the new state. The political plan which Brandeis delineated really reflected his concept of an ideal America; the Jewish homeland was to be a vicarious America on the banks of the Mediterranean; it was to be a Jewish utopia, American style. Above all else Brandeis was always the Americanizer.

In the Pittsburgh Platform Brandeis called for equal rights for all who dwelt in the country, males and females. Women were thus to have political rights well over a year before the nineteenth amendment giving suffrage to women was ratified in this country (August 1920). The people, said Brandeis, are to own and control the natural resources, the public utilities; the cooperative principle was to be introduced into new economic enterprises; education, presumably compulsory, was to be available to all, with Hebrew as the medium of instruction. Much of what he proposed was incorporated into the later State of Israel. It is curious that this radical Pittsburgh Platform had the support of his associates including men like Bernard Flexner, Felix Frankfurter, Nathan Straus, Marcus Fechheimer, a Cincinnati shoe manufacturer, and the rabbis Stephen S. Wise and Abba Hillel Silver. None of them was a socialist. Except for the two rabbis they were businessmen, attorneys, men of influence and affairs. That they approved of Brandeis's blueprint is a tribute to their vision and to the Justice's persuasiveness. In July of 1919 Brandeis made a trip to Palestine to see the Jewish settlements, to observe what the local Zionists were doing. What he saw did not make him happy; fiscal irresponsibility was palpable; the Palestine Jewish executives were slipshod in matters of finance. For Brandeis that was a crime against the Holy Ghost. A year later, 1920, Brandeis attended an important Zionist conference that met in London a few months after England was given the mandate over Palestine. The Jews were now challenged to build a state of their own. Chaim Weizmann, the new president of the World Zionist Organization, was present; Brandeis was honorary president. The two leaders no longer saw eye to eye. One of the sources of the conflict was that the delegates in London had approved of the establishment of the Keren Hayesod, the Palestine Foundation Fund, an all-purpose fund to help the proposed Jewish state. This new organization, the Fund, was to be the rock of offence on which the Brandeis ship was to founder. On the way back from the meeting in London, on the steamship *Zeeland*, the Justice sat down and wrote the so-called Zeeland Memorandum. Repeating what he had outlined in Pittsburgh in 1918 Brandeis sketched his grand design for the new state in much the same fashion that Alexander Hamilton, in the days of Washington, charted the guidelines for the new America. In the Zeeland Memorandum Brandeis succinctly announced what he hoped to achieve in the area of immigration, investments, education, research. His approach was very businesslike: "we are no longer a propaganda movement." Brandeis laid out the lines to be followed in matters of agriculture, commerce, industry, culture. It was his hope that there would be a large influx of immigrants from Russia, Poland, Galicia, and Rumania. Actually, though suffering one of the worst calamities in all Jewish history, very few of these East Europeans opted for immigration to Palestine. Knowing that they had but one last chance to come to America they flocked here in 1921, 119,000 strong; fewer than 9,000 went to Palestine. For them it was not a land of unlimited opportunity.

CLEVELAND: BRANDEIS AND WEIZMANN

The Zionist conference in Cleveland, June 1921, was very important; it was there that the differences between Weizmann and Brandeis surfaced. The Justice was not present. He was represented by his friends, his supporters. The fight between the two leaders was over the new Foundation Fund; Weizmann and his associates were traveling across the country raising money for the Keren Hayesod successfully. They would soon have the means to carry on without Brandeis. Why did the Justice and his friends object to the Fund? They disliked it because it was an all-purpose grab bag; it could be used at the discretion of the World Zionist Organization. Monies from it could even be siphoned off for party purposes, to take care of the faithful. The Brandeis group was determined to build a new type of state, an efficient one conducted like a well-run corporation; there must be a rigid stewardship of all expenditures. Under no circumstances were investment funds to be commingled with those set aside for education and propaganda. The Justice was interested in building a country, not a worldwide Zionist movement.

It boded no good for the cause that there was no trust between the two leaders. Brandeis did not like Weizmann; he felt that the latter was too much of a party man; he was not a free agent. Their goals were different. Weizmann wanted to build an even stronger political state; for him San Remo was the beginning; for Brandeis the English mandate was adequate, at least for the time being. Weizmann's reach was all-embracing; he was interested in all Jews, everywhere; he wanted to harness them all, to Zionize the whole Jewish world into one common nationalist pro-Palestine brotherhood. Brandeis limited his vision to Palestine hoping to build it according to his specifications. Weizmann and his cohorts could do nothing without money; to this end they had established the Keren Hayesod. Now that the Fund was firmly ensconced in this country, he and his East European followers were ready to break with Brandeis and his friends, to remove them as leaders of the Zionist Organization of America. Weizmann phrased it candidly; there could be no bridge between Washington and Pinsk, between the two leaders. The man from Pinsk—actually a nearby village—was riding high; his confidence was justified. When the battle was joined at Cleveland the Brandeis cohorts were soundly trounced. Numerous East European leaders of the American Zionist movement here had for years been unhappy with the Justice and his clique. They were prepared to remove the silent, the invisible leader. The émigrés wanted control of the movement. Mack, president of the ZOA, and over thirty of his colleagues resigned; Brandeis gave up his post as honorary president of the World Zionist Organization. The 1921 revolt against the elitists who led the American Zionist organization was a success. In any rebellion the motivations to overthrow the ruling authorities are diverse. There was more to this struggle than control of the Keren Hayesod. Why did the majority of the delegates in Cleveland turn against the Justice and his cohorts? What was it really all about? The Weizmann-Lipsky-Goldberg-Rothenberg coalition had a number of goals in mind. Weizmann and his followers wanted to concentrate power, authority, in the World Zionist Organization which was based in Europe. To a large degree America had ruled Zionism since the outbreak of World War I and the creation of the Provisional Executive Committee for General Zionist Affairs. Now the World Zionist Organization insisted upon resuming control. In some respects the Cleveland insurrection was a continuation of the struggle that began in 1914 when America's new Jewish immigrants insisted upon cutting the leading strings that tied them to the American old-timers. The newcomers wanted to emancipate themselves from the control of the natives; they wanted to run their own show. The new leaders appointed after the dismissal of Mack and his associates were, with one possible exception, all of East European background. With the Keren Hayesod to fund them they now had the means to implement their programs and to spend money without having Brandeis looking over their shoulders.

Cleveland is a replay of the Yidden versus the Yahudim, the masses versus the elite. In a way the conflict was an ethnic one. Weizmann spoke as a Jew who had suffered under the Russians; he was intensely Jewish, steeped in yiddishkeit; Brandeis was first and last an "American"; he had never experienced humiliating disabilities. In addition there is no question that Cleveland was the scene of a battle between two strong personalities, a power struggle; there could be but one skipper on the ship. That control may even have been primary—not the program—is documented by the fact that before the decade had run its course the Weizmann crowd in America had to reinstate some of the men who had been ousted. Their new program was essentially Brandeisian. The rejection of the Mack-Brandeis group in 1921 hurt the movement; some of the most distinguished of America's Jews were now out. These men, Frankfurter, Silver, Wise, were politically powerful; they had access to the generous rich. Yet very few of those who had been cast out, if any, cut their ties to the movement. They retained their interest in Zionism and worked to strengthen the "settlement," the *yishuv*, in the land of their fathers. Some non-Zionists who watched the changing of the guard in Cleveland were not happy; they had confidence in the men who had been rejected; they belonged to the same social class. The historian who is above party strife takes note that even before the fall of the old administration, membership in the movement had begun to decline precipitously; this was through no fault of the Brandeis or Weizmann devotees. The masses who affiliated with Zionism and paid their modest shekels were concerned primarily with the fate of their dear ones abroad. Now, after Versailles and San Remo, these American immigrants believed that the future of Polish, Rumanian, and Palestine Jewry was assured; there was no need to retain membership in any Zionist organization. It would take another crisis to excite the American Jewish masses, to breathe new life into Zionism and Jewish nationalism. The brutalities of the anti-Semitic Germans in the 1930's and 1940's would resuscitate American Zionism.[9]

LOUIS D. BRANDEIS, THE MAN

Brandeis was a man of some political importance. To be sure it is not easy to determine the extent or nature of his impact on the larger American scene but he did exercise influence on presidents and congress from the days of the first Roosevelt, Theodore, down to the time of the later Roosevelt, Franklin Delano. There are historians who believe that his impress may be detected on Wilson's New Freedom and on Roosevelt's New Deal. Sociopolitical impacts, however, are difficult to demonstrate. It is easier to comment on what he did for Zionism. It was he who really built the Federation of American Zionists and, later, the better structured Zionist Organization of America. Under Brandeis the movement in this country moved forward rapidly; circumstances and the times aided him materially. When in 1917 the British issued the Balfour Declaration Jews all over the world were thrilled. Zionism was now more than a Herzlian dream; indeed there were prospects that a state of sorts could be established. The Justice was helpful in inducing the British to accept the mandate over Palestine and he was eager to make sure that they implemented its provisions. He wanted to rebuild the ancient Jewish homeland. To reach his Zionist goals he worked quietly, effectively, as a *shtadlan*, a lobbyist. This form of approach he had in common with Marshall.

Brandeis gave the movement status in this country; it owes much to him; he made it respectable. When he first took over the Federation of American Zionists it was fortunate if it could muster 12,000 members; in 1919 it had 175,000. In 1918 at war's end, the Zionists could boast that about 185,000 men, women, and youngsters were affiliated with the movement; by 1920 their rolls were reduced to 21,000. During the years that the Justice labored to promote Zionism, Marcus Garvey tried to organize blacks everywhere into the Universal Negro Improvement Association. He wanted to develop racial pride in his people. As a black restorationist he hoped that his followers would return to Africa and there establish a new state where they could foster a culture of their own. Though he was able to rally thousands behind him he was not successful. Brandeis was far more fortunate. As long as he lived—even though he was no longer personally represented in the Zionist administration—he exercised influence through his disciples and his program which his opponents finally adopted. This man helped lay the foundations for the future State of Israel. His achievements are remarkable when it is borne in mind that he was active publicly for only two years, from 1914 to 1916; after that he went on to the Supreme Court becoming the invisible leader until 1921 when his deputies were voted out of office.

BRANDEIS, THE AMERICAN

The previous delineation of Brandeis's role in American Jewry provides intimations of what moved him to action. Since he was one of the country's most distinguished Jews, he merits further characterization. It is well to recall that he was born and raised in Kentucky before the Civil War when states' rights was still an issue; he opposed centralization in government. He rejected monopolistic restrictions when exercised by labor unions; he objected to any abuse of power, especially in the business world. Although he was not a radical he was deemed such because he was opposed to many of the practices which characterized large corporations. "The public be damned," ascribed to William H. Vanderbilt, was a concept anathema to Brandeis. Criticism of big business was heresy in middle-class circles of his day. This is why, when nominated for a seat on the Supreme Court, he evoked a bitter reaction from some of the witnesses who appeared before the Senate Judiciary Committee. Anti-Jewish prejudice was not the prime reason which prompted some individuals to move against him although Brandeis thought it motivated some of his opponents. As early as the 1880's and 1890's economic liberals, Gentiles, notables, were summarily dismissed from academic posts when they voiced so-called radical opinions. Nevertheless Brandeis's nomination was confirmed. Even Schiff was willing to have Brandeis join the Supreme Court although a few years earlier, 1913-1914, the Boston reformer had attacked Schiff's firm, Kuhn, Loeb & Company, for what he deemed to be illegal practices. Brandeis was always the democrat and it was this very democracy to which he subscribed wholeheartedly that unseated him in Cleveland in 1921. He was a liberal, voting for causes and men, not for political parties; he was concerned with society, with human beings and their welfare. For him human rights were as important as property. He was eager that labor be paid a fair wage, that women at work not be overtaxed.

The letter of the law, Brandeis taught, is not sacrosanct; law must accommodate itself to the changes demanded by the times. He wanted a just society, and as a civil libertarian he was willing to work for it. Arabs, as well as Jews in the Palestine of the future, must be treated with equity; he shared this attitude with Magnes, Henrietta Szold, Ahad Ha-Am. There was one important respect in which he differed radically from his social compeers. Most Jews of Germanic origin backed off from Zionism because they were terrified that they might open themselves to the accusation of nurturing dual loyalties. They believed that one could not be loyal to the American republic and to the Jewish commonwealth in Palestine. Many of these protestants had been born in Germany where for generations they had been denied civic equality; here in this transatlantic republic they were granted all rights; this country was very dear to them; they loved America. This loyalty, they felt, could not be shared or divided.

Dual or divided loyalty was a problem that did not disturb Brandeis, certainly not after he became a Zionist. Once he had rejected Jewish-American hyphenates. In his later years Brandeis was quite secure in his own faith, in his dual loyalties, although he was well aware that this was a problem for thousands. He addressed himself to it more than once; he told his Jewish auditors, whether acculturated natives, Central Europeans, or more recently arrived East Europeans that multiple loyalties were objectionable only if they were inconsistent. Though this leader was always to stress the right of the Jew to further his own cultural life in Palestine he and his coworkers in the movement were totally Americanistic. As an individual he was first, last, and at all times oriented to the United States, to its way of life and thought, despite the obvious imperfections of its politicoeconomic system. This complete and utter devotion to the American republic was shared by his opponents in the non-Zionist American Jewish Committee and, what is equally true, by practically all Russian, Polish, and Rumanian Jews here. Most of them prayed three times a day for the restoration of ancient Palestine but the United States was home; they were not in exile; here they were determined to stay. Very few American Jewish immigrants were Diaspora pessimists; they were convinced that Jewry had a future in the lands of Western Europe and America. Brandeis certainly believed that the Jews were safely ensconced in this country, indeed in all lands where they had been accepted as citizens and where they enjoyed all rights and privileges. Here they would survive, of this he had no doubt.

BRANDEIS, THE ZIONIST

Brandeis loved this the land of his birth, yet as a dedicated Zionist he was determined to build Palestine as a new America for his people—the East Europeans primarily; it was to be a better United States. What manner of Zionist was he? Some Jews, opposed to him because of his sociopolitical views, questioned the sincerity of his devotion to the movement. The angry William Howard Taft—resentful that Brandeis was being considered for the Supreme Court—said that he had become a Zionist to advance himself; he had been "metaphorically" recircumcised. Taft attacked him as a "muckraker" a "socialist" a man engaged in "professional crookedness." There can be no question, however, that after his conversion to Zionism in 1912-1913 Brandeis was utterly devoted to the cause. He felt keenly the sufferings of his people in Eastern Europe; decency dictated that as a just man he rally to their defense; it was his conviction that wherever Jews lived they were entitled to civic rights and economic opportunities. Over the years—it took a long generation—he developed a Jewish identity; as a Jew and as a humanitarian he set out to provide a sanctuary in the ancient homeland for all Jews in distress. Brandeis became a strong Jewish nationalist; he had ethnic pride; he gloried in the accomplishments which had distinguished his people since biblical times.

He was strongly opposed to assimilation; it was imperative that Jews survive. Was he influenced by the cultural pluralism of Horace Meyer Kallen? This is questionable; although the two had been in touch with one another since 1913. Brandeis was certainly aware of Kallen's belief that members of different ethnic or religious groups—Jews for instance—could develop their own culture within the confines of a common (American) civilization. It is not easy, however, to determine the extent of Kallen's influence; Brandeis was never a protagonist of the concept that the United States was a symphony of nationalities; the Justice did not want the Jew in this country to manifest a distinct disparate nationality, to emphasize an autonomous culture that would set Jews apart from their fellow Americans. When he stressed Jewish nationality—and he did—one suspects that he had Palestine in mind where the Jew could best develop his intrinsic ancestral values; in that ancient home, where the prophetic teachings were first heard, he hoped that the Jew would accept the challenge once again to make a cultural contribution to human society. When he thought of great Jews he did not cite the religionists Isaiah, Jeremiah, Micah, Maimonides; he recalled the names of Spinoza, Marx, Disraeli, Heine. Three of these four were converts to Christianity; Brandeis was a secularist.

BRANDEIS, PALESTINE: A BETTER AMERICA

In his thinking the Justice effected a synthesis of his Americanism and his Zionism. This country—imperfect to be sure—was his paradigm. For him America, Jewish ideals, and Zionism were to be equated. Both the United States and the Jewish national movement emphasized social justice and democracy; the word democracy was sacrosanct; it was his hope it would come to full bloom in Palestine. This man was preparing to build a new country patterned on his own mind-set. It was to be a land of refuge where a socially and ethically motivated idealism, incarnate in Jewish nationality, would and could flourish. Like Ahad Ha-Am, whom he had read in English, he hoped that the new state would become a center for the Jewish spirit based on Hebraic culture. Like the Reformers, Brandeis preached his version of the Jewish mission. The theistic Reformers posited that God had scattered them in order that they might be a light to the Gentiles; Brandeis taught that from Zion would go forth a law, a secular spiritual doctrine that would illumine the Moslem Near East with western culture and benefit mankind at large. Thus the Justice's vision of a Jewish "republic." He wanted to further and revitalize Jewry culturally. Brandeis knew no Hebrew but he had read extensively in English on Jewish subjects. His notions of Jewish culture were hazy; in all probability he was thinking primarily in Palestinian terms; that country was to be a source of scholarship and social idealism. As a political Zionist he was sui generis. In the Herzlian sense he wanted a Jewish homeland with ample guaranteed borders; he did not equivocate on that score; the Jews were entitled to a legally assured homeland where they could go as of right. However, it was to be a home for those alone who wanted to settle there. If they became a majority and achieved home rule so much the better; the Justice was not interested in the trappings of a sovereign state.

This Jewish Brahmin was thrilled by his newly found identification with Jewry in the form of Zionism. The East European Jew—the typical member of a Zionist organization—was at home in a traditional religiously based restorationism; Brandeis had no such background, yet the austere soberminded lawyer was a historical romantic. (Maybe he was reaching out to Orthodox Uncle Lewis, now long since dead.) Everyone in life has his great adventure if only in fantasy. Zionism was Brandeis's adventure; he was deadly in earnest. For Weizmann, Zionism was a passion almost religious in its intensity; for the Justice, Zionism was a politicoeconomic challenge. This social engineer was going to lay the foundations of a new country and a new nation and would see to it—if he had anything to say—that it would be built and administered efficiently. In his mind's eye he saw himself as a state builder. For him, as with the Russian and Polish American masses, the new Palestine was to be an ideal commonwealth; for the immigrant and Orthodox Jew it was to be a hearth where the fire of religion and observance would burn brightly; for Brandeis it was to be a polity that would nurture an exemplary society that would serve as a laboratory for the social problems that were still harassing the world's democracies.

BRANDEIS: HIS ESSENTIAL NATURE

And the real inner man, the real naked Brandeis? The corporation lawyer who could sit down and write the Zeeland Memorandum, blueprinting a new state that had no like in all the world, was no earthling. True, the German in him was strong, very strong. His slogan—money, discipline, efficiency—is Germanic. He had gone to a German-tinged academy as a youth in Louisville and had attended a German secondary school in Europe. He was meticulous, exact, thorough, by no means an unexacting taskmaster in his own office. He installed a time clock in the Zionist bureaus to the discomfiture of the employees. As a German he was never comfortable with East European Jews; he thought that many cut corners in economic matters. Yet he revolted against German paternalism; he objected to any form of autocracy or despotism; he despised the Nazi Germans. There was a touch of the zealot in him; this made him a poor politician; there was little give-and-take in the man. He had a strong sense of righteousness, of the inexorability of justice. It was this concept which compelled him to work for a Jewish homeland, one where Jews would be denied no opportunity.

Brandeis was consistently courteous, a gentleman who knew and observed the amenities; he was unpretentious but not humble. He lived simply, never owned a car; the fare on his table was plain; he went to court with a bag of sandwiches. However when the *Jewish Frontier*, the Labor Zionist magazine, was established he gave it a check for $25,000 to get started. Though by nature and training thrifty he made very generous gifts to the movement and its institutions. In his will he bequested a very substantial part of his estate "for the upbuilding of Palestine as a national home for the Jewish people." He demonstrated little outward warmth; his soul was not resplendent. A sense of humor? One wonders whether he was the corporation lawyer or the inwardly chuckling father when he sat down with his two young daughters and made them sign a contract to the effect that they would polish his shoes daily in exchange for a weekly allowance of five cents. (In those days one cent would buy at least two pieces of candy.) He was not a man to be loved but many admired him for his qualities of mind, for his moral courage. He was not petty or revengeful. Louis D. Brandeis never went to the synagog to pray yet he was one of America's greatest Jews.[10]

CHAPTER TWENTY-THREE

ZIONISM: CONFRONTATION AND VICTORY

NON-ZIONISM AND ANTI-ZIONISM

At no time prior to 1921 were the Zionists able to muster more than a very small number of America's Jews. By 1921—so it is estimated —there were about 3,500,000 Jews in the United States; the Zionist Organization of America could count on only about 20,000 shekel payers. Why did Jews not join the movement en masse? Most natives and acculturated Germans were indifferent; they were not interested in a Jewish nationalistic organization. America was the only state that appealed to them. The newcomers, the East European masses, Orthodox, believed in an ultimate return to the ancient Land of Promise but in the meantime they were determined to remain here. They were not anti-Zionist. Most of them, however, were too poor to join; many had to slave in a sweatshop for hours to pay even the modest fee demanded of registered Zionists. American Jewish socialists believed that a proletarian revolution would solve all problems; internationalism, not nationalism, was the answer. There was no need for Jews to bury themselves in a distant neglected corner of the Ottoman Empire where they would be subject to Moslem misrule. Since non-Zionism and anti-Zionism were typical of the American Jews all through the first two decades of the twentieth century it is necessary to study in some detail the reasons that influenced them to withhold their support from the politically-minded Zionists.[1]

ORTHODOX AND CONSERVATIVE NON-ZIONISTS AND ANTI-ZIONISTS

Orthodox religionists were Zionists, by definition at least. The majority, however, were inactive, indifferent; they had no intention to push the Holy One Blessed Be He to dispatch His Messiah and effect the return to Palestine. There was a handful of Orthodox rabbinic leaders who opposed Zionism because it set out to force God's hand; they rejected the movement because it was not committed to Orthodoxy. Abram Samuel Isaacs, a native American Orthodox rabbi, had no sympathy for Emma Lazarus's proto-Zionist preachments (1882). As early as 1912 some Torah-true traditionalists had organized themselves in Europe as the Agudat Israel; they had some followers here in the United States; they were hostile to Zionism. Rabbi Shalom (Samuel) Elhanan Jaffe of New York City rejoiced when Herzl died but Moses Simon Sivitz, the dean of Pittsburgh's Orthodox rabbinate, was sympathetic. A substantial number of American talmudic worthies were Zionists. These are the men who had fostered the Mizrachi movement here ever since the first decade of the new century; it had an enthusiastic, devoted following. One of its outstanding leaders was Rabbi Dov Ber Abramowitz of St. Louis. By 1914 there were numerous local branches of this Orthodox Zionist organization; in the next two decades it succeeded in establishing women's auxiliaries and youth groups. The Mizrachi flourished in the United States; ethnic national movements appealed to many everywhere.

Very few Conservative Jews were anti-Zionists. Theologically most Conservatives followed the standard Orthodox Book of Common Prayer, the siddur; hence they were committed to a Return, in God's good time of course. They, too, looked forward to the coming of the Messiah, the precursor of the Restoration. Like the acculturated Abram Samuel Isaacs, Sabato Morais, the minister at Philadelphia's Mikveh Israel, was opposed to the new nationalism of Emma Lazarus. You cannot renationalize the Jew, Morais insisted; Palestine could only hope to become a puny commonwealth in a pauperized land. A new Jewish state is but an antiquated fantasy. Morais was the principal of the faculty at the Jewish Theological Seminary; Schechter his successor also shied away from Zionism for years. Cyrus Adler, who succeeded Schechter as president of the seminary, remained a consistent anti-Zionist all his life. Despite their essential Orthodoxy, Isaacs, Morais, and Adler believed that the return to Palestine was a flight from the world of modernity.[2]

THE ATTITUDE OF POLITICAL LEFT-WINGERS TO ZIONISM

Most Jewish socialists and anarchists were opposed to Zionism because it was nationalist and tolerated religion; Marxists and other radicals were anti-religious and internationalist. When in 1917 the English issued the Balfour Declaration organized American labor—not the Jewish unions— welcomed the opportunity it afforded Jews to build a homeland of their own. Anti-British Irish and Catholic labor leaders here in the United States, mindful that England denied the Irish sovereignty in their homeland, rejoiced that the Jews were to have a state of their own. Indeed, a pro-Zionist resolution was passed in 1917 in Buffalo at a trade union conference; some Jewish Marxists voted against it. Jewish unions, like most anti-Zionists were always ready to help the Palestine colonists; however, they were at first adamant in their opposition to a national state. The American Federation of Labor, steadfast in favoring Zionism, remained equally steadfast in closing America's doors to immigrants from Eastern Europe. What many of the Jewish socialists, secularists, anti-Zionists, never seemed to realize was that they themselves were nationalist by virtue of the fact that they herded together as Jews, spoke Yiddish, and came together in ethnic organizations. As early as 1900 quite a number of these Marxists made a bold leap and synthesized Zionism and socialism. These were Zion's Workers, the Poale Zion. They cultivated Jewish separation, secularism, Yiddish culture. After the Balfour Declaration some of the anti-Zionists in the Workmen's Circle welcomed the establishment of a national home in Palestine; Abraham Cahan, editor of the *Forward*, softened his anti-Zionism early in the 1930's; Jews had to have a home; Palestine was one of the few lands which would admit Jews fleeing from Germany.[3]

THE ORIGINS OF ANTI-ZIONISM

As a rule the articulate demonstrative anti-Zionists were acculturated Jews, natives, "Germans," Reform Jewish religionists, and East European politicoeconomic leftists. What were the sources of this opposition to a Jewish national homeland? As pointed out above the socialists leaned on Karl Marx; they were internationalists and, like him, disdainful of all forms of revealed religion. However, the anti-Zionism that was tied up with the problem of dual loyalties goes back to the French Revolution and Napoleon. When Jews in France were granted citizenship they were expected to foreswear all loyalties to Jewry as a people (1791). The slogan of that day was: "To the Jews as human beings, everything; to Jews as a nation, nothing" (1789). In the early 1840's the German Reform Rabbi Samuel Holdheim declared that Jews who loved their German fatherland must rid themselves of all Jewish national concepts. Meeting a few years later in Frankfurt on the Main, some left-wing ministers voted for the elimination of all prayers for the restoration of the Jewish state. Four years before the Frankfurt radicals rejected the return to the land of their fathers, Rabbi Gustavus Poznanski of Charleston had dedicated the new Reformist synagog with the magniloquent phrase: "This city our *Jerusalem*, this happy land our *Palestine*" (1841). In 1845, the very year that the radical German religionists met at Frankfort, Max Sutro, the rabbi of Congregation Har Sinai in Baltimore, questioned whether Jews should assemble in prayer on the Ninth of Ab, the anniversary of the fall of the Temple. To do so might question their loyalty to the American homeland.

It was sometime in the 1860's that Jacob Clavius Levy, one of South Carolina's most cultured Jews, put the finishing touches to a manuscript which he called "Vindiciae Judaeorum" (Claims of the Jews), obviously an apologia. It was never published. Palestine, he wrote, may ultimately be restored by one of the great powers and turned over to the Jews. If this should come to pass it would be deplorable; the new state would not survive. Jews are divided in their views; there would be no political and religious freedom; constitutional checks would not be countenanced. An Oriental or North African Jew would have nothing in common with a cultured European. There is no evidence that Levy knew of the writings of Kalischer and Moritz Hess who were then publishing their brochures on the rebirth of a Palestinian commonwealth.

Rabbi David Einhorn of Baltimore and Philadelphia was fully aware of the new nationalist aspirations that were then being voiced in Europe. When he and other Reform rabbis met nationally for the first time in Philadelphia, in 1869, they denounced and rejected the hopes for a Palestine reborn. They argued that, in a way, the dispersal of the Jews after the fall of Jerusalem was a blessing; through liberal Judaism Gentiles could be led to the true knowledge of God. Jews do not want to be separated from the world's nations. Thus the Mission of Israel was preached in the United States by these early religious liberals. Edward Benjamin Morris ("Alphabet") Browne, rabbi of Atlanta in the 1870's and 1880's, said that even if Jews were offered Palestine they would not go back. A resolution proposed at a Union of American Hebrew Congregations convention condemning colonization in Palestine failed to pass in 1883 but, two years later, the Reform rabbis meeting in Pittsburgh declared categorically that the Jews were no longer a nation; they had no desire to return to the land of their fathers. In answer to this abrupt departure from tradition, the Union of Orthodox Jewish Congregations of America, meeting in solemn assembly in New York in 1898, said that the Restoration was a legitimate aspiration and in no sense in conflict with political loyalties.[4]

As the 1890's dawned Jewish nationalism increased in all lands due to Russian persecutions and expulsions, the rise of modern nationalisms in Europe, and the activities of the Lovers of Zion here in the United States. At the same time the non- and anti-Zionists made their presence felt. Paul Haupt suggested settling Jews in Mesopotamia; Cyrus Adler and some of his friends were willing to colonize Jewish refugees there; they feared the rise of a Jewish state in Palestine; that land was holy to Christians; Jews wanted no conflict with them. With few, very few exceptions American Anglo-Jewish papers were strongly anti-Zionist; a Detroit Jewish weekly said that turning to Palestine was arch-treason to the best government on earth. Those Jews who had no sympathy for Herzlian nationalism were convinced that it was only a matter of time before all Jews everywhere would be emancipated; there was no need for a separate state for the Chosen People. Like the socialists many American Jews hoped that the Russian revolution of 1917 would emancipate the Jewish millions there and preclude the necessity of a Palestinian homeland to shelter refugees. Going back to Jerusalem was a return to the ghetto.

Prior to his death in 1900 Isaac M. Wise of Cincinnati exercised a great deal of influence on Jews in the Midwest through his paper the *American Israelite*. He was hostile to political Zionism. Yet at the same time he always responded to the plight of his fellow Jews in the Holy Land. Free America was always open to émigrés; there was no need for a separatist state. Sooner or later all Jews deprived of civic rights would be emancipated. In antebellum days when Wise's American patriotism glowed ardently he said that before the end of the century the essence of Judaism would become the religion of America's Gentile intelligentsia. In his moments of prejudice he hoped that the disfranchised Russians and Poles would choose Palestine rather than the United States; he was always ready to divert the uncouth newcomers to their ancestral homeland. Colonization there met with his approval till the 1890's when the thought that the new settlements might become the core of a Jewish state alarmed him.

Why was this man so disturbed by the thought of a Jewish homeland? He was born in 1819, the very year that the Germans rioted and attacked their Jewish fellow citizens. Wise himself was a Hapsburg refugee fleeing from a land of pettiness and bigotry. Here in the United States he gradually became a notable citizen. He was pathetically eager to demonstrate his loyalty; Zionism, the movement to create a Jewish commonwealth in Palestine, threatened him. It was this fear that impelled him to make intemperate remarks in 1897 when Herzl summoned World Jewry to meet in Basel. American Judaism, Wise believed, was now being compromised in the eyes of the public; the new proposal was "a prostitution of Israel's holy cause." Who wants a "ridiculous miniature state in dried up Palestine" when he has the choice of America, blueprinted by Moses? Despite his opposition to a modern Jewish commonwealth in the Holy Land Wise did not censure his students or professors who defended the new movement in the College student paper, the *H.U.C. Journal*. Caspar Levias, one of his faculty, was sympathetic to the new Jewish nationalism; his apologies for the movement were published in the *H.U.C. Journal* and in the year book of the Central Conference of American Rabbis. When Zevi Hirsch Masliansky, the Jewish nationalist propagandist, was in Cincinnati Wise invited him to address the students in chapel. Masliansky spoke in Hebrew; Professor Deutsch, a non-Zionist, also employed the Sacred Tongue when he introduced the famous Orthodox preacher.[5]

Kaufmann Kohler, who succeeded Wise, was an anti-Zionist. He had belabored the nationalists as early as 1895 in a patriotic Fourth of July address; the attack then was directed against the pre-Herzlian Lovers of Zion. The new president of the Hebrew Union College believed in the peoplehood of Jewry but as a religionist he objected vigorously to Zionist secularism. America is the land of promise, of a new human race. In 1907 he ran into trouble, serious trouble, with three of his faculty. Two years earlier, in 1905, he had let Professor Caspar Levias go. Zionism was not the issue; Levias was no "trouble maker"; though learned he was apparently an incompetent teacher. At all events Kohler and the arch-opponent of Zionism, David Philipson, both tried to secure other employment for him. In 1907 three professors—Max Schloessinger, Max Margolis, and Henry Malter—resigned. Zionism was an issue here; for the Board of Governors who let them leave Zionism was, it would seem, the paramount issue. But there were other reasons for the bitter conflict between Kohler and the three instructors. Malter wanted more money and, so it would seem, hoped that his threat to leave would bring the Board to terms.

All three maintained that there was no *Lehrfreiheit*, freedom to speak one's mind at the College. This was true. Margolis was forbidden to teach the prophets whom he interpreted as nationalists. (After the 1905 pogroms in Russia nationalism appealed to many Jews, especially those who hailed from Eastern Europe.) Quite a number of the alumni—who had little influence at this time—agreed that Kohler was intolerant in some of his views. The problem this year—probably the real reason for this cause célèbre—was that the three professors were not loyal to the president. There is reason to suspect that they wanted him out hoping to introduce a new spirit into the school, probably a more traditional one. This was a power struggle exacerbated by the fact that Kohler, now in his middle sixties, was stubborn, inept, intolerant. He had no charisma. Margolis was ambitious. In 1903 he had written a long position paper—really a monograph—*The Theological Aspect of Reformed Judaism*, hoping that he would be recognized as a Reform Jewish leader; he had not always been a Zionist. That Zionism was not the only issue in this affair is documented by the fact that the very year the three remonstrants left Kohler hired David Neumark to teach; he was a Zionist, a noted protagonist of modern Hebrew.

The president's opposition to Zionism did not abate with the passing of time. The year 1915 was a bad year for the intractable old man. Kohler refused to let Professor Horace M. Kallen talk to the students in the College chapel. Kohler resented the fact that this philosopher was both a Zionist and an atheist. Pushed by Rabbi Max Heller, a Zionist, the Board, however, said that students could preach on Zionism at the regular Sabbath service, and when student James Heller was forbidden to speak in chapel on a nationalist theme, Papa Max intervened and Kohler was compelled to permit the brilliant youngster to mount the pulpit. That same year the local Hebrew-speaking literary society gave Neumark a testimonial dinner honoring him for his publications in the field of Jewish philosophy and theology. He wrote in Hebrew, German, and English. At the banquet hall an anti-Zionist present discovered a small paper Zionist flag; he insisted on its removal. Kohler, who was present, had prepared an attack on Zionism because he knew the literary society were honoring Neumark as a Zionist. The sponsors of the banquet appealed to a member of the Board of Governors who then forbade Kohler to read his paper; the College president in turn told his audience that he was not permitted to speak freely.[6]

THE DIEHARDS

Among those present at the banquet in honor of David Neumark was a Hebrew Union College board member, David Philipson. This rabbi of the prestigious Rockdale Temple was one of the country's most articulate anti-Zionists. He enjoyed his reputation as a man who made no concessions to the political Zionists; his attacks on the movement kept this Midwesterner in the national limelight. There were a number of these irreconcilables; for the most part they were notable Americans. Rabbi Jacob Voorsanger of San Francisco, the Pacific Coast's most distinguished Jewish clergyman, denounced Zionism as an Oriental aberration, a crime; Rabbi Emil G. Hirsch of Temple Sinai in Chicago, described New York's Gottheils, Zionists, as miserable swindlers. Simon Wolf, still American Jewry's outstanding lobbyist, was more temperate in his language. He told the Industrial Commission in 1901 that American Jews were not enthusiastic about the proposed new Jewish state but that it would well serve as a refuge for Jews from Russia, Rumania, and Austria. The former attorney general for the state of New York, Simon W. Rosendale, voiced his objection to any secular Hebrew organization; Adolph S. Ochs of the *New York Times* had no interest in a Jewish commonwealth but he did attend a luncheon in honor of the Zionist Nahum Sokolow and he did congratulate Brandeis on his seventy-fifth birthday. In this congratulatory note he was careful to avoid any mention of the Justice's Zionist activities. Though Henry Morgenthau, Sr., was always helpful to Palestine Jews he decried Jewish nationalism. He wrote a strong protest against the implications of the Balfour Declaration. Ochs, his friend, published it in *The Times*. Political Zionism, said the former ambassador to Turkey, would turn the Jews back a thousand years.

After Henrietta Szold addressed the Washington section of the Council of Jewish Women on her work in Palestine, Florence Kahn, wife of a congressman and later a member of Congress, rose and told the audience that America was her Zion and Washington her home. Samuel Schulman, the New York rabbi, was quick to admit that the pro-Palestine movement strengthened Jewish ethnic consciousness but it made the Jew a "Gentile," a nation, a goy, like all non-Jewish peoples. When Schulman, one of the country's most brilliant Jewish clergymen, voiced his objection to the new nationalism in the synagog, Nathan Straus, the philanthropist, walked out; he was a committed Zionist. With the exception of Schulman all these opponents of the movement were "Germans" but there were numerous East Europeans, left-wingers, who also rejected Jewish nationalism summarily. Morris R. Cohen, the philosopher, denounced it as tribalism, racism; it is an evasion not an answer; it revived the past but ignored the present. Like Schulman, a fellow East European, he admitted Zionism gave the Jew a sense of self-respect and encouraged him to nurture his traditional values. But a new country? Liberia had done nothing for the Negroes in the United States; Palestinianism is Balkanization. Cohen survived to read of the horrors of the Holocaust in the 1940's. He then hoped that the Jewish state in the making, nonsectarian, would accord full rights to all including Moslems and atheists.[7]

NOTABLE NON-ZIONISTS

In all probability the best known non-Zionist in all American Jewry was Jacob H. Schiff. He was very rich, generous, revered, a committed Jew. As far back as 1898 Schiff recognized that Palestine might well serve as a home for Jews leaving inhospitable Russia and Rumania; American Jews, enjoying all rights and immunities, would certainly not want to return to the home of their ancestors. Schiff was opposed to the idea of a Jewish national state as an end in itself. In 1907 he made a categorical statement: a political Zionist cannot be a true American. Reared as an Orthodox Jew, Schiff never forgot that he was a religionist; Zionists, officially, were not committed to Judaism. This Wall Street banker was fully aware, however, that as nationalists Zionists resisted assimilation. The Hebrew language strengthened Jewish identity. This pleased him. The Zionist emphasis on the Hebrew language tied them to the millions who prayed daily swaying over their Hebrew language prayer book. Schiff was happy to support the proposed new technical school in Haifa; later he gave generously to the university then in the making. In his gifts to the ancient home of his ancestors he was joined by Julius Rosenwald. Even Bernard Baruch—a marginal Jew—was helpful; his gift of $10,000 went directly to the Zionist Organization of America. By 1917 when it was obvious that the

English would soon rule Palestine as the mandatory power, Schiff moved closer to the nationalists. It was imperative that something be done to help the Jews dying by the thousands in Poland and Russia. Schiff was ready to come to the aid of a Palestine which would serve as a haven and as a cultural center for those Jews who had no future among the Slavs. A Jewish state was not an imperative in Palestine but if Jews were ever to become a majority in the land there was always the possibility that they would establish a government of their own. That eventuality was of no immediate concern. He shared the cultural Zionist views of men like Magnes, Schechter, Friedlaender but, unlike them, he joined no Zionist party.

It may well be that the real leader of American Jewry in the first three decades of the twentieth century was not Schiff, the millionaire banker, but Louis Marshall, the corporation lawyer. He and Schiff had much in common. Both were firmly anchored in the religious traditions in which they had been nurtured. Both loved America but this love never diminished their concept of *Kelal Yisrael*, their embrace of World Jewry, their identification with all Jews, particularly those in distress. Marshall was never an anti-Zionist; he always remained a non-Zionist interested in succoring fellow Jews. As early as 1907 he had begun to realize the ethnic and cultural significance of the movement. In those early days he already knew that a new haven would have to be found for European Jews in flight; it was only a matter of years before the United States would no longer serve as the asylum for the world's poor and oppressed. These are some of the reasons that moved him to help Palestine. His conviction that American Jewry would have to aid that country financially he shared with others, with Nathan and Oscar Straus, Julius Rosenwald, Schiff. This is why he also supported the Palestine agricultural experimental station of Aaron Aaronsohn and the proposed Haifa technical school. Again, like Schiff, Marshall had no interest in developing an independent Jewish state but he enjoyed his status as a leader and knew that if he wanted to remain on top he would have to come to terms with America's East European immigrant masses; it was obvious that they would ultimately dominate this country's Jewry. The victory of the American Jewish Congress movement, 1916-1918, was not lost on him. In the early 1920's farsighted Marshall moved to effect a working arrangement of the non-Zionists with the World Zionist Organization. By joining the Zionist Jewish Agency he and his wealthy friends hoped so to build Mandate Palestine that it would be able to house large numbers of impoverished East European immigrants. The virulent anti-Semitism here in the United States during the 1920's may have prompted him to push steadily for help to Palestine Jewry.[8]

THE ANTI-ZIONISM OF NATIONAL REFORM ORGANIZATIONS
AND INSTITUTIONS

The three basic Reform Jewish institutions, the Union of American Hebrew Congregations, the Hebrew Union College, and the Central Conference of American Rabbis had set their faces resolutely against any form of an independent Jewish state. The repudiation of a Jewish nationality at the 1885 Pittsburgh rabbinical conference may well have been an answer to the Lovers of Zion who were busy recruiting followers. As early as 1890 the first convention of the Central Conference of American Rabbis took note of all preceding Reform Jewish pronouncements (1807-1885) in Europe and in the United States, particularly those affirming that liberal Jews would tolerate but one civic loyalty; this was a summary rejection of any proposed new Jewish state. A resolution at this conference to the effect that there was no "Jewish nation" produced a lively debate; with the members about equally divided the question was laid on the table for the time being. From the earliest days down into the 1920's the Reform Jewish rabbinical conference persisted in rejecting political Zionism; at times the attacks were vitriolic. In consonance with the Central Conference of American Rabbis the Hebrew Union College summarily rejected the national hopes of the Zionists. The Union of American Hebrew Congregations also made it abundantly clear that "America is our Zion" (1898). Zionism, the angry anti-Zionists said, only confirms what our enemies say: We are foreigners. We cannot retreat to Palestine; the whole world is our homeland; we have a message for it; we are the bearers of good tidings. Let it not be forgotten, said one Reform Jew, that the best of Judaism came out of the Diaspora. The numerous anti-Zionist resolutions and attacks of the three basic Reform institutions prove that these men were running scared. Many of them, born in Central Europe, still remembered the disabilities under which they had labored abroad; they wished to prove they were 125 percent loyal Americans. Yet, let this caveat be uttered; they rarely objected to colonization in Palestine; the Jews there had to be succored. It is also well to recall that in the very midst of these tirades Maximilian Heller of New Orleans, an ardent Zionist, was elected vice president and later president of the Central Conference, 1907-1911.[9]

The formal reasons cited by non- and anti-Zionists for their opposition were ideological. The socialists were determined to save the world and Jewry by abolishing nationalisms; thus they were opposed to Zionism. Cutting across Jewish ethnic lines the Marxist proletarians joined hands with the bourgeois American Jewish Committee which also rejected Zionism; the latter tolerated but one nationalism, Americanism. The congruence of these two disparate groups has been referred to as the "alliance between Hester Street and Wall Street." The Reformers leaned heavily on the "mission" theory; they were internationalists, universalists theologically, American patriots politically. The mission theory? The scattering of the Jews was no curse but a blessing in disguise; religious liberals made a virtue of catastrophe. Jews have a religious mission, a message to bring to the world: justice, peace, spirituality. "And ye shall be unto me a kingdom of priests and a holy nation." (Ex.19:6). Like the Christians the Jews asserted that they were the ones who would usher in the millennium—sans Christ, of course. And until this Jewish messianic day dawned Jews must keep themselves separate and not intermarry.

What the Reform leaders, like the Jewish labor leaders, did not realize or admit was that this very separatism from the Gentile world was in itself a form of ethnicism, Jewish nationalism. Some anti-Zionists looked askance at the Jewish nationalists because, formally, they were secularists, neutrals where Judaism was concerned. One wonders to what extent Reform Jews took the mission theory seriously. It may well have been a rationale for rejecting Zionism politically. Reform Jews, with very few exceptions, wanted nothing to do with a Jewish state; a few would certainly have gone along with the German Ludwig Geiger who intimated that Zionists ought to be deprived of their German citizenship. Many American anti-Zionists were perplexed. How can these Russian refugees, fleeing from pogroms, even think of Zionism in a free America and seek a Jewish homeland elsewhere? This is implicit disloyalty to the best of all possible lands, America. This was illogical, infuriating. The Jewish Chautauqua in a syllabus proposed a debate on the subject: "Can Zionism Be Legitimately Criticized as un-American?" When Henrietta Szold came to St. Paul in 1913 the trustees of the temple refused to allow her to talk on Zionism.[10]

ANTI-ZIONISTS, 1917-1948

Most American Jews were either non-Zionists or anti-Zionists till the 1917 Balfour Declaration. After that, for reasons to be described below, they began to turn slowly toward Zionism, the need for a national Jewish home in Palestine. There was always a small group—including some very distinguished men—which was never reconciled to the concept of Jewish nationality. These intransigents had the moral support of Christian missionaries and a number of bureaucrats in the State Department. One suspects that some of the important functionaries in the foreign service were moved as much by anti-Jewish prejudice as they were by concern for the government which they served. These civil servants could point out— quite correctly—that the Moslems were Palestine's majority people as late as 1946. As oil in the Moslem lands became an important factor in developing American industry, the concern for Arab sensitivities was weighed against America's Jewish votes. Tension in the Holy Land was ever present. Most Moslems despised Jews; American Jewry was determined to protect the colonies in Palestine. In 1919 the handful of anti-Zionist notables continued to carry on a vigorous battle to convince President Wilson and the Peace Conference not to further the nationalist goals of the Zionists. The campaign failed; Wilson gave these men no encouragement.

These elite irreconcilables were important as individuals but they were not representative; they had no organized mass following; they were ignored despite an occasional splash in the *New York Times*. But even these critics never objected to the work being done in Palestine; they approved of it and were willing to support the farmers and planters. Indeed the larger part of the American funds that flowed into that country came from non-Zionists. These anti-state petitioners wanted the country to receive Jewish refugees; they argued however that the land was sacred to Moslems and Christians; trouble was inevitable if a Jewish commonwealth was established. The ideal state in Palestine, they said, would be a government patterned after European and American democracies where all inhabitants, regardless of religion, would enjoy equal rights. A dwindling number of opponents still carried on the battle in 1922 as the House Foreign Affairs Committee met to discuss the Hamilton Fish resolution approving of the Balfour Declaration; once more the dissenters met with defeat.[11]

Up until 1917, the year of the Balfour Declaration, most Jews in this country evinced little interest in the Zionist movement. England's declaration profoundly influenced American Jewry; Wilson finally voiced his approval of the proposed Jewish homeland. In 1920 the Allied Powers at San Remo had given the mandate over Palestine to England; in 1922 the Mandate and the Balfour Declaration were approved by the United States Congress and the League of Nations. If Zionism was kosher for the Gentiles, it was certainly kosher for Jews. By the 1920's the East European immigrants and their children were rising to power in American Jewry; many of them were looking forward to the ultimate rise of a Jewish state in the ancient homeland. In 1922 Stephen S. Wise opened his new Zionist oriented rabbinical seminary; in 1923 Emanuel Gamoran, an ardent Lover of Zion, was put in charge of the educational work of the Reform movement. The following year the ports of the United States were closed, tightly, against Jews; Palestine was one of the few lands to which they could immigrate. By 1933, when the Nazis had come to power in Germany, European Jewry was desperate; it needed a haven. Ten years later millions of Jews were exterminated by the Germans. There had to be one country to which the survivors could turn as of right. Palestine was their only hope. Then in 1948 the State of Israel was established. Here in America, from 1917 to 1948 there was a gradual transition from anti-Zionism and non-Zionism to enthusiastic acceptance of the State of Israel. The new Jewish settlements had already saved the lives of thousands. No notable anti-Zionist ever reproached American Jewry for the monies sent to the colonies. By 1918 Jewish labor leaders, socialists, non-religionists, began issuing statements in support of the new Jewish homeland. With certain exceptions most American Jews were sympathetic to Zionism in the 1930's; Nazi Germany had converted them. When in 1939 the British issued the Malcolm MacDonald White Paper which, in effect, would close Palestine to Jews, American Jewry was outraged for this was at a time when the German Jews were being crushed.

The gradual shift from anti-Zionism and non-Zionism to pro-Zionism can be documented in the history of the American Jewish Committee, one of the country's most prestigious and efficient Jewish organizations. As early as 1910 these New Yorkers were eager to work with Aaron Aaronsohn in his efforts to modernize agriculture in Palestine. In April of 1918 the Committee came out with a formal statement in which it interpreted the Balfour Declaration to mean that Palestine was to serve as a haven and as a cultural center. This somewhat sympathetic pronouncement may reflect the influence of individual Zionists, such as Julian Mack and Nathan Straus, who were high in the councils of the Committee. Marshall and his associates were not alarmed by the Balfour Declaration. They believed, correctly, that it did not in effect establish a Jewish state; they were of the opinion that it was a government paper, promising little; it was, in part, a British device to protect the highway to India. Marshall made clear to anti-Zionist intransigents that it was a war measure. To oppose it was an act of disloyalty. In June 1921, less than a month after the passage of the immigrant quota act, Marshall wrote a friend that Palestine had to be kept open to shelter refugees from the lands of oppression; America was no longer prepared to offer Jews a home. And when in 1920 and 1922 the Allied Powers and the United States Congress endorsed the Balfour Declaration and the Palestine Mandate, the Committee professed its readiness to go along with the Jewish nationalists. The Committee was now a non-Zionist organization; it was no longer anti-Zionist.[12]

THE UNION OF AMERICAN HEBREW CONGREGATIONS, THE CENTRAL CONFERENCE OF AMERICAN RABBIS, AND THE ZIONISTS

Marshall, the head of the Committee, was politically astute; he was a "good" Jew and knew when to stoop in order to conquer. The Union of

American Hebrew Congregations (UAHC), based in Cincinnati, was cautious, conservative, slow to change. In 1919, long after the Balfour Declaration, the UAHC reaffirmed its 1898 hostile attitude to Zionism; "we are Jews in religion and Americans in nationality." (The Union leaders loved that phrase.) Jews had a mission to the world. Suffering Jews need a homeland? Let us work for civic equality in all lands. A year later the Board of the Hebrew Union College declared unequivocally, Palestine is not our national home. In 1923 non-Zionist forces in the UAHC offered a resolution praising the pro-Zionist action taken at San Remo and in the American Congress. The resolution was defeated; the Union leaders said that they were looking forward to a religious revival, not political controversy. By the mid-1930's—about a decade after the closing of the gates to Ellis Island—the UAHC leaders were only too well aware that Germany was persecuting Jews vindictively. German Jews desperately needed a home; Palestine could become a spiritual and cultural center; it could serve as a Jewish homeland (1937). From that time on the UAHC looked kindly on the Zionists; it had no choice. And when the pro-Zionist American Jewish Conference met in 1943 the UAHC worked with it even though it was not yet ready officially to sanction a Jewish state; it wanted a democratic republic, American style, where all inhabitants and religions were placed on the same plane of equality. In 1944 it adopted a neutral stance where Zionism was concerned; in 1948, after the Holocaust, again it had no choice but to go along with the new State of Israel which was prepared to shelter hundreds of thousands of survivors who needed a home.[13]

The Central Conference of American Rabbis (CCAR), the international association of rabbis who served Reform congregations, had also been ready to aid the Palestine colonies long before the Balfour Declaration. However, it refused to join the American Jewish Congress and constantly denounced Jewish nationalism. These rabbis expressed the hope, however, that Palestine would develop as a center where the spiritual genius of the Jew would find expression. They welcomed the English Mandate but, like the Union, wanted no Jewish state; Palestine must be nonsectarian. The racist 1924 immigration act seems to have influenced their thinking. By that year a bipartisan Jewish Agency for Palestine was in the making; non-Zionists were to be co-opted in order to rehabilitate the land. The CCAR was willing to go alone with this proposed philanthropic agency. Palestine, the rabbis realized, might well serve as a beacon of hope to civically disabled Jews. The year 1932 was, in a sense, a watershed. "Ha-Tikvah" the Zionist national anthem was included in a Reform hymnal; a year later the Nazis ruled Germany and the Zionists in the Central Conference of American Rabbis staged a "palace revolution" against the non-Zionist establishment. From that day on Zionists have dominated this Reform rabbinical assembly. In 1935 the CCAR formally renounced its traditional anti-Zionist position by passing a neutrality resolution; each rabbi was encouraged to determine his own stance toward a Jewish state. Nationalism and universalism can be reconciled.

Two years later the rabbis met at Columbus, Ohio, and modified the 1885 Pittsburgh Platform; they were now willing to aid in the building of a Jewish homeland. (This was the very year, 1937, that the Union of American Hebrew Congregations expressed its sympathy for Zionist aims. The persecutions of the Jews in Germany could not be ignored; there had to be a way out.) In 1940 the revised *Union Prayer Book* offered an optional Zionist service; the mission idea and cultural rebirth were offered to a restored Zion; it was low-key nationalism. In the 1940's the Reform rabbis moved still closer to the Zionists. International assemblies meeting at Évian-les-Bains (1938) and in the Bermudas (1943) did precious little to provide an asylum for Europe's Jewish refugees. The situation of the Jews in Germany was becoming increasingly desperate. Throughout the early 1940's the Central Conference pleaded in vain with Great Britain to open wide the gates of Palestine to Jews in flight. The British, however, refused to modify substantially the 1939 White Paper.

In 1942, during World War II, the CCAR placed its stamp of approval on a Palestine Jewish army fighting under its own banner. It was at this time that the Zionists meeting in New York's Biltmore Hotel came out for a Jewish commonwealth, presumably a sovereign state. A very vigorous, articulate, and determined minority among the rabbis wanted no Zionist army, no Jewish state. These were the men who emphasized the purely religious nature of Reform. They resented the imputation of the Zionists that Palestine was the prime Jewish center; they believed that Jews had a future in lands of culture; these men were Diaspora optimists. Above all they resented what they believed was the politicization of the Conference; the Zionists were riding high. Many of these anti-Zionist rabbis knew that their laymen back home were not yet ready to embrace the Zionist goals of the CCAR leaders. It was these rabbinical dissidents who in 1942-43 formed the American Council for Judaism; they set out to emphasize religion, not the Restoration. Dozens of rabbis joined the new movement. They were sympathetic to the hope for a culturally oriented reconstituted Palestine but insisted that it be a modern liberal democratic state that was prepared to enfranchise all inhabitants. Church and State were to be separate. This demand would certainly create problems for the Zionists; the Moslems still far outnumbered the Jews. The danger of a split CCAR was ultimately resolved, for the American Council for Judaism was taken over by laymen. Intransigently anti-Zionists, they evinced little interest in Judaism and Jewish culture; as a consequence most of the rabbis, disillusioned, dropped out of the organization. The American Council for Judaism continued to flourish for a few years but without rabbinic support it gradually withered; by the late twentieth century it could muster but few followers.

One of the outstanding congregations in Texas which sympathized with the aspirations of the American Council was Beth Israel of Houston. In 1943 the board members published their Basic Principles. Proudly announcing that they proposed to offer women religious equality, that they were Jewish religionists of the Caucasian race—"our flag is the Stars and Stripes"—they pledged themselves to help the Palestine settlements spiritually, culturally, financially. But they were opposed to the establishment of a Jewish commonwealth. Following in their footsteps, apparently, Baton Rouge's B'nai Israel dispatched a general epistle to the Jews of America in which its members reaffirmed their devotion to the 1885 anti-national Pittsburgh Platform: "we are Americans of the Jewish faith." The German Holocaust murderers succeeded effectively in undermining the American Council for Judaism. After the Final Solution any American Jew who rejected Israel, the new state, found himself outside the pale of acceptance; he had violated the new sacrosanct consensus; he was no longer a "good" Jew. By 1948 there were exceedingly few anti-Zionists in the United States. In 1977, the Union of American Hebrew Congregations and the Central Conference of American Rabbis brought to birth the Association of Reform Zionists of America (ARZA); Reform anti-Zionism had finally gone the way of all flesh.[14]

SUMMARY: THE WHY OF ZIONISM IN THE UNITED STATES

In the first decades of the twentieth century most Jews in the United States were concerned for their families and their kinsmen in Eastern Europe; restoring ancient Israel was not primary. Zionism was not a mass movement; compared to the United States, Palestine offered very little; in effect, America was Zion. Prior to the 1920's, the United States was open to all; here in this country there was equality, freedom, opportunity; there was no need for Palestine. Even affiliated Zionists were not dedicated to aliyah, to immigration to Palestine; down to the present day the number of those who have left America for the Holy Land has remained minuscule. Hadassah, America's Zionist organization for women, does not even exact a pledge from its members that they will support the Basel program. The ultimate goal of Hadassah has always been to bring good medicine and hygiene to Palestine. America's Zionists, non-Zionists, and anti-Zionists had much in common; they were determined to remain in this country; Zion was to be a haven for others, for oppressed Jews. Until the 1940's Zionism was essentially a philanthropic, not a political movement.

The proto-Zionists, Mordecai M. Noah, and Emma Lazarus, and later Henrietta Szold concurred; America, first and last, was their home. Zionists and non-Zionists alike were in agreement that Palestine and America can become great Jewish cultural centers. Nearly all American Jews—Zionists too—were Diaspora optimists; Jews, Judaism can survive in all Western lands where democracy prevails.

Because of their devotion to World Jewry rather than to one community, specifically the Palestinian, American Jews responded primarily to World Jewish crises; thus there were at the most but 12,000 registered Zionists in the United States when the First World War erupted (1914). After the Balfour Declaration into the 1920's, when war and disaster faced the Jews in Europe's East, the number of shekel payers shot upward; it was said that there were over 170,000 cardholders, but when the future of Palestine as a haven was assured at San Remo membership declined precipitously. In the 1930's American Jews once more turned to Zionism; the American ports were open to but few immigrants; the Germans had begun to destroy Europe's Jews; membership in the Zionist organization rose to over 150,000. Though not affiliated with Zionism, most East European immigrant Jews in this country were Zionistic; they prayed daily for the restoration of the ancient commonwealth. Most of them were nationalists. Rejecting Pan-Slavism—and being rejected by their host nations—these East European émigrés had intensified their traditional Jewish ethnicism. Ever since talmudic times Jews were always taught that "every Jew is responsible for his fellow Jew" (Sanhedrin, 27b). Although their political loyalties were totally American, Orthodox American synagoggoers always supported the Jews in Palestine and would continue to do so. Jews in that land practiced a pure Judaism; their prayers on our behalf would guarantee us eternal bliss in the world to come!

If the United States is Zion, then why Zionism? Despite all that America offered, despite the fact that for the Jewish immigrant it was the best of all lands, America was not the fulfillment of the messianic dream. The Russian newcomers struggled and suffered as peddlers, sweatshop workers, strikers, petty shopkeepers, members of the cockroach bourgeoisie. The reality of anti-Semitism in all lands, including the United States, stimulated interest in Palestine as a homeland. Eastern Europe's violence and disabilities, France's Dreyfus Affair, shocked World Jewry and turned many to Zionism; there had to be one place in the world where anti-Semitism was absent; most Jews agreed that as Jews they would never be completely accepted anywhere in the world. Influenced by Russian traditions many of the newcomers here were agricultural romantics; the return to the soil is a spiritual experience; America's acculturated non-Zionists, generous to the Palestinians, were insistent that they follow the plough. These American philanthropists were physiocratic; land is the source of all wealth and well-being, so they said. For the East European Jew here in the United States Palestine came to symbolize an ideal, a utopia that touched on the mythical. Palestine was to be a new and better America. There is always the threat of assimilation in the Diaspora; in a Jewish Palestine there can be no assimilation, no evanescence as Jews. There, if nowhere else, a real Jewish cultural center can be developed. Because even the humblest of American East Europeans were convinced that the ancient commonwealth must be rebuilt, they tacked up Zionist contribution boxes on the walls of their homes. Rarely formal members of the Zionist organization, these men and women set out to build a new Palestine with pennies.

Two factors made Zionism an important and ultimately a popular movement in the United States: Jewish tradition and the accidents of history. These accidents are the more important of the two factors: World War I and its horrors, the efficient administration of the marginal Jew, Brandeis, American quota immigration laws, anti-Semitic pressures of the 1920's and 1930's here in the United States, increasing disabilities in Russia and Rumania, and the destruction of German Jewry. The Holocaust guaranteed that emotionally, politically, almost every American Jew would become a Zionist; this sympathy for the cause was reinforced when the Moslem lands forced the emigration of over 600,000 Jews, many of whom found a home in the new State of Israel. If there had been no oppression in East European lands, no Holocaust, there would have been no Israel. For American Jews, the unhappy events in the Europe of the second quarter of the century were a learning experience. Much to their consternation they began to realize that humanitarianism is not a concomitant of an advanced culture; the Germans were among the most civilized and educated people in the world. Some American historians in the middle decades of this century began to wonder whether modernity, the period between 1791 and 1914 was but an interlude in a medieval continuum. There were Jews, Zionists, who were convinced that the only escape from modern medievalism was a new type of state in the ancestral Land of Promise. If a new homeland was to be established—and it was— it was in large part due to America's Jewry, both the Zionists and the non-Zionists.

What did American Jewry do for Zionism? It gave the movement leaders, notables such as Richard Gottheil, Henrietta Szold, Julian Mack, Louis Brandeis, Stephen Wise, Judah Leon Magnes, Abba Hillel Silver, devoted wheelhorses like Louis Lipsky and Emanuel Neumann. The Americans brought money into the movement, at first millions, ultimately billions, through the Joint Distribution Committee, the United Palestine Appeal, and the sale of bonds. There is nothing comparable to this generosity in all American history; as late as 1984 the budget of the

American National Red Cross was about $30,000,000; that very year the Jews in the United States, through gifts and the purchase of bonds, sent Israel alone well over $500,000,000. The political aid which American Jews brought to Zionist Palestine was all important; one of the most powerful lobbys in Washington is the AIPAC, the American Israel Public Affairs Committee; it protects Zion politically and helps secure the grants and the armaments without which the country could not maintain itself. All American Jewry has joined in the effort to make of Palestine a haven for Jews in flight; it has become World Jewry's "city of refuge," a new Land of Promise. For decades the Joint Distribution Committee fed and clothed the bodies of Europe's Jews; Zionism fed their souls; it gave them hope for the future. Many Jews in the United States, conscious of the anti-Semitism which has always been present here, were eager to build a land to which they could turn in dire straits; they were building for themselves, for their children; they have no assurance that there will never be an anti-Semitic upheaval here; they are mindful that, prior to the rise of the Nazis, Germany was one of the most liberal republics.

We see that American Jewry did a great deal for Palestine; it is equally true that Zionism did a great deal for the American Jew. It intensified the Jewishness of this country's outstanding institutions—once hostile to Zionism—such as the Union of American Hebrew Congregations, the Hebrew Union College, the Central Conference of American Rabbis, the B'nai B'rith, the American Jewish Committee; it restored the balance between acculturation and Judaism. (If, however, this redressed balance forced Jews back into the mold of traditionalism at the sacrifice of liberalism then this move toward the right was no spiritual advance.) Zionism evoked pride. For many of the country's Jews the new Palestine was a Maccabean rebirth. These American romantics recalled that the five Maccabean brothers, fighting for freedom, had all died with their boots on. Palestine gave American Jews a heightened sense of dignity; they believed that the achievements of the Jew in the land of his fathers enhanced their status here in the United States. Devotion to Palestine strengthened the kinship of Jews everywhere; this was certainly true here in the United States. Zionism, Zion, appealed to American Jewry because it offered something to almost every Jew. The movement, generous in its embrace, sheltered and welcomed diverse groups. The socialists glowed in the thought that they were about to build the first real Marxist state; the agricultural romantics were happy as they surveyed the vineyards and the rural cooperatives; the Orthodox were grateful that the traditions and rites were observed meticulously. The intelligentsia hoped that the country, the universities, would develop a renascent Jewish culture; secularists were pleased because they looked forward to complete acceptance as Jews in the new polity. For many, secularism was to be the new substitute for religion. The country's civil religion was nondivisive; it emphasized culture. America's political idealists proclaimed the developing state an exemplary democracy.

No matter where a Jew stood, if he had some Jewish interests, Zionism was an acceptable form of identification. Influenced by their Orthodox training, native-born children of East European parents were not hostile to Zionism. The movement created a sense of community, gemeinschaft, that encompassed all Jews everywhere. Religion was played down because by its very nature it divided Jews. Zionism drew the secularists back into the magic circle of Jewry. It was a movement that could assimilate a secularist Supreme Court Justice like Brandeis and a humble illiterate Orthodox sweatshop worker. The all-inclusive character of Zionism is shown in the fact that in a period in which there was patent hostility between the immigrants and the natives, the real leaders of the Zionist movement from 1897 to 1921 were scions of older American Jewish families. Because of its numbers and wealth American Jews became the world's most important supporters of Palestine; this was certainly true in the middle and late twentieth century. Without the Jews of this country the State of Israel could not have come to birth; without their political and financial aid the new Jewish commonwealth might not have survived. The Palestinians and the Americans had a partner; the world, guiltridden for having tolerated the Holocaust, attempted to pay its debt to the dead and the survivors by aiding in the establishment of the new commonwealth. By the mid-twentieth century the State of Israel had become a very important Jewish cultural center, rivaled only by that of American Jewry.

It has been said that Zionism was the most successful movement in American Jewish history. This is moot. The Conservative and the Reform Movements—new and uniquely American—muster millions of followers; they reflect a religious revolution of tremendous import, the most radical change in Judaism since the rise of the Karaites in the eighth century. Zionism set out to solve the Jewish problem, this it did not, could not do; in no sense has it induced the world to accept the Jew as a Jew. However, there is no question that Zionism, Palestine, Israel have materially aided Jewry in distress and have served as an inspiration, a source of pride to Jews in every corner of the world.[15]

CHAPTER TWENTY-FOUR

THE GERMAN AND EAST EUROPEAN JEWS, 1860–1920

A SUMMARY

THE RISE AND DOMINANCE OF THE GERMAN JEWS

German Jews had been coming to North America ever since the seventeenth century but it was not until 1802 that they succeeded in establishing an Ashkenazic congregation that was destined to survive. Attempts had been made earlier in Philadelphia and Charleston to set up Ashkenazic prayer groups but they were unsuccessful. In the 1830's the Central Europeans started coming to the United States in substantial numbers. A mass immigration? Hardly. Between the 1830's and the 1880's about 150,000 German Jews may have crossed the Atlantic to settle on these shores. This is an estimate; there are no official figures for Jews at this time. Why did they come? Legal disabilities persisted in the Fatherland up to the 1870's; there were anti-Jewish riots in 1819. Most emigrants, however, left the German lands because of economic dislocations at home due to the rise of industrialism; the economic and political opportunities in this country were the lures that drew the Germans, Jews and Gentiles alike. Many of the Jews headed for the big cities but there were few towns in the country that did not shelter at least one of them. They earned their salt wherever they went by bringing and distributing consumer wares. They were peddlers, artisans, petty retailers, large-scale outfitters, wholesalers. There were a few professionals, primarily physicians.

When they first landed here they found well-established small Sephardic congregations peopled by natives; these old-timers were, for the most part, Sephardized Central Europeans. Seeking to pray in their own style, the newcomers established conventicles in almost every corner of the country; they were not welcome in the old-line synagogs in the coastal towns. In antebellum days the synagog was the basic American Jewish institution; it was serviced by a "rabbi," often a worthy man, but not infrequently a European of little learning and less character; renegades flocked to this transatlantic frontier. By the 1840's superior men were coming over to serve as rabbis; the more liberal among them protestantized the services; decorum improved; preaching in German was introduced; the interior of the synagogs came to resemble churches; in fact the synagogs were often refurbished buildings once used by Christians for worship. Without any authority to police orthodoxy, religious laxity became the rule for many; America encouraged tolerance, permissiveness.

Like the Gentile immigrant groups who were streaming in, the Jews, too, created a series of charitable institutions to protect themselves and to provide for the less fortunate. Hebrew benevolent societies, mutual-aid congeries, and immigrant relief organizations were established as early as the second decade of the nineteenth century. The Independent Order of B'nai B'rith—Covenant Brothers—a national fraternal order was founded in 1843. Political and religious discussions were frowned upon; harmony was one of the watchwords of this new benefit and insurance society. Before the Civil War started Jews in this country would boast of Jewish libraries, hospitals, hospices, homes for orphans. The federating of local philanthropies had begun in Chicago and New York in 1859. Support for all charitable institutions came from dues and an annual ball where substantial sums were raised. There was hardly a charity that was not dependent on the women; in this area they were very important. Businessmen fashioned leisure institutions. There had been a Jewish social club in Newport as early as the eighteenth century; in the mid-nineteenth century there was hardly a town of size without a purely social society. Jews wanted lodges of their own; they founded numerous Young Mens' Hebrew Associations.

Jewish culture was inextricably tied to the synagog and Jewish education. Rebbes, private teachers, abounded; some were already here in the early eighteenth century. One could secure a Jewish education—such as it was—in parochial schools, Jewish private institutions of learning, in Sunday schools, in congregational afternoon classes. Literary societies were common all through the second half of the nineteenth century; some of these were more social than cultural. There were also two unsuccessful attempts to establish a Jewish Publication Society before a permanent one was organized. The religious literature was inadequate; it included a motley collection of textbooks, apologetic works defending Judaism, prayer books with a facing German or English translation, works of fiction—borrowed or translated.

In antebellum days, no Jew, as Jew, as teacher, was more important than Isaac Leeser, a German immigrant. He it was who introduced regular preaching in the English vernacular; he translated prayer books and catechisms, published apologies for Judaism, a Hebrew Bible and an English version; he founded a national Jewish newspaper, a publication soci-

ety, and finally a rabbinical seminary. In 1841 he made a fruitless attempt
to organize all of American Jewry, nationally, religiously, culturally. The
German immigrants were too poor to support this farsighted project; the
natives opposed all hierarchical outreaching. Nineteenth-century America
gloried in a strong tradition of states' rights; Jews here always insisted on
congregational independency; crises alone could unite them.

Unlike the Christians who began to marshal their forces nationally
after the Revolution, the Jews refused to create a national church. Their
neighbors tolerated them, left them alone; political anti-Jewish disabilities disappeared by 1877. There were still problems—there would always
be problems—many Christians here never ceased to harass them. Unsuccessful attempts were made to amend, to Christianize, the Federal Constitution; governors and an occasional president invited Christians only to
observe Thanksgiving Day; Sunday laws forced Jews to close their shops
on the first day of the week; New Testament readings were common in
the public schools. In the 1850's the United States negotiated a treaty
with the Swiss which ignored the rights of American Jewish citizens.
When Pope Pius IX took an Italian Jewish child, Edgar Mortara, away
from his mother and reared him as a Christian, President Buchanan refused to raise his voice in protest. (The American Irish Catholic vote was
not to be disdained by the Democrats.) The Swiss and Mortara affairs
frightened American Jews; in 1859 they set up their first national religious organization, the Board of Delegates of American Israelites (BDAI).

Following Leeser, Isaac Mayer Wise, the stormy petrel of America's
midwestern Reform Jews, had appealed for national unity on a religious
basis in 1848 and 1855. Both attempts failed. In 1857 he set out to organize American Jewry politically to protest against the discriminatory Swiss
treaty; his following numbered but a handful. The BDAI was more successful; it brought many Eastern congregations together to plead for Jewish education and financial relief for the oppressed Jews of Europe, Asia,
and North Africa. Let it not be forgotten: these Germans always
identified with fellow Jews in distress. The BDAI fought for civic and political rights for coreligionists here and abroad but even it, a synagog organization, dared not encroach on the religious governance of the individual congregation. In 1860 when secession and war threatened,
American Jews had become a community of about 150,000 souls; they
had grown about 1,000 percent in the course of but two decades. In 1840
there may have been some twenty congregations or prayer groups; in
1860 there were at least seventy. The BDAI was never a very strong organization; it sedulously avoided national partisan political issues; it took
no stand on slavery; neither did the vast majority of the Jews north of the
line. (The Southern Jews, as far as the evidence runs, were nearly all pro-
slavery.) There were not a dozen known Jewish antislavery propagandists

in the North, and some of these took their stand publicly only when the break with the South was imminent. American Jewry, less than 1 percent of the population, sought a low profile; Northern Jewish businessmen nursed their Southern customers.[1]

When the War of 1861 finally broke out Jews went with their region. Northerners volunteered in numbers; a few officers were even brevetted as generals; Jewish chaplains were finally authorized by Congress; Jewish bankers began selling bonds in Europe just about the time that General U. S. Grant expelled Jews from the territories occupied by his armies. Jews were trading with the enemy, he complained; that is true; so were his officers and his father. Lincoln immediately revoked the expulsion edict. Though Jews in the South were held at arm's length socially, they were given high office in the Confederacy. After the war was over the South found itself sore-stricken; the brilliant educated Jewish men and women who had cast luster on the Jewries of Richmond, Wilmington, Charleston, and Savannah soon passed away; they had no successors. The Southern Jewish communities were to make little if any impress upon American Jewry again until after World War II.

The North was now very much in the ascendancy. In the first two years of the Civil War immigration to the United States fell off. By the time Gettysburg was fought Jews again began to trickle into the country; the Union forces had the upper hand. Samuel Gompers, later to be the founder of the American Federation of Labor, landed in 1863; Sigmund Shlesinger, an Indian fighter, came in 1864; Jacob H. Schiff, the future banker, arrived in 1865; they were all teenagers. Isaac Mayer Wise, a Bohemian, had come earlier, in 1846. He was the country's most important Jewish religious organizer. The Reform Movement owes much to him. He was no innovative theologian. His ideology had its roots in the eighteenth-century Enlightenment, in German Reform, and in early American Jewish religious liberalism. After he went West in 1854, to Cincinnati, he may have been influenced by Western tolerance for new religious approaches. This autodidact made his career in this country as an educator, a teacher, a leader, a builder of institutions. Beginning in Albany in 1846 he learned his craft as an American rabbi; he was a moderate liberal; his upward rise came after he moved onto Cincinnati, a large community. There he issued two national newspapers, a German and an English one. By 1855 he had opened a school to train American youth, both Jews and Gentiles. Zion College he called it. It died speedily for lack of funds. It was in 1855 also that he called a national religious conference to unite American Jewry; he succeeded only in dividing it into Orthodox, moderates, and radicals. In 1869 he traveled East to meet with a group of German immigrant Reformers; they had stolen a march on him; their conference marked the beginnings of American Classical Reform.

That same year at Promontory Point in Utah Territory, in the Rockies, the last tie was laid that created the first transcontinental railroad. Now that space and time had been annihilated and people could travel from all parts of the country speedily, Wise's followers, devoted, aggressive laymen, brought to birth the Union of American Hebrew Congregations (UAHC) and the Hebrew Union College. (One should note the avoidance of the adjective "Jewish.") Wise had been pushing for a national religious union and a college since 1848. When, because of his militancy, he made little progress, his pragmatic Cincinnati laymen snatched the reins of leadership out of his hands (1873). In 1878 the UAHC took over the Board of Delegates of American Israelites which then became the Board of Delegates on Civil and Religious Rights (BDCRR). Reform was now powerful for it had incorporated a substantial number of congregations in the eastern part of the country. The BDCRR became the public relations wing of American Reform; it continued the work of the older BDAI in that it sought to protect the rights of Jews here and in foreign lands. Simon Wolf was its lobbyist in Washington. The Reform Movement grew steadily, constantly moving away from Orthodoxy by emphasizing the late Friday night service, modifying the old liturgy, doffing the hat, introducing the family pew, the choir, and the confirmation ceremony. Reform, in the decade of the 1860's, entered its Classical Age; it remained the dominant Jewish religious group in this country up to the 1940's when the Conservatives rose to challenge it; the unorganized Orthodox East Europeans were, originally, far more numerous.

In 1880, at the height of its power, the Union published a survey that had been undertaken in the 1870's by the Board of Delegates. This showed that, all told, there were about 278 important congregations in the United States; fewer than half were Reform. Most were Orthodox; Reform was never American Jewry's majority faith. The Reformers, it is true, took the lead in making the inevitable adjustments to the larger Gentile polity. They paid lip service to the emancipation of women, encouraged cultural loans, stressed the education of children along modern lines, introduced a variety of new textbooks, and pleaded for closer relations with Gentiles. There can be no question that this acculturational movement hindered assimilation and kept many within the parameters of Jewry and Judaism. According to this national survey American Jewry could boast of four national secret orders, five hospitals, six orphan asylums, two homes for the aged, at least eighteen Jewish newspapers, including two catering to the needs of youth, twenty-five YMHA's, and dozens if not hundreds of local social and charity organizations.

In a way the creation of the Union and the College was a regional, a Midwestern attempt, to assume national Jewish leadership. It was resented in the East. Aggressive religious radicals, led by Kaufmann Kohler of New York, now moved beyond the liberal Philadelphia religious pronouncements (1869). In Pittsburgh, where the Reform rabbis foregathered in 1885, a completely rounded out platform was adopted; to this day its articles, with one notable exception, are accepted by the Reformers. The rabbis who had come together actually had no authority: they were not invested by their congregations with the right to make decisions. Yet they were not out of step with their followers; they merely formalized the beliefs and practices of their most educated and liberal members. Revelation, they said, is continuous; every generation is a Sinai; the moral not the rabbinical law is paramount; there is no need for a human Messiah; Reform, which postulates a messianic age, has undertaken the mission to preach the gospel of love and justice. Sunday services though not encouraged were permitted; proselytes to Judaism would not have to undergo the rite of circumcision; the return to Palestine was rejected. (Today in the late twentieth century there are but few Reform Jews who are not in sympathy with the State of Israel.)

Anti-Zionism now became an important issue in American Jewish life, notably so after the first Jewish World Zionist Congress in 1897. Opposition to a Jewish state was the cement that united moderate and radical Reformers, both in the East and West, until the 1930's when Germany's expulsions of her Jews induced these anti-Zionists to accept Zionism and the prospect of a Jewish national state. In 1889, four years after Reform's spiritual leaders met in conference in Pittsburgh, Isaac M. Wise organized the Central Conference of American Rabbis (CCAR), the country's first nationwide Reform institution. The Union of congregations and its rabbinical seminary both maintained that they were prepared to embrace all Jews, both Orthodox and heterodox. Wise now broke with the Orthodox; two years earlier they had rejected him definitively by opening a rabbinical seminary that hewed to the Orthodox line. The CCAR published its own prayer book in 1892; this was the instrumentality which in a positive sense united all Reformers. In 1895 the Conference formally rejected all traditional rabbinical law (halakah) in the sense that it was no longer binding. Let it be borne in mind however that the Conference as a liberal body could not impose its resolutions on its members; the Conference was a sounding board; none of its religious decisions was mandatory.

By the 1890's the "Germans" here were beginning to build a Jewish culture that was impressive. There was some English and German fiction and poetry, a series of annuals and almanacs, a rapidly growing Anglo-Jewish press, Sunday schools in all large towns, teachers' courses, rabbinic colleges, a national Jewish history organization, and a publication society that was fated to last. It was this body, the Jewish Publication Society of America, that distinguished itself by publishing several notable works;

among them was a new English version of the Old Testament which was the most accurate translation that had yet appeared in any language. Scientific works in the field of Judaica and Hebraica also began to appear in this country; these efforts were capped in 1901-1906 by the publication of the *Jewish Encyclopedia*. American Jewry was now making a bid for world Jewish cultural leadership.

The coming of the Russians and Poles after 1880 challenged the rather primitive social-welfare institutions in this country. In 1880 there were only 250,000 Jews in the United States; by 1900 there were about 1,000,000. The local charities were overwhelmed by the awesome task that faced them. Ever since the 1850's the charity institutions in the cities had begun the process of coalescing, federating. Isaac Mayer Wise had sought a national federation of all charities in that decade. The modest efforts to meld a few charities in antebellum days marks the rather uneven journey toward unity and the creation of a formal American Jewish community. The first federations in the mid-nineteenth century set out to collect funds efficiently; they resented the numerous annoying fund-raising efforts; they moved to increase the number of givers. Large sums were needed to provide for the impoverished East Europeans arriving here. By 1899 the social workers, now professionals, had organized themselves nationally. The First World War brought a real challenge. Millions of Jews in Eastern Europe were in desperate straits. The American Jewish Joint Distribution Committee, then organized, included all American Jews, the proletarians too. Thus by 1914-1915 an informal national community had come into being. In 1729 the earliest known American Jewish charity budget set aside a little less than £31 for "pious works"; in 1920 many millions were collected by American Jewry to save the suffering Jews of Europe and Palestine.

Giving money to the needy and afflicted implies a degree of affluence. This was true of the older immigration and of some of the newer settlers too. The latter had begun their rise even before the turn of the century. Jews who had means—and even some without means—built sociorecreational agencies. Beyond the family circle there were lodges, clubs, Young Men's Hebrew Associations—women's "Ys" too, later—and fancy fundraising balls where the well-to-do danced and drank. The ball was the great social occasion of the year. Jews had been an extended middle-class group in this country ever since the eighteenth century. It kept expanding with the rise of America politically, commercially, and industrially. Individuals like Joseph Pulitzer and A. S. Ochs built great newspapers. Many successful Jews in the big cities made their fortune in jewelry, tobacco, meat, leather, and liquor. The typical Jewish businessman however was a shopkeeper; others were in real estate; very few were in banking; still fewer succeeded in building department stores. More and more ambitious men turned to the professions, particularly to law and medicine. Simon Sterne, a lawyer, drafted the Interstate Commerce Act for the Senate. Jewish textile manufacturers in the South were exceptional; Jewish garment manufacturers were found in many major cities. Individuals achieved national importance—and power, too—in mining and international banking.

Despite the fact that, on the whole, Jews were good citizens they were often rebuffed by many of their fellow citizens. Though Jew-hatred goes back to pre-Christian times, Jews never learned to accept prejudice. They were constantly reminded that they were not wanted socially. Many were men and women of some culture yet they were kept out of Gentile (Christian) clubs, fraternities; there were quotas in colleges and private schools. Some hotels would not admit them. The populists of the Midwest and South damned them because, as with Karl Marx, Jews were identified as the quintessential capitalists. Some of America's most distinguished literati were pathological in their fear and hatred of Jews. The Jewish newcomers were often denounced as criminals; humble Jewish peddlers were beaten; at least two Jews were lynched in the South. Labor in America was often anti-Jewish; religious prejudice, in the guise of a pseudoscientific racist anthropology, finally triumphed in the enactment of immigration quota laws which set out deliberately to keep Jews out of this country (1921, 1924). A few Jews accepted the current Judeophobic stereotypes at their face value; they were ashamed of themselves. Most Jews, however, were deeply resentful; they reacted by working harder; they were determined to be better in order to succeed; they were wary of Gentiles. In 1913 the B'nai B'rith established an Anti-Defamation League to fight attacks on Jews in the general press; ultimately it was successful; the newspapers stopped their sniping.

On the whole the Central Europeans who came over in the nineteenth century found little difficulty in fitting themselves into the American cultural scene despite their love for the German language, literature, and customs. Most had some schooling; illiteracy among them was very low. A few moved slowly away from the Judaism in which they had been reared; in New York and other towns a handful turned to Ethical Culture. Very few intermarried; fewer still became Christian; nothing was to be gained by baptism; on rare occasions, Jews did turn to Christianity because of its mystical, its emotional, its spiritual appeal. Though given little encouragement a few individuals began to make headway as college instructors; this was in the first quarter of the twentieth century. A German immigrant, Emile Berliner, invented the first usable microphone; another American, Albert Michelson, was the first scientist to be awarded a Nobel prize in the physical sciences. Jews were very active in the theatre as writers, players, actors, entrepreneurs, they were leaders in the fields of music and medicine. Despite the fact that many Gentiles looked askance at these descendants of the biblical patriarchs they were probably accorded more acceptance than their fellows in European lands. Congress took note of the death of the German Jewish statesman, Eduard Lasker; the authorities in Washington were resentful when the Austrians declined to accept an American diplomat because his wife was a Jew.

Ever since the 1860's Jews and Gentiles had been exchanging pulpits; churches and synagogs were opened to Jews and Christians after disastrous fires. Gentiles in the major cities attended Sunday services in synagogs eagerly listening to the addresses of distinguished liberal Jewish clergymen. During World War I Jews occupied important positions in Washington; thousands of young Israelites were commissioned as officers in the army and navy. Wealthy Jewish philanthropists responded to America's hospitality by showering millions on public institutions to further the arts and sciences, to provide good milk for children, to educate blacks. Beginning with the 1790's Jews had begun to hold public office, elected in all instances by their Gentile fellow citizens. In the 1840's Jews went to the Senate and the House; soon they were dispatched to Europe to serve as ministers and ambassadors; by 1906 Theodore Roosevelt had chosen a Jew to sit in his cabinet; in Wilson's day they were elected governors; in 1916 Louis D. Brandeis moved on to the Supreme Court. In voting, Jews usually cast their ballot for the dominant party; they had no desire to roil the waters. After the Civil War many voted for the Republican Party though New York's Tammany always had a large Jewish following. Wilson attracted many Jews and in the decades that followed the Jews continued to vote for the Jeffersonians in national elections. In 1920 almost all Jewish achievers—there were thousands—were immigrants or the sons of immigrants. America had accepted them.

THE COMING AND CHALLENGE OF THE EAST EUROPEAN JEWS, 1852–1920

Why was the Pittsburgh Platform laid down in 1885? The Reformers met then because they feared that they would be swamped by newcomers from Russia, Poland, Galicia, Hungary, Rumania. The Reformers were determined to fix their liberalism: we are a different breed of Jews; we are modern, cultivated; don't compare us with these backward hordes from the Slavic lands. The Pittsburgh Platform reflected the fervent optimism of its builders; we are living in the best of all possible times. They ignored the Russian massacres, the disabling May Laws, the Tisza-Eszlar ritual murder accusation, German anti-Semitism. These were but temporary setbacks. They were convinced that it was only a matter of time before all Europe's Jews would be emancipated. God's in his heaven! Why did these

Russian Jews start pouring into America by the thousands in the 1880's? There were pogroms back home; little hope was held out for improved conditions; as in an earlier Germany, Russia was disrupted by economic dislocation; America spelt salvation, security, opportunity. How many Jews came? From 1881 to 1924, when the gates were closed, about 2,500,000 men, women, and children sought refuge here. In some respects these immigrants were different from others who landed in American ports. They came with their families; they intended to remain; they were poor; a substantial number of them were skilled artisans; many could read no language, yet as a body they were more literate than others who came from East European, Balkan, and Mediterranean lands. Few American Jews came down to Castle Garden to greet them; they resented them. These were uncouth foreigners; they were impoverished, Yiddish-speaking, Orthodox, Russian; some were political radicals. These are the people who will turn the Gentiles against us! (Actually the anti-Semites had bigger game in their sights; they were gunning for "German" millionaires.) This was an invasion of the Vandals.

If these newcomers were a problem there had to be a solution; there were, in fact, several. The obvious one was to improve conditions in Russia and Rumania so that they would not come here. The B'nai B'rith, the Board of Delegates on Civil and Religious Rights, and later American Jewish agencies made valiant efforts to emancipate Jews in their homelands; they accomplished little. If these immigrants persisted in leaving their homelands then divert them to other European lands, to Palestine. These efforts, too, met with little success. Nothing availed; the Russians were determined to come here and they did. Some individuals like Emma Lazarus, the writer, and Michael Heilprin, the scholar, were friendly. In the long run the Jewish elite resigned itself to help these unfortunates. Jews here never denied that the newcomers were fellow Jews; they had to be helped and were given aid, "we take care of our own"; they must not turn to the Gentiles for charity; that would be a reflection on us. Now that they are here and we have made some provision for the very needy what shall we do for them? They must leave New York; they must be dispersed; they are a threat to our status; ship them off to the backcountry. In formulating a policy of removal New York's Jewish social workers and leaders thought first of colonization. Put them on the soil. Well over a hundred colonies were established; not a single one was truly successful. These shtetl, small town, Jews were not farmers; they had no means; they had no capital; here in this country they were settled on poor lands, far from markets and from Jewish institutions. And the vaunted South New Jersey colonies? Hundreds—but only hundreds—eked out an existence there because they combined industry with farming. In sum, these newcomers refused to be buried in the swamps of Louisiana or in the arroyos of Colorado.

Individuals who turned to farming did better. Dozens were ultimately successful in the New England states and on the Dakota homesteads, but, on the whole, farming was no solution for hundreds of thousands in a day when farmers all over the country were trekking to the cities. There was little or no Jewish life for isolated yeomen. Two Jewish farm schools that were opened in the 1890's produced few dirt farmers; one school, in Woodbine, New Jersey, did help train a few men who became soil chemists. And the Catskill farmers? They made a living taking in boarders. In 1901 the Baron de Hirsch money set up the Industrial Removal Office (IRO) to direct incoming immigrants to the states west of the Hudson. A few years later Schiff gave generously to divert the stream of newcomers to the Southwest and transmississippi country by way of Galveston. There is no failure without some success. The thousands who were dispatched west by the IRO or Schiff's immigration bureau brought in their families and served as nuclei to expand older communities. They helped create a midwestern American Diaspora but dispersal, removal, was a failure. The immigrants stayed in the East because they had no money, no desire to travel farther; in an industrial age they opted for the sweatshop and the factory. They wanted all the advantages of a Yiddish community.

Obviously, settling Jews in colonies, on farms, or in western towns was no answer. These impoverished East European Jews sensed intuitively that their future lay in the metropolises. The Union of American Hebrew Congregations, an influential national organization, was committed to a policy of removal but accomplished very little if anything; the B'nai B'rith was equally unsuccessful. These two West-centered national organizations should have taken the initiative in helping the newcomers. They did not. The UAHC, a religious organization of acculturated American Jews, failed to build a bridge to the Russians and Poles. These immigrants were lovers of Hebrew, Yiddish-speaking, Zionists, observers of kashrut, ardent protagonists of a type of Orthodoxy that was in some respects not even congruent with that of American Jewish traditionalists. They were exuberantly noisy in their services, disdainful of the whispering silences of the protestantized Reformers. The Reformers could have opened their vestry rooms to these newcomers; this they did not do. After 1903 a group of professors at the Hebrew Union College, Zionists, may have hoped to turn Reform around and bring it closer to the East European ethos. If this was their intention they failed; they left the College. The UAHC was not equipped emotionally, conceptually to help the new masses. The Union was headquartered in Cincinnati where, in 1900, there were about 15,000 Jews; New York that year sheltered about 350,000; its Jewry was almost twenty-five times larger.

The Westerners were not confronted by the problem of coping with massive migration; the Easterners were. Thousands, ultimately hundreds of thousands of Russians, Galicians, Poles, Rumanians, and people from the Balkans remained in New York City. The self-appointed Jewish leaders in that metropolis faced their problems honestly. Removal was no answer. A new approach was formulated; these newcomers must be Americanized; their religion must be occidentalized; they must be given proper leadership. The men and women who tackled this problem were intelligent, dedicated. They were devoted Jews. Most of the men knew some Hebrew; they were the children of Germans who had all been Orthodox. They were aware of the plight of the East Side denizens; they were determined to help. The Americanization institutions they created in New York and which were also established in most major towns were settlement houses, vocational and religious schools, sections of the National Council of Jewish Women. They set out to teach civics and trades; they established libraries, they encouraged manly (!) sports, and emphasized that cleanliness was next to godliness.

And the occidentalization of the East European Orthodox? Boiled down this meant decorum and an English sermon. The inner structure, layout, of the synagog—altar and pews—resembled the typical Christian church or Reform temple. Schiff and his friends wanted to move the Hebrew Union College to New York to undertake this task of occidentalization. The Westerners refused indignantly. The New York Reformers then proceeded to build the Conservative Movement; the children of the immigrants must be reared as religionists. Socialism, anarchism, secularism were constant threats. The new Americanized Orthodoxy was built on the antebellum Orthodox synagogs some of which were to affiliate themselves with the Union of Orthodox Congregations of the United States and Canada established in 1898. Their training school was the Jewish Theological Seminary of America which opened its doors in 1887. Acculturated Orthodox rabbis—both immigrants and natives—broke with the Hebrew Union College, Wise, and the Union of American Hebrew Congregations. This rejection had been prompted, in part, by the radical Pittsburgh Platform (1885). Unfortunately the new seminary was a failure. This was the situation round 1900. Then it was that Schiff et al induced Solomon Schechter to come to America and help rebuild Conservative Judaism. This time they were successful in effecting a fusion of traditionalism and modernism; many Americanized East Europeans joined them; the new generation remained loyal to the movement; by the late twentieth century this Jewish denomination outnumbered the Orthodox and the Reformers. Its followers were loyally traditional, thoroughly American.

The New York notables who set out to win and mold the East Side masses and to establish paradigms for other American Jewish communities made progress in their Americanization programs and in furthering the Jewish Theological Seminary. More important is the support they gave America's East European Jews in every crisis that faced them and their families both here and abroad. It was Schiff, Marshall, Magnes and that crowd that stood shoulder to shoulder with the newcomers protesting the 1903 and 1905 murders in Russia. The Union of American Hebrew Congregations and the B'nai B'rith were equally responsive. In 1906 the New York leaders established the American Jewish Committee (AJC). There was need for national leadership centered in New York. Hundreds of thousands of newcomers lived there; national Jewish organizations had their offices in that city, but the UAHC and the B'nai B'rith were located in the distant West. The new organization, the AJC, an assembly of notables, made an honest effort to include representatives of all groups in the country including the Russians and Poles. Control, however, lay in the hands of a small New York inner circle. It was a very successful organization. Together with the UAHC and the B'nai B'rith— mass membership organizations—it induced Congress to urge the abrogation of the discriminatory Russian Treaty. This was a great victory for American Jews; they were now politically powerful (1911).

While protesting against the disabilities imposed by the Russian government the AJC turned to a more immediate problem. The immigrants, slum dwellers, were poor; poverty breeds crime. The Jews of Lower Manhattan now had to deal with prostitution, desertion, gangsters, juvenile delinquency. In response to attacks in the press the American Jewish Committee set out to organize all of New York Jewry—really the East Side—into a Kehillah, a community, the better to meet its problems. It was a grandiose scheme, truly bold, imaginative, visionary, but it failed. The New York elite wanted control; the East Europeans wanted autonomy. There was no homogeneity among the newcomers; the state could not and would not intervene to exercise authority; the Kehillah was based on voluntarism. The program which embraced religion, education, arbitration in industry, and demographic research was too all-inclusive, too daring. The leadership was inadequate to the task; it is questionable whether any person could have fused these peoples into a community; the First World War diverted the interest of the ghetto masses.

The War of 1914-1918 faced the American Jews with a dilemma. The government in Washington was pro-French and pro-English but these two liberal states were allied with brutal Russia. The Russian and German Jews, all American Jews, were anti-Russian; they could not conscientiously support any alliance which included this oppressor; thus there was a possibility of collision with the authorities in Washington. The dilemma was resolved in 1917 when the czar was overthrown and when the United States joined the Western allies; the Jews were loyal citizens. To help the more than 200,000 Jews who were enlisted in the armed forces the Jewish Welfare Board was established; this organization provided for the non-military needs of the men and women who served. It was particularly effective in the army encampments and base hospitals. The leadership which the older settlers gave to the new Jews was accepted and appreciated; the two disparate groups were drawn together. The unification process was speeded up, intensified, when the American Jewish Joint Distribution Committee was organized (1914-1915). The "Germans" took the lead in saving the East European myriads abroad. America now was coming into its own. Twenty-three years earlier Baron de Hirsch had established a fund to help immigrants here on the Jewish frontier; now American Jewry poured millions into the European lands to rescue war-wracked kinsmen. With the war won victorious America now began to impose a Pax Americana; imitative American Jewry would now reach out to exercise a degree of hegemony over the Jews of the world; all this but thirty-seven years after the first pogrom victims landed on these shores.[2]

Despite the ongoing Americanization of the East European Jews these men and women maintained a separate subethnic community; they were totally different from the older Jewish settlers. The natives and the Germans rejected these newcomers socially; this was inevitable, understandable. The economic and cultural differences could not be bridged easily. In order to save their souls, and bodies too, in order that they might survive comfortably, the newcomers tried to build a community of their own, one which would sustain them spiritually. In this sense they were no different than any group of immigrants who had come to North America. With their few belongings—in their baggage—came the institutions which had nourished them at home. Where necessary these were adapted to American conditions. New organizations were also created as the need rose. The ghetto, the Jewish quarter, accompanied them; it was a social, religious, cultural, physical home. They brought their religion, their Orthodoxy with them. It was their very life; it was distinctively East European. They differed one from the other but they were united by a common prayer book, the siddur. The rabbis who accompanied the immigrants struggled to avoid any compromises in the observance of their faith; the masses, too, clung tenaciously to their traditional way of life but many thousands had to work on the Sabbath. This was a terrible wrench for them. The rites of passage were observed; bar mitzvah was important; kashrut was imperative; the Holy Days were celebrated. For many the synagog services were a refuge and a solace; hundreds of conventicles were established; most often the minyan, the minimum quorum of ten males, met in a rented room.

Here, in unkosher America, the rabbi was at first not honored. There was no real need for his expertise; at home he was an ecclesiastical judge, but here in America the rabbinic codes were honored in the breach; in practice the halakah was no longer the organic law of the community; it was often bypassed. A chief rabbinate established in 1888 in the New York ghetto failed in its prime purpose of holding the immigrants together and providing them with certifiably kosher meat. Similar chief rabbinates in other major cities met with different degrees of compliance. Better treatment of Orthodox rabbis would come with Americanization. Influenced by the treatment accorded the Reform ministers and the Christian clergymen, the Jews here would do better by their spiritual leaders, financially at least; most Orthodox rabbis were poorly paid. The astute among them built little empires of their own and zealously guarded their patch and their prerogatives; poaching rival rabbis were warned off. Brilliant, aggressive leaders were able to exercise a great deal of moral authority. Facing the devastating impact of permissive America, Orthodoxy languished; the children, if religiously minded, turned to Conservatism and to Reform when they grew up. The native American Orthodox fought back at Reform by creating a union of Orthodox congregations (1898); the immigrant rabbis, disdaining the Americanized Orthodox, went off by themselves in a right-wing uncompromising union of their own. Their emphases lay on Sabbath observance, adherence to the old laws touching on marriage, divorce, diet, the ritual bath for women. They were not being unduly stubborn; they knew that if a man or woman kept kosher they would survive as Jews. These rabbis, however, were fighting a losing battle; they had no state backing, no communal support; it was difficult to transport the shtetl across 3,000 miles of water. A substantial number of these immigrant rabbis deliberately courted religious isolation; by 1912 perceptive Orthodox realized that they could not ignore the forces of Americanization; they organized as Young Israel.

The Jewish majority here, the Slavic and Balkan Jews, employed five vernaculars, Russian, Ladino, Hebrew, Yiddish, and English. Many Balkan Turkish Jews enjoyed their beloved Iberian tongue; a few Jews here could speak Russian; for the most part they were the core of the intelligentsia; English, of a sort, became a necessity for all; Yiddish was the national tongue. The Russians, Poles, Hungarians, and Rumanians loved Yiddish even as the German Jews loved their mother tongue; Yiddish bound Jews together; it was the source of the culture they held dear. For years it was the teaching language in many Hebrew schools; the instructors knew no other. And when the schismatic socialists, secularists, went off by themselves the afternoon schools they created employed only Yiddish as the language of instruction. American Yiddish culture was reflected primarily in the press, in the dailies and weeklies. The masses looked to their newspapers for titillating sensations, for romantic and Gothic fiction, as well as the always-present articles on history, economics, the sciences. Every ideology had its journal.

In the long run all readers were Americanized; no one, no thing, no journal, no institution could escape the enveloping impact of the American milieu. There was a whole host of writers and poets; some were superior, brilliant, exceptional. The New York Yiddish dailies were read in all major towns; local Yiddish papers vied with the New Yorkers for subscribers. Less important was the Yiddish theatre but thousands rushed to hear their favorite actor or actress declaim. The newcomers loved to glow, to weep, to drown themselves in maudlin sentiment. For those who loved tone and sound there were operas, operettas, musical comedies. From the vantage point of the late twentieth century much in the Yiddish theatre was bad; there was buffoonery, pathos, trash. For the generation before 1900—and often after, there was no bad theatre. But even in the early days of the immigrant theatre there was excellent serious drama and notable actors, male and female. The Yiddish language, music, theatre, literature, press sustained the masses emotionally even as the parlance of the Italian, Polish, and Scandinavian immigrants gave them the strength to survive in America, a foreign land where hardships faced them at every turn. The Yiddish culture is a transitional one; it was dying yet still alive in the 1980's; it would struggle on for decades before it would take its place with Greek and Latin as theses options in university seminars. There are millions of pages of Yiddish print locked away in the great libraries of this country; in another generation dozens of dissertations on Yiddish culture will run off the printers of personal computers.

Yiddish will ultimately die as a Jewish language, even as centuries ago Aramaic died as the lingua franca of the Chosen People. Hebrew will die only with the death of the last committed Jew. As part of the prayer ritual, Hebrew was always alive; the three Jewish denominations employed it in their prayers; it was taught in most religious schools, in the home, in the heder, the Talmud Torah, the yeshivah, and even in the Sunday schools of some Reform temples. All this before 1921. The East Europeans set up their own ghetto parochial school in 1886; in 1897 they opened a Russian style talmudic academy; in 1915 they turned it into a modern rabbinical seminary headed by a scholar with a graduate degree. It was rigidly meticulously Orthodox in belief and practice; Talmud was the basic subject. Back in Eastern Europe Jewish modernists employed Hebrew as a vehicle to transmit Western culture; those modernists, Maskilim, "Enlighteners," who came over here had no future. Before 1900 they had already published more than twenty journals; not one lived. A Hebrew press had no future here; people turned for news and information to the Yiddish and English dailies. In the ghettos of Europe one could still

make a career as a talmudist; in this land English was imperative for anyone who sought a livelihood, recognition, success. Hebrew as a modern
language saved itself through a fortuitous circumstance. Zionism, looking
forward to building a state, needed a national tongue; it encouraged the
rise of a modern Hebrew language, literature, and press. Back in Russia
the Hebraic Enlighteners were assimilators, embracing the Western world
and its culture; here in America they were rejected by anglophilic Americanizers. To save modern Hebrew, these Maskilim did an about face and
as Jewish nationalists cultivated Hebrew as the language of a state yet to
be born. Here in America Hebrew was to flourish in the seminaries, in the
synagogs, and in the hearts and on the tongues of a few Zionists.

Researchers are now beginning to discover that among the suppos-
edly intractable East European Orthodox stalwarts there was a very substantial minority ready to synthesize traditionalism and Americanism.
These perceptive men made their presence and philosophy felt as early as
1900. Orthodox synagogs built Sunday schools; the curricula included
Hebrew, history, ceremonies. A teachers' college, Gratz College, was
opened in Philadelphia in the late 1890's by the native Orthodox; Mordecai M. Kaplan, traditionalist and modernist, was put in charge of a teachers' college at the Jewish Theological Seminary in 1909; by 1917 the Orthodox Zionist rabbinate had opened its Hebrew Teachers' Institute
combining the old and the new, Talmud, grammar, and other subjects
too. The New Yorkers, attempting to forge a citywide community, a
Kehillah, included a Bureau of Jewish Education (1910). It too was not
fated to endure but it exercised a profound influence on American Jewish
education. This Bureau, led by Dr. Samson Benderly, adopted modern
American pedagogical principles, particularly those taught at Teachers'
College, Columbia. In the new schools which he supervised in New York
City Benderly insisted on qualified teachers, graded courses, a varied curriculum, instruction in English. Girls were encouraged to study. Hebrew
was taught as a living language; Palestine, Zionism, was emphasized.

Essential in the teachings of the Bureau was the conviction that education was to be community-centered, not congregationally-centered. In
this respect Benderly and his friends were reflecting the prevailing American public school system. They erred; American Jewry never accepted the
concept of community responsibility for education; that was the congregation's job; religion and education are one and inseparable. In the long
run, central bureaus had no future; their pedagogical principles, however,
were adopted. Among Benderly's several disciples was Emanuel Gamoran; as the educator for the Union of American Hebrew Congregations he
not only influenced a generation of Reform youngsters Jewishly but his
publications served as patterns for the Conservatives and the Orthodox.
He certainly helped to keep young Reformers well within the magic cir-

cle of World Jewry. Interesting, though not really important because of their lack of mass followers, were the afternoon Yiddish schools sponsored by socialists, communists, Zionists, and Yiddish literary aficionados. These schools, secularistic, emphasized variant ideological philosophies; most of them reflected political teachings current in the ghettos of Russia which could be freely vented here in America. By the late twentieth century most of these schools had long since died; some of their students, now grown up, became pillars of the American Jewish community.

One of the outstanding characteristics of the New York Bureau of Education was its emphasis on Zionism; Benderly was a native Palestinian. Zionism was to become increasingly important; it was a cement that would hold many East European Jews together. True, they did not join the movement formally, but they looked forward to the day when Palestine would rise again as a Jewish commonwealth. These immigrants looked with favor on the concept of a Jewish state because of liturgical teachings and Jewish ethnicism; some were agrarian romantics; others, influenced by Ahad Ha-Am, hoped that the new Palestine would evolve into a spiritual, a cultural, center. Most Zionists—even those who lived in America—would have agreed that they needed a secure home, a land free of all anti-Semitism, where its inhabitants would always remain Jewish, where assimilation was no threat. Palestinianism, Zionism, if you will, had a history here going back to the eighteenth century; there were political proto-Zionists and Palestinian organizations in the early nineteenth century; the degradation of Captain Alfred Dreyfus in France convinced many that Jews had no future even in liberal lands; the massacres in Russia made a Jewish state imperative. Herzlian Zionism took root here almost immediately. Devoted leaders stepped forward; among them were Orthodox talmudists, Conservative and Reform rabbis, acculturated secularists of the older and more recent migrations. Zionism spread its net wide. Professor Horace M. Kallen preached a cultural pluralism that encouraged Jews to cultivate their own way of life even in an America that embosomed a multitude of peoples. Zionism, the word, was made flesh with the coming of Brandeis into the movement actively and with the publication of the Balfour Declaration. The children of the East Europeans were not hostile to this new political philosophy which seemed to challenge the prevalent monolithic loyalty to America; the anti-Zionism that characterized hundreds of thousands abated sharply in later decades when Jews were decimated in Europe and when Palestine was their only salvation.

The new immigrants, who made up the body of true Zionist believers, found it difficult to maintain membership in their favorite Zionist groups; they were too poor. Many were humble artisans; many more worked in the garment industry. Sweatshop conditions were common;

the wages were low, hours were long, strikes were frequent; tuberculosis struck down many. As early as 1888 Jews had begun to organize into unions to advance themselves; an umbrella association of Yiddish-speaking unions, the United Hebrew Trades (UHT), was called into being. By the early twentieth century the outstanding Jewish unions were the International Ladies' Garment Workers' Union, the cloth hat, cap, and millinery workers, the furriers, the Amalgamated Clothing Workers of America. There were many others. Thousands of these laborers were women; most of them were young, unmarried. These early trade guilds were politically motivated; their leaders, socialists, emphasized the class struggle; they wanted to change the political system, to create a workers' paradise. At first they made relatively little progress in building effective unions that would improve the lot of their followers; the national milieu was hostile to all unionists. After 1910 conditions began to change for the better. Strikes were more successful; the unions became stronger; the Democratic administration of Woodrow Wilson was not unsympathetic; the good will of the workmen was needed in World War I. An effort was made to bring order into the garment industry; factories were improved hygienically; arbitration and collective bargaining were stressed.

The new Jewish leaders, Russian émigrés of the early twentieth century, were better educated, more pragmatic, less doctrinaire in their socialism. Political activism gave way, to a degree, to union statesmanship. Social security for the individual worker was stressed; a diagnostic union health center was built. Not politics but the welfare of the individual worker was constantly held in mind; in large part this reflected the influence of non-Jewish labor unions; their prime concern was the worker himself. Under the influence of men like Sidney Hillman, a former Russian talmudic student and revolutionary, some of the Jewish unions—certainly those making men's clothing—began to cooperate with management; this was an aspect of what some were pleased to call industrial democracy. As the unions grew in strength they were able to do more for their members; they helped support a Yiddish press, schools, and fraternal orders that were ideologically close. In the course of years the unions reached out to help their members after work hours in housing, education, recreation. The Jewish labor world was a protective one, solicitous of the welfare of all who bent over a machine. As late as 1921 the union bosses were still uncommitted Jews; they were anti-religious, anti-Zionists. In theory at least they were still interested in the social revolution. The mass of workers was far more to the right; they were practitioners of traditional Judaism, American style.

For a period around the turn of the nineteenth century, most Jews in New York City were artisans and factory workers, but no later than the second decade of the new century large numbers in this metropolis and in all major American cities, began to inch upward into an all-inclusive middle class. Flight from the ghetto was continuous and as these Jews moved outward and upward they became clerks, stenographers, storekeepers, manufacturers, realtors, builders, and even large-scale industrialists. Like the Germans they, too, had often begun life as peddlers and artisans before climbing into commerce, trade, and the professions. One group of entrepreneurs was sui generis; these were the men who helped develop the cinema industry; a number of them were East Europeans whose beginnings were indeed modest. They built the movie industry as producers and marketers; they pioneered in sound movies and in building movie palaces. The cultural contributions of the movies were revolutionary.

Secular education appealed to large numbers of the newcomers; in Russia and Rumania they had been denied Western learning; here they envied the Germans who had become men and women of culture and affairs; the new immigrants were eager, almost overeager, to advance themselves. Wherever they could, as the opportunity presented itself, they turned to the professions; only a handful of these foreign-born intellectuals secured posts in colleges; many succeeded, however, as lawyers, physicians, musicians. It would take another generation before the children of the émigrés would emerge as important figures in the arts and sciences.

Although there were paupers and professional beggars among those who fled here after the 1881 pogroms most of the men and women who landed knew that they would have to depend upon themselves; they would have to build their own self-help institutions. This they did. There was no major American community without its mutual-aid hometown societies, freeloan organizations, sick-care congeries, burial associations. Émigrés established lodges where they felt at home, secure in the financial benefits which protected them, luxuriating in the company of friends who shared their way of thinking. Most fraternal orders were apolitical; others were Zionist, socialist, and communist. They offered culture, sociality, a financial hedge against an evil day. The parliamentary law they learned was but one aspect of the Americanization to which they were constantly exposed. Some of these self-help societies—there were hundreds of them—built special subethnic overall organizations (verbands) to provide services for their followers such as synagogs, charities, schools. In effect they became substantial subcommunities unifying large numbers of Jews from the same East European regions or lands. Here was Horace Kallen's cultural pluralism in action. The move toward societies to protect oneself was paralleled by the desire to help others. Hospices, orphan homes, asylums for the aged, tuberculosis sanatoria, the Hebrew Immigration Aid Society all bear witness that these humble workers and petty businessmen were willing to share in order that others might live.

The United States was good to the men, women, and children who came from the East European lands; in all those regions they were oppressed; large numbers were impoverished. Here they adapted their religion in order that it might survive in a new environment; they were given papers to read; their standard of living was raised; they were accorded the opportunity through the ballot to improve themselves civically; new worlds of the arts and sciences were revealed to them. They even changed physically; they increased in stature and weight. As their social vision broadened they became better men and women, more sensitive human beings.

By 1920 there were still two separate somewhat hostile Jewish communities in the United States, the "German" and the "Russian." Conscious of their numbers and strength, the newcomers, through the American Jewish Congress, 1916-1920, impelled the natives and Germans to accept the newcomers' programs for the furtherance of Zionism and the rehabilitation of East European Jewry. In 1860 American Jewry was not notable, certainly not in a cultural or economic sense; sixty years later it had become, in many respects, the greatest Jewry in the world. New York City alone in 1917 had 3,637 Jewish organizations; 2,168 were mutual-aid societies. Millions of Jews had crossed the Atlantic to find political asylum and economic opportunity. Here they built a new life for themselves, a consensual community that would yet usher in a Golden Age unparalleled in all Jewish history.[3]

CHAPTER TWENTY-FIVE

EPILOGUE 1921–1985

THE EMERGING AMERICAN JEWISH COMMUNITY

The period following the Treaty of Versailles in 1919 ushered in years of reaction. Indeed, it is tempting to suggest that the years from the French Revolution of 1789 to the capitulation of the Germans in 1918, were but an aberrant modern episode in the long centuries of an ongoing medievalism. Here in the United States after World War I, the sad 1920's saw deportations of radicals, heightened recriminations against Jews by Henry Ford and the Ku Klux Klan, exclusion of Jewish students from colleges and universities, and racist legislation in Congress—all this before the Great Depression of 1929 which dragged on for years both here and abroad, unsettling governments and giving rise to dictatorships in Europe, South America, and Asia. The National Socialist German Workers' Party (Nazis) destroyed the liberal German Weimar republic and ultimately inaugurated World War II. Realizing the Nazi threat to Western culture and civilization, Winston Churchill and President Franklin Delano Roosevelt, architect of the socially concerned New Deal, called a halt to the advances of the new German imperialism. Before World War II was over many European states had been crushed and two powerful new world empires emerged to overshadow all others—the Soviet Union in the Old World, the United States in the New. European Jewry barely survived complete annihilation.[1]

Even before World War II, technology, civilization, resources, wealth, made America the most powerful state the world had yet known. The third decade of the century ushered in a new world of the cinema, the radio, and a sophisticated industrialism; as the post-World War II decades advanced, American technology developed nuclear energy and the jet plane. Men mounted up on wings as eagles and landed on the moon.

Rising in the shadow of this American colossus, American Jewry emerged as early as 1921 as the greatest Jewish community in all the world's history, great in size, culture, stability, wealth, generosity, and leadership. Through their insurgent American Jewish Congress, the East European immigrants here had dominated World Jewish policy at the peace conference in Paris; they spoke for the 3,600,000 souls who constituted American Jewry in 1920. Apparently, the Russian, Polish, and Rumanian newcomers were then in control of the Jewish community. Did they continue to impose their rule on the native-born and the "Germans"? Did the Germans and the old-timers recover the control temporarily lost after 1916 and continue their wonted hegemony? What happened to American Jewry during the next two generations?

THE TWO AMERICAN JEWISH COMMUNITIES: CONFLICT AND FUSION

THE ROLE OF THE JEW IN THE ARTS AND SCIENCES, POLITICS, WAR, AND SPORTS

After 1920, the original American Jewish Congress was dissolved; that was a condition imposed by the American Jewish Committee before it agreed to engage in a common effort to secure equal rights for Eastern Europe's Jews. In 1919, at the Paris Peace Conference, America's Jewish leaders had presented a united front to plead for the emancipation of Jews in Eastern Europe. But by the spring of 1920, when the American Jewish Congress was adjourned, the old-timers and the new arrivals were once more in conflict just as they had been ever since the 1880's. Thus in 1920, the United States again sheltered two separate Jewish communities—but they had already begun to merge. It is no problem to summarize briefly what would come to pass in the next generation. The quota laws, from 1921 into the 1960's, kept Jewish newcomers out; Americanization, economic and cultural advances came with startling rapidity; intramarriage between the children of the old and the new settlers reduced differences; anti-Semitism forced all groups regardless of prepossessions to work as one; the German Holocaust taught all Jews that no one was exempt from prejudice; Zionism and the struggle for Israel offered every Jew a common ideal, a common hope, a haven; raising millions for overseas relief cemented them all; wealthy, cultured Jews of Russian and Polish ancestry were invited to share community power. By World War II, one more or less consolidated Jewish community had begun to emerge; no longer were there Russians, Germans, Poles, and Rumanians; now there were only Americans.

A distinct American Jewry had come into being, evolving out of two German components (West German and East German) and at least five trans-Vistula groups (Russians, Lithuanians, Poles, Galicians, and Rumanians). The force, the culture, that integrated all these disparate elements was America itself. Inasmuch as the exclusionist immigration acts of the 1920's made it impossible for the Russian-Polish reservoirs in the American ghettos to be replenished, the East European way of life could be maintained only with great difficulty. The new American environment would not, could not, be denied; there was a new garb, a new language, new ideas, a whole new challenging world of thought. Freedom here gave the immigrants the right to differ, to rebel, to throw off the shackles of the past if they so desired, as many did. Secular education—something new to most of the émigrés—was emphasized here. Respect for learning was a Jewish tradition; knowledge brought status and prestige. Jews, both men and women, turned to the colleges; they pursued graduate study; a degree was the royal road to a career. They were ambitious. Relatively speaking, more Jews went to college and pursued graduate studies than any other group in this country. In Washtenaw County, Michigan (Ann Arbor!), a university enclave, to be sure, almost 90 percent of the Jewish adults were college graduates. It has been pointed out that there were 50,000 Jewish faculty members in colleges and universities; among them were numerous college presidents; at least one of them was a woman.

All this took shape after the Second World War. What happened? Jews are an urban people; advanced culture is resident in the cities; hundreds of Jews in the social and natural sciences are listed in the current volumes of *Who's Who in America*; a quick look into any issue of the *World Almanac and Book of Facts* will show that many Jews, both male and female, are the recipients of Pulitzer Prizes and other awards for their prose, poetry, and music. The lists of fiction and nonfiction best sellers in the *New York Times Book Review* include Jews in almost every issue. Notable Jewish poets and journalists have come to the fore in every decade; female columnists who dispense advice on any and every subject—finance, too—have readers in the millions; innovative entrepreneurs have created chains of newspapers; book publishers have made their presence felt in the industry ever since the 1920's. Jews of Russian, Polish, and Rumanian background have been writing proletarian novels—ghetto literature, if you will—since the 1890's. Some of them emphasized the seamy side of life in the Jewish quarter; they wrote with gusto of vice and evil. Jews were shocked; they denied angrily that what they perceived as a self-hating, cloacal school was producing literature of quality. After the Soviets put their satellite, their sputnik, into space, many institutions and organizations began ignoring their prejudices against Jews; it was imperative that America catch up and bypass the Russians; Jews then were given every opportunity to study, to teach, to help make technological advances. Because the first native-born generation of East European Jews was speedily acculturated and attained middle-class status, the older settlers accepted it;

these Jews became *Salonfaehig*, even marriageable. Israel Zangwill in his famous play of 1908, the *Melting Pot*, had preached the gospel of intermarriage. Jews, however, rarely intermarried with Gentiles in those early days; by the middle decades of the twentieth century, the Jewish children of the old and the recent settlers found one another; there was a Jewish melting pot. Most children today do not know of their disparate origins; they care even less.[2]

Jewish businessmen controlled America's theatres in the first quarter of the century; a number of the outstanding producers and directors were also Jews. It was obvious that the New York of 1920 with its 5,600,000 people, which included 1,500,000 Jews, would boast not only of its theatrical magnates, but also of its playwrights, actors, and comedians. The Jewish intelligentsia—and wealthy, too—crowded around the Theatre Guild, founded in 1919 and were among the first to produce the plays of Shaw and O'Neill. The theatre, certainly in the backcountry, was in large part displaced by the movie palace. The cinema, an art and an industry, owes much to daring Jewish businessmen, who at first had much to gain and little to lose. These unknowns took a nickel industry, a nickelodeon, and they parlayed it into a billion-dollar enterprise. These New York and Hollywood speculators produced good and bad pictures. Like the Yiddish newspaper owners, the motion picture pioneers produced a great deal of *shund*, trash, but let it not be forgotten that one person's trash is another person's ecstasy. Critical evaluation is subjective. Motion pictures—often the worst—have enriched the lives of millions of men, women, and children in every corner of the world. National broadcast systems that came in with radio and television were controlled by Jews. Imagine the twentieth century without these media.

Eighteenth-century Jewry, off by itself in the ghettos of Central and Eastern Europe, was to a large degree cut off from the world of art and music. The nineteenth century saw great changes as the German Jews in this country embraced the fine arts; the Russians followed in their wake. Here in the United States, Jews are today preeminent in their support of classical music, symphonies, and the opera; they are impresarios, symphony conductors, virtuosi; their violinists and pianists are household names. Wherever there is good music, there Jews are found in disproportionate numbers. Song writers penetrate the very souls of the American people. The newspapers report that millions of copies of Johnny Marks's "Rudolph the Red-Nose Reindeer" were sold. The roster of musical comedy writers includes the names of George and Ira Gershwin, Richard Rodgers, Oscar Hammerstein II, Sigmund Romberg, Jerome Kern, and the Russian immigrant Irving Berlin. It is probable that Berlin's "White Christmas" is sung more often than the traditional Yuletide carols; his "God Bless America" is more popular than the "Star Spangled Banner."

The new generation, the children of East European immigrants, turned avidly to the graphic arts and to sculpture. The rich among them became collectors; Benjamin Altman—of German background—gave his $30,000,000 collection of paintings to the Metropolitan Museum of Art. (This did not deter a later director of that museum from publishing a brochure which included an attack on Jews.) Baltimore's Jews justly brag of their collections of great paintings; Jacob Epstein, the Lithuanian immigrant who made a fortune in a mail-order wholesale house, had a fine gallery which he assembled over the years. Claribel and Etta Cone collected French contemporary art which eventually found a home in the local museum. Young Jacob Epstein—no relative of the Baltimore merchant—funded his art education in Europe by drawing sketches for Hutchins Hapgood's, *Spirit of the Ghetto*, still a popular study of the East Side, and later, in England, became the famous sculptor Sir Jacob Epstein. His marble "Genesis" and his alabaster "Adam" are overwhelmingly powerful. His rugged portraits, cast in bronze, are startlingly lifelike. Joseph H. Hirshhorn (1899-1981), a Latvian immigrant who made a fortune in uranium mining, established the Joseph H. Hirshhorn Museum and Sculpture Garden in Washington, D. C. He had purchased thousands of pieces of modern sculpture—and paintings too—and turned them over to the government.

The Guggenheim is another family whose benefactions were numerous and important; the Solomon Robert Guggenheim Foundation built the modern art museum which bears the Guggenheim name; the Fifth Avenue building housing the Foundation's collections was designed by Frank Lloyd Wright. Some scholars consider the John Simon Guggenheim Memorial Foundation one of the most significant contributions to twentieth-century America. Hundreds of brilliant men and women, scholars, writers, artists, have been given the means to study and thus enhance the culture of the American people. Those who study abroad bring back knowledge of the best in the world's arts and sciences.

The devotion of Jews to the fine arts is especially notable in view of the fact that for centuries they were not much exposed to the art of medieval Christendom; they lived in seclusion and often looked upon pictorial painting and sculpture as forms of idolatry, recalling that the Ten Commandments frowned upon "any graven image, or any likeness of anything that is in heaven above, or that is in the earth beneath, or that is in the water under the earth" (Ex.20:4). Today, almost every Jewish Community Center in every American city encourages its members to study and appreciate the graphic arts. American Jews are disappointed that many notables in the fields of art and music—especially the latter—do not identify with their people. For these musicians and artists, nothing is more important than their careers; socially acceptable in the best Gentile

homes, they are virtually untouched by anti-Semitism; most of them reject Judaism, part of a world which means very little to them. When during the days of World War II Jewish virtuosi played German music, some
American Jews were resentful, unwilling to distinguish between German
music and German cruelty.

Many Jewish academicians turned to the natural and social sciences.
There are several notable physiologists, prominent among them Rosalyn
Sussman Yalow, a Nobel prize winner who taught for a while in the University of Illinois College of Engineering, where she was the only female
teacher on the staff. Unlike most of her scientist confreres, she keeps a kosher home, if only to please her husband. By a peculiar series of circumstances, Jews have been preeminent in the development of the atomic
bomb, the hydrogen bomb, and the neutron bomb; the latter is the most
compassionate of these instruments of death: it destroys human beings but
spares property. Jonas E. Salk and Albert B. Sabin succeeded in producing
vaccines against infantile paralysis; Selman Abraham Waksman is remembered for his research in antibiotics. Jews working in the natural sciences
are frequently singled out as recipients of the National Medal of Science
Award, the country's highest honor in the biological and physical sciences. More and more, the Children of Israel in America have turned to
sociology and history. Back at the turn of the century, Jews were not welcome in the fields of American history and Anglo-American literature.
Now, in the closing decades of the twentieth century, Jews are frequently
elected to head the major American historical societies; among them was
a woman, Gerda Lerner, a German refugee who has written on blacks and
women in American history. One must bear in mind, too, that the biblical
and talmudic studies published in the seminaries and the university presses
must be seen as contributions to contemporary culture in America.[3]

In pre-World War I days, a great many Jews, reaching out for status,
voted the Republican ticket, the party of the middle class, the affluent, the
industrialists, the solid citizens. A change came with Wilson. Since then,
the majority has always voted the Democratic ticket. The Democrats, as
their name implies, were generally deemed more liberal than the Republicans, more sympathetic to the immigrants, more inclined to keep the
ports open to newcomers from Europe's Eastern lands. Frequently, Jews
voted for the best man. In New York, they preferred a Democratic Roman Catholic gubernatorial candidate to a Republican Jew; this assured
the election of the Democrat. In that same city, a substantial minority of
Jews often voted for the Socialists; in the 1920's and 1930's, many in the
labor unions, intellectuals, idealists, turned to communism hoping that it
would usher in a messianic age. But the Marxist promise of a future
workers' paradise could not compete with the realities of the New Deal,
and when Joseph Stalin joined the Germans in a nonaggression pact in

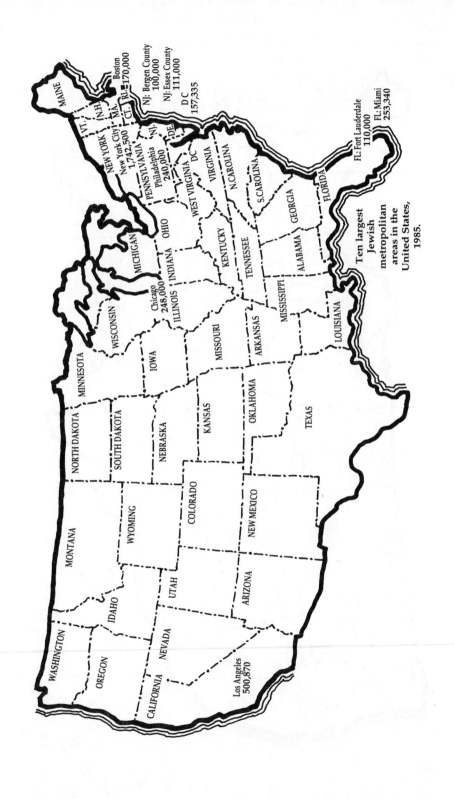

Ten largest Jewish metropolitan areas in the United States, 1985.

MAINE
N.H.
VT.
MA.: Boston
R.I.: 170,000
CT.
NJ: Bergen County 100,000
NJ: Essex County 111,000
D C 157,335
FL: Fort Lauderdale 110,000
FL: Miami 253,340

NEW YORK
New York City 1,742,500
PENNSYLVANIA
Philadelphia 240,000
N.J.
DEL.
MD.
DC
WEST VIRGINIA
VIRGINIA
N.CAROLINA
S.CAROLINA
GEORGIA
FLORIDA

MICHIGAN
OHIO
INDIANA
KENTUCKY
TENNESSEE
ALABAMA

WISCONSIN
ILLINOIS
Chicago 248,000
IOWA
MISSOURI
ARKANSAS
MISSISSIPPI
LOUISIANA

MINNESOTA
NORTH DAKOTA
SOUTH DAKOTA
NEBRASKA
KANSAS
OKLAHOMA
TEXAS

MONTANA
WYOMING
COLORADO
NEW MEXICO

IDAHO
UTAH
ARIZONA

WASHINGTON
OREGON
NEVADA
CALIFORNIA
Los Angeles 500,870

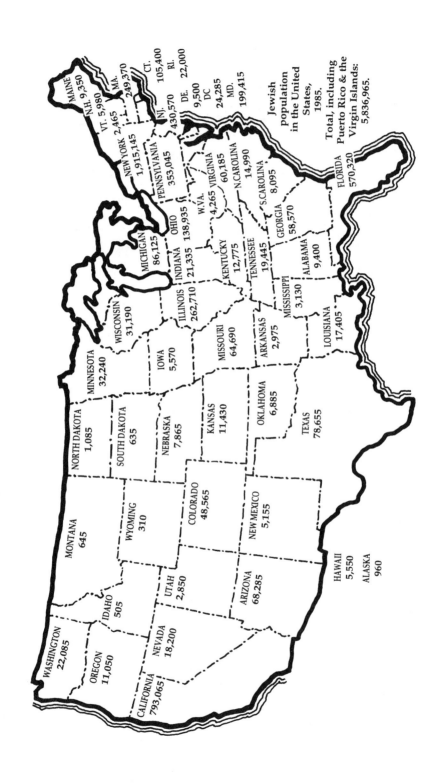

MAINE 9,350

N.H. 5,980

VT. 2,465

MA. 249,370

CT. 105,400

R.I. 22,000

NEW YORK 1,915,145

N.J. 430,570

DE. 9,500

DC 24,285

MD. 199,415

Jewish population in the United States, 1985.

Total, including Puerto Rico & the Virgin Islands: 5,836,965.

PENNSYLVANIA 353,045

VIRGINIA 60,185

N.CAROLINA 14,990

S.CAROLINA 8,095

FLORIDA 570,320

OHIO 138,935

W.VA. 4,265

GEORGIA 58,570

MICHIGAN 86,125

INDIANA 21,335

KENTUCKY 12,775

TENNESSEE 19,445

ALABAMA 9,400

WISCONSIN 31,190

ILLINOIS 262,710

MISSISSIPPI 3,130

MINNESOTA 32,240

IOWA 5,570

MISSOURI 64,690

ARKANSAS 2,975

LOUISIANA 17,405

NORTH DAKOTA 1,085

SOUTH DAKOTA 635

NEBRASKA 7,865

KANSAS 11,430

OKLAHOMA 6,885

TEXAS 78,655

MONTANA 645

WYOMING 310

COLORADO 48,565

NEW MEXICO 5,155

HAWAII 5,550

ALASKA 960

WASHINGTON 22,085

IDAHO 505

UTAH 2,850

ARIZONA 68,285

OREGON 11,050

NEVADA 18,200

CALIFORNIA 793,065

1939, Jewish enthusiasm for the Soviet Union waned. In 1953, Julius and Ethel Rosenberg, both native-born American Jews and people of culture, were executed on the charge of espionage. Both were Communists; the presiding judge who condemned them to death was also a Jew. During Franklin D. Roosevelt's presidency, the Jews emerged as a political force. They were small in numbers, forming less than 4 percent of the American population, but they turned out to vote; they valued their franchise. They were numerous in strategic states, in metropolitan areas; few though they were nationally, they could swing an election.

Jews have been elected to office since the late eighteenth century; as early as antebellum days, they sat in the House and in the Senate. By the third quarter of the twentieth century, they had occupied almost every elective and appointive office of any importance. They sat in the cabinets of presidents; in the last quarter of the twentieth century, Reubin O'-Donovan Askew, son of the Jew Leo Goldberg, presented himself as a Democratic candidate for the presidency. Askew was proud of the fact that he had been an elder in the Presbyterian church since 1960. The National Council of Jewish Women admired him enough to give him its John F. Kennedy award. Jews were influential during the administration of Franklin D. Roosevelt; they were a significant component of the coalition which helped elect him, a coalition including, among others, blacks, liberals, and the unions. The laboring classes were shepherded in Roosevelt's days by Sidney Hillman, quondam immigrant and socialist, who was one of the founders of the Congress of Industrial Organizations and its Political Action Committee.

Even before the rise of the State of Israel, the Zionist Organization of America had established a vigorous political lobby in Washington; this was later to become the American Israel Public Affairs Committee, which has been highly successful in securing loans and large grants for armaments for a beleaguered Israel surrounded by 50,000,000 hostile Moslems. In the last decades of the twentieth century, the devotion of Jews to the Democratic party has been tempered; they have given hostages to fortune; many—still a minority—have voted for the Republicans who smiled benevolently on the State of Israel and provided it with guns and dollars. As political liberals, the Jews fought valiantly and often successfully to keep the gates to America open to immigrants; they were really fighting for their kin who sought to escape the Russians, the Poles, the Rumanians, the poverty in Galicia. Ever since the American Revolution, they have been concerned with liberal legislation, with civil liberties for Jews. Because they want to survive, enjoying all rights and immunities, they have never failed to fight for the separation of church and state. (The Orthodox right-wingers are an exception; they want government grants for their religious schools.) Most Jews work together with the liberals and with large segments of the evangelicals to maintain the constitutional provisions against an established church. In their never ending effort to keep America religiously a truly free country, Jews have always served as the barometer of its conscience.[4]

As liberals, Jews were more often than not on the side of those who fought for peace. It is, therefore, somewhat ironic, if not sad, to limn the career of Lt. Raymond Zussmann, a Detroit young man who served in the tank corps during the Second World War. He was awarded the Congressional Medal of Honor for unusual bravery in action; Zussmann drove the Germans out of a French town, killed seventeen, and captured ninety-two single-handedly. Later he was himself killed in battle. Such militancy would certainly have pleased the belligerent Theodore Roosevelt and a host of others who wanted the Jews to stand out as fighting men. During World War II, about 550,000 Jews served in the armed forces. Most, of course, were soldiers; about 20 percent were commissioned officers; there were numerous generals, admirals, and chaplains, too. The latter—there were hundreds—did a magnificent job salvaging Jews who had not yet been gassed in the German death factories. Among the admirals was Hyman George Rickover, an immigrant and the man responsible for the atomic submarine, which, even when submerged could fire missiles into enemy territory. Possibly even more important is his development of the first nuclear-powered electric utility station. His was a remarkable career. Like many other Jews high in the councils of the nation, he had little interest in Jews or Judaism.

The army was a civic forcing house—immigrants emerged from the conflict completely Americanized—but sports were even more important in the job of turning newcomers into Americans. Mid-nineteenth-century German Jews of sporting bent joined the turnvereins; the world's champion rifle shot was a California Jew, Philo Jacoby; Lucius Littauer, the philanthropist, had played football for Harvard in the 1870's; there was an all-American Jewish quarterback in the 1890's. At one time a Jew owned the Pittsburgh Pirates; another owned the New York Giants; earlier, August Belmont had helped found the American Jockey Club. Always sensitive to anti-Semitic stereotypes—popular fancy held Jews to be physically weak—the Jewish elite here saw to it that the YMHA's and settlement houses had gymnasiums. Muscular Judaism was a consummation devoutly to be hoped for. In the twentieth century, Jews were frequent recipients of Olympic medals; they starred on the basketball court; dozens managed to become professional baseball players. Jewish immigrants seeking to make a career for themselves, to attain speedy recognition, turned to boxing. They were very important in pugilism in the early twentieth century; later, they were crowded out by the blacks. After World War II, Jews, now in the middle class, turned to swimming and tennis. (The intellectuals among them were masters in chess.) Sanford "Sandy" Koufax, a Brooklyn Jewish boy, became one of America's baseball heroes; pitching for the Dodgers in 1963, he struck out 306 batters. When Jews starred in sports, they were acclaimed by non-Jews; a home run by Hank (Henry) Greenberg of the Detroit Tigers was more important in combating anti-Semitism than 100,000 pamphlets distributed by a Jewish defense agency. In 1934, in a race for the American League pennant, Hank Greenberg turned to a Detroit rabbi for guidance; the High Holy Days summoned him to worship. On Rosh Hashanah, the rabbi had permitted him to play; the team won—on Yom Kippur, the rabbi forbade him; the team lost:

> We shall miss him in the infield and
> Shall miss him at the bat,
> But he's true to his religion—and I
> Honor him for that!

In the years between 1921 and the 1980's, Jews made remarkable advances in the arts and sciences. Their fathers and mothers—certainly their grandparents—had come out of the ghetto. Most Jews lived here in cities where education, culture, the arts and the sciences were at hand; they took advantage of the opportunities afforded them. Jews brought Hebrew and Jewish scholarship to America; they, more than any other Jewish group, helped build Israel; they received important political appointments. After Arthur Goldberg left the United States Supreme Court to become America's Ambassador to the United Nations, President Lyndon B. Johnson made this statement:

> When a Southerner can sit in the White House, when a Negro can aspire to the highest offices in the land, when a man of deep Jewish background can be the spokesman of this country to the world—that's what America is all about.

American Jews acculturated, yet remained Jewish; most of them met the challenge of assimilation; in their Jewishness, they added to the richness and diversity of the American setting.[5]

THE ECONOMIC LIFE OF THE AMERICAN JEW IN THE MID AND LATE TWENTIETH CENTURY

Numerous Jews were active in the apparel unions during the first two decades of the twentieth century; the numbers declined as the older generation retired or died out. These unions, however, still retained Jewish leaders in the mid and late decades of the century. By the 1930's, the union leaders and many of their Jewish members had ceased to be schismatics.

They no longer turned away from the Zionists; Palestine, they recognized, was needed as a haven for their kin now that the United States had decided to close its doors to practically all East Europeans, both Gentiles and Jews. The union notables, thoroughly Americanized, realized that they would make no friends attacking organized religion; their political radicalism abated as the New Deal cut the ground from under their feet; they were completely integrated into the American scene. The unions they led were no longer ignored by an old-line American Federation of Labor congeries. In many respects, these Jewish labor associations were exemplary. In dealing with employers, they encouraged arbitration, the peaceful settlement of grievances; they experimented with employment and retirement insurance, with medical care for members. They were concerned with their fellow workmen after they left the shop; they introduced recreational, educational, leisure programs; they established banks of their own; they erected apartment houses for their people. More importantly—and here they pioneered—they preached the gospel of cooperation with capitalism; the owner is no enemy; help him survive and make a profit so that you, the laborer, will always have a good paying job. It is probable that the Jewish unions, the International Ladies' Garment Workers, the hat, cap and millinery workers, the furriers, and the Amalgamated Clothing Workers, influenced the social legislation of the New Deal. Jews like Benjamin V. Cohen drafted laws for Roosevelt. The exact nature of the contribution that Jewish unions, sociologists, economists, and statisticians made to the sweeping changes of the 1930's is yet to be determined. One thing is sure: there is no question that the clothes manufactured by Jewish industrialists and Jewish employees made for democracy. One of the prime distinctions between gentry and commoner is dress; good garments available to all at a fair price make a great leveler; American men and women are the world's best dressed citizens.

By the third quarter of the century, most American Jews were part of an all-embracing middle class. Around the year 1900, a large percentage of the Jewish newcomers in New York, possibly 50 percent, were working in industry, many in the garment factories and sweatshops. This changed radically in the course of several decades. The disappearing apparel workers were neither the children of proletarians nor the parents of proletarians. The new generation of native-born Americans was almost completely deproletarianized; these men—and women, too—were moving upward rapidly. Some of them had "made it" in only one generation. Many were shopkeepers; others were in service industries; Jews were in trade, wholesale and retail; they were managers, proprietors, professionals. By 1979, 53 percent of the Jews were in business and the professions—more than twice the proportion for their Gentile fellow citizens. By the second half of the twentieth century, most Jews were white-collar workers; many of them, especially in the backcountry, were self-employed. To some degree, but only to a degree, Jews resorted to trade and the professions because they ran into anti-Semitic prejudice in other avenues to economic sufficiency. For years, employment agencies heeded the requests of anti-Jewish employers and refused to place Jews. In time, this type of discrimination was outlawed, but, even in the 1980's, Jews were still not welcome in many corporations. It was very difficult for qualified Jews to gain admission into the executive suite, particularly in banking, insurance, communications, transportation, and utilities. By 1981, 50 percent of New York City's college graduates were Jews; only 2 or 3 percent had jobs at the higher corporate level. There have been some changes. In recent years, Procter and Gamble of Cincinnati, Chrysler of Detroit, and Colgate-Palmolive began admitting Jews into their executive hierarchy; the board of Dupont elected a Jew as its chief executive officer. When Irving S. Shapiro became head of Dupont, he was invited to join a local exclusive country club. His response—it is reliably reported—was that the club was a generation too late.

Though the Jews today are largely a middle-class group, by no means do all of them make a decent living. A very substantial percentage, about 15 percent, struggles to make a decent living. During the years of the depression which began in 1929, large numbers of middle-class Jews suffered; they, too, managed to hold on only through the largess distributed by the new Roosevelt regime. Poverty frequently brings crime in its wake. The East Side—indeed, all the ghettos of our metropolises—saw the rise of Jews who were bootleggers, labor racketeers, gamblers, drug dealers, and professional assassins. Organized crime, often called the Syndicate, included Jews among the leaders; the execution squad, Murder, Inc., was started by Brooklyn Jews. However, 80 to 85 percent of the country's gainfully employed Jews were certainly not poor. All population studies—and they include most of America's major Jewish communities and many smaller ones—are in agreement that the Jews are one of the most affluent groups in the country. Some maintain that they are the most affluent. This is not to say that they have a substantial billionaire class; as far as it is now known, there are not a great many Jews among America's fabulously wealthy, including old and new money.

German and Russian twentieth-century Jewish fortunes in America were built on department stores, banking, catalogue houses, the construction industry, motion pictures, textiles, real estate speculation, grain trading, apparel manufacture, scrap iron, cosmetics, broadcasting empires, electronics, pet supplies, liquor, hotels, magazine and newspaper publishing, and farm produce wholesaling. Business was no longer exclusively a man's world; women, independently or with their husbands, built multimillion dollar businesses in toys, fabrics, a Catskill vacation resort, a department store, a research laboratory, apparel, and cosmetics. Tillie Lewis made a fortune growing and selling the Italian pear-shaped tomato, the pomodore; this Brooklyn-born woman, who had but one year of high school, developed a fruit and vegetable canning industry which ultimately brought her a fortune in the millions. Why were Jews successful? There is no definitive answer to this simple question, but this much is obvious: America gave them opportunity; many were well educated; they were able and ambitious; they worked hard.[6]

THE AMERICAN JEW AS PHILANTHROPIST

With wealth came philanthropy. The Germans who settled here in the mid-nineteenth century were a thrifty lot, but as they became wealthy, in some instances very wealthy, they learned to give generously to colleges, hospitals, and black institutions. The mining Guggenheims were among the most philanthropic. The East Europeans, too, parents and children, tradesmen and industrialists made large gifts, once they began to build substantial empires. The new rich vied with one another in giving the United Jewish Appeal huge sums to be sent abroad for relief purposes. Million-dollar gifts became commonplace. In 1925, the East European Jacob R. Schiff (d.1949)—no relative of the German-born banker Jacob H. Schiff—gave $200 to the Federation for the Support of Jewish Philanthropic Societies of New York. It was a generous gift for those days; when he died, a generation later, he left his multimillion dollar estate to "further the ideals of American democracy." Two Gentiles and a Jew were appointed to administer his trust funds.[7]

THE FUSION OF THE TWO DISPARATE JEWISH COMMUNITIES

OVERSEAS RELIEF

A day or two after a Russian or Polish or Galician or Balkan Jew landed at Castle Garden or Ellis Island, he started down the road to Americanization. With acculturation came integration, not only into the general culture, but into the older Jewish community as well. Ultimately, the disparate Jewish subethnic groups in this country were fused together. They melded because of the initiative taken by the newcomers who proved thoroughly imitative and socially ambitious; subconsciously at least, they wanted to be accepted by the older group, to become part of it. The day came when the young native of East European ancestry was accepted as a son-in-law; marriage is the ultimate solvent. In the meantime, the older native-born and German settlers had made a place for the newcomers in the community hierarchy; the Russians were given a role in the raising and distribution of funds for the stricken East Europeans abroad. This was recognition, power. Fusion on the Americanist level was being achieved; fusion on a Judaic level, coalescence into one overall Jewish community, had become a reality by the time of World War II.

This is what happened: the promises made by post-World War Rumania and the succession states that they would give their Jews equality were not fulfilled. The Joint Distribution Committee (JDC) sent millions to help Jewries abroad; the "Germans" and the "Russians" worked shoulder to shoulder in bringing relief, and these common efforts helped create a common, united American Jewry. All the Jewish forces in America worked together to protest the political shenanigans of the East European states and the devious practices of Great Britain in Mandatory Palestine. It is very difficult to determine whether the indictments of American Jewish agencies were effective to any degree. One suspects—this is but a guess— that the protests of the Jews put a damper on the extreme measures that the Poles and Russians as well as the English Colonial Office may have contemplated. American Jewry's political remonstrances were perhaps largely ineffective, but its philanthropic work was successful. By 1939, the United Jewish Appeal (UJA), a combined effort of the Zionists and the non-Zionists to raise money for Jews abroad, was in full swing. As the JDC was sending aid to Jews in Europe and the North African littoral, the Zionists, concerned with Palestine alone, worked through the United Palestine Appeal, later the United Israel Appeal and the Israel Bond Organization. The monies sent to Palestine were used to buy land, to establish colonies, and later, after 1948, to finance the new State of Israel. At first, the bulk of the funds raised in the United States went to help European Jews; later, as persecution abroad increased and Palestine stood out as World Jewry's only haven, the United Palestine Appeal received the larger share of American gifts.

In addition to helping needy Jews in Palestine, Europe, and North Africa, the United Jewish Appeal subsidized the work of the HIAS, the Hebrew Immigrant Aid Society, whose job was to help America-bound refugees. HIAS representatives were found as far away as Australia and New Zealand. Inasmuch as many of the new arrivals settled in New York City, special provision was made for them there. More and more the JDC also devoted its efforts to help Palestine Jewry, too. Its work in the old homeland was important; it supplied a substantial part of the funds needed to transport and settle Jews in the Holy Land; without these settlers, the new State of Israel could not have maintained itself, surrounded as it was by hostile Arab states. During the difficult 1930's, when all Central European Jews were threatened by Nazi Germany, thousands were aided by the JDC and private sponsors as they fled to the United States. These Central European émigrés were probably the most gifted immigrant group that ever sought sanctuary on these shores. They had been men of affairs and means in their native lands; among them was a number of scientists who had achieved international recognition; a few were Nobel laureates. One of the exiles was Hannah Arendt, a political theorist and the first woman to be appointed a full professor at Princeton University.

The big job of the JDC—this was before World War II—was in Eastern Europe. Millions of Jews there were helped financially and culturally. The Russians finally ordered the JDC and its affiliates out of the Soviet Union after they had expended huge sums rehabilitating Russian Jewry. It is sad that myriads who lived in these East European lands, and were sustained by the JDC, survived only to be annihilated by the Germans and their Slavic allies. Even while World War II raged, some Jews were rescued; after the conflict, the JDC was needed more than ever. Survivors were evacuated; Western European Jewish communities were given advice and funds; North African Jewish educational institutions were subsidized. Whenever permitted to do so, the JDC moved behind the Iron Curtain into Czechoslovakia, Hungary, Poland, and Rumania; later in the century it befriended the thousands of Soviet émigrés as they passed through Austria and Italy on their way to Israel or to North America; in 1985, millions were poured into famine-ridden Ethiopia; thousands of children there were fed daily. Jewish refugees lucky to find a home in the United States were exiled to paradise. It is no exaggeration; the UJA may well be acclaimed the most successful philanthropic agency in all American history. Its work—in the late twentieth century—was made possible by a Jewry which constituted less than 3 percent of the American people; this small group has a better record than the American Red Cross; over the years it has sent billions abroad.

The Americanization process, the acculturation of the East Europeans and their native-born children, their economic successes, the efforts of all American Jews to aid kinfolk and coreligionists in Europe, Asia, and Africa, cemented the relations between the pre-1880 and the post-1880 settlers; they found that, after all, they had much in common; they were becoming one community.[8]

FUSION STRENGTHENED:
ZIONISM COMES INTO ITS OWN IN THE UNITED STATES

The togetherness in American Jewry that came through engaging in a common philanthropic task was fortified by Zionism. By 1933, American Jews had begun turning toward Palestine in what was, indeed, a bouleversement. Prior to the 1920's and 1930's, the old-line settlers—with some notable exceptions—wanted nothing to do with Palestine Jewish nationalism; the "Russians" were more sympathetic than the "Germans," but even they blandly refused to join the numerous Zionist societies in any great numbers. After 1924, when America would no longer admit East European migrants, many of them turned to the ancient homeland. American Jewry knew that the doors to that land had to be kept open; Jews in Poland, Rumania, and Russia were increasingly persuaded that they had no future in the lands of their nativity. Aware of the need to work with the Zionists, the American Jewish leader Louis Marshall set out to involve this country's Jewish notables in an expanded Zionist Jewish Agency, which finally took shape in 1929. The Arabs, realizing that the settlement of Palestine would now be undertaken in earnest, protested by massacring about 100 Jews in Hebron. To keep Jews from coming into the country, the Arabs resorted to guerrilla warfare; this war of murders and reprisals has continued throughout the century. At this writing, in 1985, there is still no secure peace in Jerusalem, "City of Peace."

The murders in Hebron in 1929 only roused the sympathies of America's Jews. Four years later, the Nazis came to power in Germany and now that country's Jews had to think seriously of leaving; Palestine was still open; Hitler made more Zionists than Stephen S. Wise or Louis D. Brandeis. That same decade, in 1937, the Reform rabbis, formerly intransigent anti-Zionists, adopted at Columbus, Ohio, a new religious program emphasizing the importance of Palestine as a center of Jewish culture. The imperative need for a haven in that country was highlighted when, in 1939, England decided to scrap the Balfour Declaration and suspend Jewish immigration to Palestine. International migration conferences held at Évian-les-Bains, France, in 1939, and in Bermuda in 1943, opened few doors anywhere. In 1942, American Zionists met at the Hotel Biltmore in New York and came out baldly for an independent state in Palestine. World War II was going on; they hoped that when it was over, a new Jewish state would be established. To reinforce their demands, they called for a reborn all-American Jewish congress. It was a replay of the demands made in 1914, demands which had finally given birth to the first American Jewish Congress. Under the name of the American Jewish Conference, the new national assembly met in 1943. By that time, Jews had reliable information about the full horror of the Holocaust; surviving Jews had to have a refuge of their own. When the majority of the delegates voted for a commonwealth, the non-Zionist American Jewish Committee walked out; labor and the women of the National Jewish Council abstained from voting; most Reform Jews still hesitated to opt for a Jewish state; American nationalism ran at high tide during the war.

Angry at what they took to be the politicization of their rabbinical association by the Zionists, dozens of Reform rabbis in 1942-1943 created an anti-national organization, the American Council for Judaism; its founders set out to stress Judaism's humanitarian universalism. These dissidents summarily rejected the concept of a Jewish state and Jewish nationalism although some of them were not opposed to Palestine as a spiritual and cultural center. In 1947, guilt at having stood idly by as millions of Jews were slaughtered may have played a large part in influencing the United Nations to offer the Zionists and World Jewry a partitioned Palestine. On May 14, 1948, the Jews of Palestine proclaimed the State of Israel. The following year the Zionists dissolved the American Jewish Conference which had served its purpose. The need for a permanent American Jewish Congress was also disregarded; neither the Zionists nor any of the large American Jewish agencies were prepared to welcome a congress which might threaten their autonomy. American Jewry flocked to help the new state in the old fatherland. Most Jews here were committed not as nationalists but as sympathizers determined to assure World Jewry a home where any Jew could go as of right. They themselves would remain in the United States; this was their *patria*.

WHAT THE AMERICAN JEW DID FOR ZIONISM; WHAT ZIONISM DID FOR THE AMERICAN JEW

There can be no question that the American Jewish Conference, speaking for millions of Jews living in the powerful United States, prepared the way for the State of Israel. Jews here had been working for Zion for over fifty years. Leadership of this nationalist movement had been assumed in the early days by men like Richard Gottheil, Stephen S. Wise, and Louis Brandeis. Later, men of East European background took control: the brilliant, aggressive Abba Hillel Silver and the prophetic, sensitive Magnes, a man who would never be completely happy with the new state whose Arab minority was disadvantaged. Unlike most of his Zionist associates, Magnes realized that the status of Arabs in Israel, where Judaism was the established religion, confronted the Zionists and World Jewry with a real problem. He was also well aware that, as late as the 1950's, the Arabs were a majority in what had been the Palestine Mandate. Even before the American Jewish Conference convened, American Jews did much to bring Israel into being; they contributed money and political influence. Organized as Hadassah, the largest Zionist organization in the world, American Jewish women raised hundreds of millions of dollars for Zionist causes, saved the lives of thousands of Europe's youth brought to Mandatory Palestine before the onset of the Holocaust and developed Palestine's medical services, eradicating diseases and establishing an excellent hospital.

But Zionism did as much for the American Jew as the American Jew did for the movement. The Zionists established a haven for all Jews; American Jews have never forgotten that Israel is there for them, too—a great comfort since anti-Semitism has remained a threat in every land of substantial Jewish settlement; the United States is no exception. Before the 1940's, the Union of American Hebrew Congregations, the B'nai B'rith, the American Jewish Committee, the Jewish Labor Committee, the Joint Distribution Committee, and most Anglo-Jewish newspapers all kept their distance from Zionism. But Zionism "rejudaized" them; it restored the balance between tradition and acculturation; it gave Jews here a sense of pride, pride in the infant state, in its army, its victories, its horny-handed farmers. Jews gloried in the thought that Gentiles had learned to respect and to admire the Israelis. Some Jews here, dreading the sneers of the Gentiles if the state failed to survive, rallied to the support of the new commonwealth. American Jews are conscious of the cultural advances made in the State of Israel; they are proud of the new universities, the press, the publications, the museums, the artists, the new music. The synagogs of the United States today rock and sway to the tuneful Hebrew melodies that have come from the hills of Judea and the Philistine lowlands. The sense of kinship encouraged by working together to succor Diaspora Jewry was strengthened further by the common struggle to establish a Jewish asylum in Israel. On May 16, 1948, two days after the Palestinian Jews declared their independence, a mass meeting was held at Madison Square Garden; 100,000 people gathered there. Herbert H. Lehman and Henry Morgenthau, Jr., represented the American Jewish elite; now they, too, rejoiced with the masses. Zionism had helped unite American Jews.

ANTI-SEMITISM IN THE UNITED STATES, 1921-1985: THE ULTIMATE FORCE FOR FUSION

The ties that bound Jews together were made ever stronger by the never ending struggle against anti-Semitism; this common threat unified all Jews. Anti-Semitism and anti-Jewish prejudice are one and the same. Anti-Semitism, a pseudoscientific justification for an old social malady, maintains that Jews are an inferior, deleterious group; they must not be accepted as fellow citizens. This hatred, as proved true in Germany, may well endanger and even cost the lives of its victims. What are the sources of this hatred of Jews here in the United States? Judeophobia, already widespread in the Levantine Hellenistic world, flourished in the early Christian communes; the Jews are the villains in the gospels. Many centuries later, most European Gentiles brought their anti-Jewish prejudices with them in the impedimenta they unloaded on the American docks.

American nativism, xenophobia, stoked the older prejudices. The one Jew who came to Sir Walter Raleigh's Roanoke in 1585 was arrested on his return to England because he had blasphemously denied the divinity of Jesus. Jews have been rejected as strangers ever since they landed at Boston in 1649 and at New Amsterdam in 1654. Bias against newcomers has always characterized American life; even Benjamin Franklin had little sympathy for most immigrants; he thought them "tawny," not quite white.

Modern racist philosophies were imported from France and Germany in the 1880's. Decades later, since some of Russia's Communist leaders were Jews, American Judeophobes identified Communism with Judaism. Their attack on Jews found a receptive audience; Americans have long nursed an obsessive fear of Marxist philosophy. American labor, for its part, was opposed to Jews not as Jews but as immigrants. Workmen here wanted no competition in the labor market and for decades urged that the doors to America be closed to foreigners. Even Samuel Gompers, a Jewish newcomer himself, led the American Federation of Labor in its efforts to reduce the number of immigrants admitted. In order to justify anti-immigration legislation, labor and its cohorts in Congress looked askance at Jews seeking the shelter of America; East Europeans were not deemed desirable settlers. Some American farmers were also anti-Jewish. It was difficult for these small freeholders to compete in the new world of massive corporate enterprises; bad times found them impoverished and in need of a scapegoat. As Populists, they attacked all bankers, whom they identified as Jews despite the fact that very few midwestern Jews were moneylenders. Still another fire to feed the new-old prejudice is the fact that, on the whole, Jews were successful; envy turned many against them in America. The pious among America's Gentile masses were dismayed; why do the Christian righteous suffer while the infidel Jews prosper?

MANIFESTATIONS OF ANTI-SEMITISM

Notwithstanding the traditions of tolerance and egalitarianism which the founding fathers had cultivated, many Americans hugged their inherited anti-Jewish stereotypes. Political reaction set in after World War I; many people were now soured on the earlier Wilsonian liberalism; the pendulum had swung to the right. In 1919-1920, Attorney General A. Mitchell Palmer carried on raids against radicals; many foreign-born left-wingers were deported, Jews among them. In 1920, the anti-Jewish *Protocols of the Elders of Zion* made their appearance in this country. This forgery purported to show how the Jews were conspiring to rule the world. That same year, Henry Ford, a confirmed anti-Semite, spent millions in a public campaign attacking Jews. Threatened with a libel suit by a Jewish attorney, Aaron Sapiro, and fearing to be exposed in court as a man who was barely literate, this simpleminded populist finally apologized in 1927 for his campaign of hatred. Five years earlier, when Ford's anti-Jewish paper was being hawked on the streets of American cities, Harvard's President Abbott Lawrence Lowell set out to limit the number of Jews admitted to his school. Most of the Ivy League colleges had for years restricted the number of Jews they would accept. A few years later, in 1923, the reborn Ku Klux Klan was at its height, preaching hatred of blacks, Catholics, and Jews. The Klan, it was reported, had millions of members and for a brief period became politically powerful in several states.

The immigration acts of 1921 and 1924 marked the climax of America's nativism and anti-Jewish agitation. These bills were intended to keep East European peoples, Jews and others, out of this country. Racially motivated quotas were established; Slavs, Jews, Eastern Mediterraneans and Asians were deemed undesirable. The 1924 exclusionary bill meant that the suffering Polish and Rumanian Jews were now locked in; there were very few places to which they could turn for refuge. The years 1925 to 1929, years of prosperity, brought temporary relief, but then came the Great Depression which lasted on and off to 1941. This period saw millions impoverished; because a scapegoat was needed, many turned against the Jews. Some Gentile Germans, native-born and immigrants, carried on Nazi propaganda; American nativists, anti-Semites, organized a number of Nazi-like groups; in 1938, Father Charles Edward Coughlin, a Catholic priest, charmed millions as he attacked Jews in his radio talks. They were the country's exploiters, he said; the Jews, the bankers, and the corporate rich were responsible for the country's problems. In 1941, as war loomed on the horizon, Charles A. Lindberg, the transatlantic aviator and a world hero, denounced the Jews as warmongers; he repeated the stereotypical charges that Jews exercised undue control over government and industry.[9]

JEWISH FORCES OPPOSING ANTI-SEMITISM, 1921–1985

When Jews set out to defend themselves they could count on several agencies organized to help fight anti-Semitism. Among them were the American Jewish Committee, founded in 1906, the Anti-Defamation League (ADL), founded in 1913, the new American Jewish Congress, and the Jewish Labor Committee, established in 1934. The American Jewish Committee represented the more affluent natives; the ADL spoke for the non-Zionist provincial middle class; the Congress reflected the views of metropolitan Zionists; the Jewish Labor Committee was deputized by American Jewish unions. These organizations worked independently; since there was little liaison between them, duplication of effort and fundraising was inevitable. The agencies represented different and sometimes conflicting interests; not even the grave crisis in Nazi Germany would bring them together. One cannot but wonder; had they been more tightly knit, might they not have done more to save Europe's Jews during the Holocaust? But these groups were determined to go off on their own; self-defense was big business; millions of dollars were spent; there were vested interests. The agencies not only document different philosophies, but also a power struggle between their bureaucrats, who were influential in selecting the lay leaders. In order to make headway—there is no question of the sincerity of the men who headed these different societies—vast quantities of literature were prepared and distributed; radio and later television were employed; articles were planted in magazines. The American Jewish Committee made detailed scientific studies utilizing the very best psychological techniques.

All the defense associations tried to enlist the help and sympathy of the churches, the unions, blacks, veterans; governors and mayors' Friendly Relation Committees were organized to win the good will and cooperation of diverse local groups. These Friendly Relations Committees were often effective. Legislative enactments and court decisions were helpful. There is no way to measure the full impact of these Jewish defense institutions; certainly they did help maintain Jewish morale, but one suspects that their rational approach, their appeal to reason, did little to convert confirmed Jew-haters. A cursory reading of any anti-Semitic newspaper—there are several—will disclose that the antagonism of the writers is pathological; they are irrational, mentally and emotionally disturbed people living in a world far removed from that of the man or woman who reads a typical American newspaper.

GENERAL FORCES OPPOSING ANTI-SEMITISM
THE DECLINE OF JUDEOPHOBIA AFTER WORLD WAR II;
ITS EFFECTS ON AMERICAN JEWRY

What allies could Jews count on in those days before World War II? Not many; or at least that is what the apprehensive Jew believed when he found himself surrounded by groups who hated him and assailed him as an *Unmensch*, a monster. He felt very much alone. The Jews did have allies, but they were few; the American people in the depression years were preoccupied with their own problems. The Jewish Labor Committee warned American unions what they could expect when fascism controlled the state; the liberals and their press were sympathetic, but they were small in number. The newspapers were rarely interested in the problems of the Jews; anti-Semitism was not news. The churches were slow to respond to Jewish calls for help. In 1928, the National Conference of Christians and Jews (NCCJ) was established, primarily by laymen concerned to eliminate prejudice, to further amity, and to emphasize the ideals which Judaism and Christianity held in common. Did the National Conference of Christians and Jews effect any change in the lives of the men and women to whom they appealed? No one can say for sure. In the last decades of the twentieth century, the NCCJ staged very impressive annual banquets where a Protestant, a Jew, and a Catholic were honored. It was always a beautiful, almost euphoric experience. Men and women of diverse faiths reached out to embrace one another, if only for a night.

Ultimately, to be sure, the war against the Jews in America failed. Prosperity followed the preparations for the armed conflict against Germany; people who have jobs are not so easily roused to hate. The New Deal social legislation pacified those crushed by the depression. World War II revealed the German, the anti-Semite, as the enemy; anti-Semitism was now unpatriotic. The isolationist America First Committee, some of whose supporters were Jew-haters, was disbanded; populist senators who had reached out to attack Jews lost their following and were not reelected. Anti-Semitism affected Jews in a variety of ways. A few sought safety in low visibility; some with German or Jewish names changed them, so that Cohens became Coles and Corbetts, while Kaplans became Capps and Copelands. Most Jews refused to let Jew-hatred cow them; their Jewish nationalist instincts were aroused, and the turn to ethnicity brought some to Zionism. Many reaffirmed their Judaism, their Jewish ties.

The resurgence of anti-Semitism in the early 1930's had induced some Jews to believe that America was not yet ready to disavow this social malady; they were even more disturbed when the liberal Weimar Republic fell into the hands of the German National Socialists. Then, a decade later, came the reports of the Holocaust, the horror of the death camps. For many, this revelation was the most traumatic event of their lives; they despaired of liberalism, of humanity itself. The generation of the 1940's would have been even more disillusioned had it known how little its idol, Roosevelt, and his administration had done to save the lives of endangered Jews. The President had been most circumspect. Neither he nor his cabinet nor the Congress nor labor had wanted or thought it politically wise to open America's ports to the trapped human beings; even the legally permissible number of immigrants had been ignored; few petitioners had been admitted. The authorities in Washington and American representatives abroad thus shared responsibility for the death of hundreds of thousands of men, women, and children who might have been saved without hindrance to the war effort. Roosevelt brought his people out of the depression and crushed the Third Reich, but he was morally derelict in refusing to help Europe's Jews in the saddest hour of Jewish history since the legions of Titus stormed the walls of Jerusalem. The Jews here were paralyzed with fear; their leader Stephen S. Wise, probably already

stricken with cancer, hesitated to break with Roosevelt. Any public protest against the beloved President—and especially in wartime—might
well have been self-defeating. There were Jews in high office who did
nothing, though they knew full well the nature of the crisis; Henry Morgenthau, Jr., Secretary of the Treasury, was a notable exception. What
the government finally did was too little and too late. After the war thousands of displaced persons and refugees—among them, many Jews—were
finally brought to the United States, but by that time more than
5,000,000 Jews had been slain in German-occupied Europe.[10]

Despite the fact that anti-Jewish prejudice was in bad odor after the
Second World War, it still persisted; a social syndrome that had thrived
for over 2,000 years may become quiescent, but it never disappears. In the
second half of the twentieth century, the practitioners of this black art
were still numerous, whether as teen-age delinquents, demagogues, or
professional anti-Semites. Included in this weird crew were occasional
congressmen, who regaled their colleagues with anti-Jewish slurs; respected business executives, who worked perhaps more discreetly against
Jews; and conservative and reactionary political associations, whose views
bordered on the anti-Semitic. Addressing a group at Duke University Law
School in 1974, General George S. Brown of the Joint Chiefs of Staff implied that Jews exerted undue influence on banks, newspapers, and the
Congress. A verbatim report of his talk indicates that this man was incredibly naive, intellectually immature. When new evidence was presented
exonerating Leo Frank, who had been lynched in 1915 by a mob in Mar-
ietta, Georgia, the State Board of Pardons and Paroles refused to acknowledge the victim's innocence; such acknowledgment would have been a
reflection on the citizens who had murdered an innocent man, and the
state had to save face.

Large cities, in the course of each year, experienced numerous acts of
anti-Jewish vandalism, usually the work of youngsters. The vandals were
not always motivated by anti-Semitism; on occasion, the defacement of a
building occupied by Jews was the work of a disgruntled Jewish lad. Still,
vandals, young and old, daubed Nazi swastikas on synagogs and other
buildings and desecrated cemeteries. (Somehow, there is a constant recur-
rent penchant to destroy tombstones; students of psychopathology and
necrophilism may find this aberration worthy of study.) Congressmen
who attacked Jews were most vocal before World War II; after the war,
demagogues elected to office were less outspoken, but violence against
Jews was not uncommon in the years following World War II. Racists
bombed and burned homes and synagogs; blacks and Jews were murdered. Most, though not all, of these acts of violence occurred in the
South, where the Ku Klux Klan tradition was still alive. Anti-Semitic
booklets had made their appearance in this country as early as the 1880's;

the first anti-Jewish newspaper—it was in German—was published in the 1890's; the number of these journals increased in the mid-twentieth century. Their circulation has always been very limited; they do not appeal to the typical American reader, but one or two of them, letterpress and multicolored, are expensive productions; obviously, they have some generous supporters. One could write a fascinating doctoral dissertation analyzing the mind-set of anti-Jewish editors.

Senator Bilbo, "The Man" from Mississippi, had nothing but contempt for dagoes (Italians), kikes (Jews), and blacks. He did not live to see the victory of the blacks in the Supreme Court decision, *Brown v. Board of Education of Topeka*, which outlawed racial segregation in public schools. After this decision, blacks won other rights and immunities to which they were justly entitled as American citizens. Jews were helpful in the struggle; Jews were among the founders of the National Association for the Advancement of Colored People, and Northern Jews often fought for blacks. Although the *Brown* decision was not a new departure in American law, it served psychologically as a breakthrough for the country's blacks spurring them on to continue the battle for full emancipation. Some militants among them turned on the Jews, whom they accused, in effect, of seeking to infantilize blacks. The Jews in the larger city ghettos, especially in New York, had trouble with them as early as the 1940's, when they began rioting and looting Jewish stores. Jewish landlords and shopkeepers were numerous in the black ghettos, which had once been Jewish neighborhoods; prime examples are Harlem and the Bronx, where some Jewish businessmen had stayed on. The revolt of the New Left in the 1960's appealed to many blacks, especially the intellectuals among them; they spoke of "Black Power," "Black is Beautiful." The Metropolitan Museum of Art incorporated an anti-Jewish slur in a brochure which it published, an essay by a young black. New York Jews were angry, many not so much with the blacks as with the museum which they had generously supported. Jews were also annoyed when it was revealed that President Carter's ambassador to the United Nations, Andrew Young, a black, had met privately with an emissary of the Palestine Liberation Organization, an anti-Israel and anti-Jewish guerrilla group—it remains unclear whether the ambassador was acting on his own or following a covert administration policy.

Sharp rejection of Jews by black militants may be explained, in part at least, on the basis of black psychological needs. They have suffered oppression for centuries; their treatment as inferiors has embittered, in some instances even deranged them; the impositions of the whites have left them unsure of their own potentialities. Because of the imperative need to reassure themselves, they have become convinced that, as Christians or, in some cases, as Muslims, they are superior to Jews, whom they often affect to despise. This denigratory attitude is supported by some of their leaders, who have on occasion expressed open contempt for Jews. A member of the Congress of Racial Equality even said that Hitler had not killed enough Jews. Some blacks, particularly Muslims, are convinced anti-Semites, since Islam has looked upon Jews—and Christians, too—with barely disguised contempt. Extremes often meet; professional white anti-Semites, who always attacked blacks, have in at least one instance joined with black Muslims in verbal assaults on Jews. In February, 1962, the late George Lincoln Rockwell, a Jew-baiter, addressed thousands of Muslim blacks at a convention.

The militants, and many other blacks, eager to advance themselves in the American economy, have posited the concept of affirmative action, arguing—often with the support of white liberals—that blacks (and Hispanics, too) must be accorded economic preference because they have been abused in the past; that they are entitled to special quotas; and that competence is not necessarily decisive. This many Jews have rejected, insisting on absolute equality of opportunity and refusing to accept the imposition of quotas. The attempt by blacks to supplant Jewish teachers in some sections of New York City made for bad blood. Owing to these conflicting interests, the alliance forged in New Deal days between blacks, Jews, labor, liberals, and Democrats has been weakened, though in the 1980's, many American Jewish leaders were determined to rebuild the old Democratic coalition which had once embraced both Jews and blacks; Jews realized full well the importance of a group which numbered 26,000,000. The more perceptive leaders of the blacks know—and so do the Jews—that, if the rights of Jews are curtailed, the blacks will be the next victims. Black people have been even more consistent than Jews in the support of the Democratic Party; they know what is at stake.

Some black states of Africa and other Third World lands have adopted an anti-Israel policy. To be anti-Israel is generally understood by American Jews to be anti-Jewish, and it follows that to be anti-Jewish is to be hostile to American Jewry. All this is deemed perilously close to anti-Semitism. Such, at least, is the reasoning of most American Jews. Theoretically, anti-Semitism is the rejection of any people whose culture is "Semitic" (even though Semitic is properly a linguistic, not an ethnic, term). All this is ironic, for many Muslims, who appear irreconcilably anti-Jewish, speak a Semitic tongue and have thus developed a "Semitic" culture. The Arabs, hating and fearing the State of Israel and its well-trained troops, have used their power as suppliers of much of the world's oil to turn the Third World against Israel, Judaism, and Jews. They have carried on a propaganda war against American Jews, too, because American Jewry is seen as Israel's prime supporter. It was due to Arab influence in the United Nations that, in 1975, Zionism was equated with racism and Zionists were denounced; in this attack, the Arabs were abetted by the Soviet Union. If Leopold von Ranke was right in his theory that, regardless of rulers, a state rarely modifies its political nature and its traditional ethos, then the Soviets and their Romanov predecessors have in common a dislike of Jews. The present-day Russian regime is also anti-Israel because it wants to secure the support of the oil-rich Arab states; the primary Soviet goal is to displace the United States as the world's foremost power; the Soviets feel threatened. With some exceptions, Jews have not been permitted to leave the Soviet Union; Jewry in this country has responded to Russian prejudice by establishing nation-wide organizations to help Soviet Jewry.

It is difficult to evaluate the influence of Arab anti-Jewish propaganda in this country; its effectiveness is certainly not patent. More important is the impact of Europe-inspired anti-Semitism, a genre of Judeophobia which made its appearance here in the 1880's. Jews on this continent had been concerned with older traditional forms of prejudice. Anti-Jewish violence has never been a problem here, although bias was endemic in the North American colonies and in the United States until the third quarter of the twentieth century when its overt exercise abated. Up until this time, about a decade after World War II, Jews experienced intolerance in housing; there were neighborhoods where they were not wanted. For a time, Gentiles in the suburbs tried to keep Jews from building their synagogs; some hotels and summer resorts were also closed to them; often, there were admission quotas in private schools, colleges, and universities; Jews were frequently excluded from the Greek letter fraternities and were kept off the teaching and administrative staffs of numerous institutions of higher learning. Orthodox Jews built Yeshiva College in 1928, because they knew they were not wanted and because they wished to indoctrinate their native-born youth.

Discriminatory practices in Ivy League institutions were also responsible for the rise of Brandeis University, a Jewish sponsored institution, in 1948; the University's declaration that it wanted to make a contribution to American culture was, one suspects, a public relations ploy to justify its distinctiveness and to open the purses of wealthy Jews. Social exclusion in Gentile clubs prevails even today. Snobbery is the last bastion of socialites who have no other distinction to sustain them. This snobbery can verge on the ludicrous; the ball committee in a Scarsdale country club barred a Christian because his father was a Jew. Introspective Jews know full well that, in their own posh country clubs, they prefer to associate with coreligionists. On the whole, Jews no longer resent the exclusionary practices of Gentiles, though they realize that social rejection may well become an economic disability; if one cannot meet with elite corporate executives, one cannot do business with them. One's only recourse, then, is to storm the doors of executive suites by sheer ability, and this is now being done.

One of the hazards ambitious Jews faced in the early decades of the twentieth century was their Russian origin. This in itself made them suspect in an America which commonly believed that a Russian is a communist. With the beginning of the Cold War and the renewal of the conflict with the Soviets in the late 1940's, it was difficult for many liberal and radical Jews to escape the stigma of communism. Senator Joseph McCarthy, an anti-communist crusader—but apparently no anti-Semite—helped create a climate of opinion that forced some Jewish officeholders out of government service. The new 1952 McCarran-Walter Immigration Act retained the old racist quotas; yet, despite its continuing restrictions, hundreds of thousands of displaced persons and refugees, among them numerous Jews, were admitted to these shores in the 1940's and 1950's. The new Immigration and Nationality Act of 1965 finally shelved ethnic quotas, although the absolute numbers of those to be admitted in the future still remained limited.

A few bold Judeophobes, encouraged by a never absent anti-Jewish sentiment, ran for high office in the last quarter of the century, but were all defeated. If these anti-Semitic candidates built their hopes on anti-Jewish prejudice, they misjudged the electorate. The polls may have misled them; various polls did indicate that more than 20 percent of the people queried felt that Jews were too powerful; 37 to 48 percent, at different times, believed that Jews were more loyal to Israel than to the United States. (The specter of dual loyalties is no delusion in the minds of those American Jews who are 125 percent patriotic.) About 34 percent of individuals polled said frankly that they disliked Jews. How significant are polls? People may vent their opinion in a poll; they are more cautious in the voting booth. Some historians of little faith may dare to venture the opinion, cautiously to be sure, that polls are self-defeating. If carefully phrased questions were to be directed to a scientific sample of the populace asking what it thought of the British, the French, or the Italians, the answers might well startle polsters. Whether the prejudice expressed would eventuate in hostile acts is questionable.[11]

JEWS AND OBSERVANT CHRISTIANS

A minority of this country's citizens want to make the United States juridically a Christian state; they are quite willing to disregard the constitutional clauses forbidding religious disabilities in political life. As it now stands the Federal Constitution does not tolerate a union of church and state, but not all Christians are happy with the constitutional barriers that have been erected between Church and State. There has never been a generation in which pious Christians have not attempted to modify the neutral religious intent of the Constitution. In 1811, some congressmen tried, unsuccessfully, to prohibit the mail stages and the post riders from traveling on Sunday. Ever since that time—indeed, for well over a century—Christians in and out of Congress have attempted to baptize the Federal Constitution. If the United States were ever to establish Christianity, the Jew would be less of a citizen, though this does not necessarily mean that he would be egregiously disadvantaged. England, for example, has an established church, yet is one of the world's most liberal states. It is worthy of note, however, that when World War II broke out and the fate of England hung in the balance, public opinion or the army brass forced the Jewish secretary of war, Leslie Hore-Belisha, out of office. Here in the United States, Judah P. Benjamin suffered a similar fate.

Recent years have seen several encroachments on the concept of the separation of Church and State. The federal, state, and municipal governments, each within its own jurisdiction, have tolerated or encouraged Bible readings and prayers in the public schools, the observance of religious holidays, the opening of classrooms for religious meetings, and the banning of books in school libraries at the request of religious denominations. Private and religious schools have received government aid in busing, textbooks, food, medical treatment, and tuition credits, all at the expense of the taxpayer. In the 1980's, the Supreme Court decided that a municipality may officially celebrate Christmas and set up crèches, all this out of public funds. In the late twentieth century, large numbers of evangelical Protestants were determined to make the United States a Christian country. These religionists have gone beyond the benevolent neutrality toward religion which was traditional in this country. They want more than the acceptance of military chaplains and the pious numismatic imprint, "In God We Trust." They desire the establishment of "Christianity"—Protestant Christianity?—in this country. More than 100 Christian radio stations and 25 television outlets champion this end. They are not inevitably anti-Jewish, but, if queried, would probably maintain that a Jew cannot be as good a citizen as a Christian. For them, there is no doubt: this is a Christian country regardless of the religious neutrality required by the country's organic statute. Many of these evangelicals are sympathetic to the State of Israel; God has promised the Chosen People that they would be restored and He has made good His word; "God is not a man, that He should lie" (Num.23:19). Back of this friendliness is the unexpressed conviction that, in millenarian days, the Jews will find shelter in the bosom of Jesus. The evangelicals are not supported, however, by the National Council of Churches of Christ, a loose federation of some 40,000,000 Christians who seek ecumenical amity. The National Council is not always happy with the State of Israel; the resurgence of this commonwealth, a symbol of a risen Jewry, is an implicit denial of the ultimate worldwide victory of Christianity, but the Council is aware that a uniform Protestantism would be but a precursor of religious intolerance.[12]

ACCEPTANCE

Is the existing prejudice against the Jew dangerous to his survival? Not necessarily. After all, affluent Jews owe almost everything to their Gentile neighbors. It should be borne in mind that the hundreds of millions of dollars raised by Jewish Welfare Funds annually and sent overseas to Jews in need has been earned from Gentile clients and customers; this money has not been made by Jews taking in one another's washing. Non-Jews patronize Jewish tradespeople and professionals; they trust their Jewish doctors, dentists, and lawyers. Only in one area do Gentiles tend to keep their distance; they live their own social life; there is relatively little post-prandial fellowship. For the most part, social separation has been welcomed by Jews; they, too, have wanted to be alone with their own. Let there be no question: on the whole, Jews have been accepted by their Gentile neighbors, probably as much here as in any other country. The glass is more than half full; rejection by Gentile fellow citizens is not and never has been a real problem in the United States. As early as World War I, when the Community Chest, now the United Way, was established to provide a common charity fund for all religious and ethnic groups in a city, the Jews were automatically included. They probably received as much as they contributed. Cordell Hull, Roosevelt's Secretary of State, did little, if anything, to rescue German Jews seeking American asylum, but Henry Alfred Kissinger, a German refugee, became Richard Nixon's Secretary of State in 1973.

Even in the early 1900's, when sentiment against Jewish immigrants was strong, well over a dozen states passed laws penalizing discrimination based on color or creed. The New Deal moved to eliminate disabilities by executive order; fair employment and fair education laws were enacted by states and the federal government in the years following World War II. Restrictive housing covenants were no longer lawfully enforceable. True, these laws were often observed in the breach, but anti-Jewish and anti-black practices were no longer given free rein. The Civil Rights Act of 1964 was a great advance in guaranteeing equality for minorities, for blacks, Jews, and women, too. Even big business in the 1960's was slowly beginning to take note of Jews and to move them into positions of power.

One suspects that it was the 1964 Civil Rights Act which helped Jews enter the countinghouse; places had to be found for qualified blacks, and Jews rode in on the coattails of the blacks, as they had in 1868, when Jews were "emancipated" following the election of blacks (Christians, of course) to the North Carolina state legislature. Jews also made notable advances in the colleges of this country. Jews no longer found it difficult to matriculate at good schools and to join teaching staffs. Their percentage in some of the best American colleges rose, and it became easier to enter medical schools and to receive internships. There were now thousands of Jewish instructors in American universities. In 1900, not a single Jew was to be found in Yale's graduate and professional schools; in 1957, there were 592. In 1900, there were no Jewish professors at Yale; in 1970, there were 103; a Jew served as provost, while another Jew, a dean at Harvard, was offered the university presidency. Jewish college presidents now abound. After blacks were encouraged to establish courses in minority studies, there was no problem for Jews as they followed suit. In the late twentieth century, studies in the German Holocaust were introduced into some of the nation's largest public school systems and in a number of universities.

Of all the tangential areas where Jew and Gentile meet, none is more sensitive than religion. Contemporary Jews, still insecure in their relations with Christians, who overwhelm them by sheer numbers, continue to evince a great deal of interest in interfaith work. This is one of the reasons they have supported the National Conference of Christians and Jews liberally. Jewish theologians and social workers in this country worked closely with the American Catholic hierarchy when Vatican II was convened in the years 1962-1965. These Jews certainly influenced the Church to condemn anti-Semitism and to declare that Catholics recognize the "bond that spiritually ties the people of the New Covenant to Abraham's stock." The Jews had hoped for a stronger statement; they failed to realize that Catholics cannot jump out of their skins by repudiating fifteen hundred years of Jewish-Catholic relations. Here in the United States, the Jews enjoy semi-official status as America's third faith. In the late 1930's, Father Coughlin found many followers among Brooklyn Catholics; a generation later, Bishop Francis J. Mugavero, of Brooklyn, urged his flock to study the history of its Jewish neighbors. Not infrequently, Jews served as chairmen on the boards of Catholic institutions. There are chapels for Jews at the United States Military Academy and the Air Force Academy; the Jewish worship pennant flies from the mast of navy ships when Jewish services are in progress; the government makes provision for Jewish day schools to the same degree that it recognizes Christian private schools.

Jews give courses in Protestant seminaries and lecture on Judaism in Catholic colleges. In 1860, several American newspapers protested when Rabbi Morris J. Raphall, attired in prayer shawl and skullcap, led Congress in prayer, but since that day hundreds of Jewish chaplains have served the armed forces, and since Truman's time they have led in prayer at presidential inaugurations. Dozens of non-Jewish institutions buy Israeli bonds; Governor James Thompson of Illinois, a Christian, conducted a seder in his gubernatorial mansion during the years he held office. Charles Hodge, a Princeton theological seminary theologian, is remembered for his famous remark: "A new idea never originated in this seminary." This may be true of the theological school; it is not true of Princeton University itself. For decades, this liberal arts college frowned on the appointment of Jewish faculty; in the 1980's, it had a kosher kitchen, which served students during the year and their parents at graduation. In March, 1945, Chaplain Roland E. Darrow, a Methodist, conducted Friday night services for Jewish troops in the cathedral town of Rheims. He wore a Jewish prayer shawl and the traditional skullcap. "He broke his teeth" over the Hebrew in the ritual, but he persisted. Governor Peter Stuyvesant of seventeenth-century New Amsterdam would not have approved; in 1656, he had seen fit to refuse the Jews "the free and public exercise of their abominable religion." Because of their religion and the accidents of history, Jews are still, to a degree, a people set apart; yet their Gentile fellow citizens have learned to live with them.[13]

WHY JEWISH DEFENSE AGENCIES?

If most Americans have accepted their Jewish neighbors, why then the need for numerous defense organizations? Why should Jews be concerned with anti-Semitism and polls which reveal anti-Jewish attitudes? The answer is: Jews oppose anti-Semitism because of its potential danger. In 315 C.E. the Christian Emperor Constantine issued his first anti-Jewish law, a prologue to the later Theodosian and Justinian codes, which incorporated a number of decrees denying Jews political, economic, religious, and social equality. These codes, in effect, created the medieval Jew who was little better than a pariah. Germany of the 1930's and 1940's is a classical example of what happened to a liberal commonwealth when Jew-haters took over. Coughlin's insidious radio appeals in 1938 frightened America's Jews; the Holocaust, five years later, warned them of the evils of Judeophobia.

Most American Jews have a twofold reaction to prejudice: some are minded to "fight"; others take refuge in "flight." What is meant by fighting, by resistance? Defense agencies seeking the good will of their fellow citizens assume that human beings respond to rational appeals. All these agencies are constant in their efforts to defeat anti-Semitism. Typical of this approach is the funding of *Commentary* by the American Jewish Committee. One wonders how effective this magazine is. And the dozens of brochures published by the Anti-Defamation League and other Jewish organizations? Do America's decision makers read them? The Jewish, Protestant, and Catholic interfaith agencies may well be making headway through their propaganda meetings and literature, but it is almost impossible to determine the degree of their success. The men and women, Christians, who are gathered together under the umbrella of the National Council of Churches of Christ have to be convinced. These believers will never easily admit that Judaism is spiritually the equal of Christianity. The indoctrination to which they are exposed leaves them scant choice. At best, in the spirit of the founding fathers, they are benevolently tolerant.

More important are the social changes wrought by state and federal legislation, by presidential executive decrees, by victories in court. Fighting in the courts and in the legislatures, the concerned Jewish agencies have done away with restrictive covenants and made progress in outlawing discriminatory practices in employment, housing, and public accommodations; they have battled against encroachments on the first amendment's religion clause, as they interpreted it. Jews have been helped materially by Title VII of the Civil Rights Act of 1964, a statute which set out primarily to protect blacks and women.

In order to help Jews, associations such as the National Jewish Community Relations Advisory Council, the American Jewish Congress, the American Jewish Committee, the Anti-Defamation League, and the like have worked through presidents, Congress, state authorities, and communications media. Rabbi Meir Kahane, not content with these moderate policies, resorted to direct action; in 1968, he set out to meet violence with violence in Brooklyn. His organization—the later Jewish Defense League—began as a semi-vigilante group to protect Jews from assaults by delinquents and hooligans. In the course of time, the League directed its energies and attacks against Soviet officialdom here in the United States. Its supporters were young people; with the Holocaust in mind, it adopted the slogan, "Never Again." The Jewish defense agencies disapproved of these tactics. Later Kahane moved to Israel, secured a seat in Parliament, and began advocating the policy of expelling all Arabs from the country. A number of young American Jewish men and women rallied around him; many Israelis and most Americans, however, have disavowed him.

The majority of American Jews, so it would seem, prefer not to fight disabilities but to take refuge in "flight"; they avoid confrontation even when their liberties are threatened. Cowardice? Not necessarily; feeling the odds are against them and hesitating to protest, they circumvent disabilities whenever possible. They are often successful; they have a long experience in survival. Community relations professionals hired to fight prejudice find at times that their own lay leaders will not support them when encroachments loom on the horizon. Opposition to the singing of Christmas carols in public schools and advocating removal of crèches municipally funded can only be bad for business! Christians in the month of December are very sensitive if their celebrations are threatened. In short, there are Jews who refuse to resist the attempts to breach the wall between Church and State. This is a battle which some decline to fight. Often, when they encounter anti-Jewish pressures in the marketplace, they sedulously avoid confrontation. They crowd into the interstitial spaces where little or no competition is offered; they enter into new, even hazardous enterprises which are not yet dominated by the powerful and the privileged. The cinema industry is a classic illustration. Some take cover in the civil services hoping that they will find security under a government committed to equality; unfortunately, they are not always guaranteed a haven during periods of reaction. Most Jews are convinced that education serves more than one purpose; they believe that a B.A. degree is an instrument of survival, a passport to social and economic mobility. The free and liberal professions give them the opportunity to "merchandise" themselves; they exploit their ingenuity, their knowledge, their personalities. As businesspeople, they set out to manufacture a better mousetrap; as professionals, they are determined to excel. To survive, most of them have already become white-collar workers; they yearn to be self-employed. They have a passion for anonymity; acculturation is seen as prophylactic.

Virtually every Jew seeks to become the perfect Anglo-Saxon gentleman or lady in garb and speech. Even some Orthodox Jews do not hesitate in business hours to eat with a client and to disregard the dietary prohibition against the eating of pork (bacon) and shellfish (shrimps). Garb is no problem; dignified rabbinic expositors of talmudic law wear dinner jackets at banquets; they conform gladly. Nowhere is the passion for anonymity and accommodation more pronounced than in the use of first names. Behind many Bruces, Scotts, and Douglases lurks a Jew; no longer is Yitshak called Isidor or Irving; a presentday parent who seeks low visibility for his son does so by rendering Yitshak literally; it emerges as the Puritan beloved Isaac. Few will suspect that a Jew would deliberately name a child after a biblical patriarch. Theodore L. Adams was one of America's outstanding Orthodox rabbis; the late Henry Adams, scholar and anti-Semite, would have resented this adoption of his family name. During the depression, Milton Shapiro, a traveling salesman, changed his name to Shapp because he ran into anti-Semitism. Later in the 1970's he became governor of Pennsylvania. Irving Shapiro, a young lawyer, held on to his cognomen; despite its Jewishness, he became the head of Dupont. Mayhap the decision to retain Jewish-sounding family names heralds the dawn of a new emancipation.

Jews who seek a low profile in business have been aided by the country's ecology. The caricature Jew now exists only in anti-Jewish cartoons. Anthropologists tell us that the Jews no longer look "Jewish." In 1907, Franz Boas, the anthropologist, was asked by an immigration commission to study newcomers. In his *Changes in Bodily Form of Descendants of Immigrants*, he demonstrated the influence of environment; American-born children differ from their foreign-born parents in physical characteristics because of America's food, climate, and speech. The rate of intermarriage in the United States of the 1980's ran to about 30 percent; the children born of these marriages take on some of the physical characteristics of their Gentile-born parents. In the early 1940's, Professor Jacob R. Marcus of the Hebrew Union College lectured at Duke. He knew that Professor Judah Goldin, a fellow Jew, was in the audience and, though he had never met, he recognized him immediately. Marcus was confident; it takes a Jew to spot a Jew. After the lecture, Marcus met the man he had picked out; he was a Christian minister.[14]

THE NEW AMERICAN JEWISH COMMUNITY
THE NEW GHETTOS

The anti-Semitism of the 1920's, the 1930's, and the 1940's, both here and in Europe, had a profound effect on American Jewry; it was shaken by the Holocaust. Jews here drew together despite conflicting loyalties to local and national institutions. Jewry here was characterized by a socioemotional ghettoistic withdrawal, a psychic reaction that, in effect, resulted in something akin to the re-creation of the medieval-like defensive community. This was certainly true on the local level. The clustering together strengthened a process already underway. By the Second World War, all American Jews were one as Americans and Jews; they were Americans civically and culturally; they were Jewishly one, forged by the common problems of relief, Zionism, and the "rejection" of the Jew in Europe and on this Western continent, too. Jews here in the United States had to work together and they did; they brushed their mutual distrust aside. Pushed by fears and desires, an integrated, consolidated American Jewry set out to create local communities and a national community; even more, it reached out to assert World Jewish hegemony. Traditionally, if there was a community, there had to be a ghetto. By the 1980's, there were three huge "ghettos" in this country. One, on the East Coast, started at Miami, Florida, and—with gaps—extended north to Portland, Maine; another, on the West Coast, reached from San Diego to the north shores of San Francisco Bay. The third, on the southern shores of the Great Lakes, extended from Rochester and Buffalo, west through Cleveland, Detroit, and Chicago to Milwaukee. American Jewry had become an urban or, more correctly, a suburban people. About 55 percent lived in five towns: New York, Los Angeles, Philadelphia, Chicago, and Miami. Long before World War I, New York's Jews had already begun moving out of the East Side, starting the long arduous upward climb to modest affluence, constantly acculturating as they shifted from one ghetto to another. In 1981, there were 1,670,700 Jews in the five urban and the three suburban counties that constituted Greater New York; Jews were 31 percent of the non-black, non-Hispanic population. In 1983 some three-fourths of American Jewry lived in or around cities of a half-million or more. Some of the Northern and Midwestern Jewish towns were losing population; the Sun Belt had come into its own. Jews, in large numbers, were moving to the South, the Southwest, and on to the Pacific Coast. In 1921, Phoenix, Arizona, seems to have had but one congregation, its membership numbering seventy; in 1984, there were several synagogs, including a Reform congregation with 1,410 members. The Jews, of course, had not initiated this trek to the South and West; they had followed their Gentile fellow citizens.

Why did Jews continue to huddle together? They have been an urban white-collar folk for a long time; they had settled in the larger towns to enjoy commercial and cultural advantages. Apprehensive, they have always wanted to be near their own. Jews may sense Gentile aloofness; certainly, their ethnic sentience is very strong. It has been charged that Jews have re-created the ghetto. Their answer may well be that they have always lived in a ghetto, whether in antiquity or in twentieth-century America; they have wished to do so; it has been a voluntary act on their part. Jews are not the only people who live in ghettos. If a demographic portrait of America was drawn it would be pointillistic; every dot would represent a ghetto of some sort, each one neatly secluded according to its own ethnic, social, and economic factors.

And how shall we define this Jew who lives in an enclave of his own choosing? More precisely who is a Jew, an American Jew? There are two definitions, that of the Gentile and that of the Jew himself. The Gentile maintains that any person is a Jew if there is the slightest reminiscence of Jewish origin. Let him join a Christian church—he will always be known as "our Jewish member." And the Jewish definition? Jews are latitudinarian. Anyone is a Jew who says he is a Jew and connects himself with the Jewish people. He is accepted with few questions asked. No confession of faith is required in any synagog, not even in a right-wing Hassidic shtiebl. One might distinguish four types of American Jews. First, there are religionists of every denominational preference; then, there are secularists, civil religionists, and ethnicists, many of whom are Zionists. The third group consists of rootless Jews; among them are intellectuals who still retain tenuous ties to Jewry. Finally, there are the Israel-oriented, their bodies in the West, their hearts in the East; they are 100 (125?) percent pro-Israel, but are not ready to make aliyah to join their fellow Jews in the land of the patriarchs. Included among these Americans are the hundreds of thousands of Israelis who have migrated to the United States and have yet to make up their minds whether they will become an integral part of the American Jewish community.[15]

AMERICAN JEWISH RELIGIOUS DENOMINATIONS

More than half of this country's Jews are religionists, in principle at least. They are not always affiliated and, even when members of a synagog, insist on their God-given right not to attend services. Among all of America's religionists, the Jews stand out in that they fall behind the Catholics and the Protestant sectarians in the frequency of their visits to a house of worship. The Jews of today often emphasize the ethnic rather than the religious; the ethnic bond is strong, which is why Israel plays such a large part in the economy of Jewish thinking. The attachment to Israel is rarely to its religious leadership; indeed most Jews are not enamored of the zealous Orthodoxy which characterizes Israel's "established church." One thing is sure: the old East European type of yiddishkeit is fast disappearing; America has given birth to a new Jew and a new Judaism; every new Jewry is sui generis.[16]

THE AMERICAN COUNCIL FOR JUDAISM

In name at least, the American Council for Judaism could claim to be the most religious of the several American Jewish religious denominations. Ultimately, it was to become the least religious—it was basically a political organization. It began in 1942 as a protest of those members of Reform's Central Conference of American Rabbis who opposed the aggressive tactics of the political Zionists in the Central Conference. The year 1942 was the year of the Biltmore Declaration and its demand for a Jewish commonwealth. The unhappy rabbis then established the American Council for Judaism, but remained members of the Reform rabbinical conference and, in effect, became its left wing. Ultimately, the Council was taken over by affluent laymen determined to oppose the creation of a Jewish political state. When its politicization became evident, most of the rabbis—not all—resigned from the Council. Their prime concern had been religion, not politics. For them, Reform Judaism meant a cosmopolitan, universalist, humanitarian faith.

The lay leaders of the Council were unsympathetic to traditional forms and ceremonies as well as to Jewish ethnicism. They had no use for Jewish nationalism, though they were ardent American nationalists. The new lay leadership set out to denationalize Reform Judaism. The religion they hoped to develop would, like Christianity, have no relation to any specific people or state. Judaism for them was to be another religious denomination; they saw themselves as American citizens of the Jewish persuasion and could not accept the claim that the Jews were also a people. It is by no means improbable that a few of the Council's votaries were escapists, inverted Marranos—overtly Jews, but wishfully Gentiles. They hesitated to assimilate totally because of Jewish social pressures or a fear of being rejected by the outside Christian world. It is not easy to secede from Jewry, as many have found out. Jews who have become members of a Unitarian church have not always been happy; after all, this liberal faith has not forgotten its Christian background. Jews who have rejected all forms of Judaism are more comfortable in the Ethical Culture movement; they are relatively numerous in that group. In the course of years, many Council members, like the secularist Yiddish laborites, have rejoined the main body of Jewry. Those Council members who are still loyal to their organization buttress Classical Reform, Reform's left wing. Classical Reformers will never disappear; these are the men and women who deplore the emphasis on Jewish nationalism and prefer to emphasize religion pure and simple. They forget that the nationalist strands woven into historical Judaism are inextricably bound up with its universalist aspirations.

RECONSTRUCTIONISM

Reconstructionism is another American Jewish religious denomination, small, but much larger than the American Council for Judaism. By the 1980's, the Council had practically disappeared as a movement; the Holocaust had convinced most American Jews that World Jewry needed a homeland where any Jew could go, if persecuted. The State of Israel answers that need. Reconstructionism, the determination to reconstruct Judaism to meet the challenge of modernism and Jewish religiocultural survival, began with the Conservative Rabbi Mordecai Menahem Kaplan (1881-1983) in New York, in 1921. Kaplan then established the Society for the Advancement of Judaism, which, in 1940 became Reconstructionism. To spread his views, he published the *SAJ Review*; later, in 1935, this periodical became *The Reconstructionist*, a well-edited, interesting magazine. In 1940, Kaplan and his disciples set out to build a movement; in 1968 his followers opened the Reconstructionist Rabbinical College, a liberal theological seminary. In order to unite, organize, and further Jewry, Reconstructionism has reached out eclectically. It aspires to make the synagog a social center; the community must be tightly knit, ready to embrace all Jews and to address their religious, cultural, and social needs.

Reconstructionism, as it has developed, is humanistic, encouraging all that is cultural and ethical; it rejects supernaturalism, which has led to the quip that in Reconstructionism there is no God and Kaplan is His prophet. This new religious association is Orthodox in insisting, gently to be sure, on the observance of traditional customs and rituals; it is yiddishist in encouraging a Diaspora nationalism, and it is Zionist in emphasizing the centrality of the State of Israel. The movement is truly a broad, all-inclusive school of thought; though it has published its own prayer book and Passover liturgy, it makes no credal demands; Judaism, the total spectrum of Jewish life, practices, and aspirations, is deemed no cult, but a way of life, a religious civilization. Ideological latitude is taken for granted, although the movement itself is strongly traditional and, in this sense, has much in common with German Jewry's Liberal Judaism, the old German Jewish religious denomination of which Leo Baeck was a notable exemplar. Apparently, the Reconstructionist movement has not enjoyed numerical success; certainly, it has no large following comparable to that of the major Jewish religious groups. Kaplan long hesitated to break with the Conservatives with whom he felt very much at home and whose synthesis of tradition and modernism he respected. The real reason that Reconstructionism has failed as a large-scale movement is that much that it stands for has already been accepted by hundreds of thousands of American Jews. In practice, if not in name, they are already "Reconstructionists." The Judaism to which most American Jewish religionists subscribe is not perceptibly different from what Kaplan advocated; there is no need for most Jews to secede from their respective denominations.[17]

ORTHODOXY

It is a far cry from Reconstructionism to Orthodoxy despite the fact that Kaplan's disciples were, for the most part, observant in the traditional sense. The Orthodox are committed to belief in a personal deity who is concerned with the life and conduct of every human being, whereas Reconstructionists do not put their trust in a compassionate personal deity, "the Holy One Blessed Be He." Orthodoxy, the "mother church" of all Jewish denominations, may claim a history stretching back for at least two millennia; it hewed to the rabbinic line, although this intransigent faith could in no sense escape the impact of the environment. Acculturation has devastated Orthodoxy; it is no longer the major American Jewish religious denomination. When Jews started leaving the core city for more comfortable ghettos, many of them, predominately Orthodox, did not as yet have the means to build big schools and beautiful synagogs; small congregations, conventicles, were no longer viable. By the third quarter of the twentieth century, Orthodoxy had become the smallest of the major Jewish religious denominations. Most American-born youngsters drifted to the left, away from Orthodoxy, with the exception of those who had been reared in a Hassidic environment. Brooklyn is Rome for Hassidim, pious isolationists, living in enclaves of their own, welcoming a self-imposed segregation. There are several Hassidic factions, and they are often bitterly hostile to each other and wary of non-Hassidic Jews. Their sons and daughters are the least acculturated among American Jewish groups, but the boys play baseball and go tearing around the bases with skullcaps on and earlocks flowing.

Conscious of the threat to survival, a group of forward-looking Orthodox of East European ancestry some decades ago established Young Israel, which eventually became a national Orthodox religious group emphasizing Torah-true Judaism, but insisting that it come to terms with the amenities of American society. Among other activities, these believers subsidized kosher dining clubs and student houses for observant college youth. They employed English in all that they did; indeed, most Orthodox groups finally dropped Yiddish as the prime medium of communication; English became their language. Even the most meticulous religious communicants are completely westernized. Not only culturally, but also structurally, Orthodox organizations have patterned themselves on the Reformers, who were the first to establish a permanent union of congregations, a rabbinic assembly, a brotherhood, a sisterhood, and an auxiliary association for youth. This sort of societal network is now characteristic of all national American Jewish religious bodies. Like the others, the Orthodox, too, publish attractive religious journals in order to appeal to the new college-trained generation. Orthodox rabbis are divided into at least three rabbinic associations. Moderate rabbis, the largest group, look for guidance to New York's Rabbi Isaac Elchanan Theological Seminary, the Rabbinic Council of America, and the Union of Orthodox Jewish Congregations of America; they are graduates of Yeshiva University. On the whole, these moderates cooperate locally and nationally with the Conservatives and the Reformers; they work with the Synagogue Council of America, the umbrella organization for most of this country's Jewish denominations. The moderate Orthodox dare not break with the Conservatives and the Reformers, if they wish to enlist the political support of these larger associations in order to protect the rights of Sabbath observers and consumers of kosher meat.

Orthodoxy is divisive; its meticulosity is self-defeating; it is constantly proliferating and moving to the right. Actually, despite multiple rabbinic congeries, there are primarily two basic groups in Orthodoxy, moderates and undeviating rightists, the latter led by rabbis who make few concessions to modernity. As Passover neared in the spring of 1984, an Orthodox group in Cincinnati printed a full page ad in the *American Israelite* informing the faithful which detergents, aluminum foil, and oven cleaners would be permissible for the coming holidays. How many of the city's 22,000 Jews took this advertisement to heart as they prepared to celebrate the exodus from Egypt? In their intransigence, America's far right traditionalists denounced Conservatives and Reformers as Jews guilty of malignant spiritual pollution. Some Orthodox Jewish laymen who wanted their sons to receive a good talmudic education sent them to

Eastern Europe before World War II. These boys, accustomed to sports, were unhappy when the head of the talmudic academy in Mir, White Russia, forbade them to play football. Eager to do something for their sons abroad, American parents did succeed in inducing the academy head to permit the installation of modern plumbing. In the aftermath of the two devastating world wars, many eminent rabbinic scholars were brought to this country; they established talmudic academies in the New York area, in New Jersey, in Baltimore, Cleveland, and other cities. Talmudic studies now flourish in this country; they are comparable to the best schools in Eastern Europe and Israel.

By the late twentieth century, there were hundreds, if not thousands, of American boys bent over their Talmud folios. On a late November day in 1982, about 10,000 Orthodox Jews took their seats in Madison Square Gardens to celebrate the eighth time the reading of the Talmud had been completed by laymen in a program that required them to study a page a day, a program initiated in 1923. Orthodoxy's hard-core right, determined to survive, has become militant, yet on occasion some of its followers have genuflected in the direction of modernism when no sacrifice of principle is involved. These men have a small, but vigorous group, organized as the Association of Orthodox Jewish Scientists. They live in a world of two truths; it is no problem for them to live comfortably ensconced in the universe of science and to submit devoutly to the mandates of revealed religion. For them, consistency is no virtue when it conflicts with treasured beliefs and practices. Orthodoxy can brag that, though it is small in numbers, its pious followers observe the divine precepts. The Orthodox have even induced leaders in many cities to see that the dietary laws are observed at community banquets; for them, this is a notable victory, a far cry from the famous Cincinnati terefah (unkosher) banquet of 1883 when the tenth anniversary of the founding of the Union of American Hebrew Congregations was celebrated and forbidden foods were served. It is the proud boast of the Orthodox that they have established a large chain of all-day schools across the country. In their eagerness to secure government funding for their schools, many of these Jews do not hesitate to breach the wall between Church and State. Thus, their views are consonant with those of many Christian evangelicals, notwithstanding the likelihood that, if these orthodox Christians came to power and succeed in establishing Christianity as this country's religion, the Orthodox will find themselves second-class citizens. To be sure, such an eventuality would not especially distress them: after all, we are in exile; God is punishing us for our sins; we have broken His Law.[18]

REFORM JUDAISM

In the 1980's the Reformers were the second largest Jewish religious group in the United States. The Reform movement in this country had started modestly at Charleston, South Carolina, in the mid-1820's; the founders had been radicals. In the 1840's, other communities began to grope their way slowly, haltingly, toward Reform. By 1885, the Reformers were secure enough to fashion their classical platform; in 1895, they broke definitively, theologically, with Orthodoxy. By this time, two wings had evolved in the movement, radicals and moderates; they differed in many respects, but before the decade had passed they were united, not in theology or liturgy, but in their common determination to oppose Zionism. The two world wars, in 1917-1918 and 1941-1945, were to prove the undoing of Classical Reform: with much of the twentieth century tarnished by reaction and the world retreating spiritually, many Jews moved from universalism to particularism; Zionism, which gradually enlisted most Jews, stressed nationalism. In 1922 Stephen S. Wise opened his rabbinical seminary, the Jewish Institute of Religion, which embraced Zionism and pluralism in Judaism; though liberal, the Institute was not dedicated to Reform alone.

From the 1920's on, anti-Semitism, both in the United States and in Europe, pushed many Jews to the right. In 1924, the Central Conference of Reform Rabbis expressed its willingness to cooperate in the rehabilitation of Jewish Palestine; the next decade saw the Union of American Hebrew Congregations, no friend of Zionist goals, express the hope publicly that Palestine would serve as a haven and home for oppressed Jews. By 1937, the rabbis, Reform's spiritual leaders, made their peace with the Zionists in the form of the Columbus Platform, which recognized, inter alia, that a home was desperately needed for German refugees. The 1940 Union Prayer Book published by the Reformers' Central Conference, introduced a pro-Zionist alternative service; from this time on, Reform strongly emphasized its ties with all Jews; no longer were the Reformers determined to be so far in the van that they risked losing touch with the Jewish masses. After 1945, when the full horror of the Holocaust was revealed to American Jews, Zionism and a politically independent Jewish Palestine no longer constituted a real issue among the Reformers.

It was now, in the mid-1940's, that Reform's Union of American Hebrew Congregations, left its headquarters in provincial Cincinnati and moved to cosmopolitan New York City; it set out to win the masses, the new generation of East European ancestry. Under a dynamic new executive, Rabbi Maurice Eisendrath, the leadership deliberately led the somewhat hesitant Classical Reformers back toward traditionalism, into Neo-Reform, but templegoers moved to the right slowly. As late as 1953, a poll by the National Federation of Temple Brotherhoods indicated that about one-fifth of the respondents had Christmas trees in their homes, that about half were not opposed to the Christmas tree, and that about a third hung up stockings for their children on this Christian holiday, but over four-fifths also lit the Hanukkah lights. Obviously, many Reform Jews of that decade wanted the best of both worlds, the Jewish and the Christian. Over 90 percent wanted nothing to do with Jewish all-day schools. Ultimately, however, under prodding, bar and bat mitzvahs were emphasized; the traditional, once optional or even excised Kol Nidre prayer was restored in the liturgy of the Day of Atonement; old ceremonies and rituals were revived; Hebrew was reintroduced; families were urged to light candles on Friday night; cantors chaunted the synagog service; the skullcap was no longer banished from Reform congregations; the rabbi hung up his striped trousers and donned a black gown adorned with a praying shawl or a stole. In 1975 the Classical Reform-oriented *Union Prayer Book* was set aside in favor of *Gates of Prayer*, which now became Reform's standard liturgy; some of the old Orthodox prayers and phrases were resurrected, and congregations were given the option of an edition that opened from the right—not from the left—in imitation of the standard siddur, the Orthodox prayer book. When one compares the massive new book of 1975 with the thin pamphlet-like prayer book which Rabbi Joseph Krauskopf used for his Sunday services in the first decades of the twentieth century, it is clear that a revolution has taken place. Two years later, in 1977 ARZA, the Association of Reform Zionists of America came into being; the Reformers were now in the mainstream of World Jewry and were swimming with the current. Have some liberal universalist views been slighted in the process? That is likely.

In the late twentieth century, the Reformers began to creep up numerically on the Conservatives. The Union of American Hebrew Congregations has more than doubled its affiliated synagogs since the Second World War. Will Reform ultimately become the largest Jewish religious denomination in this country? The answer lies, of course, in the realm of prophecy; the Conservatives, a dynamic crowd, thoroughly devoted to the demands of modernity, will not be overtaken in a hurry. To a considerable degree, the UAHC was successful in its efforts to win many of the native-born men and women of East European background. The Reform synagog has become an institution of increasing importance; it furthers worship and study; it has become an associational, cultural, and, to a degree, communal center. This is true, too, of the Conservative synagogs; it is less true of the Orthodox shul. Back in pre-Holocaust days, Reform rabbis stressed social justice; they preached universalism and rationalism, but their enthusiasm for a messianic dawn has abated somewhat in a world where so many countries are ruled by dictators.

Whenever a Reform rabbi speaks to a service club, over the radio, or on television, he challenges his Gentile auditors to come to terms with his liberal Jewish views; thinking Christians are compelled to reexamine and reassess their basic beliefs in the light of what they have heard. Because of his close relations with the Gentile world, the Reform rabbi has probably increased the acceptance of the Jew and Judaism in the larger community. As far back as the 1860's, Reform rabbis pioneered in interreligious amity; they exchanged pulpits with Gentile ministers and, on rare occasions, even officiated at Gentile burials. In those halcyon days, all the stress was on universalism; now, in less sanguine decades, the Reform rabbi is pressed to maintain a balance between liberalism and particularism. Universalism is emphasized less today; convinced that they cannot save the world, many Reform Jewish leaders are content with pushing to save Jews. Despite the decline in universalist exhortation, Reform is still a powerful American religious movement. It owes much to the innovative planning and vision of Alfred Gottschalk, the president of the Hebrew Union College-Jewish Institute of Religion; in 1985 his spiritual empire embraced four seminaries; his graduates served congregations and troops westward from Boston to Taiwan. The 1980's may have seen liberalism in retreat, but American Jewish Reform, present in every American town of size, has remained an exemplary ethical force; it ordains women, encourages the conversion of unaffiliated Gentiles, seeks to expound high moral and ethical ideals, and shows itself utterly devoid of religious intolerance. In the 1980's, Reform Judaism could proclaim itself the largest liberal religious movement in the world. This is no cause for rejoicing, but one for lament; religious liberalism is at a low ebb; Reform numbers at best but a million souls, including its followers in Europe and in Israel.[19]

CONSERVATISM

Reform's chief rival is Conservatism, a movement organized in 1886 as a protest against the radical proposals of liberal Reform innovators. Conservatism made little progress in those early days. Its new school, the Jewish Theological Seminary in New York, languished for lack of means; its head, Sabato Morais, lived in Philadelphia, and young institutions cannot be run successfully by administrators at long distance. The school moved forward with the coming of Solomon Schechter, the Rumanian-born talmudist who had become a cultured Englishman. After his death, the Seminary and the Conservative movement continued to advance under the guidance of Cyrus Adler, a native Arkansan, and subsequently prospered under the brilliant, Cincinnati-born Rabbi Louis Finkelstein. A graduate of the Seminary, Finkelstein set out to win the acculturated East Europeans and their native-born children; he did so by fostering Orthodoxy, yet welcoming all that was worthwhile in the world of modernism. His wealthy Reform patrons—the source of his funding—were pleased when he initiated vigorous programs of cultural interchange with Gentile academicians. How did he and his school of thought reconcile the new sciences and the traditional rabbinic law? In what might be seen as an opportunistic approach, they adopted a policy of salutary neglect; they were nominally Orthodox, but creed was not emphasized, practice was selective, and latitudinarianism prevailed. Worship services were decorous; English was the primary medium of communication; family pews replaced separate seating; good modern music was introduced, and some congregations installed organs. The rabbis, whether foreign-born or native-born, were completely Americanized and made outstanding contributions to the scientific study of rabbinical literature.

Despite its formal attachment to Orthodox tradition, the new Conservative movement did not hesitate in the course of decades to grant women religious privileges previously accorded only to men. Women were called to the Torah, counted for a religious quorum (minyan), and finally, in the 1980's, admitted into the rabbinate—a major break with Orthodoxy. Conservative clergymen may, if they wish, join the Central Conference of American Rabbis. Yet the two denominations are distinct and separate; the Conservatives have never officially repudiated the ancient rabbinic codes; the Reformers have. How do these middle-of-the-road religionists resolve the problem of authority and freedom? Easily; they think what they wish but they adhere to many age-old traditional practices; for them, the old customs and rituals are an appealing way of life. Even so, very few Conservative Jews—the rabbis excepted—observe the dietary laws when away from home. Like their Reconstructionist brethren, Conservatives tend not to believe in the binding character of the rabbinic codes. They, too, have been influenced by Mordecai M. Kaplan, who taught at the Seminary from 1909 to his retirement many decades later. It is obvious that when the basic concept of authority is in limbo, the movement will be riven by internal struggles.[20]

THE *HAVURAH*

By the third quarter of the twentieth century, American Judaism witnessed the rise of a new religious institution, the *havurah*, a tightly-knit socioreligious fellowship, a conventicle, more often than not a commune of intellectuals. Inquiring youth and adult "seekers" established intimate groups to build a faith tailored to their individual needs. Fellowships and communes are not new in Judaism; they go back to biblical days. Centuries later, the Essenes in Palestine and the Therapeutae in Egypt gathered together to live a life apart in communities of their own. Christianity was such a Jewish *havurah*, when it first rose after the death of Jesus. Although Protestant communes were not uncommon in colonial North America during the late seventeenth century, they had no influence on Jews. The first secessionist Jewish religious fellowship made its appearance in cultured Charleston, South Carolina, in 1824; Temple Emanu-El of New York began as a Reform *havurah* in the early 1840's, and Young Israel, the modernist Orthodox fellowship, was founded in 1912. But it was in the 1960's, America's decade of ferment, that these new Jewish *havurot* multiplied producing numerous groups of intelligent, sensitive Conservatives and Reformers in rebellion against the structured denominations with their stereotypical services, practices, and beliefs. Each *havurah* constituted an extended family in which religious expression was encouraged. The new generation set out to fashion a comforting minuscule world in which it could feel at home. There are many *havurot*. How successful have they been? Emotional contentment and religious success cannot always be measured; the soul brooks no yardstick. Some of these attractive fellowships are attached to a synagog; others are independent; all of them further sociability, religion, intellectual inquiry; they offer a healthy challenge in the world of the spirit.[21]

SOME NOTES ON AMERICAN JUDAISM

Religion is basic in American Jewish life, although it is by its very nature highly proliferative. In addition to the four denominations, offshoots have appeared in Orthodoxy, Reform, and Conservatism; these dissidents who espouse new approaches may be few in number, but they are ardent devotees of the philosophies they cherish. The synagog is still more important than the charity federation; it represents Jewish tradition and Jewish history. A Jewish community can survive without a welfare federation; if necessary, the synagog can provide for those in want, as it did in early America. Here in the United States, a substantial body of Jews adheres to religion, probably about 50 percent. In matters religious, however, American Jews are not joiners; in New York City of the 1980's only about 40 percent of the Jews are synagog members whereas 75 percent identify themselves as part of a Jewish religious group. Very many men and women remain within the ancestral ambit by joining Jewish social, philanthropic, fraternal, Zionist, and cultural organizations. The Holocaust has induced many to take a second look at themselves. Suburban dwellers have turned to the synagog. In the core city, surrounded by fellow Jews, individuals may have felt no need to establish their identity; in new areas of settlement, there was an almost irresistible appeal to pattern oneself on the Catholics and Protestants. One joined a "church," a synagog; one took pride in a beautiful new sanctuary with its numerous school rooms and its spacious acreage for parking. Structurally, with all their trappings, these new sanctuaries differed little from Protestant churches. Hundreds of such magnificent synagogs have been erected in the United States in the decades since the Second World War. The awful threat of nuclear extermination may have impelled some Jews to wrestle with thoughts of eternity and may have induced them to join a temple or a synagog. Rabbis have shown themselves more often than not devoted and competent synagog leaders. Have any emerged as national religious leaders? Few, very few. Where the rabbinate as a whole is brilliant—and this is true—outstanding leaders fail to emerge. Have the professions of law and the sciences siphoned off the truly remarkable intellects?

Owing to the decline of Orthodoxy on the right as a mass movement and of Classical Reform on the left, a culturally homogeneous Jewry seems to be drawing somewhat closer together religiously. To a degree, the different denominational synagogs in the larger communities manage to cooperate; religiously there is something of a "truce of God." Sniping has decreased precipitously. In some towns, the rabbis of the different denominations are joined together in a common association. The Reformers appear most careful to respect the sensitivities of the Orthodox; the liberals go out of their way to keep the organization together. Traditionalists, for their part, hesitate to touch the sacrosanct Hebrew text of the prayer book, but they are moving to the left nonetheless; this turn is reflected in the paraphrastic translations that face the Hebrew text. Vested interests, however, will always keep the denominations apart despite the fact that, liturgically and ideologically, they are growing closer. In the smaller towns where there is but one basic institution—usually, the community center—the congregation and the center are one; here we have a completely merged religious group. When this occurs, the traditionalists and the Reformers both suffer; their principles are often violated. The problem becomes more acute in larger towns, where separate congregations are not viable and fusion is imperative. Reformers, Conservatives, and Orthodox must come to terms. The resulting worship service is a matter of negotiation. A Reform rabbi is sometimes called upon to officiate in a merged congregation, where the liturgy employed is appreciably or even totally at variance with the principles Reform rabbis have always avowed. In comparable circumstances, if the rabbi was a Christian in a community church he or she would be serving Catholics, Protestants, and Unitarians! When congregations find it possible to worship together regardless of the text of the prayers, the conclusion cannot but be drawn that ethnicity, not theology, is most important.[22]

JEWISH EDUCATION

The kinship among Jews that had been reinforced through helping the oppressed, finding a haven for them in Palestine, and fighting anti-Semitism is a relationship that owes its origin to social pathology. Jews were constrained to rescue fellow Jews—and themselves—from the threat of a sick society. Education, on the other hand, is a positive approach on the part of a Jewish community. It is stressed by Jews everywhere in this country; practically all of them are convinced that a Jewish education guarantees identification. This is not necessarily true, though most Jews believe that a common education furthers common ties. According to Jewish law and tradition, the community as such is under no obligation to educate every child; education is the responsibility of the family. The community must, however, provide schooling for the children of the poor. This is why, in colonial America, children of parents without means were given schooling at the expense of the synagog.

Jewish education may be formal or informal—or both; it can be religious or secular. Elementary education is most important; few Jewish boys and girls have been given advanced instruction in Jewish subjects. Youngsters were taught in the heder, Talmud Torah, the afternoon schools of congregations and bureaus; the Sunday schools were very popular. The curriculum included Hebrew reading, translation of the Pentateuch, proficiency in the Jewish book of common prayer (the siddur), and some knowledge of Jewish history, ceremonies, and standard blessings; contemporary schools add information on the State of Israel and the Holocaust. The Sunday schools are patronized by many because they are patterned on similar Christian schools; they seem typically American! Throughout the twentieth century, bureaus of Jewish education, modeled on the original in New York's Kehillah, have been established in every town of size and have become *the communal educational agency.* The American educational ideal assumes public school education will be communal, lay, compulsory, but when the bureaus patterned themselves on that concept, they failed. Dr. Benderly and his disciples forgot that religion and education are inseparable, that congregations were determined to control the schooling of their young and were set on indoctrinating the children of members, preparing them for membership, and training them to be good Jews. There was very little status in a bureau school; prestige lay in the synagog.

HOW SUCCESSFUL WERE THESE RELIGIOUS SCHOOLS?

Professional educators are distressed, but then they always insist that all instruction is inadequate, that, unless the boys and girls receive training at an additional secondary level, they will never be truly educated. If questioned, the father or mother would readily pay lip service to these contentions of the professionals; actually, most parents have been satisfied, glad of the children's willingness to go to an elementary school. Parents are really not demanding; they are pleased if a child can read Hebrew mechanically—understanding it is not imperative; the reading alone makes the youngster Jewish, so they believe. The bureaus have regrouped their forces; frozen out by the synagogs, they have found a raison d'être; they would offer technical advice and administer occasional classes and schools of a communal nature; they would seek to further the growth of Jewish afternoon high schools.

The most significant change in American Jewish education has been the rise of the all-day schools. These go back to colonial times, but, by the 1860's and 1870's, the all-day schools of the Germans and the native-born had petered out; they could not compete with the public schools. In the 1880's, the Russian newcomers started a new chain of all-day schools; they opened the Etz Chaim which taught more Hebrew than English. By the middle of the twentieth century, these nurseries of Jewish learning had increased in number. The isolationist mood in traditional Jewry was strong after the destruction of European Jewry, predominantly Orthodox, in the 1940's. The Reformers, too, have sponsored several all-day schools; the Conservatives many; the Orthodox even more. The right-wing Orthodox, who dominate this new educational movement, are convinced that the public schools lead to assimilation; they want so to mold their children that they will remain loyal to rabbinic tradition. The rationale justifying the establishment of a separate school system is the need to provide Jewish leaders, though there is very little evidence that this hope has been justified. The Orthodox are convinced that their day schools can teach religion and bring boys and girls closer to Judaism and the Jewish people, an expectation which may, indeed, be valid.

The first patrons of these schools, traditionalists, were reacting to anti-Semitism and the Holocaust. Others were responding to an awakened Jewish nationalism, to Zionism. Reform and Conservative Jews turned to these new schools because classes were smaller, standards were higher; they wanted to avoid the drugs and violence that were in evidence in many metropolitan public schools. By the 1980's, there were hundreds of coeducational all-day institutions, some attached to synagogs, others administered by the community. Statistics on their number leave something to be desired. It is estimated that anywhere from 20 to 25 percent of all children receiving an elementary Jewish education go to these schools. In New York and Brooklyn, so it is said, only about 50 percent of the Jewish children patronize the public schools; the many thousands of Hassidim in Brooklyn are determined to educate their youngsters according to their own lights. Some, if not all, Orthodox day schools receive subsidies from the Jewish welfare federations. This may ultimately create a problem, since it is possible that the federation leaders will attempt to exercise authority over the conduct, administration, academic standards, and even curricula of the institutions they help fund. Thus far, however, communal leaders have not imposed their views on the various Jewish educational institutions which they subsidize. All in all, the statisticians tell us, 75 percent of the country's Jewish children receive some training in ancestral lore at some time or other.

Excepting the seminaries and teachers' colleges, education on a secondary level does not have an impressive record, even though the American Jewish community has been working with its adolescents since the Civil War period, when it encouraged them to organize Young Men's Hebrew Associations. Early in the twentieth century, several denominations and agencies made an effort to federate college youth. The Judaization of these young men and women was important if religion was to have a future. The few late afternoon high schools, sponsored by bureaus or the conjoint efforts of several synagogs, have emphasized Hebrew; Jewish all-day high schools have evolved more extensive curricula. These schools—now beginning to increase in number—appeal primarily to the Orthodox, who are determined to influence their young at every step of the educational process. A new and very successful type of youth education is the summer camp. All Jewish religious denominations and a number of national associations have turned to camping. The isolationist Agudath Israel, aggressive and competent, has summer camps for youngsters in many parts of the world; here in the United States, it bring in children from Latin America. Most of the Jewish youth camps in the United States employ the English vernacular; the Conservatives have a few where Hebrew is spoken. Decades ago, the secular Yiddishists, Zionists and non-Zionists alike, developed Yiddish-speaking camps for their limited number of followers. Culturally, the Yiddishists have fallen on hard times; the English vernacular has overwhelmed them; only a handful of third-generation American Jewish youth has any inkling of a language that was once spoken and loved by millions in this country.

The innovative programs of the camps are almost without exception effective, even inspirational, and the intellect is challenged, too. These late twentieth-century Jewish youth activities and institutions do not represent a movement of protest; American Jewish youngsters are not in revolt; they are concerned with their own careers, not with the state of the universe. Boys and girls look forward to the weeks at camp; they go to learn, to have a good time, to make friends, to come away with a good feeling. There was a movement of revolt in the 1960's when the New

Left appealed to many Jewish college students; they were invariably on the side of compassion and social justice. Some of the leaders of the counterculture were Jews who rebelled against home, school, synagog, and the state; anarchistically, they rejected the old paths, the cherished traditions, the accepted mores. In the course of a year or two, the protests of the New Left were spent; Jews were shocked by the attacks on Israel and Zionism and dismayed when some black militants turned on them. This rejection may have impelled a few to realign themselves with their people.

The new teachers' colleges that sprang up as early as the 1890's have had a good record of appealing to those few young men and women interested in Jewish studies. A relatively large number of these schools have been established in the United States since Philadelphia's Gratz College opened its doors to students in 1897. Some of the colleges have succeeded in enlisting communal, federation support, but most owe their origin to the several Jewish religious denominations which seek to recruit instructional personnel. The Conservatives, led by Mordecai Kaplan, were the pioneers; under the aegis of the Jewish Theological Seminary, his Teachers' College raised up a generation with Jewish knowledge and pedagogical expertise; many of his graduates had studied at Columbia. Rabbinical seminaries and the yeshivot are the basic nurseries for advanced Jewish studies. Yeshivot, talmudic academies for the Orthodox, were first established here by the East Europeans during the late 1890's in New York on the East Side, where the observant Jewish masses were settled. For the traditionalists, Talmud study is basic; the Hebrew Bible is the inspired source of Judaism, but Talmud, the code, as it were, of rabbinic Judaism, is deemed even more worthy of study. The successful transatlantic crossing of Talmud study is an historic event of great significance; it documents the emergence of American Jewry as one of the world's important centers of rabbinic study. Hundreds of American Jewish men—a few women, too—are at home in talmudic and later rabbinic literature. All this American Jewry owes to the East European newcomers. The establishment of yeshivot in the United States is comparable to the transfer of talmudic studies from Mesopotamia to Spain and North Africa in medieval days; Europe then emerged as a rival of the authoritative academies in the Middle East.

Comparable in significance to the founding of American talmudic academies—but on an entirely different level—is the expansion of Hebraic and Judaic studies in over 300 American colleges and universities. American Jewish young men and women can now steep themselves in Jewish studies in a purely academic environment; there is virtually no limit to the educational opportunities offered them to acquire a Jewish education. This remarkable development followed in the wake of the

Holocaust and the consequent resurgence in Jewish nationalism. The blacks insisted on black studies; the Jews followed in their heels with Jewish studies. Here, too, American Jewry is indebted primarily to Jews of East European ancestry for these courses. In addition, there is a drive to reach adults who have long finished their years of formal study. All the teachers' colleges, most of the synagogs, almost every national agency, Zionists, and women's organizations, too, offer courses in Judaism and Jewish history. The B'nai B'rith has for years organized institutes for adult study in various parts of the country; the Orthodox, the Conservatives, and the Reformers carry on extension programs, lectures and classes for adults, in the major cities. These institutional offerings are reinforced by the dozens of magazines available to readers who evince any interest. Some of these publications are of high intellectual quality. Every group, every subgroup, children, youth, adults, has a paper, a magazine, a journal to which it can turn; they are published in English, Yiddish, and Hebrew, too. In 1984, New York City was the home of 100 such journals; most of them imparted information, learning. "All who are hungry may come and eat." If practically all the educational institutions described above enjoy the approval of American Jewish religionists, the Yiddish secular schools have been an exception; they were an interesting interlude in the educational history of the American Jewish community. All the Yiddishist schools in their curricula taught history, literature, folklore, music; humanistically, they emphasized ethics. Later in the century, reacting to the shock of the slaughter abroad, most of these schools ameliorated their indifference or hostility to Judaism. They developed their own secular bar mitzvah ceremonies; they observed some of the Holy Days, after their own fashion of course, and they accepted the new State of Israel which offered a home to their kinsmen.

Jewish institutions of higher learning were also opened for secular purposes, although the founders were themselves not necessarily secularists. In 1925, the Graduate School for Social Work was started to train professional personnel to administer the Jewish welfare agencies. The emphasis in the training was on Americanization, since most of America's Jews were still foreign-born. The school was a good one; several of the theses written by its graduates are of high quality and still of value to the research historian. Unfortunately, the school closed its doors in 1939; obviously, the depression was taking its toll. However, the colleges of this country were constantly graduating trained social workers; there would be no dearth of recruits. It is equally patent that the leaders of American Jewish federations believed that there was no need to employ caseworkers specially equipped to deal with Jews. Eleven years later, in 1950, the Holocaust was history and a new Jewish social workers' college was opened —the Training Bureau for Jewish Communal Service. The title is revelatory. This post-war and post-calamity generation had begun to think in terms of a "Jewish community." Despite the fact that the immigrant generation was dying out rapidly, the Bureau had an excellent curriculum in Judaica; some of the syllabi published indicate that the instruction was superior. One surmises that the problem of the 1950's was not Americanization, but the need to keep the native-born generation Jewish. Alas, the school soon closed; it is difficult to understand why the federations did not support it. Over the decades, its place has been taken by several similar Jewish schools to train personnel for communal service. These new institutions are affiliated with disparate denominations and colleges, each seeking zealously to put its own stamp on the graduates. The constantly increasing impact of Jewish nationalism as well as the destruction of European Jewry also moved American Jews to create liberal arts colleges of their own. Establishing denominational colleges has been an overall American tradition since Congregationalist Harvard was opened in 1636. Yeshiva College became a university in 1945; Brandeis was founded three years later.

Jewish institutions have always been fortified by auxiliary educational programs and agencies. Actually, almost every national Jewish institution is engaged in some form of instruction. In the course of the year, a Jew hears talks from the pulpit and attends meetings of a brotherhood, a sisterhood, Hadassah, the National Council of Jewish Women, Woman's ORT, B'nai B'rith, and a whole host of other organizations. The Jewish community centers present cultural programs; the universities have their Hillel foundations; the Jewish Publication Society distributes books; the Jewish Telegraph Agency publishes a daily news bulletin, American Jewry's substitute for a national journal. Through all these agencies and organizations, Jewish children, youth, and adults are literally taken by storm in cultural terms; their identity as Jews is heightened; they sense themselves part of a community that reaches out to fellow Jews in every corner of the world.[23]

JEWS AND CULTURE

Education and culture are obviously intertwined in Judaism. It is not easy to define the term "Jewish culture." It is a term that includes beliefs and traits, learning, literary productions, and accomplishments in the fine arts. A long theological discourse by Isaac Leeser may well be an aspect, and not an unimportant one, of Jewish culture; it explicates Leeser's religious standpoint. A brilliant study of early Judaism by the Gentile scholar George Foot Moore, of Harvard University, is not Jewish culture, although it is much more important than Leeser's lucubration. In the late twentieth century, Jewish litterateurs and scholars were busy publishing works, mostly in English, of course, but in Yiddish and Hebrew, too. Even as far back as World War I, there were American Jews, native-born and immigrants, who were trying to find a place for themselves in the world of Anglo-American letters; relatively little that they produced was of high literary quality, though writers like Abraham Cahan, Ludwig Lewisohn, and Anzia Yezierska deserved to be respected. As the century advanced, a body of writing eventuated, which may be denominated ghetto literature; it describes the attempt of the immigrant to come to terms with an awesome new America. Genius from time to time would manifest itself: Henry Roth, Daniel Fuchs, Michael Gold, Clifford Odets. As late as 1976, Irving Howe published *The World of Our Fathers*, a nostalgic farewell to a culture that had been dead for decades.

After the Second World War, Jews, who numbered a mere 2 to 3 percent of the country's population, entered the mainstream of the country's literary culture. Craftsmen of repute began to make their appearance in the 1950's and 1960's. (Their parents and their grandparents often knew little English.) Some speak of these years as the Jewish decades, and a number of these writers became household names. There are poets, dramatists, literary critics, and editors of respected journals. Saul Bellow became a Nobel laureate in 1976; he is deemed one of the country's leading novelists. His colleagues, writers of comparable capacity, would include Philip Roth, Bernard Malamud, Grace Paley, Cynthia Ozick, and Karl Shapiro, to name a few. There are other writers of the 1970's and 1980's, who wrote best sellers and whose books sell in the hundreds of thousands. They often tackle Jewish themes; non-Jews, too, write about Jews in works of fiction and biography; for many, the Chosen People remain a fascinating topic; their success in America stimulates inquiry.

In 1900, American Jewry published a total of 42 periodicals; in 1985, more than 180, most of them in English. The quality of these journals has improved perceptibly since the first decades of the century. There are dozens of weeklies, monthlies, quarterlies, and annuals but there are no dailies; the important items of Jewish interest appear in the *New York Times*, which brags that it provides "All the News That's Fit to Print." The Anglo-Jewish weeklies carry information on problems, anti-Semitism, Israel; for the most part, they are local news bulletins. Other magazines—and there are several—are filled with thoughtful essays and good book reviews. They appeal to college-trained men and women (by the 1980's, most of the younger generation had studied at institutions of higher learning). Many of the good journals are published by national Jewish agencies, which seek to win the intelligentsia to their point of view. The women, entrenched in their own organizations, make sure that their voices are heard; they all publish national magazines for their members and for those whom they hope to attract. The Anglo-Jewish periodical has a future; Jews are literate, intelligent, very curious about themselves.

Yiddish has no future as a living language despite the voluble assurance of its votaries that it is very much alive. It will still linger on for decades; languages die hard; in the 1970's, there were still about 1,600,000 Jews who recorded Yiddish as their mother tongue. Yiddish is fated to become a dead language and, like Greek and Latin, a field for linguistic and literary research in the colleges of this country; indeed, many universities already teach Yiddish. The Yiddish theatre has struggled to stay alive. In the 1920's, there was an art theatre of excellent quality, but all it succeeded in doing was to prepare the cognoscenti for Broadway theatre. One can still see Yiddish shows in New York, but this is the afterglow. The theatre began to die when the 1924 Immigration Act was passed; not many Yiddish-speaking immigrants were admitted thereafter. The old-timers and their children kept the Yiddish theatre alive, but it is only a faint shadow of its former self. Yiddish literature, however, is not dead; it is still being cultivated; as late as the middle of the twentieth century, there were numerous Yiddish poets, novelists, and dramatists; there was still momentum. Isaac Bashevis Singer received a Nobel Prize in 1978 for his Yiddish writings. Most readers know him, of course, only in translation.

Present-day Yiddish must be measured not by its litterateurs, but by its press; the dailies are all gone, but some weeklies and monthlies have survived; in the 1980's, New York still published nearly fifteen such periodicals. What a pity that this great culture has to die, a culture that brought comfort and assurance to millions. Now that the daily press is gone, an evaluation is in order. Compared to the *New York Times*, the Los Angeles *Times*, the St. Louis *Post-Dispatch*, and papers in Washington, Boston, Miami, and other cities, the few surviving Yiddish journals tend to fade in significance. The owners and publishers of the Yiddish dailies were not always idealistic or conscientious; they did not always measure up to the standards that characterized America's finest papers, but these Jewish gazettes were very important, especially as Americanizers. They explained this country to immigrant readers; they brought news from the old home, from distant lands; they guided New York Jewry politically; they offered comfort to the Jewish labor unions as they struggled to make a place for themselves alongside unions peopled in the main by non-Jews. They helped their readers make the difficult transition from a backward Russia to an enlightened America; they brought knowledge of the arts and sciences to a people which had lived in darkness; they put a brake on dejudaization and assimilation.

There was also a modest Hebrew literary movement here in the United States even before the rise of the State of Israel. A number of American litterateurs in the field of modern Hebrew immigrated to the new state, which provided a larger and more receptive setting, since mod-

ern Hebrew is Israel's vernacular. To be sure, there are still numerous Hebrew readers in North America. For years, the language was taught in
many public high schools along with French, German, and Spanish; now,
young Americans who want to learn the new Hebrew go on to spend a
year or two in Israel. Some of America's Jewish schools of higher learning
require that matriculants spend the first year of their academic program in
the reborn state so that these American students will learn Hebrew more
easily and lose their fear of the challenge involved in the study of biblical
and rabbinical Hebrew. Even now, in the 1980's, a national Hebrew Federation (Histadruth Ivrith) continues to exist in this country. Established
in 1922 with high, if unrealistic hopes, it set out to emphasize the primacy of Hebrew in Jewish life. Several Hebrew magazines are still published in New York City; among them is an English-Hebrew monthly
distributed to the youngsters who attend Orthodox day schools. All of
these American Hebrew periodicals are subsidized. Readers determined to
keep abreast of all that is new in the Hebrew literary world subscribe directly for the airmail editions of one or another Israeli daily.

The Here in the United States, Hebrew—classical and talmudic—has a
future as a sacred tongue. Hebrew, both modern and biblical, is being
taught in the universities of the country. The Psalms and the Pentateuch
were required reading for Christian students in some American colleges
during the seventeenth and eighteenth centuries; the Old Testament today is more a Christian than a Jewish book; Christians pay it more attention. Even so, as long as there are Jewish religionists, biblical and rabbinic
Hebrew will be studied by scholarly men and women. Several talmudic
academies now dot the American landscape, most of them located in or
near New York City—Brooklyn, to be more exact. This country has published some very good editions of important rabbinic classics. Yet, American scholars have not yet produced an authoritative gloss or a work codi-
fying the changes in Jewish law since the appearance of Joseph Caro's
sixteenth-century standard code.

The Talmud is generally taught in American yeshivot without
benefit of instruction in formal Aramaic grammar. (Much of the text is in
Aramaic, not rabbinic Hebrew.) Instruction in Talmud, with the exception of an occasional course in Aramaic grammar and in historical analysis, tends to be totally unscientific as measured by modern canons. The
historicocritical approach to literature, law, and history was developed in
Germany in the first quarter of the nineteenth century. Here in the
United States, in order to bring the findings of this Science of Judaism to
the attention of the typical intelligent inquirer, a body of popular
scientific data and conclusions was assembled. One aspect of this form of
education is reflected in Jewish museums. There are two major Jewish
museums in the United States, one in New York City, the other in Los

Angeles, although numerous exhibitions and displays of various types are to be encountered in almost every town of size. Most of them display pictures, paintings, and ceremonial objects in cloth, brass, and silver. Publishers of Jewish books have done much to further the culture of North American Jews. Most of the commercial bookdealers are in the New York area, but a number of universities have undertaken the task of publishing books for the Jewish market. Jews are readers and Jewish books are in demand. The number of works of a solid nature that appear annually in English, Yiddish, and Hebrew mount into the hundreds. Good magazines in English first made their appearance in 1886, when Benjamin Franklin Peixotto began to edit the *Menorah* under B'nai B'rith sponsorship; a generation later, in 1915, brilliant young college men, primarily of East European background, began publishing the *Menorah Journal*, a treasury of literature and art. It, in turn, was succeeded in the second half of the century by numerous magazines of high quality, edited for the cultured; they deal with Jewish learning, history, and problems. Frequently they advance the views of the sponsoring national agency.

The Jewish Chautauqua Society, taking its name from a Christian cultural organization, has long sent rabbis and other scholars to lecture in American colleges and universities. This organization, sponsored by the National Federation of Temple Brotherhoods, seeks to further understanding of Jews by talks on Jewish history and ideals; it also builds libraries of Judaica in academic institutions which cultivate Jewish studies. Local Jewish historical societies confine themselves to the job of exploring the history of the town, state, or region in which the members live. In the last decades of the twentieth century, at least eighty such historical and genealogical study groups were active; several publish periodicals in which they explore the history of their community in detail. A generation earlier not a single organization of this type had existed in any American town; the rise of the United States as a Jewish cultural center has made all the difference. The Jewish Welfare Board (JWB), one of the country's leading Jewish service agencies, does double duty; it serves the men and the women in the armed forces and furthers the arts at home through its book and music councils. Its *Jewish Book Annual*, now in its forty-third year (1985), lists the English, Yiddish, and Hebrew books printed in the United States; the works included—juveniles, fiction, and non- fiction—number several hundred. Over 200 volumes in Hebrew alone have been published or reprinted. Through the YMHA-YWHA's and Jewish community centers which it supervises, the JWB is in a position to influence the hundreds of thousands who frequent these sociorecreational agencies. Though the community centers are not preeminently cultural institutions, there is no "Y" or center which does not foster some cultural activity. The Jewish Publication Society (JPS), on the other hand, is a purely cultural association. The Society, which has been in existence since 1888, publishes a number of Jewish books every year in addition to the *American Jewish Year Book*, an indispensable reference book for everyone interested in Jewish studies. Many of the books published by the JPS are of a relatively popular scientific nature. In the 1960's, it gave the English-speaking world a new translation of the Holy Scriptures according to the traditional Hebrew text; when published, it was the most accurate translation of the Hebrew Bible available in English; it was a scholarly achievement of importance.

Translating the Hebrew Bible was a scientific tour de force, which took a generation to complete. The Science of Judaism in its formal sense is cultivated primarily in non-Orthodox seminaries, teachers' colleges, and universities with departments of Hebrew and Judaic studies. Apparently, there are more than 350 such schools; over thirty of them have graduate programs. American universities like Harvard and Columbia, and many others, welcome this new cultural challenge—quite a contrast with the year 1840, when the Prussian state refused to include Jewish disciplines in university curricula. Among the subjects taught in the seminaries and the universities are biblical, rabbinical, and modern Hebrew literature, Semitic languages, Jewish history, Jewish philosophy, and the sociology of the Jewish community. Formal Jewish studies are also cultivated by a number of scientific institutions such as the American Academy for Jewish Research, which gives scholars grants-in-aid and publishes an annual volume of proceedings. Many of the teachers in the Judaica programs at institutions of higher learning are members of the Association for Jewish Studies, whose roster in the mid-1980's include about 900 university teachers and researchers. In the 1930's, when anti-Semitism both here and in Europe was a constant concern, Jewish academicians created the Conference on Jewish Relations whose name was later changed to the Conference on Jewish Social Studies. In a sense, this organization was apologetic in intent, although its publications leave nothing to be desired scientifically. Like Leopold Zunz and his 1819 Association for Culture and Science, the Conference on Jewish Relations believed that a presentation of scholarly data on Jewry would further an understanding of Jews on the part of American academics. Its quality magazine *Jewish Social Studies* was widely read. Yet, the pursuit of the Science of Judaism in Germany—its hearth—would seem to indicate that scientific scholarship was not an effective instrument in warding off the evils of anti-Semitism, at least not in the circles where such a counterforce was most needed.

The YIVO Institute for Jewish Research has for decades addressed itself to the task of preserving and interpreting Yiddish literature. This organization has amassed a huge collection, millions of pages of documentary material on the literature, folkways, art, and music of the

Yiddish-speaking masses both here and in other countries where the language once flourished. (There are some lands—Israel and Argentina among them—where Yiddish is still heard.) Scholars in the field of Yiddish will never lack for resource data. Researchers in the larger field of the Science of Judaism can always turn to the virtually complete collections of Jewish books in the libraries of this country; those who study source materials on American Jewish history have access to the voluminous papers stored in the files of the American Jewish Historical Society and the American Jewish Archives; numerous periodicals in English, Hebrew, and Yiddish publish the latest findings of social scientists working in the Jewish field. Scholarly writings by these specialists are of the highest quality; there is a flood of new works on talmudic literature, Jewish history, Semitic lore, theology, and Zionism.

LATE TWENTIETH CENTURY CULTURE: A BRIEF SUMMARY

It is manifest that, with the dissolution of Europe's Jewries in the 1940's, American Jews would be given the opportunity to assume a world Jewish leadership role. Through a host of formal and informal agencies, through synagogs, schools, colleges, libraries, and a trilingual press, it was not long before a culture evolved that was both Jewish and American. With study and knowledge of the Jewish experience through the ages came a glow of identification, a feeling of oneness with all Jews on all levels; a common culture created a gemeinschaft, a community. Citizenship in the republic of Jewish letters was open to every scholarly Jew, whatever his or her country or status in life. Unfortunately, the destruction of European Jewry has sparked a sort of hyperethnicism and a desire for withdrawal which, unwittingly at least, generated hostility to an objective scientific approach in analyzing historical data; in the 1980's, the critical method was not in the ascendant.[24]

SOCIORECREATIONAL AGENCIES

Scholars have recognized merit, intellectual brilliance; in this sense, they have shown themselves to be egalitarians; social demarcations have not concerned them, but such distinctions have always characterized social clubs. America's Jewish affluent had clubs in the northern cities even in ante-bellum days; indeed, such a society is documented in colonial Newport, Rhode Island. The Newport group met to eat, drink, and play cards; the clubs later established by America's German Jews were no different. Most of these social congeries died out in the early twentieth century; a few are still left, sporting the old familiar names, the Harmonie, the Concordia. With the coming of the automobiles and good roads, Jews, like their Gentile counterparts, turned to golf and tennis. These clubs are rated not by wealth, but by social status; in many towns, the native-born of German ancestry did not wish to associate with those of Russian ancestry. In some communities, the Jewish country club was originally set up as an extension of an existing city club; like the Gentiles, the Jews wanted to play their eighteen holes of golf; exclusion from some Christian organizations was not the prime motivation for Jews to establish recreational facilities of their own.

City clubs and country clubs are for people of means, not for the typical middle-class urban Jew. However, Mr. Cohen did have a "club" at his disposal, if he was inclined to join it—the Jewish Community Center, the successor of the YMHA-YWHA and the settlement houses. Originally, the "Ys" were socioliterary associations for native-born adolescents of German background. Later, like the settlement houses, they became Americanization agencies serving East European immigrants primarily. By the second quarter of the twentieth century, Americanization was no longer imperative; the young of immigrant stock were now native-born; their problem was Judaization. The centers could not effectively address themselves to this religious challenge; that was the job of the congregations. What the centers did offer was a Jewish ambience, and that was important. By the last decades of the twentieth century, there were at least 300 of these centers in the cities and suburbs; most of them were superbly housed in beautiful and functional buildings. Ever since 1921, they have enjoyed the guidance and supervision of an experienced national organization, the Jewish Welfare Board. The centers differed from the Christian "Ys" in that they did not emphasize religion; their goals were not evangelical, and very few stood out as cultural institutions, though New York's 92d Street Y developed cultural programs which were—and are—exemplary: a poetry center, a performing arts group, and Jewish Omnibus Classes for the study of Talmud, Jewish history, Zionism, and other subjects; some of the teachers are scholars of national repute.

Centers are not concerned with the religious affiliation of their members; they cut across all Jewish religious lines, although as Jewish institutions they observe the Holy Days and make their halls and rooms available for worship services. The better equipped centers have clubrooms, a stage, an auditorium, a swimming pool, a library, game rooms, a health club, and a gymnasium. They encourage music and further the arts and crafts. Athletics, too, are not neglected. The centers cater primarily to the youth, although they also provide numerous facilities for adults. The kitchen and the snack bar may be "kosher style" or even legitimately kosher. The type of food offered is important, of course, to traditionalists. There have been problems; the young folks were eager to keep the center, especially the pool and the gymnasium, open on the Sabbath; the Orthodox opposed any activity that conflicts with Jewish law. In a few communities, the admission of Christians or blacks has been an issue; most Jews, however, live in the suburbs off by themselves and have been left alone.

Center workers have held high hopes for their institution; they have wanted it to be the organization around which the whole community would agglomerate; in this expectation, they have been disappointed. It was certainly unrealistic in a metropolitan setting, but in small communities the center served frequently as the core institution. In large cities Jews have set out to build tight well-integrated communities with the center, the "Y," as their recreational arm. Realizing the center's importance as an organization which transcends many differences, the federation supports it generously and loyally. Young men who wish to rise in the communal hierarchy often begin as advisors, workers, and club leaders in the center; it is a favorite training ground for future leaders. The importance of the center lies in its desire to serve the community as a whole; it is an all-embracing, unifying force.[25]

SOCIAL WELFARE AGENCIES, THE FEDERATION, THE COMMUNITY RELATIONS COMMITTEE, THE JEWISH COMMUNITY COUNCIL

The Jewish Community Center receives a very substantial part of its funding from the local Jewish social-welfare federation, which controls practically all relief and welfare agencies in every Jewish community. All told, there are about 200 such federations; they include about 800 Jewish communities. In 1932, they were united into a strong national Jewish organization, the Council of Jewish Federations and Welfare Funds. Though the federating of Jewish philanthropic agencies had already begun in antebellum days, it was not until the 1890's that Jewish social workers in the large towns set out in earnest to coordinate the local relief and welfare associations. The prime motivation was the need to stop the diverse and incessant campaigns for funds; under the federation, there was only one campaign. Jews responded; in most towns, more than half of the householders contributed to the single combined annual drive for money. In Cincinnati, for instance, in 1984, more than 70 percent of all Jewish householders contributed to the Jewish Welfare Fund.

Because of its financial support for many of the community's basic services and institutions, the federation was very influential everywhere. By the second decade of the twentieth century, when the federations were in full swing, they provided social service and funds for children, orphans, the family, camps, and hospitals; later, through their grants, they moved into the field of community relations (defense!) and even religious education. In subsidizing some of the social service activities of synagogs in various towns, the federations were moving toward potential conflict with the synagogs. Federations helped synagogs by providing some funding for services to single parents—a large group—as well as to senior citizens and to the handicapped. Congregational presidents are wary of federation help; they insist on autonomy; there must always be a wall between "Church and State." In the larger towns, practically all the service agencies established by the East European newcomers have now become part of the federation. There are exceptions; the Orthodox will not surrender an old-age home, if kosher food is not provided. By the middle of the century, the number of foreign-born clients served by the federation has declined; many who required aid were native-born. The burden of relief was shared by old-age survivors' disability insurance and medicare, government programs.

It was during the period of the long depression, 1929-1940, that the federations organized a Jewish vocational service; they sought to provide employment for those without jobs. One of their innovations was the creation of sheltered workshops where the sick, the retarded, and the elderly could find something to do and keep one another company. The federation set itself the task of holding the family together; counseling and psychiatric services were emphasized. The agencies were in the van of those who employed the techniques of geropsychiatry; the numbers of elderly are increasing and they need help, assurance. "Senior citizens" are provided with special facilities, housing as well as recreational and cultural services. Volunteers bring food for shut-ins; meals are served the ambulatory. No one can question the wish of the agencies to see their elderly receive excellent care; they are among the leaders in the gerontological services they offer. The agencies are creative; many years ago, a Jewish sociologist, Dr. Abraham Cronbach, pointed out that the Jewish community had pioneered in twenty-nine areas of social service. In large towns, Jews have the assurance that the community will make ample provision for them—extending from prenatal care to postmortem examinations. American Jews are exemplary in their generosity to fellow Jews both here and abroad.

During the First World War, the Community Chest was established in many cities as a common fund set up to help finance the welfare needs of all groups, Protestants, Catholics, and Jews. Many Jewish social workers went along with this innovation but were not happy with it, fearing as they did that the Community Chest would threaten their autonomy as Jewish social practitioners, their authority, and their outreach. Jewish welfare workers had vested interests which they were determined to protect. In a way, their concern was justified. For Jewish purposes, the grants from the Community Chest were inadequate. There were certain Jewish needs which the Chest could not or would not fund. Jews required subsidies for their religious schools, their bureaus of education, their national religious agencies, overseas relief, Jewish settlement in Palestine, the Hebrew University, and the Haifa Technical Institute. Consequently, it was not long before a supplementary fund was provided by Jews in the 1920's to meet the needs not covered by the Chest. Actually, Jews had to raise about twice what they received from the general funds. The new source of revenue was called the Jewish Welfare Fund. Ultimately, the Fund and the federations were coupled.

By virtue of the monies at its disposal, the federation added to its power; now it controlled most agencies in the community with the exception of the synagogs. It often happened, however, that the welfare leaders were also powers in the synagog; the two agencies were not necessarily hostile. The Fund-federation coopted every individual in the community; it united all Jews and its leaders enjoyed an enviable status. The medium of communication employed by the Fund-federation is the local Jewish newspaper. In many towns it is published by the Fund-federation; in some cities it is subsidized by this organization. On the whole, these controlled papers are well-edited; the occasional articles they publish on history, literature, and sociology are informative. There is no question, however, that these weeklies are federation organs; the local Jewish press is controlled. Completely independent Jewish local papers are few. Fortunately, there are some maverick editors and publishers who are not subject to the federation; they print and interpret the facts as they see them and criticize the local, the national Jewish establishments, and even the Jewish Agency and the State of Israel. No institution should be exempt from critical review; American Jewry wishes to know how its millions are spent.

American Jews in the 1920's and 1930's had to face a vicious anti-Semitism. The federations, though well organized, could not cope with the problem. In a crisis of this nature, there was a need for some form of effective defense, if only to reassure the Jewish masses. Little help came from the four leading national defense agencies, the American Jewish Committee, the American Jewish Congress, the Anti-Defamation League, and the Jewish Labor Committee; they themselves did not know what to do; they had no effective plans; because of their impotence, the morale of the communities was low. In response to this menace, after the Nazis had come to power in Europe and similar racist groups had made their appearance here in the United States, local Jewish communities spontaneously organized defense instrumentalities; they were called Jewish Community Relations Committees (JCRC). Because all Jews were threatened, all Jews responded. The JCRC coopted elements heretofore ignored: the religious leaders and the East Europeans; prior to this time, these two groups had not been fully represented in the councils of the federations and the Welfare Fund. The tradition of rivalry between rabbis and welfare workers dated back to the turn of the century; the rabbis looked down on social workers, while, for their part, many social workers had little sympathy for religion and its leaders; even today, the executives of the social agencies tend to keep their distance from the clergy. During the 1930's, when the community was exposed to Judeophobic assaults, the movement to organize community-wide defense agencies on a local level spread like wildfire; by the last decades of the century, there were over 100 such JCRC's organized loosely into the National Jewish Community Relations Advisory Council (NJCRAC); they were manned by professionals who were learning to cope with prejudice. The Community Relations Committees depend on the federations for their budgets; they cannot undertake any large-scale programs without the approval of the funding body.

As the all-inclusive Community Relations Committees were developing, the communities themselves were keeping pace; the rank and file, eagerly reaching out for recognition, hoped that their voices, too, would be heard. The concept of community was spreading; if we are a community, said many, then there must be social planning, coordination of all agencies, farsighted programs. Funds must be allocated according to need, according to the importance of a project. There must be one overall dominating, controlling agency that will be efficient and will further Jews and Judaism. The ultimate goal is cultural and spiritual survival. Those who pressed forward toward this goal were often the lower middle classes, the commonality of East European background; they wanted a place in the sun. These people remembered the victories of the American Jewish Congress in the years 1916-1918. The Jewish community, they pointed out, was headless. Since the city is ruled by a council, they wanted a democratically elected Jewish Community Council (JCC). Thus it was that during the 1930's and 1940's Jewish Community Councils were organized in several American towns. The JCC got its start in some places because it was identified in the late 1920's with the desire to establish one single welfare fund, to put an end to the seemingly innumerable fund-raising campaigns. To this end, all elements in the city had to be invited to join in a common effort to raise enough money at one fell stroke for all needs.

Once the Welfare Fund was established by the leaders, the Jewish masses moved in to insist that the total Jewish community meet democratically and make the important decisions. These insurgents were active in the 1930's and 1940's. Cincinnati, frequently in the forefront in matters of social welfare, had begun to employ the term Jewish Community Council as early as 1928 and had a functioning council of sorts in 1930. The concept of a Jewish Community Council as the structural head of a local American Jewish community never got off the ground, though the name was retained in some towns. Why was the Council doomed to rejection? The reason is quite obvious; 80 to 85 percent of all monies raised came from 10 to 15 percent of the people. The big givers were not going to let others tell them how to run the community. Even if there is a nominal JCC in town, the big givers still determine policy. These generous men and women who donate huge sums are not always rooted in Jewish tradition; some, unfortunately, have no philosophy of survival. The struggle for a democratic Jewish Community Council is a battle that American Jewry has lost. After all, the question might well be asked: to what extent does the Congress, sitting in Washington, actually represent the interests of the American millions.[26]

TAXATION AND SANCTIONS

In the drive toward "community," the local associations and institutions have been aided by a form of taxation, the Welfare Fund. Every Jewish householder is expected to make a contribution. One may question whether this is in any sense a tax since enforcement is impossible. Yet, Jews who refuse to give are frowned upon. This is particularly true when large-scale fund-raising is conducted in public; the affluent dare not refuse to pledge; social pressure is too strong. In some towns, the name of the donors and the amounts given are published. This happened in 1925 in New York City; 30,000 givers were listed in a fat booklet; it makes for fascinating reading. In a few communities, the local club importuned its members to be generous; there was an implicit threat here. It is difficult to determine whether coercive measures to impose taxation have been effective, but this much seems true: Jewish public opinion has formulated several unwritten sanctions; most Jews accept them. To be recognized as a Jew in good standing, one must give to Israel, help the Soviet Jews, contribute to the Welfare Fund, fight anti-Semitism, and join some Jewish organization, secular or religious. Those who do not are considered to be virtually beyond the pale. The more homogeneous the community, the more effective are these unwritten demands. The authority of the consensus increases after every crisis. There is a continuous move toward integration. Ever since the early twentieth century, there has been an inexorable fusion of the various Jewish subethnic groups, associations, institutions, and cultures. By the end of the twentieth century, the consensual community was rounded out: Jews lived in (golden) ghettos; in a latitudinarian sense, no Jew was outside the fold; every community had its spectrum of religious, cultural, educational, defense, recreational, and welfare agencies. Despite the lack of an authoritative overall community council, there was, in effect, an integrated community.

THE NATIONAL JEWISH COMMUNITY

If at first glance the local American Jewish community was headless, it was nevertheless a community that was the stronger because it was consensual. The unstructured national community was less real, less tangible —one is tempted to say, anarchic. The following bears repetition: in early biblical times, every tribe did what was right in its own eyes; this tradition has never died. Jews have always hesitated to organize their forces; if unification is a virtue, it is one to be honored in the breach. In America's early national period, in the days of George Washington, the Christian churches organized nationally, but not the Jews. Throughout the nineteenth century, the Jews moved slowly to establish national associations of lodges, denominational synagogs, rabbis, women, YMHA's, educational and social welfare groups, and a historical society. In the early twentieth century, two of the outstanding national organizations were the defense-oriented American Jewish Committee and the overseas relief combine called the Joint Distribution Committee (JDC), which subsidized Jewish institutions as far east as India. Both worked effectively. However, the national institutions have not moved to create a solid structured national community. The changes wrought by World War I made American Jewry the greatest in the world; it responded to this implicit challenge by assuming responsibilities both here and abroad. In 1921, there were fewer than 100 national organizations; in 1984, there were at least 200 serving in the areas of religion, education, defense, overseas aid —billions were raised—social welfare, mutual aid, Zionism, and recreation. They welded together, nationally, groups concerned with women, youth, students, and a distressed Soviet Jewry. All these national associations were autonomous; there was little, if any, liaison among them.

American Jewry was distraught in the 1930's; German agitators were busy here, and petty American Hitlers dressed in colored shirts carried on an unrelenting anti-Jewish propaganda. Jews here wanted one consolidated national defense institution, but rivalries and vested interests decreed that this was never to be. Various halfhearted attempts to create a central public relations agency were all unsuccessful. Finally, in 1943, the American Jewish Conference was organized—a repeat of the successful American Jewish Congress of the second decade of the century. The Conference focused its attention on reestablishing the ancient Jewish state in Palestine; it saw no other solution to the problem of Jewish insecurity. Little, if anything, was done to help American Jewry resolve its own difficulties. For this and other reasons, a number of powerful American Jewish organizations—the American Jewish Committee, for instance— did not affiliate with the Conference. In 1949 the American Jewish Conference disbanded; it had reached its goal with the establishment of the new State of Israel. As early as 1944, those Jews who had hoped for a re-structured national American Jewish community realized that nothing was to be expected from the Conference. They were disturbed. The horrors of the Holocaust had been revealed; grass root Jewries pressed for some action. The local Community Relations Committees wanted a say in the conduct of the several national defense agencies. There was waste, duplication; huge sums were involved; in 1975, over $21,000,000 was expended; and still there was no single consolidated national Jewish defense agency. In 1944, answering the cry of the local CRC groups, the national Council of Jewish Federations and Welfare Funds organized the National Community Relations Advisory Council (NCRAC) which included all the local and national defense groups. The NCRAC set out to watch American anti-Semites, to counteract anti-Jewish Arab propaganda, to help oppressed Soviet Jewry. Unfortunately, it was not destined to become an effective agency; though the most representative, it had the least funds; the major defense agencies continued to operate autonomously.

By 1951, the Council of Federations, realizing that the NCRAC needed help, tried another tack; it asked the Columbia University sociologist Robert M. MacIver to study the numerous defense agencies. In the report he presented in 1952, MacIver recommended that every problem be evaluated and that the task of coping with it be assigned to the association most competent to tackle it. Refusing to coordinate their work with the other agencies, the American Jewish Committee (AJC) and the Anti-Defamation League (ADL) withdrew. In later years, they returned—but more or less on their own terms. These two large associations insisted on autonomy; they emphasized policy differences; they represented different social and class groups; leaders and bureaucrats clashed. One suspects that the final authority in these powerful institutions rested with the bureaucrats. The AJC, the ADL, and the NCRAC each went its own way, yet they all discovered empirically that they experienced their best results by fighting disabilities through legislative acts and resort to the courts, an approach pioneered by the American Jewish Congress. These larger agencies thus adopted a somewhat similar approach in resolving the problems of American Jewry.

Faced with constant guerrilla warfare on the part of hostile Arabs, pro-Israel forces here in the United States organized the Conference of Presidents of Major American Jewish Organizations in 1955; this new group included almost every national Jewish association except the American Jewish Committee. The Presidents Conference was determined to aid the State of Israel. As an umbrella organization, the Conference is today the most impressive of all national agencies, though it remains questionable how much authority each president has to commit his group. There is no doubt, however, that the Conference is in a position to exert influence. In the next decade, in 1964, the American Jewish Conference on Soviet Jewry was organized. Jews here were concerned with the difficulties facing Soviet Jews, who suffered disabilities and whose migration from the Soviet Union was severely restricted. In the 1980's, the new Union of Councils for Soviet Jews and similar societies in this country addressed themselves to the problem of helping these unfortunates. The prime purpose of these American pressure congeries was to bring Jews out of Russia and make a home for them in Israel. For a time, thousands were rescued. Surrounded by 50,000,000 hostile Muslims, the Israelis were hungry for manpower. Many of the Soviet émigrés, divorced for two generations from Jewish influences, were not ardent Jews and opted not for Israel but for the United States; here the opportunities were more inviting.

At the present writing in the 1980's, there is no authoritative overall national American Jewish community agency. It is true, however, that power is no longer vested in the hands of a few New Yorkers; very frequently the leaders of the different national agencies are men and women from the states west of the Hudson. This is a significant step in the direction of national unity and of representativeness. It is futile to speculate on the possibility or the nature of an overall uniting American Jewish organization. There are people who would welcome a democratically elected national Jewish congress; there are others who hope the Presidents Conference may yet be in a position to speak with authority for all of its constituent agencies. Though the prospect today of an effective national organization is dim, there is no question that a crisis of significance would bring about a change. Crises crowd out differences.[27]

UNITED STATES JEWRY AND OVERSEAS COMMUNITIES

Frequently, perhaps more often than not, American Jews showed more concern for overseas coreligionists than they did for their own in America. Others came first. It is not improbable, too, that American Jews were somewhat guilt ridden; "we have it so good here." Jews took pride in helping fellow Jews abroad. It is also true that their sympathies have been heightened by the magic of almost instantaneous communication. In the late 1890's, Rabbi Isaac M. Wise required an hour to drive out to his farm on the northern outskirts of Cincinnati. Less than a century later, a Concorde plane could fly halfway to Europe in the same space of time. When a group of students was gunned down by Arabs in Hebron, the report of the killing was broadcast in the United States a few moments later. European, African, and Asian Jewry, 8,000,000 strong, all live in the backyard of every American Jew. Israel assumes World Jewish leadership; United States Jewry exercises it. In their effort to influence World Jewry, Jews here reflect the intention of the United States government itself to wield international authority, the Pax Americana; the synagog follows the flag.

American Jewry has always reached out to offer the Jews of Europe, North African, and Asia political, religious, and philanthropic help. Secure on this continent, the Orthodox and the Conservatives seek to extend their influence overseas. The right-wing Orthodox have established the Agudath Israel World Organization which has proven itself able and aggressive. Working through the United Jewish Appeal, American Jewry has spent millions supporting traditional Hebrew schools and talmudic academies in Israel and other lands. The Appeal subsidizes the American Jewish agencies that carry on cultural work in Europe, Israel, and North Africa. In a manner reminiscent of the early Christians, the modern evangelicals, and the Mormons, the Lubavitcher Hassidim—staunchly Orthodox pietists—send their apostles all over the Jewish world to preach their gospel and garner disciples; their zeal is astounding. In 1957, the Conservatives set up a World Council of Synagogues; the Reformers established a World Union for Progressive Judaism in 1926. How successful these latter two groups are numerically is difficult to determine, but they are gaining followers, especially in Israel.

It is not easy to evaluate the political influence of the American defense agencies as they set out to aid Jews who are still denied the Rights of Man. The Big Four—the American Jewish Committee, the American Jewish Congress, the B'nai B'rith-Anti-Defamation League, and the Jewish Labor Committee—have never ceased their efforts to help Jews in foreign lands. The American Jewish Committee has worked independently and with the conservative Alliance Israélite Universelle; the Congress has long been linked to the World Jewish Congress and the Zionists; the ADL and B'nai B'rith have had good relations with the Board of Deputies of British Jews and with South African Jewry; the Labor Committee has been persona grata in the socialist circles of Western and Central Europe. These American agencies have done what they could to protest the suppression of the religious and cultural practices of Jews in the Soviet empire. One suspects that their efforts are not without some influence; dictatorial regimes are often paranoid, and, at least to some degree, sensitive to world public opinion.

The political and religious work of the Big Four is overshadowed by the accomplishments of the Joint Distribution Committee (JDC) and the United Israel Appeal (UIA), both of them major relief agencies. As late as 1980, the JDC was helping half a million Jews in more than twenty different lands. Actually, most European Jews still turn to Big Brother, American Jewry, for financial aid in maintaining their welfare and cultural institutions. North Africa has been a troubled area for centuries. Before the rise of the State of Israel, some 600,000 Jews lived in Morocco,

Algiers, Tunis, Tripoli, and Egypt; in the 1980's only about 30,000 remained, most of them in Morocco, though a few were left in Tunisia and Egypt. The Jews remaining in these lands live warily; their situation is on the whole unenviable, the more so since Israel has emerged victorious in the Arab-Israel wars. There are no Jews—officially at any rate—in Saudi Arabia; the Yemenite and the Iraqi Jews fled or were airlifted to Israel a generation ago in Operation Magic Carpet and Operation Ezra-Nehemiah; thousands upon thousands were flown out and resettled in Israel—a remarkable feat. In the late 1940's, there were over 160,000 Jews in Aden, Iraq, Yemen, Syria, and Lebanon; now, no more than about 6,000 remain there. In the few Muslim lands where Jews still live, they are aided by the Joint, if in need; they are given food, clothing, and schooling. Many brought to Israel from Islamic lands face a problem: fleeing from a familiar medievalism, they are confronted by an unfamiliar modernism. One is reminded of the East Europeans who left the czarist Pale of Settlement for American shores; here, they had no choice but to come to terms with Americanism. The immigrants from the Islamic lands will ultimately do well in Israel; after all, their ancestors in the Middle Ages included distinguished scholars, some of the leading intellectuals in the Mediterranean basin and the Middle East in those centuries.

ISRAEL

The United Israel Appeal and the Joint Distribution Committee are the chief beneficiaries of America's United Jewish Appeal (UJA), which was established in 1939. The UJA may well be the largest voluntary philanthropy in all history. For decades these two relief agencies have poured millions into Jewish Palestine and, later, the State of Israel. The ancient Jewish homeland has always been given preference over all other countries by American Jewry. After 1924, when Palestine was the only real haven open to oppressed Jews, more and more money was funneled into the country. Funds were needed even more desperately after 1948, when the State of Israel came into being and had to defend itself in a series of wars that continued into the 1970's; guerrilla incursions have never ceased. Billions have been sent to shore up this little country, which is not yet self-sufficient. To be sure American Jewry is not always happy with the disposal of its largess; Israel party politics play an important part in the dispersal of these funds. Most American Jewish institutions use their political influence to help Israel survive; they never forget that the Jewish state is threatened by millions of hostile Muslims all the way from Morocco and Algeria to Iran and Pakistan. Here, too, on this side of the Atlantic, pro-Israel American Jewry has had to walk carefully; the State Department has often looked askance at the Israelis. To protect the Zionist effort, American Jewry, led by Abba Hillel Silver, organized a Washington Jewish lobby, which later, in 1954, became the really effective American Israel Political Affairs Committee (AIPAC).

THE ZIONISTS

American lovers of Zion have done much since the 1880's to nurture the hope for a Jewish state. For decades they have carried on national educational programs. Zionists here have exerted political influence to win government support and have encouraged American Jews to migrate to Israel, an effort, this last, in which they have been singularly unsuccessful. Present-day American Zionists remain relatively well organized; in addition to the Zionist Organization of America, there are over fifty national Zionist organizations in this country, all of them concerned with the welfare of Israel. This young republic is very dependent on American Jewry; practically every institution of consequence in Israel seeks or is dependent upon funds from the United States. If one is tempted to reproach these 3,000,000 Jews for their outstretched palms, let it be noted that in 1984-1985 the estimated American government budgetary deficit was well over $200,000,000,000. Despite the abundance of Zionist organizations in the United States, the movement is faced with grave problems. After Israel came to birth in 1948, there was little need for Zionism as a political organization; its mission had been accomplished. Indeed, the State of Israel has always frowned upon a vigorous Zionist organization; it brooks no conflict of authority. The strength of the movement in the United States and elsewhere will always be in inverse ratio to the strength of Israel itself. When Israel is weak, Zionism will be strong; when Israel is strong, Zionism will be weak. Today, the Jewish state is barely tolerant of Zionist pretensions.

THE ATTITUDE OF UNITED STATES JEWRY TO ISRAEL

Few Jews refuse to help Israel; World Jewry is determined: the new state must survive. Yet, at the same time, Israel and the American Jews are rivals in the field of Jewish learning and scholarship. Zionists here and a host of other American Jews talk of the centrality of Israel. Certainly, this much is true: Jews here manifest an intense interest in the reborn state; it is precious to them, but it is not central in most American Jewish lives. Indeed, most American Jews have never visited the new Israel. There are many American Jews who seek not only to further that republic but all Jewries everywhere; this is particularly true if they are in distress. Still others question the wisdom of gathering all Jews into a few great centers.

Because they believe that no Jewry anywhere is guaranteed survival, they plead for a wider dispersion, a far-flung Diaspora; they stand foursquare on a passage in the Talmud (Pesahim 87b), which says that God showed his goodness to the Jews by scattering them among the nations. The comment of the medieval scholar Rashi (1040-1105) is enlightening: if they are scattered, they cannot all be annihilated at one fell stroke. Over the centuries, omniterritoriality alone has saved the Jews. And there are others, too, who look beyond the political state; now that we have won Palestine, we must not lose Zion. Zion, they say, is our highest Jewish self in projection; Zion is what is ideally Jewish on a meta-Israel, meta-America level.[28]

THE AMERICAN JEW IN THE LATE TWENTIETH CENTURY

American Jewish historians are beginning to learn more about their subject, the American Jewish people. Demographers and sociologists have conducted about 130 Jewish communal surveys since World War II, over forty of them since 1975. The government conducts no religious census, hence the researcher is dependent on the sample polls. A great deal of data has been available, and all this is helpful, but a caveat is necessary. The pollsters accept their findings at face value. They forget to take a liberal discount in certain areas. Persons polled, eager to be on the side of the angels, frequently exaggerated. They do not tell the whole truth. Historians must use their judgment in studying the printed record.

In many respects, the Jew of today is simply another American. Few Jews look "Jewish," whatever that means; some of the new Jewish forenames are characteristically American: Sue, Peggy, William, George. Most Jews live close to one another; they are residentially integrated in physical and psychological havens, a ghetto of sorts. There is this difference: in the early twentieth century, the number of Jewish residential areas was limited. Now, in the big towns, there are several such areas where Jews congregate. Golden ghettos have multiplied. What is true of the cities is true of the country as a whole. Decades ago most American Jews clustered together in about ten large towns; now they are to be found in many more and go wherever opportunity beckons. Yet, Jews are different from other Americans. They marry later; their families are smaller. Jews in this country—some of the Orthodox excepted—are barely reproducing themselves.

Jews are now important politically; a large percentage go to the polls. Toward the end of the twentieth century, they had more than tripled their demographic percentage in the House and the Senate. Aware of Jewish political influence, the United States government hovers over Israel protectively; that small Jewish republic is, in many respects, a client state; one wonders whether it could survive without American aid. This is particularly true in periods of tension and war, when huge quantities of munitions are required. The United States government favors Israel despite the temptation to back the Arabs, who control the oil reserves so important for American industry. This country has also invested billions in Muslim lands. Despite this need for Arab oil and despite some pro-Arab forces in Washington bureaus, the United States as a rule has leaned in the direction of the Israelis. There are many other reasons why Washington favors Jerusalem; America distrusts and fears the Russians, who are making advances in the Middle East and cultivating allies there; American evangelicals are pro-Israel; God promised the land to the Jews. Moreover, the Israelis maintain the strongest army in their part of the world.

Jews are among the most highly educated groups in the United States, possibly the highest. In Washington—an exceptional community, to be sure—85 percent of all people polled replied that they had attended, or graduated from, or possessed an advanced degree from, colleges; the percentage in California was 81; it was 77 in Chicago. In general, surveys agree that the percentage of educated Jews far exceeds that of the non-Jews. In the decade of the 1970's, at least 50 percent of young American Jewish men and women were entering institutions of higher learning. In the 1980's, the percentage was probably 60. One wonders how many students seek education for its own sake; most have an eye on a career; education in the sciences or in business is a prerequisite for achievement and success. The special training which many Jews have acquired may help explain their accomplishments. The fact that some non-Jews look askance at Jews may well drive the latter to work harder. A very large percentage of Jews are in the white-collar class; they are professionals, managers, proprietors, and, increasingly self-employed, certainly more so than their non-Jewish fellow citizens. Jews are deemed affluent, because about 20 percent of them have an annual income of $50,000 or more. Many own their own homes; there are very few without an automobile. Yet, at least 30 percent are "poor," disadvantaged; many make less—considerably less —than $20,000 a year in 1980 dollars, hardly enough to sustain a family with one or two children on a decent standard of living. Despite the substantial numbers who are really in the lower or lower middle class, American Jewry as a body is very philanthropic. Approximately 50 percent of all Jewish men and women make gifts to Jewish charities. American Jews raise at least $500,000,000 annually for their philanthropies; the gross national product of all Jewish communal institutions runs to about $3,000,000,000. About one half of these funds flow in and out of the Jewish hospitals, most of whose patients are Gentile; like many similar Christian institutions throughout the country, Jewish hospitals are, in reality, general hospitals despite their denominational label.

If a very perceptible number of Jews do not give to Jewish causes, it is because they do not have the means, though, to be sure, there are some who are indifferent. Most Jews do give and give liberally, moved by a prideful sense of kinship "we take care of our own." Jews fear their Gentile neighbors will reproach them if too many Jews resort to the municipal charities; Jews glory in the Gentile image of them as people who have prospered and have few, if any, paupers. Tradition, customary and biblical law command the Jew to help a coreligionist; religion ties Jews together. When Jews help one another, the religious bond is often a motivating factor. Though only a minority are synagog and temple members, religion is central in the life of every American Jewish community. It is questionable whether a community here in the United States can survive as a purely secular complex without a religious base. The majority of Jews in the United States—and in Israel, too—are worshippers at the altar of civil religion. This is the new surrogate for theism, a compound of traditional practices where belief in God plays a lesser role or none at all.

How many American Jews are actually religionists? The polls reveal that 50 to 60 percent pay dues to Jewish houses of worship, but these polls are obviously wrong: many respondents did not tell the truth; not more than 30 percent of the Jews in this country are actually on the rolls of the synagogs. These men and women have joined, because they are believers and are eager to educate their children Jewishly. Jewish education is the synagog's job. How many Jews attend services regularly? About 10 percent occupy the pews on the Sabbath at weekly services; about 40 to 50 percent make their appearance on the High Holy Days. These statistics apply primarily to members, but there is a large number of non-members who identify with the three main Jewish denominations. They do not join because they are too poor or too thrifty. Ever since the third quarter of the nineteenth century, there have been three main denominations in this country, the Orthodox, the Reformers, and the middle group, the Conservatives. By the 1980's, the Orthodox had declined and become a smaller group. The Conservatives had the largest following; the Reformers are close on their heels and will very probably overtake the Conservatives in the next decade or two. In some large cities, the Reformers already outnumber the Conservatives; since Reform has turned back towards tradition, it has won thousands of new recruits.

On balance, most American Jews have maintained some relationship to their people and their faith; they like being Jews; it gives them a sense of security. For many, affiliation has become a form of ethnic identification. Joining a church is an American amenity, and evidence of respectability. With the increase of tension between American religionists and Slavic Marxists, fealty to the church or synagog took on added significance. The day the forces of capitalism and Marxism confront each other at Armageddon, American Jews will stand side by side with the Christians of the land. They will not dare do otherwise. Nearly every Jewish family observes some Jewish ceremony, holiday, or custom. The most popular is the Passover dinner, the seder, the festival of freedom. Why? The ritual is exotic, interesting; the traditional foods—matzo balls and all—are tempting. Four glasses of wine are de rigueur, for every participant has the biblical assurance that "wine maketh glad the heart of man" (Ps. 104:15). After the seder come these observances or practices in a descending order: lighting the eight candles at Hanukkah—coincident with the Christmas season—attaching the amulet mezuzah to the doorpost, fasting on Yom Kippur (the Day of Atonement), keeping the Sabbath with its candles, white bread, and wine, adhering to the dietary laws (kashrut), praying daily. Despite the relatively large number of Jews who are affiliated or unaffiliated religionists, there is still a substantial number who ignore all ritual and custom. Even Israel leaves them cold; nothing Jewish touches them. They are assimilationists who are on their way to breaking all ties with their people.

Though religious affiliation and affluence are in no sense a guarantee of Jewish survival, many American Jews are most generous in their support of institutions that further Jewish knowledge and education. Jewish learning in this country has made sizable progress since the Second World War. In the 1970's and 1980's, there were at least 2,000 congregations in the United States. Many of them have substantial collections of Jewish books: Cincinnati's Isaac M. Wise Temple housed about 15,000; Beth Israel in Phoenix, Arizona, over 20,000. Here in the United States, there are literally more books on Jews, Judaism, and Jewish history than in any other country in the world. American Jewish scholars and writers have produced about 1,000 solid volumes in English, Hebrew, and Yiddish every decade. The objection may be voiced that, because most are in Yiddish and English, they cannot be read by foreign students and scholars and, therefore, American Jews can exercise little cultural influence on World Jewry. The answer is that many of the best books produced on this continent are ultimately translated into foreign languages, especially into Hebrew. Throughout the centuries, the important Jewish vernacular classics have sooner or later been translated into Hebrew for the edification of learned Jews. Most of the medieval philosophic works were written originally in Arabic. *The Guide for the Perplexed* (*Moreh Nevukhim*) of Maimonides is an example; today, it can be read in Hebrew and in several modern languages. It would seem that at least 50 percent of American Jewish children are being given some training in Sunday schools and in afternoon and all-day schools. Most Jews own a Bible—which they rarely read—a Passover ritual (Haggadah), a prayer book, and a few other books of Jewish interest. There is hardly a family that does not receive the local Jewish newspaper; Jews read the social columns and the obituaries eagerly and keep in touch with Israel and with Jewish life the world over. After a fashion, this, too, is culture and strengthens identification with Jews and Judaism.[29]

The Messiah tarries; there is much to be deplored in the conduct of every state on this planet of ours; the United States is no exception. Yet, there can be no question, for the Jew this is the best country, the freest land in the world. This he knows full well; he is happy that his lines have fallen in pleasant places. There may be misgivings but he faces the future with trust, with confidence, with dogged faith.

ABBREVIATIONS, SYMBOLS, AND SHORT TITLES

IN THE NOTES

This key may be considered a virtual bibliography for it includes all the unpublished records, documents, source collections and works to which my notes refer with some frequency. Omitted here are works and manuscripts cited only once. All term papers unless otherwise marked are in the AJAr.

Abbott, *Women in Industry*
  Edith Abbott, *Women in Industry: A Study in American Economic History* (N.Y. & London, 1910).

Abrahams, *Hebraic Bookland*
  Israel Abrahams, *By-Paths in Hebraic Bookland* (Phila., 1920).

ACOAB
  Appleton's Cyclopaedia of American Biography.

Adler, *I Have Considered the Days*
  Cyrus Adler, *I Have Considered the Days* (Phila., 1941).

Adler, *Jacob H. Schiff*
  Cyrus Adler, *Jacob H. Schiff: His Life and Letters* (2 vols., Garden City, N.Y., 1928).

Adler, *Kansas City*
  Frank J. Adler, *Roots in a Moving Stream: The Centennial History of Congregation B'nai Jehudah of Kansas City, 1870-1970* (Kansas City, Mo., 1972).

Adler, *Lectures*
  Cyrus Adler, *Lectures, Selected Papers, Addresses* (Phila., privately printed, 1933).

Adler, *Recent Persecution*
  Felix Adler, *The Recent Persecution of the Jews, etc.* (N.Y., 1879).

Adler, *Selected Letters*
  Ira Robinson (ed.), *Cyrus Adler Selected Letters,* (2 vols., Phila., 1985).

Adler (ed.), *Voice of America on Kishineff*
  Cyrus Adler (ed.), *The Voice of America on Kishineff* (Phila., 1904).

Adler & Connolly, *Buffalo*
  Selig Adler and Thomas E. Connolly, *From Ararat to Suburbia: The History of the Jewish Community of Buffalo* (Phila., 1960).

Adolph Huebsch: A Memorial
  Rev. Dr. Adolph Huebsch, Late Rabbi of the Ahawath Chesed Congregation, New York. A Memorial (N.Y., 1885).

AH
  The American Hebrew.

Ahlstrom, *Relig. Hist. of Am. People*
  Sidney E. Ahlstrom, *A Religious History of the American People* (New Haven, 1972).

AHR
  American Historical Review.

AI
  The American Israelite [until 1874: *The Israelite*].

AJA
  American Jewish Archives (publication).

AJAr
  American Jewish Archives (institution), Cincinnati.

AJH
  American Jewish History.

AJHQ
  American Jewish Historical Quarterly.

AJHSL
  American Jewish Historical Society Library, Waltham, Mass.

AJYB
  American Jewish Year Book.

Allen, "Americanization of the East-European Jew"
  Harold Allen, "The Americanization of the East-European Jew as Reflected in the Anglo-Jewish Press, 1900-1905" (HUC prize essay, n.d.).

Allen, "Reform Judaism"
  Daniel Allen, "Reform Judaism as Reflected in the Proceedings of the Union of American Hebrew Congregations, 1897-1910" (HUC term paper, n.d.).

American Jews' Annual
  The American Jew's Annual (Cincinnati, Chicago and N.Y., 5645-57, A.M. [1884-1897]).

Americana
  The Americana.

Amopteil
  Yorbukh fun Amopteil (Annual of the American Branch of the Yiddish Scientific Institute) (2 vols., N.Y., 1938-1939).

Analyticus, *Jews Are Like That*
  Analyticus, *Jews Are Like That!* (N.Y., 1928).

Angel, *Sephardic Experience in the United States*
  Marc D. Angel, *La America: The Sephardic Experience in the United States* (Phila., 1982).

Arfa, "Attitudes of the American Reform Rabbinate Toward Zionism"
  Cyrus Arfa, "Attitudes of the American Reform Rabbinate Toward Zionism, 1885-1948" (Ph.D. diss., N.Y.U., 1978).

Asmonean
  The Asmonean.

Auerbach, "Nebraska"
  Ella F. Auerbach, "Jewish Settlement in Nebraska, General Survey" (n.p., n.d.), typescript, copy in Marcus Collections.

Ausubel, *Book of Jewish Knowledge*
  Nathan Ausubel, *The Book of Jewish Knowledge* (N.Y., 1964).

Avery (ed.), *Laws Applicable to Immigration and Nationality*
Edwina Austin Avery (ed.), *Laws Applicable to Immigration and Nationality* (Washington, D.C., 1953).

AZJ
Allgemeine Zeitung des Judenthums.

B. & B., *JOUS*
Joseph L. Blau and Salo W. Baron (eds.), *The Jews of the United States, 1790-1840: A Documentary History* (3 vols., N.Y., 1963).

Bachrach, "Immigrant on the Hill"
Minnie Mildred Bachrach, "The Immigrant on the Hill" (M.A. thesis, Carnegie Institute of Technology, Pittsburgh, 1921?).

Bailey, *Diplomatic History of the American People*
Thomas A. Bailey, *A Diplomatic History of the American People* (N.Y., 1950).

Baker, *Brandeis and Frankfurter*
Leonard Baker, *Brandeis and Frankfurter: A Dual Biography* (N.Y., 1984).

Baltzell, *Protestant Establishment*
E. Digby Baltzell, *The Protestant Establishment* (N.Y., 1964).

Band, *Portland*
Benjamin Band, *Portland Jewry: Its Growth and Development* (Portland, 1955).

Banks, *First-Person America*
Ann Banks (ed.), *First-Person America* (N.Y., 1981).

Barnard, *Julian W. Mack*
Harry Barnard, *The Forging of an American Jew: The Life and Times of Judge Julian W. Mack* (N.Y., 1974).

Baron Festschrift
Joseph L. Blau et al., *Essays on Jewish Life and Thought Presented in Honor of Salo Wittmayer Baron* (N.Y., 1959).

Baron, *History*
Salo Wittmayer Baron, *A Social and Religious History of the Jews* (3 vols., N.Y., 1937).

Bauer, *JDC*
Yehuda Bauer, *My Brother's Keeper, etc.* (Phila., 1974).

BDEAJ
Joseph R. Rosenbloom, *A Biographical Dictionary of Early American Jews: Colonial Times through 1800* (Lexington, Ky., 1960).

Beerman, "Rebecca Gratz"
Leonard I. Beerman, "Rebecca Gratz—An Analysis of the Life and Activity of the Foremost Jewess of the Nineteenth Century as Reflected in Hitherto Unpublished Source Materials" (rabbinical thesis, HUC, 1949).

Beifield, "Joseph Krauskopf"
Martin P. Beifield, "Joseph Krauskopf, 1887-1903" (rabbinical thesis, HUC, 1975).

Benderly, *Aims and Activities of the Bureau of Education*
S. Benderly, *Aims and Activities of the Bureau of Education of the Jewish Community (Kehillah) of New York City* (N.Y.?, 1912).

Benjamin, *Three Years*
I.J. Benjamin, *Three Years in America, 1859-1862* (2 vols., Phila., 1956).

Bentwich, *Judah L. Magnes*
Norman Bentwich, *For Zion's Sake: A Biography of Judah L. Magnes* (Phila., 1954).

Bentwich, *Solomon Schechter*
    Norman Bentwich, *Solomon Schechter* (Phila., 1938).

Berkman, *Prison Memoirs of an Anarchist*
    Alexander Berkman, *Prison Memoirs of an Anarchist* (N.Y., 1912).

Berkowitz, "Hebrew Free School Association"
    Philip Berkowitz, "The Hebrew Free School Association and the Educational Alliance,
    1879-1907" (HUC term paper, 1964).

Berkson, *Theories of Americanization*
    Isaac B. Berkson, *Theories of Americanization, etc.* (N.Y., 1920).

Berman, "East European Immigration"
    Myron Berman, "Attitudes of American Jewry Toward East European Immigration,
    1881-1914" (Ph.D. diss., Columbia University, 1963).

Berman, *Shehitah*
    Jeremiah J. Berman, *Shehitah: A Study in the Cultural and Social Life of the Jewish People*
    (N.Y., 1941).

Bernheimer, *Russian Jew in the U.S.*
    Charles S. Bernheimer, *The Russian Jew in the United States* (Phila., 1905).

Bernstein, *English Speaking Orthodox Rabbinate*
    Louis Bernstein, *Challenge and Mission: The Emergence of the English Speaking Orthodox
    Rabbinate* (N.Y., 1982).

Beth Ahabah, Richmond
    Edward N. Calisch, *The Light Burns On: Centennial Anniversary, Beth Ahabah* (Rich-
    mond, Va., 1941).

Biographical Directory of the American Congress
    Biographical Directory of the American Congress, 1774-1971 (Washington, D.C., 1971).

Birmingham, *"Our Crowd"*
    Stephen Birmingham, *"Our Crowd": The Great Jewish Families of New York* (N.Y.,
    1967).

Blau (ed.), *Cornerstones*
    Joseph L. Blau (ed.), *Cornerstones of Religious Freedom in America* (Boston, 1950).

Blaustein (ed.), *Memoirs of David Blaustein*
    Miriam Blaustein (ed.), *Memoirs of David Blaustein: Educator and Communal Worker*
    (N.Y., 1913).

Bloch, *Of Making Many Books*
    Joshua Bloch, *Of Making Many Books, etc.* (Phila., 1953).

Blum, *Baltimore*
    Isidor Blum, *The Jews of Baltimore, etc.* (Baltimore, 1910).

Bogen, *Born a Jew*
    Boris D. Bogen, *Born a Jew* (N.Y., 1930).

Bogen, *Jewish Philanthropy*
    Boris D. Bogen, *Jewish Philanthropy, etc.* (N.Y., 1917).

Boraisha, *Yiddish*
    Menahem Boraisha, *The Story of Yiddish* (offprint, *Jewish Affairs*, vol.1, no.4, March 15,
    1946).

Brandeis, *Business: A Profession*
    Louis D. Brandeis, *Business: A Profession* (Boston, 1914, 1925).

Brandeis, *Jewish Rights and the Congress*
    Louis D. Brandeis, *Jewish Rights and the Congress* (N.Y., 1916).

Brandeis on Zionism
  Brandeis on Zionism: A Collection of Addresses and Statements by Louis D. Brandeis (Washington, D.C., 1942).
Brandeis, *Other People's Money*
  Louis D. Brandeis, *Other People's Money and How the Bankers Use It* (Washington, D.C. 1933).
Brandes & Douglas, *Immigrants to Freedom*
  Joseph Brandes and Martin Douglas, *Immigrants to Freedom: Jewish Communities in Rural New Jersey since 1882* (Phila., 1971).
Breck, *Colorado*
  Allen duPont Breck, *The Centennial History of the Jews of Colorado, 1859-1959* (Denver, 1960).
Bregstone, *Chicago*
  Philip P. Bregstone, *Chicago and Its Jews* (privately published, Chicago?, 1933).
Brickner, "Jew. Com. of Cin."
  Barrett R. Brickner, "Jewish Community of Cincinnati: Historical and Descriptive, 1817-1933" (Ph.D. diss., University of Cincinnati, 1933).
Brooks, *Jews in Utah and Idaho*
  Juanita Brooks, *History of the Jews in Utah and Idaho* (Salt Lake City, 1973).
Brownstein, "Philadelphia"
  Marc Brownstein, "Jewish Life in Philadelphia as reflected in the *Jewish Exponent*, October 1888–December 1892" (HUC term paper, n.d.).
Bryson, *American Diplomatic Relations*
  Thomas A. Bryson, *American Diplomatic Relations with the Middle East, 1784-1975: A Survey* (Metuchen, N.J., 1977).
Bushee, *Boston*
  Frederick Bushee, *Ethnic Factors in the Population of Boston* (N.Y., 1903).
By Myself I'm A Book
  By Myself I'm A Book! An Oral History of the Immigrant Jewish Experience in Pittsburgh (NCJW, Waltham, Mass., 1972).
Byars, *B. and M. Gratz*
  William Vincent Byars, *B. and M. Gratz: Merchants in Philadelphia, etc., 1754-1798* (Jefferson City, Mo., 1916).

Cahan, *Rise of David Levinsky*
  Abraham Cahan, *The Rise of David Levinsky* (N.Y., 1917, reprinted in 1966).
Cambridge History of American Literature
  The Cambridge History of American Literature (3 vols., N.Y., 1943).
Catalogue of the Exhibition of 1970 on the Yiddish Press
  Catalogue of the Exhibition, One Hundred Years of the Yiddish Press in America, 1870-1970 (N.Y., 1970).
CCAR Journal
  Central Conference of American Rabbis Journal.
CCARYB
  Central Conference of American Rabbis Yearbook.
Chiel, "Jewish Life in America as Seen Through 'Hamelitz'"
  Arthur A. Chiel, "Jewish Life in America as Seen Through 'Hamelitz'" (typescript, Winnepeg, n.d.), copy in Marcus Collections.

Chiel, *Kelman Festschrift*
    Arthur A. Chiel (ed.), *Perspectives on Jews and Judaism: Essays in Honor of Wolfe Kelman* (N.Y., 1978).
Chomsky, *Hebrew*
    William Chomsky, *Hebrew: The Eternal Language* (Phila., 1957).
Clothing Workers of Chicago
    Leo Wolman (ed.), *The Clothing Workers of Chicago, 1910-1922* (Chicago, 1922).
Cohen, *American Jewish Committee*
    Naomi W. Cohen, *A History of the American Jewish Committee, 1906-1966* (Phila., 1972).
Cohen, *Jews in the Making of America*
    George Cohen, *The Jews in the Making of America* (Boston, Mass., 1924).
Cohen, *They Built Better Than They Knew*
    Julius Henry Cohen, *They Built Better Than They Knew* (N.Y., 1946).
Cole, *Irrepressible Conflict*
    Arthur Charles Cole, *The Irrepressible Conflict, 1850-1865* (N.Y., 1934).
Colton, "American Jewry, 1901-1910"
    Lawrence M. Colton, "American Jewry From the Vantage Point of the *London Jewish Chronicle* for the Years 1901-1910" (HUC term paper, 1965).
Columbia Encyclopedia
    William H. Harris and Judith S. Levy, *The New Columbia Encyclopedia* (N.Y., 1975).
Commons, *History of Labour in the U.S.*
    John R. Commons, *History of Labour in the United States* (2 vols., N.Y., 1921).
Congress Weekly
    Congress Weekly: A Review of Jewish Interests.
Cowen, *Memories of an American Jew*
    Philip Cowen, *Memories of an American Jew* (N.Y., 1932).
Curti et al., *American History*
    Merle Curti et al., *An American History* (2 vols., N.Y., 1950).
Curti, *American Philanthropy Abroad*
    Merle Curti, *American Philanthropy Abroad: A History* (New Brunswick, N.J., 1963).
Curti, *American Thought*
    Merle Curti, *The Growth of American Thought* (N.Y., 1943).

DAB
    Dictionary of American Biography.
DAH
    Dictionary of American History.
Davidson, *Jewish Farmers*
    Gabriel Davidson, *Our Jewish Farmers and the Story of the Jewish Agricultural Society* (N.Y., 1943).
Davidson, *Parody*
    Israel Davidson, *Parody in Jewish Literature* (N.Y., 1907).
Davis, *Israel*
    Moshe Davis, *Israel: Its Role in Civilization* (N.Y., 1956).
Davis, "Synagogues, Hebrew Free Schools and Other Educational Influences"
    Mrs. Ben Davis, "Synagogues, Hebrew Free Schools and Other Educational Influences," written for Bureau of Associated Charities - Seventh Ward District - 1899 (typescript, Chicago, n.d.), copy in Marcus Collections.

Davitt, *Within the Pale*
Michael Davitt, *Within the Pale: The True Story of Anti-Semitic Persecution in Russia* (Phila., 1903).

Dawidowicz, *On Equal Terms*
Lucy S. Dawidowicz, *On Equal Terms: Jews in America, 1881-1981* (N.Y., 1982).

Deborah
Die Deborah.

Degler, *At Odds*
Carl N. Degler, *At Odds: Women and the Family in America from the Revolution to the Present* (Oxford, 1980).

De Haas, *Louis D. Brandeis*
Jacob De Haas, *Louis D. Brandeis* (N.Y., 1929).

Deinard, *Koheleth America*
Ephraim Deinard, *Koheleth America: Catalogue of Hebrew Books Printed in America from 1735-1925* (St. Louis, 1925?).

Der Tog
Der Tog (The Day).

Doroshkin, *Yiddish in America*
Milton Doroshkin, *Yiddish in America: Social and Cultural Foundations* (Rutherford, 1969).

Drachman, *Neo-Hebraic Literature*
Bernard Drachman, *Neo-Hebraic Literature in America* (N.Y., 1901?).

Dresner, *Agenda for American Jews*
Samuel H. Dresner, *Agenda for American Jews: Federation and Synagogue* (n.p., 1976).

Dreyfus, *Henry Cohen*
A. Stanley Dreyfus, *Henry Cohen: Messenger of the Lord* (N.Y., 1963).

Dubnow, *History of the Jews in Russia and Poland*
S.M. Dubnow, *History of the Jews in Russia and Poland, etc.* (Phila., 1918).

Dubnow, *Weltgeschichte*
Simon Dubnow, *Weltgeschichte des juedischen Volkes* (10 vols., Berlin, 1925-1929).

Duker, *Jews in World War I*
Abraham Gordon Duker, *Jews in World War I: A Brief Historical Sketch* (N.Y., 1939).

Duker, *Non-Zionist and Anti-Zionist Groups*
Abraham G. Duker, *Non-Zionist and Anti-Zionist Groups* (Training Bureau for Jewish Communal Service, Syllabus, N.Y., 1950).

Dushkin, *Jew. Ed. in NYC*
Alexander M. Dushkin, *Jewish Education in New York City* (N.Y., 1918).

E. & L., *Richmond*
Herbert T. Ezekiel and Gaston Lichtenstein, *The History of the Jews of Richmond from 1769 to 1917* (Richmond, Va., 1917).

EAH
Richard B. Morris (ed.), *Encyclopedia of American History* (N.Y., 1953).

Eastern Union
Joseph Gale (ed.), *Eastern Union: The Development of a Jewish Community* (Elizabeth, N.J., 1958).

Education of Abraham Cahan
The Education of Abraham Cahan (Phila., 1969).

Ehrenfried, *Boston*
>   Albert Ehrenfried, *A Chronicle of Boston Jewry: From the Colonial Settlement to 1900* (Sherman Oaks, Ca., 1963).

EIAJH
>   *Essays in American Jewish History, etc.* (Cincinnati, 1958).

Eichhorn, *Evangelizing*
>   David Max Eichhorn, *Evangelizing the American Jew* (Middle Village, N.Y., 1978).

Eichhorn, *Joys of Jewish Folklore*
>   David Max Eichhorn, *Joys of Jewish Folklore: A Journey From New Amsterdam to Beverly Hills and Beyond* (N.Y., 1981).

Eisenberg, *Eyewitnesses to American Jewish History*
>   Azriel Eisenberg (ed.), *Eyewitnesses to American Jewish History: Part IV, The American Jew* (N.Y., 1982).

Eisenstadt, *Hakme Yisrael be-Amerika*
>   Ben Zion Eisenstadt, *Hakme Yisrael be-Amerika* (N.Y., 1903).

Eisenstein, *Zikhronothai*
>   Judah David Eisenstein, *Ozar Zikhronothai: Autobiography and Memoirs* (N.Y., 1929).

EJ
>   *Encyclopaedia Judaica.*

Elbogen, *Cent. of Jewish Life*
>   Ismar Elbogen, *A Century of Jewish Life* (Phila., 1944).

Ellis, *Am. Catholicism*
>   John Tracy Ellis, *American Catholicism* (2nd revised edition, Chicago, 1969).

Elovitz, *Birmingham*
>   Mark H. Elovitz, *A Century of Jewish Life in Dixie: The Birmingham Experience* (Birmingham, 1974).

Elzas, *Jews of S.C.*
>   Barnett A. Elzas, *The Jews of South Carolina* (Phila., 1905).

EOZAI
>   *Encyclopedia of Zionism and Israel.*

Epstein, *Profiles of Eleven*
>   Melech Epstein, *Profiles of Eleven* (Detroit, 1965).

Ernst, *Immigrant Life*
>   Robert Ernst, *Immigrant Life in New York City, 1825-1863* (N.Y., 1949).

ESS
>   *Encyclopaedia of the Social Sciences* (N.Y., 1949).

Essrig, "Russian-Jewish Immigration"
>   Harry Essrig, "The Contribution of the Russian-Jewish Immigration to the American Labor Movement, 1880-1914" (rabbinical thesis, HUC, 1940).

Faulkner, *Social Justice*
>   Harold Underwood Faulkner, *The Quest for Social Justice, 1898-1914* (N.Y., 1931).

Fein, *Baltimore*
>   Isaac M. Fein, *The Making of an American Jewish Community: The History of Baltimore Jewry from 1773 to 1920* (Phila., 1971).

Feingold, *Zion in America*
>   Henry L. Feingold, *Zion in America* (N.Y., 1974).

Feinsilver, *Taste of Yiddish*
Lillian Mermin Feinsilver, *The Taste of Yiddish* (N.Y., 1970).

Feinstein, *American Zionism*
Martin Feinstein, *American Zionism, 1884-1904* (N.Y., 1965).

Feldman, *Jew. Experience in Western Pa.*
Jacob S. Feldman, *The Jewish Experience in Western Pennsylvania: A History, 1755-1945* (Phila., 1968).

Felsenthal, *Bernhard Felsenthal*
Emma Felsenthal, *Bernhard Felsenthal: Teacher in Israel* (N.Y., 1924).

Fink, *Biog. Dict.*
Gary M. Fink (ed.), *Biographical Dictionary of American Labor Leaders* (Westport, Conn., 1974).

Finkelstein, *The Jews* (1949)
Louis Finkelstein (ed.), *The Jews: Their History, Culture, and Religion* (4 vols., N.Y., 1949).

Finkelstein, *The Jews* (1960)
Louis Finkelstein (ed.), *The Jews: Their History, Culture, and Religion* (3d ed., 2 vols., N.Y., 1960).

Fishberg, *The Jews*
Maurice Fishberg, *The Jews: A Study of Race and Environment* (N.Y., 1911).

Fishman, *Yiddish in America*
Joshua A. Fishman, *Yiddish in America: Socio-Linguistic Description and Analysis* (Bloomington, Ind., 1965).

Fleishaker, "Illinois-Iowa Jewish Community"
Oscar Fleishaker, "The Illinois-Iowa Jewish Community on the Banks of the Mississippi River" (Ph.D. diss., Yeshiva U., 1957).

Fliegel, *Max Pine*
Hyman J. Fliegel, *The Life and Times of Max Pine* (N.Y., 1959).

Foner, *Fur and Leather Workers Union*
Philip S. Foner, *The Fur and Leather Workers Union* (Newark, N.J., 1950).

Foner, *Labor Movement in U.S.*
Philip S. Foner, *History of the Labor Movement in the United States* (4 vols., N.Y., 1955).

Foner, *Women and the American Labor Movement* (1979)
Philip S. Foner, *Women and the American Labor Movement: From Colonial Times to the Eve of World War I* (vol. 1 of 2, N.Y., 1979).

Foner, *Women and the American Labor Movement* (1980)
Philip S. Foner, *Women and the American Labor Movement: From World War I to the Present* (N.Y., 1980).

Frank, "Jews of Lynn, Mass."
Bernard S. Frank, "A Brief History of the Jews of Lynn, Massachusetts, etc." (HUC term paper, 1960).

Frank, *Nashville*
Fedora S. Frank, *Five Families and Eight Young Men (Nashville and her Jewry, 1850-1861)* (Nashville, 1962).

Friedman, *EAJ*
Lee M. Friedman, *Early American Jews* (Cambridge, Mass., 1934).

Friedman, *Pilgrims*
Lee M. Friedman, *Pilgrims in a New Land* (Phila., 1948).

Friedman, *Philadelphia*
   Murray Friedman (ed.), *Jewish Life in Philadelphia, 1830-1940* (Phila., 1983).
Friedman & Gordis, *Jewish Life in America*
   Theodore Friedman & Robert Gordis, *Jewish Life in America* (N.Y., 1955).
Friesel, *Ha-Tenuah Ha-Tsiyonit*
   Avyatar Friesel, *Ha-Tenuah Ha-Tsiyonit be-Artsot Ha-Berit, 1897-1914* (Hebrew, Tel Aviv, 1970).
From a Ruined Garden
   From a Ruined Garden: The Memorial Books of Polish Jewry (N.Y., 1983).
Frommer, "American Jewish Congress"
   Morris Frommer, "The American Jewish Congress: A History, 1914-1950" (Ph.D. diss., Ohio State Univ., 1978).
Frumkin et al., *Russian Jewry*
   Jacob Frumkin et al., *Russian Jewry (1860-1917)* (N.Y., n.d.).
Fuchs, *Political Behavior*
   Lawrence H. Fuchs, *The Political Behavior of American Jews* (Glencoe, Ill., 1956).

Gal, *Brandeis of Boston*
   Allon Gal, *Brandeis of Boston* (Cambridge, 1980).
Gannes, *Central Community Agencies*
   Abraham P. Gannes, *Central Community Agencies for Jewish Education* (Phila., 1954).
Gartner, *Cleveland*
   Lloyd P. Gartner, *History of the Jews of Cleveland* (Cleveland, 1978).
Gartner, *Jew. Ed. in U.S.*
   Lloyd P. Gartner (ed.), *Jewish Education in the United States: A Documentary History* (N.Y., 1969).
Gaustad, *Relig. Hist. of America*
   Edwin Scott Gaustad, *A Religious History of America* (N.Y., 1966).
Geller, "Jewish Life in Boston"
   Gordon L. Geller, "Jewish Life in Boston As Reflected in the Boston *Jewish Advocate*, 1905-1910" (HUC term paper, 1965).
Ginsberg, *Jews of Virginia*
   Louis Ginsberg, *Chapters on the Jews of Virginia, 1658-1900* (Petersburg, Va., 1969).
Ginsberg, *Petersburg*
   Louis Ginsberg, *History of the Jews of Petersburg*, 1789-1950 (Petersburg, Va., 1954).
Ginzberg & Berman, *American Worker*
   Eli Ginzberg and Hyman Berman, *The American Worker in the Twentieth Century* (London, 1963).
Glanz, *Jewish Woman*
   Rudolf Glanz, *The Jewish Woman in America: Two Female Immigrant Generations, 1820-1929* (2 vols., N.Y., 1976).
Glanz, *Studies*
   Rudolf Glanz, *Studies in Judaica Americana* (N.Y., 1970).
Glanz, *The German Jew in America*
   Rudolf Glanz, *The German Jew in America: An Annotated Bibliography, etc.* (Cincinnati, 1969).
Glassman (ed.), *BEOAJ, 1935*
   Leo M. Glassman (ed.), *Biographical Encyclopaedia of American Jews, 1935* (N.Y., 1935).

Glazer, *American Judaism*
Nathan Glazer, *American Judaism* (2nd ed., Chicago, 1972).

Glazer, *Jews of Iowa*
Simon Glazer, *The Jews of Iowa, etc.* (Des Moines, 1904).

Goldberg, *Pioneers and Builders*
Abraham Goldberg, *Pioneers and Builders: Biographical Studies and Essays* (N.Y., 1943).

Golden, *Jewish Roots in the Carolinas*
Harry L. Golden, *Jewish Roots in the Carolinas* (Greensboro, N.C., 1955).

Golden & Rywell, *Jews in American History*
Harry L. Golden & Martin Rywell, *Jews in American History* (n.p., 1950).

Goldman, *Giants of Faith*
Alex J. Goldman, *Giants of Faith: Great American Rabbis* (N.Y., 1964).

Goldman, *Living My Life*
Emma Goldman, *Living My Life* (reprint, 2 vols., N.Y., 1970).

Goldmark, *Pilgrims of '48*
Josephine Goldmark, *Pilgrims of '48, etc.* (New Haven, 1930).

Goldstein, *Cent. of Jud. in NYC*
Israel Goldstein, *A Century of Judaism in New York: B'nai Jeshurun, 1825-1925, etc.* (N.Y., 1930).

Goldstein, *Jewish Colonies of South Jersey*
Philip Reuben Goldstein, *Social Aspects of the Jewish Colonies of South Jersey* (N.Y., 1921).

Gompers, *Seventy Years of Life and Labor*
Samuel Gompers, *Seventy Years of Life and Labor* (2 vols., N.Y., 1925).

Goodhart, *Five Jewish Lawyers*
Arthur L. Goodhart, *Five Jewish Lawyers of the Common Law* (London, 1949).

Goodman, "American Jewish Life"
Mark Steven Goodman, "American Jewish Life as Reflected in the Anglo-Jewish Press of Baltimore, Cincinnati, New York, Philadelphia and San Francisco from 1905-1910" (rabbinical thesis, HUC, 1975).

Goren, *American Jews*
Arthur A. Goren, *The American Jews* (Cambridge, Mass., 1982).

Goren, *Dissenter in Zion*
Arthur A. Goren (ed.), *Dissenter in Zion: From the Writings of Judah L. Magnes* (Cambridge, Mass., 1982).

Goren, *Kehillah*
Arthur A. Goren, *New York Jews and the Quest for Community: The Kehillah Experiment, 1908-1922* (N.Y., 1970).

Gorin, *Idishen Theater*
Bernard Gorin, *Di Geschichte fun Idishen Theater* (Yiddish, 2 vols., N.Y., 1923).

Gottheil, *Zionism*
Richard J.H. Gottheil, *Zionism* (Phila., 1914).

Gottschalk & Duker, *Jews in the Post-War World*
Max Gottschalk and Abraham G. Duker, *Jews in the Post-War World* (N.Y., 1945).

Grayzel, *Hist. of Contemporary Jews*
Solomon Grayzel, *A History of the Contemporary Jews, from 1960 to the Present* (Phila., 1960).

Grayzel, *History of the Jews*
    Solomon Grayzel, *A History of the Jews from the Babylonian Exile to the End of World War II* (Phila., 1947).
Grinstein, *History*
    Hyman B. Grinstein, *A Short History of the Jews in the United States* (London, 1980).
Grinstein, *New York City*
    Hyman B. Grinstein, *The Rise of the Jewish Community of New York, 1654-1860* (Phila., 1945).
Grose, *Israel in the Mind of America*
    Peter Grose, *Israel in the Mind of America* (N.Y., 1983).
Grusd, *B'nai B'rith*
    Edward E. Grusd, *B'nai B'rith: The Story of a Covenant* (N.Y., 1966).
Gurock, *Guide*
    Jeffrey S. Gurock, *American Jewish History: A Bibliographical Guide* (ADL, n.p., 1983).
Gutstein, *Chicago*
    Morris A. Gutstein, *A Priceless Heritage: The Epic Growth of Nineteenth Century Chicago Jewry* (N.Y., 1953).

Handlin, *Adventure in Freedom*
    Oscar Handlin, *Adventure in Freedom, etc.* (N.Y., 1954).
Handlin, *American People in the Twentieth Century*
    Oscar Handlin, *The American People in the Twentieth Century* (Boston, 1954).
Handlin, *Immigration*
    Oscar Handlin, *Immigration as a Factor in American History* (Englewood Cliffs, N.J., 1959).
Hapgood, *Spirit of the Ghetto*
    Hutchins Hapgood, *The Spirit of the Ghetto (Cambridge, Mass., 1967)*.
Harris, *Merchant Princes*
    Leon Harris, *Merchant Princes: An Intimate History of Jewish Families Who Built Great Department Stores* (N.Y., 1979).
H. Pereira Mendes
    H. Pereira Mendes: A Biography (N.Y., 1938).
HEAEG
    Stephan Thernstrom (ed.), *Harvard Encyclopedia of American Ethnic Groups* (Cambridge, Mass., 1980).
Hebrew Standard
    The New York *Hebrew Standard.*
Heller, *Isaac M. Wise*
    James F. Heller, *Isaac M. Wise, His Life, Work and Thought* (N.Y., 1965).
Hennig, *Columbia, S.C.*
    Helen Kohn Hennig, *The Tree of Life: Fifty Years of Congregational Life at the Tree of Life Synagogue, Columbia, S.C.* (Columbia, 1945).
Herscher, *Jewish Agricultural Utopias*
    Uri D. Herscher, *Jewish Agricultural Utopias in America, 1880-1910* (Detroit, 1981).
Hertz, *Authorised Daily Prayer Book*
    Joseph H. Hertz, *The Authorised Daily Prayer Book* (rev. ed., N.Y., 1948).
Hertzberg, *Atlanta*
    Steven Hertzberg, *Strangers Within the Gate City: The Jews of Atlanta, 1845-1915* (Phila., 1978).

Herzl Year Book
   Herzl Year Book: Essays in Zionist History and Thought (N.Y., 1958-   ).

Higham, *Send These to Me*
   John Higham, *Send These to Me: Immigrants in Urban America* (revised ed., Baltimore, 1984).

Hillquit, *Loose Leaves From a Busy Life*
   Morris Hillquit, *Loose Leaves From a Busy Life (N.Y., 1934).*

Hinchin, "Jews of Sioux City"
   Martin I. Hinchin, "A History of the Jews of Sioux City, Iowa (1857-1945)" (rabbinical thesis, HUC, 1946).

Hindus, *Old East Side*
   Milton Hindus, *The Old East Side* (Phila., 1969).

Hirsch & Doherty, *Mount Sinai Hospital*
   Joseph Hirsch and Beka Doherty, *The First Hundred Years of the Mount Sinai Hospital of New York, 1852-1952* (N.Y., 1952).

Holy Scriptures
   The Holy Scriptures According to the Masoretic Text (2 vols., Phila., 1955).

Horwich, *My First Eighty Years*
   Bernard Horwich, *My First Eighty Years* (Chicago, 1939).

Howe, *World of Our Fathers*
   Irving Howe, *World of Our Fathers* (N.Y., 1976).

Howe & Greenberg, *Treasury of Yiddish Poetry*
   Irving Howe and Eliezer Greenberg (eds.), *A Treasury of Yiddish Poetry* (N.Y., 1969).

Howe & Greenberg, *Treasury of Yiddish Stories*
   Irving Howe and Eliezer Greenberg (eds.), *A Treasury of Yiddish Stories* (N.Y., 1954).

Howe & Greenberg, *Voices From the Yiddish*
   Irving Howe and Eliezer Greenberg (eds.), *Voices From the Yiddish: Essays, Memoirs, Diaries* (Ann Arbor, 1972).

Howe & Libo, *How We Lived*
   Irving Howe and Kenneth Libo, *How We Lived* (Phila., 1979).

HUC
   Hebrew Union College, Cincinnati.

HUC Journal
   The H.U.C. Journal.

HUCA
   Hebrew Union College Annual.

HUCL
   Hebrew Union College Library, Cincinnati.

Hyams, "Memorandum for My Children"
   Henry M. Hyams, "Memorandum for My Children of My Father's Family and My Mother's Family" (typescript, Oct. 19, 1936), Marcus Collections courtesy of Mrs. Julian Hennig.

Idelsohn, *Jewish Music*
   A.Z. Idelsohn, *Jewish Music in its Historical Development* (N.Y., 1929).

Israel Vindicated
   Israel Vindicated: Being a Refutation of the Calumnies Propagated Respecting the Jewish Nation, etc. (N.Y., 1820).

Israelites of Louisiana
> *Israelites of Louisiana: Their Religious, Civic, Charitable and Patriotic Life* (New Orleans, ca. 1900).

Janowsky, *American Jew*
> Oscar I. Janowsky (ed.), *The American Jew: A Complete Portrait* (N.Y., 1942).

Janowsky, *Am. Jew. Reappraisal*
> Oscar I. Janowsky (ed.), *The American Jew: A Reappraisal* (Phila., 1964).

Janowsky, *Ed. of Am. Jew. Teachers*
> Oscar I. Janowsky (ed.), *The Education of American Jewish Teachers* (Boston, 1967).

Janowsky, *Jews and Minority Rights*
> Oscar I. Janowsky, *The Jews and Minority Rights (1898-1919) (N.Y., 1933)*.

JE
> *The Jewish Encyclopedia.*

Jenks & Lauck, *Immigration Problem*
> Jeremiah W. Jenks and W. Jett Lauck, *The Immigration Problem, etc.* (N.Y., 1917).

Jeshurin, *100 Yor Moderne Yidishe Literatur*
> Ephim H. Jeshurin, *100 Yor Moderne Yidishe Literatur* (Yiddish, N.Y., 1965).

Jew. Com. Reg.
> *Jewish Communal Register of New York City, 1917-1918* (2nd ed., N.Y., 1918).

Jew. Ed.
> *Jewish Education.*

Jew. Rev.
> *The Jewish Review.*

Jewish Chronicle
> New York *Jewish Chronicle.*

Jewish Digest
> *The Jewish Digest.*

Jewish Landsmanschaften of New York
> *The Jewish Landsmanschaften of New York* (WPA, N.Y., 1938).

Jewish Life
> *Jewish Life: A Progressive Monthly*; after 1958, *Jewish Currents.*

Jewish People
> *The Jewish People: Past and Present* (4 vols., N.Y., 1946-1955).

Jewish Post and Opinion
> New York *National Jewish Post and Opinion.*

Jewish Times
> The New York *Jewish Times.*

Jewish Tribune
> The St. Louis *Jewish Tribune.*

JJOS
> *Jewish Journal of Sociology.*

JL
> *Juedisches Lexikon.*

JM
> *The Jewish Messenger.*

JOAH
>   *The Journal of American History.*

Joselit, *Our Gang*
>   Jenna Weissman Joselit, *Our Gang: Jewish Crime and the New York Jewish Community, 1900-1940* (Bloomington, Ind., 1983).

Joseph, *Baron de Hirsch Fund*
>   Samuel Joseph, *History of the Baron de Hirsch Fund* (Phila., 1935).

Joseph, *Jewish Immigration*
>   Samuel Joseph, *Jewish Immigration to the United States* (N.Y., 1914).

Josephson, *Sidney Hillman*
>   Matthew Josephson, *Sidney Hillman: Statesman of American Labor* (N.Y., 1952).

JQR o.s. and n.s.
>   *The Jewish Quarterly Review,* old series and new series.

JRM
>   Jacob Rader Marcus.

JSS
>   *Jewish Social Studies.*

JSSQ
>   *Jewish Social Service Quarterly.*

JTA-DNB
>   *Jewish Telegraphic Agency–Daily News Bulletin.*

Judaeans
>   *Judaean Addresses* (3 vols., N.Y., 1900-1917).

Judaism at the World's Parliament of Religions
>   *Judaism at the World's Parliament of Religions* (Cincinnati, 1894).

Judenpogrome
>   *Die Judenpogrome in Russland, etc.* (Koeln and Leipzig, 1910).

JWB Circle
>   *The JWB Circle: Issued by the National Jewish Welfare Board.*

Kabakoff, *Halutse Ha-Sifrut Ha-Ivrit be-Amerika*
>   Jacob Kabakoff, *Halutse Ha-Sifrut Ha-Ivrit be-Amerika* (Tel Aviv, 1966).

Kagan, *Contributions*
>   Solomon R. Kagan, *Jewish Contributions to Medicine in America, from Colonial Times to the Present* (2nd ed., Boston, 1939).

Kaganoff (ed.), *America-Holy Land Studies*
>   Nathan M. Kaganoff (ed.), *Guide to America-Holy Land Studies, 1620-1948* (N.Y., 1982).

Kaganoff, *Essays on American Zionism*
>   Nathan M. Kaganoff (ed.), *Solidarity and Kinship: Essays on American Zionism* (Waltham, Mass., 1980).

Kallen, *Essays*
>   Horace M. Kallen, *"Of Them Which Say They Are Jews" and Other Essays on the Jewish Struggle for Survival* (N.Y., 1954).

Kaminsky, *Arbeter-Ring*
>   J. Kaminsky, *Fertsik Yor Arbeter-Ring: Geshikhte in Bilder* (Yiddish and English, N.Y., 1940).

Kane, "David Pinski"
  Gerald M. Kane, "David Pinski: The Prolific, But Still-to-Be Discovered Playwright of the American-Yiddish Theatre" (HUC term paper, 1968).

Kansas City Population Study
  The Jewish Population of the Greater Kansas City Area (Kansas City, 1977).

Kaplan Jubilee Volume
  Mordecai M. Kaplan Jubilee Volume (N.Y., 1953).

Karff, *HUC-JIR*
  Samuel E. Karff (ed.), *Hebrew Union College-Jewish Institute of Religion at One Hundred Years* (Cincinnati, 1976).

Karp, *Jew. Exp. in America*
  Abraham J. Karp (ed.), *The Jewish Experience in America, etc.* (5 vols., Waltham, Mass., 1969).

Karpf, *Jewish Community Organizations*
  Maurice Karpf, *Jewish Community Organizations in the United States* (N.Y., 1938).

Katz, *Jacob Dolnitzky Memorial Volume*
  Morris Casriel Katz (ed.), *The Jacob Dolnitzky Memorial Volume* (Skokie, Ill., 1982).

Kehillah Annual Convention, 1913
  Report of the Executive Committee and Proceedings of the Fourth Annual Convention of the Jewish Community (Kehillah), New York, April 12 and 13, 1913 (N.Y., 1913).

Kiev Festschrift
  Charles Berlin (ed.), *Studies in Jewish Bibliography History and Literature in honor of I. Edward Kiev* (N.Y., 1971).

Klaperman, *Yeshiva University*
  Gilbert Klaperman, *The Story of Yeshiva University* (London, 1969).

Kohler, *German Jewish Persecutions*
  Max J. Kohler, *The United States and German Jewish Persecutions—Precedents for Popular and Governmental Action* (N.Y., 1933).

Klausner, *Modern Hebrew Literature*
  Joseph Klausner, *A History of Modern Hebrew Literature (1785-1930)* (London, 1932).

Kohler, *Immigration and Aliens*
  Max J. Kohler, *Immigration and Aliens in the United States, etc.* (N.Y., 1936).

Kohler, *Simon Wolf Addresses*
  Max J. Kohler (ed.), *Selected Addresses and Papers of Simon Wolf* (Cincinnati, 1926).

Kohler, *Studies*
  Kaufmann Kohler, *Studies, Addresses and Personal Papers* (Phila., 1931).

Kohn, *Utica*
  S. Joshua Kohn, *The Jewish Community of Utica, New York 1847-1948* (N.Y., 1959).

Kohut, *As I Know Them*
  Rebekah Kohut, *As I Know Them* (Garden City, N.Y., 1929).

Koplin, *"Jewish Exponent"*
  Aaron Koplin, "The Eastern European Jew as Reflected in the *Jewish Exponent* for the Years 1910-1915" (HUC term paper, 1966).

Korey, "Jew. Ed. in Chicago"
  Harold Korey, "The History of Jewish Education in Chicago" (Ph.D. diss., U. of Chicago, 1942).

Korn, *Marcus Festschrift*
  Bertram Wallace Korn, *A Bicentennial Festschrift for Jacob Rader Marcus* (N.Y., 1976).

Korn, *Retrospect and Prospect*
> Bertram Wallace Korn (ed.), *Retrospect and Prospect . . . The Central Conference of American Rabbis, 1889-1964* (N.Y., 1965).

Kraus, *Immigration*
> Michael Kraus, *Immigration, the American Mosaic: From Pilgrims to Modern Refugees* (Princeton, N.J., 1966).

Kraus, *Reminiscences*
> Adolf Kraus, *Reminiscences and Comments* (Chicago, 1925).

Kraus, "Settlement House Movement in NYC"
> Harry P. Kraus, "The Settlement House Movement in New York City, 1886-1914" (Ph.D. diss., NYU, 1970).

Kull and Kull, *Chronology*
> Irving S. and Nell M. Kull, *A Short Chronology of American History, 1492-1950* (New Brunswick, N.J., 1952).

Kurland, *Felix Frankfurter*
> Philip B. Kurland (ed.), *Of Law and Life & Other Things That Matter: Papers and Addresses of Felix Frankfurter* (Cambridge, Mass., 1965).

Landau, *Louisville*
> Herman Landau, *Adath Louisville: The Story of a Jewish Community* (Louisville, 1981).

Landesman, *Brownsville*
> Alter F. Landesman, *Brownsville: The Birth, Development and Passing of a Jewish Community in New York* (N.Y., 1969).

Lang & Feinstone, *United Hebrew Trades*
> Harry Lang and Morris Feinstone (eds.), *Gewerkschaften Jubilee Book dedicated to 50 Years of Life and Labor of the United Hebrew Trades* (N.Y., 1938).

Laqueur, *History of Zionism*
> Walter Laqueur, *A History of Zionism* (N.Y., 1972).

LC
> Library of Congress, Washington, D.C.

Learsi, *Jews in America*
> Rufus Learsi, *The Jews in America: A History* (Cleveland, 1954).

Lebeson, *Pilgrim People*
> Anita Libman Lebeson, *Pilgrim People* (N.Y., 1950).

Leeser, *Discourses*
> Isaac Leeser, *Discourses on the Jewish Religion* (10 vols., Phila., 1867-1868).

Leftwich, *Anthology of Modern Yiddish Literature*
> Joseph Leftwich (ed.), *An Anthology of Modern Yiddish Literature* (The Hague, 1974).

Leket Mekorot
> *Hitpathut ha-Historit shel Yahadut Arzot ha-Brit Leket Mekorot (The Historical Development of American Jewry)* (Hebrew, Jerusalem, 1982).

Lesser, *In the Last Days*
> A.J.G. Lesser, *B'Akharith Hayamim (In the Last Days)*, etc. (Chicago, 1897).

Levin, "East European Jews in U.S."
> Herschel Levin, "The History of the East European in the United States from 1850 to 1881" (HUC prize essay, 1937).

Levin, *Jewish Socialist Movements*
> Nora Levin, *While Messiah Tarried: Jewish Socialist Movements, 1871-1917* (N.Y., 1977).

Levine, *Am. Jew. Bibliography*
  Allan E. Levine, *An American Jewish Bibliography . . . 1851 to 1875, etc.* (Cincinnati, 1959).

Levine & Miller, *American Jewish Farmer*
  Herman J. Levine and Benjamin Miller, *The American Jewish Farmer in Changing Times* (N.Y., 1966).

Levinger, *Jews in U.S.*
  Lee J. Levinger, *A History of the Jews in the United States* (Cincinnati, 1930).

Levinthal, *Message of Israel*
  Israel H. Levinthal, *The Message of Israel* (N.Y., 1973).

Levy, "Gus Karger"
  Eugene H. Levy, "Gus Karger: Taft, the Jews and Brandeis" (HUC term paper, 1971).

Lifson, *Yiddish Theatre in America*
  David S. Lifson, *The Yiddish Theatre in America* (N.Y., 1965).

Lipman, *Soc. Hist. of Jews in England*
  V.D. Lipman, *Social History of the Jews in England, 1850-1950* (London, 1954).

Lipsky, *Memoirs in Profile*
  Louis Lipsky, *Memoirs in Profile* (Phila., 1975).

Liptzin, *Eliakum Zunser*
  Sol Liptzin, *Eliakum Zunser: Poet of His People* (N.Y., 1950).

Liptzin, *Flowering of Yiddish Literature*
  Sol Liptzin, *The Flowering of Yiddish Literature* (N.Y., 1963).

Liptzin, *Generation of Decision*
  Sol Liptzin, *Generation of Decision: Jewish Rejuvenation in America* (N.Y., 1958).

Liptzin, *History of Yiddish Literature*
  Sol Liptzin, *A History of Yiddish Literature* (Middle Village, N.Y., 1972).

Lisitzky, *In the Grip of Cross-Currents*
  Ephraim E. Lisitzky, *In the Grip of Cross-Currents* (N.Y., 1959).

LNYL
  Leksikon fur der Nayer Yidisher Literatur (Yiddish, N.Y., 1956-   ).

London *Jewish Chronicle*
  The Jewish Chronicle (London).

Louisiana Inventory
  Inventory of the Church and Synagogue Archives of Louisiana: Jewish Congregations and Organizations (New Orleans, 1941).

Lurie, *A Heritage Affirmed*
  Harry L. Lurie, *A Heritage Affirmed* (Phila., 1961).

Luzzatti, *God in Freedom*
  Luigi Luzzatti, *God in Freedom: Studies in the Relation Between Church and State* (N.Y., 1930).

Lyons & De Sola, *Jewish Calendar*
  Jacques J. Lyons and Abraham De Sola, *A Jewish Calendar* (Montreal, 1854).

M. & M., *History*
  Max L. Margolis and Alexander Marx, *A History of the Jewish People* (Phila., 1956).

Madison, *Yiddish Literature*
  Charles A. Madison, *Yiddish Literature: Its Scope and Major Writers* (N.Y., 1968).

Malachy, *American Fundamentalism and Israel*
>Yona Malachy, *American Fundamentalism and Israel* (Jerusalem, 1978).

Mallinger, "Jewish Day School"
>Stephen Mallinger, "The Need for and the Beginnings of the Jewish Day School Movement Under Eastern European Leadership" (HUC term paper, n.d.), Marcus Collections.

Mallinger, "Kreiner Interview"
>Interview with Mr. Israel Kreiner, Casper, Wyoming, by student rabbi Steven Mallinger, Oct. 8, 1970, AJAr.

Manuel, *American-Palestine Relations*
>Frank E. Manuel, *The Realities of American-Palestine Relations* (Washington, D.C., 1949).

Marcus, *AJD*
>Jacob Rader Marcus, *American Jewry: Documents, Eighteenth Century* (Cincinnati, 1959).

Marcus, *AJW*
>Jacob Rader Marcus, *The American Jewish Woman, 1654-1980* (N.Y., 1981).

Marcus, *AJWD*
>Jacob R. Marcus, *The American Jewish Woman: A Documentary History* (N.Y. and Cincinnati, 1981).

Marcus, *CAJ*
>Jacob R. Marcus, *The Colonial American Jew, 1492-1776* (Detroit, 1970).

Marcus Collections
>American Hebraica and Judaica in the possession of Jacob Rader Marcus, Cincinnati.

Marcus, *EAJ*
>Jacob Rader Marcus, *Early American Jewry* (2 vols., Phila., 1951-1955).

Marcus, "Gershom Seixas"
>Jacob Rader Marcus, "The Handsome Young Priest in the Black Gown, the Personal World of Gershom Seixas," in *HUCA*, vols. 40-41 (pp.409-467).

Marcus, *Memoirs*
>Jacob Rader Marcus, *Memoirs of American Jews, 1775-1865* (3 vols., Phila., 1955-1956).

Marcus, *Studies*
>Jacob R. Marcus, *Studies in American Jewish History: Studies and Addresses* (Cincinnati, 1969).

Marcus, *United States Jewry*
>Jacob Rader Marcus, *United States Jewry, 1776-1985* (4 vols., 198-).

Marcus & Peck, *Studies in the American Jewish Experience*
>Jacob R. Marcus & Abraham J. Peck (eds.), *Studies in the American Jewish Experience* (3 vols., Detroit, 1989-1993).

Margolin, *Jews of Eastern Europe*
>Arnold D. Margolin, *The Jews of Eastern Europe* (N.Y., 1926).

Marinbach, *Ellis Island of the West*
>Bernard Marinbach, *Galveston: Ellis Island of the West* (Albany, 1983).

Markens, *Hebrews*
>Isaac Markens, *The Hebrews in America* (N.Y., 1888).

Martin, *Judaism*
>Bernard Martin, *A History of Judaism* (2 vols., N.Y., 1974).

Marx, *Studies in Jewish History*
>Alexander Marx, *Studies in Jewish History and Booklore* (N.Y., 1944).

Mason, *Brandeis*
   Alpheus Thomas Mason, *Brandeis: A Free Man's Life* (N.Y., 1946).

Masserman & Baker, *Jews Come to America*
   Paul Masserman and Max Baker, *The Jews Come to America* (N.Y., 1932).

Meites, *Chicago*
   Hyman L. Meites (ed.), *History of the Jews of Chicago* (Chicago, 1924).

Memorials Submitted to President Wilson, March 2, 1919
   *Memorials Submitted to President Wilson Concerning the Status of the Jews of Eastern Europe,
   and in Palestine, by Representatives of the American Jewish Congress, on March 2, 1919*
   (N.Y., 1919).

Menorah
   The Menorah.

Meyer (ed.), *Early History of Zionism in America*
   Isidore S. Meyer (ed.), *Early History of Zionism in America* (N.Y., 1958).

MGWJ
   Monatsschrift fuer Geschichte und Wissenschaft des Judenthums.

Michael, "Cincinnati"
   Ann Deborah Michael, "The Origins of the Jewish Community of Cincinnati, 1817-
   1860" (M.A. thesis, University of Cincinnati, 1970).

Michigan Inventory
   Inventory of the Church and Synagogue Archives of Michigan: Jewish Bodies (WPA, Detroit,
   1940).

Miliukov, et al., *History of Russia*
   Paul Miliukov, et al., *History of Russia* (3 vols., N.Y., 1969).

Mississippi Inventory
   *Inventory of the Church and Synagogue Archives of Mississippi: Jewish Congregations and Or-
   ganizations* (Jackson, Miss., 1940).

Morais, *Eminent Israelites*
   Henry Samuel Morais, *Eminent Israelites of the Nineteenth Century: A Series of Biographical
   Sketches* (Phila., 1880).

Morais, *Philadelphia*
   Henry Samuel Morais, *The Jews of Philadelphia* (Phila., 1894).

Morgenthau, *All in a Life-Time*
   Henry Morgenthau, *All in a Life-Time* (Garden City, N.Y., 1922).

Morison, *History*
   Samuel Eliot Morison, *The Oxford History of the American People* (N.Y., 1965).

Morning Freiheit
   Morning Freiheit (Morning Freedom).

Morris & Freund, *Trends*
   Robert Morris & Michael Freund (eds.), *Trends and Issues in Jewish Social Welfare in the
   United States, 1899-1952* (Phila., 1966).

MVHR
   The Mississippi Valley Historical Review.

Myers, *Bigotry*
   Gustavus Myers, *History of Bigotry in the United States* (N.Y., 1943).

Myers, *Great American Fortunes*
   Gustavus Myers, *History of the Great American Fortunes* (3 vols., Chicago, 1909-1910).

NAR
North American Review.

Nash, *Bloodletters*
Jay Robert Nash, *Bloodletters and Badmen* (Book 2, n.p., 1975).

NAW
Edward T. James et al. (eds.), *Notable American Women 1607-1950* (3 vols., Cambridge, Mass., 1971).

NCHR
The North Carolina Historical Review.

Neidle, *America's Immigrant Women*
Cecyle S. Neidle, *America's Immigrant Women* (N.Y., 1975).

Ner Ha'maarabi
Ner Ha'maarabi (The Western Light): A Hebrew Literary Review.

Neumann, *In the Arena*
Emanuel Neumann, *In the Arena: An Autobiographical Memoir* (N.Y., 1976).

Nevins & Commager, *United States*
Allan Nevins and Henry Steele Commager, *The Pocket History of the United States* (N.Y., 1942).

New York Statistics, 1981
The Jewish Population of Greater New York: A Profile (N.Y., 1984).

Niemcewicz, *Under Their Vine and Fig Tree*
Julian Ursyn Niemcewicz, *Under Their Vine and Fig Tree* (Elizabeth, N.J., 1965).

Niger, *Yidishe*
S. Niger, *Yidishe Shrayber fun Tsvantiskstn Yorhundert* (2 vols., N.Y., 1972-73).

Nodel, *The Ties Between*
Julius J. Nodel, *The Ties Between: A Century of Judaism on America's Last Frontier* (Portland, Or., 1959).

Nudelman & Slesinger, *Jew in America*
Edward A. Nudelman and Zalman Slesinger, *The Jew in America: A Syllabus for Teachers* (American Association for Jewish Education, n.p., 1954).

NYHS
New York Historical Society, N.Y.

NYHSL
New York Historical Society Library, N.Y.

Occ.
The Occident and American Jewish Advocate.

Odell, *Annals*
George C.D. Odell, *Annals of the New York Stage (N.Y., - 1949)*.

Ozar Yisrael
J.D. Eisenstein (ed.), *Ozar Yisrael, An Encyclopedia, etc.* (Berlin, 1924).

P. & K., *Tourist's Guide*
Bernard Postal and Lionel Koppman, *A Jewish Tourist's Guide to the U.S.* (Phila., 1954).

PAAJR
American Academy for Jewish Research Proceedings.

PAJHS
Publications of the American Jewish Historical Society.

Paper, *Brandeis*
Lewis J. Paper, *Brandeis* (Englewood Cliffs, N.J., 1983).

Papers of the Jewish Women's Congress
Papers of the Jewish Women's Congress Held at Chicago, September 4, 5, 6, and 7, 1893 (Phila., 1894).

Parzen, *Architects*
Herbert Parzen, *Architects of Conservative Judaism* (N.Y., 1964).

Parzen, *Zionism*
Herbert Parzen, *A Short History of Zionism* (N.Y., 1962).

Perlman & Taft, *History of Labor*
Selig Perlman and Philip Taft, *History of Labor in the United States, 1896-1932,* vol.4 (N.Y., 1935).

Philippsborn, *Vicksburg*
Gertrude Philippsborn, *The History of the Jewish Community of Vicksburg, etc.* (Vicksburg, Miss., 1969).

Philipson, *My Life*
David Philipson, *My Life as an American Jew* (Cincinnati, 1941).

Phillips (ed.), *Felix Frankfurter Reminisces*
Harlan B. Phillips (ed.), *Felix Frankfurter Reminisces* (N.Y., 1960).

Philpott, *The Slum and the Ghetto*
Thomas Lee Philpott, *The Slum and the Ghetto* (N.Y., 1978).

Pilch, *Hist. Jew. Ed.*
Judah Pilch (ed.), *A History of Jewish Education in America* (N.Y., 1969).

Pilch (ed.), *Jewish Education Register, 1951*
Judah Pilch (ed.), *Jewish Education Register and Directory, 1951* (N.Y., 1951).

Pittsburgh Platform
Proceedings of the Pittsburgh Rabbinical Conference, November 16, 17, 18, 1885 (n.p., 1923).

Plaut, *Jews in Minnesota*
W. Gunther Plaut, *The Jews of Minnesota: The First Seventy-five Years* (N.Y., 1959).

Plaut, *Mt. Zion*
W. Gunther Plaut, *Mt. Zion, 1856-1956, The First Hundred Years* (St. Paul, Minn., 1956?).

Plaut, *Reform Judaism*
W. Gunther Plaut, *The Growth of Reform Judaism: American and European Sources until 1948* (N.Y., 1965).

PMHB
The Pennsylvania Magazine of History and Biography.

Polier & Wise (eds.), *Stephen Wise*
Justine Wise Polier and James Waterman Wise, *The Personal Letters of Stephen Wise* (Boston, 1956).

Pollak, *Michael Heilprin*
Gustav Pollak, *Michael Heilprin and His Sons* (N.Y., 1912).

Pool, *Old Faith*
David and Tamar de Sola Pool, *An Old Faith in the New World* (N.Y., 1955).

Pool, *Portraits*
David de Sola Pool, *Portraits Etched in Stone* (N.Y., 1952).

Pope, *Cloth. Ind. in NYC*
Jesse Eliphalet Pope, *The Clothing Industry in New York* (N.Y., 1905, reprinted 1970).

"Proceedings of the Conference on the Writing of Regional History in the South"
"Proceedings of the Conference on the Writing of Regional History in the South, etc." (Miami Beach, Florida, 1956).

Proceedings of the NCJW, 1896
Proceedings of the First Convention of the National Council of Jewish Women Held at New York, Nov . . . 1896 (Phila., 1897).

PUAHC
Proceedings of the Union of American Hebrew Congregations.

R
A.S.W. Rosenbach, "An American Jewish Bibliography, etc.", *PAJHS*, vol. 30.

R. & E., *Charleston*
Charles Reznikoff and Uriah Z. Engelman, *The Jews of Charleston* (Phila., 1950).

RA
The Chicago *Reform Advocate.*

Rabinowitz, *Justice Louis D. Brandeis*
Ezekiel Rabinowitz, *Justice Louis D. Brandeis: The Zionist Chapter of His Life* (N.Y., 1968).

Raisin, *Great Jews I Have Known*
Max Raisin, *Great Jews I Have Known: A Gallery of Portraits* (N.Y., 1952).

Raphael, *Jews and Judaism in the U.S.*
Marc Lee Raphael (ed.), *Jews and Judaism in the United States: A Documentary History* (N.Y., 1983).

Ravitch & Goodenow, *Educating an Urban People*
Diane Ravitch and Ronald K. Goodenow (eds.), *Educating an Urban People: The New York City Experience* (N.Y., 1981).

Rawidowicz (ed.), *Chicago Pinkas*
Simon Rawidowicz (ed.), *The Chicago Pinkas* (Chicago, 1952).

Reisen, *Leksikon*
Zalmen Reisen, *Leksikon fun der judisher Literatur un Prese* (Yiddish, Warsaw, 1914).

Reisin, *Leksikon (1926-1929)*
Zalman Reisin, *Leksikon fun der Yidisher Literatur, Prese, un Filologi* (Yiddish, 4 vols., Volna, 1926-1929).

Reports, Immig. Com.
Reports of the Immigration Commission (41 vols., Washington, D.C., 1911).

Reports, Immig. Com. Abstracts
Reports of the Immigration Commission; Abstracts of the Immigration Commission (2 vols., Washington, D.C., 1911).

Reports, Ind. Com.
Reports of the Industrial Commission (19 vols., Washington, D.C., 1900-1902).

Reznikoff, *Louis Marshall*
Charles Reznikoff (ed.), *Louis Marshall, Champion of Liberty: Selected Papers and Addresses* (2 vols., Phila., 1957).

Ribalow (ed.), *Autobiographies*
Harold U. Ribalow (ed.), *Autobiographies of American Jews* (Phila., 1965).

Richards, *Organizing American Jewry*
 Bernard G. Richards, *Organizing American Jewry* (N.Y., Office of Jewish Information, 1947).

Richardson, *Messages and Papers of the Presidents*
 James D. Richardson, *A Compilation of the Messages and Papers of the Presidents, 1789-1902* (Washington, D.C.?, 1907).

Riis, *Children of the Poor*
 Jacob A. Riis, *The Children of the Poor* (N.Y., 1908).

Riis, *How the Other Half Lives*
 Jacob A. Riis, *How the Other Half Lives: Studies Among the Tenements of New York* (N.Y., 1890).

RIJHN
 Rhode Island Jewish Historical Notes.

Ringler, "Boston"
 Stanley A. Ringler, "Boston Jewish Life 1911-1914" (HUC term paper, 1967).

Rischin, *Inventory*
 Moses Rischin, *An Inventory of American Jewish History* (Cambridge, Mass., 1954).

Rischin, *Promised City*
 Moses Rischin, *The Promised City: New York's Jews, 1870-1914* (Cambridge, Mass., 1962).

Roback, *Story of Yiddish Literature*
 A.A. Roback, *The Story of Yiddish Literature* (N.Y., 1940).

Robertson, *92nd Street YMHA & YWHA*
 Nancy M. Robertson, *92nd Street Young Men's & Young Women's Hebrew Association; Inventory of Record Group 5* (N.Y., 1980).

Robinson, "Philadelphia"
 Bernard James Robinson, "The East European Jewish Immigrant: His Life, Hopes, Activities, and Reception into the Larger Jewish Community, etc." (HUC term paper, 1965).

Rockaway, *Jews of Detroit*
 Robert A. Rockaway, *The Jews of Detroit From the Beginning, 1762-1914* (Detroit, 1986).

Rogoff, "Formative Years"
 Abraham Meyer Rogoff, "Formative Years of the Jewish Labor Movement in the United States (1890-1900)" (Ph.D. diss., Columbia U., 1945).

Rosenberg, *Rochester*
 Stuart E. Rosenberg, *The Jewish Community in Rochester, 1843-1925* (N.Y., 1954).

Rosenblatt, *Mizrachi Movement*
 Samuel Rosenblatt, *The History of the Mizrachi Movement* (N.Y., 1951).

Rosenthal, *Des Moines*
 Frank Rosenthal, *The Jews of Des Moines: The First Century* (Des Moines, 1957).

Rosenthal, "Louis Marshall: Early Public Life"
 Jerome C. Rosenthal, "The Early Public Life of Louis Marshall: 1900-1912, etc." (M.A. thesis, HUC, 1978).

Rosenthal, "Public Life of Louis Marshall"
 Jerome C. Rosenthal, "The Public Life of Louis Marshall" (Ph.D. diss., U. Cincinnati, 1983).

Roskolenko, *Lower East Side*
 Harry Roskolenko, *The Time That Was Then: The Lower East Side, 1900-1914, An Intimate Chronicle* (N.Y., 1971).

Rosten, *Joys of Yiddish*
  Leo Rosten, *The Joys of Yiddish* (N.Y., 1968).

Roth, "American Jewish Congress"
  Alvin S. Roth, "Backrounds and Origins of the American Jewish Congress" (rabbinical thesis, HUC, n.d.).

Rothkoff, *Bernard Revel*
  Aaron Rothkoff, *Bernard Revel: Builder of American Orthodoxy* (Phila., 1972).

Rothschild, *Atlanta*
  Janice O. Rothschild, *As But A Day: The First Hundred Years, 1867-1967* (Atlanta, Ga., 1967).

Rudolph, *Syracuse*
  B.G. Rudolph, *From a Minyan to a Community: A History of the Jews of Syracuse* (Syracuse, 1970).

Sabsovich, *Adventures in Idealism*
  Katherine Sabsovich, *Adventures in Idealism* (N.Y., privately printed, 1922).

Sachar, *History of Israel*
  Howard M. Sachar, *A History of Israel From the Rise of Zionism to Our Time* (N.Y., 1976).

Sachar, *Modern Jewish History*
  Howard M. Sachar, *The Course of Modern Jewish History* (Cleveland and N.Y., 1958).

Sachar, *Sufferance is the Badge*
  Abram Leon Sachar, *Sufferance is the Badge* (N.Y., 1939).

Sachs, "Tales From the First Synagogue in Kansas City"
  Howard F. Sachs, "Tales From the First Synagogue in Kansas City" (typescript, n.p., 1968), copy in Marcus Collections.

Samuels, "Judah David Eisenstein"
  Robert L. Samuels, "The Life and Work of Judah David Eisenstein as Reflected Primarily in His Memoirs, etc." (rabbinical thesis, HUC, 1960).

Samuelson, "Baltimore"
  Norbert Samuelson, "The East European Jewish Immigrant as Reflected in the pages of *The Jewish Comment* of Baltimore, etc." (HUC term paper, 1960).

Sanders, *Downtown Jews*
  Ronald Sanders, *The Downtown Jews* (N.Y., 1969).

Sann, *Story of Dutch Schultz*
  Paul Sann, *Kill the Dutchman! The Story of Dutch Schultz* (N.Y., 1971).

Sarna, *Mordecai Noah*
  Jonathan Sarna, *Jacksonian Jew, The Two Worlds of Mordecai Noah* (N.Y., 1981).

Schachner, *American Jewish Committee*
  Nathan Schachner, *The Price of Liberty: A History of the American Jewish Committee* (N.Y., 1948).

Schappes, *DHJUS*
  Morris U. Schappes, *A Documentary History of the Jews in the United States, 1654-1875,* (N.Y., 1950).

Schappes, *JIUS*
  Morris U. Schappes, *The Jews in the United States, A Pictorial History* (N.Y., 1958).

Schary, *For Special Occasions*
  Dore Schary, *For Special Occasions* (N.Y., 1961).

Schiff, *Jewish Day School*
    Alvin Irwin Schiff, *The Jewish Day School in America* (N.Y., 1966).

Schlesinger, *New Viewpoints*
    Arthur Meier Schlesinger, *New Viewpoints in American History* (N.Y., 1934).

Schlesinger, *Rise of the City*
    Arthur M. Schlesinger, *The Rise of the City, 1878-1898* (N.Y., 1933).

Schmelz, *Jewish Demography*
    U.O. Schmelz et al., *Papers in Jewish Demography* (Jerusalem, 1983).

Schoener, *Lower East Side*
    Allon Schoener (ed.), *The Lower East Side: Portal to American Life (1870-1924)* (N.Y., 1966).

Schoener, *Portal to America*
    Allon Schoener (ed.), *Portal to America: The Lower East Side* (N.Y., 1967).

Schulman, *Geshikhte*
    Elias Schulman, *Geshikhte fun der Yidisher Literatur in Amerika, 1870-1900* (Yiddish, N.Y., 1943).

Seidman, *Needle Trades*
    Joel Seidman, *The Needle Trades* (N.Y., 1942).

Seller (ed.), *Immigrant Women*
    Maxine Schwartz Seller (ed.), *Immigrant Women* (Phila., 1981).

Shapiro, *Leadership of the American Zionist Organization*
    Yonathan Shapiro, *Leadership of the American Zionist Organization, 1897-1930* (Chicago, 1971).

Sherman, *A Fateful Half-Century*
    C. Bezalel Sherman, *A Fateful Half-Century* (pamphlet, N.Y., 1963?).

Shinedling, *West Virginia Jewry*
    Abraham I. Shinedling, *West Virginia Jewry: Origins and History, 1850-1958* (3 vols., Phila., 1963).

Shubow (ed.), *Brandeis Avukah Annual*
    Joseph Shalom Shubow (ed.), *The Brandeis Avukah Annual of 1932, etc.* (Boston, 1932).

Silber, *America in Hebrew Literature*
    Mendel Silber, *America in Hebrew Literature* (New Orleans, 1928).

Silberman, *A Certain People*
    Charles E. Silberman, *A Certain People: American Jews and Their Lives Today* (N.Y., 1985).

Silberschlag, *Renaissance*
    Eisig Silberschlag, *From Renaissance to Renaissance, etc.* (N.Y., 1973).

Silver Festschrift
    Daniel Jeremy Silver (ed.), *In Time of Harvest: Essays in Honor of Abba Hillel Silver, etc.* (N.Y., 1963).

Silverberg, *If I Forget Thee O Jerusalem*
    Robert Silverberg, *If I Forget Thee O Jerusalem* (N.Y., 1970).

Silverman, *Hartford Jews*
    Morris Silverman, *Hartford Jews, 1659-1970* (Hartford, Conn., 1970).

Simon, *Israel Zangwill*
    Maurice Simon (ed.), *Speeches, Articles and Letters of Israel Zangwill* (London, 1937).

Simonhoff, *Saga of American Jewry*
    Harry Simonhoff, *Saga of American Jewry, 1865-1914* (N.Y., 1959).

Singer, "American Jew in Agriculture"
Richard E. Singer, "The American Jew in Agriculture, Past History and Present Conditions" (rabbinical thesis, HUC, 1941).

Singer, *Russia at the Bar of the American People*
Isidore Singer, *Russia at the Bar of the American People* (N.Y., 1904).

Sklare, *Jew in American Society*
Marshall Sklare (ed.), *The Jew in American Society* (N.Y., 1974).

Slosson, *The Great Crusade*
Preston William Slosson, *The Great Crusade and After, 1914-1928* (N.Y., 1930).

Smill, "The Stogy Industry"
Eva Smill, "The Stogy Industry on the Hill in Pittsburgh, Pa." (M.A. thesis, Carnegie Institute of Technology, 1920).

Smucker, *History*
Samuel M. Smucker, *A History of the Modern Jews, etc.* (Phila., 1860).

Sokolow, *History of Zionism*
Nahum Sokolow, *History of Zionism, 1600-1918* (2 vols., London, 1919).

Soltes, *Contemporary Jew. Hist.*
Mordecai Soltes, *Contemporary Jewish History, etc.* (N.Y., 1931).

Soltes, *Yiddish Press*
Mordecai Soltes, *The Yiddish Press: An Americanizing Agency* (N.Y., 1925).

Statistical History of U.S.
The Statistical History of the United States from Colonial Times to the Present, etc. (Stamford, Conn., n.d.).

Stephenson, *American Immigration*
George M. Stephenson, *A History of American Immigration, 1820-1924* (Boston, 1926).

Stern, "East European Jews in the U.S."
Malcom H. Stern, "The History of the East European Jews in the United States During the Period, 1850-1881" (HUC prize essay, 1936).

Stern, *FAJF*
Malcom H. Stern (comp.), *American Jewish Families, 600 Genealogies, 1654-1977* (Cincinnati and Waltham, Mass., 1978).

Stern, *Grundriss*
M. Stern, *Grundriss zur Geschichte der Juden und ihrer Literatur, u.s.w.* (Berlin, 1908).

Stern, *Occasional Addresses*
Horace Stern, *The Spiritual Values of Life: Occasional Addresses on Jewish Themes* (Phila., 1953).

Stern, "Sephardic Jewish Community of Los Angeles"
Stephen Stern, "The Sephardic Jewish Community of Los Angeles: A Study in Folklore and Ethnic Identity" (Ph.D. diss., Indiana U., 1977).

Stern, *Temple Emanu-El*
Myer Stern, *The Rise and Progress of Reform Judaism Embracing a History Made from the Official Records of Temple Emanu-El of New York, etc.* (N.Y., 1895).

Stevens & Glazer, *CCAR Resolutions*
Elliot Stevens and Simon Glazer, *Resolutions of the Central Conference . . . 1889-1974* (N.Y., 1975).

Stocker, *Jewish Roots in Arizona*
Joseph Stocker, *Jewish Roots in Arizona* (Phoenix, 1954).

Stokes, *Church & State*
    Anson Phelps Stokes, *Church and State in the United States* (3 vols., N.Y., 1950).

Straus, *Under Four Administrations*
    Oscar S. Straus, *Under Four Administrations: From Cleveland to Taft* (Boston, 1922).

"Sulzberger," "East European Jews"
    "Mayer Sulzberger," "The Attitude of the Older Immigrants and Natives to the Immigration of the Eastern European Jews as Reflected in the Anglo-Jewish Press of New York and Philadelphia, 1891-1894" (HUC prize essay, 1959), Marcus Collections.

Suwol, *Oregon*
    Samuel N. Suwol, *Jewish History of Oregon* (Portland, Or., 1958).

Swarsensky, *Madison*
    Manfred Swarsensky, *From Generation to Generation* (Madison, Wis., 1955?).

Swichkow & Gartner, *Milwaukee*
    Louis J. Swichkow and Lloyd P. Gartner, *The History of the Jews of Milwaukee* (Phila., 1963).

Szajkowski, *Jew. Mass Settlement*
    Zosa Szajkowski, *Jewish Mass Settlement in the United States, etc.* (N.Y., 1966).

Szajkowski, *Jews, Wars, and Communism*
    Zosa Szajkowski, *Jews, Wars, and Communism, etc.* (N.Y., 1972).

Tarbell, *Nationalizing of Business*
    Ida M. Tarbell, *The Nationalizing of Business, 1878-1898* (N.Y., 1936).

Tarshish, "American Judaism"
    Allan Tarshish, "The Rise of American Judaism" (Ph.D. diss., HUC, 1939).

Tarshish, *Dawn in the West*
    Allan Tarshish, *Dawn in the West* (N.Y., 1985).

Tcherikower (ed.), *Jewish Labor Movement in the U.S.*
    Elias Tcherikower, *History of the Jewish Labor Movement in the United States* (N.Y., 1945).

Temkin, *Philadelphia Conference*
    Sefton D. Temkin, *The New World of Reform, etc.* (London, 1971).

Tennessee Inventory
    Inventory of the Church and Synagogue Archives of Tennessee: Jewish Congregations (Tennessee, 1941).

Thompson, *Jewish Missions*
    A.E. Thompson, *A Century of Jewish Missions* (Chicago, 1902).

Todd, *Louis D. Brandeis*
    A.L. Todd, *Justice on Trial: The Case of Louis D. Brandeis* (N.Y., 1964).

Turkus & Feder, *Murder Inc.*
    Burton B. Turkus and Sid Feder, *Murder Inc.: The Story of "The Syndicate"* (N.Y., 1951).

U.A.H.C. Statistics
    Statistics of the Jews of the United States, etc. (Cincinnati, 1880).

Uchill, *Pioneers*
    Ida Libert Uchill, *Pioneers, Peddlers and Tsadikim* (Denver, 1957).

UJE
    The Universal Jewish Encyclopedia.

Urofsky, *American Zionism*
> Melvin I. Urofsky, *American Zionism From Herzl to the Holocaust* (Garden City, N.Y., 1975).

Urofsky, *Mind of One Piece*
> Melvin I. Urofsky, *A Mind of One Piece: Brandeis and American Reform* (N.Y., 1971).

Urofsky & Levy, *Letters of Louis D. Brandeis*
> Melvin I. Urofsky & David W. Levy, *Letters of Louis D. Brandeis* (5 vols., N.Y., 1971).

Vorspan & Gartner, *Los Angeles*
> Max Vorspan and Lloyd P. Gartner, *History of the Jews of Los Angeles* (Phila., 1970).

Vorwaerts
> (Jewish Daily *Forward*).

W. & W., *Philadelphia*
> Edwin Wolf, 2d, and Maxwell Whiteman, *The History of the Jews of Philadelphia from Colonial Times to the Age of Jackson* (Phila., 1957).

Waldstein, *Modern Hebrew Literature*
> Abraham Solomon Waldstein, *The Evolution of Modern Hebrew Literature, 1850-1912* (N.Y., 1916).

Watters, *Utah*
> Leon L. Watters, *The Pioneer Jews of Utah* (N.Y., 1952).

Waxman, *Conservative Judaism*
> Mordecai Waxman (ed.), *Tradition and Change: The Development of the Conservative Movement* (N.Y., 1958).

Waxman, *Jew. Literature*
> Waxman, *A History of Jewish Literature* (vol 4, N.Y., 1960).

Weinberger, *Jews and Judaism*
> Jonathan D. Sarna (trans. & ed.), *People Walk on Their Heads: Moses Weinberger's Jews and Judaism in New York* (N.Y., 1982).

Weisgal (ed.), *Theodor Herzl*
> Meyer W. Weisgal (ed.), *Theodor Herzl: A Memorial* (N.Y., 1929).

Weizmann, *Trial and Error*
> Chaim Weizmann, *Trial and Error: The Autobiography of Chaim Weizmann* (Phila., 1949).

Where We Stand
> *Where We Stand: Social Action Resolutions adopted by the Union of American Hebrew Congregations* (N.Y., 1960, 1980).

Wiernik, *History*
> Peter Wiernik, *History of the Jews in America* (N.Y,, 1912).

Wilansky, *Sinai to Cincinnati*
> Dena Wilansky, *Sinai to Cincinnati, etc.* (N.Y., 1937).

Winter, *Jewish Education*
> Nathan H. Winter, *Jewish Education in a Pluralist Society: Samson Benderly and Jewish Education in the United States* (N.Y., 1966).

Winter & Wuensche, *Litteratur der Juden*
> J. Winter and Aug. Wuensche, *Geschichte der Poetischen, Kabbalistischen, Historischen und Neuzeitlichen Litteratur der Juden* (Trier, 1896).

Wirth, *Ghetto*
>   Louis Wirth, *The Ghetto* (Chicago, 1928).

Wischnitzer, *To Dwell in Safety*
>   Mark Wischnitzer, *To Dwell in Safety: The Story of Jewish Migration Since 1800* (Phila., 1948).

Wischnitzer, *Visas to Freedom*
>   Mark Wischnitzer, *Visas to Freedom* (Cleveland and N.Y., 1956).

Wise, *Challenging Years*
>   *Challenging Years: The Autobiography of Stephen Wise* (N.Y., 1949).

Wish, *Society and Thought*
>   Harvey Wish, *Society and Thought in America* (2 vols., N.Y., 1950-1952).

Wittke, *Refugees of Revolution*
>   Carl Wittke, *Refugees of Revolution: The German Forty-Eighters in America* (Phila., 1952).

Wittke, *We Who Built America*
>   Carl Wittke, *We Who Built America: The Saga of the Immigrant* (N.Y., 1939).

Wolf, *American Jew*
>   Simon Wolf, *The American Jew as Patriot, Soldier and Citizen* (Phila., 1895).

Wolf, "East European Jews in the U.S."
>   Alfred Wolf, "The History of the East European Jews in the United States from 1881 to 1890" (HUC prize essay, 1938).

Wolf, *Legal Sufferings of the Jews in Russia*
>   Lucien Wolf (ed.), *The Legal Sufferings of the Jews in Russia* (London, 1912).

Wolf, *Presidents I Have Known*
>   Simon Wolf, *The Presidents I Have Known from 1860-1918* (Washington, D.C., 1918).

Wolf, *The Jewish Question*
>   Lucien Wolf, *Notes on the Diplomatic History of the Jewish Question* (London, 1919).

Wolfe, *Iowa*
>   Jack Wolfe, *A Century of Iowa Jewry* (Des Moines, 1941).

Woods, *Americans in Process*
>   Robert A. Woods, *Americans in Process, etc.* (Boston, 1903).

WPA
>   Work Projects Administration.

WSJHQ
>   *Western States Jewish Historical Quarterly.*

WWIA
>   *Who's Who in America.*

WWIAJ
>   *Who's Who in American Jewry, 1926, 1928, 1938* (N.Y. 1927, 1928, 1955).

WWIWJ
>   *Who's Who in World Jewry.*

WWW
>   *Who Was Who in America: A Companion Volume to Who's Who in America* (6 vols., Chicago, 1943-1977).

WWW, 1607-1896
>   *Who Was Who in America, Historical Volume, 1607-1896* (Chicago, 1967).

YA
>   *Yivo Annual of Jewish Social Science.*

Yalkut Maarabi
  Yalkut Maarabi (N.Y., 1904).
Yearbook of the Leo Baeck Institute
  Yearbook of the Leo Baeck Institute (London, 1965).
Yiddishes Morgen Journal
  (*Jewish Morning Journal*).
Yiddishes Tageblatt
  (*Jewish Daily News*).

Zaretz, *Amalgamated Clothing Workers*
  Charles Elbert Zaretz, *The Amalgamated Clothing Workers of American* (N.Y., 1934).
Zola, "Zvi Hirsch Masliansky"
  Gary Phillip Zola, "The People's Preacher: A Study of the Life and Writings of Zvi Hirsch Masliansky (1856-1943)" (rabbinical thesis, HUC, 1982).
Zylbercwaig, *Leksikon fun Yidishn Teater*
  Zalmen Zylbercwaig (ed.), *Leksikon fun Yidishn Teater* (Yiddish, 6 vols., N.Y., 1931).

NOTES

CHAPTER ONE
THE EAST EUROPEAN JEWS

1. *AJHQ*, 66:479.
2. *PUAHC*, 5:4664 ff.; Joseph, *Jewish Immigration*, 93, 113; Karp, *Jew. Exp. in America*, 4:ix.
3. "Mordecai, Mordecai M.," *BDEAJ*; Elzas, *Jews of S. C.*, 163, 191; Hyams, "Memorandum for My Children"; Stern, *FAJF*, 170.
4. *AH*, Apr. 1, 1904, pp. 630-31, Apr. 8, 1904, pp. 660-61, Apr. 15, 1904, pp. 686-87; "United States," *JE*, 12:368-69; Uchill, *Pioneers*, 22, 165 ff.; Adler & Connolly, *Buffalo*, 28, 97-99, 102, 416, n. 30; Glazer, *Jews of Iowa*, 235-36. These references to East Europeans in early America are but a meager sampling of data available: James William Parkes, *How Russian Jews Came to the West* (Toronto, Canada, 1938); B. & B., *JOUS*, 3:758, 768; Marcus, *CAJ*, 2:712, 967, 1000, 1004, 1007, 1063, 1073, 1095; P. & K., *Tourist's Guide*, 174, 581; Hyams, "Memorandum for My Children"; *YA*, 9:205, 207; Niemcewicz, *Under Their Vine and Fig Tree*, 264; Elzas, *Jews of S. C.* 99, 120, 188; R. & E., *Charleston*, see Index sub "Polish Jews"; *PAJHS*, 39:143 ff., 49:222-23, 224, n. 17, 225; Grinstein, *New York City*, 22-23; *RIJHN*, 1:236; Feldman, *Jew. Experience in Western Pa.*, 19-20; Gutstein, *Chicago* 33 ff., 381 ff.; *AZJ*, Oct. 5, 1846, pp. 595-96, Mar. 29, 1858, pp. 191-93; Hennig, *Columbia, S. C.*, 11-12; Wolf, "East European Jews in the U. S."; *AJHQ*, 51:60; Stern, "East European Jews in the U. S."; Benjamin, *Three Years*, vol. 2 documents the presence of East European Jews in 1859-1862 in several towns: e. g., see 274-75, 281-82, 284-85; E. & L., *Richmond* 294, 300; *WSJHQ*, 8:33-39, 10:377; Brickner, "Jew. Com. of Cin.," 106; *Jewish Review*, 4:69, 146, 283; Fein, *Baltimore*, 141; Wirth, *Ghetto*, 146 ff.; *YIVO Bleter*, 40:224 ff.; Elbogen, *Cent. of Jewish Life*, 61-62; *JSS*, 4:291 ff.; Tarshish, "American Judaism," i, n. 14; Szajkowski, *Jew. Mass Settlement*, 6; Wischnitzer, *To Dwell in Safety*, 28 ff.; George Alexander Kohut, *Ezra Stiles and the Jews* (N. Y., 1902), 93; *Bulletin*, Missouri Historical Society, 17:64-89; Eisenstein, *Zikhronothai*, 38 ff.; *Yalkut Maarabi*, 1:128 ff.; *AJA*, 3:14; Karp, *Jew. Exp. in America*, 4:viii; Breck, *Colorado* 73-74; Auerbach, "Nebraska," 24 ff.; Herschel Levin, "The History of East European Jews in the United States from 1850 to 1881" (HUC prize essay, 1937), 38 ff.; Hinchin, "Jews of Sioux City"; Rosenthal, *Des Moines*, 25-26, 33, 52-53; Plaut, *Jews in Minnesota*, 58; *Historia Judaica*, 22:140; *Mississippi Inventory*, 29-32; "Chicago," *EJ*, 5:412; Swichkow & Gartner, *Milwaukee* 192; "Cleveland," "Evansville,"

"Indianapolis," "Iowa," "Kingston," "Mount Vernon," "New Bedford," "Saint Paul," "Savannah," "Troy," "Worcester," *UJE*; "New Orleans," *UJE*, 8:172, "Ohio," 8:288-89, "Philadelphia," 8:478-80, "Richmond," 9:160, "Saint Louis," 9:313-14, "Wisconsin," 10:534; "Wilkes-Barre," *JE, UJE*; Baltimore *Jewish Times*, Sept. 30, 1928, p. 2; Ehrenfried, *Boston*, 424, 429-30; *Commentary*, 15:497; Kohn, *Utica*, 13-14.

5. *PAJHS*, 9:63 ff., 12:144-45, 33:134, 34:285 ff.; "Ash, Abraham Joseph," "Heilprin, Phinehas Mendel," *UJE*; *AH*, Apr. 8, 1904, pp. 660-61; Wiernik, *History*, 189 ff., 309-10; Schappes, *DHJUS*, 373 ff., 671-72; "New York," *JE*, 9:275; "New York City," *UJE*, 8:180; *Ben Chananja*, 6-7(1863):652; Goldstein, *Cent. of Jud. in NYC*, 107-8; Ernst, *Immigrant Life*, 45-46, 73 ff.; Wolf, "East European Jews in the U. S."; Eisenstein, *Zikhronothai*, 38 ff. For Yiddish and Hebrew literature see infra, section on Hebrew and Yiddish; *Yalkut Maarabi*, 1:128 ff.; *Ner Ha-Maarabi*, 1/2:21 ff.; Grinstein, *New York City*, 22-23, 218-19, 528; Stern, "East European Jews in the U. S."; Fein, *Baltimore*, 142-43; M. & M., *History*, 694 ff.; *AJA*, 33:184; Martin, *Judaism*, 2:305; *Amopteil*, 2:147 ff.

6. Webster, *Guide to American History* (Springfield, Mass., 1971), 207; Leeser, *Discourses*, 10:262; M. & M., *History*, 683 ff.; Schappes, *JIUS*, 66; Elbogen, *Cent. of Jewish Life*, 41 ff.; Dubnow, *History of the Jews in Russia and Poland*, 2:46 ff.; "United States," *JE*, 12:367; Sachar, *Modern Jewish History*, 86-88; Fein, *Baltimore*, 34; *Occ.*, 2:562 ff.

7. Dubnow, *History of the Jews in Russia and Poland*, 2:309, 312, 373; *EAH*, 474; Wish, *Society and Thought*, 2:430-32; Homer Carey Hockett, *The Critical Method in Historical Research and Writing* (N. Y., 1955), 194-95; Rischin, *Promised City*, 23-24, 32; Stephenson, *American Immigration*, 81 ff.; *PAJHS*, 22:137, 29:102, 36:124, 39:153, n. 40; Sachar, *Modern Jewish History*, 89, 95, 240 ff., 256 ff.; *By Myself I'm A Book*, 13; "Rumania," *JE, EJ*; "Roumania," *UJE*; Schappes, *DHJUS*, 726, n. 3; *AH*, Oct. 19, 1900, pp. 647 ff., Oct. 26, 1900, pp. 680 ff., Apr. 1, 1904, pp. 630-31; Elbogen, *Cent. of Jewish Life*, 61; *Education of Abraham Cahan*, 196; Sklare, *Jew in American Society*, 42; *YA*, 23:160 ff., 7:255 ff., 264, 9:377 ff.; Leeser, *Discourses*, 10:262; *Jewish People*, 1:408, 428 ff., 4:73 ff.; Wittke, *We Who Built America*, 328 ff., 333 ff.; "Jews," *HEAEG*, 579 ff.; Handlin, *Adventure in Freedom*, 83 ff.; N. Y. *Jewish Tribune*, Dec. 22, 1922, pp. 2 ff.; Michael, "Cincinnati," 14; Tarbell, *Nationalizing of Business*, 14; "Russia," *JE, UJE, EJ*; *AJA*, 24:39 ff., 33:1 ff.; *AJHQ*, 53:117 ff., 56:10, 286-87, 293, 59:179 ff.; Bushee, *Boston*, 2; "United States of America," *EJ*, 15:1608; *Reports Immig. Com.*, 15:lxxxix; Cowen, *Memories of an American Jew*, 95, 287-88; "United States," *JE*, 12:358-59, 367-68; Masserman & Baker, *Jews Come to America*, 289 ff.; Ehrenfried, *Boston*, 504 ff.; Wiernik, *History*, 254 ff.; "May Laws," *JE*; Wolf, *Legal Sufferings of the Jews in Russia*; Dubnow, *History of the Jews in Russia and Poland*, 2-3, chaps. 21-37; Frumkin et al., *Russian Jewry*, 85 ff.

8. *AJHQ*, 42:208; *PAJHS*, 22:101 ff., 132 ff., 38:239 ff., 305 ff., 39:87 ff., 45:69-89; *Congress Weekly*, Dec. 10, 1956, pp. 9-11; *AJA*, 17:143 ff.; Martin Ryback, "Articles on American Jewish Life in *Ha-Karmel* and *Ha-Maggid*, 1863" (HUC term paper, 1948); Murray Blackman, "America Seen Through Two European Periodicals: An Analysis of the Attitude to America as presented in the pages of *Ha-Magid* and *Ha-Mevasser*, 1860-1865" (HUC term paper, 1947); Leo Shpall, "Selected Items of American Jewish Interest in the Yiddish Periodicals of Russia and Poland, 1862-1940" (AJA monograph, Cincinnati, 1966); *JSS*, 39:105 ff., 113, 115; Adler & Connolly, *Buffalo*, 221; Faulkner, *Social Justice*, 17; Curti et al., *American History*, 125; *Reports, Ind. Com.*, 15:xc; Rischin, *Promised City*, 24, 31; *YA*, 2-3:163 ff., 174-76, 9:63 ff.; Philip Taylor, *The Distant Magnet: European Emigration to the USA* (London, 1971).

9. *PAJHS*, 36:226, 39:232 ff., 389 ff., 46:371-76, 48:43; *RIJHN*, 3:46-47; *Reports, Immig. Com. Abstracts*, 1:215; *AJYB*, 26:583, 56:11; Tarshish, "American Judaism," 10, n. 15; Kraus, *Immigration*, 73; Sachar, *Modern Jewish History*, 309-11; Joseph, *Jewish Immigration*, 132 ff., 162, 174; "Migration," *UJE*, 7:549; *Jewish People*, 1:407, 409-15, 4:59;

"Jews," *HEAEG*, 579 ff.; Rischin, *Promised City*, 20-33; Lipman, *Soc. Hist. of Jews in England*, 41, 66, 85-87; *YA*, 6:157 ff., 9:379; Wiernik, *History*, 343; *AJHQ*, 67:298-99; Szajkowski, *Jew. Mass Settlement*, 6; Stephenson, *American Immigration*, 73; Baron, *History*, 2:264 ff.; Schlesinger, *New Viewpoints*, 13 ff.; "Jews," *DAH* (1961); Soltes, *Contemporary Jewish History*, 11; Wittke, *We Who Built America*, 332; *Jewish Life*, 9 (no. 1):18 ff.; Schappes, *JIUS*, 119; Handlin, *Adventure in Freedom*, 84-85; Levinger, *Jews in U. S.*, 263, 265, 271; Plaut, *Jews in Minnesota*, 55-56, 90 ff.; Ann Novotny, *Strangers at the Door: Ellis Island, Castle Garden, and the Great Migration to America* (abridged edition, Toronto, 1974).

10. *AJH*, 71:218, 221-22, 256 ff.; Bushee, *Boston*, 13-14; *Reports, Immig. Com. Abstracts*, 1:103-4, 112, 175, 439, 444-45; Wish, *Society and Thought*, 2:250 ff.; Sachar, *Modern Jewish History*, 197; *AH*, Mar. 4, 1904, pp. 503-4, July 12, 1907, pp. 237-38; Jenks & Lauck, *Immigration Problems*, 25-26, 409 ff.; *Reports, Ind. Com.*, 15:lxvii ff.; Seller (ed.), *Immigrant Women*, 100; Bushee, *Boston*, 16-18, 128; Joseph, *Jewish Immigration*, 132, 158, 187, 189, 192 ff.; *Jewish Life*, 9(no. 1):19-20; Isaac M. Rubinow, *Economic Condition of the Jews in Russia* (reprint ed., N. Y., 1975); Schappes, *JIUS*, 122; Nudelman & Slesinger, *Jew in America*, 2:113; *HUCA*, 23(part 2):242-43; "Migrations," *UJE*, 7:548; *Jewish People*, 1:416 ff., 425-26, 4:274; Fein, *Baltimore*, 297, n. 112; *JM*, Aug. 11, 1882, p. 5, c. 4, Aug. 18, 1882, p. 2, cs. 3-4; *PAJHS*, 40:241 ff., 44:199 ff., 48:30 ff., 44; *AJYB*, 11(1909-1910):56, 18 (1916-1917):284, 20 (1918-1919):346, 22:376, 23:294, 24:316, 25:594, 27:399, 50:753; *AJHQ*, 67:306; Walter Nugent, *Structures of American Social History* (Bloomington, Ind., 1981), 112; Schlesinger, *New Viewpoints*, 13-14; Oscar Theodore Barck, Jr. & Nelson Manfred Blake, *Since 1900: A History of the United States in Our Times* (4th ed., N. Y., 1965), 128; *PUAHC*, 5:4664 ff.; Israel Cohen, *Jewish Life in Modern Times* (N. Y., 1914), 194 ff.; Finkelstein, *The Jews* (1949), 4:1198, 1220 ff.

11. *PAJHS*, 15:48 ff., 73 ff., 19:125 ff., 24:21, 25 ff., 29 ff., 102 ff., 111-12, 29:83 ff., 109-10, 114-16; 36:99 ff., 112, 120 ff., 171 ff., 178, 195 ff., 205-6, 217 ff., 38:53-56, 39:389 ff., 412-23, 40:251 ff., 41:127 ff., 42:157 ff., 45:67 ff., 49:177; Beifield, "Joseph Krauskopf," 48-49; Elbogen, *Cent. of Jewish Life*, 61 ff., 72, 217 ff., 224 ff.; *AI*, Mar. 25, 1870, p. 9, c. 3, June 7, 1872, p. 9, cs. 3-4, Feb. 10, 1882, p. 260, cs. 3-4, Mar. 3, 1882, p. 286, cs. 1-2, Mar. 10, 1882, p. 290, cs. 1-2, May 25, 1893, p. 7, cs. 1-2, Oct. 11, 1894, p. 4, cs. 2-3; W. & W., *Philadelphia*, 376; Malcolm Stern, N. Y., to JRM, Oct. 7, 1986, re a separate Sephardic cemetery in 1681/2, Marcus Collections; Byars, *B. & M. Gratz*, 106-7; Lipman, *Soc. Hist. of Jews in England*, chaps. 5-8; Schappes, *DHJUS*, 210, 543 ff.; *Der Orient*, 7 (1846):67; Tarshish, "American Judaism," 420-21; Szajkowski, *Jew. Mass Settlement*, 6-9, 11; *JM*, Nov. 18, 1881, p. 5, c. 5, p. 6, cs. 1-2, Jan. 27, 1882, p. 3, c. 2, p. 5, c. 2, Feb. 3, 1882, p. 2, c. 4, Mar. 24, 1882, p. 4, c. 5; Wiernik, *History*, 264, 343 ff.; Philip Joachimsen, N. Y., to M. S. Isaacs, N. Y., Oct. 14, 1872, BDAI Collections, AJHSL; M. S. Isaacs, N. Y., to Isaac Seligman, London/Paris, Oct. 10, 1872, BDAI Collections, AJHSL; *YA*, 2-3:160 ff., 6:169-72; *Zion*, 26(1961):96 ff.; B.P. Poore, *A Descriptive Catalogue of the Government Publications of the United States, etc.* (Washington, D. C., 1885, reprinted, N. Y., 1970), p. 959, treatment of Israelites in Europe; Markens, *Hebrews*, 235-37, 343; "United States," *JE*, 12:358; Judaeans, 4:41 ff.; Adler, *Recent Persecution*; "Board of Delegates on Civil and Religious Rights," *UJE*; Learsi, *Jews in America*, 128-29, 217 ff.; Doctor Junius, *Die Leiden der rumaenischen Juden und Vorschlaege zur Abhuelfe ihrer Nothlage* (Leipzig, 1885); *Menorah*, 1 (1886):22 ff., 15:462-66; Records of the Department of State, Consular Despatches, Bucharest, vol.2, Jan. 10 1870 - Mar. 31, 1881; Morais, *Eminent Israelites*, 267 ff.; "Peixotto, Benjamin Franklin," *DAB*; Randi Musnitski, "America's Goodness: An Edited Translation of Leon Horowitz's *Tov Artsot Habrit*" (rabbinical thesis, HUC, 1983); Kohler, *German Jewish Persecutions*, 14 ff.; Stephenson, *American Immigration*, 81; *AH*, Apr. 9, 1880, p.

91, Jan. 12, 1923, p. 256; *Education of Abraham Cahan*, 158, 182 ff., 194-96; N.Y. *Hebrew Standard*, Nov. 3, 1922, p. 1; Sachar, *Modern Jewish History*, 240 ff.; Morais, *Philadelphia*, 206-7; Stern, *FAJF*, 164; *Hebrew Emigrant Aid Society of the United States. Report of Moritz Ellinger*, (N.Y., 1882), copy in Marcus Collections; *Hebrew Review*, 2:5; *Jewish People*, 4:245; Joseph Melamed, "'History of the Russian Exiles in America,' by J.D. Eisenstein, etc." (HUC term paper, n.d.); *AJA*, 3 (no.1):11 ff., 32:23 ff.; "Migration," *UJE*, 7:547 ff.; O. S. Straus, N. Y., to Baron de Hirsch, Paris, Aug. 8, 1890, Straus Papers, LC; *Mid-America*, 60:171-84; *Gates of Zion*, 9:22 ff.; *JSS*, 4:291 ff., 309 ff., 22: 157; Meites, *Chicago*, 687 ff.; Richardson, *Messages and Papers of the Presidents*, 8:39, 9:188; *AJHQ*, 53:99 ff., 110ff., 58:25 ff., 75, 108-12, 116, 60:344 ff., 64:236 ff., 241; *PUAHC*, 4:3354 ff.; "Jewish Colonization Association," *UJE*; Kohler, *Simon Wolf Addresses*, 215 ff., *Reports, Ind. Com.*, 15:xciv; Joseph, *Jewish Immigration*, 93, 164, 167; Oscar S. Straus, N.Y., to F. D. Mocatta, London, Apr. 14, 1902, Straus Papers, LC; George Alexander Kohut, *A Hebrew Anthology* (2 vols., Cincinnati, 1913), 1:70; Oscar S. Straus, N. Y., Apr. 2, 1902, to Jacob H. Schiff, N. Y., Straus Papers, LC; Oscar S. Straus, N. Y., to President Roosevelt, May 15, 1902, Straus Papers, LC; *U.S. Foreign Relations*, 1872, 688 ff., copy in Marcus Collections; Oscar Straus, "Memorandum As To Hay's Roumanian Note," undated, Straus Papers, LC; Wolf, *Presidents I Have Known*, 156 ff., 184 ff.; Wolf, *The Jewish Question*, 23 ff., 75 ff.; Bailey, *Diplomatic History of the American People*, 560, n. 30; *AJYB*, 7 (1905-1906):263-64, 9 (1907-1908):511, 26:420 ff., 441 ff.; Baltimore *Jewish Comment*, Nov. 7, 1902, p. 6, c. 3, p. 7, c. 2; Plaut, *Reform Judaism*, 83-84.

12. Rabbi Clifton Harby Levy interview with JRM, Marcus Collections; "Migrations," *UJE*, 7:548 ff.

13. "Gordon, Aaron David," *UJE*; *AJA*, 3 (no. 2):323; *Occ.*, 8:199.

14. Eisenstein, *Zikhronothai*, 52; *AJHS*, 60:145; *AI*, May 25, 1893, p. 7, cs. 1-2; *AJA*, 12:66-67; Rosenthal, *Des Moines*, 22-24; Sachs, "Tales from the First Synagogue in Kansas City," 4-5; Tarshish, "American Judaism," 260; *PAJHS*, 42:196.

15. Grinstein, *New York City*, 172; St. Louis *Jewish Tribune*, Nov. 2, 1883, p. 403, cs. 1-2.

16. *PAJHS*, 40:231; *Proceedings of the NCJW, 1896*, 193; Mrs. Perry Kallison, San Antonio, to JRM, June 29, 1971, Marcus Collections.

17. Myers, *Bigotry*, 140 ff.; "Canterbury," *UJE*; "Bordeaux," *JE*, 3:319; Marcus, *CAJ*, 2:798; Marcus, *EAJ*, 2:72; *PAJHS*, 35:189 ff., 40:221 ff., 50:213, 53:99 ff., 127-29, 255, n. 8; Marcus, *Memoirs*, 3:300; Grinstein, *New York City*, 538, n. 10; Joseph Jonas, Cincinnati, to I. L., Phila., Sept. 6, 1845, copy in Marcus Collections; Henry Gersoni, *Jew Against Jew* (Chicago, 1881), 27, 39; *YA*, 2-3:97 ff.; *AZJ*, July 27, 1846, pp. 448-49; H. Myers, St. Louis, to I. L., Phila., 1854, copy in Marcus Collections; *AI*, Mar. 11, 1881, p. 292, cs. 1-2, Mar. 10, 1882, p. 290, cs. 1-2, Jan. 28, 1887, p. 4, cs. 2-3, Apr. 15, 1887, p. 4, cs. 3-4; Swichkow & Gartner, *Milwaukee*, 81-87; Baltzell, *Protestant Establishment*, 60; *AH*, Aug. 5, 1881, p. 133, Apr. 3, 1908, p. 552; Uchill, *Pioneers*, 115; Henry Hart Milman, *The History of the Jews* (N. Y., 1913), 2:403; Fein, *Baltimore*, 144; *AJA*, 3 (no. 1):20-32, 18:134, 31:204-5; Ginsberg, *Jews of Virginia*, 42; Jacob Rader Marcus, "The Handsome Young Priest in the Black Gown, the Personal World of Gershom Seixas," in *HUCA*, vols. 40-41 (pp. 409-467); Handlin, *Adventure in Freedom*, 157 ff.; *AJHQ*, 60:133 ff., 144-47, 62:273, 275; "Sulzberger," "East European Jews"; Michael Gilbert, "The Jewish Community of Chicago as Viewed Through the *Occident*: 1881 and 1890" (HUC term paper, n. d.), 9-10; Sachs, "Tales from the First Synagogue in Kansas City," 4; Nodel, *The Ties Between*, 51-52; Silber, *America in Hebrew Literature*, 88 ff.; Phila. *Jewish Exponent*, July 28, 1893, p. 4, c. 3; *JM*, May 27, 1881, p. 4, c. 3, May 19, 1882, p. 3, c. 1, Aug. 11, 1882, p. 5, c. 4, Sept. 8, 1882, p. 2, cs. 4-5; Adler & Connolly, *Buffalo*, 165-67; Brownstein, "Philadelphia," 16-17, 32; R. & E., *Charleston*, 228; Harold Silver, "Some Attitudes of the East European Immigrants Toward Organizing Jew-

ish Charities in the United States in the Years 1890-1900" (typescript, New York Public Library, N. Y., 1934); Berman, "East European Immigration"; London *Jewish Chronicle*, Sept. 9, 1884, p. 5, c. l, Oct. 3, 1884, p. 6, c. 1; Rischin, *Promised City*, 95 ff., 237-41; *CCARYB*, 18:145-46; *AJYB*, 50:69; *JSS*, 25:71-72; Horwich, *My First Eighty Years*, 131, 143-44; Wischnitzer, *To Dwell in Safety*, 31-33; *Menorah*, 5:321-22; Schappes, *DHJUS*, 546; Vorspan & Gartner, *Los Angeles*, 91.

18. "Amsterdam," *AJA*, 1:286; *JM*, Jan. 27, 1882, p. 5, c. 2, Mar. 10, 1882, p. 3, c. 2, p. 4, c. 4; "Sulzberger," "East Europeans Jews"; *PAJHS*, 40:221 ff.; *AJA*, 18:137; *Der Zeitgeist* 3(1882):168-69.

19. Stern, *Temple Emanu-El*, 73 ff.; Philip S. Bernstein," Dr. Landsberg Comes to Rochester: 100 Years of Reform at B'rith Kodesh" (mimeo, sermon, 1970), copy in Marcus Collections; *AI*, May 25, 1893, p. 7, cs. 1-2; Adler, *Recent Persecution*; *Der Zeitgeist*, 3(1882):168-69; "Sulzberger," "East European Jews," 11; *WSJHQ*, 8:283-84; *AJHS*, 53:126, 62:276; *Judaism at the World's Parliament of Religions*, 342-47; *Pittsburgh Platform*, 10; Elbogen, *Cent. of Jewish Life*, 326 ff., 332-33; *AJYB*, 50:1-84; Eisenstein, *Zikhronothai*, 48-50; *AH*, June 10, 1881, p. 39; *JM*, Feb. 10, 1882, p. 4, cs. 2-3, Feb. 28, 1882, p. 4, c. 1, p. 5, c. 4, Mar. 3, 1882, p. 5, c. 2, Mar. 10, 1882, p. 3, c. 2, p. 4, c. 4, Aug. 18, 1882, p. 2, cs. 3 -4, Sept. 1, 1882, p. 2, cs. 2-3, Sept. 8, 1882, p. 2, cs. 4-5; Schoener, *Lower East Side*, 53; Blum, *Baltimore*, 15; Morais, *Philadelphia*, 131-35, 142-43, 322 ff., see Index sub Louis E. Levy, Simon Muhr, Sabato Morais, Alfred T. Jones, Michael Heilprin; "Heilprin, Michael," *JE, UJE, EJ, DAB*; Stern, "East European Jews in the U. S."; Pollak, *Michael Heilprin*; Schappes, *JIUS*, 124; AJAr Release, Aug. 1963; *Education of Abraham Cahan*, 251 ff.; *AJA*, 3 (no. 1):32 ff.; Elbogen, *Cent. of Jewish Life*, 26 ff., 240, 326 ff., 330-31; Wilhelmina Christina Pieterse, *Daniel Levi De Barrios als Geschiedschrijver van de Portuges-Israelietische Gemeente te Amsterdam, etc.* (Dutch, Amsterdam, 1968), 195; Schappes, *DHJUS*, 198 ff., 538-39; Fein, *Baltimore*, 148, 151-52; Szajkowski, *Jew. Mass Settlement*, 20; *YA*, 9:313; "United States," *JE*, 12:368; Bernheimer, *Russian Jew in the U. S.*, 64 ff.; *EAH*, 217; *Jewish People*, 4:245; New York *World*, June 4, 1882, copy in Marcus Collections; Rischin, *Promised City*, 98; Wischnitzer, *To Dwell in Safety*, 72 ff., 299-300; *Hebrew Emigrant Aid Society of the United States. Report of Moritz Ellinger* (N. Y., May 15, 1882); *Proceedings of the Hebrew Emigrant Aid Societies and Auxiliary Committees Representing the Various Cities of the United States and Canada, N. Y., June 4, 1882* (N. Y., 1882); Adler & Connolly, *Buffalo*, 169; Swichkow & Gartner, *Milwaukee*, 71 ff.; "Wisconsin," *UJE*, 10:534; Sachs, "Tales from the First Synagogue in Kansas City," 7; Rothschild, *Atlanta*, 21.

20. *PUAHC*, 3:2820-21; Sachar, *Modern Jewish History*, 310; Sklare, *Jew in American Society*, 46; Adler & Connolly, *Buffalo*, 221; *Der Zeitgeist*, 3 (1882):216-17; *AI*, May 26, 1882, p. 380, cs. 2-4; *CCARYB*, 17:160-66; *AJHS*, 53:99 ff., 119 ff.; Berman, "East European Immigration"; *AJA*, 3 (no. 1):13-14.

CHAPTER TWO
DISPERSAL AND COLONIES

1. AJA, 18:137; Michael, 3:23 ff.; Marcus, *EAJ*, 2:see Index sub "Colonization"; Marcus, *CAJ*, 3:see Index sub "Agriculture"; *PAJHS*, 23:178-79, 37:171 ff.; Sarna, *Mordecai Noah*, 61 ff.; Grinstein, *New York City*, 115 ff.; Baron, *History*, 2:339-40; *MGWJ*, 75:429 ff.; B. & B., *JOUS*, 3:906 ff.; Friedman, *EAJ*, 102 ff., 107; Schappes, *DHJUS*, 195-98; Schappes, *JIUS*, 69; P. & K., *Tourist's Guide*, 342, 365; Herscher, *Jewish Agricultural Utopias*, 28 ff.; "Agricultural Colonies in the United States," *JE*; Davidson, *Jewish Farmers*, 196 ff.; *Olde Ulster*, 8(no.6):161 ff.

2. N.M. Gelber, *Zur Vorgeschichte des Zionismus* (London, 1927), 176 ff.; *Occ.*, 1:28-32, 4:268 ff., 367; Baron, *History*, 2:339-40: *AZJ*, July 27, 1846, p.448, Mar. 2, 1857, pp.132-33, Oct. 30, 1960, p.653; *MGJW*, 75:429 ff.; *PAJHS*, 2:22-23, 11:118-19, 38:185 ff., 215 ff.; Goldmark, *Pilgrims of '48*, 207 ff.; William Rosenthall, "*Israel's Herold*: A Survey in Content & Spirit" (HUC term paper, 1956); Glanz, *The German Jew in America*, no.1820; *Amopteil*, 1:85-111; Grinstein, *New York City*, 123 ff.; Schappes, *DHJUS*, 662-64: Sigmund Watterman, *A Call to Establish a Hebrew Agricultural Society*, as cited in *Agricultural History*, 24:120-46; *AI*, June 15, 1855, p.389, c.4, Jan. 15, 1861, p.229, cs.3-4, Mar. 9, 1866, p.284, cs.3-4, Mar. 23, 1866, p.292, cs.3-4; Tarshish, "American Judaism," 85, xxiv, n.204; Herscher, *Jewish Agricultural Utopias*, 28-30; *AJHQ*, 39:61 ff.; Mrs. Perry Kallison, San Antonio, to JRM, Sept. 6, 1966, Marcus Collections.

3. *JM*, Oct. 15, 1869, p.4, cs.1-2, Dec. 10, 1869, p.4, c.1, July 25, 1879, p.3, c.1, May 28, 1880, p.4, c.2, June 4, 1880, p.4, cs.3-5; *Agricultural History*, 24:124; *AH*, Dec. 10, 1937, p.31; *AJHS*, 58:75; *AZJ*, Oct. 22, 1872, pp.854-55; *AJA*, 3 (no.1):15, 8:70-71; Schappes, *DHJUS*, 147 ff.; Tarshish, "American Judaism," 250, xxiv, n.204; Steven Alen Fox, "A Detailed Analysis of the Union of American Hebrew Congregations, Its Structure, Its Goals, And Its Accomplishments, 1873 to 1903" (rabbinical thesis, HUC, 1980), 92-93; *PUAHC*, 1:190, 249, 408, 570, 678 ff., 720 ff., 2:793, 1418-19; Clipping, July 1879, n.p., citing New York *Sun*, July 21, 1879, UAHC Scrapbook #3, p.58, AJAr; Phila. *Jewish Record*, July 25, 1879, UAHC Scrapbook, #3, p.58, AJAr; *AI*, July 25, 1879, p.4, cs.4-5, Aug. 29, 1879, p.4, c.5, p.5, c.1, May 21, 1880, p.4, c.6, p.5, c.1.

4. *Statistical History of U.S.*, 57; London *Jewish Chronicle*, Sept. 2, 1881, p.12, c.2; *AI*, Dec. 2, 1881, p.180, cs.3-6, Aug. 4, 1882, p.36, cs.4-6, Jan. 5, 1883, p.227, c.2; *PUAHC*, 2:785, 927, 1073, 1112 ff., 1129, 1143, 1156 ff., 1171 ff., 1275 ff., 1404-8, 1416-17, 1453, 1601, 1801, 3:1889; Henri E. Front, "The Union of American Hebrew Congregations and Agriculture, etc." (HUC term paper, 1955); *AJA*, 3(no.1):15.

5. *AJYB*, 4(1902-1903):115-16; *AJHS*, 60:355 ff.; Singer, "American Jew in Agriculture," Table of Contents, iv ff.

6. *AJA*, 17:150; "Proceedings of the Conference on the Writing of Regional History in the South," 117-117a; *New York History*, 54:109; *JSS*, 35:76; Joseph, *Jewish Immigration*, 164, 174; *Statistical History of U.S.*, 57, 74; Brandes & Douglas, *Immigrants to Freedom*, ix, 9; Wiernik, *History*, 266; Goldman Report, Hebrew Immigrant Aid Society, N.Y., May 31, 1882, Marcus Collections; *YA*, 4:9 ff.; *Der Zeitgeist*, 3(1882):94; *AI*, Dec. 2, 1881, p.180, cs.2-3.

7. "Agricultural Colonies in Russia," *JE*, 1:252 ff.; "Agricultural Colonies in the United States," *JE*; "Pinsker, Leo," *EOZAI*; *YA*, 4:9 ff., 20 ff., 16:356; *Jewish People*, 4:337; *AJHQ*, 39:237, 60:355 ff., 66:207; Sachar, *Modern Jewish History*, 305 ff.; *Education of Abraham Cahan*, 185-86, 198, 204 ff., 210, 246-47; "Am Olam," *EJ*, *EJ* (German); "United States," *JE*, 12:367; Singer, "American Jew in Agriculture"; *PAJHS*, 38:245 ff., 48:78 ff.

8. *AJYB*, 14(1912-1913):21 ff., 55 ff.; Bogen, *Jewish Philanthropy*, 125ff.; Brandes & Douglas, *Immigrants to Freedom*, 36ff.; *AJHQ*, 48:78 ff., 60:355 ff.; Eisenstein, *Zikhronothai*, 281; *WSJHQ*, 6:156; *Jewish People*, 4:32-33; *Amopteil*, 1:60-90; Davidson, *Jewish Farmers*, 194ff.; Grinstein, *New York City*, 115 ff.; Singer, "American Jew in Agriculture"; Levine & Miller, *American Jewish Farmer*, 7ff.; Levin, "East European Jews in U.S.," p.24; Arthur & Lila Weinberg, *Passport to Utopia: Great Panaceas in American History* (Chicago, 1968); *Agricultural History*, 24:120 ff., 145; Herscher, *Jewish Agricultural Utopias*, 28 ff.; "Agricultural Colonies in the United States," *JE*; "Colonies, Agricultural," *UJE*, 3:294 ff., "Louisiana," 7:208; *AH*, Feb. 2, 1917, p.416; Simonhoff, *Saga of American Jewry*, 143 ff.; Wiernik, *History*, 266-67; Leo Shpall, "A Jewish Agricultural

Colony in Louisiana," *Louisiana Historical Quarterly*, 20(1937):821-31; *Louisiana Inventory*, 106-7; *Hebrew Emigrant Aid Society of the United States. Report on the Formation of the First Russian Jewish Colony in the United States at Catahoula Parish, Louisiana, By J. Stanwood Menken, President*, Jan. 9, 1882, (pamphlet, London, 1882).

9. Joseph, *Jewish Immigration*, 164; *AJHQ*, 60:373 ff., 378-79, 61:325 ff.; *Jewish People*, 4:337-38; Nodel, *The Ties Between*, 64; *Education of Abraham Cahan*, 267, 339 ff.; *JM*, Jan. 26, 1883, p.2, c.5; *Yalkut Maarabi*, 1:46 ff.; *YA*, 4:28 ff.; Herscher, *Jewish Agricultural Utopias*, 37 ff., 52-55.

10. Uchill, *Pioneers*, 174-83; "Agricultural Colonies in the United States," *JE*, 1:258; *AJA*, 8:91; Breck, *Colorado*, 274 ff.; *Agricultural History*, 24:135-37; *JM*, Jan. 5, 1883, p.31, c.1; *Der Zeitgeist*, 3(1882):300-1; P. & K., *Tourist's Guide*, 72; Herscher, *Jewish Agricultural Utopias*, 55-61.

11. Uchill, *Pioneers*, 177-83; Singer, "American Jew in Agriculture," 507-9; Breck, *Colorado*, 157 ff.

12. Schlesinger, *Rise of the City*, 27; "Colonies, Agricultural," *UJE*, 3:294 ff.; "Agricultural Colonies in the United States," *JE*, 1:259; P. & K., *Tourist's Guide*, 484 ff., 581-83; *AJYB*, 14(1912-1913):55 ff., 60; Herscher, *Jewish Agricultural Utopias*, 48-52, 70 ff.; *Agricultural History*, 24:131-33, 137-38; *Jewish People*, 4:337; *AJA*, 8:105 ff., 23:47 ff.; London *Jewish Chronicle*, Oct. 3, 1884, p.7; *Jewish Digest*, 13(no.11):53 ff.; *North Dakota History*, 32:59 ff., 217 ff.; *WSJHQ*, 10:266 ff.; Curti et al., *American History*, 2:132; Plaut, *Jews in Minnesota*, chaps. 14-15.

13. P. & K., *Tourist's Guide*, 182-83; *AI*, Feb. 3, 1882, p.252, c.6, p.253, c.1, June 30, 1882, p.420, cs.1-3, July 28, 1882, p.29, c.2, Jan. 5, 1883, p.277, c.2, July 20, 1883, p.5, cs.2-4, Nov. 20, 1885, p.4, c.1; *WSJHQ*, 3:157 ff.; *PUAHC*, 2:1406 ff., see Index sub "Agricultural Pursuits"; Nathan Isaacs, Boston/Cambridge, to J.D. Eisenstein, N.Y.?, Dec. 23, 1929, copy in Marcus Collections; *AJHQ*, 60:159 ff.; *AJYB*, 14(1912-1913):62; *Agricultural History*, 24:139-40; "Colonies, Agricultural," *UJE*, 3:294; "Agricultural Colonies in the United States," *JE*, 1:259; *AJA*, 17:114 ff.; Topeka *Daily Capital*, Aug. 10, 1958, p.12A, copy in Marcus Collections.

14. Fein, *Baltimore*, 150-51; *JM*, May 25, 1883, p.5, cs.5-6; "Agricultural Colonies in the United States," *JE*, 1:259; Newsletter of the Jewish Historical Society of Maryland, Feb. 1975, p.7, copy in Marcus Collections.

15. "Agricultural Colonies in the United States," *JE*, 1:260-62; Eisenberg, *Eyewitnesses to American Jewish History*, 3:13 ff.; London *Jewish Chronicle*, Oct. 3. 1884, p.7; *AJYB*, 4(1902-1903):76, 14(1912-1913):62 ff.; Brandes & Douglas, *Immigrants to Freedom*, 6 ff., 10 ff.; Morais, *Philadelphia*, 212 ff.; *Agricultural History*, 24:140-45; Davidson, *Jewish Farmers*, 249-55; *AJHQ*, 60:360 ff.; "Colonies, Agricultural," *UJE*, 3:295-96, "New Jersey," 8:169; *Ner Ha-Maarabi*, 2:13 ff., 64 ff., 135-36; Goldstein, *Jewish Colonies of South Jersey*; Moses Klein, *Migdal Zophim (The Watch Tower). The Jewish Problem and Agriculture as its Solution* (Phila., 1889), 41 ff.; Wiernik, *History*, 269; Singer, "American Jews in Agriculture," Table of Contents, pp.247-318; "Alliance, New Jersey," *JE*; Herscher, *Jewish Agricultural Utopias*, 73 ff.; *Michael*, 3:59 ff.; Bernheimer, *Russian Jew in the U.S.*, 376 ff.; *Reports, Ind. Com.*, 15:510 ff.

16. Chiel, "Jewish Life in America as seen through 'Hamelitz' "; *AJHQ*, 63:197; *WSJHQ*, 10:159 ff., 343 ff., 13:130 ff.; Mallinger, "Kreiner Interview"; Singer, "American Jew in Agriculture," 359-74, 528-29, 540 ff.; Hertzberg, *Atlanta*, 76-77, *Michigan Jewish History*, 49(no.2):14 ff.; *Michigan History*, 56:119 ff.; Detroit *Jewish News*, Apr. 25, 1969, p.22, cs.1-4; P. & K., *Tourist's Guide*, 246-47; *PAJHS*, 29:61-74; *Agricultural History*, 24:145; Herscher, *Jewish Agricultural Utopias*, 61-70.

17. *Michael*, 3:59 ff.; Herscher, *Jewish Agricultural Utopias*, 89 ff.; Joseph, *Baron de Hirsch Fund*, 48 ff.; *AJHQ*, 56:151 ff.; P. & K., *Tourist's Guide*, 309-9, 327-28; Singer, "American Jew in Agriculture," 300-10; "Sabsovich, Hirsch Leib," "Woodbine," *UJE*;

Sabsovich, *Adventures in Idealism*; Wiernik, *History*, 269; "Colonies, Agricultural," *UJE*, 3:296; *Ner Ha-Maarabi*, 2(1897):130 ff.; *Reports, Ind. Com.*, 15(1901):lxxvi, 510 ff.; *Final Report of the Industrial Commission*, 19(1902):50-51; *American Jews' Annual for 5653 A.M.* (1892-93), 58 ff., 87-90; Elbogen, *Cent. of Jewish Life*, 337-38; *AH*, Nov. 24, 1905, pp.854-60, Mar. 12, 1915, p.492; "Agricultural Colonies in the United States," *JE*, 1:262, "United States," 12:361-62; Goldstein, *Jewish Colonies of South Jersey*, 19-24, 29, 35; Morais, *Philadelphia*, 213; *National Jewish Monthly*, 80(no.11):11.

18. P. & K., *Tourist's Guide*, 636; *AJA*, 30:3 ff.

19. "Colonies, Agricultural," *UJE*, 3:296; Singer, "American Jew in Agriculture," 511 ff.; Auerbach, "Nebraska," 8, 57-58; P. & K., *Tourist's Guide*, 657.

20. "Colonies, Agricultural," *UJE*, 3:296, "Wisconsin," 10:534; Watters, *Utah*, 168-69; Singer, "American Jew in Agriculture," 374-95; Dr. Lou Silberman, Omaha, to JRM, Sept. 13, 1948, Marcus Collections; *AH*, Dec. 10, 1937, p.31; Mallinger, "Kreiner Interview"; Auerbach, "Nebraska," 8-9, 67 ff.; P. & K., *Tourist's Guide*, 648; *AJA*, 30:3 ff.

21. Brandes & Douglas, *Immigrants to Freedom*, 350, 354-55;*Menorah*, 15:3 ff.; B. & B., *JOUS*, 3:747 ff.; London *Jewish Chronicle*, Oct. 3, 1884, p.7.

22. Singer, "American Jew in Agriculture," Table of Contents, iv-viii; *Journal of Southern History*, 48:457-58; Tarbell, *Nationalizing of Business*, chap. 13; Schlesinger, *Rise of the City*, 199; Wish, *Society and Thought*, 2:114; Herscher, *Jewish Agricultural Utopias*, 112 ff.; *Ner Ha-Maarabi*, 2:183 ff.; *AJYB*, 14(1912-1913):62-63; *AJA*, 34:117; London *Jewish Chronicle*, Oct. 3, 1884, p.7; *AJHQ*, 60:361-62, 368, 382; *WSJHQ*, 13:134; *Agricultural History*, 24:127; Goldman Report, Hebrew Immigrant Aid Society, N.Y., May 31, 1882, copy in Marcus Collections; Jewish Agricultural Society Release, Aug. 22, 1947, "Jews in Agriculture in the United States," copy in Marcus Collections.

23. Marcus, *EAJ*, 287, 291-92; Auerbach, "Nebraska," 4; *AI*, Nov. 9, 1860, p.148, cs.1-3; Morris & Freund, *Trends*, 43 ff.; Bernheimer, *Russian Jew in the U.S.*, 37, 388 ff.; Schappes, *JIUS*, 125-26; Ada Sterling, *The Jew and Civilization* (N.Y., 1924), 240 ff.; *AJA*, 33:7 ff., 35 ff.; Bogen, *Jewish Philanthropy*, 125 ff.; Davidson, *Jewish Farmers*, 6 ff.; *Agricultural History*, 24:120 ff.; *AJYB*, 14(1912-1913):21 ff.; *Commonweal*, 41:120 ff.; *Jewish People*, 2:69 ff.

24. *AH*, July 21, 1899, p.340, July 28, 1899, pp.365-66, Aug. 18, 1899, pp.462 ff.; Julius Rosenwald, Chicago, to Harry B. Hirsh, Phila., Apr. 28, 1922, Rosenwald Papers, University of Chicago, copy in Marcus Collections; P. & K., *Tourist's Guide*, 535; *AJHS*, 67:342 ff.; "National Farm School, The," *UJE*; Beifield, "Joseph Krauskopf," 45 ff.; "Krauskopf, Joseph," *DAB*; Blood, *Joseph Krauskopf*, 93 ff.; Davidson, *Jewish Farmers*, 264 ff.

25. *AJHQ*, 61:78 ff.; "Sabsovich, Hirsch Leib," *UJE*; P. & K., *Tourist's Guide*, 327-28; Herscher, *Jewish Agricultural Utopias*, 88 ff., 104; Sabsovich, *Adventures in Idealism*; Eisenberg, *Eyewitnesses to American Jewish History*, 3:57 ff.; *AH*, July 25, 1947, p.13.

26. "Hirsch, Baron de," *JE, UJE, EJ*; Samuel J. Lee, *Moses of the New World: The Work of Baron de Hirsch* (N.Y., 1970); Detroit *Jewish News*, May 6, 1983, p.26; Joseph, *Baron de Hirsch Fund*, 10-22, 275-77; Kurt Grunwald, *Tuerkenhirsch: A Study of Baron Maurice de Hirsch, Entrepreneur and Philanthropist* (N.Y., 1966), 63 ff.; "England," *EJ*, 5:173; *AH*, July 25, 1947, p.15; "Jewish Colonization Association," *JE, UJE, EJ*; Sachar, *Modern Jewish History*, 510-11; "Seattle," *UJE*, 9:450; "Memphis," *JE, UJE, EJ*, 60:26, n.74.

27. "Jewish Colonization Association," *JE, UJE, EJ*; Joseph, *Baron de Hirsch Fund*, 278 ff.; *AH*, Mar. 12, 1915, pp.491-92, July 25, 1947, pp.5 ff.; *PAJHS*, 48:236. There is correspondence on the founding of the BDHF in the Oscar Straus Papers in the LC, especially for the years, 1888-1890; P. & K., *Tourist's Guide*, 328; *AJYB*, 14(1912-1913):67 ff.; "United States," *JE*, 12:361-62; *National Jewish Monthly*, 80(no.11):11-12.

28. Joseph, *Baron de Hirsch Fund*, 116 ff.; Elbogen, *Cent. of Jewish Life*, 334-35; *PUAHC*, 2:1801; *AH*, July 25, 1947, p.14; "Jewish Agricultural Society, Inc., The," "Jewish Farmers of America, Federation of," *UJE*; *Jewish People*, 2:69-70; "New York," *JE*, 9:287; *AJYB*, 4(1902-1903):111 ff.

29. *WSJHQ*, 9:219 ff., 12:31-32, 123; Uchill, *Pioneers*, 183-84.

30. P. & K., *Tourist's Guide*, 84, 23:47 ff.; *Eastern Union*, 103; *Final Report of the Industrial Commission*, 19(1902):50-51; *Reports, Ind. Com.*, 15:510; *WSJHQ*, 10:166-67: *Ner Ha-Maarabi*, 2:179 ff.; P. & K., *Tourist's Guide*, 315; Levine & Miller, *American Jewish Farmer*, 49-70; "Agriculture," *EJ*, 2:411-12; Singer, "American Jew in Agriculture," iv-viii, 197-247; *Agriculture History*, 24:145.

31. Singer, "American Jew in Agriculture," 174-96; Advertisement of the New York, Ontario & Western Railway, copy in Marcus Collections; Joseph, *Baron de Hirsch Fund*, 164-68; *Agricultural History*, 55:31 ff., esp. 34; Marcus, *AJWD*, 671 ff.; Levine & Miller, *American Jewish Farmer*, 70 ff.; P. & K., *Tourist's Guide*, 357-58; "New York," *UJE* 8:197-98; *New York Times*, May 14, 1974, p.40, cs.3-4; *Jewish Post and Opinion*, Nov. 8, 1968, p.1; *Jewish Digest*, 1 (no.8):21 ff.; *National Jewish Monthly*, 73(no.6):17 ff., 77(no.2):16 ff.; *Commentary*, 18:147 ff.; Joel Pomerantz, *Jennie and the Story of Grossinger's* (N.Y., 1970); Harold Jaediker Taub, *Waldorf in the Catskills: The Grossinger Legend* (N.Y., 1952); *50 Golden Years: The Ellenville Hebrew Aid Society 1907-1957* (Ellenville, N.Y., 1959); Oscar Straus, Washington, to Edward B.M. Browne, Columbus, Ga., June 15, 1906, Straus Papers, LC.

32. "Heilprin, Michael," *JE*, *UJE*; Pollak, *Michael Heilprin*; P. & K., *Tourist's Guide*, 34, 48 ff.; "Lubin, David," *UJE*, *DAB*; Olivia Rossetti Agresti, *David Lubin: A Study in Practical Idealism* (Boston, 1922).

33. Leonard G. Robinson, N.Y., to J. Rosenwald, Chicago, Mar. 6, 1916, Rosenwald Papers, Univ. of Chicago, copy in Marcus Collections. Biographies of the above soil scientists are found in the standard biographical lexica; *AJYB*, 51:523-24; *New York Times*, Apr. 20, 1939, p.23, c.1; "Lipman, Jacob Goodale," *DAB*.

34. Cowen, *Memories of an American Jew*, 100-1; "Missouri," *UJE*, 7:590; *Jewish Post and Opinion*, Aug. 28, 1970, p.4. For very successful Jewish farmers in New England in the mid-twentieth century, see Levine & Miller, *American Jewish Farmer*, 51 ff.; "Fishman, Simon," Glassman (ed.), *BEOAJ 1935*; P. & K., *Tourist's Guide*, 187-88; *North Dakota History*, 32:226-27.

35. Singer, "American Jew in Agriculture," 152 ff.; *AJYB*, 14(1912-1913):63 ff., 77 ff., 50:21; Goldstein, *Jewish Colonies of South Jersey*, 29; Levine & Miller, *American Jewish Farmer*, 16, 19, 21; Jewish Agricultural Society news release, n.d., "Some Facts About the Jewish Farm Movement in the United States," copy in Marcus Collections; Soltes, *Contemporary Jew. Hist.*, 37 ff.; *JSS*, 6:405-6; *Commonweal*, 41:120 ff.; *Reports, Immig. Com. Abstracts*, 1:552, 575 ff., 760; Wittke, *We Who Built America*, 334-35; *Reports, Ind. Com.*, 15(1901):516.

36. Marcus, *EAJ*, 2:277 ff.; Fein, *Baltimore*, 150; Schappes, *DHJUS*, 196-200; *Jewish Life*, 9(no.1):2l; *PAJHS*, 40:235 ff., 272-73, 49:127; *Historia Judaica*, 22:140; Adler & Connolly, *Buffalo*, 170; Swichkow & Gartner, *Milwaukee*, 73, 158; *AJHQ*, 62:253; *AH*, July 25, 1947, p.5 ff.

37. Elbogen, *Cent. of Jewish Life*, 336; *AJHQ*, 53:127-28, 64:331 ff.; M. Kohler, N.Y., to Mortimer Schiff, Oct. 14, 1925, copy in Marcus Collections; Joseph, *Baron de Hirsch Fund*, 22, 128-29; *Jewish Charities*, 1(no.9):7-8; *AH*, Mar. 12, 1915, p 491-92; Morais, *Philadelphia*, 209. "Sulzberger," "East European Jews"; *AI*, July 26, 1900, p.7, c.2.

38. "Industrial Removal Office," *UJE*; *Michigan Jewish History*, 10(no.2):32-35; *Michael*, 3:156; Morris & Freund, *Trends*, 34 ff.; Joseph, *Baron de Hirsch Fund*, 184 ff.; *Reports, Immig. Com.*, 15:514-15; *AJYB*, 50:28; Uchill, *Pioneers*, 138, 185; "Jewish Charities," *Americana*; Handlin, *Adventure in Freedom*, 105; *Where We Stand*, 6-7; *PAJHS*, 40:235 ff.,

48:119, 49:127; Auerbach, "Nebraska," 7, 56-57; "Nebraska," *UJE*, 8:138; Rosenthal, *Des Moines*, 84-85; Adler, *Kansas City*, 87; Szajkowski, *Jew. Mass Settlement*, 12-13; Sachar, *Modern Jewish History*, 316; "New York," *JE*, 9:287; Breck, *Colorado*, 107-8.

39. *PUAHC*, 6:5640 ff.; Joseph, *Jewish Immigration*, 174; Morris & Freund, *Trends*, 39 ff.; Bernheimer, *Russian Jew in the U.S.*, 369; Jacob H. Schiff, N.Y., to Oscar Straus, Washington, D.C., Jan. 22, 1907, Straus Papers, LC; *Juedische Volkstimme*, Apr. 1, 1906, p.4; Jacob H. Schiff, N.Y., to M. Sulzberger, Phila., Sept. 27, 1906, AJAr; Jacob Schiff, N.Y., to Israel Zangwill, London, Aug. 24, 1906, AJAr.

40. *AJA*, 30:43 ff.; *AJHQ*, 60:12 ff., 14, 23, 27, 32; Dreyfus, *Henry Cohen*, 22 ff., 58-59, 72, 123; *Golden Jubilee Program in Commemoration of Fiftieth Anniversary, Dr. Henry Cohen as Rabbi, Congregation B'nai Israel, etc.* (Galveston, Texas. 1938); "Cohen, Henry," *UJE*; *AI*, Apr. 2, 1908, p.4, cs.6-7.

41. *AJA*, 30:43 ff., 75; *AJYB*, 13(1911-1912):129.

42. *WSJHQ*, 12:220 ff., 308 ff.; *CCARYB*, 33:425; *AJHS*, 60:26-36, 63:15, 19, 22-23, 29, 38-39, 67:294; *PAJHS*, 49:127; Horwich, *My First Eighty Years*, 202-3; "Kehillah Movement," *UJE*; Wischnitzer, *To Dwell in Safety*, 127 ff.; Goodman, "American Jewish Life," 37 ff.; Szajkowski, *Jew. Mass Settlement*, 12-13; "Industrial Removal Office," *UJE*; "Industrial Removal," *EJ*; Uchill, *Pioneers*, 185; Morris & Freund, *Trends*, 39 ff.; Anne Nathan & Harry I. Cohen, *The Man Who Stayed in Texas: The Life of Rabbi Henry Cohen* (N.Y., 1941), 189 ff., 198 ff., 313-14; Dreyfus, *Henry Cohen*, 58 ff.; Joseph, *Baron de Hirsch Fund*, 205 ff.; *Detroit Jewish News*, Oct. 14, 1983, p.77; Marinbach, *Ellis Island of the West*, 1 ff.; Phila. *Jewish Exponent*, Aug. 5. 1910, pp.1 ff.; Simon Wolf, Washington, D.C., to Benjamin S. Cable, July 27, 1910, AJAr; *Freeland*, 21:10 ff.; David N. Bressler, N.Y., to Israel Zangwill, London, Dec.17, 1913, Apr. 16, 1914, July 3, 1914, AJAr; Alfred Hampton, Galveston, to D.N. Bressler, N.Y., Nov. 17, 1911, copy in Marcus Collections: Henry Cohen, Galveston, to D.N. Bressler, N.Y., Nov. 15, 1911, copy in Marcus Collections; Jacob H. Schiff, N.Y., to Henry Cohen, Galveston, Nov. 22, 1911, copy in Marcus Collections; *AH*, July 25, 1947, pp.12-13; D.N. Bressler, N.Y., to Jacob Billikopf, Kansas City, Nov. 7, 1912, AJAr. The Zangwill correspondence with Oscar Straus in the Straus Papers in the LC will throw light on the Galveston Movement. Galveston *Daily News*, June 13, 1952, pp.1-2; Adler, *Jacob H. Schiff*, 2:94 ff.; *AI*, Apr. 2, 1908, p.4, cs.6-7; Henry Cohen, *The Galveston Immigration Movement, 1907-1910* (pamphlet, Galveston, 1908); Bernheimer, *Russian Jew in the U.S.*, 366, 369; *AJYB*, 57:24; Leo Shpall, *The Galveston Experiment* (N.Y., n.d.); Max Kohler, N.Y., to George W. Wickersham, Washington, D.C., Nov. 20, 1922, AJAr; *Dept. of Commerce and Labor, Bureau of Immigration and Naturalization, Washington, D.C. to Commissioners of Immigration and Inspectors in Charge of Ports of Entry*, June 21, 1910; *Wohin*, Yiddish magazine, Kiev, 1911-12. This magazine contains data on Galveston.

43. *AJYB*, 24:312, 50:28; *AJHQ*, 60:143, 64:341 ff.; Morris & Freund, *Trends*, 34 ff.; Swichkow & Gartner, *Milwaukee*, 158; Adler & Connolly, *Buffalo*, 438, n.20; P. & K., *Tourist's Guide*, 636; Sachar, *Modern Jewish History*, 316; *AH*, Mar. 31, 1911, pp.637-38, July 25, 1947, pp.5 ff.; Bernheimer, *Russian Jew in the U.S.*, 370-71; Rischin, *Promised City*, 92.

CHAPTER THREE

PART I: THE EAST EUROPEANS IN THE HINTERLAND TO 1921

1. Hertzberg, *Atlanta*, 76; *AJHQ*, 53:100.
2. *Nebraska History*, 63:476 ff.; Biography of Robert E. Segal, Newton Highlands, Mass., AJAr; *AJA*, 17:179.

3. "Seattle," *UJE*, 9:451; *AJA*, 19:3 ff.; "Oregon," "Portland," *UJE*; Nodel, *The Ties Between*, 47-48; Suwol, *Oregon*, 5.
4. *AH*, Apr. 1, 1904, pp.630-31, Apr. 8, 1904, pp. 660-61, Apr. 15, 1904, pp.686-687; "United States," *JE*, 12:369; Benjamin, *Three Years*, 1:210; *AJYB*, 21:341-42, 344, 25:340; *AI*, Nov. 21, 1856, p.154, c.4, p.155, c.1; Marcus & Peck (eds.), *Studies in the American Jewish Experience*, 1:78 ff.; *WSJHQ*, 10:24-26, 14:302 ff.; *Reports, Immig. Com. Abstracts*, 1:625.
5. *Congress Bi-Weekly*, Mar. 30, 1959, pp.13 ff.; *AI*, Sept. 25, 1913, p.5, c.1; "Hawaii," *EJ*; Arizona *Post*, Apr. 30, 1965, AJAr; St. Louis *Jewish Light*, July 14, 1982, pp.4 ff., AJAr; *AJYB*, 2(1900-1901):623, 87:167; *World Over*, Apr. 17, 1959, pp.3, 11; *AZJ*, Sept. 30, 1879, p.635; "Hawaiian Islands," *UJE*; *Dedication Temple Emanu-El, Honolulu, 1960-5720* (Honolulu, 1960), Marcus Collections; Boston *Jewish Advocate*, Mar. 26, 1959, pp.1, 14; Heinrich Kurtzig, *Ostdeutsches Judentum* (Stolp, Germany, 1927), 61-62.
6. *Jewish Digest*, 4(no.1):15 ff.; *Congress Weekly*, July 21, 1958, pp.6 ff.; *JTA-DNB*, Mar. 26, 1959, p.4; *Jewish Post and Opinion*, Apr. 1, 1960, p.4, cs.1-2, Apr. 22, 1960, p.15, cs.1-2; "Alaska," *UJE*, *EJ*; *AJYB*, 4(1902-1903):21-22, 6(1904-1905):106-7, 61:165 ff., 87:167, 180; *Keeping Posted*, 31(no.1):11 ff.; *AI*, Aug. 14, 1986, p.4, cs.3-4; *World Over*, Jan. 29, 1959, p.1; "Gruening, Ernest," *UJE*; Samuel P. Johnston (ed.), *Alaska Commercial Company, 1968-1940* (San Francisco?, 1940); Gregory Blattman, Alaska: Seven Arts Feature Syndicate release, 1937, copy in Marcus Collections; *Journal of the West*, 4:504 ff.; P. & K., *Tourist's Guide*, 635; *Jewish Frontier*, 25(no.9, sec.1):13 ff.; Robert and Jessie S. Bloom Papers, AJAr; Rudolf Glanz, *The Jews in American Alaska (1867-1880)* (N.Y., 1953); *Pacific Historian*, 28:5 ff.; John H. Davis, *The Guggenheims: An American Epic* (N.Y., 1978); Heinrich Kurtzig, *Ostdeutsches Judentum* (Stolp, Germany, 1927), 54-58; David Goldberg, "A History of the Jews of Alaska" (HUC term paper, 1988).
7. "Alexander, Moses," "Montana," *UJE*; *AJYB*, 1(1899-1900):174-75, 82:167; Brooks, *Jews in Utah and Idaho*, 136; *PAJHS*, 21:359; Marcus, *AJWD*, 2:630-38; "Wyoming," *UJE*, *EJ*.
8. "Nevada," "Wyoming," *UJE*, *EJ*; Noem Veta biography file, AJAr; *AJA*, 8:125-26; P. & K., *Tourist's Guide*, 656-58; Wyoming *Eagle*, July 21, 1959, AJAr; *AH*, Sept. 10, 1926, p.526; *U.A.H.C. Statistics*, 53.
9. Stocker, *Jewish Roots in Arizona*, 31; *AJYB*, 9(1907-1908):127, 25:338; *U.A.H.C. Statistics*, 54-55; "Arizona," "Goldwater," "New Mexico," *EJ*.
10. "Salt Lake," "Utah," *UJE*; Watters, *Utah*, 137; *WSJHQ*, 8:203 ff.; *U.A.H.C. Statistics*, 55; Brooks, *Jews in Utah and Idaho*, 109 ff.; Uchill, *Pioneers*, 294.
11. *AJA*, 11:190 ff.; *AJYB*, 21:346-47; "Denver," "Kauver, Charles Eliezer Hillel," *UJE*; Uchill, *Pioneers*, 168-71, 200 ff., 204 ff., 212 ff., 223 ff., 227-28; 284 ff.; Breck, *Colorado*, 80 ff., 88 ff., 111-13, 118, 135 ff., 145 ff., 261; "Colorado," *JE*, *UJE*; *Jewish Post and Opinion*, June 13, 1958, p.16; W. Lovelace, *Jesse Shwayder and the Golden Rule* (Denver, 1960), 3 ff., 59.
12. P. & K., *Tourist's Guide*, 580-81, 584-85; "North Dakota," "South Dakota," *UJE*; Robert J. Lazar, "From Ethnic Minority to Socio-Economic Elite: A Study of the Jewish Community of Fargo, North Dakota" (Ph.D. diss., U. of Minnesota, 1968); "United States," *JE*, 12:355-56; *AJYB*, 21:524-25; "Memoirs of [I.] Papermaster translated and edited by his son David" (typescript, Boston, 1959), AJAr.
13. Sachs, "Tales from the First Synagogue in Kansas City"; Elias Eppstein, "Diaries," MS, 1871-1903, pp.54, 224, AJAr; *AJYB*, 9(1907-1908):181-82, 21:375; "Kansas," *UJE*, *EJ*; *U.A.H.C. Statistics*, 47; Elbert L. Sapinsley interview of Myer Scrinopskie, Apr. 17, 1961, Topeka, Kansas, copy in Marcus Collections.
14. *AJYB*, 9(1907-1908):238-40; *Nebraska History*, 63:474 ff.; "Lincoln," "Nebraska," *UJE*; "Omaha," *UJE*, *EJ*; Eisenstadt, *Hakme Yisrael be-Amerika*, 30; Auerbach, "Nebraska," 7, 16, 24 ff., 39 ff.; "Sorensen," *WWIA*, 1986- 1987; Carol Gendler, "Jews of Omaha: The First Sixty Years" (MA thesis, U. of Omaha, 1968), 114-18.

15. "Oklahoma City," "Tulsa," *UJE*; Randall M. Falk, "A History of the Jews of Oklahoma with special emphasis on the Tulsa Jewish Community" (rabbinical thesis, HUC, 1946), 11, 16-19, 22; "Oklahoma," *UJE, EJ*; *AJYB*, 5(19031904):45, 21:535-36, 605; P. & K., *Tourist's Guide*, 510 ff.

16. *U.A.H.C. Statistics*, 55; Samuel Mittenthal interview by JRM, Dallas (?), Texas, Apr. 14, 1939, Marcus Collections; "Texas," *JE, UJE, EJ*; *AJYB*, 1(1899-1900):256- 63, 21:567 ff., 25:338; Galveston *Daily News*, Feb. 8, 1914, p.20; Eichhorn, *Evangelizing*, 117-18; "Dallas," "Fort Worth," "Galveston," "Houston," "San Antonio," *UJE, EJ*; "El Paso," *EJ*; "Galveston," "San Antonio," "Waco," *JE*.

17. *AJYB*, 21:340-41; "Arkansas," *JE, UJE, EJ*; *AJA*, 33:105 ff.

18. Eisenstadt, *Hakme Yisrael be-Amerika*, 9; *Bulletin*, Missouri Historical Society, 27(Oct. 1970):69 ff.; *AJYB*, 1(1899-1900):171 ff., 21:411 ff.; "Kansas City," "Sachar, Abram Leon," *UJE, EJ*; "Saint Joseph," *UJE*; "Saint Louis," *JE, UJE, EJ*; Z. Abrams, *The Book of Memories* (N.Y., 1932); Adler, *Kansas City*, 137, 142-44; Joseph P. Schultz (ed.), *Mid-America's Promise: A Profile of Kansas City Jewry* (Kansas City, 1982), 91.

19. *Louisiana Inventory*, 42, 118, 121, 127; "Shreveport," *UJE*; "Louisiana," "New Orleans," *UJE, EJ*; *AJYB*, 1(1899-1900):140 ff.; "Lisitzky, Ephraim E.," "Zemurray, Samuel," *EJ*; Benjamin Kaplan, *The Eternal Stranger: A Study of Jewish Life in the Small Community* (N.Y., 1957), 154; P. & K., *Tourist's Guide*, 205-6.

20. *AJYB*, 21:409-11, 25:339; "Alabama," "Mississippi," *UJE, EJ*; Phillipsborn, *Vicksburg*, 41 ff., 70-71; *Mississippi Inventory*, 20-24; Leo E. and Evelyn Turitz, *Jews in Early Mississippi* (Jackson, Miss., 1983); Elovitz, *Birmingham*, 53 ff., 59-61; "Birmingham," "Mobile," "Montgomery," *UJE*.

21. "Hart, Myer," *BDEAJ*; *AJYB*, 21:355-56, 25:338, 85:184; "Jacksonville," "Miami," *UJE, EJ*; "Proceedings of the Conference on the Writing of Regional History in the South," 81 ff., 117 ff.

22. *AJYB*, 1(1899-1900):122 ff., 5(1903-1904):80, 21:356-58, 605; Hertzberg, *Atlanta*, 73 ff., 86 ff., 89, 111, 125, 149, 245 ff.; *AJH*, 62:250 ff.; "Atlanta," "Georgia," "Savannah," *UJE, EJ*.

23. Elzas, *Jews of S.C.*, 188, 261, n.1; R. & E., *Charleston*, 194 ff., 207 ff., 214, 229-30; *JM*, Aug. 11, 1882, p.5, c.4; "Charleston," "South Carolina," *UJE*; Lawrenceville *News Herald*, June 17, 1898 and other newspaper cuttings on Nicholas Eugene Lugoff, Marcus Collections: Charleston *News and Currier*, July 20, 1899, Columbia, S.C. *State*, June 30, 1899, copies in Marcus Collections; *United States Official Postal Guide, July 1947* (Part 1, Washington, D.C., 1947), 380.

24. "North Carolina," *UJE, EJ*; *YA*, 16:192; Hugh Talmage Lefler & Albert Ray Newsome, *North Carolina: A History of a Southern State* (Chapel Hill, N.C., 1954), 481-82; William Kenneth Boyd, *The Story of Durham: City of the New South* (Durham, 1927), 87-88, 203-4; Eli N. Evans, *The Provincials: A Personal History of the Jews in the South* (N.Y., 1973), 13 ff.; Golden, *Jewish Roots in the Carolinas*, 44 ff.; *AJYB*, 21:523 ff.

25. "Chattanooga," "Knoxville," "Nashville," "Tennessee," *UJE*; "Memphis," "Tennessee," *JE, EJ*; *AJYB*, 1(1899-1900):254 ff., 21:565-67; Landau, *Louisville*, 52, et passim; Sam Shankman, *Baron Hirsch Congregation: From UR to Memphis* (Memphis, 1957), 37 ff.; *Tennessee Inventory*, 21-22, 25-35; Frank, *Nashville*, 103 ff., 149 ff., 155 ff.

26. "Kentucky," *JE, UJE, EJ*; "Louisville," *UJE, EJ*; *AJYB*, 1(1899-1900):138 ff., 5(1903-1904):107, 21:376-78; Landau, *Louisville*, 51 ff.; Rosenthal, *Des Moines*, 197, n.27; Eisenstadt, *Hakme Yisrael be-Amerika*, 52.

27. *AJYB*, 1(1899-1900):269, 21:578-79; Shinedling, *West Virginia Jewry*, 1:364 ff., 2:527 ff., 538, 552, 661 ff., 667, 983 ff., 1120, 3:1492 ff.; "West Virginia," *JE, UJE, EJ*. For the Marcuses of Farmington, West Virginia, see the Index to Shinedling, *West Virginia Jewry*, under the "Marcus" entries.

28. *AJYB*, 3(1901-1902):151, 21:573 ff., 26:576; Ginsberg, *Petersburg*, 65 ff.; Marcus, *AJD*, 51 ff.; "Richmond," "Virginia," *JE, UJE*; Ginsberg, *Jews of Virginia*, 82, 89; E. & L., *Richmond*, 275 ff., 279-80; Myron Berman, *Richmond's Jewry, 1769-1976* (Charlottesville, Va., 1979), 265 ff., 270.

29. *AJYB*, 1(1899-1900):142 ff., 146, 151 ff., 155, 3(1901-1902):137, 21:382 ff.; *Newsletter of the Jewish Historical Society of Maryland*, Feb. 1975, p.6; *Baltimore Jewish Times*, Sept. 30, 1928, p.2; Fein, *Baltimore*, 141, 157, 173-74, 187, 197, 221-23; "Baltimore," *JE, EJ*; "Wolman, Abel," *WWIAJ*, 1980; Blum, *Baltimore*, 181 ff., 269, 360; "Maryland," *EJ*; "Epstein, Jacob," *UJE*; Avrum K. Rifman, "Centennial of Eastern European Jewish Immigration, 1882-1982, etc." (typescript lecture, Rockville, Md., 1982), copy in Marcus Collections, 3, 8, 25-26; Constitution, Congregation Hevra B'nai Abraham, Hagarstown, Maryland, (est.) 1892, copy in Marcus Collections; *Reports, Immig. Com. Abstracts*, 1:516.

30. Grinstein, *New York City*, 145; *AJYB*, 1(1899-1900):120-21, 21:354-55; *Washington Record*, 3:5 ff., 9:16 ff., 20 ff.; "Washington, D.C.," *JE, UJE, EJ*.

CHAPTER FOUR

PART II: THE EAST EUROPEANS IN THE HINTERLAND TO 1921

1. "Mordecai, Mordecai M.," "Solomon, Hyam," *BDEAJ; JSS*, 9:152; Lois G. Michaels, "Historical Study of the Growth and Development of the Montefiore Hospital Association of Western Pennsylvania, 1906-1963" (MS thesis, U. of Pittsburgh, 1963), 22 ff.; Feldman, *Jew. Experience in Western Pa.*, 33 ff., 240-41, 252 ff., 278-79, et passim; Markens, *Hebrews*, 154 ff.; Smill, "The Stogy Industry" (M.A. thesis, Carnegie Institute of Technology, Pittsburgh, 1920); "Delaware," "Pittsburgh," *JE, UJE, EJ; AJYB*, 1(1899-1900):236-52, 3(1901-1902):131, 9(1907-1908):120-22, 21:332, 354, 537 ff., 546 ff., 555-57; "Wilmington," *UJE*; "Pennsylvania," *UJE*, 8:429-33; *Jewish Delaware: History, Sites, Communal Services* (Wilmington (?), 1976), 10 ff.; Constitution, Congregation Agudath Achim, Braddock, Pa, Oct. 14, 1894, copy in Marcus Collections; *PAJHS*, 42:196; Jacob S. Feldman, *The Early Migration and Settlement of Jews in Pittsburgh, 1754-1894* (Pittsburgh, 1959), 40-41; Jacob S. Feldman, Sharpsville, Pa., to JRM, July 1974, copy in AJAr; Samuel N. Gottlieb, *Sefer Ohole-Schem, etc.* (Pinsk, Russia, 1912), 310-13; *Journal of Urban History*, 4:296 ff., 301 ff.; *AJHQ*, 65:272 ff.; personal recollections of JRM for the years 1906-1907; *By Myself I'm A Book*, 38, 47 ff., 58-60, 62-63, 101, 143-45; *Jewish Criterion*, May 31, 1918, pp.19 ff.; Bloch, *Of Making Many Books*, 42, 55; Phila. *Jewish Exponent*, Jan. 19, 1900, p.4, c.1, Apr. 13, 1900, p.4, c.3; "Heilprin," "Levinthal," *EJ*; Eisenstadt, *Hakme Yisrael be-Amerika*, 14, 45-46, 67; "Heilprin, Michael," *JE, UJE*; "Morais, Sabato," "Rosenthal, Max," *JE, UJE, EJ, DAB*; Morais, *Philadelphia*, 215-35; Bernheimer, *Russian Jew in the U.S.*, 122 ff., 130-31, 133, 354; Robinson, "Philadelphia," 5-6, 14-17; Koplin, *"Jewish Exponent,"* 17-18, 22; Friedman, *Philadelphia*, chaps.3-5, 12; A. David Packman, "The Economic, Social, Cultural and Religious Experience of the East European Jewish Immigrant as Reflected in the Philadelphia *Jewish Exponent*, 1896-97, 1899-1900" (HUC term paper, n.d.); *AJA*, 9:32 ff.; "Pennsylvania," *JE*, 9:677-78, *UJE*, 8:480, *EJ*; "Greenfield, Albert Monroe," *WWW*, vol.4.

2. *AJYB*, 1(1899-1900):225, 229 ff., 232 ff., 3(1901-1902):146-47, 9(1907-1908):351-54, 21:525 ff., 528 ff., 26:578, 581; "Ohio," "Youngstown," *UJE*; Brickner, "Cincinnati," 1:106 ff.; P. & K., *Tourist's Guide*, 495; Gartner, *Cleveland*, 162 ff.; *American Jews: Their Lives and Achievements, etc.* (2 vols., N.Y., 1947), 1:215 ff.; "Isaacs, Nathan," *WWW*, vol.1; "Bevis, Howard Landis," "Schiff, Robert William," *WWW*, vol.5; the Isaacs-Bevis story was authenticated by Dr. H.B. Weiss of Cincinnati; Lesser, *In the Last Days*;

"Berman, Oscar," *WWIAJ*, 1938-1939, *WWW*, vol. 3; Gutstein, *Chicago*, 126, et passim, 313-14; Meites, *Chicago*, 124-25; Eisenstadt, *Hakme Yisrael be-Amerika*, 67-68; "Cincinnati," "Cleveland," *UJE, EJ*; *AJHQ*, 65:10 ff., 34-35.

3. "Indiana," *JE*; Judith E. Endelman, *The Jewish Community of Indianapolis, 1849 to the Present* (Bloomington, Ind., 1984), 57 ff., 66; "Indianapolis," *EJ*; "Fort Wayne," "South Bend," *UJE*; *AJYB*, 1(1899-1900):134 ff., 3(1901-1902):134, 21:369 ff.

4. *Journal of the Illinois State Historical Society*, 75:82 ff.; "Chicago," *JE, UJE, EJ*; "Illinois," *JE, UJE*; *AJYB*, 1(1899-1900):125 ff., 3(1901-1902):133-34, 21:359 ff, 589; Meites, *Chicago*, 113 ff., 195-96, 491; Bregstone, *Chicago*; Gutstein, *Chicago*, 41, 403 ff.; Rawidowicz (ed.), *Chicago Pinkas*; Wirth, *Ghetto*, 179 ff., 195 ff.; Korey, "Jew. Ed. in Chicago"; "Hillel Foundations, B'nai B'rith," *UJE*; Simon Litman, *Ray Frank Litman: A Memoir* (N.Y., 1957), 171 ff.; Marcus, *AJWD*, 380-83; Horwich, *My First Eighty Years*, 130, 228 ff.; "Horwich," Glassman (ed.), *BEOAJ, 1935*; Bernheimer, *Russian Jew in the U.S.*, 139 ff., 143 ff.; "Zeitlin, Jacob," *WWIAJ*, 1926, *WWIAJ*, 1938-39; "Paley, Samuel," "Silber, Saul," *WWIAJ*, 1938-39; Melvin G. Holli & Peter d'A. Jones, *The Ethnic Frontier, etc.* (Grand Rapids, Mich., 1977), 263 ff., 272 ff., 278.

5. "Iowa," *JE, UJE, EJ*; Glazer, *Jews of Iowa*, 152 ff., 203 ff., 233 ff., 257-58, 260 ff., 297 ff., 311, 316, 337 ff., 351-54; *AJYB*, 1(1899-1900):137-38, 3(1901-1902):134-35, 21:372-75; P. & K., *Tourist's Guide*, 145, 174; Rosenthal, *Des Moines*, 26 ff., 31 ff., 39, 56 ff., 67 ff.; Hinchin, "Jews of Sioux City," 113 ff., 120 ff.; Joseph, *Baron de Hirsch Fund*, 289; *Sioux City Federation News Letter*, copy in Marcus Collections; Meites, *Chicago*, 182, 195; "Glazer, Simon," *UJE*, *AJYB*, 5(1903-1904):58; Fleishaker, "Illinois-Iowa Jewish Community," 49-52; Wolfe, *Iowa*, 27 ff.; Bernard Shuman, *A History of the Sioux City Jewish Community, 1869 to 1969* (Sioux City, Iowa, 1969), 12 ff.

6. "Minneapolis," "Minnesota," *JE, UJE, EJ*; "Duluth," "Saint Paul," *UJE*; *AJYB*, 1(1899-1900):166-68, 3(1901-1902):139-40, 21:406-9; Plaut, *Jews in Minnesota*, 30, 55 ff., 90 ff., 115 ff., 119 ff., 126-28, 135 ff., 170 ff., 202, 206-8, see Index sub "Simon, Herman"; P. & K., *Tourist's Guide*, 254-55; Plaut, *Mt. Zion*, 55-58; *AJA*, 17:179; "Gordon, George Jacob," Glassman (ed.), *BEOAJ, 1935, WWIAJ*, 1938-39.

7. *AJYB*, 1(1899-1900):163 ff., 21:403 ff., 25:338, 340; *YA*, 15:82 ff.; Eisenstadt, *Hakme Yisrael be-Amerika*, 65-66; *Michigan Jewish History*, 5:7-8, 6:4 ff., 11 ff., 8:19-21, 11(no.2):29 ff., 12:19 ff., 14(no.2):24 ff., 17(no.1):3 ff., 18(no.2):20 ff., 20:4 ff., 21:3 ff., 17-19, 22(no.2):6 ff.; "Detroit," "Michigan," *JE, UJE, EJ*; "Simons, Charles Caspar," *WWIAJ*, 1938-39; P. & K., *Tourist's Guide*, 245; *Michigan Inventory*, 3 ff., 15, 39 ff., 41-42; Rockaway, *Jews of Detroit*, 80; Eli Grad, "Congregation Shaarey Zedek, Detroit, Michigan, etc." (typescript, n.p., n.d.), 15 ff., copy in Marcus Collections; *Congregation Shaarey Zedek, Detroit, Michigan, 5622-5712, 1861-1951, etc.* (Detroit, 1951), 16; *Detroit Jewish Directory* (Yiddish, Detroit, 1907); *Family Trails*, 4(no.3):10-11.

8. *U.A.H.C. Statistics*, 41, 55; *AJYB*, 1(1899-1900):269-70, 3(1901-1902):152, 9(1907-1908):425-30, 21:579-83, 25:338; "Milwaukee," *UJE, EJ*; Berman, "Wisconsin," 7, et passim; Swichkow & Gartner, *Milwaukee*, 88 ff., 164 ff., 193 ff., 197 ff., 232, 406, n.30, 424, n.88; "Wisconsin," *JE, UJE, EJ*; *New York Times*, Oct. 4, 1969, pp.1 ff.; "Mier," *EJ, EOZAI*; *Milwaukee Journal*, Mar. 27, 1938, p.2; "Anonymous MS: As Told to Charles E. Brown at New Glarus, April 30, 1930," Wisc. Hist. Soc. This is the same as the article, "Levitan, Solomon," *Dictionary of Wisconsin Biography* (Madison, 1950), 229; "Madison," *UJE*; P. & K., *Tourist's Guide*, 648-50; references for biography of S.B. Shiner now missing; Alfred D. Sumberg, "Some Notes on the History of the Jews of Wisconsin," *Wisconsin Jewish Chronicle*, Feb. 18, 1955, copy in Marcus Collections; Swarsensky, *Madison*, 26 ff., 32 ff., 41 ff., 64, 77; "Levitan, Solomon," *WWIAJ*, 1938-39; "Levitan, Sol," *UJE*; Alfred D. Sumberg, "The Fond Du Lac Jewish Community" (typescript, n.p., n.d.), copy in Marcus Collections; Alfred D. Sumberg, "Manitowoc Jewish Community" (typescript, n.p., n.d.), copy in Marcus Collections; *World Over,*

Apr. 11, 1969, p.2; Golda Meir, *My Life* (N.Y., 1975); Alfred R. Schumann, *No Peddlars Allowed* (Appleton, Wis., 1948).

CHAPTER FIVE

PART III: THE EAST EUROPEANS IN THE HINTERLAND TO 1921

1. *U.A.H.C. Statistics*, 55; "Lewiston," "Portland," *UJE*; "Maine," *UJE, EJ*; P. & K., *Tourist's Guide*, 208; *AJYB*, 1(1899-1900):142, 3(1901-1902):137, 21:381-82; "United States," *JE*, 12:372; Band, *Portland*, 8, 10 ff., 16-45, 110.

2. "New Hampshire," *JE, UJE, EJ*; *AJYB*, 1(1899-1900):176, 2(1900-1901):314, 3(1901-1902):142, 9(1907-1908):240, 21:417, 25:338; "United States," *JE*, 12:349, 373; P. & K., *Tourist's Guide*, 301.

3. *U.A.H.C. Statistics*, 6, 55; "Vermont," *UJE, EJ*; *AJYB*, 1(1899-1900):263-64, 2(1900-1901):476-77, 3(1901-1902):148-49, 151, 9(1907-1908):416-17, 21:573, 25:338; "United States," *JE*, 12:349, 374; "Burlington," "Lamport, Nathan," "Lamport, Samuel Charles," *UJE*; Myron Samuelson, *The Story of the Jewish Community of Burlington, Vermont* (Burlington, 1976), 51-165; "Lamport, Harold," *WWW*, vol.7; Friedman, *Pilgrims*, 353 ff.; P. & K., *Tourist's Guide*, 616-17.

4. *AJH*, 72:369 ff.; *PAJHS*, 27:3-5; Morris A. Gutstein, *The Story of the Jews of Newport* (N.Y., 1936), 256 ff., 268-77; "Rhode Island," *JE, UJE, EJ*; "Newport," "Providence," *UJE, EJ*; *RIJHN*, 1:72-74, 129 ff., 236-37, 3:44 ff., 5:275-88, 389 ff., 414-27, 6:83 ff., 7:189 ff., 202 ff., 236, 245 ff., 8:10 ff., 18, 82 ff., 9:127 ff., 19:236-37; "United States," *JE*, 12:369, 1373; *AJYB*, 1(1899-1900):252-53, 2(1900-1901):455-57, 3(1901-1902):148-49, 9(1907-1908):107, 120, 398-402, 21:561 ff., 23:311-12, 25:338; *U.A.H.C. Statistics*, 7; "Cutler, Harry," *UJE*.

5. "Connecticut," *JE, UJE, EJ*; *U.A.H.C. Statistics*, 55; *AJYB*, 1(1899-1900):117-20, 2(1900-1901):210 ff., 3(1901-1902):130-31, 9(1907-1908):141 ff., 147, 21:348 ff., 25:338; *AJA*, 31:196 ff.; "Hartford," "Koppleman, Herman Paul," "New Haven," *UJE, EJ*; "Bridgeport," "Kahn, Reuben Leon," "New Britian," "New London," "Norwalk," "Norwich," "Stamford," *UJE*; *Jewish Review*, 5:1 ff.; Esther Sulman, *A Goodly Heritage: The Story of the Jewish Community in New London* (New London, Conn., 1957), 9 ff.; Silverman, *Hartford Jews*, 12 ff., 206-7, 427 ff.; Arthur Goldberg, *The Jew in Norwich: A Century of Jewish Life, etc.* (Norwich, Conn., 1956), 14 ff., 22 ff., 32 ff.; Barry E. Herman (ed.), *Jews in New Haven II* (pamphlet, Hamden, Conn., 1979), 79-83; *RIJHN*, 7:88 ff., 100 ff.; "Schwartz, Joseph J.," *EJ*; Kagan, *Contributions*, 310 ff.

6. *AJYB*, 1(1899-1900):156 ff., 2(1900-1901):280 ff., 3(1901-1902):138, 9(1907-1908):201-16, 21:387 ff., 25:338; *U.A.H.C. Statistics*, 7, 55; Ehrenfried, *Boston*, 512-15, 744-47; Barbara Miller Solomon, *Pioneers in Service: A History of the Associated Jewish Philanthropies in Boston* (Boston, 1956), 7, 65, 85-86, 94-95, 108-9; "Boston," "Massachusetts," *JE, UJE, EJ*; "Springfield," "Worcester," *UJE, EJ*; Benjamin, *Three Years*, 2:285; biography of Julius Selzer by Harold T. Handley, typescript, Marcus Collections; P. & K., *Tourist's Guide*, 234; *Essex Institute Historical Collections*, 115:256 ff.; "Fall River," "Lynn," "Pittsfield," *UJE*; Pink Horwitt, *Jews in Berkshire County* (Williamstown, Mass., 1972), 1 ff.; Geller, "Jewish Life in Boston," 4 ff., 10; Wieder, *Boston's North End*, 21 ff., 57; *Jewish People*, 4:81; Frank, "Jews of Lynn, Mass.," 2 ff.; *AJA*, 29:107 ff.; *AJHQ*, 42:339-40, 54:12, 20, 22, et passim; "Margolies, Moses Sebulon," *EJ*; Eisenstadt, *Hakme Yisrael be-Amerika*, 73; *Menorah Journal*, Valedictory Issue, 1962, 136 ff.; Boston *Jewish Advocate*, Mar. 14, 1957, p.16; Solomon Schindler, *Israelites in Boston, etc.* (Boston, n.d.); "Antin, Mary," *UJE, DAB*, vol.4.

7. Marcus, *CAJ*, 1:332; *PAJHS*, 17:36-37; "New Jersey," *JE, UJE, EJ*; "Bergen County," "Essex County," *EJ*; "Bayonne," "Camden," "Elizabeth," "New Brunswick,"

"Orange," "Paterson," "Trenton," *UJE*; "Waksman, Selman Abraham," *UJE*, *EJ*; Henry R. Schnitzer, *The Goodly Tent: The First Fifty Years of Temple Emanu-El, Bayonne, N.J.* (Bayonne, 1961), 4 ff.; "Newark," *UJE*, 8:206-8; *AJYB*, 1(1899-1900):176 ff., 2(1900-1901):314 ff., 3(1901-1902):142-43, 9(1907-1908):241 ff., 21:417 ff., 25:338; Ruth Martin Patt, *The Jewish Scene in New Jersey's Raritan Valley, 1698-1948* (New Brunswick, N.J., 1978), 21-84; Ruth Martin Patt (ed.), *The Jewish Scene in New Jersey's Raritan Valley, Supplement—1980* (New Brunswick, N.J., 1980), 3 ff.; *Eastern Union*, 18, 39 ff., 49, 54, 70 ff., 86 ff., 98 ff.; Gary Klein, "A Study of the Economic Activity of the Jewish Community of Newark, New Jersey, 1861-1875" (HUC term paper, 1972); Constitution, Congregation Anshe Sefarad, Linas Ha-Tsedek, Newark, New Jersey, 1912, copy in Marcus Collections; *U.A.H.C. Statistics, 14,55*.

8. *U.A.H.C. Statistics*, 9-55; *Agricultural History*, 55:39-42; *AJYB*, 1(1899-1900):181 ff., 2(1900-1901):325 ff., 3(1901-1902):143-44, 9(1907-1908):258 ff., 260, 270-71, 21:431 ff., 517-19, 520-21, 25:338-41, 26:575; "Albany, ""Binghamton," "Buffalo," "Jolson, Al," "Kingston," "Monticello," "New York City," "Newburgh," "Rochester," "Schnectady," "Syracuse," "Troy," "Utica," *UJE*; Glazer, *Jews of Iowa*, 235; Korn, *Marcus Festschrift*, 263 ff.; *AJH*, 72:388-89; *AJA*, 16:22 ff., 18:24 ff.; "Conkling, Roscoe," *DAB*; Rudolph, *Syracuse*, 83 ff., 149 ff., 212-13, 279-80; Rosenberg, *Rochester*, 150 ff., 156, 159-60, 163 ff., 171, 182, 186 ff., 238 ff.; *Constitution, Congregation B'rith Sholem, Buffalo, N.Y.* (Yiddish, Buffalo, 1894); Adler & Connolly, *Buffalo*, 32, 171, 182-83, 187-88, 190-91, 195, 197-98, 217, 220-36, 239-40, 247 ff., 250-51, 254-58, 267-72, 323; Kohn, *Utica*, 12 ff., 21-56, 158-67, 168 ff.; B. Friedberg, *Bet Eked Sepharim* (Antwerp, Belgium, 1928-31), 200, no.168; "Zhitlowsky, Chaim," *UJE*; "New York," *UJE*, 8:197.

9. *AJHQ*, 62:264; *Now and Then*, 20(1981):46 ff.; *YA*, 15:101ff.; Hertzberg, *Atlanta*, 92; *PAJHS*, 49:125 ff.

CHAPTER SIX

THE EAST EUROPEANS DECIDE TO STAY IN THE EAST

1. Slosson, *The Great Crusade*, 196; *EIAJH*, 40, 44; Schlesinger, *Rise of the City*, xiv, 73, 425, 435-36; Faulkner, *Social Justice*, 6-7, 67-68; Morison, *History*, 768 ff.; Ray Allen Billington, *The American Frontier* (pamphlet, 2nd ed., American Historical Association, Washington, D.C., 1965), 15-16; Curti et al., *American History*, 2:134, 182 ff., 213-14; Wish, *Society and Thought*, 2:100-10, 122-23, 177; Rischin, *Promised City*, 5-6, 12, 33; *PAJHS*, 49:129; *Reports, Immig. Com. Abstracts*, 1:105 ff.; *AJYB*, 28:398, 402; Fein, *Baltimore*, 150; Sachar, *Modern Jewish History*, 31617; Handlin, *Adventure in Freedom*, 99-100, 108; *Jewish Life*, 9(no.1):20-22; *Jewish People*, 1:420; Finkelstein, *The Jews* (1960), 2:1698, (1949), 4:1229; Bernheimer, *Russian Jew in the U.S.*, 367, 370; *PUAHC*, 5:4667.

2. *Baron Festschrift*, 342; Grinstein, *New York City*, 472 ff.; *RIJHN*, 2:241 ff., 8:39, 43, 47; *PAJHS*, 37:248, 46:71 ff., 56:42 ff.; *AJYB*, 1(1899-1900):225 ff., 2(1900-1901):32, 225 ff., 3(1901-1902):133-34; "Brooklyn," *UJE*, 2:552, "Chicago," 3:140 ff.; Uchill, *Pioneers*, 196-97; Fein, *Baltimore*, 156-57; *YA*, 9:240; Janowsky, *American Jew*, 135-36; Levinger, *Jews in U.S.*, 278-79; Wiernik, *History*, 192; Lebeson, *Pilgrim People*, 243; Morais, *Philadelphia*, 226 ff., 229-30; Howard Arnold Kosovske, "Jewish Life in Philadelphia as Reflected in the *Jewish Record* for 1882-1886" (HUC term paper, 1965), 7-11; Bernheimer, *Russian Jew in the U.S.*, 83 ff., 174 ff., 197; "Philadelphia," *JE*, 9:677-78, *UJE*, 8:479, 482; *Eastern Union*, 28-29; Horwich, *My First Eighty Years*, 268 ff.; Vorspan & Gartner, *Los Angeles*, 173 ff.; *AJHQ*, 60:150; Oscar Handlin, *Immigration as a Factor in American History* (Englewood Cliffs, N.J., 1959), 84 ff.; Schlesinger, *Rise of the*

City, 65; Grayzel, *Hist. of Contemporary Jews*, 44-45; Curti, *American Thought*, 501; Lipman, *Soc. Hist. of Jews in England*, 49 ff., 120; *Jewish People*, 4:194; "New York City," *EJ*, 12:1097; Swichkow & Gartner, *Milwaukee*, 220, 228- 29, 424, n.81; Adler & Connolly, *Buffalo*, 187, 251 ff.

3. Morais, *Philadelphia*, 230; Horwich, *My First Eighty Years*, 145 ff.; Bernheimer, *Russian Jew in the U.S.*, 252; *Jew. Com. Reg.*, 961 ff., 980 ff.; Wiernik, *History*, 247-48; Swichkow & Gartner, *Milwaukee*, 244; Abraham G. Duker, *Syllabi: Labor Organizations, Landsmanshaften, and Fraternal Orders* (Training Bureau for Jewish Communal Service, N.Y., 1948-1949); Meites, *Chicago*, 195; *Baron Festschrift*, 345; *Detroit Jewish Chronicle*, Apr. 11, p.13, Apr. 18, p.13, Apr. 25, 1947, p.13; Finkelstein, *The Jews* (1949), 4:1301; *New York Times*, Nov. 3, 1965, p.39, cs.1-2; *Every Friday*, June 26, 1964, p.8; Sherman, *A Fateful Half-Century*; Levinger, *Jews in U.S.*, 499; *Jewish Landsmanshaften of New York*, 378-79.

4. *AJYB*, 1(1899-1900):62 ff., 73 ff.; "Brith Abraham Independent Order," "Workmen's Circle," *UJE*; *Jew. Com. Reg.*, 865 ff.; Adler & Connolly, *Buffalo*, 259; Swichkow & Gartner, *Milwaukee*, 248.

5. *Jew. Com. Reg.*, 732 ff., 831, 871 ff.; Doroshkin, *Yiddish in America*, 219 ff., 229 ff., 233; *AJHQ*, 53:253, 62:275; Morais, *Philadelphia*, 220 ff., 230-32; *By Myself I'm a Book*, 22, 113 ff.; *Jewish People*, 2:225, 4:64, 162-63; Wish, *Society and Thought*, 2:235, 244, 247, 259, 262, 267, 429, 432, 435; "Jacksonville," *UJE*; *Baron Festschrift*, 342- 43; Schoener, *Lower East Side*, 49-50; Janowsky, *American Jew*, 144 ff.; Schappes, *JIUS*, 112, 127; *AJYB*, 21:491 ff., 50:34 ff.; Goren, *American Jews*, 45-46; Sachar, *Modern Jewish History*, 523; Sherman, *A Fateful Half-Century*, 30-31; "New York City," *UJE*, 8:194; "Landsmannshaften," *EJ*; *YA*, 9:244; *Toledot*, 2:11 ff.; Elbogen, *Cent. of Jewish Life*, 438- 39; *Jewish Digest*, 21(no.10):73 ff.; Rischin, *Promised City*, 105; Handlin, *American People in the Twentieth Century*, 72; *Jewish Book Annual*, 10:81 (Yiddish pagination); "United States of America," *EJ*, 15:1618-19; *Jewish Landsmanshaften of New York*, 382 ff.; Bernheimer, *Russian Jew in the U.S., 84 ff.; Michigan Jewish History*, 16:39; Adler & Connolly, *Buffalo*, 302 ff.; Carl Applebaum, "A History of the Jewish 'Landsmanschaften' Organizations in New York City" (Ph.D. diss., N.Y.U., 1952); Constitution of the Chechanoffzer Unterseutzungs Verein (N.Y., English and Yiddish, n.d.); Fred M. Raskind, "A Study of the Landsmanshaften: 1900-1940" (HUC term paper, 1971); "Fraternal Orders," *UJE*; *Detroit Jewish News*, Mar. 12, 1976, p.18; *RIJHN*, 6:56 ff.

6. P. & K., *Tourist's Guide*, 385, 448; *Jew. Com. Reg.*, 1328 ff.; "Polish Jews in America, Federation of," *UJE*; *AJYB*, 21:304-5, 309-10, 24:226-27, 256, 74:77 ff.; Wiernik, *History*, 379; *YA*, 2-3:227; *Jewish People*, 4:162; Learsi, *Jews in America*, 136; Schappes, *JIUS*, 165-66; Wish, *Society and Thought*, 267; "Galician Jews of America, United," "Lithuanian Jews, Federation of," "Polish Jews in America, Federation of," "Roumanian Jews of America, United," *UJE*; Rischin, *Promised City*, 110.

7. *AJYB*, 16(1914-1915):144; "Seattle," *UJE*, *EJ*; Angel, *Sephardic Experience in the United States*, 152 ff.; Elizer Chammou, "Migration and Adjustment: the Case of the Sephardic Jews in Los Angeles" (Ph.D. diss., U. of California at Los Angeles, 1976); Stern, "Sephardic Jewish Community of Los Angeles."

8. *JSS*, 38:321 ff.; 45:186-87; *Detroit Jewish News*, Sept. 17, 1971, p.3; *New York Times*, Nov. 13, 1973, p.31; Haham Isaac Yerushalmi, *Sephardic Life in Cincinnati, 1906-1976* (Cincinnati, 1976), 3 ff.; *Jewish Digest*, 15(no.4):53 ff., 22(no.5):24 ff., 25(no.6):52 ff.; Marc D. Angel (ed.), *Studies in Sephardic Culture* (N.Y., 1980), 65 ff.; Angel, *Sephardic Experience in the United States*, 19 ff., 106 ff.; Joseph A.D. Sutton, *Magic Carpet: Aleppo-in-Flatbush* (N.Y., 1979), 3 ff., 34 ff., 63, 74; Tracy Guren Klirs, "'Turkishe Yidn' and 'Shomeho': Relations Between the Sephardic and Ashkenazic Communities of Seattle, 1903-1939" (HUC term paper, 1981); Finkelstein, *The Jews* (1949), 1:424; *AJYB*, 15(1913-1914):207 ff., 16(1914-1915):146, 21:309, 68:490, 74:77-138; "United

States," *JE*, 12:374; *Jewish Journal of Sociology*, 9:25 ff.; P. & K., *Tourist's Guide*, 447, 449-50, 457; *Congress Monthly*, 43:(no.3):15 ff.; "Brooklyn," *UJE*, 2:550, "New York City," 8:194; "Indianapolis," "Montgomery," *UJE*; Sol Beton (ed.), *Sephardim and a History of Congregation Or Ve Shalom* (Atlanta, 1981); *Louisiana Inventory*, 55, 57-58; *WSJHQ*, 6:241 ff., 7:22 ff., 29, 13:208-9, 14:187; N.Y. *Jewish Tribune*, Oct. 5, 1928, p.3, entire; Vorspan & Gartner, *Los Angeles*, 261-62; *AJA*, 25:156 ff.; Rischin, *Inventory*, 12; *Sephardi Heritage*, Winter, 1982, pp.37 ff., Winter, 1983, pp.26 ff.; *Jewish Book Annual*, 35:92 ff.; Mair Jose Benardete, *Hispanic Culture and the Character of the Sephardic Jews* (N.Y., 1953), 135 ff., 169 ff.; *History of the Etz Ahayen Congregation, 1906-1962* (Montgomery, Ala., 1962), 3 ff.; Stern, "Sephardic Jewish Community of Los Angeles"; *JSSQ*, 3(no.2):32-40; "Seattle," *UJE*, *EJ*; Washington *Record*, 8:22 ff.; *Commentary*, 25:28 ff.; "New York," *EJ*, 12:1097-98, "Sephardim," 14:1173-74; *National Jewish Monthly*, 77(no.9):12 ff.; *Present Tense*, 4:12; Brickner, "Jew. Com. of Cin.," 252 ff.; Handlin, *Adventure in Freedom*, 84; *AJHQ*, 62:253, 260; "Behar, Nissim Abraham," *JE*, *UJE*, *EJ*, *WWIAJ*, 1926; Goldberg, *Pioneers and Builders*, 188 ff.; "Ben Yehuda, Eliezer," *UJE*, *EJ*, *EOZAI*; *Jew. Com. Reg.*, 623, 1214 ff., 1220, 1339.

9. *AJYB*, 1(1899-1900):214-15, 21:313, 485 ff.; Eichhorn, *Joys of Jewish Folklore*, 164 ff.; "Arbitration," "Macht, David Israel," *UJE*; *Jew. Com. Reg.*, 204 ff., 467 ff., 989-1165, 1245 ff., 1281 ff.; P. & K., *Tourist's Guide*, 380.

10. "New York," *JE*, 9:187, 285; Morais, *Philadelphia*, 224-26; Blum, *Baltimore*, 29; Grinstein, *History*, 11; Rischin, *Promised City*, 105; "Immigrant Aid," *UJE*, 5:545; *JTA Community News Reporter*, Nov. 17, 1982, p.3; *Jew. Com. Reg.*, 1011.

11. *JTA Community News Reporter*, Aug. 18, 1966, p.3, Aug. 28, 1970, p.3, Dec. 18, 1970, p.4, Dec. 3, 1971, pp.2-3, Sept. 1, 1972, p.2; Swichkow & Gartner, *Milwaukee*, 229; Rischin, *Promised City*, 106; "Hebrew Free Loan Society," *UJE*; P. & K., *Tourist's Guide*, 389-90; *Jew. Com. Reg.*, 689 ff., 727 ff.; Bernheimer, *Russian Jew in the U.S.*, 71; *RIJHN*, 1:129 ff., 5:275, 414 ff., 7:92, 501; Blum, *Baltimore*, 31; Detroit *Jewish News*, Mar. 18, 1983, p.18; Meites, *Chicago*, 190-91, 604; Fein, *Baltimore*, 157; *AJA*, 31:194-95; Vorspan & Gartner, *Los Angeles*, 173, 333, n.13; Grinstein, *New York City*, 150.

12. Tina Levitan, *Islands of Compassion: A History of the Jewish Hospitals of New York* (N.Y., 1964), 89 ff.; Rischin, *Promised City*, 106; Bernheimer, *Russian Jew in the U.S.*, 71-72; *Jew. Com. Reg.*, 1014 ff.; M.M. Tates, Brooklyn, to JRM, Dec. 19, 1972, Marcus Collections; *Constitution of the Brownsville and East New York Hospital, Inc., 1918*, copy in Marcus Collections; Blum, *Baltimore*, 51-52, 103; *RIJHN*, 1:129 ff., 7:236-37, 242; "New York," *JE*, 9:280, *UJE*, 8:186; P. & K., *Tourist's Guide*, 395-96; *By Myself I'm a Book*, 106, 117-18; Levinthal, *Message of Israel*, 190; "Chicago," *UJE*, 3:144.

13. *Jew. Com. Reg.*, 1109 ff., 1112 ff.

14. Pool, *Portraits*, 8; Grinstein, *New York City*, 137-38; *Jew. Com. Reg.*, 334-35; Rischin, *Promised City*, 105, 111; Auerbach, "Nebraska," 85; Adler & Connolly, *Buffalo*, 255.

15. *Jew. Com. Reg.*, 1037 ff., 1051 ff.; Horwich, *My First Eighty Years*, 270-71; Blum, *Baltimore*, 29-31; Meites, *Chicago*, 616 ff.; Marcus, *AJWD*, 2:682 ff.

16. W. & W., *Philadelphia*, 136-37, 264-65; Grinstein, *New York City*, 149; "Migrations," *UJE*, 7:555-56; Morais, *Philadelphia*, 131 ff., 142-43; *Jew. Com. Reg.*, 1241; *RIJHN*, 6:209-17; Szajkowski, *Jew. Mass Settlement*, 921; "New York," *JE*, 9:287, "United States," 12:368; "Immigrant Aid," *UJE*, 5:545; Wiernik, *History*, 414; *By Myself I'm a Book*, 29; *Generations*, 1(no.5):10 ff.; Cole, *Irrepressible Conflict*, 122; *AJHQ*, 49:79; Sachar, *Modern Jewish History*, 312; *AJYB*, 21:310; "United HIAS Service," *EJ*; *Reports, Immig. Com.*, 15:lxxii; Wischnitzer, *To Dwell in Safety*, 121 ff.

CHAPTER SEVEN

MAKING A LIVING, PART I:

THE GARMENT INDUSTRY

1. *Jewish People*, 1:391 ff., 397, 4:75 ff.; "American Continent," *UJE*, 1:233, "Artisans," 1:509 ff.; "New York City," *EJ*, 12:1083 ff., "Tailoring," 15:708-9; *Zeitschrift des Institutfuer Weltwirtschaft und Seeverkehr an der Universitaet Kiel*, 27(part 2):170 ff.; Janowsky, *Am. Jew Reappraisal*, 67; *Reports, Immig. Com. Abstracts*, 1:324-25, 331, 364, 767; "United States," *JE*, 12:369, 374-75; *AJYB*, 56:12; Nudelman & Slesinger, *Jew in America*, 2:95, 112; Joseph, *Jewish Immigration*, 158-96; *AJHQ*, 65:257-65; Ravitch & Goodenow, *Educating an Urban People*, 103; Lipman, *Soc. Hist. of Jews in England*, 106 ff.; Rischin, *Promised City*, 26, 62; *JSS*, 8:219 ff.; *Jewish Review*, 3:3 ff.; Levin, *Jewish Socialist Movements*, 220-21; Schlesinger, *New Viewpoints*, 134, 148 ff.

2. J.B.S. Hardman, *The Amalgamated—Today and Tomorrow* (N.Y., 1939); Jack Kroll, *The Cincinnati Clothing Workers, 1913-1938* (Cincinnati, 1938), 6 ff.; *Profile of a Union* (Amalgamated Clothing Workers of America, N.Y., 1958); Schappes, *JIUS*, 144 ff.; *JQR*, 45:540 ff.; Tcherikower (ed.), *Jewish Labor Movement in U.S.*; Aaron Antonovsky, *The Early Jewish Labor Movement in the United States* (N.Y., 1961); Melvyn Dubofsky, *When Workers Organize* (Amherst, Mass., 1968); Foner, *Fur and Leather Workers Union*; Foner, *Labor Movement in U.S.*; *Clothing Workers of Chicago*; *Menorah Journal*, 15:293 ff., 414 ff., 526 ff., 18:303 ff.; Lang & Feinstone, *United Hebrew Trades*, 11 ff.; *Jewish Life*, 8(no.8):17 ff., 8(no.11):21 ff., 8(no.12):17 ff., 9(no.2):19 ff., 9(no.3):20 ff.; *YA*, 2-3:180 ff., 5:197-204, 7:229-67, 9:308-31, 363-96, 16:this entire volume deals with the Jewish labor movement and socialism, especially p.8; *JSS*, 8:219-44; Maximilian Hurwitz, *The Workmen's Circle* (N.Y., 1936); Kaminsky, *Arbeter Ring*; Isaac A. Hourwich, *Immigration and Labor* (N.Y., 1912); J.S. Hertz, *50 Years of the Workmen's Circle in Jewish Life* (N.Y., 1950); Seidman, *Needle Trades*; Benjamin Stolberg, *Tailor's Progress* (Garden City, N.Y., 1944); Epstein, *Profiles of Eleven*; Melech Epstein, *Jewish Labor in U.S.A., 1914-1952* (N.Y., 1953); Charles H. Green, *Headwear Workers: A Century of Trade Unionism* (N.Y., 1944); Fliegel, *Max Pine*; *PAJHS*, 41:297-355; Moshe Davis & Isidore S. Meyer, *The Writing of American Jewish History* (N.Y., 1957), 210 ff.; Jesse Thomas Carpenter, *Competition and Collective Bargaining in the Needle Trades, 1910-1967* (Ithaca, N.Y., 1972); Baron Festschrift, 63 ff.; Howe, *World of Our Fathers*, chaps.2-5, 9-10; Rogoff, "Formative Years"; *Amopteil*, 2:102-32; *AJH*, 71:188 ff.; Gurock, *Guide*, 53 ff.; Howe & Libo, *How We Lived*, 153 ff.; Zaretz, *Amalgamated Clothing Workers*, 13 ff.; A.S. Sachs, *Di Geshikhte fun Arbayter Ring, 1892-1925* (2 vols., N.Y., 1925); *Jewish Review*, 3:3 ff.; Cohen, *They Builded Better Than They Knew*, 179 ff.; *AJYB*, 31:203-4, 50:45 ff., 53:3-35; *Jewish People*, 1:391 ff.; "New York City, *UJE*, 8:184; Handlin, *Adventure in Freedom*, 91 ff.; Wiernik, *History*, 297 ff.; *Reports, Ind. Com.*: there is particularly valuable material on the conditions of Jewish workers in volumes 7, 8, 14, 15, 17, 19. There are also two volumes of *Reports, Immig. Com Abstracts*. *Reports, Ind. Com.*, 14:150 ff.; Pope, *Cloth. Ind. in NYC*, chap.3; *Jew. Com. Reg.*, 697 ff., 1264 ff., 1270 ff.; Josephson, *Sidney Hillman*; "Garment Industries," *ESS*; Rischin, *Promised City*, 62, 174-75, 243 ff.; Faulkner, *Social Justice*, 75-76; Masserman & Baker, *Jews Come to America*, 259 ff.; Rischin, *Inventory*, 40-43; Levine, *Women's Garment Workers*; *Jewish People*, 2:399 ff.; "Needle Trades," *UJE*; "Trades Union," *UJE*, 10:289-90; Perlman & Taft, *History of Labor*, 4:282 ff.; Essrig, "Russian-Jewish Immigration"; Marcus, *CAJ*, 2:677, 3:1323; Abbott, *Women in Industry*, 229, 237; Friedman, *Pilgrims*, 79 ff.; Schappes, *JIUS*, 103 ff., 110-12; Schappes, *DHJUS*, 103 ff., 561 ff.; *AH*, Apr. 15, 1904, pp.686-87; Marcus, *AJWD*, 93-94.

3. *AH*, Apr. 15, 1904, pp.686-87; Abbott, *Women in Industry*, 229; *Jewish Life*, 8(no.8):17-20, 8(no.11):21 ff.; Perlman & Taft, *History of Labor*, 4:289 ff.; *YA*, 16:8; "Philadelphia," UJE, 8:479; Eisenberg, *Eyewitnesses to American Jewish History*, 3:3 ff.; *Jewish People*, 4:346-47; Tarbell, *Nationalizing of Business*, 155; Rogoff, "Formative Years," 22 ff.; *AJYB*, 53:3-35; *PAJHS*, 48:40; Levine, *Women's Garment Workers*, chaps. 5-6:24 ff.

4. Beard, *Rise of Am. Civilization*, 760, 775; Abbott, *Women in Industry*, 237; Rischin, *Promised City*, 64, 84; Schoener, *Portal to America*, 159-60; Wish, *Society and Thought*, 1:266-67, 397-98, 2:134-35, 417; *YA*, 2-3:203-4, 5:227-28, 16:9; Curti et al., *American History*, 2:61, 201, 441; Marcus, *AJWD*, 82, 658; *Reports, Immig. Com. Abstracts*, 1:752; Faulkner, *Social Justice*, 21-23; *AJA*, 31:35 ff.; *Education of Abraham Cahan*, 397 ff.; Schappes, *DHJUS*, 509-10; Blake McKelvey, *Rochester: The Flower City, 1855-1890* (Cambridge, Mass., 1949), 103-4; Lipman, *Soc. Hist. of Jews in England*, 78; Tarshish, "American Judaism," 358; *Jewish People*, 2:400-1, 4:397; *Generations*, 1(no.5):32 ff.; *Reports, Ind. Com.*, 14(1901):73-95, 15:xxii ff.; Pope, *Cloth. Ind. in NYC*; Riis, *How the Other Half Lives*, chap. 11; Bernheimer, *Russian Jew in the U.S.*, 124-34; *AJA*, 21:149 ff.; *PAJHS*, 48:52; "United States," *JE*, 12:375; Ginzberg & Berman, *American Worker*, 123-26; *AJH*, 71:224; Milton Meltzer (ed.), *The Jewish Americans* (N.Y., 1982), 76 ff.

5. Leket Mekorot, 108-9; Schappes, *JIUS*, 128-30; Handlin, *Adventure in Freedom*, 132-33; Rischin, *Promised City*, 176; *Jewish Life*, 8(no.11):21 ff.; *YA*, 16:6-15; Meites, *Chicago*, 453 ff.; Morais, *Philadelphia*, 233-34; *AJYB*, 53:3 ff.; *Jewish People*, 4:157, 401-2; "United States," *JE*, 12:368; *Jew. Com. Reg.*, 1277-79; Foner, *Labor Movement in U.S.*, 2:35-36; "Pine, Max," Fink, *Biog. Dict.*; Fliegel, *Max Pine*. The standard histories of Jewish labor all contain data on the United Hebrew Trades.

6. *AJYB*, 6(1904-1905):58-59; Epstein, *Profiles of Eleven*, 113 ff.; *YA*, 7:283, 16:11; *Midstream*, 16(no.4):69 ff.; Rischin, *Promised City*, 192-93; "Barondess, Joseph," UJE, EJ, *WWIAJ*, 1926, Fink, *Biog. Dict.*; *AJHQ*, 64:321, 325; Masserman & Baker, *Jews Come to America*, 263 ff.; *Jew. Com. Reg.*, 72, 1222, 1228, 1443; Stanley J. Kunitz & Howard Haycraft (ed.), *American Authors, 1600-1900* (N.Y., 1938), 439.

7. Gompers, *Seventy Years of Life and Labor*, 1:6, 2:152-53; Florence Calvert Thorne, *Samuel Gompers—American Statesman* (N.Y., 1957); Stuart Bruce Kaufman, *Samuel Gompers and the Origins of the American Federation of Labor, 1848-1896* (Westport, Ct., 1973); "Gompers, Samuel," *JE*, UJE, EJ, DAB, Fink, *Biog. Dict.*; *AJHQ*, 65:220 ff.; Gaustad, *Relig. Hist. of America*, 207; Friedman, *Pilgrims*, 337 ff.; Marcus, *Memoirs*, 3:282; *Jewish People*, 4:334 ff.; *YA*, 16:12-13; Rischin, *Promised City*, 178; *Labor History*, 7:35 ff., 54, 57; Samuel Gompers, Washington, D.C., to R.F. Ely, Madison, Wis., June 21, 1915, Ely Papers, Wisconsin Historical Society, copy in Marcus Collections; Faulkner, *Social Justice*, 52 ff.; *Antioch Review*, 13:191 ff., 203 ff.; Morison, *History*, 772; Tarbell, *Nationalizing of Business*, 156-57, 167.

8. Bernheimer, *Russian Jew in the U.S.*, 115, 134; Levine, *Women's Garment Workers*, chaps. 8-14; *JSS*, 8:219 ff.; Goren, *American Jews*, 47; Schappes, *JIUS*, 122 ff., 155-56; *Jewish Life*, 8(no.11):21, 8(no.12):17 ff., 9(no.1):18 ff.; *Jewish Review*, 3:3 ff., 7 ff., 11, 19 ff.; *AJYB*, 9(1907-1908):119-22, 19(1917-1918):345, 51:55, 53:3 ff.; "New York," *JE*, 9:288-89, "Trade-Unionism," 12:217-18, "United States," 12:374-75; Grayzel, *Hist. of Contemporary Jews*, 23-28; Finkelstein, *The Jews* (1960), 2:1635 ff.; Pope, *Cloth. Ind. in NYC*, 105, 176; Nudelman & Slesinger, *Jew in America*, 2:114-15; *Jewish People*, 1:392, 4:356; "Wages and Hours of Labor," *DAH* (1942), 5:386 ff.; *Commentary*, 10:186 ff.; *Menorah Journal*, 15:293-307, 414 ff.; Phila. *Jewish Exponent*, Aug. 1, 1890, pp.3, 6, Aug. 8, 1890, p.6, Aug. 15, 1890, p.6, Aug. 29, 1890, p.4; *PAJHS*, 49:95-96; Rogoff, "Formative Years," 40 ff.; Schoener, *Portal to America*, 165 ff.; Fein, *Baltimore*, 165 ff.; Rischin, *Promised City*, 179 ff.; "Rickert, Thomas A.," Fink, *Biog. Dict.*; "White, Henry," *AJYB*, 6(1904-1905):205-6; *AJH*, 71:193, 72:369; Essrig, "Russian-Jewish

Immigration," 127 ff.; Kull & Kull, *Chronology*, 197; Curti et al., *American History*, 2:197-98; Faulkner, *Social Justice*, 57; *Jew. Com. Reg.*, 700-1, 1269; Masserman & Baker, *Jews Come to America*, 417; "United States of America," *EJ*, 15:1616; Morison, *History*, 811 ff.; *YA*, 7:229 ff., 16:16 ff.; Foner, *Fur and Leather Workers Union*, 51.

9. *Jewish People*, 4:360 ff., 365 ff.; Marcus, *AJWD*, 569-70; Rischin, *Promised City*, 247 ff.; *Jewish Life*, 9(no.1):7-11, 9(no.3):20-24; "Marks, Marcus M.," *AJYB*, 6(1904-1905):151, *WWIAJ*, 1926; *Baron Festschrift*, 63 ff.; Levine, *Women's Garment Workers*, chaps.21-29, pp.144 ff., 154, 159; Perlman & Taft, *History of Labor*, 293 ff.

10. Rischin, *Promised City*, 67, 247; *New York Times Book Review*, Feb. 1, 1976, pp.1 ff.; Perlman & Taft, *History of Labor*, 295 ff.; Cohen, *They Builded Better Than They Knew*, 181 ff.; *YA*, 16:18, 132; *Baron Festschrift*, 63 ff.; Wish, *Society and Thought*, 2:215-16; *Menorah Journal*, 15:418 ff.; Levine, *Women's Garment Workers*, chaps.21-22, pp.346 ff.; *AJYB*, 53:3; "Needle Trades," *UJE*, 8:143; *Jewish Life*, 9(no.1):7 ff., 9(no.3):20-24; "Cohen, Julius Henry," "International Ladies' Garment Workers' Union," *UJE*; Epstein, *Profiles of Eleven*, 262 ff.; Grayzel, *Hist. of Contemporary Jews*, 692; *AJA*, 3:1; Hyman Berman, "The Era of Protocol: a Chapter in the History of the International Ladies' Garment Workers' Union, 1910-1916" (Ph.D. diss, Columbia Univ., 1956); *Jewish People*, 4:365 ff.; Goren, *American Jews*, 54-55; *New York History*, 50:187 ff.; *Jewish Labor in the United States* (*This is Our Home*, no.11, American Jewish Committee Leaflet Series, 1957), 9-11; *Justice*, Sept. 1982, p.6, copy in Marcus Collections; Faulkner, *Social Justice*, 58 ff.; Schappes, *JIUS*, 160 ff.

11. *Jew. Com. Reg.*, 1275; "Schlesinger, Benjamin," *UJE, EJ, DAB*, Fink, *Biog. Dict.*; Epstein, *Profiles of Eleven*, 235 ff.; *JTA-DNB*, Sept. 24, 1956.

12. Perlman & Taft, *History of Labor*, 302 ff.; *Jew. Com. Reg.*, 961-62; Epstein, *Profiles of Eleven*, 255 ff.; Levine, *Women's Garment Workers*, chap.26; *Report, Ind. Com.*, 14:150 ff.; "Hourwich, Isaac A.," *JE, UJE, AJYB*, 6(1904-1905):120.

13. *New York Times*, July 31, 1942, G.M. Price obituary; "Price, George Moses," *UJE*; *Private Papers of George M. Price, M.D.* (2 vols., typescript copy of minutes of the Union Health Center, N.Y., 1914), copy in Marcus Collections.

14. *AJHQ*, 58:337-38; Marcus, *AJWD*, 2:590 ff.; Rischin, *Promised City*, 252-54; Leon Stein, *The Triangle Fire* (Phila., 1962); "Triangle Fire," *DAH* (1942); Schoener, *Portal to America*, 171 ff.; *Congress Bi-Weekly*, Feb. 4, 1963, pp.9 ff.; *American Heritage*, 8(no.5):54 ff.; Eisenberg, *Eyewitnesses to American Jewish History*, 3:125 ff.

15. "Schneiderman, Rose," *UJE, EJ, NAW*, Fink, *Biog. Dict.*; Marcus, *AJWD*, 2:449 ff.; *AJYB*, 74:559; *New York Times*, Aug. 13, 1972, p.59; Foner, *Women and the American Labor Movement* (1979), 279-80, 310, 390-91; Gary Edward Endelman, *Solidarity Forever: Rose Schneiderman and the Women's Trade Women League* (N.Y., 1982); *Reports, Immig. Com. Abstracts*, 1:761, 764-65; Rose Schneiderman & Lucy Goldthwaite, *All For One* (N.Y., 1967).

16. *Jewish People*, 2:419 ff.; *Jew. Com. Reg.*, 1268; Schappes, *JIUS*, 164-65; Perlman & Taft, *History of Labor*, 315; *YA*, 7:229 ff.

17. "Schlossberg, Joseph," *UJE, EJ*, Fink, *Biog, Dict.*; *Jew. Com. Reg.*, 1268-69; *JTA-DNB*, Jan. 18, 1971, p.4.

18. Masserman & Baker, *Jews Come to America*, 274 ff.; Perlman & Taft, *History of Labor*, 304, 313-14; Commons, *History of Labor in the U.S.*, 2:520 ff.; *YA*, 16:46-47; Epstein, *Profiles of Eleven*, 271-94; *Antioch Review*, 13:191 ff.; *Jewish People*, 2:419 ff., 4:370 ff.; "Amalgamated Clothing Workers of America," *UJE*; *Jew. Com. Reg.*, 1264 ff., 1268; Schappes, *JIUS*, 162 ff.; *AJH*, 71:192 ff.; *Labor History*, 4:245; George Soule, *Sidney Hillman: Labor Statesman* (N.Y., 1939), 12 ff.; Zaretz, *Amalgamated Clothing Workers*, 93 ff.; Foner, *Women and the American Labor Movement* (1979), 350 ff.; "Wages and Hours of Labor," *DAH* (1942); Josephson, *Sidney Hillman*, 86 ff.; *Commentary*, 15:312 ff.; Ella F. Auerbach, Omaha, to JRM, Dec. 4, 1969, Marcus Collections; Sachar, *Modern Jewish*

History, 330; *AJYB*, 49:67 ff.; "Hillman, Sidney," *UJE, EJ, DAB*, Supplement 4; *PAJHS*, 46:226 ff.; Wish, *Society and Thought*, 2:250-51; *Clothing Workers of Chicago, 1910-1922*, chaps.1-6; Seidman, *Needle Trades*, 115 ff.

19. Curti et al., *American History*, 2:197-98; *YA*, 7:229 ff., 16:132, 411 ff.; *Jewish Review*, 3:19 ff.; *Reports, Immig. Com. Abstracts*, 1:516-17; Lipman, *Soc. Hist. of Jews in England*, 118; Ravitch & Goodenow, *Educating an Urban People*, 103; *Jew. Com. Reg.*, 697 ff., 1270 ff.; *Jewish People*, 2:410 ff., 415 ff., 4:334 ff., 374; *Labor History*, 4:227 ff.; Elbogen, *Cent. of Jewish Life*, 446-47; Schappes, *JIUS*, 148; "United States of America," *EJ*, 16:1616 ff.; "Amalgamated Clothing Workers of America," "International Ladies' Garment Workers' Union," *UJE*.

20. *American Zionist*, 61(no.3):34 ff.; "Socialism," *UJE*, 9:584-85; "Jacobi, Abraham," *JE, UJE, EJ, DAB*; Schappes, *JIUS*, 110; *Jewish Life*, 9(no.10):30; Schappes, *DHJUS*, 539 ff., 724-25; Wittke, *Refugees of Revolution*, 167; *YA*, 16:8, 198, n.1; Korn, *Eventful Years*, 6 ff.; *PAJHS*, 17:137-38; *New York History*, 49:391 ff.

21. *New York History*, 49:392-93, 397-98, 400; *YA*, 9:325, 383 ff., 16:8 ff., 17, 342 ff.; *WSJHQ*, 10:273-74; Janowsky, *Am. Jew. Reappraisal*, 69-70; *Jewish People*, 2:404, 4:346 ff., 355 ff.; Bernheimer, *Russian Jew in the U.S.*, 272-73; *Education of Abraham Cahan*, 31; Eisenberg, *Eyewitnesses to American Jewish History*, 3:48 ff.; *AJHQ*, 53:254, n.7; Howe, *World of Our Fathers*, 75; *AH*, Sept. 27, 1889, p.125; "Anarchism," *JE, UJE*; *Midstream*, 18(no.7):63 ff.; Fein, *Baltimore*, 169 ff.; Karp, *Jew. Exp. in America*, 4:xvii.

22. "Labor Zionist Organization of America," *EJ*; *Jew. Com. Reg.*, 961 ff.; Secretary, Workmen's Circle, Branch 179 to the Jewish Settlement Extension, Cincinnati, Jan. 16, 1910, Marcus Collections; *AJA*, 12:34 ff.; Schappes, *JIUS*, 158-59; *Jewish Landsmanshaften of New York*, 382 ff.; Kaminsky, *Arbeter-Ring*; Pilch, *Hist. Jew. Ed.*, 104 ff.

23. "Liebermann, Aaron Samuel," *EJ*; *Jewish People*, 4:350; Lipman, *Soc. Hist. of Jews in England*, 131 ff.; *AJA*, 12:56-57.

24. "Socialism," UJE, 9:584-85, *EJ*, 15:46-48, *Columbia Encyclopedia*; *Leket Mekorot*, 108-9; Swichkow & Gartner, *Milwaukee*, 253; *AJHQ*, 49:82-83, 58:336, 66:298; Schappes, *JIUS*, 155; Rischin, *Promised City*, 44-46; Tarbell, *Nationalizing of Business*, 274 ff.; Morison, *History*, 811 ff.; *Jewish Life*, 9(no.2):22; *AJYB*, 53:25 ff.; Wish, *Society and Thought*, 2:212 ff.; Wiernik, *History*, 300 ff.

25. *Labor History*, 4:243-44; "Rubinow, Isaac Max," *UJE, EJ, DAB*, Supplement 2, *WWW*, vol.1; "Epstein, Abraham," *UJE, EJ, DAB*, Supplement 3.

26. *AJYB*, 22:344 ff.; Gurock, *Guide*, 53 ff.; Lipman, *Soc. Hist. of Jews in England*, 131-33; Levin, *Jewish Socialist Movements*, 38 ff.; *AH*, Sept. 27, 1889, p.125; New York, Oct. 13, 1975, p.75; Howe, *World of Our Fathers*, 287 ff., 360 ff.; *Jew. Com. Reg.*, 617 ff., 1256 ff., 1455; *AJHQ*, 62:429 ff., 66:478-79; Learsi, *Jews in America*, 143-44; *Humanistic Judaism*, 10(no.2):9 ff.; Rischin, *Promised City*, 120, 159-60; Curti et al., *American History*, 2:297; "Rostow, Eugene Victor," *WWIA*; *AJH*, 69:413 ff.; Gartner, *Cleveland*, 249-50; *Jewish Life*, 9(no.5):21-24; *Jewish Currents*, 13(no.5):24; David A. Shannon, *The Socialist Party of America: A History* (N.Y., 1955); J.S. Hertz, *Di Yidishe Sotsialistishe Bavegung in Amerika* (Yiddish, N.Y., 1954); Szajkowski, *Jews, Wars, and Communism*, vol. 1; Howe & Libo, *How We Lived*, 161 ff.; Irving Howe & Lewis Coser, *The American Communist Party: A Critical History (1919-1957)*, (Boston, 1957); Friedman & Gordis, *Jewish Life in America*, 109 ff.; Sachar, *Modern Jewish History*, 284 ff., 323 ff.; Berkman, *Prison Memoirs of an Anarchist*; Goldman, *Living My Life*; Uri D. Herscher & Stanley F. Chyet (eds.), *On Jews, America and Immigration: A Socialist Perspective* (Cincinnati, 1980); Harry W. Laidler, *History of Socialism* (London, 1968), 577 ff.; Melech Epstein, *The Jew and Communism* (N.Y., n.d.), 3 ff.; *PAJHS*, 50:202 ff., 238 ff.; Epstein, *Profiles of Eleven*: this includes profiles of Morris Winchevsky, Abraham Cahan, Joseph Barondess, Meyer London, Morris Hillquit, Benjamin Schlesinger, Isaac A. Hourwich, Sidney Hillman, Chaim Zhitlowsky, and Baruch Charney Vladeck; *AJA*, 12:37 ff., 59, 67-68, 14:138 ff.; *Commentary*, 15:336 ff.

CHAPTER EIGHT

MAKING A LIVING, PART II: NOTABLE JEWISH
SOCIALISTS, AMERICAN JEWRY, AND THE LABOR MOVEMENT

1. "De Leon, Daniel," *UJE, EJ, DAB, WWW*, vol.1; N.Y. *Jewish Reformer and Times*, Jan. 17, 1879, p.5, cs.2-3, Feb. 14, 1879, p.5, cs.3-5; Schappes, *JIUS*, 131; *AJYB*, 53:3-35; Gurock, *Guide*, 57-58; *Jewish Life*, 8(no.12):17 ff.; Commons, *History of Labour in the U.S.*, 2:517 ff.; Isaac S. and Suzanne A. Emmanuel, *History of the Jews of the Netherland Antilles* (2 vols., Cincinnati, 1970), 428-29, 449-53; *PAJHS*, 26:239; *AJHQ*, 65:245 ff.; *Wisconsin Magazine of History*, 61:210 ff.; *AHR*, 59:955-56; *Jewish People*, 4:357 ff.; Tarbell, *Nationalizing of Business*, 114-15; Rischin, *Promised City*, 225-26; L. Glen Seretan, *Daniel De Leon: The Odyssey of an American Marxist* (Cambridge, Mass., 1979).

2. *Education of Abraham Cahan*, 229-304, et passim; "Cahan, Abraham," *UJE, EJ, DAB*, Supplement 5; Gompers, *Seventy Years of Life and Labor*, 2:45; *Jewish People*, 4:358-59; Rischin, *Promised City*, 159; Theodore Marvin Pollach, "The Solitary Clarinetist: A Critical Biography of Abraham Cahan, 1860-1917" (Ph.D. diss., Columbia Univ., 1959); AJA, 23:33-46.

3. Hillquit, *Loose Leaves from a Busy Life*, 170; "Hillquit, Morris," *UJE, EJ, DAB*, Supplement 1, Fink, *Biog. Dict.*; Laurence D. Lauer, "A View of Morris Hillquit: An American (Jewish?) Socialist" (HUC term paper, 1971); *PAJHS*, 50:214 ff.; *Jewish Currents*, 35(no.11):41 ff.; *AJH*, 68:163 ff., 172 ff., 69:138 ff.; *Jewish Life*, 9(no.5):21 ff.; *AJA*, 12:46; *JSS*, 32:286 ff.; *Jew. Com. Reg.*, 1256 ff.; Epstein, *Profiles of Eleven*, 191 ff.; Norma Fain Pratt, *Morris Hillquit: A Political History of an American Jewish Socialist* (Westport, Conn., 1979); *YA*, 16:24; Gurock, *Guide*, 57.

4. "Berger, Victor Luitpold," *Biographical Directory of the American Congress*; "Berger, Victor Louis," *UJE, EJ, DAB*, Supplement 1, Fink, *Biog. Dict.*; Gurock, *Guide*, 57.

5. "London, Meyer," *UJE, EJ, DAB*, Fink, *Biog. Dict.*; "London, Meyer," *Biographical Directory of the American Congress*; *AJH*, 68:169, 73:203; *Jewish Digest*, 5(no.12):33 ff.; Epstein, *Profiles of Eleven*, 161 ff.; Harry Rogoff, *An East Side Epic: The Life and Work of Meyer London* (N.Y., 1930), 69; *Jewish People*, 4:378; William Frieburger, "The Lone Socialist Vote: A Political Study of Meyer London" (Ph.D. diss., U. of Cincinnati, 1980).

6. *American Jewish Experience*, 1:26 ff.; "Vladeck, Baruch Charney," *UJE, EJ, DAB*, Supplement 2, Fink, *Biog. Dict.*; *New York Times*, Oct. 31, 1938, Nov. 3, 1938, obituaries of Baruch Vladeck; Ephim H. Jeshurin (ed.), *B. Vladeck: In Leben un Shafen (His Life and Works)* (N.Y., 1935-36); *AJYB*, 40:530, 41:79-93.

7. "Zhitlowsky, Chaim," *UJE, EJ, EOZAI*; Epstein, *Profiles of Eleven*, 297-322; Chaim Zhitlowsky, *Zikhrononos fun Mayn Lebn* (vol.1, N.Y., 1935).

8. Schlesinger, *Rise of the City*, 142; Charlotte Baum et al., *The Jewish Woman in America* (N.Y., 1976), chap.5; Neidle, *America's Immigrant Women*, 133 ff., 156 ff., 167 ff.; Charles Reznikoff, *Family Chronicle* (N.Y., 1971), 7 ff.; Hamilton Holt (ed.), *The Life Stories of Undistinguished Americans as Told by Themselves* (N.Y., 1906), 34 ff.; *Reports, Immig. Com. Abstracts*, 1:326-27, 365, 368-69, 372-73, 376-78, 381, 390-91, 393, 398, 410, 414, 449-50, 463-66, 766; Abbott, *Women in Industry*, 232-44.

9. Lang & Feinstone, *United Hebrew Trades*, 50; Marcus, *AJWD*, 581 ff.; *YA*, 16:31; *AJH*, 68:189 ff.

10. Ricki Carole Myers Cohen, "Fannia Cohn and the International Ladies' Garment Workers' Union" (Ph.D. diss., U. of Southern California, 1976), 4 ff.; "Pesotta, Rose," "Cohn, Fannia," *NAW*; "Cohn, Fannia," "Newman, Pauline," Fink, *Biog. Dict.*; Marcus, *AJW*, 1:107, 210, 215; Marcus, *AJWD*, 581-89; Foner, *Women in the American Labor Movement* (1979), 385-87; Neidle, *America's Immigrant Women*, 156 ff.; "Oral history

interview with Pauline Newman" (U. of Michigan-Wayne State Univ., Ann Arbor, Mich., 1978).

11. "Bellanca, Dorothy Jacobs," *NAW*, Fink, *Biog. Dict.*; Marcus, *AJWD*, 797 ff.; Foner, *Women and the American Labor Movement* (1979), 219 ff.

12. Perry, *Belle Moskowitz*; "Moskowitz, Belle Lindner Israels," *UJE, DAB*, Supplement 1, *NAW*; *Labor History*, 23:5 ff.; "Moskowitz, Henry," *EJ*; Marcus, *AJWD*, 489 ff.

13. "Rosenberg, Anna M.," *UJE, WWIAJ*, 1938; Neidle, *America's Immigrant Women*, 281 ff.

14. Neidle, *America's Immigrant Women*, 167-74; "Goldman, Emma," *UJE, EJ, DAB*, Supplement 2, *NAW*; *Midstream*, 17(no.5):67 ff.; Jacob S. Feldman, "Berkman's Pittsburgh Years, 1892-1906" (typescript, n.d.), copy in Marcus Collections; Pittsburgh *Post*, July 25, 1892, p.1, Pittsburgh *Times*, July 25, 1892, p.1, Pittsburgh *Commercial Gazette*, July 25, 1892, p.1, copies in Marcus Collections; Richard Drinnon, *Rebel in Paradise: A Biography of Emma Goldman* (Chicago, 1961), 44; *National Jewish Monthly*, 96(no.9):22 ff.; Berkman, *Prison Memoirs of an Anarchist*; "Berkman, Alexander," *UJE, DAB*, Supplement 2; *New York Times*, May 15, 1940, obituary of Emma Goldman; Goldman, *Living My Life*; Tarbell, *Nationalizing of Business*, 224-25; Alix Kates Shulman (ed.), *Emma Goldman, Red Emma Speaks: Selected Writings and Speeches* (N.Y., 1972); *AJA*, 23:6 ff.; Marcus, *AJWD*, 351-59; Seller (ed.), *Immigrant Women*, 245, 259 ff.; Schappes, *JIUS*, 180; Feldman, *Jew. Experience in Western Pa.*, 243-45; Reznikoff, *Louis Marshall*, 2:977 ff.; *EAH*, 331; *AHR*, 88:1330-31.

15. Neidle, *America's Immigrant Women*, 167, 174-85; *Jewish Currents*, 37(no.6):23 ff.; "Stokes, Rose Harriet Pastor," *UJE, EJ, DAB, NAW*, Fink, *Biog. Dict.*; *New York History*, 62:415-38; *YA*, 7:290 ff.; Marcus, *AJWD*, 485-88, 538-44; Wilansky, *Sinai to Cincinnati*, 176; *AI*, Mar. 25, 1870, p.9, c.4.

16. "Leo," *EJ*, 11:22-23; Bernheimer, *Russian Jew in the U.S.*, 267; "New York City," *UJE*, 8:184; *AJHQ*, 65:209-10, 66:299-300; "United States of America," *EJ*, 15:1619; *Jewish People*, 2:401 ff., 4:349; *AJA*, 12:44; Gurock, *Guide*, 56-58; Morais, *Philadelphia*, 233 ff.

17. "Communism," *UJE*, 5:804-5; *AJYB*, 46:439, 50:562; *AJHQ*, 53:192 ff., 66:302; *AJH*, 68:245; *YA*, 16:52.

18. "New York City," *EJ*, 12:1109-10; *YA*, 9:366 ff., 16:103; *Jewish People*, 4:361-62; Glazer, *American Judaism*, 67; Dan Fogel, "The East European Immigrant as Reflected in *The Jewish Exponent*, 1893-1896" (HUC term paper, n.d.), 10; *AJHQ*, 52:79 ff.; *JQR*, 45:540 ff.; *AJYB*, 53:3 ff.

19. *YA*, 16:9, 33, 40-42, 104; *JSS*, 8:225, 33:249 ff.; *AJH*, 71:188 ff.; *AJYB*, 53:3 ff., 68 ff.; *AJHQ*, 65:203-8; *Labor History*, 4:245.

20. *The Jewish Labor Movement in America* (pamphlet, Jewish Labor Committee, Workmen's Circle, N.Y., 1958), 19 ff.; *Labor History*, 4:243; Sidney Hillman, *Labor in the United States* (N.Y., 1929); *AJHQ*, 51:14; *YA*, 9:288 ff.; 368 ff.; Levine, *Women's Garment Workers*, chaps. 35-36; *AJHQ*, 65:283; Gurock, *Guide*, 53-59.

21. "Communism," *EJ*, 5:804; Handlin, *American People in the Twentieth Century*, 73; N.Y. *Hebrew Standard*, Sept. 1, 1928, pp.1 ff.; *YA*, 16:26, 150 ff., 197; Pope, *Cloth. Ind. in NYC*, 178-79; *Jewish People*, 4:83; *JQR*, 45:540 ff.; *PAJHS*, 49:92; *AJYB*, 24:290 ff., 56:153.

22. *AJHQ*, 65:209 ff.; *Education of Abraham Cahan*, 242; *AJYB*, 53:69-71. Despite the inadequate samplings, the following statistics in *Reports, Immig. Com. Abstracts* indicate that these Russian and Polish newcomers were doing moderately well here compared to some other foreign-born: 1:367, 371, 375, 379, 384-85, 397, 400-1, 407-9, 412.

23. Levine, *Women's Garment Workers*, Frontispiece; Janowsky, *American Jew*, 97-98; Learsi, *Jews in America*, 153 ff.; Jacob Rader Marcus, *Jews in American Life* (Cincinnati, 1945), 12-14; *AJHQ*, 51:14-15, 52:79 ff., 58:334, 65:203 ff., 212 ff.; *YA*, 9:321-22, 366 ff., 16:16, 43-47, 394 ff.; *New York History*, 62:415 ff.; "New York City," *EJ*, 12:1109-10, "United States of America," 16:1619; *JOAH*, 57:475 ff.; Pope, *Cloth. Ind. in NYC*, 293

ff.; *Labor History*, 4:227 ff., 235, 242; *Menorah Journal*, 15:293 ff., 414 ff.; *JQR*, 45:540
ff.; Adler & Connolly, *Buffalo*, 245 ff.; Schoener, *Lower East Side*, 15-16; Janowsky, *Am.
Jew. Reappraisal*, 213; Essrig, "Russian-Jewish Immigration," 175 ff.; *JSS*, 8:219 ff.;
Friedman, *Pilgrims*, 309 ff., 440, n.4; *PAJHS*, 49:90 ff.; Cahan, *Rise of David Levinsky*,
444; Gurock, *Guide*, 56-59.
24. *AJH*, 73:201 ff.; "New York City," *EJ*, 12:1077, 1103-5; *Statistical History of the U.S.*,
682-83; *YA*, 9:316-17; Bernheimer, *Russian Jew in the U.S.*, 261; "New York," *JE*,
9:282, 289; "United States," *UJE*, 10:351; *Jew. Com. Reg.*, 1256 ff.; Rischin, *Promised
City*, 272 ff.; "Panken, Jacob," *UJE*; *AJYB*, 23:277-78, 70:523-24; "Hillquit, Morris,"
UJE, EJ, DAB, Supplement 1.
25. Hertzberg, *Atlanta*, 129-30; *AJYB*, 15(1913-1914):421, 23:278, 26:176-77; *PAJHS*,
48:127, 49:83, 97-98, 50:202 ff., 222-23; *Jewish Digest*, 17(no.12):50 ff.; *AJHQ*, 51:4
ff., 66:301; "Politics," *EJ*, 13:821-22; Fuchs, *Political Behavior*, 41-62; *YA*, 7:229 ff.;
New York Times, Feb. 5, 1968, obituary of Jacob Panken; Howe, *World of Our Fathers*,
360 ff.; Howe & Libo, *How We Lived*, 217 ff.; *JSS*, 8:237, 25:115 ff.; *Reviews in American
History*, 9:244 ff.; *AJH*, 71:232-33, 73:157 ff.; Gurock, *Guide*, 85-88; Bushee, *Boston*,
131 ff.; Boston *Jewish Advocate*, Nov. 2, 1916, p.8; Werner Cohn, "Sources of American
Jewish Liberalism" (Ph.D. diss., New School for Social Research, 1956); "Borofsky,
Samuel Hyman," *UJE, AJYB*, 6(1904-1905):69, *WWIAJ*, 1938-39.

CHAPTER NINE

MAKING A LIVING, PART III:

JEWS IN THE LOWER, MIDDLE AND UPPER CLASSES,

PRIMARILY IN NEW YORK CITY AND SURROUNDING AREAS

1. *Israel Vindicated*, viii; "Trade-Unionism," *JE*, 12:217-18, "United States," 12:368, 375;
Nudelman & Slesinger, *Jew in America*, 2:112; *Jewish Review*, 3:3-24, 161-86, 262-90;
Reports, Immig. Com. Abstracts, 1:339 ff., 363, 514, 517, 524-25, 529; *Jewish People*,
1:391-405, 426-27, 2:426, 4:77; Joseph, *Jewish Immigration*, 158, 188; *PAJHS*, 48:52,
124; Smill, "The Stogy Industry"; *New York Times*, Mar. 1, 1979, obituary of Abraham
Dreier; Ravitch & Goodenow, *Educating an Urban People*, 103; Ginzberg & Berman,
American Worker, 75 ff.; Banks, *First-Person America*, 43 ff.; *AJYB*, 31:203-4; *Jewish Life*,
8(no.12):17 ff.; *YA*, 16:13, 16, 98-99, 101, 18:39 ff.; *AJHQ*, 65:203 ff., 265-66, 272 ff.;
Rischin, *Promised City*, 56, 59-60, 68-69, 187, 272; Fishberg, *The Jews*, 397, 399; *Commentary*, 37(no.2); *American Heritage*, 17(no.6):78; *AH*, Mar. 4, 1904, pp.503 ff.; Bernheimer, *Russian Jew in the U.S.*, 108; Janowsky, *Am. Jew. Reappraisal*, 67-68; *Labor History*, 4:227 ff.; Bushee, *Boston*, 63 ff.; Rogoff, "Formative Years," 93-94.
2. Banks, *First-Person America*, 31 ff.; Bernheimer, *Russian Jew in the U.S.*, 109, 297; Rischin, *Promised City*, 56; *Senior Summary* (published by the N.Y. Junior League),
5(no.1):6; Friedman, *Pilgrims*, 312 ff.; Harold Friedman, *The Happiest Man: The Life of
Louis Borgenicht* (N.Y., 1942); *Sayings of the Fathers*, 2:6; Hertz, *Authorized Daily Prayer
Book*, 632-33; *AH*, Apr. 1, 1904, pp.630-31, Apr. 8, 1904, pp.660-61, Apr. 15, 1904,
pp.686-87; *AJHQ*, 53:269-72, 56:295-96; *New York Times*, Dec. 3, 1971, p.44, cs.3-4;
Moody's Investor's Fact Sheet, NYSE, Dec. 20, 1982; *Education of Abraham Cahan*, 219-
20, 233, 259-62; Learsi, *Jews in America*, 152; *YA*, 9:239; Howe & Libo, *How We Lived*,
65 ff.; *Jewish Review*, 3:3 ff.; Ribalow (ed.), *Autobiographies*, 166 ff.; Grayzel, *History of
the Jews*, 688-89; *Jewish People*, 4:82.
3. Bushee, *Boston*, 86-88, 97; "United States," *JE*, 12:376; *Reports, Immig. Com. Abstracts*,
1:741 ff., 747 ff., 759, 2:91 ff., 95 ff., 102 ff., 110-11, 130 ff., 142, 259 ff.; Seller (ed.),
Immigrant Women, 122, 158; Weinberger, *Jews and Judaism*, 84 ff.; *Jewish People*, 1:392.

4. Finkelstein, *The Jews* (1949), 1:344, (1960), 2:1730-31; *AJH*, 71:232; *AJHQ*, 53:264 ff.; Rischin, *Promised City*, 56-59, 70; Jenks & Lauck, *Immigration Problem*, 125; "United States," *JE*, 12:374; *Jewish Digest*, 17(no.7):55-56; "New York City," *EJ*, 12:1110.

5. *American Heritage*, 17(no.6):78; *U.A.H.C. Statistics*, 11; Cowen, *Memories of an American Jew*, 297, 301; *By Myself I'm A Book*, 43-44; Bachrach, "The Immigrant on the Hill"; *PAJHS*, 9:74, 49:122-23; *Papers of the Jewish Women's Congress*, 179; *AJH*, 71:225-27, 230; P. & K., *Tourist's Guide*, 445 ff., 452-53, 458-59, 464-65, 473; Howe, *World of Our Fathers*, 608; *Reports, Immig. Com.*, 15:xlv; *Jew. Com. Reg.*, 81 ff.; N.Y. *Jewish Spectator*, 30(no.1):12 ff.; *AJHQ*, 65:264; JSS, 32:172 ff.; Eisenberg, *Eyewitnesses to American Jewish History*, 4:20 ff.; Rischin, *Promised City*, 10, 59, 92-94; Jeffrey Gurock, *When Harlem Was Jewish, 1870-1930* (N.Y., 1979); Grinstein, *New York City*, 64 ff.; "New York," *JE*, 9:281, 290-91, "United States," 12:369, 373; "New York City," *UJE*, 8:182-83, 201 ff., *EJ*, 12:1078, 1080 ff., 1082, 1107-8; "Brooklyn," *UJE*, 2:547, 550, 554, "New York (State), Long Island," 8:196 ff., 200 ff.; "Mount Vernon," "New Rochelle," "Yonkers, N.Y.," *UJE*; "Westchester County," *EJ*; Fishberg, *The Jews*, 401-3; *AJYB*, 26:583, 28:402, 55:11; *Eastern Union*, 86-93. The following works have further information on Brooklyn: Ralph Foster Weld, *Brooklyn is America* (N.Y., 1950); Landesman, *Brownsville*; Alter F. Landesman, *A History of New Lots, Brooklyn* (Port Washington, N.Y., 1977); George Kranzler, *Williamsburg: A Jewish Community in Transition* (N.Y., 1961); Egon Mayer, *From Suburb to Shtetl: The Jews of Boro Park* (Phila., 1979); Samuel P. Abelow, *History of Brooklyn Jewry* (Brooklyn, 1937); Rita Seiden Miller (ed.), *Brooklyn USA: The Fourth Largest City in America* (Brooklyn, 1979); Sutton, *Aleppo-in-Flatbush*.

6. Jenks & Lauck, *Immigration Problems*, 297; Rockaway, *Jews of Detroit*, 66-67; Thomas Kessner, *Golden Door: Italian and Jewish Immigrant Mobility in New York City, 1880-1915* (N.Y., 1977), 168 ff., 170-72; *American Heritage*, 17(no.6):78; *AH*, Apr. 1, 1904, pp.330-31, Apr. 8, 1904, pp.660-61, Apr. 15, 1904, pp.686-87, Jan. 27, 1911, p.379, June 7, 1912, pp.154, 163, June 21, 1912, pp.209, 221, Aug. 7, 1914, p.387; *Reports, Immig. Com. Abstracts*, 2:22 ff., 413 ff.; *AJA*, 9:32 ff.; *Ha-Yehudi*, no.24, 1912, p.16; S. Jarmulowsky Bank, N.Y., to Felix M. Warburg, N.Y., Oct. 29, 1913, May 21, 1914, Warburg Papers, AJAr; *New York Times*, June 2, 1912, obituary of Jarmulowsky; Bernheimer, *Russian Jew in the U.S.*, 105-6, 108, 114; Pittsburgh Wholesale District: recall of J.R. Marcus, age eleven, who accompanied his father on buying trips to Pittsburgh's wholesale district, 1907; "United States," *JE*, 12:368-69, 374-76; Herbert S. Goldstein, *Forty Years of Struggle For a Principle: The Biography of Harry Fischel* (N.Y., 1928), 32-33; "Fischel, Harry," *UJE*; *Jewish Digest*, 8(no.8):33 ff.; Schary, *For Special Occasions*, 4; "Schary, Dore," *EJ*, *WWW*, vol 7; "Rosenberg, Samuel," *UJE*; "Grossinger, Jenny," *AJYB*, 74:556; Marcus, *AJWD*, 671-76; *Jew. Com. Reg.*, 145-285, 716 ff.; Memphis *Commercial Appeal*, Feb. 14-15, 1945; *AJYB*, 47:520; Gurock, *Guide*, 55-56; *PAJHS*, 48:46-47; *Jewish People*, 4:82; Goren, *American Jews*, 47-48; Finkelstein, *The Jews* (1960), 2:1637 ff.; "New York City," *JE*, 9:279, *UJE*, 8:182-84; Davis & Meyer, *American Jewish History*, 366 ff.; *JSS*, 3:41 ff.; Geller, "Jewish Life in Boston"; *AJHQ*, 66:484; Rischin, *Promised City*, 68-69; Streator, Illinois *Daily Times-Press*, Sept. 30, 1933, p.2; Illinois *Home Times*, July 12, 1912; Howe, *World of Our Fathers*, 137 ff., 159 ff., 163 ff.; Edward Alsworth Ross, *The Old World in the New, etc.* (N.Y., 1914), chap. 7; Friedman, *Pilgrims*, 309 ff.

7. "Dix, Henry A.," *UJE*; Mark H. Dix, *An American Business Adventure: The Story of Henry A. Dix* (N.Y., 1928).

8. "Horowitz, Louis Jay," *UJE, EJ, WWW*, vol.3, *WWIAJ*, 1938-1939; Baron, *History*, 2:272; Cohen, *Jews in the Making of America*, 129-30.

9. Horwich, *My First Eighty Years*; Meites, *Chicago*, 151, 231; "Horwich, Bernard," Glassman (ed.), *BEOAJ, 1935*.

10. "Greenfield, Albert Monroe," *WWIAJ*, 1938-1939; *New York Times*, July 28, 1937, obituary of Louis Blaustein, Jan. 6, 1967, obituary of Albert Greenfield; *Jewish Digest*, 7(no.6):27 ff.; "Blaustein, Louis," *UJE, EJ, WWW*, vol.1; Fein, *Baltimore*, 223; *AH*, Apr. 1, 1904, pp.630-31, May 5, 1905, pp.725 ff.

11. "Edelhertz, Bernard," "Matz, Israel," "Satenstein, Louis," *WWIAJ*, 1926; *AJYB*, 44:340; "Eisenman, Morris," *AJYB*, 50:520; *New York Times*, June 2, 1962, obituary of Nathan Posner, Nov. 7, 1968, p.47.

12. *Jewish Post and Opinion*, Aug. 7, 1970, p.12; "Paley, Samuel," *WWIAJ*, 1938-1939; *New York Times*, Nov. 29, 1958, obituary of Julius Klorfein.

13. *Moody's Investor's Fact Sheet*, Nov. 18, 1982, 5(no.86, sec.16); GHQ, Winter 1974, 511 ff.; J. Pfeffer, *Distinguished Jews of America, etc.* (2 vols., N.Y., 1917), 1:259; *New York Times*, Aug. 3, 1966, obituary of Nathan Handwerker.

14. "Himmelstein, Lena," *EJ*.

15. "Davidson, Benjamin," *WWIAJ*, 1926; Elovitz, *Birmingham*, 62-63, 125-30; "Pizitz, Louis," *WWW*, vol 3; Louis Pizitz file in the Marcus Collections.

16. *AJYB*, 53:524; "Uris, Harris H.," *AJYB*, 47:533; "Rosenthal, Joseph," *UJE*; "Hoffman, Jacob M.," "Sobel, Leon," "Winter, Benjamin," *WWIAJ*, 1926.

17. *Hattie Callner: An Autobiography as told to Bernard Levin* (n.p., n.d.), AJAr.

18. Marcus, *AJW*, 161-62.

19. *New York Times*, July 16, 1970, p.23; "Prentis, Meyer Leon," *WWIAJ*, 1938-1939.

20. *AJYB*, 73:635; "Sarnoff, David," *UJE, EJ, WWIAJ*, 1926, *WWIAJ*, 1938-1939, *WWW*, vol.5; Eugene Lyons, *David Sarnoff* (N.Y., 1966), 32-33, 39; Harris, *Merchant Princes*, 740.

CHAPTER TEN

MAKING A LIVING, PART IV:

THE CINEMA

1. *Pacific Historian*, 26(no.4):1 ff.; *AJHQ*, 54:368-69; Faulkner, *Social Justice*, 295 ff.; *WSJHQ*, 11:20-24, 14:278, 15:182, 374; "Laemmle, Carl," *UJE, EJ, DAB*, Supplement 2, *WWW*, vol.1; "Zukor, Adolph," *UJE, EJ*, Glassman (ed.), *BEOAJ*, 1935; Devils Lake, North Dakota *Journal*, Nov. 28, 1983, p.3; "Balaban, Barney," *WWIAJ*, 1938-1939, *WWW*, vol.5; Carrie Balaban, *Continuous Performance: The Story of A.J. Balaban* (N.Y., 1964); Meites, *Chicago*, 390; Simonhoff, *Saga of American History*, 355 ff.; Will Irwin, *The House That Shadows Built* (Garden City, N.Y., 1928); Adolph Zukor, with Dale Kramer, *The Public Is Never Wrong* (N.Y., 1953); Arthur Mayer, *Merely Colossal: The Story of the Movies From the Long Chase to the Chaise Lounge* (N.Y., 1953), 149-53; Bob Thomas, *Selznick* (N.Y., 1970), 6-25, et passim; "Lasky, Jesse Louis," "Marx, Julius (Groucho)," "Selwyn, Edgar," "Tucker, Sophie," *UJE*; Friedman, *Pilgrims*, 319 ff., 331 ff.; Golden & Rywell, *Jews in American History*, 442 ff.; *Every Friday*, Mar. 30, 1962, p.3; Jesse Louis Lasky, with Don Weldin, *I Blow My Own Horn* (Garden City, N.Y., 1957); "Motion Pictures," *DAH* (1942), *DAH* (1976-1978); *New York Times* Jan. 14, 1958, obituary of Jesse Lasky, Mar. 21, 1960, p.8, Oct. 23, 1961, obituary for Joseph Schenck, Mar. 5, 1969, p.41, Mar. 8, 1971, p.32, Jan. 9, 1973, p.28; Detroit *Jewish News*, Mar. 1, 1974, p.27; "Fox, William," *UJE, EJ, DAB*, Supplement 5, *WWIAJ*, 1926, *WWIAJ*, 1938-1939, Glassman (ed.), *BEOAJ, 1935*; Trinidad, Colorado *Chronicle News*, Oct. 13, 1929, p.5; *Time*, Feb. 11, 1974, p.67; "Theatre," *UJE*, 10:231 ff.; Wish, *Society and Thought*, 2:vii, 254, 291-92, 522 ff.; "Goldwyn, Samuel," *UJE, EJ, WWW*, vol.7, *WWIAJ*, 1926, *WWIAJ*, 1938-1939, Glassman (ed.), *BEOAJ, 1935*; *Land Without Peasants* (*This is Our Home*, pamphlet no.12, American Jewish Committee), 14 ff.; "Loew, Marcus," *UJE, DAB, WWW*, vol.1; "Schenck, Joseph," Glassman

(ed.), *BEOAJ, 1935*; "Schenck, Nicholas M.," *WWIAJ*, 1938-1939; Bosley Crowther, *The Lion's Share: The Story of an Entertainment Empire* (N.Y., 1957), 41; Bosley Crowther, *Hollywood Rajah: The Life and Times of Louis B. Mayer* (N.Y., 1960), 59-60; "Mayer, Louis Burt," *UJE, EJ, DAB*, Supplement 6; Sachar, *Modern Jewish History*, 345; *EAH*, 628-29; Pearl Sieben, *The Immortal Jolson: His Life and Times* (N.Y., 1962); Terry Ramsaye, *A Million and One Nights: A History of the Motion Picture* (N.Y., 1964), 300, 393, et passim, 417, et passim, 430, 585, 588-89, 594 ff., 612 ff., 712, 761 ff., 766, 771, 773; "Warner," *UJE, EJ*; Jack L. Warner, with Dean Jennings, *My First Hundred Years in Hollywood* (N.Y., 1965); "Warner, Albert," "Warner, Jack Leonard," *WWIAJ*, 1938-1939; "Warner, Harry Morris," *DAB*, Supplement 6, Glassman (ed.), *BEOAJ, 1935, WWIAJ*, 1938-1939; Werner Keller, *Diaspora: The Post-Biblical History of the Jews* (N.Y., 1969), 488-89; "Rothafel, Samuel Lionel," *UJE, DAB*, Supplement 2; *AHR*, 87:913-14; "Motion Pictures," *EJ*, 12:446 ff.; *WSJHQ*, 3:52; Handlin, *Adventure in Freedom*, 141, 239; *Judaism*, 19:482 ff.; Nevins & Commager, *United States*, 424; Marcus, *AJW*, 1:174; Cohen, *Jews in the Making of America*, 160 ff.; *EJ Year Book*, 1977-1978, 78 ff.; Lewis Jacob, *The Rise of the American Film* (N.Y., 1969); Kevin Brownlow, *The Parade's Gone By . . .* (Berkeley, 1968).

CHAPTER ELEVEN

MAKING A LIVING, PART V:

THE ARTS AND THE PROFESSIONS

1. *CCAR Journal*, 23(no.2):57 ff.; Jenks & Lauck, *Immigration Problem*, 351-52; *AJHS*, 65:257 ff.; *AJH*, 71:230; *Menorah Journal*, 3:252 ff., 260 ff.

2. Schoener, *Portal to America*, 129-30; *AJHQ*, 53:270; Nudelman & Slesinger, *Jew in America*, 2:112; *Jewish Review*, 3:11-12; "United States," *JE*, 12:369-70, 374; *Jewish People*, 4:82; *PAJHS*, 49:96; "Rabi, Isidor I.," *WWIWJ*, 1978; Rischin, *Promised City*, 71-74; "New York City," *EJ*, 12:1085; Fishberg, *The Jews*, 401 ff.; *AJYB*, 22:383-93, 50:22; *JSS*, 1:327 ff.; Bernheimer, *Russian Jew in the U.S.*, 106-7; *AH*, Mar. 4, 1904, pp.503-4; Geller, "Jewish Life in Boston," 8 ff.; Lee J. Levinger, *The Jewish Student in America* (B'nai B'rith, Cincinnati, 1937), 85 ff.

3. *Jewish People*, 1:425-27; "New York," *EJ*, 12:1085, 1110- 1111; *Reports, Immig. Com. Abstracts*, 2:49 ff., 76-83; Seller (ed.), *Immigrant Women*, 85; Jenks & Lauck, *Immigration Problem*, 311 ff.; Marcus, *AJWD*, 626-29; *Jewish Review*, 3:22, 162-73.

4. "Perlman, Selig," "Sharfman, Isaiah Leo," *WWIAJ*, 1926, Glassman (ed.), *BEOAJ, 1935, WWIAJ*, 1938-1939; Golden & Rywell, *Jews in American History*, 157, 399; "Meltzer, Samuel James," *UJE, WWW*, vol. 1; "Rosenthal, Max, *JE, EJ, DAB, AJYB*, 6(1904-1905):174-75; Kagan, *Contributions*, 39-40, 323-27, 332-34; "Levene, Aaron Theodore," *UJE, EJ, WWIAJ*, 1926, Glassman (ed.), *BEOAJ, 1935, WWIAJ*, 1938-1939; "Lipman, Charles B.," Glassman (ed.), *BEOAJ, 1935*; "Sabin, Albert Bruce," *EJ*.

5. *AJYB*, 49:49 ff., 54:540, 56:571, 60:356; "Cohen, Morris Raphael," *UJE, EJ, WWIAJ*, Supplement 4, *WWW*, vol.2; *A Dreamer's Journey: Autobiography of Morris Raphael Cohen* (Boston, 1949); Morris Raphael Cohen, *Reflections of a Wondering Jew* (Boston, 1950); Leonora Cohen Rosenfield, *Portrait of a Philosopher: Morris R. Cohen in Life and Letters* (N.Y., 1962); *AJA*, 5:34 ff.; "Perlman, Nathan D.," *WWIAJ*, 1926.

6. "Pritzker, Louis," "Pritzker, Nicholas," *WWIAJ*, 1926, *WWIAJ*, 1938-1939; Meites, *Chicago*, 619; Los Angeles *Times*, Feb. 9, 1986, part 1, p.29; "Pritzker, Jay," *American Jewish Biographies* (N.Y., 1982); "Pritzker," *WWIA*, 1982-1983; Louis Waldman, *Labor Lawyer* (N.Y., 1944); "Waldman, Louis," *WWIAJ*, 1938-1939; *New York Times*, Dec. 13, 1957, Sept. 14, 1982, obituary for Louis Waldman; Reznikoff, *Louis Marshall*, 2:979 ff.

7. *JTA-DNB*, Apr. 21, 1966, p.4; "Rabinoff, Max," *UJE*; S. Hurok, *Impresario* (N.Y., 1946); S. Hurok *Presents: A Memoir of the Dance World* (N.Y., 1953); "Hurok, Sol," *EJ*, *WWIAJ*, 1926, Glassman (ed.), *BEOAJ, 1935*; "Gest, Morris," *WWIAJ*, 1926, *AJYB*, 44:337.

8. Hapgood, *Spirit of the Ghetto*, chap.9; "Sterne, Maurice," *UJE, EJ, DAB*, Supplement 6, Glassman (ed.), *BEOAJ, 1935*; "Auerbach-Levy," *UJE, AJYB*, 66:572; *New York Times*, May 18, 1966, p.39, cs.1-3; *AJYB*, 47:525, 67:544; "Weber, Max," *UJE, EJ, AJYB*, 64:497, *WWIAJ*, 1926; *Jewish Currents*, 36(no.11):16; "Hirshhorn, Joseph Herman," "Shahn, Ben," *EJ*; "Berenson, Bernard," *UJE, EJ, DAB*, Supplement 6.

9. *New York Times*, Aug. 17, 1962, obituary of Louis I. Bloom, July 2, 1969, p.39, July 25, 1970, p.23; "Birnbaum, Martin," *WWW*, vol .5; "Zorach, William," *EJ, WWW*, vol.4.

10. "United States," *JE*, 12:368, 374; "Pasternack, Josef Alexander," *UJE*, Glassman (ed.), *BEOAJ, 1935, WWIAJ*, 1938-1939; "Sokoloff, Nikolai," *WWIAJ*, 1938-1939; "Gabrilowitsch, Ossip Salmonovitch," *UJE*, Glassman (ed.), *BEOAJ, 1935*; "Godowsky, Leopold, "*UJE, EJ, WWIAJ*, 1926, Glassman (ed.), *BEOAJ, 1935*; "Zimbalist, Efrem," *UJE, EJ, WWIAJ*, 1926, Glassman (ed.), *BEOAJ, 1935*; Marcus, *AJW*, 70; "Elman, Mischa," *UJE, EJ, AJYB*, 69:606, *WWIAJ*, 1926, Glassman (ed.), *BEOAJ, 1935*; "Heifetz, Jascha," *UJE, EJ, WWIAJ*, 1926, *WWIAJ*, 1938-1939, Glassman (ed.), *BEOAJ, 1935*.

11. "Berlin, Irving," *UJE, EJ, WWIAJ*, 1926, *WWIAJ*, 1938-1939, Glassman (ed.), *BEOAJ, 1935*; *AJYB*, 68:534.

12. "Moisseiff, Leon Solomon," *UJE, EJ, WWIAJ*, 1926; "Strauss, Joseph Baermann," *WWIAJ*, 1938-1939, *AJYB*, 46:343; P. & K., *Tourist's Guide*, 447, 459; "Radin, Adolph Moses," "Radin, Max," "Radin, Paul," *UJE, AJYB*, 52:504; "Klapper, Paul," *WWIAJ*, 1926, *WWIAJ*, 1938-1939, *AJYB*, 54:539.

13. "Strunsky, Simeon," *UJE, AJYB*, 50:524; "Tobenkin, Elias," *UJE, AJYB*, 65:438, *WWIAJ*, 1926; "Yezierska, Anzia," *UJE, WWIAJ*, 1926; Marcus, *AJWD*, 784 ff.; "Bernstein, Herman," *UJE, EJ, WWIAJ*, 1926.

14. "Bogen, Boris David," *UJE, EJ, WWIAJ*, 1926; *AJYB*, 68:527; M. Bruce Lustig, "The Life and Activity of Jacob Billikopf, etc." (rabbinical thesis, HUC, 1986); "Fink, David Ely," *WWIAJ*, 1926, *WWIAJ*, 1938-1939; "Billikopf, Jacob," *UJE, EJ, DAB*, Supplement 4, *AJYB*, 53:523, *WWIAJ*, 1926; "Loeb, Sophie Irene," *UJE, WWIAJ*, 1926; Marcus, *AJW*, 97, 124, 206, 209; Marcus, *AJWD*, 639 ff.

15. *AJYB*, 43:358, 55:455-56; "Goldenweiser" *UJE, EJ*; for Ludwig Behr Bernstein, the sociologist, see *AJYB*, 47:519; "Stone, Nahum I.," *WWIAJ*, 1926; *New York Times*, Oct. 26, 1966, obituary for Nahum Stone; "Jastrow, Joseph," "Marcus, Morris Jr.," *UJE, AJYB*, 46:339.

16. *AJYB*, 45:389, 46:339, 345, 47:532, 48:494, 497, 50:514, 518, 52:505, 53:526, 56:569, 67:537; Kagan, *Contributions*, 138-39, 446-47; "Friedman, Gedide," *WWIAJ*, 1926.

17. *New York Times*, Dec. 12, 1962, obituary for Isaiah Wechsler; *JSS*, 25:100; "Wechsler, Isaiah," *WWIAJ*, 1926; *AJYB*, 51:523, 64:496; "Brill, Abraham Arden," *DAB*, Supplement 4, *WWIAJ*, 1926.

18. "Marmer, Harry Aaron", "Silberstein, Ludwik," *WWIAJ*, 1926; "Lefschetz, Solomon," *WWIAJ*, 1926, *Jews in the World of Science: A Biographical Dictionary of Jews Eminent in the Natural and Social Sciences* (N.Y., 1956); "Gomberg, Moses," *UJE*, Glassman (ed.) *BEOAJ, 1935*; *AJYB*, 48:486; "Rosanoff, Martin André," *WWIAJ*, 1926.

19. "Finn, Julius," *WWIAJ*, 1926; "Reshevsky, Samuel Herman," *UJE, EJ, Columbia Encyclopedia*.

20. "Abelman, Max," *WWIAJ*, 1926, *WWIAJ*, 1938-1939; "Bloomfield, Meyer," *WWIAJ*, 1926; "Moskowitz, Henry," *WWIAJ*, 1928.

21. "Levine (Lorwin), Lewis L.," *WWIAJ*, 1926, *WWIAJ*, 1928, *WWIAJ*, 1938-1939; "Lorwin, Lewis L.," *WWW*, vol.5; *AJA*, 33:53 ff.; "Levine, Isaac Don," "Levine, Manuel," "Levine, Max," "Levine, Victor Emanuel," *UJE*.

22. *AJHQ*, 55:5.

CHAPTER TWELVE
TWO DIFFERENT COMMUNITIES:
THE "GERMANS" AND THE NEWCOMERS
EAST EUROPEANS AND THEIR RELIGION:
THE GHETTO AND ORTHODOXY

1. Malcom Stern, N.Y., to JRM, Oct. 7, 1986, Marcus Collections; Byars, *B. & M. Gratz*, 106-7; *PAJHS*, 49:121; S. Adler-Rudel, *Ostjuden in Deutschland, 1880-1940* (Tuebingen, 1959), 27 ff.; Adler & Connolly, *Buffalo*, 114.
2. Swichkow & Gartner, *Milwaukee*, 170-71; "Anarchism," *UJE*; *Jewish People*, 4:286; Rischin, *Promised City*, 150-51, 155, 166.
3. Grinstein, *New York City*, 460 ff.; "Conferences, Rabbinical," *JE*; Janowsky, *Am. Jew. Reappraisal*, 324; Swichkow & Gartner, *Milwaukee*, 171.
4. Wirth, *Ghetto*, Foreword, 1 ff.; "Ghetto," *UJE*; *By Myself I'm A Book*, 30 ff.; *PAJHS*, 48:108; *Midstream*, 12:11 ff.; "New York City," *UJE*, 8:182; *YA*, 15:82 ff.; P. & K., *Tourist's Guide*, 381, 387; *Reports, Ind. Com.*, 15:xlv, xlvii ff.; Levinger, *Jews in U.S.*, 268, 285; Philpott, *The Slum and the Ghetto*, 3 ff.; Adler & Connolly, *Buffalo*, 185 ff.; Ellis, *Am. Catholicism*, 167; Schoener, *Portal to America*, Introduction; *Jewish People*, 4:338; *AJYB*, 50:23 ff.; Ray Allen Billington, *American History after 1865* (Paterson, N.J., 1960), 73; Cole, *Irrepressible Conflict*, 181-82; Curti, *American Thought*, 299; *Education of Abraham Cahan*, 220 ff., 355; *Pa. Mag. of Hist.*, 93:136-37; Schappes, *DHJUS*, 217 ff.; Lipman, *Soc. Hist. of Jews in England*, 94 ff.; Grinstein, *New York City*, 32 ff.; Wish, *Society and Thought*, 2:142 ff.; "Slums," *DAH* (1942); Arthur M. Schlesinger, *Paths to the Present* (N.Y., 1949), 59-60; Hirsh & Doherty, *Mount Sinai Hospital*, 3-9; Howe, *World of Our Fathers*, 67 ff., 148 ff.; Benjamin, *Three Years*, 1:77; Smucker, *History*, 326-27; *Baron Festschrift*, 285 ff.; Ernst, *Immigrant Life*, 48 ff.; *AJH*, 70:429 ff.; Bernheimer, *Russian Jew in the U.S.*, 43 ff., 58 ff., 118, 282 ff., 304 ff., 320 ff., 322 ff.; Faulkner, *Social Justice*, 157-58; *American Heritage*, 17(no.6):78; *JM*, Feb. 15, 1884, p.5, c.4.
5. Hertzberg, *Atlanta*, 110 ff.; Gartner, *Cleveland*, 123; *AJYB*, 26:578; *YA*, 15:129; *By Myself I'm A Book*, 70, 153, 156; Blum, *Baltimore*, 28; *Generations*, 1(no.5):19; Swichkow & Gartner, *Milwaukee*, 166 ff.; *Michigan History*, 52:28 ff.; *U.A.H.C. Statistics*, 19, 40; *AJHQ*, 62:261 ff., 264, 71:225; Geller, "Jewish Life in Boston," 2; Uchill, *Pioneers*, 203; Adler & Connolly, *Buffalo*, 186; Curti, *American Thought*, 298-99; Elovitz, *Birmingham*, 64 ff.; P. & K., *Tourist's Guide*, 381, 387; Bushee, *Boston*, 25, 32-33; Wirth, *Ghetto*, 195 ff.; Morais, *Philadelphia*, 215-16; Sachar, *Modern Jewish History*, 316 ff.; Ernst, *Immigrant Life*, 45-47; Rischin, *Promised City*, 79; *Reports, Ind. Com.*, 15:xliii, 476-78; *Bulletin*, Missouri Historical Society, 33(no.2):64 ff., 71; Woods, *Americans in Process*, 63 ff.; *RIJHN*, 8:68 ff.; Vorspan & Gartner, *Los Angeles*, 203-4, 217.
6. Wittke, *We Who Built America*, 337-38; Adler & Connolly, *Buffalo*, 186, 256-58; *Generations*, 1(no.5):19; Schlesinger, *New Viewpoints*, 15-16; *AJYB*, 26:583; *PAJHS*, 48:106 ff.; Sachar, *Modern Jewish History*, 317; Bernheimer, *Russian Jew in the U.S.*, 284; Schoener, *Lower East Side*, 11; Schoener, *Portal to America*, 208 ff.; Rischin, *Promised City*, vii, 9-10, 93-94; "New York City," *JE*, 9:281; *AJA*, 33:95 ff.
7. *Michigan History*, 52:34; Adler & Connolly, *Buffalo*, 198 ff.; *Jewish Post and Opinion*, Oct. 20, 1961, p.2, cs.1-3; Rischin, *Promised City*, 76-78, 141; Handlin, *American People in the Twentieth Century*, 72; Janowsky, *Am. Jew. Reappraisal*, 397; Wittke, *We Who Built America*, 337-38; Eisenberg, *Eyewitnesses to American Jewish History*, 3:31 ff.; Schoener, *Lower East Side*, 19 ff.; *National Jewish Monthly*, 90(no.8):43; *HUCA*, 23(part 2):221 ff.

8. *From a Ruined Garden*, 111; *Education of Abraham Cahan*, 12; *National Jewish Monthly*, 90(no.8):40 ff.; Howe, *World of Our Fathers*, 148 ff.; Woods, *Americans in Process*, 40 ff.; Riis, *Children of the Poor*, 54 ff.; "New York City," *EJ*, 12:1078, 1106-8, "United States of America," 16:1615; *AJHQ*, 50:24; *Papers of the Jewish Women's Congress*, 170 ff.; Lipman, *Soc. Hist. of Jews in England*, 104; Bernheimer, *Russian Jew in the U.S.*, 304 ff.; "New York," *JE*, 9:284; *PAJHS*, 48:108, 125; Goren, *American Jews*, 44; *Jewish People*, 1:395; *AJYB*, 50:24; Baltzell, *Protestant Establishment*, 58 ff.; *Proceedings of the NCJW*, *1896*, 258 ff.; *Reports, Immig. Com. Abstracts*, 1:420-31; Riis, *How the Other Half Lives*, 85.

9. *YA*, 9:320; Schoener, *Lower East Side*, 15-16, 50 ff.; Hindus, *Old East Side*, 54 ff.; *AJYB*, 7(1905-1906):224; Gartner, *Cleveland*, 124; *Education of Abraham Cahan*, 12; *Jewish Life*, 9(no.4):15; *Reports, Immig. Com. Abstracts*, 1:753; Wish, *Society and Thought*, 1:404; *RIJHN*, 7:197 ff., 227-29, 236; Weinberger, *Jews and Judaism*, 84 ff.; *PAJHS*, 48:107-8; Rischin, *Promised City*, 259; Schoener, *Portal to America*, 57-58, 207-8; *Michigan Jewish History*, 7(no.2):8 ff.

10. Rischin, *Promised City*, 86-89, 196, 219; Markens, *Hebrews*, 190; Ernst, *Immigrant Life*, 48 ff.; Elbogen, *Cent. of Jewish Life*, 429; *AJA*, 33:3; Bushee, *Boston*, 30, 36, 40-42, 54; *Medical History*, 25:1-10; Bernheimer, *Russian Jew in the U.S.*, 136, 285-301, 329-30; *AJH*, 70:429-37, 73:134 ff.; Feingold, *Zion in America*, 137; *Reports, Ind. Com.*, 15:xlvi, lxxvi-vii; *YA*, 5:219 ff.; *Pope, Cloth. Ind. in NYC*, 193; *AJYB*, 50:25.

11. "United States," *JE*, 12:378; Franz Boas, *Changes in Bodily Form of Descendants of Immigrants* (Washington, 1911); *AJH*, 70:440; Bernheimer, *Russian Jew in the U.S.*, 58-59, 120-21, 282, 286-87, 326; *AJA*, 9:40, 33:85 ff., 101; Cowen, *Memories of an American Jew*, 298; *Jewish People*, 4:58; Myers, *Great American Fortunes*, 1:218-22; Schoener, *Portal to America*, 213 ff.; Lipman, *Soc. Hist. of Jews in England*, 95; *YA*, 9:317; *Reports, Ind. Com.*, 15:xlvii, 479; "New York," *JE*, 9:284; Oral interview of Hilda Fagelson Matzkin, copy in AJAr; *New York*, Oct. 13, 1975, pp.51 ff.; Rischin, *Promised City*, 92; Hindus, *Old East Side*, 51 ff., 251 ff.; *Generations*, 1(no.5):40 ff.; "Pobedonostsev, Konstantin Petrovich," *EJ*.

12. *New York*, Oct. 13, 1975, pp.63, 74-77; *AJYB*, 50:27; Adler & Connolly, *Buffalo*, 186, 308-9; Schoener, *Portal to America*, Introduction, 10-12; Schoener, *Lower East Side*, Introduction, 9-10; *Congress Monthly*, 42(no.7):15; "Padua," *JE*, 9:457; *Congress Bi-Weekly*, June 18, 1971, pp.17 ff.; *Reports, Ind. Com.*, 15:xlvi; Rockaway, *Jews of Detroit*, 145; *YA*, 9:319; *National Jewish Monthly*, 90(no.80):43; Howe, *World of Our Fathers*, 148 ff., 256 ff.; Howe & Libo, *How We Lived*, 48 ff.; Ribalow (ed.), *Autobiographies*, 262 ff., 303 ff.; Hindus, *Old East Side*, 51 ff., 121 ff.; Riis, *How the Other Half Lives*, 85 ff.; David R. Goldfield & James B. Lane, *The Enduring Ghetto* (Phila., 1973), 197-211; Bachrach, "Immigrant on the Hill," 2 ff.; Weinberger, *Jews and Judaism*, 40 ff.; Ida R. Zagat (ed.), *Jewish Life on New York's Lower East Side, 1912-1962* (N.Y., 1972); Roskolenko, *Lower East Side*; Diane Cavallo, *The Lower East Side: A Portrait in Time* (N.Y., 1971); Cowen, *Memories of an American Jew*, 289 ff.; Azriel Eisenberg, *The Golden Land* (N.Y., 1964), 121-22; *WSJHQ*, 11:99 ff.; Wieder, *Boston's North End*, 17 ff.; Eisenberg, *Eyewitnesses to American Jewish History*, 4:20-22; Oscar Handlin, *The Uprooted* (Boston, 1952), 144 ff.; Philpott, *The Slum and the Ghetto*, 3 ff.; *AJHQ*, 53:261, 56:150; Rawidowicz, *Chicago Pinkas*, 113 ff.; Margolin, *Jews of Eastern Europe*, 251 ff.

13. M. Friedlaender, *The Jewish Religion* (London, 1913); Janowsky, *American Jew*, 206, 213; *AJYB*, 66:28, 30; *Judaism*, 14:309; *By Myself I'm A Book*, 107 ff.; *AI*, Jan. 28, 1887, p.4, cs.2-3; article in Syracuse *Standard*, Dec. 29, 1890, reprinted from the New York *Sun*, copy in Marcus Collections; "Philadelphia," *UJE*, 8:479; Bernheimer, *Russian Jew in the U.S.*, 15; Adler & Connolly, *Buffalo*, 193 ff.; Grinstein, *History*, 83; *AJHQ*, 53:253; *AJH*, 73:169-70.

14. Levin, "East European Jews in U.S.," 6 ff.; Janowsky, *American Jew*, 214; *Baron Festschrift*, 294, 296; Grayzel, *History of the Jews*, 698; Levinger, *Jews in U.S.*, 272; Curti et al., *American History*, 268-69.

15. Weinberger, *Jews and Judaism*, 6-7, 14-15, 17-18, 20, 78 ff., 118; Finkelstein, *The Jews* (1949), 1:408; Schoener, *Lower East Side*, 49; Hertzberg, *Atlanta*, 92; *By Myself I'm A Book*, 107 ff.; Bushee, *Boston*, 137 ff., 145, 157.

16. *PAJHS*, 49:109; Eisenberg, *Eyewitnesses to American Jewish History*, 3:86-87; *By Myself I'm A Book*, 31; *AJYB*, 66:29-30; Weinberger, *Jews and Judaism*, 13, 22-23, 107 ff.; Wish, *Society and Thought*, 2:148; Learsi, *Jews in America*, 142 ff.; Marcus, *CAJ*, 2:1009; *JSS*, 2:339, n.413; Rischin, *Promised City*, 146-47; Harvey Fields, "A Description of the Cincinnati Jewish Community from 1895-1899, etc." (HUC term paper, 1961), citing *AI*, Nov. 1898, no.20; Bachrach, "Immigrant on the Hill," 18-19.

17. Schoener, *Lower East Side*, 5; N.Y. *Evening Post*, Sept. 25, 1897, copy in Marcus Collections; *PAJHS*, 9:63 ff., 49:95; *Jew. Com. Reg.*, 111 ff., 117 ff., 121, 321 ff., 330 ff.; Howe & Libo, *How We Lived*, 116 ff.; Weinberger, *Jews and Judaism*, 15, 72 ff.; Glazer, *American Judaism*, 62; Finkelstein, *The Jews* (1960), 1:538 ff.; Grinstein, *History*, 98 ff.; *AJH*, 73:163 ff. Light is thrown on the problems of Orthodoxy in Hayyim Weinschel, *Nité Naamanim* (N.Y., 1891) and Meir Rabinowitz, *Ha-Mahanaim* (N.Y., 1888).

18. Bernheimer, *Russian Jew in the U.S.*, 288, 327; *By Myself I'm A Book*, 101, 108; Weinberger, *Jews and Judaism*, 15-16; *Commentary*, 60(no.5):84 ff.; *AJH*, 70:91 ff.; *AJHQ*, 57:568-70; "Meat Inspection Laws," *DAH* (1976-78); *JSS*, 25:174 ff.; Marcus, *CAJ*, 3:see Index sub "Kashrut"; Finkelstein, *The Jews* (1949), 1:408; *By Myself I'm A Book*, 98; Chiel, "Jewish Life in America as Seen Through 'Hamelitz'"; Harold P. Gastwirt, *Fraud, Corruption, and Holiness: The Controversy Over the Supervision of Jewish Dietary Practices in New York City, 1881-1940* (Port Washington, N.Y., 1974); Schoener, *Portal to America*, 112 ff.; *PAJHS*, 25:31 ff.; Berman, *Shehitah*; *RIJHN*, 6:454 ff.; Wish, *Society and Thought*, 2:146; Sinclair Lewis, *The Jungle*; Woods, *Americans in Process*, 141; Foner, *Women and the American Labor Movement* (1980), 294 ff.; *JTA-DNB*, Apr. 24, 1984, p.4, May 3, 1984, p.3.

19. *AJYB*, 13(1911-1912):132, 16(1914-1915):147; *Jewish Digest*, 18(no.2):29; *New York Times*, Feb. 10, 1962, p.11, May 29, 1973, p.37, Nov. 19, 1973, p.44, Mar. 22, 1974, p.45, Nov. 4, 1974, p.47, May 17, 1976, p.24; *PAJHS*, 39:362, 376.

20. *Holiday*, 23(no.5):22 ff.; *Jewish Digest*, 21(no.3):70 ff.; *New York Times Magazine*, Jan. 25, 1976, pp.12 ff.; *New York Times*, Apr. 6, 1974, p.36; *Jewish Post and Opinion*, Jan. 26, 1962, p.6, entire; "Lewin-Epstein, Elias Wolf," *AJYB*, 6(1904-1905):141; Wish, *Society and Thought*, 2:262, 430; *PAJHS*, 35:192, 39:376-77; Detroit *Jewish News*, Oct. 13, 1972, p.2, c.2; Weinberger, *Jews and Judaism*, 46 ff.; *Jew. Com. Reg.*, 312 ff.; *AJYB*, 84:132.

21. *YA*, 9:326; Wiernik, *History*, 276-77; Finkelstein, *The Jews* (1949), 1:404-5; Bernheimer, *Russian Jew in the U.S.*, 40, 162 ff.; Frank, "Jews of Lynn, Mass.," 7-8; Swichkow & Gartner, *Milwaukee*, 170; Blum, *Baltimore*, 31.

22. *Michigan Jewish History*, 11(no.2):4 ff., 19(no.2):10; *RIJHN*, 3:45, 7:225, 420 ff.; "Chicago," *JE*, 4:24; *By Myself I'm A Book*, 110 ff.; Blum, *Baltimore*, 28, 31; Lipman, *Soc. Hist. of Jews in England*, 75; Benjamin, *Three Years*, 281, 285; Robinson, "Philadelphia," 15-16; Frank, "Jews of Lynn, Mass.," 7-8; Bernheimer, *Russian Jew in the U.S.*, 173-74; Hertzberg, *Atlanta*, 89; *AJA*, 9:38-39; *Constitution fuer der Congregation Bris Sholem fun Buffalo, N.Y.* (Buffalo, 1894); Adler & Connolly, *Buffalo*, 103-4, 189; *Constitutzian der Congregashan Anshe Sfard Linas Hazedek, etc.* (Newark, N.J., 1912), copy in AJAr; Korn, *Marcus Festschrift*, 263 ff.

23. Wiernik, *History*, 274 ff.; "New York," *JE*, 9:288, 291, "United States," 12:370; "New York City," *EJ*, 9:1094 ff.; Schoener, *Portal to America*, 106; *Jew. Com. Reg.*, 108 ff., graph opposite 122; *AJYB*, 3(1901-1902):144-45; "Brooklyn," *UJE*, 2:248-50, "New

York," 8:193, "New York City," 8:182; Isaac M. Wise, *Reminiscences* (Cincinnati, 1901), 165; *PAJHS*, 9:63 ff., 12:145; Lyons & De Sola, *Jewish Calendar*, 160 ff., 165; Grinstein, *New York City*, 14, et passim; Weinberger, *Jews and Judaism*, 4-5, 40 ff.; *100th Jubilee Banquet of Founding of the Congregation Beth Hamidrash Hagadol, June 3, 1952*, copy in Marcus Collections; Bernheimer, *Russian Jew in the U.S.*, 150-51.

24. *PAJHS*, 12:144; Finkelstein, *The Jews* (1949), 1:380; Levin, "East European Jews in U.S.," 12 ff.; Schoener, *Portal to America*, 65-66, 109 ff.; Howe & Libo, *How We Lived*, 111, 116; Howe, *World of Our Fathers*, 190 ff.; "New York," *JE*, 9:288; *AJYB*, 1(1899-1900):189 ff.

25. *Jewish People*, 3:345-46; N.Y. *Evening Post*, Sept. 25, 1897, as cited in Schoener, *Portal to America*, 110 ff.; Eisenstein, *Zikhronothai*, 55; *PAJHS*, 9:72 ff.; Weinberger, *Jews and Judaism*, 12 ff.; *AH*, Sept. 23, 1887, p.101; *Education of Abraham Cahan*, 393-94, 428; "Minkowsky, Pinchos," *UJE*; Boston *Jewish Advocate*, Mar. 28, 1972, p.9; *Jewish Digest*, 29(no.5):48 ff.; "Rosenblatt, Joseph," *DAB*; "Rosenblatt, Josef," *UJE*, *EJ*; Idelsohn, *Jewish Music*, 334-35; Samuel Rosenblatt, *Yossele Rosenblatt* (N.Y., 1954); "Sandler, Koppel," *EJ*, *DAB*; Kenneth Aaron Kanter, *The Jews on Tin Pan Alley* (N.Y., 1982), 133 ff.; Janowsky, *Am. Jew. Reappraisal*, 246; Weinberger, *Jews and Judaism*, 98 ff.; Schoener, *Portal to America*, 109 ff.

26. *AJA*, 35:100 ff.; Bernheimer, *Russian Jew in the U.S.*, 179-80; Weinberger, *Jews and Judaism*, 23 ff.; Curti et al., *American History*, 2:87; Handlin, *Adventure in Freedom*, 114; P. Wiernik, Chicago, to B. Felsenthal, Chicago, July 7, 1893, Felsenthal Collections, AJHSL.

27. Grinstein, *New York City*, 86 ff., 233, 253, 354, 395; Grinstein, *History*, 100-1; Tarshish, "American Judaism," 215-16; "Ash, Abraham Joseph," *JE*, *Ozar Yisrael*; Schappes, *DHJUS*, 373 ff.; *Occ.*, 14:599-601; *American Jews' Annual for 5648 A.M. (1887-88)*, 45; *PAJHS*, 9:63-74, 12:144, 44:131, 188; "Aaronson, Moses ben Aaron," *Ozar Yisrael*; *Jewish Observer*, 10(no.1):16 ff.

28. *PAJHS*, 44:129 ff., 131-33, 49:87, 231; "Malbim, Meir Loeb ben Jehiel Michael," *JE*, *UJE*, *EJ*; *Jewish Book Annual*, 36:79-87; Eisenstein, *Zikhronothai*, 45; *Jewish Observer*, 10(no.1):16 ff.; Grinstein, *History*, 142; L. Naumberg, Point Chautauqua, N.Y., to H. Berkowitz, July 23, 1888, Naumberg Collection, AJAr; *Jew. Com. Reg.*, 114; *Education of Abraham Cahan*, 424-25; "New York City," *EJ*, 12:1094 ff.; "New York," *JE*, 9:282; Janowsky, *American Jew*, 37; Schoener, *Lower East Side*, 55; Detroit *Jewish American*, Aug. 1, 1902, p.6, c.3; *AH*, Sept. 5, 1902, p.426; *Jewish Digest*, 14(no.4):57 ff.; Eisenberg, *Eyewitnesses to American Jewish History*, 3:26 ff.; Rischin, *Promised City*, 148; Weinberger, *Jews and Judaism*, 107 ff.; Wiernik, *History*, 278; Glazer, *American Judaism*, 70.

29. *AJYB*, 19(1917-1918):367, 21:413.

30. "Lichtenstein, Hillel," "Sofer, Moses," *UJE*; Chiel, *Kelman Festschrift*, 215 ff.; Horwich, *My First Eighty Years*, 205 ff.; Levinthal, *Message of Israel*, 133 ff.; *PAJHS*, 44:182 ff.; *AJHQ*, 57:557 ff.; "Willowski, Jacob David ben Ze'ev," *EJ*; Eisenstadt, *Hakme Yisrael be-Amerika*, 38-40; "Zarchy, Asher L.," *AJYB*, 5(1903-1904); Meites, *Chicago*, 494.

31. Lesser, *In the Last Days*; Leo Jung (ed.), *Guardians of Our Heritage (1724-1953)* (N.Y., 1958), 347 ff.; *AJYB*, 5(1903-1904):43, 100; Brickner, "Jew. Com. of Cin.," 106-7.

32. Uchill, *Pioneers*, 232 ff.; Bernheimer, *Russian Jew in the U.S.*, 163 ff.; *WSJHQ*, 11:99 ff.; Sachar, *Modern Jewish History*, 523-24; Wiernik, *History*, 281 ff.; Goldman, *Giants of Faith*, 160 ff.; Grinstein, *History*, 101-2; Morais, *Philadelphia*, 217-23; *AI*, Sept. 5, 1889, p.5, cs.3-4; "Hirschensohn, Chaim," *DAB*, Supplement 1; "Margolies, Morris S.," *WWIAJ*, 1926; "Margolies, Moses Z.," *AJYB*, 5(1903-1904):78-79; Eisenstadt, *Hakme Yisrael be-Amerika*, sub "Margolies, Moses Z.".

33. Hapgood, *Spirit of the Ghetto*, chap.2; Howe, *World of Our Fathers*, 190 ff.; "Margolies, Moses Sebulun," *EJ*; Goldman, *Giants of Faith*, 160 ff.; Morais, *Philadelphia*, 223-24.

34. Stern, *Grundriss*, 65; Eisenstein, *Zikhronothai*, 65-66; Karp, *Jew. Exp. in America*, 4:xx; "Union of Orthodox Jewish Congregations of America," *UJE*; *PAJHS*, 14:58 ff., 35:316 ff., 55:364 ff.; "Mendes, Henry Pereira," *DAB*, Supplement 2; Glazer, *American Judaism*, 78; Elbogen, *Cent. of Jewish Life*, 349-50; Learsi, *Jews in America*, 209; *AJYB*, 2(1900-1901):163 ff., 3(1901-1902):122-23, 40:41-60; "Conferences, Rabbinical," *JE*, 4:217; Grinstein, *History*, 99.

35. Weinberger, *Jews and Judaism*, 130, n.11; "Union of Orthodox Rabbis of the United States and Canada," *UJE*; *AJYB*, 16(1914-1915):149; *PAJHS*, 55:364 ff., 374; Glazer, *American Judaism*, 78; *Jew. Com. Reg.*, 287 ff., 1180 ff., 1189 ff.; *AH*, June 17, 1904, pp.130-31, July 1, 1904, p.180; Finkelstein, *The Jews* (1949), 1:405-6, (1960), 1:539-42; Levinthal, *Message of Israel*, 135 ff.; *H. Pereira Mendes*, 39.

36. *PAJHS*, 44:137 ff., 55:370; Bernstein, *English Speaking Orthodox Rabbinate*; Lesser, *In the Last Days*, p.1 of the preface; Hertz, *Authorized Daily Prayer Book*, 145-47; Zola, "Zvi Hirsch Masliansky," 2, 6, 67-68; Reform rabbis J.R. Marcus and Solomon A. Fineberg were students at this school in 1907; *AJYB*, 9(1907-1908):119, 21:324-25, 82:37, 61; *Jew. Com. Reg.*, 1180 ff.; *RIJHN*, 4:257-58, 8:18 ff.; Blum, *Baltimore*, 59 ff.; "Klein, Philip," *JE, UJE, EJ, AJYB*, 5(1903-1904):69; "New York City," *UJE*, 8:193, *EJ*, 12:1097; Lipsky, *Memoirs in Profile*, 237 ff.; "Aschinsky, Aaron Mordecai Halevi," "Levinthal, Bernard Louis," *UJE*; Lewis M. Barth, "The Bernard L. Levinthal Papers" (HUC term paper, 1962); Levinthal, *Message of Israel*, 144-45, 168, 178 ff., 184-86; "Schaffer," *AJYB*, 6(1904-1905):222-23; "Philadelphia," *JE*, 9:677; Goldman, *Giants of Faith*, 160 ff.; *New York Times, Sept. 25, 1952*, obituary of Levinthal; Tarshish, *Dawn in the West*, 225 ff.; Grinstein, *History*, 99-100; "Young Israel, National Council of," *UJE, EJ*; Koplin, "Jewish Exponent," 12-13; Bernheimer, *Russian Jew in the U.S.*, 168-69.

CHAPTER THIRTEEN
HEBREW AND THE EAST EUROPEAN JEWS

1. *PAJHS*, 49:98, 116 ff.; Rischin, *Promised City*, 129-30; *Education of Abraham Cahan*, 267.

2. "Ben Jehudah, Eliezer," *UJE*; "Haskalah," *JE, UJE, EJ*; "Literature, Modern Hebrew," "Maskil," *JE*; Raisin, *The Haskalah Movement in Russia* (Phila., 1913); Shalom Spiegel, *Hebrew Reborn* (Phila., 1926); Waldstein, *Modern Hebrew Literature*; Klausner, *Modern Hebrew Literature*; Janowsky, *American Jew*, 122 ff.; Waxman, *Jew. Literature*, 4:1157-58; *Jewish Digest*, 5(no.10):59 ff.; Adler & Connolly, *Buffalo*, 193, 239, 252; Rischin, *Promised City*, 131-32; *Education of Abraham Cahan*, 223-24; *Baron Festschrift*, 346; *RIJHN*, 1:262-63, 4:245, 258; Weinberger, *Jews and Judaism*, 19; Bernheimer, *Russian Jew in the U.S.*, 173; "Hebrew Literature in the United States," *EJ*, 8:208 ff.; *Jewish Book Annual*, 18:62 ff., 68; *Jewish People*, 4:270; Gutstein, *Chicago*, 396 ff.; Silber, *America in Hebrew Literature*, 7-8.

3. "Freidus, Abraham Solomon," *JE, UJE, EJ*; Kohut, *As I Know Them*, 181 ff.; *Hebrew Studies*, 22:97 ff.; "Eisenstein, (Julius) Judah David," *JE, UJE, EJ*; Eisenstein, *Zikhronothai*; Eisenstadt, *Hakme Yisrael be-Amerika*, 62-64; *YA*, 7:288 ff.; "Deinard, Ephraim," *UJE, EJ*; Waxman, *Jew. Literature*, 4:1083-1191; *Herzl Year Book*, 5:92; Katz, *Jacob Dolnitzky Memorial Volume*, 79 ff.; Drachman, *Neo-Hebraic Literature*, 86-87; Meyer Waxman, *The Story of Hebrew* (Jewish Affairs) 3 (1949).

4. "Ehrlich, Arnold Bogumil," *JE, UJE, EJ, DAB*; "Rodkinson, Michael Levi," *UJE*; "Mordell, Louis Joel," "Mordell, Phinehas," *UJE, EJ*; "Mordell, Albert," *UJE*; Drachman, *Neo-Hebraic Literature*, 75-77; Eisenstein, *Zikhronothai* in Samuels, "Judah David Eisenstein," 80-81; "Kohut, Alexander," *JE, UJE, EJ, DAB*; "Szold, Benjamin," *JE, UJE, EJ*.

5. "Schechter, Solomon," *JE, UJE, EJ, DAB*; Norman Bentwich, *Solomon Schechter* (London, 1931); "Ginzberg, Louis," *JE, UJE, EJ*; "Davidson, Israel," *UJE, EJ, DAB*, Supplement 2; Drachman, *Neo-Hebraic Literature*, 74-75, 87-91.

6. *HUCA*, 37:dedicatory page on Neumark, by JRM; "Levias, Caspar," "Neumark, David," "Rhine, Abraham Benedict," *UJE*; "Lauterbach, Jacob Zallel," "Raisin, Jacob Salman (Zalman)," "Raisin, Max," *UJE, EJ*; *New York Times*, May 29, 1973, p.37, cs.1-8; *CCARYB*, 52:266-69.

7. Waxman, *Jew. Literature*, 4:1101, 1160 ff., 1183, 1188; "Reider, Joseph," *UJE*; "Halper, Benzion," "Malter, Henry," *UJE, EJ*; "Margolis, Max Leopold," *JE, UJE, EJ*; Max Raisin, *Dapim mi-pinkaso shel Rabai* (Leaves From a Rabbi's Notebook) (Brooklyn, 1941); Samuels, "Judah David Eisenstein," 75-76.

8. Rothkoff, *Bernard Revel*; Leo W. Schwartz, *Wolfson of Harvard: Portrait of a Scholar* (Phila., 1978), 3 ff.; *Judaism*, 3:405 ff.; *Jewish People*, 4:327 ff.; "Churgin, Pinkhos," "Revel, Bernard," *UJE*; Waxman, *Jew. Literature*, 4:1137 ff., 1183, 1188; "Efros, Isaac," "Husik, Isaac," "Mann, Jacob," "Wolfson, Harry Austryn," *UJE, EJ*.

9. *Jew. Com. Reg.*, 564 ff.; "United States," *JE*, 12:370; "Society for the Promotion of Culture Among the Jews of Russia," *JE, EJ*; *Hazefirah*, 12(no.43(1885)):350-51; "Chicago," *UJE*, 3:142; Meites, *Chicago*, 151, 187, 549; "Philadelphia," *JE*, 9:677-78; Recollections of JRM then a student at the H.U.C.; Samuels, "Judah David Eisenstein," 59-60; Rischin, *Promised City*, 102-3, 131-32; Chomsky, *Hebrew*, 260 ff.; *Herzl Year Book*, 5:98, 101 ff., 105, 107; Silberschlag, *Renaissance*, 259; Davis, "Synagogues, Hebrew Free Schools and Other Educational Influences," 16; *Jewish Book Annual*, 38:42 ff.; Janowsky, *Ed. of Am. Jew. Teachers*, 3 ff.; Jacob Freid (ed.), *Jews in the Modern World* (2 vols., N.Y., 1962), 2:405 ff.

10. *Jew. Com. Reg.*, 569, 1214 ff., 1355; *AJYB*, 15(1913-1914):247, 83:288-90; "Histadruth Ivrith," *UJE*; "Histadrut Ivrit of America," *EJ*; *Judaism*, 3:161 ff.; Drachman, *Neo-Hebraic Literature*, 87-91; *Herzl Year Book*, 5:102-5; Chomsky, *Hebrew*, 261 ff., 269.

11. Gutstein, *Chicago*, 380; *AJHQ*, 59:139 ff., 157; *Jewish Book Annual*, 37:71 ff.; Samuels, "Judah David Eisenstein," 123; Drachman, *Neo-Hebraic Literature*, 87-91; "Ribalow, Menachem," *EJ*; *Herzl Year Book*, 5:83 ff.

12. "Matz, Israel," *WWIAJ*, 1926; "Rabinowitz, Louis Mayer," *UJE, WWIAJ*, 1926, *WWIWJ*, 1955.

13. *PAJHS*, 33:127 ff.; *Jewish Book Annual*, 37:71 ff.; Waxman, *Jew. Literature*, 4:1-48 ff., 1074 ff., 1297 ff., 1300 ff.; *Judaism*, 3:391 ff.; "Literature, Modern Hebrew," *JE*, 8:118 (2 lines!); "Histadruth Ivrith," "Literature, Hebrew," *UJE*; "New York City," *UJE*, 8:188, "Periodicals and Press," 8:453-54; "Hebrew Literature in the United States," *EJ*, 8:208 ff., "Newspapers, Hebrew," 12:1052 ff.; "Berkowitz, Yitzhak Dov," "Stybel, Abraham Joshua," *EJ*; *Alexander Marx Jubilee Volume* (N.Y., 1950), 2:115 ff., Hebrew Section; Wiernik, *History*, 302 ff.; Rischin, *Promised City*, 127-28; *AJHQ*, 59:140 ff., 151 ff., 165; Ezra Spicehandler, "The Ideology of the Hebrew Movement in the United States As Reflected in the Monthly *Ha-Toren*" (HUC term paper, 1944); Rawidowicz, *Chicago Pinkas*, 35 ff.; *Jewish People*, 4:324 ff.; Janowsky, *American Jew*, 122 ff.; Chomsky, *Hebrew*, 259 ff.

14. *JQR*, 45:363 ff., 374 ff., 413 ff.; *AI*, Dec. 8, 1954, p.175, c.2; Hebrew poetry holdings in Marcus Collections; Drachman, *Neo-Hebraic Literature*, 64, 66-69, 94 ff., 100 ff., 112 ff., 116-17; W. & W., *Philadelphia*, 19-20, 257; *R*, nos.28, 176, 284, 368-69, 381, 426, 428-30, 497; Levine, *Am. Jew. Bibliography*, no.119; *JM*, May 26, 1865, p.164, c.3; *AJH*, 69:364 ff.; Pool, *Portraits*, 268; "Leeser, Isaac," *JE*; *PAJHS*, 17:151, 27:89, 30:see Index sub "Leeser"; *Occ.*, 7:359-60, 10:144 ff., 13:585-86, 14:38-39; Mordecai Netter, *Salvim min ha-Yam* (Vienna, 1860); *Judaism*, 3:391 ff.

15. *PAJHS*, 9:65, 22:134-35, 137, 34:285 ff., 45:67 ff.; Joshua Bloch, *The People and the Book* (N.Y., 1954), 99; Wiernik, *History*, 256. Among those active in America during

this decade were Henry Vidaver, Simon Berman, H. Weinshel, Mordecai Jahlomstein, Leon Horowitz, James (Jacob) H. Sobel (Soble), Wolf Schur, Henry (Zevi Hirsch) Bernstein, J.D. Eisenstein, Michael Heilprin, K.H. Sarasohn, Gerson Rosenzweig, Henry Gersoni, Mayer Rabinowitz, Isaac Rabbinowitz, Arnold B. Ehrlich, Samuel B. Schwarzberg, Herman Eliassof. *YA*, 9:83 ff.; *Judaism*, 3:391 ff.; Charles L. Arian, "Jewish Traditions in Rabinowitz's *Ha-Mahanaim*" (HUC term paper, n.d.), copy in Marcus Collections; *Jewish People*, 4:270; Drachman, *Neo-Hebraic Literature*, 67, 70 ff., 77-83, 90-91, 120-27; N.Y. *Jewish Times*, July 21, 1871, p.324; Randi Musnitsky, "America's Goodness" (rabbinical thesis, HUC, 1983); Abraham Judah Loeb Horowitz, *Rumanyah ve-Amerikah: Tov Artsot Ha-Brit* (Berlin, 1874); *AJHQ*, 56:467, 58:98-99; Goldstein, *Cent. of Jud. in NYC*, 145-49, et passim; Hayyim Weinshel, *Nité Naamanim* (N.Y., 1891); *Kiev Festschrift*, 167 ff.; Chomsky, *Hebrew*, 257 ff.; Waldstein, *Modern Hebrew Literature*; JSS, 38:277 ff.; *Jewish Book Annual*, 34:26 ff., 38:42 ff.; Kabakoff, *Halutsé Ha-Sifrut Ha-Ivrit be-Amerikah*.

16. *Education of Abraham Cahan*, 279-80; Weinberger, *Jews and Judaism*, 61-62; "Harkavy, Alexander," *UJE*, *AJYB*, 6(1904-1905):110-11; *AJA*, 33:35 ff.; "Gersoni, Henry," *JE*, *UJE*, *EJ*; Eisenstadt, *Hakme Yisrael be-Amerika*, 30; Rothschild, *Atlanta*, 8-10; *AJHQ*, 45:70-71, 56:466 ff.; *Jewish People*, 4:270; *Jewish Book Annual*, 34:26 ff.; Weinberger, *Jews and Judaism*, 61-62; Samuels, "Judah David Eisenstein," 71-72; Grinstein, *History*, 77; for another Maskil of the 1880's, Hillel Malachovsky, see his *K'thabim Basepher* (Phila., 1902); Eisenstadt, *Hakme Yisrael be- Amerika*, 30, 69-70; Drachman, *Neo-Hebraic Literature*, 64, 67, 130-33.

17. "Benjaminson," *AJYB*, 6(1904-1905):60-61; Gutstein, *Chicago*, 129, 393; *PUAHC*, 3:2465-68, 4:3178; Eisenstadt, *Hakme Yisrael be-Amerika*, 91; *Jewish People*, 4:310; Gottheil, *Gustav Gottheil*, 139; *AI*, Jan. 26, 1883, p.250, cs.2-5; W.D. Miller, poem dedicated to Mr. Mittenthal, Waxahachie, Texas, Sept. 29, 1892, Marcus Collections; Mielziner, *Moses Mielziner*, 30; *Adolph Huebsch: A Memorial*, 350.

18. Fein, *Baltimore*, 197; *Kiev Festschrift*, 169; *PAJHS*, 33:140; Drachman, *Neo-Hebraic Literature*, 71-72; "Dolitscky, Menahem Mendel," *LNYL*; *Jewish People*, 4:310; Menahem Dolitsky, *Shiré Menahem* (N.Y., 1900); Eisenberg, *Eyewitnesses to American Jewish History*, 3:155 ff.; "Dolitzki, Menahem Mendel," *JE*, *EJ*; "Dolicki, Menahem Mendel," *UJE*; Lisitzky, *In the Grip of Cross-Currents*, 170 ff.

19. Drachman, *Neo-Hebraic Literature*, 72, 83-84; *PAJHS*, 6:175, 33:138; "Rosenzweig, Gerson," *UJE*, *EJ*; Rosenzweig, *Masekhet America* (N.Y., 1892); Davidson, *Parody*, 98-108, 240-41, 263; Waxman, *Jew. Literature*, 4:1050-51; JSS, 38:277 ff.; "Hebrew Literature, Modern," *EJ*, 8:210; *Jewish Book Annual*, 18:62 ff.; "Rosensweig, Gerson," *AJYB*, 6(1904-1905):175.

20. Drachman, *Neo-Hebraic Literature*, 134-37; "Schur, Zev Wolf (William)," *EJ*; "Schur, William," *JE*, *AJYB*, 6(1904-1905):182; Waxman, *Jew. Literature*, 4:1266, 1299; Eisenstadt, *Hakme Yisrael be-Amerika*, 103-4; "Schapira, Hermann (Hirsch)," *UJE*; *EIAJH*, 425 ff.

21. "Maskil," *JE*; "Buchhalter, Julius," *AJYB*, 6(1904-1905):72, "Jonathanson, Jonas A.," 126, "Judson, Solomon," 127, "Silberstein, Solomon (Sholem) Joseph," 187-88, et passim for other Maskilim; *Jewish People*, 4:1310 ff.; "Hebrew Literature, Modern," *EJ*, 8:209-11; Klausner, *Modern Hebrew Literature*, 111-12; Kabakoff, *Halutsé Ha-Sifrut Ha-Ivrit be-Amerika*; Janowsky, *Am. Jew. Reappraisal*, 180-81; "Imber," *AJYB*, 6(1904-1905):122; Goldberg, *Pioneers and Builders*, 133 ff.; Lipsky, *Memoirs in Profile*, 178 ff.; Abrahams, *Hebraic Bookland*, 359 ff.; "Imber, Naphtali Herz," *JE*, *UJE*, *EJ*, *DAB*, *EOZAI*; Kohut, *As I Know Them*, 190 ff.; Levinthal, *Message of Israel*, 137-38; *Michael*, 3:88 ff.; *AJHQ*, 60:17; *Congress Weekly*, Dec. 24, 1956, pp.10-13; Imber's doggerel: copies in Marcus Collections; Waldstein, *Modern Hebrew Literature*, 123. Waldstein has very little to say about Haskalah in the U.S. (1912).

22. "Altman, Rebecca Annetta," *AJYB*, 6(1904-1905):56; "Avinoam (Grossman), Reuven," *EJ*. Among the writers who had settled here and had begun their literary work by 1921 were: Simon Halkin, Zevi Scharfstein, Pesah Ginzburg, Mordekhai Lipson, Hillel Bavli, Nissan Touroff, Reuben Brainin, Shalom Dov Ber Maximon, Eisig Silberschlag, Abraham S. Schwartz, Abraham Hyman Friedland, Abraham Regelson, Simon Ginzburg, Daniel Persky. This list is not intended to be exhaustive. Biographies of most of these men may be found in Waxman, *Jew. Literature*, and in the *UJE* and *EJ*.

23. *Judaism*, 3:403 ff.; Grinstein, *History*, 77 ff.; *AJH*, 68:248 ff.; Waxman, *Jew. Literature*, 4:1052-53, 1060-84; *Jewish Book Annual*, 12:29 ff., 13:9 ff., 23:115 ff., 33:33 ff., 39:132 ff.; Finkelstein, *The Jews* (1960), 2:916 ff.; *Jewish People*, 4:311 ff.; *JSS*, 38:283 ff.; Learsi, *Jews in America*, 197; *JQR*, 45:413 ff., 421 ff., 426 ff.; *Herzl Year Book*, 5:86-87, 94 ff, 109; *YA*, 9:106-8; "Hebrew Literature, Modern," *EJ*, 8:211; "Berkowitz, Yitzhak, Dov," "Lisitzky, Ephraim E.," "Ribalow, Menachem," "Silkiner, Benjamin Nahum," *EJ*; *Jewish Book Annual*, 18:66 ff., 28:105 ff.; *JTA-DNB*, June 27, 1952; *JSS*, 25:159-60; *AJYB*, 64:495, 83:353; "Efros, Israel Isaac," *UJE*, *EJ*; "Literature, Hebrew," *UJE*, 7:95 ff.; Janowsky, *American Jew*, 122 ff.; Janowsky, *Am. Jew. Reappraisal*, 182 ff.; Waldstein, *Modern Hebrew Literature*; S. Spiegel, *Hebrew Reborn* (Phila., 1962).

24. *JSS*, 38:277 ff., 287; Chiel, "Jewish Life in America as Seen Through 'Hamelitz'"; *Jewish People*, 4:311 ff.; *Jewish Book Annual*, 9:30, 12:29 ff., 14:23 ff., 24:23 ff., 33:33 ff., 34:7; Hamelitz, Mar. 6, 1894, p.5; *AJHQ*, 49:85; *Hebrew Abstracts*, 15:58-67; "Literature, Hebrew," *UJE*, 7:95-96; Chomsky, *Hebrew*, 270 ff.; Silberschlag, *Renaissance*, 249 ff., 274 ff., 414; Waxman, *Jew. Literature*, 4:960 ff., 1084-85.

CHAPTER FOURTEEN
RELIGIOUS EDUCATION

1. Eisenstein, *Zikhronothai*, 51; Morais, *Philadelphia*, 228 ff.; Davis, "Synagogues, Hebrew Free Schools and other Educational Influences," p. 18; Feldman, *Jew. Exp. in Western Pa.*, 261-65; *YA*, 9:279, 15:143; *By Myself I'm A Book*, 72 ff.; Howe & Libo, *How We Lived*, 102 ff.; Weinberger, *Jews and Judaism*, 51 ff.

2. Bernheimer, *Russian Jew in the U.S.*, 166-67, 177; Pool, *Old Faith*, 212; *PAJHS*, 21:19; Weinberger, *Jews and Judaism*, 51-52; Howe & Libo, *How We Lived*, 106-7; Gartner, *Jew Ed. in the U.S.*, 125-26; *Jewish People*, 2:102 ff., 157 ff.; Fein, *Baltimore*, 185 ff.; Pilch, *Hist. Jew. Ed.*, 69; Dushkin, *Jew. Ed. in NYC*, 66 ff.; *AH*, Aug. 23, 1907, p.384; *YA*, 16:349.

3. Schlesinger, *Rise of the City*, 168; Rischin, *Promised City*, 107; *Eastern Union*, 81; *AJYB*, 50:54 ff.; Howe & Libo, *How We Lived*, 106-9; Howe, *World of Our Fathers*, 200 ff.; Bernheimer, *Russian Jew in the U.S.*, 151, 166-67, 177; *Jewish People*, 2:156 ff.; "New York," *JE*, 9:286-87; Weinberger, *Jews and Judaism*, 51-52; Finkelstein, *The Jews* (1949), 3:929; *YA*, 5:223, 9:274, 15:142; Dushkin, *Jew. Ed. in NYC*, 66 ff.; *AH*, Aug. 23, 1907, p.384; Gartner, *Jew Ed. in the U.S.*, 11, 123 ff.; Pilch, *Hist. Jew. Ed.*, 69; *AJHQ*, 53:264 ff., 274 ff.; Levinthal, *Message of Israel*, 157 ff.; *By Myself I'm A Book*, 73; "New York City," *EJ*, 12:1097 ff.; Swichkow & Gartner, *Milwaukee*, 264-65; Samuel Eliot Morison, *The Puritan Pronaos* (N.Y., 1936); *Education of Abraham Cahan*, 14, 25 ff.; Kalman Whiteman, *Bar-Mitzvah, etc.* (N.Y., 1931).

4. "Lichtenstein, Hillel," *JE*, *UJE*; Curti et al., *American History*, 2:88; *Jew. Com. Reg.*, 394-95; Schiff, *Jewish Day School*, 28 ff., 32 ff., 37 ff., 244-45; Grinstein, *History*, 109-10; Critique of Etz Hayyim sent to O. Straus, late nineteenth century, Straus Papers, LC, copy in Marcus Collections; *Jewish People*, 4:286; Klaperman, *Yeshiva University*, 23-24; Weinberger, *Jews and Judaism*, 55-56; "Yeshibah," *JE*, 12:600; "Reines, Isaac Jacob," "Yeshiva," *UJE*; Dushkin, *Jew. Ed. in NYC*, 73, 480 ff.; *AJHQ*, 54:8-9, 198-201,

57:571; "New York City," *UJE*, 8:190; *AJYB*, 50:52 ff.; "Education, Jewish," *EJ*, 6:437 ff.; Rischin, *Promised City*, 100-1, 107; Mallinger, "Jewish Day School"; Schlesinger, *Rise of the City*, 170.

5. *AH*, Aug. 23, 1907, p.384; Wiernik, *History*, 370 ff.; *AJHQ*, 54:32; Dushkin, *Jew. Ed. in NYC*, 75-76; "Yeshibah," *JE*; Schiff, *Jewish Day School*, 32 ff., 43 ff., 245 ff.; Mallinger, "Jewish Day School"; *Michigan Jewish History*, 5(no.2):7-8; *Jew. Com. Reg.*, 394-95; Fein, *Baltimore*, 192; Berkson, *Theories of Americanization*, 177 ff.; Landesmann, *Brownsville*, 155; *Reports, Immig. Com. Abstracts*, 2:66; *AJYB*, 38:33; Gartner, *Jew Ed. in the U.S.*, 28.

6. *YA*, 10:45 ff., 11:89 ff., 98; *Jewish Digest*, 15(no.5):72 ff.; Weinberger, *Jews and Judaism*, 33 ff., 51 ff., 55; Mallinger, "Jewish Day School," 5; Goren, *American Jew*, 50 ff.; *JSS*, 8:51 ff.; "Education, Jewish," *EJ*, 6:438-39; *AH*, Aug. 23, 1907, p.384; Rischin, *Promised City*, 107; *Tradition*, 19:244 ff.; Grinstein, *History*, 109; Wiernik, *History*, 376; "New York," *JE*, 9:286; "New York City," *UJE*, 8:190, *EJ*, 12:1097; *Jewish People*, 2:158; Dushkin, *Jew. Ed. in NYC*, 68-72, 472 ff.; "Sulzberger" "Eastern European Jews"; Schoener, *Portal to America*, 108-9; Pilch, *Hist. Jew. Ed.*, 56 ff.

7. *AJYB*, 16(1914-1915):102 ff., 115 ff., 124; *YIVO Bleter*, 42:284 ff.; *Jewish Education News*, 1(no.9):3-4; Gartner, *Jew Ed. in the U.S.*, 16 ff., 118 ff.; Pilch, *Hist. Jew. Ed.*, 62 ff.; *JSS*, 8:51 ff.; *YA*, 10:50-52, 62-65, 68, 11:90 ff., 94 ff., 16:349; *Tradition*, 19:244 ff.; Dushkin, *Jew. Ed. in NYC*, 130-31, 472 ff.

8. *PAJHS*, 33:150; Katz, *Jacob Dolnitzky Memorial Volume*, 13 ff.; *YA*, 11:92, 15:141, n.73; *RIJHN*, 5:399; Handlin, *Adventure in Freedom*, 119-20; Davis, "Synagogues, Hebrew Free Schools and Other Educational Influences," 14-16; Boston *Jewish Advocate*, Feb. 16, 1940, p.14, cs.3-8, p.15, cs.3-8; *Herzl Year Book*, 5:88 ff.; *Michigan Jewish History*, 5(no.2):5-6; Levinthal, *Message of Israel*, 190-91; *AJA*, 31:199; *By Myself I'm A Book*, 108; Koplin, "Jewish Exponent," 10-12; Blum, *Baltimore*, 28-29; Morais, *Philadelphia*, 228; *Jewish People*, 2:158; "Minneapolis," *UJE*, 7:571; *Generations*, 2:14 ff.; Bernheimer, *Russian Jew in the U.S.*, 167, 177-78, 214-15; Adler & Connolly, *Buffalo*, 239 ff.; *RIJHN*, 7:413-14; Fein, *Baltimore*, 186-88; Auerbach, "Nebraska," 84; *PAJHS*, 33:158; Meites, *Chicago*, 156-58, 563; Horwich, *My First Eighty Years*, 142; Swichkow & Gartner, *Milwaukee*, 264-65.

9. Pilch, *Hist. Jew. Ed.*, 68 ff.; Gartner, *Jew Ed. in the U.S.*, 121 ff.; *PAJHS*, 55:368; Swichkow & Gartner, *Milwaukee*, 263; Boston *Jewish Advocate*, Feb. 16, 1940, p.14, cs.3-8, p.15, cs.3-8; *RIJHN*, 7:225; Bernheimer, *Russian Jew in the U.S.*, 166-67; Grinstein, *History*, 110; *JSS*, 8(no.2):51 ff.; Weinberger, *Jews and Judaism*, 52 ff.

10. *JSS*, 8:51 ff.; Emanuel Gamoran, *Jewish Education in the United States* (Nashville, 1931), 502; Weinberger, *Jews and Judaism*, 51 ff.; *Jewish People*, 2:158 ff., 4:279; Gartner, *Jew Ed. in the U.S.*, 23; Finkelstein, *The Jews* 1949), 3:929 ff.; *YA*, 10:63 ff.

11. *The New Era*, 6(no.4):344-47; *AJA*, 35:100 ff., 174, n.69, 175, nn.74-76, 177, n.90; Klaperman, *Yeshiva University*, 17 ff., 48 ff., 144 ff.; *PAJHS*, 54:5 ff.; Rothkoff, *Bernard Revel*, 38-39; "Fischel, Harry," "Revel, Bernard," *UJE*, *EJ*; Lisitzky, *In the Grip of Cross-Currents*, 90-94; "Yeshibah," *JE*, 12:600; "New York City," *UJE*, 8:190, "Philadelphia," 8:482, "Yeshiva," 10:595; Weinberger, *Jews and Judaism*, 22; *Education of Abraham Cahan*, 371-72; *Jew. Com. Reg.*, 395, 1201 ff.; Gartner, *Jew Ed. in the U.S.*, 31-32, 153 ff.; Levinthal, *Message of Israel*, 152-53, 178, 190-91; Bernheimer, *Russian Jew in the U.S.*, 167; Meites, *Chicago*, 324, 550 ff.; Finkelstein, *The Jews* (1949), 1:390, (1960), 1:540 ff.; Abraham J. Karp, *Golden Door to America* (N.Y., 1976), 245-46; Grayzel, *Hist. of Contemporary Jews*, 68-69; Howe & Libo, *How We Lived*, 109-10; *Herzl Year Book*, 5:90-91; Grinstein, *History*, 100; Dushkin, *Jew. Ed. in NYC*, 75, 97; *AJYB*, 21:321, 25:287-88, 50:56-57; "Young Israel, The National Council of," *EJ*.

12. *JSS*, 8:57 ff.; Handlin, *Adventure in Freedom*, 119; *Jew. Com. Reg.*, 349; *AJYB*, 16(1914-1915):116-20, 122-24, 21:481 ff., 38:34-35, 54, 97-98, 50:55 ff., 57, 66:28; Gartner,

Jew Ed. in the U.S., 11, 21, 23, 118 ff., 122-23, 125, 132 ff.; Eisenberg, *Eyewitnesses to American Jewish History*, 3:104-5; Boston *Jewish Advocate*, Feb. 16, 1940, p.14, cs.3-8, p.15, cs.3-8; *Herzl Year Book*, 5:88-89; "Education, Jewish," *EJ*, 6:440-42, "New York City," 12:1097, 1119-20; Glazer, *American Judaism*, 72-73; *By Myself I'm A Book*, 74; Pilch, *Hist. Jew. Ed.*, 67 ff., 82-83; Janowsky, *American Jew*, 65-66; Dushkin, *Jew. Ed. in NYC*, 154-56, 413, 418, 430, 439, 487; *YA*, 9:247 ff., 271, 15:142.

13. Pilch, *Hist. Jew. Ed.*, 55, 66; *AJYB*, 16(1914-1915):90 ff., 127, 38:27 ff., 32, 78 ff.; Dushkin, *Jew. Ed. in NYC*, 63 ff.; Weinberger, *Jews and Judaism*, 21, 51 ff.; *Tradition*, 19:244 ff.; Grinstein, *History*, 100.

CHAPTER FIFTEEN

YIDDISH: THE THEATRE AND THE PRESS

1. Deinard, *Koheleth America*, 126, no.790; "Sobel, Jacob Zevi," *EJ*; "Periodicals," *JE*, 9:607; Waxman, *Jew. Literature*, 4:956, 996 ff.; *Commentary*, 52(no.6):103; Learsi, *Jew in America*, 144 ff.; "Literature, Yiddish," *UJE*, 7:125 ff., 128 ff.; "Drama, Yiddish," "Judaeo-German Literature," *JE*; Marcus, *CAJ*, 3:Index sub Yiddish; *Jewish People*, 4:267, 269 ff.; *Education of Abraham Cahan*, 9, 133-34, 396-97; Miriam Shomer Zunser, *Yesterday* (N.Y., 1939); "Zunser," *JE, UJE, EJ, DAB, AJYB*, 6(1904-1905):212-13; Hapgood, *Spirit of the Ghetto*, 91 ff.; Liptzin, *Eliakum Zunser*, 207 ff.; *YA*, 9:207 ff.; A.H. Fromenson (ed.), *A Jewish Bard Being the Biography of Eliakum Zunser, Written by Himself and Rendered into English by Simon Hirdansky* (N.Y., 1905); *U.A.H.C. Statistics*, 55; Dushkin, *Jew. Ed. in NYC*, 486; Schlesinger, *Rise of the City*, 170; *EAH*, 469.

2. Hapgood, *Spirit of the Ghetto*, 113 ff.; Liptzin, *History of Yiddish Literature*, 73 ff.; Sanders, *Downtown Jews*, 277 ff., 301 ff.; Zylbercwaig, *Leksikon fun Yidishn Teater*, 6 vols.; *Jewish Book Annual*, 18:12 ff., 34:32 ff., 40:127 ff.; Gorin, *Idishen Theater*; Howe, *World of Our Fathers*, 460 ff.; Howe & Libo, *How We Lived*, 237 ff.; Louis Lipsky, *Tales of the Yiddish Rialto* (Cranbury, N.J., 1963); "Theater," *UJE*, 10:236-38, *EJ*, 15:1064 ff.; *Jewish Heritage*, 1(no.3):39 ff.; Reisin, *Leksikon*; Reisin, *Leksikon* (1926-1929); *AJYB*, 50:61 ff.; Nahma Sandrow, *Vagabond Stars: A World History of Yiddish Theater* (N.Y., 1977); "Drama, Yiddish," *JE*; Lifson, *Yiddish Theatre in America*, 37 ff.; for biographies see *JE*, *UJE, EJ*, Reisin's lexica, and *LNYL*; *Algemayne Entsiklopedie Yidn*, 2:389 ff., 447 ff.; Schulman, *Geshikhte*, 237-44; Ignaz Schiffer (Yitzhok Shiper), *Geshikhte fun Yidisher Teater Kunst un Drame* (3 vols., Warsaw, 1923-1928); Schappes, *JIUS*, 167 ff.; *Reconstructionist*, 33(no.8):20 ff.; *Jewish Book Annual*, 34:32 ff. For early Yiddish theatre in New York City from 1879 to 1885 see Odell, *Annals*, 11(1879-1882):509-10, 12(1882-1885):74; this last reference may refer to a German Jewish production.

3. *JSS*, 10:67 ff.; Odell, *Annals*, 11(1879-1882):509-10, 12(1882-1885):74; *Education of Abraham Cahan*, 275 ff., 421; *AJYB*, 50:61; Wolf, *American Jew*, 275-76; *Jewish Life*, 9(no.1):23-24; "Goldfaden, Abraham," Reisin, *Leksikon*; "Drama, Yiddish," *JE*; Baltimore *Jewish Comment*, Nov. 1, 1901, pp.1 ff.; Eisenstein, *Zikhronothai*, 54, sub 1885; Masserman & Baker, *Jews Come to America*, 383 ff.; *Jewish Book Annual*, 18:12 ff., 34:32 ff.; Finkelstein, *The Jews* (1949), 3:878-79; Boraisha, *Yiddish*, 12; "Goldfaden, Abraham," *JE, UJE, EJ, LNYL, Concise Oxford Companion to the Theatre, AJYB*, 6(1904-1905):102; Janowsky, *Am. Jew. Reappraisal*, 204; Schappes, *JIUS*, 140; Learsi, *Jews in America*, 193-96; Goldberg, *Pioneers and Builders*, 420 ff.; *New York Times*, July 8, 1973, sec.2, pp.1 ff., Oct. 28, 1982, p.23; *Cambridge History of American Literature*, 3:607 ff.

4. Zylbercwaig, *Leksikon fun Yidishn Teater*, 3:2106; Bernheimer, *Russian Jew in the U.S.*, 227-29; "Latteiner, Joseph," *UJE*; *Education of Abraham Cahan*, 384 ff., 423-26; *Jewish Book Annual*, 6:86, 18:15; Markens, *Hebrews*, 344-45; Schappes, *JIUS*, 140; Wiernik, *History*, 393; "Horowitz, Moses Ha-Levi," *UJE, AJYB*, 6(1904-1905):120; Masserman

& Baker, *Jews Come to America*, 385-86; *Jewish Heritage*, 1(no.3):39 ff.; "Drama, Yiddish," *JE*; "Shaikewitz, Nahum Meyer," *AJYB*, 6(1904-1905):181; "Shaikewitz, Nahum Meir (Shomer)," *JE*; "Schomer, Nahum Meir," *DAB*; *YA*, 7:277 ff.; Hapgood, *Spirit of the Ghetto*, 272 ff., 277.

5. Rischin, *Promised City*, 135 ff.; "Gordin, Jacob," *JE, UJE, EJ, DAB, LNYL*, Reisin, *Leksikon*, Zylbercwaig, *Leksikon fun Yidishn Teater, Concise Oxford Companion to the Theatre*; *PAJHS*, 49:106; *YA*, 9:126 ff.; *Cambridge History of American Literature*, 3:608; *AJHQ*, 56:151 ff.; Schappes, *JIUS*, 140, 167-68; Janowsky, *Am. Jew. Reappraisal*, 204-5; *Education of Abraham Cahan*, 392, 422; Learsi, *Jews in America*, 193-94; Masserman & Baker, *Jews Come to America*, 386; *Jewish Digest*, 13(no.10):43; Epstein, *Profiles of Eleven*, 137 ff.; "Theatre," *UJE*, 10:236 ff.; "Drama, Yiddish," *JE*; *AJA*, 33:189 ff.; *Jewish People*, 4:293.

6. Biographies of Libin, Gorin, and Kobrin in *UJE, EJ*, Reisin's lexica, *LNYL*, and Zylbercwaig, *Leksikon fun Yidishn Teater*; Gorin, *Idishen Teater*; *AJYB*, 57:607; *The Bookman*, 39:631 ff.; Boraisha, *Yiddish*; *Jewish Book Annual*, 6:85; *Cambridge History of American Literature*, 3:604 ff.; Masserman & Baker, *Jews Come to America*, 368; "Kobrin, Leon," *AJYB*, 6(1904-1905):129; *AJA*, 33:192-93; Ausubel, *Book of Jewish Knowledge*, 512; Wiernik, *History*, 393.

7. *Jew. Com. Reg.*, 572 ff.; "Hirschbein, Peretz," "Pinski, David," *UJE, EJ, LNYL*; "Hirschbein, Peretz," *DAB*, Supplement 4, Zylbercwaig, *Leksikon fun Yidishn Teater*; Finkelstein, *The Jews* (1949), 3:885; Masserman & Baker, *Jews Come to America*, 369-70; *AJYB*, 51:521; *Jewish Book Annual*, 9:64, 11:178 ff., 15:84 ff., 18:12 ff., 17-18; Elbogen, *Cent. of Jewish Life*, 448-49; Wiernik, *History*, 391; Ausubel, *Book of Jewish Knowledge*, 515; Grinstein, *History*, 74; Waxman, *Jew. Literature*, 4:1016 ff.; *Cambridge History of American Literature*, 3:609; Janowsky, *Am. Jew. Reappraisal*, 203; Boraisha, *Yiddish*, 11; Schappes, *JIUS*, 168, 205-10; Kane, "David Pinski"; *AJA*, 33:193 ff.

8. *AJYB*, 62:452; *New York Times*, May 11, 1960, p.39, cs.2-3; for biographies of Ben-Ami and Schwartz consult the standard lexica; for Schwartz see also *DAB*, Supplement 6; Kane, "David Pinski," 5, 10, 11, 13; Glanz, *Jewish Woman*, 1:117; Rischin, *Promised City*, 137; Meites, *Chicago*, 389 ff.; Learsi, *Jews in America*, 195-96; *Jewish Heritage*, 1(no.3):39 ff.; *Jewish Digest*, 13(no.10):41 ff.; Janowsky, *Am. Jew. Reappraisal*, 204-6; *New York Times*, July 8, 1973, sec.2, pp.1 ff.; *Jew. Com. Reg.*, 572 ff.; Lifson, *Yiddish Theatre in America*, 185 ff., 214, 313-95, 396 ff., 402, 576 ff.; *YA*, 16:355; *Jewish Book Annual*, 34:38-39; Elbogen, *Cent. of Jewish Life*, 582; *Jewish People*, 4:302; Masserman & Baker, *Jews Come to America*, 387 ff.; Odell, *Annals*, 15:112-14, 402-3, 659.

9. "Moscovitch, Maurice," *UJE*; Odell, *Annals*, 15:112-15, 398; "Mogulesco, Sigmund," Zylbercwaig, *Leksikon fun Yidishn Teater*, 2:186; "Kalich, Bertha," *NAW*, Zylbercwaig, *Leksikon fun Yidishn Teater*; "Spachner, Bertha Kalisch," *AJYB*, 6(1904-1905):192; "Kalich, Bertha Rachel," *UJE*; Schappes, *JIUS*, 168; *Commentary*, 13:344 ff.; Lifson, *Yiddish Theatre in America*, 150; Wiernik, *History*, 393-94; *Jewish Digest*, 13(no.10):42; *Algemayne Entsiklopedie Yidn*, 2:389 ff.; *Education of Abraham Cahan*, 383 ff., 392, 415, 425, 433; Learsi, *Jew in America*, 195; "Thomashefsky," *AJYB*, 6(1904-1905):200-1; Masserman & Baker, *Jews Come to America*, 384-85; *AJA*, 33:189; "Thomashefsky, Boris (Baruch) Aaron," *UJE, EJ*, Zylbercwaig, *Leksikon fun Yidishn Teater*; Bernheimer, *Russian Jew in the U.S.*, 228-29; *AJYB*, 50:62 ff.; "Kessler, David," *EJ*, Zylbercwaig, *Leksikon fun Yidishn Teater*; "Adler, Sarah," *DAB*, Supplement 5; "Adler," *UJE, EJ*; Odell, *Annals*, vols. 9-15 for references to Yiddish theatre; *Jewish Heritage*, 1(no.3):39 ff.; Lulla Rosenfeld, *Bright Star of Exile: Jacob Adler and the Yiddish Theatre* (N.Y., 1977), 207 ff.; "Theater," *UJE*, 10:236-38; "Adler, Jacob P.," *AJYB*, 6(1904-1905):55; Schoener, *Lower East Side*, 6; "Gordin, Jacob," *DAB*.

10. Harry S. Linfield, *The Communal Organization of the Jews in the United States, 1927* (N.Y., 1930), 131; Hapgood, *Spirit of the Ghetto*, 113 ff., 126-27, 135 ff.; Odell, *Annals*, 13:86, 313 ff., 317-18, 529-30, 14:77 ff., 310 ff., 312, 338-39, 378, 618 ff., 15:112-15, 398-

401; *AJYB*, 13(1911-1912):133, 23:94, 69:610; "Muni, Paul," *UJE*; *Jewish Book Annual*, 18:17 ff., 34:32 ff., 38; *New York Times Book Review*, Feb. 1, 1976, p.29; *New York Times*, July 8, 1973, sect.2, pp.1 ff.; Lifson, *Yiddish Theatre in America*, 214 ff., 590 ff.; *PAJHS*, 49:99, 59:545 ff.; Rischin, *Promised City*, 133-37; "New York City," *EJ*, 12:1102-3, 1121; *YA*, 9:134-36, 16:102; *Jew. Com. Reg.*, 577-78; Bernheimer, *Russian Jew in the U.S.*, 226-31; *Jewish Digest*, 13(no.10):41 ff.; Learsi, *Jews in America*, 196; Handlin, *Adventure in Freedom*, 139 ff.; Eisenberg, *Eyewitnesses to American Jewish History*, 3:106, 130 ff.; Fishman, *Yiddish in America*, 38-40; *AH*, Oct. 15, 1915, pp.651 ff.; Masserman & Baker, *Jews Come to America*, 389-90; *National Jewish Monthly*, 90(no.8):40 ff.; Schappes, *JIUS*, 139-40; *Jewish People*, 4:282, 293-94; *Jewish Life*, 9(no.1):26.

11. The following works are very helpful in evaluating the development of the Yiddish press in the United States: Fishman, *Never Say Die*, 513 ff.; for biographies of Yiddish writers and journalists, see the Reisin lexica, *LNYL, JE, UJE, EJ*, and *DAB*, particularly the supplements. In the early years of the twentieth century the editions of the *DAB* were not very interested in Yiddish writers. Interest, highlighted in later decades, is reflected in the biographies which have appeared in the *DAB* supplements. Liptzin, *History of Yiddish Literature*; Liptzin, *Flowering of Yiddish Literature*, 52 ff.; Liptzin, *Generation of Decision*; Charles A. Madison, *Jewish Publishing in America* (N.Y., 1976), 101 ff., 129; Niger, *Yidishe Shrayber fun Tsvantsikstn Yorhundert*; Doroshkin, *Yiddish in America*, 97 ff.; Friedman & Madison, *Yiddish Literature*, 134 ff.; Gordis, *Jewish Life in America*, 214 ff.; Schulman, *Geshikhte*, 33-83; Howe, *World of Our Fathers*, 518 ff.; Janowsky, *Am. Jew. Reappraisal*, 195-96; *Jewish People*, 3:190 ff., 4:271 ff.; *Cambridge History of American Literature*, 3:599 ff.; Howe & Greenberg, *Voices From the Yiddish*, 191-238; *Jewish Book Annual*, 10:116 ff., 31:44 ff.; Fishman, *Yiddish in America*, 27 ff.; Goldberg, *Pioneers and Builders*, 284 ff.; Rosten, *Joys of Yiddish*; Soltes, *Yiddish Press*; *Judaism*, 3:154 ff.; *Radical History Review*, 23:8 ff.; Epstein, *Profiles of Eleven*, see the biographies of Cahan, Zhitlowsky, and Winchevsky; Heller, *Isaac M. Wise*, 586; *Jewish Digest*, 16(no.1):8-10; *Di New Yorker Yidish-daytshe Tsaytung, Hebrew Times*, Mar. 1, 1870, copy in Marcus Collections; Baron, *History*, 2:335; Schappes, *JIUS*, 113 ff.; Schappes, *DHJUS*, 730, n.3; Learsi, *Jews in America*, 188 ff.; Gutstein, *Chicago*, 381 ff.; *Catalogue of the Exhibition of 1970 on the Yiddish Press*; *Detroit Jewish News*, Apr. 3, 1970, p.20; Rischin, *Inventory*, 12 ff.; Wiernik, History, 256-59; *Amopteil*, 2:181 ff.; "New York City," *UJE*, 8:188, "Periodicals and Press," 8:453; *Jew. Com. Reg.*, 600 ff.; *Pioneer Woman*, Dec. 1970, p.3; Weinberger, *Jews and Judaism*, 63 ff.; "Periodicals," *JE*, 9:602, 607, 612; for another listing of the Yiddish press see Reisin, *Leksikon*, 665 ff.; "Sarasohn, Kasriel Hersch," *UJE*; Rischin, *Promised City*, 117.

12. Lipman, *Soc. Hist. of Jews in England*, 131; *Cambridge History of American Literature*, 3:598 ff.; Fishman, *Yiddish in America*, 28 ff.; "Periodicals," *JE*, 9:612; *Jewish People*, 3:191, 4:276-77; Waxman, *Jew. Literature*, 4:996 ff.; *Education of Abraham Cahan*, 309-10.

13. *Pioneer Woman*, Dec. 1970, p.3; *Amopteil*, 1:273 ff., 2:181 ff.; *Jew. Com. Reg.*, 600 ff., 623 ff., 633; Soltes, *Yiddish Press*, 14 ff.; *JSS*, 19:113 ff., 25:102 ff., 126; *Catalogue of the Exhibition of 1970 on the Yiddish Press*, 16; *Supplement to Abstracts of Papers Presented at 49th Annual Meeting (of the AJHS)*; Soltes on the *Jewish Morning Journal*, Marcus Collections; *PAJHS*, 46:397; Reisin, *Leksikon*, 665 ff.; Sanders, *Downtown Jews*, 97 ff.; Lipman, *Soc. Hist. of Jews in England*, 131-33; *AJYB*, 16(1914-1915):143, 50:58-59; *Jewish People*, 4:282 ff.; Weinberger, *Jews and Judaism*, 67 ff.; Boraisha, *Yiddish*, 8 ff.; Fishman, *Yiddish in America*, 28 ff.; "Press," *EJ*, 13:1046, "Yiddish Literature," 16:821 ff.; *Jewish Digest*, 21(no.4):15 ff.; *Congress Weekly*, Dec. 6, 1954, p.8; "Almanac," *JE*, 1:427; *AJA*, 33:184 ff.; Waxman, *Jew. Literature*, 4:996 ff.

14. Wiernik, *History*, 394-95; Soltes, *Yiddish Press*, 23 ff.; *Jew. Com. Reg.*, 600 ff.; *Catalogue of the Exhibition of 1970 on the Yiddish Press*; *Jewish People*, 3:190-219, 4:282-83; "New York City," *UJE*, 8:188-90; *Cambridge History of American Literature*, 3:598 ff., 606; *YA*,

9:101, 14:234 ff., 16:101-2, 351 ff.; Janowsky, *Am. Jew. Reappraisal*, 196; *AJA*, 12:34 ff., 23:33 ff.; *Judaism*, 3:161-62; Masserman & Baker, *Jews Come to America*, 410 ff.; *AJYB*, 26:168, 171, 53:527-29; Marcus *AJW*, 1:171; Marcus, *AJWD*, 529 ff.; "Cahan, Abraham," *DAB*, Supplement 5; *AJH*, 68:93-95; Epstein, *Profiles of Eleven*, 51-109; Sanders, *Downtown Jews*, 148 ff., 181 ff.; Goldberg, *Pioneers and Builders*, 284 ff.; Hapgood, *Spirit of the Ghetto*, 230 ff.; Higham, *Send These to Me*, 88 ff.; *Education of Abraham Cahan*, vii; Rischin, *Promised City*, 124 ff., 131; "Asch, Sholem," *EJ*; *PAJHS*, 43:10 ff.; Handlin, *Adventure in Freedom* 125-26; *Association for Jewish Studies Newsletter*, March 1978, p.12; Judd L. Teller (ed.), *Acculturation and Integration* (n.p., 1965), 130 ff.; Selig Perlman at the Annual Meeting of the AJHS, February 1952: *AJHQ*, 41:330; *Jewish Digest*, 11(no.2):37 ff., 16(no.1):8-10, 28(no.9):44-45; Waxman, *Jew. Literature*, 4:1045-46; *Midstream*, 16(no.4):69 ff.; *New York*, May 1, 1972, pp.36 ff.; Fishman, *Never Say Die*, 515; *New York Times*, Apr. 22, 1967, p.33; Grinstein, *History*, 71; Eisenberg, *Eyewitnesses to American Jewish History*, 3:69-70; *Jewish Book Annual*, 19:64 ff.; *Detroit Jewish News*, Apr. 23, 1971, p.48, cs.1-3; *Radical History Review*, 23:16; *Commentary*, 51:53 ff.; J.C. Rich, *60 Years of the Jewish Daily Record Forward* (N.Y., 1957).

15. Eisenstadt, *Hakme Yisrael be-Amerika*, 50, 71-72, 75-76; "Masliansky, Hirsch," *AJYB*, 6(1904-1905):152; Zola, "Zvi Hirsch Masliansky"; "Mintz, Moses Isaac," *LNYL*; "Paley, John," *AJYB*, 6(1904-1905):162-63; *JTA-DNB*, Jan. 2, 1975, p.3; "Hermalin, David Moses," *UJE*, Reisin, *Leksikon*, *AJYB*, 6(1904-1905):114; "Selikovitsch, George (Goetzel)," *UJE*, *AJYB*, 6(1904-1905):186; "Winchevsky, Morris," *DAB*; "Vinshevsky, Morris," *EJ*; for biographies of the journalists described above consult *JE*, *UJE*, *EJ*, Reisin's lexica, *LNYL*, *DAB*; "Judaeo-German Literature," *JE*, 7:310; "Adler, Jacob," *UJE*; *Cambridge History of American Literature*, 3:603; Epstein, *Profiles of Eleven*, 13 ff.; *Jewish Book Annual*, 39:177; "Wiernik, Peter," *UJE*, *LNYL*, *AJYB*, 6(1904-1905):206; Typescript biography of Peter Wiernik by Joseph Hirsch, copy in Marcus Collections; Gutstein, *Chicago*, 384, 400; Bregstone, *Chicago*, 47, 74, 333-34; Horwich, *My First Eighty Years*, 194 ff.; *EJ Year Book*, 1975-1976, p.424; Lipsky, *Memoirs in Profiles*, 251 ff.; Eisenstein, *Zikhronothai*, 54.

16. Wittke, *We Who Built America*, xiii; Soltes, *Yiddish Press*, 165, 167, 178, 192, 332-34; Rischin, *Promised City*, 119, 124 ff., 303, n.12; Learsi, *Jews in America*, 188 ff.; *Jew. Com. Reg.*, 613 ff.; *AJHQ*, 57:89; "New York City," *UJE*, 8:188-90; "United States," *JE*, 12:370; *PAJHS*, 50:208; Sachar, *Modern Jewish History*, 523; *AJYB*, 1(1899-1900):277-82, 21:587 ff., 23:270 ff., 50:60; *YA*, 14:234 ff.; *AJHQ*, 53:256; Boraisha, *Yiddish*, 8 ff., 12; *Jewish Digest*, 16(no.1):8-10; Janowsky, *Am. Jew. Reappraisal*, 195; Baron, *History*, 2:335; Doroshkin, *Yiddish in America*, 211 ff.

17. Handlin, *Immigrant in American History*, 90-93; Fishman, *Yiddish in America*, 28; *New York Times Book Review*, Feb. 1, 1976, pp.1 ff.; Learsi, *Jews in America*, 183 ff., 188-90; Curti et al., *American History*, 2:99; "New York City," *UJE*, 8:188; *AJYB*, 1:277 ff., 26:174-75, 189-91, 193, 201, 50:60; Schlesinger, *Rise of the City*, 185; Gutstein, *Chicago*, 380 ff.; Rischin, *Inventory*, 12 ff., 47; Soltes, *Yiddish Press*, 39-40, 160, 176; *Jewish People*, 4:288 ff.; Rischin, *Promised City*, 119 ff., 123 ff.; *Jew. Com. Reg.*, 612-18; *YA*, 9:101-2; Elbogen, *Cent. of Jewish Life*, 581 ff.; *AJHQ*, 59:164-65, 547; *Pioneer Woman*, Dec. 1970, p.3; *Catalog of the Exhibition of 1970 on Yiddish Press*, 5, 15; Boraisha, *Yiddish*, 12; *The Bookman*, 39:631 ff.; "Maisel, Max N.," *WWIAJ*, 1926; *Finding Lists of the Chicago Public Library* Yiddish, 7th ed., Chicago, 1907); Masserman & Baker, *Jews Come to America*, 417-19; *Jewish Book Annual*, 3:81-82, 19:60 ff.; Roskolenko, *The Time That Was Then*, 109 ff.; *Jewish Digest*, 28(no.9):43-45; *JSS*, 25:102 ff.; Hapgood, *Spirit of the Ghetto*, 177-98; *Judaism*, 3:154 ff.; Howe, *World of Our Fathers*, 518-51.

CHAPTER SIXTEEN

YIDDISH LITERATURE

1. The following works throw light on the history of Yiddish prose literature in the United State: *Jewish People*, 3:190 ff., 4:288 ff.; Liptzin, *History of Yiddish Literature*; Jeshurin, *100 Yor Moderne Yidishe Literatur; The Forward Anniversary Issue*, May 23, 1982, copy in Marcus Collections; Madison, *Yiddish Literature*, 134-381; Schulman, *Geshikhte*, 84-139; Ausubel, *Book of Jewish Knowledge*, 512 ff.; Howe & Greenberg, *Voices from the Yiddish*, 193 ff.; Niger, *Yidishe Shrayber fun Tsvantsikstn Yorhundert*, 1:36, et passim, 2:9, et passim; Doroshkin, *Yiddish in America*, 97 ff.; Roback, *Contemporary Yiddish Literature*, 24 ff., 29 ff., 72 ff.; Feinsilver, *Taste of Yiddish*, 23 ff.; Rosten, *Joys of Yiddish*; Goldberg, *Pioneers and Builders*, 380 ff.; Sol Liptzin, *The Maturing of Yiddish Literature* (N.Y., 1970), 1-81; Liptzin, *Flowering of Yiddish Literature*, 178, et passim; Howe & Greenberg, *Treasury of Yiddish Stories*; Roback, *Story of Yiddish Literature*, 192 ff., 274 ff., 298 ff.; Friedman & Gordis, *Jewish Life in America*, 214 ff.; Howe, *World of Our Fathers*, 417 ff., 460-96, 518 ff.; Janowsky, *Am. Jew. Reappraisal*, 193 ff.; Benjamin Kelson, "The Religious Life of the Eastern Jewish Immigrants to America, etc." (rabbinical thesis, HUC, 1925), 26 ff.; "Literature, Yiddish," *UJE*, 7:129 ff.; *Cambridge History of American Literature*, 3:598 ff.; Liptzin, *Generation of Decision*; Winter & Wuensche, *Literatur der Juden*, 3:612-13; "Wiener, Leo," *UJE, DAB*, Supplement 2; Margolin, *Jews of Eastern Europe*, 256-59.

2. "Wolfenstein, Martha," *UJE*; *YA*, 9:67 ff., 72 ff., 98, 101 ff., 16:355 ff.; Waxman, *Jew Literature*, 4:956 ff., 1003-4; Masserman & Baker, *Jews Come to America*, 367 ff.; Schlesinger, *Rise of the City*, 297; Winter & Wuensche, *Literatur der Juden*, 3:133; *Cambridge History of American Literature*, 3:598 ff., 604, 607-8; Learsi, *Jews in America*, 190 ff.; Elbogen, *Cent. of Jewish Life*, 448; Wiernik, *History*, 302 ff.; *AJYB*, 50:60; Rischin, *Promised City*, 130 ff.; *Education of Abraham Cahan*, 181; *Jewish Book Annual*, 1:80, 33:20 ff., 38:34; Boraisha, *Yiddish*, 10; "Dick, Isaac Meir," *EJ*; *PAJHS*, 48:132; *AJA*, 33:187-89.

3. "Moissieff, Leon," *DAB*, Supplement 3; "Spivak, Charles David," *UJE, DAB, AJYB*, 6(1904-1905):194; Ausubel, *Book of Jewish Knowledge*, 512-17; Wiernik, *History*, 392-93; "Selikovitsch, George (Goetzel)," *UJE, DAB; JSS*, 2:340, 5:311 ff.; "Schaikewitz, Nahum Meyer (Shomer)," *UJE, AJYB*, 6(1904-1905):181; Hertz Burgin, *Die Geschichte fun der idisher Arbeter Bewegung* (N.Y., 1915); *The Bookman*, 39:631; *Jewish People*, 3:190 ff., 201-2; Janowsky, *Am. Jew. Reappraisal*, 202; Masserman & Baker, *Jews Come to America*, 368-69; Wiernik, *History*, 304, 392-93; *Cambridge History of American Literature*, 3:604-6; "Miller, Louis E.," *UJE, EJ, LNYL*; "Bandes, Louis E.," "Bercovici, Konrad," "Rombro, Jacob (Philip Krantz)," *UJE*; "Richards, Bernard Gerson," *UJE, EJ, AJYB*, 6(1904-1905):168-69; Rischin, *Promised City*, 116-17, 131; "Niger, Samuel," "Reisin, Abraham," "Shomer," "Tashrak," *EJ*; "Gorin, Bernard (Isaac Goido)," *EJ*, Reisin's lexica; "Bublick, Gedaliah," "Coralnik, Abraham," "Shalom (Sholem) Aleichem," *UJE, EJ*; Simon Noveck (ed.), *Great Jewish Personalities in Modern Times* (Clinton, Mass., 1961), 207 ff.; *Congress Bi-Weekly*, Mar. 16, 1959, pp.3 ff.; *New York Times*, Dec. 21, 1961, p.24; *Wall Street Journal*, June 18, 1968, p.16, c.3; "Zevin, Israel Joseph," Reisin, Leksikon, *DAB, AJYB*, 6(1904-1905):211-12; "Libin, Z.," *UJE, EJ*, Reisin's lexica, *LNYL*; *Cambridge History of American Literature*, 3:604-5; *Atlantic Magazine*, 91:254 ff.; Learsi, *Jews in America*, 191-93; Schappes, *JIUS*, 138; Waxman, *Jew. Literature*, 4:999 ff., 1010 ff., 1040 ff.; "Opatoshu, Joseph," "Raboy, Isaac," "Zhitlowsky, Chaim," *UJE, EJ*; *AJYB*, 42:153, 57:607, 60:354; Finkelstein, *The Jews* (1949), 3:888; "Krantz, Philip," *EJ, AJYB*, 6(1904-1905):170, Reisin, *Leksikon; Judaeans*, 2:153 ff., 183; "Tannenbaum, Abner," *AJYB*, 6(1904-1905):200, *LNYL*, Reisin's lexica; Masserman & Baker, *Jews Come to America*, 368; "Harkavy," *JE*, 6:234, *UJE, EJ, AJYB*, 6(1904-1905):110-11, Re-

isin's lexica; *AJA*, 33:35 ff., 188, 197-200; *Finding Lists of the Chicago Public Library* (Yiddish, Chicago, 1907); for Sholem Asch, see the standard biographical lexica; *Jewish Book Annual*, 1:88-93 (Yiddish section), 3:77, 11:169 ff., 183 ff., 21:41 ff., 26:100 ff., 37:116 ff., 38:36; Rischin, *Promised City*, 116-17; *Education of Abraham Cahan*, 422; *Congress Weekly*, Jan. 30, 1956, pp.11-12; *Jewish Publication Society Bookmark*, 3(no.1):7; Saul Goodman (ed.), *Yorbukh Gevidmet Shmuel Niger* (N.Y., 1968); Howe & Libo, *How We Lived*, 113; *AJHQ*, 53:263; Epstein, *Profiles of Eleven*, 297 ff.; Fishman, *Never Say Die*, 291 ff.

4. *Cambridge History of American Literature*, 3:604; Waxman, *Jew Literature*, 4:1008 ff.; Finkelstein, *The Jews* (1949), 3:886 ff.; *YA*, 9:103; Liptzin, *History of Yiddish Literature*, 136 ff., 156 ff., 175 ff.; Hapgood, *Spirit of the Ghetto*, 199 ff., 230 ff.

5. *Jewish People*, 4:274 ff.; "Sobel, Jacob Zevi," *LNYL*; Waxman, *Jew Literature*, 4:956 ff., 1004 ff.; Janowsky, *Am. Jew. Reappraisal*, 193 ff.; Schappes, *JIUS*, 114.

6. Howe & Greenberg, *Treasury of Yiddish Poetry*; Schulman, *Geshikhte*, 140 ff., 155-57; "Judaeo-German Literature," *JE*, 7:310; *JSS*, 5:311-13; Sanders, *Downtown Jews*, 126 ff.; *AJA*, 33:187 ff.; Finkelstein, *The Jews* (1949), 3:878; "Literature, Yiddish," *UJE*, 7:128-29; *Jewish Book Annual*, 33:20 ff.; N.B. Minkoff, *Pionern fun Yidisher Poezie in Amerike: Dos Sotsiale Lid* (3 vols., N.Y., 1956), 1:19 ff., 71, 223 ff., 226-27; *Jewish People*, 4:288 ff.; Leftwich, *Anthology of Yiddish Literature*, 807 ff.; *Jewish Currents*, 37(no.5):12 ff.; "Winchevsky, Morris," *DAB*, the standard lexica.

7. See the biographical lexica for Edelstadt; David Edelstadt, *Geklibene Verk* (2 vols., Moscow, 1935); Uchill, *Pioneers*, 303-4; Sanders, *Downtown Jews*, 126 ff.; *Cambridge History of American Literature*, 3:603; *Jewish Book Annual*, 20:39.

8. Rose Freeman-Ishill (ed.), *To the Toilers and Other Verses by Basil Dahl* (Joseph Bovshover) (Berkeley Heights, N.J., 1928); *Jewish Book Annual*, 14:32 ff.; *Amopteil*, 2:32 ff.; *Jewish People*, 3:193; see the biographical lexica for Bovshover.

9. Schappes, *JIUS*, 136 ff.; "Rosenfeld, Morris," *DAB*; Howe & Greenberg, *Treasury of Yiddish Poetry*, 17 ff., 78-81; Leo Wiener (trans.), Morris Rosenfeld, *Songs From the Ghetto* (Boston, 1898). There are various editions of Rosenfeld's works: see the published catalogue of the HUCL. *YIVO Bleter*, 42:199 ff.; *PAJHS*, 43:23; Finkelstein, *The Jews* (1949), 3:878; *Education of Abraham Cahan*, 382, 430; *Jewish Book Annual*, 1:53 ff., 20:37 ff., 100 ff.; Masserman & Baker, *Jews Come to America*, 371; *Cambridge History of American Literature*, 3:602-3; "Rosenfeld, Morris," *AJYB*, 6(1904-1905):172; Goldberg, *Pioneers and Builders*, 123 ff.; Sanders, *Downtown Jews*, 134 ff.; Howe, *World of Our Fathers*, 422-23; *Jewish People*, 4:293; Janowsky, *Am. Jew. Reappraisal*, 197 ff.; *JSS*, 22:124; Leftwich, *Anthology of Yiddish Literature*, 141 ff.; *AJA*, 22:121 ff.; "Rosenfeld, Morris," *JE*; Waxman, *Jew Literature*, 4:1004 ff.

10. *Cambridge History of American Literature*, 3:604, 606; Roback, *Story of Yiddish Literature*, 258 ff.; "Literature, Yiddish," *UJE*, 7:130; "Yiddish Literature," *EJ*, 16:814-15, 822; "Ignatoff, David," "Leivick, H. (Leivick Halpern)," "Raboy, Isaac," "Yunge, Di," *EJ*; *Jewish People*, 4:299-300; Finkelstein, *The Jews* (1949), 3:886-88; Ausubel, *Book of Jewish Knowledge*, 515-16; Wiernik, *History*, 392; see the biographical lexica for Opatoshu; Howe & Greenberg, *Treasury of Yiddish Stories*, 88, 414 ff., 427 ff., 552 ff.; Janowsky, *Am. Jew. Reappraisal*, 202; *Jewish Book Annual*, 3:76, 21:77 ff.; Leftwich, *Anthology of Modern Yiddish Literature*, 215 ff.; *AJA*, 33:195 ff. For notes on other Young Ones who had a following: Howe & Greenberg, *Treasury of Yiddish Poetry*, 85 ff., 97-101, 115-16, 146-50, 151-59, 164 ff.; Leftwich, *Anthology of Modern Yiddish Poetry*, 147 ff., 160 ff., 173 ff., 293 ff., 323 ff., 327 ff., 373-74, 380 ff., 396 ff.; Waxman, *Jew Literature*, 4:1018 ff., 1037 ff.; *JSS*, 38:265 ff.; Learsi, *Jews in America*, 191; Madison, *Yiddish Literature*, 348-81; for women poets see Howe & Greenberg, *Treasury of Yiddish Poetry*, 160-63, 168-69.

11. *Jewish Book Annual*, 20:41-42, 38:35; Detroit *Jewish News*, Dec. 5, 1969, p.30, c.1; *Cambridge History of American Literature*, 3:606; Janowsky, *Am. Jew. Reappraisal*, 200-201; *JSS*, 38:265 ff., 275; "Literature, Yiddish," *UJE*, 7:130; *AJA*, 33:195 ff.; *AJYB*, 73:611 ff.; Roback, *Story of Yiddish Literature*, 258-321; Schappes, *JIUS*, 169-70; *Jewish People*, 3:204.

12. Liptzin, *History of Yiddish Literature*, 311 ff.; Howe & Greenberg, *Treasury of Yiddish Poetry*, 91, 245 ff., 257-59, 260 ff., 326 ff.; Ausubel, *Book of Jewish Knowledge*, 516; "Glanz-Leyeles, Aaron," "Glatstein (Gladstone), Jacob," "Minkoff, Nahum Baruch," *EJ* and the biographical lexica; "In-Zikh," *EJ*; Leftwich, *Anthology of Yiddish Poetry*, 311 ff., 332 ff., 342 ff.; *AJYB*, 68:526, 73:611 ff.; Leftwich, *Anthology of Modern Yiddish Literature*, 228 ff., 238 ff.; *Jewish Book Annual*, 25:116 ff., 33:25; Finkelstein, *The Jews* (1949), 3:887; "Literature, Yiddish," *UJE*, 7:131-32; *Jewish People*, 3:215; *Congress Bi-Weekly*, Apr. 17, 1970, pp.15 ff.; *AJA*, 33:201-2; Janowsky, *Am. Jew. Reappraisal*, 201, 206-7.

13. *Congress Bi-Weekly*, Apr. 17, 1970, pp.15 ff.; Leftwich, *Anthology of Yiddish Poetry*, 307 ff.; "Walt, Abraham," *AJYB*, 6(1904-1905):203-4; *Jewish Book Annual*, 20:40-41, 38:38 ff.; "Liessen, Abraham," *EJ* and the biographical lexica; Waxman, *Jew Literature*, 4:1021 ff.; "Bloomgarden, Solomon," *DAB*, *AJYB*, 6(1904-1905):66 and the biographical lexica, especially *LNYL*; Masserman & Baker, *Jews Come to America*, 371; *Cambridge History of American Literature*, 3:603-4; *AJA*, 33:201; Schappes, *JIUS*, 168-69; Howe & Greenberg, *Treasury of Yiddish Poetry*, 73 ff.; Goldberg, *Pioneers and Builders*, 111 ff.; Uchill, *Pioneers*, 304-5; Yehoash, Bronx, to Isaac Goldberg, N.Y.?, May 4, 1920, copy in Marcus Collections; Ausubel, *Book of Jewish Knowledge*, 512.

14. *Midstream*, 16(no.4):16 ff.; Liptzin, *History of Yiddish Literature*, 288 ff.; Hapgood, *Spirit of the Ghetto*, 90 ff.; "Literature, Yiddish," *UJE*, 7:129 ff.; Jehiel B. & Sarah H. Cooperman (eds.), *America in Yiddish Poetry: An Anthology* (N.Y., 1967); *YA*, 9:106-8; Howe & Greenberg, *Treasury of Yiddish Poetry*; Leftwich, *Anthology of Modern Yiddish Literature*, 215, et passim; Joseph Leftwich (ed.), *The Golden Peacock: A Worldwide Treasury of Yiddish Poetry* (N.Y., 1961), 7-22, 116-40, 141-79, 293-468, 737 ff. (women poets); Ruth Rubin, *Voices of a People: The Story of Yiddish Folksongs* (Phila., 1979); Liptzin, *Generation of Decision*, 160 ff.; *AJA*, 33:206.

15. *YA*, 16:353 ff.; *AJYB*, 1(1899-1900):277 ff., 21:587 ff., 23:386 ff., 26:171-72, 28:400 ff., 50:59; Horwich, *My First Eighty Years*, 143; *Jewish Digest*, 16(no.1):8-10, 21(no.4):15-16; "Baltimore," *JE*, 2:481, *UJE*, 2:57; Koplin, "Jewish Exponent," 16-17; Gutstein, *Chicago*, 380-81, 400 ff.; *Michigan Jewish History*, 14:21-22, 17:11 ff.; *By Myself I'm A Book*, 76 ff., 79 ff.; *YA*, 16:353-54; Fishman, *Yiddish in America*, 38; *Generations*, 1:46 ff., 3:45; Bernheimer, *Russian Jew in the U.S.*, 250 ff.; Fein, *Baltimore*, 172-73; *Education of Abraham Cahan*, 392; Gartner, *Cleveland*, 206 ff., 214; Janowsky, *Am. Jew. Reappraisal*, 203; *Amopteil*, 2:219 ff.; Handlin, *Adventure in Freedom*, 126, 139; Meites, *Chicago*, 358 ff.; Rawidowicz (ed.), *Chicago Pinkas*, 69 ff.; "Chicago," *UJE*, 3:142, "Philadelphia," 9:676; Hertzberg, *Atlanta*, 123-24; "Zolotkoff, Leon," *AJYB*, 6(1904-1905):212; *AJHQ*, 60:10-11, 62:268; "Selikovitsch, Goetzel," *DAB*; Schappes, *JIUS*, 114; Morais, *Philadelphia*, 198-99; *Catalogue of the Exhibition of 1970 on the Yiddish Press*; Grinstein, *History*, 71; Blum, *Baltimore*, 25; *RIJHN*, 5:406-7.

16. *Jewish Book Annual*, 33:20 ff.; Rischin, *Promised City*, 132; *AJYB*, 26:327, 329-31, 339; Winter & Wuensche, *Literatur der Juden*, 3:612 ff.; *Education of Abraham Cahan*, 241-42; *Jewish Review*, 1:169 ff. (Yiddish section), 220 (English section).

17. References for America and Yiddish: *AJYB*, 26:172, 326, 329-31, 368; Marcus, *CAJ*, 3:1186; *Jewish Review*, 1:169 (Yiddish section), 220 (English section); Riis, *Children of the Poor*, 53-55; Rischin, *Promised City*, 133; Kane, "David Pinski"; *Jewish Book Annual*, 33:20 ff.; Fishman, *Yiddish in America*, 35; *JSS*, 14:257-58; *AH*, Oct. 15, 1915, pp.651 ff.; *New York Times*, Jan. 25, 1959, p.18; Mencken, *American Language*, 633; *Jewish Digest*, 15(no.4):33 ff.; *Midstream*, 15(no.3):75 ff.; Rosten, *Joys of Yiddish*; *PAJHS*, 38:21,

39:362, 49:246; *YA*, 9:72 ff.; *Education of Abraham Cahan*, 356. For striking examples of the use of English in Yiddish advertisements in the late nineteenth century, see Winter & Wuensche, *Literatur der Juden*, 3:612 ff.

18. *AJYB*, 83:345-50; Feinsilver, *Taste of Yiddish*, 290 ff.; Howe & Greenberg, *Voices from the Yiddish*; Wish, *Society and Thought*, 2:229, 240, 253; *Basic Facts About Yiddish* (YIVO, N.Y., 1946); "New York City," *EJ*, 12:1102-3, 1117, "United States of America," 15:1627; Swichkow & Gartner, *Milwaukee*, 172; Birmingham, *Our Crowd!*, 313; B. Felsenthal, Chicago, to R. Gottheil, N.Y., July 10, 1899, copy in Marcus Collections; G. Gottheil, N.Y., to J.D. Eisenstein, N.Y., n.d., copy in Marcus Collections; "Braslau, Sophie," *UJE*; "Sandler, Jacob Koppel," *DAB*; *JSS*, 3:224-26, 33:141, 151, 155; *YA*, 7:283, 9:103, 16:346 ff., 353; *Druckerman Catalogues*, collection in HUCL covering period 1890's-1920's; Learsi, *Jews in America*, 146-47; Hapgood, *Spirit of the Ghetto*, 71 ff.; Seller (ed.), *Immigrant Women*, 74 ff.; Howe & Libo, *How We Lived*, 125-50, 279 ff.; Glanz, *Jewish Woman*, 115 ff.; *AJH*, 69:524, 70:68 ff.; *AJHQ*, 59:201 ff., 545 ff., 67:386 ff.; *AJA*, 22:107-15, 33:199-200; *RIJHN*, 7:405; *Jewish Book Annual*, 12:34 ff., 40, 44, 34:38-41, 38:33 ff.; Schappes, *JIUS*, 136 ff.; *Congress Weekly*, Nov. 15, 1954, pp.8-10; Rischin, *Promised City*, 115 ff.; "New York City," *UJE*, 8:188-90; Boraisha, *Yiddish*, 11-12; Fishman, *Yiddish in America*, 14, 27, 34, 36, 41, 47; *Jewish Life*, 9(no.4):14-15; *PAJHS*, 48:132, 49:85, 99, 110; *Labor History*, 4:235; Greenberg, "The History of the East European Jews in the United States, 1890-1900" (HUC prize essay, 1939), 96 ff.; Gutstein, *Chicago*, 389; Karp, *Jew. Exp. in America*, 4:xvi-xvii; *Congress Bi-Weekly*, May 23, 1966, p.26, June 18, 1971, pp.17 ff.; Uchill, *Pioneers*, 165 ff.; Ellis, *Am. Catholicism*, 167; *JJOS*, 12:29; C.D. Spivak, Denver, to C.H. Kauver, Denver, Sept. 28, 1917, copy in Marcus Collections; Fein, *Baltimore*, 173; Bernheimer, *Russian Jew in the U.S.*, 33-34, 173; Wiernik, *History*, 391 ff.; *Commentary*, 18:31 ff.; 52(no.6):102 ff.; Waxman, *Jew Literature*, 4:956 ff., 961, 1010; *Jewish Heritage*, 1(no.2):15-18; *Atlantic Magazine*, 91:254; *AJYB*, 26:178, 211-16, 258-59, 265, 286 ff., 302 ff., 324, 327; Sherman, *A Fateful Half-Century*, 8; Rosenthal, "Public Life of Louis Marshall," 126-27.

CHAPTER SEVENTEEN

WHAT IS TO BE DONE WITH THESE INCOMING EXOTICS

1. *PAJHS*, 48:35; *AH*, May 18, 1900, pp.69-72.
2. *Pittsburgh Platform*, 38-39.
3. *AJYB*, 26:404 ff.; *PAJHS* vol. 24 is *Jewish Disabilities in the Balkan States*; "Board of Delegates of [on] Civil and Religious Rights," *UJE*; Wolf, *Presidents I Have Known*; *AH*, Oct. 27, 1916, pp.874-75; "Wolf, Simon," *JE, UJE, EJ, DAB, WWW*, vol.1.
4. "B'nai B'rith," "Fraternities," *JE*. After the death of Wise, the disarray in Western leadership is reflected in the Joseph Stolz Papers in the Marcus Collections; Colton, "American Jewry, 1901-1910," 14 ff.; *Menorah*, 38:52; Finkelstein, *The Jews* (1949), 1:399; Karff, *HUC-JIR*, 49 ff.; "Levi, Leo N.," "Bien, Julius," *JE, UJE, DAB*; Kraus, *Reminiscences*, 151 ff.; Grusd, *B'nai B'rith*, 121 ff., 131; *CCARYB*, 14:64 ff., 179 ff., 207 ff.; Bernheimer, *Russian Jew in the U.S.*, 168-69.
5. *PUAHC*, 2:1572-74, 1602-3, 1803-4.
6. Biographies of the Eastern Jewish notables mentioned in the preceding paragraphs may be found in the *UJE*. Schoener, *Portal to America*, 132; *Papers of the Jewish Women's Congress*, 179, 194; Karpf, *Jewish Community Organization*, 36 ff.; *AJYB*, 23:84 ff., 26:235 ff., 57:34; *YA*, 14:248; Allen, "Americanization of the East-European Jew"; Howe & Libo, *How We Lived*, 193 ff.; Howe, *World of Our Fathers*, 271 ff.

7. "Straus, Oscar Solomon" or "Straus," *JE, UJE, EJ, DAB*; Straus, *Under Four Administrations*; Naomi W. Cohen, *A Dual Heritage: The Public Career of Oscar S. Straus* (Phila., 1969); Marcus, *Memoirs*, 2:237 ff.

8. Stern, *Occasional Addresses*, 88 ff.; *PAJHS*, 33:17 ff.; Adler (ed.), *Voice of America on Kishineff*; Cowen, *Memories of an American Jew*, 124; Morais, *Philadelphia*, 437; "Adler, Cyrus," *JE, UJE, EJ, DAB*, Supplement 2; Adler, *I Have Considered the Days; Holy Scriptures* (Phila., 1955), iv; *Jewish Publication Society Bookmark*, 10(no.2A):4-5.

9. *PAJHS*, 29:188 ff.; *AJYB*, 26:373 ff.; "Sulzberger, Mayer," or "Sulzberger," *JE, UJE, EJ, DAB*; Morais, *Philadelphia*, 301 ff.; Stern, *Occasional Addresses*, 106 ff.; Marx, *Studies in Jewish History*, 234; *Mayer Sulzberger: Biographical Sketch* (N.Y., 1916), (a reprint from the *National Cyclopaedia of American Biography*); Simon, *Israel Zangwill*, 143 ff.

10. *AH*, Oct. 8, 1920, p.625 ff., Oct. 15, 1920, pp.658, 665; Richard D. Messing, "The Life and Activities of Jacob H. Schiff During the Years 1918-1920" (HUC term paper, 1966); Marinbach, *Ellis Island of the West*, 111; *Jewish Home*, 10(no.1):53-54; Adler, *Jacob H. Schiff*; *New York Times*, Sept. 26, 1920, p.1, cs.5-6, p.2, entire; Max Kohler, n.p., to Mortimer L. Schiff, N.Y., Oct. 14, 1925, AJHSL; Abram Vossen Goodman, *Jacob Schiff in Retrospect* (typescript, Cincinnati, 1945); Gotthard Deutsch, *Scrolls: Essays on Jewish History and Literature, and Kindred Subjects* (2 vols., Cincinnati, 1917), 2:257 ff.; Mark Sullivan, *Our Times: The United States, 1900-1925* (3 vols., N.Y., 1927), 3:58, 425; Singer, *Russia at the Bar of the American People*, 161 ff.; Birmingham, *"Our Crowd"*, 282 ff.; *JSS*, 29:3, 8, 10, 15, 20, 75 ff., 83 ff., 89, n.196, 35:87 ff., 100, 103; for Corbin affair, see Marcus, *U.S. Jewry*, vol. 3; *AJHQ*, 61:313 ff.; Reznikoff, *Louis Marshall*, 2:674; P. & K., *Tourist's Guide*, 385-387; *AJA* 3:21; *Reconstructionist*, 33(no.18):28; *PAJHS*, 28:301 ff.; "Schiff, Jacob Henry," *JE, UJE, EJ, DAB*; *Liberal Judaism*, 14(no.9):19 ff.; Jacob Billikopf, "Jacob H. Schiff, A Statesman" (typescript, n.p., n.d.), copy in Marcus Collections; Herbert Morris, "Philanthropic Activity of J.H. Schiff, 1914" (HUC term paper, 1955); Levinger, *Jews in U.S.*, 309 ff.; Simon, *Israel Zangwill*, 138 ff.; Masserman & Baker, *Jews Come to America*, 445.

11. Markens, *Hebrews*, 229; Rosenthal, "Public Life of Louis Marshall"; Reznikoff, *Louis Marshall*, 1:12 ff., 2:881-82, 988 ff., 1175-77; "Marshall, Louis," *JE, UJE, EJ, DAB*; *AJYB*, 32:21 ff., 42; Rudolph, *Syracuse*, 103 ff.; Stern, *Occasional Addresses*, 69 ff.; *American Judaism*, 6(no.1):12 ff.; Analyticus, *Jews Are Like That*, 181 ff.; *JSS*, 25:102 ff., 30:277-78; *AH*, Sept. 13, 1929, pp.489 ff.; N.Y. *Jewish Tribune*, Dec. 10, 1926, p.13, Dec. 17, 1926, p.22; Goldberg, *Pioneers and Builders*, 302-7; Phila. *Jewish Exponent*, Sept. 7, 1956, p.51, cs.1-5, p.52, cs.2-5; *Commentary*, 23:365 ff,; *AJHQ*, 63:18; *EIAJH*, 457 ff.; Morton Rosenstock, *Louis Marshall: Defender of Jewish Rights* (Detroit, 1965).

12. *PAJHS*, 21:72, 85; *New York History*, 63:426-27; *YA*, 9:253-64; Morais, *Philadelphia*, 142-43; Joseph, *Jewish Immigration*, 174; *Festskrift i Anleding af Professor David Simonsens* (Danish, Copenhagen, 1923), 277-89; *AJYB*, 7(1905-1906):83-84, 23:99-100; Robertson, "92nd Street YMHA & YWHA Inventory," 2; "Einstein, Hannah Bachman," "Lazarus, Emma," *NAW*; "Jewish Charities," *Americana*, 9; "Hirsch, Baron Maurice de," "Sisterhoods of Personal Service," *JE*; *WSJHQ*, 14:351 ff.; *Education of Abraham Cahan*, 262; "Moskowitz, Henry," "Radin, Adolph Moses," "Richman, Julia," *UJE*; Marcus, *AJW*, 65, 84-85, 105, 209; Joseph, *Baron de Hirsch Fund*, 211 ff.; *Moral and Spiritual Foundation for the World of Tomorrow: The Centenary of Congregation Emanu-El, etc.* (N.Y., 1945), 215-16; R.L. Duffus, *Lillian Wald: Neighbor and Crusader* (N.Y., 1938), 36-37; "Wald, Lillian," *UJE, EJ, NAW, DAB*, Supplement 2.

13. Kavitch & Goodenow, *Educating an Urban People*, 106-10; Wish, *Society and Thought*, 2:141, 147; *Baron Festschrift*, 293; *New York History*, 63:427-28; *Reports, Immig. Com. Abstracts*, 1:615; Woods, *Americans in Progress*, 292, 348, 374; *AJHQ*, 54:43, 53-60, 62, 76-80, 60:142; Zola, "Zvi Hirsch Masliansky," 40, 47 ff.; Schappes, *DHJUS*, 550 ff., 730-31; Curti et al., *American History*, 2:86, 279; Lipman, *Soc. Hist. of Jews in England*,

144 ff.; Rischin, *Promised City*, 100 ff., 202, 205-9; *AJYB*, 23:84 ff., 94-100, 106 ff., 57:34 ff.; *PUAHC*, 3:2670-71, 4:3720; Joseph, *Baron de Hirsch Fund*, 13-19, 211 ff., 253 ff., 266, 278-86; *Jew. Com. Reg.*, 648 ff., 653 ff., 994 ff.; "New York," *JE*, 9:277, 279, 285-88, "United States," 12:377; *PAJHS*, 37:221 ff., for Julia Richman, see 248, 282 ff.; *Education of Abraham Cahan*, 223; "Council of Jewish Women," "Hirsch, Clara de," "Young Men's Hebrew Association," *JE*; "Americanization," "National Council of Jewish Women," *UJE*; Morris & Freund, *Trends*, 113 ff.; Schlesinger, *Rise of the City*, 351-52; Goren, *American Jews*, 63-65; *Jewish People*, 4:159-60; "Social Settlements," *DAH* (1976-1978); Kraus, "Settlement House Movement in NYC," 165 ff., 203, 214-15, 236-37; Robertson, "92nd Street YMHA & YWHA Inventory"; Adler, *Jacob H. Schiff*, 1:382 ff.; *Lillian D. Wald, 1867-1940. The Hall of Fame for Great Americans* (N.Y., 1971); "Memorandum in Support of the Candidacy of Lillian Wald of Henry Street for Admission to the Hall of Fame for Great Americans" (N.Y., 1968); Lillian D. Wald, *The House on Henry Street* (N.Y., 1915); Lillian D. Wald, *Windows on Henry Street* (Boston, 1934); Allan Edward Reznick, "Lillian D. Wald: The Years at Henry Street" (Ph.D. diss., U. of Wisconsin, 1973), 22, 32; Stanley Skolnik, "Lillian Wald: Her Work with New York's Jewish Community from 1893 to 1910" (HUC term paper, n.d.), copy in Marcus Collections; Golden & Rywell, *Jews in American History*, 317-18;ff; *New York Times*, Sept. 3-4, 1940, necrologies and tributes for Lillian Wald; P. & K., *Tourist's Guide*, 385-86; Berkowitz, "Hebrew Free School Association"; Sklare (ed.), *Jew in American Society*, 48; "Blaustein, David," *EJ*, *DAB*; Markens, *Hebrews*, 318-21; Schoener, *Portal to America*, 129 ff.; "New York City," *UJE*, 8:190, "Philadelphia," 8:479; Curti, *American Thought*, 619; Handlin, *Adventure in Freedom*, 153-54, 158-59; Wiernik, *History*, 376-77; Schoener, *Lower East Side*, 5 sub 1889; Glazer, *American Judaism*, 90-91; Howe, *World of Our Fathers*, 229-81, especially 230, 234-35; Schappes, *JIUS*, 132-33; Blaustein (ed.), *Memoirs of David Blaustein*.

14. Kraus, "Settlement House Movement in NYC," 165-67; *New York History*, 63:417 ff., 424; "Abelson, Paul," *UJE*, *EJ*; *Declaration of Independence: Deinard, Koheleth America*, p.55, no.327; Joseph Barondess, N.Y., to J.D. Eisenstein, N.Y., July 8, 1912, copy in Marcus Collections; "Thomas, Allen Clapp," *WWW*, vol. 1; "Baruch, Simon," *JE*, *UJE*, *DAB*; *The Educational Alliance: Prospectus, 1908-1909* (English and Yiddish, N.Y., n.d.), Marcus Collections; Schappes, *JIUS*, 132-33; David Blaustein, *From Oppression to Freedom. The Hebrew Immigrant is Taught his First Lessons in American Liberty at the Educational Alliance, a Place of Organized Opportunities* (reprint from *Charities*, April 4, 1903); *Bread to the Hungry* (*This is Our Home*, no.14, AJC pamphlet, N.Y., 1956), 13; "Masliansky, Zevi Hirsch," Reisin, *Leksikon*; *AJHQ*, 53:117, 54:57, 59, 63 ff., 67 ff., 72-74, 78-79; "New York City," *UJE*, 8:190; "Young Men's Hebrew Association," *JE*; Karpf, *Jewish Community Organization*, 97 ff.; *Jew. Com. Reg*, 648 ff.; *PUAHC*, 3:2670-71; *Education of Abraham Cahan*, 262; Schlesinger, *Rise of the City*, 340, 351-52; Markens, *Hebrews*, 317 ff.; *Jewish Post and Opinion*, Apr. 26, 1957, p.12, cs.13; "Jewish Charities," "Jewish Women's Council," *Americana*, vol.9; Rischin, *Promised City*, 100 ff., 133, 205 ff., 208, 240; "Social Settlements," *DAH* (1976-1978); Selma Cantor Berrol, *Immigrants at School: New York City, 1898-1914* (N.Y., 1978), 41 ff.; Sjazkowski, *Jew. Mass Settlement*, 18; John Foster Carr, *Guide to the United States for the Jewish Immigrant: A Nearly Literal Translation of the Second Yiddish Edition* (N.Y., 1916); "America, Judaism in," *JE*, 1:516, "New York," 9:287-88, "United States," 12:360, 370; M.M. Kaplan, N.Y., to Felix Warburg, N.Y., Nov. 1, 1913, copy in Marcus Collections; Elbogen, *Cent. of Jewish Life*, 337; *AJYB*, 12(1910-1911):38-42, 50:72 ff., 57:35; Allan Nevins, *The Emergence of Modern America* (N.Y., 1932), 208-9; Schoener, *Portal to America*, 133-36; *World Over*, Nov. 19, 1971, p.1; Wish, *Society and Thought*, 2:140-41, 144-45; Bernheimer, *Russian Jew in the U.S.*, 192-96; *Papers of the Jewish Women's Congress*, 178 ff.; Howe, *World of Our Fathers*, 274 ff., 279-81; Bogen, *Jewish Philanthropy*, 226 ff.;

Schoener, *Lower East Side*, 54:57; *JSS*, 25:102 ff., 38:287, n.38; *AJA*, 3:14; Blaustein (ed.), *Memoirs of David Blaustein*; *YA*, 15:141, 144, 16:342; *PAJHS*, 49:111 ff.; Ravitch & Goodenow, *Educating an Urban People*, 101 ff., 105-6; *Jewish People*, 4:302; Robertson, "92nd Street YMHA & YWHA Inventory"; Berkowitz, "Hebrew Free School Association"; Allen, "Americanization of the East-European Jew"; Steven W. Siegel, prepared by Nancy M. Robertson, *Inventory of Group 6: Clara de Hirsch Home for Working Girls, 1897-1962, Ninety-Second Street Young Men's and Young Women's Hebrew Association* (N.Y., 1980); "American Hebrew, The," "Council of Jewish Women," "Sisterhoods of Personal Service," *JE*; "National Council of Jewish Women," *JE, UJE*.

15. Schlesinger, *Rise of the City*, 340; Meites, *Chicago*, 512 ff.; *AJYB*, 23:84 ff.; Curti et al., *American History*, 86; *Bread to the Hungry (This is our Home*, no.14, AJC pamphlet, N.Y., 1956), 13; Karpf, *Jewish Community Organization*, 97-99.

16. AJYB, 2(1900-1901):137 ff., 25:337 ff.: "Kraus, Adolf," *UJE, EJ*, "Hirsch, Emil Gustav," "Rosenwald, Julius," "Selling, Benjamin," "Solomon, Hannah Greenebaum," *UJE, EJ*; "Voorsanger, Jacob," *UJE, WWW*, vol.1, *AJYB*, 5(1903-1904):104; "Billikopf, Jacob", "Freiberg", "Friend, Ida Weis," "Hackenburg, William Bower," "Krauskopf, Joseph," "Loth, Moritz," "Solis-Cohen, David," *UJE*; Meites, *Chicago*, 186, 194-95, 217, 569; Marcus, *AJW*, 83-85; Marcus, *AJWD*, 315 ff., 550 ff.; "Bettman, Bernhard," *UJE, AJYB*, 6(1904-1905):62-63; *Israelites of Louisiana*, 65-66; Morais, *Philadelphia*, 273-76, 287 ff., 301-4; *AH*, June 10, 1881, p.39; Friedman, *Philadelphia*, 165 ff.; "Levy, Louis Edward," *AJYB*, 6(1904-1905):139-40; Lurie, *A Heritage Affirmed*, 52-63; *PAJHS*, 37:294; "Bogen, Boris David," *UJE, EJ, WWIAJ*, 1926; Bogen, *Born a Jew*.

17. Kohler, *Simon Wolf Addresses*, 12 ff., 25; *AJHQ*, 62:250 ff., 277 ff.; Hertzberg, *Atlanta*, 134 ff.; *RIJHN*, 8:23; Fein, *Baltimore*, 218-19; Chyet (ed.), *Lives and Voices*, 170-71; Alan Krause, "History of B'nai Yeshurun from 1872 to 1891" (HUC term paper, n.d.); *Cincinnati Historical Society Bulletin*, 32(nos.1-2).47. ff.; Charles T. Greve, *Centennial History of Cincinnati and Representative Citizens* (Cincinnati, 1904), 1:947-48; *AJYB*, 7(1905-1906):102, 23:84 ff., 96-99, 50:72 ff.; "Senior, Max," *UJE*; "Kander, Lizzie Black," *NAW*; Marcus, *AJWD*, 517 ff.; *By Myself I'm A Book*, 54, 66 ff., 77-78, 94, 102, 130 ff., 142 ff.; *YA*, 15:130 ff.; Morais, *Philadelphia*, 157, 166; *AJA*, 9:38-39; *American Jews' Annual for 5651 A.M.* (1890-1891), 53 ff.; Marcus, *Memoirs*, 1:287-88; Meites, *Chicago*, 160 ff., 185-86, 216-26, 240-43, 280, 287, 327, 337, 391, 472, 558 ff.; *Judaism at the World's Parliament of Religions*, 334 ff., 358 ff.; Bogen, *Jewish Philanthropy*, 228-41; "Chicago," *JE*, 4:26, *UJE*, 3:146; Adler & Connolly, *Buffalo*, 99-100; Harry Bluestone, *A Historical Review of the Jewish Community Center of Wilmington, Delaware, Inc., 1901-1965* (Wilmington, 1965?), 2 ff.; Wiernik, *History*, 378; "United States," *JE*, 12:370; *PAJHS*, 13:147-49, 37:286 ff.; "Americanization," *UJE*, 1:273-74, "Massachusetts," 7:404; Charles S. Bernheimer, *Half a Century in Community Service* (N.Y., 1948), 132-34; Markens, *Hebrews*, 324.

CHAPTER EIGHTEEN

AMERICANIZATION

1. *PAJHS*, 3:91-92, 22:206 ff., 383 ff., 29:178-79, 37:286 ff., 297 ff., 49:90 ff., 111-12, 120-21; *New York History*, 63:417 ff., 430; *AJYB*, 1(1899-1900):73 ff., 12(1910-1911):38 ff., 19(1917-1918):407-8, 410, 26:349-51, 42:153 ff., 50:71 ff., 56:15, 122; Joseph Barondess, N.Y., to J.D. Eisenstein, N.Y., July 8, 1912, copy in Marcus Collections; Martin S. Scharf, "A Study of the Acculturation of the Immigrant from 1880 to 1920" (rabbinical thesis, HUC, 1978); Leo W. Schwarz, *Menorah Treasury: Harvest of Half a Century* (Phila., 1964), 528 ff.; Samuel Neal Gordon, "The Acculturation of the

Eastern European Jewish Immigrant in America, 1880-1920" (rabbinical thesis, HUC, 1980); *YA*, 9:328-29, 15:139; Riis, *How the Other Half Lives*, 85 ff.; *JSS*, 22:158, 25:102 ff., 125 ff.; *AI*, Oct. 11, 1894, p.4, cs.2-3, Feb. 2, 1905, p.4, c.2; P. & K., *Tourist's Guide*, 384-85; Kraus, "Settlement House Movement in NYC," 236-37; Soltes, *Contemporary Jew. Hist.*, 14-15; *Baron Festschrift*, 295; Faulkner, *Social Justice*, 128; Schlesinger, *Rise of the City*, 169; Blaustein (ed.), *Memoirs of David Blaustein*, 34 ff.; Rischin, *Promised City*, 102, 141, 220; "Young Israel, National Council of," *UJE*; *Papers of the Jewish Women's Congress*, 170 ff., 180, 187 ff.; *Education of Abraham Cahan*, viii-ix; *AJHQ*, 54:54 ff., 61, 67, 57:557 ff., 561; *H. Mendes Pereira*, 39; Bogen, *Jewish Philanthropy*, 226 ff., 234 ff., 276-78; Band, *Portland*, 9; Morris & Freund, *Trends*, 114-29; Wilansky, *Sinai to Cincinnati*, 181; "Fromenson, Abraham H.," *AJYB*, 6(1904-1905):99-100; Janowsky, *American Jew*, 150; *Jewish People*, 4:159-60, 354; "New York, *JE*, 9:286; Ravitch & Goodenow, *Educating an Urban People*, 111-13; *Reports, Ind. Com.*, 15:478; Karp, *Jew. Exp. in America*, 4:xvi; *Reports, Immig. Com. Abstracts*, 1:470-88, 763, 768-69, 2:16-29, 32-42, 71, 151 ff., 501-56; *AJH*, 71:230; Degler, *At Odds*, 141; Gartner, *Jew. Ed. in the U.S.*, 10-11; Howe, *World of Our Fathers*, 277-78, 282 ff.; Schoener, *Portal to America*, 120, 127 ff.; Schoener, *Lower East Side*, 50 ff.; Bushee, *Boston*, 20 ff.; Eisenberg, *Eyewitnesses to American Jewish History*, 3:64 ff., 4:10 ff.; Levinthal, *Message of Israel*, 142-43; Slosson, *The Great Crusade*, 303; "Rosalsky, Otto A.," *UJE*; *A Dreamer's Journey: The Autobiography of Morris Raphael Cohen* (Boston, 1949); "Stokes, Rose Harriet Pastor," *UJE, EJ, NAW, DAB*; for biographies of East European Jews who attained affluence and recognition before 1921, see *WWIAJ*, 1926; *RIJHN*, 6:83 ff., 7:277-93; *Jewish Digest*, 6(no.8) :57 ff.; "Loeb, Sophie Irene Simon," *DAB, NAW*; Marcus, *AJWD*, 639 ff.; Hindus, *Old East Side*, 5 ff.; "Cohen, Morris Raphael," *DAB*, Supplement 4; Leonora Cohen Rosenfield, *Portrait of a Philosopher: Morris R. Cohen in Life and Letters* (N.Y., 1962), 218; *AH*, Dec. 22, 1905, p.159; Learsi, *Jews in America*, 350; Allen, "Americanization of the East-European Jew"; "Americanization," *UJE*.

2. Lipman, *Soc. Hist. of Jews in England*, 120 ff.; Plaut, *Reform Judaism*, 192-93; *JM*, Sept. 17, 1880, p.4, cs.2-3; Eisenberg, *Eyewitnesses to American Jewish History*, 3:92 ff.; S. Schechter, N.Y., to J.H. Schiff, N.Y., Feb. 9, 1904, copy in Marcus Collections; *Jew. Com. Reg.*, 1058 ff.; "Glazer, Simon," *WWIAJ*, 1926; "Abramowitz, Dob Baer," "Ganzfried, Solomon", "Young Israel, National Council of," *UJE*; S. Druckerman, *Catalogs no.9, 11, 12* (N.Y., 1908-1909); *AJYB*, 6(1904-1905):258 ff., 86:3-61; *AJA*, 35(no.21:90 ff.); Eisenstadt, *Hakme Yisrael be- Amerika*, sub "Abramowitz, Dober"; B. Abramowitz, *Dat Yisrael* (N.Y., 1902); Herbert Rosenblum, *Conservative Judaism: A Contemporary History* (N.Y., 1983), 1-34; Waxman, *Conservative Judaism*, 3-37; Marshall Sklare, *Conservative Judaism: An American Religious Movement* (N.Y., 1972), 15 ff.; Parzen, *Architects*, 1-78; "Aschinsky, Aaron Mordecai Halevi," *UJE*; "Lewisohn, Leonard," *JE*.

3. *Judenpogrome*, 2:5-37; Schappes, *JIUS*, 145; Baltimore *Jewish Comment*, Sept. 9, 1904, pp.1 ff.; *Jewish Life*, 9(no.2):20; *AJYB*, 5(1903-1904):20-21; Adler (ed.), *Voice of America on Kishineff*; "Kishinev (f)," *JE, UJE, EJ*; Miliukov, *History of Russia*, 180; *PAJHS*, 34:280 ff., 36:261 ff.; Sachar, *Modern Jewish History*, 247 ff.; Davitt, *Within the Pale*, 91 ff., 268 ff.; Salo W. Baron, *The Russian Jew Under Tsars and Soviets* (N.Y., 1964), 67 ff.; Dubnow, *History of Jews in Russia and Poland*, 3:69 ff.; Straus, *Under Four Administrations*, 169 ff.

4. For typical protest meetings see Adler & Connolly, *Buffalo*, 220-21; Fein, *Baltimore*, 207-8; Uchill, *Pioneers*, 265; *JSS*, 33:13 ff.; "Lynch Law," *Americana*, vol.10; "Lynching," *DAH* (1942); *AJHQ*, 60:350-53, 63:262 ff., 278, 282; Richardson, *Messages and Papers of the Presidents*, 11:4714, 13:5623; *Slavic Review*, 42:409; Bailey, *Diplomatic History of the American People*, 560, n.30; Wolf, *Presidents I Have Known*, 187 ff.; Davitt, *Within the Pale*, 256 ff.; Singer, *Russia at the Bar of the American People*, 1 ff.;

Dubnow, *Weltgeschichte*, 10:368 ff., 490-91; Kohler, *German Jewish Persecutions*, 23 ff.; Wiernik, *History*, 353 ff.; Adler (ed.), *Voice of America on Kishineff*, ix ff.; Grusd, *B'nai B'rith*, 128 ff.; Leo N. Levi Papers, Marcus Collections, especially the memorandum of L.N. Levi, N.Y., July 2, 1903; Esther & David Panitz, *Liberty Under Law: The Life and Contributions of Simon Wolf* (monograph, Washington, D.C., 1950), 8; *AJYB*, 5(1903-1904):18 ff., 218-19; *Jewish People*, 4:149; *PAJHS*, 33:26, 36:261 ff.; "New York," *JE*, 9:282, "United States," 12:359; "Kishinef," *JE*; "Kishinev," *UJE, EJ*; Detroit *Jewish News*, July 9, 1971, p.2; *Jewish Digest*, 4(no.1):37; Kohler, *Immigration and Aliens*, 428; Martin Philippson, *Neueste Geschichte des juedischen Volkes* (3 vols., Leipzig, 1907), 3:182 ff.; *AJHQ*, 60:350-53, 63:262 ff., 282-83.

5. *AI*, July 11, 1974, p.8, entire; Joseph, *Jewish Immigration*, 174; *JSS*, 29:3 ff., 33:13 ff.; Goren, *American Jews*, 40-41; *AJHQ*, 61:313-24, 63:267, 283, 64:244; Rischin, *Promised City*, 163, 165-66; Cowen, *Memories of an American Jew*, 273 ff., 286; Adler & Connolly, *Buffalo*, 221, 231; Szajkowski, *Jew. Mass Settlement*, 11, nos.76-77; Philipson, *My Life*, 167; *CCARYB*, 13:23 ff.; *PUAHC*, 5:5291-92, 6:4808.

6. "Odessa," *EJ*, 12:1323, "Pogroms," 13:697-98; *AJYB*, 7(1905-1906):220 ff., 238, 8(1906-1907):34-89, esp. 70 ff.; *Judenpogrome*, 1:187-404, 2:109 ff.; *Jewish Life*, 9(no.2):20; Cowen, *Memories of an American Jew*, 189 ff., 204 ff., 282 ff.; Schappes, *JIUS*, 145; Wiernik, *History*, 358; Stern, *Grundriss*, 68; Dubnow, *History of the Jews in Russia and Poland*, 3:96-97, 124 ff.; Sachar, *Modern Jewish History*, 246 ff.; Adler, *Selected Letters*, 1:119-21; London *Times*, Mar. 13, 1906, Straus Papers, LC; Learsi, *Jews in America*, 220 ff.; *AH*, Sept. 30, 1921, pp.508 ff.; Wolf, *The Jewish Question*, 57 ff.

7. *AJYB*, 7(1905-1906):152, 220 ff., 227, 229 ff., 240, 8(1906-1907):38 ff., 90-91, 263-64; Cowen, *Memories of an American Jew*, 328 ff.; *AJHQ*, 61:313 ff.; *PAJHS*, 14:1 ff., 8, 18; *YA*, 17:54 ff., 64, 66, 68, 74-75, 80, 82, 85, 87, 107; *WSJHQ*, 11:192, 12:281; Elbogen, *Cent. of Jewish Life*, 433; Schappes, *JIUS*, 145; Wiernik, *History*, 358 ff.; *Judenpogrome*, 1:401; *Congress Weekly*, Oct. 31, 1955, pp.10-11; Finkelstein, *The Jews* (1949), 1:409; Uchill, *Pioneers*, 81; Shinedling, *West Virginia Jewry*, 3:1337; Geller, "Jewish Life in Boston," 5; *Stenographic Report of Proceedings of Mass Meeting Jewish Citizens Held on Wednesday Evening, January 17, 1906 at the Phoenix Club House, Cincinnati, Ohio to Organize a Cincinnati Branch of the Jewish Defence Association of the United States* (Cincinnati, 1906); Samuel Montague, London, to O.S. Straus, Washington, D.C., Mar. 30, 1906, Straus Papers, LC; Adler, *Kansas City*, 113-15; Henrietta Szold, N.Y., to B. Felsenthal, Chicago, Dec. 24, 1905, AJHSL; *News of the Yivo*, no.47, p.5; Sachar, *Modern Jewish History*, 249 ff.; Kraus, *Reminiscences*, 155-74; JSS, 29:3 ff., 75 ff., 91; Straus, *Under Four Administrations*, 209, 212; Masserman & Baker, *Jews Come to America*, 297-98; "Pogroms," *EJ*, 13:796-98; Dubnow, *History of the Jews in Russia and Poland*, 3:87-164.

8. Philip N. Krantz, "The Attempt to Create an Overall National Jewish Community, 1790-1943" (HUC term paper, 1969); *PUAHC*, 1:422; Francis J. Brown & Joseph S. Roucek (eds.), *One America, etc.* (Englewood Cliffs, N.J., 1959), 576 ff.; Morais, *Philadelphia*, 142-43; Liptzin, *Eliakum Zunser*, 219 ff.; Learsi, *Jews in America*, 212-14; Swichkow & Gartner, *Milwaukee*, 90 ff.; Wiernik, *History*, 286 ff.; *AJHQ*, 53:127-28; Richards, *Organizing American Jewry*, 15-16; Robert Kraus, "The Jewish Alliance of America" (HUC term paper, 1967); Wolf, *American Jew*, 559 ff.; *PAJHS*, 40:237-38, 49:86-87; *EIAJH*, 450 ff.; *YA*, 17:115, n.60.

9. *PUAHC*, 5:4322-25, 4713-14, 4718, 6:4808, 4817, 5514; *CCARYB*, 14:22 ff., 16:132 ff., 226 ff.; Rischin, *Promised City*, 241, 243; Adler, *Lectures*, 200, 206; Goodman, "American Jewish Life," 21 ff.; *YA*, 13:187 ff., 192, 17:87 ff.; *JSS*, 22:151; *AH*, Feb. 2, 1906, pp.345 ff., May 25, 1906, pp. 807-8; *AJYB*, 5(1903-1904):36-37, 9(1907-1908):331; *PAJHS*, 39:389 ff., 423 ff., 436-37.

10. "Brussels Conference," *EOZAI*; Wolf, as fossil: George Zepin, UAHC, reported to JRM, July 21, 1956, a conversation of J. Walter Freiberg, UAHC, with Marshall; Ad-

ler, *Selected Letters*, 1:108, 122 ff.; Sachar, *Modern Jewish History*, 521; Reznikoff, *Louis Marshall*, 1:23-26; Cohen. *American Jewish Committee*, chap.1; Schachner, *American Jewish Committee*, 12 ff., 23 ff., 217 ff.; Levinger, *Jews in U.S.*, 179; "Sobel, Isador," Glassman (ed.), *BEOAJ, 1935*; *PAJHS*, 40:304; *PUAHC*, 6:5779-80, 7:5878, 6254 ff., 8:7715 ff., 7722 ff.; N.Y. *Jewish Tribune*, June 8, 1906, p.6; *AJYB*, 8(1906-1907):263 ff., 9(1907-1908):25, 553, 10(1908-1909):237-38, 247, 15(1913-1914):438-39, 17(1915-1916):356 ff., 18(1916-1917) :288-90, 324 ff., 42:173 ff., 74:51; Goren, *American Jews*, 65-66; *AJHQ*, 62:88 ff.; Elbogen, *Cent. of Jewish Life*, 433-35; Wiernik, *History*, 369-70; Adler, *Lectures*, 199 ff., 206; Arthur J. Abrams, "The Formation of the American Jewish Committee" (HUC term paper, 1960); *Jewish People*, 4:143-50; "American Jewish Committee, The," *UJE, EJ*; *Jewish Frontier*, 24(no.4):33 ff.; Handlin, *Adventure in Freedom*, 166-67; Learsi, *Jews in America*, 212 ff.; Masserman & Baker, *Jews Come to America*, 295 ff.; Adler, *I Have Considered the Days*, 245-46; *YA*, 17:87 ff., 95; *The American Jewish Committee: A Brief Statement of Its Organization, Aims, and Work* (pamphlet, N.Y., 1917); Raphael, *Jews and Judaism in the U.S.*, 111 ff.; *AH*, Jan. 5, 1906, p.233 ff., Feb. 2, 1906, pp.343-44, Feb. 16, 1906, p.401, May 25, 1906, pp.803, 805-9, June 29, 1906, pp.93 ff.

11. *AJYB*, 10(1908-1909):Preface, 19(1917-1918):452 ff., 28:472 ff.; "Vatican Council, Second," *Columbia Encyclopedia*; *PAJHS*, 36:64, 148, 151 ff.; *Milestones of the American Jewish Committee, 1906-1966* (pamphlet, N.Y., 1966); *JSS*, 35:170; *Congress Bi-Weekly*, Nov. 10, 1972, pp.25-26; "American Jewish Committee, The," *UJE, EJ*.

12. *PAJHS*, 36:171 ff., 180, 187 ff., 203, 41:163 ff., 168, 46:86 ff.; *AJYB*, 6(1904-1905):284, 286-87, 290, 11(1909-1910):21 ff., 13(1911-1912):19 ff., 78; *AI*, Apr. 25, 1879, p.5, cs.1-2, May 30, 1879, p.4, c.4, Mar. 10, 1882, p.292, cs.1-2, Apr. 17, 1885, p.4, cs.1-2; *American Jews' Annual for 5648 A. M.* (1887-88), 148 ff.; Learsi, *Jews in America*, 226 ff.; "United States," *JE*, 12:358; Wiernik, *History*, 306 ff., 309 ff.: Richardson, *Messages and Papers of the Presidents*, 11:4626, 4714, 4758.

13. Wiernik, *History*, 306 ff., 309-10, 312 ff.; *Isidor Rayner Memorial Addresses, etc.* (Washington, D.C., 1914); Milton E. Altfeld, *The Jew's Struggle for Religious and Civil Liberty in Maryland* (Baltimore, 1924), 14; *PAJHS*, 39:67 ff., 40:288 ff., 291, 41:163 ff.; "Rayner, Isidor," *UJE, DAB*; *Slavic Review*, 42:411 ff. *AH*, Jan. 12, 1923, p.256; *PUAHC*, 4:3008-9, 3357 ff., 3650; Richardson, *Messages and Papers of the Presidents*, 13:5623, 14:6067; Baltimore *Jewish Comment*, Sept. 9, 1904, p.3; *AJYB*, 6(1904-1905) :28S-86; Fein, *Baltimore*, 206-7; "United States," *JE*, 12:358; Masserman & Baker, *Jews Come to America*, 304-6.

14. Wiernik, *History*, 306 ff., 315 ff.; Masserman & Baker, *Jews Come to America*, 304 ff.; *AJYB*, 6(1904-1905):283 ff., 300, 305, 11(1909-1910):21 ff., 29, 105, 13(1911-1912):19 ff., 22 ff., 35, 37, 45 ff., 51 ff., 54 ff.; *PAJHS*, 36:265, 41:163 ff., 177-78; *Where We Stand*, 9; Baltimore *Jewish Comment*, Sept. 9, 1904, pp.1 ff.; Richardson, *Messages and Papers of the Presidents*, 16:6924-25; "United States," *JE*, 12:358-59; *Slavic Review*, 42:411 ff.

15. *AI*, Nov. 27, 1913, p.1, cs.1-5.

16. *PAJHS*, 41:163 ff., 179; *AJYB*, 6(1904-1905):283 ff., 10(1908-1909):74-79, 248-54, 11(1909-1910):21 ff., 247-48, 13(1911-1912):19 ff., 51 ff., 103, 14(1912-1913):196-210, 295-98, 15(1913-1914):244; Stokes, *Church and State*, 2:442-43; *AI*, Dec. 23, 1881, p.204, cs. 3-4; Wiernik, *History*, 306 ff,; *Slavic Review*, 42:411 ff., 421; Reznikoff, *Louis Marshall*, 1:49-108, especially 78 ff.; Wolf, *Presidents I Have Known*, 264 ff., 292 ff., 302; Excerpts from the American Jewish Committee, Executive Committee Meeting Minutes, Feb. 19, 1911, cited in Robert T. Gan, "A Documentary Source Book for Jewish-Christian Relations in the United States, 1865-1914" (rabbinical thesis, HUC, 1967), 128 ff.; Adler, *Jacob H. Schiff*, 2:146 ff.; *AH*, Sept. 6, 1918, p.466; Luzzatti, *God in Freedom*, 719 ff.; Chicago *Reform Advocate*, Oct. 25, 1930, pp.318 ff.; *Zion*, 33(no.1-

2):v; *Queen City Heritage*, 42(no.1):39 ff.; Gary Dean Best, *To Free a People, etc.* (Westport, Ct., 1982), 166 ff.; Rosenthal, "Public Life of Louis Marshall," 185 ff.; *JSS*, 25:40; Masserman & Baker, *Jews Come to America*, 308; *New York Times*, Jan. 2, 1974, p.57; Kraus, *Reminiscences*, 192 ff,; *National Jewish Monthly*, 85(no.11):44.

17. Chicago *Reform Advocate*, Oct. 25, 1930, pp.318 ff.; *PAJHS*, 39:67 ff., 41:163 ff., 46:86 ff., 100, 49:96 ff.; Luzzatti, *God in Freedom*, 714 ff.; Adler, *Jacob H. Schiff*, 2:151-52; Dubnow, *Weltgeschichte*, 10:492-93; *Slavic Review*, 42:411.

CHAPTER NINETEEN

THE GHETTO: PROBLEMS AND SOLUTIONS

1. Salo Wittmayer Baron, *The Jewish Community, etc.* (3 vols., Phila., 1942), 3:387; Schappes, *DHJUS*, 20 ff.; Marcus, *CAJ*, 2:792 ff.; Ernst, *Immigrant Life*, 58; *NAR*, 188:383-94; Schappes, *JIUS*, 166; "Mafia Incident, The," *DAH* (1942); Reznikoff, *Louis Marshall*, 1:xxvi, 2:1125-27; Rosenthal, "Public Life of Louis Marshall," 142 ff.; "Kehillah Movement," *UJE*; *AJYB*, 2(1900-1901):250; *Jew. Com. Reg.*, 47; Goren, *Kehillah*, 25 ff.; *Education of Abraham Cahan*, 224-25; Rischin, *Promised City*, 89; Samuel Stern, *Thrilling Mysteries of the Rubenstein Murder Never Before Brought to Light* (N.Y., 1876); Goodman, "American Jewish Life," 76ff.; *YA*, 13:187 ff.; "Berkman, Alexander," *DAB*, Supplement 2; Berkman, *Prison Memoirs of an Anarchist*, 1 ff.; Joselit, *Our Gang*, 54 ff.

2. Marcus, *EAJ*, 1:129-30; Joselit, *Our Gang*, 12, 39-40, et passim; Rischin, *Promised City*, 89; for German Jewish arsonists see earlier volumes of Marcus, *United States Jewry*; Nash, *Bloodletters*, 345 ff.; Woods, *Americans in Process*, 146, 199 ff.; *YA*, 18:121 ff.; *AJA*, 31:200 ff.; Albert Fried, *The Rise and Fall of the Jewish Gangster in America* (N.Y., 1980), 1 ff., 1.75 ff.; Bushee, *Boston*, 117 ff.; Handlin, *Adventure in Freedom*, 102 ff.; Schlesinger, *Rise of the City*, xv, 111-12; *New York Times*, Aug. 13, 1939, p.10, c.1, Dec. 21, 1939, p.1, c.4, p.19, c.2, Jan. 3. 1940, p.1, c.3, July 9, 1941, p.22, c.5; *AJHS*, 59:386; Goren, *Kehillah*, 134 ff., 148 ff.

3. *Reports, Immig. Com. Abstracts*, 2:178 ff., 211, 214-15, 218, 281, 333, 342-43; Charles R. Snyder, *Alcohol and the Jews, etc.* (Glencoe, Ill., 1958); 189-90; *Jewish Digest*, 2(no.3):67 ff.; Bernheimer, *Russian Jew in the U.S.*, 289-90, 344 ff., 349, 351, 355-58, 362-63, 412; "New York," *JE* 9:282, 287-88, "United States," 12:369, 376-77; Reznikoff, *Louis Marshall*, 1:47; *Jew. Com. Reg.*, 1136 ff.; *New York History*, 63:431; *Reports, Ind. Com.*, 15:xlvii ff., lxix ff., 478-80, 487; *The Forum*, 15(1893):180; *YA*, 13:187 ff., 18:121 ff.; Rischin, *Promised City*, 90-91, 103-4; *Commentary*, 16:334 ff., 78:53 ff.; *Baron Festschrift*, 286-87, 296; *New York Times*, Aug. 13, 1939, p.10; Learsi, *Jews in America*, 173 ff.; Dr. Albert B. Yudelson, Chicago, to J. Rosenwald, Chicago, Oct. 14, 1915, Yudelson, Chicago, to Mr. Graves, n.d., Rosenwald Papers, Univ. of Chicago, copies in AJAr; *JOAH*, 57:619 ff.; Bushee, *Boston*, 98 ff.; Nash, *Bloodletters*, 345 ff.; Goren, *Kehillah*, 134 ff.; Joselit, *Our Gang*, 85 ff.; *AJH*, 68:552-53; London *Jewish Chronicle*, Sept. 18, 1908, p.14; Eisenberg, *Eyewitnesses to American Jewish History*, 3:84 ff.; Riis, *How the Other Half Lives*, 88; Handlin, *Adventure in Freedom*, 104; Cole, *Irrepressible Conflict*, 153; *Education of Abraham Cahan*, xi; *CCARYB*, 17:119, 21:98 ff., 24:100-101; Turkus & Feder, *Murder, Inc.*: this deals with Jewish gangsters who flourished in the second quarter of the twentieth century. Ralph Salerno and John S. Tompkins, *The Crime Confederation* (N.Y., 1969); Sann, *Story of Dutch Schultz*.

4. "Seligman, Edwin Robert Anderson," *DAB*, Supplement 2; Morison, *History*, 905-6; Edward J. Bristow, *Prostitution and Prejudice, etc.* (N.Y., 1983), 146 ff., 220, 226-27; Goren, *Kehillah*, 134 ff., 137; *Michael*, 3:188 ff.; Bernheimer, *Russian Jew in the U.S.*, 346-47, 357-59; *Reports, Immig. Com. Abstracts*, 2:332-33, 342-44; Rischin, *Promised*

City, 90-91; *AJA*, 36:1 ff.; Kraus, *Reminiscences*, 177-78; Murray T. Bloom, Great Neck, N.Y., to JRM, Nov. 10, 1972, Marcus Collections; *YA*, 5:222; Jenks & Lauck, *Immigration Problem*, 64 ff.; 383 ff.; Fein, *Baltimore*, 163; Schlesinger, *Rise of the City*, 156 ff.; *PAJHS*, 49:114-15; Marcus, *AJWD*, 472-78, 690 ff.; "New York," *JE*, 9:287; *AJH*, 73:138; *New York History*, 3:431; Ruth Rosen, *The Lost Sisterhood: Prostitution in American, 1900-1918* (Baltimore, 1982); *Commentary*, 78(no.2):53 ff.; Archibald A. Marx, New Orleans, to B. Wadel, Tyler, Texas, Dec. 20, 1912, Marcus Collections; *Baron Festschrift*, 288; Grusd, *B'nai B'rith*, 127; Samuelson, "Baltimore," 19; Faulkner, *Social Justice*, 159; Wolf, *Presidents I Have Known*, 365-66.

5. Degler, *At Odds*, 135; *Jew. Com. Reg.*, 1318; "United States," *JE*, 12:376; Morris & Freund, *Trends*, 66 ff.; *AJH*, 71:285 ff., 291; Wish, *Society and Thought*, 2:132; Bernheimer, *Russian Jew in the U.S.*, 362; Bushee, *Boston*, 44; Adler & Connolly, *Buffalo*, 226-27, 439, n.32; *JSS*, 44:1-18.

6. *CCARYB*, 20:15; *YA*, 9:104-5; Bernheimer, *Russian Jew in the U.S.*, 73-74, 344 ff., 357-59, 409-10; "United States," *JE*, 12:369; Adler & Connolly, *Buffalo*, 223, 225; *Jewish People*, 2:157; *AJYB*, 50:26; Samuelson, "Baltimore," 19; Fein, *Baltimore*, 163, 220, 296, n.97; "New York City, *UJE*, 8:186-87; Goren, *American Jews*, 44-45; *Religious Education*, 25:1-4; *Baron Festschrift*, 287-89; *AJA* 26:14; *Jew. Com. Reg.*, 1136 ff.; Marcus, *AJW*, 535-37; Learsi, *Jews in America*, 174; Breck, *Colorado*, 114, 197; Uchill, *Pioneers*, 190-91; Wish, *Society and Thought*, 2:136, 241; "Flegenheimer, Arthur," *DAB*, Supplement 1; Sann, *Story of Dutch Schultz*; Pilch, *Hist. Jew. Ed.*, 71, n.62; Rosenthal, "Louis Marshall: Early Public Life," 76 ff.; Rosenthal, "Public Life of Louis Marshall," 70 ff., 142 ff.; Morris & Freund, *Trends*, 110 ff.; Berkowitz, "Hebrew Free School Association"; *YA*, 5:224; *RIJHN*, 7:244; "United States," *JE*, 12:369; *New York Times*, Aug. 9, 1972, p.34, cs.1-3; Howe, *World of Our Fathers*, 263-64; Davidson, *Parody*, 105; "Kehillah Movement," *UJE*.

7. *Commentary*, 78:54; *YA*, 13:196 ff., 18:136; Morais, *Philadelphia*, 131 ff., 142-43; Weinberger, *Jews and Judaism*, 113-14; Rischin, *Promised City*, 103 ff., 111; Hertzberg, *Atlanta*, 76-77; *AJHQ*, 49:78 ff.; "Conferences, Rabbinical," *JE*, 4:217; "Union of Orthodox Rabbis of the United States and Canada," *UJE*; *AJA*, 35:105; Learsi, *Jews in America*, 157; Lipman, *Soc. Hist. of Jews in England*, 120.

8. Rischin, *Promised City*, 241; "New York," *JE*, 9:285; "Kahal," *JE, AJYB*, 11(1909-1910):64; *AH*, Oct. 11, 1907, pp.559-60; Goren, *Kehillah*, 35-36; *YA*, 13:187 ff.

9. *YA*, 13:187 ff.; Goren, *Kehillah*, 38 ff.; *AJYB*, 11(1909-1910):44 ff., 253-54, 12(1910-1911):341-42, 16(1914-1915):148, 18(1916-1917):329-30; *Jew. Com. Reg.*, 45 ff., 57 ff.; Reznikoff, *Louis Marshall*, 1:29 ff., 37 ff.; *Kaplan Jubilee Volume, English Section*, 73 ff.; J.H. Schiff, N.Y., to David Philipson, Cincinnati, June 10, 1909, Philipson Papers, AJAr; Schappes, *JIUS*, 166; Eisenstein, *Eyewitnesses to American Jewish History*, 3:1.39; Wiernik, *History*, 370; Goren, *American Jews*, 66.

10. Reznikoff, *Louis Marshall*, 1:31 ff.; *AJHQ*, 60:150, 317 ff.; Rischin, *Promised City*, 243; *PAJHS*, 31:257-58; *AI*, Mar. 11, 1909, p.4, cs.3-4, Apr. 1, 1909, p.4, cs.2-3, May 16, 1912, p.5, c.3; Philipson, *Reform Movement*, 361; Gartner & Vorspan, *Los Angeles*, 186, 334, n.8; *AJYB*, 16(1914-1915):144; Koplin, "Jewish Exponent"; Schappes, *JIUS*, 166; Phila. *Jewish Exponent*, Jan. 14, 1955, p.19, cs.1-3; Goren, *Kehillah*, 245 ff.; Learsi, *Jews in America*, 214-16; Feingold, *Zion in America*, 219 ff.; Goodman, "American Jewish Life," 46 ff., 56-57, 76 ff.; Rosenthal, "Louis Marshall: Early Public Life," 145 ff.; Rosenthal, "Public Life of Louis Marshall," 174 ff.; Joselit, *Our Gang*, 10, 58, 80 ff.; N.Y. *Jewish Spectator*, 36(no.10):16; "Kehillah Movement," *UJE*; Elbogen, *Cent. of Jewish Life*, 439-40; *AJYB*, 11(1909-1910):44 ff., 13(1911-1912):305-6, 14(1912-1913):298 ff., 16(1914-1915):406 ff., 17(1915-1916):377 ff., 18(1916-1917):311 ff., 329 ff., 356 ff., 19(1917-1918):482 ff., 20(1918-1919):401 ff., 21:672 ff., 22:452 ff.; Hadassah Assouline (ed.), "Judah Leib Magnes Papers, 1890-1948" (Central Archives for the His-

tory of the Jewish People, Jerusalem, 1979), copy in AJAr, the Kehillah papers are included.

11. Goren, *Kehillah*, 60 ff., 195; AJYB, 14(1912-1913):299, 15(1913-1914):445 ff., 21:673, 675, 22:452-53; *Jew. Com. Reg.*, 73.

12. *AJYB*, 13(1911-1912):305-6, 16(1914-1915):109, 17(1915-1916):210; Wiernik, *History*, 370; Dushkin, *Jew. Ed. in NYC*, 98-99; Elbogen, *Cent. of Jewish Life*, 439-40; *Jew Com. Reg.*, 55; Schappes, *JIUS*, 167; *Kaplan Jubilee Volume*, English Section, 73 ff.

13. *AJYB*, 18(1916-1917):329-30, 20(1918-1919):402-3; Feingold, *Zion in America*, 225 ff.; Goren, *Kehillah*, 223, 246 ff.; *Jew. Com. Reg.*, 45 ff., 55; Bentwich, *Judah L. Magnes*, 69-70; Elbogen, *Cent. of Jewish Life*, 440-41; *Kaplan Jubilee Volume*, English Section, 82 ff.; "Kehillah Movement," *UJE*; Jonathan Eichhorn, "The New York Jewish Community in 1918" (HUC term paper, 1960); *Journal of Jewish Communal Service*, 48(no.1):113 ff.; *Congress Bi-Weekly*, May 21, 1971, pp.9-11; Reznikoff, *Louis Marshall*, 1:43-44, 2:509-10, 971 ff.; *Commentary*, 51(no.4):92 ff.; Szajkowski, *Jews, War and Communism*, 1:79 ff.

14. Raisin, *Great Jews I Have Known*, 211 ff.; *AH*, Apr. 29, 1910, pp.677 ff., May 27, 1910, p.77; Board of Trustee Minutes, Temple Emanu-El, May 16, 23, 1910, AJAr; *AJYB*, 12(1910-1911):106, 26:585, 49:735; *Kaplan Jubilee Volume*, English Section, 157 ff.; "Magnes, Judah Leon," *DAB*, Supplement 4; Goren, *Kehillah*, Index sub "Magnes, Judah L."; Goren, *Dissenter in Zion*, 149 ff., 295-96; Bentwich, *Judah L. Magnes*; Lipsky, *Memoirs in Profile*, 224-27, 229-30; JRM interview with Rabbi George Zepin, a classmate of Magnes at the HUC, Sept. 8, 1962; Rabbi M. Friedlander, N.Y., to Louis Wolsey, Phila., Apr. 5, 1927, copy in Marcus Collections. Friedlander had once been the rabbi of young Magnes in Oakland; Nelson Glueck review of Bentwich, *Judah L. Magnes*, typescript, 1954, copy in Marcus Collections; "Magnes, Judah Leon," *EOZAI*; Detroit *Jewish News*, Dec. 31, 1982, p.48, cs.1-6; *AJHQ*, 65:105, 113 ff.; Goren, "Judah L. Magnes: The Wider Pulpit," typescript copy in Marcus Collections; *Jewish Book Annual*, 9:65; JSS, 44:337; Rischin, *Promised City*, 243.

15. "Halevi, Judah," *UJE*, 5:226; Name: memo on names of Magnes from Dr. Ida Selavan, HUCL, Sept. 1984, Marcus Collections; *PUAHC*, 5:4701, 4708, 4751, 6:5057; *AJHQ*, 65:99 ff.; Goren, *Dissenter in Zion*, 82-83; *HUCA*, 1:177 ff., 459; *AJYB*, 51:512 ff., 522-23; *AJA*, 5:38; Detroit *Jewish News*, Oct. 17, 1969, p.21; personal note to JRM from Rabbi Benjamin Friedman, Syracuse, Dec. 7-9, 1962, Marcus Collections; lecture of Arthur A. Goren on Magnes at HUC, Sept. 23, 1981; Eisenstein, *Zikhronothai*, sub 1908, p.115, sub 1910, pp.118-19; J.L. Magnes, Jerusalem, to Rabbi B.W. Korn, Cincinnati, Feb. 15, 1948, copy in Marcus Collections; *Kaplan Jubilee Volume*, English Section, 157 ff.; "Magnes, Judah Leon," *UJE, EJ*; *Jewish Digest*, 1(no.8):21 ff.; *H.U.C. Journal*, 7(1903):230-35; Plaut, *Reform Judaism*, 160; *Congress Weekly*, Dec. 27, 1954, pp. 11 ff.; *Jewish Newsletter*, Nov. 24, 1952, copy in Marcus Collections; *Judah L. Magnes: Pioneer and Prophet on Two Continents, a Pictorial Biography* (Berkeley, Calif., 1977); Beatrice L. Magnes, *Episodes: A Memoir* (Berkeley, Calif., 1977); Jonathan Frankel (ed.), *Studies in Contemporary Jewry* (Bloomington, Ind.), 1(1984):163 ff.; Reznikoff, *Louis Marshall*, Index sub "Magnes, Judah L.".

16. The following works are helpful in evaluating the work of the Bureau of Jewish Education: Dushkin, *Jew. Ed. in NYC*; Berkson, *Theories of Americanization*; Pilch, *Hist. Jew. Ed.*; Gartner, *Jew. Ed. in the U.S.*; Winter, *Jewish Education*; *Jew. Com. Reg.*, 349 ff., 367 ff., 380 ff., 1153 ff.; "New York City," *EJ*, 12:1097; Pilch (ed.), *Jewish Education Register*, 1951; Gorin, *Kehillah*, 86 ff.; *Jewish People*, 2:156 ff.; Reznikoff, *Louis Marshall*, 1:39 ff.; Janowsky, *Am. Jew. Reappraisal*, 130 ff.; *Jewish Education*, 51(no.3):3 ff.

17. *PAJHS*, 43:27; Dushkin, *Jew. Ed. in NYC*, 44 ff., 100 ff., 154-56; Pilch, *Hist. Jew. Ed.*, 72, 83; *Jew. Com. Reg.*, 349 ff., 367 ff., 380 ff., 1153 ff.; Pilch (ed.), *Jewish Education Register*, 1951, 20, 27, 39; "New York City," *EJ*, 12:1097; Winter, *Jewish Education*, 23-24;

Jewish Education, 51(no.3):5; Schiff, *Jewish Day School*, 7 ff., 30 ff., 37 ff., 45-46, 77 ff.; Goren, *Kehillah*, 86 ff.

18. Goren, *Kehillah*, 91-92, 126-27: *PUAHC*, 6:5354 ff.; Gartner, *Jew. Ed. in the U.S.*, 118 ff.; *Jewish Education*, S1(no.3):3 ff.; *YA*, 9:94; *Statistical History of U.S.*, 214; *Kaplan Jubilee Volume*, Hebrew Section, 249 ff.; *AJA*, 21:114-16; Schiff, *Jewish Day School*, 33; Winter, *Jewish Education*, 58 ff.

19. *Generations*, 4(no.2):25 ff.; Fein, *Baltimore*, 188 ff., 192; Winter, *Jewish Education*, 36, 97 ff., 104-6, 199 ff.; Reznikoff, *Louis Marshall*, 2:899; *Jewish People*, 2:158 ff.; Janowsky, *American Jew*, 68 ff.; Goren, *Dissenter in Zion*, 197-98; "Benderly, Samson," *UJE*, *EJ*; *AJHQ*, 58:515 ff.

20. Winter, *Jewish Education*, 43, 52-55, 58 ff., 99 ff., 118, 161-62, 185; Pilch, *Hist. Jew. Ed.*, 51 ff., 55 ff., 70 ff.; Janowsky, *Am. Jew. Reappraisal*, 130-31; *AJHQ*, 58:515 ff., 60:319; Goren, *Kehillah*, 86 ff., 110 ff., 119, 121-23, 144; Reznikoff, *Louis Marshall*, 40 ff., 45-46; *Conference on Perpetuation of Judaism: Thirtieth Council, Union of American Hebrew Congregation* (Cleveland, 1927), 82 ff.; *AJA*, 21:135; *JSS*, 44:135 ff.; Emanuel Gamoran, *Jewish Education in the United States*, offprint from Lotz & Crawford (eds.), *Studies in Religious Education* (Nashville, 1931); *Conservative Judaism*, 27(no.1):46 ff.; *Jewish People*, 2:158 ff.; "Education, Jewish," *EJ*, 6:440; Gartner, *Jew. Ed. in the U.S.*, 127 ff., 132 ff., 161 ff., 167 ff.; Goren, *American Jews*, 66 ff.; Dushkin, *Jew. Ed. in NYC*, 100 ff.; Pilch (ed.), *Jewish Education Register*, 1951, 10, 22; Schiff, *Jewish Day School*, 28 ff., 37 ff.; Benderly, *Aims and Activities of the Bureau of Education*.

21. *Jew. Com. Reg.*, 454 ff., 462-63, 620, 1156, 1163-64; Pilch, *Hist. Jew. Ed.*, 88 ff., 114; Dushkin, *Jew. Ed. in NYC*, 96 ff.; Goren, *Kehillah*, 86 ff., 119 ff.; Gartner, *Jew. Ed. in the U.S.*, 18; Winter, *Jewish Education*, 165 ff., 21.2 ff.; Karpf, *Jewish Community Organization*, 119-20; *Jewish People*, 2:167; *AJA*, 21:121 ff.; *Kehillah Annual Conventions*, 1913; *AJYB* 17(1915-1916):378.

22. Berkson, *Theories of Americanization*, 207 ff.; *AJA*, 21:113 ff., 132-33; Goren, *Kehillah*, 86 ff., 106 ff., 111-13, 119, 125-30; Reznikoff, *Louis Marshall*, 1:44-45; "Education, Jewish," *EJ*, 6:440-41; Pilch (ed.), *Jewish Education Register*, 1951, 24; *Jewish People*, 2:159 ff., 167; *Jew. Com. Reg.*, 349 ff., 370 ff., 380 ff., 461 ff., 1153 ff.; Pilch, *Hist. Jew. Ed.*, 72-96, 100 ff., 114; Winter, *Jewish Education*, ix, 80, 97 ff., 129, 165 ff., 186 ff., 189 ff., 212 ff., 217 ff.; *AJHQ* 58:515 ff., 60:319; *Jewish Education*, 36:44, 50 ff.; Learsi, *Jews in America*, 198; *Kehillah Annual Convention, 1913*, 12; *AJYB*, 13(1911-12):305-6, 16(1914-1915):110 ff., 17(1915-16):378, 18(1916-1917):356 ff., 38:64 ff.; Janowsky, *Am. Jew. Reappraisal*, 132-33; Reznikoff, *Louis Marshall*, 1:44-46; Dushkin, *Jew. Ed. in NYC*, 96 ff., 100 ff., 126-28, 132-33; Goren, *Dissenter in Zion*, 126 ff.; Benderly, *Aims and Activities of the Bureau of Education*; "New York City," *EJ*, 12:1097.

23. "Friedlaender, Israel," *UJE*, *EJ*; Pilch, *Hist. Jew. Ed.*, 93 ff., 100; Pilch (ed.), *Jewish Education Register*, 1951, 58 ff.; Berkson, *Theories of Americanization*, 177 ff., 187 ff.; "Kaplan, Mordecai Menahem," *UJE*; Gartner, *Jew. Ed. in the U.S.*, 161-77; "Education, Jewish," *EJ*, 6:440-44; "Reconstructionism," *EJ*; "Judaism: Reconstructionism," *UJE*, 6:245-46.

24. "Berkson, Isaac B.," "Brickner, Barnett Robert," "Chipkin, Israel S.," "Dushkin, Alexander M.," "Gamoran, Emanuel," "Honor, Leo Lazarus," *UJE*; *AJA*, 21:133; Goren, *Kehillah*, 57 ff., 114-15; Pilch, *Hist. Jew. Ed.*, 74 ff., 86; "Education, Jewish," *EJ*, 6:441; Samuel Grand and Mamie G. Gamoran (eds.), *Emanuel Gamoran: His Life and Work* (N.Y., 1979); Kerry Marc Olitzky, "A History of Reform Jewish Education During Emanuel Gamoran's Tenure as Educational Director of the Commission on Jewish Education of the Union of American Hebrew Congregations, 1923-1958" (Ph.D. diss., HUC, 1984).

25. Pilch, *Hist. Jew. Ed.*, 74 ff., 84 ff.; "Education," *EJ*, 6:441; Pilch, *Jewish Education Register*, 1951, 20, 109 ff.; *Jewish People*, 2:163-64; Schiff, *Jewish Day School*, 44; *Herzl Year*

Book, 5:90-91; *AH*, Aug. 23, 1907, p.384; *Jew. Com. Reg.*, 451 ff.; Dushkin, *Jew. Ed. in NYC*, 97-98; Janowsky, *Ed. of Am. Jew. Teachers*, 4 ff.; "New York," *JE*, 9:286-87; Gartner, *Jew. Ed. in the U.S.*, 22-23; Boston *Jewish Advocate*, Feb. 16, 1940, pp.14-15; Grinstein, *History*, 79; Recollections of JRM, an instructor in the Hebrew Union College Training School for Teachers, 1920-1922.

26. Learsi, *Jews in America*, 199; Goren, *Kehillah*, 131-33; *AJA* 21:127; Reznikoff, *Louis Marshall*, 1:44-45.

27. *Jewish People*, 2:164 ff.; "Jewish Education Committee," *UJE*; B. Franklin, Paris to Dear Nephew, May 27, 1777, facsimile in *Memorable Documents in American Jewish History* (N.Y., 1946), p.10; Pilch (ed.), *Jewish Education Register*, 1951, 17 ff., 27-39; *Jewish Education*, 36:44 ff., 52; Pilch, *Hist. Jew. Ed.*, 74 ff., 83; *AJHQ*, 58:515 ff., 60:319; *AH*, Feb. 23, 1912, pp.496-97; *Jew. Com. Reg.*, 349 ff., 1153 ff.; Janowsky, *Am. Jew. Reappraisal*, 132; Goren, *Kehillah*, 86 ff., 122; Winter, *Jewish Education*, 97; *AJA*, 21:113-34.

28. Gartner, *Jew. Ed. in the U.S.*, 102-3, 155-56; *AJHQ*, 52:241-43; "Education, Jewish," *EJ*, 6:439; Dushkin, *Jew. Ed. in NYC*, 81-85, 484; Pilch, *Hist. Jew. Ed.*, 63 ff.; *Jewish People*, 2:159-60; *Yalkut Maarabi*, 77 ff.; "United States of America," *EJ*, 15:1621-22; *Jew. Com. Reg.*, 373, 1033 ff.; *Herzl Year Book*, 5:88 ff.; Bernstein, *English Speaking Orthodox Rabbinate*, 10-13.

29. "Education, Jewish," *UJE*, 3:639-40, *EJ*, 6:440; Bernstein, *English Speaking Orthodox Rabbinate*, 10; *Michigan Jewish History*, 5(no.2):5 ff., 19(no.2):9; Handlin, *Adventure in Freedom*, 119-20; Pilch (ed.), *Jewish Education Register*, 1951, 39 ff.; Janowsky, *Am. Jew. Reappraisal*, 147; Breck, *Colorado*, 88 ff.; *AJYB*, 50:56; Weinberger, *Jews and Judaism*, 14-15; Gartner, *Jew. Ed. in the U.S.*, 18 ff.; *AJA*, 21:113 ff.; Hertzberg, *Atlanta*, 87; *Jewish People*, 2:165; Goren, *Dissenter in Zion*, 131; Simon Glazer, *Sabbath School Guide: A Systematic Work for the Instruction of Judaism, etc.* (Toledo, 1907); Simon Glazer, *Guide of Judaism, etc.* (N.Y., 1917).

30. Boston *Jewish Advocate*, Feb. 16, 1940, pp.14-15; *AJA*, 21:133; Pilch (ed.), *Jewish Education Register*, 1951, 22 ff.; Janowsky, *Ed. of Am. Jew. Teachers*, 4 ff.; "Philadelphia," *UJE*, 8:480-81; *Jew. Com. Reg.*, 371-77; Blum, *Baltimore*, 28-29; Pilch, *Hist. Jew. Ed.*, 66-67.

31. *YA*, 15:141-43; Adler & Connolly, *Buffalo*, 239, 252, 321, 323; "Abrams, Israel A.," *WWIAJ*, 1926, *WWIAJ*, 1938-1939; *By Myself I'm A Book*, 75.

32. Plaut, *Jews in Minnesota*, 118, 168, 170 ff., 216, 239, 251-52, 297; Eisenstein, *Eyewitnesses to American Jewish History*, 3:121 ff.; "Gordon, George Jacob," *WWIAJ*, 1938-1939; Deborah Michael, "Introduction for Educational Institutions" (typescript, n.p., n.d.), copy in AJAr; *Jewish Education News*, 1(no.9):3-4.

33. Glazer, *American Judaism*, 86; *AJYB*, 21:315-16, 38:60-61, 68:482, 485; *Jewish People*, 2:144-50, 170, 3:205, 4:172, 302 ff., 376-77, 405; "Zhitlowsky, Chaim," *EJ*; *By Myself I'm A Book*, 75 ff.; *Michigan Jewish History*, 5(no.2):8, 14(no.2):9 ff.; Fishman, *Yiddish in America*, 47; *Jew. Com. Reg.*, 961; Gartner, *Cleveland*, 204; Swichkow & Gartner, *Milwaukee*, 266; Boston *Jewish Advocate*, Feb. 16, 1940, pp.14-15; *RIJHN*, 7(no.3):417-18; Schiff, *Jewish Day School*, 61; Mordecai Grossman, *Jewish Experience in America* (mimeograph, National Jewish Welfare Board, N.Y., 1945), 108; Finkelstein, *The Jews* (1949), 3:931-32; *Congress Bi-Weekly*, Mar. 13, 1961, pp.7-9; Janowsky, *American Jew*, 75-76; Janowsky, *Am. Jew. Reappraisal*, 314; *Jewish Post and Opinion*, Oct. 1, 1954, p.2; Emanuel Gamoran, *Jewish Education in the United States*, offprint from Lotz & Crawford (eds.), *Studies in Religious Education* (Nashville, 1931), 504-5; Pilch, *Hist. Jew. Ed.*, 104 ff., 108 ff.; Gartner, *Jew. Ed. in U.S.*, 19 ff., 157 ff., 188 ff.; Saul Goodman (ed.), *Our First Fifty Years: Sholem Aleichem Folk Institute* (N.Y., 1972), 3-16; "Education, Jewish," *EJ*, 6:435; *JSS*, 2:534, 18:154-55; "New York City," *UJE*, 8:190-91; Pilch (ed.), *Jewish Education Register*, 1951, 20, 109; Adler & Connolly, *Buffalo*, 249; *YA*, 9:276 ff., 296, 305, 11:84, 89, 99, 15:143-44, 16:358, 366 ff., 371 ff.; Grinstein, *History*, 112-13; Sherman, *A Fateful Half-Century*, 8; Levinger, *Jews in U.S.*, 447-48; *Jewish Education*, 36:51; Dushkin,

Jew. Ed. in NYC, 332-34; Howe, *World of Our Fathers*, 204 ff.; "Communism," *EJ*, 5:804; *Jewish Education News*, 1(no.9):3-4; C.D. Spivak & Sol Bloomgarten, *Yiddish Dictionary Containing All the Hebrew and Chaldaic Elements of the Yiddish Language Illustrated with Proverbs and Idiomatic Expressions* (N.Y., 1911); Janowsky, *Ed. of Am. Jew. Teachers*, 9, 175 ff., 181; Gannes, *Central Community Agencies*, 35-36; Levin, *Jewish Socialist Movements*, 169-70; Saul Goodman, *Philosophy and Curriculum of the Sholem Aleichem Folk Schools* (pamphlet, N.Y., n.d.); *JTA-DNB*, Mar. 16, 1973, p.2. For secular Yiddish schools see Ephim H. Jeshurin, *One Hundred Years Modern Yiddish Literature: Bibliography* (N.Y., 1965); Leibush Lehrer, *The Objectives of Camp Boiberik in the Light of Its History* (N.Y., 1962).

CHAPTER TWENTY

WORLD WAR ONE AND THE AMERICAN JEWISH
JOINT DISTRIBUTION COMMITTEE

1. Birmingham, "Our Crowd", 316 ff.; Schappes, *JIUS*, 176-78; Wiernik, *History*, 417; Learsi, *Jews in America*, 241 ff.; *JSS*, 19:113 ff., 22:135, 29:79; Marcus & Peck, *Studies in the American Jewish Experience*, 2:1 ff.; *Yearbook of the Leo Baeck Institute*, 10:28; Handlin, *American People in the Twentieth Century*, 117-18.

2. Jewish People, 4:247, 284; Stephenson, *American Immigration*, 83 ff.; *The Jews in the Eastern War Zone* (American Jewish Committee, N.Y., 1916); "Anti-Semitism," *UJE*, 1:354; *AJA*, 22:69; *AH*, Feb. 11, 1916, p.386; Duker, *Jews in World War I*, 14 ff., 23; Elbogen, *Cent. of Jewish Life*, 468; Sachar, *Modern Jewish History*, 296 ff.; Masserman & Baker, *Jews Come to America*, 310 ff.; Learsi, *Jews in America*, 243; *AJYB*, 41:141 ff.

3. Finkelstein, *The Jews* (1949), 1:409, (1960), 1:562-63; *JSS*, 29:90; Grinstein, *History*, 160; "Central Relief Committee, The," *UJE*; Swichkow & Gartner, *Milwauke*, 268 ff.; L. Marshall, N.Y., to Felix Warburg, N.Y., Mar. 28, 1913, Marshall Papers, AJAr; *AJA*, 22:67 ff.; *AJYB*, 1 7(1915-1916):366-69, 19(1917-1918):198 ff., 26:574; *Jewish People*, 1:410, 4:248; Bauer, *JDC*, 3-18; Reznikoff, *Louis Marshall*, 1:xxxi; *Yearbook of the Leo Baeck Institute*, 10:33; *AJHQ*, 57:55; Kaganoff (ed.), *America-Holy Land Studies*; *PAJHS*, 50:209; *YA*, 14:99 ff., 156 ff.; Masserman & Baker, *Jews Come to America*, 312; *J.D.C. Primer*, 12 ff.; "An Appeal to the Jews of America" by the American Jewish Relief Committee, N.Y., 1914, Warburg Collections, AJAr; "Zuckerman, Baruch," *EJ*, *WWIAJ*, 1928; [Baruch Zuckerman (ed.)], *The People's Relief of America: Facts and Documents, 1915-1924* (Yiddish & English, N.Y., 1924); "Kamaiky, Leon," *WWIAJ*, 1926, *WWIAJ*, 1928; "Warburg, Felix Moritz," *UJE*, 10:445-56, *EJ*, 16:282-84; Goldberg, *Pioneers and Builders*, 461 ff.

4. Schappes, *JIUS*, 174-78, 184; J.H. Schiff, Bar Harbor, Maine, to S.O. Levinson, Kennebunk Beach, Maine, Aug. 28, 1917, Schiff Papers, AJAr; Szajkowski, *Jews, Wars and Communism*, 1:84 ff., 208 ff.; *JSS*, 32:267 ff., 37:170 ff.; Slosson, *The Great Crusade*, 7, 28-30; Wiernik, *History*, 417; "Root, Elihu," *DAB*, Supplement 2; Jacob H. Kaplan, Cincinnati, to Eli Mayer, Phila., Apr. 12, 1917, copy in Marcus Collections; *AI*, Apr. 12, 1917, p.4, cs.6-7; *AJA*, 20:129 ff., 136; *Herzl Year Book*, 5:249 ff.; *PAAJR*, 37:57 ff.; "Kahn, Julius," *UJE*; Marcus, *AJW*, 1:139; *For Max Weinreich on His Seventieth Birthday: Studies in Jewish Languages, Literature and Society* (London, 1964), 31 ff.

5. "Meyer, Eugene Isaac," *WWW*, vol.3, *DAB*, Supplement 6; "Lasker, Albert Davis," *WWW*, vol.3, *DAB*, Supplement 5; "Baruch, Bernard Mannes," "Frankfurter, Felix," *WWW*, vol.4; John Gunther, *Taken at the Flood: The Story of Albert D. Lasker* (N.Y., 1960); Learsi, *Jews in America*, 254; Wiernik, *History*, 419; Szajkowski, *Jews, Wars and Communism*, 1:220; *AJHQ*, 53:80-81; *AJYB*, 4(1902-1903):175; Jordan A. Schwarz, *The Spectator: Bernard M. Baruch in Washington* (Chapel Hill, N.C., 1981), 50 ff.; Ber-

nard M. Baruch, *My Own Story* (N.Y., 1957), 48-52, 59, 130-31; Bernard M. Baruch, *The Public Years* (N.Y., 1960), 53 ff.; James Grant, *Bernard M. Baruch: The Adventures of a Wall Street Legend* (N.Y., 1983), 15 ff.; *AJA*, 34:106 ff.; *JSS*, 13:86-87.

6. *AJYB*, 19(1917-1918):244, 20(1918-1919):88 ff., 66:290 ff.; "National Jewish Welfare Board," *EJ*; "Chaplains, Jewish," "Jewish Welfare Board," *UJE*; Morris & Freund, *Trends*, 136-37; *Jew. Com. Reg.*, 1204 ff.; Schappes, *JIUS*, 179-80; Adler, *Lectures*, 219 ff.; "Military Service," *EJ*, 11:1569-70; Bertram Wallace Korn, *American Jewry and the Civil War* (Phila., 1951), 84 ff.; Acting Chaplain David Goldberg correspondence with naval authorities, 1918-1945, copies in Marcus Collections.

7. Rabbi Eli Mayer, Phila., to Rabbi Jacob H. Kaplan, Cincinnati, Apr. 16, 1917, Harold S. Loeb, Phila., to Eli Mayer, Phila., May 26, 1917, copies in Marcus Collections; *AJYB*, 21:141 ff., 629 ff.; Schappes, *JIUS*, 179; Learsi, *Jews in America*, 250-53; Wiernik, *History*, 418; "United States of America," *EJ*, 15:1622-25; "Davis, Abel," "Dreben, Sam," "Foreman, Milton J.," "Krotoshinsky, Abraham," "Lauchheimer, Charles Henry," "Strauss, Joseph," *UJE*; Meites, *Chicago*, 262-68; Wolf, *Presidents I Have Known*, 393; Gloria R. Mosesson, *The Jewish War Veterans Story* (Washington, D.C., 1971), 31; *90th Congress, 2d Session, Medal of Honor, 1863-1968, etc.* (Washington, D.C., 1968), 447, 449, 461-62; J. George Fredman & Louis A. Falk, *Jews in American Wars* (N.Y., 1942), 55 ff., 69 ff., 76; *PAJHS*, 31:211 ff.; "Buck Private," L.C. McCollum, *History and Rhymes of the Lost Battalion* (N.Y., 1929), 44-45, 83 ff.; *Detroit Jewish News*, Oct. 7, 1983, p.20.

8. *AJHQ*, 57:56, 236, 246, 285-313, 323 ff., 348 ff.; Gartner, *Cleveland*, 255; Szajkowski, *Jew. Mass Settlement*, 14-15; Wischnitzer, *To Dwell in Safety*, 141 ff., 170; Wischnitzer, *Visas to Freedom*, 37 ff., 40, 91 ff.; Curti, *American Philanthropy Abroad*, 299.

9. McCall, *Patriotism of the American Jew*, 280 ff.; *AJYB*, 16(1914-1915):352; *WSJHQ*, 10:276 ff.; Horwich, *My First Eighty Years*, 308 ff.; Swichkow & Gartner, *Milwaukee*, 269-71; E. & L., *Richmond*, 207; Vorspan & Gartner, *Los Angeles*, 181-82; Fein, *Baltimore*, 212-13.

10. "Flaccus, L. Valerius," *JE*; "Halukkah," *UJE*; *PAJHS*, 27:157, 250; Curti, *American Philanthropy Abroad*, 241-45; *AJYB*, 19(1917-1918):220; Duker, *Jews in World War I*, 13-14, 19-20; *Detroit Jewish News*, Jan. 22, 1982, p.64, Dec. 2, 1983, p.12; Bauer, *JDC*, 7; Wiernik, *History*, 419; "American Jewish Joint Distribution Committee," *EJ*; Elbogen, *Cent. of Jewish Life*, 468; Reznikoff, *Louis Marshall*, 2:759; Learsi, *Jews in America*, 249.

11. Herbert Agar, *The Saving Remnant: An Account of Jewish Survival* (N.Y., 1960); Bauer, *JDC*, 3-18, et passim; *JSS*, 32:14-43; pages 14-15 contain a detailed bibliography on the JDC. *Jew. Com. Reg.*, 1462 ff.; Oscar Handlin, *A Continuing Task: The American Jewish Joint Distribution Committee* (N.Y., 1964), chaps. 2-3; "United Palestine Appeal (UPA)," *EOZAI*; "American Jewish Joint Distribution Committee," *EOZAI*, 1:32-33; *AJYB*, *Index to Volumes 1-50* (N.Y., 1967), 363-64. This contains numerous references to Jews in World War I, gallantry in battle, relief abroad, etc. [Julian Leavitt], "First Draft of a Memorandum on the Present Situation of the Jews in Poland, etc." (N.Y., June 30, 1919); typescript data on the problems of distributing relief in Poland, Julian Leavitt Papers, AJAr; *J.D.C. Primer*, 12 ff.; *Jewish People*, 4:248, 379; Oscar I. Janowsky, *People at Bay: The Jewish Problem in the East-Central Europe* (N.Y., 1938), 161 ff.; Wiernik, *History*, 408 ff.; Janowsky, *American Jew*, 155-56; Curti, *American Philanthropy Abroad*, 242-45, 292 ff., 298, 300, 365 ff., 457; Wischnitzer, *To Dwell in Safety*, 142 ff., 151 ff.; *AJHQ*, 53:435 ff., 57:52 ff., 73, 191 ff., 285 ff., 58:376 ff., 395 ff., 484 ff., 505, 59:83 ff., 87; Duker, *Jews in World War I*, 17 ff.; Morris & Freund, *Trends*, 141-42; McCall, *Patriotism of the American Jew*, 276 ff., 283 ff.; *Jewish Post-War Problems, Unit III: How the Jewish Communities Prepared for Peace During the First World War* (N.Y., 1943); *AJYB*, 19(1917-1918):194 ff., 242-43, 20(1918-1919):153-55, 22:343, 23:269, 24:289, 25:329, 41:141 ff., 155, 66:3 ff.; Jacob Billikopf, N.Y., to Alfred Benjamin, Kansas

City, Mo., Mar. 8, 1917, copy in Marcus Collections; Elbogen, *Cent. of Jewish Life*, 466 ff.; Vorspan & Gartner, *Los Angeles*, 180-82; "An Appeal to the Jews of America" by the American Jewish Relief Committee, N.Y., 1914, Warburg Collection, AJAr; Jacob H. Schiff, Mt. Desert Island, Maine, to Julius Rosenwald, Washington, D.C., Nov. 21, 1918, Rosenwald Papers, U. of Chicago, copy in Marcus Collections; "Joint Distribution Committee, American Jewish," *UJE*; "American Jewish Joint Distribution Committee," *EJ*; "American Jewish Joint Agricultural Corporation (Agro-Joint)," "American Joint Reconstruction Foundation," "Belz," *UJE*; Herbert H. Lehman, N.Y., to Joseph Rosen, N.Y., Sept. 21, 1922, copy in Marcus Collections; "Rosen, Joseph A.," *UJE, WWIAJ*, 1938-1939; "Cantor, Bernard," *UJE*; Hyman B. Cantor, Lvow, Poland, to G. Deutsch, Cincinnati, Apr. 2, 1920, AJAr; *JSS*, 19:113 ff., 26:126-27, 32:14 ff.; Denver *Intermountain Jewish News*, New Year Issue, Sept. 13, 1974, p.14, cs.1-5; "Friedlaender, Israel," *WWW*, vol.1; Learsi, *Jews in America*, 245-46, 273; James N. Rosenberg, Paris, to Walter Lyman Brown, London, Feb. 26, 1922, Frank F. Rosenblatt, Paris, to W.L. Brown, London, Feb. 26, 1922, copies in Marcus Collections; *YA*, 14:99 ff., 155 ff.; *AJA*, 3(no.3):51-52, 56-57, 16:80-81, 22:67, 73-76, 79, 83 ff., 88-89; Masserman & Baker, *Jews Come to America*, 312; Detroit *Jewish News*, Dec. 6, 1974, p.62, Jan. 22, 1982, p.64; *AI*, Aug. 9, 1984, p.14, entire; Sachar, *Modern Jewish History*, 527; *Yearbook of the Leo Baeck Institute*, 10:24 ff.; Swichkow & Gartner, *Milwaukee*, 230-31; Janowsky, *Am. Jew. Reappraisal*, 279; Sherman, *A Fateful Half-Century*, 11-12; "Billikopf, Jacob," *UJE, EJ, WWW*, vol.3, *WWIAJ*, 1926, *WWIAJ*, 1928, *WWIAJ*, 1938-1939; "Lehman, Herbert Henry," *UJE, WWW*, vol.4; Jacob Billikopf, N.Y., to Alfred Benjamin, Kansas City, Mo., Jan. 7, 1918, copy in Marcus Collections; Allan Nevins, *Herbert H. Lehman and His Era* (N.Y., 1963), 68 ff.; Feingold, *Zion in America*, 211 ff.; *Jew. Com. Reg.*, 1469, 1475 ff., 1486, 1489.

CHAPTER TWENTY-ONE
UNITY, CONFLICT, ZIONISM

1. *AJHQ*, 63:16 ff.; *AJYB*, 10(1908-1909):237.
2. "Herzl, Theodor," *JE, UJE, EJ, EOZAI*; Janowsky, *Am. Jew. Reappraisal*, 305-6; "Basle Program," *EOZAI*; Feingold, *Zion in America*, 196; Sachar, *Modern Jewish History*, 271 ff.; Charles Spivak, Wien, to his wife in U.S., June 22, 1920, AJAr; Sokolow, *History of Zionism*, 1:xxiv; for "Zionism" see also the *JE, UJE, EJ*, and *EOZAI*. One of the most important bibliographical aids is Sophia A. Udin et al. (eds.), *Palestine and Zionism*, vols. 1-10 (N.Y., 1949-1955). One can consult with profit Gurock, *Guide*, 77 ff. There is much useful material on Zionism in the *Herzl Year Book*, 1 (N.Y., 1958) and the following volumes. *Palestine Year Book* (N.Y., 1947), 3:383 ff. contains a number of important documents touching upon Zionism. Finkelstein, *The Jews* (1960) has material on Zionism in some detail; this is also true of the series *Jewish People*. Janowsky, *American Jews* and *Am. Jew. Reappraisal* have chapters on Zionism. The standard one-volume histories of American Jews all contain information on the history of the movement in this country. The following is a list of works on Zionism. Most of them contain data of importance on the history of the movement in the United States: Bryson, *American Diplomatic Relations*; Naomi W. Cohen, *American Jews and the Zionist Idea* (N.Y., 1975); Davis, *Israel*; Moshe Davis (ed.), *Zionism in Transition* (N.Y., 1980); Sundel Doniger, *A Zionist Primer: Essays by Various Writers* (N.Y., 1917); Feinstein, *American Zionism*; Isaiah Friedman, *The Question of Palestine, 1914-1918: British-Jewish-Arab Relations* (N.Y., 1973); Friesel, *Ha-Tenuah Ha-Tsiyonit*; Edward Bernard Glick, *The Triangular Connection: America, Israel, and American Jews* (London, 1982); Goldberg, *Pioneers and Builders*; Gottheil, *Zionism*; Grose, *Israel in the Mind of America*; Samuel Halperin, *The Political*

World of American Zionism (Detroit, 1961); Ben Halpern, *The American Jew: A Zionist Analysis* (N.Y., 1983); Kaganoff (ed.), *America-Holy Land Studies*; Laqueur, *The History of Zionism*; Learsi, *Epic Story of Zionism*; Lipsky, *Memoirs in Profile*; Manuel, *American-Palestine Relations*; Meyer (ed.), *Early History of Zionism in America*; Neumann, *In the Arena*; Parzen, *Zionism*; David A. Rausch, *Zionism Within Early American Fundamentalism, 1878-1918, etc.* (N.Y., 1979); Rosenblatt, *Mizrachi Movement*; Sachar, *History of Israel*; Sachar, *Modern Jewish History*; Shapiro, *Leadership of the American Zionist Organization*; Shubow (ed.), *Brandeis Avukah Annual*; Silverberg, *If I Forget Thee O Jerusalem*; Sokolow, *History of Zionism*; Alan R. Taylor, *Prelude to Israel: An Analysis of Zionist Diplomacy, 1897-1947* (N.Y., 1959); Urofsky, *American Zionism*; David Vital, *The Origins of Zionism* (2 vols., Oxford, 1975-1982); Weisgal (ed.), *Theodor Herzl*; Weizmann, *Trial and Error*; Nadav Safran, *The United States and Israel* (Cambridge, Mass., 1963).

3. "Zionism," *UJE*, 10:649; "Flaccus, L. Valerius," *JE*; Sokolow, *History of Zionism*, xxiv-xxv; Sachar, *Modern Jewish History*, 264-65; Baron, *History*, 2:338 ff.; "Jews in the United States," *DAH*, (1960); Levinger, *Jews in U.S.*, 290 ff.

4. "Bilu," "Hess, Moses," "Hoveve Zion," "Kalischer, Zvi Hirsch," "Kattowitz Conference," "Mikve Israel," "Petah Tikva," "Pinsker, Leo," "Rishon L'Tziyon," *EOZAI* and in other standard encyclopedias; Urofsky, *American Zionism*, 15 ff.; "Zionism," *UJE*, 10:649; Sachar, *Modern Jewish History*, 261 ff.; *Judaeans*, 1:34 ff.; *AI*, July 2, 1914, p.4, cs.6-7.

5. Grose, *Israel in the Mind of America*, 1 ff.; Meyer (ed.), *Early History of Zionism in America*, 34 ff.; *Silver Festschrift*, 136 ff.; *Historia Judaica*, 1:81 ff.; Sokolow, *History of Zionism*, 2:416-17; Lebeson, *Pilgrim People*, 308-9; *PAJHS*, 8:75 ff.; "Cresson, Warder," *UJE*; *Occ.*, 18:307-8; *JSS*, 19:25 ff.; Schappes, *DHJUS*, 404-5; John Harvard Ellis, *The Works of Anne Bradstreet* (N.Y., 1932), 196; Fein, *Baltimore*, 193 ff.; *Historian*, 46:187 ff.; Baron, *History*, 2:338 ff.; "The Restoration Movement," *EOZAI*; *PMHB*, 95:147 ff.

6. Sokolow, *History of Zionism*, 1:49-51, 133 ff., 2:476, Index sub "Restoration of Israel"; *AJYB*, 56:156 ff.; Finkelstein, *The Jews* (1949), 1:376 ff.; *Silver Festschrift*, 136 ff.; *JSS*, 5:115 ff., 142 ff.; Grinstein, *New York City*, 447 ff., 455 ff., 461; *PAJHS*, 8:75 ff., 10:114-15, 21:139, 27:34 ff., 126-43, 41:23; Marcus, *EAJ*, 2:501-2; Beerman, "Rebecca Gratz," 46-47; Urofsky, *American Zionism*, 44 ff.; M.M. Noah, *Discourses on the Restoration of the Jews* (N.Y., 1845); *Occ.*, 2:600 ff., 3:29 ff., 33-35, 6:61-72, 22:5 ff.; B. & B., *JOUS*, 1:82-83, 3:912-23; *AJHQ*, 55:194-96, 58:118 ff.; Schappes, *DHJUS*, 247 ff.; Glanz, *Studies*, 380; Meyer (ed.), *Early History of Zionism in America*, 1-108; *PAAJR*, 18:27; Malachy, *American Fundamentalism and Israel*; Wiernik, *History*, 334 ff.; Janowsky, *Am. Jew. Reappraisal*, 303 ff.; Korn, *Marcus Festschrift*, 341 ff.; Kaganoff (ed.), *America-Holy Land Studies*.

7. Sokolow, *History of Zionism*, chaps.9-10, 17, 20, 23-27, 35; Meyer (ed.), *Early History of Zionism in America*, 1-108; Urofsky, *American Zionism*, 44 ff.; *JOAH*, 71:524 ff.; *AJH*, 68:43 ff.; *Zionism: An Exposition by George Eliot from "Daniel Deronda"* (pamphlet, Boston, 1915); *JSS*, 5:230, 40:239 ff., 32:137 ff., 44:149 ff.; "Oliphant, Laurence," *JE, UJE, EJ, EOZAI*; "United States," *JE*, 12:357; Grinstein, *History*, 173; *AI*, July 9, 1970, p.15, cs.4-5, Nov. 9, 1983, p.4, c.2; James Mitchell, Atlanta, Georgia, to President Hayes, Mar. 5, 1878, Hayes Papers, Hayes Memorial Library, Fremont, Ohio, copy in Marcus Collections; Malachy, *American Fundamentalism and Israel*, 123 ff., 136 ff.; "Zionism," *EJ*; Manuel, *American-Palestine Relations*, 68 ff.; *The Peculiar People*, 4(no.1):16 ff., 18; *EIAJH*, 435-36; Gutstein, *Chicago*, 404-5; Gartner, *Cleveland*, 241 ff.; Thompson, *Jewish Missions*, 15-16, 239; Meites, *Chicago*, 164 ff., 687 ff.; "United States of America," *EJ*, 15:1657 ff.; "The Restoration Movement," *EOZAI*; Fein, *Baltimore*, 200; Oscar S. Straus, Constantinople, to Secretary of State Bayard, Jan. 28, 1888, Straus Papers, LC, copy in Marcus Collections; Oscar Straus, Constantinople, to F. de Sola Mendes, N.Y., May 28, 1888, Straus Papers, LC, copy in Marcus Collections; Oscar

Straus, Constantinople, to Secretary of State John Hay, Washington, D.C., Nov. 22, 1898, July 24, 1899, Sept. 13, 1899, Straus Papers, LC, copies in Marcus Collections; *Records of the Dept. of State, Diplomatic Despatches, Turkey*, vol.67, July 1, 1898-Sept.30, 1899, NA; Janowsky, *Am. Jew. Reappraisal*, 301 ff.; Davis, *Israel*, 266.

8. Lance Jonathan Sussman, "'Confidence in God': the Life and Preaching of Isaac Leeser, etc." (rabbinical thesis, HUC, 1980), 105; *The Peculiar People*, 4(no.1):22 ff.; *PAJHS*, 35:53 ff.; *AJHQ*, 63:220, 64:120 ff., 66:432 ff.; *Commentary*, 15:497; Meyer (ed.), *Early History of Zionism in America*, 39 ff., 155 ff., 219-27; *Herzl Year Book*, 1:232 ff., 274 ff., 5:57, 6:255 ff.; Schappes, *JIUS*, 133; Sokolow, *History of Zionism*, 1:241 ff.; Gendler, "Omaha," 116; *Education of Abraham Cahan*, 182 ff.; *Jewish People*, 4:152 ff.; B. & B., *JOUS*, 3:876-77; "Hoveve, Zion," "Rosenberg, Adam," *EOZAI*; Fein, *Baltimore*, 193 ff.; Lebeson, *Pilgrim People*, 416-17; Adler & Connolly, *Buffalo*, 215; "Szold, Benjamin," *JE*; Morais, *Philadelphia*, 232; Learsi, *Jew in America*, 175-82, 234-35; Urofsky, *American Zionism*, 83-84, 108; Levin, *Jewish Socialist Movements*, 139; Feinstein, *American Zionism*, 20 ff., 37-38, 267 ff.; Weinberger, *Jews and Judaism*, 115 ff.; *YA*, 9:95; Gartner, *Cleveland*, 246; "Zionism," *UJE, EJ*; "Bluestone, Joseph Isaac," *UJE, EOZAI*; *Congress Bi-Weekly*, Nov. 15, 1965, p.15; *JSS*, 5:225 ff., 230, 44:152; Howe, *World of Our Fathers*, 205; Swichkow & Gartner, *Milwaukee*, 237 ff.; Horwich, *My First Eighty Years*, 228 ff.; Gutstein, *Chicago*, 407; Blum, *Baltimore*, 39 ff.; *WSJHQ*, 3:120, 6:232, 8:232 ff.; *Beth Ahabah, Richmond*, 24; *PAJHS*, 29:114, 33:136-37; *AI*, Apr. 17, 1863, p.324, cs.1-2, Nov. 9, 1893, p.4, c.2; Uchill, *Pioneers*, 136-37; *JM*, Mar. 30, 1893, p.1, cs.5-6, p.2, c.1; Felsenthal, *Bernhard Felsenthal*, 74-84; Janowsky, *American Jew*, 231 ff.; Janowsky, *Am. Jew. Reappraisal*, 303; "Lazarus, Emma," *JE, EOZAI*; *EIAJH*, 425 ff., 433 ff.; *Ha-Meliz*, 26:502; "United States of America, Zionism in," *EOZAI*; Davis, *Israel*, 253 ff.

9. *NAR*, 165:487 ff.; Gottheil, *Zionism*, 108 ff.; *Herzl Year Book*, 5:61.

10. *AJYB*, 1:36 ff., 41-42, 68:489, 497; Dushkin, *Jew. Ed. in NYC*, 85 ff.; Urofsky, *American Zionism*, 86, 100, 108, 112-13; Learsi, *Jews in America*, 231 ff., 337-38; "New York," *JE*, 9:288; *Jewish People*, 4:154; "Young Judaea," *UJE, EOZAI*; David Robins, "The Political, Cultural, and Religious Goals of Zionism, 1901-1904, as Reflected in the Maccabaean" (HUC term paper, 1957); *AJHQ*, 57:490; Janowsky, *American Jew*, 235 ff.; "United States of America, Relations with Zionism and Israel," *EOZAI*, 2:1156; "Zionism," *EJ*, 16:1031 ff., *JE*, 12:684-85; *Jew. Com. Reg.*, 980, 1340 ff., 1374 ff.; "Zionist Organization of America," *EOZAI*; Janowsky, *Am. Jew. Reappraisal*, 309 ff.; Davis, *Israel*, 243 ff.; Parzen, *Zionism*, 45 ff.; *JSS*, 18:163 ff.; Feingold, *Zion in America*, 202 ff.; Meyer (ed.), *Early History of Zionism in America*, 191-218, 228-288; "Order Sons of Zion," *UJE*; Feinstein, *American Zionism*, 245 ff.; *Minutes of the Central Bureau of the Federation of Zionist Societies of Greater New York and Vicinity*, B.C. Ehrenreich Papers, AJAr; "United States of America, Zionism in," *EOZAI*, 2:1163 ff.; Wiernik, *History*, 415; "B'nai Zion," *EOZAI*.

11. "Barondess, Joseph," "Goldberg, Abraham," "Lipsky, Louis," "Richards, Bernard Gerson," *UJE*; "Rosenblatt, Bernard A.," *UJE, WWIAJ*, 1926; Analyticus, *Jews Are Like That*, 55; Goldberg, *Pioneers and Builders*, 308 ff.; Neumann, *In the Arena*; *AJYB*, 65:435; "Lipsky, Louis," *EOZAI*; Louis Lipsky, *Thirty Years of American Zionism Being Volume One of Selected Works* (2 vols., N.Y., 1927), 1:3-80; Ribalow (ed.), *Autobiographies*, 97-130.

12. *Jew. Com. Reg.*, 1350 ff.; Urofsky, *American Zionism*, 101 ff., 108; "General Zionism," "Religious Zionists of America," *EOZAI*; "Zionism," *UJE*, 10:653 ff.; Meyer (ed.), *Early History of Zionism in America*, 219 ff.; "United States of America, Zionism in," *EOZAI*, 2:1163 ff.; Learsi, *Jews in America*, 234; Levinthal, *Message of Israel*, 135-36; "Bar-Ilan (Berlin), Meir," *EOZAI, EJ*; Goldberg, *Pioneers and Builders*, 266; Zola, "Zvi Hirsch Masliansky"; Feinstein, *American Zionism*, 267 ff.; "Hirschensohn, Chaim," *DAB*, Supplement 1; *Palestine Year Book*, 3:401-3; Rosenblatt, *Mizrachi Movement*.

13. "Zionism," *UJE*, 10:660; Max Roth, "A History of the Zionist Workers' Movement in the United States" (HUC term paper, 1968); "United States of America, Zionism in," *EOZAI*, 2:1163-64; *Jewish People*, 4:156 ff., 380 ff.; *YA*, 16:357; Levin, *Jewish Socialist Movements*, 139-40; Shubow (ed.), *Brandeis Avukah Annual*, 552-53; Ben Halpern, *A Galaxy of American Zionist Rishonim: Nachman Syrkin* (N.Y., 1963); Urofsky, *American Zionism*, 103; *Jewish Review*, 3:223 ff.; "Poale Zion in America," *EOZAI*; "Syrkin, Nachman," *UJE, EJ, EOZAI*; *AJA*, 35:53 ff.

14. *Studies in Zionism*, 5:55 ff.; Israel Friedlaender, *Past and Present: A Collection of Jewish Essays* (Cincinnati, 1919), 335-36; *JSS*, 23:236 ff., 243 ff.; *Herzl Year Book*, 5:366 ff.; *AH*, Dec. 18, 1906, pp.191-94; Leon Simon (tr.), *Selected Essays by Ahad Ha-Am* (Phila., 1912); Sachar, *Modern Jewish History*, 275-76; "Ahad Haam," *UJE*; "Zionism," *UJE*, 10:658 ff.; Goren, *Kehillah*, 323-24; "Kallen, Horace Mayer," *UJE, EJ*; *Jewish Currents*, 36(no.12):17; Barnard, *Julian W. Mack*, 81; Chiel, *Kelman Festschrift*, 257 ff.; Gottheil, *Zionism*, 210 ff.; Judah L. Magnes, *What Zionism Has Given the Jews* (N.Y., 1914); Friesel, *Ha-Tenuah Ha-Tsiyonit*, 209-10.

15. *PAJHS*, 37:481 ff.; Marvin Lowenthal, *Henrietta Szold: Life and Letters* (N.Y., 1942); Joan Dash, *Summoned to Jerusalem: The Life of Henrietta Szold* (N.Y., 1979); *AJHQ*, 49:162, 61:361 ff.; Marcus, *AJW*, 65, et passim; Marcus, *AJWD*, 614, et passim; Donald H. Miller, "A History of Hadassah, 1912-1935" (Ph.D. diss., NYU, 1968); "Szold, Henrietta," *JE, UJE, EJ, EOZAI, DAB*, Supplement 3; Meyer (ed.), *Early History of Zionism*, 228 ff.; Irving Fineman, *Woman of Valor* (N.Y., 1961); Rose Zeitlin, *Henrietta Szold: Record of a Life* (N.Y., 1952); *JSS*, 16:193 ff., 23:261; *AJYB*, 2(1900-1901):38-39, 39:45, 46:50-51, 57:51; Lipsky, *Memoirs in Profile*, 46; *AJH*, 69:416 ff.; Learsi, *Jews in America*, 239; "Hadassah, The Women's Zionist Organization of America," *UJE, EJ*; Howe, *World of Our Fathers*, 208; *Palestine Year Book*, 3:405 ff.; Goldberg, *Pioneers and Builders*, 323 ff.; *Hadassah Magazine*, Bulletin no.23, pp.8 ff.; *Jew. Com. Reg.*, 1360 ff.; Eisenberg, *Eyewitnesses to American Jewish History*, 3:134 ff.; Raisin, *Great Jews I Have Known*, 165 ff.; *Jewish Book Annual*, 18:95 ff.; Urofsky, *American Zionism*, 140 ff.

16. *AJYB*, 1(1899-1900):41; *JSS*, 23:235; "Conservative Judaism and Zionism," *EOZAI*; Edward D. Coleman (ed.), *Keepsake: Dr. Herzl Zion Club, Twenty-fifth Anniversary Reunion, 1904-1929* (N.Y., 1929); *CCAR Journal*, 26:52 ff., 47:24 ff.; Benjamin Friedman, Miami Beach, Fla., to JRM, Mar. 5, 1985, AJAr; Oral statement of Abraham J. Feldman, a member of the club, to JRM; Memo of JRM; conversation with Rabbi B. Friedman, Marcus Collections.

17. Meyer (ed.), *Early History of Zionism in America*, 200; *WSJHQ*, 10:274-75; Lipsky, *Memoirs in Profile*, 51; Horwich, *My First Eighty Years*, 228 ff., 234 ff.; Bernheimer, *Russian Jew in the U.S.*, 168, 180-81; Gutstein, *Chicago*, 407 ff.; Learsi, *Jews in America*, 234-35; Meites, *Chicago*, see Index sub "Palestine Movement"; "Chicago," *UJE*, 3:142, 144; Gartner, *Cleveland*, 245-52; *Herzl Year Book*, 5:211, 218-19, 221 ff., 225; Swichkow & Gartner, *Milwaukee*, 237 ff., 244; *Louisiana Inventory*, 118-19, 125; Fein, *Baltimore*, 193 ff., 198; "Baltimore," *JE*, 4:146-47; Urofsky, *American Zionism*, 84; Blum, *Baltimore*, 39 ff.; *Book of Redemption, Sefer Ha-Geulah* (Houston, 1939), 73 ff.; for various other hinterland societies, see *Palestine Year Book*, 3:387 ff.; *By Myself I'm A Book*, 119 ff.; *AJHQ*, 62:274 ff.; Hertzberg, *Atlanta*, 131 ff.; *WSJHQ*, 6:232, 9:238 ff., 12:369; Vorspan & Gartner, *Los Angeles*, 187 ff.; Adler & Connolly, *Buffalo*, 215-16; Uchill, *Pioneers*, 280-81; Breck, *Colorado*, 212 ff.; *YA*, 15:193; Hinchin, "Jews of Sioux City," 122; "Des Moines," "Fort Wayne," *UJE*; "Saint Louis," *UJE*, 9:314-15.

18. "New York City," *EJ*, 12:1100, "United States of America," 15:1625; Wiernik, *History*, 336-37; *EIAJH*, 425 ff.; *Zionism: A Jewish Statement to the Christian World* (N.Y., 1907); Gurock, *Guide*, 78-80; *Jew. Com. Reg.*, 1340 ff.; "Zionism," *JE*, 12:681-84 for U.S. only; *Jewish People*, 4:154 ff.; *Herzl Year Book*, 5:105 ff., 147 ff., 364-65; Urofsky, *American Zionism*, 113-18; Levin, *Jewish Socialist Movements*, 139; *Judaeans*, 1:34 ff.; *AJHQ*,

64:137 ff.; "Ahuza (Achooza, Achusa, Achuza) Societies," "Jewish Legion," "Language War," *EOZAI*; "United States of America, Zionism in," *EOZAI*, 2:1163 ff.; *Michigan Jewish History*, 8(no.2):3 ff.; Eichhorn, *Joys of Jewish Folklore*, 160 ff.; Dushkin, *Jew. Ed. in NYC*, 85 ff., 131-32; *By Myself I'm A Book*, 119 ff.; *Jewish Post and Opinion*, Dec. 8, 1978, p.2, cs.3-5; Atlanta *Southern Israelite*, Sept. 4, 1979, pp.12-13; *AJYB*, 1(1899-1900):36 ff., 3(1901-1902):156, 16(1914-1915):145; "New York," *JE*, 9:288; "Jews," *HEAEG*, 585; *AJHQ*, 63:220; "Zionism," *UJE*, 10:658; *JSS*, 44:153; *AJH*, 69:34 ff.; Handlin, *Adventure in Freedom*, 169; *Menorah Journal*, 14:134 ff.

CHAPTER TWENTY-TWO
THE AMERICAN HERZL: LOUIS DEMBITZ BRANDEIS

1. Biographies of Brandeis may be found in the *UJE, EJ, EOZAI,* and the *DAB,* Supplement 3. The Louis Dembitz Papers are found in the University of Louisville Law Library; a microfilm copy of the Zionist Papers are available at the American Jewish Archives. For the letters of Brandeis, see Urofsky & Levy, *Letters of Louis D. Brandeis.* For papers and addresses of Brandeis see Ervin H. Pollack, *The Brandeis Reader* (N.Y., 1956); *Brandeis on Zionism*; Brandeis, *Business: A Profession and Brandeis, Other People's Money.* The following are a number of works on Brandeis that will be useful for the researcher: Baker, *Brandeis and Frankfurter*; De Haas, *Louis D. Brandeis.* Beginning with p.161 the author has included a series of important statements and papers by Brandeis. Irving Dilliard (ed.), *Mr. Justice Brandeis: Great American* (St. Louis, 1941); Bernard Flexner, *Mr. Justice Brandeis and the University of Louisville* (Louisville, 1938); Avyatar Friesel, *Ha-Maavak ben Brandeis u-Weizmann* (*The Struggle between Brandeis and Weizmann*) (Beersheba, 1972); Gal, *Brandeis of Boston*; Goldmark, *Pilgrims of '48*; Goodhart, *Five Jewish Lawyers*, 24 ff.; *Jewish Frontier*, 3(Nov. 1936):5 ff.; Kurland, *Felix Frankfurter*, 54 ff.; Alfred Leif, *Brandeis: The Personal History of an American Ideal (N.Y., 1936)*; Mason, *Brandeis*; Paper, *Brandeis*; Kallen, *Essays*, 131 ff.; Rabinowitz, *Justice Louis D. Brandeis*; Rosenthal, "Public Life of Louis Marshall," 2:395 ff.; Shapiro, *Leadership of the American Zionist Organization*; Philippa Strum, *Louis D. Brandeis: Justice for the People* (Cambridge, Mass., 1984); Todd, *Louis D. Brandeis*; Urofsky, *Mind of One Piece.*

2. "Frank, Jacob and the Frankists," *EJ*; "Frank, Jacob Leibovicz and the Frankist Movement," *UJE*; Barnard, *Julian W. Mack*, 179; *AJH*, 68:19 ff.; *AJHQ*, 55:199 ff., 62:303; Goldberg, *Pioneers and Builders*, 178 ff.; *Reminiscences of Frederika Dembitz Brandeis Written for Her Son Louis, in 1880-1886. Translated by Alice G. Brandeis for Her Grandchildren in 1948* (privately printed), copy in Marcus Collections; Kaganoff (ed.), *Essays on American Zionism*, 56 ff.; notes from a lecture of M.I. Urofsky, *HUC*, 1984; Isidor Busch, St. Louis, to B. Felsenthal, Chicago, May 18, 1884, copy in Marcus Collections; *JSS*, 13:263-64, 44:154; Urofsky & Levy, *Letters of Louis D. Brandeis*, 1:5, n.11, 120 ff., 386, 2:402; Phila. *Jewish Exponent*, May 6, 1955, pp.23 ff.; Solomon, *Pioneers in Service*, 176; Mason, *Brandeis*, 441 ff.; Charles A. Madison, *Eminent American Jews: 1776 to the Present* (N.Y., 1970), 133; Rabinowitz, *Justice Louis D. Brandeis*, 14-16; Denver *Intermountain Jewish News, Literary Supplement*, July 22, 1983, pp.3 ff.; Boston *Jewish Advocate*, Jan. 27, 1955, p.29, Jan. 18, 1962, section 3, p.6; De Haas, *Louis D. Brandeis*, 151 ff., 154-55; Lipsky, *Memoirs in Profile*, 201 ff.; Gal, *Brandeis of Boston*, 157 ff., 178 ff.; "Brandeis, Louis Dembitz," *UJE*; Weizmann, *Trial and Error*, 1:248; Goodhart, *Five Jewish Lawyers*, 36; *AJYB*, 44:37 ff., 42-48; *Commentary*, 60:88 ff.; *Reviews in American History*, 1:340-41; *Association for Jewish Studies, Newsletter*, June 1981, pp.15-16; Gurock, *Guide*, 78; *Congress Bi-Weekly*, Dec. 14, 1973, pp.15-16; Shapiro, *Leadership of the American Zionist Organization*, 77 ff.; Neumann, *In the Arena*, 32 ff.; Felix Frankfurter (ed.), *Mr. Justice Brandeis: Essays by Charles E. Hughes et al.* (New Haven, 1932); Ringler, "Boston" .

3. Rosenthal, "Public Life of Louis Marshall," 395 ff.; *PUAHC*, 6:4808; *Congress Bi-Weekly*, June 25, 1962, 8 ff.; Richards, *Organizing American Jewry*; "World Zionist Organization," *EOZAI*; *YA*, 2-3:222 ff., 14:156, 16:202 ff.; Urofsky, *American Zionism*, 164 ff., 231 ff.; Kaganoff, *Essays on American Zionism*, 56 ff., 64; Urofsky, "Special lecture on Zionism at the HUC," 1984; Shapiro, *Leadership of the American Zionist Organization*, 61 ff.; "Brandeis, Louis Dembitz," *UJE, EJ, EOZAI*; Janowsky, *Am. Jew. Reappraisal*, 311 ff.; Parzen, *Zionism*, 54 ff.; *PAJHS*, 49:188 ff.; "United States of America, Zionism in," "Zionist Organization of America (ZOA)," *EOZAI*; *The American Jewish Congress: What It Is and What It Does* (N.Y., 1936); Handlin, *Adventure in Freedom*, 171; Frommer, "American Jewish Congress," 528 ff.; *JSS*, 18:168; Ribalow (ed.), *Autobiographies*, 117 ff., 128-30; Brandeis, *Jewish Rights and the Congress*; *Jewish Life*, 9(no.4):16 ff.; *AJYB*, 17(1915-1916):210, 18(1916-1917):88-89, 310 ff., 19(1917-1918):245-46, 440 ff., 20(1918-1919):380; *To the Jews of America: The Jewish Congress Versus the American Jewish Committee, a Complete Statement with the Correspondence between Louis D. Brandeis and Cyrus Adler Aug. 1915, Issued by the Jewish Congress Organization Committee* (N.Y., 1915); "New York City," *EJ*, 12:1100; Newspaper Release of Provisional Executive Committee for General Zionist Affairs, New York, Oct. 15, 1915, copy in Marcus Collections; *Congress Weekly*, Mar. 16, 1945, pp. 8 ff., Nov. 24, 1958, pp.10 ff.; "American Jewish Congress," *UJE*, 1:247, "Zionism," 10:653 ff.; *Menorah Journal*, 14:139; *AJHQ*, 57:55; Janowsky, *Jews and Minority Rights*, 264 ff.; Shmarya Levin, *Childhood in Exile, Youth in Revolt, The Arena* (N.Y., 1932); "Levin, Shmarya," *UJE, EJ, EOZAI*; "Syrkin, Nachman," *UJE, EJ, EOZAI*; Raisin, *Great Jews I Have Known*, 71 ff.; Weisgal (ed.), *Theodor Herzl*, 218 ff.; Gal, *Brandeis of Boston*, vii ff.; Gartner, *Cleveland*, 253; *Herzl Year Book*, 5:374; Learsi, *Jews in America*, 260-61; recollection of Levin lecture at HUC by JRM; Duker, *Jews in World War I*; *Jew. Com. Reg.*, 1429 ff.; Roth, "American Jewish Congress," 71-133.

4. *PUAHC*, 8:7719; *Jew. Com. Reg.*, 1429 ff., 1445 ff.; *YA*, 2-3:232, 16:202 ff., 211, 223; *AJYB*, 17(1915-1916):210, 18(1916-1917):310 ff., 19(1917-1918):440 ff.; *Jewish People*, 4:168; Newspaper Release of Provisional Executive Committee for General Zionist Affairs, N.Y., Oct. 15, 1915, copy in Marcus Collections; Urofsky, *American Zionism*, 120, 182 ff.; Goren, *Kehillah*, 219 ff.; Roth, "American Jewish Congress," 134-301; *AJHQ*, 63:221; Abraham G. Duker, *The Impact of Zionism on American Jewry* (pamphlet, N.Y., 1958), 23; *Congress Bi-Weekly*, May 12, 1958, pp.4 ff.; Reznikoff, *Louis Marshall*, 2:509-10; *PAJHS*, 49:191-92; De Haas, *Louis D. Brandeis*, 213 ff.; Raphael, *Jews and Judaism in the U.S.*, 114 ff.; "Minority Rights," *UJE*; Richards, *Organizing American Jewry*; Gottschalk & Duker, *Jews in the Post-War World*, 29 ff.; Rosenthal, "Public Life of Louis Marshall," 399 ff.; Frommer, "American Jewish Congress," 83 ff., 109, 113 ff.

5. *AI*, Dec. 30, 1915, p.6, c.2, Jan. 13, 1916, p.6, c.2, Mar. 30, 1916, p.7, c.1, Apr. 6, 1916, p.1, cs.4-6, Apr. 13, 1916, p.4, c.5; Urofsky & Levy, *Letters of Louis D. Brandeis*, 3:309 and footnote, 4:3; Urofsky, *American Zionism*, 165 ff., 186-92; Philipson, *My Life*, 475-76; *AJYB*, 18(1916-1917):290; Roth, "American Jewish Congress," 302 ff., 333, 338, 356, 393; Frommer, "American Jewish Congress," 97 ff.; *Congress Bi-Weekly*, May 6, 1968, pp. 3 ff.; *Jew. Com. Reg.*, 1429-41.

6. *PAJHS*, 49:190; Reznikoff, *Louis Marshall*, 1:351-53; Sherman, *A Fateful Half-Century*, 13; Wiernik, *History*, 417; "Brandeis, Louis Dembitz," "Montagu, Edwin Samuel," *UJE*; *Studies in Zionism*, 7:49 ff.; Weizmann, *Trial and Error*, 1:193, 200, 208; *AJA*, 14:180 ff.; Leonard Stein, *The Balfour Declaration* (N.Y., 1961), 428, 664; Urofsky & Levy, *Letters of Louis D. Brandeis*, 4:318; *Judaism*, 24:296 ff.; *AJHQ*, 53:440 ff., 57:480 ff., 493, 515; *JSS*, 10:393 ff., 26:58 ff., 37:105 ff.; *Herzl Year Book*, 5:309 ff., 340-50; *The American Jewish War Congress and Zionism, etc.* (pamphlet, N.Y., 1919); Manuel, *American-Palestine Relations*, 175 ff.; Urofsky, *American Zionism*, 212 ff., 219; *Journal of Modern History*, 40(no.4):501 ff.; *PAAJR*, 37:111 ff.; Davis, *Israel*, 272 ff.; "United States

of America: Relations with Zionism and Israel," *EOZAI,* 2:1156; *Commentary,* 33:487 ff., 57(no.6):88 ff.; "Meyer, Eugene Isaac," *DAB,* Supplement 6; *Jewish Digest,* 13(no.1):9 ff., 13(no.2):77 ff., 26(no.1):45 ff., 27(no.2):66 ff.; Lipman, *Soc. Hist. of the Jews in England,* 141 ff.; *American Zionist,* 44(no.6):26 ff.; *Jewish Life,* 9(no.4):18; Elbogen, *Cent. of Jewish Life,* 477-79; Learsi, *Jews in America,* 257 ff.; Baron, *History,* 2:352 ff.; Levin, *Jewish Socialist Movements,* 210; Morgenthau, *All in a Life- Time,* 175; Meyer (ed.), *Early History of Zionism in America,* 297-325; Levinger, *Jews in U.S.,* 338; Sokolow, *History of Zionism,* 2:28-29; Szajkowski, *Jews, Wars, and Communism,* 1:138-39; Sachar, *History of Israel,* 89 ff.

7. Frommer, "American Jewish Congress," 108 ff.; "Selling, Ben," *UJE, WWIAJ,* 1928; "Abramowitz, Dov Baer," "Oklahoma," *UJE;* "Mack, Julian William," *UJE, EJ, EOZAI, DAB,* Supplement 3, *WWW,* vol. 2, *AJYB,* 6(1904-1905):147; Barnard, *Julian W. Mack,* 121 ff., 186 ff., see Index sub "Zionism"; Shapiro, *Leadership of the American Zionist Organization,* 31, 54, et passim; *PAJHS,* 37:476-77, 49:193; Kallen, *Essays,* 121 ff., 154 ff.; Voss (ed.), *Stephen S. Wise,* 13-14; Melvin I. Urofsky, *A Voice The Spoke For Justice: The Life and Times of Stephen S. Wise* (Albany, 1982); Polier & Wise (eds.), *Stephen Wise;* Wise, *Challenging Years;* Lipsky, *Memoirs in Profile,* 192 ff.; Analyticus, *Jews Are Like That,* 81 ff.; Raisin, *Great Jews I Have Known,* 223 ff.; *AJYB,* 5(1903-1904):106, 21:186 ff., 46:35 ff., 342, 51:515 ff., 525-26; "Wise, Stephen Samuel," *JE, UJE, EJ, EOZAI, DAB,* Supplement 4; Reznikoff, *Louis Marshall,* 2:509, 526 ff., 831 ff.; *Memorials Submitted to President Wilson,* March 2, 1919; Sokolow, *History of Zionism,* 2:82; *Jewish Book Annual,* 9:66; Levinger, *Jews in U.S.,* 507 ff.; Sachar, *Modern Jewish History,* 522; *AJA,* 21:3 ff.; *Minutes of Temple Emanu-El,* Oct.-Dec., 1905, copies in AJAr; Markens, *Hebrews,* 305; *AJH,* 69:41 ff., 73:110; Verbal statements of Rabbi Clifton Harby Levy to JRM in New London, Conn., June 21, 1951, Marcus Collections; *AHR,* 89:225; Julian Morgenstern, Cincinnati, to Rabbi Martin B. Ryback, Norwalk, Conn., Feb. 26, 1952, copy in Marcus Collections; Nodel, *The Ties Between,* 98 ff.; *Report of the Proceedings of the American Jewish Congress,* Phila., Pa., Dec. 1918 (n.p., n.d.); Richards, *Organizing American Jewry,* 6, 19 ff.; *Congress Weekly,* June 17, 1957, pp.9 ff.; *Congress Bi-Weekly,* June 25, 1962, pp.8 ff.; *YA,* 2-3:230 ff., 16:279 ff.; *AJHQ,* 63:242; Kaganoff, *Essays on American Zionism,* 68 ff.; Goren, *American Jews,* 71-72; "American Jewish Congress," *UJE, EJ, EOZAI;* Learsi, *Jews in America,* chap.18; Rosenthal, "Public Life of Louis Marshall," 399 ff.; Gottschalk & Duker, *Jews in the Post-War World,* 29 ff.; Janowsky, *Jews and Minority Rights,* 162 ff.

8. Phillips (ed.), *Felix Frankfurter Reminisces,* 147; *New York Times,* Feb. 11, 1960, p.37, c.6; *Judaeans,* 4:42 ff.; *Memorials Submitted to President Wilson, March 2, 1919;* "Jews," *Encyclopaedia Britannica,* 1943, p.63; Gottschalk & Duker, *Jews in the Post-War World,* 37; *AJYB,* 21:156 ff., 180, 188 ff., 192, 22:101 ff., 136-37, 143, 406-8, 23:330 ff., 24:40 ff., 48 ff., 42:100, 49:615, 67:31 ff., 535, 75:71-72; "Ukraine," *EJ,* 15:1517, *UJE,* 10:336; Duker, *Jews in World War I;* Adler & Connolly, *Buffalo,* 283-84; Stephenson, *American Immigration,* 84-86; "Pogroms," *EJ,* 13:698 ff.; Sachar, *Modern Jewish History,* 355 ff., 376 ff.; *EIAJH,* 457 ff.; Michael E. Parrish, *Felix Frankfurter and His Times: The Reform Years* (N.Y., 1982), 59, 129 ff., 141-42, 149; H.N. Hirsch, *The Enigma of Felix Frankfurter* (N.Y., 1981); Philip B. Kurland, *Mr. Justice Frankfurter and the Constitution* (Chicago, 1971); Baker, *Brandeis and Frankfurter;* Kurland, *Felix Frankfurter,* 113 ff.; "Frankfurter, Felix," *UJE, EJ, EOZAI, WWW,* vol.4; Wallace Mendelson (ed.), *Felix Frankfurter: A Tribute* (N.Y., 1964); Felix Frankfurter, AJAr microfilm nos. 1608-13, AJAr; *Congress Bi-Weekly,* Apr. 12, 1965, pp.13-14, June 25, 1962, pp.8 ff.; *Political Science Quarterly,* 85(no.1):99 ff.; Weizmann, *Trial and Error,* 1:195 ff., 245 ff.; *Jewish Digest,* 8(no.2):9 ff., 15; Grinstein, *History,* 172-73; *AJH,* 68:35, 69:41 ff.; *Jewish Currents,* 36(no.12):84 ff.; *JSS,* 22:153, 37:178 ff.; "Balfour Declaration," "Comité des Delegations Juives," "Feisal (Faysal)," "King-Crane Report," "Mandate for Palestine,"

EOZAI; *Jewish Post-War Problems, Unit III: How the Communities Prepared for Peace during the First World War* (pamphlet, American Jewish Committee, N.Y., 1943); Urofsky, *American Zionism*, 231 ff.; *Herzl Year Book*, 5:78 ff., 80-81, 249 ff., 369-70; Felix Frankfurter, Paris, to Woodrow Wilson, Paris, May 8, 1919, May 14, 1919, copies in Marcus Collections; *Congress Weekly*, June 17, 1957, pp.9 ff.; *YA*, 2-3:235-42, 16:270 ff., 17:260 ff.; "Minority Rights," "Montagu, Sir Samuel Stuart," *UJE*; Learsi, *Jews in America*, 257 ff., 261 ff.; Janowsky, *American Jew*, 231 ff., 243-44; Richards, *Organizing American Jewry*; "American Jewish Congress," *UJE, EOZAI, EJ*; *AJHQ*, 57:492 ff., 60:71 ff.; "United States of America, Relations with Zionism and Israel," *EOZAI*, 2:1156, "United States of America, Zionism in," 2:1163 ff.; Baron, *History*, 2:322-23, 354; "Zionism," *ESS*; Feingold, *Zion in America*, 254; Gottschalk & Duker, *Jews in the Post War World*, 37 ff.; Sachar, *History of Israel*, 116 ff.; *Commentary*, 23:365 ff.; Sachar, *Modern Jewish History*, 354 ff.; Schappes, *JIUS*, 184-85; "Pogroms," *EJ*, 13:698 ff.; *The Massacres and Other Atrocities Committed Against the Jews in Southern Russia: A Record Including Official Reports, Sworn Statements and Other Documentary Proof* (American Jewish Congress pamphlet, N.Y., 1920); Morison, *History*, 861 ff.; Janowsky, *Jews and Minority Rights*, 282 ff.; *Palestine*, 1(no.4):1 ff.; "United States," *UJE*, 10:350, "Zionism," 10:665 ff.; *PAJHS*, 36:79 ff., 45:35 ff., 49:190; Levinger, *Jews in U.S.*, 335 ff.; Luzzatti, *God in Freedom*, 735-94; *New York World*, Nov. 23, 1877, reprinting an item from the London *Jewish Chronicle*, Dec. 12, 1877, clippings in Marcus Collections; Oscar Straus, Constantinople, to William Seligman, Paris, Straus Papers, LC; Janowsky, *Am. Jew. Reappraisal*, 310 ff.; Elbogen, *Cent. of Jewish Life*, 505 ff.; Masserman & Baker, *Jews Come to America*, 336 ff.; Goren, *American Jews*, 70-72; *Mass Welcome to Louis Marshall on his Return from the Peace Conference, Monday Evening, July 28, 1919* (N.Y., 1919); *Final Drafts of the Mandates for Mesopotamia and Palestine for the Approval of the Council of the League of Nations, Aug. 1921, London* (London, 1921); *AJA*, 29:22 ff.; Szajkowski, *Jews, Wars, and Communism*, 2:16 ff.; Bryson, *American Diplomatic Relations*, 58 ff.; Levinger, *Jews in U.S.*, 335 ff.; Bogen, *Born a Jew*, 133 ff., 164 ff., 202 ff.; *Jewish Digest*, 8(no.2):15; H. Morgenthau, Constantinople, to Bernard G. Richards, N.Y., Jan. 23, 1923, copy in Marcus Collections; Morgenthau, *All in a Life-Time*, 298 ff., 348 ff.; Analyticus, *Jews Are Like That*, 29 ff.; Weisgal (ed.), *Theodor Herzl*, 216; "Morgenthau, Henry," *DAB*, Supplement 4; Phillips (ed.), *Felix Frankfurter Reminisces*, 13 ff., 145 ff., 154 ff.; "Samuel Commission," *EJ*; Manuel, *American-Palestine Relations*, 267 ff.; Rosenthal, "Public Life of Louis Marshall," 2:555 ff.; Morris Rothenberg, *The Works and Plans of the Congress Organization: Address Delivered Before the Preliminary Conference, Held at the Hotel Astor, N.Y., Mar. 20, 1921* (Phila., n.d.).

9. *Herzl Year Book*, 4:359, 374-75; *AJH*, 69:41 ff.; *YA*, 15:145-64; "Keren Hayesod," "London Zionist Conference of 1920," "Pittsburgh Program," *EOZAI*; De Haas, *Louis D. Brandeis*, 260 ff.; "Weizmann, Chaim," *UJE*, 10:497-98; "Zionism," *UJE*, 10:654-55, *EJ*, 16:1141 ff.; Kaganoff, *Essays on American Zionism*, 74 ff.; *AJHQ*, 60:37 ff., 63:228 ff., 65:143 ff.; Weizmann, *Trail and Error*, 1:261 ff., 2:65 ff.; *National Jewish Post*, Mar. 12, 1965, p.7, entire; "United States of America," *EJ*, 15:1625; Reznikoff, *Louis Marshall*, 1:190 ff.; Urofsky & Levy, *Letters of Louis D. Brandeis*, 4:xix; Bernard Flexner, N.Y., to F. Frankfurter, Cambridge, Mass., May 2, 1921, copy in Marcus Collections; *JSS*, 37:178 ff.; *PAJHS*, 45:37; Zola, "Zvi Hirsch Masliansky," 65 ff.; Gartner, *Cleveland*, 263; Sachar, *History of Israel*, 138 ff.; Eisig Silberschlag, "Zionism and Hebraism in America (1897-1921)" (typescript, n.d.), copy in Marcus Collections; *AJYB*, 26:594, 46:44; Mason, *Brandeis*, 441 ff.; "Zionist Organization of America (ZOA)," *EOZAI*; Janowsky, *Am. Jew. Reappraisal*, 301 ff.; Weisgal (ed.), *Theodor Herzl*, 218 ff.; "Immigration to Palestine and Israel," *EOZAI*, 1:536, "United States of America, Zionism in," 2:1165.

10. Levy, "Gus Karger," 6 ff.; Learsi, *Jews in America*, 241 ff., 257 ff., 282-84; *AJH*, 68:7 ff., 19 ff., 32 ff., 69:541 ff., 71:390 ff.; Howe, *World of Our Fathers*, 204 ff.; *Reader's Digest*, 73(no.435):65 ff.; Mason, *Brandeis*, 26, 347, 413-14, 442 ff., 470, 691; *AJHQ*, 55:199 ff., 62:76 ff., 383 ff., 63:221 ff., 227, 65:121 ff., 371, 66:548-51, 72:440; Sachar, *Sufferance is the Badge*, 512-13; Washington *Record*, 4(no.1):3 ff.; Paper, *Brandeis*, 198 ff., 259 ff., 262, 315 ff.; *AJYB*, 42:171, 44:37 ff., 75:55 ff.; *Jewish Frontier*, 3:22 ff.; Urofsky, *American Zionism*, 103-4, 118, 120 ff.; Korn, *Marcus Festschrift*, 145; Kallen, *Essays*, 131 ff.; *Commentary*, 15:499, Oct. 1945, 313 ff., 60(no.5):88; *JSS*, 19:126, 35:167 ff., 37:18 ff., 38:205 ff.; Louis D. Brandeis, *Zionism and Patriotism* (N.Y., 1915); Raphael, *Jews and Judaism in the U.S.*, 125 ff.; *AJA*, 10:3 ff., 14:180 ff., 15:6 ff., 27:78 ff., 28:59 ff.; *Brandeis on Zionism*, 59 ff., 65-66, 150-51; Gurock, *Guide*, 80-82; Brandeis, *Jewish Rights and the Congress*; *PAJHS*, 46:467 ff.; *Congress Bi-Weekly*, Dec. 14, 1973, p.15, Jan. 18, 1974, pp.6 ff.; Sachar, *Modern Jewish History*, 334-35, 370; *Jewish Book Annual*, 20:107-110, 39:119 ff.; Todd, *Louis D. Brandeis*, 74, 80, 180-82; *Historia Judaica*, 9:198; Urofsky & Levy, *Letters of Louis D. Brandeis*, 2:402, 4:382, 446-47, 551-52, 5:xv-xvi; "Brandeis, Louis Dembitz," *UJE, EJ, EOZAI, DAB*, Supplement 3; L.D. Brandeis, Boston, to Horace M. Kallen, Madison, Wisc., Feb. 23, 1913, Brandeis Papers, University of Louisville, copy in Marcus Collections; for Kallen's correspondence with Brandeis, see Urofsky & Levy, *Letters of Louis D. Brandeis*, vols.3-5; Kallen, Madison, to Brandeis, Boston, Dec. 20, 1913, copy in Marcus Collections; Schlesinger, *Rise of the City*, 227-28; *Herzl Year Book*, 5:371-72; *Atlantic Magazine*, 198(no.5):66 ff.; M.I. Urofsky, lecture at HUC, Oct. 31, 1984, Marcus notes, Marcus Collections; *American Zionist*, 43(no.3):36 ff.; *Register of the Kentucky Historical Society*, Winter 1979, pp.30 ff., AJAr; Association for Jewish Studies, *Newsletter*, June 1981, pp.15-16; Shapiro, *Leadership of the American Zionist Organization*, 77 ff.; *YA*, 15:145 ff.; *Menorah Journal*, 14:134 ff.; Brandeis, *Other People's Money*, 116, et passim; Brandeis, *Business: A Profession*, xi; *Jewish Frontier*: statement of Rabbi Jacob Weinstein to JRM, June 15, 1965. Weinstein received the check for $25,000.

CHAPTER TWENTY-THREE
ZIONISM: CONFRONTATION AND VICTORY

1. Urofsky & Levy, *Letters of Louis D. Brandeis*, 4:382; *AJYB*, 26:577; Stuart E. Knee, *The Concept of Zionist Dissent in the American Mind, 1917-1941* (N.Y., 1979); *JSS*, 39:209 ff.; "Zionism," *EJ*, 16:1143 ff.; Blau, *Reform Judaism*, 367-92; *YA*, 17:260 ff.; Duker, *Non-Zionist and Anti-Zionist Groups*.

2. *The Poems of Emma Lazarus* (2 vols., Boston, 1888), 1:27; Dan Vogel, *Emma Lazarus* (Boston, 1980), 141-43; for Shalom Elhanan Jaffe, see Eisenstadt, *Hakme Yisrael be-Amerika*, 60-61; *AJYB*, 21:318; Urofsky, *American Zionism*, 91, 102; "Mizrachi," *EJ*, 12:180; Learsi, *Jews in America*, 234; Duker, *Non-Zionist and Anti-Zionist Groups*, 12; Levinthal, *Message of Israel*, 135; *AJA*, 35:126-27, 148 ff., 157; *PAJHS*, 37:81; Feldman, *Jew. Experience in Western Pa.*, 217; *AI*, Feb. 9, 1877, p.5, c.5, p.6, cs.1-2; *JM*, Feb. 23, 1883, p.5, cs.1-2; Meyer (ed.), *Early History of Zionism in America*, 85-86.

3. Learsi, *Jews in America*, 231; *AJHQ*, 57:488 ff., 65:231 ff.; *JSS*, 44:154; Duker, *Non-Zionist and Anti-Zionist Groups*, 7 ff.; *YA*, 16:355-56, 371-72; Levin, *Jewish Socialist Movements*, 138 ff.; *AJYB*, 20(1918-1919):156-57; Wiernik, *History*, 415-16.

4. "Sanhedrin, Napoleonic," *UJE*; "France," *UJE*, 4:376-77; *CCARYB*, 16:315 ff.; "Conferences, Rabbinical," *JE*, 4:212-13, 215, 217; R. & E., *Charleston*, 140; Fein, *Baltimore*, 64-65; *PAJHS*, 40:361 ff.; Jacob Clavius Levy, "Vindiciae Judaeorum," MS, Phillips Papers, LC; Temkin, *Philadelphia Conference*, 38 ff.; Hertzberg, *Atlanta*, 131 ff.; Rothschild, *Atlanta*, 11-12, 120; *PUAHC*, 2:1418-19.

5. *JM*, Mar. 30, 1883, p.1, cs.5-6, p.2, c.1; *PAJHS*, 47:154 ff.; Blau, *Reform Judaism*, 371 ff.; *AJHQ*, 60:149; *Herzl Year Book*, 5:63; Wilansky, *Sinai to Cincinnati*, 32-33, 185, 189, 195; *CCARYB*, 7:x-xii, 9:179 ff., 52:341-42; *AJA*, 3(no.2):3 ff.; "Zionism," *UJE*, 10:665; M. Nathaniel Bension and Alton M. Winters, "Attitudes of Isaac Mayer Wise to Palestine as Reflected in the American Israelite" (HUC term paper, 1944); *H.U.C. Journal*, 3:165 ff., 4:45 ff.; Eisenberg, *Eyewitnesses to American Jewish History*, 3:71 ff.

6. Kohler, *Studies*, 229 ff., 232; Karff, *HUC-JIR*, 62 ff.; *Studies in Zionism*, 7:49 ff.; *CCARYB*, 13:185 ff. This analysis of the 1907 Kohler affair at the HUC is based primarily on a cache of contemporary letters treating of this incident. They are in the Marcus Collections. Additional data may be found in: Karff, *HUC-JIR, 65 ff.; Max Leopold Margolis: Scholar and Teacher* (Phila., 1952); Minutes of the Board of Governors, HUC, 1907, AJAr; Kenneth H. Kudisch, "And Then There Were None" (HUC term paper, 1969); Kohler, *Studies*, 453 ff.; *JSS*, 37:295 ff.; *The Maccabaean*, 12:97; *AH*, Apr. 12, 1907, p.606; Max Schloessinger, *Reform Judaism and Zionism: An Examination of Dr. David Philipson's Thesis That They Are Irreconcilable* (Baltimore, 1907); *AJYB*, 9(1907-1908):516; *Herzl Year Book*, 5:365; *AJH*, 73:375 ff., 392; *AJA*, 23:154 ff.

7. *AJHQ*, 63:200 ff.; E.G. Hirsch, Chicago, to B. Felsenthal, Chicago, Oct. 11, 1898, copy in Marcus Collections; Simon W. Rosendale, Winter Park, Fla., to Harry Cutler, NYC, Mar. 22, 1917, copy in Marcus Collections; *Herzl Year Book*, 5:368-69; Shubow (ed.), *Brandeis Avukah Annual*, 15; Morgenthau, *All in a Life-Time*, 289 ff., 294; *Washington Record*, 5(no.1):42; Lewis H. Kamrass, "The Life and Works of Rabbi Samuel Schulman As Reflected in His Writings, etc." (rabbinical thesis, HUC, 1985), 75 ff.; Cohen, *Faith of a Liberal*, 326 ff.

8. *Studies in Zionism*, 5:55 ff.; *JSS*, 20:239 ff., 23:242, 252-53, 29:83, 85-86, 89, n.196; J.H. Schiff, N.Y., to Friedenwald, Baltimore, Nov. 18, 1907, Schiff Papers, AJAr; *AH*, Aug. 23, 1907, p.385; J.H. Schiff, Bar Harbor, Me., to D. Philipson, Cincinnati, Aug. 30, 1907, AJAr; Barnard, *Julian W. Mack*, 176; *The Nation*, Apr. 26, 1919, p.654; Julius Rosenwald, Chicago, to J.H. Schiff, White Sulphur Springs, W.Va., Dec. 1, 1914, Schiff to Rosenwald, Dec. 4, 1914, Rosenwald Papers, U. of Chicago, copies in AJAr; J.H. Schiff, White Sulphur Springs, W. Va., to S.W. Rosendale, Coronado Beach, Calif., Mar. 15, 1916, Schiff Papers, AJAr; *AJYB*, 18(1916-1917):95, 21:193, 22:144; Goren, *Kehillah*, 218 ff.; Elisha M. Friedman, Washington, D.C., to J.H. Schiff, N.Y., Sept. 28, 1917, Schiff Papers, AJAr; J.H. Schiff, N.Y., to J. Rosenwald, Chicago, Dec. 18, 1919, Rosenwald Papers, U. of Chicago, copy in AJAr; *Freeland*, 21:13; *AJHQ*, 60:36; Rosenthal, "Public Life of Louis Marshall," 127 ff., 135-37; *AH*, Jan. 11, 1907, pp.246-47; *PAJHS*, 49:188 ff.; *Studies in Zionism*, 7:73; Correspondence, Oct. - Nov. 1917, between Schiff, Marshall and Elisha M. Friedman, in Eugene Meyer Papers, LC, copies in Marcus Collections.

9. Robert L. Katz, "The American Jewish Congress Movement, 1914-1918" (HUC term paper, n.d.), Marcus Collections; *CCAR Journal*, 21(no.1):17 ff.; *PAJHS*, 40:361 ff.; *CCARYB*, 1:25-26, 80 ff., 2:54, 16:315 ff., 17:31-34, 30:141-42; *AJA*, 3(no.2):3 ff., 35:263 ff.; Urofsky, *American Zionism*, 83, 96-97; Handlin, *Adventure in Freedom*, 168; *PUAHC*, 2:1418-19, 5:3981, 6:5241, 5317-18, 5324, 7:5956; *Studies in Zionism*, 7:73; Allen, "Reform Judaism"; *Herzl Year Book*, 5:57 ff.; Philipson, *My Life*, 135 ff.; "Zionism," *UJE*, 10:665 ff.; "Reform Judaism and Zionism," *EOZAI*; "Anti-Zionism," *EOZAI*, 1:49; *Judaism*, 14:310; William Rosenau, *Zionism from the Stand-Point of the Non-Zionist, etc.* (Baltimore, 1916); Philipson, *Reform Movement*, 360 ff.; *AJH*, 73:375 ff.; Blau, *Reform Judaism*, 367-92; Arfa, "Attitudes of the American Reform Rabbinate Towards Zionism," chap. 2; Harold Floyd Caminker, "Reform Judaism in the United States and Its Relationship to Zionism as Reflected in Sources Heretofore Not Researched, 1889-1948" (rabbinical thesis, HUC, 1978); A.L. Redstone, "Trends in Reform Judaism, 1875-1940," typescript analysis of attitudes of Reform rabbis to Zionism, AJAr.

10. Sheldon Harr, "From Kishinev to the Rise of the American Jewish Committee, 1903-1906 as Reflected in the *American Hebrew*: A Study of American Jewish Life" (HUC term paper, 1971); Laqueur, *History of Zionism*, 396; Rosenthal, "Public Life of Louis Marshall," 127 ff.; "Reform Judaism and Zionism," *EOZAI*; *Herzl Year Book*, 5:221 ff., 230, 369; *Studies in Zionism*, 7:66; "Zionism," *UJE*, 10:664-73, *EJ*, 16:1049 ff.; *AH*, May 7, 1897, p.18; *H.U.C. Journal*, 4:48; Henry Berkowitz, *Syllabus of American Jewish History* (Phila., 1905), 7.

11. "Zionism," *UJE*, 10:658-62, 666-67; *PAJHS*, 40:361 ff., 391, 49:199; Philipson, *My Life*, 135 ff., 299, 304-5; "Anti-Zionism," *EOZAI*, 1:49; *AJH*, 73:375 ff.; *Studies in Zionism*, 7:65-66, 82; Schachner, *American Jewish Committee*, 79-80; Morris D. Waldman, *Nor By Power* (N.Y., 1953), 199 ff.; *JSS*, 23:242; *Herzl Year Book*, 5:78 ff., 115 ff.; Jesse I. Straus, N.Y., to S.W. Rosendale, Albany, Apr. 16, 1919, copy in Marcus Collections; Wiernik, *History*, 415; *AJA*, 14:3 ff.; "Zionism," *EJ*, 16:1144 ff.; *AJHQ*, 57:476 ff.; Urofsky & Levy, *Letters of Louis D. Brandeis*, 4:388, n.1; *AJYB*, 21:178, 194; Petition of dissidents to Peace Conference, "A Statement to the Peace Conference," Wolsey Papers, AJAr; *YA*, 17:264; Gurock, *Guide*, 82; Learsi, *Jews in America*, 266.

12. Wiernik, *History*, 415; "Zionism," *UJE*, 10:658-62; "Reform Judaism and Zionism," *EOZAI*; Levin, *Jewish Socialist Movements*, 210; *PAJHS*, 31:197 ff., 49:188 ff., 196, 198; J. Rosenwald, Chicago, to J.H. Schiff, White Sulphur Springs, W. Va., Dec. 1, 1914, copy in Marcus Collections; Reznikoff, *Louis Marshall*, 1:351 ff., 560; Rosenthal, "Public Life of Louis Marshall," 417-26; Schachner, *American Jewish Committee*, 79; *AJYB*, 20(1918-1919):159; N.Y. *Hebrew Standard*, Feb. 7, 1919, pp.2-3; Avery (ed.), *Laws Applicable to Immigration and Nationality*, 397.

13. *AJYB*, 21:185; Plaut, *Reform Judaism*, 96 ff., 154-55, 158, 161; *PAJHS*, 40:361 ff., 382; *Where We Stand*, 17, 24-25; *Sixty-Third Annual Report of the Union of American Hebrew Congregations, May 9, 1937* (Cincinnati, 1937), 158; "Reform Judaism and Zionism," *EOZAI*; *71st-73rd Annual Reports of the Union of American Hebrew Congregations* (Cincinnati, 1947), 254 ff.

14. *AJH*, 73:373 ff.; *Studies in Zionism*, 7:49 ff., 82; Urofsky, *American Zionism*, 213, 218; *PAJHS*, 47:98; *AJYB*, 31:191, 48:602; Philipson, *My Life*, 136-37, 299 ff., 302; *CCARYB*, 28:133 ff., 30:140 ff., 31:79-80, 85 ff., 34:105-6, 135 ff., 38:140, 43:120, 44:131, 45:102, 110-12, 50:118, 52:169-82, 53:91 ff., 160, 54:91-92, 55:119-20; Arfa, "Attitudes of the American Reform Rabbinate Toward Zionism," 178, 459-65; Avery (ed)., *Laws Applicable to Immigration and Nationality*, 408 ff.; Plaut, *Reform Judaism*, 96 ff.; *The Union Prayerbook for Jewish Worship* (Cincinnati, 1940), 68-69; "American Council for Judaism," *EJ*; "Biltmore Program," *EOZAI*; *Basic Principles of Congregation Beth Israel, Houston, Texas, (An American Reform Congregation)* (Houston, Texas, Nov. 23, 1943), copy in Marcus Collections; "Houston," *EJ*, 8:1051; General Epistle of Congregation Beth Israel, Baton Rouge, La., Apr. 25, 1945, copy in Marcus Collections; Association of Reform Zionists of American (ARZA): *AJYB*, 84:296; Stevens & Glazer, *CCAR Resolutions*, 37 ff.; *Palestine Year Book*, 3:423 ff., 427 ff.; *Union Hymnal: Songs and Prayers for Jewish Worship* (Cincinnati, 1940), 266.

15. Friedman & Gordis, *Jewish Life in America*, 301 ff.; *AJA*, 18:107 ff.; *PAJHS*, 45:99; Horwich, *My First Eighty Years*, 258; *Commentary*, 60(no.5):88; "Zionism," *ESS*, 15:534 ff.; *JSS*, 44:153; *Menorah Journal*, 14:141; *AJYB*, 41:516.

CHAPTER TWENTY FOUR

THE GERMAN AND EAST EUROPEAN JEWS, 1860-1920:

A SUMMARY

1. *JSS*, 9:130.

2. "Soldiers," *UJE*, 9:603.
3. *AJYB*, 21:330.

CHAPTER TWENTY-FIVE

EPILOGUE: 1921-1985

1. *AJHQ*, 51:97 ff.; Learsi, *Jews in America*, 359 ff.; Wiernik, *History*, 453 ff.; Feingold, *Zion in America*, 258 ff.; Stanley Feldstein, *The Land That I Show You: Three Centuries of Jewish Life in America* (Garden City, N.Y., 1979), 254 ff.; Goren, *American Jews*, 73 ff.; Dawidowicz, *On Equal Terms*, 86 ff.; Raphael, *Jews and Judaism in the U.S.*; Abraham J. Karp, *Haven and Home: A History of Jews in America* (N.Y., 1985), 262 ff.; Robert M. Seltzer, *Jewish People, Jewish Thought: The Jewish Experience in History* (N.Y., 1980), 647 ff.; Silberman, *A Certain People*; *Face to Face*, 9:7 ff., 30 ff.; Lloyd P. Gartner, "The Midpassage of American Jewry, 1929-1945" (pamphlet, U. of Cincinnati, 1982); *Encyclopedia Judaica Decennial Book, 1973-1982*, 590 ff.; "United States of America," *EJ*; *AJYB* volumes 79 through 86 are invaluable for the study of events of recent history.
2. Marcus, *AJW*, 1:171; "United States Literature," *EJ*, 15:1574 ff.; Detroit *Jewish News*, Oct. 30, 1981, p.20; *AJYB*, 19(1917-1918):407-8, 56:28, 65:133; *AJHQ*, 55:5 ff.; *AI*, Feb. 16, 1978, p.17, cs.1-2; *Women's American Ort Reporter*, Fall 1981, 9 ff.
3. "Hirshhorn Museum," "Theatre Guild," *Columbia Encyclopedia*; *AJYB*, 26:579; "Altman, Benjamin," *UJE*; Marcus, *AJW*, 1:76; "Lerner, Gerda," *WWIA*, 1986-87; *New York Times*, Mar. 28, 1982, p.14, Sept. 4, 1985, p.17; *AJHQ*, 55:7.
4. *AJYB*, 42:222; "Rosenberg, Julius and Ethel Rosenberg," *DAB*, Supplement 5; "Rosenberg, Ethel Greenglass," *NAW, Modern Period*; "Rosenberg, Anna M.," *WWIAJ*, 1955; "Askew, Reubin O'Donovan," *WWIA*, 1985-86; Rosenthal, "Louis Marshall," 688 ff.; *AJHQ*, 56:274; *New York Times*, Nov. 12, 1978, p.27, June 1, 1983, for Askew; *Milwaukee History*, 6:70 ff.; *AJH*, 72:461 ff.; Detroit *Jewish News*, Oct. 21, 1983, p.26.
5. "Submarine," *Columbia Encyclopedia*; "Rickover, Hyman George," *WWIA*, 1986-87; Detroit *Jewish News*, June 10, 1983, p.42; *AJHQ*, 55:6 ff.; *Time Magazine*, July 30, 1965, p.11, cited in *AJHQ*, 55:149; "Sports," *EJ*, 15:300 ff.; *AJH*, 74:211 ff.; Bernard Postal et al., *Encyclopedia of Jews in Sports* (N.Y., 1965), 62, 66-67.
6. *AJYB*, 56:20 ff., 27 ff.; *YA*, 16:387 ff.; Detroit *Jewish News*, Sept. 17, 1976, p.56, Oct. 26, 1984, p.38; *New York Statistics, 1981*, 35-37; Thomas J. Cottle, *Hidden Survivors: Portraits of Poor Jews in America* (Englewood Cliffs, N.J., 1980); *Jewish Community News Reporter*, July 17, 1981, p.1; Joselit, *Our Gang*; Turkus & Feder, *Murder, Inc.*; *AJHQ*, 55:5; *Jewish Post and Opinion*, Jan. 4, 1980, p.3; C. Joseph Pusateri, *A History of American Business* (Arlington Heights, Ill., 1984), 243 ff.; *AJA*, 25:153; Marcus, *AJW*, 1:136, 161-62, 210; Marcus, *AJWD*, 650-54; Stephen L. Slavin & Mary A. Pradt, *The Einstein Syndrome: Corporate Anti-Semitism in America Today* (Washington, D.C., 1982); Silberman, *A Certain People*, 82 ff.
7. *New York Times*, Jan. 11, 1949, p.27; Release on Jacob R. Schiff by Standard Factors Corporation, Aug. 2, 1950, copy in AJAr; *Federation for the Support of Jewish Philanthropic Societies of New York City . . . List of Subscribers, 1925* (N.Y., 1925), 590.
8. "Arendt, Hannah," *Columbia Encyclopedia*; *Jewish Currents*, 35(no.5):46; *JTA-DNB*, Jan. 11, 1980, p.4; "American Jewish Joint Distribution Committee," *EJ*; *AJH*, 71:540; Bauer, *JDC*, 19 ff.
9. Koppel S. Pinson (ed.), *Essays on Anti-Semitism* (N.Y., 1942), 175 ff.; Marcus, *CAJ*, 3:1428, n.11; Silverberg, *If I Forget Thee O Jerusalem*, 410; Bernard Postal & Henry W. Levy, *And the Hills Shouted For Joy, etc.* (N.Y., 1973), 379-80; *WSJHQ*, 15:79 ff.; Richard Davis, "Radio Priest: The Public Career of Father Charles Edward Coughlin" (Ph.D. diss., U. of North Carolina, 1974); "New York City," *EJ*, 12:1114-15; Lewis S.

Feuer, *Jews in the Origins of Modern Science and Bacon's Scientific Utopia, etc.* (Cincinnati, 1987), 5 ff.

10. Dawidowicz, *On Equal Terms*, 105 ff.; "National Conference of Christians and Jews," *UJE*; Raul Hilberg, *The Destruction of the European Jew* (3 vols., N.Y., 1985); Arthur D. Morse, *While Six Million Died: A Chronicle of American Apathy* (N.Y., 1968); David S. Wyman, *The Abandonment of the Jews: America and the Holocaust, 1941-1945* (N.Y., 1984); *Journal of American Ethnic History*, 2(no.1):66 ff., 2(no.2):3 ff., 84-85; *JTA-DNB*, Passover Edition, 1982, p.4.

11. "Bilbo, Theodore Gilmore," *DAB*, Supplement 4; *Commentary*, 74(no.4):64; *AJYB*, 56:34, 84, 76:125-26; *New York Times*, Dec. 30, 1980, p.6; *Jewish Digest*, 29(no.6):56; Detroit *Jewish News*, Oct. 28, 1983, p.15; *JTA-DNB*, Rosh Hashanah Edition, 1984, p.4, Oct. 4, 1985, pp.1-2; *CCARYB*, 95:239; *Woman's American Ort Reporter*, Fall 1981, p.9; *Reviews in American History*, 11:442.

12. *American State Papers* (1949), 207-8; *AI*, Sept. 18, 1980, p.5, cs.1-3; Blau (ed.), *Cornerstones*, 106 ff.; *AJYB*, 33:70 ff., 78:157; *Wall Street Journal*, Sept. 17, 1980, p.22; Detroit *Jewish News*, May 14, 1982; "National Council of Churches of Christ in the United States of America," *Columbia Encyclopedia*; *Midstream*, 30(no.3):32-37.

13. *AJYB*, 56:88 ff.; *Journal of American Ethnic History*, 2(no.2):83 ff.; *EAH*, 475; Dan A. Oren, *Joining the Club: A History of Jews and Yale* (New Haven, 1985), 274 ff., 325-26; "Vatican Council, Second," *Columbia Encyclopedia*; *AI*, Mar. 17, 1983, p.11; *CCARYB*, 86:167 ff.; Will Herberg, *Protestant-Catholic-Jew* (N.Y., 1955); *Cross Currents*, Winter 1963, pp.34 ff.; *Jewish Post and Opinion*, Dec. 18, 1981, p.12, Apr. 30, 1982, p.5; "Hodge, Charles," *DAB, ACOAB*; Jane Priwer, *The United Hebrew Congregation, St. Louis, Mo., 1837-1963* (St. Louis, 1963); *AJA*, 22:13-14; *PAJHS*, 18:21.

14. Jacob R. Marcus, *The Jew in the Medieval World* (Cincinnati, 1938); "Commentary," *EJ*; *AJYB*, 56:89-90; "New York City," *EJ*, 12:1114-15, "New York State," 12:1127, "Self-Defence," 14:1128-29; Phila. *Inquirer*, Oct. 20, 1974, p.1 ff.; "Adams, Theodore Lionel," *WWIAJ*, 1955.

15. *AJYB*, 23:247; *Union of American Hebrew Congregations: Directory of Member Congregations, 1984* (N.Y., 1984), 5; *New York Statistics*, 1981, 4-5; Detroit *Jewish News*, June 14, 1985, pp.44-45; *In the Dispersion, Survey and Monographs on the Jewish World*, Winter 1963-64, 72.

16. *JSS*, 21:91; Detroit *Jewish News*, June 2, 1978, p.14.

17. "American Council for Judaism," "Biltmore Program," "Reconstructionism," *EJ*; "Judaism," *UJE*, 6:245-46; "Kaplan, Mordecai Menahem," *UJE, EJ*; Gurock, *Guide*, 74-75.

18. *AI*, Mar. 29, 1984, p.16; Dresner, *Agenda for American Jews*, 24; Rudolph, *Syracuse*, 219; "Young Israel, The National Council of," *EJ*; "New York City," *EJ*, 12:1097, "Students' Movements, Jewish," 15:450; *From the Ruined Garden*, 110-11; *JTA Community News Reporter*, Nov. 26, 1982, p.1, Sept. 6, 1985, p.2; Cincinnati *Enquirer*, Aug. 30, 1985, pp.13-16.

19. *Where We Stand*, 24; Arthur L. Reinhart, *The Voice of the Jewish Laity* (Cincinnati, 1928), 85 ff.; Abraham N. Franzblau, *Reform Judaism in the Large Cities* (UAHC, n.p., 1931), 47 ff.; *Proceedings: XV Biennial Convention of the National Federation of Temple Brotherhoods and the Jewish Chautauqua Society, November 8-10, 1953, Hotel Jefferson, St. Louis, Missouri, Appendix O: A Survey of Current Reform Jewish Practice; 77th-80th Annual Report of the Union of American Hebrew Congregations, December 1955* (N.Y., 1956), 530-31; *Union Prayer Book* (Cincinnati, 1945), 2:131; Tarshish, *Dawn in the West*, 265 ff.; Avi M. Schulman, "Visionary and Activist: A Biography of Maurice N. Eisendrath" (rabbinical thesis, HUC, 1984); *CCARYB*, 34:105-6.

20. "Conservative Judaism," *EJ*; Dresner, *Agenda for American Jews*, 22; Detroit *Jewish News*, Feb. 24, 1984, p.4.

21. Bernard Reisman, *The Chavurah: A Contemporary Jewish Experience* (N.Y., 1977); Jacob Neusner, *Contemporary Jewish Fellowship in Theory and Practice* (N.Y., 1974); James A. Sleeper and Alan Minitz (eds.), *The New Jews* (N.Y., 1971).
22. Tarshish, *Dawn in the West*, 275 ff.; *Michigan Inventory*, 30-40; *JSS*, 21:92 ff.; *Jewish Post and Opinion*, Aug. 24, 1979, p.11, Aug. 31, 1979, p.11, Mar. 19, 1982, p.2; *New York Statistics*, 1981, 22 ff.
23. *Encyclopedia Judaica Yearbook*, 1974, p.138, 1977-1978, p.77; Detroit *Jewish News*, Nov. 5, 1976, p.17, Aug. 3, 1979, p.2, Feb. 22, 1980, p.18, May 21, 1982, p.72; JSS, 21:106 ff.; *New York Statistics*, 1981, 25-26; "Gratz College," *EJ*; *Kansas City Population Study*, 17; Gartner, *Jew. Ed. in the U.S.*, 30; *JTA Community News Reporter*, Sept. 19, 1980, p.1; *JTA-DNB*, Oct. 1, 1984, p.4.
24. Schmelz, *Jewish Demography*, 132; "United States Literature," *EJ*; Nisson Wolpin, *The Torah World: A Treasury of Biographical Sketches* (N.Y., 1982), 184 ff.; Detroit *Jewish News*, June 11, 1982, p.15; *AJYB*, 50:90, 76:38; *JTA Community News Reporter*, Sept. 6, 1985, p.2; *Jewish Currents*, 30(no.11):22.
25. Karpf, *Jewish Community Organization*, 97 ff.; "Center, The Jewish," *UJE*; *AJYB*, 68:30, 78:201; Levinger, *Jews in U.S.*, 450; *JWB Circle*, 42(no.3):4 ff.
26. *AJA*, 3(no.2):51 ff.; Brickner, "Jew. Com. in Cin.," 246; "Community Councils," *UJE*.
27. *PAJHS*, 48:141 ff.; *AJYB*, 78:190 ff., 205; *AI*, Dec. 31, 1981, p.7; "Jews in the United States," *DAH* (1961), vol. 6 (Supplement); Korn, *Retrospect and Prospect*, 224-25; Detroit *Jewish News*, May 30, 1980, p.54, Feb. 24, 1984, p.69; "American Jewish Conference," "Conference of Presidents of Major American Jewish Organizations," *EJ*; Janowsky, *Am. Jew. Reappraisal*, 16 ff.
28. Detroit *Jewish News*, Sept. 12, 1980, p.36; *Jewish Currents*, 35(no.5):46.
29. *World Almanac*, 1984, 407 ff., 695; *World Almanac*, 1985, 37, 408 ff.
30. *AJYB*, 25:339, 68:271; *Jewish Book Annual*, 34:110 ff.
31. *AJYB*, 25:337, 339, 42:215 ff., 68:271, 78:174 ff., 190, 193, 205; *Jewish Post and Opinion*, Mar. 31, 1978, p.11, Sept. 18, 1985, p.2; *New York Statistics, 1981*, 27; *Reviews in American History*, 9:138 ff.; Detroit *Jewish News*, May 12, 1978, p.64, June 2, 1978, p.14; Dresner, *Agenda for American Jews*, 1 ff.
32. *AJYB*, 77:299; *AJA*, 22:15 ff., 26:3; Detroit *Jewish News*, Apr. 28, 1978, p.20, Jan. 26, 1979, p.25, June 6, 1980, p.21, Sept. 17, 1982, pp.38-39, Oct. 28, 1983, p.6, Oct. 26, 1984, p.38-39, June 14, 1985, pp.44-45; *JTA-DNB*, July 14, 1978, p.3, Dec. 7, 1979, p.4, *Rosh Hashanah Edition*, 1980, pp.1-3; *Encyclopedia Judaica Yearbook*, 1975-1976, 198 ff.; *New York Times*, Jan. 28, 1979, p.18, Dec. 8, 1979, p.46, Feb. 7, 1983, p.20; *Wall Street Journal*, Apr. 13, 1984, pp.1, 23, Apr. 16, 1984, pp.1, 16; Egon Mayer & Carl Sheingold, *Intermarriage and the Jewish Future* (N.Y., 1979), 29-31; Egon Mayer, *Children of Intermarriage* (N.Y., 1983), 43-45; Schmelz, *Jewish Demography*, 37 ff., 291-93; *Jewish Population of Rochester, New York* (Monroe County), 1980 (Rochester, 1980), i-iv, 10, 19, 20, 30 ff.; *Jewish Digest*, 22(no.4):68 ff., 24(no.3):3 ff., 24(no.4):17 ff., 24(no.6):50 ff., 25(no.12):16 ff.; *Jewish Education*, 44(no.3-4):25 ff.; *Reform Judaism*, 7(no.8):6 ff.; *Jewish Post and Opinion*, Dec. 15, 1978, p.11, Aug. 24, 1983, p.3; *Midstream*, 24(no.8):50 ff.; *Cincinnati Post*, Apr. 27, 1984, p.1; William Haber, *Educating Our Children Toward New Dimensions* (pamphlet, Brookline, Mass., 1968); *Jewish Currents*, 30(no.11):22, 36(no.12):4 ff.; Memorandum of Rabbi Garry Greenebaum to JRM re conversion, Mar. 23, 1978, Marcus Collections; Neil C. Sandburg & Gene M. Levine, "The Changing Character of the Los Angeles Jewish Community: A Study Sponsered by the Center for the Study of Contemporary Jewish Life of the University of Judaism" (typescript, n.p., 1980), Marcus Collections; *Denver Post*, Mar. 5, 1982, p.6; *JTA Community News Reporter*, Dec. 21, 1979, pp.1-2; Steven Huberman (ed.), "Demographic Highlights of the Los Angeles Community, Jewish Federation Council of Greater Los Angeles" (typescript, L.A., 1983), Marcus Collections; *Baron Festschrift*,

348; James McCann & Debra Friedman, *A Study of the Jewish Community in the Greater Seattle Area* (Seattle, 1979), 65-66; *PAJHS*, 47:125 ff.; Henry Lefkowitz, "Notable American Jews: An Analysis of *Who's Who in American Jewry*, 1980, edition A-L" (HUC term paper, 1985); Abraham Karp, "American Jewry Approaches the 1980's" (typescript lecture, n.d.), copy in Marcus Collections; *Metropolitan Atlanta Jewish Population Study: Summary of Major Findings* (Atlanta, 1985?); *Women's American Ort Reporter*, Fall 1981, p.9; *Kansas City Population Study*; William Wirt, Washington, D.C., to John Myers, Norfolk, June 12, 1818, copy in Myers family Papers, AJAr.

INDEX

Cohen, Benjamin V., 748
Cohen, Henry, 66, 673
Cohen, Jake, 273
Cohen, Joseph H., 531
Cohen, Julius H., 207
Cohen, Morris Raphael, 298, 429, 514, 675, 705
and Felix Frankfurter, 681
Cohn, Fannia, 237–39, 241
Cohn, Michael, 220
Cohn, Sol, 272–73
Cohodas, Aaron, 131
Cohodas Brothers Company, 132
Cohon, Emanuel S., 331
Collis, Charles H. T., 20
Colorado,
free loan societies, 80
settlement in, 10–11, 30, 43–44, 56, 79–82
Columbia, S.C., settlement in, 11
Commentary, 768
Commerce and trade, 199–226
Commercial Cable Company, 281
Community Chest drives, 752
Concerning the Settlement of the Russian Jews in the Area of the Euphrates and Tigris, 643
Condor, Claude R., 642
Cone, Claribel, 743
Cone, Etta, 743
Conference of Jewish Charities, 305
Conference on Jewish Relations, 514, 794
Conference of Presidents of Major American Jewish Organizations, 803
"The Confession of the Parents," 540
Congress of Berlin, 1878, 15, 20
Congress of Industrial Organizations (CIO), 215
Political Action Committee, 745
Conkling, Roscoe, 164
Connecticut,
colonization in, 53, 58, 148–51, 261
working conditions, 199
Connecticut Land Company, 138
Conservative Judaism,
Buffalo, N.Y., 170
Hawaiian Jewry, 74
and modern Orthodoxy, 350
Rochester, N.Y., 168
Constantine, Roman Emperor, 768
Consumptives' Relief Society, Chicago, 117
The Contemporary Jewish Record, 535
Coolidge, Calvin, 82, 103, 615

Coralnik, Abraham, 437–38
Corbin, Austin, 477
Coughlin, Charles E., 173, 757, 767–68
Council of Jewish Federations and Welfare Funds, 797, 803
Council of Jewish Women: *See* National Council of Jewish Women
The Courier, 223
Covenant of Peace, B'rit Shalom, 568
Cox, Samuel Sullivan, 13, 537–38
Crane, Charles R., 680
Crawford, Samuel Johnson, 83
Crémieux Colony, Dakota Terr., 44
Cresson, Nicholas I., 638–41
Cronbach, Abraham, 798
Crown Overall Company, 114
Cutler, Harry, 147, 532, 610

Dahl, Basil (Joseph Bovshover), 442–44
Dakota Territory,
colonization programs, 44–45
settlement in, 44–45, 57, 82–83
Dalrymple, Oliver, 45
Damascus persecutions, 1840, 526
Daniel Deronda, 641–42
Darrow, Roland E., 768
Daughters of Zion, New York City, 653
Davidson, Benjamin, 278
Davidson, Israel, *Thesaurus of Medieval Hebrew Poetry*, 359
Davis, Abel, 613–14
Davis, Allan, 158, 588, 673
Davis, Mrs. Barnett, 106–107
Davis, Mrs. Ben, 499
Davis, Freda, 588
The Day (Der Tog), 236, 304, 406–407, 417, 424, 438, 447
Deadwood, S.D., settlement in, 11
Deborah, 461, 606
Debs, Eugene V., 224–25, 242, 245, 514, 595
Deinard, Ephraim, 47, 357–58
Declaration of Independence, translation to Yiddish, 452, 454
DeCordova, Raphael, 640
DeHaas, Jacob, 661
Delaware, settlement in, 105
DeLeon, Daniel, 418
socialism, Jewry and labor movement, 204, 212–13, 227–30, 252–53
Delitzsch, Franz, 358
Dembitz family, 660